**Books are to be returned on or
before the last date below**

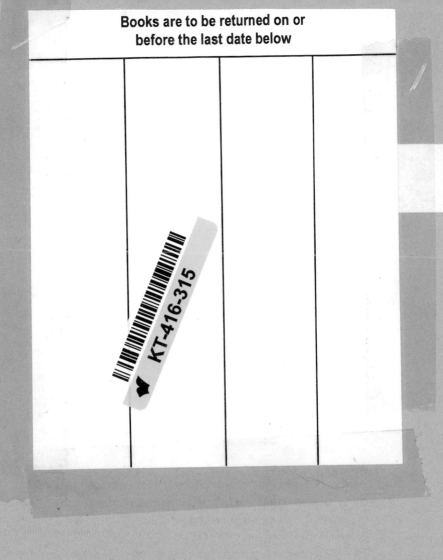

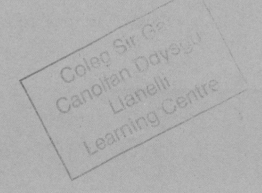

Sixteenth Edition

Smith and Keenan's
COMPANY LAW

Charles Wild

PhD, MBA, LLM, PCHE, LPC, CPE, BSc (Econ)

Dean of the School of Law at the University of Hertfordshire

Professor of Legal Education, University of Hertfordshire

Head of the Centre for International Law, University of Hertfordshire

Stuart Weinstein

JD, MBA, BA

Associate Dean (Research), School of Law, University of Hertfordshire

Solicitor, Supreme Court of England and Wales

Attorney-at-Law, New York, California, District of Columbia

PEARSON

Harlow, England • London • New York • Boston • San Francisco • Toronto • Sydney
Auckland • Singapore • Hong Kong • Tokyo • Seoul • Taipei • New Delhi
Cape Town • São Paulo • Mexico City • Madrid • Amsterdam • Munich • Paris • Milan

Pearson Education Limited
Edinburgh Gate
Harlow CM20 2JE
United Kingdom
Tel: +44 (0)1279 623623
Web: www.pearson.com/uk

First published under the Pitman imprint in 1966 (print)
Second edition published 1970 (print)
Third edition published 1976 (print)
Fourth edition published 1981 (print)
Fifth edition published 1983 (print)
Sixth edition published 1986 (print)
Seventh edition published 1987 (print)
Eighth edition published 1990 (print)
Ninth edition published 1993 (print)
Tenth edition published 1996 (print)
Eleventh edition published 1999 (print)
Twelfth edition published 2002 (print)
Thirteenth edition published 2005 (print)
Fourteenth edition published 2009 (print)
Fifteenth edition published 2011 (print)
Sixteenth edition published 2013 (print and electronic)

ISBN: 978-1-4479-2310-7 (print)
978-1-4479-2312-1 (PDF)
978-1-4479-2313-8 (eText)

British Library Cataloguing-in-Publication Data
A catalogue record for the print edition is available from the British Library

Library of Congress Cataloging-in-Publication Data
A catalog record for the print edition is available from the Library of Congress

10 9 8 7 6 5 4 3 2 1
16 15 14 13

Print edition typeset in 10/12.5pt Minion Pro by 35
Printed in Great Britain by Ashford Colour Press Ltd, Gosport, Hampshire

NOTE THAT ANY PAGE CROSS REFERENCES REFER TO THE PRINT EDITION

Brief contents

Guided tour   xvi
Preface to the sixteenth edition   xviii
Law report abbreviations   xx
Table of cases   xxi
Table of statutes   xxxvii

1   The nature of a company   1
2   The corporate veil   34
3   Companies and partnerships compared   50
4   Promotion and incorporation   64
5   The constitution of the company – the memorandum of association   87
6   The constitution of the company – the articles of association   103
7   The constitution of the company – altering the articles   124
8   The company and its contracts   138
9   The capital of a company   153
10 Capital maintenance – generally   171
11 Capital maintenance – company distributions   205
12 Company flotations   222
13 Shares – generally   236
14 Shares – transfer and transmission   254
15 Shares – payment for and insider dealing   270
16 Membership – capacity, registration, director and substantial
    holdings, annual return   287
17 The statutory derivative action   300
18 The protection of minorities   325
19 Directors and management – generally   352
20 Financial arrangements with, and fair dealing by, directors   378
21 The duties of directors   397
22 Vacation of office, disqualification and personal liability   431
23 Meetings and resolutions   462
24 Debentures and charges   500
25 Accounts and audit   527
26 Amalgamations, reconstructions and takeovers   554
27 Corporate insolvency – company rescue   577
28 Corporate insolvency – procedures other than rescue   605
29 Corporate insolvency – winding-up in context   620

Answers to test your knowledge questions   645

Appendix 1 – Companies (Model Articles) Regulations 2008, SI 2008/3229   647

Appendix 2 – Companies (Tables A to F) Regulations 1985 (SI 1985/805)
as amended by SI 2007/2541 and SI 2007/2826   694

Index   713

Contents

Guided tour   xvi
Preface to the sixteenth edition   xviii
Law report abbreviations   xx
Table of cases   xxi
Table of statutes   xxxvii

1 The nature of a company   1

General features   2
Background to limited liability   3
Classification of corporations – the company as a corporation   5
Classification of registered companies   14
Companies and human rights   30
Essay questions   31
Test your knowledge   32
Suggested further reading   32

2 The corporate veil   34

The judiciary   35
Statutory provisions   47
Limits on lifting the veil   48
Essay questions   48
Suggested further reading   48

3 Companies and partnerships compared   50

The ordinary partnership   51
Law Commission Joint Consultation Paper on Partnership
   Law Reform   54
Limited liability partnerships (LLPs)   55
The Limited Liability Partnerships (Application of Companies Act 2006)
   Regulations 2009 (SI 2009/1804)   58
LLP or private limited company?   61
Advantages and disadvantages of incorporation   62
Essay questions   63
Suggested further reading   63

4 Promotion and incorporation — 64

The promoter — 65
Incorporation — 74
Electronic incorporation — 78
Effect of incorporation — 78
Ready-made companies — 79
Publicity in connection with incorporation — 80
Post-incorporation procedures for re-registration — 80
Essay questions — 84
Test your knowledge — 85
Suggested further reading — 86

5 The constitution of the company – the memorandum of association — 87

Company names — 88
The objects clause — 92
Capital — 96
The registered office — 97
Essay questions — 100
Test your knowledge — 101
Suggested further reading — 102

6 The constitution of the company – the articles of association — 103

The traditional division of powers under the articles — 106
The legal effect of the articles — 108
The articles and insider/outsider rights — 113
The effect of the Contracts (Rights of Third Parties) Act 1999 — 117
Shareholders' agreements — 118
Essay questions — 121
Test your knowledge — 122
Suggested further reading — 122

7 The constitution of the company – altering the articles — 124

Breaches of contract arising out of alteration of the articles — 133
Alteration of the articles by the court — 135
Essay questions — 136
Suggested further reading — 137

8 The company and its contracts — 138

Public companies and the s 761 certificate — 139
Directors and others as agents — 140

Essay questions 150

Test your knowledge 151

Suggested further reading 152

9 The capital of a company 153

Ordinary shares 157

Preference shares 157

Variation and abrogation of class rights 161

Alteration of share capital 165

Redeemable shares 166

Essay questions 168

Test your knowledge 169

Suggested further reading 170

10 Capital maintenance – generally 171

Reduction of capital 172

Acquisition of own shares – generally 181

Purchase of own shares 183

Financial assistance for the purchase of shares 191

Essay questions 202

Test your knowledge 203

Suggested further reading 204

11 Capital maintenance – company distributions 205

Profits available for distribution – generally 206

What is a distribution? 206

Profits available – public and private companies 207

Realised profits and accounting standards 208

Related statutory rules 209

Special cases 211

Relevant accounts 211

Audit considerations 211

Declaration and payment of dividends 212

Consequences of unlawful distribution 215

Capitalising profits 217

Reserves 218

Essay questions 218

Aid to learning on distributions 219

Suggested further reading 221

12 Company flotations 222

The official system for listing securities on an investment exchange 223

Offers of unlisted securities 228

The remedy of rescission 229
Procedures for issuing shares 229
Underwriting 230
Brokerage 231
Reform 231
Essay questions 233
Test your knowledge 234
Suggested further reading 235

13 Shares – generally 236

Subscribers' contract 237
Allotment 238
Return of an allotment 240
Share certificates 241
Share warrants (or bearer shares) 243
Calls 244
Mortgages of shares 246
Lien 247
Forfeiture of shares 248
Surrender of shares 250
Essay questions 251
Test your knowledge 251
Suggested further reading 253

14 Shares – transfer and transmission 254

Transfer of unlisted shares 255
Transfer of listed shares 257
Companies whose articles restrict transfer 260
Transmission of shares 266
Trustees 267
Essay questions 267
Test your knowledge 268
Suggested further reading 269

15 Shares – payment for and insider dealing 270

The consideration – generally 271
Prohibition on allotment of shares at a discount 275
Shares issued at a premium 276
Insider dealing 279
Market abuse 281
Model Code for Securities Transactions by directors of listed companies 283
Essay questions 284
Test your knowledge 285

16 Membership – capacity, registration, director and substantial holdings, annual return 287

Capacity 288
The register of members 289
Director and substantial shareholdings 293
The annual return 295
Essay questions 297
Test your knowledge 298
Suggested further reading 299

17 The statutory derivative action 300

The s 33 contract revisited 302
Shareholders' agreements 302
The rule in *Foss* v *Harbottle* 302
The statutory derivative action 313
Essay questions 323
Suggested further reading 324

18 The protection of minorities 325

Statutory protection against unfair prejudice 326
Minority petition for a just and equitable winding-up 345
Essay questions 348
Test your knowledge 349
Suggested further reading 350

19 Directors and management – generally 352

Definition 353
Appointment of directors 355
Directors' share qualification 364
Division of power – directors and members 365
The chairman and executive directors 370
Publicity in connection with directors 371
The secretary 373
The company accountant 375
Essay questions 375
Test your knowledge 376
Suggested further reading 377

20 Financial arrangements with, and fair dealing by, directors 378

Remuneration 379
The power to pay directors 384

Compensation for loss of office 386
Fair dealing by directors 387
Essay questions 395
Test your knowledge 395

21 The duties of directors 397

The CA 2006 codifies the general duties of directors 398
Scope and nature of general duties 398
Duty to act within powers 399
Duty to promote the success of the company 402
Duty to exercise independent judgement 408
Duty to exercise reasonable care, skill and diligence 408
Duty to avoid conflicts of interest 412
Duty not to accept benefits from third parties 422
Duty to declare interest in proposed transaction or arrangement 422
Effects of a breach of duty 424
Ministerial 'eight-point guidance' 426
Essay questions 426
Test your knowledge 428
Suggested further reading 429

22 Vacation of office, disqualification and personal liability 431

Expiration of the period of office 432
Removal – under statute 433
Removal under the articles 434
Statutory removal – restrictions 435
Resignation 436
Winding-up 436
Appointment of an administrator/administrative receiver 437
Disqualification – generally 438
Disqualification by the court and personal liability 439
Disqualification only 439
Disqualification and personal liability 444
Personal liability only 455
Human rights and directors 457
Essay questions 458
Test your knowledge 460

23 Meetings and resolutions 462

General meetings of the company 463
Notice of meetings 467
Procedure at meetings – legal aspects 471
The chairman 474
Voting 475

Proxies 477
Adjournment of the meeting 481
Minutes 482
Class meetings 483
Company meetings and the disabled 484
Board meetings 484
Resolutions – generally 489
Ordinary resolutions requiring special notice 492
Amendments 492
Written resolutions for private companies (s 288, CA 2006 *et seq.*) 493
Meetings of single-member companies 495
Electronic communications – CA 2006 495
Essay questions 497
Test your knowledge 498

24 Debentures and charges 500

Power to borrow 501
Debentures – generally 501
Types of debentures 502
Acquisition of debentures 505
The trust deed 506
Company charges 508
Crystallisation of floating charges 510
Postponement of floating charges 510
Validity of charges 516
Registration of charges 516
Company's register 519
Avoidance of floating charges 520
Preference 522
Remedies of secured debenture holders 523
BIS consultation 523
Essay questions 524
Test your knowledge 525
Suggested further reading 526

25 Accounts and audit 527

Small and medium-sized companies 528
Accounting records 530
Annual accounts 531
Group accounts 534
The directors' report 535
Publication of accounts and reports 537
Filing of accounts and reports 538
Auditors 540
Duties of auditors 542

Rights of auditors   543
Information and the Companies (Audit, Investigations and
    Community Enterprise) Act 2004   543
Duty of care of the auditor   544
Auditors' liability   547
Essay questions   551
Test your knowledge   552

26 Amalgamations, reconstructions and takeovers   554

Generally   555
Amalgamations and reconstructions   558
Amalgamation (or reconstruction) under the Insolvency Act 1986, s 110   559
Amalgamation (or reconstruction) under the CA 2006, s 895   560
Takeovers   563
Essay questions   573
Test your knowledge   575
Suggested further reading   576

27 Corporate insolvency – company rescue   577

Voluntary arrangements   578
Administration   587
Essay questions   602
Test your knowledge   603

28 Corporate insolvency – procedures other than rescue   605

Receiverships   606
Winding-up or striking off   606
Compulsory winding-up   607
Voluntary winding-up   607
Members' voluntary winding-up   610
Alternatives to winding-up   613
Suggested further reading   619

29 Corporate insolvency – winding-up in context   620

Winding-up by the court   621
Voluntary winding-up   627
The duties of a liquidator   629
Compulsory winding-up by a company in voluntary liquidation   640
Essay questions   641
Test your knowledge   643
Suggested further reading   644

Answers to test your knowledge questions   645

Appendix 1 – Companies (Model Articles) Regulations 2008, SI 2008/3229   647

Appendix 2 – Companies (Tables A TO F) Regulations 1985 (SI 1985/805) as amended by SI 2007/2541 and SI 2007/2826   694

Index   713

Companion Website

For open-access **student resources** specifically written to complement this textbook and support your learning, please visit **www.pearsoned.co.uk/legalupdates**

Guided tour

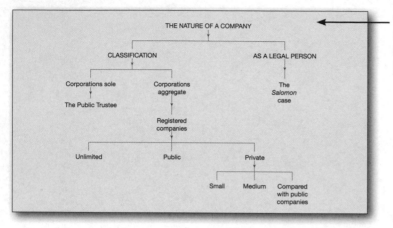

Topic maps – at the start of each chapter topic maps are used to illustrate complex legal structures and processes.

Cross references – Clear in-text cross-references come in handy to help you identify where to discover more information on key topics.

private companies. Finally, as regards a lien or charge on its own shares, this is restricted in the case of public companies by s 670 (see Chapter 13, p. 247 ○). The provisions are not applicable to private companies which may take a lien or charge on their shares.

(e) *As regards payment for shares*. In the case of public companies, any agreement under which shares are to be allotted by an undertaking to carry out work or perform services is prohibited (s 585) but is allowed in the case of private companies. The subscribers to the memorandum of a public company must pay for their shares in cash, whereas in a private company payment may be in cash or some other consideration. In public companies there is a minimum payment for shares whenever issued (i.e. at least one-quarter of the nominal value plus the whole of any share premium must be paid up), but in private companies there is no minimum payment requirement. Where shares are to be paid for by a non-cash asset, public companies are required to ensure that the asset is to be transferred by contract within five years of the allotment, whereas there is no special requirement for private companies. Furthermore, public companies must have an independent accountant's report on the value of the non-cash asset used as consideration for an issue of shares. This requirement does not apply to private companies.

(f) *Acquisition of non-cash assets*. A public company cannot validly acquire non-cash assets valued at one-tenth or more of the company's issued share capital from subscribers to

 Hickman v Kent or Romney Marsh Sheepbreeders' Association [1915] Ch 881

The defendant company was incorporated under the Companies Acts in 1895. The objects of the company were to encourage and retain as pure the sheep known as Kent or Romney Marsh, and the establishment of a flock book listing recognised sires and ewes to be bred from. The articles provided for disputes between the company and the members to be referred to arbitration. This action was brought in the Chancery Division by the claimant because the Association had refused to register certain of his sheep in the flock book, and he asked for damages for this. It also appeared that the Association was trying to expel him, and he asked for an injunction to prevent this.

Held – by Astbury J – that the Association was entitled to have the action stayed. The articles amounted to a contract between the Association and the claimant to refer disputes to arbitration. However, Astbury J, after accepting that the articles were a contract between a company and its members, went on to say:

> [. . .] No right merely purporting to be given by an article to a person, whether a member or not, in a capacity other than that of a member, as for instance, a solicitor, promoter, director, can be enforced against the company.

Case summaries – throughout the chapters essential case summaries detail key decisions in company law clearly explaining the decision.

Essay questions

1 Describe the procedure for alteration of articles and detail the considerations made in determining the validity of the alteration. *(The Institute of Company Accountants)*

2 H plc wishes to change its articles of association to add a clause which states 'any director of the company may be removed from office if all other directors give notice in writing of their desire that the named directors be so removed'.
   You are required to explain the procedure for alteration and discuss the difficulties the company might encounter in adding this new clause.
   (The Chartered Institute of Management Accountants)

3 Free Range Chickens R Us wishes to change its articles of association to add a clause which would state that 'any director of the company may be removed from office if all other directors give notice in writing of their desire that the named directors be so removed'.
   You are required to explain the procedure for alteration and discuss the difficulties which the company might encounter in adding this new clause. *(Authors' question)*

4 Perfect Puddings Ltd was incorporated to purchase the chocolate manufacturing business previously carried on by Louise. The contract of sale between the company and Louise provided, inter alia, that as long as Louise held 20 per cent of the shares of Perfect Puddings, she was entitled to be managing director of the company. The Articles of Association which otherwise follow *Table A* reproduce this provision and also contain the following:

Essay questions – end of chapter essay questions allow you to hone your essay writing skills while asking you to reflect on and consider what you have learnt from the chapter. Answer guidance may be found on the website.

Test your knowledge

Four alternative answers are given. Select ONE only. Circle the answer which you consider to be correct. Check your answers by referring back to the information given in the chapter and against the answers at the end of the text.

1 When a private company wants to re-register as a public company it must file a balance sheet with the Registrar. The balance sheet must be one which is not more than:

   A Fifteen months old at the date of re-registration.
   B Seven months old at the date of re-registration.
   C Fifteen months old at the date of application.
   D Seven months old at the date of application.

2 Thames was re-registered from a limited to an unlimited company. It wishes to re-register as a public company.

   A It must apply to the Registrar to be registered as a public limited company.
   B It must re-register as a private limited company and then re-register as a public company.
   C It must pass a special resolution to convert into a public company.
   D There is no procedure whereby Thames may become a public limited company.

3 Fred is a member of a private company at the date of its re-registration as a public company. Fred cannot profit by selling non-cash assets to the public company within an initial period of two years from the date of re-registration unless:

Test your knowledge – end of chapter test your knowledge sections challenge you to check that you understand each topic fully. Answers can be found at the back of the book.

Companion Website

For open-access **student resources** specifically written to complement this textbook and support your learning, please visit **www.pearsoned.co.uk/legalupdates**

ON THE WEBSITE

Preface to the sixteenth edition

This edition continues to explore the impact that the Companies Act 2006 has had on the regulation of small and medium-sized companies following the highly publicized 'wholesale rethink' of corporate law which the Act represents. Whilst the Act can no longer be described as being in its infancy, it is nevertheless an exciting and challenging period for practitioners, academics and students alike as the case law emerges.

Building on the previous edition, which analysed the fundamental change in approach under the 2006 Act to corporate regulation at the small and medium-sized company level, we have extended our discussion of the corporate form, together with that of other business formats such as limited liability partnerships (LLPs). As such, the front section of this edition has been reworked so as to include specific chapters focusing on the corporate form, the veil of incorporation (together with when it may be lifted), as well as a detailed analysis of LLPs and how these may present a viable alternative to the small private company format. Recent case law such as *Chandler* v *Cape Plc* [2012] is included in these new chapters, as well as the Limited Liability Partnerships Regulations (Application of Companies Act 2006) Regulations 2009 (SI 2009/1804) which completed the application of the Companies Act 2006 to limited liability partnerships.

The new Model Articles that accompany the 2006 Act, and which have replaced *Table A* as the template for corporate constitutions, represent a dramatic shift away from the 'one size fits all' mentality to that of a 'think small first' approach, providing bespoke model articles for private companies limited by shares, private companies limited by guarantee, and public companies limited by shares. However, *Table A* remains an important consideration when dealing with any company incorporated before this date. Consequently, we have sought to balance our discussion of the new Model Articles and their impact on the day-to-day management and running of both public and private companies, with maintaining a thorough analysis of *Table A* so as to provide the reader with a practical, and relevant, overview of the area. Given the complexity of this issue, copies of these documents are contained in the two Appendices to this text and readers are referred to them throughout the text so as to familarise themselves with these key provisions.

We have continued to expand and enrich reference to case law throughout. This includes current cases such as *Stainer* v *Lee* [2010], *Hughes* v *Weiss* [2012] and *Harbourne Road Nominees Ltd* v *Karvaski* [2011] which relate to the new statutory derivative action and the unfair prejudice head, as well as a broader analysis of traditional common law and equitable duties imposed on directors, which underpin the statutory duties introduced by the 2006 Act. As with the previous edition, this is supported by reference to an increased selection of academic articles at the end of chapters, in order to ensure that the text is as current and relevant as possible for readers.

We would like to thank those members of staff at Pearson Education who have helped to produce this edition, particularly Cheryl Cheasley, Gabriella Playford and Tim Parker. Our thanks are also due to those who designed, set, printed and bound the book.

Finally, we would like to thank our respective families who have shown considerable patience and understanding over the past few months. The production of any text requires a significant support network and for that we are both truly grateful.

Any errors and omissions at the level at which the text is aimed are down to the authors.

Charles Wild and Stuart Weinstein
Hatfield, May 2013

Law report abbreviations

The following table sets out the abbreviations used when citing the various series of certain law reports which are in common use, together with the periods over which they extend. Law Reports, Appeal Cases, 1891–(current)

ATC	Annotated Tax Cases, 1922–75
All ER	All England Law Reports, 1936–(current)
All ER (D)	All England Direct (an online service)
All ER Rep	All England Law Reports Reprint, 36 vols 1558–1935
App Cas	Law Reports, Appeal Cases, 15 vols 1875–90
BCC	British Company Law and Practice (CCH editions)–(current)
BCLC	Butterworths Company Law Cases, 1983–(current)
B & CR	Reports of Bankruptcy and Companies Winding-up Cases, 1918–(current)
CL	Current Law Monthly Digest, 1947–(current)
CLJ	Cambridge Law Journal
CLY	Current Law Yearbook, 1947–(current)
CMLR	Common Market Law Reports, 1962–(current)
Ch	Law Reports Chancery Division, 1891–(current)
Com Cas	Commercial Cases, 1895–1941
Fam	Law Reports Family Division, 1972–(current)
ICR	Industrial Court Reports, 1972–74; Industrial Cases Reports, 1974–(current)
IRLB	Industrial Relations Law Bulletin, 1993–(current)
IRLR	Industrial Relations Law Reports, 1971–(current)
ITR	Reports of decisions of the Industrial Tribunals, 1966–(current)
KB	Law Reports, King's Bench Division, 1901–52
LGR	Local Government Reports, 1902–(current)
Lloyd LR or Lloyd's Rep	Lloyd's List Law Reports, 1919–(current) (from 1951)
LRRP	Law Reports Restrictive Practices, 1957–(current)
LSG	Law Society Gazette Reports
NLJ	New Law Journal
P	Law Reports, Probate, Divorce and Admiralty Division, 1891–1971
P & CR	Planning and Compensation Reports, 1949–(current)
PIQR	Personal Injuries and Quantum Reports
QB	Law Reports Queen's Bench Division, 1891–1901; 1953–(current)
SJ	Solicitors' Journal, 1856–(current)
STC	Simon's Tax Cases, 1973–(current)
Tax Cas (or TC)	Tax Cases, 1875–(current)
TLR	Times Law Reports, 1884–1952
WLR	Weekly Law Reports, 1953–(current)

Table of cases

A & BC Chewing Gum Ltd, *re* [1975] 1 All ER 1017 *357*

ABC Coupler & Engineering Ltd, *re* [1961] 1 All ER 354 *623*

ASRS Establishment Ltd, *re* (1999) *The Times*, 17 November *508*

Abbott *v* Strong (1998) *The Times*, 9 July *548*

Accidental Death Insurance Co, Allin's Case, *re* (1873) LR 16 Eq 449 *263*

Adair *v* Old Bushmills Distillery [1908] WN 24 *158*

Adams *v* Cape Industries [1990] Ch 433, CA *1, 13, 34–37*

Adelaide Electric Co *v* Prudential Assurance [1934] AC 122, HL *161*

Advantage Healthcare (T10) Ltd, *re* [1999] All ER (D) 1294 *518*

Aerators Ltd *v* Tollitt [1902] 2 Ch 319 *90*

Agnew *v* Inland Revenue (The Brumark Case) [2001] All ER (D) 21 *509, 510*

Airey *v* Cordell [2006] EWHC 2728 (Ch) *315, 318*

Al Saudi Banque *v* Clarke Pixley [1989] 3 All ER 361 *547*

Albacruz (Cargo Owners) *v* Albazero (Owners), *The Albazero* [1977] AC 774 *35*

Albazero, The, see Albacruz (Cargo Owners) *v* Albazero (Owners)

Alexander *v* Automatic Telephone Co [1900] 2 Ch 56 *245*

Allen *v* Gold Reefs of West Africa Ltd [1900] 1 Ch 656 *124, 125, 126, 127, 130, 156*

Allen *v* Hyatt (1914) 30 TLR 444 *405*

Allied Carpets Group plc *v* Nethercott [2001] BCC 81 *216*

Allin's Case *see* Accidental Death Insurance Co, Allin's Case, *re*

Al-Nakib Investments (Jersey) Ltd *v* Longcroft [1990] 3 All ER 321 *228*

AluminiumIndustrieVaassen BV *v* RomalpaAluminium [1976] 2 All ER 552 *513*

American Cyanamid Co *v* Ethicon [1975] AC 396 *514*

Andrews *v* Gas Metre Co [1897] 1 Ch 361 *154*

Anglesey Colliery Co, *re* (1886) 1 Ch App 555 *622*

Anglo-American Insurance Ltd [2001] 1 BCLC 755 *560*

Antal International Ltd [2003] EWHC 1339 (Ch), [2003] 2 BCLC 406 *601*

Arab Bank plc *v* Mercantile Holdings Ltd [1994] 1 All ER 74 *196*

Arthur Rathbone Kitchens Ltd, *re* [1997] 2 BCLC 280 *582*

Ashbury *v* Watson (1885) 30 Ch D 376 *155*

Ashbury Railway Carriage and Iron Co *v* Riche (1875) LR 7 HL 653 *92, 95*

Ashpurton Estates Ltd, *re* [1982] 3 All ER 665 *519*

Asprey & Garrard Ltd *v* WRA (Guns) Ltd (2001) High Court 18 May unreported *89*

Astec (BSR) plc, *re* [1999] 2 BCLC 556 *332, 334*

Attorney-General *v* Blake [2001] 1 AC 268, HL [1998] Ch 439 *419*

Attorney-General *v* Lindi St Claire (Personal Services) Ltd [1981] 2 Co Law 69 *78, 89*

Attorney-General's Reference (No 2 of 1982) [1984] 2 All ER 216 *11*

Atwool *v* Merryweather (1867) LR 5 Eq 464 *312*

Australian Coal and Shale Employees' Federation *v* Smith (1937) 38 SR (NSW) 48 *114*

Automatic Self-Cleaning Filter Syndicate Co Ltd *v* Cuninghame [1906] 2 Ch 34 *107*

AvelingBarford Ltd v Perion Ltd (1989) 5 BCC 677 *637*

Baber v Kenwood Manufacturing Co [1978] 1 Lloyd's Rep 175 *545*

Baglan Hall Colliery Co, *re* (1870) LR 5 Ch App 346 *27*

Baily v British Equitable Assurance Co Ltd [1904] 1 Ch 374 *133*

Bairstow v Queens Moat Houses plc, High Court [2000] 1 BCLC 549 *216*

Baker v Gibbons [1972] 2 All ER 759 *415*

Ball v Eden Project Ltd, Eden Project v Ball [2001] 1 BCLC 313 *415*

Balston Ltd v Headline Filters Ltd [1990] FSR 385 *421*

Bamford v Bamford [1969] 2 WLR 1107 *368, 369, 424*

Bank of Credit and Commerce International (No 8), *re* [1997] 4 All ER 568 *517*

Bank of Tokyo Ltd v Karoon [1987] AC 45 *42*

Barclays Bank plc v Ellis (2000) *The Times*, 24 October *31*

Barclays Bank v Stuart London Ltd [2001] 2 BCLC 316 *519*

Bargate v Shortridge (1855) 5 HL Cas 297 *149*

Barnett, Hoares & Co v South London Tramways Co (1887) 18 QBD 815 *168*

Baron v Potter [1914] 1 Ch 895 *108*

Barrett v Duckett [1995] BCC 362 *323*

Beattie v E and F Beattie Ltd [1938] Ch 708 *111, 112, 114, 115, 302*

Bell v Lever Bros Ltd [1932] AC 161 *415*

Bell Houses Ltd v City Wall Properties Ltd [1966] 2 All ER 674 *94*

Bellador Silk, *re* [1965] 1 All ER 667 *328*

Bellerby v Rowland & Marwood's SS Co Ltd [1902] 2 Ch 14 *250*

Belmont Finance v Williams (No 2) [1980] 1 All ER 393 *192, 193, 194*

Berry and Stewart v Tottenham Hotspur FC Ltd [1935] Ch 718 *263, 264*

Bersel Manufacturing Co Ltd v Berry [1968] 2 All ER 552 *434*

Bhullar Bros Ltd, *re* [2003] All ER (D) 445 *414*

Biba Group Ltd v Biba Boutique [1980] RPC 413 *91*

Biosource Technologies Inc v Axis Genetics plc (in administration) [2000] 1 BCLC 286 *599*

Birch v Cropper (1889) 14 App Cas 525 *159*

Bird Precision Bellows, *re* [1984] 2 WLR 869 *339, 347*

Blackspur Group plc, *re* [1997] 1 WLR 710 *443, 444*

Blackspur Group plc (No 3), *re* (2001) *The Times*, 5 July *444*

Blaker v Herts & Essex Waterworks (1889) 41 Ch D 399 *523*

Bloom v Pensions Regulator [2011] EWCA Civ 1124, [2010] EWHC 3010 (Ch) *596*

Blue Arrow plc, *re* [1987] BCLC 585 *301, 334, 335*

Boardman v Phipps [1967] 2 AC 46 *414, 418*

Bolam v Friern Hospital Management Committee [1957] 2 All ER 118 *209, 549*

Bolitho v City and Hackney Health Authority [1997] 4 All ER 771 *209, 549*

Bonelli's Electric Telegraph Co, Cook's Claim (No 2), *re* (1874) LR 18 Eq 656 *360*

Borden (UK) Ltd v Scottish Timber Products Ltd [1979] 3 All ER 961 *514*

Borland's Trustees v Steel Bros & Co Ltd [1901] 1 Ch 279 *172*

Boulting v Association of Cinematograph, Television and Allied Technicians [1963] 2 QB 606 *408*

Bowman v Secular Society [1917] AC 406 *78*

Brac Rent-A-Car International Inc, *in re* [2003] EWHC 128 (Ch), [2003] All ER (D) 98 (Feb) *100, 626*

Bradford Banking Co Ltd v Henry Briggs, Son & Co Ltd, The (1886) 12 App Cas 29 *248, 293*

Bradman v Trinity Estates plc [1989] BCLC 757 *469*

Brady v Brady [1988] 2 All ER 617, HL *192, 193*

Bratton Seymour Service Co Ltd v Oxborough [1922] BCLC 693 *118*

Braymist Ltd v Wise Finance Company Ltd (2001) *The Times*, 27 March *72*

Brelec Installations Ltd, *re* (2000) *The Times*, 18 April *582*

Briess *v* Woolley [1954] 1 All ER 909 *405*

British America Nickel Corporation Ltd *v* O'Brien [1927] AC 369 *163*

British Diabetic Association *v* Diabetic Society Ltd [1995] 4 All ER 812 *89*

British Midland Tool Ltd *v* Midland International Tooling Ltd [2003] EWHC 466 (Ch), [2003] 2 BCLC 523 *420, 421*

British Seamless Paper Box Co, *re* (1881) 17 Ch D 467 *69*

British Thomson-Houston Co Ltd *v* Federated European Bank Ltd [1932] 2 KB 176 *146*

British Union for the Abolition of Vivisection, *re* (1995) *The Times*, 3 March *464*

Brown *v* British Abrasive Wheel Co [1919] 1 Ch 290 *307*

Brown and Green Ltd *v* Hays (1920) 36 TLR 330 *379*

Browne *v* La Trinidad (1887) 37 Ch D 1 *301, 487*

Brownlow *v* GH Marshall Ltd [2000] 2 BCLC 655 *340*

Brumark Case, *see* Agnew *v* Inland Revenue

Buchan *v* Secretary of State for Employment [1997] IRLR 80, (1997) 565 IRLB 2 *12, 355, 363, 364, 511*

Bugle Press Ltd, *re* [1960] 3 All ER 791 *570*

Bulkeley *v* Schutz (1871) LR 3 PC 764 *75*

Burland *v* Earle [1902] AC 83 *130, 305*

Burns *v* Siemens Bros Dynamo Works Ltd [1919] 1 Ch 225 *291*

Bushell *v* Faith [1970] 1 All ER 53, HL, [1970] AC 1099, [1969] 1 All ER 1002 *103, 154, 366, 433, 471, 492*

Byers *v* Yacht Bull Corp [2010] EWHC 133 (Ch) *627*

Byng *v* London Life Association Ltd (1988) *The Times*, 22 December *482*

CE King Ltd (in administration) [2000] 2 BCLC 297 *600*

CMS Dolphin Ltd *v* Simonet Ltd [2002] BCC 600, [2001] 2 BCLC 704 *415, 417, 419, 421*

CVC/Opportunity Equity Partners Ltd *v* Demarco Almeida [2002] BCC 684

Cadbury Schweppes plc *v* Somji [2001] 1 WLR 615 *581*

Cameron's Coalbrook Steam Coal, and Swansea and Kougher Railway Co, *re* Bennett's Case (1854) 5 De GM & G 284 *400*

Canadian Aero Service Ltd *v* O'Malley (1973) 40 DLR (2d) 371 (Canaero) *421*

Cancol Ltd, *re* [1996] 1 BCLC 100 *580*

Cannon *v* Trask (1875) LR 20 Eq 669 *465*

Caparo Industries *v* Dickman [1990] 1 All ER 568 *228, 547, 548, 549*

Cape Breton, *re* (1887) 12 App Cas 652 *67*

Carl Zeiss Stiftung *v* Rayner and Keeler Ltd (No 3) [1970] Ch 506 *97*

Cawley & Co, *re* (1889) 42 Ch D 209 *245*

Centrebind, *re* [1966] 3 All ER 889 *612, 631*

Centros Ltd *v* ErhvervsogSelskabsstyrelsen (Case C-212/97) [1999] ECR I-1459 *200–201*

Chandler *v* Cape plc [2012] 3 All ER 640, [2011] EWHC 951 *37–38*

Chapman's Case (1866) LR 1 Eq 346 *625*

Charge Card Services Ltd, *re* [1986] 3 All ER 289 *517*

Chettiar *v* Chettiar [1962] 1 All ER 494 *199*

Chida Mines Ltd *v* Anderson (1905) 33 TLR 27 *374*

China Jazz Worldwide plc, *re* [2003] All ER (D) 66 (Jun) *456, 457*

CiroCitterio Menswear plc *v* Thakrar [2002] 2 All ER 717 *390*

Citco Banking Corporation NV *v* Pusser's Ltd [2007] UKPC 13 *130*

City Equitable Fire Insurance Co, *re* [1925] Ch 407 *409, 410, 546*

Clayton's Case (1816) 1 Mer 572 *521*

Cleadon Trust Ltd, *re* [1939] Ch 286 *374*

Clemens *v* Clemens Bros [1976] 2 All ER 268 *128, 307, 341, 399*

Clydebank Football Club Ltd *v* Steedman 2002 SLT 109 *638*

Cobley *v* Forward Technology Industries plc [2003] All ER (D) 175 *361, 364*

Colin Gwyer & Associates Ltd *v* London Wharf (Limehouse) Ltd [2003] BCC 885 *449*

Colt Telecom Ltd, *re* (20 December 2002, unreported) *589*

Commercial Solvents *see* I stituto Chemioter apico Italiano SpA and Commercial Solvents Corpn *v* EC Commission

Company (No 002567 of 1982), *re* a [1983] 2 All ER 854 *346*

Company (No 004475 of 1982), *re* a [1983] 2 WLR 381 *336*

Company (No 007623 of 1984), *re* a [1986] BCLC 362 *341*

Company (No 005287 of 1985), *re* a [1986] 1 WLR 281 *331*

Company (No 008699 of 1985), *re* a [1986] PCC 296 *340*

Company (No 00477 of 1986), *re* a (1986) 2 BCC 99, [1986] PCC 372 *327, 335*

Company (No 00370 of 1987), *re* a (1988) 4 BCLC 506, (1988) *The Times*, 5 July *204, 215*

Company (No 004803 of 1996), *re* a (1996) *The Times*, 2 December *453*

Compaq Computers Ltd *v* Abercorn Group Ltd (t/a Osiris) [1993] BCLC 603 *513*

Conegrade Ltd, *re* [2003] BPIR 358 *392*

Connolly *v* Sellers Arenascene Ltd (2000) 633 IRLB 15 *364*

Consumer and Industrial Press Ltd, *re* [1988] BCLC 177 *588, 600*

Conti, Petitioner [1998] 11 CL 581 *617*

Conti *v* Ueberseebank AG [2000] 4 CL 698 *617*

Continental Assurance Co of London plc, *re* [1996] 28 LS Gaz 29 *443*

Contract Corporation, Gooch's Case, *re* (1872) LR 8 Ch App 266 *289*

Conway *v* Ratiu [2006] 1 All ER 571 *38*

Cook *v* Deeks [1916] 1 AC 554 *306, 308, 311, 367, 415*

Cook's Claim (No 2) *see* Bonelli's Electric Telegraph Co, Cook's Claim (No 2), *re*

Copal Varnish Co Ltd, *re* [1917] 2 Ch 349 *264, 370*

Cotman *v* Brougham [1918] AC 514 *78, 93, 94*

Cotronic (UK) Ltd *v* Dezonie [1991] BCC 200 *72*

Coulthard *v* Neville Russell (A Firm) [1998] 1 BCLC 143 *200, 548*

County Properties Ltd *v* Scottish Ministers (2000) *The Times*, 19 September; *reversed* 2002 SC 79 *30*

Cousins *v* International Brick Co Ltd [1931] 2 Ch 90 *481*

Crantrave Ltd (in liquidation) *v* Lloyds Bank plc [2000] 3 WLR 877, CA *515*

Craven Textile Engineers Ltd *v* Batley Football Club Ltd, Transcript: B2 99/1127, CA *393*

Craven-Ellis *v* Canons Ltd [1936] 2 KB 403 *380*

Crichton's Oil Co, *re* [1902] 2 Ch 86 *158*

Criterion Properties plc *v* Stratford UK Properties LLC [2002] 2 BCLC 151 *400*

Cumbrian Newspapers Group Ltd *v* Cumberland & Westmorland Herald Newspaper & Printing Co Ltd [1987] Ch 1, (1986) 2 BCC 99, [1986] 3 WLR 26 *103, 124, 153, 155, 335*

Currencies Direct Ltd *v* Ellis [2003] 2 BCLC 482 *392*

Cyona Distributors, *re* [1967] 1 All ER 281 *633*

DHN Food Distributors *v* Tower Hamlets London Borough Council [1976] 1 WLR 852; [1976] 3 All ER 462 *36, 37, 40–41, 43, 48*

DKG Contractors Ltd, *re* [1990] BCC 903 *450*

DPP *v* Dziurzynski (2002) *The Times*, 8 July *2*

D'Jan of London, *re* [1994] 1 BLCL 561 *410, 446*

Dafen Tinplate Co Ltd *v* Llanelly Steel Co (1907) Ltd [1920] 2 Ch 124 *129, 307*

Daimler Co Ltd *v* Continental Tyre & Rubber Co (Great Britain) Ltd [1916] 2 AC 307 *43–45, 97, 374*

Daniels *v* Daniels [1978] Ch 406, [1978] 2 All ER 89 *305, 310, 311*

Daniels *v* Walker [2000] 1 WLR 1382 *31*

Danmarks/Bosbaek Case [1998] All ER (EC) 112 *512*

David Moseley & Sons Ltd [1939] 2 All ER 791 *432*

Davis *v* R Bolton & Co [1894] 3 Ch 678 *143*

Dawson International plc *v* Coats Patonsplc 1988 SLT 854 *403*

Day *v* Haine [2008] EWCA Civ 626 *596*

De Courcy *v* Clements [1971] 1 All ER 681 *609*

Debtor (No 2021 of 1995), *re* a, *ex parte* IRC *v* Debtor [1996] 2 All ER 345 *479*

Debtor (No 50A SD/95), *re* a [1997] 2 All ER 789 *621*

Derry *v* Peek (1889) 14 App Cas 337 *227*

Destone Fabrics Ltd, *re* [1941] 1 All ER 545 *522*

Development Co of Central and West Africa, *re* [1902] Ch 547 *177*

Devlin *v* Slough Estates Ltd [1982] 2 All ER 273 *312*

Dimbleby & Sons Ltd *v* National Union of Journalists [1984] 1 WLR 427; [1984] 1 All ER 751 *41, 47*

Dimbula Valley (Ceylon) Tea Co Ltd *v* Laurie [1961] 1 All ER 769 *161*

Dorchester Finance Co Ltd *v* Stebbing [1989] BCLC 498 *409, 424*

Dronfield Silkstone Coal Co, *re* (1880) 17 Ch D 76 *181*

Dunderland Iron Ore Co Ltd, *re* [1909] 1 Ch 446 *506*

Duomatic Ltd, *in re* [1969] 2 Ch 365, [1969] 1 All ER 161 *62, 120, 379, 386, 425, 489, 493, 630*

EDC *v* UK [1998] BCC 370 *458*

EIC Services Ltd *v* Phipps [2003] 3 All ER 804 *141*

EW Savory Ltd, *re* [1951] All ER 1036 *158*

East *v* Bennet Bros Ltd [1911] 1 Ch 163 *474*

East Pant Du United Lead Mining Co Ltd *v* Merryweather (1864) 2 Hem & M 254 *312*

Eaton *v* Robert Eaton Ltd and Secretary of State for Employment [1988] IRLR 83 *362*

Ebrahimi *v* Westbourne Galleries [1973] AC 360, [1972] 2 All ER 492 *45–46, 53, 128, 307, 329, 345, 346, 347, 348, 357*

Eddystone Marine Insurance Co, *re* [1893] 3 Ch 9 *272, 273*

Edwards *v* Halliwell [1950] 2 All ER 1064 *301, 304, 305*

El Sombrero Ltd, *re* [1958] 3 All ER 1 *473*

Elder *v* Elder & Watson 1952 SC 49 *328*

Electronics Ltd *v* Akhter Computers Ltd [2001] 1 BCLC 433 *148*

Eley *v* Positive Government Security Life Assurance Co (1876) 1 Ex D 88, CA, *Affirming* (1875) 1 Ex D 20, Ex D *112, 114, 117, 156*

Ellis *v* Rowbotham [1900] 1 QB 740 *595*

Emmadart Ltd, *re* [199] Ch 540 *592*

Energy Holdings (No 3) Ltd (In Liquidation), *in re* [2010] EWHC 788 (Ch) *578*

Equiticorp International plc, *re* [1989] 1 WLR 1010 *592*

Eras Eil Actions [1992] 1 Lloyd's Rep 570 *343*

Erlanger *v* New Sombrero Phosphate Co (1878) 3 App Cas 1218 *66*

Esparto Trading, *re* (1879) 12 Ch D 191 *249*

Estmanco (Kilner House) Ltd *v* Greater London Council [1982] 1 All ER 437 *305*

Euro Brokers Holdings Ltd *v* Monecor (London) Ltd [2003] 1 BCLC 506 *120, 493*

Eurofood IFSC Ltd, *re* (Case C-341/04) [2006] All ER (D) 20 (May)

European Society Arbitration Acts, *re* (1878) 8 Ch D 679 *293*

Everson *v* Secretary of State for Trade and Industry [2000] All ER (EC) 29 *512*

Ewing *v* Buttercup Margarine Company Ltd [1917] 2 Ch 1 *90*

Exeter City Council *v* Bairstow [2007] EWHC 400 (Ch) *343, 595*

Fanmailuk.com Ltd *v* Cooper [2008] EWHC 2198 (Ch) *318*

Fayed *v* UK (1994) *The Times*, 11 October *457*

Fell *v* Derby Leather Co Ltd [1931] 2 Ch 252 *118*

Firedart Ltd, Official Receiver *v* Fairall, *re* [1994] 2 BCLC 340 *442*

Fireproof Doors, re [1916] 2 Ch 142 *482*

Firestone Tyre & Rubber Co Ltd v Lewellin [1957] 1 WLR 464; [1957] 1 All ER 561 *36, 43*

First Global Media Group Ltd v Larkin [2003] All ER (D) 293 *392*

Five Minute Car Wash Service Ltd, re [1966] 1 All ER 242 *348*

Fleming v Secretary of State for Trade and Industry (1998) 588 IRLB 10 *12, 364*

Flitcroft's Case (1882) 21 Ch D 519 *215*

Folkes Group plc v Alexander [2002] EWHC 51 (Ch), [2002] 2 BCLC 254 *118, 136*

Fomento (Sterling Area) Ltd v Selsdon Fountain Pen Co Ltd [1958] 1 WLR 45 *546*

Fortune Copper Mining Co, re (1870) LR 10 Eq 390 *98*

Foss v Harbottle (1843) 2 Hare 461 *110, 114, 123, 300, 301, 302–313, 316, 323, 324, 326, 328, 330, 349, 405*

Foster v Foster [1916] 1 Ch 532 *379*

Foster Bryant Surveying Limited v Bryant, Savernake Property Consultants Limited [2007] BCC 804 *416–421*

Fowler v Broads Patent Night Light Co [1893] 1 Ch 724 *625*

Framlington Group plc v Anderson [1995] 1 BCLC 475 *421*

Franbar Holdings Ltd v Patel and Others [2008] EWHC 1534 (Ch) *316, 318*

Freeman & Lockyer v Buckhurst Park Properties (Mangal) Ltd [1964] 1 All ER 630 *138, 144, 146*

Friedrich Binder GmbH & Co KG v Hauptzollamt Bad Reichenhall (Case 161/88) [1989] ECR 2415 *217*

Fulham Football Club (1987) Ltd v Richards & Anor [2011] EWCA Civ 855 *341–343*

Gaiman v National Association for Mental Health [1971] Ch 317 *105*

Galloway v Hallé Concerts Society [1915] 2 Ch 233 *369, 399*

GamlestadenFastigheter AB v Baltic Partners Ltd [2007] UKPC 26, [2007] 4 All ER 164, PC *343–345*

Garage Door Associates, re [1984] 1 All ER 434 *336*

Gardner v Iredale [1912] 1 Ch 700 *273*

Gartside v Silkstone and Dodworth Coal and Iron Co Ltd (1882) 21 Ch D 762 *502*

Gasque v Commissioner of Inland Revenue [1940] 2 KB 8 *97*

Gencor ACP Ltd v Dalby [2000] 2 BCLC 734 *414*

General Auction Estate and Monetary Co v Smith [1891] 3 Ch 432 *501*

George Newman & Co, re [1895] 1 CH 674 *379*

Gething v Kilner [1972] 1 All ER 1166, [1972] 1 WLR 337 *403, 568*

Ghyll Beck Driving Range Ltd, re [1993] BCLC 1126 *340*

Gilford Motor Co v Horne [1933] Ch 935 *38*

Glenister v Rowe (Costs) [2000] Ch 76 *596*

Gluckstein v Barnes [1900] AC 240 *66, 67*

Goldacre (Offices) Ltd v Nortel Networks UK Ltd [2010] Ch 455 *595*

Goldsmith v Sperrings [1977] 1 WLR 478 *319*

Gomba Holdings UK Ltd v Homan [1986] 3 All ER 94 *437*

Gooch's Case see Contract Corporation, Gooch's Case, re

Goodfellow v Nelson Line [1974] 1 WLR 1133 *130, 164*

Goy & Co Ltd, Farmer v Goy & Co Ltd, re [1900] 2 Ch 149 *503*

Grace v Biagioli [2005] EWCA Civ 1222 *340*

Gramophone and Typewriter Co Ltd v Stanley [1908] 2 KB 89, CA *15–16*

Grant v United Kingdom Switchback Railways Co (1888) 40 Ch D 135 *367, 368*

Gray v Lewis (1873) 8 Ch App 1035 *303*

Greene, re [1949] 1 All ER 167 *255*

Greenhalgh v Arderne Cinemas Ltd [1951] Ch 286, [1946] 1 All ER 512 *125, 127, 128, 161*

Greymouth Point Elizabeth Rail & Coal Co Ltd, re [1904] 1 Ch 32 *487*

Guinness v Saunders [1990] 1 All ER 652 *393, 394*

H and others, *re* [1996] 2 All ER 391 *42*

H & K Medway Ltd, Mackay *v* IRC [1997] 2 All ER 321 *515*

HR Harmer Ltd, *re* [1958] 3 All ER 689 *326, 330*

HR Paul & Son Ltd, *re* (1973) *The Times*, 17 November *473*

Hackney Pavilion Ltd, *re* [1924] 1 Ch 276 *264, 265*

Hague *v* Dandeson (1848) 2 Exch 741 *248*

Hale *v* Waldock [2006] EWHC 364 (Ch) *334*

Halifax plc *v* Halifax Repossessions Ltd [2004] 2 BCLC 455, CA *91*

Hallet, *ex parte* National Insurance Co, *re* [1894] WN 156 *267*

Halls *v* David and Another (1989) *The Times*, 18 February *447*

Halt Garage (1964) Ltd, *re* [1982] 3 All ER 1016 *385, 637*

Hamlet International plc, *re*; Jeffrey Rogers (Imports) Ltd, *re* [1998] 95 (16) LSG 24 *517*

Harbourne Road Nominees Ltd *v* Karvaski [2011] EWHC 2214 (Ch) *338*

Harmony and Montague Tin and Copper Mining Co, Spargo's Case, *re* (1873) LR 8 Ch App 407 *271*

Harmony Care Homes Ltd, *re* [2010] BCC 358 *522*

Hawk Insurance Co Ltd [2001] All ER (D) 289 (Feb) *560*

Heald *v* O'Connor [1971] 1 All ER 1105 *191*

Hedley Byrne & Co *v* Heller & Partners [1963] 2 All ER 575 *545*

Heffer *v* Secretary of State for Trade and Industry (EAT 355/96) *363*

Hellenic and General Trust Ltd, *re* [1975] 3 All ER 382 *40, 560*

Hely-Hutchinson *v* Brayhead [1968] 1 QB 549 *145–147, 149, 393*

Henderson *v* Bank of Australasia (1890) 45 Ch D 330 *493*

Hennessy *v* National Agricultural and Industrial Development Association [1947] IR 159 *27*

Henry Head & Co Ltd *v* Ropner Holdings Ltd [1952] Ch 124 *277, 278*

Heydon's Case (1584) 3 Co Rep 7a *327*

Hickman *v* Kent or Romney March Sheepbreeders' Association [1915] 1 Ch 881 *103, 109, 111, 115, 116, 302*

Hilder *v* Dexter [1902] AC 474 *279*

Hill and Tyler (In Administration), *re* [2004] EWHC 1261 (Ch) *197*

Hillman *v* Crystal Bowl Amusements [1973] 1 All ER 379 *481*

Hindle *v* John Cotton Ltd (1919) 56 SLR 625 *401*

Hirsche *v* Sims [1894] AC 654 *243*

Hogg *v* Cramphorn [1966] 3 All ER 420 *399, 400, 401*

Hoicrest Ltd, *re* [1999] 2 BCLC 346 *256*

Holders Investment Trust, *re* [1971] 2 All ER 289 *167*

Holdsworth (Harold) & Co (Wakefield) Ltd *v* Caddies [1955] 1 All ER 725; [1955] 1 WLR 352 *36, 41*

Holmes *v* Keyes [1959] Ch 199 *118*

Home & Colonial Insurance Co, *re* [1929] All ER Rep 231 *630*

Homer District Consolidated Gold Mines Ltd, *ex parte* Smith, *re* (1888) 39 Ch D 546 *487*

Hong Kong & China Gas Co Ltd *v* Glen [1914] 1 Ch 527 *273*

Hooley, *ex parte* United Ordnance and Engineering Co Ltd, *re* [1899] 2 QB 579 *638*

Horbury Bridge Coal, Iron & Wagon Co, *re* (1879) 11 Ch D 109 *491*

House of Fraser plc *v* ACGE Investments [1987] 2 WLR 1083 *162*

Howard Smith Ltd *v* Ampol Petroleum Ltd [1974] AC 821 *400, 402*

Hughes *v* Weiss [2012] EWHC 2363 (Ch) *322*

Hunter Kane Ltd *v* Watkins [2003] EWHC 186 (Ch) *417*

Hutton *v* Scarborough Cliff Hotel Co (1865) 2 Drew & Sm 521 *154*

Hutton *v* West Cork Railway (1883) 23 Ch D 654 *384*

IRC *v* Adams and Partners Ltd [1999] 2 BCLC 730 *578*

Idessa Ltd, *re* [2012] 1 BCLC 80 *449*

Iesini *v* Westrip Holdings Ltd [2009] EWHC 2526 (Ch), [2010] BCC 420 *318, 321*

Imperial Hydropathic Hotel Co, Blackpool *v* Hampson (1882) 23 Ch D 1 *106*

In Plus Group Ltd *v* Pyke [2002] EWCA Civ 370, [2003] BCC 332 *417, 420, 421*

Indo China Steam Navigation Co, *re* [1917] 2 Ch 100 *374*

Industrial Development Consultants *v* Cooley [1972] 1 WLR 443, [1972] 2 All ER 162 *306, 413, 416, 421*

Instrumentation Electrical Services Ltd, *re* (1988) 4 BCC 301 *592*

Interedil Srl, in liquidation *v* Fallimento Interedil Srl, Intesa Gestione Crediti SpA (Case C-396/09) (CJEU 1st Chamber, 20 October 2011)

Inverdeck Ltd, *re* [1998] 2 BCLC 242 *255*

Investors Compensation Scheme Ltd *v* West Bromwich Building Society [1998] 1 BCLC 493 *136*

Irvine *v* Irvine (No 1) [2007] 1 BCLC 622 *336*

Irvine *v* Union Bank of Australia (1877) 2 App Cas 366 *142*

Isaacs *v* Chapman (1916) 32 TLR 237 *478*

Island Export Finance Ltd *v* Umunna [1986] BCLC 460 *420, 421*

Islington Metal and Plating Works, *re* [1983] 3 All ER 218 *634*

IstitutoChemioterapicoItalianoSpA and Commercial Solvents Corpn *v* EC Commission: 6/73 and 7/73 [1974] ECR 223; [1974] 1 CMLR 309 *36*

It's a Wrap (UK) Ltd (In Liquidation) *v* Gula [2005] EWHC 2015 (Ch), [2006] BCLC 634 *216*

Ivey *v* Secretary of State for Employment (1997) 565 IRLB 2 *363*

JE Cade & Son Ltd, *re* [1991] BCC 360, [1992] BCLC 213 *333, 345*

JEB Fasteners Ltd *v* Marks Bloom & Co [1983] 1 All ER 583 *527, 549*

JRRT (Investments) *v* Haycraft [1993] BCLC 401 *256*

JSF Finance & Currency Exchange Co Ltd *v* Akma Solutions Inc [2001] 2 BCLC 307 *621*

JacobusMarler Estates Ltd *v* Marler (1913) 114 LT 640n *67*

James *v* Eve (1873) LR 6 HL 335 *356*

James *v* Kent & Co Ltd [1950] 2 All ER 1099 *362*

James McNaughton Paper Group *v* Hicks Anderson [1991] 1 All ER 134 *547, 548*

Jesner *v* Jarrad (1992) *The Times*, 26 October *347*

John *v* Rees [1969] 2 All ER 274 *482*

John Smith's Tadcaster Brewery Co Ltd, *re* [1953] Ch 308, CA *162*

Johnson *v* Gore Wood & Co [2001] BCC 820, [2002] 2 AC 1 *320*

Jones *v* Bellgrove Properties [1949] 2 All ER 198 *375*

Jones *v* Lipman [1962] 1 All ER 442 *39*

Joseph Holt plc Winpar Holdings Ltd *v* Joseph Holt Group plc, *re* [2000] 97 (44), LSG 44 *571*

Jubilee Cotton Mills *v* Lewis [1924] AC 958 *78, 79*

Jupiter House Investments (Cambridge) Ltd, *re* [1985] 1 WLR 975 *177*

Kayford, *re* [1975] 1 All ER 604 *631*

Keenan Bros Ltd, *re* [1985] 1 RLM 641 *509*

Kelner *v* Baxter (1866) LR 2 CP 174 *70*

Kent Coalfields Syndicate, *re* [1898] 1 QB 754 *290*

Kenyon Swansea Ltd, *re* (1987) *The Times*, 29 April *327*

Kerr *v* Marine Products Ltd (1928) 44 TLR 292 *380*

Kerr *v* Mottram [1940] Ch 657 *482*

Kiani *v* Cooper [2010] EWHC 577 (Ch) *319–321*

King *v* Crown Energy Trading [2003] EWHC 163 (Comm), [2003] All ER (D) 133 (Feb) *627*

Kingston Cotton Mill Co, *re* [1896] 2 Ch 279 *545*

Knightsbridge Estates Trust Ltd *v* Byrne [1940] AC 613 *505*

Konamaneni v Rolls Royce Industrial Power (India) Ltd [2002] 1 WLR 1269 *323*

Kreditbank Cassel v Schenkers Ltd [1927] 1 KB 826 *148*

Kripps v Touche Ross (1992) 94 DLR (4th) 284 *209*

Kudos Glass Ltd (in liquidation), *re* [2001] 1 BCLC 390 *582*

Kushler, *re* [1943] 2 All ER 22 *522, 637*

Lagunas Nitrate Co v Schroeder (1901) 85 LT 22 *214*

Lander v Premier Pict Petroleum Ltd [1998] BCC 248 *387*

Lee v Chou Wen Hsian [1984] 1 WLR 1202 *435*

Lee v Lee's Air Farming Ltd [1960] 3 All ER 420 *363*

Lee (Catherine) v Lee's Air Farming Ltd [1960] 3 All ER 420 *10–11, 12*

Leeds and Hanley Theatres of Varieties Ltd, *re* [1902] 2 Ch 809 *67, 68*

Leeds Estate, Building and Investment Co v Shepherd (1887) 36 Ch D 787 *545*

Legal Costs Negotiators Ltd [1998] CLY 695 *329*

Lehman Brothers International (Europe) (in administration), *re* [2009] EWHC 2545 (Ch) *595*

Lennard's Carrying Co Ltd v Asiatic Petroleum Co Ltd [1915] AC 705 *131*

Leon v York-O-Matic [1966] 3 All ER 277 *630*

Lewis v Inland Revenue Commissioners (2000) *The Times*, 15 November *633*

Lewis's Case *see* Lundy Granite Co, Lewis's Case, *re*

Liquidator of West Mercia Safetywear Ltd v Dodd [1988] BCLC 250 *407*

Lister v Romford Ice and Cold Storage Co [1957] 1 All ER 125 *409*

Lloyd Cheyham & Co v Littlejohn & Co [1987] BCLC 303 *209, 549*

Loch v John Blackwood Ltd [1924] AC 783 *345*

Lomax Leisure Ltd, *re* [1999] 1 All ER 22 *599*

London and County Coal Co, *re* (1866) LR 3 Eq 355 *348*

London and General Bank, *re* [1895] 2 Ch 166 *544*

London Flats Ltd, *re* [1969] 2 All ER 744 *472, 474, 610*

London Sack and Bag Co Ltd v Dixon and Lugton Ltd [1943] 2 All ER 763 *110*

London School of Electronics, *re* [1985] 3 WLR 474 *312, 339, 341*

Loquitur Ltd, IRC v Richmond, *re* [2003] STC 1394 *216*

Lowry v Consolidated African Selection Trust Ltd [1940] 2 All ER 545f *279*

Lubin, Rosen & Associates [1975] 1 All ER 577 *641*

Lucania Temperance Billiard Halls (London) Ltd, *re* [1966] Ch 98 *174*

Lundy Granite Co, Lewis's Case, *re* (1872) 26 LT 673, (1870–71) LR 6 Ch App 462 *380, 386, 595*

Lyle & Scott Ltd v Scott's Trustees [1959] 2 All ER 661 *262*

MP Guimaraens and Son v Fonseca and Vosconcellos Ltd (1921) 38 RPC 388 *91*

McCarthy Surfacing, *re* [2009] BCLC 622 *336*

Macaura v Northern Assurance Co Ltd [1925] AC 619 *9, 219, 237*

McConnell v Prill [1916] 2 Ch 57 *470*

MacDougall v Gardiner (1875) 1 Ch D 13 *109, 110, 303*

McKays Case *see* MorvahConsols Tin mining Co, McKays Case, *re*

Mackenzie & Co Ltd, *re* [1916] 2 Ch 450 *469*

McLean v Secretary of State for Employment (1992) 455 IRLIB 14 *362*

MacPherson v European Strategic Bureau Ltd [2000] 2 BCLC 683, (2000) *The Times* 5 September *206, 407*

Macro (Ipswich) Ltd, *re* [1994] 2 BCLC 354 *341*

Mahoney v East Holyford Mining Co (1875) LR 7 HL 869 *143*

Manton v Brighton Corporation [1951] 2 All ER 101 *368*

Marco v Thompson [1997] 2 BCLC 626 *262*

Marini Ltd (liquidator of Marini Ltd) *v* Dickinson [2003] EWHC 334 (Ch) *216*

Marquis of Bute's Case [1892] 2 Ch 100 *409*

Menier *v* Hooper's Telegraph Works Ltd (1874) 9 Ch App 350 *306, 308*

Mercer *v* Heart of Midlothian plc 2001 SLT 945 *386*

Merrett *v* Babb [2001] QB 1174 *57*

Metropolitan Coal Consumers' Association *v* Scrimgeour [1895] 2 QB 604 *231*

Migration Services International Ltd, *in re* [2000] 1 BCLC 666 *455*

Minmar (929) Ltd *v* Khalatschi [2012] 1 BCLC 798 *592*

Mission Capital plc *v* Sinclair and Another [2008] All ER (D) 225 (Mar) *316, 317*

Mitchell *v* City of Glasgow Bank (1879) 4 App Cas 624 *29*

Mitchell *v* Hobbs (UK) Ltd *v* Mill [1996] 2 BCLC 102 *371*

Modelboard Ltd *v* Outer Box Ltd (in liquidation) [1993] BCLC 623 *513*

Mond *v* Hammond Suddards [2000] Ch 405 *633*

Moore *v* Gadd [1997] 8 LSG 27 *451*

Moorgate Mercantile Holdings, *re* [1980] 1 All ER 40 *492*

Morgan *v* Gray [1953] 1 All ER 213, [1953] Ch 83 *267, 475*

Morgan Crucible Co plc *v* Hill Samuel Bank Ltd [1991] 1 All ER 148 *548*

Morphitis *v* Bernasconi [2003] 2 BCLC 53 *445*

Morris *v* Banque Arabe et Internationale D'Investissement SA (No 2) (2000) *The Times*, 26 October *445*

Morris *v* Kanssen [1946] 1 All ER 586 *146, 149*

Morvah Consols Tin Mining Co, McKays Case, *re* (1875) 2 Ch D 1 *373*

Mosely *v* Koffyfontein Mines Ltd [1904] 2 Ch 108 *275, 506*

Moss *v* Elphick [1910] 1 KB 846 *53*

Mossmain Ltd, *re* (1986) *Financial Times*, 27 June *340*

Mourant & Co Trustees Ltd *v* Sixty (UK) Ltd [2010] BCC 82 *580*

Moxham *v* Grant [1900] 1 QB 88 *216*

Multinational Gas and Petrochemical Co *v* Multinational Gas and Petrochemical Services Ltd [1983] 2 All ER 563 *41, 311*

Mumbray *v* Lapper [2005] EWHC 1152 (Ch) *323*

Murad *v* Al-Saraj [2005] EWCA Civ 959, [2005] WTLR 1573 *421*

Musselwhite *v* C H Musselwhite & Sons Ltd [1962] Ch 964 *468*

Mutual Life Insurance Co of New York *v* Rank Organisation Ltd [1985] BCLC 11 *403*

NFU Development Trust Ltd [1973] 1 All ER 135 *557, 560, 561*

NT Gallagher Ltd, *re* [2002] EWCA Civ 404 *579*

Natal Land and Colonization Co *v* Pauline Colliery and Development Syndicate [1904] AC 120 *74*

National Motor Mail Coach Co Ltd, Clinton's Claim, *re* [1908] 2 Ch 515 *70*

Nelson *v* James Nelson & Sons Ltd [1914] 2 KB 770 *134*

Neptune (Vehicle Washing Equipment) Ltd, *re* (1995) *The Times*, 2 March *394*

Netherlands South African Rly Co Ltd *v* Fisher (1901) 18 TLR 116 *44*

New British Iron Co, *ex parte* Beckwith, *re* [1898] 1 Ch 324 *112, 116*

New Bullas Trading Ltd, *re* [1994] 1 BCLC 485 *509, 510*

New Eberhardt Co *ex parte* Menzies, *re* (1889) 43 Ch D 118 *237*

Newhart Developments Ltd *v* Co-operative Commercial Bank Ltd [1978] 2 All ER 896 *437, 438*

Norman *v* Theodore Goddard [1992] BCLC 1028 *410*

Northern Counties Securities Ltd *v* Jackson & Steeple Ltd [1974] 1 WLR 1133 *130, 131*

Northern Engineering Industries plc, *re* [1993] BCLC 1151 *173*

North-West Transportation Co Ltd *v* Beatty (1887) 12 App Cas 589 *130, 369, 412*

Nottingham General Cemetery Co, re [1955] 2 All ER 504 638

Nurcombe v Nurcombe [1985] 1 All ER 65 312

O'Neill and Another v Phillips and Others [1999] 1 WLR 1092, [1999] 2 BCLC 1, [1999] BCC 600 113, 301, 332–334, 337, 338, 339, 345, 346

Oakdale (Richmond) Ltd v National Westminster Bank plc [1997] 1 BCLC 63 509

Ocean Coal Co Ltd v Powell Duffryn Steam Coal Co Ltd [1932] 1 Ch 654 262

Oliver v Dalgleish [1963] 3 All ER 330 478

Ooregum Gold Mining Co of India v Roper [1892] AC 125 271

Ord v Belhaven Pubs Ltd [1998] 2 BCLC 447 13

Oshkosh B'Gosh Ltd v Dan Marbel Inc Ltd [1989] BCLC 507 92

Ossory Estates plc, re [1988] BCLC 213 274

Otton v Secretary of State for Employment (1995) 7 February EAT 1150/94 363

Overnight Ltd (in liquidation), re [2010] BCC 796 445

Oxford Pharmaceuticals Ltd, re [2009] EWHC 1753 (Ch), [2009] 2 BCLC 485 624

P v F Ltd [2001] NLJR 284 290

PNC Telecom plc v Thomas [2003] BCC 202 479

Pamstock Ltd, re [1994] 1 BCLC 716 441

Panorama Developments (Guildford) Ltd v Fidelis Furnishing Fabrics Ltd [1971] 3 All ER 16 147, 374

Pantone 485 Ltd, Miller v Bain, re [2002] 1 BCLC 266 412

Park House Properties Ltd, re [1997] 2 BCLC 530 441

Parke v Daily News Ltd [1962] Ch 927 406

Parker v McKenna (1874) 10 Ch App 96 421

Parkes Garage (Swadlincote) Ltd, re [1929] 1 Ch 139 522

Parry v Bartlett [2011] EWHC 3146 (Ch) 323

Patent Floor Cloth Co, re (1872) LT 467 634

Pavlides v Jensen [1956] 1 Ch 565, [1956] 2 All ER 518 305, 310, 311, 314

Payne v The Cork Co Ltd [1900] 1 Ch 308 559

Peachdart Ltd, re [1983] 3 All ER 204 514

Pearce Duff Co Ltd, re [1960] 3 All ER 222 467

Pedley v Inland Waterways Association Ltd [1977] 1 All ER 209 367, 435, 436

Peel v L & NW Railway [1907] 1 Ch 5 479

Pelling v Families Need Fathers Ltd [2002] 2 All ER 440 290

Pender v Lushington (1877) 6 Ch D 70 111, 117, 304

Penrose v Official Receiver [1996] 2 All ER 96 455

Percival v Wright [1902] 2 Ch 421 280, 281, 403, 404

Peskin v Anderson [2001] 1 BCLC 372 404

Peso Silver Mines Ltd (NPL) v Cropper (1966) 58 DLR (2d) 1 415

Peveril Gold Mines Ltd, Re [1898] 1 Ch 122 104

Philip Morris Products Inc v Rothmans International Enterprises Ltd (No 2) (2000) The Times, 10 August 569

Phillips v Manufacturers' Securities Ltd (1917) 116 LT 290 129

Phoenix Contracts (Leicester) Ltd, re [2010] EWHC 2375 (Ch) 340

Phoenix Office Supplies Ltd, re [2003] BCC 11 337

Phonogram Ltd v Lane [1981] 3 All ER 182 70–72, 73

Platt v Platt [1999] 2 BCLC 745 404

Polly Peck International plc (in administration), re [1996] 2 All ER 433 42

Polly Peck International plc (in administration) v Henry [1999] 1 BCLC 407 602

Pool Shipping Ltd, re [1920] 1 Ch 251 265

Popely v Planarrive Ltd [1997] 1 BCLC 8, [1996] 5 CL 104 264

Portbase (Clothing) Ltd, Mond v Taylor, re [1993] 3 All ER 829 508, 515

Possfund Custodian Trustee Ltd v Victor Derek Diamond [1996] 1 WLR 1351, [1996] 2 All ER 774 228

Powdrill v Watson [1995] 2 AC 394 595, 601

Power v Sharp Investments Ltd [1993] BCC 609 520

Practice Direction (administration orders: reports) [2002] 3 All ER 95 590

Precision Dippings Ltd v Precision Dippings Marketing Ltd [1986] Ch 447, [1985] 3 WLR 812 212

Princess of Reuss v Bos (1871) LR 5 HL 176 75

Produce Marketing Consortium Ltd (No 2), in re [1989] 3 All ER 1 446, 449

Progress Property Co Ltd v Moore [2009] EWCA Civ 629, [2010] UKSC 55, [2010] 1 BCLC 1 637

Prudential Assurance Co Ltd v Chatterley-Whitfield Collieries Ltd [1949] AC 512, [1949] 1 All ER 1094 161, 177–179

Prudential Assurance Co Ltd v Newman Industries Ltd [1980] 2 All ER 841 308, 310, 367

Prudential Assurance Co Ltd v Newman Industries Ltd (No 2) [1982] Ch 204, [1982] 1 All ER 354, CA 306, 308, 312

Prudential Assurance Co Ltd v PRG Powerhouse Ltd [2007] EWHC 1002 (Ch), [2007] Bus LR 1771 581

Puddephatt v Leith [1916] 1 Ch 200 132

Punt v Symons & Co Ltd [1903] 2 Ch 506 125, 133, 134

Quin & Axtens v Salmon [1909] AC 442 103, 114, 117, 302

R v Corbin [1984] Crim LR 302 439

R v Doring (2002) 33 LS Gaz R 21 359

R v International Stock Exchange of the United Kingdom and the Republic of Ireland Ltd, ex parte Else (1982) Ltd [1993] BCLC 834, [1993] BCC 11 224

R v McCredie [2000] BCLC 438 632

R v Merchant Tailors Co (1831) 2 B & Ad 115 489

R v Panel on Takeovers [1987] 1 All ER 564 567

R v Registrar of Companies, ex parte Attorney-General [1991] BCLC 476 78

R v Registrar of Companies, ex parte Bowen [1914] 3 KB 1161 77

R v Registrar of Joint Stock Companies, ex parte More [1931] 2 KB 197 77

R v Secretary of State for the Environment, etc., ex parte Holding and Barnes plc (2001) The Times, 10 May 30

R (on the application of Steele) v Birmingham City Council [2006] 1 WLR 2380 596

R & H Electric Ltd v Haden Bill Electrical Ltd, re Haden Bill Electrical Ltd [1995] BCC 958, [1995] 2 BCLC 280 345

RA Noble (Clothing) Ltd, re [1983] BCLC 273 336, 340

Ransomesplc [1999] 2 BCLC 591, CA 171, 173, 174

Ratiu & Regent House Properties v Conway [2006] 1 All ER 571 42

Rayfield v Hands [1960] Ch 1, [1958] 2 All ER 194 110, 112, 262

Razzaq v Pala [1997] 1 WLR 1336 599

Read v Astoria Garage (Streatham) Ltd [1952] Ch 637 112, 116

Regal (Hastings) Ltd v Gulliver [1967] 2 AC 134n, [1942] 1 All ER 378 112, 414, 418, 419, 420, 421, 426, 572, 632

Regentcrestplc (in liquidation) v Cohen [2001] 2 BCLC 80, [2001] BCC 494 403, 449

Reigate v Union Manufacturing Co (Ramsbottom) [1918] 1 KB 592 610

Republic of Bolivia Exploration Syndicate Ltd [1914] 1 Ch 139 545

Revenue and Customs Commissioners v Holland [2010] UKSC 51, [2010] 1 WLR 2793 450

Revlon Inc v Cripps and Lee Ltd [1980] FSR 85 36

Rhondda Waste Disposal Ltd (in administration), re [2000] EGCS 25 599

Richmond Gate Property Co Ltd, re [1964] 3 All ER 936 380

Ridge Securities Ltd v Inland Revenue Commissioners [1964] 1 WLR 479 637

Roberts v Frolich [2011] 2 BCLC 625 *448*

Roberts and Cooper Ltd, re [1929] 2 Ch 383 *158*

Rolled Steel Products (Holdings) Ltd v British Steel Corporation [1985] 2 WLR 908 *93, 138, 143, 369, 399*

Romalpa *see* Aluminium Industrie Vaassen BV v Romalpa Aluminium

Rose v Lynx Express Ltd [2004] EWCA Civ 447 *118*

Ross v Telford [1998] 1 BCLC 82 *464*

Royal Bank of Scotland plc v Bannerman Johstone Maclay (a firm) 2003 SLT 181 *550*

Royal Bank of Scotland plc v Sandstone Properties Ltd (1998) *The Times*, 12 March *259*

Royal British Bank v Turquand (1856) 6 E & B 327 *138, 142–143, 149, 151, 152, 365*

Ruben v Great Fingall Consolidated [1906] AC 439 *138, 149, 243*

Russell v Northern Bank Development Corporation Ltd [1992] 1 WLR 588 *103, 119, 122, 125*

Russell v Wakefield Waterworks Co (1875) LR 20 Eq 474 *312*

Ryder Installations, re [1966] 1 All ER 453 *641*

Safeguard Industrial Investments Ltd v National Westminster Bank [1982] 1 All ER 449 *266*

Salmon v Quin & Axtens Ltd [1909] 1 Ch 311 *114*

Salomon v Salomon & Co Ltd [1897] AC 22 *1, 5, 6–9, 11, 13, 31, 33, 35, 36, 37, 39, 41, 42, 44, 47, 48, 67, 68, 113, 168, 273*

Saltdean Estate Co Ltd, re [1968] 1 WLR 1844 *161, 179*

Sam Weller & Sons Ltd, re [1990] Ch 682, [1989] 3 WLR 923 *215, 336*

Saul D Harrison & Sons plc, re [1995] 1 BCLC 14 *328, 333, 334*

Saunders v UK (1997) 23 EHRR 313 *457*

Savoy Hotel Ltd, re [1981] 3 All ER 646 *158, 561*

Scott v Frank F Scott (London) Ltd [1940] Ch 794, CA *117, 135*

Scottish Co-operative Wholesale Society Ltd v Meyer [1959] AC 324, [1958] 3 All ER 66 *36, 326, 328, 415*

Scottish Insurance Corporation v Wilsons and Clyde Coal Co [1949] AC 462 *159, 178*

Scotto v Petch (2001) *The Times*, 8 February *262*

Sea Fire and Life Assurance Co, Re (Greenwood's Case) (1854) 3 De G M & G 459 *4*

Seagon v Deko Marty Belgium NV (Case C–339/07) [2009] BCC 347, [2009] 1 WLR 2168 *627*

Seagull Manufacturing Co (No 2), re [1994] 2 All ER 767 *441*

Secretary of State for Business, Enterprise & Regulatory Reform v Neufeld & Anor [2009] EWCA Civ 280 *12*

Secretary of State for Employment v Wilson (1996) 550 IRLB 5 *512*

Secretary of State for Trade and Industry v Backhouse (2001) *The Times*, 23 February *13*

Secretary of State for Trade and Industry v Bottrill [1998] IRLR 120, (1999) 615 IRLB 12 *12, 364*

Secretary of State for Trade and Industry v Cleland [1997] 1 BCLC 437 *443, 444*

Secretary of State for Trade and Industry v Creegan [2002] 1 BCLC 99 *452*

Secretary of State for Trade and Industry v Deverell [2000] 2 BCLC 133 *354*

Secretary of State for Trade and Industry v Ivens [1997] BCLC 334 *442*

Secretary of State for Trade and Industry v Laing [1996] 2 BCLC 324 *354*

Secretary of State for Trade and Industry v Tjolle [1998] 1 BCLC 333 *353*

Selangor United Rubber Estates Ltd v Cradock (No 3) [1968] 1 WLR 1555 *198*

Sethi v Patel [2010] EWHC 1830 (Ch) *337*

Shackell & Co v Chorlton & Sons [1895] 1 Ch 378 *595*

Shackleford, Ford & Co v Dangerfield (1868) LR 3 CP 407 *245*

Shah v Shah [2010] EWHC 313 (Ch) *340*

Sharp v Dawes (1876) 2 QBD 26 *472*

Shaw & Sons (Salford) Ltd v Shaw [1935] 2 KB 113 *375*

Sheffield Corporation v Barclay [1905] AC 392 *259*

Shepherds Investments Ltd v Walters [2006] EWHC 836 (Ch), [2007] 2 BCLC 202 *420, 421*

Sheppard and Cooper Ltd v TSB Bank plc [1996] 2 All ER 654 *510*

Shuttleworth v Cox Brothers & Co (Maidenhead) Ltd [1927] 2 KB 9 *124, 125, 130, 134, 438*

Sidebottom v Kershaw, Leese & Co [1920] 1 Ch 154 *129, 293, 307*

Siebe Gorman & Co Ltd v Barclays Bank Ltd [1979] 2 Lloyd's Rep 142 *509, 510*

Simpson v Molson's Bank [1895] AC 270 *292*

Singer v Beckett [2007] 2 BCLC 287 *445*

Singh (Sajan) v Sardara Ali [1960] 1 All ER 269 *199*

Singla v Hedman [2010] BCC 684 *447*

Sisu Capital Fund Ltd v Tucker [2005] EWHC 2170 (Ch), [2006] BCC 463 *581*

Smith v Croft (No 2) [1988] Ch 114, [1987] 3 All ER 909 *308, 309*

Smith v Fawcett, re [1942] Ch 304, CA *260–261, 403*

Smith v Henniker-Major & Co (a firm) [2002] All ER (D) 310 (Jul) *142*

Smith v Paringa Mines Ltd [1906] 2 Ch 193 *465*

Smith (Administrator of Coslett (Contractors) Ltd) v Bridgend County Borough Council [2001] UKHL 58, [2002] 1 All ER 292 *519*

Smith, Stone and Knight Ltd v Birmingham Corporation [1939] 4 All ER 116 *43*

Société Anonyme des Anciens Etablissements Panhard et Lavassor v Panhard Levassor Motor Co Ltd [1901] 2 Ch 513 *90, 292*

Société Générale de Paris v Walker (1885) 11 App Cas 20 *292*

Southern Foundries v Shirlaw [1940] AC 701 *133–134, 371, 438*

Spargo's Case *see* Harmony and Montague Tin and Copper Mining Co, Spargo's Case, *re*

Spectrum Plus Ltd (in liquidation), *in re* [2004] NLJR 890 *509*

Spiller v Mayo (Rhodesia) Development Co (1908) Ltd [1926] WN 78 *481*

Stainer v Lee [2010] EWHC 1539 (Ch) *313, 319, 321, 322, 323*

Standard Chartered Bank v Pakistan National Shipping Co (No 2) [2003] 1 All ER 173 *411*

Staples v Eastman Photographic Materials Co [1896] 2 Ch 303 *158*

State of Wyoming Syndicate, *re* [1901] 2 Ch 431 *374, 465*

Stedman v UK (1997) 23 EHRR CD 168 *458*

Steen v Law [1963] 3 All ER 770 *199*

Steinberg v Scala (Leeds) Ltd [1923] 2 Ch 452 *288*

Stimpson v Southern Landlords Association [2009] EWHC 2072 (Ch) *316*

Structures and Computers Ltd v Ansys Inc (1997) *The Times*, 3 October *590*

Sunberry Properties Ltd v Innovate Logistics Ltd (in administration) [2009] BCC 164 *595*

Swabey v Port Darwin Gold Mining Co (1889) 1 Meg 385 *135*

Swaledale Cleaners, *re* [1968] 3 All ER 619 *255, 265*

Swedish Central Railway Co Ltd v Thompson [1925] AC 495 *97*

Sykes (Butchers) Ltd, *re* [1998] 1 BCLC 110 *353*

T & D Industries plc [2000] 1 All ER 333 *588*

TCB v Gray [1987] 3 WLR 1144 *140, 143*

TO Supplies Ltd v Jerry Creighton Ltd [1951] 1 KB 42 *98*

Tait Consibee (Oxford) Ltd v Tait [1997] 2 BCLC 349 *391*

Tate Access Floors Inc v Boswell [1991] Ch 512 *48*

TaupoTotara Timber Co Ltd v Rowe [1977] 3 All ER 123 387

Taurine Co, re (1883) 25 Ch D 118 474

Taylors Industrial Flooring Ltd v M & H Plant Hire (Manchester) Ltd [1990] BCLC 216 622

Teede and Bishop Ltd, re (1901) 70 LJ Ch 409 493

Thomas Gerrard & Son Ltd, re [1968] Ch 455 546, 547

Thomas Saunders Partnership v Harvey [1989] 30 Con LR 103 411

Thundercrest, re (1994) The Times, 2 August 469

Toshoku Finance UK plc (in liquidation), re [2002] UKHL 6, [2002] 1 WLR 671 595, 596

Towers v African Tug Co [1904] 1 Ch 558 312

Trevor v Whitworth (1887) 12 App Cas 409, HL 181, 183, 250

Trident Fashions plc, re (2004) The Times, 23 April 581

Trustor AB v Smallbone (2001) The Times, 30 March 13

Turquand's Case see Royal British Bank v Turquand

Tussaud v Tussaud (1890) 44 Ch D 678 89

Twycross v Grant (1877) 2 CPD 469 65

UK Safety Group Ltd v Heane [1998] 2 BCLC 208 360

United Provident Assurance Co Ltd, re [1910] 2 Ch 477 156

Virdi v Abbey Leisure Ltd [1990] BCLC 342 348

Walker v London Tramways Co (1879) 12 Ch D 705 125

Wall v London Northern & Assets Corporation [1898] 2 Ch 469 474

Wallersteiner v Moir [1974] 3 All ER 217 39–40

Wallersteiner v Moir (No 2) [1975] QB 373, [1975] 1 All ER 849 312, 322

Walter Symons Ltd, re [1934] Ch 308 158

Waring and Gillow Ltd v Gillow and Gillow Ltd (1916) 32 TLR 389 91

Warner International & Overseas Engineering Co Ltd v Kilburn, Brown & Co (1914) 84 LJ KB 365 230

Wealandsv ICLC Contractors Ltd [1999] 2 Lloyd's Rep 739 342

Webb v Earle (1875) LR 20 Eq 556 158

Webb, Hale & Co v Alexandria Water Co (1905) 93 LT 339 244

Weisgard v Pilkington [1996] CLY 3488 522

Welton v Saffery [1897] AC 299 104, 110, 120

West v Blanchet and Another [2000] 1 BCLC 795 331

West Canadian Collieries Ltd, re [1962] Ch 370 468

Westbourne Galleries see Ebrahimi v Westbourne Galleries

Western Intelligence Ltd v KDO Label Printing Machines Ltd [1998] BCC 472 519

Westmid Services Ltd, Secretary of State for Trade and Industry v Griffiths, re [1998] 2 All ER 124 456

Westminster Fire Officer v Glasgow Provident Investment Society (1888) 13 App Cas 699 9

Westminster Road Construction and Engineering Company Ltd (1932) unreported 546

Whaley Bridge Printing Co v Green (1880) 5 QBD 109 65

Wharfedale Brewery Co, re [1952] Ch 913 158, 159

Whitbread (Hotels) Ltd Petitioners 2002 SLT 178 618

Whitchurch Insurance Consultants Ltd, re [1993] BCLC 1359 464

White v Bristol Aeroplane Co Ltd [1953] Ch 65 124, 131, 156, 162

Wilkinson v West Coast Capital [2005] EWHC 3009 (Ch) 119, 415

Will v United Lankat Plantations Co Ltd [1914] AC 11 158, 160

William C Leitch Ltd (No 2), re [1933] Ch 261 632

William Metcalfe & Sons Ltd, *re* [1933]
Ch 142; 148 LT 82 *160*

Williams *v* Natural Life Health Foods Ltd
[1998] 2 All ER 577, (1998) *The Times*,
1 May *57, 411*

Wilson *v* Inverness Retail & Business Park
Ltd 2003 SLT 301 *323*

Wilson *v* Kelland [1910] 2 Ch 306 *514*

Windsor Steam Coal Ltd, *re* [1929]
1 Ch 151 *630*

Wood *v* Odessa Waterworks Co (1889)
42 Ch D 636 *109, 111*

Wood, Skinner and Co Ltd, *re* [1944]
Ch 323 *159*

Woodroffes (Musical Instruments,) *re*
[1985] 2 All ER 908 *510*

Woolfson *v* Strathclyde Regional Council
1978 SLT 159; (1978) 38 P & CR 521 *36,
41, 48*

Woolwich *v* Milne [2003] EWHC 414 (Ch)
340

Wragg Ltd, *re* [1897] 1 Ch 796 *272*

Yeovil Glove Co Ltd, *re* [1965] Ch 148 *521*

Yorkshire Enterprises Ltd *v* Robson
Rhodes New Law Online (1998) 17 June,
Transcript Case No 2980610103 *548*

Young *v* Ladies Imperial Club [1920] 2 KB
523 *468*

Zinotty Properties Ltd, *re* [1984] 3 All ER
754 *436*

Table of statutes

Access to Justice Act 1999 *633*
  s 6 *633*
  s 28 *633*
  Sch 2, para 1(g) *633*
  Sch 2, para 1(h) *633*
Apportionment Act 1870 *595*
Arbitration Act 1996
  s 1(b) *342*
  s 9(4) *342*

Bank of England Act 1998
  Pt 2 *682*
Bribery Act 2010 *63*
Business Names Act 1985 *55, 101*

Coal Industry Nationalisation Act 1946
  159, 177, 178, 179
  s 25 *178, 179*
Companies Act 1844 *109*
Companies Act 1862 *4, 6–8, 106*
  s 8 *154*
  s 14 *125*
  s 16 *111, 125, 172*
  s 30 *248*
  s 50 *125, 126, 154, 155*
  s 51 *125, 154*
Companies Act 1895 *4, 111*
Companies Act 1908 *4*
  s 13 *163*
Companies Act 1929 *4, 191*
  Table A *117, 260*
  Art 68 *116, 117*
Companies Act 1935 *4*
Companies Act 1948 *4, 5, 46, 47, 277*
  s 20 *122*
  s 54 *39, 199, 200*
  s 54(1) *199*
  s 72 *180*
  s 169(4) *198*
  s 190 *39*

s 199 *146*
  s 210 *45, 46, 326, 327, 328, 330, 335, 339*
Sch 1, Table A *23, 489*
Sch 1, Table A, Part I, art 106 *489*
Sch 1, Table A, Part II, arts 1, 5 *489*
Sch 1, Table A, Art 80 *131*
Sch 1, Table A, Art 127 *23, 24*
Sch 1, Table A, Art 130 *23, 24*
Companies Act 1980 *4, 47, 206, 276*
  s 75 *328, 339*
Companies Act 1981 *4, 47*
  s 42 *309, 310*
Companies Act 1985 *4, 27, 58, 59, 65, 73, 74,
    78, 88, 91, 104, 105, 106, 121, 122,
    163, 196, 197, 212, 237, 294, 324,
    329, 335, 365, 367, 372, 390, 407,
    410, 438, 478, 483, 488, 490, 491,
    492, 496, 501, 502, 514, 524, 548,
    550, 555, 556, 571, 572, 614, 630,
    662, 694*
  s 3A *88, 94, 101, 155*
  s 10 *355*
  s 14 *108, 109, 113, 237, 302, 324*
  s 15A *494*
  s 35 *95*
  s 35A *140, 141, 143, 148*
  s 36C *86*
  s 40 *241, 242*
  s 80(1) *238*
  s 80(2) *238*
  s 80(9) *238*
  s 80(10) *238*
  s 88 *240, 241*
  s 121 *97*
  s 125 *155, 163*
  s 132 *563*
  s 135 *173*
  s 137 *174*
  s 151 *197, 443*
  s 153(2) *194*

s 153(2)(a) *194*
s 153(2)(b) *194*
s 183(6) *264*
s 198 *294*
s 212 *295*
s 221 *442*
s 224(2) *532*
s 232 *382*
a 241A *384*
s 247(3) *583*
Pt VIII *161*
s 263 *217*
s 263(2)(d) *408*
s 270 *216*
s 271 *216*
s 277(1) *217*
s 285 *245*
s 309 *405*
s 317 *393, 394*
s 318 *381*
s 319 *382*
s 324(6) *294*
s 325 *294*
ss 330–342 *387*
s 330 *391*
s 331(3) *388*
s 334 *390*
s 341 *390*
s 346 *294*
s 351 *148*
s 359 *264*
s 360 *247, 248, 251*
s 366 *463*
s 367 *463*
s 368 *465*
s 369 *467*
s 371 *464*
s 373(2) *475*
s 374 *476*
s 380 *490*
s 390 *494*
s 395 *518, 519*
ss 425–427 *556*
s 425 *558, 561*
s 425(1) *556*
s 425(2) *557*
s 425(3) *557*

s 425(4) *557*
s 425(6) *556*
s 426 *557*
s 426(7) *557*
s 427 *561*
s 427(1)–(6) *557, 562*
s 427A *556*
s 428 *571*
s 429 *570*
s 429(1) *571*
s 430(2) *571*
s 437 *441*
s 447 *441*
s 448 *441*
s 450 *328*
ss 459–461 *350*
s 459 *326, 328, 332, 333, 335, 337, 343,*
     344, 345, 346, 347, 350, 351, 414
s 461 *337, 341*
s 461(1) *345*
s 461(2)(b) *337*
s 652 *618*
ss 652A–652F *614*
s 723B *59*
s 727 *216, 446*
s 739 *271*
Sch 6 *382*
Sch 7 *294*
Sch 7A *382*
Sch 15A *494*
Sch 15B *556*
Companies Act 1989 *95*
Companies Act 2006 *2, 4, 17, 18, 19, 23, 25,*
     29, 53, 56, 57, 58, 59, 60, 61, 62, 65,
     69, 73, 74, 75, 76, 77, 78, 83, 88,
     94–97, 101, 105, 106, 108, 119, 121,
     122, 140, 151, 155, 161, 175, 181,
     185, 192, 196, 200, 202, 207, 210,
     211, 214, 219, 223, 237, 245, 252,
     271, 276, 277, 278, 279, 284, 289,
     290, 294, 297, 298, 299, 301, 304,
     312, 316, 317, 324, 326, 336, 341,
     342, 348, 354, 362, 365, 367, 370,
     371, 373, 387, 395, 396, 397, 398,
     399, 406, 424, 426, 429, 432, 438,
     463, 464, 465, 467, 472, 477, 480,
     481, 483, 487, 488, 490, 491, 492,

495, 496, 498, 501, 502, 505, 514,
516, 518, 523, 528, 529, 530, 531,
532, 533, 534, 548, 550, 551, 552,
553, 555, 556, 557, 564, 565, 571,
572, 573, 576, 614, 630, 636, 637,
638, 648, 662, 664, 694

Part 1 (ss 1–6) 109
s 1(4) 489
s 2 647, 663
s 4 14
s 7 14
s 8 88, 104, 109, 163
s 8(2) 88
s 9 87, 88, 433
s 9(2) 75
s 9(2)(a) 88
s 9(2)(b) 97
s 9(3) 75
s 9(4) 75, 96, 155
s 10 75–76, 153, 155
s 10(2) 96
s 10(2)(c) 155
s 11 76
s 12 355
s 13 76
s 14 77
s 15 14, 77, 78
s 16 78
s 17 74, 88, 95, 103, 104, 110, 113, 122,
302
s 18 104
s 18(3) 104
s 20 104
s 20(2) 104
s 21 96, 105, 113, 124, 125, 156, 161
s 21(1) 119
s 22 96, 124, 126, 156
s 22(1) 126
s 22(3) 126
s 23 126
s 24 126
s 25 124
s 25(1) 126
s 26(1) 125
s 27(1) 125
s 27(4) 125
s 28 87, 109

s 28(1) 88, 95, 109, 110
Part 3, Ch 3 (ss 29, 30) 88, 104, 240, 302
s 29 103, 104, 118, 490, 491
s 29(1)(a) 104
s 29(1)(b) 104
s 29(1)(c) 104
s 30 490, 491, 492
s 30(4) 630
s 31 87, 555
s 31(1) 94
s 33 103, 108–112, 113, 115, 116, 117,
121, 125, 127, 130, 137, 203, 237,
300, 301, 302, 324
s 33(1) 88
s 39 87, 95, 96, 102, 140, 304, 500, 501,
637
s 40 96, 138, 140–144, 148, 149, 152, 500,
501, 637
s 40(1) 95, 140
s 40(2)(b) 140, 141
s 40(4) 95, 141
s 40(5) 95, 141
s 42 96
s 50(1) 241, 242
s 51 70–72, 73
s 53 88
s 54(1) 89
s 58 88
s 59 88
s 60 88
s 65 89
s 66 89
s 66(4) 89
s 77 92
s 78 23, 92
s 78(1) 92
s 79 92
s 79(1) 92
s 80 92
s 81(1) 92
s 82 88
ss 82–85 456
ss 90–96 80
s 95 81
ss 97–101 82
s 98 182
ss 102–104 83

ss 105–108 *83*

s 112 *313, 664*

s 112(1) *288*

s 113(1) *289*

s 113(2)(a) *289*

s 113(2)(b) *289*

s 113(2)(c) *289*

s 113(3) *289*

s 113(3)(b) *289*

s 113(4) *289*

s 113(5) *289*

s 113(6) *289*

s 113(7) *289*

s 113(8) *289*

s 114(1)(a) *289*

s 114(2) *289*

s 114(3) *290*

s 114(5) *290*

s 115 *2 89*

s 115(1) *289*

s 115(2) *289*

s 115(4) *289*

s 116 *290*

s 116(1)(a) *290*

s 116(1)(b) *290*

s 116(2) *290*

s 117(1)(a) *290*

s 117(1)(b) *290*

s 117(3)(a) *290*

s 117(3)(b) *290*

s 117(5) *290*

s 119(1) *290*

s 119(2) *290*

s 121 *290*

s 122(1)(g)

s 122(2) *288*

s 123 *16*

s 125 *256, 291*

s 125(2) *291*

s 125(4) *291*

s 126 *247, 248, 251, 291–293*

s 127 *290, 365*

s 130 *277, 285*

s 136(1)(a) *182*

s 136(1)(b) *182*

s 137 *182*

s 138 *182*

s 141 *182*

s 144 *182*

Part 10 (ss 154–259) *200, 353, 381*

Ch 1 (ss 154–169)

s 154 *16, 353*

s 155 *359*

s 157 *358*

s 158 *358*

s 159 *358, 439*

s 160 *25, 187, 355*

s 161 *245*

ss 162–165 *59*

s 162 *353, 365, 372*

s 163 *372*

s 165 *372*

s 167 *79*

s 168 *45, 46, 360, 361, 373, 432, 433, 434, 435, 436, 438, 471, 489, 491, 492, 494*

s 169 *366, 433, 435*

Ch 2 (ss 170–181) *398, 399*

ss 170–176 *314*

s 170 *397, 398*

s 170(1) *398*

s 170(2)(b) *422*

s 170(3) *399*

s 170(5) *354*

ss 171–177 *398, 399*

s 171 *93, 143, 188, 399*

s 172 *315, 316, 318, 319, 320, 321, 322, 323, 402, 403, 535*

s 172(1) *402, 405, 429*

s 172(1)(f) *322*

s 172(2) *402*

s 172(3) *402, 407*

s 173 *408*

s 173(1) *408*

s 173(2) *408*

s 174 *399, 408*

s 174(1) *408*

s 174(2) *408*

s 175 *398, 412–413, 416, 424, 572*

s 175(1) *412*

s 175(2) *412*

s 175(3) *412*

s 175(4) *412*

s 175(5) *412*

s 175(6) *413*
s 175(7) *413*
s 176 *398, 422*
s 176(1) *422*
s 176(2) *422*
s 176(3) *422*
s 176(4) *422*
s 176(5) *422*
s 177 *394, 413, 416, 422–423, 424*
s 177(1) *422*
s 177(2) *422*
s 177(3) *422*
s 177(4) *422*
s 177(5) *423*
s 177(6) *423*
Ch 3 (ss 182–187)
s 182 *393, 394, 423*
s 182(1) *423*
s 182(2) *423*
s 182(3) *423*
s 182(4) *423*
s 182(5) *423*
s 182(6) *423*
s 184 *422, 423*
s 185 *422, 423*
s 187 *399*
Ch 4 (ss 188–226)
ss 188–189 *362*
s 188 *362, 382*
s 188(5) *494*
s 189 *362, 382*
ss 190–196 *394*
ss 197–214 *387*
s 197 *388, 389*
s 198 *388, 389*
s 199 *388*
s 200 *388, 389*
s 201 *388, 389*
s 202 *389*
s 203 *389*
s 204 *389*
s 205 *389*
s 206 *389*
s 207(1) *389*
s 207(2) *389*
s 207(3) *389*
s 208 *389*

s 211(7) *390*
s 213 *390*
s 214 *390*
ss 215–222 *386*
s 215 *382*
s 215(2) *386*
s 217(1) *386*
s 218(1) *386*
s 219 *386*
s 220 *386*
s 221 *386*
s 223 *391*
Ch 5 (ss 227–230)
s 227 *381*
s 227(1)(a) *381*
s 227(1)(b) *381*
s 227(2) *381*
s 228 *381*
s 229 *381, 382*
s 230 *381, 382*
Ch 6 (s 231)
s 231 *17*
Ch 7 (ss 232–239)
s 232 *424, 425*
s 232(2) *425*
s 233 *424*
s 234 *425*
s 235(6) *662*
Ch 8 (ss 240–246) *60*
Ch 9 (ss 247–259)
s 248 *482, 484*
s 249 *484*
s 249(2) *484*
s 249A(1A) *22*
s 249A(1B) *22*
s 249A(1C) *22*
s 249AA *23*
s 249AA(2)(a) *23*
s 250 *353*
s 251 *354*
s 256 *388*
Part 11 (ss 260–269) *399*
Ch 1 (ss 260–264) *300, 313*
s 260 *314, 316, 319*
s 260(1) *313*
s 260(2) *313, 314*
s 260(3) *314, 319*

s 260(4) *314*
s 260(5) *313, 314*
s 261 *315, 319, 321, 322*
s 261(1) *314*
s 261(2) *314*
s 261(3) *314*
s 261(4) *314*
s 261(4)(c) *319*
s 262 *314, 315*
s 263 *315, 316, 317, 319, 321, 322*
s 263(2) *315, 317, 319*
s 263(2)(a) *318*
s 263(3) *315, 320*
s 263(3)(a)–(f) *317*
s 263(3)(a) *322*
s 263(3)(b) *316, 318*
s 263(4) *315, 320*
Part 12 (ss 270–280) *373*
s 270 *16, 373*
s 270(1) *353*
s 271 *16, 373*
s 273 *25, 373, 374*
s 274 *16, 375*
Part 13 (ss 281–361) *477*
Ch 1 (ss 281–287)
s 281 *489, 490, 491*
s 281(2) *489, 494*
s 281(3) *477, 491*
s 281(4) *489*
s 282 *477, 491, 647, 664*
s 282(2) *491*
s 282(5) *491*
s 283 *490, 648, 664*
s 283(2) *490, 494*
s 283(3) *490*
s 283(4) *490*
s 283(5) *490*
s 283(6) *490*
s 284 *28, 477*
s 285 *477*
s 285(1) *478, 479*
s 285(2) *478, 479*
s 285(5) *479*
Ch 2 (ss 288–300) *463, 489*
s 288 *493*
s 288(2) *489*
s 288(4) *494*

s 288(5) *494*
s 291 *494*
s 292 *494*
s 296 *494*
s 298 *494*
s 300 *489*
Ch 3 (ss 301–335) *483*
s 302 *465*
ss 303–305 *466, 483*
s 303 *237, 367, 436, 465, 466*
s 303(3) *432, 465*
s 303(4)(a) *466*
s 303(5)(a) *237*
s 303(6)(a) *466*
s 303(6)(b) *466*
s 304 *466*
s 304(2) *466*
s 305 *466*
s 305(2) *466*
s 305(3) *466*
s 305(6) *466*
s 305(7) *466*
s 306 *464, 465, 483*
s 306(2) *465, 466*
s 307 *467, 469, 490*
s 307(1) *490*
s 307(2) *490*
s 307(5) *467*
s 307(6) *467*
s 308 *469, 480*
s 309 *469, 480*
s 310 *468*
s 311 *469*
s 312 *471, 489*
s 312(4) *434*
s 313 *468*
s 314 *367, 435, 470*
s 314(4) *470*
s 315 *367*
s 316(1) *470*
s 316(2) *470*
s 317 *471*
s 318 *16, 17, 471, 472*
s 319 *474*
s 321 *475*
s 322 *475, 476*
s 322A *476*

s 323 *472, 481*
s 323(2) *481*
ss 324–331 *477*
ss 324–330 *479*
s 324 *28, 237, 475, 477*
s 324(1) *476, 477*
s 324(2) *478*
s 324A *480*
s 325 *470, 478*
s 326 *479*
s 327 *478*
s 327(2) *478*
s 327(2)(c) *477*
s 327(3) *478*
s 328 *479*
s 329 *475*
s 330(6)(c) *477*
s 331 *479*
s 333 *480*
s 333(1) *480*
s 333(4) *480*
s 333A *480*
s 333A(4) *480*
s 334 *472, 473, 474*
s 334(1) *483*
s 334(2)(a) *483*
s 334(2)(b) *483*
s 334(4) *483*
s 334(6) *483*
s 335 *474*
s 335(1) *483*
s 335(4) *483*
s 335(5) *483*
Ch 4 (ss 336–340B)
s 336 *463*
s 337 *470*
s 337(2) *467*
s 338 *436*
s 339 *470*
Ch 5 (ss 341–354) *476*
s 341 *476, 477*
s 342 *476*
s 343 *476*
s 344 *476*
s 347 *477*
s 348 *477*
s 349 *477*

s 351 *477*
Ch 6 (ss 355–359)
s 355 *483*
s 357 *17, 483*
s 358 *237, 483*
Ch 7 (ss 360–361)
s 360 *292, 467*
s 361 *476*
Part 15 (ss 380–474) *533, 540*
ss 381–384 *18*
s 381 *528*
ss 382–384 *527, 528*
s 382 *19*
s 382(1) *528*
s 382(2) *529*
s 382(3) *528*
s 382(5) *528*
s 382(6) *528*
s 382(7) *529*
s 383 *20, 529*
s 383(1) *529*
s 383(3) *529*
s 383(4) *529*
s 383(6) *529*
s 384 *529*
s 384(1) *529*
s 384(2) *529*
s 385 *476*
s 386 *23, 24, 442, 530*
s 386(1) *530*
s 386(2) *530*
s 386(3) *530*
s 386(4) *530*
s 387 *442*
s 387(1) *531*
s 387(3) *531*
s 388(1) *530, 531*
s 388(2) *531*
s 388(3) *531*
s 388(3)(b) *530*
s 388(4) *531*
s 388(4)(a) *531*
s 388(4)(b) *531*
s 388A *24*
ss 390–392 *527, 531*
s 390(2) *531*
s 390(3) *531*

s 391 *531*

s 391(2) *532*

s 391(4) *532*

s 391(5) *532*

s 391(6) *532*

s 392 *538*

s 392(1) *532*

s 392(2) *532*

s 393 *527*

s 393(1) *533*

s 394 *532*

ss 395–397 *214*

s 395(1) *532*

s 395(3) *532*

s 395(4) *532*

s 396 *208, 532*

s 396(1) *532*

s 396(2) *533*

s 396(3) *533*

s 396(4) *533*

s 396(5) *533*

s 397 *533*

s 399(2) *534*

s 400 *535*

s 401 *535*

s 404 *529, 534*

s 404(1) *534*

s 404(2) *534*

s 404(3) *534*

s 404(4) *533*

s 404(5) *533*

s 405 *47*

s 405(1) *535*

s 405(2) *535*

s 405(3) *535*

s 406 *534*

s 407 *535*

s 407(1) *535*

s 411 *533*

s 412 *382*

s 413 *382*

s 413(1) *533*

s 413(2) *534*

s 414 *23, 214, 527*

s 414(1) *534*

s 414(2) *534*

s 414(3) *534*

s 414(4) *534*

ss 415–419 *527*

s 415(1) *535*

s 415(4) *535*

s 416 *535*

s 416(1) *535*

s 416(3) *535*

s 417 *535*

s 417(2) *535*

s 417(3) *535*

s 417(4) *535*

s 417(5) *535*

s 417(6) *536*

s 417(7) *536*

s 417(8) *536*

s 417(10) *536*

s 417 (11) *536*

s 418 *536*

s 418(1) *536*

s 418(2) *536*

s 418(4) *536*

s 418(5) *536*

s 419(1) *536*

s 419(2) *513, 536*

Ch 6 (ss 420–422) *382*

s 420 *382*

s 421 *382*

s 421(3) *382*

s 421(4) *382*

s 422 *382*

s 422(1) *383*

s 423 *25, 537, 542*

s 423(1) *537*

s 424(2) *537*

s 424(3) *537*

s 424(4) *537*

s 425 *537*

s 426 *537*

s 426(4) *537*

s 427 *383, 537*

s 428 *537*

s 429 *537*

s 430 *384*

s 431 *25, 29*

s 433 *537*

s 433(2) *537*

s 433(3) *537*

s 433(4) *537*
s 434 *537*
s 434(3) *537*
s 435 *537*
s 435(2) *538*
s 436(2) *538*
s 437 *540*
s 438 *540*
s 439 *383, 384*
s 439(4) *383*
s 440 *384*
s 440(2) *384*
s 440(3) *384*
s 441 *537, 538, 540*
s 442(2)(a) *538*
s 442(2)(b) *538*
s 442(3) *538*
s 442(4) *538*
s 444 *538*
s 444(1) *538*
s 444(2) *538*
s 444(4) *538*
s 444(5) *18, 538*
s 444(6) *539*
s 444(7) *539*
s 445 *538*
s 445(1) *539*
s 445(2) *539*
s 445(3) *539*
s 445(5) *539*
s 445(6) *539*
s 446 *538*
s 447 *538, 539*
s 447(1) *539*
s 447(2) *539*
s 447(3) *539*
s 447(4) *539*
s 448 *29*
s 449 *538*
s 451 *540*
s 451(1) *539*
s 451(2) *540*
s 451(3) *540*
s 452 *540*
s 453 *23, 540*
s 453(3) *540*
s 463 *384*

ss 465–467 *18, 527, 529*
s 465 *19, 20, 529*
s 465(1) *530*
s 465(2) *530*
s 465(3) *530*
s 465(5) *530*
s 465(6) *530*
s 465(7) *530*
s 466 *530*
s 467(1) *530*
s 467(2) *530*
s 472(1) *533*
s 472(2) *533*
Part 16 (ss 475–539) *531, 536, 541*
s 475(1) *531*
s 475(2) *531*
s 475(3) *531*
s 476 *24, 531*
s 477 *21, 531*
s 479 *22*
s 480 *22, 23, 24, 531*
s 482 *531*
ss 485–526 *540*
s 489 *540*
s 489(2) *540*
s 489(3) *540*
s 489(4) *540, 541*
s 490 *541*
s 491 *541*
s 491(1) *541*
s 491(2) *541*
s 495 *550*
s 498(1)(c) *383*
s 498(2) *538*
s 498(3) *538*
s 502 *494*
s 506 *539*
s 510 *436, 489, 494, 541*
s 511 *471, 491, 492, 541*
s 511(3) *541*
s 511(4) *541*
s 511(5) *541*
s 511(6) *541*
s 512 *541*
s 516 *541*
s 516(3) *542*
s 517 *542*

s 518 *464*

s 519 *464, 542*

s 520 *542*

s 520(2)(a) *542*

s 520(3) *542*

s 520(4) *542*

s 520(5) *542*

s 521 *542*

s 522 *542*

s 522(5) *542*

s 523 *542*

s 523(3) *542*

Part 17 (ss 540–657) *237*

s 540 *237*

s 540(1) *237*

s 540(2) *237*

s 540(3) *237*

s 540(4)(a) *237*

s 540(4)(b) *237*

ss 549–551 *236, 238*

s 549 *238*

s 549(2) *238*

s 550 *238*

s 551 *238*

s 552 *275, 276*

s 552(3) *231*

s 553 *230, 231*

s 553(2) *230*

s 554 *240*

s 555 *240, 241*

s 555(2) *96*

s 555(3)(b) *96*

s 555(4) *96*

s 556 *241*

s 560 *190, 229*

s 561 *229, 236, 238, 239, 308*

s 561(5)(a) *229*

s 568 *239*

s 569 *239, 308*

s 570 *229, 239*

s 571 *229, 239*

s 571(7) *494*

s 573(5) *494*

Ch 5 (ss 580–592) *271*

s 580 *271, 275*

s 581 *271*

s 582 *271*

s 583 *271*

s 584 *275*

s 585 *25, 272, 273, 275*

s 586 *240*

s 587 *273, 275*

s 588 *275*

s 590 *273*

s 592 *240, 272, 275*

s 593 *81, 240, 273, 274*

s 597 *80, 240, 274*

s 598 *69, 274*

s 600 *69, 275*

s 601 *275*

s 603 *69*

s 606 *274*

s 606(1) *274*

s 610 *230, 276, 277*

ss 611–615 *277*

s 611 *278, 563*

s 611(2) *279*

s 613 *278*

s 617 *153, 165*

s 617(2)(b) *172*

ss 618–619 *166*

s 618 *165*

s 619 *165*

s 619(2) *165*

s 619(3) *165*

s 620 *237*

s 629(1) *155*

s 629(2) *155*

s 630 *124, 131, 135, 153, 155, 156, 157, 161, 163, 171, 173, 216, 217, 324*

s 630(2) *131, 163*

s 630(2)(b) *163, 173*

s 630(4) *131, 163, 173*

s 630(5) *164*

s 633 *131, 153, 164, 326*

s 633(3) *165*

s 633(4) *164*

s 635(1) *165*

Ch 10 (ss 641–653) *172, 195*

ss 641–651 *555*

s 641 *29, 166, 171, 172, 176, 555*

s 641(1)(a) *175*

s 641(1)(b) *173*

s 641(2) *173*

s 641(3) *173*
s 641(4) *176*
s 641(6) *555*
ss 642–644 *166, 173*
s 642(2) *176*
s 642(3) *176*
s 643 *175, 186*
s 643(2) *175*
s 643(3) *175*
s 643(5) *175, 176*
s 644(1) *176*
s 644(2) *176*
s 644(3) *176*
s 644(4) *176*
s 644(5) *176*
s 644(7) *176*
ss 645–651 *166, 173*
s 645 *173*
s 645(2) *174*
s 646 *171, 174, 176*
s 646(2) *174*
s 646(4) *174*
s 647 *174*
s 648(1) *174*
s 648(2) *174*
s 649 *175*
s 649(2) *175*
s 649(3) *174*
s 649(4) *175*
s 650 *175*
s 653 *174*
s 656 *25, 464*
Part 18 (ss 658–737) *181*
s 658 *171, 181*
s 658(2) *181*
s 659 *182*
s 659(1) *182*
s 660(2) *181*
s 661 *182*
s 661(4) *182*
s 662 *250*
s 669(1) *182*
s 670 *25, 182, 247*
ss 677–683 *192*
s 677 *171, 193*
s 677(1) *193*
s 677(1)(d) *193*

s 677(2) *193*
s 678 *171, 193, 194, 196, 197, 443*
s 678(1) *192*
s 678(3) *192*
s 678(4) *194*
s 680 *196*
ss 681–682 *171*
s 681 *195*
s 681(2)(a) *195*
s 681(2)(b) *195, 196*
s 681(2)(c) *195*
s 681(2)(d) *195*
s 681(2)(f) *195*
s 682(2)(a) *195*
s 682(2)(d) *196*
s 683 *193*
Ch 3 (ss 684–689) *195, 206*
s 684 *166*
s 684(1) *166*
s 684(2) *166*
s 684(3) *166*
s 684(4) *166*
s 685 *167*
s 686(1) *166*
s 686(2) *166*
s 687(2) *166*
s 687(4) *167*
s 687(5) *167*
s 688 *167*
s 689 *166, 168*
s 689(5) *168*
Ch 4 (ss 690–708) *183, 195, 206*
s 690 *183*
s 691(1) *183*
s 693(5) *183*
s 694 *171, 184*
s 694(4) *184*
s 694(5) *184*
s 695(2) *184, 185, 494*
s 695(3) *184*
s 695(4) *184*
s 696 *184*
s 696(2) *185, 494*
s 696(3) *185*
s 698(2) *494*
s 699(2) *494*
s 701 *171*

s 701(1) *183*
s 701(2)(a) *184*
s 701(2)(b) *184*
s 701(3)(a) *184*
s 701(3)(b) *184*
s 701(4) *184*
s 701(5) *184*
s 701(6) *184*
s 701(8) *184*
Ch 5 (ss 709–723) *185, 206*
s 709 *185*
s 709(2) *185*
s 710 *171, 185*
s 710(2) *185*
s 711 *185*
s 712 *185*
s 713 *185*
s 714 *185, 186, 189*
s 714(2) *185*
s 714(3)(a) *186*
s 714(3)(b) *186*
s 714(4) *186*
s 714(5) *185*
s 714(6) *186*
s 715 *186, 189*
s 716 *52, 185, 186*
s 716(1) *186*
s 717(2) *494*
s 718(2) *494*
ss 719–720 *171*
s 719 *185, 186*
s 720 *185, 186*
s 720(3) *186*
s 720(4) *186*
s 721 *171, 186, 186*
s 721(6) *182*
s 723(1) *186*
Ch 6 (ss 724–732) *189, 190*
s 724(1)(b) *189*
s 725(1) *190*
s 725(2) *190*
s 734 *187, 188*
s 734(4) *187*
s 735 *505*
s 735(2) *186*
s 735(3) *187*
s 735(4) *187*

s 735(5) *187*
s 739 *505*
s 740 *506*
s 741 *241*
ss 743–748 *503*
s 752 *504*
Part 20, Ch 1 (ss 755–760) *14*
s 759 *182*
s 761 *14, 25, 47, 138, 139, 373, 621*
s 761(4) *139*
s 762 *139, 500, 501, 622*
s 763 *139*
s 767 *47, 139*
s 767(3) *139*
Part 21 (ss 768–790)
Ch 1 (ss 768–782) *241*
s 768 *241*
s 769 *241, 258*
s 770 *241, 255*
s 771 *17, 241*
s 771(4)(b) *241*
s 774 *266*
s 775 *258*
s 778 *664*
s 779 *236, 240, 241, 243*
Ch 2 (ss 783–790) *241, 242*
s 784 *242*
s 786 *242*
Part 23 (ss 820–853) *185, 206, 214, 215*
s 829 *206*
s 830(1) *207*
s 830(2) *207*
s 831 *207*
s 831(3) *208*
s 831(5) *208*
ss 832–835 *211*
s 832(4) *208*
s 836 *214*
s 836(1) *214*
s 837 *216*
s 838 *214*
s 838(3) *214*
s 838(4) *214*
s 838(5) *214*
s 847 *215, 217*
s 847(2) *215*
s 847(3) *216*

s 853(3) *217*

Part 24 (ss 854–859) *23, 295*

s 854 *60, 295*

s 854(2) *295*

s 854(3)(b) *295*

s 855 *60, 295, 297*

s 855A *60*

s 855(1) *60*

s 856 *297*

s 856(1) *296*

s 856(2) *296*

s 856(3) *296*

s 856(4) *296*

s 856(5) *296*

s 856(6) *296*

s 857(1) *297*

s 857(2) *297*

s 858(1) *296*

s 858(2) *297*

s 858(3) *297*

s 858(4) *60, 296*

Part 25 (ss 860–894) *508*

ss 860–877 *514*

s 860 *513, 516, 518, 519*

s 861 *516*

s 866 *517*

s 867(3) *167*

s 870 *517*

s 877 *519*

s 881 *518*

s 885 *518*

s 887 *519*

s 892 *519*

Part 26 (ss 895–901) *554, 556, 578, 594, 598, 615*

s 895 *556, 558, 560, 561, 564, 575, 608, 615*

s 896 *556, 560*

s 896(2) *557*

s 897 *557*

s 898 *557*

s 899 *556, 557, 560, 561*

s 899(2) *557, 598*

s 899(4) *557*

s 900 *557, 558, 560, 561, 562, 608*

s 901 *557, 561, 598*

s 901(3) *557*

Part 27 (ss 902–941) *556, 594*

s 933 *60*

Part 28 (ss 942–992) *563*

Ch 1 (ss 942–965) *563*

ss 942–963 *566*

s 942 *563*

s 951 *567*

s 952 *567*

s 955 *567*

s 979 *570*

s 979(1)–(4) *556*

s 981 *571*

s 993 *440, 444*

ss 994–996 *68, 182, 336, 341, 342, 344, 347*

Part 30 (ss 994–999) *182*

s 994 *45, 46, 52, 116, 119, 121, 193, 215, 218, 266, 301, 312, 313, 314, 316, 317, 320, 321, 323, 325, 326, 327, 328, 329, 332, 334, 335, 336, 337, 340, 341, 342, 348, 349, 350, 395, 415*

s 994(1) *329, 342*

s 996 *320, 325, 330, 331*

s 996(1) *331, 342*

s 996(2)(a) *330*

s 996(2)(b) *330*

s 996(2)(c) *320, 330*

s 996(2)(e) *331*

ss 1000–1011 *614*

s 1000 *607, 613, 615, 618*

s 1001 *618*

s 1003 *60, 614*

s 1004 *607, 609, 615*

s 1004(1) *614*

s 1005 *607, 609, 615*

s 1006 *615*

s 1006(1) *615*

s 1009 *608*

s 1025 *618*

s 1066 *77*

s 1077 *240*

s 1078 *240*

s 1135 *483*

s 1136 *381, 483, 519*

s 1136(2) *520*

ss 1143–1148 *480, 495*

s 1144(2) *480*

s 1144(3) *480*
s 1145 *497*
s 1146 *497*
s 1159 *648, 664*
s 1168 *495, 647, 664*
s 1169 *495*
s 1173 *373*
s 1177 *382*
s 1266 *294*
s 1295 *295*
Sch 4 *78, 207, 211, 480, 495*
Sch 5 *78, 480, 495, 496*
Sch 5, Pt 4 *496*
Sch 13, Part IV, para 29 *463*
Companies (Audit, Investigations and
      Community Enterprise) Act 2004
      543
Companies (Jersey) Law 1991 *343–345*
Art 141 *343–345*
Art 143 *344, 345*
Art 143(1) *343–345*
Company Directors Disqualification Act
      1986 *5, 61, 359, 439, 440, 441, 443,
      459*
s 1 *359, 454*
s 2 *439, 440*
s 3 *440*
s 4 *440*
s 5 *440*
s 6 *359, 440, 441, 442, 455*
s 6(1)(b) *442, 453*
s 7 *440*
s 8 *441*
s 9 *440, 454*
s 10 *444*
s 11 *358*
s 15 *455*
s 17 *456*
Sch 1 *440, 441, 455*
Sch 1, Pt I *440*
Sch 1, Pt II *440*
Competition Act 1998 *558, 570*
Ch I *454*
Ch II *454*
Contracts (Rights of Third Parties) Act 1999
      70, 72, 74, 117, 237
s 6(2) *117*

Courts and Legal Services Act 1990
s 58B *633*
Criminal Justice Act 1993 *270, 279, 280,
      281, 282, 283, 404, 543, 563, 565,
      567*
Part V *279*
Sch 2 *279, 281*

Dentists Act 1878 *77*
Deregulation and Contracting Out Act 1994
s 13 *614*
Sch 5 *614*

Electronic Communications Act 2000
      694
Employment Act 1980
s 17 *41*
Employments Rights Act 1996 *361,
      512, 640*
s 98 *361*
ss 166–168 *639*
s 166 *362, 363*
ss 167–170 *512*
s 167 *512*
s 182 *363*
Enterprise Act 2002 *2, 437, 454, 511, 570,
      588, 589, 598, 599, 601, 606, 626,
      639*
s 251 *598*
Part 10 *587*
Sch 16 *588, 593*
Equality Act 2010 *361, 484*

Family Law Reform Act 1969
s 1 *289*
Financial Services and Markets Act 2000 *20,
      21, 22, 61, 65, 190, 223, 225, 228,
      229, 231, 233, 234, 281, 282, 294,
      457, 528, 530, 564, 565, 567*
Part IV (ss 40–55) *530*
Part VI (ss 72–103) *223, 502*
s 72 *223*
s 75 *223, 224*
s 76 *224*
s 77 *224*
s 78 *224*
s 79(3) *225, 227*

s 80 *226*
s 80(1) *224*
s 80(2) *224*
s 81 *225, 226*
s 82 *226*
s 83 *224*
s 85 *225*
s 85(1)–(3) *225*
s 86 *225*
s 86(1) *225*
s 88 *225*
s 89 *225, 226*
ss 89A–89G *294*
s 90 *226*
s 90(3) *226*
s 90(6) *227*
s 90(7) *227, 228*
s 91 *225*
ss 92–94 *225*
s 96A(2)(f) *294*
s 96B(1) *294*
s 96B(2) *294*
s 97 *225*
s 114(8) *283*
s 118(1) *282*
s 118(2) *282*
s 118(10) *282*
s 122 *283*
s 123(1) *282*
s 123(2) *283*
s 123(3) *282*
Part IX (ss 132–137) *224*
ss 134–136 *283*
s 174(2) *283*
s 382 *225*
s 382(1) *283*
s 382(8) *283*
s 383 *225*
s 383(1) *283*
s 383(3) *283*
s 383(10) *283*
s 384(1) *283*
s 384(6) *283*
Sch 10 *215, 226*
Sch 10, para 1 *226*
Sch 10, para 2 *226*
Sch 10, para 3 *226*

Sch 10, para 4 *226*
Sch 10, para 5 *226*
Sch 10, para 6 *226*
Sch 10, para 7 *226*
Sch 10, para 8 *226*
Sch 11A *225*

German Codetermination Act 1976 *5*

Health and Safety at Work Act 1974
439
Henry Johnson, Sons & Co., Limited Act
1996 (Ch v) (Private Act) *97*
Housing Act 1957 *41*
Human Rights Act 1998 *30, 31, 457–458*
s 6 *30, 31*

Insolvency Act 1986 *2, 5, 47, 58, 61, 348,*
438, 451, 459, 472, 492, 511, 516,
578, 586, 594, 602, 606, 609, 621,
624, 627, 637, 638, 641
Pt I *195, 562*
ss 1–7 *578*
s 6 *578*
s 6(1) *581*
s 8 *590*
s 19 *601*
s 22 *374*
s 35 *523*
s 40 *523*
s 47 *374*
s 74 *622*
s 74(3) *27*
s 76 *189*
s 77 *556*
s 77(2) *84*
s 79 *348*
s 84 *582, 628*
s 89 *627, 628*
s 91 *436*
s 95 *628*
s 103 *436*
s 110 *195, 293, 554, 556, 558, 559, 564,*
575
s 112 *407, 631, 633*
s 114 *436*
s 115 *633*

s 116 *641*

s 122 *167, 621*

s 122(1)(g) *45, 46, 79, 301, 326, 345, 357*

s 123 *621, 622, 623*

s 123(1)(e) *175*

s 124 *348, 622, 623, 641*

s 124A *584*

s 125(2) *348*

s 127 *256, 584, 624*

s 129(2) *348*

s 130 *625*

s 131 *374, 624*

s 132 *624*

s 133 *625*

s 135 *623*

s 136 *624*

s 139 *624*

s 140 *624*

s 141 *624*

s 143 *629*

s 146 *640*

s 156 *633*

s 165 *631*

s 166 *612, 631*

s 167 *406, 631*

s 175 *373*

s 176A(5) *599*

s 178 *638*

s 179 *638*

s 187 *406*

s 189 *636*

s 195 *623*

s 201 *640*

s 208 *632*

s 208(1) *632*

s 212 *68, 385, 450, 546, 547, 597, 630, 633*

s 212(3)(a) *450*

s 212(3)(b) *450*

s 213 *444, 445*

s 213(1) *445*

s 213(2) *445*

s 214 *410, 444, 445, 446, 447, 448, 450, 451, 453*

s 214(2)(b) *448*

s 216 *455*

s 217 *455*

s 237 *632*

s 238 *448*

s 239 *522*

s 241 *636*

s 245 *520, 521, 522*

s 315 *267*

s 320 *267*

s 382(1)(b) *596*

s 423 *448*

Sch B1 *513, 576, 588, 591, 592, 593, 601*

Sch B1, para 3 *587*

Sch B1, para 5 *594*

Sch B1, para 14 *588, 591, 593*

Sch B1, para 18(6) *591*

Sch B1, para 22 *592*

Sch B1, para 26 *591, 592, 593*

Sch B1, para 35 *589*

Sch B1, para 36 *589*

Sch B1, para 36(2) *589*

Sch B1, para 40 *599*

Sch B1, para 43 *599*

Sch B1, para 43(4) *516, 600*

Sch B1, para 44 *593*

Sch B1, para 49 *593*

Sch B1, para 51 *594*

Sch B1, para 52 *594*

Sch B1, para 59 *602*

Sch B1, para 59(c) *602*

Sch B1, para 65 *594*

Sch B1, para 65(2) *594*

Sch B1, para 66 *594*

Sch B1, para 68 *602*

Sch B1, para 69 *594, 601*

Sch B1, para 70 *594, 600*

Sch B1, para 71 *594, 600*

Sch B1, para 72 *594*

Sch B1, para 73 *594*

Sch B1, para 74 *597*

Sch B1, para 76 *597*

Sch B1, para 77 *597*

Sch B1, para 78 *597*

Sch B1, para 83 *598*

Sch B1, para 84 *598*

Sch B1, para 96 *598*

Sch B1, para 99 *601*

Sch B1, para 105 *592*

Sch B1, para 108(2) *594*

Sch 1 *588, 594, 594*

Sch 4, Part I 562
Sch 6 373, 511, 598, 639
Sch 6, para 11 511
Insolvency Act 2000 444, 454, 580, 583
  s 1 583
  s 4 579
  s 6 444
  Sch 1 583–586
  Sch 1, para 7 583
  Sch 1, para 8 583
  Sch 1, para 27 585
  Sch 1, para 28 585
  Sch 2 579
  Sch 2, para 5 582
  Sch 2, para 6 580
  Sch 2, para 7 580
  Sch 2, para 8 581
  Sch 2, para 10 581
  Sch 2, para 12 581
Interpretation Act 1978 118

Joint Stock Companies Act 1844 3, 4
Joint Stock Companies Act 1856 3, 4
Judgements Act 1838 627
  s 17 636

Land Compensation Act 1961 41
Law of Property Act 1925 507
  s 85(1) 508
  s 101 523
Law of Property (Miscellaneous Provisions)
    Act 1989 634, 635
  s 2(1) 72
  s 2(3) 72
Limitation Act 1980 611, 617, 634
  s 8 245
  s 9(1) 451
Limited Liability Act 1855 3, 4
Limited Liability Partnerships Act 2000 2,
    50, 51, 54, 55
  s 1 56
  s 1(1) 57
  s 1(5) 58
  s 2(1) 55
  s 2(2) 56
  s 2(3) 56
  s 3 56

s 5(1) 58
s 14 56
s 15 58
s 17 58
s 17(4) 58
s 17(5)(b) 58
Limited Partnerships Act 1907 51, 53, 54
Lotteries Act 1823 77
  s 41 77

Mental Health Act 1983 266
Mental Health Act 2007 266
Minors' Contracts Act 1987 288
Misrepresentation Act 1967 229
  s 2 67
Moneylenders Act 1927 410
Moneylenders Act 1991 410

New Zealand Workers' Compensation Act
    1922 10, 11

Partnership Act 1890 50, 51, 52, 54, 55, 58
  s 1 51
  s 24(5) 46
Pensions Act 1995
  s 47 543
  s 48 543
Pensions Act 2004 596
Protection from Harassment Act 1997 2
Public Interest Disclosure Act 1998 543
Public Trustee Act 1906 5

Royal Exchange and London Assurance
    Corporation Act 1719 (The Bubble
    Act) 4

Sale of Goods Act 1979 288
Social Security Act 1998 456
  s 64 456
Social Security and Administration Act 1982
  s 121C 456
  s 121D 456
Stannaries Act 1869 472
Statute of Frauds 1677
  s 4 112
Stock Transfer Act 1963 257
  Sch 1 256

Supply of Goods and Services Act 1982
s 13 *411*

Third Parties (Rights Against Insurers) Act
1930 *635*
Third Parties (Rights Against Insurers) Act
2010 *635*
Trade Marks Act 1994
s 25 *516*
Trade Union and Labour Relations
(Consolidation) Act 1992
s 117(1) *22*
s 224 *41*
Trustee Act 1925 *630*
s 40 *267*
s 61 *630*

Statutory Instruments

Civil Procedure Rules 1998 (SI 1998/3132
L.17) *91, 98, 314*
Companies (Acquisition of Own Shares)
(Treasury Shares) Regulations 2003
(SI 2003/1116) *189*
Companies Act 1985 (Electronic
Communications) Order 2000 (SI
2000/3373) *462, 492*
Companies Act 1985 (International
Accounting Standards and Other
Accounting Amendments)
Regulations 2004 (SI 2004/2947)
530
Art 4 *534*
Companies Act 2006 (Annual Return and
Service Addresses) Regulations
2008 (SI 2008/3000) *528*
Companies Act 2006 (Commencement
No 5, Transitional Provisions and
Savings) Order 2007 (SI 2007/3495)
556
Sch 5, para 2(5) *491*
Companies (Company Records) Regulations
2008 (SI 2008/3006) *520*
Companies Consolidation (Consequential
Provisions) (Northern Ireland)
Order 1986 (SI 1986/1035) (NI 9)
618

Companies (Cross-Border Mergers)
Regulations 2007 (SI 2007/2974)
59
Companies (Model Articles) Regulations
2008 (SI 2008/3229) *23, 25, 58, 62,
75, 104–106, 118, 121, 122, 144,
353, 359, 368, 380, 385, 473, 480,
647–693*
Sch 1 (Private Companies Limited by
Shares) *432, 433, 484, 485, 647*
Part 1 *647*
Arts 1–2 *105, 647, 648*
Part 2 *648*
Arts 3–6 *105*
Art 3 *106, 365, 367, 648*
Art 4 *106, 648*
Art 4(1) *106*
Art 4(2) *106*
Art 5 *368, 371, 648*
Art 6 *649*
Arts 7–16 *105*
Art 7 *17, 484, 649*
Art 8 *484, 649*
Art 9 *484, 649*
Art 10 *485, 650*
Art 11 *368, 485, 650*
Art 12 *370, 485, 650*
Art 13 *485, 650*
Art 14 *381, 485, 650, 651*
Art 15 *485, 651*
Art 16 *485, 651*
Arts 17–20 *105*
Art 17 *356, 439, 651, 652*
Art 18 *652*
Art 19 *371, 379, 652*
Art 20 *379, 652, 653*
Part 3 *653*
Arts 21–29 *105*
Art 21 *653*
Art 22 *653*
Art 23 *653*
Art 24 *241, 653*
Art 25 *654*
Art 26 *654*
Art 26(5) *17*
Art 27 *654*
Art 28 *654, 655*

Art 29 *655*
Arts 30–35 *105*
Art 30 *213, 214, 655*
Art 31 *480, 655, 656*
Art 32 *480, 656*
Art 33 *656*
Art 34 *656*
Art 35 *657*
Art 36 *105, 657*
Part 4 *658*
Arts 37–47 *105*
Art 37 *658*
Art 38 *473, 658*
Art 39 *658*
Art 40 *658, 659*
Art 41 *659*
Art 41(5) *482*
Art 42 *659*
Art 43 *659*
Art 44 *660*
Art 45 *647, 660*
Art 45(3) *478*
Art 46 *660, 661*
Art 47 *661*
Part 5 *661*
Arts 48–51 *105*
Art 48 *661*
Art 49 *662*
Art 50 *662*
Art 51 *662*
Arts 52–53 *105*
Art 52 *662*
Art 53 *663*
Sch 2 (Private Companies Limited by
    Guarantee) *484, 485*
Art 7 *484*
Art 8 *484*
Art 9 *484*
Art 10 *485*
Art 11 *485*
Art 12 *485*
Art 13 *485*
Art 14 *381, 485*
Art 15 *485*
Art 16 *485*
Art 19 *379*
Art 20 *379*

Sch 3 (Public Companies) *358, 433, 485*
Part 1 *663*
Art 1 *663, 664*
Art 2 *664*
Part 2 *665*
Art 3 *365, 367, 665*
Art 4 *665*
Art 5 *368, 371, 665*
Art 6 *665*
Art 7 *665*
Art 8 *666*
Art 9 *666*
Art 10 *666*
Art 11 *368, 666*
Art 12 *370, 486, 663, 667*
Art 13 *667*
Art 14 *667*
Art 15 *486, 667*
Art 16 *486, 667, 668*
Art 17 *486, 668*
Art 18 *486, 668, 669*
Art 19 *381, 669*
Art 20 *356, 669*
Art 21 *669*
Art 22 *669*
Art 23 *371, 379, 670*
Art 24 *379, 670*
Art 25 *663, 670*
Art 26 *670, 671*
Art 27 *671*
Part 3 *671*
Art 28 *671*
Art 29 *671, 672*
Art 30 *473, 672*
Art 31 *663, 672*
Art 32 *672*
Art 33 *672, 673*
Art 33(5) *482*
Art 34 *673*
Art 35 *673*
Art 36 *673, 674*
Art 37 *674*
Art 38 *664, 674, 675*
Art 39 *675*
Art 40 *675, 676*
Art 41 *676*
Art 42 *676*

Part 4 *676*
Art 43 *676*
Art 44 *676*
Art 45 *480, 677*
Art 46 *480, 677*
Art 47 *241, 664, 677*
Art 48 *677, 678*
Art 49 *678*
Art 50 *678, 679*
Art 51 *243, 679, 680*
Art 52 *663, 680*
Art 53 *664, 680, 681*
Arts 54–62 *245*
Art 54 *663, 681*
Art 55 *682*
Art 56 *682*
Art 57 *682*
Arts 58–62 *245*
Art 58 *683*
Art 59 *249, 683*
Art 60 *249, 683*
Art 61 *684*
Art 61(3) *249*
Art 62 *250, 684*
Art 63 *684, 685*
Art 64 *685*
Art 65 *685*
Art 66 *685*
Art 67 *685, 686*
Art 68 *686*
Art 69 *213, 214, 686*
Art 70 *686, 687*
Art 71 *687*
Art 72 *687, 688*
Art 73 *688*
Art 74 *688*
Art 75 *688*
Art 76 *688, 689*
Art 77 *689*
Art 78 *689, 692*
Part 5 *690*
Art 79 *690*
Art 80 *690*
Art 81 *691*
Art 82 *691, 692*
Art 83 *692*
Art 84 *692*

Art 85 *692*
Art 86 *692, 693*
Companies (Share Capital and Acquisition by Company of its Own Shares) Regulations 2009 (SI 2009/2022)
Reg 2 *238*
Companies (Shareholders' Rights) Regulations 2009 (SI 2009/1632) *491*
Companies (Tables A–F) Regulations 1985 (SI 1985/805) *694–712*
Sch 1, Table A *23, 25, 58, 104–106, 144, 212, 213, 214, 215, 217, 218, 241, 243, 244, 245, 248, 249, 250, 255, 353, 356, 357, 358, 359, 360, 365, 366, 368, 370, 371, 373, 375, 379, 380, 381, 385, 394, 432, 438, 439, 463, 468, 469, 470, 474, 475, 476, 478, 481, 482, 486, 487, 488, 489, 491, 501, 524, 694–712*
Art 1 *105*
Arts 2–35 *105*
Arts 36–63 *105*
Arts 64–98 *105*
Art 70 *106, 359, 367*
Art 72 *371*
Art 79 *433*
Arts 99–101 *105*
Arts 102–110 *105*
Arts 111–116 *105*
Art 1 *694*
Art 2 *434, 694*
Art 3 *695*
Art 4 *695*
Art 5 *247, 695*
Art 6 *695*
Art 7 *695*
Art 8 *695*
Art 9 *695*
Art 10 *695*
Art 11 *696*
Art 12 *696*
Art 13 *696*
Art 14 *696*
Art 15 *696*
Art 16 *696*
Art 17 *696*
Art 18 *696*

Art 19 *696*

Arts 20–22 *245*

Art 20 *696, 697*

Art 21 *697*

Art 22 *697*

Art 23 *697*

Art 24 *266, 697*

Art 25 *697*

Art 26 *697*

Art 27 *697*

Art 28 *697*

Art 29 *698*

Art 30 *266, 267, 698*

Art 31 *266, 698*

Art 32 *698*

Art 33 *698*

Art 34 *698*

Art 35 *699*

Art 36 *463*

Art 37 *463, 699*

Art 38 *699*

Art 39 *699*

Art 40 *473, 699*

Art 41 *699*

Art 42 *700*

Art 43 *700*

Art 44 *700*

Art 45 *700*

Art 46 *700*

Art 47 *700*

Art 48 *700*

Art 49 *700*

Art 51 *700, 701*

Art 52 *701*

Art 54 *476, 701*

Art 55 *701*

Art 56 *701*

Art 57 *701*

Art 58 *701*

Art 59 *701*

Art 60 *479, 701, 702*

Art 61 *702*

Art 62 *479, 702, 703*

Art 63 *703*

Art 64 *703*

Art 65 *703*

Art 66 *703*

Art 67 *703*

Art 68 *703*

Art 69 *703*

Art 70 *365, 379, 703, 704*

Art 71 *704*

Art 72 *474, 704*

Art 73 *704*

Art 74 *704*

Art 75 *704*

Art 76 *704*

Art 77 *705*

Art 78 *356, 705*

Art 79 *705*

Art 80 *705*

Art 81 *705*

Art 82 *385, 706*

Art 83 *706*

Arts 84–86 *706*

Art 87 *707*

Arts 88–98 *487*

Art 88 *707*

Arts 89–93 *707*

Arts 94–99 *708*

Arts 100–105 *709*

Art 102 *215*

Art 106 *709, 710*

Arts 107–110 *710*

Art 111–116 *711*

Art 115 *469*

Art 117 *711, 712*

Art 118 *712*

Companies (Table A to F) (Amendment) Regulations 2007 (SI 2007/2541) *694*

Companies (Table A to F) (Amendment) (No 2) Regulations 2007 (SI 2007/2826) *694*

Companies (Trading Disclosure) Regulations 2008 (SI 2008/495) *520*

Directors' Remuneration Report Regulations 2002 (SI 2002/1986) *383*

Employment Rights (Increase of Limits) Order 2008 (SI 2012/3007) *364*

European Public Limited-Liability Company Regulations 2004 (SI 2004/2326) *29*

Financial Services and Markets Act 2000 (Regulated Activities) (Amendment) (No 3) Order 2003 (SI 2003/2822) *190*

Fixed-Term Employees (Prevention of Less Favourable Treatment) Regulations 2002 (SI 2002/2034) *360*

Information and Consultation of Employees Regulations 2004 (SI 2004/3462) *29–30*

Insolvency Act 1986 (Amendment) (No 2) Regulations 2002 (SI 2002/1240) *100, 626*

Insolvency Act 1986 (Prescribed Part) Order 2003 (SI 2003/2097) *598*

Insolvency (Amendment) Rules 2002 (SI 2002/1307) *626*

Insolvency (Amendment) Rules 2010 (SI 2010/686) *587, 630*

Insolvency Rules 1986 (SI 1986/1925) *478, 595, 634*
   rule 2.2 *589, 590*
   rule 2.20(2) *593*
   rule 2.67(1)(a) *595*
   rule 2.67(1)(f) *595*
   rule 4.218(1)(a) *595*
   rule 7.31 *590*
   rule 7.31(4) *317*
   rule 7.31(5) *590*
   rule 8.1(3) *478*
   rule 8.2(3) *479*
   rule 133.12(1)(a), (b) *596*

Judgment Debts Rate of Interest Order 1993 (SI 1993/564) *636*

Large and Medium-sized Companies and Groups (Accounts and Reports) Regulations 2008 (SI 2008/410) *528*
   Sch 8 *383*
   Sch 8, Pt 3 *383*

Large and Medium-sized Limited Liability Partnerships (Accounts) Regulations 2008 (SI 2008/1913) *58*

Limited Liability Partnerships Regulations 2001 (SI 2001/1090) *58, 59*

Reg 7 *3, 46*

Reg 8 *3*

Limited Liability Partnerships (Accounts and Audit) (Application of Companies Act 2006) Regulations 2008 (SI 2008/1911) *58*

Limited Liability Partnerships (Application of Companies Act 2006) Regulations 2009 (SI 2009/1804) *3, 50, 58–61*
   Part 5, Ch 1 *59*
   Part 5, Ch 2 (reg 19) *59, 60*
   Part 8 *60*
   Part 11 (reg 47) *60*
   Part 12 (regs 48, 49) *60*
   reg 48 *60, 61*
   Part 13 *60*
   Sch 3, para 7(3) *58*

Partnerships (Accounts) Regulations 2008 (SI 2008/569) *528*

Prospectus Regulations 2005 (SI 2005/1433) *228*
   Sch 1, para 4 *224*

Public Offers of Securities Regulations 1995 (SI 1995/1537) *228, 502*

Regulatory Reform (Removal of 20 Member Limit in Partnerships) Order 2002 (SI 2002/3203) *52*

Rules of the Supreme Court (SI 2009/1603) *54, 247*
   Ord 14a *39*
   Ord 18, r 9 *309*
   Ord 18, r 19 *309*
   Ord 33, r 3 *309*
   Ord 45, r 5(1) *131*
   Part 73 *247*

Small Companies and Groups (Accounts and Directors' Report) Regulations 2008 (SI 2008/409) *528, 534*

Small Limited Liability Partnerships (Accounts) Regulations 2008 (SI 2008/1912) *58*

Supply of Services (Exclusion of Implied Terms) Order 1982 (SI 1982/1771) *411*

Uncertificated Securities Regulations 2001
 (SI 2001/3755) *257, 258*
Unregistered Companies Regulations 2009
 (SI 2009/2436) *563*

EU Legislation

Coventions and Treaties

European Convention on the Protection of
 Human Rights and Fundamental
 Freedoms 1950 *30, 31, 99, 282,
 457–458*
 Art 6 *30, 457–458*
 Art 8 *458*
 Art 9 *458*
 Art 10 *458*
 Art 14 *458*

Treaties of the European Union
 Art 81 *454, 509*
 Art 82 *454, 509*
 Art 189 *71*
Treaty of Utrecht 13 July 1713 *3*
Treaty on European Union
 Art 52 *201*
 Art 58 *201*

Directives

Fifth Company Law Directive (2001/86/
 EC) *5*
First Council Directive (68/151/EEC) *71*

Ninth Company Law Directive *43*

Second Council Directive (77/91/EC)
 Art 15 *217*
 Art 16 *217*

Takeover Bids Directive (2004/25/EC) *563,
 564, 566, 576*
Transparency Directive (2004/109/EC) *223,
 294–295*
 Art 9(1) *294*

Prospectus Directive (2003/71/EC)
 231–233

Regulations

Insolvency Proceedings Regulation
 1346/2000/EC *98, 625, 626, 627*
 Art 3 *98, 99*
 Art 3(1) *99*
 Art 3(2) *100*
 Art 16 *98, 99*
 Art 26 *98, 99*
Judgments Regulations 44/2001/EC *627*
 Art 1(2)(b) *627*
Statute of a European Company Regulation
 2157/2001/EC *5, 29*

Miscellaneous

City Code on Takeovers and Mergers *190,
 191, 554, 563, 564–569, 571–573,
 575, 576*
 Rule 2 *567, 568*
 Rule 2.5(c) *569*
 Rule 4 *567, 568*
 Rule 6.2 *572*
 Rule 7.1 *572*
 Rule 8.1 *572*
 Rule 9 *568*
 Rule 9.7 *569*
 Rule 21 *565, 566*
 Section J *564, 568*
 Rules 23–27 *564, 568*
 Rule 23 *564, 568*
 Rule 24.2 *564*
 Rule 26 *573*
 Rule 36 *568*
 Rule 36.1 *568*
 Rule 36.5 *568*
 Rule 36.8 *568*
 Appendix 7 *573*
 Code Rules *564*
 General Principles *564*
 Principle 7 *565, 566*
Corporate Governance Code (FRC, June
 2010) *381*

Disclosure and Transparency Rules *223, 294*
 DTR 3.1.2 *294*
 DTR 3.1.3 *294*
 DTR 3.1.4 *294*

DTR 5 *295*
DTR 5.8.3 *295*

Financial Services Authority Handbook of
    Rules *233*
Pt VI *223*
Disclosure Rules *223, 233*
Listing Rules *190, 215, 223, 224, 225, 226,
    230, 231, 232, 233, 239, 283, 284,
    405*
    LR 2.2.7R *224*
    LR 2.2.8G *224*
    LR 5 *223*
    LR 6.1.19R *223*
    LR 9.3.11R *229*
    LR 9.3.12R *229*

LR 9.8.8R *381*
LR 13.8.2R *229*
LR 14.2.2R *223*
Model Code for Securities Transactions
    by Directors (CBI) *190, 283, 284,
    405*
Prospectus Rules *224, 225, 233*
    r 1.2.2 *225*
    r 1.2.3 *225*

International Accounting Standards (IAS)
    529, 530, 532, 533, 538
IAS 36 *278*

Rules Governing Substantial Acquisitions of
    Shares (SARs) *564*

1 The nature of a company

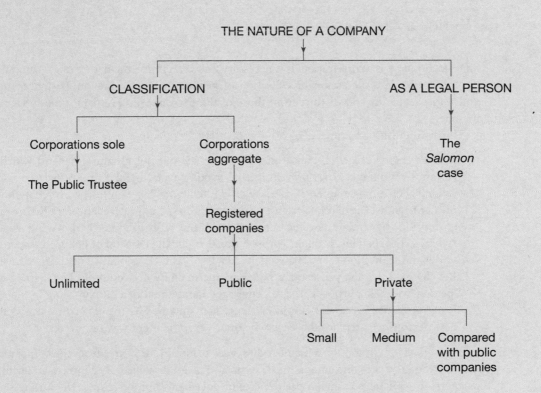

T his text is concerned almost entirely with the law relating to registered companies which, in turn, are governed in the main by the Companies Act 2006 and relevant case law. Section references have been cut to a minimum, but those that do appear relate to the Companies Act 2006 unless otherwise indicated.

As regards corporate insolvency, section references are to the Insolvency Act 1986. Here, again, a number of the sections quoted were not in the original Act but have been inserted by subsequent statutory instruments and, in particular, by the Enterprise Act 2002. Furthermore, where a case is quoted and its date is before the company legislation that it illustrates, it was decided on identical (or similar) legislation which is now consolidated into the 2006 Act. This is why a case decided in 1936 can still be used to illustrate a provision in the 2006 Act.

General features

Since a company is a corporation, it is necessary first to examine the nature of a corporation. A corporation is a succession or collection of persons having at law an existence, rights and duties, separate and distinct from those of the persons who are from time to time its members.

The distinguishing features of a corporation are:

(a) It is a persona at law (i.e. an artificial legal entity and not a natural person) which in certain circumstances may prevent it from making a successful claim for harm inflicted upon it. For instance, in *DPP* v *Dziurzynski* (2002) *The Times*, 8 July, a prosecution was brought against D, an animal-rights protestor, for harassing a company (B & K Universal Group Ltd) by filming its vehicles going in and out of its premises and making abusive remarks. The company brought a prosecution through the Director of Public Prosecutions under the Protection from Harassment Act 1997. The Divisional Court of the Queen's Bench ruled that the prosecution failed because a company could not be regarded as a 'person' for these purposes. The Act envisaged harassment of a human being.

(b) It has perpetual succession, i.e. its existence is maintained by the constant succession of new persons who replace those who die or are in some other way removed.

This means that even though a member dies, goes bankrupt, or retires from the company by transferring his shares, the company carries on and is not dissolved. By contrast, an ordinary partnership is dissolved when a partner dies or goes bankrupt, or retires. The business will usually continue under the remaining partners but the retiring partner is entitled, subject to what the partnership agreement says, to be paid his share in the firm. The executor of a deceased partner and the trustee in bankruptcy of a bankrupt partner are also entitled to payment of the relevant share.

This results in a return of capital in a partnership and can effect some dislocation of the business, but although this can be reduced by clauses in the articles of partnership, e.g. deferred payment, the problem cannot be totally eliminated, and provision must be made. The same does not happen in companies. A retiring shareholder must find a purchaser for the shares, as must the executors and trustee in bankruptcy. A company can purchase its own shares but is not forced to do so.

A limited liability partnership (LLP) registered under the Limited Liability Partnerships Act 2000 is more like a company than an ordinary partnership in that it has a separate existence at law, i.e. is a persona at law with its own property and liabilities separate from its members (not partners). The retirement of a member, therefore, will not effect a dissolution of the LLP but there may be problems in terms of the repayment of the retiring member's capital. It is important, therefore, that the members of the LLP make an effective and valid agreement between themselves before the LLP is registered and incorporated. That failing, the default provisions of the Limited Liability Partnerships Regulations 2009 (SI 2009/1804) apply under which all members of an LLP are entitled to share equally in the capital and profits of the firm, and in the absence of a special member agreement would be entitled to the return of it on retirement. The members of an LLP do not hold saleable shares in the LLP and the procedure for the retirement of members and the admission of new members should appear in the pre-registration agreement, otherwise the retirement of a member and the admission of a member take place 'in accordance with any agreement made in a particular case with the other members of the LLP'. (Partnerships and LLPs will be discussed in greater depth within Chapter 3. ◑)

Background to limited liability

Company law in its modern form may be traced back to the mid-nineteenth century and the enactment of the Limited Liability Act and Joint Stock Companies Acts. However, an array of business associations developed long before this time, among which was the common law construct of the partnerships. However, as England sought to expand its international trade activities across the globe, the government sought to create corporations under Royal Charters and Acts of Parliament, granting monopolies over specified territories; the best known example being the East India Company.

A similar chartered company, the South Sea Company, was established in 1711 in order to undertake trade with the Spanish South American colonies. However, it met with far less success than the British East India Company. The South Sea Company's monopoly rights were based on the Treaty of Utrecht which purported to grant the United Kingdom an *assiento* to trade in the region for thirty years. In reality the company was unable to undertake extensive business, though such problems did not permeate back to the UK for quite some time and, in the interim period, investors were encouraged to purchase large quantities of shares based on extravagant promises of profit. Consequently, as it was undertaking little actual business, the South Sea Company became extremely rich on the basis of shareholder investment.

Following the company's agreement to take on a considerable proportion of the UK's public debt in 1717, share prices continued to rise so rapidly that people began buying them merely in order to sell such shares later at a higher price. (This new breed of investors who traded in shares were called the 'stockjobbers' and were based around the coffee houses of Exchange Alley.) Shares were also sold to politicians, enabling the company to publicise a growing list of elite stockholders, further enhancing the legitimacy of its claims of lucrative trade and, in turn, speculative investment. On 21 January 1720, an announcement was made that the company would take over the entire national debt, taking on annuities of around £30 million. (Given the current global financial crisis in 2010, it is worth noting the creative solution that the government sought to use in the 1700s – using the South Sea Company as a means of reducing the cost of servicing the public debt by converting government annuities into lower-yielding shares.)

The 'South Sea bubble' was, in essence, the first speculative bubble that the UK had experienced. However, by late 1720 the bubble had 'burst' resulting in the company's share price falling from around £1,000 to less than £100. Inevitably, this burst led to widespread bankruptcies and, more importantly, impacted directly on members of the government and political classes of the country which, in turn, led to calls for greater control and regulation of companies and their directors. The estates of the company's directors were confiscated and used to offset some of the losses suffered by investors while the South Sea Company's stock was divided between the Bank of England and the East India Company; in essence, the government nationalised the company in order to protect the financial system.

The prohibition on establishing joint-stock companies with a Royal Charter set down in the Bubble Act (also known as the Royal Exchange and London Assurance Corporation Act 1719), remained in force until 1825. By this stage the Industrial Revolution had gathered momentum and, with it, a growing sense that the time was right for legal change to be effected in order to facilitate business activity. Restrictions were gradually lifted on ordinary people being permitted to incorporate businesses. However, little success was enjoyed until 1843 when William Gladstone took chairmanship of a Parliamentary Committee on Joint Stock Companies; the resultant piece of legislation being the Joint Stock Companies Act 1844.

The Joint Stock Companies Act 1844 first introduced the possibility of incorporation of companies via registration. Due to the fact that the concept of 'limited liability' remained rather a contentious issue that ran contrary to the established business practice of the time (i.e. that an individual – e.g. merchant, trader, etc. – should be personally liable for debts incurred in the course of his/her business), the Joint Stock Companies Act 1844 imposed a form of direct and unlimited liability for debts (*Re Sea Fire and Life Assurance Co, Greenwood's Case* (1854) 3 De G M & G 459).

However, the debate as to whether limited liability ran contrary to accepted business practice designed to maintain certain standards of behaviour in society or that many members in such joint-stock companies were simply passive investors who sought no active involvement in the day-to-day running of the business (and as such should not be held accountable for any resultant debts accrued) continued, fuelled by the needs of the Industrial Revolution. The growing sense was that in order to attract capital from private investors into the hands of industrialists and/or entrepreneurs, and as such fuel the growing economy, a certain level of protection needed to be provided to these people. The Limited Liability Act 1855 marked the pivotal moment in this debate, allowing any registered company with at least 25 members to limit the liability of its members to the amounts unpaid on their shares. However, as a warning to those external to the company seeking to undertake business with it, such companies were required to place 'limited' as the last word of its name.

The Joint Stock Companies Act 1856 subsequently reduced the minimum number of members to seven. The Act also provided for the fact that the liability of members of a registered company should only be to the company and not directly to the creditors of the company. However, the 1856 Act is significant in terms of bringing together the concepts of a simple registration process coupled with limited liability in the form of the world's first modern company law legislation. All subsequent Companies Acts, even the Companies Act 2006, have sought to retain these same fundamental principles.

It is worth noting that while this new concept of limited liability encouraged private investors to invest capital into companies in which they would not undertake any active management roles, the legislation did not specify that such companies were expected to have investors who did not take part in the day-to-day running of the company. As such, the opportunity for groups of investors, who were also the managers of the company, to adopt the limited liability format began to be increasingly pursued by the late 1800s. This, in turn, gave rise to the growth of quasi-partnership companies (discussed in greater depth within Chapters 5 and 6 ●) as well as one of the leading cases in Company Law – *Salomon* v *Salomon& Co Ltd* [1897] AC 22.

The growth of the corporate form and its subsequent dominance as the preferred organisational form have led to ongoing concerns regarding the accountability of managers to shareholders and attempts to reform this area of the law, even up to the present day. For example, following the Great Depression the Companies Act 1948 sought to provide greater 'shareholder democracy' within companies by ensuring that a number of member-authorisations were introduced alongside the ability of shareholders to remove directors via a simple majority vote. However, such procedures have come at the expense of time and money in compliance with such procedures. The UK government's Bullock Report published in 1977 proposed further reform in the shape of allowing employees to participate in the selection process for a company's board of directors, as exemplified by the German Codetermination Act 1976. Under this system there is a two-tier management structure (consisting of a managerial/executive board and a supervisory board), the former being responsible for the day-to-day management of the company and the latter overseeing the executive board – and having the power of appointment and removal of its personnel. (In most German public companies around one-third of the supervisory board's membership is elected by the employees of the company, with the remaining two-thirds being appointed by the shareholders.) However, the UK never implemented these reforms, driven in part by the UK's limited concern for the interests of employees. (It should be noted that the Draft Fifth EU Directive on Company Law would have introduced this two-tier model for all public companies of EU member states. However, this proposal was resisted by a number of governments, with the introduction of the Societas Europaea being the compromise position. See: Regulation (EC) 2157/2001.)

The Cork Report subsequently sought to curtail the actions of directors who negligently ran companies at a loss, resulting in the Insolvency Act 1986 and the Company Directors Disqualification Act 1986. More recently, the focus of reform has been upon internal control mechanisms (e.g. auditing processes, remuneration committees, etc.).

Classification of corporations – the company as a corporation

The main classification is between corporations sole and aggregate.

Corporation sole

A corporation may be a corporation sole (i.e. it may consist of only one member at a time holding a perpetual office). Here the office is personified to distinguish it from the person who is from time to time the holder of it.

The concept has little commercial application but a useful and practical example is provided by the Public Trustee which is a corporation sole created by the Public Trustee Act 1906. The Public Trustee is a civil servant who, while in post, is the sole member of the corporation. The corporation is trustee of much property and it would be inconvenient if all the trusts had to be transferred into the ownership of the new holder of the office every time there was a change. The office of Public Trustee, therefore, was personified as a corporation sole and the trust property is vested in the corporation and is not affected when the human holder of the office changes.

The role of Public Trustee has now been assumed by the Official Solicitor and the Public Trust Office no longer exists. The posts of Official Solicitor and Public Trustee are held by the same person, although some types of work can only be accepted by that person in the role of Public Trustee, and other types of work only in the role of Official Solicitor. The Office of the Official Solicitor and Public Trustee handles relevant business.

Corporation aggregate

A corporation aggregate consists of a number of persons so associated that in law they form a single person, e.g. a registered company. Here the undertaking is personified so that it may be distinguished from its members. A registered company is, like any other corporation, an entity separate from its members, as the following cases illustrate.

Salomon v Salomon & Co Ltd [1897] AC 22

Salomon carried on business as a leather merchant and boot manufacturer. In 1892 he formed a limited company to take over the business. The memorandum of association was signed by Salomon, his wife, his daughter, and four of his sons. Each subscribed for one share. The subscribers met and appointed Mr Salomon and his two elder sons as directors. The company paid £39,000 to Salomon for the business, and the mode of payment was to give Salomon £10,000 in debentures, secured by a floating charge on the company's assets, and 20,000 shares of £1 each and the balance in cash. Less than one year later the company fell on hard times and a liquidator was appointed. If Salomon's debenture was valid, he was, as a secured creditor, entitled to be paid before the unsecured trade creditors. The assets were sufficient to pay off the debentures but in that event the trade creditors would receive nothing. The unsecured creditors claimed all the remaining assets on the ground that the company was a mere alias or agent for Salomon.

Held – A company is, at law, a distinct and separate person from the people who set the company up. Once an association has incorporated, the company is an independent entity, separate from those who had set it up. Any fully paid-up shareholders could not be required to pay any more. The debentures were perfectly valid, and Salomon was entitled to the remaining assets in payment of the secured debentures held by him. Lord MacNaughten stated:

> When the trial came on before Vaughan Williams J., the validity of Mr Broderip's claim was admitted, and it was not disputed that the 20,000 shares were fully paid up. The case presented by the liquidator broke down completely; but the learned judge suggested that the company had a right of indemnity against Mr Salomon. The signatories of the memorandum of association were, he said, mere nominees of Mr Salomon – mere dummies. The company was Mr Salomon in another form. He used the name of the company as an alias. He employed the company as his agent; so the company, he thought, was entitled to indemnity against its principal. The counter-claim was accordingly amended to raise this point; and on the amendment being made the learned judge pronounced an order in accordance with the view he had expressed.
>
> The order of the learned judge appears to me to be founded on a misconception of the scope and effect of the Companies Act 1862. In order to form a company limited by shares, the Act requires that a memorandum of association should be signed by seven persons, who are each to take one share

at least. If those conditions are complied with, what can it matter whether the signatories are relations or strangers? There is nothing in the Act requiring that the subscribers to the memorandum should be independent or unconnected, or that they or any one of them should take a substantial interest in the undertaking, or that they should have a mind and will of their own, as one of the learned Lords Justices seems to think, or that there should be anything like a balance of power in the constitution of the company. In almost every company that is formed the statutory number is eked out by clerks or friends, who sign their names at the request of the promoter or promoters without intending to take any further part or interest in the matter.

When the memorandum is duly signed and registered, though there be only seven shares taken, the subscribers are a body corporate 'capable forthwith', to use the words of the enactment, 'of exercising all the functions of an incorporated company'. Those are strong words. The company attains maturity on its birth. There is no period of minority – no interval of incapacity. I cannot understand how a body corporate thus made 'capable' by statute can lose its individuality by issuing the bulk of its capital to one person, whether he be a subscriber to the memorandum or not. The company is at law a different person altogether from the subscribers to the memorandum; and, though it may be that after incorporation the business is precisely the same as it was before, and the same persons are managers, and the same hands receive the profits, the company is not in law the agent of the subscribers or trustee for them. Nor are the subscribers as members liable, in any shape or form, except to the extent and in the manner provided by the Act. That is, I think, the declared intention of the enactment. If the view of the learned judge were sound, it would follow that no common law partnership could register as a company limited by shares without remaining subject to unlimited liability.

Mr Salomon appealed; but his appeal was dismissed with costs, though the Appellate Court did not entirely accept the view of the Court below. The decision of the Court of Appeal proceeds on a declaration of opinion embodied in the order which has been already read.

I must say that I, too, have great difficulty in understanding this declaration. If it only means that Mr Salomon availed himself to the full of the advantages offered by the Act of 1862, what is there wrong in that? . . .

It has become the fashion to call companies of this class 'one man companies'. That is a taking nickname, but it does not help one much in the way of argument. If it is intended to convey the meaning that a company which is under the absolute control of one person is not a company legally incorporated, although the requirements of the Act of 1862 may have been complied with, it is inaccurate and misleading: if it merely means that there is a predominant partner possessing an overwhelming influence and entitled practically to the whole of the profits, there is nothing in that that I can see contrary to the true intention of the Act of 1862, or against public policy, or detrimental to the interests of creditors. If the shares are fully paid up, it cannot matter whether they are in the hands of one or many. If the shares are not fully paid, it is as easy to gauge the solvency of an individual as to estimate the financial ability of a crowd. One argument was addressed to your Lordships which ought perhaps to be noticed, although it was not the ground of decision in either of the Courts below. It was argued that the agreement for the transfer of the business to the company ought to be set aside, because there was no independent board of directors, and the property was transferred at an overvalue. There are, it seems to me, two answers to that argument. In the first place, the directors did just what they were authorised to do by the memorandum of association. There was no fraud or misrepresentation, and there was nobody deceived. In the second place, the company have put it out of their power to restore the property which was transferred to them. It was said that the assets were sold by an order made in the presence of Mr Salomon, though not with his consent, which declared that the sale was to be without prejudice to the rights claimed by the company by their counter-claim. I cannot see what difference that makes. The reservation in the order seems to me to be simply nugatory.

I am of opinion that the appeal ought to be allowed, and the counter-claim of the company dismissed with costs, both here and below.

Furthermore, Lord Halsbury stated:

My Lords, the important question in this case, I am not certain it is not the only question, is whether the respondent company was a company at all – whether in truth that artificial creation of the

Legislature had been validly constituted in this instance; and in order to determine that question it is necessary to look at what the statute itself has determined in that respect. I have no right to add to the requirements of the statute, nor to take from the requirements thus enacted. The sole guide must be the statute itself.

Now, that there were seven actual living persons who held shares in the company has not been doubted. As to the proportionate amounts held by each I will deal presently; but it is important to observe that this first condition of the statute is satisfied, and it follows as a consequence that it would not be competent to any one – and certainly not to these persons themselves – to deny that they were shareholders.

I must pause here to point out that the statute enacts nothing as to the extent or degree of interest which may be held by each of the seven, or as to the proportion of interest or influence possessed by one or the majority of the shareholders over the others. One share is enough. Still less is it possible to contend that the motive of becoming shareholders or of making them shareholders is a field of inquiry which the statute itself recognises as legitimate. If they are shareholders, they are shareholders for all purposes; and even if the statute was silent as to the recognition of trusts, I should be prepared to hold that if six of them were the *cestuis que* trust of the seventh, whatever might be their rights inter se, the statute would have made them shareholders to all intents and purposes with their respective rights and liabilities, and, dealing with them in their relation to the company, the only relations which I believe the law would sanction would be that they were corporators of the corporate body.

I am simply here dealing with the provisions of the statute, and it seems to me to be essential to the artificial creation that the law should recognise only that artificial existence – quite apart from the motives or conduct of individual corporators. In saying this, I do not at all mean to suggest that if it could be established that this provision of the statute to which I am adverting had not been complied with, you could not go behind the certificate of incorporation to show that a fraud had been committed upon the officer entrusted with the duty of giving the certificate, and that by some proceeding in the nature of *scire facias* you could not prove the fact that the company had no real legal existence. But short of such proof it seems to me impossible to dispute that once the company is legally incorporated it must be treated like any other independent person with its rights and liabilities appropriate to itself, and that the motives of those who took part in the promotion of the company are absolutely irrelevant in discussing what those rights and liabilities are.

I will for the sake of argument assume the proposition that the Court of Appeal lays down – that the formation of the company was a mere scheme to enable Aron Salomon to carry on business in the name of the company. I am wholly unable to follow the proposition that this was contrary to the true intent and meaning of the Companies Act. I can only find the true intent and meaning of the Act from the Act itself; and the Act appears to me to give a company a legal existence with, as I have said, rights and liabilities of its own, whatever may have been the ideas or schemes of those who brought it into existence.

I observe that the learned judge (Vaughan Williams J) held that the business was Mr Salomon's business, and no one else's, and that he chose to employ as agent a limited company; and he pro-ceeded to argue that he was employing that limited company as agent, and that he was bound to indemnify that agent (the company). I confess it seems to me that that very learned judge becomes involved by this argument in a very singular contradiction. Either the limited company was a legal entity or it was not. If it was, the business belonged to it and not to Mr Salomon. If it was not, there was no person and no thing to be an agent at all; and it is impossible to say at the same time that there is a company and there is not.

Comment

(i) There was no fraud upon creditors or shareholders. The creditors of the old business had been paid off. The unsecured creditors concerned in this case were creditors of the new company. The House of Lords took the view that they must be deemed to know the risk they were taking if the company went into liquidation with insufficient funds. The members who had fully paid shares could not be required to pay more. Any profit which Mr Salomon might have made as a promoter selling his business to the company, and in fact the price of some of the assets was fixed prior to sale at figures exceeding their balance sheet value by some £8,000, was fully disclosed and approved by the shareholders, i.e. his family.

(ii) The decision in *Salomon* was of vital importance at the time. Shortly after the industrial revolution, commerce and capitalism were on the increase and this decision encouraged individuals to provide money for businesses, without the threat of liability if the company became insolvent. This in turn increased the country's economic prosperity as more people were willing to take risks with their money within the safety buffer of limited liability.

Judicial pronouncement has also been firm in support of the principle that if people choose to conduct their affairs through the medium of corporations, they are taking advantage of the fact that in law those corporations are separate legal entities, whose property and actions are in law not the property or actions of their incorporators or shareholders.

Macaura v Northern Assurance Co Ltd [1925] AC 619

Macaura was the owner of a timber estate in County Tyrone and he formed an estate company and sold the timber to it for £42,000. The purchase money was paid by the issue to Macaura and his nominees of 42,000 fully paid shares of £1 each. No other shares were issued. He also financed the company and was an unsecured creditor for £19,000, its other debts being trifling. Macaura effected an insurance policy on the timber in his own name, and not in that of the company or as agent for the company, and on 23 February 1922 most of the timber was destroyed by fire. Macaura claimed under his policies, but he was held not to have an insurable interest. He could only be insuring either as a creditor or as a shareholder of the company, and neither a simple creditor nor a shareholder has an insurable interest in a particular asset which the company holds, since the company is an independent entity. Lord Sumner stated:

> My Lords, this appeal relates to an insurance on goods against loss by fire. It is clear that the appellant had no insurable interest in the timber described. It was not his. It belonged to the Irish Canadian Sawmills Ltd, of Skibbereen, Co Cork. He had no lien or security over it and, though it lay on his land by his permission, he had no responsibility to its owner for its safety, nor was it there under any contract that enabled him to hold it for his debt. He owned almost all the shares in the company, and the company owed him a good deal of money, but, neither as creditor nor as shareholder, could he insure the company's assets. The debt was not exposed to fire nor were the shares, and the fact that he was virtually the company's only creditor, while the timber was its only asset, seems to me to make no difference. He stood in no 'legal or equitable relation to' the timber at all. He had no 'concern in' the subject insured. His relation was to the company, not to its goods, and after the fire he was directly prejudiced by the paucity of the company's assets, not by the fire . . .

Lord Wrenbury also noted:

> My Lords, this appeal may be disposed of by saying that the corporator even if he holds all the shares is not the corporation, and that neither he nor any creditor of the company has any property legal or equitable in the assets of the corporation.

Comment

Unlike a shareholder, a debenture holder can insure the property of the company on which his debenture is secured (*Westminster Firer Officer v Glasgow Provident Investment Society* (1888) 13 App Cas 699). The difference in the debenture holder's position is justifiable since as a secured creditor he has an interest by way of a charge on the company's property which, of course, the shareholder does not have.

Lee (Catherine) v Lee's Air Farming Ltd [1960] 3 All ER 420

In 1954 the appellant's husband formed the respondent company which carried on the business of crop spraying from the air. In March 1956, Mr Lee was killed while piloting an aircraft during the course of top-soil dressing, and Mrs Lee claimed compensation from the company, as the employer of her husband, under the New Zealand Workers' Compensation Act 1922. Since Mr Lee owned 2,999 of the company's 3,000 £1 shares and since he was its governing director, the question arose as to whether the relationship of employer and employee could exist between the company and him. One of his first acts as governing director had been to appoint himself the only pilot of the company at a salary arranged by himself. The judgment of their Lordships was delivered by Lord Morris of Borth-Y-Gest, who stated:

> The Court of Appeal recognised that a director of a company may properly enter into a service agreement with his company, but they considered that, in the present case, inasmuch as the deceased was the governing director in whom was vested the full government and control of the company he could not also be a servant of the company. After referring in his judgment to the delegation to the deceased of substantially all the powers of the company, North J said: 'These powers were moreover delegated to him for life and there remained with the company no power of management whatsoever. One of his first acts was to appoint himself the only pilot of the company, for, although article 33 foreshadowed this appointment, a contract could only spring into existence after the company had been incorporated. Therefore, he became in effect both employer and worker. True, the contract of employment was between himself and the company . . . but on him lay the duty both of giving orders and obeying them. In our view, the two offices are clearly incompatible. There could exist no power of control and therefore the relationship of master–servant was not created.'
>
> The substantial question which arises is, as their Lordships think, whether the deceased was a 'worker' within the meaning of the Workers' Compensation Act, 1922, and its amendments. Was he a person who had entered into or worked under a contract of service with an employer? The Court of Appeal thought that his special position as governing director precluded him from being a servant of the company. On this view it is difficult to know what his status and position was when he was performing the arduous and skilful duties of piloting an aeroplane which belonged to the company and when he was carrying out the operation of top-dressing farm lands from the air. He was paid wages for so doing. The company kept a wages book in which these were recorded. The work that was being done was being done at the request of farmers whose contractual rights and obligations were with the company alone. It cannot be suggested that when engaged in the activities above referred to the deceased was discharging his duties as governing director. Their Lordships find it impossible to resist the conclusion that the active aerial operations were performed because the deceased was in some contractual relationship with the company. That relationship came about because the deceased as one legal person was willing to work for and to make a contract with the company which was another legal entity. A contractual relationship could only exist on the basis that there was consensus between two contracting parties. It was never suggested (nor in their Lordships' view could it reasonably have been suggested) that the company was a sham or a mere simulacrum. It is well established that the mere fact that someone is a director of a company is no impediment to his entering into a contract to serve the company. If, then, it be accepted that the respondent company was a legal entity their Lordships see no reason to challenge the validity of any contractual obligations which were created between the company and the deceased . . .
>
> Nor in their Lordships' view were any contractual obligations invalidated by the circumstance that the deceased was sole governing director in whom was vested the full government and control of the company. Always assuming that the company was not a sham then the capacity of the company to make a contract with the deceased could not be impugned merely because the deceased was the agent of the company in its negotiation. The deceased might have made a firm contract to serve the company for a fixed period of years. If within such period he had retired from the office of governing director and other directors had been appointed his contract would not have been affected. The circumstance that in his capacity as a shareholder he could control the course of events would not in

itself affect the validity of his contractual relationship with the company. When, therefore, it is said that 'one of his first acts was to appoint himself the only pilot of the company', it must be recognised that the appointment was made by the company, and that it was none the less a valid appointment because it was the deceased himself who acted as the agent of the company in arranging it. In their Lordships' view it is a logical consequence of the decision in *Salomon's* case that one person may function in dual capacities. There is no reason, therefore, to deny the possibility of a contractual relationship being created as between the deceased and the company. If this stage is reached then their lordships see no reason why the range of possible contractual relationships should not include a contract for services, and if the deceased as agent for the company could negotiate a contract for services as between the company and himself there is no reason why a contract of service could not also be negotiated. It is said that therein lies the difficulty, because it is said that the deceased could not both be under the duty of giving orders and also be under the duty of obeying them. But this approach does not give effect to the circumstance that it would be the company and not the deceased that would be giving the orders. Control would remain with the company whoever might be the agent of the company to exercise it. The fact that so long as the deceased continued to be governing director, with amplitude of powers, it would be for him to act as the agent of the company to give the orders, does not alter the fact that the company and the deceased were two separate and distinct legal persons. If the deceased had a contract of service with the company then the company had a right of control. The manner of its exercise would not affect or diminish the right to its exercise. But the existence of a right to control cannot be denied if once the reality of the legal existence of the company is recognised. Just as the company and the deceased were separate legal entities so as to permit of contractual relations being established between them, so also were they separate legal entities so as to enable the company to give an order to the deceased . . .

Ex facie there was a contract of service. Their Lordships conclude, therefore, that the real issue in the case is whether the position of the deceased as sole governing director made it impossible for him to be the servant of the company in the capacity of chief pilot of the company. In their Lordships' view, for the reasons which have been indicated, there was no such impossibility. There appears to be no greater difficulty in holding that a man acting in one capacity can give orders to himself in another capacity than there is in holding that a man acting in one capacity can make a contract with himself in another capacity. The company and the deceased were separate legal entities. The company had the right to decide what contracts for aerial top-dressing it would enter into. The deceased was the agent of the company in making the necessary decisions. Any profits earned would belong to the company and not to the deceased. If the company entered into a contract with a farmer, then it lay within its right and power to direct its chief pilot to perform certain operations. The right to control existed even though it would be for the deceased in his capacity as agent for the company to decide what orders to give. The right to control existed in the company, and an application of the principles of *Salomon's* case demonstrates that the company was distinct from the deceased. As pointed out above, there might have come a time when the deceased would remain bound contractually to serve the company as chief pilot though he had retired from the office of sole governing director. Their Lordships consider, therefore, that the deceased was a worker and that the question posed in the case stated should be answered in the affirmative.

Held – Mrs Lee was entitled to compensation because her husband was employed by the company in the sense required by the Act of 1922, and the decision in *Salomon v Salomon & Co* was applied.

Comment

(i) In *AG's Reference (No 2 of 1982)* [1984] 2 All ER 216 the Court of Appeal held that two directors who were also shareholders of several companies were capable of stealing from those companies. Money from the companies, which had raised large loans from various institutions, had been used, it was alleged, to support the extravagant lifestyle of the directors and their wives. There had, it was alleged, been a spending of the company's money in hotels and restaurants and on cars, yachts, and house improvements, silver and antiques. The effect on creditors was obviously uppermost in the mind of the court, which felt that a criminal sanction was needed. By applying the rule of corporate personality the directors could, as a matter of law, be liable for stealing from a company which they owned.

(ii) This case has been distinguished in employment/insolvency law. When a company becomes insolvent, directors, who are regarded for many purposes as employees, i.e. the executive directors such as the finance director, are preferential creditors for salary due up to defined limits. These will be discussed in later chapters on company charges and insolvency. If the insolvent company cannot meet these payments, there may be a claim through the government's Department for Business, Innovation and Skills (BIS), which in turn will try to recoup any payments made from the company. However, where the director concerned is also a controlling shareholder, the Employment Appeal Tribunal has refused to support claims on the BIS. Lee's case has been distinguished because claims on the BIS are met from public funds whereas in Lee's case the funds were supplied by the company's insurers (see *Buchan v Secretary of State for Trade and Employment* (1997) 565 IRLB 2). The tribunal approach is based upon the fact that the definition of an employee still requires an element of employer control which is not present where the worker in effect controls himself. However, in *Fleming v Secretary of State for Trade and Industry* (1998) 588 IRLB 10 the Scottish Court of Session rejected the view expressed in Buchan that a controlling shareholder/director could never as a matter of law be an employee. However, the director's claim in *Fleming* was turned down on the facts. He worked alongside the employees but was a majority shareholder and had guaranteed the company's debts. The *Fleming* approach was also approved by the Employment Appeal Tribunal in *Secretary of State for Trade and Industry v Bottrill* [1998] IRLR 120 where Morison J said that the reasoning in Buchan was 'unsound'. The decision of the EAT was affirmed by the Court of Appeal in *Secretary of State for Trade and Industry v Bottrill* (1999) 615 IRLB 12. In *Connolly v Sellers Arenascene Ltd* (2000) 633 IRLB 15 the EAT ruled that the controlling shareholder of a company could be an employee. He had a contract of employment with the company. The contract was not a sham and he had been treated and rewarded as an employee.

It seems then from the case law that a director/controlling shareholder will be regarded as an employee where there is a written contract of employment and all the usual hallmarks of employment are present. Certainly the original, almost blanket, ban on controlling shareholder/directors as employees has been much eroded. However, it is worth noting the more recent case of *Secretary of State for Business, Enterprise & Regulatory Reform v Neufeld & Anor* [2009] EWCA Civ 280, in which a majority shareholder was not recognised by the court as an employee of a company. The court noted that Mr Neufeld 'certainly had a contract of employment albeit oral' and noted that it had not been suggested that it was a sham or was otherwise unusual save that it was not in writing. In addition, the court stated that 'a large shareholding in itself does not debar that person from being an employee; it is just one of the factors to be taken into account in the overall picture'. However, whilst the evidence was that all three directors had worked together over 20 years in a collegiate atmosphere and had together resolved to put A & N into liquidation, nevertheless as a 90 per cent shareholder Mr Neufeld held the ultimate control and, in the face of disagreement with his co-directors, could have removed them and obstructed any efforts by them to remove or discipline him. Furthermore, Mr Neufeld had given guarantees to A & N's bank manager: one for £10,000 in relation to a machine and another for up to some £25,000 in relation to sales financing, to which it was noted by the judge: 'In my view [Mr Neufeld] has endeavoured to put a gloss on these issues. If a factoring company has advanced money and the sales do not materialise because of insolvency, it can have recourse to any guarantee. [A & N] itself may not be worth pursuing. There is no doubt in the Tribunal's mind that in arriving at these arrangements [Mr Neufeld] was seeking to give an advantage to [A & N]. However at the same time in the Tribunal's view he was involving himself in potential losses and liability. Very few employees would enter into such an arrangement where their own capital is at risk. In my view it points to [Mr Neufeld] running his own business as a manager and major shareholder of that business seeking commendably to secure on-going finances through its bankers. I have also taken into account against the overall background the very significant shareholding of [Mr Neufeld]. I am clear that the preponderance of characteristics of the relationship between [A & N] and [Mr Neufeld] point very much away from one of employer/employee particularly against the dimension of the personal guarantees. It follows that as [Mr Neufeld] has been adjudged not to be an employee of [A & N] his claim against the Secretary of State must fail.'

(iii) The courts continue to be willing to draw aside the corporate veil where the circumstances warrant it. Thus, in *Secretary of State for Trade and Industry* v *Backhouse* (2001) *The Times*, 23 February, Mr Backhouse was ordered to pay the costs of the Secretary of State in connection with a winding-up petition presented by him against North West Holdings plc, a company controlled by Mr Backhouse. It appeared that Mr Backhouse had caused the company to defend the petition not in the interests of the company but in order to protect his own personal reputation. His personal business affairs were bound up with those of the company and money the company earned had been treated as if it belonged to Mr Backhouse. The court drew aside the corporate veil so as to make the company's liability to pay costs that of Mr Backhouse personally. The court would obviously bear in mind that if the company was required to pay the costs, they would in effect be paid by the company's creditors who would be denied access to the funds required to pay them.

Again, in *Trustor AB* v *Smallbone* (2001) *The Times*, 30 March, Mr Smallbone, a director of Trustor AB, opened a bank account in London for the company and without the approval of the board paid money belonging to Trustor AB from its account in Sweden to the London account. Mr Smallbone then paid £38 million from Trustor AB's account in London to the account of a company called Introcom (International) Ltd that he controlled. When this was discovered by the members of the board of Trustor AB, they caused the company to claim the funds back from Introcom and also claimed that Mr Smallbone should be regarded as having received the money personally so that he was liable to repay the money personally if Introcom did not. The High Court ruled that the corporate veil could be drawn aside in this case to make Mr Smallbone personally liable.

On the other hand, the Court of Appeal refused to draw aside the veil in *Ord* v *Belhaven Pubs Ltd* [1998] 2 BCLC 447. The Ords purchased a 20-year lease of a pub, the Fox Inn. Belhaven Pubs Ltd owned the freehold and was the landlord. The Ords later alleged misrepresentation by Belhaven as to the turnover and profitability of the Fox Inn. They wished to make a claim. However, the holding company of the group in which Belhaven was a subsidiary carried out a reconstruction of the group, leaving Belhaven with only the Fox Inn as an asset. Belhaven ceased trading. The Ords wanted to claim against Ascot Holdings as the true owner (they said) of the Belhaven business. The Court of Appeal refused to draw aside the Belhaven veil and the Ords were unable to make Ascot a defendant. The reconstruction was genuine, ruled the Court of Appeal. There was no justification for ignoring the *Salomon* principle. (See p. 6. ◐)

As a separate legal entity, the courts to a very large degree will allow companies to operate as they see fit within the boundaries of the law. (This will be explored further in Chapter 6. ◐) The courts are very protective of the Salomon decision and the corporate form. Without it, company law would virtually collapse as limited liability would no longer act as an incentive for investors to be able to restrict the risks associated with their 'passive' investment; the consequence being the grinding to a halt of the corporate-capitalist machine.

However, on some occasions the courts and the legislature have found it necessary to lift the corporate veil, or to remove the protection (in the form of limited liability) that is afforded shareholders. This means that the courts or statutes will lift the veil of incorporation to reveal the people who stand behind the company. They will look to make those people responsible for the actions of the company. This will be examined further later in this chapter. However, it is worth reading some of the academic opinion in the area. (See Ottolenghi (1990). Note: this article provides a useful overview of cases, but does not take into account *Adams* v *Cape Industries*.)

Classification of registered companies

Public companies

Section 4 defines a public company as a company limited by shares or by guarantee with a share capital whose certificate of incorporation states that the company is a public company. The name of a public company must end with the words 'public limited company', or the Welsh equivalent if the registered office is situated in Wales. The abbreviation plc may be used and the equivalent in Welsh may be given where the registered office is to be in Wales.

If the company is to be a public company, the minimum capital must be at least £50,000, or such other sum as the Secretary of State, in the future by statutory instrument, specifies instead. As we have seen, the certificate of incorporation of a public company states that it is (a public company) and is conclusive evidence that the Act has been complied with and that the company is a public company (s 15).

Under s 761 a public company formed as such cannot commence business or borrow money unless the Registrar has issued a s 761 certificate, which private companies do not require. The certificate is issued if the nominal value of the company's allotted share capital is at least £50,000 and not less than one-quarter of the nominal value of each issued share and the whole of any premium has been received by the company whether in cash or otherwise. A share allotted under an employees' share scheme cannot be taken into account in determining the company's allotted share capital unless it is paid up as to one-quarter of the nominal value and the whole of any premium on the share.

In order to show the extent to which the company's starting capital might be watered down, the obtaining of a s 761 certificate requires disclosure to the Registrar of the amount of preliminary expenses (including the cost of allotting shares) and by whom these were paid or are payable because if not by the company such persons will normally require reimbursement and the benefits given or intended to be given to the company's promoters.

The s 761 certificate is conclusive evidence that the company is entitled to do business and exercise any borrowing powers. It is unusual for a company to incorporate as a public company. It is more common to incorporate as a private company and go public at a later stage (e.g. when the business has expanded sufficiently to benefit from going to the market so that the public can subscribe for its shares). This obviates the need for a s 761 certificate in most cases.

Private companies: generally

These are intended for the smaller business. Chapter 1 of Part 20 of the Companies Act 2006 (ss 755–760) prohibits public offers by private companies. A private purchaser must be found.

The single-member private limited company

Section 7 of the Companies Act 2006 permits the formation of single-member limited liability companies. It is now no longer necessary to have an 'artificial' member, who exists in many private companies which in fact have a sole proprietor but where, for example, a spouse holds a nominee share to fulfil the previous two-member requirement.

The same is true of subsidiaries whether trading or dormant where someone such as the group secretary or a separate nominee company has in the past had to hold a share or shares in the subsidiary, normally under a declaration of trust and a blank transfer form in favour of the parent company so that the shareholding can be recalled from the nominee at any time.

A further useful application is that where one shareholder in a two-member company dies, the remaining shareholder can seek to acquire the deceased's shares from the personal representatives and convert the company into a single-member private company.

Gramophone and Typewriter Co Ltd v Stanley [1908] 2 KB 89 (Court of Appeal)

In this case the appellant company (resident in England) held all of the shares in a German company (Deutsche Grammophon Aktiengesellschaft). The appellant had then been assessed, for income tax purposes, on the monies retained by the German company (and subsequently transferred to a depreciation fund) as well as the actual profits which had been remitted to it in England. The case was dependent upon whether the unremitted funds were the gains of a business 'carried on' by the English company as opposed to a separate entity.

Held – the Court of Appeal rejected this view. The fact that all of the shares in a company are held by one person does not, without additional factors, make the company's business the business of that person. Buckley LJ stated:

> The question is, I think, one of fact, and one upon which we are not concluded by any findings of fact on the part of the Commissioners. The question of fact is whether the business in Germany is carried on by the appellant company. If it is, the respondents do not dispute that the Attorney-General is right. If, on the contrary, the German business is not carried on by the English company, then equally the Attorney-General cannot dispute but that the English company is assessable only upon the dividends which it may receive upon its shares in the German company.
>
> In order to succeed the Attorney-General must, I think, make out either, first, that the German company is a fiction, a sham, a simulacrum, and that in reality the English company, and not the German company, is carrying on the business; or, secondly, that the German company, if it is a real thing, is the agent of the English company. As regards the former of these, there are no facts at all to show that the German company is a pretence. It was formed in January 1900 by the union of three other companies, each of which brought in substantial properties, and of two individuals. It is duly constituted and governed according to German law, and there is no ground whatever for saying that it is other than a real German corporation carrying on business in Germany under circumstances in which the company and its officers are amenable to German law and with a view to the acquisition of profit. The only remaining question, therefore, is whether the German company is agent of the English company, whether the English company is really carrying on the business and is employing the German company to do so on its behalf. Upon this point the Attorney-General relies principally upon the fact that, as stated in paragraph 17 of the case, the appellant company now holds all the shares of the German company. In my opinion this fact does not establish the relation of principal and agent between the English company and the German company. It is so familiar that it would be waste of time to dwell upon the difference between the corporation and the aggregate of all the corporators. But I may point out the following considerations as bearing upon the question whether the possession of all the shares is evidence of agency. Suppose that during the year whose accounts are under review the appellant company had held no shares at all in the first six months and had held all the shares in the last six months, or suppose that, having held all the shares but ten today, it became the holder of all tomorrow and again parted with ten the next day, it cannot seriously be suggested that each time one person becomes the holder of all the shares an agency comes into existence which dies again when he parts with some of them.
>
> Further it is urged that the English company, as owning all the shares, can control the German company in the sense that the German company must do all that the English company directs. In my opinion this again is a misapprehension. This Court decided not long since, in *Automatic Self-Cleansing Filter Syndicate Co Ld v Cunninghame*, that even a resolution of a numerical majority at a general meeting of the company cannot impose its will upon the directors when the articles have

15

confided to them the control of the company's affairs. The directors are not servants to obey directions given by the shareholders as individuals; they are not agents appointed by and bound to serve the shareholders as their principals. They are persons who may by the regulations be entrusted with the control of the business, and if so entrusted they can be dispossessed from that control only by the statutory majority which can alter the articles. Directors are not, I think, bound to comply with the directions even of all the corporators acting as individuals. Of course the corporators have it in their power by proper resolutions, which would generally be special resolutions, to remove directors who do not act as they desire, but this in no way answers the question here to be considered, which is whether the corporators are engaged in carrying on the business of the corporation. In my opinion they are not. To say that they are involves a complete confusion of ideas.

Registration of single-member companies

The documents which are sent to Companies House are the same as those required for multi-member companies (which are considered in Chapter 4; see p. 74 ◐). The necessary amendments to company legislation are considered below but it should be noted at this stage that a public single-member company requires two directors and a secretary so such companies can have one member but need three officers (i.e. two directors and a secretary). In a private single member company the sole member can be the sole director and a secretary is not a legal requirement. Such companies need only one member and one officer (i.e. the sole member) though if a secretary was appointed that individual would be regarded as an officer of the company which would then have one member and two officers (ss 154, 270, 271 and 274 apply).

Conversion to single-member status

There are no re-registration requirements. Conversion is achieved by transferring the nominee holding to the then sole proprietor. No resolutions of the company are required and there are no filing requirements at Companies House. Under s 123, when the number of members falls to one, or if an unlimited company with only one member becomes a limited company on re-registration, a statement that this is the case must be entered on the Register of Members at the side of the name and address of the sole member, together with the date on which this occurred. No special form of words is given but a statement saying 'The company became a single-member company on . . . (date–month–year)' would appear to suffice. If the membership increases to two or more, then when that happens, a statement that the company has ceased to have only one member must be entered in the Register of Members alongside the name and address of the person who was formerly the sole member. The date when this occurred is also required. A statement saying 'The company ceased to be a single-member company on . . . (date–month–year)' would suffice. A default fine is imposed on the company and its officers in default if the relevant statement is not made.

Accounts and audit

The requirements are no different from those applying to other companies.

Meetings of the single-member company

Section 318 provides that notwithstanding any provision to the contrary in the articles (so that no changes in the articles are required) one member present in person or by proxy shall be a quorum. Section 357 provides that if the sole member takes any decision which could have been taken in general meeting he shall (unless it is a written resolution) provide the company with a written record of it and although it would seem desirable for the sole member to sign it in case of dispute there is no requirement of signature in the regulations. Section 318 is not a significant change since all the formalities of calling and holding a meeting will have to be gone through. However, s 357 is significant in that it allows the sole member to conduct business informally without notice or formal minutes.

Filing requirements still apply when, for example, the articles are altered informally, and an annual general meeting must still be held unless the company is a private company. The Companies Act 2006 does not require a private company to hold an Annual General Meeting (AGM) nor need it lay its accounts and reports before a general meeting, thus there need not be any member meetings. However, board meetings and board resolutions are required although even here the written resolution procedure for directors provided for by Reg 7 of the Model Articles for private companies may be used.

Single-member companies may conduct business by written resolution. There is no provision in the Companies Act 2006 for a public company to conduct business by written resolution. However, in multi-member companies written resolutions cannot be used to remove a director or auditor from office. In single-member companies the s 357 procedure would seem to be available. Removal of a non-member director or the auditor without a meeting and without receiving representations from them could be achieved in that way, although the regulations are silent on this.

Contracts with a sole member who is also a director

Section 231 provides that the terms of a contract with a sole member/director must either be set out in a written memorandum or be made the subject of a report to the next available board meeting and be recorded in the minutes.

This provision does not apply if the contract is in writing or if it is entered into in the ordinary course of business, as where the company buys raw materials from the sole member/director.

Death of the sole member: private companies

If a sole member/director of a private company dies, there is no board to approve the transfer of his or her shares under the terms of the will or on intestacy. The company is then in effect paralysed, being without a board or shareholders. The articles should therefore be altered so as to allow, for example, the company secretary, if one has been appointed, to authorise a transfer or allow the personal representatives of the deceased member to appoint a director if the company has none. The director could then approve the transfer and the business of the company could proceed.

There is also a common law rule that the directors must actively refuse a transfer within a reasonable time. Under s 771 any power of veto vested in the directors must be exercised within two months after the lodging of the transfer and after that time the court can compel the registration of the transfer (as is further described in Chapter 14; see p. 263 ○). Nevertheless, it is better that the articles address this matter. In fact, a power of refusal is not given by s 771 and must be in the articles. A power of refusal is given in the Model Articles in Reg 26(5) – private limited companies model – and Reg 62 – public limited companies model.

Small and medium-sized companies

Private companies are further subdivided by ss 381–384 (small companies including parent companies and groups), which introduce the accounting exemptions. They give the benefit of confidentiality of information but involve the preparation of two sets of accounts – one for members and one for the Registrar of Companies. These exemptions then draw a distinction between the reporting requirements in regard to the accounts which small or medium-sized companies prepare for their members and those which they file with the Registrar of Companies. They are allowed to file what the Act refers to as 'abbreviated' and 'modified' accounts with the Registrar.

The 2006 Act permits (but does not require) a small company to dispense with the filing of its directors' report and profit and loss account and allows the filing of an abbreviated balance sheet only. Fuller particulars of the exemptions are given below, but the major result is that members of the public examining these abbreviated accounts at Companies Registration Office will have no trading information and will know nothing about directors' emoluments or the company's dividends.

If a small company files accounts made up in accordance with International Accounting Standards (IAS accounts) or Companies Act accounts that are not abbreviated accounts but the directors wish to exercise the option of not providing a copy of the director's report and/or profit and loss account, then s 444(5) states that the balance sheet shall include in a prominent place a statement that the accounts have been delivered in accordance with the provisions relating to small companies.

Sections 465–467 set out which companies, parent companies and groups qualify as medium sized. A medium-sized company may modify only its profit and loss account. Apart from this, full accounts and reports must be filed.

The modifications to the profit and loss account of a medium-sized company are as follows:

- Instead of showing turnover, cost of sales, gross profit or loss and other operating income as separate figures, they can be combined into one figure under the heading Gross Profit or Loss.
- In addition, the analysis of turnover and profit among different classes of business and different markets need not be given in the notes to the profit and loss account.

The reason for this is that the details of turnover profits and markets were sometimes used to the unreasonable disadvantage of medium-sized companies by their larger competitors. It should be noted, however, that this requirement is now removed for all companies where, in the opinion of the directors, the disclosure of such information would seriously prejudice the company's interests and the fact that it has not been disclosed is stated.

In the case of medium-sized companies, a full and unmodified set of accounts must be prepared for members. The full accounts and reports will be sent to the members, though any member, or the company's auditor, is given the right to require the accounts and reports to be laid before a general meeting of members.

It may be taken as a general view that there is in many cases little benefit in filing abbreviated accounts for medium-sized companies. Unless there are special reasons for not disclosing details of turnover and cost of sales, the cost of preparing such accounts may outweigh the benefits.

Summary of abbreviations applicable

The abbreviations in Table 1.1 are applicable where the accounts of small and medium-sized companies are filed at Companies House.

Table 1.1

	Directors' report	Profit and loss a/c	Balance sheet	Cash flow statement	Notes to the accounts	Auditors' report
Small	Not required	Not required	Required with special directors' statement	Not required	Limited information only	Special report (unless audit exempt)
Medium-sized	Required in full	Required but may start at 'Gross Profit'	Required with special directors' statement	Required	All except analysis of turnover and profit	Special report

Note: Companies that are audit exempt do not need any form of audit or accountants' report, although exempt charitable companies must file a copy of the statutory accountants' report.

Financial reporting standard for smaller entities

The Accounting Standards Board (see now the Financial Reporting Council) decided to free small companies from the burden of complying with many of the accounting standards. By conforming to the Financial Reporting Standard for Smaller Entities (FRSSE) such companies are able to ignore other accounting standards. They may choose not to adopt it, in which case they remain subject to the full range of standards and abstracts.

Small and medium-sized companies: definitions

(a) Small companies

A small company is one which has been within the limits of two of the following thresholds since incorporation or, if not within the limits at incorporation, then for the current financial year and the one before:

> Turnover £5.6 million or less
> Balance sheet total (i.e. total assets) £2.8 million or less
> Employees 50 (average) or less.

(b) Medium-sized companies

A medium-sized company is one which has been within the limits of two of the following thresholds since incorporation or, if not within the limits at incorporation, then for the current financial year and the one before:

> Turnover £22.8 million or less
> Balance sheet total (i.e. total assets) £11.4 million or less
> Employees 250 (average) or less.

As regards both small and medium-sized companies, the employee average is to be ascertained on a monthly basis and not a weekly basis as it was initially. The average is derived by dividing the sum of the number of employees employed under contracts of service in each month by the number of months in the financial year.

The authority for the above thresholds is the Companies Act 2006: s 382 for small companies and s 465 for medium-sized companies.

Subsequent failure to qualify

If a company ceases to satisfy the exemption requirements for two successive years, it must file full accounts for the second year.

Exemptions inapplicable: small and medium-sized companies

The exemptions do not apply if the company concerned is or at any time during its financial year was:

(a) A public company (whether listed or unlisted).
(b) A banking or insurance company.
(c) An organisation authorised to conduct investment business under the Financial Services and Markets Act 2000. (However, small authorised firms and appointed representatives whose only regulated activities are mortgage and insurance activities may take the Companies Act 2006 exemption. An appointed representative is a person in a contractual relationship with an authorised person to carry out authorised activities with the principal having proper control and for whose activities the authorised principal has accepted responsibility in writing.)
(d) A member of an 'ineligible group', i.e. a group containing any of the companies in (a) to (c) above.

A company which has subsidiaries, i.e. it is a holding or parent company, although it satisfies the definition of a small or medium-sized company, cannot be treated as one unless the group as a whole is small or medium-sized within the definitions given below. Thus if the parent company qualifies as a small company but the group is medium-sized, the parent would only be entitled to the exemptions available to a medium-sized company when preparing individual accounts.

Small and medium-sized groups

This is a further division into small and medium-sized groups of private companies. Normally, where a company, say A Ltd, is the holding (or parent) company of B Ltd, e.g. because A Ltd owns more than half of the voting share capital of B Ltd – generally more than half of B Ltd's ordinary shares – then A Ltd and B Ltd have to prepare individual accounts. However, A Ltd has an extra duty which is to prepare group accounts (or consolidated accounts) showing, for the benefit of outsiders who might invest in or do business with either company, the financial position of A Ltd and B Ltd together in one set of financial statements.

However, a parent company, such as A Ltd, need not prepare group accounts for a financial year in relation to which the group headed by that company qualifies as a small or medium-sized group and is not an ineligible group. This is a further example of the deregulation of private companies running the smaller business.

The qualifying conditions are met by a group which satisfies two or more of the following thresholds: (a) in the parent company's first financial year as a parent company; and (b) in its second or subsequent financial year as a parent company in that year and the preceding year. If it fails to satisfy the exemption requirements for two successive years, it must prepare group accounts in the second year. The thresholds under s 383 (small) and s 465 (medium-sized) are given in Table 1.2.

Table 1.2

	Small	Medium-sized
Aggregate turnover	£5.6 m (net) or less *or* £6.72 m (gross) or less	£22.8 m (net) or less *or* £27.36 m (gross) or less
Aggregate balance sheet total	£2.8 m (net) or less *or* £3.36 m (gross) or less	£11.4 m (net) or less *or* £13.68 m (gross) or less
Number of employees	50 (average) or less	250 (average) or less

A group can choose to meet the gross or net formula for any item; thus, say, turnover may be gross and balance sheet total net. The net formula is calculated after adjustments are made in the consolidation of the accounts, e.g. elimination of inter-company balances. Thus, if B Ltd owes A Ltd £20,000, this £20,000 will be shown as an asset in A Ltd's individual balance sheet and as a liability in the individual balance sheet of B Ltd but not at all in the group balance sheet. The transaction is cancelled out on consolidation because it is of no interest to outsiders. Where there are extensive inter-company balances, it may be difficult for the group to meet the gross formula but the exemptions apply if the net formula is complied with.

In the case of a small or medium-sized group, the average number of persons that the company employs can now be calculated on a monthly average basis instead of a weekly average as before.

Where a parent company is not exempt and, therefore, is required to prepare group accounts, it is not required to file a profit and loss account with the annual accounts. However, where a small or medium-sized company is exempt but chooses voluntarily to prepare group accounts, it must file a profit and loss account. It is not able to take advantage of the exemption because it is not 'required' to prepare group accounts.

Exemptions inapplicable

A group is ineligible if any of the companies in it is a plc (listed or unlisted) or a company carrying on an insurance market activity or an authorised person under the Financial Services and Markets Act 2000 (though see earlier comment on this point for small groups). A special auditors' report is required for accounts delivered to the Registrar when small and medium-sized companies and groups take advantage of the exemptions referred to above. The purpose of the report is to say that the company concerned is entitled to them. This report is not required where the company has taken advantage of the audit exemption referred to below.

Criteria for exemption

Under s 477, the following conditions must apply in respect of the financial year:

- The company must qualify as a small company though even where it does it need not take advantage of the exemption and can have an audit.
- For these companies:
  (a) turnover must not be more than £5.6 million, and
  (b) the balance sheet total (assets) must not be more than £2.8 million.

- The company must not at any time during the financial year have been an ineligible company, for example:
  (a) a public company (listed or unlisted);
  (b) a parent or a subsidiary undertaking unless a member of a small group (see below) or where the subsidiary is dormant (s 249A(1A), (1B) and (1C));
  (c) a company carrying on an insurance market activity;
  (d) an authorised person or appointed representative under the Financial Services and Markets Act 2000 (subject to exceptions considered above in regard to accounting exemptions);
  (e) a trade union special registered body under the Trade Union and Labour Relations (Consolidation) Act 1992, s 117(1), which are treated as corporate entities.

Members holding 10 per cent or more of the issued share capital (or any class thereof) may require the company to have an audit for the financial year by depositing a written notice at the company's registered office not later than one month before the year end.

Audit exemption and small groups

A parent or non-dormant subsidiary company can claim exemption from audit if the group of which it is a member satisfies all of the following conditions throughout the financial year into which the period of group membership falls (s 479):

- the group qualifies as a small group for the purposes of s 479 and is not at the time of preparing accounts or at any time in the financial year an ineligible group (see above);
- the group's aggregate turnover in that year is not more than £5.6 million net (or £6.72 million gross);
- the group's aggregate balance sheet total for that year is not more than £2.8 million net (or £3.36 million gross).

Effect on dormant companies

Exemption from audit is available to small dormant companies that are not ineligible under the dormant company provisions (see below) or the audit exemption procedure. Dormant companies automatically qualify by being dormant and so long as 10 per cent of the members do not request an audit (s 480).

Disclosure in annual report and accounts

The balance sheet of a company taking advantage of the relevant audit exemptions must include a statement to the effect that:

- the company is eligible to claim the exemption;
- no notice has been deposited at the company's registered office by members holding 10 per cent or more of the issued capital (or a class thereof) requiring that the company shall have an audit for the financial year; and
- the directors acknowledge their responsibilities for:
  (a) ensuring that the company keeps proper accounting records; and
  (b) preparing accounts which give a true and fair view.

The statement must appear on the face of the balance sheet above the signature required by s 414 (i.e. by a director of the company on behalf of the board). The name of the signatory must also be stated.

Format of accounts

Even if the accounts are not audited they should comply with the provisions of the Companies Act 2006. The format should follow the relevant regulations as issued by the Secretary of State.

References to audit in the articles

Companies with articles based on the 1985 version of *Table A* are unlikely to have problems in dispensing with the audit requirement since the 1985 version does not impose an obligation to appoint auditors. Article 130 of *Table A* to the 1948 Act does and companies with that or a similar article should review the contents of their articles to see that they are not precluded from implementing the audit exemption. Furthermore, Article 127 which requires that the accounts be sent to members accompanied by an auditor's report will also require amendment.

No such problems arise with companies adopting their relevant Model Articles for the Companies Act 2006.

Dormant companies

When is a company dormant? Under s 480 a company is dormant if:

- it has been dormant since its formation; or
- it has been dormant since the end of the previous financial year; and
- it is a small company; and
- it is not required to prepare group accounts;
- during the dormant period there have been no significant accounting transactions that, by s 386, are required to be entered in the company's accounting records.

Transactions that are exempt from the above and do not prevent dormant status are transactions arising from the taking of shares in the company by a subscriber to the memorandum as a result of an undertaking in the memorandum, a fee to the Registrar of Companies on a change of name under s 78, a fee to the Registrar on the re-registration of a company under the Companies Act 2006 (e.g. limited to unlimited), a penalty under s 453 for failure to deliver accounts, or a fee for the registration of the annual return under Part 24 of the Companies Act 2006.

Ineligible companies

A company cannot be regarded as dormant if it is ineligible in terms already considered for audit and accounting exemptions. However, a public company can qualify as a dormant company if it meets the basic s 249AA requirements and is a small company but cannot prepare small company accounts because of its public company status (see s 249AA(2)(a)) or because it is a member of an ineligible group. This means that free-standing public limited companies may have dormant status. If they are members of an ineligible group because the group contains one or more plcs, they may become dormant only if they are subsidiaries. Parent companies cannot be dormant because no company can be dormant under the general definition (see above) if it is required to prepare group accounts. Examples of transactions which could prevent dormant status are as follows:

- bank charges even where the account is inactive;
- payment of audit fee for the audit of the last period during which the company traded.

The problem can be solved by, say, a holding company or an individual paying the relevant fees.

Loss of exemption

The directors, or failing them the members, must appoint auditors if the company ceases to be dormant or otherwise becomes ineligible. Details of the method of appointment appear in s 388A, which should be referred to.

Form of dormant accounts

The accounts must include:

- A profit and loss account but only if the company traded in the previous period, the comparative figures being put in.
- A directors' report to include a statement that the company has not traded during the financial year. It should also state, if relevant, that a profit and loss account has not been prepared for the year.
- In place of the previous requirement on directors to make a statement on the balance sheet that the company has been dormant throughout the year, they must now make the following statements which bring them into line with the requirements on other trading audit exempt companies:
  1 For the year ended . . . the company was entitled to exemption under s 480 of the Companies Act 2006.
  2 Members have not required the company to obtain an audit of its accounts for the year in question in accordance with s 476.
  3 The directors acknowledge their responsibility for:
    (a) ensuring that the company keeps accounting records which comply with s 386; and
    (b) preparing accounts which give a true and fair view of the state of the affairs of the company as at the end of its financial year in accordance.

Standard format for accounts

Provided the company has been dormant since it was incorporated, it may use Companies House Form DCA to file its accounts. The form which is available free is only suitable for dormant companies where the only transaction has been the issue of subscribers' shares and the company is not a subsidiary.

A dormant company can file abbreviated accounts in which case there is no need to file the directors' report or the comparative profit and loss account if applicable.

Articles of association

The company's articles should be referred to. Articles 127 and 130 of *Table A* to the Companies Act 1948 require the appointment of auditors unless altered by special (or written) resolution.

There is no similar provision in *Table A* to the Companies Act 1985 or in the Companies Act 2006 Model Articles.

Provisions of company law applicable to dormant companies

These are as follows:

(a) rights to receive or demand copies of accounts and reports under ss 423 and 431 continue but there is obviously no need for an auditors' report if there is no audit;

(b) it is not necessary to lay or circulate a copy of the auditors' report if there is one nor deliver a copy to the Registrar.

Dormant companies: agency arrangements

It is common in a wide variety of businesses to operate under agency arrangements where the agent company has no economic interest in the transactions but merely brings together the principal company and the third party into a contractual arrangement. Where the agency is disclosed to the third party, no entries need to be made in the agent company's accounting records and it may submit dormant company accounts. If the agency is not disclosed, the agent company should record the transactions in its records and, therefore, cannot submit dormant company accounts. Where the agency is disclosed, the agent company will have to submit memorandum accounts to the principal and will therefore need to record transactions but this does not give rise to entries in its own records and so it can be regarded as dormant.

Dormant companies that act as agents must disclose this in their annual accounts. This applies also to the abbreviated accounts.

Distinctions between a public and a private company

(a) As we have seen, a private company need have only one director and need not have a secretary; a public company must have at least two directors and a secretary. The secretary of a private company, if one is appointed, need not be qualified in the terms required of a secretary of a public company (see s 273).

(b) In a private company two or more directors may be appointed by a single resolution. In a public limited company they must be voted on as individuals (see s 160).

(c) *As regards registration.* The name of a public company must include 'public limited company' or 'plc'. A private limited company's name must only include 'limited' or 'Ltd'. Furthermore, a public company can only commence business and borrow on the issue of a s 761 certificate by the Registrar of Companies, whereas a private company can commence business and borrow on incorporation.

(d) *As regards share capital.* The minimum allotted share capital of a public company is £50,000, whereas there is no minimum capital requirement for a private company. A public company has an unrestricted right to offer shares or debentures to the public, whereas this is prohibited in the case of a private company. The pre-emption rights of the 2006 Act apply to public companies which must offer equity share capital first to existing shareholders. These provisions apply also to a private company though they may be excluded by the articles. Under s 656 where a public company has lost half or more of its share capital it must call a general meeting, whereas this provision is not applicable to private companies. Finally, as regards a lien or charge on its own shares, this is restricted in the case of public companies by s 670 (see Chapter 13, p. 247 ⬤). The provisions are not applicable to private companies which may take a lien or charge on their shares.

(e) *As regards payment for shares*. In the case of public companies, any agreement under which shares are to be allotted by an undertaking to carry out work or perform services is prohibited (s 585) but is allowed in the case of private companies. The subscribers to the memorandum of a public company must pay for their shares in cash, whereas in a private company payment may be in cash or some other consideration. In public companies there is a minimum payment for shares whenever issued (i.e. at least one-quarter of the nominal value plus the whole of any share premium must be paid up), but in private companies there is no minimum payment requirement. Where shares are to be paid for by a non-cash asset, public companies are required to ensure that the asset is to be transferred by contract within five years of the allotment, whereas there is no special requirement for private companies. Furthermore, public companies must have an independent accountant's report on the value of the non-cash asset used as consideration for an issue of shares. This requirement does not apply to private companies.

(f) *Acquisition of non-cash assets*. A public company cannot validly acquire non-cash assets valued at one-tenth or more of the company's issued share capital from subscribers to the memorandum in the first two years of its existence as such unless an independent accountant's report is received and the members approve by ordinary resolution. These restrictions do not apply to private companies.

(g) *As regards distribution of profits and assets*. Where interim accounts are used to support a proposed distribution these accounts must, in the case of a public company, be filed with the Registrar of Companies, whereas there is no filing requirement for private companies. Private companies need only fulfil the basic requirement of profits available for distribution. Public companies must also comply with the capital maintenance rule whereas private companies need not (see further Chapters 10, p. 175, and 11 ⬤).

(h) *As regards loans to directors, etc*. Quasi-loans and credit transactions, etc. for directors and the directors of the company's holding company are prohibited with certain exceptions in the case of public companies, as are loans, etc. to persons connected with the directors and the directors of any holding company. Quasi-loans and credit are not so restricted in private companies nor are, in general, such dealings with connected persons (see further Chapter 20, p. 387 ⬤).

(i) An essential feature of more recent company legislation has been the move towards the deregulation of private companies. In particular, company legislation now provides for written resolutions of private companies which can be passed by members without the need to call or hold a meeting. Private companies may also opt out of the audit requirement. These matters are considered in more detail in appropriate parts of the text.

Limited and unlimited companies

A registered company may be:

(a) Limited by shares

First it should be noted that limitation of liability refers to the members and not to the company itself. The liability of the company is always unlimited in the sense that it must discharge its liabilities so long as it has assets to do so.

Limitation of liability by shares may occur on formation, i.e. the company is registered as such. Where this is so the liability of each member to contribute to the capital of the company is limited to the nominal value of the shares that he has agreed to take up or, if he has agreed to take up such shares at a premium (i.e. at more than their nominal value), to the total amount agreed to be paid for such shares. Once the member has paid the company for his shares, his liability is discharged completely and he cannot be made responsible for making up the deficiencies of the company or of other shareholders. Furthermore, he has no liability whatever in respect of unissued shares. Indeed, in *Re Baglan Hall Colliery Co* (1870) LR 5 Ch App 346, Giffard LJ stated that it 'is the policy of the Companies Act to enable business people to incorporate their businesses and so avoid incurring further personal liability'.

However, in the case of a small private company, the advantages of limited liability tend to be illusory, since those who give the company a significant amount of credit and bank overdraft facilities will in practice require personal guarantees from its directors and major shareholders.

(b) Limited by guarantee

Formerly, companies limited by guarantee could be registered with or without a share capital. Companies limited by guarantee with a share capital may now not be registered, though, of course, companies which had registered with a share capital before the 1985 Act forbade this remain in existence. Since they cannot now have a share capital, they must of necessity be formed as private companies because the presence of a share capital is fundamental to the definition of a public company. Where there is no share capital the members have no liability unless and until the company goes into liquidation. When this happens those who are members at the time are required if necessary to contribute towards the payment of the company's debts and liabilities and the costs of winding-up in accordance with the guarantee. The amount guaranteed will be whatever sum is stated in the statement of guarantee on formation and it is frequently a small sum such as £100, although in some cases the agreed liability may be substantial and much depends upon the type of company.

The guarantee is not an asset of the company but a mere contingent liability of its members until winding-up. Consequently it cannot be charged by the company as a security nor can it be increased or reduced by an alteration of the memorandum or by agreement with the members or by any procedure equivalent to the increase or reduction of share capital (*Hennessy* v *National Agricultural and Industrial Development Association* [1947] IR 159).

If those who are members at the date of winding-up cannot meet their obligations under the guarantee or the debts exceed what they are liable to contribute, then the liquidator may have access to those who were members during the year prior to the commencement of the winding-up but only in respect of debts and liabilities incurred while they were members.

If a company limited by guarantee has a share capital, its members have two liabilities. They must pay the issue price of their shares, and must honour their guarantee in the event of the company being liquidated (Insolvency Act 1986, s 74(3)). There is no benefit to the company in having such a dual liability and in practice companies limited by guarantee with a share capital were not formed. The device of the guarantee company is only used where no share capital is to be issued but the members of the company wish to limit their liability to contribute towards the company's debts and liabilities. Obviously, the members are not shareholders (except in some of the earlier companies) and membership will often be acquired by application. Provision is usually made in the articles for a member to resign. These companies provide a suitable organisation for professional bodies and trade associations which have not received a Royal Charter, particularly since under certain circumstances there is no need to show the word 'limited' – which denotes commerciality – as part of the name (see further Chapter 5, p. 88 ◑).

Once incorporated as a guarantee company, there is no provision in company legislation for re-registration as a company limited by shares or vice versa.

It is worth noting that each member has one vote at general meetings (s 284) and is entitled to appoint a proxy to represent him (see s 324).

As regards accounts and audit, accounts must be prepared and audited, and filed at Companies House. The audit report is similar to that required for other companies but is addressed to the members, not the shareholders. The audit exemption is available as for other companies on the turnover, etc., basis.

(c) Unlimited

The personal liability of members of this type of company is the reason why not many of them exist. They are sometimes formed by those who wish to keep the company's accounts away from the public gaze (see below). In addition, there are advantages in having separate corporate status and perpetual succession even though these are not accompanied by limited liability.

Unlimited companies must be private companies since a public company is by definition a company limited by shares (or by guarantee with a share capital).

Unlimited companies may be formed as such, either with or without a share capital. A share capital may be used, for example, if the company is trading and making profits, since the shares are a basis for the distribution of that profit. As regards liability, where there is a share capital, the members must, even while the company is a going concern, pay for their shares in full, and if on a liquidation this is not adequate to satisfy all the debts and liabilities of the company together with the costs of winding-up, the members must contribute rateably according to the nominal value of their shareholding. Where there is no share capital, the members contribute equally until all the debts and liabilities of the company plus the costs of winding-up are paid. In the event of any members defaulting the others are liable to make good the deficiency as much as is necessary to pay the whole of the company's liabilities and the costs of liquidation.

If the members at the time of commencement of the winding-up cannot collectively contribute enough to pay off the debts and liabilities, the liquidator can go to those who were members during the 12 months prior to winding-up, but only in respect of debts incurred while they were members.

Special features of unlimited companies

There are certain special features relating to unlimited companies. For example, an unlimited company may reduce its capital by extinguishing liability on partly paid shares or even repaying capital to the members by passing a special resolution to that effect and the permission of the court is not required. In addition, although an unlimited company cannot issue redeemable shares it may, if its articles permit, reduce its capital by buying back the shares of its members even from out of its capital.

These practices, in theory at least, do not reduce the funds available to creditors on a winding-up because the members are liable to pay the debts and liabilities of the company in full on winding-up. However, as regards reduction of capital by purchase of shares, if the company knew at the time of purchase that the members would not be able to meet their liabilities on winding-up, the purchase would be set aside as a fraud on the creditors (*Mitchell v City of Glasgow Bank* (1879) 4 App Cas 624).

It will be noted later in the text (see Chapter 10, p. 175 ◐) that the difference between the unlimited company and the private limited company are not now so marked in terms of reduction of share capital, and purchase by the company of its own shares, because of deregulation features in the Companies Act 2006. For example, under a new procedure in s 641, private companies may pass a special resolution to reduce capital without an application to the court.

In addition, an unlimited company enjoys privacy in regard to its financial affairs because it need not deliver copies of its annual accounts and the relevant reports to the Registrar (s 448), not even abridged or modified ones, though it must, under s 431, prepare audited accounts for its members unless it has taken the audit exemption when unaudited accounts will suffice.

However, the price of privacy is the unlimited liability of its members. The provision in regard to the annual accounts does not apply if the company concerned is a subsidiary or holding company of a limited company or is potentially under the control of two or more limited companies, including a foreign company, because of share or voting rights which they hold even though these have not been exercised in concert for the purposes of control.

European company

The EU Council (formerly the Council of Ministers) reached agreement on 20 December 2000 on the legislative framework necessary to establish a European Company Statute. The legislation came into force on 8 October 2004. Under the statute, a European Company, called a *Societas Europaea* (SE), will operate on a Europe-wide basis governed by Community law directly applicable in all member states. The statute provides for the creation of European companies in one of four ways:

1 by merging two or more existing public companies from at least two different member states;
2 by forming a holding company promoted by public or private limited companies from at least two different member states;
3 by forming a subsidiary of companies from at least two member states;
4 by the conversion of a public limited company which for at least two years had a subsidiary in another member state.

Each SE will be registered on the same register as national companies. Registration will be in the member state in which the SE has its administrative head office. SEs do not have to have a public quotation. The minimum capital requirement is 120,000 ECUs to enable medium-sized companies from different member states to create an SE.

The creation of an SE requires negotiations on worker involvement. If it is not possible to negotiate a satisfactory arrangement with worker representatives, a set of standard principles laid down in an annexe to the legislation will apply. Employment contracts and pensions are subject to national law in the member states where headquarters operate. The European Public Limited-Liability Company Regulations 2004 (SI 2004/2326) implement the above materials in the UK from 8 October 2004.

The idea is not new but has been held up for some 25 years because of the question of no worker participation in business decisions in the UK. However, this was changed from 6 April 2005 when employers with at least 150 employees became obliged to inform and consult with employees on certain of these matters under the Information and Consultation of

Employees Regulations 2004 (SI 2004/3462). This was extended to employers with at least 100 employees from 6 April 2007 and to those with at least 50 from 6 April 2008. The application form for registration of an SE requires confirmation to be given that employee participation procedures are in place.

Companies and human rights

The Human Rights Act 1998 came into force on 2 October 2000. It implements the European Convention on Human Rights into UK law. The Convention is available to companies in terms of their dealings with emanations of the state, e.g. government and local authorities. This is because the initial effect of the Act is vertical. Whether the Convention will be extended by the courts horizontally into areas of private business remains to be seen, though s 6 of the 1998 Act provides that the courts and tribunals of the UK must not act contrary to the Convention. Problems have arisen in connection with the lack of independence in UK courts and tribunals in that Crown Court recorders were appointed part time and paid by the state and removable by the state with no security of tenure. The same was true of appointments to employment tribunals in cases involving the state as an employer or an emanation of the state, such as a local authority. The solution here has been to give these part-time judicial officers fixed-term contracts of, say, five years during which time they are not dismissible except for misconduct, and this gives some security of tenure. That a company can complain about the infringements of its human rights in this context (and others no doubt) is illustrated by *County Properties Ltd* v *Scottish Ministers* (2000) *The Times*, 19 September, which, although a Scottish case, is applicable in the rest of the UK. The company, in effect, had been refused permission by the Crown to obtain the release of the listed building restrictions on one of its properties and the matter was referred for decision to an inspector appointed by the Crown. The company objected to this procedure because it infringed Art 6 of the Convention that provides: 'In the determination of his civil rights and obligations [. . .] everyone is entitled to a [. . .] hearing [. . .] by an independent and impartial tribunal.' The Court of Session held that this was an infringement of the company's rights. That part of the procedure was invalid and the matter would have to be dealt with by appeal to the courts as the relevant legislation allowed. The case was overturned on appeal (*County Properties Ltd* v *Scottish Ministers* 2002 SC 79) the court following the same line as in the Barnes case.

The House of Lords took a different view in an appeal from the Divisional Court of Queen's Bench in England. Their Lordships felt that the hearing of planning matters by a government-appointed inspector did not flout Art 6 of the Convention because the inspector's decision could always be brought before the ordinary courts by means of a procedure called judicial review (see *R* v *Secretary of State for the Environment, etc., ex parte Holding and Barnes plc* (2001), *The Times*, 10 May). Nevertheless, the cases show that companies can argue human rights matters before our courts.

Action against companies based on human rights

Implementation of the Human Rights Act 1998 on 2 October 2000 raised the spectre of the litigation floodgates opening since it made the European Convention on Human Rights available to litigants in UK courts, thus avoiding the need to take the matter to the European Court of Human Rights at Strasbourg, previously the only option. It has already been noted that the initial effect is against public authorities with the possibility of some expansion into the private sector through s 6 of the 1998 Act. In this connection, a statement by the Lord Chief Justice in **Daniels v Walker** [2000] 1 WLR 1382, CA is of interest. He expressed the hope that judges would be robust in resisting attempts to allow inappropriate arguments on human rights. These he defined as arguments that lead the court down blind alleys. There has also been the suggestion that adverse costs may be awarded against those who raise spurious questions and points on human rights. Furthermore, the Court of Appeal observed in **Barclays Bank plc v Ellis** (2000) *The Times*, 24 October that legal representatives seeking to rely on the Human Rights Act 1998 should supply the court with any decisions of the European Court of Human Rights on which they intend to rely or which might assist the court. This should operate as a deterrent to those lawyers who may think of raising human rights issues unless, where possible, supported by authority.

The specific effect of the Convention on directors is considered, in terms of their functions as individuals and managers, in Chapter 9 ●.

Essay questions

1. (a) In the celebrated case of *Salomon v Salomon & Co Ltd* [1897] AC 22, Lord Halsbury LC observed: 'Either the limited company was a legal entity or it was not. If it was, the business belonged to it and not to Mr Salomon. If it was not, there was no person and no thing to be an agent at all and it is impossible to say at the same time that there is a company and there is not.'

   Comment.

   (b) Tiedeman was the owner of a large bulk-carrier called *Ocean-Star*. The ship was valued at £1 million and was insured for that sum with Lloyd's in Tiedeman's name. Subsequently, Tiedeman incorporated Tiedeman Ltd in which he held all the shares but one which was held by his wife as his nominee. *Ocean-Star* was then sold to Tiedeman Ltd and the purchase price was secured by a debenture issued in favour of Tiedeman giving as a security a fixed charge on the only asset of the company *Ocean-Star*. While carrying a valuable cargo on charter to a Kuwait company the *Ocean-Star* was attacked by Iranian gun-boats and sunk.

   Consider whether Tiedeman or in the alternative Tiedeman Ltd could claim to be indemnified by Lloyd's for the loss of the bulk-carrier. *(University of Plymouth)*

2. '. . . a fundamental attribute of corporate personality . . . is that the corporation is a legal entity distinct from its members' – Gower.

   Which do you consider are the two outstanding advantages of incorporation? Give reasons for your choice and explain their dependence upon this fundamental attribute.

   (The Institute of Chartered Accountants in England and Wales)

3. John, who runs Trent Ltd, a small manufacturing company, has heard that he may not have to appoint auditors in regard to future accounts and is keen to save the audit fees. Advise John as to the relevant law.

   (Authors' question)

Test your knowledge

Four alternative answers are given. Select ONE only. Circle the letter beside the answer which you consider to be correct. Check your answers by referring back to the information given in the chapter and against the answers at the end of the text.

1 The members of a social club wish to form a legal entity. There is no commercial risk but they do not want too much disclosure of their affairs to the public. What type of company should they form?

   A   A company limited by guarantee.
   B   An unincorporated association.
   C   A private company limited by shares.
   D   A private unlimited company.

2 Fred has been allotted 200 £1 ordinary shares in Ark Ltd with a nominal value of £1 and a premium of 0.40 pence. Fred has paid 0.85 pence. What is Fred's maximum liability if the company is wound up?

   A   £30   B   £110   C   £2,000   D   £280

3 To what extent is a member of a company which is limited by guarantee personally liable for the company's debts?

   A   He is personally liable for all the company's debts at any time.
   B   He is personally liable for all the company's debts if the company is wound up.
   C   His personal liability is limited to the amount set out in the memorandum on a winding-up.
   D   His personal liability is limited to the amount set out in the memorandum at any time.

4 Three friends own and are also directors of a limited company carrying on the family business. They have it in mind to change the organisation to an ordinary partnership. What aspect of the business would be affected if this change were carried out?

   A   The right to sue in the business name.
   B   The right to mortgage the business assets.
   C   The right of the partners to examine the firm's accounts.
   D   The ability to create a floating charge over the business assets.

The answers to test your knowledge questions appear on p. 645.

Suggested further reading

Adeyeye, 'The limitations of corporate governance in the CSR agenda' (2010) 31 *Company Lawyer* 114.

Drury, 'The Delaware Syndrome: European fears and reactions' (2005) JBL 709.

Hicks, 'Corporate form: Questioning the unsung hero' [1997] JBL 306.

Kahn-Freud, 'Some reflections on Company Law reform' (1944) 7 MLR 54.

Keay, 'Ascertaining the corporate objective: An entity maximisation and sustainability model' (2008) 71 MLR 663.

Ottolenghi, 'From peeping behind the corporate veil to ignoring it completely' (1990) 53 MLR 338.

Pickering, 'The company as a separate legal entity' (1968) 31 MLR 481.

Schmitthoff, 'Salomon in the shadow' [1976] JBL 305.

Wolff, 'On the nature of legal persons' (1938) 54 LQR 494.

2 The corporate veil

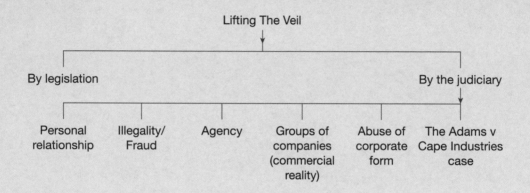

The principle set out in *Salomon* v *Salomon & Co Ltd* (1897) (i.e. that a body corporate is a separate entity, separate that is from its members), led to the use of the phrase 'the veil of incorporation', which is said to hang between the company and its members and, in law at least, acts as a screen between them.

However, the principle can cause difficulty and in a number of cases is lifted by the law so that the human and commercial reality behind the corporate personality can be taken account of. The veil may be lifted by the judiciary or by statute.

The judiciary

It is difficult to be precise about the circumstances in which a judge will lift the corporate veil. However, what is clear is that on occasions the *Salomon* decision has caused problems and the courts have had to remove the veil of incorporation to enable them to see the commercial reality behind the corporate personality. But, it is important to bear in mind that there are only a few examples of the courts removing the veil of incorporation. The overriding concern is to protect the corporate form; there is a great reluctance by the courts to depart from the *Salomon* principle.

Yet, it is clear that the courts will remove the veil of incorporation in cases where the incorporator is trying to avoid an obligation or achieve an unfair advantage. In other words, where there is an abuse of the corporate form. There are some occasions where it is clear that the courts will 'remove' the veil, yet the important thing to remember is that any list, including the one that follows, is not exhaustive and it is not known where the boundary lies between a court lifting/removing a veil of incorporation and leaving it intact. One of, if not *the* important case, in this area is that of *Adams* v *Cape Industries*.

Adams v *Cape Industries plc* [1990] Ch 433, CA

Until 1979, Cape, an English company, mined and marketed asbestos. Its worldwide marketing subsidiary was another English company, Capasco. It also had a US marketing subsidiary incorporated in Illinois, NAAC. In 1974, some 462 plaintiffs sued Cape, Capasco, NAAC and others in Tyler, Texas, for personal injuries allegedly arising from the installation of asbestos in a factory. These actions were settled. Between 1978 and 1979, a further 206 similar actions were commenced and default judgments entered against Cape and Capasco. In 1978, NAAC ceased to carry on business and other subsidiaries replaced it. The plaintiffs sought to enforce the judgments in England. The defendants denied that the Texas court had jurisdiction over them for the purposes of English law.

Held – by the Court of Appeal – that the defendants were neither present within the USA, nor had they submitted to the jurisdiction there. The method of computing damages of the individual plaintiffs was contrary to the English law concept of natural justice. Accordingly, the actions would be dismissed. Slade LJ stated:

The 'single economic unit' argument

There is no general principle that all companies in a group of companies are to be regarded as one. On the contrary, the fundamental principle is that 'each company in a group of companies (a relatively modern concept) is a separate legal entity possessed of separate legal rights and liabilities': The Albazero [1977] AC 774, 807, *per* Roskill LJ.

It is thus indisputable that each of Cape, Capasco, NAAC and CPC were in law separate legal entities. Mr Morison did not go so far as to submit that the very fact of the parent–subsidiary relationship existing between Cape and NAAC rendered Cape or Capasco present in Illinois. Nevertheless, he submitted that the court will, in appropriate circumstances, ignore the distinction in law between members of a group of companies treating them as one, and that broadly speaking, it will do so whenever it considers that justice so demands. In support of this submission, he referred us to a number of authorities . . .

Principally, in reliance on those authorities and the case next to be mentioned, Mr Morison submitted that in deciding whether a company had rendered itself subject to the jurisdiction of a foreign court it is entirely reasonable to approach the question by reference to 'commercial reality'. The risk of litigation in a foreign court, in his submission, is part of the price which those who conduct extensive business activities within the territorial jurisdiction of that court properly have to pay . . .

We have some sympathy with Mr Morison's submissions in this context. To the layman at least the distinction between the case where a company itself trades in a foreign country and the case where it trades in a foreign country through a subsidiary, whose activities it has full power to control, may seem a slender one . . . It is not surprising that in many cases such as *Holdsworth* [1955] 1 WLR 352, *Scottish Co-operative* [1959] AC 324, *Revlon* [1980] FSR 85 and *Commercial Solvents* [1974] ECR 223, the wording of a particular statute or contract has been held to justify the treatment of parent and subsidiary as one unit, at least for some purposes. The relevant parts of the judgments in the *DHN* case [1976] 1 WLR 852 must, we think, likewise be regarded as decisions on the relevant statutory provisions for compensation, even though these parts were somewhat broadly expressed, and the correctness of the decision was doubted by the House of Lords in *Woolfson* v *Strathclyde Regional Council* 1978 SLT 159 in a passage which will be quoted below.

Mr Morison described the theme of all these cases as being that where legal technicalities would produce injustice in cases involving members of a group of companies, such technicalities should not be allowed to prevail. We do not think that the cases relied on go nearly so far as this. As Sir Godfray submitted, save in cases which turn on the wording of particular statutes or contracts, the court is not free to disregard the principle of *Salomon* v *A Salomon & Co Ltd* [1897] AC 22 merely because it considers that justice so requires. Our law, for better or worse, recognises the creation of subsidiary companies, which though in one sense the creatures of their parent companies, will nevertheless under the general law fall to be treated as separate legal entities with all the rights and liabilities which would normally attach to separate legal entities.

In deciding whether a company is present in a foreign country by a subsidiary, which is itself present in that country, the court is entitled, indeed bound, to investigate the relationship between the parent and the subsidiary. In particular, that relationship may be relevant in determining whether the subsidiary was acting as the parent's agent and, if so, on what terms. In *Firestone Tyre and Rubber Co Ltd* v *Lewellin* [1957] 1 WLR 464 (which was referred to by Scott J) the House of Lords upheld an assessment to tax on the footing that, on the facts, the business both of the parent and subsidiary were carried on by the subsidiary as agent for the parent. However, there is no presumption of any such agency. There is no presumption that the subsidiary is the parent company's alter ego. In the court below the judge, ante, p. 484B, refused an invitation to infer that there existed an agency agreement between Cape and NAAC comparable to that which had previously existed between Cape and Capasco and that refusal is not challenged on this appeal. If a company chooses to arrange the affairs of its group in such a way that the business carried on in a particular foreign country is the business of its subsidiary and not its own, it is, in our judgment, entitled to do so. Neither in this class of case nor in any other class of case is it open to this court to disregard the principle of *Salomon* v *A Salomon & Co Ltd* [1897] AC 22 merely because it considers it just so to do . . .

The 'corporate veil' point

Quite apart from cases where statute or contract permits a broad interpretation to be given to references to members of a group of companies, there is one well-recognised exception to the rule prohibiting the piercing of 'the corporate veil'. Lord Keith of Kinkel referred to this principle in *Woolfson* v *Strathclyde Regional Council*, 1978 SLT 159 in the course of a speech with which Lord Wilberforce,

Lord Fraser of Tullybelton and Lord Russell of Killowen agreed. With reference to the *DHN* decision [1976] 1 *WLR* 852, he said, at p. 161: 'I have some doubts whether in this respect the Court of Appeal properly applied the principle that it is appropriate to pierce the corporate veil only where special circumstances exist indicating that it is a mere façade concealing the true facts' . . .

Mr Morison submitted that the court will lift the corporate veil where a defendant by the device of a corporate structure attempts to evade (i) limitations imposed on his conduct by law; (ii) such rights of relief against him as third parties already possess; and (iii) such rights of relief as third parties may in the future acquire. Assuming that the first and second of these three conditions will suffice in law to justify such a course, neither of them applies in the present case. It is not suggested that the arrangements involved any actual or potential illegality or were intended to deprive anyone of their existing rights. Whether or not such a course deserves moral approval, there was nothing illegal as such in Cape arranging its affairs (whether by the use of subsidiaries or otherwise) so as to attract the minimum publicity to its involvement in the sale of Cape asbestos in the United States of America. As to condition (iii), we do not accept as a matter of law that the court is entitled to lift the corporate veil as against a defendant company which is the member of a corporate group merely because the corporate structure has been used so as to ensure that the legal liability (if any) in respect of particular future activities of the group (and correspondingly the risk of enforcement of that liability) will fall on another member of the group rather than the defendant company. Whether or not this is desirable, the right to use a corporate structure in this manner is inherent in our corporate law. Mr Morison urged on us that the purpose of the operation was in substance that Cape would have the practical benefit of the group's asbestos trade in the United States of America without the risks of tortious liability. This may be so. However, in our judgment, Cape was in law entitled to organise the group's affairs in that manner and (save in the case of AMC to which special considerations apply) to expect that the court would apply the principle of *Salomon* v *A Salomon* in the ordinary way [. . .] We reject the 'corporate veil' argument . . .

The 'agency argument' in relation to NAAC

We now proceed to consider the agency argument in relation to NAAC on the footing, which we consider to be the correct one, that NAAC must for all relevant purposes be regarded as a legal entity separate from Cape/Capasco . . .

Having regard to the legal principles stated earlier in this judgment, and looking at the facts of the case overall, our conclusion is that the judge was right to hold that the business carried on by NAAC was exclusively its own business, not the business of Cape or Capasco, and that Cape and Capasco were not present within the United States of America, through NAAC at any material time. We see no sufficient grounds for disturbing this finding of fact.

Comment

For the purpose of enforcement of a foreign judgment, the defendant would only be regarded as falling under the jurisdiction of the foreign court where it was present within the jurisdiction or had submitted to such jurisdiction.

The Court of Appeal has recently outlined the circumstances in which it could impose responsibility on a parent company for the health and safety of employees of a subsidiary company which was no longer in existence. In the case of *Chandler* v *Cape Plc* [2012] 3 All ER 640, the parent company owed a duty of care to the subsidiary's employee, who had developed asbestosis after exposure to asbestos dust.

 Chandler v Cape Plc [2012] 3 All ER 640

The appellant (D) appealed against a decision ([2011] EWHC 951 (QB)) that it owed a duty of care to the respondent (C). C had been employed by a company (X) between 1959 and 1962. X was a wholly owned subsidiary of D and was in the business of manufacturing incombustible asbestos. In 2007 C discovered he had contracted asbestosis as a consequence of exposure to asbestos dust whilst employed by X. By that time X no longer existed and had had no policy of insurance that would indemnify it against claims for asbestosis. C issued proceedings against D on the basis that D and X were joint tortfeasors who were jointly and severally liable to pay him damages. The judge held that D owed a duty of care to C on the basis of the common law concept of assumption of responsibility.

Appeal dismissed. D owed a direct duty of care to the employees of X and it had omitted to advise on precautionary measures given its state of knowledge about the nature and management of asbestos risks. In appropriate circumstances the law could impose on a parent company responsibility for the health and safety of its subsidiary's employees. Those circumstances included a situation such as the instant case where: (a) the businesses of the parent and subsidiary were in a relevant respect the same; (b) the parent had, or ought to have had, superior knowledge on some relevant aspect of health and safety in the particular industry; (c) the subsidiary's system of work was unsafe as the parent company knew, or ought to have known; (d) the parent knew, or ought to have foreseen, that the subsidiary, or its employees, would rely on it using that superior knowledge for the employees' protection although it was not necessary to show that the parent was in the practice of intervening in the health and safety policies of the subsidiary. The court had to look at the relationship between the companies more widely and could find that the element of reliance on it using superior knowledge was established where the evidence showed that the parent had a practice of intervening in the trading operations of the subsidiary.

It may be said that the judiciary's power to lift the veil is a tactic used by the courts in a flexible way so as to counter fraud, sharp practice, oppression and illegality. In *Conway v Ratiu* [2006] 1 All ER 571, Auld LJ noted the 'readiness of the courts, regardless of the precise issue involved, to draw back the corporate veil to do justice when common sense and reality demand it'. However, this view must be tempered by the vast amount of case law in the area which indicates that the judiciary's focus is upon safeguarding the corporate form and preventing fraudulent practice as opposed to dispensing 'justice for all' via this avenue (see below). As noted earlier, there is no substitute for reading the academic articles in this area which are outlined at the end of this chapter. Examples of special areas of application are as follows:

(a) Abuse of the corporate form

One of the fundamental areas where the courts appear willing to lift the corporate veil is where the corporate form is being used as a 'façade', 'sham' or as a 'mask' so as to evade existing liabilities or to defeat the law.

Here the courts have been prepared to investigate sharp practice by individuals who are trying to hide behind a company front. Thus, in *Gilford Motor Co v Horne* [1933] Ch 935 a former employee bound by a restraint of trade set up a company in order to evade its provisions, claiming that he as a person might be bound by the restraint but the company, being a separate entity, could not be. An injunction to prevent solicitation of Gilford's customers was granted against both him and his company which the court described as 'a device, a stratagem [. . .] a mere cloak or sham'. In this regard, Lord Hanworth MR observed:

Farwell J heard the evidence about that company and had these documents before him. He says this: 'The defendant company is a company which, on the evidence before me, is obviously carried on wholly by the defendant Horne. Mrs Horne, one of the directors, is not, so far as any evidence I have had before me, taking any part in the business or the management of the business.

The son, whose initials are "J M", is engaged in a subordinate position in that company, and the other director, Howard, is an employee of the company. As one of the witnesses said in the witness-box, in all dealings which he had had with the defendant company the "boss" or the "guvnor", whichever term is the appropriate one, was the defendant Horne, and I have not any doubt on the evidence I have had before me that the defendant company was the channel through which the defendant Horne was carrying on his business. Of course, in law the defendant company is a separate entity from the defendant Horne, but I cannot help feeling quite convinced that at any rate one of the reasons for the creation of that company was the fear of Mr Horne that he might commit breaches of the covenant in carrying on the business, as, for instance, in sending out circulars as he was doing, and that he might possibly avoid that liability if he did it through the defendant company. There is no doubt that the defendant company has sent out circulars to persons who were at the crucial time customers of the plaintiff company.'

Now I have recalled that portion of the judgment of Farwell J, and I wish in clear terms to say that I agree with every word of it. I am quite satisfied that this company was formed as a device, a stratagem, in order to mask the effective carrying on of a business of Mr E B Horne. The purpose of it was to try to enable him, under what is a cloak or a sham, to engage in business which, on consideration of the agreement which had been sent to him just about seven days before the company was incorporated, was a business in respect of which he had a fear that the plaintiffs might intervene and object.

Now this action is brought by the plaintiffs, the Gilford Motor Company Ltd, to enforce the terms of clause 9 of the agreement of 30 May 1929, on the ground that the defendant Horne, and the company, as his agent and under his direction, have committed breaches of the covenant which I have read.

Jones v Lipman [1962] 1 All ER 442

Lipman sold a house to Jones but ultimately refused to complete the sale. In order to ensure that he would not have to sell the house to Jones, Lipman executed a sham transfer of the house to a company controlled by him (which was in fact a shelf company he had purchased) just before completion of the sale contract to Jones. Lipman and a clerk of his solicitors were the only shareholders and directors. Jones applied under Ord 14a for specific performance against Lipman and the company.

Held – specific performance should be ordered against both. Russell J stated:

> The defendant company is the creature of the first defendant, a device and a sham, a mask which he holds before his face in an attempt to avoid recognition by the eye of equity. The case cited illustrates that an equitable remedy is rightly to be granted directly against the creature in such circumstances [. . .] The proper order to make is an order on both the defendants specifically to perform the agreement between the plaintiffs and the first defendant.

Wallersteiner v Moir [1974] 3 All ER 217

In 1967, the plaintiff (Dr Wallersteiner), a financier, issued a writ claiming damages from the defendant (Mr Moir) for libel contained in a circular letter sent out by the defendant, alleging a series of unlawful activities on the part of the plaintiff. The defendant served a defence whereby he also counterclaimed for breaches of the Companies Act 1948 s 54 and s 190, and claimed declarations that the plaintiff had been guilty of fraud. The plaintiff failed to deliver a reply or defence to counterclaim. Nevertheless, he used the proceedings to stop investigation into his conduct by the company at meetings, on the grounds that the matter was *sub judice*.

Held – the plaintiff's delays were 'intentional and contumelious and the proceedings could not be used as a gag to prevent discussion'. The action for libel should be struck out, and there would be judgment on the counterclaim. Lord Denning MR took the opportunity to make the following observations with respect to the corporate veil:

> Mr Browne-Wilkinson, as *amicus curiae*, suggested that all these various concerns were used by Dr Wallersteiner as a façade: so that each could be treated as his alter ego. Each was in reality Dr Wallersteiner wearing another hat. Mr Lincoln, for Dr Wallersteiner, repudiated this suggestion. It was quite wrong, he said, to pierce the corporate veil. The principle enunciated in *Salomon* v *Salomon* was sacrosanct. If we were to treat each of these concerns as being Dr Wallersteiner himself under another hat, we should not, he said, be lifting a corner of the corporate veil. We should be sending it up in flames.
>
> I am prepared to accept that the English concerns were distinct legal entities [. . .] Even so, I am quite clear that they were just the puppets of Dr Wallersteiner. He controlled their every movement. Each danced to his bidding. He pulled the strings. No one else got within reach of them. Transformed into legal language, they were his agents to do as he commanded. He was the principal behind them. I am of the opinion that the court should pull aside the corporate veil and treat these concerns as being his creatures – for whose doings he should be, and is, responsible. At any rate, it was up to him to show that anyone else had a say in their affairs and he never did so.

(b) Groups of companies: the human and commercial reality of the group

The court has, on occasion, lifted the veil of incorporation to allow a group of companies to be regarded as one, because in reality they were not independent either in human or commercial terms.

Re Hellenic and General Trust Ltd [1975] 3 All ER 382

A company called MIT was a wholly-owned subsidiary of Hambros Ltd and held 53 per cent of the ordinary shares of Hellenic. A scheme of arrangement was put forward under which Hambros was to acquire all the ordinary shares of Hellenic for a cash consideration of 48p per share. The ordinary shareholders including MIT met and over 80 per cent approved the scheme, MIT voting in support. However, the National Bank of Greece, which was a minority shareholder, opposed the scheme because it would be liable to meet a heavy tax burden under Greek law as a result of receipt of cash for its shares. Templeman J refused to approve the scheme on a number of grounds. However, the one which interests us here is that he ruled that there should have been a separate class meeting of ordinary shareholders excluding MIT; thus, in effect, regarding the holding company, Hambros, and the subsidiary, MIT, as one economic unit in the class meeting and not two independent companies with independent interests.

DHN Food Distributors v Tower Hamlets London Borough Council [1976] 3 All ER 462

DHN Food Distributors (DHN) was a holding company which ran its business through two wholly-owned subsidiaries, Bronze Investments Ltd (Bronze) and DHN Food Transport Ltd (Transport). The group collected food from the docks and distributed it to retail outlets. Bronze owned the premises in Bow from which the business was conducted and Transport ran the distribution side of the business. Tower Hamlets compulsorily acquired the premises in Bow for the purpose of building houses. This power of compulsory acquisition arose under the Housing Act 1957 and compensation was payable under the Land Compensation Act of 1961 under two headings: (a) the value of the land; and (b) disturbance of business. Tower Hamlets was prepared to pay £360,000 for the value of the land but refused to pay on the second heading because DHN and Transport had no interest in the land. This was unfortunate for the group as a whole since the loss of the premises had caused all three companies to go into liquidation, it being impossible to find other suitable premises. The practical answer would have been, of course, to have conveyed the premises from Bronze to DHN when compulsory acquisition was threatened. This had not been done, although the conveyance would have been exempt from stamp duty since it would have been a transfer between associated companies. However, Lord Denning in the Court of Appeal drew aside the corporate veil and treated DHN as owners of the property whereupon Tower Hamlets became liable to pay for disturbance of business. The basis of Lord Denning's judgment was that company legislation required group accounts and to that extent recognised a group entity which he felt the judiciary should do also. Lord Denning did not feel that it was necessary to imply an agency between the holding and subsidiary company.

Lord Denning observed 'This case might be called the "Three in one". Three companies in one. Alternatively, the "One in three", one group of three companies', going on to note:

> . . . A further very interesting point was raised by Mr Dobry on company law. We all know that in many respects a group of companies are treated together for the purpose of general accounts, balance sheet, and profit and loss account. They are treated as one concern. Professor Gower in *Modern Company Law*, 3rd edn (1969), p. 216 says: 'there is evidence of a general tendency to ignore the separate legal entities of various companies within a group, and to look instead at the economic entity of the whole group.'

> This is especially the case when a parent company owns all the shares of the subsidiaries – so much so that it can control every movement of the subsidiaries. These subsidiaries are bound hand and foot to the parent company and must do just what the parent company says. A striking instance is the decision of the House of Lords in *Harold Holdsworth & Co. (Wakefield) Ltd* v *Caddies* [1955] 1 W.L.R. 352. So here. This group is virtually the same as a partnership in which all the three companies are partners. They should not be treated separately so as to be defeated on a technical point. They should not be deprived of the compensation which should justly be payable for disturbance. The three companies should, for present purposes, be treated as one, and the parent company DHN should be treated as that one. So DHN are entitled to claim compensation accordingly. It was not necessary for them to go through a conveyancing device to get it.

> I realise that the President of the Lands Tribunal, in view of previous cases, felt it necessary to decide as he did. But now that the matter has been fully discussed in this court, we must decide differently from him. These companies as a group are entitled to compensation not only for the value of the land, but also compensation for disturbance. I would allow the appeal accordingly.

Comment

(i) It cannot be said from this case that there is a general principle of group entity. Much depends upon the circumstances of the case. Thus, in *Woolfson* v *Strathclyde Regional Council* (1978) 38 P & CR 521 the House of Lords did not follow DHN Foods in what was a similar situation because in Woolfson the subsidiaries were active trading companies and not, as in DHN Foods, mere shells. Again, in *Multinational Gas and Petrochemical Co* v *Multinational Gas and Petrochemical Services Ltd* [1983] 2 All ER 563 the Court of Appeal held, following *Salomon*, that wholly owned subsidiaries in a group were separate entities and not the agents of the holding company or each other in the absence of a specific agency agreement. Furthermore, in *Dimbleby & Sons Ltd* v *NUJ* [1984] 1 All ER 751, a group of companies was regarded as a series of separate entities so that the picketing of one company within the group by workers employed by another company within the group was regarded as unlawful secondary picketing for the purposes of s 17 of the Employment Act 1980. (See now s 224 of the Trade Union and Labour Relations (Consolidation) Act 1992.)

(ii) Additional examples in the group situation are to be found in *Re H and Others* [1996] 2 All ER 391 where in an action by Customs and Excise to restrain defendants who had been charged with various offences of evading excise duty from dealing with assets pending trial the Court of Appeal was prepared to restrain subsidiary companies' assets, refusing to regard the companies as separate entities under the *Salomon* rule even though the evasions were alleged to have been committed by the holding company. However, in *Re Polly Peck International plc (In Administration)* [1996] 2 All ER 433 the High Court applied the *Salomon* rule in a corporate insolvency, holding that the separate legal existence of group companies was important where the companies were creditors of the holding company and each wished to make a separate claim in the holding company's insolvency and be paid what is called a dividend on that claim.

(iii) More recently, the court has drawn aside the corporate veil in order that the defence of justification to a claim for defamation could succeed. See *Ratiu & Regent House Properties* (below).

Ratiu & Regent House Properties v *Conway* [2006] 1 All ER 571

Regent instructed Mr Conway, a solicitor, to act in the purchase and development of a site in London and related matters. Mr Conway's retainer was with the subsidiary. Relationships deteriorated when Mr Conway made a bid for a property in competition with Regent. Following this, Regent made an allegation of misconduct in regard to his proposed property purchase in that he was in breach of his fiduciary duty to Regent. Mr Conway brought a claim for defamation against Regent, contending that his fiduciary duty was owed only to the subsidiary and not to Regent.

Regent defended the claim on the basis of justification (i.e. that the allegations they had made were true because Mr Conway owed Regent a duty of care as a fiduciary as well as the subsidiary and that duty of care had been broken as regards Regent also. That, of course, was not the contractual position and to accept that fiduciary duties were owed to Regent it was necessary for the court to draw aside the corporate veil in favour of Regent and so sustain its defence. This the Court of Appeal did. It found that throughout the relevant period, Regent had been the 'moving spirit' behind the relevant transactions. In reality, said the court, Mr Conway well knew that his client was Regent and that the subsidiary was merely a vehicle controlled by Regent. Mr Conway was in breach of a fiduciary duty to Regent. The decision of the jury in the lower court that Regent's defence of justification failed was set aside.

The current approach was set down by Robert Goff LJ in *Bank of Tokyo Ltd* v *Karoon* [1987] AC 45, stating 'Counsel suggested beguilingly that it would be technical for us to distinguish between parent company and subsidiary in this context; economically, he said, they were one. But we are concerned not with economics but with law. The distinction between the two is, in law, fundamental and cannot be abridged.'

(c) Groups of companies: the concept of agency

The concept of agency has sometimes been used by the courts under which a subsidiary is regarded as the agent of its holding company, even though there is no agency agreement as such between them in regard to the transaction concerned. The effect is that transactions entered into by a subsidiary are regarded as those of the holding company for which the holding company is liable. This doctrine has been implemented for purposes of liability to tax.

Firestone Tyre & Rubber Co Ltd v Lewellin [1957] 1 All ER 561

An American company formed a wholly owned subsidiary in England to manufacture and sell its brand of tyres in Europe. The American company negotiated agreements with European distributors under which the latter would place orders with the American company which the English subsidiary would carry out. In fact, the distributors sent their orders to the subsidiary direct and the orders were met without any consultation with the American company. The subsidiary received the money for the tyres sold to the distributors and, after deducting its manufacturing expenses plus 5 per cent, it forwarded the balance of the money to the American company. All the directors of the subsidiary resided in England (except one who was the president of the American company) and they managed the subsidiary's affairs free from day-to-day control by the American company.

Held – by the House of Lords – that the American company was carrying on business in England through its English subsidiary acting as its agent and it was consequently liable to pay United Kingdom tax.

Comment

(i) The principle of presumed agency, or agency in fact, of the subsidiary was used in *Smith, Stone & Knight Ltd* v *Birmingham Corporation* [1939] 4 All ER 116. Premises belonging to Smith, Stone were compulsorily acquired by the Corporation. The question to be resolved was whether the business of waste paper merchants, for which the premises were used, was carried on by Smith, Stone or by its subsidiary, Birmingham Waste Co Ltd. This was vital because an owner/occupier could get compensation, but a tenant/occupier like the waste company could not. The court decided that the waste company occupied the premises as a mere agent of Smith, Stone because, among other things, it was a wholly owned subsidiary and the directors were the same in both companies. Smith, Stone was entitled to compensation. This case can be distinguished from *DHN Food Distributors* because, as we have seen in the *DHN* case, Lord Denning did not find it necessary to imply an agency.

(ii) The theories of the economic reality of the group and the implied agency approach have not been used to control abuses in the area of holding and subsidiary companies in regard to trade creditors. If a subsidiary is insolvent, only public and stock market opinion prevents the holding company from liquidating the subsidiary leaving its creditors' claims unsatisfied even though the group as a whole is solvent. In some cases even public and market opinion and criticism do not prevent it. The EC Ninth Directive, which has yet to be implemented, does in certain situations make the dominant company within the group liable for losses incurred by a dependent company.

(d) Illegality

The courts have been prepared to draw aside the veil of incorporation in order to establish that a company was owned by nationals of an enemy country so that to do business with it would be illegal because it would be trading with the enemy.

Daimler Co Ltd v Continental Tyre & Rubber Co (Great Britain) Ltd [1916] 2 AC 307

After the outbreak of war with Germany, the tyre company, which was registered in England and had its registered office there, sued the Daimler Company for money due in respect of goods supplied to Daimler before the outbreak of war. Daimler's defence was that, since the tyre company's members and officers were German, to pay the debt would be to trade with the enemy, and that, therefore, the claim by the tyre company should be struck out, i.e. not allowed to go to trial. Evidence showed that all the members of the tyre company save one were German. The secretary of the company, who held one share, lived in England and was a British subject. He brought the action in the name of, and on behalf of, the company. Lord Parker of Waddington stated:

No one can question that a corporation is a legal person distinct from its corporators; that the relation of a shareholder to a company, which is limited by shares, is not in itself the relation of principal and agent or the reverse; that the assets of the company belong to it and the acts of its servants and agents are its acts, while its shareholders, as such, have no property in the assets and no personal responsibility for those acts. The law on the subject is clearly laid down in a passage in Lord Halsbury's judgment in *Salomon* v *Salomon & Co* 'I am simply here', he says, 'dealing with the provisions of the statute, and it seems to me to be essential to the artificial creation that the law should recognise only that artificial existence – quite apart from the motives or conduct of individual corporators . . . Short of such proof' – i.e., proof in appropriate proceedings that the company had no real legal existence – 'it seems to me impossible to dispute that once the company is legally incorporated it must be treated like any other independent person with its rights and liabilities appropriate to itself, and that the motives of those who took part in the formation of the company are absolutely irrelevant in discussing what those rights and liabilities are.' I do not think, however, that it is a necessary corollary of this reasoning to say that the character of its corporators must be irrelevant to the character of the company; and this is crucial, for the rule against trading with the enemy depends upon enemy character.

A natural person, though an English-born subject of His Majesty, may bear an enemy character and be under liability and disability as such by adhering to His Majesty's enemies. If he gives them active aid, he is a traitor; but he may fall far short of that and still be invested with enemy character. If he has what is known in prize law as a commercial domicil among the King's enemies, his merchandise is good prize at sea, just as if it belonged to a subject of the enemy Power. Not only actively, but passively, he may bring himself under the same disability. Voluntary residence among the enemy, however passive or pacific he may be, identifies an English subject with His Majesty's foes. I do not think it necessary to cite authority for these well-known propositions, nor do I doubt that, if they had seemed material to the Court of Appeal, they would have been accepted.

How are such rules to be applied to an artificial person, incorporated by forms of law? As far as active adherence to the enemy goes, there can be no difference, except such as arises from the fact that a company's acts are those of its servants and agents acting within the scope of their authority. An illustration of the application of such rules to a company (as it happens a company of neutral incorporation, which is an a fortiori case) is to be found in *Netherlands South African Ry Co* v *Fisher*.

In the case of an artificial person what is the analogue to voluntary residence among the King's enemies? Its impersonality can hardly put it in a better position than a natural person and lead to its being unaffected by anything equivalent to residence. It is only by a figure of speech that a company can be said to have a nationality or residence at all. If the place of its incorporation under municipal law fixes its residence, then its residence cannot be changed, which is almost a contradiction in terms, and in the case of a company residence must correspond to the birthplace and country of natural allegiance in the case of a living person, and not to residence or commercial domicil. Nevertheless, enemy character depends on these last. It would seem, therefore, logically to follow that, in transferring the application of the rule against trading with the enemy from natural to artificial persons, something more than the mere place or country of registration or incorporation must be looked at.

My Lords, I think that the analogy is to be found in control, an idea which, if not very familiar in law, is of capital importance and is very well understood in commerce and finance. The acts of a company's organs, its directors, managers, secretary, and so forth, functioning within the scope of their authority, are the company's acts and may invest it definitively with enemy character. It seems to me that similarly the character of those who can make and unmake those officers, dictate their conduct mediately or immediately, prescribe their duties and call them to account, may also be material in a question of the enemy character of the company. If not definite and conclusive, it must at least be prima facie relevant, as raising a presumption that those who are purporting to act in the name of the company are, in fact, under the control of those whom it is their interest to satisfy. Certainly I have found no authority to the contrary. Such a view reconciles the positions of natural and artificial persons in this regard, and the opposite view leads to the paradoxical result that the King's enemies, who chance during war to constitute the entire body of corporators in a company registered in England, thereby pass out of the range of legal vision, and, instead, the corporation, which in itself is incapable of loyalty, or enmity, or residence, or of anything but bare existence in contemplation of law and registration under some system of law, takes their place for almost the most important of all purposes, that of being classed among the King's friends or among his foes in time of war.

What is involved in the decision of the Court of Appeal is that, for all purposes to which the character and not merely the rights and powers of an artificial person are material, the personalities of the natural persons, who are its corporators, are to be ignored. An impassable line is drawn between the one person and the others. When the law is concerned with the artificial person, it is to know nothing of the natural persons who constitute and control it. In questions of property and capacity, of acts done and rights acquired or liabilities assumed thereby, this may be always true. Certainly it is so for the most part. But the character in which property is held, and the character in which the capacity to act is enjoyed and acts are done, are not in pari materia. The latter character is a quality of the company itself, and conditions its capacities and its acts. It is not a mere part of its energies or acquisitions, and if that character must be derivable not from the circumstances of its incorporation which arises once for all, but from qualities of enmity and amity, which are dependent on the chances of peace or war and are attributable only to human beings, I know not from what human beings that character should be derived, in cases where the active conduct of the company's officers has not already decided the matter, if resort is not to be had to the predominant character of its shareholders and corporators . . .

Held – by the House of Lords – that the action must be struck out. Although the place of registration and the situation of the registered office normally governs the company's nationality and domicile for the purposes of actions at law, the court has a jurisdiction to draw aside the corporate veil in some cases to see who the persons in control of the company's affairs are. If, as here, the persons in actual control of the company were enemy aliens, the company could be so regarded for the purposes of the law relating to trading with the enemy.

(e) The personal relationship company

A breakdown in the management of the company or the complete exclusion of a member director from participation in management have been redressed by winding up the company on the just and equitable ground by regarding the company as in fact, if not in form, a partnership.

Ebrahimi v Westbourne Galleries [1972] 2 All ER 492

Since 1945 Mr Ebrahimi and Mr Nazar had carried on a partnership which dealt in Persian and other carpets. They shared equally the management and profits. In 1958 they formed a private company carrying on the same business and were appointed its first directors. Soon after the company's formation, Mr George Nazar, Mr Nazar's son, was made a third director. By reason of their shareholdings, Mr Nazar and George had the majority of votes at general meetings. The company made good profits, all of which were distributed as directors' remuneration and no dividend was ever paid. In 1969 Mr Ebrahimi was removed from the position of director by a resolution at a general meeting in pursuance of what is now s 168. Mr Ebrahimi presented a petition seeking an order under s 210 of the Companies Act 1948 (see now s 994, 2006 Act) that Mr Nazar and George should purchase his shares or, alternatively, an order under what is now s 122(1)(g) of the Insolvency Act 1986 that the company be wound up. At first instance Plowman J refused the order under s 210 because the oppression alleged was against Mr Ebrahimi in his capacity as director and not that as member. However, the petition for a compulsory winding-up was granted because, in the opinion of Plowman J, it was just and equitable that the company should be wound up. The Court of Appeal affirmed the decision of Plowman J under s 210 but dismissed the petition for a compulsory winding-up, regarding it as an unjustifiable innovation in the company situation. On further appeal, the House of Lords reversed the Court of Appeal and restored the decision of Plowman J that an order for winding-up should be made. The major points arising from the case are as follows:

(a) The majority shareholders, Mr Nazar and George, had made use of their undisputed right under what is now s 168, CA 2006 to remove a director, namely Mr Ebrahimi. Could such use of a statutory right be a ground for making a compulsory winding-up order under what is now s 122(1)(g) of the Insolvency Act 1986? In other words, could the exercise of a legal right be regarded as contravening the rules of equity which are the basis of what is now s 122(1)(g)?

(b) The House of Lords answered these questions in the affirmative, at least for companies founded on a personal relationship, i.e. for companies which in essence were partnerships, though in form they had assumed the character of a company: '[. . .] a limited company is more than a mere judicial entity, with a personality in law of its own: [. . .] there is room in company law for recognition of the fact that behind it, or amongst it, there are individuals, with rights, expectations and obligations *inter se* which are not necessarily submerged in the company structure. That structure is defined by the Companies Act [. . .] and by the articles of association by which shareholders agree to be bound. In most companies and in most contexts, this definition is sufficient and exhaustive, equally so whether the company is large or small. The "just and equitable" provision does not, as the respondents suggest, entitle one party to disregard the obligations he assumes by entering a company, nor the court to dispense him from it. It does, as equity always does, enable the court to subject the exercise of legal rights to equitable considerations; considerations, that is, of a personal character, arising between one individual and another, which may make it unjust, or inequitable, to insist on legal rights, or to exercise them in a particular way', said Lord Wilberforce.

(c) The decision makes an important contribution to the movement for harmonisation of European company law. The concept of the private company founded on a personal relationship has been approximated to the continental European concept. For example, it is accepted in Germany and France that the private company is a special association and not merely a variety of a general concept of companies and they are governed by different enactments.

(d) The partnership analogy is an example of the drawing aside of the corporate veil, i.e. treating a company as a partnership. Once this has been done, partnership law applies and under this each general (not salaried) partner is, in the absence of contrary agreement, entitled to a say in management (see Partnership Act 1890, s 24(5)). The same is true of a limited liability partnership under Reg 7 of the Limited Liability Partnership Regulations 2001. Furthermore, the definition of partnership requires that the partners be in business 'in common' which they obviously are not if one or more of them is deprived of a say in management. A general partner who is deprived of a say in management is, in the absence of a contrary agreement, entitled to dissolve the firm.

However, the partnership analogy would not necessarily be applied to all private companies. The analogy is most likely to be used where, as in the **Westbourne** case, the proprietors (members) and the managers (directors) are one and the same, as full general partners in a partnership are.

Comment

(i) For the possibility, in more recent times, of using the more versatile remedy of 'unfair prejudice' under s 994, see later in the text (Chapter 18, p. 326 ⬥).

(ii) It should also be noted that the Nazars did not offer to buy Mr Ebrahimi's shares. If they had done so, e.g. at a fair price to be decided by the company's auditors, the court may not have wound the company up so that Mr Ebrahimi could get his share capital back. A pretty drastic remedy, though, to wind up a solvent company just to achieve this (see also Chapter 18, p. 345 ○).

Statutory provisions

A good starting point for the discussion of such statutory provisions is Lord Diplock's statement in *Dimbleby & Sons Ltd* v *National Union of Journalists* [1984] 1 WLR 427 when he observed: 'The corporate veil in the case of companies incorporated under the Companies Acts is drawn by statute and it can be pierced by some other statute if such statute so provides; but, in view of its raison d'être and its constant recognition by the courts since *Salomon* v *A. Salomon & Co Ltd*, one would expect that any parliamentary intention to pierce the corporate veil be expressed in clear and unequivocal language.'

(a) Section 761, Companies Act 2006

It will be recalled that by reason of s 761 a plc cannot commence trading or exercise borrowing powers unless and until it has received a s 761 certificate from the Registrar. If it does so, the transactions are enforceable against the company but if the company fails to meet its obligations within 21 days of being called upon to do so the directors are, under s 767, jointly and severally liable to indemnify a person who has suffered loss or damage by reason of the company's failure to meet its obligations. This is a further example of liability in the directors to pay, e.g. the company's debts, and no proof of fraud is required.

(b) Section 405, Companies Act 2006

This provides that where there is a holding and subsidiary relationship between companies the holding company is required, subject to certain exceptions already referred to, not only to prepare its individual accounts but also group accounts. This suggests that for financial purposes the companies within a group are one.

Finally, there are a number of examples to be found in the law relating to corporate insolvency. Thus, when a company goes into liquidation and the evidence shows that the directors have negligently struggled on for too long with an insolvent company in the hope that things would get better but which has, in the end, gone into insolvent liquidation, there are provisions in the Insolvency Act 1986 under which the directors concerned may, if the company goes into liquidation, be required by the court, on the application of the liquidator, to make such contribution to the company's assets as the court thinks proper. This means in effect that the directors will be paying or helping to pay the company's debts. Further and more detailed considerations will be given to this concept, which is called wrongful trading, and others in the chapters on directors and corporate insolvency which is where they really belong.

It is worth noting that when offering s 767 together with the insolvency situations as examples of drawing aside the veil to make the members liable for the debts of the company, these are examples of director liability. They are therefore only truly legitimate examples if the

47

directors are also members. Since most of the problems in this area occur in private companies where the directors are normally also members, the examples can be given provided it is made clear that we assume we are dealing with director/members.

Limits on lifting the veil

It should be noted though that concepts such as 'fairness' and 'justice' do not play a leading role in the court's consideration of whether or not the corporate veil should be lifted. The prevailing attitude of the judiciary is that those individuals who adopt the corporate form should expect to take 'the highs with the lows'. Indeed, this has been highlighted by Browne-Wilkinson VC who observed in *Tate Access Floors Inc* v *Boswell* [1991] Ch 512: 'If people choose to conduct their affairs through the medium of corporations, they are taking advantage of the fact that in law those corporations are separate legal entities, whose property and actions are in law not the property or actions of their incorporators or controlling shareholders. In my judgment controlling shareholders cannot, for all purposes beneficial to them, insist on the separate identity of such corporations but then be heard to say the contrary when discovery is sought against such corporations.' Thus, as noted earlier, in *Woolfson* v *Strathclyde Regional Council* (1978) 38 P& CR 521 the House of Lords did not follow DHN Foods in what was a similar situation.

Essay questions

1 The principle of law set out in *Salomon v Salomon & Co Ltd* is not always applied. Give the facts of this case and give its principle of law, and discuss when the judiciary or statutory provisions will not take account of that principle.   *(University of Paisley)*

2 Explain by reference to statutory and common law examples what is meant by the term 'lifting the veil of incorporation'.   *(The Chartered Institute of Management Accountants)*

Suggested further reading

Arthurs, 'To pierce or not to pierce? The Court of Appeal protects the corporate veil' (2012) Co. LJ 17.

Gallagher and Zieger, 'Lifting the Corporate Veil in the Pursuit of Justice' (1990) JBL 292.

Lowry, 'Lifting the Corporate Veil' [1993] JBL 41.

Mitchell, 'Piercing the corporate veil to impose contractual liability on a director' (2012) BJIB & FL 27(3) 149.

Mohanty and Bhandari, 'The evolution of the separate legal personality doctrine and its exceptions: A comparative analysis' (2011) *Company Lawyer* 32(7) 194.

Moore, 'A Temple Built on Faulty Foundations: Piercing the Corporate veil and the Legacy of *Salomon v Salomon*' (2006) JBL 180.

Ottolenghi, 'From Peeping Behind the Corporate Veil to Ignoring It Completely' (1990) 53 MLR 338.

Rixon, 'Lifting the Veil between Holding and Subsidiary Companies' (1986) 102 LQR 415.

Samuels, 'Lifting the Veil' [1964] JBL 107.

Vlasov, 'Liability of a puppeteer for a puppet: A recent development in law on piercing the corporate veil' (2012) *Company Lawyer* 33(11) 356.

3 Companies and partnerships compared

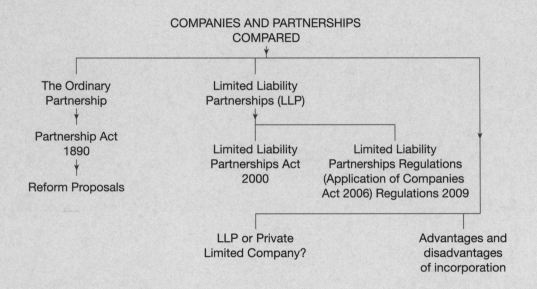

COMPANIES AND PARTNERSHIPS
COMPARED

The Ordinary
Partnership

Partnership Act
1890

Reform Proposals

Limited Liability
Partnerships (LLP)

Limited Liability
Partnerships Act
2000

Limited Liability
Partnerships Regulations
(Application of Companies
Act 2006) Regulations 2009

LLP or Private
Limited Company?

Advantages and
disadvantages
of incorporation

Whilst the focus of this book is the law of corporations, it is nevertheless useful to take the opportunity to appreciate comparisons with other business formats such as the partnership. The first and the oldest form of partnership is governed by the Partnership Act 1890 and is referred to here as the ordinary partnership. There is also the limited partnership governed by the Limited Partnerships Act of 1907, and finally the limited liability partnership governed by the Limited Liability Partnerships Act 2000. These will be discussed in greater detail below.

The ordinary partnership

A partnership is defined in s 1 of the Partnership Act 1890 as 'the relationship which subsists between persons carrying on a business in common with a view of profit'. It will be noted that there must be a business; that it must be carried on in common by the members (whether by all of them, or by one or more of them acting for the others, will depend on the agreement subsisting between them); and that there must be the intention to earn profits.

An association of persons formed for the purpose, say, of promoting some educational or recreational object to which the whole of the funds of the association shall be devoted, and from which no advantage in the nature of a distribution of a profit shall accrue to the members, is not a partnership.

Sharing profits

Participation in the profits of a business may be regarded as *prima facie* evidence of a partnership, but it is not conclusive – the intention of the parties must be examined. Thus, an employee whose remuneration is based on a share of profits, or the widow or child of a deceased partner receiving an annuity in the form of a share of profits, would not legally be deemed to be partners. Neither does the common ownership of property constitute a partnership (see further Chapter 29 ○), nor the lending of money in consideration of an agreement to pay the interest, or to repay the capital, as a share or percentage of profits as they accrue. (But in such a case the lender should take the precaution of having the agreement embodied in writing, signed by all the parties, and setting out clearly the fact that he is not to be considered a partner.)

Liability

The liability of a general partner is unlimited. In a limited partnership one or more of the partners may limit his liability for the firm's debts to the amount of capital he has contributed, though even a limited partnership must have at least one general partner. In this connection it should be noted that a partnership can consist entirely of limited companies in order, for example, to further a joint venture between them which stops short of merger, and a limited company can be a partner with individuals as the other partner(s). This will not in either case make the partnership a limited partnership unless the firm is registered as such under the Limited Partnerships Act 1907. The liability of a limited company for debt is unlimited in that it is liable for debt down to its last asset. It is the liability of the members which is limited.

As will be noted later in this text, the liability of a member of a company may be limited by shares or by guarantee.

Citation as partner

The question of citation as a partner is of great importance because the existence of a partnership, if such is proved, will involve all parties cited as partners in unlimited liability for the debts of the firm. Partners are agents for the firm, and can bind the other partners in contracts concerning the business of the firm whether they are specifically authorised to make them or not.

No formalities

Two or more persons can combine to form a partnership, which can be brought into existence in a highly formal or a very casual manner. Whilst no legal formalities are required, it is desirable and usual for the rights and liabilities of the partners to be defined in a formal Deed of Partnership, or at least in a written Partnership Agreement. On the other hand, a mere oral agreement is equally binding, and in extreme cases a relationship of partnership may be inferred from the conduct of the parties. The partners are at liberty to vary the arrangements made between them and, where the conduct of the parties has for a lengthy period been inconsistent with the terms as originally agreed, it will be presumed that they intend that the new arrangements shall be binding on them.

Management

The Partnership Act 1890 makes provisions as to contribution of capital, division of profits, rights of partners to participate in active management, and so on, but these only apply in so far as they are not varied by agreement between the partners. General partners are entitled to share in the management of the firm unless the articles provide otherwise.

By contrast, members of a company are not entitled to take part in the management of the company unless they become directors. It is worth bearing this in mind when looking at the issue of 'quasi-partnerships' (see Chapter 6 ◐) as it is such expectations of participation which are frequently carried over by people from partnerships into small private companies when incorporation occurs. This in turn leads to a number of challenges for the courts in terms of reviewing a company's articles of association and determining whether a provision represents an 'insider' or 'outsider' right and/or a 'legitimate expectation' which may form the basis of an action under s 994 of the Companies Act 2006.

Number of partners

The Regulatory Reform (Removal of 20 Member Limit in Partnerships) Order 2002 disapplied the prohibition contained in s 716 of the Companies Act 1985, which prevented the formation of a partnership consisting of more than 20 persons for the purpose of carrying on any business for gain. It therefore removes entirely the 20-member limit from all unlimited and limited partnerships. By contrast, a company whether public or private has no upper limit of membership.

Capacity to contract

There is no limitation on the activities of partners, provided that these are legal, nor is there any limit to the liability of the individual partners for the debts of the firm, each partner being liable to the full extent of his personal estate for any deficiencies of the partnership. However, provision is made for the introduction of limited partners whose liability is limited to the amount of capital they have introduced, though there must always be at least one general partner who is fully liable for the debts of the firm. Such a partnership must be registered as a limited partnership under the Limited Partnerships Act 1907 (and see below).

By contrast, the affairs of a company are closely controlled by company legislation and the company, if it has stated objectives, can only operate within those objects as laid down in its articles of association, though these can be altered to some extent by special resolution. Equally under the Companies Act 2006, a company is not required to have objects clauses and, as such, this brings them closer to the partnership position whereby it may carry on any business so long as it is not illegal.

Partnership as a business organisation

The partnership was the normal form of business organisation for operations on a fairly large scale before the advent of the joint stock company (refer to Chapter 1 ◔), but it is now largely restricted to the type of enterprise requiring intimate personal collaboration between the members, or where incorporation is not possible or desirable, as among doctors, though the increasing control over companies including, in particular, private companies, may see some revival of the partnership as a more general business organisation. However, in the legal and accounting professions particularly, negligence liability is encouraging a move towards incorporation of firms to achieve limited liability or the formation of limited liability partnerships (see below).

Lack of continuity

One of the defects of the partnership is its lack of continuity. No one member of a company can wind up the company (but see exceptionally *Ebrahimi*), and the death, bankruptcy or insanity of a member does not mean that the company must be wound up. However, a partnership may be dissolved by any partner giving notice to the others at any time unless the partnership is entered into for a fixed period of time. Dissolution by notice depends upon what the partnership agreement, if any, says. If, as in *Moss* v *Elphick* [1910] 1 KB 846, the agreement says that dissolution is only to be by mutual consent of the partners, then dissolution by notice as described above does not apply. A partnership is, subject to any agreement between the partners to the contrary, dissolved by the death or bankruptcy of a partner. The partnership agreement will normally provide that the business is to continue under the remaining partner(s), so the dissolution is only a technical one, though it does leave the continuing partner(s) to deal with the paying out of the former partner's share in the business, usually in line with provisions in the partnership agreement.

In addition, on the death of a partner the continuing partners must account to his personal representatives for the amount of his interest in the firm. This difficulty may be met to some extent by providing funds out of the proceeds of an insurance policy on the deceased partner's life, or by arranging for the balance of his capital account to be left in the business as a loan, but failing these measures the sudden withdrawal of a large amount of capital may well cause serious dislocation of the smaller business, or even end its operations. The most serious defect of a partnership, however, is the difficulty of providing additional funds for expansion, and this may induce partners to admit new members for the sake of their capital, regardless of their fitness for taking an active part in controlling the business.

Not a persona at law

A partnership firm is not a persona at law; a partnership is an aggregate of its members. In the matter of procedure, the Supreme Court Rules 2009 (SI 2009/1603) make it possible for the firm to sue and be sued in its own name, but this does not confer upon it a legal personality as is possessed by a corporation. This makes the holding of property more difficult in the partnership. For example, land cannot be conveyed to the firm. Instead it is conveyed to some or all of the partners as legal owners who declare a *trust of land* for all the partners in equity.

Law Commission Joint Consultation Paper on Partnership Law Reform

The Law Commission issued a Consultation Paper on Partnership Law in response to a request from the DTI and in conjunction with the Scottish Law Commission. The review was conducted in respect of the provisions of the Partnership Act 1890, many but not all of which operate as default provisions in the absence of a contrary agreement of the partners, and the Limited Partnerships Act 1907. The Limited Liability Partnerships Act 2000 (see below) was not involved. The reforms would, however, if implemented, narrow the present distinction between ordinary partnerships and the new limited liability partnership.

Main reform proposals

The three main proposals are:

1 Proposals to introduce separate legal personality. There are two sub-proposals here:
  (a) to confer legal personality on all partnerships without registration. There would be a transitional period to allow the parties to a partnership agreement to organise their affairs or to opt out of the continuing aspect of separate personality of the firm.
  (b) to make legal personality depend on registration. Under this sub-proposal only a registered partnership would have legal personality capable of continuing regardless of changes in the membership of the firm. Under this option non-registered partnerships would not have legal personality.
  The Commission feels that having a system of registration would create a more complex situation in which there would be a legal environment for registered partnerships and another for non-registered firms. The Commission also feels that many small firms would not register and so lose the benefits of legal personality. On balance therefore the provisional view of the Commission is the first option, i.e. continuity of legal personality without registration, and views are invited on this. The creation of a registered partnership regime would bring partnership law in the UK closer to those legal systems in Europe in which legal personality is conferred by registration.
2 Proposals to avoid the unnecessary discontinuance of business caused by the dissolution of the firm under the 1890 Act default rules when one person ceases to be a partner.
3 Proposals to provide a more efficient and cheaper mechanism for the dissolution of a solvent partnership.

Other reform proposals

The following suggestions for reform are, according to the Commission, intended to clarify some of the uncertainties in the 1890 Act; to update provisions which are outdated or spent and to propose adaptations of existing provisions if in the event consultees support the separate and continuing legal personality of the firm.

(a) *Partnership and agency.* With the concept of legal entity the partners would be agents of the firm but not each other.

(b) *Ownership of property.* With separate personality the firm would be able to hold property in its own name. It would not be necessary, as now, to use the device of the trust. Also, the firm and not the partners would have an insurable interest in partnership property.

(c) *Partners' liability for the obligations of the firm.* As a result of separate personality, the firm would be primarily liable. A partner's liability would be subsidiary but unlimited. Creditors would normally need to get a judgment against the firm before enforcing the claim against the assets of the firm or the partners. The liability of partners would be joint and several for the debts and obligations of the firm.

(d) *Partners' duties.* Partners have a duty to act in good faith in equity already. The Commission proposes to include the duty in a reformed statute and possibly also a duty of skill and care in negligence. There is a suggestion that partners be relieved of the duty of good faith when, on the break-up of a firm, they are competing for its client base provided they act honestly and reasonably.

(e) *Litigation.* A partnership with a separate legal personality would be sued in its own name and the partners could be sued in the same action.

(f) *Information about the firm including former partners who may have subsidiary liability at the time of a claim would be available if the partnership was registered.* If this is not so, the Commission proposes an extension to the Business Names Act 1985 requiring display of such information by the firm administratively.

(g) *Floating charges.* Currently, partnerships cannot grant floating charges over the firm's assets. The Commission makes no proposals on this but invites views.

Limited liability partnerships (LLPs)

The Limited Liability Partnerships Act 2000 creates a new kind of partnership arrangement that is of major importance to those in the professions and in business generally. Its main characteristics are set out below.

Formation

Section 2(1) of the Act states that an LLP may be incorporated when two or more persons associated for the purpose of carrying on a lawful business subscribe their names to an incorporation document. That incorporation document, or an approved copy of it, has been delivered to the Companies Registrar at Companies House and a statement either by a solicitor or one of the subscribers that the formalities have been complied with has also been delivered to the Registrar.

An LLP is registered at Companies House using form LLPIN01. The registration fee is £20. From 19 August 2010, Companies House electronic filing services have been enhanced so as to enable Limited Liability Partnerships to file their information on-line. LLPs will be able to join the PROOF Scheme (protected on-line filing). Transactions available via the filing service include annual returns, the appointment of corporate members, any changes to members' details, and the termination of appointment of members. (See: **http://www.companieshouse.gov.uk/onlinefilingLLP/index.shtml**).

According to LLPA 2000 s 2(2), the incorporation document must take either the prescribed form or a form as close to the prescribed form as possible. It must contain the address of the registered office of the LLP (see below), state the name of the LLP, state the name of the members of the LLP on incorporation, state which of those members are to be 'designated members' or that all members will be 'designated members' and also say whether the LLP's registered office is to be situated in England and Wales, Wales or Scotland. LLPA 2000 Section 2(3) goes on to provide that if a person makes a false statement under the subsection, which he knows to be false, or does not believe to be true, he commits an offence.

LLPA 2000 Section 3 provides that once the formalities have been complied with the Registrar retains the incorporation document or a copy of it and issues a certificate of incorporation. That certificate is regarded as conclusive evidence that the incorporation formalities have been complied with.

Status at law

Section 1 of LLPA 2000 provides that an LLP is a legal person. It is a body corporate formed by incorporation (see below). It has an unlimited capacity and is able to undertake the full range of business activities which an ordinary partnership can undertake. The matter of *ultra vires* transactions will not therefore arise. An LLP is separate and distinct from its members. However, the members may be liable to contribute to its assets if it is wound-up. The extent of that liability is set out in regulations. Since an LLP will be a corporate body partnership law will not in general apply to an LLP. The basic principles of corporate law and the Companies Act 2006 apply with appropriate modifications. Section 14 of LLPA 2000, however, provides that elements of partnership law may be applied to LLPs by regulations. (It will be noted later that a company is an artificial legal person with perpetual succession and is an entity distinct from its members. As such, a company may own property, make contracts, and sue and be sued.)

The LLP format is not confined to those practising a profession but is open to other persons who may wish to use it as a business organisation. The new form of limited liability partnership also addresses liability of the partners individually in terms of their private estate. The members of the new organisation will benefit from limited liability because the LLP is a separate person. Thus the LLP and not its members personally will be liable to third parties. However, under the general law a professional person owes a duty of care to a third party or may do. Therefore negligent advice given to a client will result in liability of the LLP and may result in the professional giving the advice having personal liability but the other members will not be personally liable. Where the person injured by negligent advice is not a client then, provided there is a duty of care when the advice was given and it was in the course of business, the LLP will be liable and the professional giving the advice will be personally liable but not the other members.

This is a principal aim of LLPs, i.e. to provide protection against 'Armageddon' legal claims, as they are called, that are capable of bringing even a substantial practice to its knees in terms of insolvency as the result of a negligent act by *one* of the partners, since in the ordinary partnership liability for such acts lies also with the other partners under the rule of joint *and several* liability.

Personal liability of the partners

It should be noted that an outsider may not find it easy to establish this personal liability. There will have to be evidence that the partner concerned was not merely acting as an agent for the firm but was also assuming personal liability to the outsider, e.g. a client. This could occur where the partner (or member as they may be called) has signed letters and documents in a personal capacity and not merely as an agent in the firm's name or on behalf of the firm. There is at the moment no specific case law, though company directors who performed a professional service on behalf of the company, e.g. a valuation, have escaped personal liability for a negligent performance where it was made clear that they were acting on behalf of the company as an agent (see *Williams* v *Natural Life Health Foods Ltd* [1998] 2 All ER 577).

However, where the evidence shows that the partner or even a qualified employee has signed documents and conducted certain business apparently in a personal capacity without indicating that he was acting as an agent of the firm there may be personal liability (see *Merrett* v *Babb* [2001] QB 1174: a case involving an ordinary partnership that is nevertheless applicable to the LLP situation). This attempt to make an individual partner or member liable will arise crucially where the firm is insolvent and there are no liability insurance arrangements to cover the loss.

Names

The name of an LLP must end with 'limited liability partnership' or llp or LLP. There are equivalents in Welsh where the registered office is situated in Wales. An LLP cannot have a name which is already used by a registered company nor one that the Secretary of State thinks constitutes a criminal offence or is offensive. A name may not be registered if it gives the impression that it is connected with central or local government authorities. An LLP may change its name at any time. If it has been registered in a name which is the same or similar to a registered name, the Secretary of State may direct a change within 12 months of registering the name. Where the LLP has given misleading information to obtain a sensitive name such as 'charity', the Secretary of State may direct a change within five years of it being registered and where it is misleading and likely to cause harm to the public the Secretary of State can direct a change *at any time* but the LLP may appeal to the court.

The above matters are for all practical purposes like those rules for company names.

Registered office

An LLP must have a registered office at all times and this must be situated in either England and Wales, Wales or Scotland. The details, e.g. the address of the registered office, must appear in the incorporation document. On change of address of the registered office, the Registrar must be notified on the approved form to be signed by a designated member. For the next 14 days documents may be validly served at the old address.

The need for a membership agreement

The need for the LLP to have a carefully drafted agreement covering all eventualities cannot be overstressed. Although the LLP regulations apply many Companies Act 2006 provisions it must be remembered that an LLP is not a species of company. Section 1(1) of the LLP Act

2000 states: 'There shall be a new form of legal entity . . .' Furthermore, the law relating to ordinary limited partnerships (see below) does not apply. Section 1(5) of the LLP Act 2000 states that in general terms and unless there is a provision in statute law to the contrary the law relating to partnerships does not apply to an LLP.

The general internal procedures of a registered company are governed by special articles or *Table A* which is a statutory instrument designed for companies. Ordinary partnerships are governed by more extensive fallback provisions in the Partnership Act 1890 that apply in the absence of partnership articles. There is no equivalent support for the LLP and so an agreement is vital to determine the internal governing rules that are to apply as outlined by s 5(1) of the Act:

> Except as far as otherwise provided by this Act or any other enactment, the mutual rights and duties of the members of a limited liability partnership, and the mutual rights and duties of a limited liability partnership and its members, shall be governed:
> (a) by agreement between the members, or between the limited liability partnership and its members, or
> (b) in the absence of agreement as to any matter, by any provision made in relation to that matter by regulations under section 15(c).

The Limited Liability Partnerships (Application of Companies Act 2006) Regulations 2009 (SI 2009/1804)

The Limited Liability Partnerships (Application of Companies Act 2006) Regulations 2009 completed the application of the Companies Act 2006 to limited liability partnerships, replacing and repealing much of the Limited Liability Partnerships Regulations 2001 (SI 2001/1090), which set out most of the detailed provisions for LLPs by applying large parts of the Companies Act 1985, the Insolvency Act 1986 and other enactments to LLPs. The accounts and audit provisions of the 2006 Act were already applied to LLPs with effect from 1 October 2008 by virtue of the Limited Liability Partnerships (Accounts and Audit) (Application of Companies Act 2006) Regulations 2008 (SI 2008/1911); the Small Limited Liability Partnerships (Accounts) Regulations 2008 (SI 2008/1912); and the Large and Medium-sized Limited Liability Partnerships (Accounts) Regulations 2008 (SI 2008/1913).

These Regulations apply as appropriate (with modification) the remaining provisions of the 2006 Act and came into force on 1 October 2009, to coincide with the final implementation of the 2006 Act for companies. Section 17 of the Limited Liability Partnerships Act 2000 provides that regulations made under s 15 of that Act applying provisions of company law to LLPs do not require an affirmative resolution if they consist entirely of the application of specified provisions of the Companies Act 1985 (s 17(4) and (5)(b) of the LLP Act). Accordingly, the affirmative resolution procedure applies to the Regulations which are the subject of this Memorandum as they apply provisions of the 2006 Act to LLPs. Paragraph 7(3) in Schedule 3 to the Regulations contains a consequential amendment to the LLP Act so that, for the future, regulations under that Act which apply specified provisions of the 2006 Act (which correspond to the specified provisions of the 1985 Act) would be subject to negative rather than affirmative resolution. The effect of this amendment is to reproduce the position under s 17 of the LLP Act so far as the Companies Act 1985 is concerned.

The 2001 Regulations (SI 2001/1090) applied large parts of the 1985 Companies Act with modifications of varying degrees made by textual amendment in the Schedules to those regulations, which created a complex set of regulations that had to be read in conjunction with the 1985 Act or the 1986 Order (SI 1986/1032 (N.I.6)). As noted earlier (see Chapter 1 ⊙), one of the key objectives of the 2006 Act was to ensure better regulation and to 'think small first'. In line with this, and the approach taken in the LLP regulations applying the accounts and audit provisions of the 2006 Act to LLPs, the 2009 Regulations (SI 2009/1804) (see below) set out the 2006 Act provisions applied to LLPs in full, as modified to take account of the particular characteristics of LLPs.

By applying the 2006 Act to LLPs in the manner outlined above, the aim is for LLPs to be able to take advantage of the benefits to business of modernising and simplifying company law, thereby ensuring that LLPs remain an attractive corporate vehicle for businesses, whilst retaining their distinctive characteristics. As with the 2006 Act, key to this approach is to ensure that the regulations for LLPs remain up to date and fit for purpose. The new approach to legislating for LLPs results in a stand-alone set of regulations that can be read without reference to the 2006 Act. The Regulations apply to LLPs (with appropriate modifications to take account of the particular characteristics of LLPs) as regards provisions of the 2006 Act governing:

- the formalities of doing business
- names and trading disclosures
- registered offices
- the register of directors and protection from disclosure of residential addresses
- debentures (including their certification and transfer)
- annual returns
- the registration of charges
- arrangements and reconstructions (including application of the Companies (Cross-Border Mergers) Regulations 2007 (SI 2007/2974)
- fraudulent trading
- protection of members against unfair prejudice
- dissolution and restoration to the Register
- trading disclosures of overseas companies
- the Registrar of companies.

Register of members

Chapter 1 of Part 5 of the Limited Liability Partnerships (Application of Companies Act 2006) Regulations 2009, SI 2009/1804 applies, with modification, ss 162 to 165 of the 2006 Act on registers of directors. Consequently, from 1 October 2009 an LLP has to keep a register of its members containing certain particulars, including a service address for each individual member and stating whether a member is a designated member. The LLP must give notice to the Registrar of Companies of the place at which the register is kept available for inspection and any changes in that place (unless it is kept at all times at the LLP's registered office). It must also be open for inspection by any member of the LLP without charge and by any other person for a fee. In addition, with effect from 1 October 2009 under Chapter 2 of Part 5 of the 2009 Regulations (2009/1804), an LLP has to keep a register of each member's usual residential address. However, where a confidentiality order under s 723B of the 1985 Companies Act, as applied to LLPs, was in force prior to 1 October 2009, particulars of the usual residential address, if contained in the register of members, do not have to be available for inspection. The new provisions on protection from disclosure of addresses in ss 240 to 246 of the 2006 Companies Act are also applied to LLPs by Regulation 19 (2009/1804).

Finally, Part 13 of the Regulations applies to LLPs the 2006 Act provisions on dissolution and restoration to the register. If an LLP carries on business without at least two members for more than six months, the remaining member is liable (jointly and severally with the LLP) for the debts contracted during the period. However, under the current law, an LLP with fewer than two members is not able to apply for voluntary strike-off of the LLP. Section 1003 on voluntary striking-off has therefore been applied to LLPs, modified to enable a sole remaining member to dissolve the LLP.

Annual return

Part 8 of the Regulations applies ss 854, 855, 855A(1) and 858 of the 2006 Act to LLPs with respect to the contents and delivery of its annual return. Consequently, every LLP must deliver to the Registrar successive annual returns each of which is made up to a date not later than the LLP's return date. The return date is usually the anniversary of the LLP's incorporation.

Each return must state the date to which it is made up and contain the following information: (a) the address of the LLP's registered office; (b) the required particulars of the members of the LLP (see s 855A); (c) if any LLP records are kept at a place other than the LLP's registered office, the address of that place and the records that are kept there. The return must also be delivered to the Registrar within 28 days after the date to which it is made up. If an LLP fails to deliver an annual return before the end of the period of 28 days after a return date, an offence is committed by (a) the LLP, and (b) subject to subsection 858 (4), every designated member of the LLP.

Fraudulent trading

Part 11 Regulation 47 provides that s 933 applies, subject to modifications, to LLPs in terms of the offence of fraudulent trading. As such, under Part 11 of the Regulations, if any business of an LLP is carried on with intent to defraud creditors of the LLP or creditors of any other person, or for any fraudulent purpose, every person who is knowingly a party to the carrying on of the business in that manner commits an offence. This applies whether or not the LLP has been, or is in the course of being, wound up. A person guilty of an offence under this section is liable: (a) on conviction on indictment, to imprisonment for a term not exceeding ten years or a fine (or both); (b) on summary conviction in England and Wales or Scotland, to imprisonment for a term not exceeding twelve months or a fine not exceeding the statutory maximum (or both).

Protection of members from unfair prejudice

The issue of unfair prejudice will be discussed in greater detail in relation to companies later in this text (see Chapter 18 ⊙). However, it is worth noting at this point that Part 12 of the Regulations sets out the position with respect to a claim for unfair prejudice in LLPs.

Regulations 48 and 49 provide that a member of an LLP may apply to the court by petition for an order under Part 12 of the Regulations on the ground that (a) the LLP's affairs are being or have been conducted in a manner that is unfairly prejudicial to the interests of members generally or of some part of its members (including at least himself), or (b) that an actual or proposed act or omission of the LLP (including an act or omission on its behalf) is or would be so prejudicial.

However, Regulation 48 goes on to provide that the members of an LLP may by unanimous agreement exclude the rights outlined above either indefinitely or for such period as is specified in the agreement. The agreement must be recorded in writing.

Accounts and audit exemption

Most of the relevant provisions of the Companies Act 2006, the Company Directors Disqualification Act 1986, the Insolvency Act 1986 and the Financial Services and Markets Act 2000 are applied to LLPs with appropriate modifications. In particular, the requirements relating to the keeping and retaining of accounting records and the preparation and publication of annual accounts, the form and content of annual accounts and the audit requirement are applied to LLPs in the same way as to companies with the members of the LLP taking on the duties of directors and their responsibilities.

There is, however, no requirement to prepare the equivalent of a directors' report. A period of ten months is given for delivery of accounts to the Registrar of Companies from the end of the financial year. Small LLPs and medium-sized LLPs will be able to take advantage of the provisions of the Companies Act 2006 applying to small and medium-sized companies, and the qualifying thresholds are the same. The usual company audit exemptions will apply as will the dormancy rules.

Financial disclosure: a disadvantage

So far as clients are concerned, one of the major disadvantages to the adoption of LLP status is the company-style financial disclosure. Even under the regime of abbreviated accounts financial disclosure may make an LLP vulnerable to commercial pressure. Furthermore, where it is necessary to disclose the income of the highest paid member of the LLP (which is where the aggregate profit exceeds £200,000) there may be repercussions from clients, creditors and staff. The government is being pressed to remove the disclosure requirements and, in general terms, the company analogy is not perfectly made out because disclosure and audit and accounting rules in a company are to a large extent to protect the shareholders against the directors. This is not the case with the members/managers of the LLP. In this connection it is worth noting that American LLPs do not need to disclose financial information at all, although some states do not permit the formation of LLPs.

LLP or private limited company?

Legal uncertainty. The company structure is a long-standing business organisation that is tried and trusted by advisers. It is set in a well-developed body of law which, over the years, has acquired a high degree of legal certainty. By contrast, the LLP is a new structure that has not been tried and tested in terms of its legal framework and legal uncertainty is often undesirable in business organisations.

Limited liability. This is, for all practical purposes, the same in the corporate and LLP organisations.

Internal flexibility. Greater flexibility in internal matters and management is claimed for the LLP as against the private company law requirements. However, this problem is often overstated in the case of the private limited company where the Companies Act 2006 now allows a high degree of flexibility in decision making, e.g. by the calling of meetings at short notice and by using the written resolution procedure. Also, the *Duomatic* principle (discussed in Chapter 6, p. 120 ○) operates to validate the informal unanimous consent of all the members, even where there has been no written resolution.

The private company does not require the equivalent of an LLP agreement. The articles of association (the Model Articles) provide standard default arrangements. However, company-specific articles are filed with the Registrar of Companies on incorporation, as are alterations to them, so that privacy is lost. The LLP agreement is not filed, nor are any alterations that may be made to it. However, these LLP agreements have not yet been challenged by disputing parties in the courts and their operation is not certain.

In conclusion, the number of LLP registrations continues to be small compared with the private limited company registrations. Business, in general, would seem to prefer the corporate route, although LLPs have found favour with organisations of professionals because they provide for a form of limited liability within the partnership ethos.

Advantages and disadvantages of incorporation

The main advantages put forward by professional advisers for the conversion of a business into a limited company for those who do not wish to incorporate as an LLP can be summarised as follows:

1　Perpetual succession of the company despite the retirement, bankruptcy, mental disorder or death of members.
2　Liability of the members for the company's debts limited to the amount of their respective shareholding.
3　Contractual liability of the company for all contracts made in its name.
4　Ownership of property vested in the company is not affected by a change in shareholders.
5　The company may obtain finance by creating a floating charge (see Chapter 24, p. 508 ○) with its undertaking or property as security yet may realise assets within that property without the consent of the lenders during the normal course of business until crystallisation (see Chapter 24, p. 510 ○) occurs. As we shall see, no other form of business organisation except an LLP can sensibly use such a charge.

It is generally thought that the above advantages outweigh the suggested disadvantages of incorporation which are:

1　Public inspection of accounts (with exceptions in the case of some unlimited companies and abbreviated or modified disclosure in the case of small and medium companies).
2　Administrative expenses in terms, for example, of filing fees for documents.
3　Cost of compulsory annual audit (unless the company is a dormant company or in a position to opt out).

Essay questions

1 Thomas Taylor-Wright is a sole trader, based in Savile Row in London, where he has a very lucrative business making men's exclusive formal suits. Thomas has decided that he would like to expand his business and is having discussions with a fellow tailor, Terry Thimble, about possibly going into business together and renting larger premises in Savile Row. Thomas comes to you for advice as he cannot decide whether he and Terry should set up as a partnership or a limited company.

   Answer ALL PARTS.

● Advise Thomas and Terry which type of business medium you would recommend and why.
● Thomas and Terry have decided to set up as a limited company, but they have no idea how they should go about doing so. Advise them of the procedure for incorporating as a limited company.
● They would like to use the name Savile Row Tailors Ltd. Advise them on their suggested choice of name.

(*University of Hertfordshire*)

Suggested further reading

Bull, 'Wheels of fortune' (2012) *Managing for Success* 57 (Aug) 18.

Foggo and Ahmed, 'When the partnership fails' (2011) *Accountancy* 147(1412) 83.

Linskell, 'Still not an employee' (2012) *Employment Lawyers Association Briefing* 19(2) 2.

Marshall, Colbridge and Cawley, 'Legal uncertainty: The criminal liability of partnerships for bribery under the Bribery Act 2010 (2012) BJIB & FL 27(3) 139.

Mather, 'Call of fiduciary duty? Members obligations in an LLP' (2012) BJIB & FL 27(1) 16.

Miller, 'Regulatory risk: The unknown unknowns' (2012) LCB 18 (Mar) 8.

Williams, 'The test of true partnership – when are LLP members also employees?' (2012) *Corporate Briefing* (March) 8.

4 Promotion and incorporation

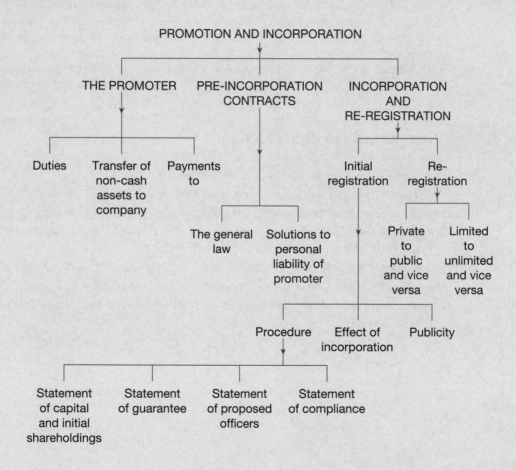

The promotion of a company consists in taking the necessary steps to incorporate it by registration under the Companies Act, to see that it has share and loan capital, and to acquire the business or property which the company is formed to control.

The promoter

There is no general definition of a promoter in the Companies Act 1985. However, Treasury regulations under the Financial Services and Markets Act 2000 exempt from liability for false statements in listing particulars, or a prospectus, those who merely give advice in a professional capacity but do not give specific reports for inclusion as experts. Thus, a solicitor or accountant who merely advises the promoters on legal and financial matters respectively will not be considered as a promoter in respect of misrepresentations which appear in any prospectus issued to raise capital. Nevertheless, accountants, in particular, may be liable as experts if any of their financial statements are included with their consent in a prospectus and turn out to be false (see further Chapter 12, p. 226 ○).

In addition, the courts have not given the expression 'promoter' a precise definition although Cockburn CJ, in *Twycross v Grant* (1877) 2 CPD 469, called a promoter 'one who undertakes to form a company with reference to a given project, and to set it going, and who takes the necessary steps to accomplish that purpose'. In addition, Bowen J in *Whaley Bridge Printing Co v Green* (1880) 5 QBD 109 said:

> The term promoter is a term not of law, but of business, usefully summing up in a single word a number of business operations familiar to the commercial world by which a company is generally brought into existence.

Thus, it can be said that whether a person is a promoter or not is a matter of fact and not of law. However, a promoter will usually be in some sort of controlling position with regard to the company's affairs, both before it is formed and during the early stages of its existence and will be in a position analogous to that of a director during that period. Basically a promoter is a person who promotes a business project through the medium of a company.

Those who would normally be regarded as promoters would include persons who authorise the drafting of legal documents such as the articles of association, and who nominate directors, solicitors, bankers and other agents, together with those who arrange for the placing of shares and who purchase property for the proposed company. The purchaser of a ready-made company is a promoter because such a person is promoting a company through the medium of a company.

During the nineteenth century there was in existence a class of professional company promoters whose methods of raising capital from the investing public were often unscrupulous and thus it was necessary for the legislature and the courts to impose rigorous duties upon such persons to protect the public from fraud.

Those days have gone and in modern times most companies are promoted as private companies by persons with an interest in the business who become directors and remain so. Obviously, some protection is still required because such persons could defraud the company by, for example, selling property to it at exorbitant rates. However, they are not likely to do so because in the modern situation the promoter retains an interest in the company and would merely be defrauding himself, whereas the old professional promoter either did not take any shares in the company at all or if he did unloaded them to others shortly after its incorporation.

If, after incorporation as a private company, there is a need to raise capital from the public then there would be a conversion to a public company. In such a situation there is no need for a promoter but there would be a need for the services of a specialist organisation such as a merchant bank to raise the necessary capital from the public.

Duties of a promoter

In equity a promoter stands in a fiduciary relationship towards the company he is promoting but is not a trustee. Thus he is not absolutely forbidden to make a profit out of the promotion so long as he has disclosed his interest in the transaction out of which the profit arose and the company consents to the retention of the profit. As a general rule, any profits which he makes on the promotion and fails to disclose must be surrendered to the company. This is illustrated by the following case.

Gluckstein v Barnes [1900] AC 240

In 1893 the National Agricultural Hall Co Ltd owned a place of entertainment called the Olympia Company which was being wound up. A syndicate was formed to raise funds to buy Olympia and resell it, either to a company registered under the Companies Act for the purpose, or to another purchaser. If a company was formed, the appellant Gluckstein and three other persons, Lyons, Hart and Hartley, who were members of the syndicate, had agreed to become its first directors and to promote it. In the event a company was formed, called the Olympia Company Ltd, and the promoters issued a prospectus stating that the syndicate which was promoting the company had purchased Olympia for £140,000 and was selling it to the company for £180,000 thus quite properly disclosing a profit of £40,000. What they did not disclose but referred to vaguely as 'interim investments', was the fact that they had purchased certain mortgage debentures in the old Olympia Company for less than their face value, and that these mortgage debentures were to be redeemed at their face value out of the proceeds of the issue of shares. This meant that the syndicate made a further £20,000 on the promotion. The company afterwards went into liquidation, Barnes being the liquidator, and he sought to recover the undisclosed secret profit.

Held – the profit of £20,000 should have been disclosed and the appellant was bound to account to the liquidator for it.

Comment

The following points of interest arise from this case:

(i) There had been disclosure by the promoters in regard to the £40,000 and £20,000 profit to themselves as directors but of course this was useless because disclosure must be to an independent board (see below).

(ii) The prospectus said that the £40,000 profit did not include profits on 'interim investments' but the court held that this was not a disclosure of the profit of £20,000.

(iii) The case also illustrates that liability of promoters is joint and several for recovery of profit because Mr Gluckstein tried to defend himself by saying he was only liable for a proportion of the profits. The House of Lords held him liable to account for it all with a right of contribution against his fellow promoters.

In *Erlanger v New Sombrero Phosphate Co* (1878) 3 App Cas 1218, the House of Lords took the view that the disclosure mentioned above had to be made to an independent board of directors. This view was, however, too strict. The boards of private companies, for example, are unlikely to be entirely independent of the promoter of the company and since *Salomon*, where it was held that the liquidator of the company could not complain of the sale to it at an obvious over-valuation of Mr Salomon's business, all the members having acquiesced therein, it has been accepted that disclosure to the members is equally effective. Thus, if the company issues a prospectus disclosure to the shareholders may be made in it and the shareholders give their consent by conduct when they apply for the shares being issued under the prospectus. Disclosure by a person, in his capacity as promoter, to himself, in his capacity as director, is not enough (*Gluckstein* v *Barnes*, 1900, above).

A promoter will perhaps most often make a secret profit by selling his own property to the company at an enhanced price and this is further considered below. However, other forms of profit are possible, e.g. where the promoter takes a commission from the person who is selling property to the company (and see also *Gluckstein* v *Barnes*, 1900). All such profits are subject to the rules of disclosure. The liability of promoters as vendors of property may be considered under two headings:

(a) Where the property was purchased by the promoter before he began to act as a promoter

If the promoter does not disclose his interest in the sale, the company may rescind the contract, i.e. return the property to the promoter and recover the purchase price. If the company wishes to keep the property it may do so, but cannot recover the profit as such (*Re Cape Breton* (1887) 12 App Cas 652). The remedy is to sue the promoter for damages in tort at common law for negligence if damage has been suffered, as where the company has paid a price in excess of the market price. That this can be done follows from the decision of the court in *Jacobus Marler Estates Ltd* v *Marler* (1913) 114 LT 640n, and in *Re Leeds and Hanley Theatres of Varieties Ltd* [1902] 2 Ch 809.

There may be, according to circumstances, an action for fraud, or under s 2 of the Misrepresentation Act 1967 where the promoter's misstatements, e.g. as to value, are made negligently. Therefore, if P acquired some land in 2008 for £10,000 and became the promoter of X Co in 2009, selling the land to the company for £20,000 through a nominee and without disclosing his interest, then the company may:

(a) rescind the contract; or
(b) keep the property and recover damages for P's breach of duty of skill and care.

If the property was worth only £18,000 in 2009, the company could recover £2,000, but in no circumstances could it recover the £10,000 profit.

(b) Where the property was purchased by the promoter after he began to act as a promoter

Here, again, the remedy of rescission is available, but if the company does not wish to rescind it is possible to regard the promoter as agent for the company when he purchased the property, and the company can recover the profit made by the promoter. Thus, in the example given above, if P had been the promoter of X Co when he purchased the land, the company could have recovered the profit made, i.e. £10,000.

One of the first acts in promotion is normally to negotiate for the purchase of property. However, the courts have been reluctant to hold that the promoter's contract to buy property is the start of his promotion and this has deprived the rule about secret profits of much of its practical value. Obviously, if the public has been invited to subscribe for shares when the property is purchased, the courts will regard the promotion as having commenced, but things rarely happen in this way.

The remedy of rescission is not, in general, available against the promoter if it is not possible to restore the company and the promoter to the position they were in before the contract was made, as where the company has resold the property to a third party. In such a case the company must go on with the contract and sue the promoter for the profit made, depending on the promoter's position when he bought the property which he later sold to the company. However, where the property has been merely used and not sold, as where the company has worked a mine purchased from a promoter, the rule of full restoration to the former position does not appear to operate as any real restriction on rescission in view of the wide powers now exercised by the courts to make financial adjustments when granting rescission. This is particularly true where the promoter has been fraudulent.

The duties of a promoter to the company are derived from common law and have not yet been fully developed by the judiciary. They are not contractual duties because the company is not incorporated and cannot contract with the promoter. Nevertheless, a promoter can be regarded as a quasi-agent working without a contract and as such would at common law owe a general duty in negligence to exercise reasonable skill and care in the promotion, i.e. to show reasonable business acumen in regard to transactions entered into.

Thus, if he allows the company to buy property – including his own – for more than it is worth, he may be liable to the company in damages for negligence (*Re Leeds and Hanley Theatres of Varieties Ltd* [1902] 2 Ch 809).

Again, if a promoter issues a prospectus which he knows to be false so that the company is liable to be sued by subscribers, the company may sue him at common law for damages. In the *Leeds* case the court proceeded on the basis of fraud but since the company does not itself act upon the fraud by subscribing for shares, the decision is felt to be based on negligence.

In other areas, e.g. the purchase by a promoter of a business which loses money, the standard required presumably depends upon the experience and/or qualifications of the promoter in business fields. A higher standard would be expected of a promoter who was, for example, an experienced and/or qualified accountant, than would be of a person of no great experience or qualification in the field of business. The duty may well be analogous to that of directors (see Chapter 21 ⊙).

The equitable and common law duties of a promoter are owed to the company, which may enforce them by a claim form served by the company on the promoter. Also, by s 212 of the Insolvency Act 1986, the court may in a liquidation, on the petition of the liquidator or a creditor, or a member, order a promoter to repay or restore property obtained by breach of duty.

A claim by a member of the company under ss 994–996 (unfair prejudice) is, in modern company law, the way to proceed. Under these sections a member may, regardless of the size of his shareholding, ask the court to authorise a claim to be brought by the company against a person who has caused loss to the generality of its members.

The duties are not owed to shareholders who are unable to bring a personal action unless this relates to false statements made by the promoter in a prospectus.

Trade creditors and debenture holders cannot sue for breach of duty. There was, for example, no action by trade creditors in *Salomon* although he did not disclose to them his interest in the promotion. However, secret profits or damages recovered by the liquidator in a winding-up are used to pay the company's debts.

The duties of disclosure and skill and care upon promoters do not end on the incorporation of the company, nor indeed on the appointment of a board of directors. However, once the company has acquired the property and/or business which it was formed to manage, the initial capital has been raised and the board of directors has effectively taken over management from the promoters, the latter's duties will terminate. Thus, in *Re British Seamless Paper Box Co* (1881) 17 Ch D 467, a promoter disclosed a profit which he had made out of the company's promotion to those who provided it with share capital when it commenced business. It was held that he was under no duty to disclose that profit to those who were invited to subscribe further capital some 12 months later and in these circumstances the company could not recover the profit from him by reason of his failure to do so.

Promoters' dealings with the prospective company: rules of capital maintenance

Although a promoter is not bound to be a subscriber to the memorandum on incorporation of a public company, it is very likely that he will be. In these circumstances certain provisions of the Companies Act 2006 relating to capital maintenance apply.

Section 598 provides that for two years following the date of issue of the certificate that a company registered as a public company is entitled to commence business, the company may not acquire (whether for cash or shares) non-cash assets from subscribers to the memorandum having an aggregate value equal to one-tenth or more of the nominal value of the issued share capital unless:

(a) the valuation rules set out in s 600 are complied with. This means that the asset must have been valued by an independent accountant who must state that the value of the consideration to be received by the company is not less than the value of the consideration to be given by it; and

(b) the acquisition of the asset and the terms of the acquisition have been approved by an ordinary resolution of the company.

Under s 603, the above provisions also apply when a private company converts to a public company and the non-cash asset is acquired from a person who is a member of the private company on the date of conversion, i.e. re-registration. The period is two years beginning with that date. Such members are also, in a way, promoters of the public company.

The above matters are considered in more detail later in the text (see Chapter 10 ◐) but it will be appreciated that they do operate as a form of control on promoters/subscribers/members, as the case may be, off-loading property on a public company at above its real value, since if the transaction has gone through in breach of s 598 the company can recover what it has paid for the asset and, if it has not gone through, it is not enforceable against the company.

Payment to promoters

Since a company cannot make a valid contract before incorporation, a promoter cannot legally claim any remuneration for his services, or an indemnity for the expenses incurred in floating the company.

Re National Motor Mail Coach Co Ltd, Clinton's Claim [1908] 2 Ch 515

A company, called the Motor Mail Coach Syndicate Ltd, promoted another company, called the National Motor Mail Coach Co Ltd, to acquire the business of a motor mail contractor named Harris. The promoters paid out £416 2s 0d in promotion fees. The two companies were subsequently wound up and Clinton, who was the liquidator of the syndicate, proved in the liquidation of the National Motor Mail Coach Co Ltd for the promotion fees.

Held – Clinton's claim on behalf of the syndicate could not be allowed because the company was not in existence when the payments were made, and could not have requested that they be made. The syndicate was not acting as the company's agent or at its request, and the fact that the company had obtained a benefit because the syndicate had performed its promotion duties was not enough.

However, since the promoters or their nominees are likely to be the first directors, the payment will usually be made by the director under their general management powers.

Pre-incorporation contracts: generally

Another consequence of the company having no legal existence and therefore no capacity to make contracts is that if a promoter, or some other person purporting to act as its agent, makes a contract for the company before its incorporation then:

(a) the company when formed is not bound by it even if it has taken some benefit under it (see *Re National Motor Mail Coach*, etc., above);

(b) the company is unable to sue the third party on the agreement unless the promoter and the third party have given the company rights of action under the Contracts (Rights of Third Parties) Act 1999 (see below);

(c) the company cannot ratify the agreement even after its incorporation (*Kelner v Baxter* (1866) LR 2 CP 174);

(d) unless the agreement has been made specifically to the contrary, it will take effect as one made personally by the promoter or other purported agent and the third party (s 51 CA 2006). This is illustrated by the following case.

Phonogram Ltd v Lane [1981] 3 All ER 182

In 1973, a group of pop artists decided that they would perform under the name of 'Cheap Mean and Nasty'. A company, Fragile Management Ltd (Fragile), was to be formed to run the group.

Before the company was formed, there were negotiations regarding the financing of the group. Phonogram Ltd, a subsidiary of the Hemdale Group, agreed to provide £12,000, and the first instalment of £6,000, being the initial payment for the group's first album, was paid. Fragile was never formed; the group never performed under it; but the £6,000 was not repaid.

The Court of Appeal was asked who was liable to repay it. It appeared that a Brian Lane had negotiated on behalf of Fragile and a Roland Rennie on behalf of Phonogram Ltd.

A letter of 4 July 1973 from Mr Rennie to Mr Lane was crucial. It read:

In regard to the contract now being completed between Phonogram Ltd and Fragile Management Ltd concerning recordings of a group [. . .] with a provisional title of 'Cheap Mean and Nasty', and further to our conversation of this morning, I send you herewith our cheque for £6,000 in anticipation of a contract signing, this being the initial payment for initial LP called for in the contract. In the unlikely event that we fail to complete within, say, one month you will undertake to pay us £6,000 [. . .] For good order's sake, Brian, I should be appreciative if you could sign the attached copy of this letter and return it to me so that I can keep our accounts people informed of what is happening.

Mr Lane signed the copy 'for and on behalf of Fragile Management Ltd'. The money was paid over, and went into the account of Jelly Music Ltd, a subsidiary of the Hemdale Group, of which Mr Lane was a director.

The court had first to consider whether or not Mr Lane was personally liable on the contract. Clearly, Fragile could not be sued, since it never came into existence. Lord Denning took the view that Mr Lane was, as a matter of construction, liable on the contract without recourse to what is now s 51, because the letter, which was in effect the contract, said: 'I send you herewith our cheque for £6,000', and 'in the unlikely event that we fail to complete within, say, one month, you will undertake to repay us the £6,000'.

However, Mr Justice Phillips at first instance had decided on the basis of a lot of evidence which he had heard that Mr Lane was not, as a matter of construction, liable personally, and Lord Denning and the rest of the Court of Appeal proceeded on the assumption that Mr Lane was not liable on the basis of intention and construction.

Lord Denning then turned to what is now s 51. This states:

A contract that purports to be made by or on behalf of a company at a time when the company has not been formed has effect, subject to any agreement to the contrary, as one made with the person purporting to act for the company or as an agent for it, and he is personally liable on the contract accordingly.

This seemed to Lord Denning to cover the case before him and render Mr Lane liable. Mr Lane made the contract on behalf of Fragile at a time when the company had not been formed, and he purported to make it on behalf of the company so that he was personally liable on it.

Mr Lane's counsel drew the attention of the court to the Directive (68/151) on which s 51 is based. This states that its provisions are limited to companies en formation (in course of formation), whereas Fragile never commenced the incorporation process.

Lord Denning rejected this submission saying an English court must under Art 189 of the Treaty of Rome abide by the statute implementing the Directive, and that contained no restriction relating to the need for the company to be en formation.

Article 189 states:

A Directive shall be binding, as to the result to be achieved, upon each member State to which it is addressed, but shall leave to the national authorities the choice of form and method.

Counsel for Mr Lane also suggested that the word 'purports' must mean that there has been a representation that the company already exists. Lord Denning did not agree with this, saying that a contract can purport to be made on behalf of a company, or by a company, even though both parties knew that the company was not formed and was only about to be formed.

The court also decided that the form in which a person made the contract – e.g. 'for and on behalf of the company' as an agent, or merely by signing the company's name and subscribing his own, e.g. 'Boxo Ltd, J Snooks, managing director', where the form is not that of agency – did not matter and that in both cases the person concerned would be liable on the contract.

As regards the words 'subject to any agreement to the contrary', the court dealt with academic opinion which had suggested that where a person signs 'for and on behalf of the company' – i.e. as agent – he is saying, in effect, that he does not intend to be liable and would not be on the basis of the words 'subject to any agreement to the contrary'.

On this, Lord Denning said:

If there was an express agreement that the man who was signing was not to be liable, the section would not apply. But, unless there is a clear exclusion of personal liability, [the section] should be given its full effect. It means that in all cases such as the present, where a person purports to contract on behalf of a company not yet formed, then however he expresses his signature he himself is personally liable on the contract.

Comment

(i) The court did not consider, because it did not arise, whether an individual such as Mr Lane could have sued upon the contract. Section 51 talks about the person or agent being 'personally liable' on the contract. Perhaps it should say 'can sue or be sued'. However, lawyers have generally assumed that the court would give an individual like Mr Lane a right to sue if it arose, since it is, to say the least, unusual for a person to be liable on a contract and yet not be able to sue upon it.

(ii) In fact, the matter was raised in *Braymist Ltd* v *Wise Finance Company Ltd* (2001) *The Times*, 27 March. In that case a solicitor signed a pre-incorporation contract for the sale of land to be owned by Braymist before that company was incorporated. Later the other party, Wise Finance, refused to go on with the contract and Braymist after incorporation sued for damages. The solicitor was also a party to the action as a claimant. The High Court ruled that the claim succeeded. The solicitor was not merely liable on the contract but could also sue for its breach. Such a ruling, said the court, was workable and fair. Furthermore, the contract did not infringe s 2(1) and (3) of the Law of Property (Miscellaneous Provisions) Act 1989, which requires a contract concerning land to be in writing and signed by the parties to it. It was signed by the solicitor who was, under the provisions of what is now s 51 of the Companies Act 2006, a party to it.

(iii) As we have seen, s 51 can apply to make the promoter or other purported agent liable even though the company has not actually begun the process of formation. However, it was held in *Cotronic (UK) Ltd* v *Dezonie* [1991] BCC 200 that there must at least be a clear intention to form the company as there was in Phonogram. In the *Cotronic* case a contract was made by Mr Dezonie on behalf of a company which had been struck off the register for five years at a time when nobody concerned with its business had even thought about re-registering it. The Court of Appeal held that the contract was a nullity and Mr Dezonie was not personally liable on it under what is now s 51.

The above difficulties do not worry, for example, a garage proprietor in a small way of business who is promoting a limited company to take over the garage business. Such a person will obviously be a director of the new company and will usually hold most of the shares in it. Being in control, he can ensure that the company enters into the necessary contracts after incorporation. However, where the promoter is not in control of the company after its incorporation, the difficulties outlined above are very real.

Pre-incorporation contracts: the Contracts (Rights of Third Parties) Act 1999

Under the above Act, the promoter and the third party are able to give the company when it is incorporated the right to sue and be sued upon a pre-incorporation contract. The Act makes clear that a party given such rights in a contract (in this case the particular pre-incorporation contract(s)) does not have to be in existence when the contract is made. Third-party rights may be applied by the court even in the absence of an express provision in the contract between the promoter and the third party if a term of the contract confers a benefit on the company which, of course, it will do. Nevertheless, an express term should be used to avoid doubt.

Pre-incorporation contracts: solutions to promoter's liability

A promoter may overcome the difficulties facing him in the matter of pre-incorporation contracts in the following ways:

(a) He may incorporate the company before he makes contracts, in which case the problems relating to pre-incorporation contracts do not apply. There is no reason why a promoter should not take this course since the expenses of incorporation are not prohibitive. There is, of course, no problem in the case of a ready-made or shelf company. The company exists and contracts can be made which will be binding on it from the beginning.

(b) He can settle a draft agreement with the other party so that when the company is formed it enters into a contract on the terms of the draft; but the parties are not bound other than morally by the draft. However, in order to ensure that the company does enter into the contract after incorporation the articles of the new company can be drafted to include a provision binding the directors to adopt it. The promoter is never liable here because there is never any contract with him.

(c) The promoter may make the contract himself and assign the benefit of it to the company after it is incorporated. Since English law does not allow a person to assign the burden of his contract, the disadvantage of this method is that the promoter remains personally liable for the performance of his promises in the contract after the assignment to the company. Thus, it is desirable for the other party to the contract to agree that the promoters shall be released from their obligations if the company enters into a new, but as regards terms identical, contract with the other party after incorporation. Since the promoters will usually control the company at this stage, they should be able to ensure that the company does make such a contract with the other party and so procure their own release.

(d) Where the promoter is buying property for the company, he may take an option on it for, say, three months. If the company, when it is formed, wishes to take over the property, the promoter can assign the benefit of the option to the company or enforce the option personally for the company's benefit. If the company does not wish to take the property, the promoter is not personally liable to take and pay for it, though he may lose the money he agreed to pay for the option.

(e) It should also be noted that s 51 states that the promoter is personally liable 'subject to any agreement to the contrary'. Thus the promoter could agree when making the contract that he should not be personally liable on it. (See the remarks of Lord Denning in *Phonogram Ltd* v *Lane*, 1981.) This may not satisfy a third party who wants a form of initial binding agreement but it is sanctioned by the 1985 Act.

Nevertheless, the general legal position is unsatisfactory and the Jenkins Committee on Company Law Reform which reported in June 1962 (Cmnd 1749) recommended legislation under which a company when formed could validly adopt a pre-incorporation contract by unilateral act, and Clause 6 of the Companies Bill 1973, which never became law, permitted a company after incorporation to ratify contracts which purported to have been made in its name or on its behalf before incorporation without the consent of the other party involved. At the present time such an act or ratification operates only as an offer to be bound which the other party must accept if there is to be an enforceable contract.

Perhaps surprisingly there is no provision under the Companies Act 2006 for ratification of a pre-incorporation contract by the company after its formation.

Natal Land and Colonization Co v Pauline Colliery and Development Syndicate
[1904] AC 120

Prior to incorporation, the P Company contracted to take an option to lease land belonging to Mrs de Carrey if it was coal bearing. After incorporation, the company entered on the land and made trial borings. The land was found to be coal bearing and the P company asked for a lease. Mrs de Carrey had by then transferred her interest in the property to the N company and it would not grant a lease. The P company sued at first instance for specific performance of the contract.

Held – the P company could not enforce the option because:

(a) its own conduct in merely boring did not unequivocally evidence an intention to take a lease; and

(b) even if it had, it was merely an offer, and there was no evidence of acceptance either by Mrs de Carrey or the N company.

Comment

Courts in the United States are more generous. They take the view that a contract made before incorporation is an offer open for acceptance by the company. So any act done by the company after incorporation which is unequivocally referable to the offer operates as an acceptance and not an offer as in English company law.

Promoter's liability and the Contracts (Rights of Third Parties) Act 1999

It should be noted that the provisions of the above Act are no help to the promoter in avoiding liability on the pre-incorporation contract because, where third-party rights are given, in this case to the company when formed, the original parties, of whom the promoter is one, remain liable on the contract.

Incorporation

Application for registration is made by filing certain documents with the Registrar of Companies. The main Registry is in Cardiff (Crown Way, Cardiff, CF14 3UZ) and further information about Companies House, together with details of the procedure for registering new companies, is available at: **www.companieshouse.gov.uk**. The documents to be filed are as follows:

1 The memorandum of association must be delivered to the Registrar together with an application for registration and a statement of compliance.

The memorandum is a significantly abridged document when compared with the former requirements of the Companies Act 1985 and previous company legislation (see Chapter 5 ◗). Its function under the Companies Act 2006 is to evidence the intention of the person or persons who subscribe to it that he/she/they have the intention to form a company and to take at least one share each in the company. A company, even a public company, can be registered with one member and, since the memorandum is reduced to a formation document, it is no longer part of the company's constitution (see s 17) and is no longer subject to alteration, amendment or update. The memorandum must be in the prescribed form and authenticated by each subscriber.

Note that there is no requirement for subscribers to a company to be domiciled in the part of the UK in which the company is to be registered (*Princess of Reuss* v *Bos* (1871) LR 5 HL 176). However, a business which is already completely constituted as a partnership or a corporation under another legal system cannot be registered as a company under the Companies Act 2006 (*Bulkeley* v *Schutz* (1871) LR 3 PC 764).

2   The application for registration. According to s 9(2) this must state:

(a)   the proposed name of the company;

(b)   whether the registered office is to be situated in England and Wales (or in Wales) or in Scotland or Northern Ireland;

(c)   whether the liability of the members of the company is to be limited and, if so, whether by shares or guarantee; and

(d)   whether the company is to be public or private.

Where the company is being formed by an agent of the subscribers to the memorandum, the application must contain his or her address (s 9(3)).

The required contents of the application for registration are outlined in s 9(4) and are as follows:

(a)   where the company is to have a share capital, a statement of capital and initial shareholdings;

(b)   where the company is to be limited by guarantee, a statement of the guarantee;

(c)   a statement of the proposed officers of the company;

(d)   a statement of the intended address of the registered office;

(e)   a copy of any company-specific articles of association.

Where no articles are filed, or insofar as the company specific articles do not modify or exclude them, the Companies Act 2006 Model Articles will apply as default articles. (See Appendix 1 of this book for a copy of these provisions.)

The application, together with a statement of compliance, must be delivered to the Registrar of Companies for England and Wales (if the registered office can be situated in England or Wales, or solely in Wales). The Registrars in Scotland and Northern Ireland deal with registrations of companies in those jurisdictions.

A fee of £20 is payable for the registration of a company non-electronically and the process normally takes five working days. For a fee of £50, the process may be undertaken on the same day so long as the documents are presented before 3pm. A reduced fee of £15 is payable for the electronic registration of a company.

Statement of capital and initial shareholdings

According to s 10 of the Companies Act 2006, this must state:

(a)   The total number of shares in the company that are to be taken by those who are subscribers to the memorandum and the total nominal value of those shares taken together.

(b)   For each class of shares, such particulars of the rights attached to them as the Secretary of State may require and prescribe; the total number of shares of the class and the total nominal value of those shares taken together and the amount to be paid up and the amount, if any, to be unpaid on each share, whether on account of the nominal value of the share or by way of premium.

(c) The statement must contain such information as the Secretary of State may require and prescribe to identify the subscribers to the memorandum. This need not be a home address; a contact address will be sufficient (e.g. the office of the subscriber's solicitors or accountants).

(d) In regard to each subscriber, the number, nominal value of each share, and the class of share to be taken by the subscriber on formation, assuming there are different classes of shares and the amount to be paid, or left unpaid, on the shares either on account of the nominal value or premium for each class, where there are different classes of shares.

Statement of guarantee

Section 11 states that this must contain:

(a) A provision that each member undertakes that if the company is wound up whilst he or she is a member, or within one year after ceasing to be a member, he or she will contribute to its assets such amount as may be required for the payment of the debts and liabilities of the company contracted before he or she ceased to be a member, and the costs, charges and expenses of winding up, as well as the adjustment of the rights of members as between themselves not exceeding a specified amount.

(b) Information, as required by the Secretary of State, sufficient to identify the subscribers; a contact address will be sufficient.

Statement of proposed officers

Under s 12 of the Companies Act 2006, this must contain details of the company's proposed officers/directors and secretary. This information must appear in the register of directors and the register of secretaries which a company keeps. For example, for directors this is as follows:

(a) name and any former names;
(b) a service address (e.g. the company's registered office);
(c) the country or state or part of the UK in which the director is usually resident;
(d) nationality;
(e) business occupation (if any);
(f) date of birth.

In addition, the usual residential address must be supplied for inclusion on the company's register of residential addresses and the Registrar's register of residential addresses, but these are not open to inspection by the public, but only to certain groups (i.e. a police authority).

The above procedure in regard to residential addresses is to protect directors against such things as violent demonstrations against them and their companies due to their line of business. The provisions apply to all directors now and also to company secretaries. (This matter is further considered in Chapter 19, p. 372. ●)

Statement of compliance

Section 13 deals with this. It is a statement that the requirements of the Act as regards registration have been complied with. The Registrar may accept this as sufficient evidence of compliance.

Registration

If the Registrar is satisfied that the requirements of the Act have been complied with, he will register the documents and issue a certificate of incorporation (ss 14, 15), together with a registered number (s 1066).

The Registrar has no discretion in the matter. He must grant a certificate of incorporation and, since the Registrar is here acting in a quasi-judicial capacity, the subscribers may enforce registration through the courts by asking the court to order the Registrar to make the registration (*R v Registrar of Companies, ex parte Bowen* [1914] 3 KB 1161).

R v Registrar of Companies, ex parte Bowen [1914] 3 KB 1161

An application was submitted to register the following proposed company name: 'The United Dental Service Ltd'. The Registrar refused to register the company unless the memorandum was amended so as to indicate that work should be undertaken only by registered dentists, or the name of the company was amended so as to omit the word 'dentist'. The applicants (seven unregistered dental practitioners) sought a writ of mandamus to compel the Registrar to register the company. Lord Reading CJ noted:

> In my opinion the question turns in the main . . . upon whether the use of these words, 'The United Dental Service', would amount to an offence under the Dentists Act 1878 . . . I think these words, 'United Dental Service', imply a description of the acts to be performed, and do not imply that the persons who will perform them are persons specifically qualified under the statute of 1878. The Registrar of Companies would be entitled, if the use of the proposed name would be an offence under the statute, to refuse to register the company with that name; but, having arrived at the conclusion that that would not be the effect of the use of the words, 'United Dental Service', I hold that the registrar was wrong in refusing registration upon that ground.

Held – The Registrar's refusal was unjustified.

However, the Registrar may refuse to register a company whose objects are unlawful. In *R v Registrar of Joint Stock Companies, ex parte More* [1931] 2 KB 197, Scrutton LJ noted:

> This is a short point involving the construction of s 41 of the Lotteries Act, 1823. Two gentlemen proposed to sell tickets in England in connection with an Irish lottery. For some reason they did not propose to do this themselves; they proposed to form a private company to do it. It is merely conjecture on my part that this may be due to the fact that the provisions in the Act of 1823 making offenders liable to be punished as rogues and vagabonds do not apply to a company, and so the two gentlemen intending to form this company wished in this way to avoid the risk of being prosecuted under the Act. They accordingly lodged the memorandum and articles of association of the proposed company with the Registrar of Companies, who, when he saw that the object of the company was to sell tickets in a lottery known as the Irish Free State Hospitals Sweepstake, refused to register the company. Thereupon an application was made to the Court for a writ of mandamus directing the Registrar to register the company. To succeed in that application the applicant must show that it is legal to sell in England tickets for the Irish Free State Hospital Sweepstake authorised by an Act of the Irish Free State. The only Act which can be supposed to authorise the selling in England is an Irish Act, but the Irish Parliament has no jurisdiction in England, and that being so, the Irish Parliament cannot authorise lottery tickets to be sold in England. The authority to sell in any place must be given by the Parliament having jurisdiction in that place, and the Imperial Parliament has given no authority to sell lottery tickets in England . . . The appeal must be dismissed.

As to the effect of registration, the subscribers to the memorandum become members of the company, which has a legal personality, and the persons named in the statement of proposed officers (i.e. directors and secretary) are deemed appointed. The certificate is also conclusive evidence that the registration requirements have been complied with so that the valid and legal existence of the company cannot be challenged in court, even if in the event they have not been (ss 15, 16).

Note, however, that the Registrar's decision to incorporate a company is subject to judicial review, as per the case of *R v Registrar of Companies, ex parte AG* [1991] BCLC 476 which dealt with the attempted registration of a company to carry on the business of prostitution.

Electronic incorporation

Companies House has introduced a service whereby presenters who incorporate companies regularly can conduct the process electronically. A citizens' incorporation service is not yet available. There is a system of electronic authentication where documents are delivered electronically. This procedure for electronic incorporation is permitted under Schedules 4 and 5 to the Companies Act 2006.

Effect of incorporation

The issue of a certificate of incorporation incorporates the members of the company into a persona at law (legal person), and limits their liability if the application for registration requires this. This takes effect from the first moment of the date of incorporation stated on the certificate (*Jubilee Cotton Mills Ltd v Lewis* [1924] AC 958). As we have seen, the certificate of incorporation is conclusive evidence that all the requirements of the Companies Act as to registration have been complied with, and if any irregularity had occurred in the registration procedure, it would not be possible to attack the validity of the company's incorporation. The evidence which was available to prove the irregularity would not be admissible (*Cotman v Brougham*, 1918; see Chapter 5 ➲). This means that all English companies registered under the Act are companies *de jure* (as a matter of law). In the jurisdictions where this rule does not apply, actions have been brought in the courts attacking the validity of a company's formation many years after incorporation. This cannot happen in England and Wales.

However, the certificate of incorporation is not conclusive evidence that all the company's business is legal; and if a company is registered with illegal or immoral business, the House of Lords decided in *Bowman v Secular Society* [1917] AC 406 that the Crown could apply, through the Attorney-General, for a quashing order to cancel the registration made by the Registrar. In *Attorney-General v Lindi St Claire (Personal Services) Ltd* [1981] 2 Co Law 69 the High Court quashed a decision by the Registrar of Companies to register the business of a prostitute as Lindi St Claire (Personal Services) Ltd. The name was registered in 1979 after the Registrar had rejected Miss St Claire's alternative titles, i.e. Prostitutes Ltd, Hookers Ltd and Lindi St Claire French Lessons Ltd. Miss St Claire's accountants advised her to register a company after receiving a letter from the Revenue's policy division stating that it considered prostitution to be a trade. The Attorney-General contended that the company should not have been registered because it was formed for sexually immoral purposes and was consequently against public policy and illegal. The High Court agreed and the registration was quashed.

In addition, a company incorporated for unlawful purposes may be ordered by the court to be wound up on the petition of a creditor or member, the ground for the petition being that it is just and equitable that the company should be wound up (Insolvency Act 1986, s 122(1)(g)), or on the petition of the Department for Business, Innovation and Skills (BIS) where it has appointed an inspector to investigate the company's affairs and he has reported adversely on the legality of the business for which it was formed.

From the date impressed upon the certificate the company becomes a body corporate with perpetual succession, and with the right to exercise the powers given in its memorandum. The company's life dates from the first moment of the day of incorporation (*Jubilee Cotton Mills v Lewis*, 1924, see below).

There is no statutory requirement that the certificate should be displayed at the registered office or kept at any particular place.

Jubilee Cotton Mills v *Lewis* [1924] AC 958

Lewis was a promoter of a company formed to purchase a cotton mill and to carry on the business of cotton spinning. The memorandum and articles of the company were accepted by the Registrar of Companies on 6 January 1920, and the certificate of incorporation was dated on that day. However, the certificate, it appeared, was not signed by the Registrar until 8 January 1920. On 6 January a large number of fully paid shares were allotted to the vendors of the mill, and were later transferred to Lewis. The question of the validity of the allotment arose in this case, and it was held that the certificate was conclusive as to the date on which the company was incorporated. A company is deemed to be incorporated from the day of the date on its certificate of incorporation, and from the first moment of that day. Therefore, the allotment was not void on the ground that it was made before the company came into existence.

Ready-made companies

It will be appreciated that where a ready-made company is used the registration procedures will have been gone through. Indeed, it has been estimated that approximately 60 per cent of company registrations are undertaken via the 'shelf company' route (see: Company Law Review Steering Group, *Modern Company Law for a Competitive Economy: Developing the Framework*, URN 00/656, London: DTI, 2000). Such companies are also relatively economic to purchase, usually being around £50 in price and simple to acquire.

Once purchased, the promoters may wish to change the ready-made company's name and will have to appoint directors and a secretary and notify these appointments to the Registrar. The ready-made company will have had directors and a secretary on formation but these persons will have resigned on the purchase of the ready-made company.

The notification of the new directors and secretary is under s 167 as changes in the directorate and secretariat since they are replacements and not original appointments.

Publicity in connection with incorporation

The Registrar is required to publish in the *London Gazette*:

(a) the issue of any certificate of incorporation (but there is in fact no statutory requirement to display the certificate at the registered office, though it is often so displayed);

(b) any report as to the value of a non-cash asset under s 597 where a non-cash asset has been acquired from a subscriber.

Post-incorporation procedures for re-registration

Conversion of companies from private to public (ss 90–96)

A private company may be re-registered as a public company if not previously re-registered as an unlimited company if:

(a) the members pass a special or written special resolution which alters the company's articles so that they fit the statutory requirements of a public company. The name must be changed on conversion to reflect the fact that the company will be a public company. Companies House will only permit a change to the suffix plc under the re-registration procedure. If any other change in the name is required, the members must pass a special resolution (which may be in written form) and file the resolution with the re-registration documents with the relevant name change fee. The re-registration certificate will carry the new name;

(b) the requirements as regards share capital are met. This means that the nominal value of the allotted share capital is not less than £50,000 and in respect of all the shares, or as many as are needed to make up the authorised minimum, the following conditions are satisfied:

   (i) no less than one-quarter of the nominal value of each share and the whole of any premium on it is paid up;

   (ii) none of the shares has been fully or partly paid up by means of an undertaking to do work or perform services where this has not already been performed or otherwise discharged; and

   (iii) where any share has been allotted as fully or partly paid up for a non-cash consideration which consists solely or partly of an undertaking to do something other than to perform services, i.e. usually an undertaking to transfer a non-cash asset, either the undertaking has been performed or otherwise discharged or there is a contract between the company and the person involved under which the undertaking must be performed within five years.

   Shares allotted under an employees' share scheme which are not one-quarter paid up can be disregarded for the purpose of deciding whether the above requirements have been met;

(c) an application for the change is made to the Registrar accompanied by a statement of compliance;

(d) the application is accompanied by the following documents:

(i)   a printed copy of the articles as altered and added to by the special or written resolution and a copy of the resolution unless already forwarded to the Registrar;

(ii) a copy of a balance sheet prepared as at a date not more than seven months before the date of the application, but not necessarily in respect of an accounting reference period. The balance sheet must be accompanied by a copy of an unqualified report of the company's auditor in relation to the balance sheet. If there is a qualification, the auditor must state in writing that it is not material in determining whether at the date of the balance sheet the company's net assets were at least equal to the sum of its called-up capital and non-distributable reserves, such as its share premium account and capital redemption reserve;

(iii) a copy of a written statement by the company's auditors that in their opinion the balance sheet referred to in (ii) above shows that the amount of the company's net assets at the date of the balance sheet was not less than the aggregate of its called-up share capital and non-distributable reserves;

(iv) the statement of compliance that: (a) the requirements in regard to the making of necessary changes in the company's constitution have been complied with; and that (b) between the balance sheet date and the application for re-registration there has been no change in the financial position of the company which has caused the net assets to become less than the aggregate of called-up share capital plus non-distributable reserves.

It should be noted that audit exemption regulations do not dispense with the requirement of an audit report on the balance sheet. This means that small companies can exempt themselves from the requirement to appoint an auditor unless and until it becomes necessary to do so for certain purposes other than the audit of financial statements. Re-registration is one of those purposes. Other areas where an auditor is required will be picked up as they occur.

Statement of proposed secretary

This is a s 95 requirement which arises as a result of the abolition of the requirement for private companies to have a company secretary. On re-registration as a public company, and on the assumption that the company does not have a secretary, details of the person or persons who will act as secretary or joint secretaries must be given together with consent to act. Where, for example, a firm acts, consent can be given by one partner on behalf of the others.

Additional requirements relating to share capital

If between the date of the balance sheet and the passing of a special (or written) resolution to convert to a public company the company has allotted shares which are wholly or partly paid for by a non-cash consideration, then it shall not make an application for re-registration unless before application is made:

(a) the consideration has been valued in accordance with s 593 (i.e. by a person or persons who are qualified by law to audit a public company's accounts who may themselves appoint other suitable persons to assist them);

(b) a report regarding the value has been made to the company by the persons referred to in (a) above during the six months immediately preceding the allotment of the shares.

If the Registrar is satisfied with the application for re-registration and provided that there is not in existence any court order reducing the company's share capital below the authorised minimum, he will, on payment of a fee, retain the documents which have been sent to him and issue a certificate of incorporation stating that the company is a public company.

The company then becomes a public company and the alterations in its constitution take effect. The certificate of incorporation is conclusive evidence that the re-registration requirements have been complied with and that the company is a public company.

Conversion of companies from public to private: generally (ss 97–101)

This is permitted and the procedure is as follows:

(a) the members must pass a special resolution altering the memorandum so that it no longer states that the company is a public company and also in terms of the name. The provisions regarding change of suffix from 'plc' to 'Ltd' and any further name change are with the necessary changes the same as those set out above for private to public conversion; and

(b) application is then made on the prescribed forms accompanied by a statement of compliance. The application is delivered to the Registrar together with a copy of the articles as altered or added to by the special resolution and the resolution to re-register.

It should be noted that because this type of conversion may well result in the loss of a market (i.e. a listing or quotation on the Stock Exchange) in which to sell the shares there are as regards the special resolution dissentient rights. Within a period of 28 days after the passing of the resolution dissentient holders of at least 5 per cent in nominal value of the company's issued share capital or any class thereof, or not less than 50 members, may apply to the court to have the resolution cancelled and the court may cancel or affirm it. If there is no application to the court or if it is unsuccessful and the court affirms the special resolution, the Registrar will issue a new certificate of incorporation as a private company.

It should also be noted that the court may, in addition, adjourn the proceedings brought by dissentients in order that satisfactory arrangements may be made for the purchase of the shares of those dissentients. The purchase may obviously be by other shareholders but the company's money may also be used for this purpose and if this is the intention the court will make the necessary order to provide for the purchase by the company of its own shares and to reduce its share capital. The order may also make any necessary alterations in or additions to the articles of the company.

Conversion of companies from public to private: reduction of share capital

If the court reduces the share capital of a public company to below £50,000, it must re-register as a private company. To speed up this process the court may authorise re-registration without the company having followed the above procedures and the court order may specify and make the necessary changes in the company's constitution. Thus, a reduction of capital may now have the further consequence of changing the company's status from public to private.

Conversion of private limited company to private unlimited company (ss 102–104)

A company limited by shares or by guarantee may be re-registered as an unlimited company.

However, no public company may apply to be re-registered as an unlimited company because a public company cannot be an unlimited company and therefore such a conversion involves a reduction in status from public to private. A public company which wishes to re-register as unlimited must use the procedure laid down in the 2006 Act for conversion of a public company to a private company.

If, however, the company is private, all the members must consent in writing and if this can be achieved there must be sent to the Registrar of Companies a statement of compliance that all the members of the company have consented together with a copy of the articles as altered. The Registrar will then issue a new certificate of incorporation which is conclusive evidence that the conversion is in all respects valid. In addition, the Registrar must publish the issue of the new certificate in the *London Gazette*. There can be no conversion back to a limited company. In addition, a company is excluded from re-registering as unlimited if it has previously re-registered as limited.

As we have seen, unlimited companies do not in general have to file accounts and re-registration back and forth between limited and unlimited status is not allowed in order to prevent selective filing of accounts, e.g. by re-registration as unlimited in a year in which the directors did not wish to file accounts and then back to limited status subsequently.

Conversion of private unlimited company to private limited company (ss 105–108)

It is also possible to re-register an unlimited company as a limited one but, as we have seen, this does not apply to a company which was previously a limited company but has re-registered as an unlimited one. If the conversion is to a private limited company, the conversion must be authorised by special or written resolution of the members. Following this a copy of the articles as altered and a statement of compliance are sent to the Registrar who will issue a new certificate of incorporation which is conclusive evidence that the conversion is in all respects valid. The Registrar will also advertise the issue of the new certificate in the *London Gazette*.

If an unlimited company wishes to re-register as a public company which is by definition a company limited by shares, the procedure to be followed is that for the re-registration of a private company as a public company except that the special resolution to convert must include two additional matters as follows:

(a) it must state that the liability of the members is to be limited by shares and what the share capital of the company is to be; and
(b) it must make such alterations in the company's constitution as are necessary to bring it in substance and in form into conformity with the requirements of the Companies Act in regard to a public company limited by shares. This involves, for example, changes in the company's name and capital.

The re-registration as a public company is not available to unlimited companies which have re-registered as such having been previously limited companies.

The effect on the liability of members of such a conversion is that those who become members after conversion are liable only to the extent of capital unpaid on their shares. Those who were members at the date of the conversion, and are still members at the date of winding-up, are fully liable for debts and liabilities incurred before conversion. Those who were members at the date of conversion but have transferred their shares after conversion and before winding-up are liable for debts and liabilities incurred before conversion up to three years after it took place (Insolvency Act 1986, s 77(2)).

Essay questions

1 The directors of Balkan Ltd have decided that it is necessary to convert their company into a public limited company. Advise them on:

(a) the differences between a private and public limited company;

AND

(b) the procedures to be followed during re-registration.

2 Brian, who had decided to transfer his existing wholesale food business to a private limited company called Brian Foods Ltd, delivered the necessary documents to the Registrar of Companies and received the Certificate of Incorporation (dated 1 April) on 6 April 2005.

On 15 March 2005, Brian agreed to purchase a quantity of coffee from Benco Ltd in a letter which he signed 'For and on behalf of Brian Foods Ltd, B Brian, Director'.

At the first meeting of the board of directors of Brian Foods Ltd the contract with Benco Ltd was approved and the company took delivery of the first consignment. The board later found that the Benco brand of coffee was more difficult to sell than had been anticipated and decided to cancel any subsequent consignments.

(a) Advise Brian Foods Ltd on its liability to Benco Ltd.

AND

(b) How far, if at all, will your answer to (a) differ if on 10 April 2005 the two companies re-negotiated the contract and agreed on a different contract price?

AND

(c) How far, if at all, will your answer to (a) differ if in the letter of 15 March 2005 Brian expressly excluded his personal liability?   *(Glasgow Caledonian University)*

3 Bill and Ben trade in partnership as garage mechanics. They are considering changing their form of business association and trading as a private registered company limited by shares.

Explain to them the legal procedures that they must follow in order to form such a company, and advise them on the advantages of trading as a private company as opposed to a partnership.

(The Association of Chartered Certified Accountants)

4 Philip, who is in the process of forming a company, wishes to avoid personal liability upon any contracts he may enter into on behalf of the proposed company. Advise Philip.

(The Institute of Chartered Accountants in England and Wales)

Test your knowledge

Four alternative answers are given. Select ONE only. Circle the answer which you consider to be correct. Check your answers by referring back to the information given in the chapter and against the answers at the end of the text.

1 When a private company wants to re-register as a public company it must file a balance sheet with the Registrar. The balance sheet must be one which is not more than:

A Fifteen months old at the date of re-registration.
B Seven months old at the date of re-registration.
C Fifteen months old at the date of application.
D Seven months old at the date of application.

2 Thames was re-registered from a limited to an unlimited company. It wishes to re-register as a public company.

A It must apply to the Registrar to be registered as a public limited company.
B It must re-register as a private limited company and then re-register as a public company.
C It must pass a special resolution to convert into a public company.
D There is no procedure whereby Thames may become a public limited company.

3 Fred is a member of a private company at the date of its re-registration as a public company. Fred cannot profit by selling non-cash assets to the public company within an initial period of two years from the date of re-registration unless:

A The sale is approved by a resolution of the board and the consideration is not an allotment of shares.
B The property is valued by an independent accountant and the members approve the sale by ordinary resolution.
C The property is independently valued and approved by a resolution of the board.
D The sale is approved by an ordinary resolution of the members and the consideration is not an allotment of shares.

4 Before the incorporation of Ouse Ltd, its promoter Bob entered into a contract on behalf of the company. The contract gave the unformed company third-party rights. Who is liable if the contract is later breached?

A Ouse Ltd.
B Bob and Ouse Ltd.
C The shareholders of Ouse Ltd.
D The directors of Ouse Ltd.

5 Joe and Fred wished to form a company. On 1 March 20XX they filed the appropriate documents with the Registrar. On 10 May 20XX they received a certificate of incorporation dated 1 May 20XX. Later they found out that the company had been registered on 4 May 20XX. On what date was the company incorporated?

A 1 March 20XX B 1 May 20XX C 10 May 20XX D 4 May 20XX

6 Meg used to be employed by Trent Ltd. Her contract contained a clause under which she agreed not to compete with Trent Ltd. The clause was reasonable in terms of its duration and

area. Meg has now formed a company called Meg (Corporate Services) Ltd and has started to compete against Trent Ltd through the company. Will Trent Ltd be able to obtain an injunction to prevent Meg (Corporate Services) Ltd from competing against Trent Ltd?

A No, because Meg (Corporate Services) Ltd is a separate entity.

B Yes, because the company has been formed as a device to avoid the restraint clause.

C No, since the company is not liable for the actions of its shareholders.

D Yes, because Meg (Corporate Services) Ltd is engaged in wrongful trading.

The answers to test your knowledge questions appear on p. 645.

Suggested further reading

Green, 'Security of transactions after Phonogram' (1984) 47 MLR 671.

Griffiths, 'Agents without principals: Pre-incorporation contracts and section 36C of the Companies Act 1985' (1993) 13 *Legal Studies* 241.

Gold, 'The liability of promoters for secret profits in English Law' (1943) *University of Toronto Law Journal* 21.

McCrea, 'Disclosure of promoters' secret profits' (1968) *University of British Columbia Law Review* 183.

5 The constitution of the company – the memorandum of association

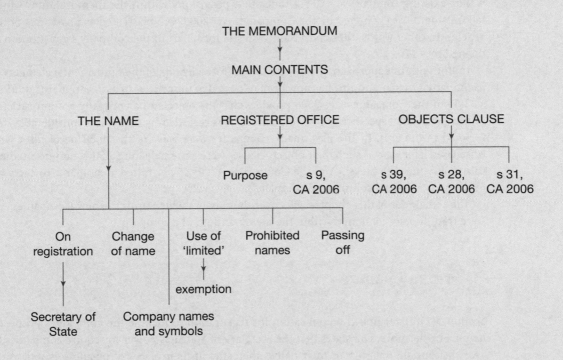

Under the Companies Act 1985, the constitution of a registered company consisted of two documents called the memorandum of association and the articles of association. However, this situation has been changed under s 17 of the Companies Act 2006, which now states that a company's constitution consists of the articles of association and any resolutions and agreements to which Chapter 3 of Part 3 of the 2006 Act applies.

The memorandum is still required for registration under s 9 of the Companies Act 2006, but is reduced significantly in its role, complexity and length. According to s 8, the document simply states the intention of the subscribers to form a company and to be members of the company on formation as well as to take at least one share each in the company (if limited by shares). The memorandum must be in the prescribed form and authenticated by each subscriber (s 8(2)).

For existing companies, s 28(1) states that provisions within the memorandum which fall outside those envisaged by the Companies Act 2006, will be treated as provisions of the articles. In other words, these provisions will still form part of the company's constitution as defined by s 17.

In line with this approach, the objects clause (formally one of the fundamental elements of a company's memorandum) has now been relocated to the articles of association. In addition, s 33(1) of the Companies Act 2006 provides that the objects of a company are unrestricted unless the articles specifically restrict them. This is regarded by many as a considerable step forward in the area. In the past, many companies were wary of the doctrine of *ultra vires* (discussed later) and as such their objects clauses were extremely long affairs, despite attempts to simplify the area (i.e. s 3A of the Companies Act 1985 permitted a company 'to carry on business as a general commercial company').

The remainder of this chapter will cover those issues which until the new Companies Act were traditionally contained within the memorandum of a company.

Company names

Section 9(2)(a) requires the application for registration to include the company's proposed name. Furthermore, s 82 states that the Secretary of State has power to require companies to give appropriate publicity to their names thereafter at their places of business as well as on business correspondence and related documentation.

A company's choice of name is subject to a number of limitations. First of all, ss 58 and 59 state that if the company is a limited company, then its name must end with the prescribed warning suffix 'limited'/'Ltd' (if it is a private company) or 'public limited company'/'plc' (if it is a public company). This requirement is subject to limited exemptions outlined in s 60 (i.e. if the private company is a charity). The purpose of this requirement is to act as a warning to anyone dealing with the company that it is an entity which has limited liability (though many feel that this is a little outdated and not very effective in practice).

In addition, under s 53, there are certain prohibited names which limit a company's choice. These include anything that is regarded offensive or which, in the opinion of the Secretary of State, would constitute an offence. This category of restriction will not often be met with in business but the Registrar turned down the names 'Prostitutes Ltd', 'Hookers Ltd' and 'Lindi St Claire French Lessons Ltd' when application was made for the registration of the business of a prostitute (*Attorney-General* v *Lindi St Claire (Personal Services) Ltd* [1981] 2 Co Law 69).

Furthermore, s 54(1) states that the approval of the Secretary of State is required for the use of a name that would be likely to give the impression that the company is connected with Her Majesty's Government, a local authority, or any public authority. Equally, the name of a company must not include indications of company type or legal form (i.e. public limited company) except in accordance with the requirements outlined above (s 65).

Finally, and probably most importantly, the proposed name of a company must not be the same as any name that already exists on the Registrar's index of names (s 66). This may appear easily avoidable, but when one considers the fact that there are currently over 2 million names on the Registrar's index, then the process becomes a little more complicated, especially when one considers the possibility for 'passing off'. Once again, a limited exception has been introduced by way of s 66(4) for groups of companies.

Where the approval of the Secretary of State is required, the necessary evidence must be submitted with the incorporation documents or with the relevant resolution on a change of name. Where the approval of a particular body or organisation is required, a statement that an approach to that body or organisation has been made, together with a copy of any response received, must be included. This would be the case where the word 'charity' was to be used and the Charity Commissioners had been approached.

Once a suitable name has been decided upon though, the company may progress the process of registration. However, a final word of caution must be noted. Even if the company successfully registers its chosen name, the Secretary of State may, within 12 months of registration, direct a change because a name has been registered which is the same or too like that of an existing company. This permits an existing company to pursue a more cost effective mode of challenging a newly registered company name that is causing confusion, than that of a 'passing off' action. If the Secretary of State so directs a company to change its name then non-compliance is a criminal offence on the part of the company and every officer in default. Once that time has passed and the existence of a company with a 'too like' name has not been discovered by the first company to have the name, then the first company is left with the only other remedy, i.e. to seek redress at common law in the law of tort.

A company or other business organisation which carries on or proposes to carry on business under a name calculated to deceive the public by confusion with the name of an existing concern commits the civil wrong (or tort) of passing off, and will be restrained by injunction from doing so from the moment of incorporation. Consequently, in the case of *Tussaud* v *Tussaud* (1890) 44 ChD 678, the court granted an injunction in favour of the company which owed Madame Tussaud's waxworks so as to prevent a member of the Tussaud family from carrying on a similar waxworks show under the name of 'Louis Tussaud Ltd'. Where the offending business is a proposed company, an injunction can be obtained to prevent registration, if information is available in time. If an injunction is made against an existing company for passing off, it must either change its name or its business or wind up. In addition, it is not necessary to demonstrate that the deception was intentional (*British Diabetic Association* v *Diabetic Society Ltd* [1995] 4 All ER 812).

It has already been noted that the mere fact of using one's own name in business will not necessarily prevent a successful passing-off claim by an organisation already in business under that name (*Asprey & Garrard Ltd* v *WRA (Guns) Ltd* (2001)).

La Société Anonyme des Anciens Etablissements Panhard et Lavassor v *Panhard Levassor Motor Co Ltd* [1901] 2 Ch 513

In this case, which we can call the *Panhard* case, the claimant was a French company and its cars were sold in England. The French company wished to set up an English company to act as an agent in England to improve the sales of its cars there. To try to stop this the defendant English company was registered, its promoters hoping that the French company would not be able to register its name for its English corporate agent, there being a company of 'too like' name on the register already, and that this would prevent increased competition in the car market. It was held that the members of the English company must change the name of their company or wind it up or the company would be taken off the register.

To constitute the tort of passing off the business carried on by the offending concern must be the same as that of the claimant, or it must be likely that custom will come to the offending concern because the public will be deceived and associate it with the claimant. An interesting contrast is provided by the following cases.

Ewing v *Buttercup Margarine Company Ltd* [1917] 2 Ch 1

The claimant had since 1904 been carrying on a business dealing in margarine and tea, and had upwards of 150 shops of his own selling 50 tonnes of margarine a week in all. The claimant's concern was called 'The Buttercup Dairy Co'. The claimant's shops were situated in Scotland and in the North of England, but he was planning to expand his business into the South of England. The defendant company was registered in November 1916, and as soon as the claimant heard about it, he complained to the management of the concern, and later brought this action for an injunction to prevent the defendant company from trading in that name. It appeared that although the defendant was in the business of selling margarine, it was a wholesaler, whereas the claimant was a retailer, and the defendant put this forward as a defence suggesting that there would be no confusion. Another defence was that the company would operate only around London and there would be no confusion with a Northern concern.

Held – by the Court of Appeal – that an injunction would be granted to the claimant restraining the defendant company from trading in that name. Although the defendant was at the moment a wholesaler, the objects clause of the memorandum did give power to retail which it might exercise in future. Further, the claimant intended to open up branches in the South of England where there would be confusion.

Aerators Ltd v *Tollitt* [1902] 2 Ch 319

The claimant company was formed to work a patent for the instantaneous aeration of liquids. The defendants were the subscribers of the memorandum and articles of a proposed new company to be called Automatic Aerator Patents Ltd. The claimant sought an injunction to restrain the defendants from registering that name because it would deceive the public, the word 'Aerator' being associated with the claimant company. The claimant's patent was a portable aerator for use in syphons, whereas the defendants' company was concerned with large installations in public houses where a large amount of aeration of beer was required.

Held – there was no evidence of the probability of deception, and an injunction would not be granted. The action was an attempt to monopolise a word in ordinary use and must be dismissed.

As a general rule, an injunction will not be granted where the offending concern is trading in the name of its proprietor though where a company is trading in a name which is merely that of one only of its members then an injunction will be granted if confusion with an existing concern is likely to result (*MP Guimaraens and Son* v *Fonseca and Vosconcellos Ltd* (1921) 38 RPC 388). Neither will an injunction be granted where a company uses a name which consists of that of the person from whom the company bought its business, even though confusion results.

Waring and Gillow Ltd v *Gillow and Gillow Ltd* (1916) 32 TLR 389

W and G Ltd, well-known furniture, carpet and rug dealers and auctioneers, sought an injunction restraining G and G Ltd from carrying on a business as auctioneers of carpets (formerly the business belonged to L C Gillow, an auctioneer, who continued to be actively concerned with the business).

The court held that on the facts the two businesses were not likely to be taken one for the other and the injunction sought was not granted. In addition, since L C Gillow was actively concerned with the business, the company was allowed to incorporate his name. Furthermore, since the defendant company had purchased the business from L C Gillow, it was allowed to use his name in order to take advantage of the goodwill purchased.

Comment

There is no similar protection for a first name or nickname. In *Biba Group Ltd* v *Biba Boutique* [1980] RPC 413 the defendant whose surname was Gill had been known since infancy by the nickname 'Biba' and she ran a boutique in that name. The claimants, who were in a similar line of business, obtained an injunction against her. Whitford J said that whatever the right of a person to use his own surname, it did not extend to the use of a first name or nickname.

It should be noted that only the members can change a company's name. The Court of Appeal has considered whether the court has jurisdiction to order and empower the Registrar of Companies to change the name of the company as it appears on the register in a situation where no special resolution of its members to that effect has been passed. The Court of Appeal ruled that there is no such jurisdiction.

Halifax plc v *Halifax Repossessions Ltd* [2004] 2 BCLC 455, CA

The claimants had brought proceedings against the defendants for infringement of trade mark and passing off and the court granted relief in terms preventing the defendant group companies from using the word 'Halifax' in their names. However, there was no change of name. The claimants then sought a court order under the Civil Procedure Rules to order the Registrar to change the names to any name not including 'Halifax'. Two such orders were made but not acted upon by the Registrar. In the Court of Appeal it was decided that the relevant rule did not give the court jurisdiction to make such a change in the absence of a special resolution of the members. The Companies Act scheme for change must be followed. There were serious consequences to a change of company name. Signing company cheques where the company's name was not properly stated could result in personal liability in the signer. There were penalties for failing to display the proper name on places of business and on stationery and so on. The Registrar could not effectively be required to go beyond her statutory functions. She could not become involved in private litigation.

Finally, according to s 77 of the Companies Act 2006, a company may change its name by special resolution (see s 78) or by other means provided for by the company's articles (see s 79). On a change of name, the company must notify the Registrar who will enter the new name on the register in place of the old one and issue an amended certificate of incorporation (s 80). Notification must be accompanied by either a copy of the resolution (s 78(1)) or a statement that the change of name has been made by means provided for by the company's articles (s 79(1)).

A change of name has effect from the date on which the new certificate of incorporation is issued (s 81(1)), though one should also bear in mind some of the more practical implications of such a change; the cost of changing letterheads and signs and, more generally, the way in which customers, suppliers and bankers are to be informed. Equally, it should be stressed that a change of name does not impact on the company's rights or obligations. In other words, the company which has an altered name and altered certificate of incorporation is still the same company as when it was first registered under its previous name; it is not reformed at the point of the change of name taking effect (*Oshkosh B'Gosh Inc v Dan Marbel Inc Ltd* [1989] BCLC 507).

The objects clause

The objects clause lists the things which the company can do (i.e. the capacity of the company). If it enters into a transaction which is not included in the clause, that transaction will, at least at common law, be *ultra vires* (that is, beyond its powers) and void (that is, of no effect).

It should be noted that what we are looking at in this chapter is the company's capacity as revealed by the objects clause of its memorandum. It will be discovered that even where the company has capacity a transaction made on its behalf may still not be enforceable against it because the agent who made it had no authority to do so. The problems presented by lack of authority in the agent are looked at later in the text (see Chapter 8 ⭕) but the reader should, even at this early stage, bear in mind the distinction between the two areas of company capacity and agent authority.

The leading case on the operation of the *ultra vires* rule at common law appears below.

Ashbury Railway Carriage and Iron Co v *Riche* (1875) LR 7 HL 653

The company bought a concession for the construction of a railway system in Belgium, and entered into an agreement to finance Messrs Riche to construct a railway line. Messrs Riche commenced the work, and the company paid over certain sums of money in connection with the contract. The company later ran into difficulties, and the shareholders wished the directors to take over the contract in a personal capacity, and indemnify the shareholders. The directors thereupon repudiated the contract on behalf of the company, and Messrs Riche sued for breach of contract. The case turned on whether the company was engaged in an *ultra vires* activity in financing the building of a complete railway system because, if so, the contract it had made with Messrs Riche would be *ultra vires* and void, and the claim against the company would fail. The objects clause of the company's memorandum stated that it was established: 'to make or sell or lend on hire railway carriages, wagons and all kinds of railway plant, fittings, machinery and rolling stock; to carry on the business of mechanical engineers and general contractors, to purchase and sell as merchants timber, coal, metal and other materials, and to buy and sell such materials on commission or as agents'.

Held – by the House of Lords – that the financing of the concession to build a complete railway system from Antwerp to Tournai was *ultra vires* and void because it was not within the objects of the company. The words empowering the company to carry on the business of general contracting must be construed *ejusdem generis* with the preceding words, and must therefore be restricted to contracting in the field of plant, fittings and machinery only. In other words, the company could use its funds to make things for railways, but not make railways as such. The contract with Messrs Riche was therefore void, and the directors were entitled to repudiate it.

The company should not carry out acts or enter into transactions which are beyond the company's objects clause and a shareholder, upon discovering the intention of the company's directors to enter into such an agreement, may obtain an injunction so as to prevent it from going ahead (though not if it has already been ratified by way of special resolution of the general meeting).

However, it should be noted that if the transaction has already been carried out, the shareholder may only seek to gain damages from the wrongdoer directors for the company. (It is also worth pointing out at this stage that if a director has exceeded his/her powers then this may be taken as a breach of the terms of his/her contract of employment as well as a breach of his/her directors' duties; s 171 imposes a duty on directors to abide by the company's constitution. This will be discussed later within the context of directors' duties.)

It is also worth noting that the reader should be aware of the distinction to be made between a transaction undertaken by the directors which beyond the capacity of the company (i.e. *ultra vires* the company's objects clause) but which is rather an abuse of power by the directors: *Rolled Steel Products (Holdings) Ltd* v *British Steel Corporation*.

Rolled Steel Products (Holdings) Ltd v British Steel Corporation
[1985] 2 WLR 908

A Mr Shenkman was a 51 per cent shareholder and director in Rolled Steel and held all the issued share capital in another company called Scottish Steel of which he was also a director. Scottish Steel owed a lot of money to Colville Ltd (a company controlled by the defendant company, British Steel Corporation) and Mr Shenkman had given his personal guarantee of that debt. Later BSC wanted more security and Mr S caused Rolled Steel to enter into a guarantee of the Scottish Steel debt. There was no benefit to Rolled Steel in this and BSC knew there was not. Rolled Steel went into liquidation as did Scottish Steel, and the court was asked to decide whether BSC could prove in the liquidation of Rolled Steel on the guarantee.

Eventually the Court of Appeal decided that it could not. Slade LJ stated:

The relevant transactions were not beyond the corporate capacity of the plaintiff and thus were not *ultra vires* in the proper sense of that phrase. However, the entering into the guarantee and, to the extent of the sum guaranteed, the debenture was beyond the authority of the directors, because they were entered into in furtherance of purposes not authorised by the plaintiff's memorandum. Despite this lack of authority, they might have been capable of conferring rights on Colvilles if Colvilles had not known of this lack of authority. Colvilles, however, did have such knowledge and so acquired no rights under these transactions.

Comment

The transaction was not *ultra vires* Rolled Steel because its objects clause contained a paragraph giving an express power to enter into guarantees. Rolled Steel also had an independent objects paragraph on the lines of that in the *Cotman* case, so the giving of guarantees was, in effect, an object of the company which it could exercise whether there was a benefit or not.

Understanding the modern objects clause

By way of explanation of the above decision, it should be said that the *ultra vires* rule of the common law was brought in by the courts to protect shareholders. It was thought that if a shareholder bought shares in a company which had as its main object publishing and allied activities, he would not want the directors of that company to start up a different kind of business because he wanted to put money in publishing.

In more recent times it has been realised that shareholders are not so fussy about the business the directors take the company into so long as it is ethical and makes profits from which to pay dividends and the price of the company's shares rises on the Stock Exchange as a result of its success.

The people most affected by the *ultra vires* rule of the common law in more recent times were creditors who had supplied goods or services to a company for a purpose not contained in its objects clause. If the company was solvent, no doubt such creditors would be paid, but if it went into insolvent liquidation, they would not even be able to put in a claim. The liquidator would reject it as being based on a void transaction. Other creditors might get paid some part of their debts if the company had some funds but the *ultra vires* creditors would get nothing.

For this reason it became, and has remained until the Companies Act 2006, usual to put in the objects clause a large number of objects and powers so that the company could do a wide variety of things apart from its main business, if at any time it wished to do so. It also became common to insert a paragraph in the objects clause which stated that each clause contains a separate and independent main object which can be carried on separately from the others. The House of Lords decided in **Cotman v Brougham** [1918] AC 514 that this type of clause was legal so that, for example, a company whose main object was publishing could use a clause giving investment powers for any kind of investment and not just investment in publishing.

Also, the decision of the Court of Appeal in **Bell Houses Ltd v City Wall Properties Ltd** [1966] 2 All ER 674 is to the effect that a subjective objects clause can be drafted in such a way as to allow the company to carry on any additional business, not provided for in the objects clause, which the directors think can be conveniently pursued by the company. If this is thought to put too much power in the hands of the directors, the objects clause may make the decision depend upon an ordinary resolution of the members.

In this way the limitations which are placed by the common law on a company's business activities by the *ultra vires* rule were much reduced. In fact, with a large number of clauses in the objects clause, with an independent objects subclause and/or a type of *Bell Houses* clause, the modern company's contractual capacity approached that of a natural person prior to the new Act, with the *ultra vires* rule as a method of controlling the activities of the board of directors being largely abandoned for quite a long time.

The Companies Act 2006

In an attempt to simplify further this area, the Company Law Review Steering Groups proposed the repeal of s 3A of the Companies Act 1985, together with the removal of the objects clause from a company's memorandum and insertion into the articles of association. Indeed, the Companies Act 2006 goes further than this and states that unless a company's articles specifically restrict its objects, then according to s 31(1) its objects are unrestricted. Consequently, for companies formed under the new Act, they are not required to have an objects clause and the doctrine of *ultra vires* (as outlined above) should be irrelevant to their operation.

However, for a company that decides to adopt an objects clause so as to limit the capacity of the company, then the doctrine of *ultra vires* will still remain relevant internally (i.e. with respect to deciding whether its directors have exceeded their powers and entered into a transaction that is *ultra vires* the company's objects clause).

It is also worth noting at this point that s 28(1) of the Companies Act 2006 provides that provisions within the memorandum of existing companies (i.e. formed before the new Act came into force) which fall outside those envisaged by the new Act, will be treated as provisions of the articles. In other words, provisions such as their objects clauses will still form part of the company's constitution as defined by s 17 and as such will be subject to the limitations outlined in the preceding paragraph.

The capacity of the company remains much the same as it did under s 35 of the Companies Act 1985 (as inserted by the Companies Act 1989), and is contained in s 39 of the Companies Act 2006. The intention of this provision was to eliminate the effect of the *ultra vires* rule on the claims of creditors, though it has less of an impact today than it would have had in the past since, as we have seen, fewer transactions are likely to be *ultra vires* at common law. However, on the assumption that the narrow scope of a particular company's objects clause may still allow for this, a review of certain of the statutory provisions appears below.

We shall deal at this stage only with the effect of legislation upon the rules relating to the company's capacity. It should also be borne in mind that legislation only reforms the *ultra vires* rule – it has not been abolished, though so far as trade creditors of a company are concerned little should now be heard of it. There is a continuing relevance of the rule in other areas as we shall see.

(a) The company's capacity

Section 39 provides that the validity of an act of a company shall not be called into question on the ground of lack of capacity by reason of anything in the company's constitution. Section 40(1) goes on to state that 'in favour of a person dealing with a company in good faith, the power of the directors to bind the company, or authorise others to do so, is deemed to be free of any limitation under the company's constitution'.

Thus, in the *Ashbury* case the contents of the objects clause only allowed the company to make things for railways and not railways as such. The contract with Messrs Riche should now have been enforceable against the company, since so far as outsiders are concerned, the contents of (what is in) the constitution do not affect the validity of the transaction in terms of the company's capacity to enter into it.

(b) The rights of members

As noted above, under the common law any member may ask the court for an injunction to prevent the directors from making (or continuing with) an *ultra vires* transaction, subject to the provisions of the Companies Act 2006. Indeed, s 40(4) states that this provision 'does not affect any right of a member of the company to bring proceedings to restrain the doing of an action that is beyond the powers of the directors'. Section 40(5) goes on to state that it does not affect any liability incurred by the directors by reason of them exceeding their powers.

However, given the fact that no objects clause is now required for private companies, this process should, in the future, become of less importance; though existing companies will still need to be wary of this possibility.

(c) Special regime for charities

Obviously charities need to be dealt with separately because people give not to the charity as such but rather to the objects of that particular charity. Consequently, under s 42 of the Companies Act 2006, ss 39 and 40 do not apply to the acts of a company that is a charity unless a person:

(a) does not know at the time the act is done that the company is a charity; or
(b) gives full consideration in money or money's worth in relation to the act in question and does not know that (i) the act is beyond the company's constitution, or (ii) the act is beyond the powers of the directors.

Altering the objects clause

The movement of the objects clause to a company's articles of association means that this provision may be changed in the same way as any other provision within the articles which have not been the subject of entrenchment (see s 22), and can be freely changed, or amended, under s 21 by way of a special resolution.

Capital

On an application for registration, s 9(4) requires a statement of capital and initial shareholdings if the company is to be limited by shares. Section 10(2) goes on to provide that the statement of capital and initial shareholdings must state:

(a) the total number of shares of the company to be taken on formation by the subscribers to the memorandum of association;
(b) the aggregate nominal value of those shares;
(c) for each class of shares: (i) prescribed particulars of the rights attached to the shares; (ii) the total number of shares of that class; and (iii) the aggregate nominal value of shares of that class; and
(d) the amount to be paid up and the amount (if any) to be unpaid on each share (whether on account of the nominal value of the share or by way of premium).

On registration this information will usually be very simple. In the case of a shelf company, this information will generally consist of two people taking one £1 share each, upon which nothing is paid. However, once a company is in the process of issuing larger, more significant numbers of shares, this information must be provided to the Registrar of Companies via a 'return of allotments'. In this regard, s 555(2) provides that within one month of making an allotment of shares, the company must deliver a return of allotment to the Registrar for registration. This return must be accompanied by a statement of capital (s 555(3)(b)) which must according to s 555(4) contain an updated version of the information required under s 10(2) discussed above.

One significant development under the Companies Act 2006 is that it has removed the notion of 'authorised capital' which had increasingly become regarded as a somewhat out-dated and irrelevant concept in practice. Indeed, as will be noted in subsequent chapters, this concept could pose problems for the directors of a company in that, once shares had been issued up to the amount of the company's authorised share capital, they were obliged to go back to the shareholders so as to gain approval to increase the authorised amount (see s 121 of the Companies Act 1985). In one sense, this provided shareholders with a certain amount of protection from having their holdings diluted. However, since the Companies Act 2006 has introduced shareholder control of share-related matters into other sections of its provisions and, with a number of the provisions formerly located in the memorandum now being included into the company's articles, this opens up possibilities for shareholders to place stronger controls in the company's constitution to the alteration of capital rather than via concepts such as 'authorised capital' as in the past.

The registered office

Section 9(2)(b) requires that on application to be registered, a company must state in which of the three United Kingdom jurisdictions its registered office will be located. If it is to be in England and Wales or Wales, then registration is effected by the Registrar of Companies in London, and if in Scotland, by the Scottish Registrar of Companies in Edinburgh. The situation of the registered office in England and Wales or Wales or Scotland fixes the company's nationality as British and its domicile as English or Scottish, as the case may be (but see *Daimler Co Ltd* v *Continental Tyre & Rubber Co Ltd*, 1916), though not its residence. Therefore, the legal system under which a company is incorporated is its domicile (*Gasque* v *Commissioners of Inland Revenue* [1940] 2 KB 8) but the company is not free to abandon one domicile in favour of another one, as per a human being under the principles of Private International Law (Conflict of Laws) (*Carl Zeiss Stiftung* v *Rayner and Keeler Ltd* (*No 3*) [1970] Ch 506). The only way in which a company may move from one jurisdiction to another is if the members of that company promote a private Act of Parliament for that sole purpose (e.g. the Henry Johnson, Sons & Co Limited Act 1996).

Residence is fixed by ascertaining where the company's centre of control and management is. Thus, a company may be resident in a number of countries where it has several centres of control in different countries. The residence of a company is important in connection with its liability to pay UK taxation.

Swedish Central Railway Co Ltd v *Thompson* [1925] AC 495

The company was incorporated in 1870 to construct a railway in Sweden, the registered office of the company being in London. Later the management of the company was moved to Sweden but the registered office remained in London, dealing only with formal administrative matters such as share transfers. All dividends were declared in Sweden, and no part of the profits was ever sent to England, except payment of dividend to English shareholders. The Commissioners of Income Tax assessed the company for tax on income received in Sweden.

Held – a company could have more than one residence, though only one nationality and domicile. This company was resident in Sweden and London, and since residence was relevant for income tax purposes, the assessment of the Commissioners was affirmed.

A company must in all its business letters and order forms state whether it is registered in England or Scotland, the registration number assigned to it (as shown in the certificate of incorporation), and the address of its registered office. There are penalties in case of default.

A company's registered office may be, and often is with private companies, the office of its accountants, and this is where formal communications will be sent. A Post Office box address cannot be used because people (members and in some cases the public) have a right to visit the registered office to inspect documents.

Purpose of registered office

The registered office is the company's official address. It provides a place where legal documents, notices and other communications can be served. A document can be served on a company by leaving it at, or sending it by registered or ordinary post to, the registered office. (*T O Supplies Ltd* v *Jerry Creighton Ltd* [1951] 1 KB 42.) If the company has no registered office, claim forms and summonses may be served on the directors or the secretary at an office which is not registered. Thus, in *Re Fortune Copper Mining Co* (1870) LR 10 Eq 390 the registered office of the company had been pulled down and a claim form was served on the secretary and the directors at an unregistered office. The court held that this was good service.

In an interesting development a change in the Civil Procedure Rules (60th update 1 April 2013) allows service of claim forms, and other legal process, on a company not only at the company's registered office but also at any place of business, such as a branch, which has some real connection with the cause or matter at issue. So if business has been conducted through a branch office which has resulted in the supply of defective goods or services, legal process could be served on the branch office. This assists the consumer, in particular, who will probably be more familiar with the branch through which he has dealings than the situation of the registered office.

When the Registrar of Companies receives a communication returned as undeliverable at the registered office, he will eventually set in motion the procedures for striking the company off the Register as a defunct company (see further Chapter 29 ◗).

The registered office and insolvency proceedings

Council Regulation (EC) No 1346/2000 on insolvency proceedings applies to insolvency proceedings, whether the debtor is a natural person or a legal person, as listed in its Annexes. The term 'insolvency proceedings' does not necessarily involve the intervention of a judicial authority and, as such, the expression 'court' contained in the Regulation includes a person or body empowered by national law to open insolvency proceedings. The Regulation enables the main insolvency proceedings to be opened in the Member State where the debtor has the centre of his main interests. These proceedings have universal scope and aim at encompassing all the debtor's assets. The 'centre of main interests' should correspond to the place where the debtor conducts the administration of his interests on a regular basis and is therefore ascertainable by third parties.

The case of *Re Eurofood IFSC Ltd (Case C-341/04)* [2006] All ER (D) 20 (May) is important in terms of the interpretation of Articles 3, 16 and 26 of the Regulation. On 24 December 2003, Parmalat was placed under administration in Italy. However, at the request of the Bank of America NA seeking the liquidation of Eurofood, the Irish High Court appointed Mr Farrell as the provisional liquidator of Eurofood in January 2004. On 9 February 2004, Eurofood was placed under the administration in Italy of Enrico Bondi. On 23 March 2004 though, the High Court found Eurofood insolvent and ordered its liquidation, appointing Mr Farrell as liquidator. It held that the proceedings opened in Ireland were the 'main' proceedings, since the centre of main interests of Eurofood was in Ireland. Mr Bondi appealed that judgment. The Supreme Court of Ireland referred several questions to the European Court of Justice.

Article 3 of the Regulation states that the court with jurisdiction to open the 'main' insolvency proceedings is the court of the Member State where the centre of the debtor's main interests is situated. In the case of a company, the place of the registered office shall be presumed to be the centre of its main interests. The Court of Justice held that that presumption can be 'rebutted only if factors which are both objective and ascertainable by third parties enable it to be established that an actual situation exists which is different from that which locating it at that registered office is deemed to reflect.' Article 16 of the Regulation goes on to provide that:

> Any judgment opening insolvency proceedings handed down by a court of a Member State which has jurisdiction pursuant to Article 3 shall be recognised in all the other Member States from the time that it becomes effective in the State of the opening of proceedings.

The Court held that this rule is based on the principle of mutual trust and, as such, insolvency proceedings opened by a court of a Member State must be recognised by the courts of the other Member States. However, Article 26 states that such recognition may be refused by a Member State where the effects of such recognition would be manifestly contrary to its public policy, in particular its fundamental principles or the constitutional rights and liberties of the individual. In this regard, the Court reiterated that it is a general principle of Community law that everyone is entitled to a fair legal process. As such, it stated that:

> the principle is inspired by the fundamental rights which form an integral part of the general principles of Community law which the Court of Justice enforces, drawing inspiration from the constitutional traditions common to the Member States and from the guidelines supplied, in particular, by the European Convention for the Protection of Human Rights and Fundamental Freedoms.

The Court held that the right to be notified of procedural documents and the right to be heard 'occupy an eminent position in the organisation and conduct of a fair legal process'. It argued that in the context of insolvency proceedings, the right of creditors or their representatives to participate in accordance with the equality of arms principle is of particular importance, and hence constitutes a ground to refuse recognition in the sense of Article 26.

In the case of *Interedil Srl, in liquidation* v *Fallimento Interedil Srl, Intesa Gestione Crediti SpA* (**Case C-396/09**) (CJEU 1st Chamber, 20 October 2011), the Court of Justice held that EU law precludes a national court from being bound by a national procedural rule under which that court is bound by the rulings of a higher national court, where it is apparent that the rulings of the higher court are at variance with European Union law, as interpreted by the Court of Justice. In addition, the court clarified the fact that the term 'centre of a debtor's main interests' in Article 3(1) of the Regulation must be interpreted by reference to European Union law. For the purposes of determining a debtor company's main centre of interests, the second sentence of Article 3(1) must be interpreted as follows:

● A debtor company's main centre of interests must be determined by attaching greater importance to the place of the company's central administration, as may be established by objective factors which are ascertainable by third parties. Where the bodies responsible for the management and supervision of a company are in the same place as its registered office and the management decisions of the company are taken, in a manner that is ascertainable by third parties, in that place, the presumption in that provision cannot be rebutted. Where a company's central administration is not in the same place as its registered office, the presence of company assets and the existence of contracts for the financial exploitation of those assets in a Member State other than that in which the registered office is situated cannot be regarded as sufficient factors to rebut the presumption unless a comprehensive assessment of all the relevant factors makes it possible to establish, in a manner that is ascertainable by third parties, that the company's actual centre of management and supervision and of the management of its interests is located in that other Member State.

- Where a debtor company's registered office is transferred before a request to open insolvency proceedings is lodged, the company's centre of main activities is presumed to be the place of its new registered office.

Finally, the court clarified the fact that the term 'establishment' within the meaning of Article 3(2) of the Regulation must be interpreted as requiring the presence of a structure consisting of a minimum level of organisation and a degree of stability necessary for the purpose of pursuing an economic activity. The presence alone of goods in isolation or bank accounts does not, in principle, meet that definition.

It is also necessary to mention the Insolvency Act 1986 (Amendment) (No 2) Regulations 2002. Before these regulations came into force it was possible for a UK court to deal with insolvency proceedings in regard to foreign companies provided that the company concerned had assets here. Under the 2002 regulations that are numbered SI 2002/1240, the territory in which the corporate debtor has its centre of main interests will have jurisdiction to open insolvency proceedings against it. These are referred to as the main proceedings and the registered office is presumed but not conclusively to be the centre of main interests. The courts of other countries can institute insolvency proceedings but only in regard to assets of the corporate debtor that are within the jurisdiction of the court. These are called territorial proceedings which would not result in, for example, the winding up of the company. This would be a matter for the main proceedings. These matters receive further consideration in the sections on corporate insolvency and company rescue. However, the importance here is the role of the registered office in deciding which country is entitled to conduct the main proceedings. The main thrust of the regulations is to deal with companies within the EU but as will be seen in the insolvency sections a UK court has regarded itself as entitled to deal with insolvency matters where the corporate debtor was an American company, ruling that its centre of main interests was the UK even though its registered office was in the United States (see *Re Brac Rent-A-Car International Inc.* [2003] All ER (D) 98 (Feb)).

Essay questions

1 'There are occasions when the courts will look behind the formality of legal personality and will appear to disregard it, but it is impossible to find any consistent principle upon which they will do so.' Discuss. *(Kingston University)*

2 In 2005 Archie, Bert, Colin and David, as shareholders and directors, set up a company to acquire a disused mill to renovate into single-person flats. David had bought the mill in 2004 and sold it to the company once it was formed. Bert has now become concerned that this deal has caused the company to suffer a loss. Advise Bert on what the common law position is regarding the company, the transaction and the protection of his interests. *(University of the West of Scotland)*

3 Eric and Stanley have been carrying on business in partnership as building contractors in a small town for some years. They carry out most of the work themselves and only occasionally employ labour. They have no plans to enlarge the area of their operations. It has been suggested to them that they ought to trade as a private registered company limited by shares. They ask your advice on the following matters.

(a) What are the alleged advantages of trading as a private registered company limited by shares? Are there any disadvantages in so trading?

(b) At present they trade as 'Ericstay'. They would like to retain the name because of the business connection attached to it. Advise them on their suggested choice of name.

(c) They have been informed that as a registered company they will need a certificate to commence business. Explain to them what a certificate to commence business is and advise them whether they will need such a certificate.

(The Association of Chartered Certified Accountants)

4 The objects clause as traditionally contained in the memorandum of association of a company has been the subject of considerable debate and disagreement, even with the introduction of s 3A of the Companies Act 1985. The only way in which this area could be clarified once and for all was to pursue the approach taken by the Companies Act 2006. Discuss.

(Authors' question)

5 Jane is a promoter dealing with the formation of a private limited company. You are required to advise Jane on the following matters.

(a) The restrictions which exist upon the choice of corporate name.

(b) The documentation which must be sent to the Registrar of Companies in order to obtain incorporated status.

(c) The liability for Jane personally if she enters into any contracts on the company's behalf before the issue of the certificate of incorporation.

(The Chartered Institute of Management Accountants)

6 Explain the term 'business name' and describe the relevance of the Business Names Act 1985. *(The Institute of Company Accountants)*

7 For several years Jay Ltd has been carrying on the business of managing night clubs. The directors are now proposing that the company should operate a chain of pizza restaurants but, because some of the shareholders are objecting to the proposal, they wish to know if it would be permissible.

Advise the directors. *(The Institute of Chartered Accountants in England and Wales)*

Test your knowledge

Four alternative answers are given. Select ONE only. Circle the answer which you consider to be correct. Check your answers by referring back to the information given in the chapter and against the answers at the end of the text.

1 A transaction with a trade creditor which falls outside a company's express objects set out in the articles is:

A Valid under s 39 of the CA 2006.

B Void as being *ultra vires* the company.

C Void as being *ultra vires* the directors.

D Void at the instance of the members.

2 On 1 February Mersey Ltd passed a special resolution changing its name to Trent Ltd. On the same day the managing director made a contract with Thames Ltd to sell it some goods. On 1 March the company received its new certificate of incorporation and on 1 April Trent Ltd failed to deliver the goods in breach of contract. What is the effect on the contract of the change of name?

A It is enforceable against the managing director as a pre-incorporation contract.

B It cannot be enforced because Mersey Ltd no longer exists.

C The contract is enforceable against the company and proceedings can be mmenced against it in its new name.

D The contract cannot be enforced unless ratified by the company in the new name.

3 Ribble Ltd has a share capital of 1,000,000 ordinary shares. The holders of 800,000 shares vote on a resolution to change the company's name. The minimum number of votes which must be cast in favour of the resolution for it to be effective is:

A 400,001 B 500,000 C 600,000 D 750,000

4 Promoters wish to form a company to be called 'Barchester City Council Tuition Services Ltd'. What is the legal position as to the permissibility of that name in company law?

A The name cannot be registered because it is unlawful.

B It can be registered if the Secretary of State gives permission.

C Permission must be obtained from the Department for Education and Employment.

D The name may be registered with the permission of the Barchester City Council.

The answers to test your knowledge questions appear on p. 645.

Suggested further reading

Keay, 'Ascertaining the Corporate Objective: An Entity Maximisation and Sustainability Model' (2008) 71 MLR 663.

Lewis, 'Corporate Redomicile' (1995) 16 Co Law 295.

6 The constitution of the company – the articles of association

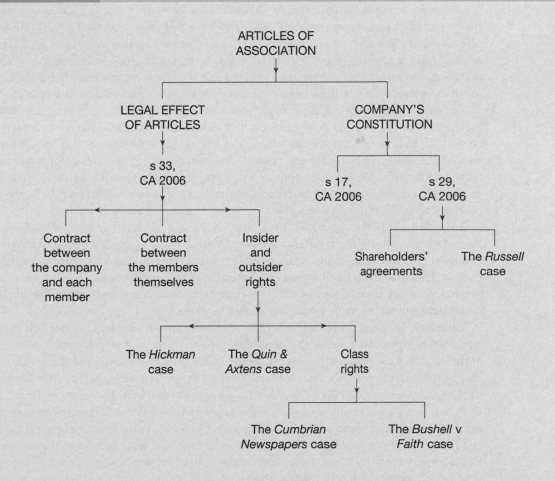

Section 17 of the Companies Act 2006 defines a company's constitution as including the articles of association and 'any resolutions and agreements to which Chapter 3 applies (see s 29)'. The most important aspects of the latter point being any special resolutions of the shareholders (s 29(1)(a)); any unanimous resolution or agreement adopted by the members of a company, that it would not otherwise be binding on them unless passed by a special resolution (s 29(1)(b)); and any resolution or agreement of a class of members binding all members of the class (s 29(1)(c)). Two points should be made at this point. First of all, given the reduced role of the memorandum of association under the Companies Act 2006, it does not form part of the company's constitution (see s 8); a contrast to the position under the Companies Act 1985. Secondly, as will be discussed later, there is the suggestion that s 29 now takes account of shareholder agreements as part of the company's constitution.

The articles of association regulate the internal affairs of a company subject to those matters which are otherwise specifically regulated by way of other sources of law. This in turn offers an incredible amount of freedom and flexibility to a company to regulate its internal affairs. Unfortunately, as will be noted later in this section, such freedom has led to academic debate, not so much as to what may be inserted into the articles of association, but rather as to which portions of the articles will be subsequently recognised and enforced by the courts.

Section 18 states that a company 'must have articles of association prescribing regulations for the company' unless it is a company to which model articles apply by virtue of s 20. It goes on to note that the articles should be contained in 'a single document' and 'divided into paragraphs numbered consecutively' (s 18(3)). In many respects, this latter point is common sense and follows accepted good practice when drafting any legal document; so as to avoid confusion of interpretation or application a contractual document should aim to utilise short, concise and self-contained paragraphs.

Turning to s 20, the Act states that if articles are not registered on the formation of a limited company, or if the registered articles 'do not exclude or modify the relevant model articles' (i.e. by way of the inclusion of a special provision expressly excluding their application), then such model articles will form part of the company's articles as if they had been duly registered at the time of formation. This is an important point and one which anyone involved in the formation of a company should be aware.

Therefore, a company may under s 18 have its own articles or adopt the relevant Model Articles (see Appendix 1, below ◯) 'prescribed for a company of that description as in force at the date on which the company is registered' (s 20(2)). It should be noted though that for many existing companies, the relevant model articles that will be encountered will still remain Table A (see Appendix 2, below ◯). A not uncommon use of special provisions in the articles of private companies is where they are subsidiaries and the holding company wants to add extra provisions, not found in the model articles (or Table A), to the articles of the subsidiary as a means of control over that subsidiary. The most usual clauses inserted into the articles of the subsidiary are to the effect that certain transactions of the subsidiary, e.g. borrowing over a set limit, require the approval of the shareholders of the subsidiary (the holding company being, of course, the controlling shareholder) by ordinary resolution (a 'general meeting' provision) or the consent of a nominated director who is a representative of the holding company (the 'special director' provision).

When amending or modifying the articles of association, a company must ensure that any new provisions are not inconsistent with the legislation governing companies (*Re Peveril Gold Mines Ltd* [1898] 1 Ch 122) and in line with the general law (*Welton* v *Saffery* [1897] AC 299) otherwise they will be void. Aside from these restrictions, members may seek to include any provisions which they feel to be appropriate to the company (*Gaiman v National Association for Mental Health* [1971] Ch 317), though the issue of insider/outsider rights should also be borne in mind when considering such provisions (see discussion later in this chapter ⊙).

The articles deal with such matters as the appointment and powers of directors, general meetings of the company, the voting rights of members, the transfer of shares, and dividends. The rights of the different classes of shareholders may also be found in the articles if included by way of special provisions. This has led many to refer to the articles as being equivalent to the 'instruction book' of a company. The contents of both *Table A* and the new Model Articles are outlined below.

Table A is a comprehensive document which deals with virtually every aspect of the internal workings of a company and applies to a company incorporated under the Companies Act 1985 unless it was specifically excluded or modified. The main areas of operation are presented.

Table A (Companies Act 1985)

Articles	Corporate issues
1	Interpretation
2–35	Shares
36–63	Members and General Meetings
64–98	Directors and Board Meetings
99–101	Administration
102–110	Profits
111–116	Notices

As noted earlier, the emphasis of the Companies Act 2006 has been to '*think small first*' and this approach is reflected in the fact that the new Model Articles have 53 provisions compared with 118 under the 1985 Act's *Table A*. The new Model Articles apply to all companies incorporated after 1 October 2009 and, importantly, provide the same freedom to companies to amend them (s 21 CA 2006).

Model Articles for Private Companies Limited by Shares (CA 2006)

Articles	Corporate issues
1–2	Definition and Members' liability limitation
3–6	Directors' powers and responsibilities
7–16	Directors' decision making
17–20	Appointment of directors
21–29	Shares
30–35	Dividends and other distributions
36	Capitalisation of profits
37–47	General meetings
48–51	General provisions re communication, seal, etc.
52–53	Directors' indemnity/insurance

The traditional division of powers under the articles

A company's articles of association determine the manner in which power within a company is divided between the shareholders in General Meeting and the Board of Directors. The relevant articles from both *Table A* and the new Model Articles are set out below and illustrate the 'default' setting for the division of powers though, as noted above, this may be amended by the company by altering its articles of association (see Chapter 7, p. 125 ○).

Table A (CA 1985) – Article 70

70. Subject to the provisions of the Act, the memorandum and the articles and to any directions given by special resolution, the business of the company shall be managed by the directors who may exercise all the powers of the company. No alteration of the memorandum or articles and no such direction shall invalidate any prior act of the directors which would have been valid if that alteration had not been made or that direction had not been given. The powers given by this regulation shall not be limited by any special power given to the directors by the articles and a meeting of directors at which a quorum is present may exercise all powers exercisable by the directors.

Model Articles for private companies limited by shares (CA 2006) – Articles 3 and 4

3   Subject to the articles, the directors are responsible for the management of the company's business, for which purpose they may exercise all the powers of the company.
4   (1)   The shareholders may, by special resolution, direct the directors to take, or refrain from taking, specified action.
    (2)   No such special resolution invalidates anything which the directors have done before the passing of the resolution.

It is worth bearing in mind at this stage that any division of powers that takes place via the articles of association has significant implications for the running of a company. If shareholders subsequently wish to retract certain powers/responsibilities that have been granted to directors, the only way forward is to amend the company's articles of association by way of a special resolution in General Meeting.

Imperial Hydropathic Hotel Co, Blackpool v Hampson (1882) 23 Ch D 1

The articles of association provided that the directors could hold office for a period of three years and then retire by rotation. At a general meeting which had been called for this purpose along with other matters, resolutions were passed to remove two directors who were not due to retire under the terms of the articles. Furthermore, they were to be replaced by two other individuals. The company claimed that the directors had been validly removed from office. Cotton LJ stated:

> There is nothing in the Act or in the articles which directly enables a general meeting to remove directors; but the way it is put is this – that there is power in these articles, as there is power in the Act, by a meeting duly called to pass a resolution altering the articles; and it is said that here there was a resolution which would have been effectual to alter the articles that these directors whom the articles did not authorise to be removed should be removed. Now in my opinion it is an entire fallacy to say that because there is power to alter the regulations, you can by a resolution which might alter the regulations, do

that which is contrary to the regulations as they stand in a particular and individual case. It is in no way altering the regulations. The alteration of the regulations would be by introducing a provision, not that some particular director be discharged from being a director, but that directors be capable of being removed by the vote of a general meeting. It is a very different thing to pass a general rule applicable to everyone who comes within it, and to pass a resolution against a particular individual, which would be a *privilegium* and not a law. Now here there was no attempt to pass any resolution at this meeting which would affect any director, except those who are aimed at by the resolution, no alteration of the regulations was to bind the company to those regulations as altered; and assuming, as I do for the present purpose, as the second meeting seems to have been regular according to the notice, that everything was regularly done, what was done cannot be treated in my opinion as an alteration first of the regulations, and then under that altered regulation as a removal of the directors. . . .

[In the present case] there is not a general alteration of the regulations of the company, but simply an attempt, without altering the rules for the purpose, to remove a director, his removal being, unless there is a general alteration, an illegal act on the part of those who attempt to remove him – by illegal I mean an act *ultra vires* and not supported by any regulation of the company. Therefore, I think that the appeal ought to be dismissed with costs.

Held – The company's articles of association could not be disregarded in this matter.

Similarly, where the articles provide that the company's directors are responsible for the day-to-day running of the business, the shareholders have no power by way of ordinary resolution to give directions to the board of directors or to overrule its decisions.

Automatic Self-Cleaning Filter Syndicate Co Ltd v *Cuninghame* [1906] 2 Ch 34

A company had power under its memorandum of association to sell its undertaking to another company having similar objects, and by its articles of association the general management and control of the company were vested in the directors, subject to such regulations as might from time to time be made by extraordinary resolution, and, in particular, the directors were empowered to sell or otherwise deal with any property of the company on such terms as they might think fit. At a general meeting of the company a resolution was passed by a simple majority of the shareholders for the sale of the company's assets on certain terms to a new company formed for the purpose of acquiring them, and directing the directors to carry the sale into effect. The directors, being of opinion that a sale on those terms was not for the benefit of the company, declined to carry the sale into effect.

Held – Upon the construction of the articles, that the directors could not be compelled to comply with the resolution. Collins MR stated:

The point arises in this way. At a meeting of the company a resolution was passed by a majority – I was going to say a bare majority, but it was a majority – in favour of a sale to a purchaser, and the directors, honestly believing, as Warrington J thought, that it was most undesirable in the interests of the company that that agreement should be carried into effect, refused to affix the seal of the company to it, or to assist in carrying out a resolution which they disapproved of; and the question is whether under the memorandum and articles of association here the directors are bound to accept, in substitution of their own view, the views contained in the resolution of the company. Warrington J held that the majority could not impose that obligation upon the directors, and that on the true construction of the articles the directors were the persons authorised by the articles to effect this sale, and that unless the other powers given by the memorandum were invoked by a special resolution, it was impossible for a mere majority at a meeting to override the views of the directors. That depends, as Warrington J put it, upon the construction of the articles. First of all there is no doubt that the company under its memorandum has the power in clause 3(k) to sell the undertaking of the company or any part thereof. In this case there is some small exception, I believe, to that which is to be sold, but I do not think that that becomes material. We now come to clause 81 of the articles, which I think it is important to refer to in this connection. [His Lordship read the clause.] Then come the two clauses which are most material, 96 and 97, whereby the powers of the directors are defined. [His Lordship read clause 96 and clause 97(1).] Therefore in the matters referred to in article 97(1) the view of the directors as to the fitness of the matter is made the standard; and furthermore, by article 96 they are given in express terms the full powers which the company has, except so far as they 'are not hereby or by statute expressly directed or required to be exercised or done by the company', so that the directors have absolute power to do all things other than those that are expressly required to be done by the company; and then comes the limitation on their general authority – 'subject to such regulations as may from time to time be made by extraordinary resolution'. Therefore, if it is desired to alter the powers of the directors that must be done, not by a resolution carried by a majority at an ordinary meeting of the company, but by an extraordinary resolution. In these circumstances it seems to me that it is not competent for the majority of the shareholders at an ordinary meeting to affect or alter the mandate originally given to the directors, by the articles of association. It has been suggested that this is a mere question of principal and agent, and that it would be an absurd thing if a principal in appointing an agent should in effect appoint a dictator who is to manage him instead of his managing the agent. I think that that analogy does not strictly apply to this case. No doubt for some purposes directors are agents. For whom are they agents? You have, no doubt, in theory and law one entity, the company, which might be a principal, but you have to go behind that when you look to the particular position of directors. It is by the consensus of all the individuals in the company that these directors become agents and hold their rights as agents. It is not fair to say that a majority at a meeting is for the purposes of this case the principal so as to alter the mandate of the agent. The minority also must be taken into account. There are provisions by which the minority may be over-borne, but that can only be done by special machinery in the shape of special resolutions. Short of that the mandate which must be obeyed is not that of the majority – it is that of the whole entity made up of all the shareholders. If the mandate of the directors is to be altered, it can only be under the machinery of the memorandum and articles themselves. I do not think I need say more.

 Baron v Potter [1914] 1 Ch 895

The company's two directors had reached deadlock whereby they no longer spoke to one another. This in turn impacted on the ability to conduct effective board meetings. The plaintiff had called a general meeting which had sought to appoint additional directors to the company's board. The defendant objected to this course of action, stating that the power to appoint new directors was vested, according to the terms of the articles of association, in the directors.

Held – Due to the deadlocked position of the current directors of the company the power to appoint reverted to the general meeting. Consequently, the appointment of additional directors was valid.

The legal effect of the articles

One aspect of the articles of association which has, until the coming into force of the new Companies Act 2006, traditionally caused confusion for both scholars and students alike has been their legal effect. Section 14 of the Companies Act 1985 has now been replaced by s 33 of the Companies Act 2006 which, significantly, has updated the wording of this traditionally awkward section.

Section 33 of the Companies Act 2006, states that 'the provisions of a company's constitution bind the company and its members to the same extent as if there were covenants on the part of the company and of each member to observe those provisions'. Under s 14 of the Companies Act 1985, the memorandum and articles, when registered, bound 'the company and its members to the same extent as if they respectively had been signed and sealed by each member, and contained covenants on the part of each member to observe all the provisions of the memorandum and articles'.

The first point that needs to be made is that s 33 now includes the phrase '*on the part of the company and each member*' as opposed to simply '*on the part of each member*'. The wording of this section, subject to slight variations, may be traced back to the Companies Act 1844, which adopted the method of forming an unincorporated joint-stock company in existence at that time. In effect, the wording of previous versions of s 33 appeared to suggest that the articles bound only the members, ignoring the fact that the company was a separate legal entity. The updated wording of the Companies Act 2006 appears to have eventually addressed this oversight. However, it has long since been assumed that the articles were binding as between members and the company. Stirling J noted in **Wood v Odessa Waterworks Co** (1889) 42 Ch D 636 that 'the articles of association constitute a contract not merely between the shareholders and the company, but between each individual shareholder and every other'. Nevertheless, it is generally acknowledged that the situation was clarified, once and for all, in the case of **Hickman v Kent or Romney Marsh** discussed below.

Secondly, s 33 makes reference to the company's constitution as opposed to 'the memorandum and articles'. This reflects the careful consideration with which this area has been revised by the Companies Act 2006. While the memorandum has effectively been reduced in its significance, and as such its role within the s 33 statutory contract, there is recognition of the role that other agreements may play within the day-to-day running of a company, particularly private limited companies. It is also worth noting at this point that, according to s 28, provisions which were contained in a company's memorandum immediately before the commencement of Part I of the Companies Act 2006, and are 'not provisions of the kind mentioned in s 8 (provisions of the new-style memorandum), are to be treated after the commencement of this Part as provisions of the company's articles' (s 28(1)).

The results of the statutory contract, as evidenced under s 14, were as follows:

(a) The memorandum and articles constituted a contract between the company and each member. Thus, each member, in his capacity as member, was bound to the company by the provisions in the articles. Furthermore, although s 14 did not state that the articles bind the company to the members but only the members to the company, the company was regarded as bound to each member in his capacity as member to observe the provisions in the articles.

(b) The memorandum and articles were also, by reason of case law, a contract between the members themselves. Thus, one member can sue another if that other fails to observe a provision in the memorandum or articles. However, the method by which this may be undertaken is discussed in greater detail below in terms of the decision in **MacDougall v Gardiner** (1875) 1 Ch D 13.

(c) No right given by the memorandum or articles to a member in a capacity other than that of member (e.g. as solicitor or director) can be enforced against the company. The memorandum and articles are not a contract with outsiders but merely with the members in respect of their rights as members.

To a large extent these points remain relevant for the s 33 statutory contract, though it is suggested that both (a) and (b) have now been clarified by the rewording of this section under the Companies Act 2006. Point (c) remains the subject of debate and will be examined in the next section in the context of 'insider' and 'outsider' rights. Nevertheless, the case law in relation to the statutory contract still remains of considerable use. For example, in *London Sack and Bag Co Ltd* v *Dixon and Lugton Ltd* [1943] 2 All ER 763, when considering the effect of the statutory contract on the legal relationship between a company's members, Scott LJ observed '. . . the statutory result may not be to constitute a contract between them about rights of action created entirely outside the company relationship, such as trading transaction between members' but rather to be restricted to membership matters. In many respects this reinforces the view that the purpose of the articles of association is to outline the way in which the proper functioning of the company is to take place.

This is echoed in *Welton* v *Saffery* [1897] AC 299, when Lord Herschell observed:

> It is quite true that the articles constitute a contract between each member and the company, and that there is no contract in terms between the individual members of the company; but the articles do not any the less, in my opinion, regulate their rights inter se. Such rights can only be enforced by or against a member through the company, or through the liquidator representing the company, but I think that no member has, as between himself and another member, any right beyond that which the contract with the company gives.

However, this also introduces the notion that rights may only be enforced via the company as opposed to directly between members and is based on the internal management principle outlined in *MacDougall* v *Gardiner* (1875) 1 Ch D 13 in which James LJ stated:

> I think it is of the utmost importance in all these companies that the rule which is well known in this court as the rule in . . . *Foss* v *Harbottle* should be always adhered to; that is to say, that nothing connected with internal disputes between the shareholders is to be made the subject of a bill by someone shareholder on behalf of himself and others, unless there be something illegal, oppressive, or fraudulent – unless there is something *ultra vires* on the part of the company qua company, or on the part of the majority of the company, so that they are not fit persons to determine it; but that every litigation must be in the name of the company, if the company really desire it.

Consequently, when considering membership rights, it would appear that not only is there a restriction on the type of actions which may be brought by members against other members, but also upon the mode by which such actions should take place. However, with an eye on the notion of quasi-partnerships, which will be discussed further in this chapter, it is perhaps worth noting the comments of Vaisey J in *Rayfield* v *Hands* [1960] Ch 1 when, having granted an order in favour of Mr Rayfield which required the directors to take his shares in accordance with the terms of the company's articles, he stated: 'The conclusion to which I have come may not be of so general application as to extend to the articles of association of every company, for it is, I think, material to remember that this private company is one of that class of companies which bears a close analogy to a partnership.'

The implications of this discussion will be examined in greater detail later in the text (see Chapters 17 and 18, ◐).

Finally, it is important to note that the term 'memorandum and articles', has been updated under the Companies Act 2006 to that of the company's constitution (see s 17). Also note the effect of s 28(1) as outlined above and in the previous chapter (see p. 88 ◐).

Wood v Odessa Waterworks Co (1889) 42 Ch D 636

The articles of association empowered the directors with the approval of the general meeting to declare 'a dividend to be paid to the members'. The directors recommended that instead of paying a dividend, members should be given debenture-bonds bearing interest repayable at par, by annual drawings, extending over 30 years. The recommendation was approved by the company in general meeting by an ordinary resolution. The plaintiff successfully sought an injunction restraining the company from acting on the resolution on the ground that it breached the articles. Stirling J stated:

> . . . the rights of the shareholders in respect of a division of the profits of the company are governed by the provisions of the articles of association. By s 16 of the Companies Act 1862 (now s 33 of the Companies Act 2006), the articles of association 'bind the company and the members thereof to the same extent as if each member had subscribed his name and affixed his seal thereto, and there were in such articles contained a covenant on the part of himself, his heirs, executors, and administrators, to conform to all the regulations contained in such articles, subject to the provisions of this Act.' . . . Those articles provide that the directors may, with the sanction of a general meeting, declare a dividend to be paid to the shareholders. Prima facie, that means to be paid in cash. The debenture-bonds proposed to be issued are not payments in cash; they are merely agreements or promises to pay: and if the contention of the company prevails a shareholder will be compelled to accept in lieu of cash a debt of the company payable at some uncertain future period. In my opinion that contention ought not to prevail.

Hickman v Kent or Romney Marsh Sheepbreeders' Association [1915] 1 Ch 881

The defendant company was incorporated under the Companies Acts in 1895. The objects of the company were to encourage and retain as pure the sheep known as Kent or Romney Marsh, and the establishment of a flock book listing recognised sires and ewes to be bred from. The articles provided for disputes between the company and the members to be referred to arbitration. This action was brought in the Chancery Division by the claimant because the Association had refused to register certain of his sheep in the flock book, and he asked for damages for this. It also appeared that the Association was trying to expel him, and he asked for an injunction to prevent this.

Held – by Astbury J – that the Association was entitled to have the action stayed. The articles amounted to a contract between the Association and the claimant to refer disputes to arbitration. However, Astbury J, after accepting that the articles were a contract between a company and its members, went on to say:

> [. . .] No right merely purporting to be given by an article to a person, whether a member or not, in a capacity other than that of a member, as for instance, a solicitor, promoter, director, can be enforced against the company.

Comment

(i) It was held, by the Court of Appeal, applying *Hickman*, in *Beattie v E and F Beattie Ltd* [1938] Ch 708, that a provision in the articles that disputes between the company and its members must be referred to arbitration did not apply to a person whose dispute was between the company and himself as director even though he was also a member.

(ii) In *Pender v Lushington* (1877) 6 Ch D 70, the chairman of a meeting of members refused to accept Pender's votes. The articles gave one vote for every 10 shares to the shareholders. This caused a resolution proposed by Pender to be lost. He asked the court to grant an injunction to stop the directors acting contrary to the resolution.

Held – Pender succeeded. The articles were a contract binding the company to the members.

Rayfield v *Hands* [1958] 2 All ER 194

The articles of a private company provided by Art II that 'Every member who intends to transfer his shares shall inform the directors who will take the said shares equally between them at a fair value'. The claimant held 725 fully paid shares of £1 each, and he asked the defendants, the three directors of the company, to buy them but they refused. He brought this action to sue upon the contract created by the articles without joining the company as a party.

Held – by Vaisey J – that the directors were bound to take the shares. Having regard to what is now s 33, the provisions of Art II constituted a binding contract between the directors, as members, and the claimant, as a member, in respect of his rights as a member. The word 'will' in the article did not import an option in the directors. Vaisey J did say that the conclusion he had reached in this case may not apply to all companies, but it did apply to a private company, because such a company was an intimate concern closely analogous with a partnership.

Comment

(i) Although the articles placed the obligation to take shares of members on the directors, Vaisey J construed this as an obligation falling upon the directors in their capacity as members. Otherwise, the contractual aspect of the provision in the articles would not have applied. (See *Beattie* v *E and F Beattie Ltd* [1938] Ch 708.)

(ii) The company's Art II was a pre-emption clause. Many such clauses use the expression 'may take the said shares'. If so, no contract is formed. The word 'may' indicates that there is an option whether to accept or not.

Eley v *Positive Government Security Life Assurance Co* (1876) 1 Ex D 88

The articles contained a clause appointing the claimant as solicitor of the company. The claimant was not appointed by a resolution of the directors or by any instrument under the seal of the company, but he did act as solicitor for some time and took shares in the company at a later stage. The company ceased to employ him, and he brought an action for breach of contract.

Held – by the Court of Appeal – that the action failed because there was no contract between the company and Eley under the articles. He was an outsider in his capacity as a solicitor, and presumably even though he was also a member, he could not enforce the articles since they gave him rights in his capacity as solicitor only, though his rights as a member to enforce the articles are not dealt with specifically in the judgment.

Comment

It was held by the court of first instance that a service contract on the terms set out in the articles was created because Eley had actually served the company as its solicitor. However, the contract was unenforceable because the articles contemplated his employment for an indefinite period of time, possibly longer than a year, and there was no written memorandum of the contract signed on behalf of the company as was then required by s 4 of the Statute of Frauds 1677. This statute is now repealed so that the case may have been decided differently today. This view is reinforced by the decision in *Re New British Iron Co, ex parte Beckwith* (see below) because surely when Eley took office he did so on the terms of the articles and had an implied contract based upon the terms of those articles. Thus, if a term as to tenure could be implied in the way that a term as to salary was in Beckwith, then Eley should have been able to sue for breach of the implied contract. *Read* v *Astoria* (see p. 116) suggests also the tenure of office may be based on the articles.

The articles and insider/outsider rights

The case of *Salomon* v *Salomon* has been described as both a blessing and a curse to modern company law. (Refer to suggested further reading at the end of this chapter.) Although the article is a little dated and the proposals for reform are not relevant, some good criticisms of the *Salomon* decision are offered. While the case confirmed the fact that, once registered, a company is a separate legal entity in the eyes of the law, it has also had a negative impact on the s 33 statutory contract.

Until *Salomon*, it was generally accepted that the company format was an inappropriate vehicle for small commercial enterprises. Rather, such enterprises should adopt the partnership format. However, this case changed the corporate landscape forever. In essence, it encouraged the growth of small private companies, which over time evolved into the widely accepted genre of 'quasi-partnership' companies (*O'Neill* v *Phillips* [1999] 2 BCLC 1). As the name suggests 'quasi-partnership' companies are operated internally on a basis far closer to that of a partnership than a 'pure' corporate structure. In other words, they contain a small number of shareholders some, or all, of whom have expectations as to their role in the company. This may include expectations such as being one of the directors. In *O'Neill* v *Phillips*, Lord Hoffmann stated that:

> In a quasi-partnership company, there will usually be understandings between the members at the time they entered into the association. But there may be later promises, by words or conduct, which it would be unfair to allow a member to ignore. Nor is it necessary that such promises should be independently enforceable as a matter of contract. A promise may be binding as a matter of justice and equity, although for one reason or another . . . it would not be enforceable in law.

These expectations may be evidenced in a number of ways – ranging from clauses in the articles of association to separate shareholders' agreements (mentioned below) and possibly a driving force behind s 17.

Today, this type of company is widely recognised and acknowledged as being a fundamental part of modern company law. However, a hundred years ago the development of this type of company led to many problems – the most significant of which centred on the use and 'misuse' of s 33 (or rather its equivalent section under previous Companies Acts).

As quasi-partnership companies became more popular, the members of these enterprises wished to evidence their expectations (e.g. to be a director) and as such wished to include additional clauses into the company's constitution to this effect. As noted above, s 21 provides the ideal method by which members may update the company's constitution. A General Meeting is called, at which a special resolution (75 per cent) is passed and the articles are duly amended. Everyone agrees because (usually) everyone is on an amicable and cooperative footing.

The problem arises when there is a dispute. At that point in time, the disgruntled individual will attempt to enforce his/her contractual right, under s 33, to be (as per the example above), a director of the company. An action is then brought before the courts to determine whether such a right may, or may not, be enforced.

This may not appear to be a particularly significant problem. However, in reality it is. Remember, the purpose of the articles of association is to regulate the internal affairs of a company (i.e. to provide detailed instructions as to how the company is to work/function).

Furthermore, as Drury notes (see suggested further reading at the end of Chapter 7 ●), one must bear in mind that the lifespan of a company may be several hundred years. In the overall scheme of things, the issue as to who is entitled to be a director and/or company solicitor is irrelevant to the continued existence and operation of a company.

Therefore, a significant number of the clauses which were added to the articles of association over the years were irrelevant to the operation of the company in question. As such, the question needed to be asked as to whether or not the court should recognise such clauses as being valid and furthermore whether they should enforce these clauses. Two cases provide alternative views on this subject: *Quin & Axtens* v *Salmon*; *Eley* v *Positive Life*.

Salmon v Quin & Axtens Ltd [1909] 1 Ch 311

The memorandum of the company included among its objects the purchasing of real or personal property. By the articles the business was to be managed by the directors, but no resolution of the board to purchase or lease any premises of the company was to be valid unless two conditions were satisfied, namely notice in writing must be given to each of the two managing directors named in the articles, and neither of them must have dissented therefrom in writing before or at the meeting at which the resolution was to be passed. In August 1908 the board passed resolutions for the purchase of certain premises by the company, and for leasing part of the company's property. The claimant, who was one of the managing directors, dissented, but at an extraordinary general meeting of the company held in November 1908, resolutions similar to those passed by the board were passed by an ordinary resolution of the members. The claimant brought this action for an injunction to stop the company from acting on the resolutions as they were inconsistent with the articles.

Held – eventually by the House of Lords (see *Quin & Axtens* v *Salmon* [1909] AC 442) – an injunction would be granted.

Comment

The claimant sued on behalf of himself and other shareholders to prevent the majority and the company from acting contrary to the company's constitution. This is in line with the contractual right highlighted by Jordan CJ in *Australian Coal and Shale Employees' Federation* v *Smith* (1937) 38 SR (NSW) 48, as the 'shareholder's right to have the articles observed by the company'.

It is worth looking at Wedderburn (1957) 'Shareholder Rights and the Rule in *Foss v Harbottle*', CLJ 193 in which he suggests that this judgment supports his view that every member has a personal right under the statutory contract (as it forms a contract between the company and its shareholders) to ensure that the company is run according to its articles of association. He goes on to suggest that a member could bring a personal claim to enforce this right, even though this may have the effect of enforcing a right conferred on this individual in a capacity other than as a member. However, the action must be brought in his/her capacity as a member. This is an interesting proposition and raises the question as to whether this case may be used to enable a solicitor who was also a shareholder indirectly to enforce a provision in the company's articles that he is to be the company's solicitor by saying to the company 'conduct business in accordance with the articles'. (See *Eley v Positive Life*.) According to Prentice, though (see (1980) 'The Enforcement of Outsider Rights', 1 Co Law 179) only those articles 'definitive of the power of the company to function' have contractual effect. Another view offered by Goldberg is that 'a member of a company has . . . a contractual right to have any of the affairs of the company conducted by the particular organ of the company specified in the Act or the company's memorandum or articles'.

Another case which is relevant to this debate is *Beattie v E and F Beattie Ltd* [1938] Ch 708, which involved an action against an individual who was both a member and director of the company in question. The director sought to rely on a clause in the articles which required all disputes between the company and a member to be referred to arbitration. The court held that the article did not constitute a contract between the company and the defendant director in his capacity as a director. Consequently, he was not entitled to rely upon the provision. The decision was affirmed by the Court of Appeal. The question is whether the outcome would have been different if the defendant director had been sued in his capacity as a member rather than that of director.

A solution was required which would alleviate the pressure on the courts to recognise and subsequently enforce additional clauses which had been validly (and legally) added to the articles of association, while at the same time ensuring that the articles remained focused on the internal regulation of the company, free of additional and irrelevant clauses. In the case of *Hickman v Kent or Romney Marsh* the courts attempted to reconcile the debate as to what could, or could not, be enforced under the s 33 statutory contract. In this case, Astbury J stated:

> First, no article can constitute a contract between the company and a third person; secondly, no right merely purporting to be given by an article to a person, whether a member or not, in a capacity other than that of a member, as for instance a solicitor, promoter or director can be enforced against the Company; thirdly, articles regulating the rights and obligations of the members generally as such do create rights and obligations between them and the company respectively.

The effect of this judgment is predominantly twofold. First of all, it poses the question as to who is attempting to enforce a provision contained within the articles of association. This essentially goes back to a privity of contract issue – the parties to the statutory contract are the company and the members (now clarified under the newly worded s 33 of the Companies Act 2006). As Astbury J observed:

> An outsider to whom rights purport to be given by the articles in his capacity as such outsider, whether he is or subsequently becomes a member, cannot sue on those articles treating them as contracts between himself and the company to enforce those rights. Those rights are not part of the general regulations of the company applicable alike to all shareholders and can only exist by virtue of some contract between such person and the company, and the subsequent allotment of shares to an outsider in whose favour such an article is inserted does not enable him to sue the company on such an article.

Consequently, non-members cannot enforce the statutory contract, no matter how closely involved with the running of the company they may appear to the outside world (i.e. directors).

Secondly, it poses the question as to the type of right that the individual is attempting to enforce. It draws a distinction between those rights given to an individual in his/her capacity as a member and those rights given to a person in a capacity other than that of a member. It is this aspect of the judgment which introduced the concept of insider and outsider rights into company law. As Greene MR observed in *Beattie v E and F Beattie Ltd* [1938] Ch 708, 'the contractual force given to the articles of association by the section is limited to such provisions of the articles as apply to the relationship of the members in their capacity as members'.

While this would appear to provide quite an elegant solution to the problem outlined above, it nevertheless introduced a number of new problems/questions. These include:

(a) Can a judicial limitation be placed on a statutory provision? In other words, s 33 states that 'those provisions' within the company's constitution must be observed by the company and each member whereas the *Hickman* judgment states that only membership (insider) rights should be observed.

(b) Where does one draw the distinction between membership (insider) rights and non-membership (outsider) rights? It is an artificial line which has been the subject of considerable academic debate over the years. Equally, as with any rule, it is subject to exceptions. Indeed, there is a suggestion that *Hickman* may be 'side-stepped' in many instances through the identification of membership rights (see Gower and Davies (2008) *Principles of Modern Company Law*).

(c) With respect to quasi-partnerships, members may have entered into a commercial relationship and amended the articles of their companies in good faith so as to evidence the true basis of the internal management structure of their business. What is a member to do if, in the event of a dispute, the courts refuse to recognise and enforce this 'legitimate' right? If a member is provided with no forum in which to express a complaint or potential remedy then this will in turn have a negative impact on the corporate sector – after all, who would invest in a company which had no method of recourse in the event of a dispute over bona fide (legitimate) expectations? This will be discussed later (see Chapter 18, p. 332) and s 994 of the Companies Act 2006.

In order to appreciate the academic debate surrounding the s 33 statutory contract and the implications of the *Hickman* judgment, there is no substitute for reading the main academic articles. (Refer to the suggested further reading at the end of this chapter.) A provision in the articles can become part of a contract between the company and a member or outsider in the following ways:

(a) where there is an express contract and a provision in the articles is expressly incorporated into that contract by a provision therein;

(b) where a provision in the articles is incorporated by implication arising out of the conduct of the parties, or where an express contract between the parties is silent on a particular aspect, e.g. in the case of a director, the length of his appointment. In such a case reference may be made to the articles in order to fill the gap, if those documents contain a relevant provision.

Re New British Iron Co, ex parte Beckwith [1898] 1 Ch 324

Beckwith was employed as a director of the company, relying for his remuneration on the company's articles which provided that the directors should be paid £1,000 per annum. In this action by Beckwith for his fees, it was *held* – by Wright J – that, although the articles did not constitute a contract between the company and Beckwith in his capacity as director, he had nevertheless accepted office and worked on the footing of the articles, and as such the company was liable to pay him his fees on that basis. Actually the company was liable on an implied contract, the articles being merely referred to for certain of its terms.

Read v Astoria Garage (Streatham) Ltd [1952] Ch 637

The defendant company was a private company which had adopted Art 68 of *Table A* of the Companies Act 1929. The articles provided for the appointment of a managing director, and said that he could be dismissed at any time and without any period of notice, if the company so resolved by a special resolution. The claimant's contract made in 1932 appointed him managing director at a salary of £7 per week but said nothing about notice. The directors dismissed him on 11 May 1949 at one month's notice, and later called an extraordinary general meeting of the shareholders and got the necessary resolution. The special resolution was passed on 28 September 1949, and Read's salary was paid until that date but not afterwards. Read now sued for wrongful dismissal, suggesting that he ought to have had more notice because a person holding his position would customarily have more notice than he had been given.

Held – by the Court of Appeal – that since the claimant's contract was silent on the point, Art 68 was incorporated into the express contract. Once this was done, the notice he had been given was most generous and his claim therefore failed, his tenure of office being based on the articles.

Although the above decisions are concerned with a member enforcing or being bound by a provision in the articles which was personal to himself as a member (e.g. a right to the vote attaching to his shares as in *Pender* v *Lushington*, 1877), the principles involved may go further than this. There is some authority for the view that each member has a right under the articles to have the company's affairs conducted in accordance with the articles; *Quin & Axtens* v *Salmon*.

Finally, it is worth noting that such matters involving 'outsider rights' could be dealt with in a separate contract such as a shareholder's agreement, which we shall examine in the next section.

The effect of the Contracts (Rights of Third Parties) Act 1999

The above Act does not apply to the statutory contract between a company and its members in terms of the provisions in a company's constitution, as set out in s 33.

According to s 6(2) of the Act it specifically excludes its application so as to prevent third-party rights from arising. Thus, the decision in *Eley* v *Positive Government Security Life Assurance Co*, 1876 still stands and would not or could not be affected by the 1999 Act.

Interpretation of the articles

As noted, section 33, CA 2006 provides that the articles form a contract between the company and its members. As such, when considering the interpretation of the articles, the traditional rules of contractual interpretation should apply. However, as also noted above, the articles form a unique type of statutory contract which is subject to certain limitations.

Scott v Frank F Scott (London) Ltd [1940] Ch 794 (Court of Appeal)

The company adopted as its articles of association *Table A* with certain modifications, and the whole of the share capital was issued to the three brothers in equal shares. The control of the company was in the hands of the ordinary shareholders, the preference shareholders only having a right of voting at a general meeting upon such questions as reduction of capital, winding-up of the company, sanctioning a sale of the undertaking or altering the regulations of the company so as to affect directly the rights of the preference shareholders. Frank Stanley Scott died on 10 September 1937, and his widow, who was the sole executrix of his will, became entitled thereunder to all his preference and ordinary shares in the company. No question arose in regard to the preference shares, but she claimed the right to be placed on the register of members in respect of his ordinary shares. The two surviving brothers, however, claimed that under the articles of association, she was bound to offer to them her testator's ordinary shares and that they had the right to acquire them at par. She therefore commenced an action against the company and the two surviving brothers, in which she sought a declaration that she was entitled to have her name entered on the register of members of the company as the holder of 100 ordinary shares. The defendants in their counter-claim sought a declaration that, upon the true construction of the articles of association, the two brothers had the right to acquire from the plaintiff these 100 ordinary shares at par and, if the construction they asked the Court to put on the articles of association should not be the correct construction, then they sought rectification of the articles so as to give them the right to acquire these shares from the plaintiff at par. Luxmoore LJ stated:

> The next question which falls to be considered is whether the defendants are entitled to have the articles of association rectified in the manner claimed by them. Bennett J said he was prepared to hold that the articles of association as registered were not in accordance with the intention of the three brothers who were the only signatories of the memorandum and articles of association, and down to the date of Frank Stanley Scott's death the only shareholders therein. Bennett J, however, held that the Court has no jurisdiction to rectify articles of association of a company, although they do not accord with what is proved to have been the concurrent intention of all the signatories therein at the moment of signature. We are in complete agreement with this decision. It seems to us that there is no room in the case of a company incorporated under the appropriate statute or statutes for the application to either the memorandum or articles of association of the principles upon which a Court of Equity permits rectification of documents whether inter partes or not . . .

Held – The Court has no jurisdiction to rectify the articles of association of a company even if those articles do not accord with what is proved to have been the concurrent intention of the signatories at the moment of signature.

Due to the fact that the model articles are prescribed in subordinate legislation (SI 2008/3229), they must be interpreted in accordance with the Interpretation Act 1978. If additional articles are adopted alongside the model articles then these provisions should also be interpreted in accordance with the Interpretation Act 1978 (*Fell v Derby Leather Co Ltd* [1931] 2 Ch 252). The courts will not consider the effect which the additional or amended articles were intended to have (*Rose v Lynx Express Ltd* [2004] EWCA Civ 447), though it will add words so as to avoid absurdity (*Folkes Group plc v Alexander* [2002] EWHC 51 (Ch)). Equally, the court will not exercise its power to imply terms into the articles so as to provide business efficacy to a scheme which the shareholders had in mind but which may not be readily apparent from the wording of the articles (*Bratton Seymour Service Co Ltd v Oxborough* [1992] BCLC 693). However, the court will seek to construe the words used in the articles so as to give them reasonable business efficacy (*Holmes v Keyes* [1959] Ch 199).

Shareholders' agreements

It is worth noting the increase in shareholders' agreements which often, in private companies, supplement the articles of association and which, it is suggested, have been included within the meaning of a company's constitution under the new Companies Act 2006: s 29.

A shareholders' agreement operates as a binding contract and deals with the rights and duties of members of a particular company to which it applies. It may be made by all members of the company, or be limited to a portion of them. Equally, given the fact that this is a traditional contract, individuals who are not shareholders in that particular company may be a party to the agreement if it is felt appropriate. The agreement can be made orally and does not need to be in writing, though of course this will impact on the practicability of an individual's ability to rely upon it should the need arise.

Such an agreement may be made at any time during the lifetime of a company, but it is most commonly made when a new company is established, thereby establishing areas of agreement between those involved. An excellent example of where one may find such an agreement is in a quasi-partnership company. However, it should be stressed at the outset that to be truly effective as a constitutional document, all members of the company should be made parties to the agreement.

The main benefit to be derived from a shareholders' agreement is the fact that it is not restricted in the same way as the articles of association (i.e. limited to the enforcement of membership rights). Therefore, if members wish to agree between themselves some matter which is unrelated to their membership rights, they may enter into this type of agreement to that effect. For example, in *Wilkinson* v *West Coast Capital* [2005] EWHC 3009 (Ch), a shareholders' agreement provided (a) in Clause 5 that specific actions could only be pursued by the company if 65 per cent of the shareholders provided their consent; and (b) in Clause 7 that the shareholders should use all reasonable and proper means to promote the interests of the company. The combination of these two clauses meant that shareholder-directors are to use their vote so as to prevent the company from pursuing certain opportunities and thereby preventing them from being classified as 'corporate opportunities' and subsequently enabling them to pursue them themselves. A minority shareholder unsuccessfully brought an action under s 994, CA 2006 on the grounds that this was unfairly prejudicial conduct.

Equally, given the fact that shareholder agreements are governed by common law, their terms can only be altered if there is 100 per cent agreement by those who signed the contract. This differs to the alteration of the articles, which under s 21(1) only requires a special resolution (75 per cent). Furthermore, as per *Russell* v *Northern Bank* (below), the courts appear to accept the existence of shareholders' agreements, providing them with a degree of legitimacy, power and scope.

Another significant advantage of such an agreement is that the contents remain private and the agreement does not have to be registered at Companies House along with the other formal constitutional documents. Therefore, the shareholders' agreement is not available for public inspection.

The key problem with these agreements is that they, in effect, create another branch of the company's constitution. As such, it is not surprising that the Companies Act 2006 has sought to include shareholder agreements within the meaning of the constitution of the company.

If there is a dispute between shareholders, it will often be the case that the shareholders' agreement will be referred to first, between the constitutional documents. This could cause a problem, however, if there is a conflict between the terms of the articles and the terms of the external agreement. The key case concerning shareholder agreements is *Russell* v *Northern Bank*.

Russell v Northern Bank Development Corporation Ltd [1992] 1 WLR 588

Five individuals agreed to refrain from voting to increase the company's share capital, unless all parties agreed to the increase (in writing). Subsequently, the company sought to increase capital, but one member of the agreement was against this increase. In court, he argued that the fellow members were acting contrary to the terms of the membership agreement. The other members of the agreement counter-claimed by saying that by enforcing the terms of the shareholders' agreement, the court would in effect restrict the court from acting within its statutory power.

The House of Lords (reversing the decision of the Court of Appeal) stated that shareholders' agreements were valid and enforceable. Lord Jauncey provided a quotation from Lord Davey in *Welton* v *Saffery* [1897] AC 299, who stated:

> Of course, individual shareholders may deal with their own interests by contract in such a way as they may think fit. By such contracts, whether made by all or only some of the shareholders, would create personal obligations, or an exception personalis against themselves only, and would not become a regulation of the company, or be binding on the transferees of the parties, or upon new or non-assenting shareholders.

Comment

Although, strictly speaking, the judgment says that a company may not be bound by one, it is without doubt that the company (practically speaking) is restricted, as it is the members who guide the company. Potentially, a member of a company could obtain an injunction to prevent other members of the company (party to a membership agreement) to restrain from allowing the company to perform an act, which it is statutorily able to do.

In *Euro Brokers Holdings Ltd* v *Monecor (London) Ltd*, 2003 the court applied the *Duomatic* principle to such a shareholders' agreement. The principle which is derived from the decision in *Re Duomatic* [1969] 2 Ch 365 states that the informal and unanimous assent of all the company's shareholders can override formal requirements as where a particular course of action requires a meeting and resolution of the shareholders, either under statutory provisions or because of the requirements of the company's articles, and no such meeting and/or resolution has been held or passed or written resolution made.

Nevertheless, if there is evidence that the shareholders were unanimously agreed on the matter, the court may accept the resulting transaction as valid.

 Euro Brokers Holdings Ltd v Monecor (London) Ltd [2003] 1 BCLC 506

So far as the facts of *Euro Brokers* are concerned, the matter in issue was a call made on the company's two shareholders requiring them to advance more capital. The finance director made the call by means of an email though the shareholders' agreement required that the call be made by a notice from the board. Nevertheless, both shareholders regarded the call as valid and agreed to send the sums required to the company. Later, one of the shareholders failed to forward the full amount. Under the shareholders' agreement this triggered a right in the other shareholder to acquire the shares of the defaulter at an agreed price. The defaulter was not prepared to accept this situation and challenged the validity of the call in terms that it had not been made by the formal notice of the board. This defence was rejected by the Court of Appeal. The shareholders had accepted the call in the manner in which it was made and the Duomatic principle could therefore be applied. In consequence, the defaulting shareholder could be required to sell his entire holding to the claimant.

A typical shareholders' agreement may include:

● Undertakings and agreements from prospective shareholders before the company is formed.
● Matters that it would be inappropriate to put on the public record such as confidentiality undertakings and non-competition restrictions, the right of certain shareholders to appoint directors and dispute resolution.

● Protection of minority shareholders if required. Thus, although alteration of the articles requires a special resolution, i.e. a 75 per cent majority of votes, a shareholders' agreement can require written consent from all shareholders so protecting those with minority holdings.

● Internal management issues which the members wish to keep off the public record, e.g. who should be entitled to appoint a director, choice of bankers, and the policy of the company on loans and borrowing together with cheque signatories.

Finally, it is worth noting in relation to the protection of minority shareholders under s 994, CA 2006, that a shareholders' agreement will carry a considerable amount of weight in terms of the court determining whether or not 'unfairly prejudicial' conduct has occurred. (Refer to Chapter 18, p. 326 for further discussion of this point. ◐)

Essay questions

1 Discuss how the Companies Act 2006 approaches the notion of a company's constitution with specific reference to the change in approach taken since the Companies Act 1985.
Explain how the Model Articles can be utilised. *(University of Hertfordshire)*

2 Success Limited has been trading profitably for 10 years, with capital provided by each of its four directors and their families. The directors consider that the company could be even more profitable, if it were able to make a public issue of securities, and they are advocating the re-registration of the company as a public limited company. However, some of the members are not enthusiastic, as they believe that there are disadvantages to trading as a public company.
Explain to the members the advantages and disadvantages of trading in the form of a public company, and the statutory procedure for re-registration of a private limited company as a public limited company. *(Napier University)*

3 (a) Section 33 of Companies Act 2006 provides that the company's constitution constitutes an agreement between the company and its members as if they have signed and sealed a contract to abide by its provisions. Comment.

(b) A, B and C are members of X Ltd. The company has now discovered that C is also a major shareholder in a rival company. It is causing concern that C might be extracting information about X Ltd's business which could confer unfair advantage on its rival. X Ltd wishes to alter its articles of association so as to require any member competing with X Ltd, to sell his or her shares as required to any person or persons named by the directors of the company, or to the directors themselves. Advise X Ltd. *(University of Plymouth)*

4 'The company's constitution forms a contract between a company and its members. This contract is, however, an unusual one, limited both in its scope and permanence despite the best efforts of the Companies Act 2006 to clarify matters.' Discuss.
(The Institute of Chartered Secretaries and Administrators)

Test your knowledge

Four alternative answers are given. Select ONE only. Circle the answer which you consider to be correct. Check your answers by referring back to the information given in the chapter and against the answers at the end of the text.

1 Fred bought some shares in Tyne Ltd on 1 February 20XX. To whom does Fred become bound in contract?

   A The company only.
   B The members of Tyne on 1 February 20XX.
   C Tyne and those who are at present its members.
   D Tyne and those who were members of Tyne on 1 February 20XX.

2 The Model Articles will apply automatically except where it is excluded or modified by special articles of association in the case of:

   A private companies limited by shares only.
   B public companies limited by shares only.
   C all companies limited by shares.
   D all limited companies.

3 The articles of association of a company on a paper incorporation must be signed by:

   A each one of the directors.
   B a majority of the directors.
   C all the subscribers to the memorandum.
   D one of the subscribers to the memorandum.

4 Under the Companies Act 1985, the capital clause of a company limited by shares was contained in the memorandum. Where is it located under the 2006 Act?

   A The memorandum of association.
   B The company's constitution as defined by s 17 of the 2006 Act.
   C A statement of capital and initial shareholdings.
   D It is no longer required under the 2006 Act.

The answers to test your knowledge questions appear on p. 645.

Suggested further reading

Brookes and Davies, 'When are pre-emption rights triggered?' (2012) *Accountancy* 148(1424), 57.

Cheung, 'Shareholders' agreements: Shareholders' contractual freedom in company law' (2012) JBL (6) 504.

Ferran, The decision of the House of Lords in **Russell v Northern Bank Development Corporation Limited**' [1994] CLJ 343.

Finn, 'Shareholder agreements' (1978) 6 *Australian Business Law Review* 97.

Goldberg, 'The enforcement of outsider rights under the section 20 contract' (1972) 35 MLR 363.

Goldberg, 'The controversy on the section 20 contract revisited' (1985) 48 MLR 158.

Gower, 'The contractual effect of article of association' (1958) 21 MLR 401.

Gregory, 'The section 20 contract' (1981) 44 MLR 526.

Kahn-Freund, 'Some reflections on company law reform' (1944) 7 MLR 54.

Marsden, 'Does a shareholders' agreement require filing with the Registrar of Companies?' (1994) 15 *Company Lawyer* 19.

Prentice, 'The enforcement of outsider rights' (1980) 1 Co Law 179.

Rixon, 'Competing interests and conflicting principles: An examination of the power of alteration of articles of association' (1986) 49 MLR 446.

Sealy, '"Bona fides" and "proper purposes" in corporate decisions' [1989] *Monash University Law Review* 16.

Van Duzer, 'Shareholder agreements' (2011) *Company Secretary's Review* 35(18), 143.

Wedderburn, 'Shareholder rights and the Rule in *Foss v Harbottle*' (1957) CLJ 193.

7

The constitution of the company – altering the articles

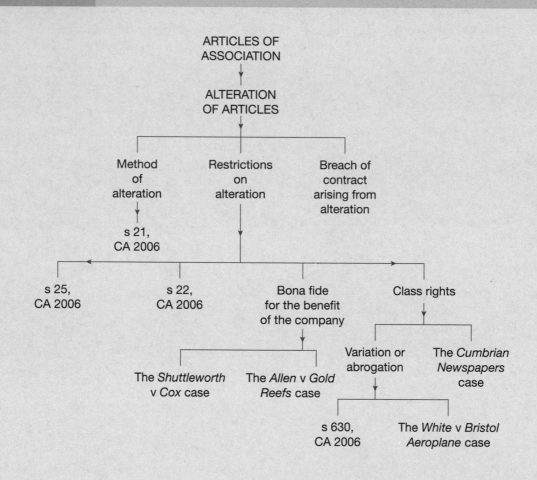

The articles of association may be amended by a special resolution in general meeting (s 21 of the Companies Act 2006). A copy of the revised articles must be sent to the Registrar 'not later than 15 days after the amendment takes effect' (s 26(1)). If the company fails to comply with this requirement, then under s 26(1) an offence is committed by the company and every officer of the company who is in default. Section 27(1) goes on to note that the Registrar may give notice to the company to comply with this requirement within 28 days of issue. Continued failure by the company to comply may result in a civil penalty of £200 in addition to criminal proceedings (s 27(4)).

The important point to appreciate is that any member of a company enters into a contract, the terms of which may be amended by the company in general meeting at any time in the future. While this may appear to go against the most basic principles of contract law, it is important to remember that this is a statutory contract by virtue of s 33 of the Companies Act 2006. Indeed, as noted in *Greenhalgh v Arderne Cinemas*, 1951 by Evershed MR '[...] when a man comes into a company, he is not entitled to assume that the articles will always remain in a particular form'. If one takes time to reflect on the situation and to bear in mind the observations of Drury (see the suggested reading at the end of the chapter ◯), the company represents a separate legal entity whose existence will, in most instances, extend far beyond either the involvement or life expectancy of the current members. As such, the company is subject to specific decision-making processes (in this instance s 21) that enable it to respond to its environment and to update its constitution accordingly (*Shuttleworth v Cox*, 1927). Indeed, this is reinforced by the case of *Russell v Northern Bank*, 1992, in which the House of Lords stated that 'a provision in a company's articles which restricts its statutory power to alter those articles is invalid'. Any contract by a company which purports to agree that its articles will not be amended in the future will not be enforced by the courts.

Punt v Symons & Co Ltd [1903] 2 Ch 506

GG Symons was given the power, under articles 95 and 97 of the company's articles, to appoint and remove directors. This power would continue to exist after his death for exercise by his executors. A separate agreement stated that the company would refrain from amending these articles in the future. In time, the relationship between the executors and the company's directors deteriorated, resulting in a proposal to amend the articles by way of a special resolution. The executors sought an injunction to prevent this action. In this regard, Byrne J said:

> The first point taken is that passing the resolution would be a breach of the contract which was entered into with the testator; and that the plaintiffs as executors are entitled to enforce the terms of the agreement by restraining any alteration of the articles. I think the answer to this argument is – that the company cannot contract itself out of the right to alter its articles, though it cannot, by altering its articles, commit a breach of contract. It is well established as between a company and a shareholder, the right not depending upon a special contract outside the articles, that this is the case. It has not been, so far as I know, the precise subject of reported decision as between a contractor and a company where the contract is independent of and outside the articles; but in the case of *Allen v Gold Reefs of West Africa* Lord Lindley, then Master of the Rolls, says: 'The articles of a company prescribe the regulations binding on its members: Companies Act, 1862, s 14. They have the effect of a contract (see s 16); but the exact nature of this contract is even now very difficult to define. Be its nature what it may, the company is empowered by the statute to alter the regulations contained in its articles from time to time by special resolutions (ss 50 and 51); and any regulation or article purporting to deprive the company of this power is invalid on the ground that it is contrary to the statute: *Walker v London Tramways Co.* The power thus conferred on companies to alter the regulations

contained in their articles is limited only by the provisions contained in the statute and the conditions contained in the company's memorandum of association . . . I am prepared to hold that in the circumstances of the present case the contract could not operate to prevent the article being altered under the provisions of s 50 of the Companies Act, 1862, whatever the result of that alteration may be.'

Held – On this particular point the executors failed and the court refused to enforce the terms of the contract preventing an amendment of the articles. However, they did succeed on another point, which related to the directors' misuse of power in terms of issuing new shares so as to dominate the General Meeting.

This process of amendment is subject to the principle of majority rule, a topic that will be discussed later (see Chapter 17, p. 303 ◐), but which raises the immediate concern of how this process is governed so as to ensure that the majority may not take advantage of their position to the detriment of a minority within the company. First of all, s 25(1) provides that a member will not be bound by an alteration of the articles if it requires him to subscribe for more shares than the number currently held, or in any way increases his liability to contribute to the company's share capital.

Secondly, even though the general rule is that a company cannot restrict its power to amend its articles, s 22 of the Companies Act 2006 permits members to entrench provisions within the company's articles. In other words, the articles may contain provisions which may be 'amended or repealed only if conditions are met, or procedures complied with, that are more restrictive than those applicable in the case of a special resolution' (s 22(1)). For example, this may include the consent of a particular member of the attainment of a higher percentage of the members in general meeting than that required for a special resolution. However, given the potential impact that entrenched provisions within a company's constitution may have, s 22(3) goes on to state that such provisions may be amended subject to the agreement of all the members of the company or by order of the court. In addition, under s 23, the Registrar must be given notice of the existence of entrenched provisions as well as of their removal from the articles of association. Section 24 also requires the company to submit a statement of compliance with the entrenched provisions whenever it amends its articles.

Third of all, as stated in *Allen* v *Gold Reefs of West Africa Ltd* [1900] 1 Ch 656 by Lindley MR, there is the suggestion that members must exercise their votes 'bona fide for the benefit of the company as a whole'. As such, this case would appear to indicate that the court jurisdiction to regard an alteration of the articles as invalid unless it is made for the benefit of the company as a whole. The court does not in fact look solely at the company as it is at the time of the action (which would be a subjective test) but tries to see the company in equilibrium. That is to say the court envisages the company in a hypothetical situation in which shares and voting power are evenly distributed among the members, and assumes that members will vote independently of each other and not, as it were, combine to coerce other members. Having viewed the company in this situation, the court then decides on the validity of the alteration. This is an objective test and is really the only one the court can adopt. If it were to test the validity of the alteration against the present state of the shareholding, then the day after the resolution was approved the shareholding may alter and there may be a shift in the centre of power in the company. Rather than cope with so many imponderables, the court decides the question by putting the company into a state of equilibrium (hypothetically at least) and then looking at the alteration.

However, the objective test is not altogether satisfactory and can sometimes operate unfavourably towards particular shareholders. The difficulty is that the court sometimes assumes, probably rightly, that those who are managing the company's affairs and, on occasion, a majority of the shareholders, know better than the court what is for its benefit. Thus shareholders may sometimes feel that they have not been dealt with fairly and yet the court will accept the alteration to the articles as valid and for the benefit of the company as a whole (see *Greenhalgh* v *Arderne Cinemas*).

Allen v *Gold Reefs of West Africa Ltd* [1900] 1 Ch 656

The articles originally gave the company a lien on partly paid shares. The claimant was the only member with fully paid shares but he also owed calls on certain other partly paid shares which he owned. The company altered its articles to give itself a lien on fully paid shares, thus putting itself in a position where it could refuse to transfer the claimant's fully paid shares unless and until he had paid calls owing on his partly paid shares. It was held that the alteration was valid and for the benefit of the company, even though the claimant was the only person practically affected at the time by the alteration. Lindley MR stated:

> Wide as the language of [s 33 Companies Act 2006] is, the power conferred by it must, like all other powers, be exercised subject to those general principles of law and equity which are applicable to all powers conferred on majorities and enabling them to bind minorities. It must be exercised, not only in the manner required by law, but also bona fide for the benefit of the company as a whole, and it must not be exceeded. These conditions are always implied, and are seldom, if ever, expressed. But if they are complied with I can discover no ground for judicially putting any other restrictions on the power conferred by the section than those contained in it.

Comment

While this would initially appear to question the bona fides of the company, given the fact that only one shareholder was affected by this alteration of the articles, it is important to realise that the altered articles were intended to apply to all holders of fully paid shares; it just so happened that the complaining shareholder was the only holder of fully paid-up shares at that time who was in arrears of calls.

Greenhalgh v *Arderne Cinemas Ltd* [1951] Ch 286

The articles of the company originally required any member who wished to sell his shares to offer them to his fellow members before selling them to a stranger. A majority group of the shareholders procured an alteration enabling a member to sell his shares without first offering them to his fellow members if the company so resolved by ordinary resolution. The purpose was so that the majority could sell their shares to an outsider, a Mr Sheckman, for 6s per share and so give Mr Sheckman a controlling interest. Mr Greenhalgh, a minority shareholder, objected to the alteration although Mr Sheckman was prepared to pay 6s per share to any shareholder of the company, including Mr Greenhalgh.

Held – by the Court of Appeal – that the alteration was valid even though its immediate effect was to enable the majority group to sell their shares to outsiders without first offering them to the minority shareholders, though the minority shareholders, not being able to pass an ordinary resolution, were still bound to offer their shares to the majority group before selling elsewhere.

Comment

(i) Perhaps the alteration of the articles could be justified in this case under the objective test adopted by the courts since the hypothetical member might benefit equally with any other member in the future by the extension of his power to sell his shares to strangers. Furthermore, the alteration represented a relaxation of the very stringent restrictions on transfer in the article which had existed before the change.

(ii) In earlier litigation between the same parties [1946] 1 All ER 512 what would now be 10p ordinary shares had one vote per share and so did each 50p ordinary share. Greenhalgh held 10p shares and controlled 40 per cent of the vote and could block special resolutions. The holders of the 50p shares procured an ordinary resolution (as company legislation requires) to subdivide each 50p share into five 10p shares with one vote each, thus reducing G's voting power. It was held that the voting rights of the original 10p shares had not been varied. They still had one vote per share.

The result of the objective test which the court uses is that most alterations are allowed, though if the court feels that a decision is oppressive of the minority then it may set aside such a resolution (*Clemens v Clemens Bros Ltd* [1976] 2 All ER 268).

Clemens v Clemens Bros Ltd [1976] 2 All ER 268

A majority shareholder in a company has not an unfettered right to vote in any way he pleases; that right must be exercised fairly and so as not to cause injustice to other shareholders. The plaintiff held 45 per cent of the issued share capital of a family company, the remaining 55 per cent being held by her aunt, who was also a director of the company. A scheme was proposed by the directors whereby the company's issued share capital would be increased and some new shares would be issued to the directors (other than the aunt) the balance being placed on trust for long-service employees. The effect of the scheme was that the plaintiff's shareholding would be reduced to under 25 per cent. Despite the plaintiff's objections, the scheme was approved, by reason of the aunt's majority shareholding. The plaintiff thereupon sought to have the restrictions set aside as oppressive of her. Foster J noted:

> There are many cases which have discussed a director's position. A director must not only act within his powers but must also exercise them bona fide in what he believes to be the interests of the company. The directors have a fiduciary duty, but is there any similar restraint on shareholders exercising their powers as members at general meeting? . . .
>
> I think that one thing which emerges . . . is that in such a case as the present Miss Clemens is not entitled to exercise her majority vote in whatever way she pleases. The difficulty is in finding a principle, and obviously expressions such as 'bona fide for the benefit of the company as a whole', fraud on a 'minority' and 'oppressive' do not assist in formulating a principle.
>
> I have come to the conclusion that it would be unwise to try to produce a principle, since the circumstances of each case are infinitely varied. It would not, I think, assist to say more than that in my judgment Miss Clemens is not entitled as of right to exercise her votes as an ordinary shareholder in any way she pleases. To use the phrase of Lord Wilberforce [*Ebrahimi v Westborne Galleries Ltd*], that right is 'subject . . . to equitable considerations . . . which may make it unjust . . . to exercise it in a particular way'.

Held – Setting aside the resolutions, that whatever other purposes there may have been behind the scheme, there was an irresistible inference that it was designed in order to diminish the plaintiff's voting rights; that accordingly the aunt had used her majority voting power inequitably.

Similarly, alterations which give the company power to expel members without cause are not acceptable to the court. However, expulsion is allowed where it would benefit the members as a whole, as where the member expelled is competing with the company or defrauding it.

Dafen Tinplate Co Ltd v *Llanelly Steel Co (1907) Ltd* [1920] 2 Ch 124

The principal shareholders of the defendant company were other steel companies, and it was hoped that the member companies would buy their steel bars from the defendants, though there was no contract to this effect. In the main the member companies did buy their steel from the defendants, but the claimant company began in 1912 to get its steel from a concern called the Bynea company in which the claimant had an interest. The defendant company then sought to alter its articles to expel the claimant company. The alteration provided that the defendant company could by ordinary resolution require any member to sell his shares to the other members at a fair price to be fixed by the directors. The claimant sought a declaration that the alteration was void.

Held – by Peterson J – that the claimant company was entitled to such a declaration. The power taken by the articles was a bare power of expulsion, and could be used to expel a member who was not acting to the detriment of the defendant company at all. Therefore, whatever its merits in the circumstances of the case, it could not be allowed.

Comment

This power of expulsion was to be written in the articles and would last indefinitely. In addition, it would permanently discriminate between shareholders of the same class and as such could not benefit the future hypothetical member and was therefore void.

Sidebottom v *Kershaw, Leese & Co* [1920] 1 Ch 154

The defendant company, which was a small private company, altered its articles to empower the directors to require any member who carried on a business competing with that of the company, to sell his shares at a fair price to persons nominated by the directors. The claimant was a member of the defendant company, and ran mills in competition with it, and this action was brought to test the validity of the alteration in articles. The court of first instance found for the claimant, regarding the alteration as a bare power of expropriation, though there was no dispute that the price fixed for the purchase of the shares was fair.

Held – by the Court of Appeal – that the evidence showed that the claimant might cause the defendant company loss by information which he received as a member, and as the power was restricted to expulsion for competing, the alteration was for the benefit of the company as a whole and was valid.

Comment

(i) It was obviously in the interest of the company as a whole and of the 'hypothetical member' that the company's trade secrets should not be available to its competitors.

(ii) As Lord Sterndale MR made clear in his judgment in this case, the power of compulsory purchase of shares is valid if contained in the original articles. Such a provision would not be set aside on the 'benefit' ground; the concept is applicable only to changes in the articles as *Phillips v Manufacturers' Securities Ltd* (1917) 116 LT 290 decides.

(iii) Lord Sterndale MR also made the following comment:

> Now it does not seem to me to matter as to the validity of this altered article, whether it was introduced with a view to using it against the plaintiff firm or not, except to this extent, that it might be that if it had been introduced specifically for the purpose of using it against the plaintiffs' firm some question of bona fides might possibly have arisen, because it might have been argued that it was introduced to do them harm, and not to do the company good [. . .] I come to the conclusion that the

directors were acting perfectly bona fide; that they were passing the resolution for the benefit of the company; but that no doubt the occasion of their passing it was because they realised in the person of Mr Bodden that it was a bad thing to have members who were competing with them.

Shuttleworth v Cox Brothers & Co (Maidenhead) Ltd [1927] 2 KB 9

The company's articles provided that Shuttleworth and four other persons should be permanent directors of the company, to hold office for life, unless disqualified by any one of the events specified in Art 22 of the company's articles. These events were bankruptcy, insanity, conviction of an indictable offence, failure to hold the necessary qualification shares, and being absent from meetings of the board for more than six months without leave. The company conducted a building business, and Shuttleworth, on 22 occasions within 12 months, failed to account for the company's money which he had received on its behalf. The articles were altered by adding another disqualifying event, namely, a request in writing by all the other directors. Having made the alteration, the directors made the request to Shuttleworth, and he now questioned the validity of his expulsion from the board.

Held – by the Court of Appeal – that the alteration and the action taken under it was valid, because it was for the benefit of the company as a whole since Shuttleworth was defrauding it. Shuttleworth also claimed that no alteration of the articles could affect his contract with the company, but the Court of Appeal held, on this point, that since part of his contract (the grounds for dismissal) was contained in the articles, he must be taken to know that this was in an alterable document and he must take the risk of change.

However, there are also cases which would appear to run contrary to the *Allen v Gold Reefs* 'bona fide' principle: *North-West Transportation Co v Beatty* (1887) 12 App Cas 589; *Burland v Earle* [1902] AC 83; *Goodfellow v Nelson Line* [1912] 2 Ch 324. (See also: *Northern Counties Securities Ltd v Jackson & Steeple Ltd* [1974] 1 WLR 1133 below.) In these instances, the courts have stated that votes are proprietary rights which the owner may exercise according to his own interests, even though these may run contrary to the interests of the company itself. Consequently, it is important to note that the shareholders' power to vote is not to be likened to the power exercised by directors which is in turn fiduciary in nature. Rather, shareholders are free to vote in whatever manner they wish to do so.

The issue is rather one whereby such proprietary rights are subject to review by the courts so as to ensure that a majority does not exploit its position against a minority within the company. In other words, the courts are adopting a very fine balance between respecting the freedom of shareholders to use their proprietary rights within the context of majority rule in the company, while at the same time ensuring that this system does not lead to an abuse of position or exploitation of minority shareholders. Indeed, this is reflected in Lord Hoffmann's discussion of the area in the recent Privy Council case of *Citco Banking Corporation NV v Pusser's Ltd* [2007] UKPC 13, in which he approved passages from both *Allen v Gold Reefs* as well as *Shuttleworth v Cox* and emphasised the subjective nature of the bona fide test and stated that the court is only justified in interfering when there is evidence impugning the honesty of the shareholders or where no reasonable shareholder could consider the proposed amendment to be beneficial to the company. (For further discussion on this point see Williams (2007) 'Bona Fide in the Interest of Certainty', CLJ 500.)

Fourthly, where the rights of different classes of shareholders are contained in the articles, then, as noted above, s 33 would appear to permit these rights to be changed by way of a special resolution of the members of the company. However, this is another area in which the law aims to protect minorities within a company from the potential oppression of majority rule. As such, the general principle is that rights attaching to a class of shares should not be altered by the holders of another class of shares without gaining the consent of the class in question for the alteration to take place. This is covered by s 630 of the Companies Act 2006 which states that rights attached to a class of a company's shares may only be varied (a) in accordance with provision in the company's articles for the variation of those rights; or (b) where no such provision exists then by way of a special resolution passed at a separate general meeting of the holders of that class sanctioning the variation, or by consent in writing (s 630(2), (4)).

It should also be noted that according to s 633, the holders of not less than 15 per cent of the issued shares of the class, who did not vote for the variation, may apply to the court within 21 days of the consent of the class being given, whether in writing or by resolution, to have the variation cancelled. Once such an application has been made, usually by one or more dissentients on behalf of the others, the variation will not take effect unless and until it is confirmed by the court.

As will be examined further (see Chapter 13, p. 238 ○), an issue which is frequently explored is whether the issue of further shares, which do not remove the current rights of a particular class but simply enjoy the same rights as the existing ones (effectively expanding the class and, as such, diluting the voting power of the original holders of that class of shares), may amount to a variation of class rights; *White* v *Bristol Aeroplane Co Ltd* [1953] Ch 65. This is also an area in which s 633 may prove useful to those shareholders who suddenly find their position diluted within a particular class and outvoted on a s 630 resolution.

Northern Counties Securities Ltd v *Jackson & Steeple Ltd* [1974] 1 WLR 1133

The defendant company has agreed to use its best endeavours to allot a certain number of shares to the plaintiffs resulting from a Stock Exchange quotation for its shares. However, it was necessary for the company to gain consent via its General Meeting. After a period of inactivity the plaintiffs successfully gained an order from the court against the company. Nevertheless, the court emphasised that fact that even though a General Meeting must be called, together with a circular inviting members to support the resolution, the members could not be compelled to vote in favour of the resolution and would not be in contempt of court if they opposed it. Per Walton LJ:

Mr Price argued that, in effect, there are two separate sets of persons in whom authority to activate the company itself resides. Quoting the well known passages from Viscount Haldane LC in *Lennard's Carrying Co Ltd* v *Asiatic Petroleum Co Ltd* [1915] AC 705, he submitted that the company as such was only a juristic figment of the imagination, lacking both a body to be kicked and a soul to be damned. From this it followed that there must be some one or more human persons who did, as a matter of fact, act on behalf of the company, and whose acts therefore must, for all practical purposes, be the acts of the company itself. The first of such bodies was clearly the body of directors, to whom under most forms of articles – see article 80 of Table A, or article 86 of the defendant company's articles which is in similar form – the management of the business of the company is expressly delegated. Therefore, their acts are the defendant company's acts; and if they do not, in the present instance, cause the defendant company to comply with the undertakings given by it to the court, they are themselves liable for contempt of court. And this, he says, is well recognised: see RSC, Ord 45, r 5 (1), whereunder disobedience by a corporation to an injunction may result directly in the issue of a writ of sequestration against any director thereof. It is of course clear that for this purpose there is no distinction between an undertaking and an injunction: see note 45/5/3 in *The Supreme Court Practice* (1973).

This is, indeed, all well established law, with which Mr Instone did not quarrel, and which indeed his first proposition asserted. But, continues Mr Price, this is only half of the story. There are some matters in relation to which the directors are not competent to act on behalf of the company. The relevant authority being 'the company in general meeting', that is to say, a meeting of the members. Thus in respect of all matters within the competence – at any rate those within the exclusive competence – of a meeting of the members, the acts of the members are the acts of the company, in precisely the same way as the acts of the directors are the acts of the company. Ergo, for any shareholder to vote against a resolution to issue the shares here in question to the plaintiffs would be a contempt of court, as it would be a step taken by him knowingly which would prevent the defendant company from fulfilling its undertaking to the court. Mr Price admitted that he could find no authority which directly assisted his argument, but equally confidently asserted that there was no authority which precluded it.

Mr Instone indicted Mr Price's argument as being based upon 'a nominalistic fallacy'. His precise proposition was formulated as follows: 'While directors have special responsibilities as executive agents of the defendant company to ensure that the company does not commit a contempt of court, a shareholder, when the position has been put before the shareholders generally, who chooses to vote against such approval will not himself be in contempt of court' . . .

In my judgment, these submissions of Mr Instone are correct. I think that, in a nutshell, the distinction is this: when a director votes as a director for or against any particular resolution in a director's meeting, he is voting as a person under a fiduciary duty to the company for the proposition that the company should take a certain course of action. When a shareholder is voting for or against a particular resolution he is voting as a person owing no fiduciary duty to the company and who is exercising his own right of property, to vote as he thinks fit. The fact that the result of the voting at the meeting (or at a subsequent poll) will bind the company cannot affect the position that, in voting, he is voting simply in exercise of his own property rights.

Perhaps another (and simpler) way of putting the matter is that a director is an argent, who casts his vote to decide in what manner his principal shall act through the collective agency of the board of directors; a shareholder who casts his vote in general meeting is not casting it as an agent of the company in any shape or form. His act therefore, in voting as he pleases, cannot in any way be regarded as an act of the company . . .

I now come to paragraph 4 of the notice of motion, which seeks an order restraining the individual respondents and each of them from voting against the resolution. Mr Price says that, as the executive agents of the defendant company, they are bound to recommend to its shareholders that they vote in favour of the resolution to issue the shares, and hence, at the least, they cannot themselves vote against it, for they would thereby be assisting the defendant company to do that which it is their duty to secure does not happen. If, as executive officers of the defendant company, they are bound to procure a certain result if at all possible, how can they, as individuals, seek to frustrate that result?

I regret, however, that I am unable to accede to Mr Price's arguments in this respect . . . I think that a director who has fulfilled his duty as a director of a company, by causing it to comply with an undertaking binding upon it is nevertheless free, as an individual shareholder, to enjoy the same unfettered and unrestricted right of voting at general meetings of the members of the company as he would have if he were not also a director.

It is also worth bearing in mind the fact that a shareholder may have agreed to vote subject to certain restrictions and/or guidelines contained in a separate contract. If this is the case then the agreement is binding on the member and may be enforced by way of an injunction.

Puddephatt v Leith [1916] 1 Ch 200

The case involved the transaction of a loan of £2,500 the payment of which, with interest at the rate of 5.5 per cent per annum, was secured to the defendant by an agreement under seal dated 14 February 1913, whereby the plaintiff transferred to the defendant by way of mortgage 2,500 fully-paid shares of £1 each in a company called the London and Cosmopolitan Mining Company, Limited. That mortgage was preceded by a collateral agreement which took the form of a letter addressed by the defendant to the plaintiff in which the defendant said that the plaintiff's voting rights in virtue of the shares held in mortgage by him during the period of the loan would be untouched though the shares would be in his name and his voice might give the vote; that he would give no such vote without consulting the plaintiff; and that he would vote in all cases where a vote was necessary in respect of those shares as the plaintiff wished him to do. A general meeting of the company was approaching, and the defendant threatened to vote as he thought fit in respect of the shares and to disregard, as he had done once before, the plaintiff's expressed wishes on this subject. As such, the plaintiff commenced this action in the Chancery Division claiming an injunction to restrain the defendant from voting upon a poll at any meeting of the company in respect of the 2,500 shares otherwise than in accordance with her directions. *Per* Sargent J:

> In my opinion, therefore, the right of the plaintiff is clear, and the only remaining question is whether she is entitled to a mandatory injunction to enforce her right. It is not disputed that she is entitled to a prohibitive injunction, and in my opinion she is also entitled to a mandatory injunction. Prima facie this court is bound . . . to give effect to a clear right by way of a mandatory injunction. There are no doubt certain exceptions from this rule, as in the case of a contract of service, because in such cases, it is impossible for the court to make its order effective, but . . . in the present case, in as much as there is one definitive thing to be done, about the mode of doing which there can be no possible doubt, I am of the opinion that I ought to grant not only the prohibitive but also the mandatory injunction claimed by the plaintiff, and I make an order accordingly.

Held – The Court ordered the defendant to comply with the undertaking.

Breaches of contract arising out of alteration of the articles

A company cannot by altering its articles escape liability for breach of a contract into which it has entered. The difficulty has arisen with regard to the remedies of the other party to the contract. In *Punt* v *Symons & Co Ltd* [1903] 2 Ch 506 it was said that the other party to the contract could sue the company for damages for breach, but could not obtain an injunction to prevent the alteration taking effect. Then followed a series of cases which revealed considerable judicial indecision on this point. For example, in *Baily* v *British Equitable Assurance Co Ltd* [1904] 1 Ch 374 the Court of Appeal seems to have been prepared to grant an injunction to restrain an alteration of the articles in breach of contract although in fact it was only asked to give a declaratory judgment as to the state of the law. However, in *Southern Foundries* v *Shirlaw*, 1940 (below), Lord Porter in an obiter dictum gave support to the view that the other party to the contract can sue the company for damages only, and cannot obtain an injunction to prevent the alteration from taking effect. It may be said, therefore, that a company is quite free to alter its articles, though if in doing so it breaks a contract which it has made, it must face an action in damages by the party aggrieved. There may also be an action against those who voted for the alteration.

 Southern Foundries (1926) Ltd v Shirlaw [1940] AC 701

The appellant company was incorporated in 1926 as a private company, and was engaged in the business of iron founders. The respondent, Shirlaw, became a director of the company in 1929

under a provision in the articles. In 1933 he became managing director under a separate contract, the appointment to be for 10 years, and containing restraints under which Shirlaw agreed that he would not, for a period of three years after leaving the employment of the appellants, engage in foundry work within 100 miles of Croydon. In 1935 there was a merger between the appellant company and ten other concerns, and the group was called Federated Industries. The members of the group agreed that they should make certain alterations in their articles regarding directors; the articles of each member were altered, and in their new form gave Federated Industries power to remove any director of the company, and also stipulated that a managing director should cease to hold office if he ceased to be a director. In 1937 Shirlaw was removed from office as a director, under the provision in the articles, by an instrument in writing, signed by two directors and the secretary of Federated Industries. This meant that Shirlaw could no longer be managing director of Southern Foundries, and since his contract had still some time to run, he brought this action for wrongful dismissal. The trial judge found for Shirlaw and awarded him £12,000 damages, and the Court of Appeal affirmed that decision. The company now appealed to the House of Lords.

Held – by a majority – that Shirlaw's contract as managing director contained an implied term that the article making him a director would not be altered. Since it had been altered, there was a breach of contract and the company was liable for it. Lord Wright took the view that since there was no privity of contract between Shirlaw and Federated Industries, it was difficult to see how they could dismiss him. Lord Romer, dissenting, did not think a term against alteration of the articles could be implied and thought that Shirlaw took the risk of alteration. Lord Porter lent support in this case to *Punt v Symons*, 1903, and said that a company could not be prevented by injunction from altering its articles but that the only remedy for an alteration which has caused a breach of contract was damages.

Comment

(i) From statements made in this case it appears that any member who votes for the alteration will also be liable to the claimant for inducing the company to break its contract if the inevitable consequence of the alteration is that the contract will be broken.

(ii) In *Shirlaw* the articles said that a managing director was to be subject to the same provisions for removal as any other director 'subject to the provisions of any contract between him and the company'. There was an implied term in the contract of service which overrode the power of removal without compensation in the articles.

(iii) In *Nelson v James Nelson & Sons Ltd* [1914] 2 KB 770 a service contract appointing the claimant to act as managing director 'so long as he shall remain a director of the company' was also held to override an article giving a power of removal without compensation. Damages were awarded to the claimant because his contract was terminated by his removal from office as a director. That was a breach by the company of his contract as managing director which he could then no longer perform.

The position is different where a person contracts with a company and the contract incorporates a provision of the articles by implication. In such a case the other party is deemed to know that the company may alter its articles, and therefore takes the risk of the contract failing because of such an alteration, even to the extent of failing in an action for damages (*Shuttleworth v Cox Bros & Co (Maidenhead) Ltd*, 1927, see above). However, there are certain limitations upon the above rule:

(a) Rights which have already accrued under the contract cannot be disturbed by the alteration.

Swabey v Port Darwin Gold Mining Co (1889) 1 Meg 385

Swabey had served the company as a director under a provision in the company's articles which provided for his salary. The articles were altered so as to reduce that salary and it was *held* – by the Court of Appeal – that, although the alteration was effective to reduce the salary for the future, Swabey could not be deprived of his salary at the original figure for the period he had served prior to the alteration of the articles. Lord Esher MR stated:

> The articles do not themselves form a contract, but from them you get the terms upon which the directors are serving. It would be absurd to hold that one of the parties to a contract could alter it as to service already performed under it. The company has power to alter the articles, but the directors would be entitled to their salary at the rate originally stated in the articles up to the time the articles were altered.

(b) It is felt that the obligations of the other party cannot be made more onerous by an alteration of the articles. Thus, if the articles appoint a director to serve for a period of years on a part-time basis, he cannot be required to give his full time to the company by the company altering its articles so as to require him to do so.

(c) As we have already seen, where the company has shares of more than one class, it cannot vary the rights of a class of shares merely by altering them in the memorandum or articles. Section 630 applies and requires the consent of three-quarters of the class and there are dissentient rights.

Alteration of the articles by the court

As discussed above, the articles are a contract between the company and each member and in this connection the court has power to rectify contracts. For example, if parties have agreed for a lease of land for 25 years that is written down in the lease by mistake as 21 years then if one of the parties is not prepared to co-operate in changing this provision of the lease the court can be asked to rectify the lease by an order inserting 25 years as the term of the lease provided the evidence shows to the satisfaction of the court that this was the intention of the parties. The court has ruled however that it does not have power to rectify the statutory contract set out in the articles.

Scott v Frank F Scott (London) Ltd [1940] Ch 794

The defendant company was a private company with three members, Frank, Stuart and Reginald Scott, the business of the company being that of butchers. On the death of Frank Scott, his widow, Marie Scott, became entitled under his will to certain preference shares and ordinary shares in the company, as executrix. When she sought to be registered in respect of the shares, Stuart and Reginald Scott claimed that under a provision in the articles the shares must on the death of a member be offered to the other members at par, but the article was not so well drafted as to make this clear beyond doubt. This action was brought to interpret the article, and also to ask the court to rectify the article to carry a right to pre-emption if the article was not so drafted as to achieve this.

Held – by the Court of Appeal – that the article did give the right of pre-emption claimed by Stuart and Reginald Scott. However, if it had not done so, the court could not have rectified it; the alteration could only be carried out by special resolution.

However, the High Court departed from this general ruling when faced with an absurd result of bad drafting.

Folkes Group plc v *Alexander* [2002] 2 BCLC 254

The Folkes family held a substantial proportion of the voting shares in the listed plc. The other shareholders had no voting rights unless the Folkes family holdings fell below 40 per cent. An article to ensure that this could never happen was drafted and agreed and became part of the articles. Later it was noticed that certain holdings of the Folkes family were excluded from the voting category so that their voting holdings fell to 23.9 per cent, thus triggering the voting rights of the other members. The former non-voting shares would not use their newly acquired voting power to change the articles to what was originally intended. The court did however do so by ordering the insertion of five words into the altered article to give it the effect intended. The judge's justification was that to leave the article as it was would flout business common sense and legal decisions might on occasion have to yield to business common sense following comments in the House of Lords in *Investors Compensation Scheme Ltd* v *West Bromwich Building Society* [1998] 1 BCLC 493.

Essay questions

1 Describe the procedure for alteration of articles and detail the considerations made in determining the validity of the alteration. *(The Institute of Company Accountants)*

2 H plc wishes to change its articles of association to add a clause which states 'any director of the company may be removed from office if all other directors give notice in writing of their desire that the named directors be so removed'.

   You are required to explain the procedure for alteration and discuss the difficulties the company might encounter in adding this new clause.
   (The Chartered Institute of Management Accountants)

3 Free Range Chickens R Us wishes to change its articles of association to add a clause which would state that 'any director of the company may be removed from office if all other directors give notice in writing of their desire that the named directors be so removed'.

   You are required to explain the procedure for alteration and discuss the difficulties which the company might encounter in adding this new clause. *(Authors' question)*

4 Perfect Puddings Ltd was incorporated to purchase the chocolate manufacturing business previously carried on by Louise. The contract of sale between the company and Louise provided, inter alia, that as long as Louise held 20 per cent of the shares of Perfect Puddings, she was entitled to be managing director of the company. The Articles of Association which otherwise follow *Table A* reproduce this provision and also contain the following:

David shall be entitled to be the company's deputy managing director for life. On any resolution to remove him from office, the shares held by him shall carry three votes per share.

Louise, David, George, John and Claire each hold 20 per cent of the issued share capital of Perfect Puddings and George as well as Louise and David are the directors. Louise and David wish to develop a new product, but George, John and Claire are opposed to this. At a forthcoming meeting, George, John and Claire are planning to propose a resolution to remove Louise and David from their directorships.

Advise Louise and David. *(University of Hertfordshire)*

Suggested further reading

Drury, 'The Relative Nature of a Shareholder's Right to Enforce the Company Contract' (1986) CLJ 219.

Griffin, 'Companies Act 2006 s 33 – altering the contractual effect of the articles of association?' (2010) *Company Law Newsletter*.

8

The company and its contracts

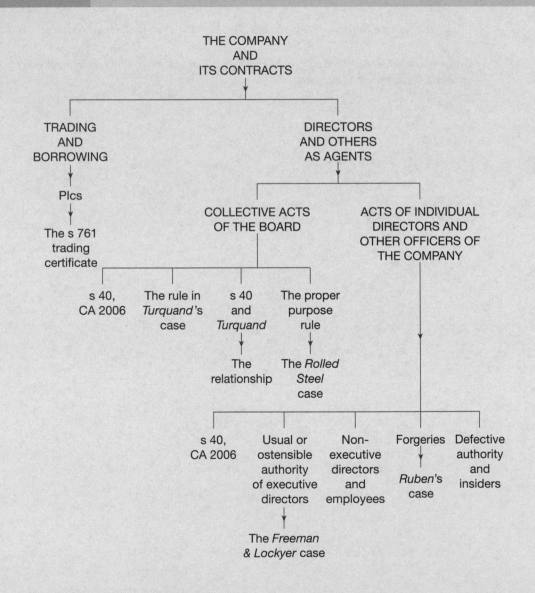

A company necessarily contracts through agents such as its directors and other officers, and senior employees. This chapter is, in the main, concerned with the problems which can arise when these agents enter into transactions which they are not authorised to make or use their powers for an improper purpose, or exercise them by irregular procedures. First, however, this is an appropriate place to deal with transactions entered into by public companies before receipt of a s 761, CA 2006 certificate from the Registrar.

Public companies and the s 761 certificate

Under s 761 a public company, registered as such on its initial incorporation, cannot commence business or exercise any borrowing powers unless the Registrar has issued what is known as a s 761 trading certificate. A private company does not require such a certificate.

The trading certificate will be issued when the Registrar is satisfied that the nominal value of the company's allotted share capital is at least £50,000 (s 763) and not less than one-quarter of the nominal value of each issued share in the company plus the whole of any premium on such shares has been received by the company, whether in cash or otherwise. A share allotted in pursuance of an employees' share scheme may not be taken into account in determining the nominal value of the company's allotted share capital unless it is paid up at least as to one-quarter of the nominal value of the share and the whole of any premium on the share.

In order to obtain a s 761 certificate, the company must file with the Registrar a statement of compliance and application specifying the following items as detailed in s 762:

(a) that the nominal value of the company's allotted share capital is not less than the authorised minimum;

(b) the amount, or estimated amount, of the preliminary expenses of the company and the persons by whom any of those expenses have been paid or are payable; and

(c) any amount or benefit paid or given or intended to be paid or given to any promoter of the company and the consideration for the payment or benefit.

The object of the ss 761–762 provisions is to ensure that a plc has some significant starting capital. The disclosure of preliminary expenses and promoter payments is required because if these are large and paid from the initial capital, then the provision for a significant initial capital is defeated.

When a trading certificate is issued it is conclusive evidence that the company is entitled to commence business and exercise borrowing powers (s 761(4)). Failure to comply with s 761 may, according to s 767, result in a fine on the company and any officer in default.

If a public company has not obtained a s 761 certificate within a year of registration, the Secretary of State for Business, Innovation and Skills may present a petition to the court to wind it up.

If a company does commence business or borrow without a s 761 certificate, transactions with traders and lenders are nevertheless enforceable against the company. However, if the company cannot meet its obligations in terms of payment of a debt or repayment of a loan incurred during the period of unlawful trading, within 21 days of being called upon to do so, the directors of the company are jointly and severally liable to indemnify the trader or lender in respect of his loss resulting from the company's failure to meet its obligations. Therefore, s 767(3) leaves the company liable and the directors become personally liable if the company does not pay, as where it goes into insolvent liquidation without discharging its liability on a transaction.

Directors and others as agents

If the board acting together (that is collectively), or one director or other officer of the company acting on his own, has actual authority to make a particular contract on behalf of the company, and that contract is within the company's powers (or if not the transaction is protected by s 39 – see Chapter 5, p. 95 ○), then the contract, when made, will be binding on the company. However, where the directors act together, or as individuals, beyond their authority the position for them and other officers is as set out below.

Collective acts of the board

(a) The Companies Act 2006

Section 40(1) provides that in favour of a person dealing with the company in good faith, the power of the board of directors to bind the company or authorise others to do so shall be deemed free of any limitation under the company's constitution (see further Chapter 19 ○), and a person shall not be regarded as acting in bad faith just because he knows that an act is beyond the powers of the directors (s 40(2)(b)). In addition, under s 40(2)(b) there is no duty to enquire as to the directors' authority and there is no constructive notice of any provision of the company's constitution limiting authority. Therefore, provided the above requirements are met, a transaction entered into by the board beyond its powers will bind the company. This applies not only where the directors are acting beyond their powers but also where they are within their powers but have failed to observe proper internal procedures.

TCB v Gray [1987] 3 WLR 1144

A company issued a debenture to secure a loan. The transaction was within the company's powers and within the authority of the board. The debenture was issued under the company's seal. On this the articles of the company said 'every instrument to which the seal shall be affixed shall be signed by a director'. In this case it was signed by a solicitor to whom one of the directors had given a power of attorney to act as his agent. The question of the validity of the debenture arose and the court held that it was valid under s 35A which protected not only against lack of authority but also against the use of incorrect procedures.

In addition, it will be noted that the section deals with a situation where the directors authorise other persons to make contracts on behalf of the company. This is to overcome the common law rule that a company can only act through organs of the company. At common law the board of directors is an organ of the company but only if acting collectively. Section 40(1) overcomes this by making it clear that an act done by a person authorised by the board is in effect an act of the board and therefore an act by an organ of the company. For example, if the board authorises the company's purchasing officer to buy materials from outsiders for use in the company's manufacturing process, each purchase within the officer's authority will be a transaction decided upon by the directors and therefore a transaction decided upon by a common law organ of the company. There is no longer an assumption as in previous legislation that all commercial decisions are made at boardroom level. If, therefore, the board collectively makes a decision and enters into a transaction which is beyond its powers, s 40 will make the transaction enforceable, and the same is true if an individual authorised by the board exceeds the powers of the directors by a contract which he as an authorised individual has made.

Good faith. Under s 40(2)(b) a person is to be regarded as acting in good faith unless the contrary is proved. Thus the burden of proof will be on the company if it wishes to avoid a transaction on the 'bad faith' ground.

Member injunctions. A member of a company is not prevented by s 40 from asking the court for an injunction to stop the directors from acting beyond their powers, but this cannot be done if the transaction has been entered into (see s 40(4)).

Director liability. The directors are liable to compensate the company as they always have been if they cause the company loss by acting outside their powers (s 40(5)).

Section 40: use by shareholders. The section has been viewed as essentially an outsider's protection as where a creditor relies on the section to validate a contract entered into by the directors without authority. However, in the following case it was held to be available to shareholders in regard to a disputed issue of bonus shares.

EIC Services Ltd v Phipps [2003] 3 All ER 804

A shareholder in the company challenged a bonus issue of shares that it had made by capitalising the sum standing to the credit of its share premium account because, if his claim had succeeded, he would have owned a substantially greater proportion of the company. The challenge was based upon the company's articles which provided that the bonus shares should be applied in proportion to the amounts paid up on the shares and following an ordinary resolution of the members. The contention was that a very substantial number of the bonus shares were issued to shareholders whose shares were not paid up and that no resolution of members was passed but only a resolution of the board. The High Court ruled, however, that the bonus issue was enforceable. The relevant shareholders were entitled to rely on the CA 1985, s 35A (now s 40 of the Companies Act 2006) which provides that, in favour of a person dealing with the company in good faith, the power of the board of directors to bind the company or authorise others to do so shall be deemed free of any limitation under the company's constitution, e.g. its articles. Regarding the fact that certain of the recipients of the bonus shares were directors, the judge referred to the further provisions of what is now s 40 which state that a person shall not be regarded as acting in bad faith because he knows that the act is beyond the powers of the directors. The judge felt that they did not know that the issue of the bonus shares was beyond their powers, though as directors they should have done. In any case, the judge felt that they had acted in good faith. The issue of all the bonus shares was therefore valid.

Comment

The issue was also challenged on the ground that the directors made it under a misapprehension of their powers. The contract for the shares, therefore, was void at common law for operative mistake. The court rejected this on the grounds that the mistake was not sufficiently fundamental to avoid the contract.

Section 40: use by directors. Section 40 states that it applies 'in favour of a person dealing with the company in good faith'. The matter of whether a director could claim to be included in the word 'person' arose in the following case.

Smith v Henniker-Major & Co (a Firm) [2002] All ER (D) 310 (Jul)

A director of a company who was in dispute with the other directors wished to bring a claim by the company against the defendant solicitors. The company was not pursuing the claim. The director, believing that he had power under the company's articles, acted alone and, without a quorate board meeting, made an agreement as agent of the company under which the company's claim against the solicitors was assigned to him personally. The assignment was later ratified by deed, presumably to prevent a ruling that the assignment was ineffective as lacking consideration. On the issue of the authority of the director to make the assignment for the company, the solicitors contended that since the company's board did not hold a quorate meeting the assignment was invalid and ineffective, so the claimant's case against them should not proceed. On the question whether a director of the company could claim to be included in the word 'person' in what is now s 40, the majority of the Court of Appeal said no. The words were wide enough to cover a director but not in this case. The claimant, Mr Smith, was the chairman of the company and it was his duty to see that the company's constitution was adhered to. The articles did not permit him to turn himself into a one-man board and he could not rely on his own error as to the company's constitution to validate a transaction with himself. His appeal against a decision striking out his claim against the defendants was dismissed.

Comment

It may be that a director not so senior as Mr Smith but, say, a more junior director – perhaps only recently appointed – might have succeeded. The decision does not rule this out.

(b) The rule in *Turquand*'s case: the indoor management rule

This rule is best explained by looking straightaway at the facts of the case (below).

Royal British Bank v Turquand (1856) 6 E & B 327

The claimant bank lent £2,000 to a joint stock company called Cameron's Coalbrook Steam Coal & Swansea and London Railway Company, which was at the time of the action in course of winding-up. Turquand was the general manager of the company and was brought into the action to represent it. The company had issued a bond under its common seal, signed by two directors, agreeing to repay the loan. The registered deed of settlement of the company (which corresponded to the articles of a modern company) provided that the directors might borrow on bond such sums as they should be authorised by a general resolution of the members of the company to borrow. In the case of this loan it appeared that no such resolution had been passed.

Held – by the Court of Exchequer – that the bond was nevertheless binding on the company, because the lenders were entitled to assume that a resolution authorising the borrowing had been passed. There was no need to go indoors the management to make active enquiries.

Comment

This case succeeded because the ordinary resolution involved did not have to be filed with the Registrar of Companies. Therefore, there was no constructive notice of it. During the period when there was constructive notice of a company's memorandum and articles and the contents of its file at the Registry, it was decided that *Turquand* could not apply where the resolution required was a special or extraordinary resolution because these have to be filed and an outsider would have constructive notice that they had not been. The relevant decision is *Irvine v Union Bank of Australia* (1877) 2 App Cas 366.

Since the enactment of the Companies Act 2006, s 40 and the abolition of constructive notice, the importance of the rule in *Turquand*'s case should now be diminished.

(c) The relationship between s 40 and the rule in *Turquand*'s case

Section 40 gives the same protection as *Turquand* in regard to unauthorised collective acts of the board and also where correct internal procedures were not followed as in *TCB* v *Gray*, 1987 (above).

While one could argue that *Turquand*'s case would appear to be wider than s 35A under the Companies Act 1985, because it applied to make a transaction by the company enforceable against it in *Mahoney* v *East Holyford Mining Co* (1875) LR 7 HL 869, where the directors who made the transaction had never been appointed at all, and again in *Davis* v *R Bolton & Co* [1894] 3 Ch 678 the rule was applied where the directors made a transfer of shares without a quorum at the meeting. The transfer was nevertheless held to be valid. This position has now been affected by the new wording of s 40 (Companies Act 2006), which refers to any 'limitation under the *company's constitution*' on the power of the board to bind the company.

Although s 40 has not been fully interpreted by the courts, it seems logical to suppose that it would not apply in the circumstances of either *Mahoney* or *Davis* because the court will presumably expect that when an English statute says 'the power of the directors to bind the company' it means directors who are properly appointed and have a quorum at the relevant meeting. Until s 40 has been more fully interpreted, it is perhaps safer to assume that *Turquand*'s case still has a role to play.

(d) The proper purpose rule

The directors must use their agency powers for the proper purpose, that is, for the benefit of the company and which is now outlined in s 171, CA 2006 (see Chapter 21, p. 399 ◗). If they do not do so, the transactions which they have entered into, while not *ultra vires* themselves or the company, are not enforceable against the company provided that the person with whom the directors dealt was aware of the improper use of the power.

> **_Rolled Steel Products (Holdings) Ltd_ v _British Steel Corporation_** [1985] 2 WLR 908

A Mr Shenkman was a 51 per cent shareholder and director in Rolled Steel and held all the issued share capital in another company called Scottish Steel of which he was also a director. Scottish Steel owed a lot of money to BSC and Mr Shenkman had given his personal guarantee of that debt. Later BSC wanted more security and Mr S caused Rolled Steel to enter into a guarantee of the Scottish Steel debt. There was no benefit to Rolled Steel in this and BSC knew there was not.

The Court of Appeal decided that BSC could not enforce the guarantee. The transaction was not *ultra vires* Rolled Steel because its objects clause contained a paragraph giving an express power to enter into guarantees (see Chapters 5 and 6 ◗). However, the power of the directors to bind the company as agents was a different matter. Mr Shenkman and the other director of Rolled Steel, Mr Shenkman's father, had exercised their powers of giving guarantees for an improper purpose (i.e. a purpose which was of no benefit to the company). The guarantee could therefore be avoided by the liquidator of Rolled Steel provided that those to whom it was given were aware of the improper purpose. Since BSC knew that there was no benefit to Rolled Steel in the guarantee, it could not enforce the guarantee and prove in the liquidation.

Comment

(i) If BSC had not been on notice of the circumstances in which Rolled Steel had been made to enter into the guarantee, it could have claimed in the liquidation.

(ii) It should be noted that if the members of Rolled Steel had passed an ordinary resolution ratifying the making of the guarantee, then it would have been enforceable against the company. Where the directors act for an improper purpose, this can be put right by an ordinary resolution of the members even if, as here, the 'wrongdoer' can himself obtain an ordinary resolution. This would not apply if the 'wrongdoer' acted fraudulently, which was not the case here.

Acts of individual directors and other officers of the company

We must now consider the extent to which a company will be bound by a transaction entered into by an individual director or other officer, e.g. the company secretary, who has no actual authority to enter into it. There are the following possibilities:

(a) The Companies Act 2006

As we have seen, s 40 states that in favour of a person dealing with a company in good faith the power of the directors to authorise other persons to bind the company shall be regarded as free from any limitation under the company's constitution. Therefore, an individual director, company secretary, employee or other agent, authorised by the directors to bind the company, will do so even if he exceeds the powers given to the board itself or other agents of the company by the articles. Once again, knowledge of the lack of power in the individual making the transaction on behalf of the company is not bad faith and does not prevent the transaction from binding the company.

(b) The rules of agency: the doctrine of holding out

Where a director or other officer of a company has no actual authority, or authorisation under s 40, an outsider may be able to regard a transaction entered into by such an individual as binding on the company if the person with whom he negotiated was held out by the company as having authority to enter into it, in regard to all commercial activities relating to the running of the business.

Since it is usual to delegate wide powers to a managing director and other executive directors, and *Table A* (replaced by the new Model Articles in newly incorporated companies) allows the board to delegate widely to such persons, an outsider will normally be protected and the transaction will bind the company if he has dealt with a managing director or other executive director (e.g. a sales director) or other officer (e.g. the company secretary) and this applies even if the person concerned has not actually been appointed to the post.

Freeman & Lockyer v Buckhurst Park Properties Ltd [1964] 1 All ER 630

A Mr Kapoor carried on a business as a property developer, and entered into a contract to buy an estate called Buckhurst Park at Sunninghill. He did not have enough money to pay for it, and obtained financial assistance from a Mr Hoon. They formed a limited company with a share capital of £70,000, subscribed equally by Kapoor and Hoon, to buy the estate with a view to selling it for development. Kapoor and Hoon, together with two other persons, comprised the board of directors. The quorum of the board was four, and Hoon was at all material times abroad. There was a power under the articles to appoint a managing director but this was never done. Kapoor, to the knowledge of the board, acted as if he were managing director in relation to finding a purchaser for the estate; and again, without express authority of the board but with its knowledge, he employed on behalf of the company a firm of architects and surveyors, the claimants in this case, for the submission of an application for planning permission which involved preparing plans and defining the estate boundaries. The claimants now claimed from the company the fees for the work done, and the company's defence was that Kapoor had no authority to act for the company. The Court of Appeal found that the company was liable, and Diplock LJ said that four conditions must be fulfilled before a third party was entitled to enforce against a company a contract entered into on its behalf by an agent without actual authority to make it:

(a) A representation must be made to the third party that the agent had authority. This condition was satisfied here because the board knew that Kapoor was making the contract as managing director but did not stop him.

(b) The representation must be made by the persons who have actual authority to manage the company. This condition was satisfied because the articles conferred full powers of management on the board.

(c) The third party must have been induced to make the contract because of the representation. This condition was satisfied because the claimants relied on Kapoor's authority and thought they were dealing with the company.

(d) Under the memorandum and articles the company is not deprived of the capacity either to make a contract of the kind made or to delegate authority to an agent to make the contract. This condition was satisfied because the articles allowed the board to delegate any of its functions of management to a managing director or a single director.

The court also decided that although the claimants had not looked at the articles, this did not matter: for the rule does not depend upon estoppel arising out of a document, but on estoppel by representation.

Hely-Hutchinson v Brayhead [1968] 1 QB 549

Under the articles of the company the directors were empowered to decide who should draw bills of exchange on behalf of the company. A Mr Clarke, who was the Manchester branch manager of Schenkers, drew bills of exchange on the company's behalf in favour of Kreditbank. He had no authority to do so. The court later held that the bills were not binding on the company because it was, on the evidence, unusual for a branch manager.

Richards, the chairman of the defendant company, Brayhead, acted as its de facto managing director. He was the chief executive who made the final decision on any matters concerning finance. He often committed the company to contracts without the knowledge of the board and reported the matter afterwards. The board knew of and acquiesced in that. In July 1964 the plaintiff, the chairman and managing director of a public company, Perdio, gave a personal guarantee to bankers for a loan of £50,000 to Perdio. Towards the end of 1964 Perdio was sustaining losses and needed financial assistance. Brayhead was prepared to help, with the intention eventually to obtain control of Perdio. In January 1965 Brayhead bought 750,000 Perdio ordinary shares from the plaintiff for over £100,000 and proposed to inject £150,000 into Perdio. About the same time the plaintiff became a director of Brayhead, but did not attend any board meetings until 19 May 1965. After that meeting, in an office outside, in a discussion between Richards and the plaintiff, the plaintiff agreed to put more money into Perdio if Brayhead would secure his position. To that end Richards, on behalf of Brayhead, as chairman signed two letters on Brayhead's paper dated 19 May 1965, and addressed to the plaintiff. In one Brayhead purported to indemnify the plaintiff against loss on his personal guarantee of £50,000 and in the other Brayhead purported to guarantee to repay money lent by the plaintiff personally to Perdio. In reliance on those letters the plaintiff advanced £45,000 to Perdio.

Article 99 of Brayhead's articles of association provided that 'A director may contract with and be interested in any contract . . . with the company . . . and shall not be liable to account for any profit made by him by reason of any such contract . . . provided that the nature of the interest of the director in such contract . . . be declared at a meeting of the directors as required by . . . section 199 of the Companies Act, 1948', but no disclosure of the two contracts was in fact made to the board.

Despite the plaintiff's and other advances by Brayhead, Perdio's financial position remained hopeless and it went into liquidation. The plaintiff was called on to honour his guarantee. He paid the bankers £50,000 and claimed that sum and the £45,000 lent to Perdio, from Brayhead. Brayhead denied liability contending that Richards had no authority to sign the letters, alternatively, that since the plaintiff had not disclosed his interest in the contracts as required by article 99 of Brayhead's articles of association and section 199 of the Companies Act 1948, the contracts were unenforceable.

Roskill J held that although Richards had no actual authority to enter into contracts, he had ostensible or apparent authority to do so; that the plaintiff's breach of article 99 of Brayhead's articles of association and section 199 of the Act of 1948, only rendered the contracts voidable, not void or unenforceable; and that the plaintiff was entitled to recover.

On appeal, Denning MR stated:

I need not consider at length the law on the authority of an agent, actual, apparent, or ostensible. That has been done in the judgments of this court in *Freeman & Lockyer* v *Buckhurst Park Properties (Mangal) Ltd*. It is there shown that actual authority may be express or implied. It is *express* when it is given by express words, such as when a board of directors pass a resolution which authorises two of their number to sign cheques. It is *implied* when it is inferred from the conduct of the parties and the circumstances of the case, such as when the board of directors appoint one of their number to be managing director. They thereby impliedly authorise him to do all such things as fall within the usual scope of that office. Actual authority, express or implied, is binding as between the company and the agent, and also as between the company and others, whether they are within the company or outside it.

Ostensible or apparent authority is the authority of an agent as it *appears* to others. It often coincides with actual authority. Thus, when the board appoint one of their number to be managing director, they invest him not only with implied authority, but also with ostensible authority to do all such things as fall within the usual scope of that office. Other people who see him acting as managing director are entitled to assume that he has the usual authority of a managing director. But sometimes ostensible authority exceeds actual authority. For instance, when the board appoint the managing director, they may expressly limit his authority by saying he is not to order goods worth more than £500 without the sanction of the board. In that case his actual authority is subject to the £500 limitation, but his *ostensible* authority includes all the usual authority of a managing director. The company is bound by his ostensible authority in his dealings with those who do not know of the limitation. He may himself do the 'holding-out'. Thus, if he orders goods worth £1,000 and signs himself 'Managing Director for and on behalf of the company', the company is bound to the other party who does not know of the £500 limitation, see *British Thomson-Houston Co Ltd* v *Federated European Bank Ltd*, which was quoted for this purpose by Pearson LJ in *Freeman & Lockyer*. Even if the other party happens himself to be a director of the company, nevertheless the company may be bound by the ostensible authority. Suppose the managing director orders £1,000 worth of goods from a new director who has just joined the company and does not know of the £500 limitation, not having studied the minute book, the company may yet be bound. Lord Simonds in *Morris* v *Kanssen*, envisaged that sort of case, which was considered by Roskill J in the present case.

Apply these principles here. It is plain that Mr Richards had no express authority to enter into these two contracts an behalf of the company: nor had he any such authority implied from the nature of his office. He had been duly appointed chairman of the company but that office in itself did not carry with it authority to enter into these contracts without the sanction of the board. But I think he had authority implied from the conduct of the parties and the circumstances of the case. The judge did not rest his decision on implied authority, but I think his findings necessarily carry that consequence. The judge finds that Mr Richards acted as de facto managing director of Brayhead. He was the chief executive who made the final decision on any matter concerning finance. He often committed Brayhead to contracts without the knowledge of the board and reported the matter afterwards. The judge said 'I have no doubt that Mr Richards was, by virtue of his position as de facto managing director of Brayhead or, as perhaps one might more compendiously put it, as Brayhead's chief executive, the man who had, in Diplock LJ's words, "actual authority to manage", and he was acting as such when he signed those two documents.' And later he said: 'The board of Brayhead knew of and acquiesced in Mr Richards acting as de facto managing director of Brayhead.' The judge held that Mr Richards had ostensible or apparent authority to make the contract, but I think his findings carry with it the necessary inference that he had also actual authority, such authority being implied from the circumstance that the board by their conduct over many months had acquiesced in his acting as their chief executive and committing Brayhead Ltd to contracts without the necessity of sanction from the board.

Held – appeal dismissed but on the grounds that Richards had actual authority to bind his company.

Panorama Developments (Guildford) Ltd v *Fidelis Furnishing Fabrics Ltd* [1971] 3 All ER 16

The claimant company trading as Belgravia Executive Car Rental sued the defendant company for £570 in respect of car hiring. Belgravia had a fleet of Rolls Royce, Jaguar and other cars. Fidelis was a company of good reputation which employed a new man, X, as its secretary. He got in touch with Belgravia and booked cars which he wanted to drive for the company to meet important customers when they arrived at Heathrow Airport. On the first occasion, X wrote a cheque on his own account and it was met. In January 1970 he gave a list of dates for which he required cars on hire to Belgravia. It confirmed that the cars would be available and sent a written confirmation to Fidelis and not to X. Belgravia allowed the cars to go out on credit, asking for references. X gave references of the company which proved to be satisfactory. The printed forms of hiring and insurance agreements showed that X, the company secretary, was the hirer. These forms were signed by X or the sales manager of Fidelis. X used the cars which were never paid for. Belgravia sent the statement of account to Fidelis but it did not pay. Later the managing director of Fidelis found many unpaid bills in the company's name and disputed X's authority to act on behalf of the company.

Held – by the Court of Appeal – that the defendant company was liable for the hire because, among other things, X as company secretary had ostensible authority to enter into the contracts for the hire of the cars on behalf of the defendant.

Comment

(i) The observations of Lord Denning on the position of a company secretary are of interest. He said:

> He is no longer a mere clerk. He regularly makes representations on behalf of the company and enters into contracts on its behalf which come within the day to day running of the company's business. So much so that he may be regarded as held out as having authority to do such things on behalf of the company. He is certainly entitled to sign contracts connected with the administrative side of the company's affairs such as employing staff and ordering cars and so forth.

(ii) It should be noted that the judges in this case referred to the power of the company secretary to bind the company in this limited way as being based on ostensible authority. The reader should, however, be aware that it is sometimes referred to as 'usual' authority', i.e. being what, for example, a managing director or company secretary can 'usually do'.

Non-executive directors and employees

Where the outsider deals with a non-executive director or employee not occupying a designated office within the company-law structure, neither of whom have been authorised under s 40, the position of the outsider is much less secure and there is little authority in case law which deals with the ostensible or usual authority of middle and lower management: such as there is would suggest that their unauthorised acts are unlikely to bind the company.

Of course, where the company allows an employee to hold himself out as an executive director, he may assume the actual ostensible or usual authority of such a director in regard to an outsider who is not aware of the true position, as the following case illustrates.

Electronics Ltd v Akhter Computers Ltd [2001] 1 BCLC 433

Mr David Bennett was employed by Skynet, a division of Akhter, as 'director PSU sales'. In fact, he was not a director of any company in the Akhter Group. He worked from a small sales office in Basingstoke with two other people, his assistant Andy Wall and a secretary. Mr Bennett's primary duty was to promote sales and he was paid large commissions when he was successful. He was given a very high degree of autonomy. He even had the habit, known to and permitted by his employers, of writing on Skynet notepaper and describing himself as a 'director'. This Skynet notepaper, in breach of s 351 of the Companies Act 1985, omitted to contain the registered name, company number, and address of Akhter, leaving the reader no indication as to whom David Bennett might answer. Mr Bennett made a contract on behalf of Skynet to arrange for the supply of power-supply units to Pitney-Bowes and share the commission with SMC, which had passed the procurement contract on to Akhter through Mr Bennett. Later Akhter contended that it was not required to pay SMC a share of the commission because Mr Bennett had no authority to make the commission-splitting deal.

Held – by the Court of Appeal – that since the agreement was reasonably associated with his job, Mr Bennett had actual authority to enter into the deal. In any event, he had ostensible authority to enter into commission agreements generally because that was ordinarily incidental to his duties. Furthermore, SMC was not on notice of any lack of authority.

Comment

There was no argument in the case that this contract was beyond the powers of the company or the board, so that it was presumably not necessary to use s 35A of the Companies Act 1985 to validate Mr Bennett's actions. The court was merely applying the common rules of agency. The provisions of Mr Bennett's employment contract were also of crucial importance. The relevant provision was in the following terms: 'Job title: Director PSU sales. You must perform such duties as may be reasonably associated with your job title.' Perhaps Akhter should have been more restrictive.

Kreditbank Cassel v Schenkers Ltd [1927] 1 KB 826

Under the articles of the company the directors were empowered to decide who should draw bills of exchange on behalf of the company. A Mr Clarke, who was the Manchester branch manager of Schenkers, drew bills of exchange on the company's behalf in favour of Kreditbank. He had no authority to do so. The court later held that the bills were not binding on the company because it was, on the evidence, unusual for a branch manager to have such authority.

Where the company document which the outsider relies upon is a forgery

The rules of law laid down in *Turquand* and the other general rules of agency described above together with the statutory contribution of s 40 will not validate a forgery. A forgery is a crime and in no sense a genuine transaction.

Ruben v Great Fingall Consolidated [1906] AC 439

Rowe was the secretary of the company and he asked the appellants, who were stockbrokers, to get him a loan of £20,000. The appellants procured the money and advanced it in good faith on the security of the share certificate of the company issued by Rowe, the latter stating that the appellants were registered in the register of members, which was not the case. The certificate was in accordance with the company's articles, bore the company's seal, and was signed by two directors and the secretary, Rowe; but Rowe had forged the signatures of the two directors. When the fraud was discovered, the appellants tried to get registration, and when this failed, they sued the company in estoppel.

Held – by the House of Lords – a company secretary had no authority to do more than deliver the share certificates, and in the absence of evidence that the company had held Rowe out as having authority to actually issue certificates, the company was not estopped by a forged certificate. Neither was the company responsible for the fraud of its secretary, because it was not within the scope of his employment to issue certificates. This was a matter for the directors. The Lord Chancellor, Lord Loreburn, said:

> The forged certificate is a pure nullity. It is quite true that persons dealing with limited liability companies are not bound to inquire into their indoor management, and will not be affected by irregularities of which they had no notice. But this doctrine, which is well established, applies only to irregularities that might otherwise affect a genuine transaction. It cannot apply to a forgery.

Defective authority and insiders

The rule in *Turquand*'s case, and the ostensible or usual authority rules of agency which have been considered above, are in general designed to protect persons who deal with the company from outside against defects in the internal management of the company's affairs. Members of a company can take advantage of the rule and in *Bargate v Shortridge* (1855) 5 HL Cas 297 it was held that a member could rely upon a written consent purporting to be given by the board, as required by the articles, allowing him to transfer his shares, even though it was given by the managing director alone. The company could not set aside the transfer and restore the member's name to the register.

Directors and persons who act as such in regard to the transaction in question are regarded as insiders and cannot rely on the rule. Thus, an allotment of shares made to a director at a meeting at which he was present by a board, some or all of whom were not properly appointed, would be invalid. As Lord Simonds said in *Morris v Kanssen* [1946] 1 All ER 586 (the case in point) in regard to directors: 'To admit in their favour a presumption that that is rightly done which they themselves have wrongly done is to encourage ignorance and careless dereliction from duty.'

However, if a director does not act as such in connection with a transaction, he may be able to rely on the rule. Thus in *Hely-Hutchinson v Brayhead* [1968] 1 QB 549 it was held that a director who lent money to his company's subsidiary, and also guaranteed loans to it by other persons, could enforce an agreement to indemnify him given in the company's name by a fellow director who had assumed the functions of managing director on an irregular basis but with the acquiescence of the board. The company was represented in the transaction only by the fellow director, and the director who made the loan was not therefore prevented from relying on the rule. Lord Denning MR observed:

> The judge held that Mr Richards had ostensible or apparent authority to make the contract, but I think that his findings carry with them the necessary inference that he had also actual authority, such authority being implied from the circumstance that the board, by their conduct over many months, had acquiesced in his acting as their chief executive and committing Brayhead to contracts without the necessity of sanction from the board.

Essay questions

1 (a) State the legal rules applying to a transaction within the powers of the company, but entered into by directors in excess of their authority.

 AND

 (b) Bob is chairman of Light Ltd. He functions as the company's chief executive and makes most decisions regarding its business. He reports his various decisions to the board in order to inform them of what has happened. The articles of Light Ltd provide that:

 > The directors may from time to time appoint one or more of their body to be managing director. The directors may entrust to and confer upon a managing director any of the powers exercisable by them, subject to such restrictions as they think fit.

 Bob has on a number of occasions given Light Ltd's guarantee of loans from finance companies to Light Ltd's customers. Each of these transactions was later reported to the board. In June 1999 in a boardroom dispute, the directors resolve that in future such guarantees may only be given after approval by the full board. On 1 August Bob as a matter of urgency acts on his own initiative to give Light Ltd's guarantee to Slow Ltd, a new and potentially valuable customer. The lender is Sharp Ltd, a finance house with whom Light Ltd has had previous dealings. Sharp Ltd has a copy of Light Ltd's articles. The board refuses to adopt Bob's action and Light Ltd disclaims liability on the guarantee.
 Advise Sharp Ltd on the enforceability of the guarantee.

 (University of Central Lancashire)

2 In what circumstances will an agent bind a company to a contract made with a third party? What effect does the company's constitution have on the power of agents to bind companies to such contracts? *(The Institute of Chartered Secretaries and Administrators)*

3 B is the managing director of T Ltd. He has decided that the company should have a new factory built. He arranges for P Ltd to carry out the building work on the usual standard term contract for the building industry which requires that T Ltd makes progress payments on a three-monthly basis.
 The articles of association of T Ltd provide that the directors of the company may negotiate any contract on the company's behalf up to a value of £100,000 but contracts in excess of this sum must be approved by the company passing an ordinary resolution in general meeting.

The value of this building contract is £500,000. B did not obtain the approval of the general meeting. The first progress payment has now fallen due and the other directors of T Ltd have resolved not to pay it on the grounds that the contract was not properly authorised by the shareholders.

You are required to explain whether T Ltd is bound to pay this progress payment and more generally whether T Ltd is bound to the contract with P Ltd.

(The Chartered Institute of Management Accountants)

4 (a) What is the rule in **Royal British Bank v Turquand** (1856), and what defences against its application are available to a company?

(b) Beetlecrush Ltd was a company involved in pest control. In 1999 Pellet was appointed as managing director of the company by a board resolution, which gave him exclusive power to manage the company, subject only to a requirement to get the approval of the board for all contracts in excess of £50,000.

On behalf of the company, Pellet began negotiating for the purchase of insecticides from Toxin, who had supplied the company with similar products for a number of years. Before these negotiations were concluded, Toxin accepted an invitation to become a member of the board of Beetlecrush Ltd, and thenceforth duly attended its board meetings. Some months after this, Pellet, without getting the approval of the board, signed a contract with Toxin for the supply of £80,000 worth of insecticides.

Preliminary trials with these insecticides have revealed that they are not as effective as the company had been hoping. The board, with the exception of Pellet and Toxin, is now seeking some way in which the company can claim that it is not bound by its obligations under the contract.

Advise the board. *(The Association of Chartered Certified Accountants)*

5 Contrast the rules governing contracts purporting to be made on behalf of a company before it has been incorporated under the Companies Act with those governing contracts made by or on behalf of an incorporated company before it is entitled to do business.

(The Institute of Company Accountants)

6 The company secretary of Beech Ltd has in the past been permitted to order office equipment and stationery for the company but no single transaction has exceeded £500. Recently, without the knowledge of the directors, he ordered a computer installation costing £200,000. The board does not wish to proceed with the purchase but the supplier is claiming that the company is bound by the contract.

Advise the directors. *(The Institute of Chartered Accountants in England and Wales)*

Test your knowledge

Four alternative answers are given. Select ONE only. Circle the answer which you consider to be correct. Check your answers by referring back to the information given in the chapter and against the answers at the end of the text.

1 Delta plc and Ullswater Ltd have each recently received their certificates of incorporation.

A Delta plc and Ullswater Ltd can now both commence trading and borrow.

B Only Delta plc can trade and borrow.

C Only Ullswater Ltd can trade and borrow.

D Neither Delta nor Ullswater can trade or borrow.

2 A transaction with another company entered into by Tom, a director of Thames Ltd, with the authority of the board is outside the authority of the board under the articles of Thames Ltd but within its objects. The transaction is:

A valid under s 40 of the Companies Act 2006.

B void as being beyond the powers of the board.

C voidable at the option of the members.

D void at the instance of the other party.

3 A managing director of a company has usual (or ostensible) authority to bind the company by his acts. Which of the following sets out the full limit of this authority?

A All commercial activities relating to the running of the business.

B All activities of the company whether commercial or not.

C Such commercial activities as the board chooses to delegate.

D Those commercial activities which the members direct in general meeting.

4 Bob, a non-executive director of Test Ltd, who has no responsibility for the purchasing department, makes a contract on behalf of Test (which is unknown to his fellow directors) to buy goods from a new supplier. What is the legal position of Test?

A It is bound because all matters decided upon by any director bind the company under s 40 of the Companies Act 2006.

B It is not bound because a non-executive director as such does not have usual (or ostensible) authority by reason of office to bind the company.

C It is bound because all the acts of an ordinary director bind the company under *Turquand*'s case.

D It is not bound because a company is never bound by the acts of one director.

Answers to test your knowledge questions appear on p. 645.

Suggested further reading

Campbell and Armour, 'Demystifying the civil liability of corporate agents' [2003] CLJ 290.

Grantham and Rickett, 'Directors' "tortious" liability: Contract, tort or company law' (1999) 62 MLR 133.

Omerod and Taylor, 'The corporate manslaughter and corporate homicide act 2007: Legislative comment' (2008) *Criminal Law Review* 589.

Stevens, 'Vicarious liability or vicarious action' (2007) 123 LQR 30.

Williams, 'Vicarious liability: Tort of the master or of the servant?' 72 LQR 522.

9 The capital of a company

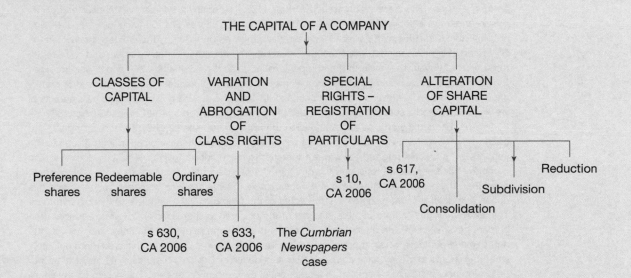

A company may confer different rights on different classes of shares, the main types being preference and ordinary shares. Shares may also be non-voting or have multiple voting rights. In the most extreme situations, shares may also carry additional voting rights on particular resolutions (i.e. to remove a director) as in the case of *Bushell v Faith* [1970] AC 1099.

There is no implied condition in a company's articles that all of its shares shall be equal (*Andrews v Gas Meter Co* [1897] 1 Ch 361).

 ## *Andrews v Gas Meter Co* [1897] 1 Ch 361

Per Lindley LJ:

The question raised by this appeal is whether certain preference shares issued by a limited company as long ago as 1865 were validly issued or not . . . The company's original capital as stated in its memorandum of association was '£60,000, divided into 600 shares of £100 each, every share being sub-divisible into fifths, with power to increase the capital as provided by the articles of association'. By the articles of association which accompanied the memorandum of association, and were registered with it, power was given to the company to increase the capital (Art 27), and it was provided that any new capital should be considered as part of the original capital (Art 28). The issue of preference shares was not contemplated or authorised. In 1865 the company desired to acquire additional works, and passed a special resolution under the powers conferred by the Companies Act 1862, ss 50 and 51, altering the articles and authorising the issue of 100 shares of £100 each, fully paid, and bearing a preferential dividend of 5 per cent per annum. Those shares were accordingly issued to the vendors of the works referred to, and are the shares the validity of which is now in question. The company has been prosperous, and the ordinary shareholders have for years received a higher dividend than the preference shareholders. A considerable reserve has also been accumulated, and this action has been brought to determine the rights of the preference shareholders to this reserve fund. The learned judge has held that the creation of the preference shares was *ultra vires*, and that their holders never became and are not now shareholders in the company, and that they have none of the rights of shareholders, whether preference or ordinary. He has not, however, declared more definitely what their rights are. They have appealed from this decision; but on the appeal they only claimed to be preference shareholders entitled to a preferential dividend of 5 per cent. Their claim to any share of the reserve fund was dropped. The judgment against the validity of the preference shares is based upon the well-known case of *Hutton v Scarborough Cliff Hotel Co* which came twice before Kindersley V-C in 1865, and which Kekewich J very naturally held to be binding on him. Kindersley V-C's first decision was that a limited company which had not issued the whole of its original capital could not issue the unallotted shares as preference shares unless authorised so to do by its memorandum of association or by its articles of association. This decision was affirmed on appeal and was obviously correct; and would have been correct even if the whole of the original capital had been issued and the preference shares had been new and additional capital. The company, however, afterwards passed a special resolution altering the articles and authorising an issue of preference shares. This raised an entirely different question, and led to the second decision. The Vice-Chancellor granted an injunction restraining the issue of the preference shares, and he held distinctly that the resolution altering the articles was *ultra vires*. He did so upon the ground, as we understand his judgment, that there was in the memorandum of association a condition that all the shareholders should stand on an equal footing as to the receipt of dividends, and that this condition was one which could not be got rid of by a special resolution altering the articles of association under the powers conferred by ss 50 and 51 of the Act . . .

These decisions turned upon the principle that although by s 8 of the Act the memorandum is to state the amount of the original capital and the number of shares into which it is to be divided, yet in other respects the rights of the shareholders in respect of their shares and the terms on which additional capital may be raised are matters to be regulated by the articles of association rather than by the memorandum, and are, therefore, matters which (unless provided for by the memorandum, as in

Ashbury v *Watson* may be determined by the company from time to time by special resolution pursuant to s 50 of the Act. This view, however, clearly negatives the doctrine that there is a condition in the memorandum of association that all shareholders are to be on an equality unless the memorandum itself shows the contrary. That proposition is, in our opinion, unsound.

As noted earlier (see Chapter 4, p. 75) under s 9(4), the required contents of the application for registration include a statement of capital and initial shareholdings if the company is to have a share capital. The details of this statement are outlined in s 10 of the Companies Act 2006, providing (under s 10(2)(c)) that for each class of shares it must state:

(a) prescribed particulars of the rights attached to the shares;
(b) the total number of shares of that class; and
(c) the aggregate nominal value of shares of that class.

The importance of this process is reinforced by the wording of s 629(1), which states that 'for the purposes of the Companies Acts, shares are of one class if the rights attached to them are in all respects uniform'. Section 629(2) goes on to note that 'for this purpose the rights attached to shares are not regarded as different from those attached to other shares by reason only that they do not carry the same rights to dividends in the twelve months immediately following their allotment'.

However, beyond these references of 'class rights' the Companies Act 2006 does not provide any further clarification as to the meaning of the term. In this respect, one needs to refer to the case law in the area, in particular that of *Cumbrian Newspapers* (below).

Cumbrian Newspapers Group Ltd v *Cumberland & Westmorland Herald* [1986] 3 WLR 26

A company which issued shares to a shareholder and amended its articles to grant the shareholder particular rights to prevent a takeover could not later cancel the articles since the shareholder had rights attached to a class of shares which could not be abrogated. The plaintiff and defendant were both publishers of newspapers. They negotiated a transaction whereby D would acquire one of P's papers and P would acquire 10 per cent of D's share capital. D duly issued the 10 per cent shareholding and as part of the agreement under which the shares were issued amended its articles to grant P rights of pre-emption over other ordinary shares, rights in respect of unissued shares, and the right to appoint a director. The purpose of such rights was to enable P as a shareholder to prevent a takeover of D. After several years, the directors of D proposed to convene an extraordinary general meeting and to pass a special resolution to cancel the articles which gave special rights to P. P sought a declaration that the rights were class rights which could not be abrogated without his consent, and an injunction restraining D from holding the meeting.

Held – granting the declaration – that the special rights granted by the articles were rights which although not attached to any particular shares were conferred on P as a shareholder in D and were attached to the shares held for the time being by P without which it was not entitled to the rights. Accordingly, P had 'rights attached to a class of shares' and since the Companies Act 1985 s 125 (now s 630 under the Companies Act 2006) provided that class rights could not be varied or abrogated without the consent of the class members, the special rights enjoyed by P could not be varied or abrogated without his consent.

In this case Scott J made the following observations with respect to class rights:

Rights or benefits which may be contained in articles can be divided into three different categories. First, there are rights or benefits which are annexed to particular shares. Classic examples of rights of this character are dividend rights and rights to participate in surplus assets on a winding up. If articles provide that particular shares carry particular rights not enjoyed by the holders of other shares, it is easy to conclude that the rights are attached to a class of shares [. . .] A second category of rights or benefits which may be contained in articles would cover rights or benefits conferred on individuals not in the capacity of members or shareholders of the company but, for ulterior reasons, connected with the administration of the company's affairs or the conduct of its business. *Eley* v *Positive Government Security Life Assurance Co Ltd* (1875) 1 Ex D 20 was a case where the articles of the defendant company had included a provision that the plaintiff should be the company solicitor [. . .] It is, perhaps, obvious that rights or benefits in this category cannot be class rights. They cannot be described as rights attached to a class of shares [. . .] That leaves the third category. This category would cover rights or benefits that, although not attached to any particular shares, were nonetheless conferred on the beneficiary in the capacity of member or shareholder of the company. The rights of the plaintiff fall, in my judgment, into this category [. . .] In the present case, the rights conferred on the plaintiff were, as I have held, conferred on the plaintiff as a member or shareholder of the defendant. The rights would not be enforceable by the plaintiff otherwise than as the owner of ordinary shares in the defendant. If the plaintiff were to divest itself of all its ordinary shares in the defendant, it would not then, in my view, be in a position to enforce the rights in the articles. But the rights were not attached to any particular share or shares. Enforcement by the plaintiff of the rights granted under the articles would require no more than ownership by the plaintiff of at least some shares in the defendant. Enforcement by the plaintiff of the rights granted under article 12, require the plaintiff to hold at least 10 per cent of the issued shares in the defendant. But any shares would do. It follows, in my judgment that the plaintiff's rights under the articles in question fall squarely within this third category.

Comment

(i) The case is unusual because one generally thinks of rights attaching to a whole class of shares and not to the holder of part only of a class.

(ii) A similar and earlier decision is that in *Re United Provident Assurance Co Ltd* [1910] 2 Ch 477 where it was held that shareholders within a class who have paid up different amounts on their shares must be regarded as a separate class and on a variation must meet separately as a class.

The general principle is that the rights enjoyed by one particular class should not be varied by the holders of another class of shares within the company (i.e. it is necessary to gain the consent of the members of the class whose rights are the subject of proposed variation to agree to this process). This process is covered by s 630 of the Companies Act 2006 and necessarily raises the question as to what amounts to a 'variation of rights' for the purposes of this provision (see *White* v *Bristol Aeroplane* below). It should be noted that this process is over and above that outlined in s 21 (amendment of the company's articles of association) and provides an important protective function. For example, if the class in question involves preference shares which are non-voting, then without s 630 they may never have an input into the proposed changes to the rights attached to their shares (i.e. the process would be open to exploitation by the majority in general meeting; a majority comprised holders of ordinary shares). As such, the class in question must vote in favour of the proposed amendment in a separate class meeting, followed by the s 21 process in the context of the general meeting. (It is perhaps worth considering the case of *Allen* v *Gold Reefs* in this context – see Chapter 7, p. 127. ◐)

In addition to this, it may be observed that s 22 provides for the entrenchment of provisions of the articles. In other words, that specified provisions may only be amended or repealed if conditions are met, or procedures are complied with that are more restrictive than a special resolution.

Ordinary shares

The nature of an ordinary share is perhaps best understood by comparing it with a preference share. In this way we can ascertain the distinguishing features, and the advantages and disadvantages which arise from the holding of ordinary shares.

Disadvantages

The main perceived disadvantage is the fact that the ordinary shareholder is entitled to a dividend only after the preference dividends have been paid. Furthermore, where the preference shares have preference as to capital, the ordinary shares rank behind the preference shares for repayment of capital on winding-up or where there is a reduction of capital by repayment. The preference shares must be fully repaid first (see further Chapter 10, p. 176 ○).

It is perhaps because of the above priorities given to preference shareholders that the ordinary shareholders are said to hold the equity share capital of the company, presumably by analogy with the equity of redemption held by a mortgagor in the law of mortgages. A mortgagor who pays off all the charges on his property has the right to redeem or recover it by virtue of this equity; indeed it is the last right he retains, for when that is gone, he has lost his property. Similarly, the equity shareholders are entitled to the remaining assets of the company after the claims of creditors and of preference shareholders have been met.

Advantages

Here we may observe that the voting power of the ordinary shareholders in general meetings is such as to allow them to control the resolutions at such meetings. In fact, this means that the directorate really represents, or can be made to represent, the ordinary shareholders.

It is not uncommon for companies to issue preference shares with no voting rights at general meetings, though if such shares are to be listed on the Stock Exchange, they must be given adequate voting rights by the company's articles. It would seem, however, that the voting rights of preference shareholders are adequate if they can vote:

(a) when their dividend is in arrear;
(b) on resolutions for reducing share capital and winding up the company; and
(c) on resolutions which are likely to affect their class rights (s 630).

A further advantage of ordinary shareholders is that their dividends are not fixed and may rise considerably with the profitability of the company.

A final advantage is that a company may issue bonus shares for which the shareholder does not pay in cash, or make new issues (called rights issues) at prices lower than outsiders would have to pay, and both of these are generally offered to the company's existing ordinary shareholders.

Preference shares

These shares are entitled to preferential treatment when dividends are declared. Thus, a 10 per cent preference share must receive a dividend of 10 per cent out of profits before anything can be paid to the ordinary shares. Since there may be several classes of preference shares ranking one after the other, it is essential to ascertain the precise rights of a holder of a particular preference share.

However, a right to preferential dividend without more is deemed a right to a cumulative dividend (i.e. if no dividend is declared on the preference shares in any year, the arrears are carried forward and must be paid before any dividend can be declared on ordinary shares (*Webb* v *Earle* (1875) LR 20 Eq 556)). Thus, if the 10 per cent preference shares mentioned above received dividends of 5 per cent in 1999; 5 per cent in 2000; and nothing in 2001; they would be entitled at the end of 2002 to **5 + 5 + 10 + 10**, or 30 per cent before the ordinary shareholders could have a penny.

However, it may be expressly provided by the terms of issue that they are to be non-cumulative but it is rare nowadays to find such a provision in the case of shares issued by public companies; and they may be held to be non-cumulative by implication, as where the terms of issue or the articles provide that dividends shall be paid 'out of yearly profits' (*Adair* v *Old Bushmills Distillery* [1908] WN 24) or 'out of the net profits of each year' (*Staples* v *Eastman Photographic Materials Co* [1896] 2 Ch 303).

Preference shares do not carry the right to participate in any surplus profits of the company unless the articles so provide (*Will* v *United Lankat Plantations Co* [1914] AC 11). However, it is possible to create cumulative and participating preference shares, conferring on the holders of such shares a right to participate in surplus profits up to a given percentage, e.g. a right to a preferential dividend of 6 per cent plus a further right, after, say, 10 per cent has been paid to ordinary shareholders, to participate in surplus profits until a further 6 per cent has been paid but no more.

Arrears of preference dividend in a winding-up

In the absence of an express provision in the articles, no arrears of preference dividend are payable in the winding-up of a company unless the dividend has already been declared (*Re Crichton's Oil Co* [1902] 2 Ch 86) and this is so even where the articles provide for the payment of dividends due at the date of winding-up, for a dividend is not due until declared (*Re Roberts and Cooper Ltd* [1929] 2 Ch 383). Where the articles do provide for payment of arrears, they may be paid out of the surplus assets after payment of the company's debts, even though those assets do not contain any undistributed profits (*Re Wharfedale Brewery Co* [1952] Ch 913). Thus, the general rule that dividends must not be paid out of capital does not apply in this sort of situation. However, unless there is a specific provision which says so, the right to arrears ceases at the date of liquidation (*Re E W Savory Ltd* [1951] All ER 1036).

Even where the articles or terms of issue do contain a provision regarding the repayment of dividend and/or capital to preference shareholders in a winding-up, problems of construction arise, i.e. problems arise with regard to the meaning of the words used. For example, in *Re Walter Symons Ltd* [1934] Ch 308, preference shares were issued with 'the right to a fixed cumulative preferential dividend at the rate of 12 per cent per annum on the capital for the time being paid up thereon [. . .] and to rank both as regards dividends and capital in priority to the ordinary shares *but with no right to any further participation in profits or assets*'. The court took the view that the italicised words envisaged a winding-up, because it is only in winding up that the question of participation in assets arises. Therefore, the rest of the clause must also apply in a winding-up, and the preference shares had priority in a winding-up for repayment of dividends unpaid at that date.

However, in *Re Wood, Skinner and Co Ltd* [1944] Ch 323, the preference shareholders had 'the right to a fixed cumulative dividend of 6 per cent per annum on the capital paid up on the shares', and were expressed to rank 'both as regards dividends and capital in priority to the ordinary shares'. In this case the court decided that since the latter part of the clause did not refer solely to the winding-up situation, the priority conferred was restricted to dividends declared while the company was in operation, and did not give the right to arrears of dividend once a winding-up had commenced.

Of course, a person drafting terms of issue today would normally make his intentions more clear than was done in the two cases cited above, and would certainly not use the phrases which were used then. Nevertheless, problems do arise out of bad draughtsmanship and the cases show how the court might deal with such situations.

A typical modern clause in the terms of issue of preference shares which more clearly expresses the rights intended to be conferred is as follows.

> The holders of preference shares shall be entitled to a fixed cumulative preferential dividend at the rate of X per cent per annum upon the amount paid up thereon, and in the event of the winding up of the company, to repayment of the amount paid up thereon together with any arrears of dividend calculated to the date of such repayment in priority to the claims of ordinary shares, but shall have no other right to participate in the assets or profits of the company.

It should be noted that under such a clause unpaid preference dividends will be payable for periods up to the repayment of the preference capital, even though the dividends have not been declared and in spite of the fact that the company may not have earned sufficient profits to pay them while it was a going concern (*Re Wharfedale Brewery Co* [1952] Ch 913).

Repayment of capital on winding-up

Preference shares have no inherent priority as to the repayment of capital in a winding-up. If the assets are not enough to pay the preference and ordinary shares in full then, unless the articles or terms of issue provide to the contrary, preference and ordinary shares are paid off rateably according to the nominal value of their shares (*Birch v Cropper* (1889) 14 App Cas 525). Where, as is usual, the preference shares have priority either by the articles or terms of issue, they are entitled to repayment of their capital in full before the ordinary shareholders receive anything by way of repayment of capital. Where there are surplus assets left after the discharge of all the company's liabilities and the repayment of capital to all shareholders, the surplus is divided among ordinary and preference shareholders unless the articles provide to the contrary. Any rights given by the articles are exhaustive. Thus, where the articles give preference shareholders priority of repayment of capital in a winding-up, but do not refer to any further rights in the capital of the company, the preference shareholders have no right to participate in surplus capital (*Scottish Insurance v Wilsons*).

 Scottish Insurance Corporation Ltd v Wilsons & Clyde Coal Co Ltd [1949] AC 462

The articles of a company provided *inter alia* that, in the event of the company being wound up, the preference shares 'shall rank before the other shares of the company on the property of the company to the extent of repayment of the amounts called upon and paid thereon'. The company, whose colliery assets had been transferred to and vested in the National Coal Board, had postponed liquidation till the compensation provided under the Coal Industry Nationalisation Act 1946 had been settled and paid, but as a preliminary step towards liquidation had passed a special resolution for the reduction of capital by which the whole paid-up capital was to be returned to the holders of preference stock.

Held – the holders of preference stock had no right to share in the surplus assets and that consequently it could not be said that the proposed reduction was not fair and equitable between the different classes of shareholders, and that it should therefore be confirmed.

Per Lord Simonds:

Reading these articles as a whole [. . .] I would not hesitate to say, first, that the last thing a preference stockholder would expect to get (I do not speak here of the legal rights) would be a share of surplus assets, and that such a share would be a windfall beyond his reasonable expectations and, secondly, that he had at all times the knowledge, enforced in this case by the unusual reference in Art 139 to the payment off of the preference capital, that at least he ran the risk, if the company's circumstances admitted, of such a reduction as is now proposed being submitted for confirmation by the court. Whether a man lends money to a company at 7 per cent or subscribes for its shares carrying a cumulative preferential dividend at that rate, I do not think that he can complain of unfairness if the company, being in a position lawfully to do so, proposes to pay him off. No doubt, if the company is content not to do so, he may get something that he can never have expected but, so long as the company can lawfully repay him, whether it be months or years before a contemplated liquidation, I see no ground for the court refusing its confirmation . . .

It is clear from the authorities, and would be clear without them, that, subject to any relevant provision of the general law, the rights *inter se* of preference and ordinary shareholders must depend on the terms of the instrument which contains the bargain that they have made with the company and each other. This means, that there is a question of construction to be determined and undesirable though it may be that fine distinctions should be drawn in commercial documents such as articles of association of a company, your Lordships cannot decide that the articles here under review have a particular meaning, because to somewhat similar articles in such cases as *In Re William Metcalfe & Sons Ltd* that meaning has been judicially attributed. Reading the relevant articles, as a whole, I come to the conclusion that Arts 159 and 160 are exhaustive of the rights of the preference stockholders in a winding up. The whole tenor of the articles, as I have already pointed out, is to leave the ordinary stockholders masters of the situation. If there are 'surplus assets' it is because the ordinary stockholders have contrived that it should be so, and, though this is not decisive, in determining what the parties meant by their bargain, it is of some weight that it should be in the power of one class so to act that there will or will not be surplus assets . . .

But, apart from those more general considerations, the words of the specifically relevant articles, 'rank before the other shares . . . on the property of the company to the extent of repayment of the amounts called up and paid thereon', appear to me apt to define exhaustively the rights of the preference stockholders in a winding up. Similar words, in *Will v United Lankat Plantations Co Ltd* 'rank, both as regards capital and dividend, in priority to the other shares', were held to define exhaustively the rights of preference shareholders to dividend, and I do not find in the speeches of Viscount Haldane LC or Earl Loreburn in that case any suggestion that a different result would have followed if the dispute had been in regard to capital. I do not ignore that in the same case in the Court of Appeal the distinction between dividend and capital was expressly made by both Cozens-Hardy MR and Farwell LJ, and that in *In re William Metcalfe & Sons Ltd* Romer LJ reasserted it. But I share the difficulty, which Lord Keith has expressed in this case, in reconciling the reasoning that lies behind the judgments in *Will*'s case and *In re William Metcalfe & Sons Ltd* respectively.

The following is, therefore, a summary of the position:

(a) Where the preference shareholders have no priority in regard to repayment of capital, they share the assets rateably with the ordinary shareholders, including any surplus assets left after repayment of share capital and other liabilities.

(b) If the articles or terms of issue give the preference shareholders priority for repayment of capital, they are repaid the nominal value of their shares before the ordinary shareholders but no more.

In addition, it should be noted that if the articles give preference shareholders an express right to participate equally with the ordinary shareholders in surplus assets, they are entitled to share in such assets even though they include ploughed back profits of former years which could have been distributed as dividend to ordinary shareholders but which instead were placed in reserve (*Dimbula Valley (Ceylon) Tea Co Ltd* v *Laurie* [1961] 1 All ER 769). The fact that the ordinary shareholders are, while the company is a going concern, in charge of the profit, i.e. they can resolve upon a distribution within the provisions of Part VIII of the Companies Act 1985, does not prevent the preference shareholders having a right to participate in those profits which the ordinary shareholders have left undistributed.

Variation and abrogation of class rights

If the shares of a company are divided into different classes (e.g. ordinary and preference), the expression 'class rights' refers to the special rights of a particular class of shareholder concerning, e.g. dividends and voting and rights on a winding-up. The Companies Act 2006 makes it clear that abrogation of class rights is included. This means that class rights can be extinguished entirely as well as merely varied provided the appropriate procedures of s 630 as set out below are followed. However, the process outlined in s 630 must be complied with, over and above that outlined in s 21 which deals with the amendment of the company's articles by way of a special resolution. Consequently, there is a built-in protective mechanism for those within the company who enjoy class rights.

1 Meaning of variation

Case law decided that class rights are to be regarded as varied only if after the purported act of variation they are different in substance from before as where the company proposes to make its existing cumulative preference shares non-cumulative. Unless this is so, consent of the particular class or classes of shareholders is not required. The courts have in general taken a narrow and, perhaps, over-literal approach to the meaning of variation of rights. For instance, in *Adelaide Electric Co* v *Prudential Assurance* [1934] AC 122, HL, the court held that the alteration of the place of payment of a preferential dividend did not vary the rights of the preference shareholders (despite the fact that the exchange rate acted in favour of the company and against the preference shareholders).

Another example has already been given in *Greenhalgh* v *Arderne Cinemas*, 1946. In particular, the creation of new rights in others does not amount to a variation if existing rights are preserved. Thus, Boxo Ltd has 'A' ordinary shares with one vote each and 'B' ordinaries with one vote each. If the company increases the voting power of the 'A' ordinaries to two votes per share, is that a variation of the rights of the 'B' ordinary shares? From the decision in *Greenhalgh*, it would seem not.

Other cases which are worth reading so as to gain an interesting insight into the approach adopted by the courts in this area are as follows: *Re Saltdean Estate Co Ltd* [1968] 1 WLR 1844 (see Chapter 7 ○); *Prudential Assurance Co* v *Chatterly-Whitfield Collieries* [1949]

AC 512; *Re John Smith's Tadcaster Brewery Co* [1953] Ch 308, CA. The following cases are also of interest.

House of Fraser plc v ACGE Investments [1987] 2 WLR 1083

In this case the House of Lords decided that where a company pays off and cancels cumulative preference shares (which have priority for repayment of capital in the company's articles) in a capital reduction there is no need for a class meeting of the preference shareholders to approve this. In the circumstances their rights have not been varied but merely put into effect. One of the rights attached to the preference shares was the right to a return of capital in priority to other shareholders when any capital was returned as being in excess of the company's needs. That right was not being affected, modified, dealt with or abrogated. It was merely being put into effect. The company was granting the preference shareholders their rights, not denying them.

White v Bristol Aeroplane [1953] Ch 65

The defendant company had sent out notices of proposed resolutions to increase the ordinary and preference stock of the company from GBP 3,900,000 to GBP 5,880,000, of which GBP 660,000 preference stock was to be distributed to the ordinary shareholders by new issues. There was a certain equilibrium between the ordinary stock and the preference stock, and it was objected that that equilibrium would be upset when the new shares were issued to the detriment of the preference stockholders and that their rights were 'affected' within the meaning of Art 68 of the company's articles and that the company could not carry out the proposed plan without first obtaining a vote of the preference stockholders. Art 68 provided:

> All or any of the rights or privileges attached to any class of shares forming part of the capital for the time being of the company may be affected modified varied dealt with or abrogated in any manner with the sanction of an extraordinary resolution passed at a separate meeting of the members of that class. To any such separate meeting all the provisions of these articles as to general meetings shall *mutatis mutandis* apply [. . .]

Held – on appeal – the provisions of the articles were inconsistent with the view that any variation which in any manner touched or affected the value of the preference stock or the character or enjoyment of any of the holders' privileges was within the contemplation of Art 68; the question was whether the rights of the preference stockholders were 'affected', not as a matter of business, but according to the meaning of the articles when construed according to the rules of construction and as a matter of law; those rights would not be affected by the proposed resolution, and, consequently, the appeal must be allowed.

In this regard, Evershed MR noted:

> The question then is – and, indeed, I have already posed it – are the rights which I have already summarised 'affected' by what is proposed? It is said in answer – and I think rightly said – No, they are not; they remain exactly as they were before; each one of the manifestations of the preference stockholders' privileges may be repeated without any change whatever after, as before, the proposed distribution. It is no doubt true that the enjoyment of, and the capacity to make effective, those rights is in a measure affected; for as I have already indicated, the existing preference stockholders will be in a less advantageous position on such occasions as entitle them to register their votes, whether at general meetings of the company or at separate meetings of their own class. But there is to my mind a distinction, and a sensible distinction, between an affecting of the rights and an affecting of the enjoyment of the rights, or of the stockholders' capacity to turn them to account.

2 Method of variation or abrogation

The method by which the variation or abrogation was effected under the Companies Act 1985 depended upon the source of the class rights. In other words, the process under s 125 of the 1985 Act was dependent upon whether the rights were conferred by the company's memorandum, articles of association, or even by way of the resolution setting out the terms of issue. This inevitably led to a rather complex process.

By contrast, s 630 of the Companies Act 2006 sets down a single, straightforward rule. (This has been made possible in part by the reforms surrounding the reduced role which the memorandum now plays in the day-to-day running of a company under s 8.) Consequently, s 630(2) states that variation of the rights attached to a class of shares may only be varied:

(a) in accordance with provisions in the company's articles for the variation of class rights; or

(b) where the company's articles contain no such provision, if the holders of shares of that class consent to the variation in accordance with this section.

Section 630(4) goes on to provide that the consent required under s 630(2)(b) is either (a) consent in writing from the holders of at least three-quarters in nominal value of the issued shares of that class; or (b) a special resolution, passed at a separate general meeting of the holders of that class, sanctioning the variation.

Consequently, a resolution to vary the rights of a particular class is of no legal effect unless the consent of the class is obtained. However, it should be borne in mind that any vote on a resolution to modify class rights must be undertaken for the purpose (or predominant purpose) of benefiting the class as a whole (*British America Nickel Corporation Ltd v O'Brien* [1927] AC 369).

British America Nickel Corporation Ltd v O'Brien [1927] AC 369

A company, incorporated in Canada, issued mortgage bonds secured by a trust deed, which gave power to a majority of the bondholders, consisting of not less than three-fourths in value, to sanction any modification of the rights of the bondholders. A scheme for the reconstruction of the company provided for the mortgage bonds being exchanged for income bonds subject to an issue of first income bonds; also that a committee, one only of whom was to be appointed by the mortgage bondholders, should have power to modify the scheme without confirmation by the bondholders. The scheme was sanctioned by the majority of the bondholders requisite under the trust deed. The required majority would not have been obtained but for the vote of the holder of a large number of bonds, whose support of the scheme was obtained by the promise of a large block of ordinary stock, an arrangement which was not mentioned in the scheme. Viscount Haldane stated:

> To give a power to modify the terms on which debentures in a company are secured is not uncommon in practice. The business interests of the company may render such a power expedient, even in the interests of the class of debenture holders as a whole. The provision is usually made in the form of a power, conferred by the instrument constituting the debenture security, upon the majority of the class of holders. It often enables them to modify, by resolution properly passed, the security itself. The provision of such a power to a majority bears some analogy to such a power as that conferred by s 13 of the English Companies Act of 1908, which enables a majority of the shareholders by special resolution to alter the articles of association. There is, however, a restriction of such powers, when conferred on a majority of a special class in order to enable that majority to bind a minority. They must be exercised subject to a general principle, which is applicable to all authorities conferred on majorities

of classes enabling them to bind minorities; namely, that the power given must be exercised for the purpose of benefiting the class as a whole, and not merely individual members only. Subject to this, the power may be unrestricted. It may be free from the general principle in question when the power arises not in connection with a class, but only under a general title which confers the vote as a right of property attaching to a share. The distinction does not arise in this case, and it is not necessary to express an opinion as to its ground. What does arise is the question whether there is such a restriction on the right to vote of a creditor or member of an analogous class on whom is conferred a power to vote for the alteration of the title of a minority of the class to which he himself belongs . . .

[T]heir Lordships do not think that there is any real difficulty in combining the principle that while usually a holder of shares or debentures may vote as his interest directs, he is subject to the further principle that where his vote is conferred on him as a member of a class he must conform to the interest of the class itself when seeking to exercise the power conferred on him in his capacity of being a member. The second principle is a negative one, one which puts a restriction on the completeness of freedom under the first, without excluding such freedom wholly.

The distinction, which may prove a fine one, is well illustrated in the carefully worded judgment of Parker J in *Goodfellow* v *Nelson Line*. It was there held that while the power conferred by a trust deed on a majority of debenture holders to bind a minority must be exercised bona fide, and while the Court has power to prevent some sorts at least of unfairness or oppression, a debenture holder may, subject to this vote in accordance with his individual interests, though these may be peculiar to himself and not shared by the other members of the class. It was true that a secret bargain to secure his vote by special treatment might be treated as bribery, but where the scheme to be voted upon itself provides, as it did in that case, openly for special treatment of a debenture holder with a special interest, he may vote, inasmuch as the other members of the class had themselves known from the first of the scheme. Their Lordships think that Parker J accurately applied in his judgment the law on this point . . .

Their Lordships are of opinion that judgment was rightly given for the respondents in this appeal. It is plain, even from his own letters, that before Mr JR Booth would agree to the scheme of 1921 his vote had to be secured by the promise of $2,000,000 ordinary stock of the Nickel Corporation. No doubt he was entitled in giving his vote to consider his own interests. But as that vote had come to him as a member of a class he was bound to exercise it with the interests of the class itself kept in view as dominant. It may be that, as Ferguson JA thought, he and those with whom he was negotiating considered the scheme the best way out of the difficulties with which the corporation was beset. But they had something else to consider in the first place. Their duty was to look to the difficulties of the bondholders as a class, and not to give any one of these bondholders a special personal advantage, not forming part of the scheme to be voted for, in order to induce him to assent.

Held – that the resolution was invalid, both because the bondholder in voting had not treated the interest of the whole class of bondholders as the dominant consideration, and because the scheme, so far as it provided for a committee, was *ultra vires*.

It is also worth noting at this point that according to s 630(5), any attempt to amend a provision contained in the articles for the variation of the rights attached to a class of shares is to be treated as a variation of those rights.

3 Right to object to variation

Dissentient members of a class may object to variation. The holders of not less than 15 per cent of the issued shares of the class, being persons who did not consent to or vote for the resolution to vary, may apply to the court to have the variation cancelled (s 633). If such application is made, the variation has no effect until confirmed by the court.

Application to the court must be made within 21 days after the date on which the resolution was passed or the consent given (s 633(4)). It may be made on behalf of all the dissentients by one or more of them appointed in writing. The variation then has no effect unless and until confirmed by the court (s 633(3)). The court's power on hearing a petition for cancellation of a variation of class rights is limited to approving or disallowing the variation. The court cannot amend the variation or approve it subject to conditions.

The company must send to the Registrar within 15 days of the making of the court order, a copy of that order embodying the court's decision on the matter of variation (s 635(1)).

Alteration of share capital

A company's share capital may be altered or increased provided the company follows the appropriate methods and procedures.

1 Alteration of share capital

A limited company, having a share capital, may not alter its share capital except in the ways outlined in s 617 of the Companies Act 2006.

2 Consolidation of capital

According to s 618, a limited company may consolidate its capital by amalgamating shares of smaller amount into shares of larger amount (e.g. by consolidating groups of 20 shares of nominal value 5p into shares of nominal value £1). It is rarely that a company needs to consolidate, the tendency being to subdivide and go for lower nominal values which makes the shares easier to sell, since shares in public companies generally sell on the Stock Exchange for more than nominal value.

Section 619 goes on to note that notice of consolidation must be given to the Registrar within one month, specifying the shares affected. In addition, s 619(2) states that this must be accompanied by a statement of capital, which under s 619(3) must state:

(a) the total number of shares of the company;
(b) the aggregate nominal value of those shares;
(c) for each class of shares; (i) prescribed particulars of the rights attached to the shares; (ii) the total number of shares of that class; and (iii) the aggregate nominal value of shares of that class; and
(d) the amount paid up and the amount unpaid on each share.

3 Subdivision of shares

This would occur, for example, where a company subdivides every £1 share into 10 shares of 10p each. However, the proportions of amounts paid and unpaid must remain the same where the shares are partly paid. For example, if before subdivision every £1 share was 50p paid, then the new shares of 10p each must be treated as 5p paid. The company cannot regard some of the new shares as fully paid and some as partly paid. A company may wish to subdivide shares to make them more easily marketable, e.g. a share having a nominal value of £1 may have a market value of £8 and this may restrict market dealings. If the company subdivides its shares into shares of 10p each, the market price would be 80p per share and dealings would be facilitated.

This is covered by ss 618–619 and follows a similar process to that outlined above for the consolidation of capital.

4 Reduction of share capital

A limited company may reduce its share capital, by special resolution confirmed by the court (see ss 645–651), or in the case of a private company limited by shares, by special resolution supported by a solvency statement (see ss 642–644). Furthermore, s 641 provides that a company may not reduce its share capital if, as a result of the reduction, there would be no longer any member of the company holding shares other than redeemable shares (see below).

Redeemable shares

Sections 684 and 689 of the Companies Act 2006 allow the issue of redeemable shares whether equity or preference.

The provisions are designed, among other things, to encourage investment in the equity of small businesses in circumstances where the proprietors, often members of a family, can at an appropriate stage buy back the equity investments without parting permanently with family control.

Issue of redeemable shares

A limited company may issue redeemable shares (s 684(1)) and may be issued as redeemable at the option of the company or the shareholder. Under s 684(2), the articles of private limited companies may either exclude or restrict the issue of redeemable shares, but a public limited company may only issue redeemable shares if authorised to do so by its articles (s 684(3)).

Redeemable shares may be issued only if there are in issue other shares which cannot be redeemed (s 684(4)). If a company's shares were all redeemable it could redeem the whole of its capital and end up under a board of directors with no members. This would circumvent provisions which have already been considered (see Chapter 1 ⬤) and which are designed to prevent a company continuing in existence without any members.

The redemption of redeemable shares

Redeemable shares may not be redeemed unless they are fully paid (s 686(1)). The issued capital is the creditors' buffer and it is this figure and not the paid-up capital which must be replaced.

The terms of the redemption may, under s 686(2), provide that the amount payable on redemption may, by agreement between the company and the holder of the shares, be paid on a date later than the redemption date.

Financing the redemption

Redeemable shares may only be redeemed out of distributable profits or out of the proceeds of a fresh issue of shares (which need not be redeemable) made for the purpose (s 687(2)).

Any premium payable on redemption must be paid out of distributable profits of the company (s 867(3)), unless the shares being redeemed were issued at a premium (see below).

Section 688 provides that shares, when redeemed, are to be cancelled and this will reduce the issued share capital of the company by the nominal value of the shares redeemed.

If the shares being redeemed were themselves issued at a premium, then s 687(4) provides that any premium on their redemption may be paid out of the proceeds of a fresh issue of shares made for the purposes of redemption up to an amount equal to:

(a) the aggregate of the premiums received by the company on the issue of the shares redeemed; or
(b) the current amount of the company's share premium account (including any sum transferred to that account in respect of premiums on the new shares) whichever is the less.

Furthermore, under s 687(5), the amount of the company's share premium account shall be reduced by a sum corresponding (or by sums in the aggregate corresponding) to the amount of any payment made out of the proceeds of the issue of the new shares.

The object of the above provisions is to tighten protection for creditors on a redemption (or purchase; see Chapter 10 ●) of shares.

In company law the creditors' buffer, as it is called, is the company's share capital plus non-distributable reserves (i.e. reserves that cannot be written off to pay dividends, such as the capital redemption reserve and the share premium account). Under the above formula the share premium account can only be written down to the extent of the amount of the new issue of shares that will replace the amount so written down, thus replacing with share capital what has been written off the share premium account and so preserving the buffer.

Miscellaneous matters relating to redeemable shares

Time of redemption

Redeemable shares can be made redeemable between certain dates. The holder thus knows that his shares cannot be redeemed before the earlier of the two dates, which is normally a number of years after the issue of the shares, in order to give him an investment which will last for a reasonable period. He also knows that the shares are bound to be redeemed by the later of the two dates mentioned.

However, there are no legal provisions requiring the company to fix the time of redemption at the time of issue though as we have seen there is no reason why this should not be done by, for instance, making the shares redeemable at the option of the company between stated dates. Section 685 provides that the redemption of shares may be effected in such a manner as may be provided by the company's articles or by a resolution of the company.

As regards failure to redeem (or purchase) its shares, a company cannot be liable in damages for such a failure. The shareholder may obtain an order for specific performance unless the company can show that it cannot meet the cost of redemption out of distributable profits.

In addition, following statements by Megarry J in *Re Holders Investment Trust* [1971] 2 All ER 289, a shareholder whose shares are not redeemed on the agreed date may be able to obtain an injunction to prevent the company from paying dividends either to ordinary shareholders or to any subordinate class of preference shareholder until the redemption has been carried out. *Re Holders* also confirms that such a shareholder may petition for a winding-up under s 122 of the Insolvency Act 1986 – the just and equitable ground.

If the company goes into liquidation and at the date of commencement of the winding-up has failed to meet an obligation to redeem (or purchase) its own shares, and this obligation occurred before the commencement of the winding-up, the terms of the redemption (or purchase) can be enforced by the shareholder against the company as a deferred debt in the liquidation, but not if during the period between the due date for redemption (or purchase) and the date of commencement of the winding-up the company could not have lawfully made a distribution (see further Chapter 10 ◐) equal in value to the price at which the shares were to have been redeemed (or purchased).

Any money owed is deferred to claims of all creditors and preference shareholders having rights to capital which rank in preference to the shares redeemed (or purchased) but ranks in front of the claims of other shareholders.

Notice to the Registrar of redemption

Notice of redemption must be given, under s 689, to the Registrar within one month of the redemption. Failure to do so is an offence covered by s 689(5).

Essay questions

1 (a) Distinguish between ordinary and preference shares.

   (b) Shark plc has a share capital of £150,000. It is divided into 50,000 £1 preference shares and 100,000 £1 ordinary shares. All shares have been issued. The rights attached to the preference shares include the right to have capital repaid before the ordinary shareholders in the event of the company being wound up. The articles contain no such provision. The articles are also silent on how to vary class rights.

   Advise Shark plc on whether and how it may convert its preference shares into ordinary shares.   *(Glasgow Caledonian University)*

2 Distinguish between preference shares, participating preference shares and ordinary shares.
                                                  (The Institute of Chartered Accountants in England and Wales)

3 'A company is contractually bound by the actions of its directors when those directors act within their authority.'
   You are required to discuss this statement.
                                                          (The Chartered Institute of Management Accountants)

4 With specific reference to the facts and principle of law in *Salomon v Salomon & Co Ltd*, discuss corporate identity and the occasions when it is set aside.   *(University of Paisley)*

5 Tom and Dick wish to form a company to manufacture wooden hen houses to be called Cluck Ltd. Explain the procedure for incorporation and commencement of business.
                                                                     (The Institute of Company Accountants)

6 'A secretary is a mere servant; his position is that he is to do what he is told, and no person can assume that he has any authority to represent anything at all . . .' *per* Lord Esher in *Barnett Hoares & Co v South London Tramways Co* (1887).
   To what extent does the statement reflect the current status of a company secretary?
                                                  (The Institute of Chartered Accountants in England and Wales)

Test your knowledge

Four alternative answers are given. Select ONE only. Circle the answer which you consider to be correct. Check your answers by referring back to the information given in the chapter and against the answers at the end of the text.

1 Where rights are attached to a class of shares set out in a company's statement of capital and initial shareholdings and the company's constitution and the articles do not contain any provision regarding the way in which the rights may be varied then they may be varied by:

   A a special resolution of the company.
   B a special resolution of the company and the consent of the holders of three-quarters of the class of shares in question.
   C the agreement of all the members of the company in general meeting.
   D an extraordinary resolution of the holders of the class in question.

2 Boxo Limited has varied the class rights of one of its classes of shares. What proportion of the owners of those shares who did not consent to or vote for the variation can make an application to the court to have the variation cancelled, and within what time must they apply?

   A The holders of not less than 15 per cent of the issued shares of the class whose rights were varied within 21 days of the passing of the resolution.
   B The holders of not less than 10 per cent of the issued shares of the class within 28 days of the resolution being passed.
   C The holders of not less than 15 per cent of the issued shares of the class within 28 days of the resolution being passed.
   D The holders of 21 per cent of the issued shares of the class within 15 days of the resolution being passed.

3 Where would a preference shareholder go to ascertain the rights attaching to the shares?

   A To the share certificate.
   B To the share certificate and the memorandum of association.
   C To the articles of association only.
   D To the articles of association and/or the terms of issue.

4 What type of resolution is required at a general meeting to increase the nominal capital?

   A An ordinary resolution.
   B A special resolution following special notice.
   C A special resolution.
   D An extraordinary resolution.

5 What type of resolution must be passed in general meeting in order that there may be a valid alteration of the company's articles?

   A A special resolution with special notice to the company.
   B An ordinary resolution following special notice to the company.
   C A special resolution.
   D An ordinary resolution.

Answers to test your knowledge questions appear on p. 645. ◗

Suggested further reading

Armour, 'Legal capital: An outdated concept?' (2006) *European Business Organization Law Review* 7, 5.

Armour, 'Share capital and creditor protection: Efficient rules for a modern company law' (2000) MLR 63, 355.

Daehnert, 'The minimum capital requirement – an anachronism under conservation' [2009] *Company Law* 30, 3.

Pennington, 'Can shares in companies be defined?' (1989) *Company Lawyer* 10, 140.

Worthington, 'Shares and shareholders: Property, power and entitlement' (2001) *Company Lawyer* 22, 258.

Capital maintenance – generally

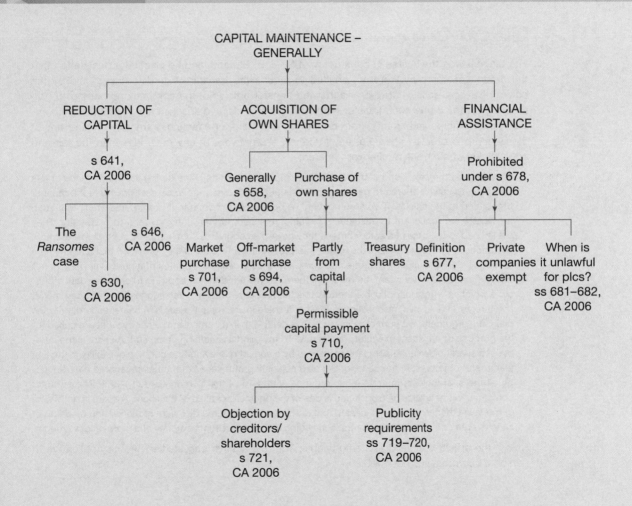

The acceptance by English company law of the concept of limited liability has led to a need to protect the capital contributed by the members of such a company since those members cannot be required to contribute funds to enable the company to pay its debts once they have paid for their shares in full.

A creditor of a company must expect that the company's capital may be lost because of business misfortune. However, he can also expect that the company's shares will be paid for in full and that the company will not return the capital to its members.

Company legislation therefore deals with the legal freedom which companies have to reduce their share capital, focusing on such issues as the protection of the creditors' fund and the class rights of members such as preference shareholders; for which both groups would appear vulnerable within the context of capital reduction.

Borland's Trustee v *Steel Bros & Co Ltd* [1901] 1 Ch 279

The plaintiff was the trustee in bankruptcy of Mr J. E. Borland, and he claimed a declaration that the defendant company were not entitled to require the transfer of certain shares held by the bankrupt at any price whatever, and that the transfer articles of the company purporting to give them power to compel such transfer were void. He also claimed an injunction to restrain the company, their officers and agents, from calling for, enforcing, or effecting, a transfer of all or any of the bankrupt's ordinary shares at any price, or, alternatively, at any price less than the fair and actual value of such shares. Farwell J stated:

> It is said that the provisions of these articles compel a man at any time during the continuance of this company to sell his shares to particular persons at a particular price to be ascertained in the manner prescribed in the articles. Two arguments have been founded on that. It is said, first of all, that such provisions are repugnant to absolute ownership. It is said, further, that they tend to perpetuity. They are likened to the case of a settlor or testator who settles or gives a sum of money subject to executory limitations which are to arise in the future, interpreting the articles as if they provided that if at any time hereafter, during centuries to come, the company should desire the shares of a particular person, not being a manager or assistant, he must sell them. To my mind that is applying to company law a principle which is wholly inapplicable thereto. It is the first time that any such suggestion has been made, and it rests, I think, on a misconception of what a share in a company really is. A share, according to the plaintiff's argument, is a sum of money which is dealt with in a particular manner by what are called for the purpose of argument executory limitations. To my mind it is nothing of the sort. A share is the interest of a shareholder in the company measured by a sum of money, for the purpose of liability in the first place, and of interest in the second, but also consisting of a series of mutual covenants entered into by all the shareholders inter se in accordance with s 16 of the Companies Act, 1862. The contract contained in the articles of association is one of the original incidents of the share. A share is not a sum of money settled in the way suggested, but is an interest measured by a sum of money and made up of various rights contained in the contract, including the right to a sum of money of a more or less amount.

Held – the article was valid and enforceable. The rule against perpetuities had no application to personal contracts such as this.

Reduction of capital

A company limited by shares may only reduce its share capital in accordance with the procedures outlined in ss 641–653 (Chapter 10 of Part 17) of the Companies Act 2006 as stated in s 617(2)(b). In this regard, s 641 states that a limited company may reduce its share capital:

(a) in the case of a private company limited by shares, by special resolution supported by a solvency statement (ss 642–644);

(b) in any case, by a special resolution confirmed by the court (ss 645–651).

Once again, as noted earlier (see Chapter 9 ○), s 641(2) underlines the fact that a company may not reduce its share capital if, as a result of the reduction, the only remaining shares held by members consisted entirely of redeemable shares.

Section 641(3) of the 2006 Act states that a company may reduce its share capital 'in any way', which may, in certain instances, lead to issues surrounding the possible variation or abrogation of class rights. Indeed, there are many examples of variations in share capital being linked with class rights. For instance, in *Re Northern Engineering Industries plc* [1993] BCLC 1151 the High Court decided that the rights of preference shareholders were to be regarded as varied by a reduction of capital in which the capital paid up on their shares was to be paid off and the shares cancelled. It could not be successfully argued that the word 'reduction' referred only to a situation in which the reduction was to a figure above zero. Therefore, the reduction had to be approved by class meetings of the company's three classes of preference shareholders.

General procedure for a reduction of capital

Section 641(1)(b) states that all limited companies may reduce their share capital by a special resolution confirmed by the court (ss 645–651). It is worth noting two points at this stage. First of all, the involvement of the court is designed so as to protect the interests of the company's creditors as well as those of any minority shareholders who may suffer as a result of such proposals. Secondly, it is worth noting that the previous requirement under s 135 of the Companies Act 1985 that the company has power under its articles of association to reduce its capital has been removed, streamlining the process involved.

The most obvious point to note is the fact that securing a special resolution may prove difficult for a company to achieve, especially where it chooses to undertake a reduction of capital which does not impact on all classes of shares in a similar fashion (see discussion in the previous chapter ○). There is also the added complication of s 630 which states that if class rights are to be varied or abrogated then the company may be accomplished this only:

(a) in accordance with provisions in the company's articles for the variation of class rights; or

(b) where the company's articles contain no such provision, if the holders of shares of that class consent to the variation in accordance with this section.

Furthermore, s 630(4) goes on to provide that the consent required under s 630(2)(b) is either (a) consent in writing from the holders of at least three-quarters in nominal value of the issued shares of that class; or (b) a special resolution, passed at a separate general meeting of the holders of that class, sanctioning the variation. Consequently, a resolution to vary the rights of a particular class is of no legal effect unless the consent of the class is obtained.

The question arises as to whether the reduction of share capital, in particular the reduction of a company's preference shares, falls within the scope of s 630. In this regard, it may be noted that s 645 only requires a copy of the resolution of the company (and not of the specific class). As such, there is an argument that the court could, in theory, approve such a reduction that impacts on class rights. However, in practice, this would not take place as the general principle is that the court will require that the proposed reduction treats all shareholders equitably; *Re Ransomes Plc* [1999] 2 BCLC 591, CA.

Re Ransomes Plc [1999] 2 BCLC 591, CA

T agreed to take over RIC. The deal was structured so that a subsidiary of T, A, would acquire all of the ordinary shares in the company, most of its preference shares, and most of its convertible stock. An Australian company, W, was holder of preference shares. The proposal was to distribute shares to A and, *inter alia*, to cancel the share premium account. An extraordinary general meeting was called to approve this plan. W petitioned the court under the Companies Act 1985 s 137 to object that the proposal had not been explained in sufficiently clear terms and that the proposals had been generally put forward with undue haste. W further contended that the cancellation of the share premium account benefited the ordinary shareholders to the detriment of the preferred shareholders.

Held – dismissing the application – an application under s 137 was not equivalent to ordinary litigation, given that many such applications were made by one party only. The court was required to give its approval under s 137 to proposed restructurings and therefore the applicant would be subject to a duty of full and frank disclosure which should not be diluted in any way. It was within the ambit of the discretion of the trial judge to decide, as he had done, that the proposal was fair and that it did not prejudice the rights of preferred shareholders to receipt of future dividends. There had not been any deliberate lack of openness in the company's dealings with the court and therefore the judge was entitled to sanction the cancellation on the material before him.

Comment

The judge approved a reduction even though there was short notice of the meeting to pass the special resolution (without formal member approval). He did so, he said, because, in fact, the vast majority of the shareholders approved of the reduction. However, he warned that other companies would not be advised to infringe the procedural rules, especially where a significant minority was likely to withhold their consent.

If one considers the interests of the company's creditors, then according to s 645(2), if a proposed reduction of capital involves either (a) diminution of liability in respect of unpaid share capital; or (b) the payment to a shareholder of any paid-up share capital, then s 646 will apply unless the court directs otherwise.

Section 646 goes on to outline that every creditor of the company who at the time is entitled to any debt or claim, that would be admissible in proof against the company if it were to be wound up, is entitled to object to the reduction in capital. In this regard, s 646(2) provides that the court shall settle a list of creditors entitled to object and is supported by s 647 which outlines the fact that it is an offence for an officer of the company to intentionally or recklessly conceal the name of a creditor entitled to object to the reduction of capital. If such an omission does in fact occur and a creditor discovers that they have been omitted from the list, s 653 provides that every person who was a member of the company at the date on which the resolution took effect under s 649(3) is liable to contribute for the payment of the debt or claim.

The general position under s 648(2) is that the court must not confirm the reduction of capital unless all of the creditors who have objected to the proposed reduction have consented, or their claims have been discharged or secured by the company (see **Re Lucania Temperance Billiard Halls (London) Ltd** [1966] Ch 98).

However, it should also be noted that s 646 does not automatically guarantee the position of creditors, since s 646(4) provides that the court may, if it thinks fit, dispense with the consent of a creditor securing payment of his debt or claim. Equally, s 648(1) provides that the court may make an order confirming the reduction of capital 'on such terms and conditions as it thinks fit'. With respect to this latter section, it may work both for and against the company, in essence providing that it is up to the court to determine the basis for a proposed reduction of its share capital.

Following confirmation by the court, s 649 provides on production of an order of the court confirming the reduction of a company's share capital and the delivery of a copy of the order and of a statement of capital approved by the court, the Registrar shall register the order and statement. (This is subject to the effect of s 650 on public limited companies.) Furthermore, under s 649(2), the statement of capital must outline:

(a) the total number of shares of the company;
(b) the aggregate nominal value of those shares;
(c) for each class of shares; (i) prescribed particulars of the rights attached to the shares; (ii) the total number of shares of that class; and (iii) the aggregate nominal value of shares of that class; and
(d) the amount paid up and the amount unpaid on each share.

Finally, according to s 649(4), notice of the registration of the order and statement of capital must be published in such a manner as the court may direct. Once registration has taken place, the order confirming the reduction will take effect (s 649).

Procedure available to private companies

The Companies Act 2006 introduces an alternative procedure for the reduction of capital by private companies, for which court confirmation is not needed and as such seeks to minimise the cost and time associated with securing confirmation from the courts. However, with respect to public limited companies, the law remains unchanged.

Section 641(1)(a) states that a private company may reduce its share capital by special resolution supported by a solvency statement.

The solvency statement must be in the prescribed form (s 643(3)) and the details required within it are outlined in s 643 and are based on the company's current and future financial positions. First of all, each of the directors must form the opinion that there is no ground on which the company could be found to be unable to pay its debts. Secondly, the statement requires them to form an opinion relating to one year into the future, in that:

(a) if it is intended to commence the winding up of the company within 12 months of that date, that the company will be able to pay its debts in full within 12 months of the commencement of winding-up; or
(b) in any other case, that the company will be able to pay its debts as they fall due during the year immediately following the date of this statement.

This is further supported by s 643(2) which outlines the fact that when forming these opinions, the directors must take into account all of the company's liabilities including any contingent or prospective liabilities. (It is worth comparing this requirement with the wording of s 123(1)(e) of the Insolvency Act 1986 whereby there is a noticeable similarity in approach.)

In addition, s 643(5) provides that an offence is committed by every officer who makes a solvency statement without having reasonable grounds for the opinions expressed therein. This reinforces the responsibility that has been placed on directors if this particular choice of approach is pursued by a company as opposed to seeking confirmation by the courts; the criminal sanctions outlined in s 643(5) reinforce the importance attached to the accuracy of the solvency statement.

Following the resolution to reduce its share capital, the company must within 15 days, deliver to the Registrar a copy of the solvency statement and a statement of capital (s 644(1)). With regards to the statement of capital, it must state with respect to the company's share capital as reduced by the resolution (s 644(2)):

(a) the total number of shares of the company;

(b) the aggregate nominal value of those shares;

(c) for each class of shares; (i) prescribed particulars of the rights attached to the shares; (ii) the total number of shares of that class; and (iii) the aggregate nominal value of shares of that class; and

(d) the amount paid up and the amount unpaid on each share.

With respect to the solvency statement, s 644(5) provides that the directors must deliver to the Registrar within 15 days after the resolution is passed, a statement confirming that the solvency statement was (a) not made more than 15 days before the date on which the resolution was passed; and (b) provided to members in accordance with s 642(2) or (3). If this latter issue is not complied with, then s 644(7) provides that an offence is committed by every officer of the company who is in default. Equally, if there is a delay in the process which takes the solvency statement outside the parameters set down by this section, the directors will be required to review and republish their solvency statement so as to comply with s 644(1).

Finally, s 644(3) provides that the Registrar must register the documents delivered to him under s 644(1) on receipt, with the resolution taking effect once registration (and, in essence, once the documentation has been made public) has taken place (s 644(4)).

Types of reduction

Under s 641 share capital can be reduced 'in any way'. The section, however, envisages three forms of reduction in particular (see s 641(4)):

(a) to extinguish or reduce the liability on any of its shares in respect of share capital not paid up;

(b) either with or without extinguishing or reducing liability on any of its shares, cancel any paid-up share capital that is lost or unrepresented by available assets;

(c) either with or without extinguishing or reducing liability on any of its shares, repay any paid-up share capital in excess of the company's wants.

In the first and third forms of reduction, it is clear that the creditors of the company are potentially in a worse position than prior to the reduction, thus falling within the intended scope of s 646 as outlined above. However, the second situation would appear to involve the company bringing its legal capital in line with its net asset position and as such not having the same impact on creditors. It is worth considering that s 641(4) enables a company to reduce for the reasons set out below:

(a) The company may have more capital than it needs and may wish to return some of it to shareholders. For example, a company may wish to return paid-up capital which is in excess of its requirements where it has sold a part of its undertaking and intends in the future to confine its activities to running the remaining part of its business. The company may achieve its purpose by reducing the nominal value of its shares. Suppose that before the reduction the company had a share capital of 50,000 shares of £1 each, fully paid. On reduction it could substitute a share capital of 50,000 shares of 50p each fully paid, and return 50p per share in cash to the members.

(b) Share capital already issued may not be fully paid and yet the company may have all the capital it needs. Reduction in these circumstances may be effected as follows. If the company's share capital before reduction was 50,000 shares of £1 each, 50p paid, the company may reduce it to 50,000 shares of 50p each fully paid. However, liability for unpaid capital cannot be reduced by crediting a partly paid share as paid up to a greater extent than it has in fact been paid up (*Re Development Co of Central and West Africa* [1902] Ch 547). Thus, it is not possible to leave the nominal value of the shares at £1 and cancel one share from every two held by shareholders, regarding the remaining one of the two as fully paid.

(c) Where the assets have suffered a realised loss as in *Re Jupiter House Investments (Cambridge) Ltd* [1985] 1 WLR 975 where the company had incurred a substantial loss on the sale of some of its property. In such a case a share capital of 50,000 shares of £1 each fully paid could be reduced to 50,000 shares of 50p each fully paid and no capital would be returned to shareholders.

(d) To comply with the law relating to distributions. The provisions relating to reduction have been increasingly used in more recent times to comply with the law relating to distributions, under which companies cannot pay a dividend unless and until any deficit on the profit and loss account is made good. In such a situation the company may wish to cancel a share premium account in order to offset a capital loss. Let us suppose that there is a balance of £5,000 in the P and L account, but the company has sold assets at a loss and suffered a realised loss of £6,000. There is, in effect, a deficit of £1,000 on the P and L account and no dividend can be paid. But if the company has a share premium account of £2,000, it can ask the court to approve a reduction in that account and write off the capital loss against it.

Payment of shareholders on reduction

The matter of repayment of shareholders should be treated as if the company was being wound up. Thus, if the capital is being repaid for the reasons given in methods (a) and (b), the preference shareholders should be paid or reduced first if they have priority in a winding-up. If the reduction is due to loss of assets, the ordinary shareholders should be paid or reduced before the preference shareholders. This order, however, may be varied if the preference shareholders consent. The court has no discretion to confirm a reduction without separate class meetings of the shareholders affected.

Prudential Assurance Co Ltd v *Chatterley-Whitfield Collieries Ltd* [1949] AC 512

Under the Coal Industry Nationalisation Act 1946, the undertaking of a colliery company carrying on business in England became vested in the National Coal Board, subject to the payment of compensation, the amount of which had not yet been assessed. The company intended thereafter to carry on a colliery business in Eire and Northern Ireland and engaged in prospecting with that end in view. Its capital being considered larger than was required, it was proposed to reduce it by paying off, out of reserves, the whole of the preference capital. By Art 7 of the articles of association the holders of preference shares had the right, in the event of a winding-up of the company, to repayment of capital in priority to the claims of the holders of ordinary shares but they were given no other rights to participate in the assets of the company. Viscount Maugham stated:

My Lords, the facts in this appeal are sufficiently stated in the speech of my noble and learned friend Lord Simonds and no useful purpose would be served by my repeating them. It is not in dispute that if the company had thought fit to pass a voluntary resolution for a winding up or to do so in the near future the rights of the preference shareholders (apart from any possible action by the Tribunal appointed under s 25 of the Coal Industry Nationalisation Act 1946) would be to receive a repayment of their share capital together with any arrears of preference dividend and they would have no other right to participate in the assets of the company. The unusual position is that the appellants as holders of a substantial number of preference shares object to the proposed reduction of capital by a repayment in full of their preference capital. Desiring to retain their preference shares though the undertaking of the company has been entirely changed, they invite the court to hold that the proposed repayment is unfair and inequitable and that the reduction ought not therefore to be approved. They acquired their shares on the footing that, subject no doubt to the approval of the court, they might be paid off under Art 43; but this they urge at the Bar is not the occasion or the method which should be adopted for such a reduction. They perhaps wisely do not tell us when that course would in their view be appropriate.

My Lords I do not propose to restate the grounds on which the majority in the Court of Appeal or my noble friends in this House have declined to accept this contention; but I should like to add a few observations of my own; for the simplest arguments sometimes escape attention merely because they are assumed. In the present case the main fact is that the undertaking of the company has been compulsorily acquired by the National Coal Board under the Coal Industry Nationalisation Act. There is no longer therefore any reason for the retention by the company of the assets and funds of great value which have been slowly added to year by year with a view to meeting contingencies or spending enormous sums in improving or reconstructing or enlarging the colliery undertaking. The obvious thing to do would be to wind up and distribute all the assets after paying debts and liabilities in accordance with the articles. It is not I think suggested that the holders of preference shares could properly object to such a course. They would cease to own a well-secured 6 per cent investment, and the ordinary shareholders would no longer possess shares paying in recent years double that amount in dividend. The object of the Coal Industry Nationalisation Act was not of course the benefit of shareholders, but if we ask whether in this case preference or ordinary shareholders are the most injured by the transfer, subject to compensation, of the colliery undertaking to a State enterprise, I think the current view of commercial men would probably be that the ordinary shareholders are the greater victims.

The company, however, does not propose to go into liquidation, at any rate at present, but to embark on two entirely new ventures in Eire and Northern Ireland, one of them a new colliery, if prospective operations should prove satisfactory, and the other the business of digging for clay and the manufacture of tiles and like articles. The working capital necessary for those enterprises is only a fraction of the available existing funds of the company; accordingly the special resolution duly passed by the company in general meeting on 30 October 1947, provided for the reducing the capital of the company from £400,000 to £200,000 by returning to the preference shareholders the amounts paid up on their shares. It is in my opinion from the point of view of those shareholders an accidental circumstance that a large majority of the ordinary shareholders have approved of the starting of two entirely new and it may be highly speculative enterprises with which the preference shareholders, if the reduction goes through, will obviously have no concern. If the preference shares are not paid off, and the new undertaking proved to be a success, the preference shares would become more and more valuable as the assets of the company became increasingly substantial. If on the other hand the undertaking were unsuccessful, those shares might nevertheless be worth par in a winding up while the ordinary share might have become valueless. The risk in short would be the risk of the ordinary shareholders, while the gain might well be that of the preference shareholders. That proposal does not commend itself to me as a fair one; and the same objection, with smaller figures affected, must apply to a proposal for a *pari passu* reduction of the ordinary and the preference shares. In short, like my noble friend Lord Simonds, I am at a loss to see what other method of reduction is to be preferred as more fair and equitable in the circumstances of this case.

The question of the effect of s 25 of the Coal Industry Nationalisation Act on the present case is one with which your Lordships have dealt in the very recent case of the *Scottish Insurance*

Corporation Ltd v *Wilsons & Clyde Coal Co Ltd*. That was also the case of a company whose undertaking was a colliery; and the dispute, as here, was between two classes of shareholders; but that company proposes to go into liquidation as soon as the amount of compensation payable under the Coal Industry Nationalisation Act has been ascertained, and the preference shareholders were claiming (but unsuccessfully) to be entitled to rank equally in the winding up with the ordinary shareholders in the surplus assets of the company, that is, in the assets available after payment of debts and liabilities and the amounts of capital paid on the ordinary and preference shares. Counsel for the preference shareholders there, as here, relied on s 25 of the Coal Industry Nationalisation Act and said that the proposed reduction of capital deprived the preference shareholders of their right to an adjustment of their interest in the company's assets. Your Lordships have now dealt with the appeal in that case and have considered the regulations which have now been made under s 25. They have held that there was no ground in that case for postponing the decision of the court on the petition before the court; and they were not persuaded that there was good reason for thinking that the apparent fairness of the proposal before the court would be affected or displaced by any order which was in the least likely to be made under the jurisdiction derived from s 25. The reduction here proposed, in my opinion, is in itself fair and equitable, and there is here, as in the previous case, no real ground for the speculation that the Tribunal might give the preference shareholders anything more than they would become entitled to receive in a liquidation.

In my opinion therefore this appeal should be dismissed with costs.

Held – the reduction proposed was fair and equitable and should be confirmed and that there was no ground to suppose that under s 25 of the Act of 1946 that preference shareholders might receive anything more than they would have been entitled to receive in a liquidation.

If priority is given to the different classes of shares in accordance with their terms of issue, then no separate class meeting is necessary to approve a reduction of the company's share capital, (subject to the specific terms of a company's articles of association) (*Re Saltdean Estate Co Ltd* [1968] 1 WLR 1844).

Re Saltdean Estate Co Ltd [1968] 1 WLR 1844

A company's capital consisted of 20,000 preferred shares of 10 shillings each, and 50,000 ordinary shares of 1s each. By Art 8 of the articles of association, in order to 'affect, modify, deal with or abrogate in any manner' the rights and privileges attaching to any particular class of shares, an extraordinary resolution, passed at a separate general meeting of the members of that class, was required, the quorum necessary at such meeting being members holding or representing by proxy three-fourths of the capital paid up, or credited as paid up, on the issued shares of that class. Article 21 provided that 'the net profits of the company which the directors shall determine to distribute by way of dividend in any year' should be applied, first, in paying a dividend of 10 per cent on the preferred shares, secondly, in distributing to the ordinary shareholders an amount equivalent to the total sum paid as dividend to the preferred shareholders, and thirdly, 'the balance of profits' was to be divided equally between the preferred and ordinary shareholders.

Article 24 provided that, on a winding up, the preferred shareholders were first to receive the capital paid up on their shares, then 'the surplus assets (if any)' were to be applied in repayment of the capital paid up, or credited as paid up, on the ordinary shares, 'the excess (if any)' to be distributed among the ordinary shareholders in proportion to their shareholding, at the commencement of the winding-up. Every share carried one vote at a general meeting and consequently the ordinary shareholders could carry an ordinary resolution, but not a special or extraordinary resolution, against the holders of the preferred shares, if all the latter opposed it.

On 8 July 1968, at an extraordinary general meeting of the company, a special resolution was passed to reduce the capital of the company by repaying the capital paid up on the preferred shares, together with a premium of 5s per share out of money surplus to the company's needs. No separate meeting of the preferred shareholders had been held, but the owner of all, or virtually all, of the ordinary shares approved the proposal, and a large number of the preferred shares were held by the holder or holders of the ordinary shares. The company's business was very profitable, and dividends totalling 1,000 per cent had been paid to the preferred shareholders during the seven years ending 30 September 1966, and a further 100 per cent gross had been proposed for the period from 1 October 1966, to 31 March 1968, at which date £324,924 stood to the credit of the revenue reserve, from which, if it were to be distributed, the preferred shareholders would receive 1,625 per cent on their shares. Some preferred shares had, however, been sold during 1966 and 1967 at 11s per share.

A petition seeking the court's sanction to the proposed reduction was opposed by the holder of 80 preferred shares on the grounds (1) that it was an abrogation of the rights attached to the preferred shares which required an extraordinary resolution to be passed at a separate class meeting, and that no such meeting had been held; (2) that the failure to obtain the preferred shareholders' approval prevented the dissentient minority from availing themselves of the protection intended to be given by s 72 of the Companies Act 1948, and (3) that it was unfair in that it discriminated against the holders of the preferred shares by preventing them from sharing in the fruits either of the company's future or its past prosperity; that the preferred shares were, in truth, a form of 'equity' capital, and that the undistributed trading profits belonged to the two classes of shares equally, and were not included in the 'surplus assets' referred to in Art 24. It was further contended that there was no present prospect of the company being wound up and that continued large distributions of profits were to be anticipated.

Held – (1) The proposed reduction of the company's capital, by means of the cancellation of the preferred shares, was in accordance with the rights attaching to the preferred shares, and was not an abrogation of those rights within the meaning of Art 8 of the company's articles of association, and that the liability to prior repayment, forming as it did an integral part of the bundle of rights which went to make up a preferred share, was a liability, of which a person had only himself to blame if he were unaware.

(2) Section 72 of the Companies Act 1948 had no application, since it related to a variation and not to a cancellation of share rights.

(3) That on the true construction of the company's articles of association, Arts 21 and 24 were not inconsistent with each other; that the 'balance of profits', which, under Art 21, was divisible equally between the preferred and ordinary shareholders, related solely to the 'net profits which the directors' should 'determine to distribute' and not to the undistributed profits, and that the natural meaning of Art 24 was that all the property of the company available for distribution in a winding-up, and remaining, after repaying all the paid-up capital, belonged to the ordinary shareholders.

(4) That, therefore, despite the fact that there was no prospect of a winding-up of the company, and that continued large distributions of profits, were to be anticipated, the proposed reduction of capital was not discriminatory or unfair to the preferred shareholders.

It should also be noted that if a company has created reserves by the transfer of retained profits and subsequently suffers a loss of assets, it is the usual practice to write off the loss against the reserves and to reduce share capital only if the reserves are insufficient. Again, where the company has capital reserves such as a share premium account or a capital redemption reserve, the practice is to write off losses against them before reducing share capital. Losses may be written off against revenue reserves by making an appropriate adjustment in the accounts but as we have seen, losses may only be written off by reducing the share premium account or capital redemption reserve if the same steps are taken as are required for reducing share capital.

Acquisition of own shares – generally

Section 658 of the Companies Act 2006 prohibits a company (whether public or private) from acquiring its own shares (whether by purchase, subscription or otherwise), except in accordance with the provisions of Part 18 of the Act. This confirms the common law rule that a company cannot purchase its own shares; *Trevor v Whitworth* (1887) 12 App Cas 409 HL, in which Lord Watson observed:

> One of the main objects contemplated by the legislature, in restricting the power of limited companies to reduce the amount of their capital as set forth in the memorandum, is to protect the interests of the outside public who may become their creditors. In my opinion the effect of these statutory restrictions is to prohibit every transaction between a company and a shareholder, by means of which the money already paid to the company in respect of his shares is returned to him, unless the Court has sanctioned the transaction. Paid-up capital may be diminished or lost in the course of the company's trading; that is a result which no legislation can prevent; but persons who deal with, and give credit to a limited company, naturally rely upon the fact that the company is trading with a certain amount of capital already paid, as well as upon the responsibility of its members for the capital remaining at call; and they are entitled to assume that no part of the capital which has been paid into the coffers of the company has been subsequently paid out, except in the legitimate course of its business.
>
> When a share is forfeited or surrendered, the amount which has been paid upon it remains with the company, the shareholder being relieved of liability for future calls, whilst the share itself reverts to the company, bears no dividend, and may be re-issued. When shares are purchased at par, and transferred to the company, the result is very different. The amount paid up on the shares is returned to the shareholder; and in the event of the company continuing to hold the shares (as in the present case) is permanently withdrawn from its trading capital. It appears to me that, as the late Master of the Rolls pointed out in *In re Dronfield Silkstone Coal Company*, it is inconsistent with the essential nature of a company that it should become a member of itself. It cannot be registered as a shareholder to the effect of becoming debtor to itself for calls, or of being placed on the list of contributories in its own liquidation.

Under s 658(2) if a company purports to act in contravention of this section, an offence is committed by the company and every officer in default. The purported acquisition is also void. It should also be noted that the Companies Act 2006 reinforces this rule with further restrictions:

(a) First of all, according to s 660(2), if the company seeks to avoid the restriction imposed by s 658 by getting a nominee to purchase the shares in question, the shares will be treated as being held by that nominee on his own account and that the company is to be regarded as having no beneficial interest in them. This is particularly relevant as such arrangements could in the past be engineered by the directors to keep themselves in secret control so that when faced with a takeover bid they could frustrate the bidder by arranging for shares to be acquired by nominees of the company, sometimes without too much attention as to when and how they were to be paid for, who would, of course, refuse to accept the bid.

Section 661 goes a stage further and provides that if the nominee fails to meet his financial responsibilities associated with the shares within 21 days of being called on to do so, then:

(i) In the case of shares that he agreed to take as a subscriber to the memorandum, the other subscribers to the memorandum are jointly and severally liable with him to pay that amount; and

(ii) In any other case, the directors of the company when the shares were issued to or acquired by him are jointly and severally liable with him to pay that amount.

Relief may be granted by the court under s 661(4) in cases where a subscriber or a director would otherwise be liable, if it appears to the court that he acted honestly and reasonably and he ought fairly to be excused, taking into account all the circumstances of the case. The relief may be granted either in any proceedings for the recovery of any amount due or upon the application of a subscriber or a director in anticipation of such proceedings.

(b) According to s 670, a lien or other charge of a public company on its own shares is void, except as permitted by this section.

(c) Section 136(1)(a) provides that a company cannot be a member of its holding company, either directly or indirectly by way of a nominee (s 144). Furthermore, under s 136(1)(b), any allotment or transfer of shares in the holding company to the subsidiary or its nominee is void. Exceptions to this rule are outlined in s 138 (subsidiary acting as personal representative or trustee), and s 141 (subsidiary acting as authorised dealer in securities). In addition, s 137 provides that this prohibition does not apply where a company is not a subsidiary at the time of acquisition of the shares but at a later stage becomes one.

(d) Where a public limited company, or nominee of the company, acquires its own shares and those shares are shown in a balance sheet of the company as an asset, then s 669(1) provides that 'an amount equal to the value of the shares must be transferred out of the profits available for dividend to a reserve fund; this amount not being available for distribution'. In other words, this amount is available to protect the interests of the company's creditors.

The exceptions to the rule prohibiting a limited company from acquiring its own shares are contained in s 659 and may be summarised as follows:

(a) the acquisition of shares in a reduction of capital duly made;

(b) the purchase of shares in accordance with a court order under s 98, s 721(6), s 759, and Part 30 of the Act (see below for discussion of unfair prejudice and protection of members);

(c) the forfeiture of shares or the acceptance of shares surrendered in lieu under provisions in the articles for failure to pay any sum payable in respect of those shares.

In addition, s 659(1) provides that a company may acquire any of its own fully paid shares otherwise than for valuable consideration. In other words, the company may acquire them by way of a gift.

The issue of redeemable shares has already been covered in the previous chapter as an exception to this general rule.

Finally, as noted above, under Part 30 of the 2006 Act, a company may be ordered by the court to acquire shares from a shareholder as a remedy under the unfair prejudice provisions contained in ss 994–996.

Purchase of own shares

Generally

Formerly the rule of capital maintenance designed to protect creditors prevented a limited company from using its resources to purchase its own shares from its shareholders. This principle first appeared in case law, the leading case being *Trevor* v *Whitworth* (1887) 12 App Cas 409, and later in company legislation. The strictness of that rule was later relaxed and purchase by a company of its own shares is allowed subject to safeguards. The procedures to be followed are set out in ss 690–708.

Section 690 provides that a limited company having a share capital may purchase its own shares subject to the provisions of Chapter 4 of Part 18 of the Companies Act 2006 and any restrictions or prohibitions that may be contained in the company's articles. Furthermore, s 691(1) sets down the same restrictions as for the redemption of shares; the shares must be fully paid.

Why purchase own shares?

Among the most important reasons for a company's purchase of its own shares are the following:

1 So far as private companies are concerned, it gives their shares some marketability. Individuals may be more easily persuaded to invest in private companies if they know that the company can buy them out even if the other shareholders have insufficient resources to do so.

2 In family companies a shareholder may die or want to, in effect, resign or retire. Perhaps the other shareholders cannot agree how many shares each should take, or they cannot afford to buy them anyway. In order to avoid an outsider taking them the company can buy them.

3 In the case of shareholder disputes, there is now the possibility of reaching a compromise with a member or members whereby they are bought out by the company thus avoiding the introduction of an outsider as the price of getting rid of a disenchanted member.

4 The provision is useful also in the case of executive directors who have taken shares in the company. Suppose a finance director has taken shares in the company but leaves at the end of his contract for, say, a better position. The company can buy his shares so that he truly severs his connection with the company. The shares must be cancelled, but this does not affect the authorised capital and new shares can be issued to the next finance director on appointment.

Types of purchase: generally

There is a 'market purchase' and an 'off-market' purchase. A market purchase includes only purchases of shares subject to a marketing agreement on a recognised investment exchange (i.e. one authorised by the Financial Services Authority: see s 693(5)). An off-market purchase is a purchase of any other types of shares.

Market purchase

According to s 701(1), a company may make a market purchase of its own shares provided that the purchase has been authorised by an ordinary resolution of the members in general meeting. The authority must:

(a) specify the maximum number of shares which the company may acquire under the resolution (s 701(3)(a));

(b) state the maximum and minimum prices which the company may pay for those shares. There will normally be a minimum price set out in the resolution, but for the maximum a formula would be used (e.g. an amount equal to 105 per cent of the average of the upper and lower prices shown in the quotations for ordinary shares of the company in the daily list of the London Stock Exchange on the three business days immediately preceding the day on which the contract to purchase is made) (s 701(3)(b));

(c) specify a date when the authority given by the resolution will expire. This must not be later than 18 months after the passing of the resolution (s 701(5)).

In addition, the authority may:

(a) be general or limited to the purchase of shares of a particular class or description (s 701(2)(a));

(b) be unconditional or subject to conditions (s 701(2)(b)).

The authority given may be varied, revoked or renewed by a further ordinary resolution of the members (s 701(4)).

Section 701(6) provides that a company may complete a purchase after the date of the authority given by the ordinary resolution has expired, given that the contract for the purchase was made before the expiry date and the terms of the ordinary resolution cover execution of the contract after the expiry date.

The ordinary resolution giving the authority must be filed with the Registrar within 15 days of being passed and a copy must be embodied in or annexed to every copy of the articles issued thereafter (s 701(8)). This ensures that the market is aware of the company's intentions as well as the specific limits within which the directors may operate in terms of price, quantity and timescale.

Off-market purchases

Section 694 provides that a company may make an off-market purchase only under a specific contract which has received advance authorisation by a special resolution of the company. That authorisation may be varied, revoked or, if subject to a time limit, renewed by special resolution under s 694(4) and with regard to a public company the resolution must give a date on which the authority will expire, this being not later than 18 months after the date on which the resolution was passed (s 694(5)).

The shareholder whose shares are being purchased should not vote the shares being purchased on a special resolution to confer, vary, revoke or renew an authority, though there is nothing to prevent him from voting against the resolution if he has changed his mind (s 695(2)). If he does, the authority will not be effective unless the resolution would have been passed with the requisite majority without his votes (s 695(3)). If he holds other shares, then he cannot vote at all on a show of hands but can vote those shares on a poll (see further Chapter 21 ➲). Any member of the company may demand a poll on the resolution (s 695(4)).

According to s 696, a copy of the contract of purchase, or a memorandum of its terms if it is not in writing, must be available for inspection by any member at the registered office for at least 15 days prior to the date of the meeting at which the special resolution is to be passed and available at the meeting itself, otherwise the resolution is of no effect.

The contract, or the memorandum of it, must include or have annexed to it a written memorandum giving the names of the shareholders to which the contract relates, if they do not appear in the contract or memorandum (s 696(3)).

The above provisions might appear to rule out the use by private companies of the unanimous written resolution procedure, since the member whose shares were being purchased would, of necessity, be voting for the purchase in respect of all his shares. However, s 695(2) of the 2006 Act states that the person whose shares are being purchased is not to be regarded as a person who can vote in respect of any of his shares. So, the resolution must be agreed unanimously by the other members and the one whose shares are being purchased is not included.

Furthermore, where the 2006 Act requires contracts or documents of one sort or another to be laid before the meeting at which the resolution is passed, that provision does not apply if the written resolution procedure is used. Instead the relevant documents must be supplied to each member at or before the time at which the resolution is supplied to him (s 696(2)).

A written resolution will therefore shorten the procedure since the relevant documents are sent to the members with the resolution.

Private companies: financing the purchase out of capital

Section 709 of the Companies Act 2006 provides that a private limited company may, in accordance with Chapter 5 of Part 18 of the Act, and subject to any restriction or prohibition in the company's articles, make a payment in respect of the redemption or purchase of its own shares otherwise than out of distributable profits or the proceeds of a fresh issue of shares.

Thus, a private family company could purchase the shares of a retiring member and so keep out non-family members even though profits were insufficient to make the purchase in full and the members of the family did not wish to subscribe to a fresh issue which would be enough to pay the full purchase price.

This type of payment is referred to as being a payment 'out of capital' (s 709(2)) but is restricted in scope by way of s 710 which provides that payment may be made by a company out of capital after first applying for that purpose (a) any available profits of the company; and (b) the proceeds of any fresh issue of shares made for the purposes of the redemption or purchase, in order to meet the price of redemption or purchase. In other words, the permissible capital payment (PCP) as per s 710(2).

Available profits are defined under s 711 of the Act as being the profits of the company that are available for distribution (within the meaning of Part 23 of the Act) and are determined according to the procedure outlined in s 712.

According to s 713, in order to be lawful, a payment out of capital by a private company must satisfy the requirements of ss 714 (directors' statement and auditor's report), 716 (approval by way of a special resolution), 719 (public notice or proposed payment) and 720 (directors' statement and auditor's report to be available for inspection).

Section 714 states that the company's directors must make a statement, in the prescribed form (s 714(5)), which must:

(a) specify the amount of the permissible capital payment for the shares in question (s 714(2));
(b) state that having made full inquiry into the affairs and prospects of the company, the directors have formed the opinion:

(i) as regards its initial situation immediately following the date on which the payment out of capital is proposed to be made, that there will be no grounds on which the company could then be found unable to pay its debts (s 714(3)(a)); and

(ii) as regards its prospects for the year immediately following that date, that having regard to (a) their intentions with respect to the management of the company's business during that year; and (b) the amount and character of the financial resources that will in their view be available to the company during that year, that the company will be able to continue to carry on business as a going concern throughout that year (s 714(3)(b)).

In many respects these issues are similar to those found in the solvency statement to be submitted by the directors of a private limited company on a proposed reduction of capital out of court (see discussion of s 643 above) in that the company's directors are required to take into account both contingent and prospective liabilities (s 714(4)). The statement must also have annexed to it a report from the company's auditor (s 714(6)). It is also interesting to note that the Act, under s 715, applies the same criminal liability for negligence as under the insolvency statement.

A special resolution of the company is required to approve the payment out of capital (s 716(1)) and this must be passed on, or within the week immediately following, the date which the directors make the statement required by s 714.

Publicity

Section 719 states that within the week immediately following the date of the resolution under s 716, the company must publish in the *Gazette*, a notice stating that the company has approved a payment out of capital for the purpose of acquiring its own shares by purchase (or redemption) and specify the amount of the permissible capital payment in question and the date of the resolution. The notice must also state where the directors' statement and auditor's report are available for inspection and that any creditor may, within five weeks following the date of the resolution, apply to the court under s 721 for an order preventing the payment.

Section 720 provides that the directors' statement and auditor's report must be kept available for inspection at the company's registered office and give notice to the Registrar as to the place at which these documents are being kept for inspection by any member or creditor of the company (ss 720(3), (4)).

Dissentient shareholders/creditors

If a member who has not consented to, or voted in favour of, the resolution or any creditor of the company wishes to object, then s 721 provides that they may apply to the court for the cancellation of the resolution.

In line with the time requirements contained in s 719, s 723(1) goes on to state that the payment out of capital must be made no earlier than five weeks after the date on which the resolution under s 716 is passed and no more than seven weeks after that date.

Failure by company to purchase shares

Section 735(2) provides that a company is not liable to pay damages in respect of a failure to purchase (or redeem) its shares. However, a shareholder may apply to the court for specific performance of the contract of purchase (or the terms of redemption) but no order is to be made if the company can show that it could not pay the price from distributable profits (s 735(3)).

In a liquidation a shareholder may enforce a contract of purchase (or the terms of redemption) against the company as a deferred debt provided that the due date for purchase (or redemption) was before the date of commencement of the winding-up, unless it is shown that the company could not at any time between the due date for purchase (or redemption) and the commencement of the winding-up have paid for the shares from distributable profits (ss 735(4) and (5)).

In a winding-up, because it is a deferred debt all other debts and liabilities are paid in priority to the purchase price (or redemption price) as are shareholders with a prior right to return of capital (e.g. preference shareholders). Subject to that the purchase or redemption price is paid in priority to amounts due to other members as members, e.g. share capital in a winding-up.

Provisions to ensure preservation of capital

As noted above, companies may purchase (or redeem) shares from profits or from a fresh issue of shares. Where the purchase or redemption is from profits, an amount equivalent to the nominal value of the shares purchased or redeemed must be transferred to a capital redemption reserve. Thus, the creditors' fund is protected because the shares purchased (or redeemed) are replaced by a new issue of shares or a capital reserve.

However, where a private limited company has made a payment out of capital, then a transfer to the capital redemption reserve is only required to the extent that distributable profits have been used in part to fund the purchase of shares (s 734(4)).

Permissible capital payment (PCP)

The following examples show how this is calculated in practice.

(a) Where the PCP is less than the nominal amount of the shares purchased

Here the difference must, under s 734, be transferred to Capital Redemption Reserve (CRR).

Shareholders' funds before purchase

	£
Share capital	100
Share premium	10
Total capital	110
Profit and loss balance	20
Net assets	130

Assume that there is now a purchase of 20 shares of £1 each at a premium of 50p and there is no fresh issue of shares.

The PCP is – cost of purchase £30 less all available profits of £20. **PCP = £10**. The premium is written off to P& L under s 160 and the £10 difference between the nominal value and the PCP is transferred to CRR as s 734 requires.

The journal entries would be as follows:

	£	£
Dr Share capital	20	
Dr Profit and loss a/c	10	
Cr Cash		30
	30	30

(Being purchase of shares at a premium of 50%)

	£	£
Dr Profit and loss a/c	10	
Cr CRR		10
	10	10

(Being transfer to CRR *per* s 171)

Shareholders' funds after purchase

	£
Share capital	80
Share premium	10
CRR	10
Net assets	100

Net assets are reduced because we have used £30 of our cash to buy the shares.

(b) Where the PCP is greater than the nominal amount of the shares purchased

Here, under s 734, the difference is written off to CRR or share premium account or revaluation reserve (if any) or even in the last analysis share capital. Suppose that in the example given in (a) above the company had purchased 30 shares of a nominal value of £1 each at £2 each with no fresh issue.

The PCP is – cost of purchase £60 less all available profits of £20. **PCP = £40**. The nominal amount of the shares purchased is £30, so £10 must be written off against a capital account. We shall take the share premium account because we do not have any other capital reserve, but if that had not been enough we should have had to proceed to reduce the share capital.

The journal entries would be as follows:

	£	£
Dr Share capital	30	
Dr Profit and loss a/c	20	
Dr Share premium a/c	10	
Cr Cash		60
	60	60

(Being purchase of 30 shares at £2 each in accordance with s 734)

Shareholders' funds after purchase

	£
Share capital	70
Share premium	–
Total capital	70
Profit and loss balance	–
Net assets	70

The net assets have been reduced because we have used £60 of our cash to buy the shares.

The above examples apply also, with the necessary changes in nomenclature, to a redemption from capital.

Civil liability of past shareholders and directors

Section 76 of the Insolvency Act 1986 contains a limited procedure for unravelling the acquisition, outlined above. If the company goes into liquidation within one year of the payment being made to the shareholder, that person is liable to return the amount made out of capital to the company to the extent outlined below:

(a) if winding-up takes place within 12 months of a purchase (redemption) from capital and the company's assets are not sufficient to pay its debts and liabilities; then

(b) the person(s) from whom the shares were purchased (or redeemed) and the directors who signed the statutory declaration; are

(c) jointly and severally liable to contribute to the assets of the company, to the amount of the payment received by the shareholder(s) when the company purchased (or redeemed) the shares. There is a right of contribution between those liable in such an amount as the court thinks just and equitable;

(d) those in (b) above, are given a right to petition for a winding-up on the grounds:

    (i) that the company cannot pay its debts; and

    (ii) that it is just and equitable for the company to be wound up.

The purpose of this is to enable them to limit the amount of their liability by initiating a winding-up before the company's assets are further dissipated leading to an increase in the contribution required of them.

Directors are not liable if they had reasonable grounds for the opinion given in the directors' statement under s 714, though the Companies Act 2006 contains its own penalties in this regard under s 715.

Treasury shares

In general terms shares which are purchased by a company must be cancelled and the amount of the company's share capital account reduced by the nominal value of the cancelled shares (s 706). As noted earlier, a company cannot usually become a member of itself.

An exception was introduced under the provisions of the Companies (Acquisition of Own Shares) (Treasury Shares) Regulations 2003 (SI 2003/1116). These have subsequently been restated in Chapter 6 of Part 18 of the Companies Act 2006.

These regulations allow companies listed on the Stock Exchange or the Alternative Investment Market (but not private companies) to buy, hold and resell their shares. The regulations apply only to 'qualifying shares'. These are shares listed on the London Stock Exchange or traded on the AIM or listed on any other European Economic Area Stock Exchange.

Other main points to note are as follows:

- The shares must be purchased from distributable profits since it was thought unlikely that a company would wish to finance the purchase of shares to be held in treasury from the proceeds of a fresh issue of share capital (s 724(1)(b)).

- The company having bought shares to hold in treasury may cancel or sell them at any time including a sale for a non-cash consideration.
- Cancellation will involve a reduction of capital but there is no need for a special resolution of the members or authorisation by the court.
- Consideration received on a sale of treasury shares is to be treated as profits for distribution purposes.
- The maximum number of treasury shares held at any one time must not exceed 10 per cent of the nominal value of the issued share capital of the company. Where there is more than one class of shares each class is subject to a separate 10 per cent limit. Shares held in breach of the 10 per cent limit are subject to mandatory cancellation (ss 725(1) and (2)).
- A company holding treasury shares must not exercise any voting rights attached to them and if it does the votes are void. No dividend or other form of distribution can be made in respect of them.

Disclosure of dealings in treasury shares

Dealings in treasury shares must be disclosed to the market under arrangements made with the Financial Services Authority and the London Stock Exchange. The Listing Rules were amended with effect from 1 December 2003 to take account of treasury shares. The rules state that shares in treasury will remain listed so that new applications for listing are not required when shares are sold out of treasury. However, to protect the market a company will normally be prohibited from buying or selling treasury shares at a time when its directors would be prevented from dealing in the company's shares under the Model Code of Directors' Dealings (see Chapter 15 ◯). A company is prohibited from buying or selling its treasury shares when in possession of price-sensitive information as by insider dealing (see Chapter 15 ◯). Treasury shares may be included or excluded from a takeover offer and the prohibition on directors dealing in share options will not extend to the purchase of options in treasury shares.

Company dealing in treasury shares: not regulated

The Financial Services and Markets Act 2000 (Regulated Activities) (Amendment) (No 3) Order 2003 (SI 2003/2822), as restated in Chapter 6 of Part 18 of the Companies Act 2006, provides that purchasing its own shares to keep in treasury and the subsequent dealing in those shares is not a regulated activity under FSMA 2000 so that the company does not require FSA authorisation, at least for these activities.

Pre-emption rights

The pre-emption rights of existing shareholders on a new issue of shares apply to the sale of shares held in treasury (s 560). These must therefore be offered first to existing shareholders unless the procedures for disapplying pre-emption rights have been followed.

The City Takeover Panel

So far as the Panel and the City Code are concerned the position is as follows:

- Since treasury shares have few rights attached to them the provisions of the City Code and the rules governing substantial acquisitions of shares will not apply to them.
- A sale and transfer by the company of treasury shares will normally be treated like a new issue.

Financial assistance for the purchase of shares

Previous position

The prohibition on the giving by companies of financial assistance for the purchase of their own shares or the shares of their holding companies by someone other than the company was introduced by the Companies Act 1929 and retained in subsequent legislation until 1981.

The object was largely to defeat the asset stripper who might, for example, acquire shares in a company by means of a loan from a third party so that he came to control it and once in control could repay the loan from the company's funds and then sell off its assets leaving the company to go into liquidation with no assets to meet the claims of creditors. The company concerned was usually one whose shares were, perhaps because of the management policies of the board, undervalued.

The sanction of the law designed to deter this sort of activity was a default fine which could be levied following criminal proceedings.

However, following cases such as *Heald* v *O'Connor* [1971] 2 All ER 1105, it was realised that there were civil law consequences since the transactions surrounding the acquisition of the company were illegal. Thus, the loan by the third party was void and irrecoverable at law; if the company had given the lender a debenture to secure the loan, or a guarantee to repay it, these securities were void and unenforceable, as was any guarantee or other security given by anyone else including the asset stripper himself.

The same civil law consequences would apply in so far as a person infringed the present law set out below. Breach of the present law is stated to be 'unlawful' and is attended as before by criminal sanctions, the maximum penalty being a term of imprisonment of two years and/or a fine of unlimited amount.

Problems created by previous legislation

The rule against the giving of financial assistance struck potentially at ordinary commercial transactions of companies as follows:

(a) Management buy-outs

This is the disposal of a company to its management. A holding company may use a buy-out to sell off a subsidiary whose business though successful does not fit the current development plan of the group.

However, the buy-out is more common in the case of private free-standing companies. Suppose that in a family business senior management has reached the age of retirement and is unable to find any purchaser of the business, who knows and can run it successfully other than those employees who are coming up as the next generation of management. In such a case those in management below the owner/directors may use a buy-out technique to acquire the business with the blessing of the owner/directors (but see *Brady* v *Brady* [1988] 2 All ER 617, below).

A management buy-out is commonly achieved by a bank lending the managers the money to buy the shares. Typically the managers can only provide between 10 and 20 per cent of the funds required. The loan is often secured on the assets of the company which management is acquiring and this is the giving of financial assistance and was an infringement of previous legislation.

Nevertheless, it was a popular and useful technique which regrettably operated outside the law.

(b) Other transactions

It was held by the Court of Appeal in *Belmont Finance* v *Williams (No 2)* [1980] 1 All ER 393 that there was an infringement of then existing legislation when Company A bought the share capital of Company B at an over-inflated price and the former owner of Company B used the money to buy shares in Company A.

Belmont Finance was a member of the Williams group of companies and engaged in property development. The directors of Belmont were anxious to get the 'expertise and flair in property development' of a Mr Grosscurth on the Belmont board, but he wanted to be a substantial shareholder in Belmont as well. Mr Grosscurth owned Maximum Finance which was worth £60,000. Belmont agreed to buy Maximum Finance for £500,000 and Mr Grosscurth used that money to buy a substantial stake in Belmont. In later proceedings this transaction, which obviously reduced the net assets of Belmont, was regarded as unlawful financial assistance by Belmont.

Finally, there were even lawyers prepared to state that the purchase of shares in a company by an innocent recipient of dividends from it might be infringing the financial assistance rule.

Thus, some not uncommon commercial transactions were rendered illegal by a rule which was not, it seems, intended to catch all of them.

The Companies Act 2006

The Companies Act 2006 eventually did not implement a number of the Company Law Review proposals to amend the rules relating to financial assistance as applicable to public limited companies. As such, the law is only slightly amended to that found in the previous Act. However, the main change that has taken place under the 2006 Act has been to take private limited companies out of the scope of this rule as contained in ss 677–683.

The prohibition

Under s 678(1) of the Companies Act 2006, it is unlawful for a public company to give a person financial assistance for the purchase of its own shares or those of its holding company, directly or indirectly, for the purpose of the acquisition before or at the same time as the shares are acquired. Section 678(3) goes on to provide that where a person has acquired shares in a company and a liability has been incurred for the purpose of the acquisition, it is not lawful for that company to give financial assistance, directly or indirectly, for the purpose of reducing or discharging the liability if, at the time the assistance is given, the company in which the shares were acquired is a public company.

There is no prohibition on a subsidiary company providing financial assistance for the purchase of shares in its fellow subsidiaries or in a holding company providing assistance for the purchase of shares in one of its subsidiaries. As we have seen, the prohibition is extended to assistance after acquisition as where A borrows money to acquire shares in B Ltd and B Ltd later repays the loan or reimburses A after A has repaid the loan. In this regard, the reference to 'a person' is not confined to individuals but includes registered companies and other corporate bodies.

Section 683 goes on to provide definitions for the following terms outlined within the chapter of the Act: 'distributable profits'; 'distribution'; 'a person incurring liability'; and 'a company giving financial assistance'.

However, a considerable amount relating to the prohibition under s 678 relies upon the definition of the term 'financial assistance' as outlined in s 677 of the Companies Act 2006.

Meaning of financial assistance

Financial assistance is provided if the company concerned makes a gift of the shares or a gift of funds to buy them; or guarantees a loan used to buy its shares; or gives an indemnity to the lender; or secures the loan by giving a charge over its assets to the lender. A company would also give assistance if it waived or released, for example, its right to recover a debt from a person A so that A could use the funds to buy shares in the company.

The 2006 Act also contains a 'sweep-up' provision contained in s 677(1)(d), which refers to 'any other financial assistance given by a company where (i) the net assets of the company are reduced to a material extent by the giving of the assistance; or (ii) the company has no net assets'. In other words, this provides a 'catch-all' provision that may include anything not specifically mentioned elsewhere within s 677(1). The test is not liquidity but net worth based on the actual value of the assets. Thus, a purchase by a company for cash at market value of a fixed asset from a person who later bought its shares would not be financial assistance because the company's net assets would not be reduced and cash would be replaced by the assets.

However, the section would catch artificial transactions affecting a company's assets, as where the company paid twice the market value for an asset in order to enable the seller to buy its shares.

Thus, as we have seen, in *Belmont* the actual transaction was artificial and designed purely to assist the owner of Company B to acquire shares in A at the expense of the assets of A, because Company A paid far more for the shares of B than they were worth, i.e. £500,000 against a valuation of £60,000. The actual deal in *Belmont* would thus infringe this, although what happened is not otherwise a forbidden transaction.

'Net assets' is defined under s 677(2) as the aggregate assets less the aggregate liabilities determined by reference to their actual rather than their book value. With respect to interpreting s 678, it is worth looking at the case of *Brady v Brady*, 1988, where the House of Lords held unanimously that the 'good faith' requirements had been complied with whilst the purpose ones had not.

 Brady v Brady [1988] 2 All ER 617 HL

The first plaintiff and first defendant were brothers who carried on a family business through B Ltd. They argued, and the first plaintiff petitioned under what is now s 994 of the Companies Act 2006 for an order to buy out the first defendant or for the company to be wound up. An agreement was reached whereby one brother (Jack) would acquire the haulage side of the business and the other (Bob) the drinks business, the assets being divided equally with B Ltd left in existence. The defendants then took the view that the assets had not been divided equally and refused to complete. The plaintiffs sued for specific performance. At the trial, the defendants contended only that the agreement had been illegal and *ultra vires* since it required B Ltd to dispose of its assets without consideration, and that the proposed arrangements constituted the giving by B Ltd of financial assistance in connection with the purchase of its own shares contrary to what is now s 678 of the Companies Act 2006. The judge held that the principal purpose of the giving of financial assistance was not to reduce or discharge any liability incurred by any person for the acquisition of shares, but was incidental to the larger purpose of the arrangement and fell within the exception in s 153(2) of the Act. He granted the order of specific performance.

Held – by the House of Lords – that the transfer of assets from B Ltd was *intra vires* and made in good faith and so came within the scope of s 153(2)(b) of the Companies Act 1985 (now s 678(4) of the 2006 Act). But the financial assistance had not been an incidental part of some larger purpose of the company within s 153(2)(a) and so prima facie it did not fall within the exception to the prohibition of what is now s 678 of the Companies Act 2006 against a company giving financial assistance for the acquisition of its own shares. However, there was a conclusive answer to the agreement being rendered unlawful, whereby a private company could give financial assistance for the acquisition of its own shares if the assets of the company providing the assistance were not reduced by the provision of the assistance, or if the assistance was provided out of distributable profits. Since B Ltd could satisfy those provisions, a decree of specific performance would be granted, subject to the defendants being given an opportunity to reinstate defences they had abandoned.

Comment

(i) The House of Lords said that it was not enough to show that there were 'other reasons' for the assistance being given. Reasons were not the same as 'a larger purpose of the company'. In this regard, Lord Oliver noted:

> The ambit of the operation of the section is, however, far from easy to discern, for the word 'purpose' is capable of several different shades of meaning. This much is clear, that paragraph (a) is contemplating two alternative situations. The first envisages a principal and, by implication, a subsidiary purpose. The inquiry here is whether the assistance given was principally in order to relieve the purchaser of shares in the company of his indebtedness resulting from the acquisition or whether it was principally for some other purpose – for instance, the acquisition from the purchaser of some asset which the company requires for its business. That is the situation envisaged by Buckley LJ in the course of his judgment in the **Belmont Finance** case as giving rise to doubts. That is not this case, for the purpose of the assistance here was simply and solely to reduce the indebtedness incurred by Motoreal on issuing the loan stock. The alternative situation is where it is not suggested that the financial assistance was intended to achieve any other object than the reduction or discharge of the indebtedness but where that result (i.e. the reduction or discharge) is merely incidental to some larger purpose of the company. Those last three words are important. What has to be sought is some larger overall corporate purpose in which the resultant reduction or discharge is merely incidental.

(ii) Although the decision is not concerned with a management buy-out but rather a company reconstruction, it could be said that a management buy-out is the 'reason' for the assistance and not 'a larger purpose of the company'.

As we have seen, it is necessary to find 'a larger purpose of the company' of which the giving of assistance is merely an incident. Clearly, if A sells an asset to B Ltd at the proper market price and uses the money to buy shares in B Ltd, then the assistance is exempt because B Ltd has 'a larger purpose' (i.e. the acquisition of the asset), but in the management buy-out it may be a struggle to convince the court that there is a 'larger purpose of the company'.

When is financial assistance lawful?

1 The giving of financial assistance is lawful if the principal purpose of the company's action is not to give financial assistance OR such assistance is given as an incidental part of some larger purpose of the company. In addition, the assistance MUST be given in good faith and in the best interests of the company giving the assistance.

The company's defence, therefore, is founded upon the purpose in giving assistance and since this is a matter of fact to be decided on the evidence it would be as well for the purpose to be set out clearly in the relevant board minutes. A purpose must be established other than the mere giving of assistance and there is also a good faith and best interests of the company requirement. This should prevent the kind of asset stripping referred to at the beginning of this section although there is little doubt that some, seeking to gain profit from purely artificial transactions at the expense of a company's assets, will try to dress up their dealings as some form, for example, of 'reconstruction'.

However, a legitimate management buy-out is hopefully allowed and other ordinary commercial transactions are no longer threatened by illegality. For example, A acquires B. B wishes to transfer its bank balances to A to effect a more efficient disposition of funds within the group. The boards of A and B may both know that A intends to use those balances to reduce indebtedness, e.g. a loan incurred as a result of acquiring B, but this is permitted because reduction of such indebtedness is merely incidental to a larger corporate purpose.

2 The following are also permitted under s 681:

(a) A distribution of assets in Company A by way of dividend or in a winding-up where the distribution is used to buy shares in A or in its holding company or in the case of winding-up A's former holding company (s 681(2)(a)).

(b) An allotment of bonus shares – which in a sense the company assists the shareholders concerned to acquire (the provisions relating to assistance cover acquisition of shares other than for cash but bonus shares are specifically exempt) (s 681(2)(b)).

(c) Any arrangement or compromise under s 110 and Part I of the Insolvency Act 1986, which results, for example, in a liquidator transferring the assets of Company A to Company B so that the shareholders of A receive shares in B into which A is merged which in a sense A's assets have assisted them to acquire (s 681(2)(f)).

Where the funds used for the purchase of the shares in the company or its holding company arise from:

● a reduction of its capital under Chapter 10 of Part 17 of the 2006 Act (s 681(2)(c)); or

● a redemption or purchase of its shares under Chapter 3 and Chapter 4 of Part 18 of the 2006 Act (s 681(2)(d)).

In the case where a company is reducing its share capital the money received by the shareholder in the reduction is most likely to be used to buy shares in the holding company.

(d) A company may lend money to a person which he uses to acquire shares in it or its holding company if lending money is part of the ordinary business of the company as is the case with a bank (s 682(2)(a)). The fact that a company has power to lend money by its memorandum does not make lending money part of its ordinary business unless making loans is one of its main business activities. Neither the loans it ordinarily makes nor the loan which facilitates the acquisition of the shares must be made for the specific purpose of acquiring the shares. The borrower must be free to use the loan as he wishes, and it must be merely coincidental that the borrower uses it to buy shares in the company. So if a person gets a general loan or an overdraft from a bank and uses it or part of it to buy shares in the bank, there is no illegal financial assistance.

(e) The provision by a company, in good faith in the interests of the company, of financial assistance for the purposes of an employees' share scheme is permitted (s 681(2)(b)). This means that assistance is not limited to the provision of money for the acquisition of shares but applies to all forms of assistance for the purposes of an employees' share scheme, e.g. repaying some or all of the borrowings taken out by the scheme in order to buy the company's shares. The giving of guarantees of loans to acquire the company's shares would also be included. A company may finance an employees' share scheme which benefits employees of the group and their dependants and not merely employees of the company. Employee/directors may be included in such a scheme.

(f) A company may make loans to its employees, other than directors, to enable them to subscribe for or purchase fully paid shares in the company or its holding company to be held by them in their own right (s 682(2)(d)).

It should be noted that the lending set out in points (d)–(f) above is permissible in the case of a public company only if the company's net assets are not thereby reduced, or, to the extent that those assets are thereby reduced, if the financial assistance is provided out of profits which are available for dividend. 'Net assets' in relation to a company for this purpose means the aggregate of that company's assets less the aggregate of its liabilities, including provisions, determined by their book value.

Finally, if shares are acquired by a nominee for a public company (not any other person) with financial assistance from the company, then (apart from any infringement of the general law) no voting rights may be exercised by that nominee and any purported exercise of such rights is void. Secondly, the company must dispose of the shares within one year and if this is not done it must cancel them. If the shares are cancelled and the cancellation has the effect of reducing the company's allotted share capital below the authorised minimum, the directors must apply for the company to be re-registered as a private company. Only a directors' resolution is required to make the necessary reduction, application and any alterations to the memorandum that are necessary. There is no need to apply to the court to obtain confirmation of the reduction but any resolution passed by the directors must be filed with the Registrar.

It is worth noting at this point that the 2006 Act does not prohibit a foreign subsidiary from giving financial assistance for the acquisition of shares in its English parent company. There is no need in such a case to follow the 1985 Act procedures. The authority for this is *Arab Bank plc* v *Mercantile Holdings Ltd* [1994] 2 All ER 74.

Relaxation of restrictions: private companies

As noted at the beginning of this section, the Companies Act 2006 has removed the financial assistance prohibition from private companies. Consequently, s 678 only applies to the provision of financial assistance being provided in relation to a public company.

Sanctions for breach of financial assistance rules

Under s 680, the consequences of a breach of the financial assistance rules are considerable, as the following summary shows:

- It is a criminal offence. The company giving the assistance is liable to a fine and the officers in default are liable to imprisonment and/or a fine.
- The company and its officers can be sued and required to compensate any person who suffers loss as a consequence of their unlawful actions.
- Breach of the rules is a breach of fiduciary duty by a director for which the company can claim damages.

Re Hill and Tyler Ltd (In Administration) [2004] EWHC 1261 (Ch)

This was an application by the administrators of a company for directions as to whether arrangements made in the course of the purchase of shares in the company by another company, and in particular security given to the respondents as part of those arrangements, constituted unlawful financial assistance by the company under s 151 of the Companies Act 1985 (now s 678 of the Companies Act 2006); the issues included the validity of a statutory declaration by the company's director and, if it was invalid, the consequence of this on the security provided by the company to the respondents and a loan made by the second respondent to the company. Richard Sheldon QC stated:

The argument can be broken down into three questions: (1) Is a contract involving the provision of financial assistance in contravention of s 151, even where the whitewash procedure is available but not properly complied with, void and unenforceable as a matter of statutory interpretation of s 151? (2) If not, under the common law, is such a contract illegal as to its formation? (3) If not, is such a contract illegal as to its performance?

I consider first whether every contract which constitutes financial assistance within s 151 is rendered void and unenforceable as a matter of statutory interpretation. In *Chitty on Contracts* [29th edn, 2004, Sweet & Maxwell] the following is stated [citations omitted]:

'Unenforceability by statute . . . arises where a statute itself on its true construction deprives one or both of the parties of their civil remedies under the contract in addition to, or instead of, imposing a penalty on them. If the statute does so, it is irrelevant whether the parties meant to break the law or not . . . Where the statute is silent as to the civil rights of the parties but penalises the making or performance of the contract, the courts consider whether the Act, on its true construction, is intended to avoid contracts of the class to which the particular contract belongs or whether it merely prohibits the doing of some particular act . . . It is important to note that where a contract or its performance is implicated with a breach of statute this does not entail that the contact is avoided. Where the Act does not expressly deprive the plaintiff of his civil remedies under the contract the appropriate question to ask is, whether, having regard to the Act and the evils against which it was intended to guard and the circumstances in which the contract was made and to be performed, it would in fact be against public policy to enforce it.

If, on the true construction of the statute, "the *contract* be rendered illegal, it can make no difference, in point of law, whether the statute which makes it so has in mind the protection of the revenue or any other object. The sole question is whether the statute *means to prohibit the contract*." If, on the other hand the object of the statute is the protection of the public from possible injury or fraud, or is the promotion of some object of public policy the inference is that contracts made in contravention of its provisions are prohibited.'

Applying these principles, and having regard to the mischief to which s 151 is directed, I consider that contracts which are entered into in breach of s 151 are rendered illegal by that section. The section provides that it is 'not lawful' for a company to give financial assistance directly or indirectly for the purpose of the acquisition of its own shares. It seems to me to follow that contracts which are entered into in contravention of that section are illegal. In consequence, such contracts are void and unenforceable. Although the consequences on an innocent party may be harsh, it is well recognised that the courts will not lend their assistance to transactions which are rendered unlawful by statute.

Selangor United Rubber Estates Ltd v *Cradock (No 3)* [1968] 1 WLR 1555

In 1957 a company, with an issued capital of £90,000, which carried on business as a rubber company in the Malay States was without a business, having sold its rubber estates, but had liquid assets of about £235,800. B & T Ltd, acting for an undisclosed principal, C, made an offer for the company's stock. The offer was accepted by 79 per cent of the stockholders. The total amount payable for the stock and expenses was £195,000.

The first transaction

It was arranged by C that the company's account with a credit of £232,500 at N Bank should be transferred to a new account at a branch of D Bank where C had an account with a very small credit. At a meeting on 25 April 1958, two draughts for a total of £232,764 were received by D Bank for the company's new account. The company's board resolved to lend 232,500 to W T Ltd at 8 per cent interest and a cheque for £232,500 was drawn on the company's new account in favour of W T Ltd; W T Ltd lent that amount at 9 per cent interest to C and the cheque was indorsed by W T Ltd in favour of C and was paid into his account with D Bank, thus covering the payment of £195,000 to B & T Ltd. The bank made no inquiries before paying that cheque. The 79 per cent of the company's stock was in due course registered in one of D Bank's nominee companies as nominee for C. Both B & T Ltd and W T Ltd knew that C's purpose was to misapply the company's moneys to finance the purchasing of its stock. By 25 April 1958, the company's board of directors had been reshuffled and L and J had been appointed. Later in 1958 L resigned. Both L and J acted exactly as told by C and exercised no discretion or volition of their own. On 26 August 1958, the company's account was transferred to N S Bank where it was opened with a credit of about £700. The usual documents authorising directors to sign for the company's cheques drawn were sent.

The second transaction

On 26 January 1960, it was resolved at a meeting that the indebtedness of W T Ltd to the company and the indebtedness of two nominee companies of C should be taken over, as to £207,500 by C and as to £42,000 by H B Ltd; that a cheque for £207,500 in settlement of C's liability be paid into the company's account; and that bills for a total of £42,000 payable on future specified dates be drawn on H B Ltd in settlement of its liability. There was a further reshuffle of the board of directors. J and one A. J resigned, and B and S were appointed directors. At another meeting held on either 26 January or on 27 January 1960, S was appointed chairman and B secretary. It was resolved that the company should open an account with N S Bank, although it already had opened an account with that bank. The usual banking resolution was passed and a mandate valid for the opening of the account was signed by B and S authorising, *inter alia*, cheques drawn on the account to be signed by the chairman and secretary or any two directors. A cheque for £207,500 was drawn for B from the company's account in accordance with the mandate by S and B and B drew a cheque for the same amount on his own account in favour of C. At an interview with an official of the N S Bank in charge of the branch in the manager's absence it was explained that the cheques were being exchanged for 'internal accounting reasons' or 'internal book-keeping reasons' and all three cheques were debited and credited as directed. On 19 February 1960, C sent the company a cheque for £42,000 in place of the bills drawn on H B Ltd which had been refused. That cheque was part of another series of three cheques and on 25 February 1960, they were debited and credited to the three accounts in the same way as the three cheques for £207,500. The purpose of the second transaction was to finance the purchase by B from C of the stock in the company. S, though he knew the purpose, handed over the company's cheque, without security, to B, but it was not intended that the money paid to the company by the cheques should belong to it, the company serving a conduit pipe for the passage of that money.

On 12 August 1964, following investigations by its inspectors, the Board of Trade issued a writ in the name of the company pursuant to s 169(4) of the Companies Act 1948, claiming, *inter alia*, a declaration that the defendants C, L, J, B and S, being directors, B & T Ltd and W T Ltd, being other parties concerned with the transactions, and D Bank and N S Bank, being the company's bankers, were jointly and severally liable to replace moneys of the company which had been misapplied contrary to s 54 (1) of the Act of 1948. Ungoed-Thomas J noted:

. . . does the principle prevent an action succeeding for breach of trust in doing what is illegal?

In *Steen* v *Law* directors of a company, incorporated in New South Wales, lent the company's funds which the directors had to give financial assistance to purchase the company's shares. The liquidator of the company claimed that there had thus been a breach of a New South Wales section, which, so far as material, was in the terms of s 54 of the Act of 1948; and that the directors had thereby committed a breach of their fiduciary duty to the company and should reimburse the company the sums so illegally applied. It was not contended that the directors were absolved from accounting by reason of the illegality of the loan by the company. Such illegality was clearly before the Privy Council and, if available against such a claim, provided a complete answer to it. Yet the point was neither taken by the defendants nor by the Privy Council; and it seems to me for the very good reason that the company was not relying for its claim on the unlawful loan and the relationship of creditor and debtor thereby created, but upon the misapplication by the directors of the company's moneys by way of the unlawful loan. That is the position with regard to the plaintiff's claim in our case. It was founding its claim, as in our case, not on a wrong done by it as a party to the unlawful loan, but as a wrong done to it by parties owing a fiduciary duty to it. The courts were being invited, as in our case, not to aid illegality but to condemn it. If this were not so, the courts would give redress to companies against directors for misapplication and breach of fiduciary duty which did not involve the company in illegality, but no redress if they were so serious as to involve the company in illegality.

I appreciate that, in the ordinary case of a claim by a beneficiary against a trustee for an illegal breach of trust, the beneficiary is not a party to the illegality; but that, when directors act for a company in an illegal transaction with a stranger, the company is itself a party to that transaction and therefore to the illegality. The company, therefore, could not rely on that transaction as 'the source of civil rights' and, therefore, for example, it could not successfully sue the stranger with regard to rights which it was claimed that the transaction conferred. If, however, property had passed under the illegal transaction, it is common ground that the right which the holding of that property conferred would be good against all the world, since the court would not assist the only party which had a better title, namely the party from whom it passed under the illegal transaction, to recover it. The right of the holder would be assisted by the courts, because it would be a right established by the holding, without having to rely on any right claimed to be conferred by the illegal transaction – and nonetheless because it was in pursuance of the illegal transaction, to which the holder was a party, that the holding in fact arose: (see particularly *Singh* v *Ali*, and *Chettiar* v *Chettiar*). In a claim based on an illegal breach of trust the claimant does not rely on a right conferred or created by that breach. On the very contrary, he relies on a right breached by the breach, as the very words 'breach of trust' indicate. It is only on the footing that there is a breach of trust that the defence of illegality becomes relevant. So it is assumed, for present purposes, that there is a breach of trust against the plaintiff by those who are directors and by those who are claimed to be constructive trustees. The constructive trustees are, it is true, parties with the plaintiff company itself to the transaction which is illegal. The plaintiff's claim, however, for breach of trust is not made by it as a party to that transaction, or in reliance on any right which that transaction is alleged to confer, but against the directors and constructive trustees for perpetrating that transaction and making the plaintiff company party to it in breach of trust owing to the plaintiff company. The breach of trust includes the making of the plaintiff a party to the illegal transaction. So it seems to me clear on analysis that the plaintiff is not precluded from relying on breach of trust by a party to an illegal transaction to which the plaintiff itself is a party, when the breach includes the making of the plaintiff a party to that very transaction. Those who proved to be constructive trustees, sharing the responsibility with the directors for the breach of trust, share the liability too.

The result is that the plaintiff in this case would not, by reason of illegality, be prevented from being reimbursed money paid by it unlawfully under a transaction to which it is a party. But this does not mean that this would nullify the ordinary operation of illegality with regard to companies and parties outside the company, and not being or treated as being a trustee to it. But it would prevent such operation shielding those whose position or conduct makes them responsible as owing a fiduciary duty or as constructive trustee.

Held – although an illegal transaction in a contract or consensual arrangement, itself being forbidden, could not give rise to civil rights a claim could be based on an illegal breach of a right; that, therefore, as against the directors and constructive trustees, the company was not precluded from relying on breach of trust by an illegal transaction to which the company was itself a party when the breach included the making of the company a party to that very transaction; and that, accordingly, the fact that both the transactions in the present case were unlawful and avoided by s 54 of the Act of 1948 did not defeat the company's claims.

Management buy-outs and fair dealing by directors

Schemes of financial assistance given to directors to achieve a management buy-out would be caught and rendered illegal by Part 10 of the 2006 Act – loans, etc. to directors. Thus financial assistance for such a buy-out could only be given personally to management who were not at the time at board level. However, if they later became directors, the outstanding loan would not be illegal unless, for example, unpaid interest was added to the capital sum. However, if the directors of, say, A Ltd, or some of them, wished to buy out the major shareholders of A Ltd, a legal procedure would be for the acquiring directors to form another company, say B Ltd, and borrow money from a bank in B Ltd's name, letting A Ltd give a security over its assets to the bank to secure the loan to B Ltd of which the acquiring directors would form the board. The loan would be used to buy the shares in A Ltd thus making it a wholly owned subsidiary of B Ltd. Although A Ltd would have given financial assistance for the purchase of its own shares, this would be within the law because the assistance would not be the 'principal purpose' but part of a management buy-out.

Financial assistance: auditors' duty

In *Coulthard* v *Neville Russell (A Firm)* [1998] 1 BCLC 143, the Court of Appeal decided that as a matter of principle auditors have a duty of care, not only to the company as client, but also to its directors to advise them that a transaction which the company and its directors intend to carry out might be a breach of the financial provisions of the Companies Act 2006. It will be appreciated that the giving of unlawful financial assistance may affect the contracts concerned with it at civil law and can result in criminal proceedings under which the company may be required to pay an unlimited fine, and its officers, if convicted, may receive a custodial sentence of up to two years and/or an unlimited fine. Because auditors are often asked to advise, and do advise, directors on the treatment of items in the accounts and their likely attitude as auditors to particular future transactions, it may well be that the duty to give advice on the statutory legal position could frequently arise. The decision seems to widen the scope of potential liability of auditors for negligence. The allegations accepted as a basis for a duty of care in this case seem to depend on an omission, i.e. the failure to advise that a particular transaction which the directors tell the auditors they intend to do may be illegal.

Share capital requirements and European law

Finally, it is worth noting the case of *Centros Ltd* v *Erhvervsog Selskabsstyrelsen (Case C-212/97)* [1999] ECR I-1459 in which Centros, a private limited company registered in

England and Wales, applied to the Trade and Companies Board to register a branch of the company in Denmark. The application was turned down by the Board on the grounds that Centros, which did not trade in the United Kingdom and whose share capital had not been paid up, was in fact seeking to establish its principal establishment in Denmark by circumventing the national rules concerning, in particular, the paying up of a minimum capital.

The company subsequently brought proceedings before the national court contending that it satisfied the conditions imposed under national law on private limited companies relating to the registration of a branch of a foreign company, and that it was therefore entitled to set up a branch in Denmark pursuant to the freedom of establishment conferred on it by Articles 52 and Article 58 EC. The Board submitted that its refusal to grant registration was justified by the need to protect creditors and to endeavour to prevent fraudulent insolvencies. The national court stayed proceedings and referred to the Court of Justice for a preliminary ruling the question whether it was contrary to Articles 52 and 58 for a Member State to refuse to register a branch of a company formed in accordance with the legislation of another Member State in which it had its registered office but where it did not carry on any business when the purpose of the branch was to enable the company to carry on its entire business in the State in which that branch was to be set up, thus avoiding the formation of a company in that State, and evading the application of national rules governing the minimum paid-up capital.

The Court of Justice held that the practice of a Member State of refusing, in certain circumstances, to refuse to register a branch of a company which had its registered office in another Member State constituted an obstacle to the exercise of the freedoms guaranteed by Articles 52 and 58. Therefore, even though Member States were entitled to take measures designed to prevent its nationals from attempting improperly to circumvent their national legislation under cover of rights created by Community law, the fact that a national of a Member State chose to form a company in the Member State whose rules of company law seemed to him the least restrictive and to set up branches in that other Member State could not in itself constitute an abuse of the right of establishment. Moreover, the fact that a company did not conduct any business in the Member State in which it had its registered office and pursued its activities only in the Member State where its branch was established was not sufficient to prove the existence of abuse or fraudulent conduct which would entitle the latter Member State to deny the company the benefit of the provisions of Community law relating to the right of freedom of establishment.

Furthermore, the refusal of a Member State to register a branch of a company formed in accordance with the law of another Member State in which it had its registered office on the grounds that the branch was intended to enable the company to carry on all its economic activity in the host State, with the result that the secondary establishment escaped national rules on the provision for and the paying up of a minimum share capital, was incompatible with Articles 52 and 58, in so far as it prevented any exercise of the right to set up a secondary establishment which Articles 52 and 58 were specifically intended to guarantee.

Essay questions

1 Soapstone Ltd has agreed with a merchant bank that the bank is to take a £50,000 equity stake in the company in the form of ordinary shares which will be redeemable in 2011 or earlier at the option of Soapstone Ltd.

Advise the directors as to the funds which can be used for the redemption, and as to the statutory procedure for the issue of redeemable shares. *(Napier University)*

2 Microchip is a public limited company. Allan and Bill are directors of the company who own 85 per cent of its equity shares between them. In addition, Allan also owns certain debentures issued by the company. The remaining 15 per cent of the equity shares is owned by Charles. Allan now wishes to dispose of his shares and debentures so as to enable him to retire to the south of France. Bill and Charles are concerned that the shares and debentures should not fall into the hands of strangers who might disrupt the smooth running of the company. They consult their accountant who devises the following scheme:

(a) Microchip uses reserves in the profit and loss account to purchase the shares and raise the necessary funds from its bank to purchase the debentures; or

(b) Microchip guarantees a private loan which Bill will arrange with his bank so as to purchase the shares and debentures as a gift to his wife; or

(c) Charles obtains a private loan, guaranteed by Microchip, to purchase Allan's shares and debentures.

Advise Microchip plc as to the legal validity of each of the proposed schemes. Would your answers be different if Microchip were a private company? *(University of Plymouth)*

3 Identify and explain the three specific circumstances envisaged by the Companies Act 2006 for a reduction of share capital.

(The Institute of Chartered Accountants in England and Wales)

4 Assume you are the management accountant reporting to the finance director of a public listed company. The finance director has recently undertaken a financial review as part of the company's strategic review process. In his report he has suggested that the company has more funds than are necessary to support its planned growth and that capital should be reduced.

You are required to write a report for the finance director explaining the methods which may be adopted to reduce the capital of the company.

(The Chartered Institute of Management Accountants)

5 (a) State the exceptions to the general rule that a public company must not give financial assistance to any person for the purpose of the acquisition of its own shares.

(b) Milk Bottles Ltd is a profitable small family company whose principal activity is the retail distribution of milk. The elderly directors appoint Kevin, a younger man, to the board. The articles of association require each director to hold 1,000 £1 qualification shares and allow a director two months from the date of his appointment to acquire his qualification shares. Kevin has not got the money to enable him to do this and the company is willing to lend him the necessary finance.

Advise:

(i) the directors as to the procedures they should observe to effect the loan;

(ii) Steven, a director who disapproves of the arrangement, of any action he may take.

(The Association of Chartered Certified Accountants)

6 Section 33 of the Companies Act 2006 provides that the company's constitution shall, when registered, bind the company and the members to the same extent as if they respectively had been signed and sealed by each member, and contained covenants on the part of each member to observe all the provisions of the memorandum and articles.

Explain the effect of this section on the relationships between shareholders and their company, persons acting in another capacity than that of shareholders and the company and between the shareholders themselves. Illustrate your answer with decided cases.

(Glasgow Caledonian University)

7 (a) The general legal principle is that a company has a separate legal existence from that of its members. In what circumstances does that general principle not apply? Give examples of such situations.

(b) Walter is employed as a managing director by Clipse Ltd whose main object is to retail office equipment. His contract of employment contains a clause which states that in the event of his leaving the employment of Clipse Ltd he will not solicit its customers for a period of two years. He resigns his employment and together with his wife Jean forms a new company, Desks Ltd, whose main object is also retailing office equipment. Bill is a salesman employed by Desks Ltd. He is given customer lists by Walter and immediately begins soliciting Clipse Ltd's customers.

In order to raise cash for his new business, Walter enters into a contract to sell his house to Wilf for £450,000. Bill, who has always admired the house, approaches Walter and makes him an offer of £460,000. Walter transfers ownership of the house to Desks Ltd, and on behalf of the company enters into negotiations to sell the house to Bill.

Advise Clipse Ltd and Wilf on any action they can take.

(The Association of Chartered Certified Accountants)

Test your knowledge

Four alternative answers are given. Select ONE only. Circle the answer which you consider to be correct. Check your answers by referring back to the information given in the chapter and against the answers at the end of the text.

1 Jock wants Trent Ltd to give a security over its assets to the Derwent bank so that the bank may lend Jock money to buy shares in Trent Ltd. The position regarding this proposal is:

A It is lawful if the court approves.
B It is lawful if approved by an ordinary resolution in general meeting.
C It is lawful if approved by a special resolution in general meeting or a written resolution.
D It is always unlawful for a company to give financial assistance for the purchase of its shares.

2 The directors of Humber Plc are intending that the company should purchase some of its own shares partly from capital. Amongst other things they must make a statutory declaration containing a statement that in their opinion the company will be able to carry on business as a going concern and will be able to pay its debts as they fall due during a stated period not exceeding:

A Twelve months
B Six months
C Eighteen months
D Two years

3 The directors of Tyne Ltd intend a purchase by the company of its own shares from John, a member, but partly out of Tyne's capital. They have made an appropriate statutory declaration and have also called an extraordinary general meeting of the members. Which of the following resolutions must be passed to approve the proposal?

   A An ordinary resolution.
   B A special resolution.
   C An extraordinary resolution.
   D An ordinary resolution following special notice.

4 What is the maximum permitted period between the passing of a resolution sanctioning a purchase of own shares partly from capital and the date of payment?

   A Fifteen days
   B One week
   C Five weeks
   D Seven weeks

5 The assets of Derwent plc are less than one-half of its called-up share capital. The directors must call an extraordinary meeting of the members to be held not later than 56 days from the date:

   A On which the auditor informed the directors in writing of the capital loss.
   B On which all the directors became aware of the capital loss.
   C On which a director became aware of the capital loss.
   D Of the deposit of a requisition by 15 per cent of the voting members.

Answers to test your knowledge questions appear on p. 645.

Suggested further reading

Armour, 'Share Capital and Creditor Protection: Efficient Rules for a Modern Company Law?' (2000) 63 MLR, 355.

Armour, 'Legal Capital: An Outdated Concept' (2006) 7 *European Business Organisation Law Review* 5.

Daehnert, 'The Minimum Capital Requirement – An Anachronism under Conservation, Parts 1 and 2' [2009] 30 Co Law 3 and 34.

Proctor, 'Financial assistance: New proposals and New Perspectives?' (2007) *Company Lawyer* 28, 3.

Worthington, 'Shares and Shareholders: Property, Power and Entitlement, Parts 1 and 2' (2001) 22 Co Law 258 and 307.

11 Capital maintenance – company distributions

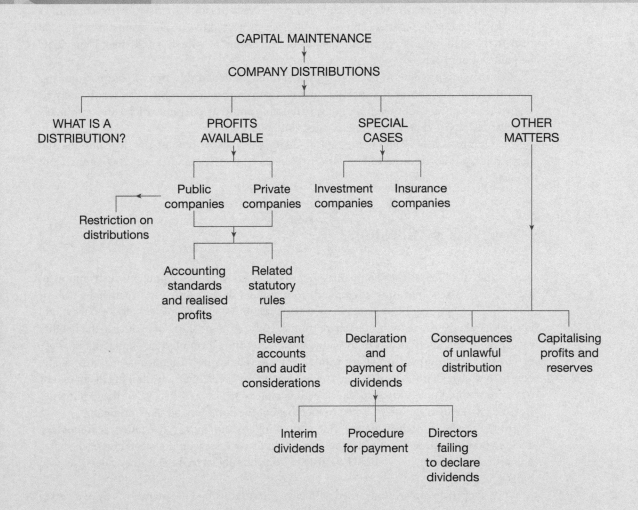

The matter of company distributions is a specific and rather special aspect of capital maintenance. The relevant rules are considered below together with the rules relating to the declaration and payment of dividends.

Profits available for distribution – generally

In earlier times when the narrower term *dividend* was used rather than the current expression *distributions*, it was said that 'dividends may not be paid out of capital'. This meant simply that share capital which the company had received from its shareholders could not be used to pay dividends to them. As we have said before, the creditors take the risk that the company's capital will be lost by business failure but they are protected by the law against it being paid back to the shareholders. An alternative way of expressing the rule is that 'dividends may only be paid out of profits'.

A continuing problem in protecting the creditors' buffer in this area of company law has been the identification of that portion of a company's resources which can legitimately be regarded as capital and, therefore, not distributable and that portion which can legitimately be regarded as profit and consequently distributable.

The Companies Act 1980 made radical changes in regard to company distributions and these rules, which are now to be found in Part 23 of the Companies Act 2006, are set out below.

What is a distribution?

According to s 829 of the Companies Act 2006, it is every description of distribution of a company's assets (not only a dividend) to members of the company, whether in cash or otherwise, except distributions made by way of (a) an issue of shares as fully or partly paid bonus shares; (b) the reduction of share capital: (i) by extinguishing or reducing the liability of any of the members on any of the company's shares in respect of share capital not paid up; or (ii) by repaying paid-up share capital; (c) the redemption or purchase of any of the company's own shares out of capital (including the proceeds of any fresh issue of shares) or out of unrealised profits in accordance with Chapters 3, 4 or 5 of Part 18 of the Companies Act 2006; (d) a distribution of assets to members of the company on its winding up.

Thus, if Boxo Ltd, a television and video hire company, run by, say, five family shareholders, decided that instead of paying shareholders a cash dividend it would instead give each shareholder free equipment, that would be a distribution and subject to the statutory rules discussed below.

Since the provisions are concerned with payments of *dividend* payments by way of *deferred remuneration* to directors, even though there are no realised profits available, they are not caught by the distribution rules (see *MacPherson* v *European Strategic Bureau Ltd* [2000] 2 BCLC 683). However, such payments would be void and recoverable by the company if it was insolvent. Then the creditors' interests would be paramount.

Profits available – public and private companies

The basic rule outlined in s 830(2) of the Companies Act 2006 is that a company's profits available for distribution are: (a) its accumulated realised profits (both revenue and capital) not previously distributed or capitalised (as by being applied in financing a bonus issue or the purchase or redemption of the company's shares with a transfer to a capital redemption reserve), LESS (b) its accumulated realised losses (both revenue and capital) not written off in a reduction or reorganisation of capital. It is also worth noting the wording of s 830(1) which states that a company may only make a distribution out of profits available for the purpose.

From the above provisions it follows that:

1 Unrealised profits, either revenue or capital, are no longer distributable.
2 A realised capital loss following, for example, the actual sale of an asset at a loss will reduce the profit available for distribution. The 2006 Act requires the making good of unrealised capital losses following, for example, the downward revaluation of an asset retained by the company, but only for public companies (see below).

   The depreciation of fixed assets is required and realised losses to be taken into account when calculating the sum available for dividend include amounts written off or retained for depreciation. This ensures that dividends will be restricted to allow for depreciation, subject to what is said below.
3 The use of the word 'accumulated' is important. It means that the position in the current year cannot be regarded in isolation. The profit and loss account is a continuous account. Thus, if Boxo Ltd makes a trading loss of £1,000 in year 1 and £2,000 in year 2, but a trading profit of £1,000 in year 3, it must make a profit in excess of £2,000 in year 4 before any dividend can be paid, unless the company applies to the court for a reduction of capital, so cancelling the losses.
4 Undistributed profits of previous years cannot be brought forward and distributed without taking into account a revenue loss on the current year's trading.
5 An unrealised capital profit cannot be applied in writing off a realised revenue loss.

The provisions also introduce other concepts which are set out below. Insofar as these relate to realised profits reference should be made to the fourth Schedule which states, in effect, that references in the Schedule to realised profits are to such profits as fall to be treated as realised profits, in accordance with principles generally accepted with respect to the determination for accounting purposes of realised profits, at the time when the relevant accounts are prepared.

This implies that it is for the accounting profession to specify in more detail the meaning of realised profits and that the term may be amended from time to time so as to encompass changes in accounting practice.

Restriction on distributions by public companies

Furthermore, with respect to public companies, s 831 of the Act states that a public company may only make a distribution if the amount of its net assets (i.e. the aggregate of the company's assets less the aggregate of its liabilities) is not less than the aggregate of its called-up share capital and undistributable reserves, and if the distribution does not reduce the amount of those assets to less than that aggregate. This means in effect that a plc must deduct any net

		Company A		Company B
		£		£
Share capital		50,000		50,000
Surplus or deficit on revaluation of fixed assets		4,000		(4,000)
Realised profits	7,000		7,000	
Realised losses	(2,000)	*5,000*	(2,000)	5,000
Total share capital and reserves/net assets	=	59,000		51,000
Distributable profit				
(*a*) if private company		5,000		5,000 (no capital maintenance rule)
(*b*) if public company		5,000		1,000 (capital maintenance rule applies)

Figure 11.1 The capital maintenance rule

unrealised losses from net realised profits before making a distribution. A private company need not do so.

Section 831(3) goes on to define the term 'liabilities' as including where the relevant accounts are Companies Act accounts, provisions of a kind specified for the purposes of this subsection by regulations under s 396; and where the relevant accounts are IAS accounts, provisions of any kind.

Furthermore, s 832(4) defines the term 'undistributable reserves' as a company's share premium account; capital redemption reserve; the amount by which its accumulated, unrealised profits (so far as not previously utilised by capitalisation) exceed its accumulated, unrealised losses (so far as not previously written off in a reduction or reorganisation of capital duly made); and any other reserve that the company is prohibited from distributing: (i) by any enactment (other than one contained in this Part); or (ii) by its articles. Section 831(5) goes on to provide that a public company must not include any uncalled share capital as an asset in any accounts relevant for purposes of this section.

Although the above rule applies only to plcs, it should be noted that none of the reserves listed above is distributable by private companies.

An illustration of the capital maintenance rule appears in Figure 11.1.

Realised profits and accounting standards

There are several possible meanings of the expression 'realised' starting with the obvious one of realised in cash. The conclusion reached following research by the accounting bodies was that the preferable approach would be to treat an item as realised if its occurrence can be established from sufficiently reliable measurements. The profit and loss account should be confined to *legally* distributable profits. The treatment of individual items should follow the guidance set out in the relevant Statements of Standard Accounting Practice (SSAPs) and, more recently, Financial Reporting Standards (FRSs), issued by the Accounting Standards Board.

These are not considered further here because they are part of accounting rather than legal practice and should be studied in the accounting context. As a legal point, however, it should be noted that it was stated in *Lloyd Cheyham & Co* v *Littlejohn & Co* [1987] BCLC 303 that 'SSAPs are very strong evidence as to what is the proper standard which should be adopted and unless there is some justification a departure [. . .] will be regarded as constituting a breach of duty'.

While the following of appropriate standards will continue to be a vital part of accountancy practice it will be possible for a court to find liability in negligence even though a relevant standard has been followed if the implication of a decision of the House of Lords in *Bolitho* v *City and Hackney Health Authority* [1997] 4 All ER 771 is taken to its logical conclusion. The Law Lords qualified the long-established principle laid down in *Bolam* v *Friern Hospital Management Committee* [1957] 2 All ER 118 that so long as medical practitioners relied on 'a responsible body of professional opinion' they would not be liable in negligence. The court was not bound, their Lordships said in *Bolitho*, to hold that a defendant doctor would escape liability for negligent treatment or diagnosis just because he leads evidence from a number of medical experts who are generally of the opinion that the defendant's treatment or diagnosis accorded with sound medical practice. The court has to be satisfied that the exponents of the body of opinion relied upon can demonstrate that such an opinion has a logical basis.

Although the *Bolitho* case is a medical one, it is likely to be given general application. It seems now that it will not necessarily be enough to meet an allegation of negligence with the response that the actions complained of are accepted and practised by many others. The court will wish to be satisfied that the practice stands up to logical scrutiny. Canadian courts have already pronounced on the position regarding accountants: the Court of Appeal of British Columbia in *Kripps* v *Touche Ross* (1992) 94 DLR (4th) 284 held against Touche on the ground 'that the accountants had known that a simple application of [a Canadian accounting standard] would omit material information'.

While *Bolitho* is an important case, it is in practice unlikely that the courts will often find that existing accounting standards are illogical, although they have now acquired the right to do so in appropriate circumstances. The decision is perhaps not too surprising. Professional persons cannot really expect to be judges in their own cause.

Related statutory rules

The relevant statutory provisions, running alongside accounting practice, are summarised below.

1 An unrealised profit cannot be applied in paying up debentures or any amounts outstanding on partly paid shares.

2 As we have seen, provisions for depreciation (and contingencies) are to be regarded as realised losses when considering profits available for distribution. In addition, a deficit on the revaluation of an asset gives rise to a provision which must be treated as a realised loss except in two situations when the provision may be treated as an unrealised loss – (a) where

	Dr	Cr
	£	£
Fixed asset at cost (2002)	2,000	
Revaluation (end 2002)	1,200	
Revalued amount before depreciation	3,200	
Revaluation reserve		
Fixed asset revaluation		
realised		1,200
unrealised		(120)
		1,080
Provision for depreciation		
Charge to P and L Account for 2002 (10 per cent of revalued figure at end 2002) (Excess depreciation over 2001 = £120		320

Figure 11.2 Realised profits – provisions for depreciation

the deficit offsets an unrealised profit previously recorded on the same asset; (b) where the deficit arises on a revaluation of all the fixed assets. This applies even though goodwill is not revalued, notwithstanding that goodwill is treated by the formats of the 2006 Act, which deal with the way in which company accounts are to look, as a fixed asset.

The revaluation does not necessitate the changing of the amounts of every fixed asset, but that every such asset be considered for revaluation by the directors. They must be satisfied that those assets whose values have not been changed have an aggregate value not less than their aggregate amount as stated in the financial statements.

The above will not apply unless the notes to the relevant accounts state:

(a) that the directors have considered the value at any time of any fixed assets of the company without actually revaluing those assets;

(b) that they are satisfied that the aggregate value of those assets at the time in question is, or was, not less than the aggregate amount at which they are, or were for the time being, stated in the company's financial statements;

(c) that the relevant items affected are accordingly stated in the relevant accounts on the basis that a revaluation of the company's fixed assets which included the assets in question took place at that time.

It will be noted that the 'aggregate' approach enables losses on some assets to be compensated for by increases in the value of others.

3 Where a fixed asset is revalued upwards and subsequently depreciated, only that part of the depreciation applicable to the value of the asset before its revaluation is treated as reducing realised profits. The excess may be added back to distributable profits.

The entries in accounting terms are set out in Figure 11.2.

4 Development costs, e.g. the costs of developing a saleable company product before any revenue is received from its sale or use, must in general be treated as a realised loss. If they are shown as an asset, i.e. capitalised, they are to be treated as a realised loss, except insofar as the development costs represent an unrealised profit made on a revaluation of those costs. The basic rule of realised loss does not apply either if the directors justify, in the light of special circumstances, that the amount carried forward shall not be treated as a realised loss. For example, the directors may feel that future benefits in terms of revenue from the product can be reasonably anticipated in the near future and may wish to set off the expenditure on development against future revenue from its sale or use rather than treat it as a realised loss in a particular year. The grounds of justification must be included in the notes to the accounts on capitalised development costs as required by the fourth Schedule.

Special cases

Investment and insurance companies are subject to different rules contained in ss 832–835. Basically, the 2006 Act gives an investment company (i.e. a public listed company whose business consists of investing its funds mainly in securities with the object of spreading investment risk and giving its members the benefits of the management of its funds), an option when making a distribution of using either the capital maintenance rule or an asset/liability ratio test under which it can make a distribution *but only out of its accumulated realised revenue profits less accumulated revenue losses* so long as this does not reduce the amount of its assets to less than one and a half times the aggregate of its liabilities immediately after the proposed distribution.

An amount properly transferred to the profit and loss account of an insurance company from a surplus on its long-term business, e.g. life assurance, shall be considered as realised profit and available for distribution provided it is supported by actuarial investigation showing a surplus in the sense of assets over liabilities attributable to the long-term business.

Relevant accounts

The Companies Act 2006 requires companies to decide the question whether a distribution can be made and the amount of it by reference to 'relevant accounts'. The relevant accounts, which must have been prepared to give a true and fair view, will most usually be the last annual accounts. The accounts must have been laid before the company in general meeting, though a private company may elect to dispense with this requirement. In any case the accounts must have been prepared in accordance with the provisions of the Companies Act, or have been so prepared subject only to matters which are not material for the purpose of determining the legality of a proposed distribution.

Audit considerations

The auditors of a company must have made an unqualified report on the accounts. If the report is qualified, then the auditors must state in writing whether, in their opinion, the substance of the qualification is material for the purpose of determining the legality of the proposed distribution. A copy of any statement by the auditors relating to the qualification must have been laid before the company in general meeting, or in the case of a private company, which is not laying the accounts before a general meeting, circulated to the members.

In the case of a holding company, the latest annual accounts would normally be group accounts and reported profit will have been determined by consolidation. If the consolidated accounts are qualified, it may be necessary for the auditors to state whether or not the qualification is material to the calculation of distributable profits of the holding company. From a legal point of view, the distributable profits are the realised profits of the holding company. In *Re Precision Dippings Ltd* [1985] 3 WLR 812 it was held that compliance with these provisions was not a mere procedural matter.

In this case the company paid a dividend of £60,000 to its holding company. This payment exhausted the subsidiary company's cash resources, and some months later it went into voluntary liquidation. The liquidator sought recovery of the payment plus interest since it had contravened the Companies Act and so was *ultra vires*.

For the year in question the auditors' report contained a qualification as to the basis of valuing work in progress. The auditors had not made the statement required by the 1985 Companies Act and the directors were unaware that it was required.

After the company had gone into liquidation, the auditors issued a statement that, in their opinion, the basis of the valuation of work in progress referred to was not material for the purpose of determining whether the dividend of £60,000 would have been in contravention of the Act. This statement was subsequently accepted by a resolution of the shareholders.

The court *held* that the distribution rules are a major protection for creditors, and the requirement for an auditor's written statement when the audit report is qualified is an important part of that protection. This statement has to be available before the distribution is made. The payment of the dividend was *ultra vires* and the holding company held the £60,000 as constructive trustee for the subsidiary.

The resolution of the shareholders could not ratify or confirm the dividend payment. The shareholders could not dispense with or waive the legal requirements.

The above provisions regarding the functions of the auditor do not apply to companies which have dispensed with the audit requirement. For these companies there is therefore no audit or reporting requirement for the last accounts on distribution of profit.

Declaration and payment of dividends

There is no absolute right to a dividend. The question of declaration of dividends is usually dealt with by the articles and the entitlements, as between shareholders, are determined by the class rights attached to the shares. As noted in the case of *Precision Dippings Ltd* v *Precision Dippings Marketing Ltd* [1986] Ch 447, the statutory procedure prescribed for the declaration of a dividend is mandatory and a subsequent resolution of the shareholders cannot rectify matters.

Where the articles follow the pattern of *Table A*, the members can declare dividends by ordinary or written resolution but cannot declare a dividend higher than that recommended by the directors, and if the directors do not recommend payment of dividend, the members cannot declare one either on the preference or ordinary shares. Under such a provision the members in general meeting can reduce the dividend recommended by the directors. As regards the dividend payable in a particular year, the matter is usually already decided because the dividend has been paid before the general meeting is held. However, the members could reduce the dividend recommended and paid which would involve adjustments in the accounts for the following year.

The new model articles for both public (Art 69) and private companies (Art 30) limited by shares require a recommendation from the board of directors for a dividend to be declared together with approval from the shareholders. Once again, the shareholders cannot approve a level of dividend above that recommended by the directors of the company.

Dividend payments have in the past been put to the members for approval at the annual general meeting but where a private company has elected not to hold annual general meetings, approval to the payment of dividend can be sought from the members at any time to suit the administrative convenience of the company in terms of the date on which a dividend payment is to be made but member approval by written resolution is required.

Table A provides that all dividends shall be declared and paid according to the amounts paid up on the shares. Under such an article, no amount credited as paid in respect of calls in advance could be counted as paid for this purpose. Where the company's articles exclude *Table A* and yet do not provide for the method of payment of dividend, dividends are paid on the nominal value of the shares.

A dividend must be paid in proportion to the shares held and at a uniform rate on all shares of the same class. It is not possible, therefore, for the holders of a majority of the shares to pass a resolution to the effect that a larger dividend (or a smaller one) shall be paid on their shares than on those of other members.

Thus if a company has two shareholders, A and B, who hold 60 per cent and 40 per cent respectively of the issued and paid-up ordinary share capital and they both agree that they should be paid the same amount of dividend in regard to the last year's accounts, this is illegal unless the shareholdings are amended to a 50/50 proportion. Thus, a total dividend of £20,000 cannot be split as to £10,000 each. The split must be £12,000/£8,000 unless the shareholding is changed.

Unless the articles otherwise provide, dividends are payable in cash, but *Table A* provides that the company may distribute specific assets in whole or in part satisfaction. *Table A* also provides that payment may be made by cheque sent through the post to the registered address of the holder. In the case of joint holders, it is sent to the one whose name appears first on the register of members, or alternatively as the joint holders may direct *in writing*. Any one of two or more joint holders may give an effectual receipt.

Table A further provides that no dividend shall bear interest against the company, unless otherwise provided by the rights attached to the shares.

Dividends, when declared, are in the nature of a specialty debt and can be sued for up to 12 years from the date of declaration.

Interim dividends

When the directors can see that the company is going to make a sufficient profit by the end of the financial year, they may declare a dividend part way through the year which is in the nature of a part payment of the dividend for the year as a whole. At the end of the year a final dividend is declared in respect of the balance. *Table A* provides that the directors may from time to time pay to the members such interim dividends as appear to the directors to be justified by the distributable profits of the company. Under *Table A* an interim dividend does not require the approval of a general meeting of the members, and is not in the nature of a debt due from the company. Thus, if it is not paid, it cannot be sued for, and there is nothing to prevent the directors subsequently rescinding or varying the dividend (***Lagunas Nitrate Co*** v ***Schroeder*** (1901) 85 LT 22).

Where the directors propose to pay an interim dividend, reference may have to be made to interim accounts (s 836), which in the case of a public company must be such 'as are necessary to enable a reasonable judgment to be made', i.e. accounts complying with the 2006 Act (true and fair view) and signed by a director.

In this regard, s 838 states that interim accounts must be accounts that enable a reasonable judgment to be made as to the amounts of the items mentioned in s 836(1). Where interim accounts are prepared for a proposed distribution by a public company, the following requirements apply. Section 838(3) provides that the accounts must have been properly prepared, or have been so prepared subject to matters that are not material for determining whether the distribution would contravene Part 23 of the 2006 Act.

In this respect, 'properly prepared' means prepared in accordance with ss 395 to 397 (requirements for company individual accounts), applying those requirements with such modifications as are necessary because the accounts are prepared otherwise than in respect of an accounting reference period (s 838(4)). Furthermore, s 838(5) states that the balance sheet comprised in the accounts must have been signed in accordance with s 414. Finally, a copy of the accounts must have been delivered to the Registrar.

It is worth noting that the articles of a company normally provide for interim dividends to be paid solely on the authority of the board of directors, rather than requiring the approval of the shareholders in addition. This approach is replicated in the model articles under the 2006 Act in the form of Art 69 (public companies) and Art 30 (private companies).

Procedure for payment of dividend

The company may close its register for a short time before payment is made in order that the register shall remain static while the procedure for payment is carried out. *Dividend warrants* are prepared in favour of those persons whose names appear on the register, the dividend being declared according to the recommendation of the directors. The warrants are posted to the shareholders as soon as possible after the dividend is declared. However, companies encourage the use of a dividend mandate system under which the payment is direct into the shareholder's bank account.

In the case of *share warrants*, the company will advertise that the dividend is payable in exchange for a coupon bearing a certain number, these coupons being attached to the share warrant. A dividend warrant is then made out in the name of the present holder of the share warrant.

It is current practice not to close registers but to declare a dividend payable to shareholders registered as at close of business on a given date (the striking date). It should be noted that companies are not concerned with equities when paying dividends. The registered shareholder (or the first named of joint holders) on the striking date or the first day on which the register is closed is the person to whom the dividend is paid. If such a person has recently sold his holding *cum* (with) dividend, the buyer's broker will claim it through the seller's broker. If the sale was *ex* (without) dividend, the seller keeps it and no claim arises. The purchase price of the share will take into account the *cum* or *ex* dividend element.

Many companies include a power in their articles to forfeit unclaimed dividends after a reasonable period. However, in the case of quoted companies Stock Exchange regulations insist that such a power shall not be exercised until 12 years or more have passed since the dividend was declared. *Table A* provides that any dividend which has remained unclaimed for 12 years from the date when it became due for payment shall, if the directors so resolve, be forfeited and cease to remain owing by the company.

In the case of public listed companies, the requirements of the listing agreement as appearing in the Listing Rules issued by the Financial Services Authority, which deals with the listing of companies on the London Stock Exchange, would have to be considered. This specialist area is considered in outline later in the text (see Chapter 12 ○).

Directors failing to declare dividends

It may well be that in a private company the directors are happy to take their salaries from the company and refuse to declare dividends. Members who are not on the board may seek advice as to the availability of remedies in this situation. Where the company has articles similar to those of *Table A* nothing can be done under the constitution. Members who find themselves in this situation are usually minority shareholders and so cannot change the articles. Regulation 102 allows the members by ordinary resolution to declare dividends not exceeding the amount recommended by the directors. So if the directors' 'recommendation' is nil, that is it.

However, a failure to pay a dividend may, in certain instances, amount to grounds for the court ordering the winding-up of a company on the 'just and equitable' ground, if it has pursued a restrictive dividend policy and prevented shareholders receiving a return on their investments which they are reasonably entitled to expect (***Re a Company*** (1988) 4 BCLC 506). The court also indicated in ***Re Sam Weller & Sons Ltd*** [1990] Ch 682 that a restrictive dividend policy may justify relief being granted by the courts under s 994 of the Companies Act 2006. Under s 994 (see Chapter 18 ○) a minority could ask the court for a declaration that they have been and are being unfairly prejudiced by the conduct of the board. Any order made by the court would normally be a requirement for the majority or the company to purchase the shares of the minority at a price to be determined usually by the company's auditors or advising accountants. The court is unlikely to declare and continue to declare dividends. As a minority such members would not have sufficient power to remove the board and so s 994 is the only real way of getting out of the company with their capital.

Consequences of unlawful distribution

Section 847(2) provides that if a member of a company knows or has reasonable grounds to believe at the time a distribution was made to him that it contravened Part 23 of the 2006 Act he is liable to repay it (or the illegal part) to the company. Section 847 does not deal with the civil liability of the directors who made the improper distribution. However, since they have misapplied the company's property they are in breach of their fiduciary duty to the company and therefore are jointly and severally liable to the company to replace the dividend paid. This was decided in ***Flitcroft's Case*** (1882) 21 Ch D 519 and means that each director can be called upon to repay the whole amount, and if he does he has a right of contribution against the others. Thus, there are three directors – A, B and C. The dividend wrongly paid is £3,000. A is called upon to pay and does. He may then recover by a claim at law if necessary £1,000 from B and £1,000 from C. Section 847(3) makes it clear that the liability of the members at common law is preserved, and according to the decision in *Moxham* v *Grant* [1900] 1 QB 88 directors who have repaid the dividend to the company have a right of *indemnity* against each shareholder who received the dividend to the extent of the dividend received whether the shareholder concerned *knew or not* that it was paid out of capital.

It may be possible for the directors to claim relief if they have acted honestly and reasonably (see Chapter 21 ○), and there may be a claim against negligent auditors.

Allied Carpets Group plc v *Nethercott* [2001] BCC 81

In this case the High Court ruled that a former managing director who had received dividends that he knew were paid on the basis of inadequate accounts held the dividends on a constructive trust for the company and he was required to repay them to the company. The accounts deliberately overstated both sales and profits by the inclusion of uncompleted transactions. The accounts failed therefore to comply with ss 270 and 271 of the CA 1985 there being also no auditor's report or statement as required by s 271 (s 837 of the CA 2006).

Comment

(i) In this connection, the High Court has also ruled that the directors of a plc who had authorised the payment of dividends other than out of distributable profits were personally liable to repay them to the company, regardless of whether they themselves were the recipients of the dividend (see *Bairstow* v *Queens Moat Houses plc*, High Court [2000] 1 BCLC 549). The amounts were not inconsiderable, being £27.7 million of dividend and £14 million in interest.

(ii) In the matter of *Marini Ltd (liquidator of Marini Ltd)* v *Dickinson* [2003] EWHC 334 (Ch) the High Court was asked to excuse directors, who had paid dividends that exceeded available profits, under s 727 CA 1985 because they had acted honestly and reasonably on accountants' advice. The court agreed that they had so acted but would not exercise its discretion to excuse because the directors had themselves received the benefit of the dividend and could not be left with what was a default benefit.

(iii) In *Re Loquitur Ltd, IRC* v *Richmond* [2003] STC 1394 the High Court ruled that the directors of a company were liable to repay to the company certain dividends declared on the basis of improperly prepared accounts which they had drawn up. The accounts did not make provision for a potential corporation tax liability if a rollover relief scheme failed, which it did. The directors' plea to be excused because they had been assisted by what the court called 'a raft of advisers' in terms of an appropriate scheme failed because they used an alternative scheme not referred back to the advisers before declaring the dividend.

In the situation of an insolvent company, directors and shareholders may be required to pay back certain dividends that have been made in contravention of s 630 of the Companies Act 2006.

It's a Wrap (UK) Ltd (In Liquidation) v *Gula* [2006] BCLC 634

The appellant company (W) appealed against the decision ([2005] EWHC 2015 (Ch)) that the respondents (G) were not liable to repay dividends which they had paid to themselves when the company had had no profits out of which it could lawfully have paid the dividends. In the relevant years W had made trading losses. Despite the fact that there were no profits out of which to pay dividends, G, as the shareholders and directors of W, had caused W to pay them substantial dividends in contravention of the Companies Act 1985 s 263 (now s 630 CA 2006). W brought proceedings for return of the dividends relying on s 277(1) of the 1985 Act (now s 847 CA 2006) which implemented the Second Council Directive 77/91 Art 16 and provided a statutory remedy against a shareholder for recovery of an unlawful distribution paid to him if he knew or had reasonable grounds to believe that it had been made in contravention of the Act. G's case was that the dividends described as such in the company's accounts had been paid as salary and shown as dividends as a tax efficient method of drawing the salaries, which was normal practice for small businesses and had been done on the advice of an accountant. The judge held that s 277(1) required G to know that they were contravening the Act when they paid the dividends and that since they were ignorant of its provisions they were not liable to repay the dividends. G submitted that a shareholder had to have knowledge of the requirement of the Act that the distribution contravened.

Held – allowing the appeal – that s 277(1) had to be interpreted in accordance with Art 16 of the Directive which provided that any distribution made contrary to Art 15 had to be returned by shareholders who received it if the company proved that the shareholders knew of the irregularity of the distribution or could not have been unaware of it. A person was taken to know the content of Community law as soon as it was published in the Official Journal, *Friedrich Binder GmbH & Co KG* v *Hauptzollamt Bad Reichenhall* (161/88) [1989] ECR 2415 applied. Accordingly the right approach to the interpretation of Art 16 was to proceed on the basis that when implemented the general presumption that ignorance of the law was no defence would apply unless on the true interpretation of the Directive it was excluded. On its true interpretation Art 16 meant that a shareholder was liable to return a distribution if he knew or could not have been unaware that it was paid in circumstances which amounted to a contravention of the restrictions on distributions in the Directive, whether or not he knew of those restrictions. The expression 'the irregularity' of the distributions referred to the fact that they had been made contrary to Art 15. It followed that all the company had to show was that the shareholders knew the facts constituting the contravention. In the instant case since G had been aware that the company had no profits they knew that the distributions had been made in contravention of the Act for the purposes of s 277(1).

Capitalising profits

The company may, as an alternative to paying a cash dividend, capitalise its profits (see s 853(3)). This may be achieved by the allotment of fully paid-up bonus shares (or scrip issue, or capitalisation issue as it is sometimes called) by transferring to the capital account undistributed profit equal to the nominal value of the shares issued.

Profits, including unrealised profits, cannot be capitalised unless the articles so provide because, as we have already seen, in the absence of such a provision a shareholder is entitled to the payment of dividend in cash. *Table A* provides for the capitalisation of profits by an ordinary resolution of the members in general meeting (or a written resolution) upon the recommendation of the directors.

Where there is an allotment of bonus shares, the company must make a return of the allotment and since the shares are allotted for a consideration other than cash, the contract constituting the title of the allottees must be registered. *Table A* allows the directors to authorise any person to enter into an agreement on behalf of the members who are to be allotted bonus shares, and this would obviate the need to make a contract with them all.

The actual distribution of the bonus shares among the various classes of shareholders will be based on their right to receive dividend unless the articles or terms of issue otherwise provide.

Reserves

A company is not in general bound to allocate certain of its profits to reserves, although it must *on a redemption or purchase of shares* out of profits set up a *capital redemption reserve*, and it may be that the company is bound under a contract with its debenture holders to set aside a certain sum by way of a reserve to redeem the debentures.

Nevertheless, the articles may provide for the directors to set up *reserve funds for dividend equalisation* or *to meet future liabilities. Table A* does not give such a power, it being implied that provided the reserves are distributable the shareholders are entitled to them. However, where such a power exists, the directors may decide to set aside all the profits, even if this means that no dividend is paid on the preference or ordinary shares, though in such circumstances there may be a petition under s 994 by a member or members on the grounds of 'unfair prejudice' (see Chapter 18 ○).

Essay questions

1 Explain the rules of company law which regulate the making of distributions by public companies, private companies and investment companies. Indicate also the consequences which can follow the making of an unlawful distribution.

(The Association of Chartered Certified Accountants)

2 The summarised draft balance sheet of a company as on 31 March 200X was as follows:

	£000
Fixed assets at cost less depreciation	
Land and buildings	1,500
Machinery	60
Fixtures	15
	1,575
Net current assets	925
	2,500
Ordinary share capital	1,600
Profit and loss account	900
	2,500

An independent professional valuation undertaken on 31 March 200X showed valuations of £1,400,000 and £50,000 for the land and buildings and machinery respectively which the directors decided to incorporate into the company's accounting records. They considered that the value of the fixtures was not less than £15,000.

Advise the directors of the maximum amount of profit *legally* available for distribution explaining fully the relevant statutory requirements.

(The Institute of Chartered Accountants in England and Wales)

3 Fred, George and Harry, who run a business buying and selling antiques, have been advised to form a private company to run the business. They seek your advice on the major differences between their present general partnership and the proposed company, and in particular as to the rules relating to company names, contracts entered into prior to the formation of the company and the concept of maintenance of share capital.

(The Institute of Chartered Secretaries and Administrators)

4 Explain the rules applicable to the determination and payment of dividends.

(The Institute of Company Accountants)

5 Give the facts in *Macaura v Northern Assurance Co Ltd* [1925] AC 619 and explain the importance of its *ratio decidendi*. *(University of Paisley)*

6 H plc wishes to change its articles of association to add a clause which states 'any director of the company may be removed from office if all other directors give notice in writing of their desire that the named director be so removed'. You are required to explain the procedure for alteration and discuss the difficulties the company might encounter in adding this new clause.

(The Chartered Institute of Management Accountants)

7 (a) Why must every company have a registered office? What information about the registered office must be published? To what extent can the registered office of the company be changed and what procedures must be observed when it is so changed?

(b) In the absence of a company taking advantage of alternative provisions under the Companies Act 2006, what statutory records must be kept at a company's registered office?

(The Association of Chartered Certified Accountants)

Aid to learning on distributions

These objective testing questions are taken from pilot papers on objective testing published by the Institute of Chartered Accountants in England and Wales and are retained because of their high quality. They take the place in this chapter of the test your knowledge questions devised by the author.

Question A

A dividend may not be paid by reference to a set of financial statements which carry a qualified audit report unless the auditor states in writing that the matter is not material in determining whether the proposed dividend is illegal under the Companies Act. Which of the following might be considered material?

A A qualification disagreeing with certain reorganisation costs being classified as extraordinary.
B A qualification disagreeing with the carrying forward of goodwill arising on consolidation in the consolidated balance sheet.
C A qualification for the non-disclosure of loans to directors.
D A qualification arising from a disagreement as to the book value of stocks.

Answer to question A

The answer is D since disagreement as to the book value of stocks will affect the amount of realised profits in the profit and loss account.

A is a matter of classification, but the requirement for profits available for dividend is whether or not they have been realised.

B is a qualification affecting the consolidated accounts, but the write-off of goodwill on consolidation will not affect the distributable profits of the holding company.

C The auditors are required to disclose loans to directors if not included in the accounts or notes, but this will not affect the distributable profits.

Question B

With reference to the following information, answer questions 1 to 6.

The table below shows the financial status of two companies, Alpha and Beta, at the year ending 31 March 20XX.

	Alpha £m	Beta £m
Unrealised revaluation surplus/(deficit)	350	(300)
Realised capital profits	250	150
Realised revenue profits brought forward	150	150
Realised revenue profits/(loss) for the year	50	(50)

At all times the net assets of the companies after distribution will exceed the statutory minimum.

1 If Alpha is a limited but not a public limited company, what are the profits available for distribution as dividend of Alpha Ltd?

A £50m   B £200m   C £450m   D £800m

2 If Alpha is a public limited company, what are the profits available for distribution as dividend of Alpha plc?

A £50m   B £200m   C £450m   D £800m

3 If Alpha is a public limited company treated as an investment company, what are the profits available for distribution as dividend of Alpha plc?

A £50m   B £200m   C £450m   D £800m

4 If Beta is a limited but not a public limited company, what are the profits available for distribution as dividend of Beta Ltd if the revaluation deficit arises on a revaluation of all the fixed assets?

A Nil   B £50m   C £100m   D £250m

5 If Beta is a public limited company, what are the profits available for distribution as dividend of Beta plc?

A Nil   B £50m   C £100m   D £250m

6 If Beta is a public limited company treated as an investment company, what are the profits available for distribution as dividend of Beta plc?

A Nil   B £50m   C £100m   D £250m

Answers to question B

Q1 The answer is C, £450m.

A only takes account of the current year's realised profits but it is accumulated realised profits that are taken into account.

B excludes capital profits which are available if realised.

D includes revaluation surplus which is not available.

Q2 The answer is **C**. There is no difference between a public and private company in such a case.

Q3 The answer is **B**, i.e. realised *revenue* profits.

Q4 The answer is **D**, £250m. Realised losses must be taken into account but revaluation deficit need not be so long as it relates to all the fixed assets (excluding goodwill).

Q5 The answer is **A**. In a public company a further limitation is that the net assets must not be reduced below the capital and non-distributable reserves.

Q6 The answer is **C**, £100m, since capital profits and losses need not be taken into account provided the company qualifies as an investment company.

Suggested further reading

Niranjan and Navavane, 'A reassessment of fundamental dividend principles' [2009] *International Company and Commercial Law Review* 88.

Payne, 'Unjust enrichment, trusts and recipient liability for unlawful dividends' (2003) LQR 119, 583.

Company flotations

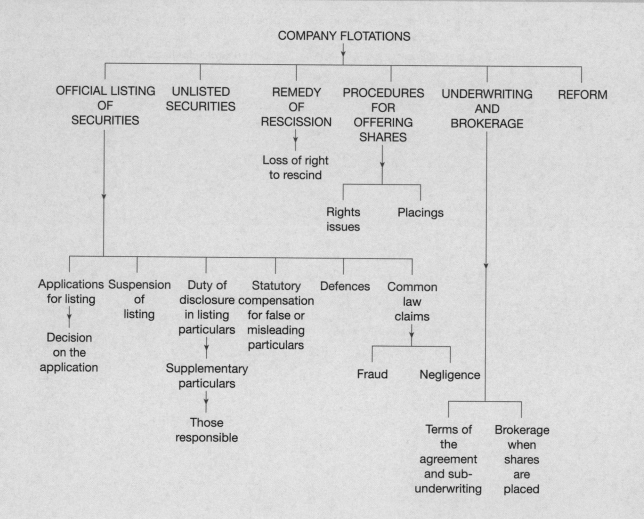

The Financial Services and Markets Act 2000 made major and important changes in the regulation of listing particulars and prospectuses as part of the new regime of investor protection. Section and other references are to the Act of 2000 (FSMA) unless otherwise indicated.

The official system for listing securities on an investment exchange

Under s 72 the UK Listing Authority (UKLA) is part of the Markets and Exchanges division of the Financial Services Authority (FSA) under the Director of Markets and Exchanges. This merger took effect in November 2003. Its main task is to determine whether securities meet the requirements to be admitted to and retained on the Official List of the relevant investment exchange, the London Stock Exchange. Permission to actually trade the securities when they have been admitted to the List is a matter for the London Stock Exchange.

The EC Transparency Directive (Directive 2004/109/EC of the European Parliament and of the Council of 15 December 2004) went into effect in the UK on 20 January 2007. The EC Transparency Directive is wide-ranging dealing with areas such as notification of major share-holdings, dissemination of information, new requirements on the content and timing of financial information such as annual reports and half-yearly reports. Under the Companies Act 2006, the FSA has been given the power to make rules for the purposes of implemented the EC Transparency Directive. As part of this, the FSA has amended the Listing Rules and updated the Disclosure Rules Sourcebook which is now known as the Disclosure and Transparency Rules.

The new Listing Rules, Prospectus Rules and Disclosure and Transparency now make up the Part VI Rules of the FSA's *Handbook of Rules* replacing the former *UKLA Listing Rules* (the 'Purple Book') which were substantially the same as the former *London Stock Exchange Listing Rules* (the 'Yellow Book'). These were adopted when the FSA took over the function of competent authority for listing from the London Stock Exchange in 2000. When the FSA performs functions as the competent authority under Part VI of FSM, in that context the name UKLA is used.

Applications for listing

The Listing Rules (LR) apply to issuers listed, or applying for listing, on the FSA's Official List and to their sponsors. There is a two-tier listing regime: premium listings for equity shares with super-equivalent standards; and standard listings for all other securities listed on an EU directive minimum basis (LR 5). An issuer with a standard listing has fewer obligations under the LR than an issuer with a premium listing. Issuers must comply with the rules that are applicable to every security in the category of listing which applies to each security the issuer has listed.

The application by a company must comply with the LR. However, an application may be refused if granting it would be detrimental to the interests of investors (s 75). Of particular importance is that, in the case of both premium and standard listing, 25 per cent of the company's shares must be in public hands and not, for example, in those of the directors (LR 6.1.19R and LR 14.2.2R, respectively). In addition the expected market value of the securities to be listed must be at least £700,000 in the case of shares and £200,000 in the case of debt securities (LR 2.2.7R (1)). Securities of a lower value can be admitted to listing if the relevant authority is satisfied that adequate marketability can be expected (LR 2.2.8G). The Treasury, which has regulatory powers in the field of financial services, has, for example, designated private companies as being unlistable.

Decision on the application

The FSA has six months to consider an application. Where listing is granted, the applicant must be given written notice. If the FSA refuses the application, there are rejection procedures that the FSA must follow, including the right of the applicant to appeal to the Financial Services and Markets Tribunal set up under Part IX of the FSMA (ss 75 and 76).

Discontinuance and suspension of listing

The FSA has discretion to suspend a listing for a while or discontinue it altogether where it is satisfied that there are special circumstances that preclude normal dealing in the shares, as where there appears to be insider dealing in them on the basis of inside information, e.g. a bid for the company not known to the public. The FSA will often need to act quickly and so need not use its rejection procedures, but if it refuses to cancel its decision to suspend a listing, it will have to follow rejection procedures. In any case, the holders of the securities cannot challenge the decisions of the FSA by judicial review through the courts (see ss 77 and 78 and *R v International Stock Exchange of the United Kingdom and the Republic of Ireland, ex parte Else (1982) Ltd* [1993] BCC 11).

Listing particulars and other documents

Prospectuses and listing particulars must be approved by the FSA. Publication and advertising before the shares can actually be listed is covered in the Prospectus Rules. The requirements for publication of a prospectus are set out in the Prospectus Rules. The requirement to file a copy of a prospectus or listing particulars with the Registrar of Companies however is no longer applicable (s 83 repealed by Prospectus Regulations 2005/1433, Sch 1, para 4).

General duty of disclosure in listing particulars

In addition to detailed information required by the Listing Rules and any special conditions imposed by the FSA that are beyond the scope of this text, listing particulars must contain all such information as investors and their professional advisers would reasonably require and reasonably expect to find there for the purpose of making an informed assessment of:

- the assets and liabilities, financial position, profits and losses and prospects of the issuer of the securities; and
- the rights attaching to the securities (s 80(1) and (2)).

Once a class of securities has been issued, further issues still require new listing particulars unless it is, for example, a bonus issue.

Supplementary listing particulars

Those responsible for the original particulars are under a duty to notify any change or new matter of which they become aware (s 81). Supplementary particulars must be submitted by the issuer for approval and then filed with the Registrar of Companies and published.

Those responsible are defined by the Treasury in statutory instruments (s 79(3)). They include the issuer or sponsor, such as a merchant (or investment) bank and, of course, the directors of the issuing company.

Default sanctions

The FSA can publicly censure (name and shame) or fine anyone who was a director at the time and was knowingly concerned in the contravention of the Listing Rules. Sponsors such as investment banks may be censured but not fined (ss 89 and 91). In imposing a public reprimand or fine, the FSA must follow its disciplinary procedures (ss 89 and 92–94). Offering securities to the public before a prospectus is issued is an offence punishable by up to two years' imprisonment as well as a fine (s 85(1)–(3)).

The FSA can launch an *investigation* into suspected contravention of the rules (s 97) and institute legal proceedings on behalf of investors for compensation and/or disgorgement of profits for breach of any obligation under the FSMA 2000 and can order an authorised firm to make payment without taking court action (ss 382 and 383).

So far as *investors* are concerned, there is a *separate civil action* for them against anyone responsible for misleading listing particulars and prospectuses (see below).

Prospectuses

When will a prospectus, as distinct from listing particulars, be used to make an issue of shares? Generally, a prospectus must be produced when securities are being issued to the public while the company is still seeking a listing, provided the shares are being offered for the first time. More specifically in order to evaluate the need for a prospectus in conjunction with any issue or offering of shares, one must consider:

1 whether the securities are of a kind to which the Prospectus Rules apply (Sch 11A); or
2 whether the securities are of a kind being offered in circumstances falling within the s 86(1) private placement exemption for which Prospectus Rules 1.2.2 R offers exemption; or
3 whether the Prospectus Rules 1.2.3 R exemption in relation to admissions to trading apply; or
4 whether an application for admission to trading is being made.

If so, a prospectus will be required unless one of the exemptions described above applies (ss 85 and 86).

Sponsors

The FSA requires all applicants for listing to use the services of a sponsor, e.g. an FSA-authorised investment bank, to ensure that the applicant company complies with all its obligations. The FSA may refuse an application to be an approved sponsor (s 88). Sponsors may be censured by the FSA but not fined for breaching any rules on listing imposed on them (s 89).

Compensation for false or misleading statements

Errors in listing particulars and prospectuses make any person responsible for the relevant document liable for any loss caused thereby to anyone acquiring the securities that the document covers (s 90).

Errors include:

- untrue or misleading statements in the document;
- the omission of any matter requiring inclusion by the Listing Rules, except:
  (a) a case where there is no such matter; or
  (b) an omission that has been authorised by the FSA.

The fact that matter required by the Listing Rules is omitted is to be taken as a statement that there is no such matter (ss 82 and 90(3)).

Statutory defences

A person responsible (see below) can avoid liability where he made such enquiries as were reasonable and reasonably believed that the statement was true and not misleading (or properly omitted) when the document was submitted for approval by the FSA, provided that when the securities were later acquired:

- he continued in that belief;
- it was not reasonably practicable to bring the correction to the attention of those likely to acquire the securities;
- he had taken all reasonable steps to bring a correction to their attention; or
- he ought reasonably to be excused because he believed it when the dealings began and now too much time has elapsed (Sch 10, para 1).

There is also a defence where, although no correction was made, the person responsible did not reasonably believe the matter was material and where he reasonably believed a correction had been published. Furthermore, no one is liable to a person who acquired the securities knowing of the error (Sch 10, paras 3, 6 and 7).

Statements by experts

If the statement is made by or on the authority of an expert, such as an accountant, valuer or engineer, and is included with his consent, other persons responsible for the document have only to prove that they reasonably believed that the expert was competent and had consented. There is no need to show that there was reasonable belief in their truth. A correction need only be to the effect that the expert was not competent or had not consented. There is no liability for statements by public officials or in official documents, provided that they have been fairly and accurately reproduced (Sch 10, paras 2, 4, 5 and 8).

The duty to report significant changes continues until dealings begin and after that there is a duty to make reasonable endeavours to issue a correction notice unless, given lapse of time, the document is no longer relevant (ss 80, 81, 90 and Sch 10).

Dealings in the after-market

Acquiring securities includes contracting to acquire them or any interest in them not merely at the time of listing but seemingly also in secondary dealings after issue called the after-market (s 90(7)).

Persons responsible

Under s 79(3) the Treasury defines by statutory instrument those responsible for listing particulars and prospectuses. Currently it is the following:

- the issuer of the securities, e.g. the sponsoring investment bank;
- the directors and proposed directors of the issuing company;
- consenting experts for their own part of the particulars or prospectus.

Common law claims

These are expressly preserved by s 90(6). The position is as follows:

- The normal contractual remedies for breach of contract or misrepresentation apply, including rescission of the contract (but see below). These remedies are against the company.
- Actions against directors, auditors or sponsors will have to be based on the tort of deceit or the tort of negligence since there is no contractual nexus with these persons.

It is not easy to prove deceit since some form of dishonesty must be shown. The burden of proof in negligence is on the claimant but is not so difficult to prove. However, the defendant will only be liable if a duty of care exists and is broken and the loss was within the contemplation of the defendant. The general rule of foreseeable loss is probably too wide for this type of case. The relevant case law appears below.

(a) Fraud claims

Derry v Peek (1889) 14 App Cas 337

The Plymouth, Devonport and District Tramways Co had power under a special Act of Parliament to run trams by animal power and, with the consent of the Board of Trade, by mechanical and steam power. Derry and the other directors of the company issued a prospectus inviting the public to apply for shares in the company and stating that the company had power to run trams by steam power and claiming that considerable economies would result. The directors assumed that the Board of Trade would grant its consent as a matter of course, but in the event the Board refused permission for certain parts of the tramway, and the company went into liquidation. Peek, who had subscribed for shares under the prospectus, brought this action against the directors for fraud.

Held – by the House of Lords – that before a statement can be regarded as fraudulent at common law, it must be shown that it was made knowing it to be untrue, or not believing it to be true, or recklessly, not caring whether it be true or false. On the facts of the case, it appeared that the directors honestly believed that permission to run the trams by steam power would be granted as a matter of course by the Board of Trade, and thus they were not liable for fraud.

Comment

Fraud must be proved to the criminal standard, i.e. beyond a reasonable doubt; not to the civil standard, i.e. on a balance of probabilities. It is thus not easy to sustain an action based on fraud. Furthermore, it will be noticed from this case that the mere fact that no grounds exist for believing a false statement does not of itself constitute fraud. Dishonesty is required.

(b) Negligence claims

As regards *claims in negligence* by those who have purchased in the market, it appears that there is no duty of care on the part of the makers of false statements in listing particulars to those who make market purchases, though there is a duty to subscribers direct from the company. This follows from the restrictive approach to liability in negligence by the House of Lords in *Caparo Industries* v *Dickman*, 1990 (see Chapter 25 ○). This restrictive approach was applied by Mervyn Davies J in the High Court in *Al-Nakib Investments (Jersey) Ltd* v *Longcroft* [1990] 3 All ER 321. The claimant company sued the directors of a company, claiming that it had bought shares in the company under an allegedly false prospectus. This it was said had induced the purchase of 400,000 shares in the newly floated company under the prospectus and directly from the company and had also induced the purchase of other shares in the company on the stock market. The judge held that since the purpose of the prospectus was to invite subscriptions direct to the company and not purchases through the stock market there was no duty of care in negligence in regard to the market purchases, though there was a duty in regard to the shares purchased directly from the company.

There has been some movement in the position at common law since *Possfund Custodian Trustee Ltd* v *Victor Derek Diamond* [1996] 1 WLR 1351. Mr Justice Lightman in the High Court stated that nowadays it is at least arguable that those who are responsible for issuing listing particulars and prospectuses owe a duty of care to subscribers and those who purchase in what may be described as the after-market in reliance on the prospectus. This could place liability on the company's directors and its advisers if they are negligent.

Purchasers in the after-market following an issue with a listing are protected by s 90(7) in terms of statutory remedies. The only advantage of claiming at common law under *Possfund* is that not all of the FSMA 2000 statutory defences are available to the defendant (see above). The only defence at common law is a reasonable belief in the truth of the statement.

Offers of unlisted securities

In previous editions we have discussed offers on the Unlisted Securities Market, which has been replaced by the Alternative Investment Market (AIM). These securities are not part of the FSMA 2000. The Prospectus Regulations 2005/1433 repeal the Public Offers of Securities Regulations 1995 which have governed public offers of unlisted securities in both unquoted and AIM companies for some 10 years. The contents of prospectuses issued by any companies in the UK (whether they be listed, AIM, Ofex or unquoted companies) are now governed by the Prospectus Regulations.

The remedy of rescission

The main remedy for loss resulting from a misstatement in listing particulars is, as we have seen, damages based either on breach of a statutory duty under the FSMA and the Misrepresentation Act 1967, or at common law under the principles of liability for negligent misstatements.

The remedy of rescission involves taking the name of the shareholder off the register of members and returning money paid to the company by him. This is against the modern trend because it goes contrary to the principle of protection of the creditors' buffer which is the major purpose of the many statutory rules relating to capital maintenance.

The modern trend is to leave the shareholder's capital in the company but allow him a remedy for money compensation if the shares are less valuable because of the misstatement and against those who were responsible for the misstatement, such as directors or experts.

The cases which are illustrative of the remedy of rescission are rather old and are not referred to here. Suffice it to say that in order to obtain rescission, the shareholder must prove a material misstatement of fact not opinion (the principles in negligence cover actions for damages for opinions), and that the misstatement induced the subscription for the shares. The action can only be brought by the subscriber for the shares under the prospectus.

The right to rescind is a fragile one, being lost unless the action is brought quickly; or if the contract is affirmed, as where the shareholder has attended a meeting and voted the shares; or where the company is in liquidation or liquidation is imminent.

Procedures for issuing shares

As we shall see in Chapter 13, shareholders in companies today have pre-emption rights, i.e. a right to have new issues offered to them first (s 561, CA 2006). A company that is proposing to allot equity securities (defined in s 560, CA 2006) must offer them to existing shareholders first (that is, on a pre-emptive basis). In essence, a shareholder should be able to protect his proportion of the total equity of a company by having the opportunity to subscribe for any issue of equity securities. This is subject to various exceptions categorised in s 561(a)(5), CA 2006. The company can disapply this right by special resolution (or in the case of private companies by the articles). Listed companies usually propose resolutions to disapply statutory pre-emption rights at each annual general meeting under CA 2006 ss 570 and 571. Listed companies must also comply with pre-emption rules contained in LR 9.3.11R and LR 9.3.12R.

However, in the case of listed companies, since the major shareholders of listed companies are institutions, such as insurance companies, which like to receive offers of new shares, listed companies are in general restricted to a disapplication of only up to 5 per cent of the existing shares. Therefore, *rights issues to existing shareholders* are the major way of financing listed companies in capital terms and not offers directly to the public. The circular that accompanies the rights issue to shareholders is a prospectus and must be approved by the FSA. The circular must contain the detailed requirements set out in the Listing Rules (LR 13.8.2R). The shares are allotted to the shareholders under provisional allotment letters and these can be traded in the market nil paid while the rights offer is open for acceptance. Thus the shareholder can sell his rights without paying the company for them. The purchaser from the shareholder will pay the market price to the shareholder and since rights issues are at a discount to the market value, but not, of course, less than par value, the shareholder will make a profit and will be left with money when he has later paid the company the discounted price. Any shares remaining, as where a shareholder does nothing, will be *placed* by the company's brokers with their clients and any not so taken up will be left with the merchant or investment bank that has underwritten the issue or any sub-underwriters. These are then the two main methods these days of raising equity finance by listed companies. A placing will be on the terms of the rights issue particulars but will not even require those, in full form at least, if the offer is to no more than 50 persons or to professional investors.

Underwriting

Before a company's shares or debentures are issued, agreement is reached with an investment bank that is prepared for a commission to take up (or underwrite) the whole or a part of the shares being offered if not all of the shares are taken up. Under the LR, the underwriting agreement is a material contract. Moreover, where the circular is a prospectus the under-writing agreement must be included into the circular through a summary of its material sections.

It is usual to underwrite even when a company is sound and the shares are popular, since changes, for example in the international situation or the financial state of the country, can affect an issue adversely.

Due to the fact that the payment of underwriting commission could be used as a device to issue shares at a discount, the payment of underwriting commission is controlled by s 553(2) of the CA 2006. Section 553 of the CA 2006 provides that a company may pay a commission to a person in consideration of his subscribing or agreeing to subscribe (whether absolutely or conditionally) for shares in the company, or procuring or agreeing to procure subscriptions (whether absolute or conditional) for shares in the company if: (a) the payment of the commission is authorised by the company's articles; and (b) the commission paid or agreed to be paid does not exceed (i) 10 per cent of the price at which the shares are issued; or (ii) the amount or rate authorised by the articles, whichever is the less.

If there is in existence a *share premium account*, this may be applied to pay the commission on an issue of shares or debentures (s 610, CA 2006).

Terms of the agreement

The underwriter agrees to underwrite a stated number of shares on the terms of a specified prospectus or particulars so that an alteration in these documents before issue may render the underwriting agreement void if it materially increases the risk taken by the underwriters. Thus, in *Warner International & Overseas Engineering Co Ltd* v *Kilburn, Brown & Co* (1914) 84 LJ KB 365 a company altered the draft prospectus on which an underwriting agreement was based by reducing the minimum subscription to be received before allotment from £15,000 to £100 and by stating also that, instead of buying a business it was to acquire by one payment from the proceeds of the issue, it would buy the business by instalments out of future issues. It was held by the Court of Appeal that the underwriters were released from their contract.

The underwriter agrees to take up the balance of shares (if any) not taken up in the issue, and authorises a director or other agent of the company to apply for the shares on the underwriter's behalf. This means that the company can ensure the allotment of the shares to the underwriter, and thus have an action for the full price, and not merely an action for damages if the underwriter merely refuses to apply for them. The authority to apply is expressed to be irrevocable.

Finally, the company agrees to pay a certain percentage of the nominal value of the underwritten shares as commission. The amount of the commission is a matter between the parties and the UKLA, but it must be in line with the risk and not excessive in terms of it if listing is to be obtained.

The liability of the underwriter ends when persons subscribe for the shares, and he cannot be called on to pay if allottees do not meet their liabilities.

Sub-underwriting

Underwriters may enter into sub-underwriting contracts to relieve themselves of the whole or part of their liability. The underwriter pays a commission to the sub-underwriters.

Brokerage

This is a commission paid over to a bank, stockbroker, or issuing house for placing shares. The difference between brokerage and underwriting is that the broker does not agree to take the shares himself, but merely agrees to try to find purchasers. The payment of brokerage could also lead to an issue of shares at a discount and yet it is not controlled by the CA 2006, s 552(3), providing that s 553 shall not affect the power of any company to pay brokerage. However, it can only be paid to a bank, market maker, or issuing house and the rate must be reasonable, though the precise rate is a matter for negotiation according to the degree of risk (*Metropolitan Coal Consumers' Association* v *Scrimgeour* [1895] 2 QB 604).

Reform

The Prospectus Directive: EU developments

This background note is included mainly because of the effect that the EU Prospectus Directive has had on the position of the AIM. As already noted this is a market that has proven quite attractive to the smaller plc wishing to trade its shares on a public market perhaps on conversion from a private company.

The Prospectus Directive came into force on 31 December 2003. Member states were required to implement the new regime by 1 July 2005. On 1 July 2005, the Prospectus Directive was implemented in the UK. In addition to changes to the FSMA and to the Listing Rules of the FSA necessitated by these directives, the FSA introduced further changes to the listing regime.

The main principle

This is that if an issuer is making an offer of securities to the public or its securities are being admitted to trading on a regulated market in the EU it must publish a prospectus and get it approved by the competent authority in what is called its 'home member state'. When the prospectus has been approved in that state it may then be used to offer shares or gain admission to regulated markets in all EU member states without the issuer having to publish any further information or having to get further approval for the document in those member states. The Directive sets out the procedure for identifying an issuer's home member state and states when a prospectus is required and what it should contain. The Directive relates only to the prospectus and does not govern admission criteria and continuing obligations. The UK and other member states will be able to impose additional obligations in those areas but cannot impose any additional disclosure requirements so far as the prospectus is concerned.

Home member state for EU issuers

The home member state for an EU issuer will be the member state in which it has its registered office.

Example

A German company decides to list its shares on the London Stock Exchange. It is not offering shares in Germany or seeking admission of the shares to a regulated market in Germany. Its home member state will be Germany and so the German competent authority will approve the prospectus. The competent authority in England will then have to accept that prospectus as approved and will not be able to require the issuer to publish any additional information. It will have discretion to assess whether the issuer satisfies any eligibility criteria for admission to listing or trading set by it.

The effect on the AIM

The Directive covers secondary markets such as the AIM and in fact one of the European Commission's objects is to catch start-up and high-tech companies and apply more onerous requirements to them. This could have affected the AIM, however, the London Stock Exchange made the AIM an unregulated market from 12 October 2004 in order to avoid the application of the Directive.

Non-EU issuers

These issuers have also been affected by the Prospectus Directive. In regard to non-EU issuers whose securities are already admitted to trading on an EU regulated market the issuer has to choose as its home member state the member state where its securities are first offered to the public or where its securities are first admitted to trading in the EU after the Directive comes into force, i.e. after 31 December 2003. The issuer had to notify its decision to the competent authority of its chosen member state by 31 December 2005.

For non-EU issuers whose securities are not already admitted to a regulated market in the EU the home member state will be the member state where the securities are offered to the public or admitted to trading in the EU for the first time (this is at the choice of the issuer whether or not the issuer has to publish a prospectus) after the date of entry into force of the Directive, i.e. 31 December 2003.

FSA Listing Rules review

The FSA has reviewed the UK Listing Rules resulting in an overhaul of the listing regime on the London Stock Exchange. This review was to some extent driven by the Prospectus

Directive and the result has been the issuance of the FSA Handbook containing the Disclosure Rules, Listing Rules and the Prospectus Rules. As a result of that review, the FSA has made a number of changes to the listing regime that have come into effect.

The two-tier listing regime still stays; however, the two branches are now called 'premium' and 'standard'. Premium listing issuers must meet 'super-equivalent' standards (which also existed previously). These are standards imposed by the FSA that go beyond relevant EU directive standards. Those issuers who have securities that do not meet premium listing standards will have to undertake standard listing. A standard listing involves the EU directive minimum standards (just as it did before). One of the major reform goals which the new requirements attempt to promote is increased harmonisation of obligations within a listing segment regardless of whether the issuer is incorporated in the UK or overseas.

Essay questions

1 'The Financial Services and Markets Act 2000 has provided a more rational and fair procedure to compensate investors who are misled by a misrepresentation in a prospectus (or listing particulars) on an issue of shares by a company. Nevertheless, the common law remedies remain of importance.'

   Discuss. *(The Institute of Chartered Secretaries and Administrators)*

2 Explain 'rescission' and the loss of the right to rescind in respect of prospectuses. *(The Institute of Company Accountants)*

3 Harriet subscribed for shares in Overseas plc on the basis of the prospectus which showed that for the previous five years the company had earned substantial and increasing profits. Shortly after allotment she sold half her shares to Georgina at a large profit. The information in the prospectus was correct but it omitted to mention that much of the business was in the Middle East and, because of various wars, the profits had been materially reduced. The shares are now worth only half the price paid by Harriet. Compare and contrast the remedies available to Harriet and Georgina. *(The Institute of Company Accountants)*

4 (a) 'The law treats a registered company as a separate legal person from its members. To this general rule there are several exceptions.'

   Examine the statement, giving two examples of circumstances in which the court will look at the reality behind the legal façade.

   (b) Dairy Products Limited employed Roundsman to distribute their products in and around Saltash. A clause in the contract of employment provided that in the event of his leaving the employment he would not solicit the company's customers for a period of three years. Roundsman assiduously collected the names and made a list of all their customers, left his employment after three months and formed a company, Farm Produce Limited, which competed with Dairy Products. All the shares in Farm Produce were allotted to Mrs Roundsman and her father, both of whom began soliciting the customers of Dairy Products with the help of the list produced by Roundsman.

   Advise Dairy Products Ltd. *(University of Plymouth)*

5 J is the managing director of Z plc, a listed company. She has recently seen the end of year accounts for Z plc which are to be published in three weeks' time. These accounts show the

company to have substantial liquid assets and J believes that Z plc is likely to attract takeover bidders when the accounts are published. J has decided that she should build up her own personal shareholding in Z plc and has asked you, the company's finance director, whether she can borrow £30,000 from the company and use it to purchase more equity shares in the company.

You are required to advise J. *(The Chartered Institute of Management Accountants)*

Test your knowledge

Four alternative answers are given. Select ONE only. Circle the answer which you consider to be correct. Check your answers by referring back to the information given in the chapter and against the answers at the end of the text.

1 A public company wishes to have its shares listed on the London Stock Exchange. What percentage of its shares must be in the ownership of the public?

   A 10 per cent   B 20 per cent   C 25 per cent   D 30 per cent

2 Fylde plc has issued listing particulars containing a material misrepresentation in a report by an accountant who did not consent to the inclusion of the report in the form in which it was included. Fred purchased shares on the stock market from Joe who was an original subscriber under the listing particulars. Fred is now suing the directors of Fylde plc for monetary compensation.

   A Fred's action against the directors will succeed because the directors are liable for all statements in listing particulars without any defence.
   B Fred's action against the directors will fail because the directors have a defence under the Financial Services and Markets Act 2000.
   C Fred's action against the directors will succeed because the accountant did not consent to the inclusion of his report.
   D Fred's action will fail because he was not an original subscriber.

3 Tay plc has issued listing particulars containing a material misrepresentation. Relying on the particulars, Alf, Bert and Clare subscribed for shares. Alf sold half of his shares immediately. Bert went to an extraordinary general meeting of Tay and voted on a number of matters. Who can rescind the contract to take the shares?

   A Clare   B Clare and Bert   C Bert   D Alf and Bert

4 Which of the following expressions best describes the relationship of company promoter to the company?

   A Fiduciary   B Equitable   C Agent to a principal   D Commercial

5 Prior to the incorporation of Ouse Ltd, Mark, its promoter, made a contract on behalf of the company. Who will be liable if the contract is breached?

   A Mark.
   B Ouse Ltd.
   C The shareholders of Ouse Ltd.
   D The directors of Ouse Ltd.

6 Alf and Bert formed a company called Tyne Ltd. They became the sole directors and took up 50 per cent of the shares, the other shares being allotted to 15 other people. Alf and Bert sold

their business to Tyne Ltd for £130,000, although it was valued at £120,000. How should the profit be dealt with?

A Alf and Bert may keep it.

B Alf and Bert may keep it if they disclose it to the board of directors and obtain the consent of the board.

C Alf and Bert may keep it if they disclose it to all the other shareholders and obtain their consent.

D Alf and Bert cannot keep it in any circumstances.

Answers to test your knowledge questions appear on p. 645.

Suggested further reading

Alcock, 'Five years of market abuse' (2007) *Company Law* 28, 163.

Davies, 'Liability for misstatements to the market: Some reflections' (2009), *Journal of Corporate Law Studies* 9, 295

Haynes, 'Market abuse: An analysis of its nature and regulation', (2007) *Company Law* 28, 323.

Villiers, 'Implementing the transparency directive: A further step towards consolidating the FSAP' (2007) *Company Lawyer* 28, 257.

13 Shares – generally

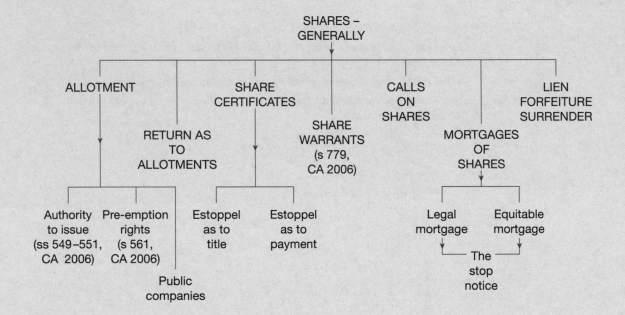

Section 540 of the CA 2006 defines the term 'shares'. Section 540(1) of the CA 2006 identifies that the term 'share', in relation to a company, means share in the company's share capital. A company's shares may no longer be converted into stock (CA 2006, s 540(2)). Section 540(3) of the CA 2006 provides that stock created before the commencement of Part 17 of the CA 2006 may be reconverted into shares. The procedure for this is set forth in s 620, CA 2006. CA 2006, s 540(4)(a) provides that in the Companies Acts references to shares include stock, except where a distinction between share and stock is express or implied. CA 2006, s 540(4)(b), provides that where references to a number of shares include an amount of stock where the context admits the reference to shares shall be read as including stock. References to 'shares' in the Companies Act 1985 and 2006 includes stock. However, now under s 540(2) of the CA 2006 it is no longer possible for a company that has stock at the date this provision came into force (1 October 2009) to reconvert its stock back into shares (s 620, CA 2006).

Prior to passage of the Companies Act 2006, CA 1985, s 14 provided that the memorandum and articles when registered bind the company and its members to the same extent as if they respectively were signed and sealed by each member and contained covenants on the part of each member to observe all the provisions of the memorandum and of the articles. Under the CA 2006, s 33, the provisions of a company are still a unique kind of contract that binds the company and its members. CA 2006, s 33 remains exempt from the Contracts (Rights of Thirds Parties) Act 1999 just as CA 1985, s 14 did. This is so that provisions of a company's constitution will not give rights to persons other than the company and its members.

Under CA 2006, s 303, members may require directors to call general meetings and move resolutions (CA 2006, s 303(5)(a)). They also have the right to inspect certain records and documents which a company is obliged to keep (CA 2006, s 358) and the right to appoint a proxy to represent them at meetings of the company (CA 2006, s 324). Financially, it represents what a member must pay or has paid for the share, and it provides a basis for the calculation of distributions of profits by means of dividends. The assets of the company are owned *by the company*. The members do not have a legal or equitable interest in them (*Macaura* v *Northern Assurance*, 1925, see Chapter 1 ○), and although share capital is in a sense a liability, it is not in the nature of a debt owed by the company, and on a winding-up the shareholders will receive what is left, if anything, after payment of the company's debts and liabilities. Shares are personal estate and not real estate. They are, therefore, in the same category as money or goods. The section removes doubts raised by early cases as to whether shares in companies formed mainly to hold and manage land were not themselves of the legal nature of realty.

Subscribers' contract

Where shares or debentures are offered to existing members, which is obligatory unless waived by special resolution of the members in plcs, the letter of rights or *provisional letter of allotment* is an offer, and no notification of acceptance is required. Acceptance is by conduct, as where the member pays an instalment of the purchase price or renounces the allotment to another person, as where he sells his rights (*Re New Eberhardt Co ex parte Menzies* (1889) 43 Ch D 118). Where there is a *placing* of any balance not taken up, the company's brokers offer the shares to their clients who can accept the offer.

Allotment

Authority to issue

CA 2006, ss 549–551

The CA 2006 removes for private companies the requirement for prior authorisation in certain situations (CA 2006, s 550). The CA 2006 also removes the requirement that a company's constitution have to contain a limit on the number of shares that the directors are authorised to issue.

CA 2006, s 549 states that the directors of a company must not exercise any power of the company to allot shares in the company except as provided for in CA 2006, s 550 (private company with a single class of shares) or CA 2006, s 551 (authorisation by a company). CA 2006, s 549 replaces 80(1), (2), (9) and (10) of the CA 1985. It requires that the directors not allot shares (or grant rights to subscribe for shares or to convert any security into shares) except in accordance with ss 550 and 551 respectively. Under the CA 2006, s 550, where a private company has only one class of shares, the directors may exercise any power of the company to allot shares of that class or to grant rights to subscribe for or to convert any security into such shares, except to the extent that they are prohibited from doing so by the company's articles. CA 2006, s 551 is the provision that covers authorisation by the company to allow directors power to allot shares. The directors of a company may exercise power to allot shares in the company or to grant rights to subscribe for or to convert any security into shares in the company, if they are authorised to do so by the company's articles or by resolution of the company. The special provision in the CA 1985 (s 80(2)) respecting the allotment of shares to employees remains and is now part of the CA 2006, s 549(2).

Allotments made in contravention of the above provisions will not be invalid but the directors are liable to prosecution. Furthermore, the provisions do not apply to shares taken by subscribers to the memorandum or to shares allotted as part of an employees' share scheme. If members refuse to authorise directors to allot shares, the power of allotment, except in relation to employees' shares, lies in the members themselves by ordinary resolution in general meeting. Before leaving the topic of authority to issue shares, it is worth noting that, because of the fiduciary duties which the directors owe the company, they must use the power of allotment for the 'proper purpose', which means to raise capital for the company and not, for example, to put off a takeover bid to keep themselves in control of the company.

Pre-emption rights

As regards ordinary (or equity) shareholders, the CA 2006, s 561 gives a right of pre-emption. This is designed to ensure that the rights of ordinary shareholders are not necessarily affected by the issue of further ordinary shares to others, which has never been regarded as a variation of rights. The section gives pre-emption rights to all equity shareholders in both public and private companies. Each ordinary shareholder must be offered a part of the issue pro rata to his existing holding. The offer must be in writing and delivered to the shareholders personally or by post. Equity shares may be offered to outsiders if they have not been taken up by existing shareholders within the offer period, which must be at least 21 days. Regulation 2 of The Companies (Share Capital and Acquisition by Company of its Own Shares) Regulations 2009

(SI 2009/2022) amended the minimum notice period for pre-emption rights from 21 days to 14 days. The Listing Rules were changed to reduce the minimum rights issue subscription period to 10 business days. Only when this date has expired or when the company has received a reply from every shareholder accepting or refusing the offer may the securities be allotted freely.

If CA 2006, s 561 is not complied with, the company and any officer knowingly in default is liable under the CA 2006, s 568 to compensate shareholders for their loss. Claims by shareholders must be brought within two years of the filing of the return of allotments under which the section was contravened.

A private, but not a public, company may disapply pre-emption rights *without a time limit* by a provision in the memorandum or articles stating this, or by having a provision in the memorandum or articles about pre-emption rights which is inconsistent with the statutory rules CA 2006, s 569. The pre-emption right is disapplied until such time, if any, as the memorandum or articles, as the case may be, are amended to remove the disapplication provision.

Both public and private companies may under CA 2006, ss 570 and 571 disapply pre-emption rights by a provision in the articles or by a special (or written if a private company) resolution of the members. *In either event, the maximum period for disapplication is five years or such shorter period as the articles or special resolution may state.*

Even in a private company which has given the directors a power of allotment for an indefinite period, the members must still approve the disapplication of pre-emption rights though the written resolution procedure can be used to do this. This assumes that the private company has not opted out of the pre-emption provisions altogether (see above).

The pre-emption provisions are triggered by an issue of equity shares for *cash*. Thus pre-emption rights would not apply, e.g. to an issue of preference shares for cash or to the issue of equity shares for a non-cash consideration, as in a merger of two companies where the shares in the company to be acquired are exchanged for shares in the acquiring company and the company to be acquired is then wound up following the transfer of its assets to the acquiring company. In addition, pre-emption rights do not apply where shares are allotted under an employees' scheme. Thus, if the company allots shares to employees under an employees' scheme, it is not obliged to make an offer of shares to the ordinary shareholders who are not employees. However, employees in a share scheme are entitled to participate in the pre-emption rights where an offer of equity shares is made to shareholders generally.

Thus, if a company, A, has an authorised and issued share capital of £100,000 divided into 100,000 ordinary shares of £1 each and 50,000 of those shares are held under an employees' share scheme, then on an increase of capital and a proposal to issue 50,000 additional ordinary shares, each member will be entitled to an offer to subscribe for one share for every two ordinary shares which he currently holds.

The directors must recommend the disapplication of pre-emption rights, and no special resolution to allow it or a special resolution to renew a period of disapplication previously approved may be proposed, unless with the notice of the meeting the directors have circulated a written statement giving their reasons for recommending disapplication and stating the amount which will be paid when the equity shares which are the subject of the disapplication are allotted and giving the directors' justification of that price. There are penalties for the inclusion of misleading matter in this statement.

A shareholder may waive his pre-emption rights, in which case he will not be entitled to receive shares under a pre-emptive offer. In addition, shares which are offered on a pre-emptive basis may be allotted to a person in favour of whom the shareholder entitled to the offer has renounced his rights.

A copy of the resolution must be filed with the Registrar of Companies within 15 days of it being passed (ss 29–30, CA 2006).

The Registrar must under CA 2006, ss 1077 and 1078, publish a notice in the *London Gazette* of the receipt by him of a resolution passed in connection with disapplication of pre-emption rights.

It will be seen from what is said above that even when the directors have been given authority to issue shares they must still observe the pre-emption provisions outlined above.

Public companies: the 25 per cent rule

CA 2006, s 586 provides that shares in a public company cannot be allotted until 25 per cent of the nominal value and 100 per cent of any premium have been received (in cash or otherwise) by the company, and also that the CA 2006, s 593 contains restrictions upon the allotment of shares for a non-cash consideration (see Chapter 15 ●).

An allottee who takes shares in a public company which are not paid up as required is liable to pay the company the balance up to the minimum the company should have received plus interest, which is at present 5 per cent per annum (CA 2006, s 592).

Allotment is usually made by the directors at a properly constituted board meeting, or by a committee of the board where the directors have power to delegate their powers to such a committee.

CA 2006, s 554 sets forth the requirements with respect to registration of allotment. In particular, such registration must take as soon as practicable but in no event later than two months after the date of the allotment. This registration requirement within two month is not applicable where the company has issued a share warrant pursuant to CA 2006, s 779.

Return of an allotment

Under CA 2006, s 555 (as under CA 1985, s 88), whenever a company makes an allotment of its shares, it must within one month of allotment deliver to the Registrar of Companies a *return of the allotments* stating the number and nominal value of the shares comprised in the allotment, the names and addresses of the allottees, and the amount paid up and unpaid on each share, whether on account of the nominal value of the share or by way of premium.

Where shares have been allotted as fully or partly paid up otherwise than in cash, as where, for example, the shares form the whole or part of the purchase price on a sale of land to the company, the consideration must be specified in the return, and if the contract is written, it must be sent with the return. If the contract is not written, a written memorandum of its terms must be made out and filed with the Registrar. These provisions are, of course, strengthened for public companies by CA 2006, s 597 (requirement to file with return of allotment an expert's report on the value of non-cash consideration) (see Chapter 15 ●).

Compliance with these requirements is enforced by a substantial fine on every director, manager, secretary or other officer of the company who is a party to the default. The court may grant relief where the omission to deliver any document within the time prescribed is accidental or due to inadvertence or it is just and equitable to grant relief, and may make an order extending the time for the delivery of the document for such period as the court thinks proper.

Return of allotments and Companies House

CA 2006, s 555 replaces CA 1985, s 88. As under both, within one month of an allotment of new shares in a limited company, the company is required to make a return of allotments to the registrar. Such return must now be accompanied by a statement of capital which is a new requirement. CA 2006, s 556 is applicable to an unlimited company that allots shares of a class with rights not uniform with shares previously allotted.

Share certificates

The CA 2006 contains the provisions with respect to the certification and transfer of securities. Part 21 is divided into Chapters 1 (general provisions on certification and transfer of securities) and 2 (evidencing and transfer of title to securities without written certificate). Share certificates are evidence of a title (CA 2006, s 768). CA 2006, s 769 sets out responsibilities of a company as to issue of certificates on allotment. CA 2006, s 770 covers the procedure for registration of a transfer, namely, that a company may not register a transfer of shares in or debentures of a company unless a proper instrument of transfer is issued. CA 2006, s 771 provides that when a transfer of shares in or debentures of a company has been lodged with the company, the company must either register the transfer or give the transferee notice of refusal to register transfer of shares (or debentures) together with its reasons for the refusal. CA 2006, s 771 is not applicable with regard to a transfer of shares if the company has issued a share warrant in respect of the shares (CA 2006, s 779) or in relation to the transmission of shares or debentures by operation of law (CA 2006, s 771(4)(b)). CA 2006, s 771 is new and implements the recommendations of the Company Law Review. Under CA 2006, s 779 a company limited by shares may if permitted in its articles issue a share warrant stating that the bearer of the warrant is entitled to the shares specified in it.

Every company must, under the penalty of a fine for every officer of the company for each day of the default, within two months after allotment or transfer of shares or debentures have ready for delivery a certificate, unless in the case of an issue of shares the terms of the issue otherwise provide (CA 2006, s 769). CA 2006, s 741 obliges a company to register an allotment of debentures as soon as practice but in any event within two months after their allotment.

The form of the certificate is governed by the articles which may provide for the issue of share certificates under seal, though a seal is not required by law. The certificate will also specify the shares to which it relates and the amount paid up on the shares. It will be signed by at least one director and the secretary (CA 2006, s 768). If the current *Table A* applies, every certificate must be under the 'common seal' of the company especially for use on securities, if it has a seal (CA 2006, s 50(1) (restating CA 1985, s 40)). This requirement can also be found in the Model Articles for Private Companies Limited by Shares (*Article 24*) and the Model Articles for Public Companies (*Article 47*) but it can be a 'common seal' or a 'securities seal'.

Shares must be distinguished by an appropriate number, but if all the shares of the company are fully paid, or all the shares in a particular class are fully paid and rank *pari passu* in all respects, the distinguishing numbers can be dispensed with.

A share certificate under the common seal of the company or the seal kept (if any) by virtue of CA 2006, s 50(1) (restating CA 1985, s 40) specifying any shares held by any member is prima facie, but not conclusive, evidence of the title of the member to the shares.

The articles usually empower the directors to renew share certificates which have been lost or destroyed. A small fee is charged, but the shareholder must give the company an indemnity in case any liability should fall upon it by reason of the possibility of two share certificates in respect of the same holding being in existence. Where the certificate is defaced or worn out, delivery of the old certificate to the company is required.

Chapter 2 to Part 21 concerns the provisions evidencing and transferring of title to securities without written instrument. CA 2006, s 784 sets out the power of HM Treasury and Secretary of State to make regulations about transfer of title to securities without written instrument. CA 2006, s 786 provides that regulations may be made enabling members of a company or of any designated class of companies, to adopt, by ordinary resolution, arrangements under which title to securities is required to be evidenced or transferred (or both) without a written instrument.

The doctrine of estoppel

By reason of the doctrine of *estoppel* a company may be unable in certain circumstances to deny the truth of the particulars in the certificate even though they are incorrect. Once again, it will be appreciated that the law relating to estoppel presupposes the existence of a share certificate. It will be relevant mainly in private companies whose shares will not be transferred through the CREST system. It will also be relevant to those members of public companies using CREST who have opted for a share certificate which will be transferred through the company itself by sending the certificate to the company together with an instrument of transfer.

(a) Estoppel as to title

The mere fact that at some time the company has issued to X a share certificate stating that he is the holder of, say, 100 shares does not prevent the company from denying that X is the holder at some future date. The certificate is only prima facie evidence that X was entitled to the shares *at the date of issue of the certificate.*

However, if the company recognises the validity of X's title by registering or certifying a transfer to Y on the basis of the certificate, the company is estopped from denying Y's title, because it has held out to Y that X has a title.

Where the transfer is a forgery, the original transferee under it will not normally obtain a good title and the company will not normally be estopped from denying his title even if it has issued a share certificate to him. But a purchaser from the original transferee, though not getting a good title, can hold the company estopped by the certificate issued to him because he did not take it under a forged transfer, the signature of the apparent owner being on the transfer form.

Thus, if X owns some shares in a company and his clerk forges X's signature on a form of transfer and sells the shares to Y, then Y will not get a good title to the shares and the company will not be estopped by the certificate issued to him, because at this stage the share certificate is one which the company issued to the true owner, X, and the company has played no part in the deception. If, however, Y transfers the shares to Z before the forgery is discovered, and Z is issued with a share certificate, then the company will be estopped as against Z, and will have to pay him the value of the shares as damages if he chooses to sue the company rather than Y. This is because the company issued a share certificate to Y who was not the owner, thereby facilitating the deception. Nevertheless, Z will not become a member by virtue of estoppel and X's name must be restored to the register.

(b) Estoppel as to payment

In similar circumstances to those outlined above, the company may be estopped from denying that the shares are fully paid, or paid up to the extent stated on the certificate, even though the effect of this is that the shares are issued at a discount. However, the directors who issue the certificate are liable to the company for the unpaid share capital which cannot now be recovered (*Hirsche* v *Sims* [1894] AC 654). This estoppel does not apply to a person such as an original allottee under a prospectus who knows how much he has paid up on the shares.

The doctrine of estoppel does not operate if the certificate itself is a forgery and in addition is issued by a person without apparent authority (*Ruben* v *Great Fingall Consolidated*, 1906).

The estoppel does not seem to be defeated by the fact that the entries in the register of members show who the true owner is even though the register is accessible to the public for inspection, but there can certainly be no estoppel in favour of a person who actually knows the true facts.

Finally, there can, in general, be no claim on an estoppel without some detriment to the person making the claim. The detriment usually arises because the claimant has bought the shares or lent money on a mortgage of them. It is not normally available to a person who has received the shares as a gift.

Share warrants (or bearer shares)

Section 779 of the CA 2006 applies to the issuance of share warrants or bearer shares. A company limited by shares may issue with respect to any fully paid shares a warrant stating that the bearer of the warrant is entitled to the shares specified in it. Public and also private companies may, if authorised by their articles, issue in respect of fully paid shares a share warrant under the common seal stating that the bearer of the warrant is entitled to the shares specified in it.

Article 51 of the Model Articles for Public Companies authorises the issuance of share warrants at the discretion of the board. *Table A* does not authorise the issue of share warrants. Although share warrants could be issued under a prospectus, it has been the case in the past that they have been exchanged for registered shares and the procedures described below relate to that situation. When a share warrant is issued the company must strike out of the register of members the name of the holder of the shares and make the following entries in the register:

(a) the fact of the issue of the warrant;
(b) a statement of the shares included in the warrant, distinguishing each share by its number, if the shares had numbers; and
(c) the date of issue of the warrant.

The bearer of the warrant is, unless the articles provide to the contrary, entitled to be registered as a member on surrender of the warrant.

Difficulties arise as to the rights of holders of warrants because, although they are always shareholders, they are not members, since they are not entered on the register of members, though the bearer of a share warrant may, if the articles so provide, be *deemed* to be a member of the company either to the full extent or for any purpose defined in the articles. Their rights are in fact governed by the articles, but *dividends* are usually obtained by handing over to the company coupons which are detachable from the warrant, the payment of dividend being advertised.

The articles may deprive the holders of share warrants of their *voting rights*, but usually they are given the right to vote if they deposit their warrants with the company, or, if the warrant is deposited at a bank, on production of a certificate from the bank. The holding of share warrants is not sufficient to satisfy a director's share qualification.

A share warrant operates as an *estoppel* that the holder has a title now, and not that he once did when the warrant was issued. Hence, *the company must recognise the holder* unless the warrant is a forgery issued by a person without apparent authority.

A share warrant is also *negotiable*, so that a title to it passes free from defects in the title of previous holders on mere delivery (**Webb, Hale & Co v Alexandria Water Co** (1905) 93 LT 339).

The main advantages of share warrants are anonymity, i.e. no one can find out from the company's public records who the owner of a warrant is, and the ease of transfer. Warrants are merely handed to the purchaser avoiding the formality and expense involved in transferring a registered share. The main disadvantage is that company law leaves it entirely to the company as to how it communicates with its warrant holders. Advertisements, e.g. of meetings, may not always be seen by warrant holders who may therefore not attend and vote.

Calls

It is usual today for a company to specify in the terms of issue that money due on the shares is payable by stated instalments. These are not really calls but are contractual instalments which the member is bound to pay on the dates mentioned by virtue of taking an allotment of the shares. Where the method of instalments is used, the company cannot ask for the money sooner by relying on a general power to make calls under the articles.

A *call proper* is made in a situation where the company did not lay down a date for payment in the terms of issue of the shares. Since shares are generally fully paid up now within a short time after allotment under a fixed instalment arrangement, calls are not common today.

The articles usually give the directors power to make calls subject to certain restrictions, e.g. *Table A* provides that subject to the terms of allotment, the directors may make calls upon the members in respect of any moneys unpaid on their shares (whether in respect of nominal value or premium) and each member shall (subject to receiving at least 14 days' notice specifying when and where payment is to be made) pay to the company as required by the notice the amount called on his shares. A call may be required to be paid by instalments.

A call may, before receipt by the company of any sum due thereunder, be revoked in whole or part and payment of a call may be postponed in whole or part. A person under whom a call is made shall remain liable for calls made upon him notwithstanding the subsequent transfer of the shares in respect of which the call was made. *Table A* must be complied with, otherwise there can be no action against the shareholders in respect of the call.

Table A also provides that a call shall be deemed to have been made at the time when the resolution of the directors authorising the call was passed. Joint holders of a share are jointly and severally liable to pay all calls in respect thereof.

The Model Articles for Public Companies (*Articles 54–62*) cover the procedures involved in the issuance of calls, liability of members to pay a call when asked, forfeiture procedures, etc. The directors may send a call notice to a member requiring the member to pay the company a specified sum of money (the 'call') which is payable in respect of shares which that member holds at the date when the directors decide to send the call notice. A call notice may not require a member to pay a call which exceeds the total sum unpaid on that member's shares (whether as to the share's nominal value or any amount payable to the company by way of premium); must state when and how any call to which it relates is to be paid; and may permit or require the call to be paid by instalments. A member must comply with the requirements of a call notice, but no member is obliged to pay any call before 14 days have passed since the notice was sent.

In those cases where the articles do not give the directors power to make calls, then the company may make them by ordinary resolution in general meeting. The resolution of the board or the members must state the amount of the call and the *date* on which it is payable (**Re Cawley & Co** (1889) 42 Ch D 209). It is essential that calls be made equally on all the shareholders of the same class unless the terms of issue and the company's articles otherwise provide. *Table A* authorises such an arrangement, but that does not entitle directors to make calls on all shareholders except themselves (**Alexander** v **Automatic Telephone Co** [1900] 2 Ch 56) unless the other shareholders *know* and *approve* of the arrangement.

An irregularity in the making of the call may make the call invalid. Any major irregularity in procedure, as where there is no quorum at the meeting, or where the directors are not properly appointed, will have that effect, although CA 2006, s 161 (replacing CA 1985, s 285) may validate the call since it provides that the acts of a director or manager shall be valid notwithstanding any defect which may afterwards be discovered in his appointment or qualification. Minor irregularities will not invalidate a call (**Shackleford, Ford & Co** v **Dangerfield** (1868) LR 3 CP 407).

All money payable by any member to the company under the memorandum or the articles is in the nature of a *specialty debt*. This allows the company to sue for unpaid calls up to 12 years after the date upon which payment became due (Limitation Act 1980, s 8). The directors may charge interest on calls unpaid, and *Table A* provides that if a call remains unpaid after it has become due and payable, the person from whom it is due and payable shall pay interest on the amount unpaid from the day it became due and payable until it is paid at the rate fixed by the terms of allotment of the share or in the notice of the call or, if no rate is fixed, at the appropriate rate (as defined by the Companies Act and currently 5 per cent) but the directors may waive payment of the interest wholly or in part.

The company may also accept payment in advance of calls if the articles so provide. Such payments are loans, and interest is usually paid on them.

Default in payment gives the company a lien over the shares for the amount unpaid.

Table A, Regs 20–22 provide for forfeiture of shares for non-payment of a call or instalment as well as do *Articles 58–62* of the Model Articles for Public Companies.

Mortgages of shares

Mortgages of shares may be either legal or equitable.

Legal mortgages

In order that there shall be a legal mortgage, the mortgagee or lender must be entered on the register of members. To achieve this, the shares which are being used as a security must be transferred to him or his nominee. A separate agreement will set out the terms of the loan, and will also contain an undertaking by the lender to retransfer the shares to the mortgagor when the loan and interest are repaid. A legal mortgage gives the lender maximum security.

With a legal mortgage the lender (mortgagee) or his nominee is on the register and therefore appears to the outside world to be the absolute owner whereas he has a duty to transfer to the borrower on the repayment of the loan. Thus the borrower (mortgagor) should serve a 'stop notice' (see below) upon the company to prevent an unauthorised sale of the shares by the lender.

During the period that the loan is outstanding the lender will be entitled to all of the rights attaching to the shares, e.g. dividends. Because he is registered he will receive all communications from the company and is thus in a better position to reach decisions affecting the value of his security, e.g. whether to subscribe for a rights issue or cast his vote against or in favour of such important issues as reorganisation or takeover bids.

Equitable mortgages

Such a mortgage is more usual than a legal mortgage, particularly in the case of a short-term loan and in the case of shares in a private company where pre-emption provisions in the articles (see above) may prevent the registration of the lender, and may be achieved in the following ways.

(a) Mere deposit of the share certificate with the lender

This is sufficient to create an equitable mortgage, given that the intention to do so is present, but if the lender wishes to enforce his security, he must ask the court for an *order for sale*, and having sold the shares under the order, he must account to the borrower for the balance if the proceeds exceed the amount of the loan. Alternatively, the lender can apply for an *order of foreclosure* which vests the ownership of the shares in him, and if such an order is made, the lender is not obliged to account to the borrower for any excess. For this reason foreclosure is difficult to obtain.

(b) Deposit of share certificate plus a blank transfer

Where the borrower deposits the share certificate along with a transfer form, signed by him but with the transferee's name left blank, the seller has an implied authority to sell the shares by completing the transfer in favour of a purchaser, or in favour of himself if he so wishes, and in such a case there is no need to go to the court. Once again, a separate agreement will set out the terms of the loan, and provide for the delivery of the certificate and blank transfer on repayment of the loan plus interest.

The methods of equitable mortgage outlined above do not necessarily ensure the priority of the lender as against other persons with whom the borrower may deal in respect of the shares. Where the borrower obtains another certificate from the company and sells to a *bona fide purchaser for value* who then obtains registration, that purchaser will have priority over the original lender.

It is no use in the borrower in a legal mortgage or the original lender in an equitable mortgage (L) writing to the company telling it of his interest, because by s 126 of the CA 2006, restating s 360 of the CA 1985 and Reg 5 of *Table A*, a company cannot take notice of any trust or similar right over its shares. However, a borrower or lender, as appropriate, may protect himself by serving on the company a stop notice under the Rules of the Supreme Court. He will file at the Central Office of the Supreme Court an affidavit declaring the nature of his interest in the shares, accompanied by a copy of the notice addressed to the company and signed by the applicant. Copies of the affidavit and the notice are then served on the company.

It is, however, unusual for lenders to take legal mortgages (where the shares are registered in the name of the lender or its nominee). Equitable mortgages are more common (where the lender holds the share certificate(s) and a blank, executed stock transfer form in respect of the charged shares and the shares are only registered in the name of the lender or its nominee on enforcement of the security).

Once the stop notice has been served, the company cannot register a transfer or pay a dividend, if the notice extends to dividends, without first notifying L. However, after the expiration of 14 days from the lodgement of the transfer or notice of payment of a dividend, the company is bound to make the transfer or pay the dividend unless in the meantime L has obtained an injunction from the court prohibiting it.

A judgment creditor of a registered owner of shares may obtain an order charging the shares with payment of the judgment debt. Notice of the making of the order, or demand for the dividend, when served upon the company, has a similar effect to a stop notice (see above), in that until the charging order is discharged or made absolute the company cannot allow a transfer except with the authority of the court. A charging order has no priority over a mortgage created by deposit of the share certificate and a blank transfer *before* the date on which the charging order was made.

The relevant specifics can be found at RSC Part 73, *Charging Orders, Stop Orders and Stop Notices* available at: **http://www.justice.gov.uk/civil/procrules_fin/contents/parts/part73. htm#IDAEVOVB.**

Lien

CA 2006, s 670 provides that a lien or other charge on a company's own shares (whether taken expressly or otherwise) is void except as permitted in the section. With respect to any kind of company, a charge is permissible if the shares are not fully paid up and the charge is for an amount in respect of the shares. However, if the company is one whose ordinary business includes lending of money or consists of provision of credit or bailment, a charge is permissible if it arises in connection with a transaction entered into by the company in the ordinary course of business.

The articles often give the company a first and paramount lien over its shares for unpaid calls, or even for general debts owed to the company by shareholders, but the Stock Exchange will not give a listing where there is a lien on fully paid shares. However, a lien is permitted over partly paid shares for amounts called or payable on the shares. It is usual also for the articles to give a power of sale. *Table A* gives such a power of sale, but requires 14 days' notice in writing to the shareholder or his representatives before the sale takes place, during which time the money owed can be paid and the sale prevented. Since on a sale the shareholder or his representatives will probably not co-operate in the necessary transfer, the articles usually provide, as *Table A* does, that a purchaser shall get a good title if the transfer is signed by a person nominated by the directors. If the articles create a lien but give no power of sale, the company would have to obtain an order for sale from the court.

A lien, other than for amounts due on the shares, cannot be enforced by forfeiture even if a power to forfeit is contained in the articles. Thus a company cannot enforce a lien for general debts by forfeiture even if its articles so provide.

The company's lien takes priority over all equitable interests in the shares, e.g. those of equitable mortgages, unless, when the shareholder becomes indebted to the company, it has actual notice of the equitable interest.

The Bradford Banking Co Ltd v *Henry Briggs, Son & Co Ltd* (1886) 12 App Cas 29

The respondent was a trading company carrying on the business of a colliery. The articles of the company provided that it should have 'a first and permanent lien and charge available at law and in equity upon every share for all debts due from the holder thereof'. John Easby, a coal merchant, became a shareholder in the respondent company, and deposited his certificates with the bank as security for the overdraft on his current account. The bank gave notice to the company that the shares had been so deposited. Easby owed the respondent company money, having done trade with it, and he also owed money to the bank. The question for decision was whether the company was entitled to recoup its debts by exercising a lien and sale on the shares, or whether the bank was entitled to sell as mortgagees.

Held – by the House of Lords – that the respondent company could not claim priority over the bank in respect of the shares for money which became due from Easby after the notice given by the bank. The notice served by the bank was not a notice of trust under s 30 of the Companies Act 1862 (CA 1985, s 360 replaced by CA 2006, s 126), but must be regarded in the same light as notice between traders regarding their interests.

Comment

A company is not ordinarily bound to take notice of a trust or other equitable interest over its shares. It is, however, bound by such a notice when the company itself is also claiming an interest, e.g. a lien, over the shares in competition with the person who gives notice.

The lien attaches to dividends payable in respect of the shares subject to the lien (*Hague* v *Dandeson* (1848) 2 Exch 741).

Forfeiture of shares

Shares may be forfeited by a resolution of the board of directors if, *and only if*, an express power to forfeit is given in the articles. Where such an express power exists, it must be strictly followed, otherwise the forfeiture may be annulled. The Model Article for Public Companies provides for express power to forfeit in *Article 59*. Further, the object of the forfeiture must be for the benefit of the company and not to give some personal advantage to a director or shareholder, e.g. in order to allow him to avoid liability for the payment of calls where the shares have fallen in value as in *Re Esparto Trading* (1879) 12 Ch D 191.

The articles usually provide that shares may be forfeited where the member concerned does not pay a call made upon him, whether the call is in respect of the nominal value of the shares or of premium.

The usual procedure is for a notice to be served on the member asking for payment, and stating that if payment is not made by a specific date, not earlier than 14 days from the date of the notice, the shares may be forfeited. If payment is not so made, the company may forfeit the shares and make an entry of forfeiture on the register of members. Once the shares have been forfeited, the member should be required to return the share certificate or other document of title so as to obviate fraud. A forfeiture operates to reduce the company's issued capital, since it cancels the liability of the member concerned to pay for his shares in full, but even so the sanction of the court is not required; a mere power in the articles is enough.

Shares cannot be forfeited except for non-payment of calls and any provision in the articles to the contrary is void.

Reissue of forfeited shares

Forfeited shares may be reissued to a purchaser so long as the price which he pays for the shares is not less than the amount of calls due but unpaid at forfeiture.

Suppose X is the holder of 100 shares of £1 each on which 75p per share has been called up, and X does not pay the final call of 25p per share, as a result of which the shares are forfeited. If they are reissued to Y, then Y must pay not less than £25 for them, and any sum received in excess of that amount from Y will be considered as *share premium* and must be credited to a *share premium account*. Thus, although Y appears to have bought the shares at a discount, this is not so because the company has received the full amount of the called-up capital, i.e. £75 from X and £25 from Y.

The company's articles usually provide (as *Table A* does) that if any irregularity occurs in the forfeiture procedure, the person to whom the forfeited shares are reissued will nevertheless obtain a good title. This is found in *Article 61(3)* of the Model Articles for Public Companies.

Liability of person whose shares are forfeited

Forfeiture of shares means that the holder ceases to be a member of the company, but his liability in respect of the shares forfeited depends upon the articles.

(a) *Where there is no provision in the articles* with regard to liability, the former holder is discharged from liability, and no action can be brought by the company against him for calls due at the date of the forfeiture unless the company is wound up within one year of it. In such a case the former holder may be put on the *B list of contributories* in the winding-up, and may be called upon to pay the calls due at the date of the forfeiture unless they have been paid by another holder.

(b) *The articles may provide* (as does *Table A* and *Article 60* of the Model Articles for Public Companies) that the former holder shall be liable to pay the calls due but unpaid at the date of forfeiture, whether the company is in liquidation or not, unless they have been paid to the company by a subsequent holder.

Surrender of shares

The directors of a company cannot accept a surrender of shares unless the articles so provide. There is no provision in *Table A* (in contrast to *Article 62* of the Model Articles for Public Companies) but it would seem from decided cases that directors may accept surrender:

(a) where the circumstances are such that the shares could have been forfeited under the articles (*per* Lord Herschell in **Trevor v Whitworth** (1887) 12 App Cas 409); and

(b) where shares are surrendered as part of a scheme to exchange existing shares for new shares of the same nominal value, the new shares having perhaps slightly different rights and the old shares being either cancelled or available for reissue.

In other circumstances surrender is not allowed (see below).

Bellerby v Rowland & Marwood's SS Co Ltd [1902] 2 Ch 14

Three directors of the company, Bellerby, Moss and Marwood, agreed to surrender several of their shares to the company so that they might be reissued. The object of the surrender was not that the directors could not pay the calls, the shares being of nominal value £11 with £10 paid, but to assist the company to make good the loss of one of its ships, the *Golden Cross*, valued at £4,000. The surrender was accepted but the shares were not in fact reissued. The company survived the loss and became prosperous, and in this action the directors sought to be returned to the register as members, claiming that the earlier surrender was invalid.

Held – by the Court of Appeal – that it was invalid since the surrender was not accepted because of non-payment of calls or inability to pay them, and so the directors must be restored to the register of members.

Comment

This decision is essentially to the effect that a company cannot evade the rules relating to reduction of capital by taking a surrender of its partly paid shares.

Treatment of forfeited and surrendered shares in public companies

The above material relating to forfeiture and surrender is still valid because it relates to the source of the power to forfeit or surrender and the surrounding circumstances. However, the treatment of forfeited and surrendered shares once this has happened is a matter for the CA 2006, s 662. CA 2006, s 662 provides that no voting rights may be exercised by the company so long as the shares are forfeited or surrendered and also that the company must dispose of the shares within three years. If they are not disposed of, they must be cancelled. If the shares are cancelled and the cancellation has the effect of reducing the company's allotted share capital below the authorised minimum, the directors must apply for the company to be re-registered as a private company. There are, however, certain relaxations in the procedures in this event. In particular, only a directors' resolution is required to make the necessary reduction application, and any alterations to the memorandum that are necessary. The company does not need to apply to the court to obtain confirmation of the reduction in capital but any resolution passed by the directors must be filed with the Registrar. If a company fails to comply with either the requirement to cancel or the requirement to re-register as a private company, the company and its officers in default become liable to a fine.

Essay questions

1 (a) Sam has 2,000 fully paid shares in X Ltd. The articles of X Ltd give a first and paramount lien over shares in respect of any debts owed by a member to the company. On 3 January, Sam borrowed £1,500 from George and secured the loan by giving George his share certificate and a blank transfer form. George notified the company of these facts. The company informed George they could not take cognisance of his interest as this would be contrary to s 126 of the Companies Act 2006. On 10 February, Sam became indebted to the company for goods delivered to him invoiced at £800. He has not paid for these and the company seeks to enforce its lien.

   Advise George of the legal position.

   (b) T stole M's share certificate and forged a transfer to B, who was a bona fide purchaser. B was registered and received a new share certificate from the company. He later sold the shares to C, but T's fraud was discovered and the company refused to register C.

   What is the legal position of M, C and B?   *(Kingston University)*

2 Describe and discuss the significance of each of the following:

   (a) The pre-emption rights of existing shareholders.

   (b) Preference shares.

   (c) Redeemable shares.   *(The Association of Chartered Certified Accountants)*

3 Dee Ltd has an authorised and issued share capital of £15,000 in £1 shares. The directors have decided to issue for cash at par a further 10,000 £1 shares.

   What procedures must the directors follow to implement their decision?
                         (The Institute of Chartered Accountants in England and Wales)

4 'Although they may not be in the strict sense agents or trustees for the company, promoters stand in a fiduciary relation to it' – *Northey and Leigh*.

   Discuss by looking at the promoter's relationship with the company he is forming and the remedies available for failure to discharge the fiduciary duty.
                         (The Institute of Company Accountants)

5 Explain by reference to statutory and common law examples what is meant by the term 'lifting the veil of incorporation'.   *(The Chartered Institute of Management Accountants)*

Test your knowledge

Four alternative answers are given. Select ONE only. Circle the answer which you consider to be correct. Check your answers by referring back to the information given in the chapter and against the answers at the end of the text.

1 The Companies Act 2006 gives shareholders a statutory right of pre-emption:

   A On the allotment of any shares. ˙
   B Where shares are transferred from one member of a company to another.
   C On the transmission of shares on the death of a member of the same company.
   D On the allotment for cash of equity shares.

2 The board of Mersey plc has authorised the allotment of shares to the public in contravention of the statutory pre-emption rights of Mersey's shareholders. What is the legal position as regards the allotment?

   A It is invalid and the allottees have no right to compensation.
   B It is valid and the shareholders can ask for compensation from the directors and the company.
   C It is invalid and the allottees can ask for compensation from the directors and the company.
   D It is valid and the original shareholders have no right to compensation.

3 The shareholders of Test Ltd are Ann who holds 600 shares, Barbara who has 100 shares, and Clare and Diana who have 250 shares each. The shares carry one vote each. A resolution to exclude the statutory pre-emption right of the shareholders of Test Ltd, given that all members attend the meeting and that voting is by poll, requires the minimum support of:

   A Ann alone.
   B Ann and Barbara.
   C Ann and Barbara and Clare.
   D Ann and Barbara and Clare and Diana.

4 Under the provisions of the Companies Act 2006, where there is to be an allotment of unissued share capital for cash the notice of the offer to existing shareholders must remain open for not less than:

   A 28 days   B 21 days   C 15 days   D 14 days

5 Which of the following resolutions requires the directors of a private company to give a statutory declaration of solvency? A resolution to:

   A Commence a creditors' voluntary winding-up.
   B Reduce the company's share capital.
   C Approve the giving of financial assistance for the purchase of its own shares from distributable profits.
   D Approve a contract for the purchase of its own shares out of distributable profits.

6 What is the minimum percentage of shareholders required to make an application to the court to set aside an alteration of the objects clause of a company?

   A Not less than 15 per cent of the total number of shareholders.
   B Those holding not less than 15 per cent in nominal value of the issued share capital of the company or any class thereof.
   C Not less than 15 per cent of the total number of shareholders or any class thereof.
   D Those holding not less than 15 per cent in nominal value of the issued share capital of the company.

The answers to test your knowledge questions appear on p. 645.

Suggested further reading

Drury, 'The relative nature of the shareholder's right to enforce the company contract' [1986] CLJ 219.

Grantham, 'The doctrinal basis of the rights of company shareholders' [1998] CLJ 554.

Rixon, 'Competing interests and conflicting principles: An examination of the power of alteration of articles of association' (1986) 49 MLR, 446.

Worthington, 'Shares and shareholders: Property, power and entitlement' (2001) 22 *Company Lawyer*, 258.

14 Shares – transfer and transmission

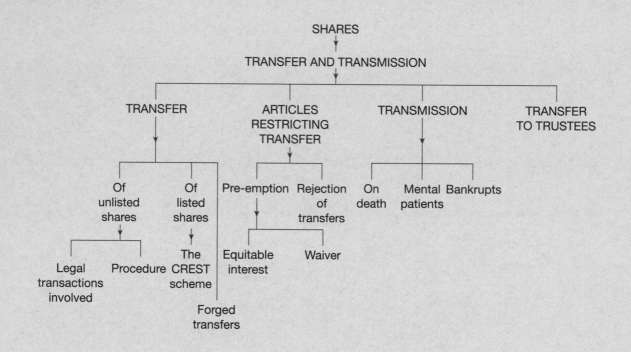

This chapter is concerned with the way in which shares are transferred from one person to another. It is necessary to distinguish between the transfer of unlisted shares and shares which are listed on an investment exchange such as the Stock Exchange. Basically the material in this chapter covers the transfer of shares in a private company which cannot have a listing on an investment exchange. The rules, however, could apply to a plc which had not sought a listing on an investment exchange.

Transfer of unlisted shares

As we have seen, shares are personal property and are transferable subject to any restriction contained in the articles. A company cannot register a transfer of shares or debentures unless a proper instrument of transfer, duly stamped, has been delivered to the company and executed by or on behalf of the transferor (CA 2006, s 770). No formal transfer is required when a company purchases its own shares, though stamp duty is payable. Thus an article which provided for the automatic transfer of shares to a director's widow on his death was held invalid (*Re Greene* [1949] 1 All ER 167). The directors usually have power under articles such as *Table A* to decline to register the transfer of a share, other than a fully paid share, to a person of whom they do not approve, e.g. a minor or person of unsound mind who cannot be bound by the contract; and also to decline to register the transfer of a share on which the company has a lien, e.g. for calls made but not paid. Any power of veto on transfer vested by the articles in the directors must be exercised within two months after the lodging of the transfer for registration and the transferee notified. If not, the company may be compelled to register the transferee as a member.

 Re Swaledale Cleaners [1968] 3 All ER 619

On 3 August 1967 the shareholding of the company was: H (deceased) 5,000; S 4,000; A (deceased) 500; L 500. S and L were directors of the company which was a private one. The company's articles provided that the quorum of directors should be two although a sole continuing director had power to appoint an additional director. At a combined board meeting and annual general meeting held on 3 August 1967, L retired by rotation and was not re-elected a director. The personal representatives of H and A had executed transfers of H and A shareholdings in favour of L, but S as director refused to register them purporting to exercise a power of refusal contained in the articles. There was no resolution either of the board or of the shareholders on the matter of refusal to register the transfers. On 11 December 1967 L began proceedings for rectification of the register, and on 18 December 1967 S appointed an additional director and the two directors formally refused to register the transfers.

Held – by the Court of Appeal – the register must be rectified to show L as the holder of the shares of H and A. The power to refuse a transfer must be construed strictly because a shareholder ordinarily has a right to transfer his shares. Furthermore, the delay in exercising the power of refusal, i.e. four months, had been unreasonable and the power was no longer capable of being exercised.

Comment

The above case was followed by the High Court in **Re Inverdeck Ltd** [1998] 2 BCLC 242. This later case stresses the need for directors in private companies as Inverdeck Ltd was to observe the relevant corporate formalities in their day-to-day transactions. The power in private companies to refuse to register a transfer is a valuable one in that it can be used to prevent persons from acquiring rights in the company which the directors believe are contrary to its interests. Failure to observe formalities can lead to this valuable power being lost.

Court's power to rectify the register where no instrument of transfer

It was held by the Court of Appeal in *Re Hoicrest Ltd* [1999] 2 BCLC 346 that the power of the court to rectify the membership register of a company could be used to effect a transfer where there was no instrument of transfer so that the company had not had an opportunity to refuse the transfer. Although CA 2006, s 125 has traditionally been used in disputes between a would-be shareholder and the company where following transfer the company refuses registration, the section was not confined to that situation and could be used to settle a dispute as to the ownership of shares between two members.

The legal transactions involved

The purchase and sale of shares involves the following separate and distinct legal transactions:

(a) An unconditional contract is agreed between the transferor and transferee. The transferor then holds the shares as a trustee for the transferee (who has an equitable interest) until registration but is still a member of the company and retains the right to vote as he chooses.

(b) The transferee pays for the shares. The position remains as in (a) above except that the transferor must now vote as the transferee directs. An unpaid transferor has the right to vote the shares free from any obligation to comply with the transferee's requirements (*JRRT (Investments)* v *Haycraft* [1993] BCLC 401).

(c) The position remains as in (b) above while the transfer is approved by the directors and the transfer is stamped.

(d) The transferee's name is entered on the register of members. At this stage the transferor ceases to be a member of the company. The transferee becomes the member and acquires the legal title to the shares. Since membership and membership rights are only effective when the transferee is on the register of members, it may be necessary to ask the court to rectify the register of members under CA 2006, s 125 where the company is refusing to register the transferee, *but only if this is contrary to the powers of the board*.

The rights of persons to obtain registration or to claim under an equitable title are set out later in the text. Section 127 of the Insolvency Act 1986 declares void any transfer of shares after the commencement of winding-up by the court, unless the court otherwise orders.

Form of transfer

Schedule 1 to Stock Transfer Act 1963 introduced a new transfer form – a *stock transfer form*, which is for general use with unlisted shares.

Registrars are required to accept for registration transfers in the form introduced by the Act because it overrides any contrary provision regarding transfer, whether statutory or not. Thus, the 1963 Act overrides any other provisions relating to the *form* of transfer in the company's articles. The signature of the transferor need not be witnessed, and the transferee need not sign the transfer, nor need it be in the form of a deed.

It should be noted that the 1963 Act does not override provisions in the articles relating to the rights of the directors to refuse registration.

The stock transfer form is not available to transfer partly paid shares or shares in an unlimited or guarantee company. If such companies are encountered, reference should be made to the articles for the form of transfer to be used.

Procedure on transfer of unlisted shares

The method of transferring fully paid shares or stock is as follows.

The shareholder executes (signs) a stock transfer form in favour of the purchaser, and hands it to the purchaser or his agent, together with the share certificate. The purchaser, or his agent, sends the stock transfer form along with the certificate to the company for registration. The purchaser need not sign the stock transfer form, nor need it be in the form of a deed. The company secretary, following approval by the board, deletes the transferor's name from the register of shareholders and replaces it with the transferee's name and, within two months, sends the share certificate to the transferee.

Transfer of listed shares

Transfers of shares with a listing on the London Stock Exchange are covered by the Uncertificated Securities Regulations 2001 (SI 2001/3755). This area of the law is rather specialised and only an outline of the system called CREST is given here.

The regulations provide for the system to be run by an approved operator which is CRESTCo Ltd, a private company owned by a number of firms connected with all sectors of the equities market. CRESTCo merged with Euroclear Bank in September 2002.

The system, which is known as CREST, is an electronic system which allows shareholders to hold and transfer their securities in dematerialised form, i.e. without a share certificate. A statement not unlike a bank statement reveals purchases and sales by the intermediaries concerned.

CREST does not impose dematerialisation of shares on shareholders. Shareholders who wish to become or remain uncertificated are able to do so. Institutional shareholders, such as insurance companies, that are frequent traders will go for dematerialisation but less sophisticated shareholders will in many cases opt for the paper certificate regime, follow the method of transfer described above and be on a separate register of members.

Uncertificated shareholders will appoint a custodian broker to hold the shares. The broker will appear on the electronic register of members but can only deal with shares in accordance with the customer agreement between the shareholder and the custodian broker. Shareholders who wish to retain paper certificates in listed companies may be forced to appoint custodian brokers as nominees because of the Stock Exchange three-day rolling settlement system under which an entire share transfer transaction must be completed in three days. This is difficult to achieve under a paper certificate regime but easy under an electronic transfer regime. It is possible to opt for a ten-day settlement regime though it will be necessary to find a stockbroker who operates it – some do.

Once a nominee is installed, the shareholder will receive dividends and benefit from capital growth but rights will be lost such as the right actually to attend meetings unless the nominee can make arrangements for this, nor will the shareholder receive the annual report and accounts unless the nominee asks for enough to send out to all his members, but this would be a concession not a right.

The regulations make dematerialisation lawful and disapply CA 2006, s 769 under which a share certificate must be provided to the transferee within two months after allotment or transfer where the uncertificated regime applies, but not in the paper certificate regime. Companies that wish to allow their shares to be transferred via CREST will have to change their articles to add a relevant provision.

Finally, a company any of whose securities can be transferred through CREST must subdivide its register of members (or debenture holders) to show how many of those securities each person holds in uncertificated form and certificated form respectively. An issuer of securities can only rectify a register of securities in relation to uncertificated units with the consent of CRESTCo or by order of the court.

Certification of transfers: unlisted shares

The above procedure assumes that on completion of the sale of registered unlisted shares the seller delivers his share certificate to the purchaser together with the instrument of transfer. Where he is selling all the shares represented by the certificate the seller will do this, but if he is selling only part of his holding, or the whole of his holding but to more than one person, he will instead send the share certificate and the executed transfer of the shares which the purchaser is buying to the company so that the transfer may be certificated.

The company secretary or registrar or transfer agent will compare the share certificate and the transfer with the register of members and if it appears that the seller is the owner of the shares mentioned in the certificate and some of those shares are comprised in the transfer, the secretary, registrar, or agent, as the case may be, will write in the margin of the transfer a note that the share certificate has been lodged and will sign it on behalf of the company.

The certificated transfer is then returned to the seller, the share certificate being retained by the company or the transfer agents. The seller will complete the sale by delivering the certificated transfer to the purchaser who will accept it as equal to delivery of an uncertificated transfer accompanied by the share certificate. The purchaser will then lodge the transfer with the company or its transfer agents for registration and the company will issue a new share certificate to him for the shares he has bought and a new certificate showing the seller as the registered holder of the balance of the shares which he retains if he retains any. Obviously, the seller will not get a new certificate where he has sold his whole holding but to more than one person.

Liability arising out of certification

This is covered by CA 2006, s 775 and although a certification is not a warranty by the company that the person transferring the shares has any title to them, it is a representation by the company that documents have been produced to it which show prima facie title in the transferor.

Where, therefore, the company or its agent fraudulently or negligently makes a false certification, a purchaser who acts upon the false certification may sue the company for any loss he may have incurred as a result.

For example, if the company certifies a transfer without production of a certificate, it may be that the certificate has been used to make an uncertificated transfer to another purchaser. If so, two purchasers now exist and both are eligible for entry on the register of members. If the later purchaser achieves registration first, he will establish priority over the certificated transferee who will not then be registered and the company will be liable in damages to the certificated transferee for the loss he suffers thereby. However, if the company registers the certificated transferee and refuses the other purchaser, it will not be liable to the latter because the share certificate does not operate as an estoppel except as on the date of issue, which will have been some time ago.

Forged transfers

If a company transfers shares under a forged instrument of transfer, the transferor whose name has been forged must be restored to the register, and in so far as this puts the company to expense or loss, it can claim an indemnity from the person presenting the transfer for registration, even though he is quite innocent of the forgery.

 ### *Sheffield Corporation* v *Barclay* [1905] AC 392

Two persons, Timbrell and Honnywill, were joint owners of corporation stock. Timbrell, in fraud of Honnywill, forged a transfer of the stock and borrowed money from the respondents on the security of the stock. The respondents sent the transfer to the corporation asking for registration, and they were duly registered. Later the respondents sold the shares and the corporation issued certificates to the purchasers who were also registered. Honnywill, after the death of Timbrell, discovered the forgery, and the corporation replaced the stock which was the best course open to them, because if they had taken the ultimate purchasers off the register of stockholders, they would have had to pay damages to them by virtue of the doctrine of estoppel. The corporation now sued the respondents for an indemnity on the grounds that they had presented the forged transfer.

Held – by the House of Lords – the corporation succeeded. The person presenting a transfer warrants that it is good, and the fact that he is innocent of any fraud does not affect this warranty. The corporation, therefore, was entitled to recover from the respondents the value of the stock replaced, leaving them to such remedies as they might have against Timbrell's estate.

Comment

(i) Where a person requests the registration of a share transfer which a company is under a duty to effect there is implied in that request a warranty that the transfer is genuine. The rule applies whether the transfer is in favour of the person presenting it or someone else, as where a broker presents a transfer on behalf of a client.

(ii) The company's loss, for which it needs an indemnity, will normally consist in buying in or issuing for no consideration new shares to recompense the original holder. The innocent transferee will stay on the register of members by reason of the rules relating to estoppel that are described above. The indemnity may be made by the fraudster if he presents the transfer but it may be presented by a broker on behalf of the fraudster where the company is listed. In these circumstances the broker must give the indemnity, even though he may be innocent of the fraud, leaving him to claim against the fraudster. This was the situation in the *Barclay* case and in *Royal Bank of Scotland plc* v *Sandstone Properties Ltd* (1998) *The Times*, 12 March, where the facts were similar and the *Barclay* case was followed.

If the company issues a share certificate to the transferee under a forged transfer, the company is not estopped from denying his title to the shares, but it may become estopped if it issues a new certificate to a non-owner as part of a subsequent transfer transaction.

A company may inform the transferor that a transfer has been received for registration so as to give him a chance to prevent a fraudulent transfer but a transferor is not prejudiced by the fact that he has received notice, and may still deny the validity of the transfer.

Death of a holder in a joint account

A transfer is not needed to a surviving joint holder or holders on the death of one. In such cases, it is usual for the company to receive a death certificate certified by the Registrar of Births and Deaths. Photocopies are not official documents but some companies will accept them if presented by a person of professional standing. Sometimes a grant of probate or administration may be received and this is satisfactory evidence of death. The necessary alterations in the register of members are made on the basis of these documents and not on the basis of the conventional instrument of transfer. The procedure is a form of transmission of shares which is considered later in this chapter.

Companies whose articles restrict transfer

In the case of a company whose articles restrict transfer a transfer must be submitted to and approved by the board and any restriction must be the decision of the directors.

Re Smith v *Fawcett* [1942] Ch 304 (Court of Appeal)

Article 10 of the articles of association of a private company provided: 'The directors may at any time in their absolute and uncontrolled discretion refuse to register any transfer of shares, and cl. 19 of *Table A* shall be modified accordingly.' The issued capital of the company consisted of 8002 ordinary shares of which the two directors of the company, J F and N S, held 4001 each. J F died, and his son as his executor applied to have the testator's shares registered in his name. N S refused to consent to the registration, but offered to register 2,001 shares and to buy 2,000 at a fixed price. The executor applied to the court by way of motion that the register of members of the company might be rectified by inserting his name as the holder of the 4,001 shares. Lord Greene MR observed:

> The principles to be applied in cases where the articles of a company confer a discretion on directors with regard to the acceptance of transfers of shares are, for the present purposes, free from doubt. They must exercise their discretion bona fide in what they consider – not what a court may consider – is in the interests of the company, and not for any collateral purpose. They must have regard to those considerations, and those considerations only, which the articles on their true construction permit them to take into consideration, and in construing the relevant provisions in the articles it is to be borne in mind that one of the normal rights of a shareholder is the right to deal freely with his property and to transfer it to whomsoever he pleases. When it is said, as it has been said more than once, that regard must be had to this last consideration, it means, I apprehend, nothing more than that the shareholder has such a prima facie right, and that right is not to be cut down by uncertain language or doubtful implications. The right, if it is to be cut down, must be cut down with satisfactory clarity. It certainly does not mean that articles, if appropriately framed, cannot be allowed

to cut down the right of transfer to any extent which the articles on their true construction permit. Another consideration which must be borne in mind is that this type of article is one which is for the most part confined to private companies. Private companies are in law separate entities just as much as are public companies, but from the business and personal point of view they are much more analogous to partnerships than to public corporations. Accordingly, it is to be expected that in the articles of such a company the control of the directors over the membership may be very strict indeed. There are, or may be, very good business reasons why those who bring such companies into existence should give them a constitution which confers on the directors powers of the widest description.

The language of the article in the present case does not point out any particular matter as being the only matter to which the directors are to pay attention in deciding whether or not they will allow the transfer to be registered. The article does not, for instance, say, as is to be found in some articles, that they may refuse to register any transfer of shares to a person not already a member of the company or to a transferee of whom they do not approve. Where articles are framed with some such limitation on the discretionary power of refusal as I have mentioned in those two examples, it follows on plain principle that if the directors go outside the matters which the articles say are to be the matters and the only matters to which they are to have regard, the directors will have exceeded their powers.

Mr Spens, in his argument for the plaintiff, maintained that whatever language was used in the articles, the power of the directors to refuse to register a transfer must always be limited to matters personal to the transferee and that there can be no personal objection to the plaintiff becoming a member of the company because the directors are prepared to accept him as the holder of 2,000 of the shares which have come to him as legal personal representative of his father. Mr Spens relies for his proposition on observations in several authorities, but on examination of those cases it becomes clear that the form of article then before the court by its express language confined the directors to the consideration of the desirability of admitting the proposed transferee to membership on grounds personal to him . . .

There is nothing, in my opinion, in principle or in authority to make it impossible to draft such a wide and comprehensive power to directors to refuse to transfer as to enable them to take into account any matter which they conceive to be in the interests of the company, and thereby to admit or not to admit a particular person and to allow or not to allow a particular transfer for reasons not personal to the transferee but bearing on the general interests of the company as a whole – such matters, for instance, as whether by their passing a particular transfer the transferee would obtain too great a weight in the councils of the company or might even perhaps obtain control. The question, therefore, simply is whether on the true construction of the particular article the directors are limited by anything except their bona fide view as to the interests of the company. In the present case the article is drafted in the widest possible terms, and I decline to write into that clear language any limitation other than a limitation, which is implicit by law, that a fiduciary power of this kind must be exercised bona fide in the interests of the company. Subject to that qualification, an article in this form appears to me to give the directors what it says, namely, an absolute and uncontrolled discretion.

Held – affirming Simonds J – that Article 10 gave the directors the widest powers to refuse to register a transfer, and that, while such powers are of a fiduciary nature and must be exercised in the interests of the company, there was nothing to show that they had been otherwise exercised.

In practice these restrictions are normally found only in the articles of private companies. Most plcs have their shares listed, or quoted, on a recognised investment exchange such as the Stock Exchange, and the rules of the listing or quotation agreement do not permit restrictions on transfer following sale. Consideration will be given to the right of pre-emption in private companies and the general rules relating to rejection of transfers.

The right of pre-emption: generally

This means that when a member of a private company wishes to sell his shares, he must, under a provision in the articles, first offer them to other members of the company before he offers them to an outsider. The price is usually to be calculated by some method laid down in the articles, e.g. at a price fixed by the auditors of the company. In this context it should be noted that the auditor can be sued by the seller of the shares if the valuation is lower than it should be because of the auditor's negligence. This is an important claim because the seller will not normally be able to avoid the contract of sale because that contract usually makes the auditor's valuation final and binding on the parties.

However, a distinction must be made where the accountant or valuer has not merely made a mistake in the valuation of the shares, but has not done what he was appointed to do. In such a case the court can intervene and set the contract of purchase aside. Thus, in *Marco* v *Thompson* [1997] 2 BCLC 626 an accountant/valuer was asked to value the shares in two private companies for the purpose of a pre-emption purchase. In reaching conclusions as to the valuation of company A's shares, he mistakenly transposed the assets of company B, which was less valuable. This transposition appeared in the judgment of an earlier decision of the court in these proceedings. The contract to buy the shares of company A at the lower price was set aside by the court even though the purchaser had paid for the shares. The accountant/valuer had been asked to value the shares of company A but by mistake had valued the shares of company B, which represented not merely an error in the valuation, but an error in terms of his instructions.

If the other members do not wish to take up the shares, the shares may then be sold to an outsider. The other members must apparently be prepared to take *all* the shares that the vendor member is offering (*Ocean Coal Co Ltd* v *Powell Duffryn Steam Coal Co Ltd* [1932] 1 Ch 654).

The right of pre-emption can, if appropriately worded, be enforced as between the members (*Rayfield* v *Hands* [1960] Ch 1), and also by the company, which may obtain an injunction against a member who is not complying with the articles in this matter (*Lyle & Scott Ltd* v *Scott's Trustees* [1959] 2 All ER 661). The decision in *Lyle & Scott Ltd* could make it very difficult for a takeover bidder to take over a private company because if there is a pre-emption clause the board can ask the court for an injunction requiring a member to offer his shares to another member rather than to the bidder.

Effect of transfer of equitable interest in shares

A method of effectively transferring control over the shares without triggering a pre-emption clause can be seen in the following case.

Scotto v Petch (2001) *The Times*, 8 February

The company owned Sedgefield racecourse, and an offer to buy all the shares in the company was made by Northern Racing Ltd. Mrs Scotto, a 21 per cent shareholder, refused to sell. The other shareholders were willing to do so. The victim company had a pre-emption clause in its articles under which pre-emption rights in other shareholders were triggered if a shareholder 'intends to transfer shares'. The shareholders other than Mrs Scotto made an agreement under which they would remain on the register as legal owners of their shares but the equitable interest would belong to Northern Racing. The agreement went on to say that if they were ever required to transfer the legal interest, it would be to another member, i.e. it would be a permitted transfer under the article. The arrangement gave Northern Racing effective control since under the agreement the shareholders, who were parties to it, would obviously vote as Northern Racing required. Mrs Scotto said that the arrangement triggered the pre-emption clause so that the shares had to be offered to her.

Held – by the Court of Appeal – the pre-emption clause was not triggered. There had been no transfer of the legal interest in the shares and if ever there was, it would be to other members and would, therefore, be a permitted transfer under the articles.

Pre-emption: members' waivers

The other members of the company may be prepared to give written waivers of their rights to pre-emption, bearing in mind that a private company will normally have articles giving the directors power to reject a transferee. However, where shares are transferred in breach of a pre-emption clause without unanimous waiver of the other members, the directors have no power to register the transfer and no question of discretion arises. A person wishing to sell his shares in a private company with a pre-emption clause will normally notify the company secretary, who will advise the other members of the wish to sell.

Rejection of transfers

Where the articles give the directors power simply to refuse or approve the registration of transfers, that power must be exercised in good faith, and this may be tested in the courts if it appears that the directors have rejected a transfer for purely personal reasons as where they simply do not like the proposed transferee (and see *Re Accidental Death Insurance Co, Allin's Case*, 1873, below); but where the power to reject is exercisable for reasons specified in the articles, the transferee need not be told which is the reason for this rejection if the articles so provide (see *Berry and Stewart* v *Tottenham Hotspur FC*, 1935, below). The position is the same where the articles merely provide that the directors may reject a transfer 'without assigning reasons therefor'. These provisions are much stronger because the directors cannot be required to give reasons and therefore it is difficult, if not impossible, to prove before a court that they acted in bad faith.

Re Accidental Death Insurance Co, Allin's Case (1873) LR 16 Eq 449

The company's deed of settlement provided that when a shareholder wished to transfer his shares, he should leave notice at the company's office, and the directors should consider the proposal and signify their acceptance or rejection of the proposed transferee. If they rejected the proposed transferee, the proposed transfer would still be considered approved unless the directors could find someone else to take the shares at market price. The company arranged to transfer its business to the Accident and Marine Insurance Corporation Ltd. The shareholders acquiesced in an arrangement to exchange their shares for shares in the corporation, but the company was not wound up. A year later, the former directors of the company reversed the procedure, and the company proposed to resume its former business. Notice of this was given to shareholders, and shortly afterwards the corporation was wound up. Under an arrangement to release certain shareholders of liability, Allin transferred 200 shares in the company to Robert Pocock for a nominal consideration. He gave notice to the directors at a meeting at which he was present, and the transfer was agreed. Later the company was wound up.

Held – by the High Court – the transfer was invalid, and Allin must be a contributory. The clauses were not intended to be in operation for the purpose of enabling individuals to escape liability when the company had ceased to be a going concern.

Berry and Stewart v *Tottenham Hotspur FC Ltd* [1935] Ch 718

Berry held one ordinary share in Tottenham Hotspur and he transferred his share to Stewart, both of them subsequently trying to register the transfer. Registration was refused, and Art 16 of the company's articles specified four grounds on which this was allowable, and also stipulated that the directors were not bound to divulge the grounds upon which registration was declined. The claimants brought an action for a declaration that the company was not entitled to decline to register the transfer, and sought interrogatories directed to find out which of the four grounds was the basis of the refusal.

Held – by Crossman J – Article 16 excused the directors from the need to disclose this information, and this was binding not only on Berry, as a member, but also on Stewart who was applying to be a member. An action coupled with a demand for interrogatories could not be used to oust the agreement.

Comment

A more recent example of the use of this much stronger power of rejection is to be found in *Popely* v *Planarrive Ltd* [1997] 1 BCLC 8. Article 14 of the articles of association of Planarrive Ltd (P Ltd), a private company, gave its directors the power 'in their absolute discretion and without assigning any reason therefor' to 'decline to register the transfer of a share'. If the directors took such an action, they were required, under Art 25, to notify the transferee of their refusal to register his interest within two months after the date on which the transfer was lodged. Darren Popely validly transferred 15 shares in P Ltd to his father Ronald. The directors of P Ltd exercised their powers under Art 14 and refused to register the transfer. Ronald Popely then applied to the Chancery Division under s 359 of the Companies Act 1985 for an order rectifying the register of members of P Ltd by registering him as the owner of the shares transferred by his son. It was not disputed that notice of the refusal to register had not been sent to Mr Popely within the time set out in Art 25. Counsel for Mr Popely attempted to argue that this breach made the whole decision void. Mr Justice Laddie said that it did not nullify the decision although it might expose the directors to some civil or criminal liability (see s 183(6)). With regard to the actual refusal to register the transfer, Mr Popely's counsel said that this refusal was based on the strong feelings of hostility felt by the directors towards his client. However, the judge said that such feelings did not render the decision invalid. Where directors have such wide powers as these in the articles, the only restriction placed on them was that they must act bona fide in the best interests of the company and not outside their powers. Mr Popely was refused his application.

When is a transfer rejected?

Where there is an equality of votes, a transfer cannot be deemed rejected, but must be accepted (see *Re Hackney Pavilion Ltd*, 1924, below), though it is usual for the chairman to have a casting vote which he can use to decide the issue. Similarly, a transferee can ask the court to rectify the register so that his name is included on it where one director, by refusing to attend board meetings, is preventing a directors' meeting from being held to consider the registration because of lack of quorum (*Re Copal Varnish Co*, 1917). In addition, the powers vested in directors to refuse to register a transfer must be exercised within a reasonable time (see *Re Swaledale Cleaners*, 1968).

Re Hackney Pavilion Ltd [1924] 1 Ch 276

The company had three directors, Sunshine, Kramer and Rose, each of whom held 3,333 shares in the company. Sunshine died, having appointed his widow as his executrix. Her solicitors wrote to the company, enclosing a transfer of the 3,333 shares from herself as executrix to herself in an individual capacity. At a board meeting at which Kramer, Rose and the secretary were present, Rose proposed that the shares be registered, but Kramer objected in accordance with a provision in the articles. There was no casting vote. The secretary then wrote to the solicitors informing them that his directors had declined to register the transfer.

Held – by the High Court – the board's right to decline required to be actively expressed. The mere failure to pass the proposed resolution for registration was not a formal active exercise of the right to decline. The right to registration remained, and the register must be rectified.

Unless the articles otherwise provide, rights of pre-emption and rejection apply only on a transfer by a member, and do not arise on transmission through death or bankruptcy. Neither do they arise where the shares are still represented by a renounceable letter of allotment.

Re Pool Shipping Ltd [1920] 1 Ch 251

The applicants were shareholders of the company which had capitalised £125,000, part of a reserve fund, for distribution among the registered shareholders or their nominees, at the rate of one share for every four shares issued. All but one of the shareholders renounced their right to allotments, and requested the company to allot the shares to Coulson who had agreed to accept them. The managers refused to issue the shares or register them to him when he presented the letters of renunciation in his favour, so the applicants moved for rectification of the register by the insertion of Coulson's name. The company had no directors but was controlled by Sir R Ropner & Co Ltd, who were described as managers and who relied on various clauses in the articles as grounds for refusal.

Held – by the High Court – letters of renunciation do not amount to transfers of shares so as to come within the provisions of the articles of association dealing with the transfer of shares already registered. The managers were wrong in thinking they could refuse to register Mr Coulson, and the register must be rectified.

Special articles may allow rejection of executors' transfers to themselves as members pending the winding-up of the estate as an alternative to dealing with them in a representative capacity, and where this is so, they will *not* be able to vote the deceased's shares. A trustee in bankruptcy in the same situation will at least be able to direct his living debtor on how to vote.

A restriction in a company's articles upon the transfer of shares covers only the transfer of the legal title, i.e. a transfer in the title of the person on the register of members, and does not include transfer of the beneficial interest. Thus, if A and B are the only shareholders in a company and B has a majority holding, then if on the death of B his executor, C, who has obtained registration, holds the shares on trust for beneficiaries, X and Y, and C proposes to vote in accordance with the wishes of X and Y so that X and Y will control the company, then

A cannot claim that there has been a transfer of the shares of B entitling A to the implementation of a pre-emption clause under which A might require the shares held by C to be offered to him (A) (see *Safeguard Industrial Investments Ltd* v *National Westminster Bank* [1982] 1 All ER 449).

Of course, if C had been refused registration under a provision in the company's articles allowing this, he could not vote and so the above situation would not apply.

Transmission of shares

This occurs where the rights encompassed in the holding of shares vests in another by operation of law and not by reason of transfer. It occurs in the following cases.

(a) Death of a shareholder

The shares of the deceased shareholder vest, in terms of the rights they represent, in executors (or administrators if there is no will) who can sell or otherwise dispose of them, e.g. to a beneficiary, without actually being registered, subject to any restrictions on transfer which the articles may contain. CA 2006, s 774 provides that the company must accept probate of the will, or in the case of administrators, letters of administration, as sufficient evidence of the title of the personal representatives notwithstanding anything in its articles.

Personal representatives can insist on registration as members in respect of the deceased's shares unless the articles otherwise provide. Under *Table A*, Reg 30, the directors have the same power to refuse to register personal representatives as they have to register transfers, provided the shares are not fully paid, i.e. Reg 24 applies and they may refuse the transfer on the grounds that the personal representative is a 'person' of whom they do not approve. The company cannot insist that personal representatives be registered as members, but Reg 30 of *Table A* allows them to elect to be registered subject to the above restriction. If they are registered as members, they become personally liable for capital unpaid on the shares with an indemnity from the estate, but they do receive the benefit of being able to vote the shares at general and class meetings and to participate in written resolutions. *Table A*, Reg 31 excludes voting rights unless personal representatives are registered. They receive all the benefits attaching to the shares without registration except voting rights. Where, under the articles, they are refused registration, they may now apply to the court for relief, e.g. an order to the company to register them under CA 2006, s 994 on the grounds of unfair prejudice.

(b) Mental Health Act patients

Transmission also occurs to a receiver appointed by the Court of Protection to the estate of a person becoming a patient under the Mental Health Act 1983 (as amended by the Mental Health Act 2007). The authority of the receiver is established by production of the protection order of the court appointing him. The position of the receiver is similar to that of personal representatives.

(c) Bankruptcy of a shareholder

On the bankruptcy of a member, the right to deal with the shares passes to the trustee in bankruptcy, and he can sell them without actually being registered or he can elect to register subject to any restrictions in the articles. Regulation 30 of *Table A* allows him to elect to register. He would then be personally liable to pay any calls on the shares subject to a right of indemnity against the estate. When the trustee sells the shares, the sale is effected by production to the company of the share certificate together with the Department of Business, Innovation and Skills' certificate appointing the trustee and a transfer signed by him. A trustee cannot vote unless he is registered but can direct the bankrupt on the way he must vote (*Morgan* v *Gray* [1953] 1 All ER 213).

A trustee in bankruptcy has a right of disclaimer under which he may disclaim shares as onerous property where there are calls due on them and they would have little value if sold. This power is given by s 315 of the Insolvency Act 1986. Disclaimer is effected by the trustee serving upon the company a notice in writing disclaiming the shares, and he is then not personally liable to pay any calls if registered and the estate of the bankrupt member is no longer liable as such. The company may claim damages, which in the case of shares of little value, which was the reason for the disclaimer, are unlikely to be as much as the calls due but unpaid (*Re Hallet, ex parte National Insurance Co* [1894] WN 156). Shares disclaimed may be reissued as paid up to the extent to which cash has been received on them. However, the company would have to ask the court for an order temporarily vesting the shares in the company so that it could reissue them. Section 320 of the Insolvency Act 1986 applies. This is because on disclaimer the shares vest in the Crown (Treasury Solicitor) as *bona vacantia* (property without an owner). The situation is one of legal difficulty and doubt and legal advice would have to be sought from a firm specialising in insolvency practice.

Trustees

The shares, if trust property, are transferred to the trustees by the settlor (in a lifetime trust), or by his personal representatives where the trust is by will. If new trustees or replacement trustees are appointed once the trust has begun, the shares must be transferred to the new trustees by the surviving former trustees in the usual way, i.e. by stock transfer form. There is no transfer by operation of law on the appointment of the new trustee, nor under s 40 of the Trustee Act 1925 where the trustee is appointed by deed.

Section 40 provides for the automatic transfer of property without a transfer or conveyance to include a new trustee where his appointment is by deed. However, the section specifically excludes company shares, which must be transferred into the joint names of the trustees including the new one(s) in the ordinary way.

Essay questions

1   Edward owns a small number of shares in Severn Ltd, a private company. He wishes to transfer these shares to a charity but fears that the directors may object.

    For what reasons may the directors refuse to register such a transfer and for how long may they delay their decision?   *(The Institute of Chartered Accountants in England and Wales)*

2 Write explanatory notes on TWO of the following:

(a) The doctrine of *ultra vires*.
(b) Promoters.
(c) Certification of transfer forms.
(d) Ways in which shares may be mortgaged.

(Kingston University)

3 (a) What is the procedure for varying the rights attached to a class of shares if the memorandum and articles are silent on the matter? What safeguards are there for a minority of that class?

(b) Explain the liability of a person who presents a forged share transfer to the company for registration and is registered accordingly. Can the company ever be liable in this situation?

(The Institute of Chartered Secretaries and Administrators)

4 Sprouts Ltd wishes to change its name to Greenstuff Ltd and trade under the name of Brassica Wholefoods. What steps must be taken to achieve this result?

(The Institute of Company Accountants)

5 Write notes on TWO of the following:

(a) The name clause of the memorandum.
(b) The transfer of shares.
(c) Variation of class rights.
(d) Promoters.

(The Institute of Chartered Secretaries and Administrators)

Test your knowledge

Four alternative answers are given. Select ONE only. Circle the answer which you consider to be correct. Check your answers by referring back to the information given in the chapter and against the answers at the end of the text.

1 When is it necessary to certify a transfer of shares?

A Where there are pre-emption rights in the articles.
B When a part holding of shares is being transferred to the transferee(s).
C When shares are being transferred to an existing member.
D On all transfers of unlisted shares.

2 What is the legal position of a person who buys shares on the faith of a share certificate issued by a company to a transferee on the basis of a forged transfer?

A The person gets an equitable interest in the shares.
B The transfer is valid and the person gets a good title if he has acted in good faith.
C The transfer is void and the person cannot claim against the company.
D The transfer is void but the person has a claim for compensation against the company.

3 Conwy Ltd has a provision in its articles which allows a transfer of shares to be made orally. This provision is:

A Invalid

B Valid

C Voidable

D Valid if the transfer is to an existing member

4 Botham dies and leaves all his shares in Thames Ltd to Gower. Under the articles the shares in Thames 'can only be transferred by the directors'. What must Botham's executor do to pass the shares to Gower?

A Become a member and sign a transfer deed.

B Sign a transfer in the form of a deed.

C Sign a stock transfer form.

D Become a member and sign a stock transfer form once on the register of members.

5 Maurice has become bankrupt. What is the legal effect of his bankruptcy on his shareholding in Mersey Ltd?

A Maurice retains his title and control of the shares but his trustee can file a stop notice.

B Maurice retains his title but the control of the shares is transmitted to his trustee in bankruptcy.

C The title to the shares passes to Maurice's trustee in bankruptcy.

D Maurice retains his title and control of the shares.

6 In which of the following circumstances is Fred not a member of a company?

A Fred subscribed the memorandum but his name is not as yet on the register of members.

B Fred has been allotted shares and entered on the register but has not received a letter of allotment.

C Fred has lodged a transfer with the company as transferee but has not yet been entered on the register of members.

D Fred has sold all his shares in the company to Bill but Fred's name has not yet been removed from the register of members.

The answers to test your knowledge questions appear on p. 645.

Suggested further reading

Hannigan, 'Altering the articles to allow for compulsory transfer – Dragging minority shareholders to a reluctant exit' [2007] JBL 471.

15

Shares – payment for and insider dealing

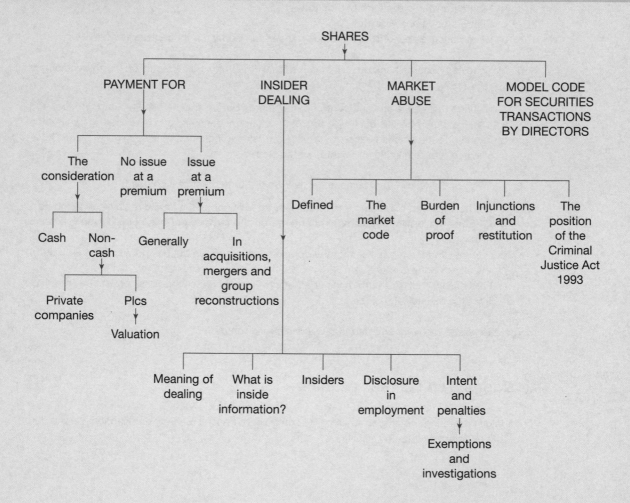

In this chapter we shall deal with the methods of payment for shares and the rules which apply according to the consideration offered, together with the rules relating to insider dealing. Companies Acts 2006, Chapter 5 to Part 17 is the applicable provisions that deal with payment for shares.

The consideration – generally

A member of a company must pay for his shares in full, and no arrangement between the company and the members can affect this rule (*Ooregum Gold Mining Co of India* v *Roper* [1892] AC 125). However, payment need not be in cash but may be for some other consideration. Where this is so issues at a discount may still in effect be made in private companies. CA 2006, s 580 requires that shares must not be allotted at a discount. CA 2006, s 581 considers provision for different amounts to be paid on shares.

Payment in cash

This is generally affected by handing cash or a cheque to the company, but if the company pays an existing debt by an issue of shares to the creditor, this set-off arrangement is deemed to be a payment in cash. CA 2006, s 582 provides that shares allotted by a company and any premium on them may be paid up in money or money's worth (including goodwill and know-how). CA 2006, s 583 provides the definition for payment in cash: a share in a company is deemed paid up in cash, or allotted for cash, if the consideration received for the allotment or payment up is a cash consideration.

Re Harmony and Montague Tin and Copper Mining Co, Spargo's Case
(1873) LR 8 Ch App 407

A company purchased a mine from Spargo and he made an agreement to buy shares in the company. The moneys owed by Spargo to the company for his shares and by the company to Spargo for the mine were payable immediately. Under a further agreement between Spargo and the company, he was debited with the amount payable on the shares and credited with the purchase price of the property making up the difference in cash. It was *held* by the Court of Appeal in Chancery that Spargo must be deemed to have paid for his shares in cash.

Comment

The provisions of the Companies Act relating to an issue of shares for a non-cash consideration seem not to apply to set-offs of this kind which are regarded as cash transactions. Section 582 of the 2006 Act provides, in effect, that the issue of shares to satisfy a liquidated sum, i.e. an existing quantified debt, as in this case, is not an issue for a consideration other than cash.

Considerations other than cash

(a) In private companies

Such considerations are legal, and the consideration very often consists in the sale of property to the company or the rendering of services. The consideration offered must be sufficient to support the contract in law and must not, for example, be past, though in private companies, at least, it need not be adequate.

Re Eddystone Marine Insurance Co [1893] 3 Ch 9

The company proposed to raise capital from the public, but passed a resolution before going to the public to allot £6,000 worth of fully paid shares to the existing directors and shareholders for a consideration other than cash. A copy of the agreement was filed in which the consideration was said to be services rendered by the allottees to the company during its formation. There was in fact no such rendering of services. Eighteen months later the company was wound up, and the liquidator proposed to regard the shares as unpaid on the grounds that there was no consideration given for them.

Held – by the Court of Appeal – the allottees must contribute the nominal value of the shares. There was in fact no consideration because the services had not been rendered, but even if they had, they would not have supported the contract to take the shares because the consideration would have been past.

Comment

CA 2006, s 585 provides that a public company shall not accept at any time in payment up of its shares or any premium on them, an undertaking given by any person that he or another should do work or perform services for the company or any other person. If shares are issued for services by a public company the holder is liable to pay the nominal value and any premium to the company plus interest set by the authorities pursuant to CA 2006, s 592. This applies whether the services are rendered or not. If services are rendered the person who renders them must pay for his shares and submit an account for the services.

Re Wragg Ltd [1897] 1 Ch 796

Messrs Wragg and Martin were the proprietors of a livery stable business and they agreed to sell it to a company, Wragg Ltd, which they formed. The business was sold to the company for £46,300, among the assets being horses and carriages valued for the purposes of the sale at £27,000. The company paid for the business by issuing shares and debentures to Wragg and Martin, and later, when the company was being wound up, the liquidator asked the court to declare that the shares were not fully paid up because it appeared that the horses and carriages had been overvalued and were really worth only £15,000 at the date of sale.

Held – by the Court of Appeal – that:

(a) Where fully paid shares are allotted to vendors under a contract registered in accordance with the Companies Acts, it is not illegal for the said vendors or promoters to make a profit, though disclosure is required. In this case disclosure did not arise, since Wragg and Martin and certain nominees of theirs became the only shareholders in Wragg Ltd, and they were aware of the details of the transaction.

(b) The court will not go behind a contract of this sort and enquire into the adequacy of the consideration unless the consideration appears on the face of the contract to be insufficient or illusory. This was not the case here for if the company had received advice on the purchase of the business, some advisers might have thought that, looking at the business as a whole, it was a good bargain at £46,300.

(c) Where persons, as vendors, make an agreement with themselves and their nominees in the character of a limited company it is, following *Salomon v Salomon & Co*, 1897, an agreement between independent legal entities and is valid.

Comment

The CA 2006, s 585 places restrictions on public companies in regard to the allotment of shares for a non-cash consideration by requiring, among other things, a valuation of that consideration. However, in private companies the company's valuation of the consideration will still be accepted as conclusive in the absence of, for example, fraud.

It should be noted, however, that the court will enquire into the agreement where the consideration does not really exist.

Hong Kong & China Gas Co Ltd v *Glen* [1914] 1 Ch 527

The company agreed that in return for a concession to supply gas to the city of Victoria, Hong Kong, it would allot the vendor of the concession 400 shares of £10 each, fully paid; and it further agreed that if and when it increased its capital in the future, the vendor or his executors, administrators or assigns should have as fully paid, one-fifth of the increased capital. In this action the company asked the court to decide whether the part of the agreement relating to the one-fifth share of any increase in the capital of the company was binding.

Held – by the High Court – it was not. The insufficiency of the consideration appeared on the face of the contract, for the company had agreed to give at any future time or times a wholly indefinite and possibly unlimited value for the purchase of the concession.

An agreement to allot shares for future services, even in a private company, may mean that the allottee will become liable to pay for the shares in full, since if he does not render the services, the company would otherwise be reduced to a mere action for damages, and would not have an action for the actual price of the shares, and it is doubtful whether a company can replace the liability of a member to pay for his shares in full with a mere action for damages (*Gardner v Iredale* [1912] 1 Ch 700).

Where shares are issued for a consideration other than cash, the contract, or if the contract is not in writing written particulars of it, must be sent to the Registrar for registration within one month of the allotment of the shares. If there is no such registration within the time prescribed, the officers of the company are liable to a fine under the CA 2006, s 590, but the allotment is not affected. It should be noted that *mere registration* of a contract will not make it binding on the company if there is no consideration for it (*Re Eddystone Marine Insurance Co*, 1893, see above).

(b) In public companies

Under s 587 of the CA 2006 a public company is only allowed to allot shares as fully or partly paid by an undertaking to transfer a non-cash asset to the company if the transfer is to take place within five years of the date of the allotment.

In addition, under CA 2006, s 593 an allotment for a non-cash consideration is not to be made unless the non-cash asset has been valued by an independent accountant who would be qualified to be the auditor of the company (or by someone else approved by that

> **Independent Accountants' Report issued in accordance with s 597 of the Companies Act 2006 to Dove plc**
>
> As required by s 597 of the Companies Act 2006, we report on the valuation of the consideration for the allotment to H Hawke of two hundred thousand shares of a nominal value of one pound issued at a premium of 50 pence per share. The shares and the share premium are to be treated as fully paid up.
>
> The consideration given by H Hawke is freehold building land situated at Meadow Drift, Chelmsford, Essex. The land was valued on the basis of its open market value by R Robin, FRICS, on 1 December 2004, and, in our opinion, it is reasonable to accept that valuation. In our opinion, the method of valuation of the freehold building land was reasonable and there appears to have been no material change in the value since it was made. On the basis of this valuation, in our opinion, the value of the consideration is not less than £300,000.
>
> Accountants & Co.

Figure 15.1 A typical report to satisfy CA 2006, s 597

independent accountant). In addition, the independent accountant must have reported to the company on his valuation during the six months prior to the allotment, and must state that the value of the consideration is at least equal to the value of the shares being allotted. A copy of the report must also have been sent to the allottee and filed at the Companies Registry with the return of allotments (CA 2006, s 597). A typical report to satisfy s 597 appears in Figure 15.1.

A valuation of the kind set out above is not required in a share exchange as in a takeover bid where Predator is acquiring Victim by exchanging Predator shares for Victim shares so that the consideration for Predator shares is the assets of Victim, but all the holders of shares in Victim must be able to take part in the arrangement (CA 2006, s 593). The valuation is not a mere formality since failure to obtain a valuation when shares in a plc are allotted for a non-cash consideration introduces the rather startling provisions of CA 2006, s 606, i.e. that the recipient of the shares must pay for them. This is in the nature of a penalty and there are no provisions in the Act for recovery of the property. This result can be mitigated under s 606(1) which allows the recipient to apply to the court for exemption.

An exemption was granted in *Re Ossory Estates plc* [1988] BCLC 213 where shares were issued for a non-cash consideration, i.e. property, without an accountant's valuation. However, there was evidence before the court that the company had sold some of the properties at a profit. This suggested that they were at least as valuable as the shares issued for them and the recipient of the shares was excused from paying the cash penalty.

Under CA 2006, s 598 for two years following the date of issue of the certificate that a company registered as a public company is entitled to commence business, the company may not acquire assets from subscribers to the memorandum having an aggregate value equal to 10 per cent or more of the nominal value of the issued share capital unless:

(a) the valuation rules set out above are complied with; and

(b) the acquisition of the asset(s) and the terms of the acquisition have been approved by an ordinary resolution of the company. A copy of that resolution must be filed at the Companies Registry within 15 days of its passing.

The report under CA 2006, s 600 is similar to that under CA 2006, s 601 except that the consideration need not be shares and approval in general meeting is required.

Similar rules apply on re-registration as a public company where non-cash assets equal to at least 10 per cent of the nominal value of the issued share capital at that time are acquired from persons who are members of the company at the time of re-registration. These provisions do not apply to assets acquired in the ordinary course of business.

In addition, under CA 2006, s 584, the shares which a subscriber of the memorandum of a public company agrees in the memorandum to take must be paid up in cash, and under CA 2006, s 585 a public company must not accept at any time in payment up of its shares or any premium on them, an undertaking given by any person that he or another should do work or perform services in the future for the company or any other person.

Where the above requirements are contravened, CA 2006, s 587 provides that the allottee and his successors, but not purchasers for value without notice, will be liable to pay to the company the amount outstanding in respect of the allotment with interest which is currently 5 per cent per annum. The company and any officer in default may also be liable to a fine. However, as we have seen, the court may grant relief where the applicant has acted in good faith and it is just and equitable to grant relief.

Prohibition on allotment of shares at a discount

Companies Acts 2006, s 580 prohibits the issue of shares at a discount, though, as we have seen, this may happen in private companies where there is a *non-cash consideration* for the reason that the directors' valuation is accepted, so that there is in law no issue at a discount. A private company that issued shares for *cash at a discount* would be acting illegally. The power to pay underwriting commission under CA 2006, s 552 is not affected. Where shares are allotted in contravention of CA 2006, s 580 those shares shall be treated as paid up by the payment to the company of the amount of the nominal value of the shares less the amount of the discount, but the allottee shall be liable to pay the company the latter amount and shall be liable to pay interest thereon at the appropriate rate which is currently 5 per cent per annum (s 592). Persons who take the shares from the original allottee are jointly and severally liable with the original allottee to pay the amount mentioned above unless they are purchasers for value, and even a purchaser for value may be liable if he has actual knowledge of the contravention of s 588 at the time of the purchase.

Debentures may be issued at a discount, though where there is a right to exchange the debentures for shares at par value the debentures are good but the right to exchange is void.

 Mosely v Koffyfontein Mines Ltd [1904] 2 Ch 108

The company proposed to issue to its shareholders certain debentures at a discount of 20 per cent, the debentures to be repayable by the company on 1 November 1909. The debenture holders were to have the right at any time prior to 1 May 1909, to exchange the debentures for fully paid shares in the company on the basis of one fully paid share of £1 nominal value for every £1 of nominal value of debentures held. The court was asked in this case to decide whether the proposed issue of debentures was void.

Held – by the Court of Appeal – it was void, because the exchange of debentures for fully paid shares would lead to the issue of shares at a discount whenever the right was exercised.

Comment

Issue of shares at a discount was permitted prior to the Companies Act 1980, but only if, amongst other things, there had been an ordinary resolution of the members, together with the permission of the court. Issue at a discount is now forbidden by CA 2006, s 552.

Shares issued at a premium

Share premiums: generally

There is nothing to prevent a company issuing shares at a premium, e.g. £1 shares at a price of £1.25p; and, indeed, where it is desired to issue further shares, of a class already dealt in on the Stock Exchange at a substantial premium, it is a practical necessity to do so except perhaps in a rights issue.

However, CA 2006, s 610 requires that such premium must be credited to a 'share premium account' to be treated as capital except in so far as it may be written down to pay up fully paid bonus shares, to write off preliminary expenses, commissions and discounts in respect of new issues, and to provide any premium on the redemption of any debentures. It may also be used in a very restricted way to charge the premium on redemption of shares if this premium has been paid out of the proceeds of a fresh issue of shares made for the purpose.

The above rules prevent such premiums which are capital by nature from being paid away as dividends. Any balance on the share premium account must be shown in the balance sheet.

Section 610 in fact recognises that the real capital of a company is the price which subscribers pay for its shares and not the somewhat artificial nominal value. This results, in effect, in an admission that shares are really of no par value. If no par value shares were issued, the capital of the company would simply be the total paid for its shares by subscribers. This is known in the United States as the company's paid-in capital. Where the whole of the issued price has not been paid, the total amount paid plus the total amount remaining to be paid is in the United States called the company's stated capital.

If it were possible to issue no par shares in England, the accidental payment of dividends out of capital would automatically be precluded by the company's obligation to keep in hand assets worth at least the amount paid by subscribers plus the amount of the company's outstanding debts. However, until no par value shares are allowed, the law can ensure that the issue price of the shares is not dissipated in paying dividends only by using the somewhat inelegant device of the share premium account.

The Companies Act 2006 requires share premiums to be credited to a share premium account whether the shares are issued for cash or otherwise. In consequence, the Act always applies whether premiums are paid in cash or kind and so if a company issues shares for a consideration in kind which is worth more than the nominal value of the shares, a sum equal to the excess value of the consideration has to be transferred to a share premium account.

Henry Head & Co Ltd v Ropner Holdings Ltd [1952] Ch 124

Ropner Holdings was formed as a holding company, its main object being to acquire the whole of the issued share capital of the Pool Shipping Co Ltd and the Ropner Shipping Co Ltd for the purposes of amalgamation. Ropner Holdings issued the whole of its authorised capital of £1,759,606 (this being equal to the sum of the issued capitals of the two shipping companies) to the shareholders of Pool Shipping and Ropner Shipping on the basis of £1 share for each £1 share held in the two shipping companies. The value of the assets of the two shipping companies, when Ropner Holdings acquired the shares, was £6,830,972, and the difference between this figure and £1,759,606, less formation expenses, was shown on the balance sheet of Ropner Holdings as 'Capital Reserve – Share Premium Account' so as to comply with the Companies Act 1948. The claimants, who were large shareholders in Ropner Holdings, asked that the company be required to treat the reserve as a general and not a capital reserve because otherwise no payment out of the reserve could be made unless the procedure for reduction of capital was followed.

Held – by Harman J – Ropner Holdings had, in effect, issued its shares at a premium within the meaning of what is now s 130, and was bound to retain the reserve as a capital reserve.

Comment

The case is still authority for the statement that a share premium account must be raised even where the consideration is not cash. However, in the circumstances of the case merger relief would presumably have been available.

Share premiums – acquisitions, mergers and group reconstructions

Companies Acts 2006, ss 611–615 give relief, in certain circumstances, from the requirement to set up a share premium account under s 610.

Acquisitions and mergers

(a) Acquisitions. This involves a takeover where the predator company P makes an offer to the shareholders of the Victim company V either with or without the consent of the board of V. The price offered is usually above the market price. If V is acquired, i.e. if there are sufficient acceptances from the shareholders of V, the investment of P in V must be shown in the books of P at its true value, i.e. the value of the consideration given. This has the effect of treating the reserves of V as pre-acquisition and therefore as undistributable and in particular pre-acquisition profits are locked up.

This position is unchanged by the CA 2006 and pre-acquisition profits must be locked up because if V pays a dividend to P out of pre-acquisition profits and P uses it to pay dividend to its shareholders P is returning the capital it used for the purchase of V's shares to its members because the pre-acquisition profits were represented in the price which P paid for V's shares.

(b) Mergers. In the case of a merger between P and V involving a share-for-share exchange, e.g. P issues its equity shares to the members of V on a one-for-one basis, in exchange for the shares of the members of V, as a result of which P becomes the holder of 90 per cent or more of the equity shares of V, then there is no need to value the investment in V at its true value. The value may simply be the nominal value of the shares exchanged and so no share premium account is created as was the case in *Henry Head* under the old law (see above). Thus, the reserves of V need not be treated as pre-acquisition and pre-acquisition profits are not locked up.

Section 613 sets out the minimum conditions which must be met before a company can use the merger method of accounting. The conditions are:

1 The parent company must acquire at least 90 per cent by nominal value of relevant shares in the target company. This is then a genuine 'pooling of assets'. Relevant shares are shares carrying unrestricted rights to participate both in distributions and in the assets of the undertaking on liquidation.
2 The 90 per cent must be achieved under an arrangement for the issue of shares by the parent company, i.e. merger accounting is appropriate only where there is substantially a share-for-share exchange. It is permissible to have a prior holding but the 2006 Act does not restrict its size.
3 The issue of equity shares must be the dominant element in the consideration offered by the parent company for the relevant shares in the company to be acquired. The fair value of the consideration which may be given in a form other than equity shares is limited to 10 per cent of the nominal value of the equity shares issued.
4 Finally, merger accounting is not available as of right even if (1)–(3) are satisfied but only where its use accords with generally accepted accounting principles and practice.

Students who are also taking accounting courses will appreciate that this area of the law is subject to Accounting Standards issued by the Accounting Standards Board. It would not be appropriate to deal with these here and an examination in company law would not require knowledge of them. They would normally be examined in accounting papers.

However some of them are so important that they have a major effect on statutory provisions and must be noted in outline here. Corporate mergers will in regard to business combinations agreed on or after 31 March 2004 always be treated as if one party is buying the other (an acquisition) under amendments to International Accounting Standard 36 issued by the International Accounting Standards Board. As already noted merger accounting enables the enlarged group to take a full year of profits from both companies. Under the amended IAS 36, companies will have to treat mergers as takeovers so the enlarged organisation can only count profits since the date of acquisition (acquisition accounting).

The need to write down goodwill following a takeover is abolished. In future all goodwill is to be valued according to the profits that are actually earned from the business and projected to be earned in the future.

Group reconstructions

Companies Acts 2006, s 611 provides limited relief in the case of certain group reconstructions. The reconstructions to which the CA 2006 applies are those where the transactions are as follows:

(a) a wholly-owned subsidiary (the issuing company) has allotted some of its shares either to its holding company or to another wholly-owned subsidiary of its holding company;
(b) the allotment is a consideration for the transfer to it of shares or any non-cash assets in another subsidiary of the holding company. This other subsidiary need not necessarily be wholly owned.

The purposes of reconstruction and the variety of changes that can be achieved by the use of the reconstruction sections of the CA 2006 are further described later in the text (see Chapter 26 ●).

However, let us assume that our holding company (H) holds 100 per cent of the shares in company A and 75 per cent of the shares in company B. A allots 1,000 £1 ordinary shares (valued at £6 per share) to H; in return H transfers its 75 per cent holding in B to A. If there was no relief in this situation, A would have had to raise a share premium account in its books. However, under s 611(2) A need only transfer to a share premium account an amount equal to the 'minimum premium value'.

This is the amount, if any, by which the base value of the shares in the subsidiary (B) exceeds the aggregate nominal value of the shares that the issuing company (A) allotted in consideration for the transfer.

Base value is the lower of:

(a) the cost to the holding company (H) of the shares in B;
(b) the amount at which the shares of B were stated immediately prior to this transfer in the accounting records of H.

Thus, if in our example the shares in B cost £4,000 but are standing in the accounting records of H at £3,000 the base value is £3,000. The nominal value of the shares allotted by A is £1,000 so the minimum premium value is £2,000 and this must be transferred to A's share premium account, but not, of course, the true value of the consideration it received from B by allotting 1,000 shares to H.

Finally, it should be noted that the CA 2006 imposes no obligation on a company to issue its shares at a premium when a premium could be obtained. Consequently, the issue of shares at par is valid even though a premium could have been obtained (*Hilder* v *Dexter* [1902] AC 474) but directors who fail to require subscribers to pay a premium which could have been obtained are guilty of breach of duty to the company and will be liable to pay the premium themselves as damages (*Lowry* v *Consolidated African Selection Trust Ltd* [1940] 2 All ER 545). Nevertheless, there are some exceptions to this ruling. For example, directors may issue shares at a price below their market value to existing shareholders in pursuance of a rights offer made to all the shareholders of the company, or to all the ordinary shareholders in proportion to the nominal values of their existing holdings. The reason for this is that all the shareholders concerned can avail themselves of the offer and if they do none of them will suffer a diminution of their percentage interest in the net assets or earnings of the company and consequently none of them will be harmed.

Insider dealing

Part V of the Criminal Justice Act 1993 applies and Sch 2 to that Act sets out the securities covered by its provisions. It is not necessary at this level to list all of these, but obviously shares issued by companies are covered, and the prosecutions that have been brought under the insider-dealing rules, which are very few, have been concerned with dealings in company shares. However, the 1993 Act also covers gilts, which are interest-bearing securities as distinct from shares which pay a dividend, and where insider dealing could consist of dealing in such securities with inside information as to changes in interest rates either up or down.

The securities must also be listed on a regulated market such as the Stock Exchange, but dealing in differences is covered too. Those who deal in differences do not buy shares or even take an option on them. The deal consists of a forecast of the price of a particular security at a given future time, and those who enter into such deals with inside information which helps them better to predict the price will commit an offence.

The Act does not apply to unlisted securities or face-to-face transactions, so that cases such as *Percival* v *Wright*, 1902 (see Chapter 21 ◑) are unaltered on their own facts.

Meaning of dealing

A person deals in securities if he acquires or disposes of the securities himself, whether for himself or as the agent of some other person, *or* procures an acquisition or a disposal of the securities by someone else. Therefore, A could acquire shares for himself, or acquire shares as a broker for his client or dispose of them in the same contexts. Alternatively, A may simply advise B to purchase or dispose of shares and still be potentially liable if he has inside information. B may also be liable in this situation if he is a tippee (see below).

What is inside information?

Basically, this is information which relates to the securities themselves or to the state of the company which issued them. It must be specific and precise so that general information about a company, e.g. that it was desirous of moving into the field of supermarkets, would not be enough. In addition the information must not have been made public and must be the sort of information which, if it had been made public, would be likely to have had a significant effect on the price of those securities, e.g. falling or rising profits or decisions to pay a higher dividend than expected, or a lower one or no dividend at all.

Insiders

In order to be guilty of the offence of insider dealing, the individual concerned must be an insider. A person has information as an insider if:

● the information which he has is and he knows it is 'insider information';
● he has the information and he knows that he has it from an 'inside source'.

A person is in possession of information from an 'inside source' if:

● he has the information through being a director, employee or shareholder of a company or by having access to it by reason of his employment, e.g. as auditor; or
● the source of the information is a person within the above categories.

So A is a director of Boxo plc. He has inside information that Boxo's profits when announced in ten days' time will be up (or down). He buys (or sells) Boxo shares himself and is potentially liable. He advises his friend Fred to buy (or sell) Boxo shares but does not tell him why. A is potentially liable but Fred is not – he does not have the inside information. If A tells Fred about the future profit announcement and then Fred deals, Fred is potentially liable, as is A. If Fred advises his son to buy (or sell) Boxo shares but does not tell him why, A and Fred are potentially liable but Fred's son is not. If Fred gives his son the inside information and the son deals, then A and Fred and Fred's son are potentially liable.

Disclosure in the course of employment

Sometimes it is necessary for a person to pass on inside information as part of his employment, as may be the case with an audit manager who passes on inside information to a senior partner of the firm who is in charge of the audit. If the senior partner deals he will be potentially liable, but the audit manager will not since the 1993 Act exempts such persons.

Necessity for intent

Since insider dealing is a crime, it requires, as most but not all crimes do, an intention to see a dealing take place to secure a profit or prevent a loss. It is unlikely that an examiner would go deeply into what is essentially the field of the criminal lawyer, but consider this example: A's son was at college and broke. He asked his father for a loan and his father said, 'Look, son, you're not getting any more money from me – pity you cannot buy some shares in Boxo plc of which I am a director. Next month's profit announcement will be way up on last year's. You could make a killing.' If for some reason A's son was able to scrape up sufficient funds to buy shares in Boxo plc, it is unlikely that his father would be liable because he had no idea that his son would be in a position to buy the shares.

Penalty for insider dealing

The contract is unaffected as in *Percival* v *Wright*, 1902. The sanctions are criminal, the maximum sentence being seven years' imprisonment and/or a fine of unlimited amount. In order to be found guilty, the offence must in general terms be committed while the person concerned was in the UK or the trading market was.

Exemptions

Schedule 2 to the Criminal Justice Act 1993 sets out in particular an exemption for persons operating as market makers, so that, for example, those engaged in making a market for shares on the Stock Exchange are exempt because they would find it difficult to operate markets in shares if they had to stop dealing in them when in possession of what might be inside information about some of them. It should be noted, however, that the exemption covers only the offence of dealing. They are not exempt from the offence of encouraging another to deal.

Market abuse

The Financial Services and Markets Act 2000 introduced the concept of market abuse. Under the relevant provisions, the Financial Services Authority has power to reprimand publicly or impose an unlimited fine on authorised and unauthorised persons for engaging in market abuse. The Financial Services Authority is the sole regulator for the financial services industry and has the power to authorise persons and organisations to operate in it. Its power extends to non-authorised persons and this would include members of professions such as lawyers and accountants who are, for example, authorised by their own professional bodies to give advice incidentally to the practice of their profession, as where an accountant gives a client advice on investments as part of a tax-planning arrangement. Such persons are not authorised by the FSA unless investment advice is their main line of business and yet are covered by the market-abuse rules. Indirect market abuse is covered as where a person requires or encourages another to engage in behaviour that if done by the defendant would amount to market abuse FSMA 2000 (s 123(1) and (3)).

Market abuse defined

FSMA 2000 Section 118(1) defines market abuse as:

- behaviour in relation to any qualifying investments;
- likely to be regarded by regular users of the market as falling below the standard reasonably expected of a person in that position; and
- that falls within at least one of three categories (see below).

In general terms, the behaviour will be in a UK investment market, such as the London Stock Exchange. The regular-user concept is hypothetical and is defined as 'a reasonable person who regularly deals on the market in investments of the kind in question' (FSMA 2000 s 118(10)). The behaviour referred to is set out in FSMA 2000 s 118(2) as:

- based on information not generally available to users of the market which, if available to a regular user, would be likely to be regarded by him as relevant in regard to the terms on which to deal in those investments. *In other words, insider information*;
- likely to give a regular user a false or misleading impression as to the market value of such investments. *In other words, misleading statements and practices*; or
- regarded by a regular user as likely to distort the market in such investments. *In other words, rigging the market*, as where a company makes funds available to a person so that he can buy its shares in order to raise the market price by increased demand so that the shares will be more acceptable as part of takeover consideration by an exchange of shares.

There is a major defence that the person concerned exercised all due diligence to avoid market abuse, and there is a 'safe haven' where the Takeover Panel has ruled that the dealing may go ahead, as where a person with inside knowledge deals as part of a rescue operation to save the company concerned.

The market code

The FSMA gives only a broad definition of abuse but the FSA has drawn up, as the Act requires, a Code of Market Conduct to help particularise abuse. For example, the Code mentions persons using Internet bulletin boards to post misleading information and journalists using inside knowledge to trade in shares.

Burden of proof

Unlike the provisions of the Criminal Justice Act 1993, which are obviously criminal in nature and where proof beyond a reasonable doubt is required (this being the cause of its failure to provide convictions in many cases), the FSA operates under *a civil regime* so that abuse need be proved only on a balance of probabilities. However, because the proceedings might be viewed as criminal in nature under the Convention on Human Rights, the government has excluded the admission of compelled evidence emanating, for example, from a BIS inspection. It has also granted safe harbours and a due diligence defence under the Code and made some legal aid available (ss 114(8), 122, 123(2), 134–136 and 174(2)).

Injunctions and restitution

In order not to disturb the proper working of the market when the FSA imposes a fine, the transaction is not made void or unenforceable. However, for any form of market abuse or misconduct, the FSA can seek to prevent anticipated abuse by a court injunction and ask the court for a restitution order on behalf of victims of abuse to make up their loss. There are defences of reasonable belief and due diligence (ss 382(1) and (8); 383(1), (3) and (10); and 384(1) and (6)).

Position of the Criminal Justice Act 1993

This measure is not repealed and continues to be available for the pursuit of criminal prosecutions.

Model Code for Securities Transactions by directors of listed companies

The Financial Services Authority set up a Model Code for Securities Transactions, to give guidance as to when it is proper for directors of listed companies to deal in the securities of the company. The Code received widespread acceptance and is part of the Listing Rules. The main principles of the Code are:

(a) Directors should not engage in short-term dealings, e.g. purchases and sales over short periods, because it is difficult to avoid the suggestion that such dealing is based on inside knowledge.
(b) Directors should not deal for a minimum period prior to the announcement of reports and results. Where results are announced half-yearly, the closed period for dealings should be the previous two months but, if announcements are more frequent, e.g. quarterly, the period is one month immediately preceding the announcement of the quarterly results.

    Directors should not deal either when an exceptional announcement is to be made which would probably affect the market price of the company's shares, or when they are in possession of knowledge which when accessible to the public will affect the market price of the shares.
(c) A director must obtain clearance from the chairman (or other designated director) before dealing. The chairman must obtain clearance either from the board or the designated director before dealing. Clearance must not be given in a closed period.
(d) A written record of dealings should be kept by the company and the board as a whole should see that directors comply with a practice to be established within the company on the above lines. In this respect a director should ensure that where he is a beneficiary under a trust, the trustees notify him after dealing so that it can be recorded. In addition, a director must return dealings of a spouse or for minor children.

The above rules apply also to 'relevant employees', i.e. those whose work within the company may cause them to be in possession of price-sensitive information in regard to its securities and to dealings by a director's 'connected' person, e.g. a spouse.

Full details of the Model Code appear in the Listing Rules (the 'Purple Book') as an appendix to Chapter 16 of those rules.

Essay questions

1 Give an account of the statutory restrictions which seek to ensure that when shares are issued by a company, they are paid for either in money or in money's worth. *(Napier University)*

2 'A survey of price movements . . . showed clearly that there was a general tendency for the price of shares in bid-for companies to rise sharply before the announcement of takeover bids, which is in itself *prima facie* evidence of "inside buying". And there has been a continuing series of cases in which specific allegations of improper conduct by insiders have been made. The question of control over insider trading has consequently been a matter of general concern in recent years.' (Hadden)

How far has legislation alleviated this concern? *(University of Central Lancashire)*

3 (a) Druid Ltd has recently issued an additional one thousand shares. Five hundred of these were issued to its former employee, Edwin, in return for his past services and his agreement not to set up a competing business in the same locality. The other 500 were issued to Francis in return for the use for a year of his garage as storage space. Previously, Francis had let his garage for this purpose for £100 per annum.

Discuss. How would your answer be different if Druid Ltd had been a public company?

(b) Gorgon Ltd has an issued share capital of £2 million. In 1999 it made a trading profit of £100,000 but the value of its assets fell to £1 million. In 1998, it made a trading loss of £50,000.

Advise the directors whether, and how much of, the 1999 profit is available for distribution as dividend. How would your answer differ if Gorgon Ltd was a public company?

(The Institute of Chartered Secretaries and Administrators)

4 (a) Explain what is meant by the term 'capital maintenance'.

(b) Discuss how the provisions of the Companies Act 2006 attempt to ensure capital maintenance by regulating:
(i) the payment of dividends,
(ii) the issue of shares at a premium.

(The Chartered Institute of Management Accountants)

5 Who is an 'insider' and what is 'inside information' for the purposes of the laws relating to insider dealing? What prohibitions are imposed on the activities of insiders? State the main exemptions to these prohibitions. *(Authors' question)*

6 James agrees to pay £2m for a controlling interest in Sapphire plc providing the company transfers £3m deposited with its present bankers to Emerald Bank from which James has

arranged to borrow £2m. After the transfer Emerald Bank honours the cheque drawn by James to pay for the shares in Sapphire plc.

Discuss the legality of the above transactions.

(The Institute of Chartered Accountants in England and Wales)

7 Rich and Wealthy are partners in a firm which they wish to convert into a limited company, but they are undecided between incorporating with private status or public status. Advise them as to the advantages and restrictions of each type of company.

(The Institute of Company Accountants)

Test your knowledge

Four alternative answers are given. Select ONE only. Circle the answer which you consider to be correct. Check your answers by referring back to the information given in the chapter and against the answers at the end of the text.

1 Boxo plc was formed five years ago. It now proposes to issue 100,000 shares of £1 each to Alan in return for freehold land in Barchester. In order that the transaction should conform with company law:

   A There must be a valuation of the land by the company's auditor.
   B There must be a valuation by the company's auditor but only if the land is estimated to be worth more than 10 per cent of the company's issued share capital.
   C There must be a valuation by an independent accountant qualified to be the company's auditor, regardless of the estimated value of the land.
   D No valuation is required.

2 Which of the following is a permissible use of the share premium account under s 130 of the Companies Act 2006?

   A Writing off a premium on redemption of any ordinary shares.
   B Writing off goodwill.
   C Writing off a premium on the redemption of debentures.
   D Writing off a deficit on the profit and loss account.

3 Trent plc has issued convertible debentures to Bill at a discount. The legal position is:

   A the issue is valid but the right to convert to shares is void.
   B the issue is valid and so is the right to convert to shares.
   C the issue is void and so therefore is the right to convert to shares.
   D the issue is valid and so is the right to convert to shares if the members of Trent agree by ordinary resolution.

4 John is a director of Derwent plc, a listed company. The board of Derwent received at its last meeting a report by Joe, the finance director of Derwent, that Derwent's profits would be up by 30 per cent and that this would appear in the press report of the annual results in two weeks' time. Next day John told Sid, his golfing companion, that Derwent's profits would be 30 per cent up and Sid bought shares in Derwent. On the same day Sid said to his son Ronald, who was a well-paid consultant engineer, that he 'really ought to have some shares in Derwent because they seem to be a good thing'. Ronald also bought shares in Derwent. When the

results were announced the shares in Derwent increased in price by 0.5p per share. Which of the following statements represents the legal liability of the parties?

A Only John is liable.
B John and Sid are liable.
C John and Joe are liable.
D John, Joe and Ronald are liable.

5 George, who is a creditor of Tees Ltd, can object to the court, regardless of the amount of his debt, about a resolution of the company which has the effect of:

A Writing off goodwill against the share premium account.
B Repaying debenture holders.
C Writing off a deficit on profit and loss account to share capital.
D Repaying non-redeemable share capital.

6 George, a director and member, proposes to transfer his shares in Moorgate Ltd in breach of a pre-emption clause in the articles of Moorgate which provides that members will offer their shares to other members first and that the other members may purchase them. What action can the other shareholders take?

A Restrain the transfer through an action by the company.
B Bring an action against George through the company for breach of his fiduciary duties as a director.
C Bring a personal action to prevent the transfer as being in breach of contract.
D They can take no action.

The answers to test your knowledge questions appear on p. 645.

16

Membership – capacity, registration, director and substantial holdings, annual return

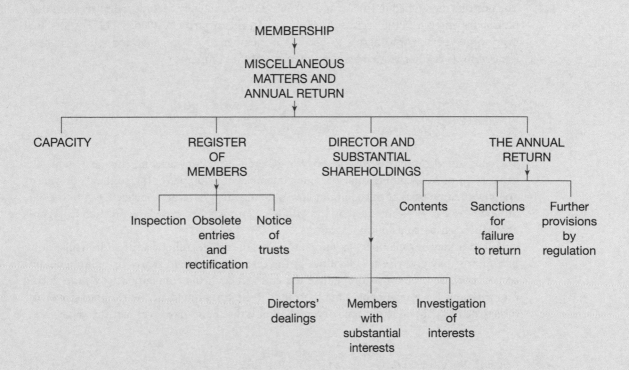

There are several ways in which membership of a company may be acquired. These are as follows:

(a) *By subscribing the memorandum.* When the company is registered, the persons who subscribed the memorandum automatically become members on subscription, and must be put on the register of members on registration of the company (s 112(1), Companies Act 2006).

(b) *By making an application* on the basis of listing particulars or a prospectus for an allotment of shares.

(c) *By taking a transfer* from an existing member.

(d) By succeeding to shares on the death or bankruptcy of a member.

The persons mentioned in (b), (c) and (d) above do not actually become members until their names are entered in the register of members. In this regard CA 2006, s 122(2) states that every other person who agrees to become a member of a company, and whose name is entered in its register of members, is a member of the company.

Capacity

The question of capacity is governed by the general law of contract, and anyone who has the capacity to make a contract may become a member of a company. The contracts of minors are governed by rules of the common law some of which have been enacted, e.g. in the Sale of Goods Act 1979 as amended by the Minor's Contracts Act 1987. The position as regards company membership appears below.

A minor may be a member of a company unless the articles otherwise provide. Registration of a minor may give rise to difficulties in the case of partly paid shares or unlimited companies, because a minor can repudiate the contract with the company at any time during minority and for a reasonable time thereafter. If he does repudiate, he cannot recover the money he has paid up to the time of repudiation if the shares have ever had any value.

 Steinberg v Scala (Leeds) Ltd [1923] 2 Ch 452

The claimant, Miss Steinberg, purchased shares in the defendant company and paid certain sums of money on application, on allotment and on one call. Being unable to meet future calls, she repudiated the contract while still a minor and claimed:

(a) rectification of the register of members to remove her name therefrom, thus relieving her from liability on future calls; and

(b) the recovery of the money already paid.

The company agreed to rectify the register and issue was joined on the claim to recover the money paid.

Held – the claim under (b) above failed because there had not been total failure of consideration. The shares had some value and gave some rights even though the claimant had not received any dividends and the shares had always stood at a discount on the market.

The Family Law Reform Act 1969, s 1 reduced the age of majority from 21 to 18 years. There is a general provision in the Act that a person attains a particular age, i.e. not only the age of majority, on the first moment of the relevant birthday.

A company always has power to refuse to accept a minor as a transferee or shareholder where it knows his age and can probably set aside a transfer to a minor once it learns the position (*Re Contract Corporation, Gooch's Case* (1872) LR 8 Ch App 266). However, if a company registers a minor knowing him to be such it cannot afterwards repudiate him.

The register of members

Section 113(1) requires every company to keep a register of its members. The register must contain the following information:

(a) the names and addresses of the members (s 113(2)(a));
(b) the date on which each person was entered in the register as a member (s 113(2)(b));
(c) the date on which each person ceased to be a member (s 113(2)(c)).

Section 113(3) goes on to state that in the case of a company having a share capital there must be entered in the register, with the names and addresses of the members, a statement of:

(a) the shares held by each member, distinguishing each share
   (i) by its number if it has one; and
   (ii) where the company has more than one class of issued shares, by its class, and
(b) the amount paid or agreed to be considered as paid up on the shares of each member (s 113(3)(b)).

Section 113(4) states that if the company has converted any of its shares into stock, and given notice of the conversion to the Registrar, the register of members must show the amount and class of stock held by each member instead of the amount of shares and the particulars relating to shares.

In the event of joint holders of shares or stock in a company, the company's register of members must, according to s 113(5), state the names of each joint holder.

Failure to keep a register of members renders the company and every officer in default liable to a fine and also to a daily fine for each day during which the default continues (s 113(7) and (8)).

The register may be kept in any form, e.g. in the form of a loose leaf system, so long as proper precautions are taken to guard against falsification. The 2006 Act allows the use of computers for company records, including the register of members, so long as the records can be reproduced in legible form. According to s 115, a company with more than 50 members must keep an index of its members, and if there is any alteration in the register, the index must also be altered within 14 days of such alteration (s 115(2)). The above provisions do not apply if the register is kept in the form of an index (s 115(1)). Section 115(4) outlines the fact that the index must be at all times kept available for inspection at the same place as the register of members.

Section 114(1)(a) states that the register and index must be kept available for inspection at the registered office of the company, or at a place specified in regulations under s 113(6) of the CA 2006. Section 114(2) goes on to note that a company must give notice to the Registrar of the whereabouts of the register and of any changes in that place. If a company makes default for 14 days in complying with this requirement, then s 114(5) states that an offence is committed by the company and every officer of the company who is in default. However, s 114(3) states that no such notice is required if the register has, at all times since it came into existence, been kept available for inspection at the company's registered office.

Inspection of register

During business hours the register and the index must under s 116 of the CA 2006 be kept open for inspection by any member free of charge (s 116(1)(a)), and by any other person on payment of a fee (s 116(1)(b)). Under s 116(2), the company must make available either to a member or to any other person a copy of any part of the register, and may make a charge for this. The company must either send the copy (s 117(1)(a)) or apply to the court (s 117(1)(b)) within five days of receiving a s 116 request.

If a company makes an application to the court and the court is satisfied that the inspection or copy is not sought for a proper purposes, then it shall direct the company not to comply with the request (s 117(3)(a)), and it may order that the company's costs on the application be paid in whole or in part by the person who made the request (s 117(3)(b)). Indeed, s 119(1) states that it is an offence for a person to knowingly or recklessly to make in a request under s 116 a statement that is misleading, false or deceptive in a material particular. This gives the court a discretion and it may refuse to make an order, e.g. in the case of a pro-hunting charity which felt that a disclosure of members might be detrimental. A compromise might be achieved by the company offering to act as a post-box for confidential communication to and from members (see *P v F Ltd* [2001] NLJR 284). The Court of Appeal accepted a similar post-box undertaking from a company and refused to make an order for inspection in *Pelling* v *Families Need Fathers Ltd* [2002] 2 All ER 440 where the defendant company was a charity with the object of helping parents to stay in touch with their children after separation or divorce.

If on application under s 117(1)(b), the court does not direct the company not to comply with the s 116 request, the company must comply with the request immediately upon the court giving its decision (s 117(5)).

According to s 119(2), it is an offence for a person in possession of information obtained by exercise of either of the rights conferred by s 116 to do anything that results in the information being disclosed to another person, or to fail to do anything with the result that the information is disclosed to another person, knowing or having reason to suspect that person may use the information for a purpose that is not a proper purpose.

The right of inspection terminates on the commencement of winding-up (*Re Kent Coalfields Syndicate* [1898] 1 QB 754). Any rights then existing are derived from the insolvency rules, and not from the Act, and may require an order of court.

Obsolete entries in the register

Section 121 states that a company may remove from the register any entry which relates to a former member where the person concerned has not been a member for at least 10 years.

Rectification of the register

The register of members is under s 127 prima facie evidence of the matters which the Companies Act requires it to contain.

However, the court has power under s 125 to rectify the register if application is made to it where:

(a) the name of any person is without sufficient cause entered in or omitted from the register; or

(b) default is made, or unnecessary delay takes place, in entering on the register the fact that a person has ceased to be a member.

As well as rectification, the court may order the payment by the company of any damages sustained by any party aggrieved (s 125(2)). Notice of rectification must be given to the Registrar of Companies under the terms of the court's order (s 125(4)).

The circumstances set out in (a) and (b) above are not the only ones in which the court can order rectification. For example, rectification will be ordered where joint holders wish to split the holding because in general terms the rights attaching to the shares, e.g. voting rights, are vested in the first-named person on the register (see below). The company should therefore in ordinary circumstances agree to a request to split the holding.

Burns v Siemens Bros Dynamo Works Ltd [1919] 1 Ch 225

The claimants, Burns and Hambro, were the joint owners of shares in the defendant company. The shares were entered in the company's register in the joint names of Burns and Hambro. The company's articles provided that, where there were joint holders, the person whose name appeared first in the register of members, and no other, should be entitled to vote in respect of the shares. The result was, of course, that Hambro had no voting rights. This action was brought by Burns and Hambro asking that the register be rectified so as to show roughly half of the joint shareholding in the name of each joint holder.

Held – by the High Court – the court had jurisdiction to make such an order, and the company was required to rectify the register, showing shares numbered 1 to 10,000 in the names of Burns and Hambro, and shares numbered 10,001 to 19,993 in the names of Hambro and Burns.

Comment

Rectification will also be granted where an allotment of shares is set aside following, for example, a false statement in a prospectus. The consequent action for rescission – if that is the course the claimant chooses to pursue – is accompanied by a request for rectification of the register.

Notice of trusts

Under s 126 of the Companies Act 2006, no notice of any trust shall be entered on the register of members of companies registered in England and Wales. The rule laid down by the section has two branches:

(a) *The company is entitled to treat every person whose name appears on the register as the beneficial owner of the shares even though he may in fact hold them in trust for another.* Thus, if the company registers a transfer of shares held by a trustee, it is not liable to the beneficiaries under the trust even though the sale of the shares by the trustee was fraudulent or in breach of the powers given to him in the trust instrument.

Simpson v Molson's Bank [1895] AC 270

This was an appeal to the Privy Council in England from the Court of Queen's Bench for Lower Canada. It appeared that the bank was incorporated by an Act of Parliament, and that by s 36 of that Act the bank was not bound to take notice of any trust over its shares. (The provision was similar to the one contained in s 360.) The executors of the Hon John Molson were given 10 years by his will to wind up his estate. After the expiration of that time, and in breach of the terms of the will, they made a transfer of certain shares in the bank. The claimants, who had an interest in the residuary estate of John Molson, brought this action claiming damages from the bank because it had registered a transfer knowing that transfer to be in breach of trust, such knowledge being derived from the fact that a copy of the will was deposited at the bank, and that William Molson, the testator's brother, was one of the executors who signed the transfer and was also the president of the bank.

Held – the bank was not liable for registering the transfer although it had notice that it was in breach of trust, because s 36 of the Act of Parliament incorporating the bank provided specifically that it should not take notice of any trust over its shares.

(b) *Where persons claim rights in shares under equitable titles, such as an equitable mortgage, the company is not made into a trustee if those persons merely serve notice on the company of the existence of their equitable claims.* The correct way of protecting such an interest is by serving a stop notice on the company.

It follows from this branch of the 'no trusts' rule that where there are two or more lenders on the security of the same shares by way of equitable mortgage, the first in date has priority, not the first to give notice to the company.

Société Générale de Paris v Walker (1885) 11 App Cas 20

James Walker was the registered owner of 100 shares in Tramways Union Ltd, and he created two charges over the shares, one on 9 March 1881 in favour of James Scott Walker, who took the certificates and a blank transfer, and one on 1 December 1882 in favour of the appellants, the latter charge being created by means of a blank transfer, duly executed but without the deposit of the share certificate. The appellants tried to obtain registration first, but Tramways Union Ltd would not register the transfer without the certificates, and later the executors of James Scott Walker informed the Tramways Union that they had the certificates. This action was brought to decide who had the title to the shares. The articles of Tramways Union Ltd provided that the company should not be bound to recognise any equitable interest in its shares. The appellants claimed that because they notified first the fact of their equitable interest in the shares, they were entitled as against the executors of James Scott Walker.

Held – by the House of Lords – they were not, because neither the company nor its officers could be treated as trustees for the purpose of notifying equitable interests over the shares. The title to the shares was in the person eventually registered by the company, and the company was right in refusing to register a person who could not produce the share certificates. The respondents were entitled to the shares.

It should be noted that s 126 only protects the company, and where directors register a transfer, *knowing it is being made in breach of trust or in fraud of some person having an equitable right*, they may incur personal liability to the person suffering loss.

The rule also means that there can be no registration of a trust as such. An entry on the register such as 'The ABC Family Trust' would be an infringement of s 126. The correct entry and the share certificate should show merely the names of the individual trustees without any reference to the fact that they are trustees or the nature of the trusts. If a note of the existence of the trust is required for administrative purposes this can be recorded outside the register possibly with a coded cross-reference.

If a trustee of shares is entered on the register, he is personally liable for the calls made by the company, though he can claim an indemnity to the extent of the trust property and, if this is not sufficient, from the beneficiaries personally. A company cannot put a beneficiary on the list of contributories in a winding-up, though it can enforce the trustee's right of indemnity against the beneficiaries by the doctrine of *subrogation* (*per* James LJ in **Re European Society Arbitration Acts** (1878) 8 Ch D 679).

A company claiming a *lien* on its shares will be affected by a notice of any charge which arose prior to the debt in respect of which the company's lien is being exercised. As we have seen, this is not regarded as a notice of trust, but is more by way of a notice of lien as between one trader and another (see **Bradford Banking Co v Briggs**, 1886).

Termination of membership

Termination of membership is complete when the name of a former member is removed from the register. This may occur by:

(a) transfer of the shares to a purchaser or by way of gift (subject to liability to be put on the list of members for one year if the company goes into liquidation) (see further Chapter 29 ○);

(b) forfeiture, surrender, or a sale by the company under its lien;

(c) redemption or purchase of shares by the company;

(d) the registration of a trustee in bankruptcy, or by his disclaimer of the shares;

(e) death of the member;

(f) rescission of the contract to take the shares arising out of fraud or misrepresentation in the prospectus, or by reason of irregular allotment;

(g) dissolution of the company by winding-up or amalgamation or reconstruction under Insolvency Act 1986, s 110 (see Chapter 26 ○);

(h) compulsory acquisition (see further Chapter 26 ○);

(i) under the provisions of the company's constitution, e.g. expulsion under the articles for competing with the company (see **Sidebottom v Kershaw Leese**, 1920).

Director and substantial shareholdings

As we have seen, the register of members merely gives the identity of the person in whose name the shares are registered. No indication is given of any interests in the shares which persons other than the registered holder might have. Furthermore, no notice of trust is to be entered on the register of members of a company registered in England. Where share warrants are in issue the position is, of course, worse since the names of the holders at any point of time are unknown, there being no form of registration.

This situation is capable of abuse. For example, it enables directors to traffic in the securities of their companies without this being known, or someone secretly to acquire control of a sizeable holding on which to base a bid for control.

The Companies Act deals with the above problems as follows.

The purchase and sale of the company's securities by the directors

Section 96A(2)(f) of the Financial Services and Markets Act 2000, states that anyone who discharges managerial responsibilities must disclose transactions conducted on their own account in shares of the company or derivatives or any other financial instrument relating to those shares.

Section 96B(1) goes on to clarify that the term 'discharging managerial responsibilities' means a director, a senior executive who has regular access to inside information relating directly or indirectly to the company, and to a senior executive who has power to make managerial decisions affecting the future development and business prospects of the company. This wording extends the scope of the regime beyond that outlined by the Companies Act 1985, but it would appear that the term 'shadow director' has been omitted under the reforms (see s 324(6), CA 1985).

Nevertheless, s 96B(2) goes on to state that the obligation extends to persons connected with anyone who discharges managerial responsibilities within the company. This covers those previously envisaged as falling within the remit of 'connected person' outlined in s 346 of the Companies Act 1985, as well as to a relative who has on the relevant date shared the same household as that person for at least 12 months, and a body corporate in which a person 'discharging managerial responsibilities' is a director or senior executive.

The Disclosure and Transparency Rules (DTR) require information about the transactions to be disclosed to the company, including under DTR 3.1.3, the price and volume of the transaction, within 4 business days of the transaction taking place (DTR 3.1.2). This information must then be passed on by the company to both the market as well as to the Financial Services Authority (FSA) within one business day (DTR 3.1.2 and 3.1.4).

Unlike under s 325 of the Companies Act 1985, the company is no longer required to maintain a register of directors' interests and dealings, or to report the position on directors' interests at the end of the financial year in the directors' report (Sch 7, CA 1985). However, the company is required to file an annual statement with the FSA making reference to all the information made public over the previous 12 months.

Substantial share interests

The current European Community principles regarding the disclosure of interests in share holdings is contained in Directive 2004/109/EC, known as the Transparency Directive (TD). This has seen the removal of the automatic disclosure requirements under the Companies Act and the transfer of a substantial part of these disclosure requirements to the Financial Services and Markets Act 2000 (FSMA). Indeed, the Companies Act 2006 has amended the FSMA to permit the area to be regulated by the FSA. In this respect, s 1266 of the CA 2006 inserts ss 89A–89G in to the FSMA 2000. In addition, the FSA has introduced the DTR to deal with this area.

This regime applies to companies which trade on a regulated market (Art 9(1) TD) as opposed to all public companies as *per* s 198 of the CA 1985. The domestic regime which has implemented the Directive applies to all companies with securities traded on a prescribed market, including any market operated by a Recognised Investment Exchange.

The disclosure requirements deal with the percentage of voting rights held in a company as opposed to the actual holdings of shares. Consequently, according to DTR 5, holdings of non-voting shares do not have to be disclosed under this regime, nor do shares which are only entitled to vote in certain circumstances (i.e. variation of class rights). However, it should be noted that those exercising managerial responsibilities within the company are required to disclose holdings in non-voting shares as this could give rise to insider dealing.

The notifiable percentage is 3 per cent of the total voting rights in the company and every 1 per cent thereafter. Once these thresholds have been crossed, the individual is required to disclose the interest to the company within two days (DTR 5.8.3).

Notification must be made, therefore, whenever a known change brings about a known increase or decrease above or below 3 per cent or a known increase or decrease to the next percentage point occurs in an interest exceeding 3 per cent. Thus, if a person has an interest in, say, 10.5 per cent of relevant capital, there is no requirement to notify a change in the interest unless and until it falls below 10 per cent or increases to 11 per cent.

The company must be notified within two days of the change and the company must record the details in a register of interests in shares. The register must be available for inspection without charge by any member or by any other person.

A person who fails to notify as required or gives false or misleading information is liable to a fine or imprisonment or both.

Power of public company to investigate interests

Section 1295 of the Companies Act 2006 repealed s 212 of the CA 1985, which had enabled a public company to previously make enquiries of *any person* (not merely a member) whom it knew or had reasonable cause to believe to be *interested* in any of its voting shares either at the present time or at any time during the preceding three years. This repeal impacts on any s 212 notice issued after 20 January 2007.

The annual return

Under s 854 of the Companies Act 2006, a company must file an annual return with the Registrar. It must be made up to a date 12 months after the previous return or in the case of the first return 12 months after incorporation (s 854(2)).

The return must be delivered to the Registrar within 28 days of the make-up date (s 854(3)(b)) and must contain the information required by or under the provisions of Part 24 of the 2006 Act.

Contents of annual return

Section 855 of the Companies Act 2006 states that every annual return must state the date to which it is made up and contain the following information:

(a) the address of the company's registered office;

(b) the type of company it is and its principal business activities;

(c) the prescribed particulars of (i) the directors of the company, and (ii) in the case of a private company with a secretary or a public company, the secretary or joint secretaries;

(d) if the register of members is not kept available for inspection at the company's registered office, the address of the place where it is kept available for inspection;

(e) if any register of debenture holders is not kept available for inspection at the company's registered office, the address of the place where it is kept available for inspection.

Furthermore, s 856(1) goes on to provide that the annual return of a company having share capital must also contain a statement of capital and the particulars required by s 856(3) to 856(6) about the members of the company. In this regard, s 856(2) states that the statement of capital must state with respect to the company's share capital at the date to which the return is made up:

(a) the total number of shares of the company;

(b) the aggregate nominal value of those shares;

(c) for each class of shares: (i) prescribed particulars of the rights attached to the shares; (ii) the total number of shares of that class; and (iii) the aggregate nominal value of shares of that class, and;

(d) the amount paid up and the amount (if any) unpaid on each share.

Section 856(3) goes on to state that the return must contain the prescribed particulars of every person who: (a) is a member of the company on the date to which the return is made up, or (b) has ceased to be a member of the company since the date to which the last return was made up (or, in the case of the first return, since the incorporation of the company).

The subsection also sets down that the return must conform to such requirements as may be prescribed for the purpose of enabling the entries relating to any given person to be easily found.

In addition, s 856(4) requires that the return must also state: (a) the number of shares of each class held by each member of the company at the date to which the return is made up; (b) the number of shares of each class transferred: (i) since the date to which the last return was made up; or (ii) in the case of the first return, since the incorporation of the company, by each member or person who has ceased to be a member; and (c) the dates of registration of the transfers.

Finally, s 856 (6) sets out that where the company has converted any of its shares into stock, the return must give the corresponding information in relation to that stock, stating the amount of stock instead of the number or nominal value of shares.

Sanctions if return not made

Section 858(1) provides that if a company fails to deliver an annual return before the end of the period of 28 days after a return date, an offence is committed by the company and, subject to s 858(4), every director of the company, and in the case of a private company with a secretary or a public company, every secretary of the company, and every other officer of the company who is in default.

Section 858(2) goes on to state that a person guilty of such an offence is liable to a fine and, for continued contravention, a daily default fine. The contravention continues until such time as an annual return made up to that return date is delivered by the company to the Registrar (s 858(3)).

Power to make further provision by regulations

Section 857(1) states that the Secretary of State may by regulations make further provision as to the information to be given in a company's annual return. The section goes on to note that the regulations may amend or repeal the provisions of ss 855 and 856, and provide for exceptions from the requirements of those sections as they have effect from time to time (s 857(2)).

Essay questions

1 Describe an annual return and state the particulars which must be given in the annual return of a company which has a share capital. *(The Institute of Company Accountants)*

2 Every public company is required to maintain a register of 'substantial holdings and interests' in shares which it has issued.

   (a) What duties are imposed upon persons to notify such holdings and interests?

   (b) What is the purpose of the requirement?
   (The Institute of Chartered Accountants in England and Wales)

3 Privatus Ltd was a private company which owed the sum of £4,000 to Alex for goods which he had sold to it. As the company was short of cash, its directors allotted to Alex 6,000 £1 shares in the company credited as fully paid. The share certificate issued to Alex stated that the shares were fully paid.

   Alex contracted to sell these shares to Bertram and duly handed him the share certificate and a signed stock transfer form. When Bertram sent these documents to the company in order to have the transfer registered, the directors became concerned that problems might arise over the original issue to Alex. They discussed the matter over a four-month period and then wrote to Bertram informing him that in accordance with Art 24 of the company's articles of association they refused to register his transfer. Article 24 reads, 'The directors may refuse to register the transfer of a share which is not fully paid to a person of whom they do not approve.' Bertram has now begun a court action to secure his registration as a member.

   Advise the company of its position with regard to the issue of the shares to Alex and the action brought by Bertram. *(The Association of Chartered Certified Accountants)*

4 The Companies Act 2006 places upon public companies certain controls over the type and value of the consideration which such companies may receive for an issue of their shares. You are required to select any three of these controls and explain in each instance how the control restricts the company and why, in your view, the provision was enacted.
   (The Chartered Institute of Management Accountants)

5 The following is a summarised balance sheet of C Ltd:

	£	£
Authorised Capital		
100,000 Ordinary Shares of £1 each	100,000	
10,000 – 10 per cent Redeemable Preference		
Shares of £1 each	10,000	110,000
Total Assets (including Cash at Bank of £50,000)		400,000
Liabilities		200,000
Net Assets		200,000
Represented by:		
Issued Capital		
100,000 Ordinary Shares of £1 each		100,000
10,000 – 10 per cent Redeemable Preference Shares		10,000
		110,000
Capital Reserve (Share Premium a/c)	10,000	
Revenue Reserves	80,000	90,000
		£200,000

The directors seek your advice as to how they may redeem the Preference Shares and whether they may issue 20,000 bonus Ordinary Shares of £1 each. Advise them on these matters and redraft the balance sheet as it would appear after implementing your advice.

(Kingston University)

6 (a) 'A company cannot issue shares at a discount.' Discuss.

(b) False Ltd and Gorgon Ltd both have an issued share capital of £500,000 and a share premium account of £50,000. The directors of False Ltd have recently decided that it is over-capitalised and wish to return £55,000 to the shareholders. Gorgon Ltd has recently made a loss of £55,000 and its directors wish to reduce the company's capital accordingly. Advise the directors of both companies.

(The Institute of Chartered Secretaries and Administrators)

Test your knowledge

Four alternative answers are given. Select ONE only. Circle the answer which you consider to be correct. Check your answers by referring back to the information given in the chapter and against the answers at the end of the text.

1 A person who acquires an interest in the shares of a public company must notify the company of that interest when it equals or exceeds:

A 20 per cent of the voting shares.
B 10 per cent of the voting shares.
C 5 per cent of the voting shares.
D 3 per cent of the voting shares.

2 Tees plc has an issued share capital of £100,000 and recently issued another 100,000 £1 ordinary shares. Fred, his wife, his son (aged 18) and a private company in which Fred is the majority shareholder each acquired 10,000 shares. What is the interest which Fred must notify to the company under the Companies Act 2006?

A 40,000 shares   B 30,000 shares   C 20,000 shares   D 10,000 shares

3 The Companies Act 2006 requires that when equity shares are allotted for cash they must be offered first to existing shareholders in proportion to their holding in the company. Such an issue of shares is known as:

   A A rights issue.
   B A preference issue.
   C An issue of bonus shares.
   D An issue of founders' shares.

4 How is a share warrant validly transferred?

   A By any writing.
   B By writing and delivery.
   C By delivery.
   D By instrument of transfer.

5 The articles of private companies often provide that members wishing to sell their shares must offer them first to existing members. What is such a clause called?

   A An expropriation clause.
   B A compulsory purchase clause.
   C A pre-emption clause.
   D A statutory pre-emption clause.

The answers to test your knowledge questions appear on p. 645.

Suggested further reading

Gong, 'The role of institutional shareholder activism in corporate governance: A comparative analysis of China and the UK' (2012) *Company Lawyer* 33(6), 171.

Worthington, 'Corporate governance: Remedying and ratifying directors' breaches' (2000) LQR 116, 638.

17

The statutory derivative action

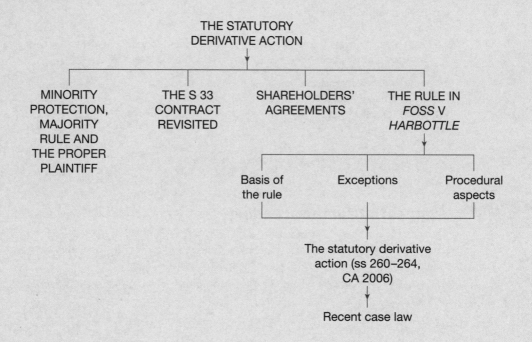

THE STATUTORY
DERIVATIVE ACTION

MINORITY
PROTECTION,
MAJORITY
RULE AND
THE PROPER
PLAINTIFF

THE S 33
CONTRACT
REVISITED

SHAREHOLDERS'
AGREEMENTS

THE RULE IN
FOSS V
HARBOTTLE

Basis of
the rule

Exceptions

Procedural
aspects

The statutory derivative
action (ss 260–264,
CA 2006)

Recent case law

The following two chapters are concerned with the various remedies available to minority shareholders. It should be noted from the outset that many of these remedies are concerned with the actions or conduct of the company's officers (e.g. directors), which infringe the rights or affect the interests of shareholders. Equally, it should be noted that not all of these remedies provide a personal remedy to the shareholder in question. Rather, actions under the exceptions to the rule in *Foss* v *Harbottle* (now in statutory form), are referred to as being 'derivative actions'. In other words, the minority shareholder undertakes such an action on behalf of, and for the ultimate benefit of, the company and not himself/herself.

This chapter will revisit briefly the s 33 statutory contract, the wording of which suggests that the parties (i.e. shareholders) to it are in a position to enforce the provisions of the company's constitution. Therefore, in terms of shareholder remedies, if a member has a right that is contained in the articles and is a party to the statutory contract, that member may enforce their right. Equally, if a member has a right contained in the articles that is being thwarted, that individual may sue for breach of contract, (see *Browne* v *La Trinidad*). Consequently, it is recommended that this heading should be the first option that is considered when addressing issues of shareholder remedies as it is potentially:

1 a straightforward enforcement of a contractual right/obligation;
2 far less expensive and time consuming for the minority shareholder.

We then go on to examine the rule in *Foss* v *Harbottle* and the minority shareholders' actions which are permitted by the exceptions to it, as set out in the case of *Edwards* v *Halliwell* and how this rule has, under the Companies Act 2006, been moved into statutory form. The case of *Foss* v *Harbottle* represents the general principle of company law that minority shareholders cannot sue for wrongs done to the company or complain of irregularities in the conduct of its internal affairs. This rule rests on two related propositions:

1 the right of the majority to bar a minority action whenever they might lawfully ratify the alleged misconduct (the principle of majority rule); and
2 the normally exclusive right of the company to sue upon a corporate cause of action (the principle of the proper plaintiff).

The next chapter will continue the discussion of 'minority protection' with an examination of two interrelated statutory remedies. First of all, s 994 of the Companies Act 2006, which permits a member (shareholder) of a company to petition on the ground of unfair prejudice as well as s 122(1)(g) of the Insolvency Act 1986, which provides a 'just and equitable' ground for a member to petition to have the company wound up.

These statutory remedies (particularly s 994) evolved in response to the undue technicality and doctrinal obscurity of the rule in *Foss* v *Harbottle*, aiming to provide a broader and more liberal judicial discretion to the area of shareholder remedies (see the case of *O'Neill* v *Phillips*). However, despite this rather positive development in the law, it should be noted that their beneficial effect is largely restricted to small and/or medium-sized private companies. Quite simply, these two remedies are not an appropriate method of dealing with issues such as corporate abuse in public listed companies (see the case of *Re Blue Arrow plc* in Chapter 18 ◐).

The s 33 contract revisited

Unlike s 14 of the Companies Act 1985, s 33 refers to '*a company's constitution*', rather than its '*memorandum and articles*'. This reflects the new division of formation and constitutional information between the memorandum, articles and other constitutional documents noted above.

However, as outlined in earlier chapters, this option is not without its problems. As such, you should try to address the following issues. First of all, is the individual in question a party to the statutory contract (***Hickman*** v ***Kent or Romney Marsh Sheepbreeders Association***)? Secondly, does the right in question fall within the scope of enforceable rights under s 33? In other words, is it an insider or outsider right (see ***Quin & Axtens*** v ***Salmon***, 1909; ***Eley*** v ***Positive Life Association***, 1876; ***Beattie*** v ***E and F Beattie Ltd***, 1938)?

In many instances, there may not be a straightforward answer to these questions. Nevertheless, you should always consider this process at the beginning of any minority protection question. Do not automatically dismiss the possibility of enforcement under the statutory contract.

Shareholders' agreements

As noted in previous chapters, many small private companies have converted from partnerships where a partnership contractual agreement has governed the business affairs. Such an agreement has a vital role to play in terms of s 17 of the Companies Act 2006, which now states that a company's constitution consists of the articles of association and any resolutions and agreements to which Chapter 3 of Part 3 of the 2006 Act, ss 29–30 applies. In addition, it plays an invaluable role in terms of evidencing the expectations of a company's members at the time the agreement was drawn up as it will normally contain provisions on how decisions are to be made on matters such as directors' pay, dividends and the employment of key staff. The agreement is designed so that shareholders with big holdings cannot in all cases impose their will through majority voting power, and is of particular importance where shareholder voting can result in damaging deadlock. One of the most important aspects of the agreement will be the provisions for share valuation on the sale of shares, on leaving the company by retirement or by death (see Chapter 6 above ➲).

The rule in *Foss* v *Harbottle*

Although many functions are delegated to the directorate, the eventual power and control in a company rests with those shareholders who can command a majority of the voting power. Thus, a person or group of persons controlling three-quarters of the votes would have complete control of the company, and a little more than half the votes would give considerable influence allowing, for example, control over appointments to the board.

The principle of majority rule is well established and is emphasised in the matter of litigation by the rule in ***Foss*** v ***Harbottle***, 1843 (see below). Generally it does little harm since most companies are managed fairly, even if at times there is not due concern for the rights of minorities which might lead to oppression. The problem is at its greatest in private companies because the shares of such companies are not listed on the Stock Exchange, the protection of the Stock Exchange rules is not available, and there is rarely any press comment on their activities.

The rule in *Foss* v *Harbottle*, 1843, states that in order to redress a wrong done to a company or to the property of the company, or to enforce rights of the company, the proper claimant is the company itself, and the court will not ordinarily entertain an action brought on behalf of the company by a shareholder.

Foss v *Harbottle* (1843) 2 Hare 461

The claimants, Foss and Turton, were shareholders in a company called 'The Victoria Park Company' which was formed to buy land for use as a pleasure park. The defendants were the other directors and shareholders of the company. The claimants alleged that the defendants had defrauded the company in various ways, and in particular that certain of the defendants had sold land belonging to them to the company at an exorbitant price. The claimants now asked the court to order that the defendants make good the losses to the company.

Held – by Vice-Chancellor Wigram – since the company's board of directors was still in existence, and since it was still possible to call a general meeting of the company, there was nothing to prevent the company from obtaining redress in its corporate character, and the action by the claimants could not be sustained.

Basis of the rule

Four major principles seem to be at the basis of the rule as the decided cases show:

1 **The right of the majority to rule.** The court has said in some of the cases that an action by a single shareholder cannot be entertained because the feeling of the majority of the members has not been tested, and they may be prepared, if asked, to waive their right to sue. Thus the company can only sue (a) if the directors pass a resolution to that effect where the power is delegated to them; or (b) if the company expresses its desire to sue by an ordinary resolution in general meeting, whether the power is delegated to the directors or not, since the power of the members to bring the company into court as a claimant is concurrent with that of the directors, and if the members wish to bring the company into court and the directors do not, the wish of the members by ordinary resolution will prevail.

2 **The company is a legal person.** The court has also said from time to time that since a company is a *persona at law*, the action is vested in it, and cannot be brought by a single member.

3 **The prevention of a multiplicity of actions.** This situation could occur if each individual member was allowed to commence an action in respect of a wrong done to the company. See James LJ in *Gray* v *Lewis* (1873) 8 Ch App 1035 at p 1051 – a judgment which is particularly supportive of the multiplicity problem.

4 **The court's order may be made ineffective.** It should be noted that the court order could be overruled by an ordinary resolution of members in a subsequent general meeting, provided that the general meeting is not controlled by the wrongdoers (see below). As Mellish LJ said in *MacDougall* v *Gardiner* (1875) 1 Ch D 13 at p 25:

[. . .] if the thing complained of is a thing which in substance the majority of the company are entitled to do [. . .] there can be no use in having a litigation about it, the ultimate end of which is only that a meeting has to be called, and then ultimately the majority gets its wishes.

It will be seen, therefore, that the rule in *Foss* is in no sense helpful to the minority. This rule means that, for good or bad, the decision-making power within a company lies with those in control of more than half of the votes in general meetings or boards of directors. In fact, if there were no exceptions to the rule, the minority could never bring a claim at all. It is to the exceptions that we must now turn. Consequently, at common law, if the minority shareholder disagrees with the majority, he has little room to complain. In many instances, the unhappy shareholder in a public limited company is encouraged to use his 'power of exit' – in other words to sell his shares on the Stock Market.

However, consider the position of a minority shareholder within a private limited company: Where is the available market? Is the shareholder able to sell his shares to individuals external to the company? (Consider pre-emption clauses.) How will the shares be valued? The main exception to this restriction on the ability of the minority shareholder to object to the actions of the majority arises in instances where there is a 'fraud on the minority'. However, even in these circumstances success is not guaranteed.

The obscure nature of the rule in *Foss* v *Harbottle* has meant that in the past individuals have been refused a remedy, despite the merits of the case.

However, since October 2007, minority shareholders have been allowed a new statutory derivative action. The two rules in *Foss* v *Harbottle* will continue to apply, although the absence of one or the other will no longer be a bar to commence proceedings. Before exploring the new statutory derivative action, it is necessary to provide some context for the rule (and the exceptions to the rule contained in *Edwards* v *Halliwell*) in *Foss* v *Harbottle*.

Acts infringing the personal rights of shareholders

These actions are not so much genuine exceptions to the rule in *Foss*, they are more in the nature of situations which are outside it. Thus, in *Pender* v *Lushingon*, 1877 (see Chapter 6 ◐), the court dealt with the attempted removal of the claimant's right to vote without suggesting that the rule in *Foss* in any way prevented the action from being brought.

Exceptions to the rule – generally

Although the courts have not developed an entirely clear pattern of exceptions, those set out below appear to be the main areas in which the court will allow claims to be brought by shareholders as an exception to the rule in *Foss* (which has now been replaced by the new provisions of the CA 2006).

1 **Acts which are *ultra vires* or illegal.** No simple majority of members can confirm or ratify an illegal act. Section 39 of the Companies Act 2006 gives an individual member a *statutory* right to ask the court for an injunction to restrain the directors from entering into *ultra vires* transactions but *not* if the members of the company have ratified a particular transaction by special resolution. So far as illegality is concerned, the minority could bring an action to force the directors to comply with the law restricting, for example, loans, quasi-loans and credit given by the company to directors and their connected persons.

2 **Where the act complained of can only be confirmed by a special or extraordinary resolution.** *Foss* is based on the principle that the majority, i.e. those who can obtain an

ordinary resolution, should decide whether or not a complaint relating to the company should be brought before the court. Clearly, therefore, a simple majority of the members cannot be allowed to confirm a transaction requiring a greater majority.

Edwards v *Halliwell* [1950] 2 All ER 1064

A trade union had rules, which were the equivalent of articles of association, under which any increase in members' contributions had to be agreed by a two-thirds majority in a ballot of members. A meeting decided by a simple majority to increase the subscriptions without holding a ballot. The claimants, as a minority of members, applied for a declaration from the court that the resolution was invalid.

Held – the rule in *Foss* did not prevent a minority of a company, or as here, an association of persons, from suing because the matter about which they were suing was one which could only be done or validly sanctioned by a greater than simple majority. This was broken down as follows:

(i) On the construction of the rules, the alteration in the rates of contribution was invalid;

(ii) The rule in **Foss** v **Harbottle** did not afford the trade union a defence because it protected only irregularities concerning matters which were *intra vires* the union and pertained to its internal management; a mere irregularity meant something not involving fraud, oppression or unfairness, but the action complained of here was strongly tinctured with oppression or unfairness;

(iii) The rule did not apply where a matter was in issue which could only be sanctioned by some special majority;

(iv) The case was not within the ambit of the rule, for the substance of the complaint was that the majority had invaded the individual rights of members.

3 **Where there is a fraud on the minority.** The rule in *Foss* would create grave injustice if the majority were allowed to commit wrongs against the company and benefit from those wrongs at the expense of the minority simply because no claim could be brought in respect of the wrong. Thus, there is a major and somewhat ill-defined exception referred to as 'fraud on the minority'. For example, in *Estmanco (Kilner House) Ltd* v *Greater London Council* [1982] 1 All ER 437, Megarry V-C noted that: 'It does not seem to have yet become very clear exactly what the word "fraud" means in this context; but I think it is plainly wider than fraud at common law . . .' Equally, in *Burland* v *Earle* [1902] AC 83, the court stated that a straightforward example of fraud is '. . . where a majority are endeavouring directly or indirectly to appropriate to themselves money, property or advantages which belong to the company'. However, in *Pavlides* v *Jensen*, 1956 (see below), it was held that a loss caused to a company through the negligence of its directors who had derived no personal gain through the transaction did not constitute a fraud on the minority. Finally, in *Daniels* v *Daniels* [1978] Ch 406 (below) it was held that a derivative claim arose where a substantial profit was made upon the resale of company land sold to a director. Therefore, it should be noted that fraud in this context is not confined to literal or common law fraud and may include the misappropriation of corporate property; mala fide abuse of power (refer to directors' duties); discrimination against a section of the membership; as well as errors of judgment from which the directors have benefited. The following headings describe the main areas of fraud.

(a) **Where the company is defrauded.** Examples of this exception are to be found in the following cases which involved misappropriation of the company's property.

Menier v *Hooper's Telegraph Works Ltd* (1874) 9 Ch App 350

Company A (European and South American Telegraph Co) was formed to lay a transatlantic cable to be made by Hooper's, the majority shareholder in company A, from Portugal to Brazil. Hooper's found that they could make a greater profit by selling the cable to another company B, but B did not have the government concession to lay the cable which company A had. After much intrigue with the Portuguese government trustee of the concession, he agreed to transfer the concession to company B, and company B then bought the cable from Hooper's. To prevent company A from suing for loss of the concession Hooper obtained the passing of a resolution to wind up company A voluntarily and arranged that a liquidator should be appointed whom Hooper could trust not to pursue the claim of company A in respect of the loss of its contract. Menier, a minority shareholder of company A, asked the court to compel Hooper to account to company A for the profits made on the sale of the cable to B.

Held – by the Court of Appeal in Chancery – where the majority shareholders of a company propose to gain a benefit for themselves at the expense of the minority, the court may interfere to protect the minority. In such a case one shareholder has a right to bring a derivative claim to seek relief and the claim is not barred by the rule in *Foss* v *Harbottle*. This was a blatant case of fraud and oppression and Hooper's were trustees of the profit and had to account to company A for it.

Comment

It seems that in cases like *Menier* and *Cook* (below) it is the company which is defrauded. It might therefore be better to rename the jurisdiction as 'fraud upon the company'. The claim is, after all, brought on behalf of the company and is therefore derivative (see below), and the company takes the benefit of any damages recovered. The value of the shares may fall giving a loss to individual shareholders but since the Court of Appeal held in *Prudential Assurance Co Ltd* v *Newman Industries* [1982] 1 All ER 354 that this loss was not recoverable by individual shareholders, at least where it is caused by fraud or negligence, it seems that the claim is basically for defrauding the company.

Cook v *Deeks* [1916] 1 AC 554

This action was brought in the High Court Division of the Supreme Court of Ontario by the claimant, suing on behalf of himself and other shareholders in the Toronto Construction Co Ltd, against the respondents, who were directors of the company. The claimant sought a declaration that the respondents were trustees of the company of the benefit of a contract made between the respondents and the Canadian Pacific Railway Co for construction work. It appeared that the respondents, while acting on behalf of the company in negotiating the contract, actually made it for themselves and not for the company, and by their votes as holders of three-quarters of the issued share capital, subsequently passed a resolution at a general meeting declaring that the company had no interest in the contract.

Held – by the Privy Council:

(a) that the contract belonged in equity to the company, and the directors could not validly use their voting powers to vest the contract in themselves, in fraud of the minority;

(b) in cases of breach of duty of this sort, the rule in *Foss* v *Harbottle* did not bar the claimant's claim.

Comment

In *Industrial Development Consultants* v *Cooley*, 1972 (see Chapter 21 ○) there was a not dissimilar misappropriation of a corporate opportunity. However, in the *Cooley* case there was no need to resort to a derivative claim because Mr Cooley had made the profit for himself. The whole board was not involved and was clearly anxious to bring the company into court in order to sue Mr Cooley for recovery of the profit.

(b) **Where the minority as individuals are defrauded:**

(i) *Expulsion of minority*. This will amount to fraud unless it is done bona fide and for the benefit of the company.

Brown v *British Abrasive Wheel Co* [1919] 1 Ch 290

The company required further capital. The majority, who represented 98 per cent of the shareholders, were willing to provide this capital but only if they could buy up the 2 per cent minority. The minority would not agree to sell and so the majority shareholders proposed to alter the articles to provide for compulsory acquisition under which nine-tenths of the shareholders could buy out any other shareholders.

Held – by Astbury J – that the alteration of the articles would be restrained because the alteration was not for the benefit of the company. In addition, the rule in *Foss* v *Harbottle* did not bar the claimant's claim.

Comment

A contrast is provided by *Dafen Tinplate Co Ltd* v *Llanelly Steel Co (1907) Ltd*, 1920, and *Sidebottom* v *Kershaw Leese & Co*, 1920 (see Chapter 9 **◯**).

(ii) *Inequitable use of majority power*. An example of this jurisdiction is to be found in the following case:

Clemens v *Clemens Bros* [1976] 2 All ER 268

In this case the issued share capital of £2,000 in a small but prosperous family company was held between the claimant (45 per cent) and her aunt (55 per cent), the aunt being one of the five directors of the company. The directors proposed to increase the company's share capital to £3,650 by the creation of a further 1,650 voting ordinary shares. The four directors, other than the aunt, were to receive 200 shares each, and the balance of 850 shares was to be placed in trust for the company's long-service employees. The claimant objected to the proposed resolution to put this scheme into effect since the result would be to reduce her shareholding to under 25 per cent. At the extraordinary general meeting called to approve the scheme, the aunt voted in favour of the resolutions which were passed. The claimant sought a declaration against both the company and the aunt that the resolutions should be set aside on the ground that they were oppressive of the claimant. The defendant contended that if two shareholders honestly hold differing opinions, the view of the majority should prevail, and that shareholders in general meeting were entitled to consider their own interests and to vote in any way they honestly believed proper in the interest of the company. In giving judgment in favour of the claimant, Foster J made it clear that in the circumstances of this case Miss Clemens (the aunt) was not entitled to exercise her majority vote in whatever way she pleased. The judge found difficulty, however, in expressing this as a general principle of law, in terms, for example, of expressions such as 'bona fide for the benefit of the company as a whole', 'fraud on a minority', and 'oppressive'. He came to the conclusion that it would be unwise to try to produce a principle because the circumstances of each case are infinitely varied. He did say, however, following a phrase of Lord Wilberforce in *Westbourne Galleries* (see Chapter 1 ◑), that the right of a shareholder to exercise voting rights in any way whatever is subject always to equitable considerations which may in particular circumstances make it unjust to exercise votes in a certain way. Dealing with the facts before him, Foster J then went on to say:

> I cannot escape the conclusion that the resolutions have been framed so as to put into the hands of Miss Clemens and her fellow directors complete control of the company and to deprive the [claimant] of her existing rights as a shareholder with more than 25 per cent of the votes, and greatly reduce her rights. They are specifically and carefully designed to ensure not only that the [claimant] can never get control of the company, but to deprive her of what has been called her negative control. [Here the judge is referring to her ability to block special and extraordinary resolutions.] Whether I say that these proposals are oppressive to the [claimant] or that no-one could honestly believe that they are for her benefit, matters not. A court of equity will in my judgment regard these considerations as sufficient to prevent the consequences arising from Miss Clemens using her legal right to vote in the way she has and it would be right for a court of equity to prevent such consequences taking effect.

Comment

(i) The case is quoted to show the very wide power which equity reserves to itself to control the activities of majority shareholders. On the particular facts of this case, of course, the pre-emption rights given to shareholders by s 561 should prevent the sort of prejudicial conduct towards a minority which was alleged in this case. The claimant could, of course, have prevented the other members from effecting the disapplication of pre-emption rights under s 569 because a special resolution is required for this (see further Chapter 21).

(ii) Although Foster J was not prepared to put the case into any existing category of *Foss* exceptions, fraud on the minority seems a possible one.

(iii) The allotment was presumably also invalid because it was an improper exercise of the directors' powers.

The exception of fraud on the minority depends *where the company is defrauded* on 'wrongdoer control', i.e. the individual shareholder must show that the wrongdoers control the company as where they control the board and general meetings and will not permit an action to be brought in the company's name. Furthermore, wrongdoer control is essential because cases of misappropriation of property and breach of duty can be ratified by a 51 per cent majority of the members which is not controlled by the wrongdoers. However, how does a shareholder demonstrate this? In other words, what is the process by which the shareholder establishes *locus standi* – the right to bring a derivative action on behalf of the company against these alleged wrongdoers in a particular case?

The wrongdoers will obviously be in the above position if they have voting control as they had, for example, in *Menier* and *Cook*. However, in *Prudential Assurance Co Ltd* v *Newman Industries Ltd* [1980] 2 All ER 841 Vinelott J held that *de facto* control was enough, i.e. the company does what the wrongdoers want even though the wrongdoers do not have voting control. They are able to persuade the majority to follow them. The Court of Appeal did not accept this reasoning because it requires a trial to see if there is evidence of control, whereas voting control is obvious from shares held and voting rights. However, they gave no guidance as to what might be meant by control. This was followed by *Smith* v *Croft (No 2)* [1987] 3 All ER 909 in which it was noted that the court can investigate the conduct of the voting and count heads in order to assess the views of other shareholders, independent of the plaintiffs and the wrongdoers, and in essence what they think should be done in the circumstances. In this scenario the organ capable of reviewing the matter will usually be the General Meeting. Following this, where the majority of independent shareholders would vote against legal proceedings, then no claim in the company's name should lie.

Smith v Croft (No 2) [1988] Ch 114

The articles of F Ltd provided that a director should be remunerated for his services at the rate of £150 per annum, the chairman receiving an additional £100 per annum, but the rate of remuneration could be increased by an ordinary resolution. The directors were also empowered to appoint one or more of their number to be holders of an executive office, and any director appointed to such office was to receive such additional remuneration by way of salary, lump sum, commission or participation in profits as the directors might determine. During the course of 1982 the appointed executive directors and companies with which they were associated acquired sufficient shares in F Ltd to give them overall voting control. The shares were bought by means of payments made to three of the associated companies in August 1982 of £33,000 each, part of which was then lent to the fourth to discharge a bank loan taken out for the purpose of obtaining cash to buy shares in F Ltd and the remainder was used for the purchase of shares by the three associated companies.

The plaintiffs, who held a minority of shares in F Ltd, brought an action against F Ltd, three executive directors and the chairman, a non-executive director, and four companies closely associated with one or other of the three executive directors, claiming that the directors had paid themselves excessive remuneration, that the payments in 1982 to the associated companies were contrary to section 42 of the Companies Act 1981 and that certain payments of expenses to directors were excessive. The plaintiffs between them held 11.86 per cent of the issued shares in F Ltd; the defendants between them held 62.54 per cent; of the remaining shares 2.54 per cent were held by a company which actively supported the plaintiffs, while 3.22 per cent were held by persons or companies which, it was common ground, were to be treated as supporting the defendants. W Ltd, a company not under the control of either the plaintiffs or the defendants, held 19.66 per cent of the shares in F Ltd and was opposed to the continuance of the plaintiffs' action.

The chairman and F Ltd sought a motion to strike out the plaintiffs' action under RSC, Ord 18, r 19 or under the inherent jurisdiction as vexatious, frivolous or an abuse of process.

Held – (1) that the defendants' application raised the issue whether the plaintiffs could proceed with their minority shareholders' action and, although that raised difficult questions of law, the defendants, by invoking the procedure under RSC, Ord 18, r 9 rather than the procedure for determining a preliminary issue of law under RSC, Ord 33, r 3, had not adopted such an inherently defective procedure that the court should not proceed to determine the issues raised; and that since the effect of the court deciding those issues against the plaintiffs would be determinative of the action, the court would entertain the application and consider whether prima facie the company was entitled to the relief claimed in the action and whether the action was within the exception to the rule in *Foss* v *Harbottle*.

(2) That although excessive remuneration paid to directors might be an abuse of power, where the power to decide remuneration was vested in the board, it could not be *ultra vires* the company; and that in view of the uncontradicted evidence about the specialised field in which the company operated and the high levels of remuneration obtaining there it was more likely that the plaintiffs would fail than succeed on the issue of quantum; that likewise no prima facie case had been shown that the executive directors' expenses were excessive; and that, prima facie, the payments to associated companies were not *ultra vires* since payments at the request of an executive director to an outside entity were capable of being payments in respect of services rendered by the executive director, save that there was a prima facie case of irregularity regarding certain payments

not fully cured by subsequent adoption of the accounts at the annual general meetings at which those payments should have been disclosed; that since the admitted payments of £33,000 to associated companies had not been shown to be reasonably necessary for the purpose of providing for amounts likely to be incurred by way of directors' remuneration there was a prima facie case of infringement of s 42 of the Companies Act 1981.

(3) That although a minority shareholder had locus standi to bring an action on behalf of a company to recover property or money transferred or paid away in an *ultra vires* transaction, he did not have an indefeasible right to prosecute such an action on the company's behalf; that it was proper to have regard to the views of the independent shareholders, and their votes should be disregarded only if the court was satisfied that they would be cast in favour of the defendant directors in order to support them rather than for the benefit of the company, or if there was a substantial risk of that happening; that there was no evidence to suggest that the votes of W Ltd would be cast otherwise than for reasons genuinely thought to be for the company's advantage; and that, accordingly, since the majority of the independent shareholders' votes, including those of W Ltd, would be cast against allowing the action to proceed, the statement of claim should be struck out.

4   **Fraud and negligence.** It is still not entirely certain whether damage caused by *negligence* can be brought under the heading of 'fraud' for the purposes of the exception of 'fraud on the minority'. In *Pavlides* v *Jensen*, 1956 (below) the court held that negligence, however gross, was not included. However, in *Daniels* v *Daniels*, 1978 (below) Templeman J, in distinguishing *Pavlides*, said that a minority shareholder who had no other remedy should be able to sue whenever directors use their powers intentionally or unintentionally, fraudulently or negligently, in a manner which benefits them at the expense of the company. Vinelott J accepted this view in the *Newman* case. The Court of Appeal in that case did not give any guidance but the general approach of the court was restrictive and suggests that negligence *which does not result in personal benefit* to the wrongdoers might still be ratifiable by a general meeting even with the votes of the wrongdoers and, therefore, not within the definition of fraud on the minority.

 Pavlides v Jensen [1956] 2 All ER 518

The directors of the Tunnel Asbestos Cement Co Ltd sold an asbestos mine to the Cyprus Asbestos Mines Ltd in which the TAC Ltd held 25 per cent of the issued capital. The mine was sold for £182,000 but the sale was not submitted to a general meeting of TAC for approval. The claimant, who was a minority shareholder in TAC, claimed that the defendant directors were negligent because the mine was worth £1,000,000, and this price or something like it should have been obtained. He sued the directors with the company as a nominal defendant for a declaration that the directors were in breach of duty, and for an enquiry into the damage caused to TAC by their negligence and for payment of that sum by the directors to TAC. On the preliminary point as to the competence of the claimant as a minority shareholder to bring a derivative action in these circumstances, it was *held* – by Danckwerts J – that the action was not maintainable because the sale was *intra vires* and, since no acts of a fraudulent character were alleged by the claimant, the sale could be approved by the majority of shareholders and it was a matter for them.

Comment

(i) The claimant was alleging negligence which is a common law claim and derivative actions are creatures of equity, the judiciary being reluctant to extend them to common law claims such as negligence.

(ii) This line of reasoning was followed in **Multinational Gas v Multinational Gas Services** [1983] 2 All ER 563 where two judges in the Court of Appeal were of opinion that a claim for negligent mismanagement could not be brought even by a liquidator against directors whose actions had been approved by a majority of the members who were not a disinterested majority because they had appointed the directors as their nominees.

Daniels v Daniels [1978] 2 All ER 89

Mr Douglas Daniels, Mr Gordon Daniels and Mrs Soule, three minority shareholders in Ideal Homes (Coventry) Ltd, wished to bring an action against the majority shareholders (who were also the directors), Mr Bernard Daniels, Mrs Beryl Daniels and the company. In their claim the minority alleged that in October 1970 Ideal Homes, acting on the instructions of the majority shareholders, sold and conveyed freehold property in Warwick to Mrs Beryl Daniels for £4,250 when they knew, or ought to have known, that the correct value of the land was higher. The majority, in reply to these allegations, said that they adopted a valuation made for probate purposes in June 1969 on the occasion of the death in that month of Mr Joseph Daniels, the father of the minority share-holders and Mr Bernard Daniels. Against this the minority shareholders alleged that probate valuations were conservative as to amount and usually less than the value obtainable on open market between a willing seller and buyer.

In 1974 the land was sold by Mrs Daniels for £120,000 and although the majority had every intention of denying the allegations, they asked at this stage that the claim of the minority be struck out as disclosing no reasonable cause of action or otherwise as an abuse of the process of the court. It was argued, on behalf of the majority, that since the minority was not alleging fraud against the majority no action on behalf of the alleged loss to the company could be brought because under the decision in **Foss v Harbottle**, 1843 the court could not interfere in the internal affairs of the company at the request of the minority. The minority said they were unable to allege fraud because they were not able to say precisely what had happened beyond the matters set out in their claim.

Templeman J, who had not been asked to try the action but only to say whether there was an action at all, reviewed the decisions under the rule in **Foss v Harbottle**, 1843 and his judgment made clear that if the breach of duty alleged turned out to be a breach of fiduciary duty, then it should be allowed to proceed under the rule in **Cook v Deeks**, 1916 because the majority could control general meetings. Furthermore, if the breach of duty alleged was one of skill and care, i.e. negligence at common law, then it should also be allowed to proceed as an exception to **Foss v Harbottle**, 1843 because the alleged negligence had resulted in a profit to one of the directors which distinguished this case from **Pavlides v Jensen**, 1956.

Procedural aspects

When a shareholder is suing to restrain the majority from acting illegally or continuing to commit a personal wrong upon him he has a choice. He may sue in his own name or in the representative form on behalf of himself and other shareholders with whom he enjoys the right allegedly denied to him. The relief asked for will normally be a *declaratory judgment* saying what the law is and by which the parties intend to abide, or an *injunction* to restrain the conduct complained of if it is thought the majority will still continue to act unfairly.

Where the individual member is seeking a claim against third parties for the company's benefit so that he is trying to enforce a claim which belongs to the company, his claim is call-ed *derivative*.

In a *personal* or *representative* claim the company is a real and genuine defendant. In a *derivative* action the company is joined as a nominal defendant because the directors and the majority of the members of the company will not bring the company into court as a claimant. The company is made a party to the action so that the judge may grant it a remedy by being brought in as a nominal defendant, the claimant naming the company as a defendant in his claim form.

The remedy of damages is available in a derivative claim. The damages go to the company and not to the claimant. However, the claimant is entitled to an indemnity for his costs from the company (*Wallersteiner* v *Moir (No 2)* [1975] 1 All ER 849).

A derivative action is not available to challenge the form in which a company's accounts are prepared. The Companies Act requires the appointment of auditors who must report upon the accounts and this is the protection which statute law gives to the exclusion of other remedies (*Devlin* v *Slough Estates Ltd* [1982] 2 All ER 273). It should be noted, however, that the courts may distinguish the *Devlin* case and intervene where the company concerned has taken advantage of the audit exemption.

A derivative action for fraud in the minority is an equitable remedy. Thus, the plaintiff must come with clean hands (*Towers* v *African Tug Co* [1904] 1 Ch 558). The plaintiff must not have been involved in the wrongdoing (*Nurcombe* v *Nurcombe* [1985] 1 All ER 65). This contrasts with petitions under s 994 where, according to Nourse J in *Re London School of Electronics*, 1985 (discussed in Chapter 18 ◐), there is no overriding requirement that the petitioner should come to court with clean hands.

The rule in *Foss* is a *rule of procedure*. It is a matter to be decided *before* the trial of the allegations as to whether the claimant can be allowed to proceed to a trial under an exception to the rule.

There is a firm statement to this effect by the Court of Appeal in *Prudential Assurance* v *Newman (No 2)* [1982] 1 All ER 354 where the court was critical of the approach of the trial judge in taking evidence in proof of the allegations for many days and at great cost to the defendants before deciding that a claim could proceed as an exception to *Foss*.

Prudential Assurance Co Ltd v Newman Industries Ltd (No 2) [1982] Ch 204, CA

Cumming-Bruce, Templeman and Brightman LJ took it in turns to read the following judgment of the Court of Appeal:

It is commonly said that an exception to the rule in *Foss v Harbottle* arises if the corporation is 'controlled' by persons implicated in the fraud complained of, who will not permit the name of the company to be used as plaintiffs in the suit: see *Russell v Wakefield Waterworks Co* (1875) LR 20 Eq 474, 482. But this proposition leaves two questions at large, first, what is meant by 'control', which embraces a broad spectrum extending from an overall absolute majority of votes at one end, to a majority of votes at the other end made up of those likely to be cast by the delinquent himself plus those voting with him as a result of influence or apathy. Secondly, what course is to be taken by the court if, as happened in *Foss v Harbottle*, in the *East Pant Du* case and in the instant case, but did not happen in *Atwool v Merryweather* (1867) LR 5 Eq 464, the court is confronted by a motion on the part of the delinquent or by the company, seeking to strike out the action? For at the time of the application the existence of the fraud is unproved. It is at this point that a dilemma emerges. If, upon such an application, the plaintiff can require the court to assume as a fact every allegation in the statement of claim, as in a true demurrer, the plaintiff will frequently be able to outmanoeuvre the primary purpose of the rule in *Foss v Harbottle* by alleging fraud and 'control' by the fraudster. If, on the other hand, the plaintiff has to prove fraud and 'control' before he can establish his title to prosecute his action, then the action may need to be fought to a conclusion before the court can decide whether or not the plaintiff should be permitted to prosecute it. In the latter case the purpose of the rule in *Foss* v *Harbottle* disappears. Either the fraud has not been proved, so *cadit quaestio*; or the fraud has been proved and the delinquent is accountable unless there is a valid decision of the board or a valid decision of the company in general meeting, reached without impropriety or unfairness, to condone the fraud [. . .]

We desire, however, to say two things. First, as we have already said, we have no doubt whatever that Vinelott J erred in dismissing the summons of 10 May 1979. He ought to have determined as a preliminary issue whether the plaintiffs were entitled to sue on behalf of Newman by bringing a derivative action. It cannot have been right to have subjected the company to a 30-day action (as it was then estimated to be) in order to enable him to decide whether the plaintiffs were entitled in law to subject the company to a 30-day action. Such an approach defeats the whole purpose of the rule in *Foss* v *Harbottle* and sanctions the very mischief that the rule is designed to prevent . . .

The second observation which we wish to make is merely a comment on Vinelott J's decision that there is an exception to the rule in *Foss* v *Harbottle* whenever the justice of the case so requires. We are not convinced that this is a practical test, particularly if it involves a full-dress trial before the test is applied. On the other hand, we do not think that the right to bring a derivative action should be decided as a preliminary issue upon the hypothesis that all the allegations in the statement of claim of 'fraud' and 'control' are facts, as they would be on the trial of a preliminary point of law. In our view, whatever may be the properly defined boundaries of the exception to the rule, the plaintiff ought at least to be required before proceeding with his action to establish a prima facie case (i) that the company is entitled to the relief claimed, and (ii) that the action falls within the proper boundaries of the exception to the rule in *Foss* v *Harbottle*. On the latter issue it may well be right for the judge trying the preliminary issue to grant a sufficient adjournment to enable a meeting of shareholders to be convened by the board, so that he can reach a conclusion in the light of the conduct of, and proceedings at, that meeting.

The statutory derivative action

The new action is found within ss 260–264 of the Companies Act 2006. It is worth noting though that in the Explanatory Notes to the CA 2006, it is noted that 'the sections in this Part do not formulate a substantive rule to replace the rule in *Foss* v *Harbottle*, but instead reflect the recommendations of the Law Commission that there should be a "new derivative procedure with more modern, flexible and accessible criteria for determining whether a shareholder can pursue an action" (Shareholder Remedies, paragraph 6.15).' However, in *Stainer* v *Lee* [2010] EWHC 1539 (Ch), Roth J stated: 'The jurisdiction governing derivative claims in England and Wales is now comprehensively governed by Chapter 1 of Part 11 of the Act: sections 260–264. Such claims may be brought only under the provisions in that chapter or pursuant to a court order in proceedings on an "unfair prejudice" petition under section 994; section 260(2).'

Section 260(1) defines a derivative claim as '[. . .] proceedings by a member of a company (a) in respect of a cause of action vested in the company, and (b) seeking relief on behalf of the company'. Accordingly, there are three elements to the derivative claim: the action is brought by a member of the company; the cause of action is vested in the company; and relief is sought on the company's behalf. With respect to the term 'member', while this is defined in s 112 of the 2006 Act, s 260(5) extends the scope of this to include 'a person who is not a member but to whom shares in the company have been transferred or transmitted by operation of law'. This would include, for example, where a trustee in bankruptcy or the personal representative of a deceased member's estate acquires an interest in a share as a result of the bankruptcy or death of a member.

Section 260(2) goes on to state that a derivative claim may only be brought under this chapter (of the 2006 Act) or s 994 (unfairly prejudicial conduct).

However, a key provision in relation to the statutory derivative action is s 260(3) which states that: 'A derivative claim under this chapter may be brought only in respect of a cause of action arising from an actual or proposed act or omission involving negligence, default, breach of duty or breach of trust by a director of the company.' This section states that the cause of action must be against the director or another person (for instance if a third party dishonestly assisted a director in breaching his fiduciary duties). Therefore, s 260(3) provides shareholders with a statutory right to sue directors for negligence (in itself a change from pre-existing common law; *Pavlides v Jensen* [1956] 1 Ch 565), default, breach of duty (see directors' duties, ss 170–176) or breach of trust.

The remaining subsections in s 260 read as follows. Section 260(4) goes on to state that 'it is immaterial whether the cause of action arose before or after the person seeking to bring or continue the derivative claim became a member of the company'. Section 260(5) clarifies those persons whom may be included within the terms used by the section. For example, for the purposes of this chapter (of the 2006 Act), the term 'director' includes a former director; a shadow director is treated as a director; and references to a member of a company include a person who is not a member but to whom shares in the company have been transferred or transmitted by operation of law.

However, it is important to realise that members do not have unfettered discretion to bring a derivative action. The member must apply to the court for permission to bring the action. Section 261(1) states that 'a member of a company who brings a derivative claim under this chapter must apply to the court for permission to continue it'. Section 261(2) goes on to note that if it appears to the court that the application and the evidence filed by the applicant in support of it do not disclose a prima facie case for giving permission (or leave), the court (i) must dismiss the application; and (ii) may make any consequential order it considers appropriate.

Section 261(3) goes on to note that if the application is not dismissed under s 261(2) then the court may give directions as to the evidence to be provided by the company, and may adjourn the proceedings to enable the evidence to be obtained.

On hearing the application, the court may according to s 261(4) give permission to continue the claim on such terms as it thinks fit; refuse permission and dismiss the claim; or adjourn the proceedings on the application and give such directions as it thinks fit.

As such, this clause provides that, once proceedings have been brought, the member is required to apply to the court for permission to continue the claim. This reflects the current procedure in England and Wales under the Civil Procedure Rules. The applicant is required to establish a prima facie case for the grant of permission, and the court will consider the issue on the basis of his evidence alone without requiring evidence to be filed by the defendant. The court must dismiss the application at this stage if what is filed does not show a prima facie case, and it may make any consequential order that it considers appropriate (for example, a costs order or a civil restraint order against the applicant). If the application is not dismissed, the court may direct the company to provide evidence and, on hearing the application, may grant permission, refuse permission and dismiss the claim, or adjourn the proceedings and give such directions as it thinks fit.

Section 262 concerns the alternative scenario of a company commencing an action, only for a member to take it forward as a derivative action. This section is unlikely to be relied upon to a great extent. Under both s 261 and s 262, the member must demonstrate two points before action can commence. First, the member has sufficient evidence to establish a prima facie case and secondly, the member needs to persuade the court that a derivative action is appropriate. The advantages of this two-stage test are that it will limit actions and minimise the initial expenditure of the company.

Section 263 outlines the considerations which the court must weigh up under an application from both s 261 and s 262. Section 263(2) states that a court must refuse permission for a derivative action if the court is satisfied:

(a) that a person acting in accordance with s 172 would not seek to continue the claim; or
(b) where the cause of action arises from an act or omission that is yet to occur, that the act or omission has been authorised by the company; or
(c) where the cause of action arises from an act or omission that has already occurred, that the act or omission (i) was authorised by the company before it occurred, or (ii) has been ratified by the company since it occurred.

If any of these three situations are met, then the court must refuse to allow the derivative action to proceed.

If the situation the court is presented with does not fall within one of the three situations as listed in s 263(2), then the court can proceed to consider a number of discretionary factors listed in s 263(3), which states that in considering whether to give permission (or leave) the court must take into account, in particular:

(a) whether the member is acting in good faith in seeking to continue the claim;
(b) the importance that a person acting in accordance with s 172 (duty to promote the success of the company) would attach to continuing it;
(c) where the cause of action results from an act or omission that is yet to occur, whether the act or omission could be, and in the circumstances would be likely to be –
    (i) authorised by the company before it occurs; or
    (ii) ratified by the company after it occurs;
(d) where the cause of action arises from an act or omission that has already occurred, whether the act or omission could be, and in the circumstances would be likely to be, ratified by the company;
(e) whether the company has decided not to pursue the claim;
(f) whether the act or omission in respect of which the claim is brought gives rise to a cause of action that the member could pursue in his own right rather than on behalf of the company.

The case of *Airey v Cordell* [2006] EWHC 2728 (Ch) considers the approach courts should take in deciding whether or not to permit a derivative action. In this case the court decided that where a shareholder applies to the court for permission to bring a derivative claim he is required to establish both that there is a prima facie case that the company is entitled to the relief sought and that the action falls within the boundaries of one of the exceptions to the rule that a member cannot bring an action on behalf of a company. If no reasonable board would bring proceedings then, even if there is a prima facie case, the court should not sanction proceedings. Where, however, the court is satisfied that a reasonable board of directors could bring the action; the court should not shut out the shareholder on the basis of its own view of what it would do if it were the board.

Section 263(4) reads as follows: 'In considering whether to give permission the court shall have particular regard to any evidence before it as to the views of members of the company who have no personal interest, direct or indirect, in the matter.' It is interesting to note that the court must pay particular regard to the views of the 'independent' members of the company and there is not merely a requirement to take into account their views. It could be argued that this should be the most prevalent thought in the mind of the judges as they decide whether a derivative action should proceed or not.

Interpretation and implementation of s 260

During the early stages of the Companies Bill, there was concern that this new statutory derivative action would open the floodgates to litigation. However, it seems that the 'checks' provided by the court will prevent this. Earlier concerns that the rule, together with the exceptions to *Foss* v *Harbottle*, would be removed are unfounded and it seems that the Companies Act 2006 has merely established a new derivative procedure.

To date, there have been a small number of reported cases which have considered the new derivative action. In the first couple of reported cases, *Franbar Holdings Ltd* v *Patel and Others* [2008] EWHC 1534 (Ch), *Mission Capital plc* v *Sinclair and Another* [2008] All ER (D) 225 (Mar), and *Stimpson* v *Southern Landlords Association* [2009] EWHC 2072 (Ch), permission to continue derivative actions was refused.

 Franbar Holdings Ltd v Patel and Others [2008] EWHC 1534 (Ch)

Following consideration of the matters contained within s 263 of the Companies Act 2006, the court ruled that the claimant had not been shown that the hypothetical director would have attached great importance to the continuation of the derivative claim at the instant stage in the proceedings. In this regard, considerable weight had to be given to the fact that the claimant could achieve all that it could properly want through the s 994 petition and the shareholders' action. Accordingly, the application for permission to continue the derivative action would be dismissed.

In this respect, Mr William Trower QC noted:

[. . .] I am required to take into account is the importance that a person acting in accordance with section 172 would attach to continuing the derivative claim. I have already concluded that I cannot be satisfied that such a person would not seek to continue it, but section 263(3)(b) requires me to form a judgment as to how important the hypothetical director would regard the continuation of the proceedings as being. This is not a particularly easy exercise, but if he would not attach very much importance to the continuation of the claim, that is likely to count against the grant of permission. If, in fulfilling his duty to promote the success of the company, he would attach substantial importance to the continuation of the claim, that factor is likely to count in favour of granting permission.

In my judgment, the hypothetical director acting in accordance with section 172 would take into account a wide range of considerations when assessing the importance of continuing the claim. These would include such matters as the prospects of success of the claim, the ability of the company to make a recovery on any award of damages, the disruption which would be caused to the development of the company's business by having to concentrate on the proceedings, the costs of the proceedings and any damage to the company's reputation and business if the proceedings were to fail. A director will often be in the position of having to make what is no more than a partially informed decision on continuation without any very clear idea of how the proceedings might turn out [. . .]

In conclusion, I take the view that there is substance in the complaints which have been made by Franbar and that some of those complaints would, if established, give rise to breaches of duty which are incapable of ratification on the votes of Casualty Plus. I also take the view that there is work still to be done in formulating a clear claim for breaches which have caused actionable loss to Medicentres, and that it would be open to the hypothetical director to decline to proceed with the derivative claim at this stage. While he may attach importance to its continuation at some stage in the future, I am not satisfied that he would attach great importance to its continuation now. I also give considerable weight to the fact that Franbar should be able to achieve all that it can properly want through the section 994 petition and the shareholders' action. Having regard to all of these considerations, and carrying out the balancing exercise as best I can on the information currently available, it is my judgment that justice is best achieved by refusing permission to continue.

Comment

The acquisition of evidence relating to the affairs of an insolvent debtor for use in other proceedings was capable of being a legitimate use of Rule 7.31(4) of the Insolvency Rules so long as that evidence was probative of (or at least related to) a fact or matter in issue in those proceedings, and so long as the person to whom material on the court file related was not able to point to any countervailing prejudice. Inspection in those circumstances was consistent with the purpose for which the right was given, that was to enable persons with a legitimate interest in a particular insolvency proceeding to discover what had taken place. Those criteria were met in this case.

Accordingly, the order would be made subject to the condition that, in the absence of further order, the copies and the information obtained were to be used only for the purposes of the s 994 petition and the shareholders' action.

Mission Capital plc v *Sinclair and Another* [2008] All ER (D) 225 (Mar)

The defendants had been the executive directors of the claimant company and clause 16.1.6 of their contracts provided that the board could terminate them if they engaged in conduct that was unacceptable in the reasonable opinion of the board. Clause 18 provided that if the defendants' contracts were so terminated they were immediately to resign all directorships. At a board meeting in February 2008, the three non-executive directors of the company purported to remove the defendants from the board pursuant to cl 16.1.6 and on the basis that they had allegedly failed to submit financial information and to meet financial forecasts. Those allegations were disputed by the defendants. P was appointed to the board as a new director with executive powers. Subsequently, the company issued a claim against the defendants and obtained interim injunctive relief. The defendants issued a counterclaim by which they sought injunctions obliging the company to continue to employ them and to re-appoint them to the board. The defendants also issued a derivative claim under the Companies Act 2006. A number of interim applications in both actions fell to be determined.

The principal issues that fell to be determined were: (i) whether the defendants were to be granted interim injunctions restoring them to their positions before the meeting of February 2008; (ii) whether the non-executive directors and P were to be joined as parties to the defendants' counterclaim in the company's action; and (iii) whether the defendants were to be granted permission to continue their derivative action under s 263 of the 2006 Act.

The court ruled that the injunctions sought by the defendants essentially amounted to orders for specific performance of their service contracts with the company. In relation to the injunction pertaining to their employment, the defendants had failed to show, on the evidence, that there was a seriously arguable case that they would succeed in obtaining the relief sought at trial. In relation to the injunction as regards the directorships, while the defendants had demonstrated an arguable case, the balance of justice weighed against the grant of the interim injunctions sought. The non-executive directors and P would be joined as parties to the defendants' counterclaim.

Furthermore, the court held that the basis for the mandatory refusal of permission to continue the defendants' derivative claim under s 263(2) of the 2006 Act had not been made out. However, having considered the discretionary factors set out in s 263(3)(a)–(f) of the 2006 Act, and the circumstances of the instant case, the defendants' application for permission to continue the derivative action would be refused.

Other cases have included *Iesini* v *Westrip Holdings Ltd* [2009] EWHC 2526 (Ch) and *Fanmailuk.com Ltd* v *Cooper* [2008] EWHC 2198 (Ch), in which applications for permission to continue derivative claim were adjourned.

Iesini v *Westrip Holdings Ltd* [2009] EWHC 2526 (Ch)

The first applicant shareholder and director (X) and the second, third and fourth applicant share-holders (Y) applied for permission to continue a derivative claim on behalf of the first respondent company (W) in which they sought to reverse the alleged stripping of W's assets and claimed declarations about W's ownership of assets. The sixth respondent company (R) held an exclusive mineral exploration licence. W agreed with R's shareholders (B), the second and third respondents, that W would purchase B's shares in return for the allotment of redeemable preference shares in W to B, so that W could exploit the licence. W resolved to issue such shares without voting, divi-dend or winding-up rights. However, W's articles of association did not permit the share issue. W and B later entered into an agreement which stated that R held its licence on trust for W. If the agreement was breached by W, B were entitled to rescind it and opt to retain the shares in R and sue for damages. W adopted new articles of association enabling directors to allot and issue com-pliant redeemable preference shares. W entered a joint venture with another company to exploit the licence. X was later suspended as W's director. W became financially unable to redeem the preference shares and it was discovered that the shares had not been issued. The board was legally advised that B had a right to rescind. B gave notice exercising that right and sought to have the shares in R retransferred to them. W accepted the rescission and offered to settle R's claims to be substituted to the joint venture agreement. X and Y claimed that W's board had breached its duty by failing to consider defences which W might advance to challenge the rescission, that W had a claim for restitution in respect of costs incurred in developing the licence, and that W held the licence on trust and so R did not have the right to be substituted to the joint venture agreement. B and R submitted that the Companies Act 2006 s 263(2)(a) required permission to be refused because a person acting in accordance with the s 172 duty to promote the success of the com-pany would not seek to continue the claim. W and the fourth and fifth respondent board members argued that B and R were not seeking to pursue the derivative action for W's benefit, but for the benefit of the joint venture company, which had provided them with an indemnity for costs and damages in relation to the claim. Application for permission adjourned.

(1) The Act provided for a two-stage procedure where a member wished to bring a derivative claim. The applicant was first required to make a prima facie case for permission to continue a derivative claim. Then the court had to find that the cause of action arose from an act or omission involving negligence, default, breach of duty or breach of trust by a director. At that second stage it was not simply a matter of establishing a prima facie case. It was wrong to embark upon a mini trial of an action, *Fanmailuk.com Ltd* v *Cooper* [2008] EWHC 2198 (Ch) applied. However, the court would have to form a provisional view on the strength of the claim to properly consider the requirements of s 263(2)(a) and s 263(3)(b). Section 263(2)(a) applied only where the court was satisfied that no director acting in accordance with s 172 would seek to continue the claim, *Airey* v *Cordell* [2006] EWHC 2728 (Ch) [2007] Bus LR 391 and *Franbar Holdings Ltd* v *Patel* [2008] EWHC 1534 (Ch) considered. If some directors would, and others would not, seek to continue the claim, s 263(3)(b) should be applied, when many of the same considerations would apply.

(2) As a matter of strict legal right, B had been entitled to rescind or terminate the agreement when they had done so. The board of W had taken advice from eminent and specialist counsel on that matter and followed that advice. It was therefore impossible to say that it had been negligent or in breach of duty in doing so. Further, if the old board, including X, had done what the agreement required it do, there would have been no question of rescission. The strength of the claim against

the board was so weak that no director, acting in accordance with s 172, would seek to continue the claim against the directors in respect of their actions in accepting the rescission. Alternatively, a person acting in accordance with s 172 would attach little weight to continuing it.

(3) The restitutionary claim contained no allegation of default or breach of duty by a director. It was therefore not a derivative claim.

(4) Using the powers in s 261(4)(c), the board were directed to reconsider W's defence to R's claim for substitution, on the basis that there might be a strong claim that W held the licence on trust. If the board decided to defend that claim, there would be no need for a derivative action. The application was adjourned pending the board's decision.

(5) Although there were collateral benefits for R and B, the dominant purpose of the claim was to benefit W, *Goldsmith v Sperrings Ltd* [1977] 1 WLR 478 considered. They had brought the claim in good faith.

However, in more recent cases, *Kiani v Cooper* [2010] EWHC 577 (Ch) and *Stainer v Lee* [2010] EWHC 1539 (Ch), the courts have appeared far more open to the prospect of granting permission to minority shareholders to continue with derivative actions, though permission extended only to the conclusion of disclosure, at which point further permission to continue should be sought.

Kiani v Cooper [2010] EWHC 577 (Ch)

The applicant shareholder and director (K) of the second respondent company (X) applied under s 261 of the Companies Act 2006 for permission to continue a derivative claim under s 260 of the Act on behalf of X against the first respondent shareholder and director (C) of the same company for breach of duty. K and C were the sole directors and equal shareholders in X, a property development company. C was also the director of another company (D) which billed X for services. A dispute arose between K and C. K alleged that C had wrongly allowed a judgment in default to be entered against X in respect of a debt allegedly owed to D. The default judgment was later withdrawn. K also alleged that, through his control of X's accounts, C had caused a further debt to be entered into X's accounts in respect of unsubstantiated services rendered to it by another company. K further obtained an injunction restraining C from presenting a winding-up petition in respect of monies allegedly owed to him in his personal capacity by X. Proudman J stated:

> A derivative claim is defined by s 260 as a claim brought by a member seeking relief on behalf of a company in respect of a cause of action vested in the company. Although the cause of action may be against a director of the company or another person or both, it must arise from an actual or proposed act or omission by the director involving negligence, default, breach of duty or breach of trust (see s 260(3)).
>
> Permission to continue a derivative action is required by s 261. The court must by that section dismiss the application for permission if there is no prima facie case for giving permission. Otherwise it may give directions as to the evidence to be provided and adjourn the proceedings to enable such evidence to be obtained. It has very wide powers to adjourn the application, to give directions and to give or refuse permission. It has wide powers to impose terms on the grant of permission.
>
> Section 263 specifies the criteria for permission. Section 263(2) is mandatory and states that permission must be refused if the court is satisfied that a person acting in accordance with the duty imposed by s 172 to promote the success of the company would not seek to continue the claim, or where the cause of action arises from an act or omission which has been pre-authorised or has been ratified by the company.

Section 263(3) sets out the factors which the court must in particular take into account in deciding whether to give permission. They are: whether the member is acting in good faith in seeking to continue the claim, the importance that a person acting in accordance with s 172 would attach to continuing it, whether the cause of action could be authorised or ratified by the company, whether the company has decided not to pursue the claim and whether the act or omission in respect of which the claim is brought gives rise to a cause of action that the member could pursue in his own right rather than on behalf of the company. Further, the court is required by s 263(4) to have particular regard to any evidence before it as to the views of members of the company who have no personal interest, direct or indirect, in the matter. In this case there are no such persons.

Although Mrs Kiani and Mr Cooper were the only two directors and members of the company, Mr Kiani was the driving force behind his wife's involvement and for present purposes they have an identity of interest. No question of authorisation or ratification arises or is likely to arise. The crucial factors of those listed in s 263(3) are therefore likely to be good faith, the availability of an alternative remedy and, in particular, the attitude of a person acting in accordance with the duties imposed by s 172 of the Act . . .

In all the circumstances of this case it seems to me is that Mrs Kiani is acting in good faith in making the present application.

Another factor prescribed by s 263(3) is the availability to Mrs Kiani of an alternative remedy in respect of the alleged breaches of duty. Mr Irvin submits that one proper remedy would be a personal action under the shareholders' agreement. However, it seems to me that such an action could meet real difficulties in that the loss claimed could be viewed as loss reflective of the company's loss, irrecoverable under the principle enunciated in *Johnson* v *Gore Wood & Co* [2001] BCC 820; [2002] 2 AC 1.

Mr Irvin's principal submission is however that Mrs Kiani's proper remedy is an unfair prejudice petition under s 994 of the Companies Act 2006. Under s 996 the court has a very wide discretion as to the relief it may grant, including, by s 996(2)(c), authorising civil proceedings in the name of and on behalf of the company.

There is a lot to be said for this procedure in a case of a two-person company where the real dispute is between those two persons alone. However, the jurisdiction to make an order under s 996(2)(c) can only be exercised if the court is first satisfied that the unfair prejudice petition is well-founded. Mrs Kiani would not therefore have standing on behalf of the company to restrain a winding-up petition. It may well be the case that the court would have jurisdiction on her application to restrain a winding-up petition pending the outcome of s 994 proceedings. I have not been addressed on that issue. Moreover, yesterday Mr Cooper and DPM, through Mr Irvin, said for the first time that they were willing to offer an undertaking not to present creditors' petitions pending s 994 proceedings.

Taking all those factors into consideration, it seems to me that Mrs Kiani's position is this. She says that she and the company have been deprived of the opportunity to pursue the development venture. She does not want the company to be wound up on the petition of Mr Cooper, at whose door she places responsibility for the deadlock which has occurred. She wants her opportunity to be preserved. She wishes to pursue Mr Cooper on behalf of the company in a derivative action. It seems to me that the fact that she could in a more roundabout way achieve the relief she seeks does not mean that she ought not to be granted permission in the present case . . .

It seems to me that, balancing all the relevant factors, Mrs Kiani's application to continue the action in the name of the company ought to be granted. However, I am prepared to give permission only down to disclosure in the action, for the reasons I have already explained.

Held – application granted.

(1) C had failed to adduce any corroborative evidence in support of his defence to the allegations against him. In respect of X's dealings with D, C should, as one of X's signatories, at least have ensured that cogent evidence of any transaction between those parties was well documented in light of the possible conflict of interests. In pursuing the case it was clear that K had been acting in good faith; C's actions having deprived her of an opportunity to pursue a number of development ventures. Although it was possible for K to pursue a petition under the Companies Act 2006,

s 994 as opposed to bringing her derivative action, the existence of an alternative remedy was only one factor to consider. Finally, it was obvious that a notional director, acting in accordance with his duties under s 172 would wish to continue with the claim against C, at least, down to the disclosure stage where corroborative documents might be produced. Balancing those facts together, K would be allowed to pursue her derivative claim.

(2) In a case where the dispute was between two people, the court ought to take a reasonable view as to whether to grant the petitioner an indemnity in respect of her costs. In the instant case it was fair, in light of the court's conclusion, that K should be indemnified for her costs but that she should have no indemnity in respect of a potential adverse costs order.

Stainer v Lee [2010] EWHC 1539 (Ch)

The applicant (S) applied under the Companies Act 2006, s 261 for permission to continue a derivative claim seeking relief on behalf of the relevant company (C) against the respondents, being C's two directors and a company (E) of which one of the directors (L) was the sole shareholder and director. S had a small shareholding in C. E had been established by L as a special-purpose vehicle for the acquisition of shares in C. By 2002, it had acquired a 65 per cent shareholding in C with the aid of a bank loan exceeding £4 million. The discharge of E's liability to its bank was achieved by a loan made by C to E. Between 2002 and 2008, C made substantial additional loans to E. S argued that L and his fellow director had acted in breach of their duties to C in allowing the lending to E to be on an interest-free basis and in lending sums to E for some purpose other than discharging or reducing the liability which E had incurred for the acquisition of shares in C, which purpose had not been approved by C's members and was not in its interests. E, S asserted, was a constructive trustee for C as regards the sums received by way of the additional lending.

Held – application granted.

(1) The test to be applied was that set out by Lewison J in *Iesini v Westrip Holdings Ltd* [2009] EWHC 2526 (Ch), [2010] BCC 420, *Iesini* applied. As to the standard to be applied generally under s 263, Lewison J held that something more than simply a prima facie case was required and that the court had to form a view on the strength of the claim, albeit on a provisional basis. The necessary evaluation was not mechanistic and a range of factors would have to be considered to reach an overall view. If the case seemed very strong, it might be appropriate to continue it even if the likely level of recovery was not so large, as such a claim stood a good chance of provoking an early settlement or might qualify for summary judgment. On the other hand, it might be in the company's interests to continue a less strong case if the amount of potential recovery was very large.

(2) The failure to obtain interest over a period of almost nine years on lending to E that rose from £4.6 million to £8.1 million constituted very strong grounds for a claim that the directors were in breach of their fiduciary duties. It had been asserted that the outstanding interest had been repaid, but it was not clear whether that was so. It would therefore be appropriate to grant S permission to continue the derivative claim until the conclusion of disclosure.

(3) There was at least a well arguable case that the additional lending to E was made in breach of the directors' relevant duties. L's witness statement fell far short of explaining the purpose of the additional loans or why they were thought to be in C's best interests. There was no indication whatever of why E needed the sums in question or indeed what it was using the money for. L had sought to rely on a 'new loan agreement' between C and E, but that did not constitute ratification of the additional lending. It could not be said that the shareholders who had voted in favour of the resolution approving the agreement had given their informed consent: they appeared not to have been told the purpose of the agreement or of L's interest in E. If the resolution were vitiated for this

reason, the entry into the new loan agreement might itself be contrary to C's best interests and the promotion of the agreement might be a further breach of the directors' duties.

(4) As the derivative action was to proceed, S was entitled to be indemnified by C as to his reasonable costs, subject to a limit of £40,000, *Wallersteiner v Moir (No 2)* [1975] QB 373 applied.

Hughes v Weiss [2012] EWHC 2363 (Ch)

The applicant (H) applied for permission to continue derivative claims against the first respondent (W) that were vested in the second respondent company (C). H, a barrister, and W, a solicitor, formed C to provide commercial legal consultancy services in relation to asset finance and had agreed, as co-directors, to draw the same modest salary with an entitlement to potential dividends. Their relationship became strained when W felt that he was putting in more effort than H and they terminated their quasi-partnership. H sought to advance three derivative claims, namely that (a) W had wrongly transferred £100,000 from C's bank account to his personal account; (b) W carried on a business in competition with C in breach of his fiduciary duties; (c) W had, in breach of fiduciary duty, diverted the payment of invoices from C to himself and had failed to account for those funds. H knew of a single invoice where C's funds had been allegedly diverted to W. W contended that the removal of the £100,000 was within his authority as a director on the bank mandate and had been pursuant to discussions with H relating to the more advantageous investment of those funds; he later contended that £30,000 of that sum had been on the basis of his entitlement to a dividend, and that payment of the remaining funds could be justified on various bases, including a quantum meruit. The issues were whether (i) there was a prima facie case for H's claims; (ii) there were any statutory mandatory bars to granting permission; (iii) H was acting in good faith and there was justification for the derivative claim on the ground that it was in C's interests; (iv) there was an alternative remedy which stood as a bar to a grant of permission.

Application granted.

(1) Although an applicant for permission to carry on a derivative action under the Companies Act 2006 s 261 had to establish a prima facie case that a company had a good cause of action arising out of a defendant's breach of duty, there was no requirement that a merits test be satisfied before permission could be given, *Stainer v Lee* [2010] EWHC 1539 (Ch), [2011] BCC 134 applied. In the instant case, H had good prospects of establishing that C had a claim against W for breach of duty. In relation to the first claim, H had a strong case for saying that W had misappropriated C's moneys and was trying to find ways to justify his wrongdoing and avoid repayment. Similarly, although the evidence was incomplete in relation to the second claim, the court reached the provisional view that H's claim was strong. In respect of the third claim, there was clear evidence of wrongdoing in relation to the relevant invoice.

(2) There were no mandatory bars to permission under s 263. W's contention that the relevant funds had been withdrawn with prior authorisation was rejected. There was no agreement that C's moneys should be placed in a more advantageous account. Further, the existence of a bank mandate permitting a single director to effect transactions on C's account did not constitute authorisation for the transfer of C's funds to W's personal bank account. Additionally there was no ground for refusing permission on the basis that there was no director acting in accordance with s 172 who sought to continue the derivative claims.

(3) As H brought the claim in order to vindicate C's rights, she acted in good faith for the purposes of s 263(3)(a); the fact that the claims might benefit her did not convert the purpose of the litigation into an improper purpose. The justification for the litigation, if any, had to be the need to act fairly as between members of the company under s 172(1)(f); the claim of diversion had sufficient merit to justify its pursuit by a person acting in accordance with s 172. The position was different with

the claim for diversion of payments as H had failed to establish that there was a substantial likelihood that other examples would come to light. Accordingly, on the basis that the claim did not stand alone, a person acting in accordance with s 172 would only attach some limited importance to continuing that claim in conjunction with other heads of claim. The fact that C would not resume trading and would be dissolved was not a compelling objection to the conclusion that a person, acting in accordance with s 172 would attach importance to continuing the proceedings. Additionally, the prima facie rule that a person acting on behalf of a company in vindicating its rights with court approval was displaced where the substance of the dispute was between H's and W's respective entitlements to C's assets; H and W were to conduct the litigation at their own risk in relation to costs. There was also no hope of ratification as C was effectively deadlocked.

(4) There was no absolute bar to a grant of permission where there was an alternative remedy under the law, *Barrett v Duckett* [1995] BCC 362 explained, *Wilson v Inverness Retail & Business Park Ltd* 2003 SLT 301 and *Konamaneni v Rolls Royce Industrial Power (India) Ltd* [2002] 1 WLR 1269 considered, *Mumbray v Lapper* [2005] EWHC 1152 (Ch) and *Parry v Bartlett* [2011] EWHC 3146 (Ch) applied. The issues H raised were more appropriately dealt with by a derivative claim than a s 994 petition under which she would seek an order that W buy her shares in C; rather, H sought financial remedies for C for misfeasance, and the proper way of obtaining that was by way of a derivative claim, *Stainer v Lee* applied. Finally, the availability of voluntary liquidation was not a basis for refusing permission; it was highly unlikely that a liquidator would fund the litigation given C's limited assets, and there was no point in pursuing what would be a convoluted solution to resolve the issues between H and W.

Essay questions

1 Ben is a minority shareholder in App plc, whose directors are Charles, David and Edward. Though not the controlling shareholders the directors control the company in practice.

   (a) Last year one of the company's employees was convicted of stealing property belonging to the company and was given a suspended sentence. A general meeting instructed the directors to bring civil proceedings to recover the value of property stolen but they refused to do so.

   (b) It has also come to light that the directors have diverted to themselves contracts obtained by the company. Fearing litigation the directors called a general meeting and persuaded the shareholders to approve their actions by passing a simple resolution. The directors cast their votes in favour of the resolution.

   Advise Ben whether he could sue the directors personally or on behalf of the company in respect of the two matters.
   (University of Plymouth)

2 Explain the rule in *Foss v Harbottle* and describe the limits to this rule.
   (The Institute of Company Accountants)

3 'For a minority shareholder who has suffered a wrong at the hands of the majority to establish a case under the alternative remedy he must show both that he suffered "unfairly prejudicial conduct" and that this was suffered in his capacity as a member of the company.' Discuss.
   (The Institute of Chartered Secretaries and Administrators)

4   Explain how the provisions of the Companies Act 2066 attempt to ensure that majority share-holders do not conduct the affairs of a company with complete disregard for the interests of minority shareholders.   *(The Chartered Institute of Management Accountants)*

5   At first sight, the statutory contract may be viewed as an effective method of enforcing a share-holder's rights, especially when considered alongside s 630 and the application of General Equitable Principles. However, once other aspects of company law are examined and factored into this process, then it may be seen that there is a real need for other avenues of minority protection to be made available to shareholders, given their vulnerable position under CA 2006 s 33 (ex CA 1985 s 14). Discuss the accuracy of this statement.   *(University of Hertfordshire)*

Suggested further reading

Almadani, 'Derivative actions: does the Companies Act 2006 offer a way forward?' (2009) 30 Co Law 131.

Baxter, 'The true spirit of *Foss v Harbottle*' (1987) 38 NILQ 6.

Boyle, 'The Prudential, the Court of Appeal and *Foss v Harbottle*' (1981) 2 Co Law 264.

Boyle, 'The new derivative action' (1997) 18 Co Law 256.

Drury, 'The relative nature of a shareholder's right to enforce the company contract' [1986] CLJ 219.

Gibbs, 'Has the statutory derivative claim fulfilled its objectives?' (2011) 32(3) *Company Lawyer* 76.

Gregory, 'What is the rule in *Foss v Harbottle*?' (1982) 45 MLR 584.

Hirt, 'Ratification of breaches of director's duties: the implications of the reform proposal regarding the availability of derivative actions' (2004) *Company Lawyer* 25(7) 197.

Keay and Loughrey, 'Something old, something new, something borrowed: an analysis of the new derivative action under the Companies Act 2006' [2008] LQR 469.

Keay and Loughrey, 'Derivative proceedings in a brave new world for company management and shareholders' [2010] JBL 151.

Milman, 'Resolution of internal disputes within solvent business organisations: the legal options' (2012) *Company Law Newsletter* 314, 1.

Mujih, 'The new statutory derivative claim: a delicate balancing act' (2012) *Company Lawyer* 33(3), 76.

Prentice, 'Shareholders' actions: the rule in *Foss v Harbottle*' (1988) 104 LQR 341.

Reisberg, 'Derivative actions and the funding problem: the way forward' [2006] JBL 445.

Roberts and Poole, 'Shareholder remedies: corporate wrongs and the derivative action' [1999] JBL 99.

Sullivan, 'Restating the scope of the derivative action' [1985] CLJ 236.

Wedderburn, 'Shareholders' rights and the rule in *Foss v Harbottle*' (1957) CLJ 194.

Wedderburn, 'Derivative actions and *Foss v Harbottle*' (1981) 44 MLR 202.

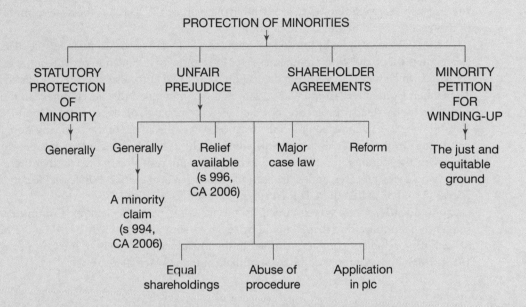

There are several other sections in the Companies Act 2006 which enable a number of shareholders to defy the majority, as discussed in previous chapters (e.g. s 633 where dissentient holders of 15 per cent of the issued shares of the class can apply for cancellation of the variation).

Statutory protection against unfair prejudice

Section 994 exists as an alternative to the statutory derivative action discussed in the previous chapter. This was of particular importance prior to the 2006 Act as it provided a relatively more accessible and straightforward route for shareholders than the complex and restrictive rule in *Foss* v *Harbottle*. However, given the changes under the 2006 Act, the relative importance of this section could be called into doubt.

Section 994 was originally introduced in the form of s 210 of the Companies Act 1948 (and subsequently as s 459 of the Companies Act 1985) and was intended to provide more flexible remedies which were also free from the harshness of s 122(1)(g), also discussed in this chapter. The Cohen Committee (Cmnd 6659, 1945) had recommended this development in the area of minority shareholder protection but their views were based on the concept of 'oppression'. In other words, a member could bring an action where the affairs of the company were being conducted in a manner oppressive to some of the members (including the petitioner). However, the wording in s 210 proved to be a problem, resulting in the fact that there were only two successful cases under the section (*Scottish Co-operative Wholesale Society Ltd* v *Meyer* [1958] 3 All ER 66; *Re H R Harmer Ltd* [1958] 3 All ER 689).

Consequently, s 210 was regarded as unsuccessful with the Jenkins Committee subsequently recommending that it should be replaced with a new remedy based on the notion of 'unfairly prejudicial conduct'. This led to the introduction of s 459 of the Companies Act 1985, which has been replaced by s 994 of the Companies Act 2006.

Scottish Co-operative Wholesale Society Ltd v *Meyer* [1958] 3 All ER 66

Per Lord Denning:

Such being 'the matters complained of' by Dr Meyer and Mr Lucas, it is said: 'Those are all complaints about the conduct of the co-operative society. How do they touch the real issue – the manner in which the affairs of the textile company were being conducted?' The answer is, I think, by their impact on the nominee directors. It must be remembered that we are here concerned with the manner in which the affairs of the textile company were being conducted. That is, with the conduct of those in control of its affairs. They may be some of the directors themselves, or, behind them, a group of shareholders who nominate those directors or whose interests those directors serve. If those persons – the nominee directors or the shareholders behind them – conduct the affairs of the company in a manner oppressive to the other shareholders, the court can intervene to bring an end to the oppression.

What, then, is the position of the nominee directors here? [. . .] It is said that these three directors were at most only guilty of inaction – of doing nothing to protect the textile company. But the affairs of a company can, in my opinion, be conducted oppressively by the directors doing nothing to defend its interests when they ought to do something – just as they can conduct its affairs oppressively by doing something injurious to its interests when they ought not to do it.

The question was asked: What could these directors have done? They could, I suggest, at least on behalf of the textile company, have protested against the conduct of the co-operative society.

They could have protested against the setting up of a competing business. But then it was said: What good would that have done? Any protest by them would be sure to have been unavailing, seeing that they were in a minority on the board of the co-operative society. The answer is that no one knows whether it would have done any good. They never did protest and it does not come well from their mouths to say it would have done no good, when they never put it to the test [. . .] So I would hold that the affairs of the textile company were being conducted in a manner oppressive to Dr Meyer and Mr Lucas [. . .]

One of the most useful orders mentioned in the section – which will enable the court to do justice to the injured shareholders – is to order the oppressor to buy their shares at a fair price: and a fair price would be, I think, the value which the shares would have had at the date of the petition, if there had been no oppression. Once the oppressor has bought the shares, the company can survive. It can continue to operate. That is a matter for him. It is, no doubt, true that an order of this kind gives to the oppressed shareholders what is in effect money compensation for the injury done to them: but I see no objection to this. The section gives a large discretion to the court and it is well exercised in making an oppressor make compensation to those who have suffered at his hands.

True it is that in this, as in other respects, your Lordships are giving a liberal interpretation to section 210. But it is a new section designed to suppress an acknowledged mischief. When it comes before this House for the first time it is, I believe, in accordance with long precedent – and particularly with the resolution of all the judges in *Heydon*'s case – that your Lordships should give such construction as shall advance the remedy and that is what your Lordships do today. I would dismiss the appeal.

Generally

Any member or personal representative may petition the court on the grounds that the affairs of the company are being, or have been, or will be, conducted in a manner unfairly prejudicial to the interests of its members generally, or of some part of its members, including the petitioner himself. The court must, among other things, be satisfied that the petition is well founded.

The provision relating to a petition by personal representatives of a deceased shareholder is important because a major form of abuse in private companies has been the refusal by the board, under powers in the articles, to register the personal representatives of a major deceased shareholder and also to refuse to register the beneficiaries under the will or on intestacy. Although personal representatives have some rights, e.g. to receive dividends, they cannot vote unless they are registered, nor can a beneficiary. The holding is therefore rendered powerless and the motive of the board is often to purchase the holding themselves at an advantageous price.

The provisions apply to conduct past, present or future. In *Re Kenyon Swansea Ltd* (1987) *The Times*, 29 April, the High Court decided that it was sufficient to support a petition that an act had been proposed which if carried out or completed would be prejudicial to the petitioner. Thus the giving of notice of a meeting at which the directors propose to use their majority power to introduce policies allegedly unfair to the minority is probably enough for the minority to commence a claim under s 994. The court also decided that it was enough that the affairs of the company had, in the past, been conducted in such a way as to be unfairly prejudicial to the petitioner, even though at the date of the petition the unfairness had been remedied. The court could still make an order to check possible future prejudice.

The use of the word 'conduct' is important since it covers both acts and omissions, e.g. failure to pay proper dividends when profits allow.

Of even greater importance, however, at least in terms of the case law, is the interpretation placed by the courts, in particular by Mr Justice Hoffmann in *Re A Company (No 00477 of 1986)* [1986] PCC 372, on 'interests of its members'. Many of the petitions presented under the unfair prejudice provisions have been in regard to the removal of a director from the board of a private company. The director concerned has been able to establish that the conduct relating to him as a director was also unfairly prejudicial to him as a member because the 'interest' of a member in a private company legitimately includes a place on the board.

The requirement that the petition be 'well founded' is to ensure that the provisions are not abused or used for a wrongful purpose. An earlier case under different legislation provides a valid illustration. In *Re Bellador Silk Ltd* [1965] 1 All ER 667 a member of the company presented a petition to the court for relief, but mainly as a form of harassment of the board in order to make them pay an alleged debt to one of his companies. The court decided that the petition had a collateral purpose and dismissed it as not a bona fide attempt to get relief.

The test for unfairness is objective and thus the fact that the minority feel that they are being unfairly treated is not enough. The starting point is whether or not the conduct of the majority is in accordance with the articles (as Hoffmann LJ said in *Saul D Harrison* [1995] 1 BCLC 14). The matter often turns upon whether the powers which the shareholders have entrusted to the majority shareholder/directors which are fiduciary powers have been exercised for the benefit of the company as a whole.

Re Saul D Harrison and Sons plc [1995] 1 BCLC 14

Hoffmann LJ observed:

'Unfairly prejudicial' is deliberately imprecise language which was chosen by Parliament because its earlier attempt in s 210 of the Companies Act 1948 to provide a similar remedy had been too restrictively construed. The earlier section had used the word 'oppressive', which the House of Lords in *Scottish Co-operative Wholesale Society v Meyer* [1959] AC 324 said meant 'burdensome, harsh and wrongful'. This gave rise to some uncertainty as to whether 'wrongful' required actual illegality or invasion of legal rights. The Jenkins Committee on Company Law, which reported in 1962, thought that it should not. To make this clear, it recommended the use of the term 'unfairly prejudicial', which Parliament somewhat tardily adopted in s 75 of the Companies Act 1980. This section is reproduced (with minor amendment) in s 994 (previously s 450 of the Companies Act 1985) [. . .]

In deciding what is fair or unfair for the purposes of s 994 (previously 459), it is important to have in mind that fairness is being used in the context of a commercial relationship. The articles of association are just what their name implies: the contractual terms which govern the relationships of the share-holders with the company and each other. They determine the powers of the board and the company in general meeting and everyone who becomes a member of a company is taken to have agreed to them. Since keeping promises and honouring agreements is probably the most important element of commercial fairness, the starting point in any case under s 994 (previously 459) will be to ask whether the conduct of which the shareholder complains was in accordance with the articles of association [. . .]

Although one begins with the articles and the powers of the board, a finding that conduct was not in accordance with the articles does not necessarily mean that it was unfair, still less that the court will exercise its discretion to grant relief. There is often sound sense in the rule in *Foss v Harbottle*. In choosing the term 'unfairly prejudicial', the Jenkins Committee (at para 204) equated it with Lord Cooper's understanding of 'oppression' in *Elder v Elder & Watson* 1952 SC 49 at p 55: 'a visible departure from the standards of fair dealing, and a violation of the conditions of fair play on which every shareholder who entrusts his money to a company is entitled to rely'. So trivial or technical infringements of the articles were not intended to give rise to petitions under s 994 (previously 459).

Not only may conduct be technically unlawful without being unfair: it can also be unfair without being unlawful. In a commercial context, this may at first seem surprising. How can it be unfair to act in accordance with what the parties have agreed? As a general rule, it is not. But there are cases in which the letter of the articles does not fully reflect the understandings upon which the shareholders are associated . . .

Thus, the personal relationship between a shareholder and those who control the company may entitle him to say that it would in certain circumstances be unfair for them to exercise a power conferred by the articles upon the board or the company in general meeting. I have in the past ventured to borrow from public law the term 'legitimate expectation' to describe the correlative 'right' in the shareholder to which such a relationship may give rise. It often arises out of a fundamental understanding between the shareholders which formed the basis of their association but was not put into contractual form, such as an assumption that each of the parties who has ventured his capital will also participate in the management of the company and receive the return on his investment in the form of salary rather than dividend. These relationships need not always take the form of implied agreements with the shareholder concerned; they could enure for the benefit of a third party such as a joint venturer's widow. But in *Re Westbourne Galleries* Lord Wilberforce went on to say: 'It would be impossible, and wholly undesirable, to define the circumstances in which these considerations may arise. Certainly the fact that the company is a small one, or a private company, is not enough. There are very many of these where the association is a purely commercial one, of which it can safely be said that the basis of association is adequately and exhaustively laid down in the articles. The superimposition of equitable considerations requires something more [. . .]

Thus, in the absence of 'something more', there is no basis for a legitimate expectation that the board and the company in general meeting will not exercise whatever powers they are given by the articles of association.

In this case, as the judge emphasised, there is nothing more. The petitioner was given her shares in 1960 pursuant to a reorganisation of the share capital which vested the entire control of the company in the A shareholders and the board whom they appointed. This scheme is binding upon her and there are no special circumstances to modify its effects. Although the petition speaks of the petitioner having various 'legitimate expectations', no grounds are alleged for saying that her rights are not 'adequately and exhaustively' laid down by the articles. And in substance the alleged 'legitimate expectations' amount to no more than an expectation that the board would manage the company in accordance with their fiduciary obligations and the terms of the articles and the Companies Act.

Essentially a minority claim – s 994

Section 994 of the Companies Act 2006 is essentially designed to protect the minority against unfairly prejudicial conduct by the majority. Indeed, s 994(1) states 'A member of a company may apply to the court by petition for an order under this Part on the ground (a) that the company's affairs are being or have been conducted in a manner that is unfairly prejudicial to the interests of members generally or of some part of its members (including at least himself); or (b) that an actual or proposed act or omission of the company (including an act or omission on its behalf) is or would be so prejudicial.'

The provisions will not normally be available to enable the majority to acquire the shares of a minority under a court order, even though there is evidence that the minority concerned is acting in an unfairly prejudicial way. This is because the majority control the company and can remove directors and so on and, in effect, put matters right without the aid of the court. Thus in *Re Legal Costs Negotiators Ltd* [1998] CLY 695 two partners converted their business into a limited company in which one held 75 per cent of the shares and the other 25 per cent. The majority shareholder alleged that the minority shareholder was not carrying out his duties properly and obtained his resignation from the board. He was also dismissed from his employment with the company. The majority shareholder then asked the court to use s 994 to grant him an order requiring the minority to sell his shares to him. The High Court refused the claim as an inappropriate use of the provisions. After all, the majority shareholder had removed his ex-partner from the board and from his employment, and to that extent had removed any problems to the company that might have resulted from the alleged conduct of the minority.

Relief available under s 996

(a) Specific relief

This is as follows:

(i) The court may make an order regulating the company's affairs for the future (s 996(2)(a)).
(ii) The court may restrain the doing of or the continuing of prejudicial acts (s 996(2)(b)).

The above two heads are illustrated quite validly by the following case decided under earlier legislation.

Re H R Harmer Ltd [1958] 3 All ER 689

The company was formed in July 1947, to acquire a business founded by Mr H R Harmer, who was born in 1869. The business of the company was stamp auctioneering and dealing in and valuing stamps. Two of Mr Harmer's sons, Cyril and Bernard Harmer, went into the business on leaving school. The nominal capital of the company was £50,000, and Mr Harmer senior and his wife were between them able to control the general meetings of the company, and could even obtain special and extraordinary resolutions. Mrs Harmer always voted with her husband. The father and his two sons were life directors under the articles, the father being chairman of the board with a casting vote. The sons claimed that their father had repeatedly abused his controlling power in the conduct of the company's affairs so that they were bound to apply for relief. Mr Harmer senior had, they said, always acted as though the right of appointing and dismissing senior staff was vested in him alone, and this right he also extended to the appointment of directors. He also considered that no director should express a contrary view to that expressed by himself, and had generally ignored the views of his sons and the other directors and shareholders. In particular he had opened a branch of the company in Australia in spite of the protests by the other directors, and the branch had not proved profitable. In addition, he dismissed an old servant and procured the appointment of his own 'yes men' to the board. He drew unauthorised expenses for himself and his wife and engaged a detective to watch the staff. He also endeavoured to sell off the company's American business which severely damaged its goodwill. Roxburgh J, at first instance, granted relief under s 210 (see below), and the Court of Appeal confirmed the order, saying that the relief was properly granted because the circumstances were such that the court would have been justified in ordering a winding-up. Roxburgh J's order provided *inter alia* that the company should contract for the services of Mr Harmer senior as philatelic consultant at a salary of £2,500 per annum; that he should not interfere in the affairs of the company otherwise than in accordance with the valid decisions of the board; and that he be appointed president of the company for life, but that this office should not impose any duties or create any rights or powers to him.

Comment

The court's order had the effect of changing the provision in the articles under which Mr Harmer was a director for life with a casting vote. The order also restrained him for the future from interfering with the valid decisions of the board.

(iii) The court may authorise a claim to be brought by the company under s 996(2)(c). This would appear to allow a minority to obtain redress for the company where it had been injured by the wrongful acts of the majority. It seems to provide another approach to that found in *Foss* v *Harbottle*, though the claim would not be derivative because the court would authorise the company to commence the action as a claimant.

(iv) The court may, according to s 996(2)(e), order the purchase of the minority shares at a fair price either by other members or by the company itself, in which case the court would also authorise a reduction of capital. This remedy has been by far the most popular and has largely substituted for winding-up under the just and equitable rule which was formerly the only real way of compelling the majority to return the share capital of the minority (see below). The court will also give directions as to the basis of the valuation of the shares to produce a fair value. The court will often, for example, direct that the shares should not be valued as a minority interest for this purpose since this would depress the value in view of the lack of power in minority shareholders. Since the companies being dealt with by the courts in these minority problem areas are usually private companies with no stock market share price, the valuation is normally carried out by the company's auditors.

(b) General relief

In addition to the above, the court may make such order as it thinks fit for giving relief in respect of the matters complained of under s 996(1). Thus, in *Re a Company (No 005287 of 1985)* [1986] 1 WLR 281, the controlling shareholder took all the profits in management fees and was ordered to account for the money to the company and this although at the time of the action he had sold all his shares in the company concerned to his Gibraltar company. Thus, a petition can be presented even against a person who has ceased to be a member.

Where the shareholding is equal

The court has been faced with a claim under the unfair prejudice provisions where the members of a private company were equal shareholders and in deadlock in terms of their relationship. They could not agree who should buy out whom where each had made an offer to buy the other's shares.

West v Blanchet and Another [2000] 1 BCLC 795

The company's business was teaching English under the name of Leicester Square School of English Ltd. It was a joint venture between Jason West, the petitioner, and Stephen Blanchet. The nominal capital was £100 divided into 100 £1 shares. The paid-up capital was £2, of which West and Blanchet held one share each. West was responsible for marketing and Blanchet for management. The second respondent, who was a director with no shares, was responsible for teaching.

The parties' relationship broke down and the respondents terminated West's employment. He played no part in management after this but continued as a director/shareholder. West later offered to buy Blanchet's shares and Blanchet made an offer for West's. However, they could not agree who should leave the company. West applied to the court for an order under s 996 that Blanchet be required to sell him the shares, alleging that the two respondents had conducted the company's affairs in a manner prejudicial to him in that they had excluded him from the company's affairs and management decisions. The respondents asked the court to strike out the claim as an abuse of court process.

The judge reached the conclusion that in a case such as this the issue was which offer was the more reasonable and realistic. Blanchet had funds readily available to buy West's shares, but West had no available personal funds and his offer was short on details. Blanchet's offer was therefore the more reasonable and realistic, so the court should strike out West's claim.

Comment

The case perhaps illustrates the need to resolve disputes such as these by alternative dispute resolution. The High Court decision does not resolve the deadlock problem in the context of this case. It simply identifies a good defence against a s 994 claim brought with a request for an order for the purchase of the respondent's shares. To avoid being forced out of the company, all the respondent needs to do is make a more reasonable and realistic counter-offer, and then ask the court to strike out the petitioner's claim.

Maybe the petitioner in this case will now accept the respondent's offer. However, he has not been ordered to do so. The court was merely asked to strike out his claim.

The motives of the minority: abuse of procedure

The unfair prejudice procedures cannot be used where they would achieve a collateral purpose, as where the board of a company would be required to make a takeover bid at a higher price than that intended.

 Re Astec (BSR) plc [1999] 2 BCLC 556

In 1989, Emerson Electric, a US company, acquired 45 per cent of the Astec shares. It made further acquisitions over the subsequent period so that in March 1997 it held 51 per cent of Astec. In January 1998, Emerson issued a press release stating that it would buy the remainder of the shares in Astec at no premium to market value, and would stop making dividend payments.

The minority shareholders petitioned the court under s 459, accusing Emerson of bullying tactics and asking the court to order it to purchase the remaining shares in Astec at a fair value – in effect, to undertake a takeover of Astec at an increased price.

Mr Justice Jonathan Parker decided, among other things, that the petition was an abuse of process and should be struck out. He said:

> I fully accept that the petitioners genuinely desire the relief claimed, that is to say an order for the buy-out of their own shares. Equally, however . . . they desire that relief not for itself but because they hope that, if granted, it will lead to something else, that something else being something which the court would not order under s 459, namely a takeover bid by Emerson. The petition is, in my judgment, being used for the purposes of exerting pressure in order to achieve a collateral purpose, that is to say, the making of a takeover bid by Emerson.

Comment

The court's ruling was a severe blow for the minority, who had costs awarded against them, and should give pause for thought to those minorities who may see the unfair prejudice procedures as available, not merely to achieve their own purposes, but to accomplish wider aims.

It is also an abuse of the unfair prejudice procedures to seek to obtain an order for purchase of shares simply because the claimant has lost trust and confidence in the way in which the company is being run by the other members. There must be some breach of the terms on which it has been agreed the company should be run.

 O'Neill and Another v Phillips and Others [1999] 1 WLR 1092

The company, which provided specialist services for stripping asbestos from buildings, employed Mr O'Neill as a manual worker in 1983. Mr Phillips, who held the entire issued share capital of 100

£1 shares, was so impressed by Mr O'Neill that in 1985 he gave him 25 shares and appointed him a director. Shortly afterwards, Mr Phillips had informally expressed the hope that Mr O'Neill would be able to take over the day-to-day running of the company and would allow him to draw 50 per cent of the profits. Mr O'Neill took over on Mr Phillips' retirement from the board, and was duly credited with half the profits.

In 1991, the industry went into recession, the company struggled and Mr Phillips, who had become concerned by Mr O'Neill's management, resumed personal command. He told Mr O'Neill that he would only be receiving his salary and any dividends on his 25 shares, but would no longer receive 50 per cent of the profits.

In January 1992, Mr O'Neill petitioned the court for relief against unfair prejudice in respect both of his termination of equal profit-sharing and the repudiation of an alleged agreement for the allotment of more shares.

The House of Lords unanimously allowed an appeal by Mr Phillips and others from the Court of Appeal. Lord Hoffmann said that, as to whether Mr Phillips had acted unfairly in respect of equality of shareholding, the real question was whether in fairness or equity Mr O'Neill had had a right to the shares. On that point, one ran up against the insuperable obstacle of the judge's finding that Mr Phillips had never promised to give them. There was no basis consistent with established principles of equity for a court to hold that he had behaved unfairly in withdrawing from the negotiations. The same applied to the sharing of profits.

A member who had not been dismissed or excluded from management could not demand that his shares be purchased simply because he felt that he had lost trust and confidence in the others and in the way the company was run.

Per Lord Hoffmann:

In section 459 Parliament has chosen fairness as the criterion by which the court must decide whether it has jurisdiction to grant relief. It is clear from the legislative history (which I discussed in *In re Saul D. Harrison & Sons plc* [1995] 1 BCLC 14, 17–20) that it chose this concept to free the court from technical considerations of legal right and to confer a wide power to do what appeared just and equitable. But this does not mean that the court can do whatever the individual judge happens to think fair. The concept of fairness must be applied judicially and the content which it is given by the courts must be based upon rational principles. As Warner J said in *In re J E Cade & Son Ltd* [1992] BCLC 213, 227: 'The court [. . .] has a very wide discretion, but it does not sit under a palm tree.'

Although fairness is a notion which can be applied to all kinds of activities its content will depend upon the context in which it is being used. Conduct which is perfectly fair between competing businessmen may not be fair between members of a family. In some sports it may require, at best, observance of the rules, in others ('it's not cricket') it may be unfair in some circumstances to take advantage of them. All is said to be fair in love and war. So the context and background are very important.

In the case of section 459, the background has the following two features. First, a company is an association of persons for an economic purpose, usually entered into with legal advice and some degree of formality. The terms of the association are contained in the articles of association and sometimes in collateral agreements between the shareholders. Thus, the manner in which the affairs of the company may be conducted is closely regulated by rules to which the shareholders have agreed. Secondly, company law has developed seamlessly from the law of partnership, which was treated by equity, like the Roman *societas*, as a contract of good faith. One of the traditional roles of equity, as a separate jurisdiction, was to restrain the exercise of strict legal rights in certain relationships in which it considered that this would be contrary to good faith. These principles have, with appropriate modification, been carried over into company law.

The first of these two features leads to the conclusion that a member of a company will not ordinarily be entitled to complain of unfairness unless there has been some breach of the terms on which he agreed that the affairs of the company should be conducted. But the second leads to the conclusion that there will be cases in which equitable considerations make it unfair for those conducting the affairs of the company to rely upon their strict legal powers. Thus, unfairness may consist in a breach of the rules or in using the rules in a manner which equity would regard as contrary to good faith [. . .].

In *In re Saul D. Harrison & Sons plc* [1995] 1 BCLC 14, 19, I used the term 'legitimate expectation', borrowed from public law, as a label for the 'correlative right' to which a relationship between company members may give rise in a case when, on equitable principles, it would be regarded as unfair for a majority to exercise a power conferred upon them by the articles to the prejudice of another member. I gave as an example the standard case in which shareholders have entered into association upon the understanding that each of them who has ventured his capital will also participate in the management of the company. In such a case it will usually be considered unjust, inequitable or unfair for a majority to use their voting power to exclude a member from participation in the management without giving him the opportunity to remove his capital upon reasonable terms. The aggrieved member could be said to have had a 'legitimate expectation' that he would be able to participate in the management or withdraw from the company.

It was probably a mistake to use this term, as it usually is when one introduces a new label to describe a concept which is already sufficiently defined in other terms. In saying that it was 'correlative' to the equitable restraint, I meant that it could exist only when equitable principles of the kind I have been describing would make it unfair for a party to exercise rights under the articles. It is a consequence, not a cause, of the equitable restraint. The concept of a legitimate expectation should not be allowed to lead a life of its own, capable of giving rise to equitable restraints in circumstances to which the traditional equitable principles have no application. That is what seems to have happened in this case.

Comment

As seen in *Re Astec (BSR) plc* (above), the unfair prejudice provisions are not a 'cure-all' remedy for shareholders who are not satisfied for a variety of reasons with the way in which the company is run. In a quasi-partnership company, one 'partner' should not be entitled at will to require the other partners to buy his shares at a fair value. There is no support in previous decisions for such a right of unilateral withdrawal under the provisions. The courts will not construe the requirement of 'unfairly prejudicial conduct' so narrowly.

However, it is worth noting that such a breach does not have to be as straightforward as the breach of a prior agreement (either written or oral) as to the way in which the company is to be run. As per Mann J in *Hale* v *Waldock* [2006] EWHC 364 (Ch):

Lord Hoffmann was demonstrating that unfairness does not arise only out of a failure to comply with prior agreements or to fulfil prior expectations. The relationships between shareholders are more subtle than that, and Lord Hoffmann was recognising that unfairness can come out of a situation where the game has moved on so as to involve a situation not covered by the previous arrangements and understanding. In those circumstances the conduct of the affairs of the company can be unfairly prejudicial within [s 994] notwithstanding the absence of the prior arrangements, and the court can thus intervene.

Application in a public limited company

Re Blue Arrow plc (below) is one of the rare cases which involved the application of s 994 to a public limited company. It is worth noting that in this case the court took a far more restrictive view of the way in which the company was to be run and less willing to look beyond the company's memorandum and articles of association.

Re Blue Arrow plc [1987] BCLC 585

Vinelott J *held*:

The petitioner claims that the affairs of the company are being conducted in a way unfairly prejudicial to some part of the members – that is herself – in that putting the resolution and the proposed amendments to the articles of association to the members, and if they are passed then removing her from the office of president, would be the culmination of the efforts of Mr Berry to exclude her.

Mr Heslop, on behalf of the petitioner, has put forward three grounds in support of the petition. The first is that, it is said, her right to remain as president is a class right, and he referred me to a decision of Scott J in *Cumbrian Newspapers Group Ltd* v *Cumberland & Westmorland Herald Newspaper & Printing Co Ltd* [1987] Ch 1; (1986) 2 BCC 99, 227. I can see nothing in that case which supports the proposition that a right conferred on an individual by the articles of a company to remain as president until removed in general meeting, and which is unrelated to any shareholding, can, by any stretch, be described as a class right. A class right is a right attaching, in some way, to a category of the shares of the company. So far as that decision is material at all, it seems to me plainly against the submission advanced by Mr Heslop. The right claimed, to remain as president, falls, to my mind, quite clearly within the second category distinguished by Scott J and explained at p 99, 236 of the report. The article did not confer any right on the petitioner as a member of the company. She would in fact retain the right, even if she sold all her shares; and the office is not, in fact, an exclusive one.

The second ground is that if the article is looked at in the light of the whole of the history, it becomes clear, it is said, that the petitioner has a legitimate expectation that she will remain president, unless and until she is removed by the machinery provided – that is by resolution of the members – and that an alteration to the articles which gives the power to the directors transgresses that legitimate expectation.

As was pointed out by Hoffmann J in *Re a Company (No 00477 of 1986)* (1986) 2 BCC 99, 171, the interests of a member are not limited to his strict legal rights under the constitution of the company. There are wider equitable considerations which the court must bear in mind in considering whether a case falls within s 459, in particular in deciding what are the legitimate expectations of a member. If I may say so, I respectfully accept that approach, but it is to my mind impossible, on the face of the allegations in the petition, to apply it here. Of course, the petitioner had a legitimate expectation that the affairs of the company would be properly conducted within the framework of its constitution. I wholly fail to understand how it can be said that the petitioner had a legitimate expectation that the articles would not be altered by special resolution in a way which enabled her office to be terminated by some different machinery. No doubt there are cases where a legitimate expectation may be inferred from arrangements outside the ambit of the formal constitution of the company, but it must be borne in mind that this is a public company, a listed company, and a large one, and that the constitution was adopted at the time when the company was first floated on the USM. Outside investors were entitled to assume that the whole of the constitution was contained in the articles, read, of course, together with the Companies Acts. There is in those circumstances no room for any legitimate expectation founded on some agreement or arrangement between the directors and kept up their sleeves and not disclosed to those placing the shares with the public through the USM.

As regards those first two grounds, therefore, I think that the petition, on its face, is so hopeless that the only right course would be to strike it out.

The Jenkins Committee and unfair prejudice

Section 994 of the Companies Act 2006 (previously s 459, CA 1985) results from recommendations made by the Jenkins Committee which advocated the repeal of s 210 of the 1948 Act and the substitution of new statutory arrangements. It is of value, therefore, to consider what sort of conduct the Jenkins Committee thought would be 'unfairly prejudicial'. It mentioned the following:

(a) directors appointing themselves to paid posts within the company at excessive rates of remuneration, thus depriving the members of a dividend or an adequate dividend – and indeed it was exactly this sort of scenario which caused the court to find unfair prejudice to a non-director member in *Re Sam Weller* [1989] 3 WLR 923;

(b) directors refusing to register the personal representatives of a deceased member so that, in the absence of a specific provision in the articles, they cannot vote, as part of a scheme to make the personal representatives sell the shares to the directors at an inadequate price;

(c) the issue of shares to directors and others on advantageous terms;

(d) failure of directors to declare dividends on non-cumulative preference shares held by a minority.

Obviously, some matters affect all the shareholders and not merely a minority, e.g. non-payment of dividends. However, the provisions as reworded by the Companies Act 2006 clearly now include acts affecting the members *generally*.

It is not clear, however, whether failure to pay a dividend would amount to unfair prejudicial conduct in every case. Much will depend upon the circumstances. It could be argued, for example, that ploughing back profits into building up the assets of the company was not in the circumstances of the case a breach of duty by the directors. Indeed, in the case of *Irvine* v *Irvine (No 1)* [2007] 1 BCLC 622, it was held that in the absence of any special agreement, a minority shareholder has no legitimate expectation that dividends will be paid simply due to the fact that they are shareholders of the company. This is the case even with quasi-partnerships. However, this should be contrasted with the situation where payment of no dividends, or extremely low dividends, may amount to unfairly prejudicial conduct (*Re McCarthy Surfacing* [2009] BCLC 622). Furthermore, the case of *Re Sam Weller & Sons Ltd* [1990] BCLC 80 indicated the fact that the courts will look at internal disparities caused due to one group obtaining their return via the payment of directors' remuneration, or other benefits, whilst another group is excluded from any substantial return.

Illustrative case law

In *Re a Company (No 004475 of 1982)* [1983] 2 WLR 381 Lord Grantchester QC held that no prejudice arose under what is now s 994 of the Companies Act 2006 simply because the directors of a company refuse to exercise their power to buy the company's shares; nor because they fail to put into effect a scheme which would have entitled the petitioners to sell their shares at a higher price than they might have been able to otherwise; nor because they proposed to dissipate the company's liquid resources by investing them in a partly owned subsidiary. Lord Grantchester also said that it would usually be necessary for a member claiming unfair prejudice to show that his shares had been seriously diminished in value. However, in *Re R A Noble (Clothing) Ltd* [1983] BCLC 273, Nourse J said that the jurisdiction under s 994 was not limited to such a case and that diminution in the value of shares was not essential. In *Re Garage Door Associates* [1984] 1 All ER 434, Mervyn Davies J held that a member could present a petition for a winding-up on the just and equitable ground *and* petition for the purchase of his shares under ss 994–996. Such a procedure is not an abuse of the process of the court. (However, the current Practice Direction indicates that the two claims should not be made as a matter of course but only where there is a chance that one or the other will fail.)

With respect to the valuation to be placed on an individual's shareholding, a member cannot force other shareholders to buy him out at the proportionate share of the company's value which his investment represents (*Re Phoenix Office Supplies Ltd* [2003] BCC 11). The issue of valuation was explored further in *Sethi v Patel* [2010] EWHC 1830 (Ch). The court ordered one of two shareholders in a company to buy the shares of the other where unfair prejudice was conceded for the purposes of a petition under s 994. The court also gave directions as to the basis on which the shares should be valued.

Re Phoenix Office Supplies Ltd [2003] BCC 11

This was an appeal against a decision of Blackburne J that by treating a director of a quasi-partnership company as if he had resigned as a director and refusing him access to certain financial information to enable him to ascertain whether an offer by the majority to buy his shares was fair, the majority's actions were unfairly prejudicial to his interests as a member under s 459 of the Companies Act 1985 and the majority was ordered to purchase his shares under s 461 valued as at the date of the court order at full value with no discount for the minority holding.

Held – allowing the appeal – (1) The unfair prejudice for which ss 459 and 461 provided a remedy was that suffered in the capacity of a company member but a partner in a quasi-partnership company who had not been dismissed or excluded could not require his partners to purchase his shares at a fair value simply because he had lost trust and confidence in them (dicta of Lord Hoffmann in *O'Neill v Phillips* [1999] BCC 600 applied).

(2) In ruling that a consequence of the quasi-partnership was that L was entitled to the full undiscounted value of his shares, the judge appeared to have proceeded on the basis that it had been P and O who had taken the initiative to sever the association rather than, as was the case, L. It was true that P and O refused to recognise L as a director after 14 September 2000, or to give him access to certain company information, but that was only after he had made plain that he wanted to sever all relationship with the company and them and to take the value of his shareholding with him. Accordingly it did not follow from the fact the company was a quasi-partnership that L was entitled to insist on leaving with an undiscounted value of his minority holding, and the judge was wrong so to find and, in large part on the basis of such finding, to conclude that P and O's denial of such entitlement amounted to unfair prejudice entitling L to relief.

(3) To the extent that L might have been unfairly prejudiced by lack of information as to the valuation of his interest in the company, his remedy under s 461(2)(b) would have been for the wrong done in failing to furnish that information, not for the refusal to acknowledge his claim for a 'put-option' for his shares.

(4) It was common ground that s 459 would afford protection to a member of a quasi-partnership company who had been unfairly excluded from participating in the management of the company. But that did not happen in the instant case; L made crystal clear in his resignation letter that he wanted to sever all connection with the company and start a new life, with a new job, elsewhere. In these circumstances it was impossible to place the instant case in that category of cases which typically qualified for relief under s 459, where a member who wished to participate in the management of a company was unfairly prevented from doing so.

(5) The issue was whether s 459 extended to affording a member of a quasi-partnership company who wished, for entirely his own reasons, to sever his connection with the company (and who de facto had done so) an opportunity to 'put' his shareholding onto the other members as its full undiscounted value when he had no contractual right to do so. There was no basis for concluding that s 459 could have such an effect. Further, L could not assert his rights as a director, by complaining of a failure on the part of his co-directors to supply him with financial information to which he was entitled as a director, in circumstances where it was plain that he had no intention whatever

of discharging any of his duties as a director. The plain inference was that L was using his position as a director simply as an aid to achieving as high a price as possible for his shares. Even if unfair prejudice had been established by reason of the withholding of financial information to which L was entitled as a director, the remedy which the judge granted – a buy-out of his shares at their full, undiscounted, value – was wholly disproportionate to any possible prejudice suffered.

The case of *Harbourne Road Nominees Ltd* v *Karvaski* [2011] EWHC 2214 (Ch) explored the principle established in *O'Neill* v *Phillips*, that where a majority shareholder in a company offered to purchase a minority shareholding at a fair value determined by a competent expert, any subsequent petition alleging unfair prejudice would be negated and was liable to be struck out as an abuse of process. In this instance, the court held that this did not apply in the case of equal shareholders. Rather, the question was whether the shareholder had been offered a sale on terms that gave him all the advantages he could reasonably expect to achieve from issuing an unfair prejudice petition: only then would it be an abuse to continue those proceedings in the face of such an offer.

 Harbourne Road Nominees Ltd v Karvaski [2011] EWHC 2214 (Ch)

The applicants (K and S) applied for an order that the unfair prejudice petition brought by the respondent (H) be struck out as an abuse of process, or for summary judgment in their favour. S was a private company whose shares were registered in H's name. H held half the shares as nominee for one individual (M) and the other half as nominee for K. M and K each owned companies and in 2001 they incorporated S as a joint-venture company to provide their services together. K became a director of S and was to receive a salary, but it was agreed that he and M would operate S jointly and, as shareholders, each would receive dividends. In 2010 K informed M that since S had received little return business from M's company, S would no longer utilise its services, that S was unlikely to declare any dividends in the current or next financial year, and that it would be in S's best interests if M no longer remained a shareholder and that K was willing to purchase his shareholding. M was also to be excluded from any participation in S's management. M indicated his concern that K's threatened actions would unfairly prejudice M's interests as shareholder. The parties were unable to agree a price for M's shares in S and M raised the issue of appointing an accountant, agreed by both parties, to value S's assets and determine the share price. K informed M that, where an offer was made by the majority shareholder in the format set out in *O'Neill* v *Phillips* [1999] 1 WLR 1092, in that there was an offer to purchase shares at a fair value which, if not agreed, should be determined by a competent expert, that would negate any claim for unfair prejudice and any petition M presented would be liable to be struck out or stayed with him suffering the costs consequences associated with that. Offers and counter-offers followed, expressed to be made in the *O'Neill* format, but there was no agreement and M, through H, issued his petition alleging unfair prejudice affecting his shareholding in S. K and S contended that M's refusal to accept K's offers to purchase his shares in S was unreasonable and that, consequently, the continued prosecution of the petition was either an abuse or was bound to fail, in accordance with the principles established in *O'Neill*. Application refused. The guidance in *O'Neill* did not have the status of legislation. The correspondence and argument between the parties in the instant case, and K's reference to an offer in the '*O'Neill* format' appeared to approach the matter as if what had to be considered was the extent to which the offer made complied with those guidelines, and that if a sufficient degree of compliance was achieved, K would inevitably be protected from any petition that M might issue. That was a cardinal error.

The question for the court was always whether in all the circumstances of the case the applicant had satisfied the conditions required to have the petition struck out, or summary judgment in his favour given on it, in that it had been shown that the continued prosecution of the petition after the making of the offer amounted to an abuse of process, or was bound to fail. The issue was highly sensitive to the facts and circumstances of each case, and consideration of the nature and terms of any offer made could only ever be an intermediate step in the process. One obvious difference between the instant case and *O'Neill* was that M was not a minority shareholder but an equal 50 per cent shareholder, and in such cases it was by no means obvious which of two equal shareholders should sell to the other, *O'Neill* distinguished. The reasoning in *O'Neill* expressly concerned cases where there was a majority shareholder. In the case of equal shareholders, particularly if they were quasi partners as in the instant case, there was a clear potential for injustice if one of them was able to seize de facto control of the company and effectively force the other either to accept his offer to buy or be forever excluded from the participation that he bargained for and cut out from any remedy in respect of what would be a continuing breach of the quasi-partnership arrangement originally made. The real question in the instant case was whether M had been offered a sale on terms that gave him all the advantages he could reasonably expect to achieve from the petition proceedings: if so, it would then be an abuse to continue those proceedings in the face of such an offer.

In all the circumstances, the court could not be satisfied that that requirement had been met since M might well obtain an order which was more advantageous to him in material respects than the offers made.

In *Re Bird Precision Bellows* [1984] 2 WLR 869 and again in *Re London School of Electronics* [1985] 3 WLR 474, Nourse J said that the removal of a member from the board was unfairly prejudicial conduct within what is now s 994, CA 2006. He made an order for the purchase of the shares of the petitioners in both cases by the majority shareholders and decided that in valuing the shares there should be no discount in the price because the holdings were minority holdings, unless the minority were in some way to blame for the situation giving rise to the alleged unfair prejudice. Indeed, Nourse J's approach for the valuation of shares has become a popular view.

Re Bird Precision Bellows [1984] 2 WLR 869

Nourse J:

> The question in this case is whether the price of shares in a small private company which were ordered to be purchased [. . .] should be fixed pro rata according to the value of the shares as a whole or should be discounted on the ground that they constitute a minority in number [. . .] Although both sections 210 and 75 are silent on the point, it is axiomatic that a price fixed by the court must be fair. While that which is fair may often be generally predicated in regard to matters of common occurrence, it can never be conclusively judged in regard to a particular case until the facts are known. The general observations which I will presently attempt in relation to a valuation of shares by the court under section 75 are therefore subject to that important reservation.
>
> Broadly speaking, shares in a small private company are acquired either by allotment on its incorporation or by transfer or devolution at some later date. In the first category it is a matter of common occurrence for a company to be incorporated in order to acquire an existing business or to start a new one, and in either event for it to be a vehicle for the conduct of a business carried on by two or more shareholders which they could, had they wished, have carried on in partnership together. Although it has been pointed out on the high authority to which I will soon refer that the description may be confusing, it is often convenient and it is certainly usual to describe that kind of company as a quasi-partnership. In the second category, irrespective of the nature of the company, it is a matter of common occurrence for a shareholder to acquire shares from another at a price which is discounted because they represent a minority holding. It seems to me that some general observations can usefully be made in regard to each of these examples [. . .]

I would expect that in a majority of cases where purchase orders are made in relation to quasi-partnerships the vendor is unwilling in the sense that the sale has been forced upon him. Usually he will be a minority shareholder whose interests have been unfairly prejudiced by the manner in which the affairs of the company have been conducted by the majority. On the assumption that the unfair prejudice has made it no longer tolerable for him to retain his interest in the company, a sale of his shares will invariably be his only practical way out short of a winding-up. In that kind of case it seems to me that it would not merely not be fair, but most unfair, that he should be bought out on the fictional basis applicable to a free election to sell his shares in accordance with the company's articles of association, or indeed on any other basis which involved a discounted price. In my judgment the correct course would be to fix the price pro rata according to the value of the shares as a whole and without any discount, as being the only fair method of compensating an unwilling vendor of the equivalent of a partnership share [. . .]

Next, I must consider the example from the second category of cases in which, broadly speaking, shares in a small private company are acquired. It is not of direct relevance for present purposes, but I mention it briefly in order finally to refute the suggestion that there is any rule of universal application to questions of this kind. In the case of the shareholder who acquires shares from another at a price which is discounted because they represent a minority it is to my mind self-evident that there cannot be any universal or even a general rule that he should be bought out on a more favourable basis, even in a case where his predecessor has been a quasi-partner in a quasi-partnership [. . .]

In summary, there is in my judgment no rule of universal application. On the other hand, there is a general rule in a case where the company is at the material time a quasi-partnership and the purchase order is made in respect of the shares of a quasi-partner.

The dismissal of a member of a quasi-partnership from the post of director may amount to unfairly prejudicial conduct if it breaches a mutual understanding that the member in question would be a director (*Re Ghyll Beck Driving Range Ltd* [1993] BCLC 1126; *Brownlow v GH Marshall Ltd* [2000] 2 BCLC 655; *Shah v Shah* [2010] EWHC 313 (Ch)). However, in *Re R A Noble (Clothing) Ltd*, 1983 (see above), Nourse J decided that a director who had been excluded from management could claim unfair prejudice but not in the particular circumstances of the case because his exclusion was to a large extent due to his own disinterest in the company's affairs so that the other members of the board felt that they had to manage without him. Similarly, if such an alleged breach of mutual understanding (legitimate expectation) is undertaken with a view to protecting the company from that person's conduct which would prove detrimental to the company (*Grace v Biagioli* [2005] EWCA Civ 1222) or that member's misconduct which would impact on the company's viability (*Woolwich v Milne* [2003] EWHC 414 (Ch)), then the court will not regard such breaches as being unfair. More recently, the case of *Re Phoenix Contracts (Leicester) Ltd* [2010] EWHC 2375 (Ch) highlighted the fact that unfairly prejudicial conduct arose for the purposes of the s 994 CA where an individual, who was one of two shareholders and executive directors and was also an employee of a company, was suspended and later made redundant after he contacted a potential customer of the company and informed it that the company was being investigated by the Office of Fair Trading. The court held that he could not be criticised for his actions and his exclusion from the company was prejudicial to his interests as a shareholder.

In *Re a Company (No 008699 of 1985)* [1986] PCC 296, the High Court held that it was unfairly prejudicial to minority shareholders where, on a takeover bid for the company, the directors recommended acceptance of a bid by a company in which they had an interest while ignoring a much more favourable alternative offer.

In *Re Mossmain Ltd* (1986) *Financial Times*, 27 June, four persons agreed to form a company. Two of these were husband and wife. Because the husband had a restrictive covenant in a contract of employment which might be infringed if he became a member/director of the company, his shares were held by his wife for the duration of the covenant, he becoming an employee only for the time being. The wife was made a director. Later the husband was dismissed and his wife was removed from the board. Husband and wife petitioned under s 994 and the court held that the husband's name must be struck out of the petition. He did not qualify to petition since he was not a member as s 994 requires.

In *Re a Company (No 007623 of 1984)* [1986] BCLC 362 it was held that there was no unfair prejudice where the company made a rights issue to all members pro rata to their shareholding which the petitioner could not afford even though his interest in the company after the issue would be reduced from 25 per cent to 0.125 per cent. The company genuinely needed capital. The case can be contrasted with *Clemens* v *Clemens Bros Ltd*, 1976 where the fresh issue of shares was not a rights issue offered to all members but to members *other* than Miss Clemens in order to reduce her voting power in the company.

In certain circumstances, serious mismanagement of a company may justify the court providing relief to a minority shareholder as per *Re Macro (Ipswich) Ltd* [1994] 2 BCLC 354, in which Arden J stated:

> All of these matters are within the responsibility of Thompsons as the companies' managing agent but they are attributable to the lack of effective supervision by Mr Thompson on behalf of the companies. It is this conduct of the companies' affairs by Mr Thompson which, in my judgment, is prejudicial in the respects I have mentioned. As the conduct is prejudicial in a financial sense to the companies, it must also be prejudicial to the interest of the plaintiffs as holders of its shares . . . In my judgment, viewed overall, those acts are sufficiently significant and serious to justify intervention by the court under s 461.

In *Re London School of Electronics*, 1985 (see above), Nourse J held that there was no overriding requirement under what is now ss 994–996, CA 2006 that the petitioner should come to court with clean hands.

The case of *Fulham Football Club (1987) Ltd* v *Richards & Anor* [2011] EWCA Civ 855 clarified the operation of s 994 where there is an agreement to refer to arbitration the question of whether the affairs of a company are being run in an unfairly prejudicial manner.

Fulham Football Club (1987) Ltd v Richards & Anor [2011] EWCA Civ 855

Lord Justice Longmore observed:

> I agree with Patten LJ that there are three questions which need to be determined, although I would prefer to consider them in a slightly different order:
>
> (i) Whether the arbitration agreements contained in the FAPL Rules and the FA Rules purport, on their true construction, to refer to arbitration the issues which arise between the parties namely; (i) whether Sir David acted as an agent on behalf of Portsmouth in and about the procurement of Mr Crouch's transfer to Tottenham rather than to Fulham or in any other way in breach of his duties as chairman of the FAPL in relation to that transfer and (ii) whether Sir David's conduct constituted such unfair prejudice on the part of the FAPL as to entitle Fulham to invoke section 994 of the CA 2006;
>
> (ii) Whether, if so, the CA 2006 expressly or impliedly prohibits the reference to arbitration of such matters;
>
> (iii) Whether, if there is no statutory prohibition of such a reference, public policy of the law of England and Wales prohibits such a reference.

In relation to the first question, my Lord has set out the terms of the FAPL Rules which bind the clubs and the Premier League itself and the FA Rules which bind Sir David and the clubs as participating in activity sanctioned by the FA. These rules are very wide being, in the case of the FAPL and its members, an agreement 'to submit all disputes which arise between them . . . to final and binding arbitration' and in the case of the FA and its participants an agreement that 'any dispute or difference between any two or more Participants . . . shall be referred to and finally resolved by arbitration'.

The phrases 'all disputes' and 'any dispute or difference' mean what they say and must cover the disputes that have arisen between Fulham on the one hand and Sir David and the Premier League on the other.

In relation to the second question, it is clear that there is no express requirement in the CA 2006 that matters arising on an unfair prejudice petition under section 994 should not be referred to arbitration. Nor do I consider that there is any implied prohibition of arbitration. It is true that section 994(1) empowers a company member 'to apply to the court by petition' and section 996(1) provides that 'if the court is satisfied that a petition . . . is well-founded, it may make such order as it thinks fit for giving relief'. But the fact that a statutory power, which a court would not have at common law apart from the statutory provision, is given to the court does not mean that an arbitrator, to whom a dispute is properly agreed to be referred, does not have a similar power. Power to make awards of monetary sums as between joint tortfeasors and between those who together have acted in breach of separate contracts are given to 'the court' by various statutory provisions but it cannot be suggested that arbitrators are prohibited from making such awards: see *Wealands* v *ICLC Contractors Ltd* [1999] 2 Lloyd's Rep 739 paras. 16–18. Such awards are frequently made. If, therefore, one looks at the actual wording of the relevant sections of the CA 2006, there is no ground for supposing that there is any implicit prohibition on agreeing to refer an allegation of unfair prejudice to arbitration.

Thirdly, does public policy prohibit or invalidate an agreement to refer to arbitration the question whether a company's affairs are being (or have been) conducted in a manner that is unfairly prejudicial to the interest of at any rate some of its members? If public policy does prohibit such an agreement, there could of course be no question of the court staying any petition seeking relief under sections 994–996 of the CA 2006 because the court would be satisfied (within the meaning of section 9(4) of the AA 1996) that the arbitration agreement would, to the extent that it purported to apply to unfair prejudice petitions, be 'null and void' or, perhaps, 'inoperative'.

It is this question that is at the heart of the appeal and I would, for my part, derive some guidance from the principle set out in section 1(b) of the AA 1996 namely 'the parties should be free to agree how their disputes are resolved, subject only to such safeguards as are necessary in the public interest'. To the extent therefore that public policy has a part to play it can only be as a 'safeguard . . . necessary in the public interest'.

This is a demanding test and I cannot see that it is necessary in the public interest that agreements to refer disputes about the internal management of a company should in general be prohibited; nor can I see any reason why it is necessary to prohibit arbitration agreements to the extent that they, in particular, apply to disputes whether a company's affairs are being (or have been) conducted in a manner unfairly prejudicial to the interests of its members.

Mr Philip Marshall QC for Fulham suggested two reasons why there might be good reason for public policy to prohibit agreements to refer unfair prejudice disputes to arbitration. The first was that an arbitrator might feel inhibited from making an award in favour of a petitioner because there was no way in which he could assess whether any conduct of the company was unfairly prejudicial to the interests of any member who was not a party to the arbitration. The second reason was that, if the arbitrator did issue an award, it might or would affect such members and there would be a risk that the award would be unenforceable because it would purport to affect the interests of members of the company who were not parties to the arbitration.

For my part I find it difficult to see why an arbitrator should feel any such inhibition as Mr Marshall suggested since there is no reason why any member of the FAPL who considered that its interests might be affected should not be able to give such evidence to the arbitrator as it wanted to. But even if any inhibition did exist, that could not amount to a reason why in the public interest an agreement to refer an unfair prejudice dispute should be prohibited. It would just be an incident of the agreement and an example of a reason why in some circumstances arbitration could be less satisfactory than court proceedings. The risk of that occurring cannot mean that it is necessary in the public interest to prohibit such agreements.

The second reason is likewise somewhat fanciful but, again, the risk that an award might ineffectively purport to affect parties other than the immediate parties to the arbitration and, to that extent, be unenforceable cannot render it necessary that agreements to refer unfair prejudice allegations should be banned as a matter of public policy.

It is well settled that the fact that an arbitrator cannot give all the remedies which a court could does not afford any reason for treating an arbitration agreement as of no effect, see *Eras Eil Actions* [1992] 1 Lloyd's Rep 570, 610. The inability to give a particular remedy is just an incident of the agreement which the parties have made as to the method by which their disputes are to be resolved. The reason put forward by Mr Marshall for regarding the FAPL Rules and FA Rules as inapplicable to unfair prejudice petitions (because of the effect any award might have or might not have on third parties) is of even less substance than the supposed inability of an arbitrator to give any particular remedy.

For these reasons and those given by Patten LJ I agree the judge reached the right conclusion. I would also commend his reluctance to treat the hearing before him as a foregone conclusion in the light of the decision of *Exeter City Council* v *Bairstow* [2007] EWHC 400 (Ch) merely because it was a second decision of a judge at first instance which had taken into account (and differed from) an earlier decision of a first instance judge. First instance judges have the luxury (which we do not) of not being bound by each other's decisions and, particularly in a specialist jurisdiction, it is usually useful to this court to have a considered view even if it is at variance with the latest first instance decision. I must confess to being much assisted by the views of Vos J in coming to my own conclusion in this case.

I would also dismiss this appeal.

Finally, as seen in the case of *Gamlestaden Fastigheter AB* v *Baltic Partners Ltd* [2007] UKPC 26 (Privy Council), the remedy for unfair prejudice may be used to protect the interests of creditors.

Gamlestaden Fastigheter AB v *Baltic Partners Ltd* [2007] UKPC 26

Lord Scott of Foscote observed:

Baltic is insolvent and the main issue for decision is whether it is open to a member of a company to make an unfair prejudice application for relief in circumstances where, as here, the company in question is insolvent, will remain insolvent whatever order is made on the application and where the relief sought will confer no financial benefit on the applicant *qua* member. The main relief now sought by Gamlestaden on its art 141 application is an order under art 143(1) ordering the directors to pay damages to Baltic for breaches of the duty they owed to Baltic as directors. But it is accepted that the damages, assuming the claim succeeds, will not restore Baltic to solvency. It will, however, if it does succeed, produce a considerable sum which will be available to Baltic's creditors. Gamlestaden, either itself or as representing its parent company Gamlestaden AB, is a substantial creditor. The indebtedness in question was a major part of Gamlestaden's investment in Baltic's business ventures. So, it is said, Gamlestaden has a legitimate interest, in the particular circumstances of this case, justifying the making of the art 141 application.

The directors, however, applied to have the application struck out on the ground that it was bound in law to fail. They contended before the Bailiff of the Royal Court and before the Court of Appeal, and have repeated the contention before the board, that the alleged improprieties in the management of Baltic of which Gamlestaden complain cannot be shown to have caused Gamlestaden any financial loss in its capacity as shareholder. Its loss, if any, is suffered as a creditor. An application under art 141 (or under s 459 of the 1985 Act) is, it is argued, a shareholder's remedy, not a creditor's remedy. Once it becomes clear that the only benefit to be derived from the relief sought in an unfair prejudice application would be a benefit to the company's creditors, and that no benefit would be obtained by the company's shareholders, it becomes clear that the application is an abuse of process, cannot succeed and should be struck out. The learned Bailiff agreed and struck out the application. The Court of Appeal dismissed Gamlestaden's appeal. The point is now before the board for a final decision. It must be emphasised that, since this appeal arises out of a strike out of the art 141 application, the facts pleaded in support of the application must be taken as true (save for any that can be shown by incontrovertible evidence to be untrue). The Bailiff and the Court of Appeal approached the case on that footing and so must their Lordships.

The point at issue depends, first, upon the scope of the power of the court under arts 141 and 143, properly construed, in dealing with the unfair prejudice application and, secondly, upon the particular circumstances that are relied on for bringing this application within that scope . . .

The first question to be addressed, therefore, is whether an order for payment of damages to the company whose affairs have allegedly been conducted in an unfairly prejudicial manner can be sought and made in an unfair prejudice application. . . .

There is nothing in the wide language of art 143(1) to suggest a limitation that would exclude the seeking or making of such an order: the court 'may make such order as it thinks fit for giving relief in respect of the matters complained of'.

That leaves the important issue regarding Baltic's insolvency. Here, too, it is appropriate to start by noting the breadth of the art 143(1) discretion conferred on the court. The court 'may make such order as it thinks fit for giving relief in respect of the matters complained of . . .'.

Bar the relatively trivial sum that Gamlestaden must have paid in subscribing for its 1,100 shares in Baltic, Gamlestaden's investment took the form of the provision of loans to Baltic to enable Baltic to fund SPK. Baltic was the corporate vehicle through which the joint venture enterprise of Gamlestaden and Mr Karlsten of investment in German commercial property was to be pursued. If mismanagement by the directors of that corporate vehicle has led to loss it seems to their Lordships somewhat artificial to insist that the qualifying loss, for art 141 (or s 994) purposes, must be loss which has reduced the value of the investor's equity capital and that it is not sufficient to show that it has reduced the recoverability of the investor's loan capital . . .

Mr Moss QC's . . . submission comes to this, that it is a fatal and insurmountable bar in any and every application for art 141 (or s 459) relief if the relief sought cannot be shown to be of some benefit to the applicant shareholder in his capacity as shareholder.

Mr Moss supported his submission by reference, in particular, to the well-established rule that a shareholder cannot petition for a winding-up order to be made in respect of a company that is insolvent. The reason is that the petitioning shareholder cannot obtain any benefit from the winding-up. The company's assets will be realised; dividends may be paid to creditors but nothing, if the company is insolvent, will go to the members. The rule that Mr Moss prays in aid is a long-established one and one on which their Lordships cast no doubt. But there is a significant difference between a creditor's winding-up petition and an art 141 (or s 459) application. The former is seeking an order to put the company into an insolvent liquidation that will affect the interests of all creditors as well as of all members. It will involve the administration of the liquidation either by the Viscount [of the Royal Court of Jersey] (or, in England, the official receiver) and his officials or by a professional liquidator who, in carrying out his duties, will be an officer of the court. The liquidation, although from a financial point of view carried out for the benefit of creditors, is a public act or process in which the public has an interest. It seems to their Lordships quite right that a member with no financial interest in the process or its outcome should be denied *locus standi* to initiate the process.

Where relief is sought via an unfair prejudice application, on the other hand, the position is quite different. There is no public involvement or interest in the proceedings, other than the natural interest that may attend any proceedings heard in open court. The purpose of art 141, or of s 459, or of their counterpart in Hong Kong, is to provide a means of relief to persons unfairly prejudiced by the management of the company in which they hold shares. If the company is a joint-venture company and the joint venturers have arranged that one, or more, or all of them, shall provide working capital to the company by means of loans, it would, in their Lordships' opinion, be inconsistent with the purpose of these statutory provisions to limit the availability of the remedies they offer to cases where the value of the share or shares held by the applicant member would be enhanced by the grant of the relief sought. If the relief sought would, if granted, be of real, as opposed to merely nominal, value to an applicant joint venturer, such as Gamlestaden, in facilitating recovery of some part of its investment in the joint-venture company, that should, in their Lordships' opinion, suffice to provide the requisite *locus standi* for the application to be made.

Mr Moss placed reliance on *Re J E Cade & Son Ltd* [1991] BCC 360 where Warner J refused s 459 relief because the applicant was 'pursuing his interests as a freeholder of the farm and not his interests as a member of the company' (p 374C). But there was no counterpart in that case with the feature in this case that the loans made by Gamlestaden were made pursuant to and for the purposes of the joint venture to be carried on by Gamlestaden and Mr Karlsten via Baltic.

There are several cases in which judicial approval is given to affording a wide scope to s 459. Some of these were referred to by Robert Walker J in *R & H Electrical Ltd* (*supra*) . . . And in *O'Neill* v *Phillips* [1999] BCC 600 at p 612; [1999] 1 WLR 1092 at 1105 Lord Hoffmann said that: 'As cases like *R & H Electrical Ltd* v *Haden Bill Electrical Ltd* [1995] BCC 958 show, the requirement that prejudice must be suffered as a member should not be too narrowly or technically construed.'

In their Lordships' opinion arts 141 and 143 properly construed do not *ipso facto* rule out the grant of relief simply on the ground that the relief sought will not benefit the applicant in his capacity as member. In many cases such a feature might justifiably lead to the refusal of relief . . . Their Lordships do not accept that the benefit must be a benefit to Gamlestaden in its capacity as a shareholder but they do accept that there must, where the only purpose of the application is to obtain payment of a sum of money to Baltic, be some real financial benefit to be derived therefrom by Gamlestaden.

In particular, in a case where an investor in a joint-venture company has, in pursuance of the joint-venture agreement, invested not only in subscribing for shares but also in advancing loan capital, the investor ought not, in their Lordships' opinion, be precluded from the grant of relief under art 143(1) (or s 461(1)) on the ground that the relief would benefit the investor only as loan creditor and not as member.

In the present case the provision of loan capital to Baltic seems to have been mainly, if not wholly, made by Gamlestaden AB, rather than by Gamlestaden, although procured by Gamlestaden pursuant to its obligation to do so under its joint-venture agreement with Mr Karlsten. But their Lordships, in agreement with the view expressed by Robert Walker J in relation to similar arrangements made by the applicant for s 459 relief in the *R & H Electrical Ltd* case, conclude that that feature should not bar Gamlestaden from relief under art 141.

Their Lordships take the view that the learned Bailiff and the Court of Appeal construed art 143(1) too narrowly and that this appeal against the strike-out of Gamlestaden's art 141 application ought to be allowed.

Minority petition for a just and equitable winding-up

The court has a jurisdiction under s 122(1)(g) of the Insolvency Act 1986 to wind up a company on the petition of a minority on the ground that it is 'just and equitable' to do so.

This ground is subjected to a flexible interpretation by the courts. In the context of minority rights, however, orders have been made where the managing director who represented the majority shareholder interests in his management of the company refused, for example, to produce accounts or pay dividends (*Loch* v *John Blackwood Ltd* [1924] AC 783) and where, in the case of a small company, formed or continued on the basis of a personal relationship, involving mutual confidence and which is in essence a partnership, the person petitioning is excluded from management participation and the circumstances are such as would justify the dissolution of a partnership. This, it will be remembered, was the approach in *Ebrahimi* v *Westbourne Galleries* (see Chapter 2 ○). However, since the enactment of the unfair prejudice provisions and following the case of *Re a Company (No 002567 of 1982)* [1983] 2 All ER 854 other matters have been brought to the fore. These are:

(a) that if the majority make an offer to buy out the shares of the director who has been removed at a fair price, e.g. to be decided on by the company's auditor, the court is not perhaps likely to wind up the company because the ex-director's capital is available by other means. No such offer was made in *Ebrahimi* v *Westbourne Galleries* [1973] AC 360;

(b) that even if no such offer is made the better approach these days might be by petition under the unfair prejudice provisions. The court can, as we have seen, order the purchase of the ex-director's shares, at a fair price, either by the other members or by the company in reduction of capital.

CVC/Opportunity Equity Partners Ltd v Demarco Almeida [2002] BCC 684

The company carried on business as general manager of a venture capital limited partnership established under Cayman Islands law by a bank and its associated companies and said to have invested funds in excess of US$1 billion largely in Brazilian enterprises. The company had no beneficial interest in the funds and derived its substantial income from fees and commissions for making deals and acquisitions on behalf of the partnership. The company could be removed as general manager for cause by a simple majority of the limited partners or without cause by a 75 per cent majority of such partners ('cause' was defined to include the institution of proceedings seeking the liquidation or winding up of the company where the proceedings were not dismissed within 30 days of their institution). 'D' was engaged by the company full time as a deal maker. He was a director of the company and held one its 100 shares. The remaining shares were held as to one each by three other deal makers and 96 by another company, 'Opportunity'. D was dismissed by Opportunity for alleged bad performance and excluded from any part of the management of the company. He accepted that he could not challenge his dismissal or exclusion from management, but challenged Opportunity's right to exclude him without offering him a fair price for his share. He unsuccessfully sought to negotiate the withdrawal of his interest in the company and was given to understand that Opportunity was not willing to acquire his interest or pay anything for it. In the circumstances his only remedy under Cayman Islands law was to petition to wind up the company. He emphasised that this was not the remedy he wanted but that it was the only remedy he had (Cayman Islands law did not have the equivalent of the unfairly prejudicial conduct remedy in s 459 in the British Companies Act 1985). He wished to petition for the company's winding up on the just and equitable ground under s 94 of the Cayman Islands Companies Act (1998 Revision) as a means of bringing Opportunity to the negotiating table. The company and Opportunity applied for an injunction to restrain him presenting the petition. Opportunity argued that it would be wrong to allow a winding-up petition to be presented when it had made an offer to buy D's shares 'at an appropriate price'. Graham J granted the injunction. The company would however only consider as an appropriate price the par value of US$1. D appealed and the Cayman Islands Court of Appeal allowed his appeal on the basis that the offer for D's shares was not shown to be a fair one. The company appealed to the Judicial Committee of the Privy Council.

Held, dismissing the appeal: (1) It was impossible in the present state of the evidence to say that the petition was manifestly unfounded.

(2) In the context of an unfairly prejudicial conduct petition, *O'Neill* v *Phillips* [1999] BCC 600 was authority that unfairness did not lie in the exclusion of a petitioner from the management of a company but in his exclusion without a reasonable offer for his shares. There was no difference in principle with the position of a winding-up petition on the just and equitable ground. In a quasi-partnership company it was unfair for the majority to insist on their legal right to exclude the petitioner without

making a reasonable offer for his shares. It was no less accurate to describe such conduct as unjust or inequitable than it was to describe it as oppressive or unfairly prejudicial to the interests of the minority.

(3) Opportunity offered to acquire D's share at a price that he would have obtained as a contributory on the liquidation of the company. Under Cayman Islands law the only statutory relief available to D was to have the company wound up but Opportunity's argument that the value of D's shares should reflect the remedy available to him was unsound as in cases such as this Opportunity were unwilling purchasers. They did not want to buy his shares and would not make him an offer at all were it not for their concern to have the winding-up proceedings aborted. The amount that D would obtain in respect of his share on a winding up represented the least it could be worth to him but it did not represent the fair value as between the parties. The fairness of the offer should be judged by reference to what would happen if it was accepted, not if it was refused.

(4) As an unwilling seller D's share should normally be valued as a rateable proportion of the value of the company as a going concern without any discount for a minority holding (*Re Bird Precision Bellows Ltd* (1985) 1 BCC 99, 467). In the case of a quasi-partnership company the corporate structure represented the legal medium by which a business was carried on as a joint venture. The petitioner's interest in the joint venture could not be determined by a sale of his shareholding to his co-venturers unless the price reflected his share in the underlying business. The subject matter of the notional sale which formed the basis of the valuation was, therefore, not the petitioner's minority holding but the entire share capital of the company. Opportunity's offer to purchase D's interest at a valuation based on the company's break-up or liquidation value fell far short of a fair offer and failed to remedy his complaint. It was not entitled on this ground to restrain the presentation of a winding-up petition.

(5) The special nature of winding-up proceedings and the loss which they might cause the company and its shareholders made in incumbent on the court to ensure that they were not brought for an improper purpose, in particular not brought simply to bring pressure on the respondents to yield to the petitioner's demands, however unreasonable, rather than suffer the losses consequent upon the presentation of a petition or the making of a winding-up order. However D had no other remedy available to him. He did not want the company wound up, but he had no choice but to initiate winding-up proceedings if he was to have any hope of receiving a reasonable offer for his shares. The fact that the court lacked the necessary power to make a more suitable order did not mean that a winding-up order would be unjust if Opportunity declined to make a fair offer for D's share. By presenting a winding-up petition D was invoking the traditional jurisdiction of equity to subject the exercise of legal rights to equitable considerations. D had not acted unreasonably in rejecting Opportunity's offer to buy his interest and by continuing to hold out for a fair offer he was not threatening to abuse the process of the court.

However, the procedure through just and equitable winding-up is not specifically repealed and there is no rule of law preventing that approach, and indeed it was held in *Jesner* v *Jarrad* (1992) *The Times*, 26 October, that a lack of unfair prejudice under s 994 (formerly s 459 of the CA 1985) will not prevent the court from winding-up a company on the just and equitable ground. In that case a family company was being run in good faith and without prejudice to the claimant who was a family member. Nevertheless, the claimant and his brother and the other members of the family had lost that mutual confidence required in what was really a quasi-partnership, and on the basis of the *Westbourne Galleries* case it was just and equitable that it should be wound up, given the disputes within the family as to how it should be run.

Further instances where the courts have considered that it was just and equitable to order the winding-up of the company include cases where the company was promoted fraudulently

(*Re London and County Coal Co* (1866) LR 3 Eq 355); situations where there was a 'deadlock'; where the management and conduct of the company are such that it is unfair to require the petitioner to remain a member (*Re Five Minute Car Wash Service Ltd* [1966] 1 All ER 242); as well as cases where the company is a quasi-partnership and where there has been a sufficiently serious breach of mutual understanding not expressed on the company constitution (*Virdi* v *Abbey Leisure Ltd* [1990] BCLC 342).

Finally, it is worth briefly mentioning that the 'winding-up' by the court commences on presentation of the petition (s 129(2)) and as soon as a prayer for winding-up has been made, the company becomes paralysed, resulting in the fact that no transactions relating to the company's property can be entered into after this point. Consequently, this is a drastic course of action and as such should be viewed as one of last resort for any minority shareholder. This is reinforced by the fact that the court, under s 125(2), may refuse to grant a winding-up order if it is of the opinion that (i) some other remedy is available to the petitioners; and (ii) the petitioners are acting unreasonably by seeking to have the company wound up instead of pursuing that other remedy.

There are other procedural limitations. A 'contributory' has standing to make an application to the court with a view to obtaining the winding-up of the company (s 124). According to s 79 of the Insolvency Act 1986, a contributory is any person who is liable to contribute to the assets of a company in the event of its being wound up.

As this is an equitable remedy, the petitioner must come with 'clean hands' (*Ebrahimi* v *Westbourne Galleries*), which may be contrasted with s 994 of the Companies Act 2006, whereby the petitioner does not have to come with 'clean hands'.

Essay questions

1 In certain areas the Companies Act 2006 and to a limited extent the Insolvency Act 1986 give special protection to minority shareholders with various holdings of shares. The most important of these statutory provisions seems to be s 994 of the Companies Act 2006 which gives any member the right to complain to the court on the ground that the affairs of the company are being or have been conducted in a manner which is unfairly prejudicial to the concerns of the members generally or of some part of the members including himself.

   (a) Explain and, by making reference to decided cases, illustrate the operation of s 994 of the Companies Act 2006.

   AND

   (b) Select TWO OTHER statutory examples of minority protection and in each selected area explain the size of holding and the rights given to a minority.

   (Glasgow Caledonian University)

2 The directors of Merchanting Ltd, a very successful business, have allocated most of the profits to themselves as remuneration and as donations to a charitable institution established by the founder of the company. Sheila, a shareholder, wishes to challenge the amount of the directors' remuneration, to discontinue the charitable donations and to increase the dividends.

   Explain how she could make her proposed challenge.

   (The Institute of Chartered Accountants in England and Wales)

3 Give an account of the legal procedure which must be followed in order to effect the registration of a new public limited company which is entitled to do business.

(The Association of Chartered Certified Accountants)

4 '. . . I think that one useful cross-check in a case like this is to ask whether the exercise of the power in question would be contrary to what the parties, by word or conduct, have actually agreed. Would it conflict with the promises which they appear to have exchanged? . . . In a quasi-partnership company [these promises] will usually be found in the understandings between the members at the time they entered into association . . . a promise may be binding as a matter of justice and equity although for one reason or another it would not be enforceable in law.'

   In the light of this statement, discuss the interrelationship between quasi-partnership companies and the remedy available under section 994 of the Companies Act 2006 for 'unfairly prejudicial' conduct.

(University of Hertfordshire)

5 Sven is a minority shareholder in the Finnish Company Ltd. Alf, Bob and Carl are the Chairman, Managing Director and Export Director respectively and together they control the company. Sven complains that:

● The company has just sold a ten-acre site to someone (believed to be Alf's father) for half the price which the company paid for it a year ago.

● No dividend had ever been declared by the company since Sven acquired his shares in the company. Nevertheless, Alf and Bob regularly take £30,000 per annum as directors' remuneration.

● £50,000 compensation was paid to Carl's predecessor, Albert, to secure his early vacation from office.

   Advise Sven as to the options available to him and his chances of success with regard to each complaint.

(University of Hertfordshire)

Test your knowledge

Four alternative answers are given. Select ONE only. Circle the answer which you consider to be correct. Check your answers by referring back to the information given in the chapter and against the answers at the end of the text.

1 The directors of Ouse Ltd have been selling off certain of the company's assets negligently at what the minority shareholders regard as too low a value. The directors have not made any gain themselves. What action can the minority shareholders bring on behalf of the company?

A An action could be brought on the basis that the directors acted *ultra vires*.

B The minority could apply to the court in the company's name for rescission of the contract.

C An action can be brought if the articles allow this.

D Under the rule in *Foss v Harbottle* no action can be brought.

2 Tom is the majority shareholder in Ribble Ltd and is also a director. Recently Tom sold freehold land belonging to the company to his wife who is also a director, and two months later his wife sold it to the local council at a profit of £30,000. The sale was ratified by an ordinary resolution. What action can the minority bring to recover the profit for the company?

A A derivative action under an exception to *Foss v Harbottle*.

B A representative action against Tom on the ground of fraud.

C No action can be brought because the sale was ratified.

D No action can be brought on behalf of the company except by the majority shareholders.

3 Which of the following can petition the court for relief under CA 2006, s 994?

A The company.

B Members holding not less than 10 per cent in number of the company's issued shares.

C A member of the company.

D A creditor of the company.

4 A derivative action is one which is brought by:

A The company.

B A member of the company on behalf of all the other members.

C A member of the company on his own account.

D A member of the company on behalf of the company.

5 John has just formed a limited company. Which of the following details can John exclude from its business stationery?

A The names of all of the company's directors.

B The company's registered number.

C The full name of the company.

D The address of the registered office.

The answers to test your knowledge questions appear on p. 645.

Suggested further reading

Acton, 'Just and equitable winding up: The strange case of the disappearing jurisdiction' (2001) 22 *Company Lawyer* 134.

Cheung, 'The use of statutory unanimous shareholder agreements and entrenched articles in reserving minority shareholders' rights: A comparative analysis' (2008) 29 *Company Lawyer* 234.

Chiu, 'Contextualising shareholders' disputes – a way to reconceptualise minority shareholder remedies' (2006) *Journal of Business Law* (May) 312–38.

Goddard, 'Closing the categories of unfair prejudice' (1999) 20 Co Law 333.

Hannigan, 'Section 459 of the Companies Act 1985 – A code of conduct for the quasi-partnership?' (1988) LMCLQ 60.

Hirt, 'In what circumstances should breaches of directors duties give rise to a remedy under ss 459–461 of the Companies Act 1985?' (2003) *Company Lawyer* 24, 100.

Keay and Loughrey, 'Derivative proceedings in a brave new world for company management and shareholders' [2010] JBL151.

Paterson, 'A criticism of the contractual approach to unfair prejudice' (2006) *Company Lawyer*, 27(7) 204

Prentice, 'Winding up on the just and equitable ground: the partnership analogy', (1973) 89 LQR 107.

Riley, 'Contracting out of company law: Section 459 of the Companies Act and the role of the courts' (1992) 55 MLR 702.

Thomas and Ryan, 'Section 459, public policy and freedom of contract' (2001) 22 Co Law 177.

Walters, 'Section 459: "Shareholder" or "investor" remedy?' (2007) *Company Lawyer* 28(10) 289.

19 Directors and management – generally

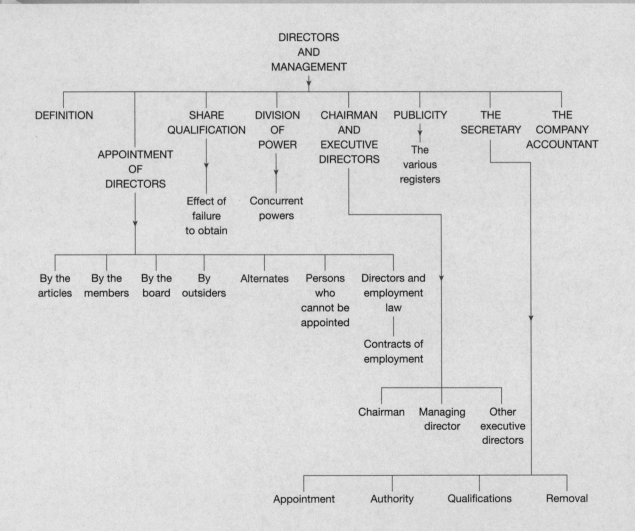

The management of a company is usually entrusted to a small group of persons called directors, supported, in the main, by the company secretary and the company accountant. It should be noted that a private company does not have to have a secretary (CA 2006, s 270(1)). Part 10 of the CA 2006 sets forth the provisions with respect to directors.

A company must have a board of directors numbering at least two in the case of a public company; one will suffice in the case of a private company (CA 2006, s 154). The previous exception for public companies registered before 1 November 1929 (or before 1 January 1933 in Northern Ireland) has been eliminated.

Apart from this, the number of directors and the way in which they are to be appointed is left to be regulated by the articles. Given the fact that the articles of association used by the vast majority of companies, to date, will follow *Table A* (see Appendix 2 ◗), this chapter will continue to outline these provisions alongside those of the new Model Articles which apply to companies incorporated after 1 October 2009 (for further discussion see Chapter 6 ◗). *Table A* (replaced by the new Model Articles in newly incorporated companies) provides that unless otherwise determined by ordinary resolution, the number of directors (other than alternate directors) shall not be subject to any maximum but shall not be less than two. *Table A*, as well as the new Model Articles (see Appendix 1 ◗), provides, in effect, that the company may from time to time by ordinary resolution increase or reduce the number of directors, and determine in what rotation the increased number is to retire.

Definition

Although the persons managing the company are usually called directors, other names are sometimes used, e.g. managers, governors, or committee of management. In this connection it is important to note the provisions of CA 2006, s 250 which are that the term 'director' when used in the Act is taken to include any persons occupying the position of director by whatever name called. Thus a director is anyone occupying the role of director regardless of his title within the company. This could include a person not actually appointed to the board, i.e. a *de facto* director. Thus, CA 2006, s 162 provides that the acts of a director are valid regardless of any defect in his or her appointment and this must of necessity apply to *de facto* directors (or directors *in fact*). A director is also an officer of the company.

It was held in **Re Sykes (Butchers) Ltd** [1998] 1 BCLC 110 that a person who denied that he was a director and whose appointment had not been notified to Companies House could nevertheless be disqualified as a *de facto* director following various defaults, including a preference in which he paid off a bank overdraft with the company's money to the detriment of other creditors where he had guaranteed the overdraft. He then went on trading with the company in a situation of inevitable insolvency. The court said that it was difficult to lay down one decisive test of whether a person is a *de facto* director. All the relevant facts relating to an involvement in management must be considered.

However, in **Secretary of State for Trade and Industry v Tjolle** [1998] 1 BCLC 333 a woman who called herself a director was not regarded as such for the purposes of disqualification because, on the facts of the case, she had no involvement with anything financial and did not form part of the company's real governance.

Shadow directors

It should also be noted that s 251 extends certain provisions of the CA 2006 to a 'shadow director', being a person in accordance with whose directions or instructions the directors of a company are accustomed to act unless the directors are accustomed so to act only because the person concerned gives them advice in a professional capacity. Professional advisers such as accountants and lawyers are not, therefore, for that reason alone, shadow directors. However, those who give advice other than purely in a professional capacity may be included. In *Secretary of State for Trade and Industry* v *Deverell* [2000] 2 BCLC 133 the Court of Appeal gave a ruling that appears to extend the definition. The court said that the concepts of 'direction' and 'instruction' in the definition did not exclude the concept of the giving of advice. The company concerned was in the travel business. It went into voluntary liquidation owing creditors an estimated £4.46 million. Disqualification proceedings were brought against three of its directors and two of its advisers or consultants who were persons with experience in the travel business. The consultants were held to be shadow directors and disqualification orders could be made against them.

Whether a person is or is not a shadow director is a matter of fact to be decided on the circumstances of the case, but some indications are: (a) being a signatory to the company's bank account and/or attendance at interviews with bank officials; (b) the ordering by the person concerned of goods and/or services for the company; (c) the signing of contracts and/or letters in the capacity of director; (d) attendance at meetings of the board; (e) possession of detailed information about the company.

The case of *Secretary of State for Trade and Industry* v *Laing* [1996] 2 BCLC 324 strengthens and points to the fact that it is not easy to persuade a court that a person has acted either as a shadow or *de facto* director. It is necessary to present to the court specific evidence of the alleged 'directions' given by the person concerned, plus evidence that they were acted upon by the company to satisfy the test for a shadow director and, for a *de facto* director, that there was a sufficient pattern of activities which could constitute acting as a *de facto* director. Thus in *Laing*, one of the directors had actually signed a contract on behalf of the company but the court concluded that this was not enough to make him a *de facto* director. The evidence did not establish that he had continued to act as a director for a sufficiently long period of time after that act.

The significance of being a shadow director is that such persons are caught by certain statutory provisions in the same way as a formally appointed or *de facto* director. The provisions are:

(a) long-term service contracts;
(b) substantial property transactions;
(c) loans and similar dealings;
(d) interests in contracts made with the company;
(e) requirements relating to disclosures in the accounts;
(f) the rules relating to wrongful trading;
(g) entry on the register of directors and secretaries.

In addition, it is necessary for a company to keep, generally at its registered office, a copy of any service contract made with a shadow director (see below).

The CA 2006 statutory duties will apply to shadow directors where, and to the extent that, the common law rules or equitable principles which they replace so apply (CA 2006, s 170(5)).

In other words, if there is a common law rule or equitable principle that currently applies to a shadow director, the statutory duty replacing that common law rule or equitable principle will also apply to the shadow director (in place of that rule of principle). However, where the rule or principle does not currently apply to a shadow director, the statutory duty replacing that rule or principle will not apply either. (For further discussion of directors' duties refer to Chapter 21. ◗)

Different types of director may exist on a single board. There may be full-time executive directors employed for their expertise under a contract of service, e.g. a finance director. Other non-executive directors may be appointed not to work full time under a contract of service, but to give general advice and business skill and experience to the board or the goodwill attached to their name. They may also carry out a service for the company below board level as in *Buchan* v *Secretary of State for Employment* (1997) 565 IRLB 2 where Mr Buchan who was a director of Croydon Scanning Centre Ltd was also the operator of the scanner and the sales manager.

Appointment of directors

Directors may be appointed in the following ways:

(i) By being named in the articles

This method is sometimes used for the appointment of the company's first directors as an alternative to following the procedure laid down in the articles.

(ii) By the subscribers to the memorandum

As we have seen, the subscribers (or subscriber in the case of a single-member company) to the memorandum, or a majority of them, may appoint directors; and again this method is sometimes used to appoint the first directors of the company.

However the first appointment is made, it is not effective unless the person concerned is named in the statement of officers which is required by CA 2006, s 12. This statement which is filed with other documents on incorporation must be signed by or on behalf of the subscribers (or subscriber) of the memorandum and must contain a consent signed by each of the directors named in it to act in that capacity. Any appointment by any articles delivered with the memorandum of a person as director is void unless he is named as a director in the statement.

CA 2006, s 12 replaces CA 1985, s 10 and makes two modifications: first, directors now have an option to withhold their home address from public access and, second, the requirement for private companies to have a secretary was eliminated.

(iii) By an ordinary resolution of the members in general meeting

In a public company the appointment of each director must be by a separate resolution, unless the meeting resolves with no dissentients that a composite resolution appointing several directors be put forward. This is to prevent the board from coercing members into voting for the appointment of an unpopular director by putting him up for election along with others who are more popular. The directors of a private company may by implication be appointed by a composite resolution and the written resolution procedure could be used (CA 2006, s 160).

In addition, subject to any restrictions in the articles, which would be improbable, all members of companies, whether public or private, can vote on a resolution for the election of directors whether they are themselves directors or not (see: Article 17 of the new Model Articles for private limited companies and Article 20 for public limited companies).

(iv) By the board of directors

The board may make appointments in two cases:

(a) to fill casual vacancies which may occur on resignation, disqualification, removal or death;
(b) to appoint *additional* directors up to a given maximum which may be set out in the company's articles. Any such appointment in excess of the permitted maximum is void.

Persons appointed in these two ways usually hold office until the next annual general meeting. However, if *Table A* applies the director concerned is not automatically eligible for re-election. The usual procedure under *Table A* requires that the director concerned be recommended by the board or that, before voting on the appointment the members have received, usually with the notice of the meeting, details of the person to be appointed which, if an appointment was made, would have to appear in the company's register of directors and secretaries. Private companies using the written resolution procedure would circulate the relevant information.

Table A, Reg 78 gives the members a concurrent power to appoint directors to fill casual vacancies and appoint additional directors, but this would involve the calling of a general meeting unless the written resolution procedure was followed. The new Model Articles for private companies is far more straightforward, with the process being covered by Article 17 (see Appendix 1 ○).

Qualifications

No general qualifications are required in order to become a company director. However, the Institute of Directors has introduced a professional qualification for directors. They are called 'Chartered Directors', and are able to use the letters 'CDir' after their names. There is an examination and normally three years' board experience before obtaining the title. Candidates also need a proposer and two seconders, and undergo a one-hour interview. After reaching chartered status, directors have to submit to 30 hours of professional development courses each year. The Institute of Directors also has power to discipline directors who fail to keep up proper standards. The Institute is considering offering some form of accreditation for non-executive directors. The object of the qualification is to enable qualified directors to distinguish themselves from those without any recognised training, or from those who run smaller companies, who may call themselves directors but who do not attend formal board meetings with agendas and formal procedures as would be required in larger companies.

Contractual rights to appoint directors

If by a company's articles directors are to be appointed by the members in general meeting, the board cannot make a valid contract by which an outsider is empowered to appoint directors (*James* v *Eve* (1873) LR 6 HL 335).

However, if the company is governed by *Table A* it seems that the board may delegate its power to appoint additional directors and this may prove useful when the board wishes, for example, to raise a loan or share capital from persons who are only willing to lend or invest if they can nominate a certain number of directors to the board to protect their interests.

If the articles expressly empower an outsider to appoint directors, the power to do so is undoubtedly valid, but whether the court would enforce the power by specific performance is doubtful. Generally, the court will not enforce contracts of personal service in this way.

However, if the company refuses to accept an appointee in these circumstances there is, of course, always the solution in a quasi-partnership company of asking for a winding-up. This method was adopted in the following case.

Re A & B C Chewing Gum Ltd [1975] 1 All ER 1017

The petitioners, Topps Chewing Gum, held one-third of the ordinary shares in A & B C on the basis of a shareholders' agreement that they should have equal control with the two Coakley brothers, Douglas and Anthony, who were directors of and held a two-thirds interest in the ordinary shares of A & B C. In order to achieve equality of control, the company adopted a new set of articles which allowed Topps to appoint and remove a director representing them in A & B C, and for board decisions to be unanimous. On the same day Topps, the Coakleys and A & B C signed and sealed the shareholders' agreement setting out the terms referred to above. Topps appointed Douglas Coakley to represent them but later removed him and appointed John Sullivan, their marketing director. Douglas and Anthony Coakley refused to accept the change so that Topps were effectively prevented from participating in management.

Held – by Plowman J – that it was just and equitable that the company be wound up under what is now s 122(1)(g) of the Insolvency Act 1986. The Coakleys had repudiated the relationship in the agreement and the articles. The case was one of expulsion and **Westbourne Galleries** (see Chapter 1 ◖) applied. It is interesting to note that in applying **Westbourne Galleries** Plowman J took the view that Lord Wilberforce's judgment spoke of entitlement to management participation as being an obligation so basic that if broken the association must be dissolved, even though it is not a company arising out of a partnership.

Comment

(i) Although Plowman J purported to be applying the equitable principles of **Westbourne**, he was in fact merely enforcing the petitioner's contract rights set out in the shareholders' agreement. He could have granted an injunction to prevent the breach of that contract by the Coakley brothers, a less drastic remedy than winding the company up.

(ii) Also less drastic, if return of share capital was required, would be an application to the court by petition for unfair prejudice. It will be recalled that earlier we gave cases in which the courts had decided that in a private company, such as this was, it was part of the interest of a member (such as Topps) to have a place on the board (see Chapter 18 ◖). Presumably this ruling would be applied to a corporate member in terms of entitling the company to have a nominee on the board where this has been agreed.

Alternate directors

These can be useful if the director has many outside commitments which may from time to time result in prolonged absences from the board. The appointment of an alternate can solve problems relating to quorum, cheque-signing and so on. There is no statutory authority for a director to appoint an *alternate* to act in his place in the event of his absence and alternate directors can only be appointed if the articles so provide. *Table A* provides that any director (other than an alternate director) may appoint any other director, or any other person approved by the directors and willing to act, to be an alternate director and may remove from office an alternate director so appointed by him. (This procedure is replicated in the new Model Articles for public limited companies – see Appendix 1. ◐) An alternate director is entitled to receive notice of all meetings of directors and of all meetings of committees of directors of which his appointer is a member, to attend and vote at any such meeting at which the director appointing him is not personally present, and generally to perform all the functions of his appointer as a director in his absence but is not entitled to receive any remuneration from the company for his services as an alternate director. But it is not necessary to give notice of such a meeting to an alternate director who is absent from the United Kingdom.

An alternate director ceases to be an alternate director if his appointer ceases to be a director, but, if a director retires by rotation or otherwise but is reappointed or deemed to have been reappointed at the meeting at which he retires, any appointment of an alternate director made by him which was in force immediately prior to his retirement continues after his reappointment. Any appointment or removal of an alternate director is by notice to the company signed by the director making or revoking the appointment or in any other manner approved by the directors. Finally, and save as otherwise provided in the articles, an alternate director is deemed for all purposes to be a director and is alone responsible for his own acts and defaults and is not deemed to be the agent of the director appointing him.

An alternate director is a director of the company in his own right and his particulars should be lodged with the Registrar if he is not already a director of the company. All the other provisions relating to directors in company legislation apply to an alternate including, for example, disclosure of interests in shares and debentures and material contracts.

Persons who cannot be appointed

This is to some extent a matter for the articles and they may, for example, provide that a minor or an alien shall not be appointed a director of the company. *Table A* does not contain any such restrictions, but the following statutory provisions apply.

(i) Age limit

CA 2006, s 157 requires that a person may not be appointed director of a company unless he has attained the age of 16. One may be appointed director below the age of 16. However, one may not serve as director until the age of 16 is reached. CA 2006, s 158 provides for certain exceptions to s 157 of the CA 2006. CA 2006, s 159 requires that a person already a director but is not the age of 16 as of the date CA 2006, s 157 comes into force (1 October 2008) must cease to be a director. There is no statutory maximum age limit for a director.

(ii) Bankruptcy

The Company Directors Disqualification Act 1986, s 11 makes it an offence for an undischarged bankrupt to act as a director of a company unless the court gives him the necessary permission to act. If he has such permission, he may take up an appointment unless the articles forbid his appointment with or without permission, in which case he cannot take the appointment. *Table A* provides that a director who becomes bankrupt vacates office. The article does not prevent the appointment of a director who is already bankrupt, but such an appointment would not normally be made since the director could not act in that capacity.

The offence created by s 11 is one of strict liability which means that it does not require a guilty mind. Therefore it is no defence for the director concerned to claim that he or she did not realise that management functions were being performed.

Thus, in *R v Doring* (2002) 33 LS Gaz R 21 the defendant said in her defence that she was only concerned with publicity and design in regard to the products of Cabouchon Europe Ltd of which she was a director. She said that she did not hire or fire staff or make financial decisions or contracts on behalf of the company. The judge directed the jury that since the offence was strict they were not required to consider whether the defendant had acted dishonestly in carrying out her duties (which she had not) but only whether her acts looked at objectively amounted to being concerned in the management of the company. The jury found her guilty and she was sentenced to 120 hours of community service. Her appeal to the Court of Appeal was dismissed.

(iii) Persons disqualified by court order

The court *may*, and in some cases under s 6 of the 1986 Act *must*, make a disqualification order. This is an order to the effect that a named person may not (unless the court gives leave) perform any of the following activities during the period specified by the order:

(a) be a director (or liquidator, or administrator receiver, or receiver and manager) of a company;
(b) be concerned with or take part in, directly or indirectly, the promotion, formation or management of a company (s 1 of the 1986 Act).

The 1986 Act requires the Registrar of Companies to keep a register of all persons against whom disqualification orders are made and they remain on the register for the period in which the order is in force. The register is open to inspection by members of the public.

(iv) Articles of association

Further disqualifications may be imposed by a company's articles. Neither *Table A* nor the Model Articles impose such disqualifications, merely specifying the grounds on which directors will vacate office. Thus, unless there are such express provisions, a person is not disqualified merely because he is a minor or an alien and a company may be a director of another company.

(v) Directors

Section 155 of the CA 2006 states that a company must have at least one director who is a natural person.

Directors and employment law: generally

Directors may be fee-paid supervisors acting in some ways as trustees for the shareholders, or senior executives or managers who work the whole time as directors of the company and who sometimes combine this with the giving of a professional service to the company, as in the case of an accountant who takes up an appointment as finance director. Under *Table A* directors are allowed to enter into service contracts which may be made by the board. They then become known as executive directors.

Under Article 70 of *Table A* the directors are empowered to enter into a service contract with an executive director, provided that the term is not for more than five years when member approval is required (see below). In addition, the normal procedures relating to the appointment of the executive as a director must be followed.

In making the contract of appointment, the board must follow requirements of the company's articles (see below).

UK Safety Group Ltd v Heane [1998] 2 BCLC 208

The problem in this case arose because of a failure by the directors to observe provisions in the company's articles. In this connection, the directors of the company can in general terms bind the company and a third party in contractual rights and duties only if the provisions of the articles in regard to contractual agreements are followed.

The main relevant article of UK Safety provided as follows in terms of the appointment of directors to an executive office. 'Any such appointment, agreement or arrangement may be made upon such terms as the directors determine and they may remunerate any such director for his services as they think fit.'

It appeared that an agreement between Mr Nicholas Heane as sales and marketing director and UK Safety was made in effect by the chief executive of UK Safety, a Mr Newman, on his own initiative and not by following the relevant article of the company. In evidence he said that he did not feel it appropriate to discuss the terms at a board meeting but that the contract and its contents had been made known to, and approved by, the remuneration committee of the board – but not the full board.

Mr Heane resigned to set up another company, which was the second defendant and UK Safety was, in this action, seeking to enforce covenants in the alleged contract with Mr Heane restraining his activities after leaving the company and in particular restraining his use of confidential information.

The judge accepted that it may not be necessary for a board to meet formally in order to transact business. He said:

> I entirely accept [. . .] that it may not be necessary for a company to have a formal board meeting and, consistently with the decision in *Re Bonelli's Electric Telegraph Co, Cook's Claim (No 2)* (1874) LR 18 Eq 656 it may be possible for all the directors informally to consider the terms of a contract [. . .] That, however, is not what occurred in the present case. The initiative for the contracts came from Mr Newman himself.

He went on to hold that the agreement with Mr Heane was not binding on him and, therefore, the restraints were unenforceable.

Comment

It is all too easy for the directors of a busy company to neglect corporate formalities but this may result in unfortunate consequences for the company, such as in this case an inability to protect the company's confidential information.

The case also makes clear that if the appointment is to the office of director or executive director of a subsidiary approval by the group board is not enough. This, of course, does not mean that the matter of the appointment by the subsidiary should not be raised with the group board in order to satisfy corporate governance requirements.

The termination of the contract of service, of itself, does not terminate the directorship. It is therefore advisable for the contract of service of an executive director to provide that the director concerned will resign the directorship on termination of the contract of employment for any reason. That failing, the director would have to be removed under a provision in the articles, if any (there is no such provision in *Table A*) or under s 168 of the CA 2006.

Removal does not prevent the director concerned from bringing an action for damages for wrongful dismissal. As regards claims for redundancy before employment tribunals, directors who are employed under service contracts may have been engaged for a fixed term of two years or more and may have been required in the contract to waive the right to claim for redundancy.

However, from 1 October 2002 it has not been possible to make a contract of fixed-term employment where the right to a redundancy payment is waived (see Fixed-Term Employees (Prevention of Less Favourable Treatment) Regulations 2002 (SI 2002/2034)).

It had been assumed that a director serving under a contract as an executive of the company could claim unfair dismissal. However, in *Cobley* v *Forward Technology Industries plc* [2003] All ER (D) 175 the Court of Appeal ruled that the chief executive of a public listed company was not unfairly dismissed when the shareholders removed him from office by a resolution in general meeting. This effected his dismissal as CEO because his contract said that he could not continue as CEO unless he was also a director of the company. His dismissal was, ruled the court, 'for some other substantial reason' under s 98 of the Employment Rights Act 1996. The removal followed a successful hostile takeover and business reorganisations are capable of amounting to 'some other substantial reason'. The judgment notes that Mr Cobley had reserved his right to claim at common law for wrongful dismissal by breach of contract. This was not an issue before the Court of Appeal.

Comment

Presumably therefore where the company can establish one of the reasons justifying dismissal under the ERA 1996 Act, i.e. incapability, misconduct, redundancy, contravention of statutory provision or 'some other substantial reason' a claim for unfair dismissal will fail. Since removal from the board is a substantial reason as a 'business reorganisation' and presumably always will be the claim for unfair dismissal seems ruled out. The statutory defence of substantial reason does not apply in wrongful dismissal claims though misconduct does. Claims for wrongful dismissal can be brought before employment tribunals but there is a cap on the award of £25,000. There is no cap in claims before the County Court or High Court.

Employee/directors may claim a redundancy payment (if they have not contracted-out before 1 October 2002) or insolvency payment as a preferential creditor. The fees of an office-holder/director are not so protected. Director/employees are also covered by the Equality Act 2010 and regulations relating to discrimination on the grounds of sexual orientation and religion or belief and employment legislation generally. The wider definition of 'employee' in the discrimination legislation brings within their scope directors who have a contract for services, as where they contract with the company to act as a consultant.

Directors' contracts of employment

As regards contracts of employment of directors, both public and private companies may not incorporate into any agreement a term under which a director's employment with the company or, if he is a director of a holding company, his employment with the group is to continue, or may be continued, except by the agreement of the members by ordinary (or written) resolution, for a period that exceeds five years, if during that period the company cannot terminate his contract by notice or his employment can be terminated by notice but only in specified circumstances.

A contract for services is included and so the provisions relating to contracts of employment cannot be circumvented by directors who enter into long-term consultancy arrangements instead of contracts of employment. These arrangements could nullify to a large extent the provisions of the CA 2006, s 168 in that directors could be removed from office under that section but long-term arrangements which they may have given themselves could involve massive compensation so that the company would, in practice, be unable to remove them.

The prohibition on long-term contracts applies to agreements between a director of a holding company and any of its subsidiaries. Thus a director is prevented from avoiding the provisions by entering into agreements with a company that is controlled by the company of which he is a director.

There are provisions to prevent avoidance of the long-term contracts rules by the device of entering into a series of agreements. Thus, if a director during the first year of a five-year contract which cannot be terminated by notice enters into a further five-year contract which cannot be terminated by notice, the period for which he is employed would be regarded as 10 years and, therefore, a term would be implied into both contracts making the employment terminable by reasonable notice.

The provisions do not apply if the agreement continues after five years, but once five years have passed, it can be terminated at the instance of the company by notice. In addition, a term longer than five years may be valid if it has been first approved by a resolution of the company and in the case of a director of a holding company, by a resolution of that company also. However, in such a case a written memorandum setting out the proposed agreement and incorporating the term regarding length, must be available for inspection by the members of the company at the registered office for not less than 15 days ending with the date of the meeting and also the meeting itself, or circulated in the case of a written resolution. Finally, the provisions do not apply to contracts given to the directors of a wholly owned subsidiary. The Act regards the subsidiary as a mere unit of management of the holding company so that the directors of these management units can have their conditions of service settled by the directors of the holding company. If a director of a wholly owned subsidiary is also a director of the holding company, any contract in excess of five years will be caught by the above provisions and will be affected unless one of the exceptions applies.

A contract which contravenes the above provisions is void and can be terminated by the company at any time after reasonable notice. Reasonable notice is not defined by the Act but in *James* v *Kent & Co Ltd* [1950] 2 All ER 1099 it was held to be an implied term of a company director's contract that he should be entitled to three months' notice.

Any term in the agreement, e.g. salary, which is distinct from the term relating to duration is valid and enforceable.

Sections 188–189 of the CA 2006 require member approval of long-term service contracts. Contracts under which a director is guaranteed at least two years of employment with the company of which he is a director or with any subsidiary of that company are required to be approved by members. The length of term was reduced from five years to two years for this requirement.

The desirability of written contracts

As we have seen, executive directors can have a double function – one as an officer of the company and the other as an employee. However, the general attitude of the courts has been to regard them as holders of an office rather than employees unless there is satisfactory evidence to the contrary (see *Eaton* v *Robert Eaton Ltd and Secretary of State for Employment* [1988] IRLR 83 and *McLean* v *Secretary of State for Employment* (1992) 455 IRLIB 14). These cases emphasise the general desirability of executive directors, particularly in small businesses, having written contracts of service. Where this is so, the court would normally recognise the employee aspect of the dual role and, in particular, allow claims to be made under s 166 of the Employment Rights Act 1996 to the Department for Business, Innovation and Skills (BIS) for a redundancy payment if the business goes insolvent. The written contract of service should not exclude employment protection rights if it is for a fixed term. Once the BIS has made the payment, the remedies of the employee against the employing company are transferred to the Secretary of State for Business, Innovation and Skills for what they might be worth. The right of an employee to apply directly to the DTI thus becomes very important in an insolvency situation. However, this right only applies to employees and many directors of small family companies who are acting in an executive role but without written contracts of employment may find themselves without any financial recompense if the business fails.

Controlling members as employed directors

Before leaving the topic of directors as employees, it is worth mentioning that a director who has a controlling interest in the shares of a company may not be regarded as an employee of the company. Control is still a major factor in establishing a contract of employment and a majority shareholder is not, as a worker, subject to any effective control by the company (see *Otton* v *Secretary of State for Employment* (1995) 7 February, EAT 1150/94). More recent case law appears below. The provisions referred to above were then administered by the Department of Employment.

Buchan v *Secretary of State for Employment* (1997) 565 IRLB 2

Mr Buchan was one of two working directors of Croydon Scanning Centre Ltd. He was also the operator of the scanner and the sales manager and had a 50 per cent shareholding in the company. He worked full time for a salary of £35,000 pa and had an entitlement of five weeks' holiday per year. He had no written contract of service and no written record of his engagement or conditions of service. The company went into administrative receivership and Mr Buchan tried unsuccessfully to obtain from the Secretary of State a redundancy payment from the National Insurance Fund under ss 166 and 182 of the Employment Rights Act 1996. As we have seen, this course of action is available to an employee where, for example, the employer is insolvent and the whole or any part of a redundancy payment remains unpaid. If the Secretary of State makes a payment, he takes over the employee's rights and remedies in the insolvency.

An employment tribunal upheld the Secretary of State's decision and Mr Buchan appealed to the EAT. The EAT dismissed Mr Buchan's appeal, concluding on the evidence that he was not an employee. As beneficial owner of 50 per cent of the shares, he could block any company decisions with which he did not agree, including decisions as to his own terms of service or dismissal. The appointment of an administrative receiver did not and could not alter Mr Buchan's status within the company. The EAT distinguished the case of *Lee* v *Lee's Air Farming Ltd* [1960] 3 All ER 420 (see Chapter 1 ◐) where a controlling shareholder was held to be an employee. He was killed while crop-spraying and a claim was brought against the company for workmen's compensation, the company being indemnified in this respect by an insurance company. The claim succeeded but the EAT did not think it would have done if it had been made under employment protection legislation. Policy considerations were involved. Employment protection claims on insolvency are met by the state and not by a company backed up by an insurer.

Comment

(i) The EAT followed this decision in a case heard contemporaneously with *Buchan*, i.e. *Ivey* v *Secretary of State for Employment* (1997) 565 IRLB 2 where Mr Ivey was managing director owning 99 per cent of the company shares and also had a written contract. The two decisions were then followed in *Heffer* v *Secretary of State for Trade and Industry* (EAT 355/96) where it was held that an individual with a 70 per cent shareholding in the company was not an employee.

(ii) There was a further development in *Fleming* v *Secretary of State for Trade and Industry* (1998) 588 IRLB 10. The decision in *Buchan* had carried the suggestion that there was a rule of law that a controlling shareholder could never be an employee. That proposition was rejected by the Court of Session in *Fleming*. The court held that the fact that a director holds a majority shareholding in the company is a relevant factor in deciding whether he is or is not an employee for the purposes of employment protection legislation but it is not in itself decisive. Nevertheless, the court held that Fleming was not an employee because, even though he worked alongside the company's employees, he was a majority shareholder and, in addition, had guaranteed the company's debts. The *Fleming* approach was also approved by the Employment Appeal Tribunal in *Secretary of State for Trade and Industry* v *Bottrill* [1998] IRLR 120 where Morison J said that the reasoning in *Buchan* and *Ivey* was 'unsound'.

(iii) The decision of the EAT was affirmed by the Court of Appeal in *Secretary of State for Trade and Industry* v *Bottrill* (1999) 615 IRLB 12. The Court of Appeal stated that whether or not a controlling shareholder could also be an employee can be decided only by having regard to all the relevant facts. His controlling shareholding is likely to be a significant fact in all situations and in some cases may be decisive. However, it is only one of the relevant facts and is not to be taken as determining the relationship without taking into account all the relevant circumstances.

(iv) Following *Bottrill*, the EAT has ruled that a controlling shareholder of a company could be regarded as an employee even though he stood to gain if the company did well. The fact that he was a skilled entrepreneur was also irrelevant to the question of whether or not he was an employee. He had a contract of employment with the company that was not a sham and he had been treated and rewarded as an employee (see *Connolly* v *Sellers Arenascene Ltd* (2000) 633 IRLB 15).

(v) It seems that a director will be regarded as an employee where there is a written contract of employment and all the usual hallmarks of employment are present. Certainly the original, almost blanket, ban on controlling shareholders as employees has been considerably eroded.

Statutory employment claims

Directors are, in general, the best paid employees in a company and they have in the past shown little interest in claims for unfair dismissal because of the existence of a cap on the amount of compensation recoverable. This limit was increased under the Employment Rights (Increase of Limits) Order 2008 SI 2012/3007, in force from February 2013, to £74,200. Since a claim for wrongful dismissal may be limited to the sum which the director would have received during the relevant period of notice, there may be more claims by directors of smaller companies for unfair dismissal where this can be sustained in the circumstances of the case.

However, in this context the decision of the Court of Appeal in *Cobley* and the comment thereto should be noted.

Directors' share qualification

The articles may require the directors to take up a certain number of shares as a share qualification. The general purpose of this is said to be that, since they are to manage the company's affairs on behalf of the other shareholders, they should have a stake in it themselves to induce them to act diligently to ensure the company's progress. However, since it is not possible to ensure that directors have a beneficial interest in their qualification shares it seems that no useful purpose is served by a requirement of qualification shares.

It is the duty of every director who is required to hold a share qualification, and who is not already qualified, to obtain the necessary shares within two months after his appointment, or such shorter time as may be fixed by the articles.

A *director must be entered on the company's register* as the holder of his qualification shares, but he need not hold them beneficially and could, for example, hold them on trust for others so long as his name appears on the register of members in respect of them. A director is not allowed to hold his qualification shares in the name of a nominee, since it would involve the company receiving notice of trust which is forbidden by CA 2006, s 127. A director is not qualified by holding a share warrant.

The modern trend is for articles of association not to require a share qualification for directors since it is now a generally held view that no useful purpose is served by the requirement. It does, of course, help to ensure a quorum at general meetings, though it carries a distinct risk that directors will become disqualified and therefore automatically vacate office, either by transfer, or during the currency of a takeover bid, where they have accepted an offer in respect of their own holdings.

It is almost certain that far more cases of disqualification occur than might be supposed and that when the fact comes to light the directors concerned merely buy sufficient shares and carry on as before. In fact, of course, having been disqualified, and thereby vacated office, they ought to be reappointed by the board or the members as the case may be, but probably very few are so reappointed and it is unlikely that CA 2006, s 162 can be relied upon. The section does admittedly provide that the acts of a director shall be valid, notwithstanding any defect that may afterwards be discovered in his appointment or qualification. However, it is possible that CA 2006, s 162 does not apply if there is no attempt at reappointment, though the rule in *Turquand*'s case may be of assistance. An unqualified person acting as director may be fined for each day that he continues to act.

Division of power – directors and members

The board of directors and meetings of members of a company can between them exercise all of the company's powers. In a private company there is the option of a unanimous written resolution of members. The distribution of those powers as between the members and the directors is, subject to the provisions of the Companies Act, left entirely to the discretion of those who frame the articles of association.

The board's powers can be as broad or as narrow as is desired, but if *Table A*, Reg 70 applies, then this confers on the board all the powers of the company, except those which the Companies Acts and the articles require to be exercised by the members. Under the new Model Articles, Article 3 confers the same powers for both public and private limited companies (see Appendix 1 ○).

The powers reserved to the members by the Companies Acts are mainly the power to alter the memorandum and articles, the power to alter share capital, the power to appoint auditors and remove directors and the power to put the company into liquidation (see Chapter 6 ○). Additionally, *Table A* reserves to the members the power to fix the rights to be attached to a new issue of shares and to effect variations of such rights, the power to appoint directors and the power to declare dividends, though not in excess of the percentage recommended by the board, and to capitalise profits and reserves.

In addition, directors of public and private companies must have the authority of the members by ordinary resolution in general meeting, or written resolution, or of the company's articles, before they exercise a power of allotment of shares or grant rights to subscribe for, or convert securities into, shares. Furthermore, public and private companies must offer new shares to existing members before they are allotted to others. However, a private company may exclude this requirement by its memorandum or articles or by special (or written) resolution and a plc may achieve the disapplication of pre-emption rights by a special resolution of its members.

Concurrent powers

Certain powers, even though given to the directors, will be regarded as concurrent and exercisable by the members unless the articles make it clear that the power is exclusive to the directors. Thus a power for directors to appoint additional directors and to fill casual vacancies on the board or to fix the remuneration of the managing director will be treated as concurrent powers, unless the articles clearly show that it is to be exclusive to the directors (which *Table A* does not) and so resolutions passed by the members in respect of such matters will prevail over the directors' own decision. Although the directors have power to sue in the company's name, there is also a concurrent power in the members so that if the board decides not to sue in a particular case the members may by ordinary resolution resolve that the company shall sue.

Control of the company's business

If the members are dissatisfied with the way in which the directors are running the company's business, there are the following ways in which the members can deal with the situation:

(a) by overriding decisions of the board by ordinary (or written) resolution where the power is concurrent. Thus if the directors have refused to bring a claim to court on behalf of the company the members may initiate it by ordinary (or written) resolution; or

(b) by altering the memorandum by special (or written) resolution to take away the company's capacity to continue the activity concerned; or

(c) by altering the company's articles by a special (or written) resolution so as to cut down the directors' powers; or

(d) by refusing to re-elect directors of whose actions they disapprove. The procedure would involve replacing the directors by others with different policies and this would require an ordinary (or written) resolution; or

(e) by recourse to the provisions of CA 2006, s 169, which provides that a company may by *ordinary resolution* remove a director before the expiration of his period of office, notwithstanding anything in the articles or in any agreement between the company and him. Such a resolution requires *special notice* of 28 days to be given to the company of the intention to propose it. The section does not deprive a director so removed of any claim he may have for damages or compensation payable to him as a result of the termination of his appointment. The section would be satisfied by a majority of one, but a small minority would be unlikely to succeed in carrying such a resolution, and removal may be impossible if the directors have weighted voting rights on the resolution to remove them (*Bushell* **v**

Faith, 1969). Company legislation does not allow the use of a written resolution by private companies for removal of directors.

In addition, *Pedley* v *Inland Waterways*, 1977 decides that a minority wishing to remove a director must be of sufficient size to comply with CA 2006, ss 314 and 315 (if the directors are to be compelled to put a resolution on the agenda for removal at an AGM), or CA 2006, s 303 (if the directors are to be required to call an extraordinary general meeting to consider the removal);

(f) where there is a regulation such as Article 70 of *Table A*, the members may give a direction by a special (or written) resolution under which the directors are required to act differently for the future. Article 70 provides that subject to the provisions of the Companies Acts, the memorandum and the articles, *and to any directions given by special resolution*, the business of the company shall be managed by the directors who may exercise all the powers of the company. (This is replicated in Article 3 of the new Model Articles for both public and private limited companies – see Appendix 1 ◗.) No alteration of the memorandum or articles *and no such direction* shall invalidate any prior act of the directors which would have been valid if that alteration had not been made *or that direction* had not been given.

Directors' irregular acts – validation

Directors who carry out acts which are initially defective can have them validated by an ordinary (or written) resolution. If the transaction is *ultra vires* the company, a special (or written) resolution is required (see Chapters 5 and 6 ◗).

Grant v *United Kingdom Switchback Railways Co* (1888) 40 Ch D 135

The articles of association of Thompson's Patent Gravity Switchback Railways Co (the second defendant) disqualified any director from voting at a board meeting in regard to any contract in which he was interested. The directors of Thompson's agreed to sell the company's undertaking to the United Kingdom Co (the first defendant) despite the fact that they were also the promoters of the purchasing company. An action was brought by a shareholder in Thompson's for an injunction to restrain Thompson's from carrying into effect the contract of sale on the grounds that they had no authority to enter into it since the articles prohibited a director from voting upon a contract in which he was interested, and here all the directors but one were interested. However, it appeared that a general meeting of the shareholders of Thompson's had been properly held and that they had passed an ordinary resolution approving and adopting the agreement and authorising the directors to carry it into effect.

Held – by the Court of Appeal – that the contract was valid and an injunction was refused.

The directors cannot cure acts which are in breach of their fiduciary duty to the company by obtaining an ordinary resolution of the members in general meeting if they control the voting at general meetings (*Cook* v *Deeks*, 1916, see Chapter 17, p. 306 ◗) or possibly control general meetings in fact, even though they do not have a majority of voting shares (*Prudential Assurance* v *Newman*, 1980, see Chapter 17, p. 312 ◗).

A unanimous written resolution would presumably cure such acts in the sense that there would be no member wishing to object. However, in a situation of insolvency the creditors, through an insolvency practitioner, may wish to contest the validity of a written resolution as a cure for the directors' breach of duty.

Delegation of powers by the directors

The well-known maxim of the law of agency – '*delegatus non potest delegare*' (a delegate cannot delegate) – applies to directors, so that they cannot delegate their functions and powers to others without the permission of the members or the articles. Articles do usually allow delegation of powers to a committee of the board (as per *Table A* and the new Model Articles), though such delegation is revocable even if made for a fixed period of time (***Manton v Brighton Corporation*** [1951] 2 All ER 101). *Table A* also allows delegation to any managing director or any director holding any other executive office of such of the directors' powers as they consider desirable to be exercised by him.

In addition, *Table A* also allows the board to employ agents and professional persons to carry out any functions which the board may itself carry out. In many respects this is covered by Article 5 of the new Model Articles for public and private companies (see Appendix 2 ⬤).

Board unable or unwilling to act

This situation may arise in the following circumstances:

(a) Where the act is beyond the powers of the board

Authority for the transaction must be sought from the members in general meeting and the authorisation may be given by ordinary (or written) resolution.

The members may authorise directors to do an act which is outside the directors' own powers, but within the company's power, by passing an ordinary (or written) resolution either before or after the directors' act (*per* Bowen LJ in ***Grant v United Kingdom Switchback Railways Co***, 1888, see above). In such a situation the members can, of course, revoke or vary the authority by ordinary (or written) resolution at any time. It is only necessary to amend the articles if the members wish to add the particular power to the powers of the board.

(b) Lack of quorum at board meetings

Directors may be unable to exercise the powers given to them by the articles because they have become so few in number that they cannot constitute a quorum, or because so many of them are, in a legal sense, interested in the transaction in question and are consequently disabled from voting by the articles, that a quorum of competent directors cannot be found.

As regards quorum, *Table A* empowers the remaining directors to fill vacancies so as to make up a quorum (this is replicated in Article 11 of the new Model Articles). If there are no directors at all, or if the remaining directors are unwilling to fill the vacancies, the members may exercise their powers until a board is properly constituted.

When a quorum of competent directors (i.e. directors who are not interested in the transaction) cannot be found, the board's powers temporarily revert to the members who may then authorise the remaining directors to act either in advance of their acting or by ratification afterwards.

(c) The proper purpose rule

If directors are unable to exercise their powers in a lawful manner because to do so would be a breach of their duty to exercise those powers for the purpose for which they were given, i.e. for the benefit of the company (alternatively expressed as the proper purpose rule), the members may by ordinary (or written) resolution ratify what the directors have in fact done (***Bamford*** v *Bamford* [1969] 2 WLR 1107), and it would seem that they may also authorise the directors in advance to do the act in question (*Bamford* v *Bamford*, 1969, *per* Russell LJ). It appears from cases such as *North-West Transportation Co Ltd* v *Beatty* (1887) 12 App Cas 589 that the directors are not under any legal duty to abstain from voting in order to achieve ratification or authorisation.

If there is no such ratification or authorisation by the members and the act of the board contravenes the proper purpose rule, it is invalid.

It is important to note that directors may fall foul of the proper purpose rule even when they are exercising a power for the benefit of the company.

Galloway v *Hallé Concerts Society* [1915] 2 Ch 233

The defendant society was registered in 1899 as a company limited by guarantee without the addition of the word limited to its name, as being formed for the promotion of art and with the intention that its profits should be applied in promoting its objects without payment of dividends to its members. Its object was the promotion of concerts known as the 'Hallé Concerts' in Manchester. Under the provisions of the memorandum each member was to contribute on a winding-up such amount as should be required to pay the company's liabilities, not exceeding £5 per member. Article 7 of the company's articles provided that each member should be liable to contribute, and should pay on demand to the society, any sum or sums not exceeding in the aggregate £100 (called the contribution) as and when called. The claimants, Galloway and Holt, were members of the society but disagreed with certain of its policies. They objected to calls being made upon them in respect of the contribution and had not paid previous calls made, although one such call had been recovered by the society in a county court. On 31 March 1915, the committee of the society resolved to call up the whole of the contributions of Galloway and Holt, but no corresponding call was made on the other members. The claimants sought a declaration that the resolution was invalid and the call unenforceable.

Held – by Sargant J – there is an implied condition of equality between shareholders in a company, and it is generally improper for directors to make a call on part of a class of members without making a similar call on all the members of the class. Further, even if the articles give power to discriminate, the fact that the members are dilatory in paying previous calls would not be sufficient reason for enforcing a discriminatory power in the articles.

Comment

(i) It should be noted that the act of making the call was not in any sense beyond the powers of the directors and was even in a sense exercised for the benefit of the company because, having called up the whole of the share capital of Galloway and Holt, they could have been sued once and for all for its recovery if they had not paid it. However, in spite of the fact that the directors had the power and were probably motivated in the company's benefit, the power was not exercised for the proper purpose and was struck down for this reason.

(ii) More commonly perhaps the proper purpose rule is used where the directors have used their powers for a purpose which does not benefit the company as in the *Rolled Steel* case (see Chapter 8, p. 143 ◐).

(d) Dissension between members of the board

If directors are unable to act because of a dissension between themselves, the members may exercise the powers of the board until a board is elected which can act. However, the dissension must result in deadlock before the members can intervene. It must, for example, be shown either that so many directors persistently absent themselves from board meetings that a quorum cannot be found, or that the dissenting parties have equal voting power at board meetings and resolutions cannot therefore be passed.

(e) Powers of the court

Where the board is unable to act because the directors are so few in number that a quorum cannot be found, or because of deadlock between the directors, the court may appoint a receiver of the company's business to manage it until a competent board can be constituted. Furthermore, if the power of the board which the members wish to have exercised is one which the court can conveniently exercise itself, the court may exercise the power and give any decision which the board could have given (see *Re Copal Varnish Co Ltd* [1917] 2 Ch 349 where the court exercised a power to approve the transfer of shares).

The chairman and executive directors

Consideration will now be given to the special position of the chairman and executive directors.

Chairman

Companies are not required by the law to appoint a chairman and, given the fact that the requirement for a private company to hold an Annual General Meeting (AGM) has been abolished by the Companies Act 2006, there would appear to be little need for a chairman to control proceedings (see further Chapter 23, p. 474 ⟳).

However, a chairman is appointed. *Table A* gives the board specific power to appoint a chairman of the board and states that the chairman of the board shall preside as chairman of general meetings, though provisions are made in each case for the chairman's absence and in practice a deputy chairman is often appointed. This approach has been repeated in Article 12 of the new Model Articles for private and public limited companies – see Appendix 1 ⟳).

The chairman is normally regarded as a non-executive director even though he may be closely involved with the affairs of the company. Where he is in receipt of fees and is not employed at a salary but is concerned solely with running the board and representing the company as a figurehead, he is properly described as a non-executive director. However, he may not qualify as an 'independent' director where such independence may be required. There is in recent times a tendency to refer to non-executive directors as 'outside directors' and in many cases the chairman would not truly fit that description.

Managing director

It is usual to make one or more of the full-time directors managing director (or directors) and to give him powers relating to the management of the business which are exercisable without reference to the full board.

Before such an appointment can be made, the articles must so provide. *Table A* provides for the appointment of a member of the board to the office of managing director, and further states that he shall not be subject to retirement by rotation, but that he shall cease to be a managing director if for any other reason he ceases to be a director, e.g. where he is removed or becomes disqualified (*Southern Foundries* v *Shirlaw*, 1940, see Chapter 6 ◐). Thus, under *Table A*, a managing director must also be a director, as must the chairman of the board. *Table A* allows the directors to fix the managing director's remuneration and in Article 72 allows the board to delegate any of their powers to him, subject to a right to review these powers from time to time. Where the articles are in the form of *Table A*, then the managing director is not wholly independent of the board, as he will be if his powers are outlined expressly in the articles. In practice, *Table A* gives the board flexibility to give a managing director a specific portfolio of powers and review the situation from time to time.

The fact that Article 72 allows the board to delegate any of its powers to the managing director has given the holder of such office wide ostensible or usual authority as an agent on the assumption perhaps by the outsider that the relevant powers have been delegated. This means that the managing director may bind the company, at least in business contracts, even where he exceeds actual authority. However, the case of *Mitchell & Hobbs (UK) Ltd* v *Mill* [1996] 2 BCLC 102 decides that such ostensible or usual authority does not extend to instructing solicitors to commence an action on behalf of the company without the consent of the board.

It is worth noting that the new Model Articles for public and private limited companies do not make specific provision for the role of managing directors. However, it is arguable that the broad wording of Article 5, coupled with Article 19 for private companies or Article 23 for public companies, may permit companies to pursue a similar course of management of the company's affairs as that set down by Article 72 of *Table A* (see Appendix 1 ◐).

Appointment of directors to executive posts

Under *Table A* the directors may appoint one or more of their number to any executive office, e.g. finance director, under the company and may enter into an agreement or arrangement with any director for his employment by the company or for the provision by him of any services outside the scope of the ordinary duties of a director. Any such appointment, agreement or arrangement may be made on such terms as the directors determine, and they may remunerate any such director for his services as they think fit. Any appointment of a director to an executive office will terminate if he ceases to be a director but without prejudice to any claim for damages for breach of the contract of service between the director and the company. A director holding executive office is not subject to retirement by rotation.

Furthermore, the board may delegate to any director holding executive office such of their powers as they consider desirable to be exercised by him. Any such delegation may be subject to any conditions the directors may impose and either collaterally with, or to the exclusion of, their own powers may be revoked or altered. This extension of the power of delegation to directors holding executive office may well have increased their ostensible or usual authority (see further Chapter 8, p. 144 ◐).

Publicity in connection with directors

Certain provisions of the Companies Act 2006 are designed to make available details regarding the executive of the company which may be of assistance to members and persons dealing with it. The following should be noted:

(a) The register of director

The company must keep at its registered office a register of directors and secretaries and must notify the Registrar of any changes within 14 days of the happening thereof (CA 2006, s 162).

The contents of the register as to directors are set forth in s 163 of the CA 2006 and include:

(i)   present name and nationality;
(ii)   any former name;
(iii)   a service address which may be stated to be 'The company's registered office';
(iv)   business occupation (if any);
(v)   date of birth;
(vi)   the country or state (or part of the United Kingdom) in which he is usually resident.

The register must be open to inspection by members free and to other persons on payment of a fee. Shadow directors are included in the above provisions.

CA 2006, s 165 covers the present status with respect to the use of directors' residential address which is a noted change from the CA 1985 position.

A service address must have a physical presence which excludes a Post Office box number but does not preclude the use of the company's registered office as the service address.

(b) Trade catalogues and circulars

Every company registered on or after 23 November 1916 must state on all letter headings, on which the company's name appears, the names of all their directors *or none of them*. This does not apply to a name quoted in the text of a letter or to the signatory. Companies incorporated before 23 November 1916 do not come within these provisions and may, if they wish, show some and not all of the names of the directors.

(c) Register of directors' interests in shares and debentures

The provisions relating to this register were considered previously.

(d) Inspection of directors' service contracts

Every company must keep a copy of each of its directors' service contracts at its registered office or at its principal place of business in England, Scotland or Wales (depending on where it is registered), or the place where its register of members is kept.

If a director has no written contract, a written memorandum of the terms on which he serves must be kept instead. This means, in practice, that directors are given written contracts if they are employed (or executive) directors. There is little point in employing a director under an oral contract if it is necessary, as it is, to draft a written memorandum of its terms.

The copy or memorandum must show all changes in the terms of the contract made since it was entered into.

The company must notify the Registrar of Companies where the copies or memoranda of its directors' service contracts are kept unless they are kept at its registered office.

There is no need for a copy or memorandum to be kept if the contract has less than 12 months to run, or if it can be brought to an end by the company within that time without payment of compensation.

Members of the company may inspect such copies or memoranda without charge. If inspection is refused, the person wishing to inspect the contract may apply to the court which will make an order compelling inspection.

The intention of the above provisions is to assist members who wish to remove a director under s 168 of the CA 2006. This publicity enables members to see what the cost of removal will be.

The CA 2006 also provides that:

(i)   A director's service contract with a subsidiary (or a memorandum of it if it is not in writing) must also be open for inspection.

(ii) The *contract* of a director who works with the company or a subsidiary wholly or mainly outside the United Kingdom need not be available for inspection. In such a case there need only be available for inspection a memorandum containing:

    (a) the director's name;

    (b) the name and place of incorporation of the subsidiary (if any) with which the contract is made; and

    (c) the provisions in the contract as to its duration.

(iii) Shadow directors, i.e. persons other than professional advisers, in accordance with whose instructions directors of a company are accustomed to act, are to be treated as directors for the purposes of this section.

The secretary

The CA 2006 sets forth a statutory basis for a company secretary. Part 12 of the CA 2006 deals with company secretaries and draws a distinction between the role of the secretary in the private company and the public company. There are common provisions that are applicable to both the private and public company secretary. The status of the company secretary has been greatly diminished under the CA 2006 for the private company.

A secretary owes fiduciary duties to the company which are similar to those of a director. Thus he must not make secret profits or take secret benefits from his office and if this happens he can be required to account for them to the company as a constructive trustee (*Re Morvah Consols Tin Mining Co, McKay's Case* (1875) 2 Ch D 1).

The criminal law regards him as an organ of the company and a higher managerial agent whose fraudulent conduct can be imputed to the company in order to make it liable along with him for crimes arising out of fraud and the falsification of documents and returns.

Under CA 2006, s 270, a private company need not have a company secretary (though the new Model Articles do, nevertheless, make several references to the post of 'secretary'). Under CA 2006, s 271, a public company must have a secretary. CA 2006, s 273 sets forth the qualifications of the secretaries of public companies. A public company must keep a register of secretaries. There is no requirement that a company secretary be a natural person.

Appointment

It is usual for the secretary to be appointed by the directors who may fix his term of office and the conditions upon which he is to hold office. *Table A* confers such a power upon the board together with the power to remove him. The secretary is an employee of the company. He is regarded as such for the purpose of preferential payments in liquidation (Insolvency Act 1986, s 175 and Sch 6). The secretary is also within the CA 2006, s 1173's definition of 'officer' of a company.

Authority

The civil courts now recognise that the modern secretary is an important official who enjoys the power to contract on behalf of the company, even without authority. This is, however, confined to contracts in the administrative operations of the company, including the employment of office staff and the management of the office together with the hiring of transport (*Panorama Developments (Guildford) Ltd* v *Fidelis Furnishing Fabrics Ltd*, 1971, see Chapter 8 ❍). However, his authority is not unlimited. He cannot without authority borrow money on behalf of the company (*Re Cleadon Trust Ltd* [1939] Ch 286). He cannot without authority commence litigation on the company's behalf (*Daimler Co Ltd* v *Continental Tyre and Rubber Co Ltd* [1916] 2 AC 307). He cannot summon a general meeting himself (*Re State of Wyoming Syndicate* [1901] 2 Ch 431) nor register a transfer without the board's approval (*Chida Mines Ltd* v *Anderson* (1905) 22 TLR 27) nor may he without approval strike a name off the register (*Re Indo China Steam Navigation Co* [1917] 2 Ch 100). These are powers which are vested in the directors.

Certain duties are directly imposed upon the secretary by statute. These include the submission of certain statutory declarations, e.g. before commencing business, in order to obtain a CA 2006, s 761 certificate (see Chapter 1 ❍), and the annual return; and also as an officer, the verification of certain statements, e.g. under s 131 of the Insolvency Act 1986 in relation to the statement of affairs to be submitted to the Official Receiver in a compulsory winding-up; under ss 22 and 47 of the same Act in relation to the statement of affairs to be submitted to an administrator and administrative receiver respectively (see further Chapter 29 ❍).

Qualifications of the secretary of a public company

CA 2006, s 273 updates the requirements of a public company secretary. It is the duty of the directors of a *public company* to take reasonable steps to secure that the company secretary or each joint secretary, where appropriate, has the requisite knowledge and experience and comes within one of the following categories:

(a) He has been the secretary of a public company for at least three out of the five years immediately preceding his appointment as secretary.
(b) He is a member of either the Institute of Chartered Accountants in England and Wales, or the Institute of Chartered Accountants of Scotland, or the Association of Chartered Certified Accountants, or the Institute of Chartered Accountants of Ireland, or the Institute of Chartered Secretaries and Administrators, or the Chartered Institute of Management Accountants, or the Chartered Institute of Public Finance and Accountancy.
(c) In addition, he will be suitable if he is a barrister, or an advocate, or a solicitor who qualified in the UK. Furthermore, a person who 'by virtue of his holding or having held any other position or his being a member of any other body, appears to the directors to be capable of discharging' the duties and functions of a secretary is also acceptable.

Thus, the directors of a public company may appoint a person who does not hold any of the specified formal qualifications.

It would seem that the duty of the board in regard to the secretary's qualification is a continuing one. Thus, if the secretary, being a member of one of the professional bodies listed, was struck off, then the directors would probably have to reconsider his position.

The word 'person' in the above provisions includes a company.

Removal

Table A allows the directors to remove the secretary before his term of office has expired but, depending on the circumstances, the secretary will retain a right to sue for damages for breach of his contract, provided that this was a separate contract and not merely contained in the articles (see further Chapter 6 ⟳).

Assistant and deputy secretary: joint secretaries

Statutory recognition of these offices is given by CA 2006, s 274, the relevant part of which provides 'Anything required or authorised to be done by or to the secretary may, if the office is vacant or there is for any other reason no secretary capable of acting, be done by or to any assistant or deputy secretary'.

Special articles may delegate the power to appoint assistant or deputy secretaries to the secretary. Otherwise the appointment and removal can be effected by the board in the same way as for the secretary but there is no need to notify appointment, removal or resignation to Companies House. Companies which have joint secretaries are required to give details of them in the register of directors and secretaries and notify Companies House of any appointments and changes in particulars within 14 days of the occurrence.

The company accountant

The accountant is an officer of the company. He owes a contractual duty to the company to prepare the accounts properly and like the auditor may, in some cases, owe a duty of care to third persons who act in reliance on his skill in their preparation. Seemingly, the accountant can acknowledge a debt on behalf of the company (*Jones* v *Bellgrove Properties* [1949] 2 All ER 198).

Essay questions

1 The articles of association of a public limited company provide as follows:

   A101 'the directors shall appoint a person to hold the office of company secretary at their discretion but subject to the provison that any such appointment must be made for a period of at least five years from the date of appointment'.

   (a) Does the inclusion of A101 in the articles really mean that the directors can appoint anyone to the office of secretary?

   (b) What could a secretary do if he were appointed and then removed from his office before the expiration of the five-year term? *(The Chartered Institute of Management Accountants)*

2 'If powers of management are vested in the directors, they and they alone can exercise these powers . . .' *per* Greer LJ in *Shaw & Sons (Salford) Ltd* v *Shaw* (1935).

   Discuss the above statement in relation to the powers of the shareholders in general meeting.

   (The Institute of Chartered Accountants in England and Wales)

3 Write notes on TWO of the following:

(a) the name clause of the memorandum;
(b) the transfer of shares;
(c) variation of class rights;
(d) promoters. *(The Institute of Chartered Secretaries and Administrators)*

4 Name FOUR ways in which the facility to purchase its own shares may be useful to a company and briefly outline the safeguards provided by the legislature when using this facility.

(Kingston University)

5 Detail the contents of the memorandum of association of a public limited company and state the importance of having a registered office. *(The Institute of Company Accountants)*

Test your knowledge

Four alternative answers are given. Select ONE only. Circle the answer which you consider to be correct. Check your answers by referring back to the information given in the chapter and against the answers at the end of the text.

1 Jones is a director of Shannon Ltd which is a subsidiary of a public company. At what age will Jones have to vacate office and seek re-election at the next annual general meeting?

A No age limit B 75 C 70 D 65

2 Fred is a director of Bray Ltd and holds 500 shares in that company. His wife is also a director and holds 400 shares. He has two children – John, aged 19 and Jane, aged 15 – who hold 50 shares each. What is the maximum number of shares which Fred must disclose as his shareholding?

A 1,000 shares B 550 shares C 950 shares D 500 shares

3 The register of directors and secretaries of a company must be available to inspection by:

A Members without charge and other persons on payment of a fee.
B Members only.
C Members and other persons without charge.
D Members and other persons on payment of a charge.

4 The register of directors and secretaries contains particulars of directors and secretaries. In the case of a director these must include his:

A Usual residential or confidentiality service address.
B Usual residential and business address.
C Usual business address only.
D Usual residential address only.

5 The managing director of a company has usual or ostensible authority to bind the company by transactions he enters into on its behalf. Which of the following statements represents the limit of this authority?

A All commercial matters which relate to the running of the business.
B All activities of the company whether commercial or not.

C Such commercial activities as the company may direct in general meeting.

D Such commercial activities as the board may delegate to him.

6 Madonna was employed as a hair stylist by Manecut Ltd. She entered into an agreement not to compete with Manecut for six months after leaving the company's employment. That agreement is a reasonable restraint of trade. Madonna left and formed a company called Topcut Ltd and began to trade in hair styling 100 yards away from the Manecut branch at which she had worked. Will Manecut Ltd be able to get an injunction to prevent Madonna and Topcut Ltd from trading?

A No, since Topcut has a separate legal entity.

B No, since a company is not liable for the acts of its shareholders.

C Yes, because the Topcut company was formed as a device to cover up Madonna's trading.

D Yes, because Topcut is engaged in fraudulent trading.

The answers to test your knowledge questions appear on p. 645.

Suggested further reading

Keay, 'Company directors behaving poorly: Disciplinary options for shareholders' [2007] JBL 656.

McGlynn, 'The constitution of the company: *Mandatory statutory provisions* v *Private Agreements*' (1994) 15 *Company Lawyer* 301.

Park and Lee, 'The business judgment rule: The missing piece in the developing Korean puzzle of Korean corporate governance reform' (2003) 3(2) *Journal of Korean Law* 15.

West, 'Challenging the "Golden Goodbye"' [2009] JBL 447.

Williams, 'Disqualifying directors: A remedy worse than the disease' (2007) 7 *Journal of Corporate Law Studies* 213.

Wooldridge, 'The management board of German public companies' (2012) 33(5) 152.

Financial arrangements with, and fair dealing by, directors

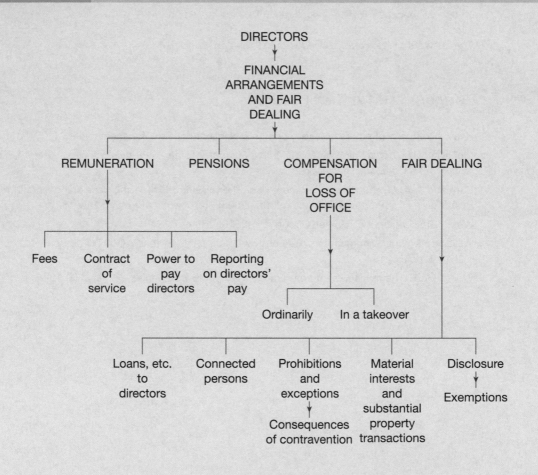

In this chapter we shall first consider those provisions of company law which relate to payments to directors, e.g. by way of remuneration and compensation for loss of office. Consideration will then be given to requirements relating to transactions with directors and persons connected with them which provide a legal safeguard against directors abusing their position in the company.

Remuneration

Fees

If a director is to receive remuneration by way of fees, the articles must expressly provide for it, and in the absence of such provision, no remuneration is payable even if the members resolve in general meeting that it shall be (*Re George Newman & Co* [1895] 1 Ch 674). Their proper procedure is to alter the articles or give the director concerned a contract so that he no longer relies on fees.

The Model Articles for Private Companies Limited by Shares, the Model Articles for Private Companies Limited by Guarantee and the Model Articles for Public Companies set forth the regulations concerning directors' remuneration in their respective Article 19 for the two kinds of private companies and Article 23 for public companies. Directors may undertake any services for the company that the directors decide. Directors are entitled to such remuneration as the directors determine: (a) for their services to the company as directors, and (b) for any other service which they undertake for the company. A director's remuneration may (a) take any form, and (b) include any arrangements in connection with the payment of a pension, allowance or gratuity, or any death, sickness or disability benefits, to or in respect of that director. Unless the directors decide otherwise, directors' remuneration accrues from day to day. Unless the directors decide otherwise, directors are not accountable to the company for any remuneration which they receive as directors or other officers or employees of the company's subsidiaries or of any other body corporate in which the company is interested.

Article 20 of the Model Articles for private companies and Article 24 for public companies governs directors' expenses in that the company may pay any reasonable expenses which the directors properly incur in connection with their attendance at: (a) meetings of directors or committees of directors, (b) general meetings, or (c) separate meetings of the holders of any class of shares or of debentures of the company, or otherwise in connection with the exercise of their powers and the discharge of their responsibilities in relation to the company.

Table A provides that the remuneration of the directors shall from time to time be determined by the company in general meeting. It should be noted that a provision in the articles is not enough; there must also be an authorising resolution by the company in general meeting (*In Re Duomatic Ltd*, 1969, see Chapter 23, p. 493 ●). A written resolution will suffice. The ability to fix the fees of directors is not within Reg 70 of *Table A* (delegation of powers to board) (see *Foster* v *Foster* [1916] 1 Ch 532). However, special articles could allow the directors to fix their own remuneration by a specific provision.

Directors are not entitled to any remuneration unless the articles so provide and if they pay themselves remuneration out of the company's funds they may be compelled to restore it, even though they believed that the payment was permissible (*Brown and Green Ltd* v *Hays*

(1920) 36 TLR 330). The directors cannot evade the rule by appointing themselves to salaried posts within the company. If they do, the appointment is valid but it appears that the director would not be entitled to the salary applicable to the post (*Kerr* v *Marine Products Ltd* (1928) 44 TLR 292). *Table A* provides for the payment of directors' expenses of office.

Where there is a provision for remuneration, it is *payable whether profits are earned or not* (*Re Lundy Granite Co* (1872) 26 LT 673), and in a winding-up the directors rank for their remuneration with ordinary creditors and are not deferred, though they are not preferential creditors, except in respect of a salary which may be payable to them as where they occupy a non-board managerial position, e.g. a company secretary, in addition to membership of the board.

Whether a director who vacates office before completing a year in office is entitled to a proportionate part of his yearly remuneration will depend upon the wording of the articles. Where *Table A* applies (replaced by the new Model Articles in newly incorporated companies), there is no problem since under *Table A* directors' remuneration accrues from day to day so that they are entitled to a proportionate part of yearly remuneration.

If the director works for the company without a contract, he can recover a sum of money for his service under a *quantum meruit* but this remedy is not available where the director has a contract which has used inappropriate words.

Craven-Ellis v *Canons Ltd* [1936] 2 KB 403

The claimant was employed as managing director by the company under a deed which provided for remuneration. The articles provided that directors must have qualification shares, and must obtain these within two months of appointment. The claimant and other directors never obtained the required number of shares so that the deed was invalid. However, the claimant had rendered services, and he now sued on a *quantum meruit* for a reasonable sum by way of remuneration.

Held – by the Court of Appeal – he succeeded on a *quantum meruit*, there being no valid contract.

Re Richmond Gate Property Co Ltd [1964] 3 All ER 936

The company was incorporated on 19 January 1962, and a resolution for a voluntary winding-up was passed on 20 September 1962, a declaration of insolvency being filed. Walker, one of the two joint managing directors, lodged proof of a salary claim which the liquidator rejected. Walker was appointed on terms that he should receive 'such remuneration as the directors may determine', and in fact no remuneration was fixed. He claimed £400 either in contract or on *quantum meruit*.

Held – by Plowman J – the liquidator was right in rejecting the proof. There was no claim under the contract which was only for 'such remuneration as the directors may determine' and none had been so determined. Moreover, the existence of an express contract in regard to remuneration automatically excluded a claim on a *quantum meruit*.

Comment

Although the decision seems harsh and represents the law, in this case there had been an understanding that until the company got on its feet, which it never did, no remuneration should be paid.

Contract of service

Remuneration by way of contract of service is governed by different rules. *Table A* provides that service contracts may be made by the board with individual directors thus ousting the general fiduciary rule that a director may not contract with his company. *Table A* allows the director concerned to be counted in the quorum at the meeting at which the company through its board decides to contract with him, though he cannot vote on his own appointment. Directors have, therefore, even under *Table A*, a largely unsupervised freedom to fix their own salaries and other terms of employment by using the contract of service approach.

The Model Articles for Private Companies Limited by Shares, the Model Articles for Private Companies Limited by Guarantee and the Model Articles for Public Companies set forth the regulations concerning conflict of interest and directors' contracts in Articles 14 (for the first two) and Article 19 (for the last). All three Model Articles specifically exempt a director's contract from being considered a conflict of interest. A director who is interested in an actual or proposed transaction or arrangement with the company is to be counted as participating in the decision-making process for quorum and voting purposes when the director's conflict of interest arises from a permitted cause such as arrangements pursuant to which benefits are made available to employees and directors or former employees and directors of the company or any of its subsidiaries which do not provide special benefits for directors or former directors.

In addition, the UK Corporate Governance Code (Financial Reporting Council, June 2010) which applies to all companies with a Premium Listing of equity shares regardless of whether they are incorporated in the UK or elsewhere also contain provisions concerning the level and make-up of directors' remuneration and the procedure for determining an individual director's remuneration. LR 9.8.8R of the Listing Rules also has information that a report to shareholders by the board must contain on directors' remuneration.

CA 2006, s 227 has introduced a definition of a director's service agreement for the purposes of Part 10 of the CA 2006 which includes contracts of service, contracts for services and letters of appointment to the office of director. While s 227(1)(a) covers contract between the director and the company to perform services for the company and s 227(1)(b) covers those services the director might make available through a third party entity such as his or her personal services company, in either case, the contract must require the director personally to perform the service or services in question. Moreover, s 227(2) ensures that the definition includes arrangements under which the director performs duties within the scope of the ordinary duties of the director, and contracts to perform duties outside the scope of the ordinary duties of a director.

CA 2006, ss 228 to 230 replaced CA 1985, s 318 which provided that directors' service agreements must be open to inspection by the shareholders, unless at the relevant time the unexpired portion of the term was less than 12 months or the company could terminate the contract within 12 months without payment of compensation. A company must keep available for inspection copies of all directors' service agreements (or, where the contracts are not in writing, memoranda of their terms) entered into by the company or one of its subsidiaries for a period of at least one year from the date of termination or from the date they expire. The copies must be retained at the company's registered office (or a place specified in regulations made under CA 2006, s 1136). This includes directors' services agreements regardless of the length of any service agreement, e.g. whether or not it is terminable within 12 months as well as those in respect of directors working overseas. On payment of a fee, shareholders have the right to inspect a director's service agreement pursuant to CA 2006, s 229 and those of shadow directors as well under CA 2006, s 230.

CA 2006, s 188 requires shareholder approval for directors' service agreements that are fixed for at least two years replacing CA 1985, s 319. However, such approval is not required by the members of a company which is either a non-UK company or a wholly owned subsidiary. CA 2006, s 189 provides that if the company agrees to a provision in contravention of s 188, the provision is void to the extent of the contravention, and the contract is deemed to contain a term entitling the company to terminate it at any time on reasonable notice.

Taxation of director's fees

As an 'officeholder' for tax purposes, a non-executive director's fees must be paid after deduction of tax and national insurance contributions at source under the HMRC's PAYE scheme. CA 2006, s 1177 provides that it is now possible for a company to agree to pay fees gross to a director, or to guarantee a fixed net value, although the obligation under PAYE remains.

Waiver of remuneration

If in, say, difficult times the directors wish to waive all or any of their remuneration, then in order to protect the company from possible claims, e.g. by personal representatives following the death of a director who had waived, the waiver should be absolute and by irrevocable deed since the company will not normally be able to show that it gave consideration for the waiver. A mere minute of the waiver following a resolution at a board meeting is not enough.

Reporting on directors' pay – listed companies

CA 2006, s 412 mandates disclosure of information about directors' benefits with special reference to remuneration. CA 2006, s 413 mandates disclosure of information about directors' benefits such as advances, credit and guarantees. Together they replace CA 1985, s 232. CA 1985, s 232 with Schedules 6 and 7A mandated disclosure of specified information on directors' remuneration in notes to a company's annual report.

CA 2006, s 412 provides that the Secretary of State may make provision by regulations requiring information to be given in notes to a company's annual accounts about directors' remuneration including: (a) gains made by directors on the exercise of share options; (b) benefits received or receivable by directors under long-term incentive schemes; (c) payments for loss of office (as defined in CA 2006, s 215); (d) benefits receivable, and contributions for the purpose of providing benefits, in respect of past services of a person as director or in any other capacity while director; and (e) consideration paid to or receivable by third parties for making available the services of a person as director or in any other capacity while director.

Chapter 6 of Part 15, CA 2006 deals with quoted companies directors' regulations. Section 420 of the CA 2006 requires the directors of a quoted company to prepare a director's remuneration report for each financial year of the company. Section 421 of the CA 2006 states that the Secretary of State may promulgate regulation as to what may be included in the report. CA 2006, s 421(3) requires that the directors and any person who was a director in the previous five years must provide information to the company to be included in the directors' remuneration report. CA 2006, s 421(4) provides that failure to do so is an offence punishable by a fine. Section 422 of the CA 2006 sets forth the requirements for approval and signing of a directors' remuneration report.

Schedule 8 of The Large and Medium-sized Companies and Groups (Accounts and Reports) Regulations 2008 (2008/410) replaced The Directors' Remuneration Report Regulations 2002 (SI 2002/1986) (the 2002 Regulations) which were introduced to improve disclosure on quoted companies' pay policies for directors and to give shareholders a say on those policies at the AGM by introducing a compulsory annual shareholders' vote on directors' remuneration packages as set out in the directors' remuneration report.

Directors' remuneration reports must contain the following information:

- The names of the persons on the company's remuneration committee who have considered matters relating to directors' remuneration and the name of any person who provided material advice or services to the committee.
- The company's policy on directors' remuneration for future financial years, including details and explanations of performance criteria for share options and long-term incentive schemes.
- A statement of how pay and employment conditions of employees of the company and of other undertakings within the same group as the company were taken into account when determining the directors' remuneration for the relevant financial year.
- A performance graph providing historic information on the company's performance against the relevant criteria showing the company's total shareholder return compared with that of a broad equity market index over a period of the five most recent financial years (or, if fewer, the number of years since the company obtained its listing).
- Details of the directors' service contracts (such as date, unexpired term, notice periods, compensation provisions, provisions on company's liability for early termination, significant awards made to former directors).
- The amount of each director's emoluments and compensation.
- Details of the directors' share options.
- Details of long-term incentive schemes.
- Details of pensions.
- The amounts of excess retirement benefits of directors and past directors.
- Details of significant compensation for former directors.
- Details of sums paid to third parties in respect of a directors' services.

Part of the directors' remuneration report is subject to audit and this is the information that is required by Part 3 of *Schedule 8 to the Large and Medium-sized Companies Regulations*, e.g. the amount of each director's emoluments and compensation in the relevant financial year; details on share options, long-term incentive schemes and pensions. CA 2006, s 498(1)(c) requires the company's auditor to investigate and confirm that the auditable part of the directors' remuneration report is in line with the company's accounting records and returns and to include any information that has been omitted and which was required to be included. CA 2006, s 422(1) requires that the board must approve the directors' remuneration report and it must be signed on behalf of the board by a director or the company secretary.

CA 2006, s 427 requires quoted companies to lay copies of its annual accounts and reports before the company in general meeting. Additionally, CA 2006, s 439 provides that a quoted company must, prior to its accounts meeting, give its members notice of an ordinary resolution approving the directors' remuneration report, although entitlement of a person to remuneration is not conditional on the resolution being passed.

CA 2006, s 439(4) requires all persons who were directors of the company immediately before the general meeting to ensure that the resolution is put to the vote of the meeting. As with other fine provisions in the CA 2006, failure to comply with s 439 makes every officer in default liable to a fine. Moreover, as with other fault schemes in the CA 2006, s 440(2) provides that if the resolution is not put to the vote of the accounts meeting, an offence has been committed by each existing director subject to a 'reasonable steps' defence provided for under CA 2006, s 440(3).

CA 2006, s 463 provides that directors will be liable to the company in relation to the whole of the directors' remuneration report (or summary financial statement derived from it) but will not have liability to anyone else relying on these reports in the absence of civil penalties or criminal liability.

CA 2006, s 430 mandates that quoted companies now must also make their annual accounts and reports available to the public on their website, until their accounts and reports for the next financial year are so made available.

Comment

Paragraph 686 of the *Explanatory Notes to CA 2006* provides that s 440 restates the requirement under s 241A of CA 1985 that a quoted company circulate a resolution approving the directors' remuneration report for the preceding financial year to its shareholders prior to its annual general meeting. However, the comment emphasises that the vote is advisory: 'as such, it does not require directors to amend contractual entitlements, nor to amend their remuneration policy, but the result of the vote will send a very strong signal to directors about the level of support among shareholders for the board's remuneration policy. In practice, directors will wish to take notice of the views of the company's members, and to respond appropriately.'

The power to pay directors

As regards the power to pay, a company may remunerate its directors where this is 'reasonably incidental to the carrying on of the company's business', *per* Bowen LJ in *Hutton v West Cork Railway* (1883) 23 Ch D 654.

Directors and the national minimum wage

It may be that while a business is being built up a director pays himself nothing while paying other employees a reasonable wage. The director may have a spouse at work or savings, or may simply get by on very little until the business is established. What is the position in regard to the payment to the director of the minimum wage (NMW)?

The NMW does not apply to company directors unless they also have contracts that make them workers. Company directors are office holders in common law and can do work and be paid for it in that capacity. This is true no matter what sort of work is done or how it is rewarded. However, company directors who also have employment contracts will need to be paid the NMW for work done under that contract.

Guidance on the NMW and directors and family members working for a family company is given in Issue 50 of the *Inland Revenue Tax Bulletin*. It is in the form of an article written by the Tax Faculty of the Institute of Chartered Accountants in England and Wales. The guidance confirms that directors and company secretaries who are paid less than the minimum wage should ensure that there is *no contract of employment with them*. That being so, the NMW is unlikely to apply. Other family members working in a family company who are not office holders may need to have their wages increased to comply with the NMW. There is, of course, the possibility that the law might *imply a contract* with a working office holder, such as a director. However, the BIS has informed the Revenue (now HMRC) that if there is no written contract of employment or other evidence of an intention to create an employer/employee relationship, it will not contest the relationship on the implied-contract ground.

Where the power to pay remuneration is expressly set out in the company's constitution, as it is in *Table A* or the Model Articles, it would seem that it can be made even though the company is not a going concern. There is no requirement that directors' remuneration should be paid only from distributable profits.

Re Halt Garage (1964) Ltd [1982] 3 All ER 1016

The entire issued share capital of the company was owned by a husband and wife, Mr and Mrs Charlesworth, who were also the only directors. During its early years the company prospered. Both husband and wife worked very hard. Later, the company got into financial problems and went into what eventually became compulsory insolvent liquidation.

The liquidator issued a summons against husband and wife under what is now s 212 of the Insolvency Act 1986. He wanted the court to decide that they were jointly and severally liable to repay to him certain sums paid to them both as directors under an express power now in Reg 82 of *Table A* which provides that: 'The directors shall be entitled to such remuneration as the company may by ordinary resolution determine [. . .]' during the period when the company had been making a loss. In regard to the husband's remuneration, the liquidator wanted repayment of that part of it which it was alleged had exceeded the market value of the work he had done. In regard to the wife, repayment was sought of the whole of her remuneration during the periods when she could not work by reason of illness. Counsel for the liquidator said quite simply that the payments to Mr and Mrs C were presents which the company had no power to make and which could not be ratified by the shareholders. Counsel for Mr and Mrs C said that the company had an express power to determine and pay directors' remuneration and that in the absence of fraud on the creditors or on minority shareholders, the amount of such remuneration was a matter for the company.

Mr Justice Oliver (as he then was) decided that:

(i) The amount of remuneration awarded to a company director was a matter of company management. Provided there has been a genuine exercise of the company's power to award remuneration and in the absence of fraud on the creditors or minority shareholders, it was not for the court to determine it or to decide to what extent it was reasonable.

(ii) Since there was no evidence, having regard to the company's turnover, that Mr C's drawings were obviously excessive or unreasonable or that they were disguised gifts of capital, the court would not enquire whether it would have been more for the benefit of the company if he had taken less. That was a matter for the company. The claim for misfeasance in regard to Mr C's drawings failed.

(iii) As regards Mrs C's drawings, the company's articles (now Reg 82 of *Table A*) gave power to award remuneration to a director on the mere assumption of office. It was not necessary that he should be active in any sense. To this extent the liquidator's claim that he should recover everything paid to Mrs C during periods of absence failed. However, where a director was not active, the court could examine the amount of the drawings. In the circumstances Mrs C was entitled to £10 per week (she had drawn £30) merely for being a director even during the period in which she was not active. Amounts drawn in excess of this were repayable to the liquidator.

Comment

It would appear from this decision, which affirms **Re Lundy Granite Co Ltd, Lewis's Case** (1872) 26 LT 673, that there is no need for directors' remuneration to come from profits. Any requirement that it must would bring some companies to a standstill and prevent those which had fallen on hard times from being brought round. The creditors' right to have the capital kept intact is subject to the consideration that directors may be paid remuneration.

Compensation for loss of office

CA 2006, ss 215–222 set out the provisions on payments for loss of office. These scenarios might include the retirement of a director from a company or other situation when an individual loses his position as director. It is important to note that the sections cover both loss of employment in connection with the management of company affairs as well as the loss of office as director including both payments made in connection with retirement and non-cash benefits which count towards compensation under CA 2006, s 215(2). Shareholder approval (CA 2006, ss 217(1) and 218(1)) is required where a company wishes to make a payment for loss of office to a director of the company or a payment for loss of office to a director of the company in connection with the transfer of the whole or any part of the undertaking or property of the company. CA 2006, s 219 mandates shareholder approval for payments for loss of office to a director in connection with a share transfer in relation to shares in the company or a subsidiary, resulting from a takeover bid. CA 2006, s 220 exempts payments made in good faith in discharge of an existing legal obligation, e.g. damages for breach of such an obligation by way of settlement or compromise of any claim arising in connection with the termination of a person's office or employment from approval by shareholders. If the company or any of its subsidiaries is making only a small payment to the director which does not exceed £200 then this payment needs no shareholder approval pursuant to CA 2006, s 221. All payments made to directors for loss of office or for anything to which a director is entitled under the service agreement are not included in the substantial property transaction regime to be discussed below whereby shareholders' approval is required.

If a payment is not disclosed and approved by shareholders where required, the director holds the money on trust for the company, and must repay the sum involved to the company (**In Re Duomatic Ltd**, 1969, see Chapter 23 ◯). Furthermore, a director is also by reason of CA 2006, s 219 under a duty to disclose payment for loss of office made in connection with a transfer of shares on an offer, for example, to take over the company. In so far as the amount a director is to receive is not disclosed and approved by the shareholders, the director concerned holds the money on trust for persons who have sold their shares as a result of the offer. The director concerned must bear the expense of distributing the compensation to them.

A payment will be treated as compensation for loss of office only if the company is under no legal obligation to make it. Thus payment of damages to a director who is dismissed in breach of his service contract, whether the damages are settled out of court or assessed by the court, does not require the approval of members. It was held in **Mercer v Heart of Midlothian** *plc* 2001 SLT 945 that payments by way of compensation are not confined to cash payments but can cover also the transfer of a company asset.

In addition, an amount which a director receives under the terms of his service contract on his resignation or removal from office in terms of severance pay is not treated as compensation for loss of office because the company is obliged by the contract to pay it. Thus, it is payable unconditionally when the resignation or removal takes place and it does not require the approval of the members in general meeting (*Taupo Totara Timber Co Ltd* v *Rowe* [1977] 3 All ER 123). The decision of the Privy Council in *Taupo* was affirmed by the Court of Session in *Lander* v *Premier Pict Petroleum Ltd* [1998] BCC 248.

Fair dealing by directors

This section is concerned with the basic rules relating to loans, quasi-loans and credit to directors, along with material interests and substantial property transactions. CA 2006, ss 197–214 (replacing CA 1985, ss 330–342) introduced major changes some of which we will explore herein. Most critically, the CA 2006 abolished the general prohibition on loans to directors and replaced it with a requirement of shareholder approval for all companies. CA 2006 also introduced provisions to ensure that public companies, and any private company associated with a public company, may only make quasi-loans to directors, loans or quasi-loans to connected persons or enter into credit transactions with directors or connected persons, if shareholder approval is obtained. CA 2006 also abolished the criminal penalty for breach of the provisions on loans, raised the maximum amounts for the exceptions for expenditure on company business, small loans, small quasi-loans and small credit transactions, abolished the maximum amounts for the money lending companies exception and allowed for affirmation of loans, quasi-loans and credit transactions entered into by the company in line with the substantial property transaction provisions. Most critical to note is that the CA 2006 made significant changes to the regime that applies to loans made by a company to its directors by replacing the general prohibition on loans to directors with a requirement for member approval.

Loans, etc. to directors

CA 2006 made significant reforms to the regulatory structure that applies to loans made by a company to its directors. It replaced the general prohibition on loans to directors with a requirement for member approval. Restrictions still exist for public companies (and private companies associated with public companies) with respect to quasi-loans and credit transactions. A description of loans, quasi-loans, credit and connected persons may be useful at this point.

Loans and quasi-loans

Basically a quasi-loan occurs when a director incurs personal expenditure but the company pays the bill. The director pays the company back later. In a loan situation the company would put the director in funds: he would buy, say, personal goods with the money, and then repay the loan. In some cases, for example, quasi-loans arise when the company buys a yearly railway season ticket for a director of the company or its holding company and he then repays the company; or a director uses a company credit card to pay for personal goods, e.g. a video, and the company pays the credit card company and then the director reimburses the company. CA 2006, s 199 defines 'quasi-loan', adapting the CA 1985, s 331(3) definition.

Credit

Examples are: (1) a furniture company sells furniture to a director of the company (or its holding company) on terms that payment be deferred for 12 months; (2) the company services a director's personal car in its workshops and the director is given time to pay; (3) Motor Sales plc sells a BMW to the wife of one of its directors under a hire-purchase agreement. The wife is a 'connected person' and in some cases transactions with such persons are controlled.

Connected persons

In broad terms, a person who is not a director of the company concerned is regarded as connected with a director of the company if the person is the spouse, child or stepchild (under 18 years of age) of that director. Also connected are companies (called associated companies) in which the director and his connected persons have together a one-fifth or more interest in the equity share capital or control one-fifth or more of the voting power.

Trustees of trusts whose beneficiaries include the director or the director's spouse or any child or stepchild (under 18) or any associated company are also connected, as is a partner of the director or a partner of the director's connected persons.

CA 2006, s 197 enables all companies to make loans to directors of the company or holding company, or give guarantees or provide security for loans made by any person to such directors, with shareholder consent. Where the director is a director of the company's holding company, the members of the holding company must also approve the transaction. No approval is required by members of a company which is not a UK-registered company or is a wholly owned subsidiary.

Relevant statutory provisions

CA 2006, s 198 prohibits a public company or a company associated with a public company, from making a quasi-loan to a director of the company or its holding company, or from giving a guarantee or providing security in connection with a quasi-loan to such a director, unless shareholder consent has been given (including consent of the members of the holding company where the director concerned is a director of the holding company). No approval is required by members of a company which is not a UK-registered company or is a wholly owned subsidiary. Under CA 2006, s 256, companies are associated if one is a subsidiary of the other or both are subsidiaries of the same body corporate.

CA 2006, s 200 considers loans or quasi-loans to persons connected with directors. A public company or company associated with a public company may not make a loan or quasi-loan to a person connected with a director of the company or its holding company or give a guarantee or provide security in connection with a loan or quasi-loan made to such a connected person, unless shareholder approval is obtained (including consent of the members of the holding company where the connected person is connected with a director of the holding company). No approval is required by members of a company which is not a UK-registered company or is a wholly owned subsidiary.

CA 2006, s 201 covers credit transactions in that it states that a public company or a company associated with a public company may not enter into credit transactions or give a guarantee or provide security in connection with a credit transaction entered into for the benefit of a director of the company or its holding company or a person connected with such a director, unless shareholder consent is obtained (including consent of the members of the holding company where the director or connected person is a director of the holding company or a person connected with such a director). No approval is required by members of a company which is not a UK-registered company or is a wholly owned subsidiary. A 'credit transaction' is defined in CA 2006, s 202.

CA 2006, s 203 requires shareholder approval in relation to related arrangements. A related arrangement is one in which another person enters into a transaction that would have required shareholder approval under CA 2006, ss 197, 198, 200 or 201 if the company had entered into the transaction and under that arrangement, that person obtains a benefit from the company or a company associated with it. Alternatively, it can be where the company arranges for the assignment to it, or assumption of rights, obligations or liabilities under a transaction that, if it had been entered by the company, would have required shareholder approval.

CA 2006, ss 197, 198, 200 and 201 mandate additional requirements that must be met with respect to related transactions in addition to obtaining shareholder consent. For instance, a written memorandum setting out the nature of the transaction or arrangement, the amount and purpose of the loan, guarantee or credit transaction and the extent of the company's liability connected with it must be made available to shareholders before they give their approval by way of ordinary or written resolution.

However, shareholder consent need not be obtained under CA 2006, ss 197, 198, 200 or 201 if the transaction falls into one of the following exceptions:

- CA 2006, s 204 applies where (i) expenditures are made on company business and (ii) the value of the transaction in question and the value of relevant transactions or arrangements, do not exceed a maximum of £50,000. Expenditures here include funds provided to directors of the company's holding company and connected persons.
- CA 2006, s 205 applies where expenditures covered by this exception are restricted to expenditure in defending criminal or civil proceedings in connection with any alleged negligence, default, breach of duty or breach of trust by the director in relation to the company or an associated company.
- CA 2006, s 206 applies where expenditures in connection with regulatory action or investigation are made. Where anything is done by a company to provide a director (or director of its holding company) with funds to meet (or avoid) expenditure incurred or to be incurred by him in defending himself in an investigation by a regulatory authority, or against action proposed to be taken by a regulatory authority, in connection with any alleged negligence, default, breach of duty or breach of trust by him in relation to the company or an associated company, this exception is triggered.
- CA 2006, s 207(1) provides an exception for minor business expenses and transactions, loans of small amounts remains and quasi-loans (not just short-term quasi-loans) in and up to £10,000.
- CA 2006, s 207(2) provides an exception for minor credit transactions up to £15,000.
- CA 2006, s 207(3) provides an exception where the credit transaction is in the ordinary course of the company's business and is not on more favourable terms than would be offered to an unconnected person of the same financial standing.
- CA 2006, s 208 covers intra-group transactions made by associated body corporates which is where one body corporate is a subsidiary of the other or both are subsidiaries of the same body corporate.

- CA 2006, s 211(7) provides that where the value of a transaction or arrangement is unascertainable, it is deemed to exceed £50,000.
- CA 2006, s 214 provides that where the transaction or arrangement is affirmed by the shareholders within a reasonable period, the transaction may no longer be avoided.

Consequences of contravention

There are consequences in civil law as follows.

A loan which contravenes the provisions set out above is voidable at the instance of the company but no one else (CA 2006, s 213). In consequence, the company will be able to recover the funds from those into whose hands they have passed and there would appear to be no limit in time for avoiding the transaction. However, there are exceptions where:

- it is no longer possible to make restitution, as where the loan has been spent on a cruise;
- the company has been indemnified, e.g. by the borrowing director;
- avoidance of the loan would affect rights which were acquired in good faith and for value and without actual notice by a person other than the person for whom the loan was made. This is the usual protection for third parties and would, for example, cover the shipping company which had provided the cruise referred to above so that the loan would not be recovered from such a company.

It appears from case law that the existence of the above-mentioned tracing of funds remedies depends upon whether or not the company has actually avoided the contract of loan.

Ciro Citterio Menswear plc v *Thakrar* [2002] 2 All ER 717

In this case the High Court ruled that an illegal loan to a director which had been used to purchase a house could not be recovered by the company's administrator by an order for a sale of the property to extract the amount of the loan from the proceeds. At the time the property was purchased the company had not rescinded the loan so that the director was still the owner of the loan. Therefore no tracing remedy was available.

Comment

The administrator presumably did not rate highly his chances of getting repayment from the director and went instead for a tracing remedy into the property purchased with the loan. It would seem that the tracing remedy could be used if the loan was used to buy the property *after* the company had provided evidence, e.g. a board resolution that it had rescinded the loan.

In addition, whether or not the transaction has been rescinded, the director who is a party to it is liable to account to the company for any gain made from the loan and to indemnify the company against any loss or damage it has suffered which has not been put right by rescinding the loan. This liability is extended also to any other director who authorised the transaction, though such a person will not be liable if he can show that he did not know the relevant circumstances constituting the contravention at the time the transaction was made.

As an example of the above-mentioned civil remedies, the Court of Appeal has decided that a company is entitled under CA 1985 to demand from a director immediate repayment of an illegal loan made to the director, regardless of any other terms of the contract of loan which may provide differently.

Tait Consibee (Oxford) Ltd v Tait [1997] 2 BCLC 349

On 1 February 1994 the claimant company made a loan of £10,000 to the defendant, who was at that time a director of the company. In July 1994 the defendant's employment terminated and in October 1994 he ceased to be a director. By a letter dated 9 January 1995 the company demanded repayment of the loan. The defendant admitted that he received that letter of demand. Since the loan was not repaid, the company commenced an action for its recovery. The defendant said that it was agreed that the loan was to be repaid from dividends declared by the company, and since no dividends had been declared the loan was not repayable, at least at the relevant point in time.

The terms of the loan agreement, which was not recorded in writing, were disputed by the company. However, the company also contended in support of its claim that the loan was recoverable anyway, regardless of the terms of any agreement (in this case, repayment from dividends), since the loan was illegal under s 330 and therefore recoverable under s 341. The Court of Appeal accepted the company's contention. The only section that might have applied to make the loan valid was s 334 which exempts loans of small amounts but applies only to loans which do not exceed £5,000. The loan in this case, being £10,000, was prohibited and recoverable. The decision of the lower court which gave the company judgment for that sum plus interest was affirmed by the Court of Appeal.

Shadow directors

By reason of CA 2006, s 223, shadow directors are included in both the civil and criminal sanctions.

Material interests

Material interests of directors and their connected persons must also be disclosed in a note to the accounts. A material interest could be, for example, a contract to build a new office block which the company had entered into with a building firm run by a director, or by the spouse of a director. It might also be a loan to the brother of a director. A brother is not a connected person but the loan might be a material interest.

The treatment of directors' loan accounts

The materials set out above may have to be applied in regard to a not uncommon feature of private companies: the directors' loan accounts. Two situations may arise as follows.

(a) The loan account is overdrawn

In this case the directors owe money to the company and problems may arise either during the company's lifetime, as on a director's resignation, and even more likely on its insolvent liquidation. The directors may have made drawings against the company's funds that have been allocated to a loan account. Consideration needs to be given to the following matters:

● Are the drawings to be regarded as loans to directors? If so, then there are issues to be addressed in terms of compliance with company law requirements. If the drawings are unlawful loans the company or a liquidator can set them aside and require repayment to the company by the director.
● Are the drawings dividends received by the director in regard to a shareholding? If so, the distribution rules in company law must be addressed. Drawings may sometimes be justified on the basis that they are made in expectation of dividends though this is a risky

strategy if the dividends do not materialise and it is a pointless strategy if the company was not in a position to pay dividends.

- Are the drawings remuneration? If they are, as where the director has carried out work or given services to the company, then the drawings are perfectly permissible given that the work or services have been rendered, though issues of taxation must be addressed.
- Are the drawings a misappropriation of corporate assets? If so, the company and its liquidator can seek recovery of the sums paid.

(b) The loan account is in credit

In this case the directors have lent money to the company which has not repaid it fully or at all. The problems that arise here are in connection with impending insolvency where the directors have arranged for the repayment of the loans and have been required to repay the sums to the company upon commencement of its liquidation as preferences. Since the directors are connected persons for the purposes of the repayment any repayment that is made within two years immediately prior to the commencement of winding-up may well amount to a preference that can be challenged by the liquidator.

The case law

There is instructive case law on the above matters, as follows.

First Global Media Group Ltd v *Larkin* [2003] All ER (D) 293 (Nov)

In this case a director tried to establish his drawings as remuneration but this was not acceptable to the court because there was a directors' agreement that in order to minimise tax no remuneration would be paid to directors. A further attempt to establish the drawings as dividends failed since, at the time the sums were drawn, the company was incurring losses and there were no distributable profits. The drawings were repayable to the liquidator.

Currencies Direct Ltd v *Ellis* [2003] 2 BCLC 482

Here a director was successful in establishing drawings as remuneration. He had done work and rendered services to the company and the Court of Appeal was satisfied that the drawings were the consideration. The court also stated that remuneration could take different forms and need not be in the nature of a regular wage or salary cheque or credit. Remuneration might consist in payment of the consideration to a third party in discharge of the debts of the person who had done or was to do the work or render services. It could take the form of commissions, fees or bonuses. It could be a lump sum payment or be spread over a period and the payment need not be backed by a formal contract. It might arise from the company's obligation to pay reasonable remuneration under an implied contract. The company could not recover the sums paid. They were not loans.

Re Conegrade Ltd [2003] BPIR 358

In this case the directors' loan account was in credit to the extent of some £65,000. At a time when the company was insolvent the directors purchased an asset from the company at the market value of £125,000. The consideration was a payment by the directors of £60,000 to the company and the cancellation of the credit balance on the loan account. The company went into insolvent liquidation and the liquidators challenged the transaction as a preference. The High Court ruled that it was. The directors were put in a better position in terms of their loans to the company of £65,000 than they would have been if they had been reduced to proving for that sum as unsecured creditors in the liquidation. The directors were ordered to pay the sum of £65,000 to the company. They would then have to prove as unsecured creditors in the liquidation for that sum.

Advice to directors

The following are some major points for consideration:

- Directors who have lent money to the company through a loan account should be apprised of the legal rules regarding preference. They should not repay any amounts due to them in the two years immediately prior to an insolvency.
- With regard to drawings made by directors it is important to ensure:
  (a) that the date and amount of the drawings are properly documented; and
  (b) that the basis on which they have been made is clearly stated.

Directors' contracts with the company

Under CA 2006, s 182 which replaces CA 1985, s 317, a director must declare the nature and any direct or indirect interest that he has in any transaction or arrangement entered into by the company. In *Guinness* v *Saunders* [1990] 1 All ER 652 the House of Lords ruled that disclosure had to be made at a full meeting of the board and not at a meeting of a committee of the board.

If the director is a member of another concern which is doing business with the company, he may give a general notice of interest, either orally to the board, or in writing to the company, and this will cover a series of contracts made with the other concern. If a director fails to make proper disclosure of his interest, he is liable to a fine.

The provisions are extended to cover any transaction or arrangement of the type set out under the loans, quasi-loans and credit heading and it should be noted that the interest of a connected person, unless the connected person is also a director, is treated for these purposes as an interest of the director. The above rules are extended to shadow directors.

Although the major sanction is a default fine, the company can in any case rescind the contract made with the director because of the fiduciary duty that exists, but it must be possible to restore the status quo (*per* Lord Denning MR in *Hely-Hutchinson* v *Brayhead* [1968] 1 QB 549). The articles may provide otherwise or the members in general meeting may, by ordinary resolution, waive the company's rights to rescind, but there can be no waiver by the board.

In this regard, *Craven Textile Engineers Ltd* v *Batley Football Club Ltd*, Transcript: B2 99/1127, CA is of interest. A director of the claimant company was also a former director of the football club. The claimant did work for and supplied goods to the football club during the period of the dual directorship. The football club purported to avoid the contract because it appeared that the director concerned had not declared his interest in the contracts to the companies. The Court of Appeal noted that s 317 does not deal with the civil consequences of a breach but at common law the contracts could be avoided by the company. However, it must be possible to restore the parties to their pre-contractual positions before this could be done. In this case that was not possible as the goods and services had already been supplied. The claimant was therefore entitled to payment of the invoices.

In *Re Neptune (Vehicle Washing Equipment) Ltd* (1995) *The Times*, 2 March, the High Court had to decide whether a sole director must hold a board meeting and formally declare his interest in a contract with the company and record it in the minutes. The High Court said he must and if not the company could rescind the contract. So, in effect, s 317 applies in this situation even though the director is disclosing what he already knows to himself.

It should also be noted that under *Table A* a director who has disclosed an interest cannot count towards the quorum of the board on the item in which he is interested nor vote upon it. These provisions of *Table A* should be amended or excluded where a private company intends to operate through a sole director since otherwise he cannot approve any transaction in which he is interested.

In addition, in the absence of disclosure, a director who has received a payment under an undisclosed contract with his company is regarded as holding that payment in the capacity of a constructive trustee for the company and is bound to repay the sum received although he may have a claim for compensation for any services actually rendered under the undisclosed contract (*Guinness* v *Saunders* [1990] 1 All ER 652).

Substantial property transactions

Under CA 2006, ss 190–196, in both public and private companies, the approval of the members by ordinary (or written) resolution of any contract to transfer to, or receive from, a director (or connected person) a non-cash asset, e.g. land, exceeding £100,000 or exceeding 10 per cent of the company's net assets, whichever is the lowest, is required. The provision does not apply, however, to non-cash assets of less than £5,000 in value.

Thus a company whose assets less its liabilities amounted to £200,000 would have to comply with this provision in respect of a transaction with a director or connected person for a non-cash asset worth more than £20,000.

The provisions are designed to prevent directors (at least without member approval) from buying assets from the company at less than their true value or transferring their own property to the company at more than market value. At least if they are to do this the members must be aware of it and approve by ordinary (or written) resolution. If the above provisions are infringed the contract is voidable by the company but not by the director.

The asset would not require valuation by an independent accountant (see Chapter 14 ◐) unless it was the acquisition of a non-cash asset by the company from a director; the company was a plc; and the consideration to the director was shares in the company.

Board minutes

Disclosure of material transactions is the responsibility of the director concerned. Such matters must be disclosed to the board of directors and recorded in board minutes. Inspection of directors' minute books should identify such transactions and any discussion that took place regarding materiality. CA 2006, s 177 requires directors to declare their interests in transactions or arrangements which are proposed but have not yet been entered into by the company. CA 2006, s 182 covers declaration of interests in relation to existing transactions or arrangements that the company has already entered into. The declaration must be of both the nature and extent of the director's direct or indirect interest. In other words, a further declaration must be made if an earlier declaration proves to be or becomes inaccurate or incomplete.

There is no need to make a declaration of interest if the interest cannot reasonably be regarded as likely to give rise to a conflict of interest. Similarly, there is also no need to disclose anything the other directors already know about or ought reasonably to have known. A declaration of an interest in an existing transaction or arrangement must be made as soon as reasonably practicable. In the last resort, if materiality cannot be agreed between the auditor and the directors, legal advice must be sought.

Essay questions

1 Dives is chairman and controlling shareholder of Cashloans plc. You are company secretary. Dives informs you he wishes to buy a seaside cottage for himself and his wife and that, to finance the transaction, he will propose to the next board meeting that the company lend him £60,000 for 10 years at 9 per cent per annum on a mortgage of the property. He asks for your comments.
    Advise Dives and the board.   *(The Institute of Company Accountants)*

2 The Companies Act 2006 contains provisions regulating 'substantial property transactions' between a company and any of its directors. What are 'substantial property transactions' and what procedure is required to approve such transactions?
                        (The Institute of Chartered Accountants in England and Wales)

3 How does s 994 of the Companies Act 2006 provide an alternative remedy to a winding-up order for the minority shareholders in a company?
                        (The Chartered Institute of Management Accountants)

4 In what circumstances may a shareholder bring a derivative action on behalf of his company? What procedure is available to deal with the procedural problems presented by such actions?
                        (The Institute of Chartered Secretaries and Administrators)

Test your knowledge

Four alternative answers are given. Select ONE only. Circle the answer which you consider to be correct. Check your answers by referring back to the information given in the chapter and against the answers at the end of the text.

1 Test Ltd is reducing the size of the board and Fred is to leave it. Test Ltd wishes to pay Fred compensation for loss of office. This payment must be approved by:

    A The Inland Revenue.
    B The shareholders by ordinary or written resolution.
    C The board of directors.
    D The creditors.

2 Tees Ltd is engaged in the catering business. It has lent John, a director, £6,000 interest free, to buy a car. It has also lent Jane, another director, £10,000 at 8 per cent per annum interest to assist in the purchase of her place of residence. What is the legal status of the loans?

    A The loans are valid.
    B The loan to Jane is valid because the company has charged interest. The loan to John is voidable because it is interest free.

c The loan to John is void since a director cannot borrow from his company. The loan to Jane is valid because it is for house purchase on commercial terms.

D Both loans are illegal because each of them exceeds £5,000.

3 Windermere Ltd has entered into a transaction with one of its directors to purchase from him freehold land exceeding £100,000 in value. Given that the transaction has not been approved by the members it is:

A Void.

B Valid.

c Voidable at the instance of the company.

D Voidable at the instance of the director.

4 Coniston Ltd holds board meetings once a month, on the first day of the month. At the August meeting the board discussed a contract with Ullswater Ltd. On 15 August John, a director of Coniston, bought shares in Ullswater. The contract was eventually signed between Coniston and Ullswater on 12 October. When should John declare his interest?

A On 12 October   B On 1 October   c On 1 September   D On 15 August

5 Manfred is a director of Thames Bank plc. He has borrowed £40,000 under the bank's directors' and employees' cheap loans scheme to carry out repairs to his main residence. His son, Adolf, who is aged 30 and is employed by the bank, has also got a loan under the scheme and his wife has borrowed money at normal commercial rates to set up a hairdressing salon. In order to calculate whether the CA 2006 borrowing limits have been exceeded, which do you include?

A Manfred's loan only.

B Manfred's loan plus Adolf's.

c Manfred's loan plus that of his wife.

D All three loans.

Answers to test your knowledge questions appear on p. 645.

21 The duties of directors

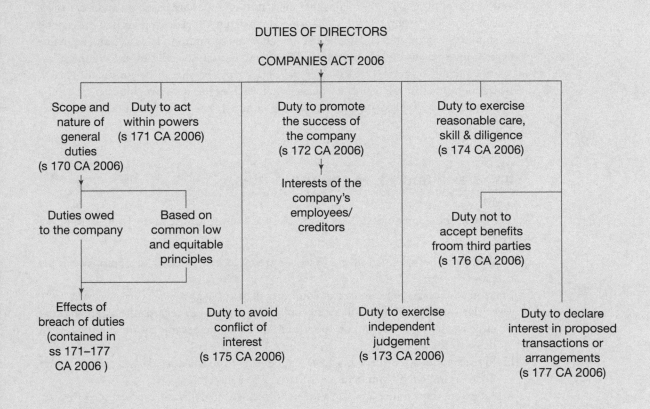

DUTIES OF DIRECTORS
↓
COMPANIES ACT 2006
↓

Scope and nature of general duties (s 170 CA 2006)

Duty to act within powers (s 171 CA 2006)

Duty to promote the success of the company (s 172 CA 2006)
↓

Duty to exercise reasonable care, skill & diligence (s 174 CA 2006)

Duties owed to the company

Based on common low and equitable principles

Interests of the company's employees/ creditors

Duty not to accept benefits froom third parties (s 176 CA 2006)

Effects of breach of duties (contained in ss 171–177 CA 2006)

Duty to avoid conflict of interest (s 175 CA 2006)

Duty to exercise independent judgement (s 173 CA 2006)

Duty to declare interest in proposed transactions or arrangements (s 177 CA 2006)

The CA 2006 codifies the general duties of directors

In this chapter, we shall consider the duties which directors owe to the company, to employees, to individual shareholders and to outsiders. The CA 2006 has taken a major step forward to codify the general duties of directors. For instance, directors' fiduciary and common law duties have now been partly codified and governed by the CA 2006. In twelve sections applying to directors, Chapter 2 of Part 10 of the CA 2006 sets out their general duties. These general duties now are a code of conduct for how directors must behave. They are not however all the duties that directors owe his or her company as a number are found elsewhere in the CA 2006 and in other statutes. Other duties are still not codified although commonly accepted.

Section 170 of the CA 2006 explains that the statutory duties are based on and have effect in place of certain common law rules and principles of equity. It also explains that the general duties should be interpreted and applied in the same way as common law rules and equitable principle. Moreover, when interpreting and applying the statutory duties, the common law rules and equitable principles that the general duties replaced should be consulted. Finally, s 170 also identifies that the civil consequences of breach of the statutory duties are the same as those that would apply if the corresponding common law rule or equitable principles were applied.

Scope and nature of general duties

Section 170 of the Companies Act 2006 provides the context for the newly codified duties of directors.

1 The general duties specified in ss 171 to 177 are owed by a director of a company to the company.
2 A person who ceases to be a director continues to be subject:
   (a) to the duty in s 175 (duty to avoid conflicts of interest) as regards the exploitation of any property, information or opportunity of which he became aware at a time when he was a director, and
   (b) to the duty in s 176 (duty not to accept benefits from third parties) as regards things done or omitted by him before he ceased to be a director.
   To that extent those duties apply to a former director as to a director, subject to any necessary adaptations.
3 The general duties are based on certain common law rules and equitable principles as they apply in relation to directors and have effect in place of those rules and principles as regards the duties owed to a company by a director.
4 The general duties shall be interpreted and applied in the same way as common law rules or equitable principles, and regard shall be had to the corresponding common law rules and equitable principles in interpreting and applying the general duties.
5 The general duties apply to shadow directors where, and to the extent that, the corresponding common law rules or equitable principles so apply.

It is clear from s 170(1) that these general duties are owed by a director to the company. Thus, only the company or members acting on behalf of the company (derivative claims such as those contained in Part 11 of the CA 2006) can enforce them. The duties apply to directors of the company, *de facto* directors and, in some cases, to former directors.

It is important to note a number of key issues at this stage. First of all, s 170(3) emphasises the fact that these general duties are based on common law rules and equitable principles and, as such, should be interpreted and applied in the same way as the previous rules. This is not only significant in terms of using the case law so as to support the implementation of these codified duties of directors but also suggests a rather smoother transition from one era to another (i.e. common law to statute) in this area. Secondly, when considering the consequences of any breach of these statutory duties, or the way in which they are to be enforced, s 187 provides:

1 The consequences of breach (or threatened breach) of ss 171–177 are the same as would apply if the corresponding common law rule or equitable principle applied.
2 The duties in those sections (with the exception of s 174 (duty to exercise reasonable care, skill and diligence)) are, accordingly, enforceable in the same way as any other fiduciary duty owed to a company by its directors.

Consequently, in order to appreciate fully the general duties embodied in the Companies Act 2006, as well as to gain an insight into how the courts are likely to interpret and subsequently apply these statutory legal obligations, it is necessary to review the fiduciary duties which, until recently, bound directors. In this regard, a review of the common law duties which have led to the development of Chapter 2 of Part 10 of the Companies Act 2006 will be undertaken alongside the statutory duties of directors.

Duty to act within powers

The statutory duty

Section 171 of the Companies Act 2006 states:

A director of a company must:

(a) act in accordance with the company's constitution, and
(b) only exercise powers for the purposes for which they are conferred.

The related common law and equitable principles

One of the main considerations to be borne in mind is that directors use their powers for the proper purpose (i.e. for the benefit of the company and not to further their own interests). Consideration has already been given to this rule which is illustrated by the decisions in the *Rolled Steel* case (see Chapter 8, p. 143 ◐), *Clemens* v *Clemens* (see Chapter 17, p. 307 ◐) and *Galloway* v *Hallé Concerts Society* (see Chapter 19, p. 369 ◐) among others.

A further example of improper use of power by directors is to be found in situations where directors have issued new shares to persons who were their nominees, e.g. the company's pension trustees, not because the company needed more capital (the proper purpose of a company's directors issuing shares) but to defeat a genuine takeover bid by another company. The nominees they knew would not accept the bid so that the bidder would not get an adequate majority of shares and so not proceed with the bid, thus keeping the directors in power (see *Hogg* v *Cramphorn* [1966] 3 All ER 420). There is, of course, statutory protection in this area in that the directors require the authority of the members to allot shares, and there are also pre-emption rights given to existing shareholders unless the shareholders have disapplied them. Nevertheless, cases such as *Hogg* have a continuing relevance since in private companies these rights may be disapplied by the articles. In such a situation, the case law would have to be used to render the allotment of shares to the nominees invalid. A further 'poison pill' device was before the High Court in the following case.

Criterion Properties plc v Stratford UK Properties LLC [2002] 2 BCLC 151

The managing director of the claimant company made an agreement with a substantial shareholder that required the company to buy out the shareholder at a high price should there be a change of control or composition of the board of directors of the company. The managing director was later removed from office and the company asked the court to set aside the agreement because it was entered into for an improper purpose. The High Court ruled that the agreement, which was intended to put off an unwelcome bidder, in a predatory takeover, had been made for an improper purpose. The damage that would be caused to the company by making the substantial shareholder buy-out would be greater than any harm likely to be inflicted on it by an acquisition. The agreement was not a proper exercise of a director's powers and could not be enforced against the company.

Comment

A 'poison pill' is North American jargon for a legal device of any form put in place by the management of a company that feels vulnerable to predatory acquisition, designed as a defence mechanism to eliminate or reduce that risk. Other expressions such as 'shark repellent' are also used.

Therefore, a director has a duty to exercise the company's powers for the purposes for which they were allocated to him and the Board of Directors (see discussion in Chapter 6 ●). This is reinforced by Turner LJ's statement in *Re Cameron's Coalbrook Steam Coal, and Swansea and Kougher Railway Co, Bennett's Case* (1854) 5 De GM & G 284:

> . . . in the exercise of the powers given to them . . . they must, as I conceive, keep within the proper limits. Powers given to them for one purpose cannot, in my opinion, be used by them for another and different purpose. To permit such proceedings on the part of directors of companies would be to sanction not the use but the abuse of their powers. It would be to give effect and validity to an illegal exercise of a legal power.

The question naturally arises as to where the limits of a director's powers end and when an individual starts to overstep what is deemed to be an acceptable use of their powers. In many instances, a common sense approach will suffice as a company's articles should outline the various powers/day-to-day decision-making activities which have been given to the board of directors. However, this will not always be the case and, in those instances, it will be necessary to look at the specific facts of the case and for the court to decide if a power has been exercised for a proper or improper purpose and as to whether the director has acted in accordance with the company's constitution (*Howard Smith Ltd v Ampol Petroleum Ltd* [1974] AC 821).

Howard Smith Ltd v Ampol Petroleum Ltd [1974] AC 821

Two companies, A and B, held 55 per cent of the issued shares of company M, which required more capital. A made an offer for all the issued shares of M, and another company, H, announced an intention to make a higher offer for those shares. M's directors considered A's offer too low and decided to recommend that the offer be rejected. A and B then stated that they intended to act jointly in the future operations of M and would reject any offer for their shares. H then applied to M for an allotment of 4.5 million ordinary shares; M's directors decided by a majority to make the allotment and immediately issued the shares. The effect of that issue was that M had much needed capital; A and B's shareholding was reduced to 36.6 per cent of the issued shares and H was in a position to make an effective takeover offer. A challenged the validity of the issue of the shares to H and sought an order in the Supreme Court for the rectification of the share register by the removal of H as a member of M in respect of the allotted shares. M's directors contended that the primary reason for the issue of the shares to H was to obtain more capital. On Appeal Lord Wilberforce stated:

> To define in advance exact limits beyond which directors must not pass is, in their Lordships' view, impossible. This clearly cannot be done by enumeration, since the variety of situations facing directors of different types of company in different situations cannot be anticipated. No more, in their Lordships' view, can this be done by the use of a phrase – such as 'bona fide in the interest of the company as a whole', or 'for some corporate purpose'. Such phrases, if they do anything more than restate the general principle applicable to fiduciary powers, at best serve, negatively, to exclude from the area of validity cases where the directors are acting sectionally, or partially: i.e. improperly favouring one section of the shareholders against another . . .
>
> In their Lordships' opinion it is necessary to start with a consideration of the power whose exercise is in question, in this case a power to issue shares. Having ascertained, on a fair view, the nature of this power, and having defined as can best be done in the light of modern conditions the, or some, limits within which it may be exercised, it is then necessary for the court, if a particular exercise of it is challenged, to examine the substantial purpose for which it was exercised, and to reach a conclusion whether that purpose was proper or not in doing so it will necessarily give credit to the bona fide opinion of the directors, if such is found to exist, and will respect their judgment as to matters of management; having done this, the ultimate conclusion has to be as to the side of a fairly broad line on which the case falls.

Held – dismissing the appeal, that, although the directors had acted honestly and had power to make the allotment, to alter a majority shareholding was to interfere with that element of the company's constitution which was separate from and set against the directors' powers and, accordingly, it was unconstitutional for the directors to use their fiduciary powers over the shares in the company for the purpose of destroying an existing majority or creating a new majority; and that, since the directors' primary object for the allotment of shares was to alter the majority share-holding, the directors had improperly exercised their powers and the allotment was invalid.

In addition, the state of mind of the directors at the time that an alleged abuse or misuse of powers took place is an important consideration for the courts. In the case of *Hogg* v *Cramphorn* [1966] 3 All ER 420, it was acknowledged by the courts that while Colonel Cramphorn had exceeded the true purpose for which the power to allot shares had been conveyed to the company's directors, his intentions were, nevertheless, bona fide in what he considered to be the best interest of the company. However, there may be instances where the rationale behind a director's improper use of a power may be multi-faceted and, in such instances, the courts will seek to identify the 'dominant purpose behind the act'. This issue was considered by Viscount Finlay in *Hindle* v *John Cotton Ltd* (1919) 56 SLR 625, when he noted:

> Where the question is one of abuse of powers, the state of mind of those who acted, and the motives on which they acted, are all important, and you may go into the question of what their intention was, collecting from the surrounding circumstances all the materials which genuinely throw light upon that question of the state of mind of the directors so as to show whether they were honestly acting in discharge of their powers in the interests of the company or were acting from some by-motive, possibly of personal advantage, or for any other reason.

This is reinforced by Lord Wilberforce's observation in *Howard Smith Ltd* v *Ampol Petroleum Ltd* [1974] AC 821 (see above):

> When a dispute arises whether directors of a company made a particular decision for one purpose or for another, or whether, there being more than one purpose, one or another purpose was the substantial or primary purpose, the court, in their Lordship's opinion, is entitled to look at the situation objectively in order to estimate how critical or pressing, or substantial or, *per contra*, insubstantial an alleged requirement may have been. If it finds that a particular requirement, though real, was not urgent, or critical, at the relevant time, it may have reason to doubt, or discount, the assertions of individuals that they acted solely in order to deal with it, particularly when the action they took was unusual or even extreme.

Duty to promote the success of the company

The statutory duty

Section 172 of the Companies Act 2006 provides that:

(1) A director of a company must act in the way he considers, in good faith, would be most likely to promote the success of the company for the benefit of its members as a whole, and in doing so have regard (among other matters) to:
   (a) the likely consequences of any decision in the long term,
   (b) the interests of the company's employees,
   (c) the need to foster the company's business relationships with suppliers, customers and others,
   (d) the impact of the company's operations on the community and the environment,
   (e) the desirability of the company maintaining a reputation for high standards of business conduct, and
   (f) the need to act fairly as between members of the company.
(2) Where or to the extent that the purposes of the company consist of or include purposes other than the benefit of its members, subsection (1) has effect as if the reference to promoting the success of the company for the benefit of its members were to achieving those purposes.
(3) The duty imposed by this section has effect subject to any enactment or rule of law requiring directors, in certain circumstances, to consider or act in the interests of creditors of the company.

The decision as to what will promote success and what is success is one for the director's good faith judgement and will be discussed further below in relation to the case law in the area. However, a look at the director's motive and intent will be essential for divining such judgement on a director's part. It is also worth noting that the 'six factors' set forth in s 172 must find their way into every decision a director makes on behalf of a company and they are only subservient to the duty of directors to promote the success of the company.

The related common law and equitable principles

In many respects, the case law already discussed in relation to a director's duty to act in accordance with the company's constitution and to use the powers available to him for their proper purposes overlaps with this statutory duty. However, it is worth considering some of the case law which relates to the decision-making process and, more importantly, whether the actions of a director will be second-guessed by a court which has the benefit of hindsight.

In *Re Smith and Fawcett Ltd* [1942] Ch 304, Lord Greene MR observed that directors must act 'bona fide in what they consider – not what a court may consider – is in the interests of the company, and not for any collateral purpose'. Consequently, if this approach is applied to s 172 then a director is expected to behave in a fashion that he himself honestly considers will be most likely to promote the success of the company. The court will not intervene so as to impose what it considers, with the benefit of hindsight and expert evidence, to be the appropriate actions. As Jonathan Parker J observed in *Regentcrest Plc v Cohen* [2001] 2 BCLC 80:

> The question is not whether, viewed objectively by the court, the particular act or omission which is challenged was in fact in the interests of the company; still less is the question whether the court, had it been in the position of the director at the relevant time, might have acted differently. Rather the question is whether the director honestly believed that his act or omission was in the interests of the company. The issue is as to the director's state of mind. No doubt, where it is clear that the act or omission under challenge resulted in substantial detriment to the company, the director will have a harder task persuading the court that he honestly believed it to be in the company's interest; but that does not detract from the subjective nature of the test.

Turning to the concept of 'success of the company', then s 172 includes an important phrase which has, for some time, been the subject of debate; 'for the benefit of its members as a whole'. In other words, the actions of a company's directors must take account of not only the shareholders but also the company as a separate legal entity. This latter aspect, though relatively easy to understand, is nevertheless quite challenging to analyse, especially in terms of posing the question '*What is best for the company as a separate legal entity*?' This in turn usually leads to a consideration of the interests of current and future shareholders, before being extended so as to consider other stakeholders in the company. Section 172 addresses this issue by focusing upon the 'members as a whole' and then, separately, as an additional list of considerations, itemises the company's stakeholders.

The result is that with this new statutory duty, a court may, at least initially, follow the reasoning set out by Goulding J in *Mutual Life Insurance Co of New York v Rank Organisation Ltd* [1985] BCLC 11, in that the powers outlined in a company's constitution to its directors are subject to two implied considerations: 'First, the time-honoured rule that the director's powers are to be exercised in good faith in the interests of the company, and secondly, that they must be exercised fairly between different shareholders.'

However, while directors do not, in general, owe any contractual or fiduciary duties directly to members of their company (*Percival v Wright*, 1902, see below), the situation becomes slightly more complex in situations involving a takeover situation. First of all, there appears to be a duty to shareholders in regard to the advice, if any, given by directors to those shareholders in regard to the acquisition or rejection of a takeover bid. Company legislation does not deal with this. However, in *Gething v Kilner* [1972] 1 All ER 1166, it was said that in a takeover the directors of the 'victim' company owe a duty to their shareholders to be honest and not to mislead as by suppressing, for instance, professional advice recommending rejection, and that the court might grant an injunction where this had happened, to prevent the bid going ahead. Where there are competing offers then the directors are not under a positive duty to recommend and facilitate the acceptance of the highest offer (*Dawson International plc v Coats Patons plc* [1988] SLT 854).

Percival v *Wright* [1902] 2 Ch 421

The claimant wished to sell shares in the company and wrote to the secretary asking if he knew of anyone willing to buy. After negotiations, the chairman of the board of directors arranged the purchase of 253 shares, 85 for himself and 84 for each of his fellow directors at a price based on the claimant's valuation of £12 10s per share. The transfers were approved by the board and the transactions completed. The claimant subsequently discovered that prior to and during the negotiations for the sale, a Mr Holden was also negotiating with the board for the purchase of the company for resale to a new company, and was offering various prices for shares, all of which exceeded £12 10s per share. No firm offer was ever made, and the negotiations ultimately proved abortive, and the court was not satisfied that the board ever intended to sell. The claimant brought this action against the directors asking for the sale of his shares to be set aside for non-disclosure.

Held – by Swinfen Eady J – the directors are not trustees for the individual shareholders and may purchase their shares without disclosing pending negotiations for the sale of the company. A contrary view would mean that they could not buy or sell shares without disclosing negotiations, a premature disclosure of which might well be against the best interests of the company. There was no unfair dealing since the shareholders in fact approached the directors and named their own price.

Comment

(i) The Criminal Justice Act 1993 would not seem to affect this decision since it does not apply its insider dealing provisions to private dealings in shares but only to dealings on a recognised stock exchange. In any case, the Act gives no civil claim but merely contains criminal sanctions.

(ii) It should not be assumed that an obligation of trust and good faith may not arise if the circumstances require it. In *Platt* v *Platt* [1999] 2 BCLC 745 the High Court ruled that although the relationship between a company director and the shareholders of the company does not of itself give rise to fiduciary duties, special circumstances may require the imposition of such a duty. Three brothers – Colin, Denis and Keith Platt – were shareholders in an Essex company holding a BMW dealership. Keith ran the business and held ordinary shares. Colin and Dennis, the claimants, did not work in the business and held preference shares. The company did badly in the recession of the early 1990s. By 1992 Keith was the only brother in touch with BMW and the only director of the company. Keith misled his brothers by telling them that BMW was about to withdraw the franchise and was urging him to sell. As a result, Colin and Denis transferred their preference shares to Keith for £1. These transfers were said to be necessary to enable the business to be sold. Subsequently profitable trading resumed and the business was not sold. Later BMW terminated the franchise and the business was sold leaving net profits after all expenses of some £770,000. Colin and Denis, who could not participate in those profits, claimed damages for misrepresentation and breach of fiduciary duty by Keith.

In particular, the court accepted the existence of a fiduciary duty in the circumstances. The interpretation of *Percival* v *Wright* [1902] 2 Ch 421 as deciding that directors owe no fiduciary duties to shareholders was not followed on the ground that the *Percival* case had been interpreted too widely. Such a wide interpretation did not follow from the underlying facts in *Percival*.

(iii) In *Peskin* v *Anderson* [2001] 1 BCLC 372 the Court of Appeal affirmed that, in the absence of a special relationship, directors do not owe a duty to individual shareholders to keep them constantly informed of all matters that might affect their position. Mr Peskin claimed damages against the directors of the RAC because he resigned his membership before its demutualisation and failed to get the consequent cash benefit. The directors had not disclosed from the beginning the negotiations about and proposals for the demutualisation and the Court of Appeal ruled that they were not required to do so. They had not been directed by the members to demutualise and were not therefore negotiating on their behalf. This was a sensible decision because in such matters the board must be left to formulate proposals which may at some stage be put to the members but not as soon as the idea occurs and is moved forward.

Secondly, where a listed company is concerned, the Stock Exchange has introduced a code of dealing for directors. The rules which the City Panel has laid down now have the force of law. In addition, the Panel on Takeovers and Mergers may issue and publish a reprimand for insider dealing in the shares of a company prior to its takeover and this could have an adverse effect upon the career, particularly of a professional person (see Chapter 26 ○). The Stock Exchange, in consultation with the CBI, published a Model Code for Securities Transactions, to give guidance as to when it is proper for directors of listed companies to deal in the securities of the company. This Code received widespread acceptance and became part of the Listing Agreement. The main principles of the Code have already been considered (see Chapter 15 ○).

Directors may become agents of the members for a particular transaction, in which case the situation of agency gives rise to fiduciary duties.

Allen v *Hyatt* (1914) 30 TLR 444

In this case the directors induced the shareholders to give them options for the purchase of their shares so that the directors might negotiate a sale of the shares to another company. The directors used the options to purchase the shares themselves and then resold them at a profit to the other company.

Held – by the Privy Council – that the directors had made themselves agents for the shareholders and must consequently account for the profit which they had obtained.

Comment

There are disadvantages in this agency arrangement. It was held by the House of Lords in *Briess v Woolley* [1954] 1 All ER 909 that where shareholders employ the directors to negotiate a sale of their shares, the shareholders will be vicariously liable in damages to the purchaser if the directors fraudulently misrepresent the state of the company's affairs to the purchaser of the shares.

Interests of the company's employees

Turning now to the list of stakeholders contained in s 172(1), to whom the directors should have regard when making decisions, it is important to emphasise the fact that while, for example, the interests of employees must be considered, the duty is owed not to the employees but directly to the company. (The same situation existed under s 309 of the Companies Act 1985.)

It would, for example, be within the provision for the directors so to arrange the company's business as to save jobs, provided the company's interests were also served in a reasonable fashion. It would not be within it for the directors to carry on the company's business at a loss and put it at risk of liquidation in order to save jobs. There must be a balance of interests but the interests of the employees must be considered.

The provisions cannot be enforced by employees unless they are also shareholders and even then a shareholder will have to bring himself within one of the exceptions to *Foss* v

Harbottle (see Chapter 17 ⊙). In normal circumstances a shareholder should be able to do this on the grounds that if the directors are ignoring the employee provisions they are doing an act contrary to law, i.e. an act contrary to the Companies Act 2006. However, unless there is damage to the company the most which a shareholder would be entitled to would be a declaration that the directors had failed to consider the interests of the employees in breach of the Act. While accepting that one cannot predict how the courts will interpret these provisions it does appear to be a declaration of good intent and little more. It is unlikely that the company will take action to enforce the duty.

The CA 2006 also provides that the powers of a company are deemed to include, if they do not otherwise do so, the power to make provisions for its own or a subsidiary's employees or former employees when the company itself or that subsidiary:

(a) ceases to carry on the whole or any part of its undertaking; or
(b) transfers the whole or any part of its undertaking.

The Act specifically states that the exercise of that power need not be in the best interests of the company. This provision therefore reverses the decision in *Parke v Daily News Ltd* [1962] Ch 927. Briefly, the facts of that case were that the defendant company had sold the major part of its business and proposed to use the proceeds to make payments to employees by way of redundancy pay before such payments were required by law. However, the court held that such payments were not for the benefit of the company, but rather for the benefit of the employees and, therefore, the company had no power to make the payments.

Where a company has power to make provision for its employees only by reason of the CA 2006, then the exercise of the power must normally be approved by an ordinary (or written) resolution. However, this does not apply if the memorandum or the articles contain a provision whereby the power can be exercised by a directors' resolution or require its sanction by a resolution other than an ordinary resolution of the company in general meeting, e.g. a special resolution.

The resolution can be implemented by a liquidator even though it was passed before the winding-up (Insolvency Act 1986, s 187). Furthermore, the power may be exercised by the liquidator if the following conditions are complied with:

(a) the company's liabilities have been fully satisfied;
(b) provision has been set aside for the costs of the winding-up;
(c) the exercise of the power has been approved either by such a resolution of the company as is required by the company's constitution or, if there is no such requirement, by an ordinary (or written) resolution of the members; and
(d) any other relevant requirements of the memorandum or the articles have been complied with.

It should be noted that if any payment is made before the commencement of a winding-up, then it must be made out of profits available for dividend as defined in the Companies Act 2006. In any other situation it must be made out of those assets of the company that are available to its members on its winding-up. In other words a payment cannot be made in order to prejudice creditors.

In connection with the power of the liquidator to implement the above provisions, it should be noted that s 167 of the Insolvency Act 1986 applies so that in a compulsory winding-up the liquidator exercises this power like all his others subject to the control of the court, and any creditor or contributory of the company may apply to the court with respect to the liquidator's exercise or proposed exercise of these powers if he does not agree with the way in which things are being done. In a voluntary winding-up the liquidator may make an application to the court for directions under s 112 of the 1986 Act if he is in any doubt as to whether he should exercise the above powers.

Since a company employer is bound in any case today to make basic redundancy payments a common application of the above provisions would be where the company intends to make redundancy payments, on a transfer of its business, which are in excess of the basic statutory requirements.

Interests of the company's creditors

In a solvent company the shareholders are entitled, as a general body, to be regarded as 'the company' when questions of the duty of directors arise. However, where a company is insolvent the interests of the creditors intrude. They have power, through insolvency procedures, to control the company's assets which are, in a practical sense, their assets and not the shareholders' assets.

Consequently, s 172(3) of the Companies Act 2006 makes it quite clear that the focus of a director's duties will shift away from the 'members as a whole' to that of the creditors when the company becomes insolvent.

Liquidator of West Mercia Safetywear Ltd v *Dodd* [1988] BCLC 250

Mr A J Dodd was a director of two companies, West Mercia and A J Dodd Ltd. The bank account of West Mercia was in credit while that of A J Dodd Ltd was considerably overdrawn. Both companies eventually went into insolvent liquidation and it then emerged that Mr Dodd had paid away £4,000 of West Mercia's money to discharge a debt which it owed to A J Dodd Ltd at a time when both companies were proceeding towards liquidation and the liquidator had instructed the directors not to operate either bank account. The advantage to Mr Dodd was that he had personally guaranteed the overdraft of A J Dodd Ltd and the payment reduced his liability on the guarantee. The Court of Appeal ordered Mr Dodd personally to repay the money to the liquidator of West Mercia on the basis that he was in breach of his duty to the creditors of West Mercia.

Comment

A further example of a breach of duty to creditors and the company is to be found in the ruling of the Court of Appeal in *MacPherson* v *European Strategic Bureau Ltd* (2000) *The Times*, 5 September. In that case three persons were members of the company. The relationship between them broke down and the company was not a success. The director/shareholders made an agreement under which two of them were to leave the company under a contract that repaid money owed to them being loans to finance the company and the profit from certain contracts of the company. All of this was expressed to be for payment of consultancy services to the company. The company later went to court to challenge the validity of the contracts. The Court of Appeal eventually ruled:

● that the contractual arrangement though supported by consideration in terms of the consultancy was not binding on the company because it was not for its benefit. It amounted to an informal distribution of assets as on a winding-up without making provision for all the company's creditors. It was a breach of the directors' duties and outside the powers of the company;

● although the matter did not arise because the contractual arrangements were not binding on the company, they were basically an infringement of the distribution rules of the 1985 Act since they were not distributions of profit alone but also distributions of the company's assets, which was permitted by law only in a winding-up (see s 263(2)(d)), but, being *remuneration* not *dividend*, they were valid;

- although it was not necessary in the circumstances to reach a definitive view, the arrangements appeared to constitute unlawful assistance for the purchase of shares since it was clearly envisaged that the departing shareholders would transfer their shares to the remaining shareholder with a material reduction in the net assets of the company.

Duty to exercise independent judgement

The statutory duty

Section 173 of the Companies Act provides:

(1) A director of a company must exercise independent judgement.
(2) This duty is not infringed by his acting:
  (a) in accordance with an agreement duly entered into by the company that restricts the future exercise of discretion by its directors, or
  (b) in a way authorised by the company's constitution.

The related common law and equitable principles

One of the most useful cases with respect to this duty is that of *Boulting v Association of Cinematograph, Television and Allied Technicians* [1963] 2 QB 606, in which Lord Denning MR noted:

> It seems to me that no one, who has duties of a fiduciary nature to discharge, can be allowed to enter into an engagement by which he binds himself to disregard those duties or to act inconsistently with them. No stipulation is lawful by which he agrees to carry out his duties in accordance with the instructions of another rather than on his own conscientious judgment; or by which he agrees to subordinate the interests of those whom he must protect to the interests of someone else.

Duty to exercise reasonable care, skill and diligence

The statutory duty

Section 174 of the Companies Act 2006 requires a director of a company to exercise reasonable care, skill and diligence. It provides:

1 A director of a company must exercise reasonable care, skill and diligence.
2 This means the care, skill and diligence that would be exercised by a reasonably diligent person with:
  (a) the general knowledge, skill and experience that may reasonably be expected of a person carrying out the functions carried out by the director in relation to the company, and
  (b) the general knowledge, skill and experience that the director has.

The related common law and equitable principles

It has been an accepted part of a director's duties to the company that he owes a duty of care to the company at common law not to act negligently in managing its affairs. The standard is that of a reasonable man in looking after his own affairs, and it might fairly be said that the earlier cases show that the duty is not a high one.

Re City Equitable Fire Insurance Co [1925] Ch 407

In this case the chairman of the company committed frauds by purporting to buy Treasury bonds just before the end of the accounting period and selling them just after the audit. By this method a debt due to the company from a firm in which the chairman had an interest was considerably reduced on the balance sheet by increasing the gilt-edged securities shown as assets. With regard to the duty of auditors it was *held* that they might have been negligent in that they had not asked for the production of the Treasury bonds but appeared to have trusted the chairman. However, they were held not liable mainly because this was one item in a very large audit. The case does, however, show a movement towards a situation in which the auditors cannot necessarily implicitly trust the company's officers. The case is also concerned with the duties of directors in that it appeared that the directors of this insurance company had left the management of its affairs almost entirely to the chairman and it was perhaps because of this that he had more easily been able to perpetrate his frauds. In the course of his judgment, Romer J laid down the following duties of care and skill required of directors, and the general view is that these are not unduly burdensome:

[. . .] (1) A director need not exhibit in the performance of his duties a greater degree of skill than may reasonably be expected from a person of his knowledge and experience. A director of a life insurance company, for instance, does not guarantee that he has the skill of an actuary or of a physician [. . .] (2) A director is not bound to give continuous attention to the affairs of his company. His duties are of an intermittent nature to be performed at periodical board meetings . . . He is not, however, bound to attend all such meetings though he ought to attend whenever, in the circumstances, he is reasonably able to do so. (3) In respect of all duties that, having regard to the exigencies of business, and the articles of association, may properly be left to some other official, a director is, in the absence of grounds for suspicion, justified in trusting that official to perform such duties honestly.

Comment

A classic illustration of the above principles is to be found in the earlier *Marquis of Bute's Case* [1892] 2 Ch 100 where the Marquis was made president of the Cardiff Savings Bank at six months old by inheriting the office from his father. He attended one board meeting in 38 years and was held by Stirling J not liable for certain irregularities in the lending operations of the bank.

However, in modern times when the directors of companies are often experts in certain fields, e.g. accounting, finance or engineering, a higher standard of competence may now be expected of them in their own sphere. Certainly directors employed by companies in a professional capacity, i.e. executive directors, have a higher objective standard of care to comply with (see *Lister* v *Romford Ice and Cold Storage Co* [1957] 1 All ER 125), and so have non-executive directors who are qualified or experienced in a relevant discipline.

Dorchester Finance Co Ltd v *Stebbing* [1989] BCLC 498

On 22 July 1977 Foster J dealt, in the Chancery Division, with this case which concerned the duties of skill and care of company directors. The decision was not initially reported, which is unfortunate since it seems to be the first decision in this area of the law since *Re City Equitable Fire Insurance Co Ltd*. The case concerned a money lending company, Dorchester Finance, which at all material times had three directors. Only one, S, was involved in the affairs of the company on a full-time basis. No board meetings were held and P and H, the other directors, made only rare visits to the company's premises. S and P were qualified accountants and H had considerable accountancy experience, though he was in fact unqualified. It appeared that S caused the company to make loans to other persons and companies with whom he had some connection or dealing, and that he was able to achieve this, in part at least, because P and H signed cheques on the company's account in blank at his request. The loans did not comply with the Moneylenders Acts and adequate securities were not taken so that the loans could not be recovered by the company which then brought an action against the three directors for alleged negligence and misappropriation of the company's property.

Held – by Foster J – that all three directors were liable to damages. S, who was an executive director, was held to have been grossly negligent and P and H were also held to have failed to exhibit the necessary skill and care in the performance of their duties as non-executive directors, even though the evidence showed that they had acted in good faith throughout. The decision is of particular importance in regard to P and H because the judge appears to have applied a higher standard for non-executive directors than that laid down in the *Re City Equitable* case. In particular, the judge rejected any defence based upon non-feasance, i.e. the omission of an act which a person is bound by law to do. Contrary to *Re City Equitable*, therefore, it would seem from this case to be unreasonable for a non-executive director not to attend board meetings or to show any interest in the company's affairs and merely rely on management, or, according to the judge, on the competence and diligence of the company's auditors.

Comment

It is not possible to say with certainty whether this decision affects the liability of non-executive directors who are not qualified or experienced in a discipline relevant to company administration. It was obviously of importance that P and H were experienced accountants and one would have expected a more objective and higher standard to be applied to such persons, even in their capacity as non-executive directors. The matter is really one which should be dealt with by legislation but there is nothing which is relevant to this problem in the Companies Act 1985. However, it is worth noting that Foster J did not make any distinction between executive and non-executive directors, stating that their duties were the same.

The UK standard of care is also being derived from the law relating to wrongful trading by directors. In particular, s 214 of the Insolvency Act 1986 (see further Chapter 27) provides for personal liability for directors in such amount as the court may decide in an insolvent liquidation as a contribution to the company's debts. The section is based on negligence and the standard is objective. The qualified/experienced (or talented) director is judged by the higher standard he ought to have but other directors are required to reach a level of competence to an objective standard. The court will consider current practice.

Of course, s 214 of the Insolvency Act 1986 can only be applied specifically when the company is in insolvent liquidation but the standard required by the section has been cited particularly in *Norman* v *Theodore Goddard* [1992] BCLC 1028 and *Re D'Jan of London* [1994] 1 BLCL 561 as being an accurate statement of a director's duty at common law which could be applied more widely than in wrongful trading; in the *D'Jan* case, for example, to make a director, who failed to read but signed an insurance proposal, which contained inaccurate information and which was repudiated by the insurance company, potentially liable in negligence. Lord Justice Hoffmann accepted that a director's duty at common law is the same as that set out in s 214.

Section 13 of the Supply of Goods and Services Act 1982 imposes an implied contractual term that a supplier of a service acting in the course of business will carry out that service with reasonable care. SI 1982/1771 provides that s 13 shall not apply to the services rendered by a company director to his company. It is evidently thought to be enough that they have to act in good faith, carry out fiduciary duties and meet the common law standard of reasonable skill and care.

As regards the duty of directors not to act negligently so as to injure outsiders, the following case is relevant.

Thomas Saunders Partnership v *Harvey* [1989] 30 Con LR 103

The claimants were architects who were retained on a project to refit office premises, one requirement being for raised access flooring. The defendant was a director of a subcontracting flooring company. He was asked whether the flooring his company offered conformed to the relevant specifications. He confirmed in writing that it did. In fact it did not and the architects were sued by the end users for £75,000, the claim succeeding. They sought an indemnity from the defendant, his company having gone into liquidation. The claim, part of which was based on negligence, succeeded even though the written confirmation had been given on behalf of and in the name of the company. The defendant was a specialist in the field and had assumed a duty of care when making the statement. He was liable in negligence. The judge did not see why the cloak of incorporation should affect liability for individual negligence.

Comment

(i) The decision has implications for companies whose products or services depend to a considerable extent on the skills and expertise of individual directors. In particular, firms of accountants who are transferring from the partnership regime to the limited company regime may not find that this affects their personal liability for negligence.

(ii) Much depends upon the facts of the case and in *Williams* v *Natural Life Health Foods Ltd* (1998) *The Times*, 1 May, the House of Lords decided that a managing director was not liable for a negligent statement as to the profits likely to be made by the claimant under a franchise agreement. He made the statement on behalf of the company as its agent. Their Lordships said that in order for the MD to be liable the claimant must show that he could reasonably rely on an assumption of personal liability by the MD so that a special relationship was created between the claimant and the MD. The claimant had not, they said, established such a relationship. In particular, he did not know the MD and had no significant pre-contractual dealings with him. Furthermore, there had been no conduct by the MD which would have suggested to the claimant that the MD was accepting liability nor did the evidence show that the claimant believed he was. Nevertheless, if the special relationship can be established the court will in effect go behind the corporate structure and find liability in those who are effectively in charge of the company. This, of course, gets around limited liability and is particularly useful where the company is insolvent.

(iii) As the above materials show, directors cannot be held personally liable for negligent misstatements unless a special relationship can be established between themselves and the claimant. However, directors may be personally liable for fraudulent misstatements (the tort of deceit) irrespective of whether a special relationship is found to exist (see *Standard Chartered Bank* v *Pakistan National Shipping Co (No 2)* [2003] 1 All ER 173). The criminal standard of proof applies to civil claims for fraud, i.e. proof beyond a reasonable doubt so that it is notoriously difficult to prove. It follows that it remains difficult to impose personal liability upon directors whether in respect of negligent or fraudulent misstatements.

Where a person is a director of a number of companies that are within the same group duties are owed to each company within the group individually (see *Re Pantone 485 Ltd, Miller v Bain* [2002] 1 BCLC 266).

What action can directors take to reduce the risk of claims for damage to the company following 'bad' business decisions? The following steps should be taken where it is thought that, although the transaction is in general terms for the benefit of the company, there are some risks:

- take all proper advice which it is thought necessary;
- document fully and clearly the reasons for the various decisions made;
- enshrine these in the board minutes or other written document; and
- in difficult cases consult the shareholders and ask them to formally approve the decisions by ordinary (or written) resolution. Ratification by the shareholders should protect the directors from the risk of subsequent proceedings by the company against them. Directors/ shareholders may vote and give this ratification unless, for example, they are seeking to approve their own fraud.

If the above steps are taken, the directors could hardly be regarded as in breach of their management duties and so could ratify the action as shareholders even if they held a majority of the membership votes (*North-West Transportation Co v Beatty* (1887) 12 App Cas 589).

Duty to avoid conflicts of interest

The statutory duty

Section 175 of the Companies Act 2006 states:

(1) A director of a company must avoid a situation in which he has, or can have, a direct or indirect interest that conflicts, or possibly may conflict, with the interests of the company.
(2) This applies in particular to the exploitation of any property, information or opportunity (and it is immaterial whether the company could take advantage of the property, information or opportunity).
(3) This duty does not apply to a conflict of interest arising in relation to a transaction or arrangement with the company.
(4) This duty is not infringed:
    (a) if the situation cannot reasonably be regarded as likely to give rise to a conflict of interest; or
    (b) if the matter has been authorised by the directors.
(5) Authorisation may be given by the directors:
    (a) where the company is a private company and nothing in the company's constitution invalidates such authorisation, by the matter being proposed to and authorised by the directors; or
    (b) where the company is a public company and its constitution includes provision enabling the directors to authorise the matter, by the matter being proposed to and authorised by them in accordance with the constitution.

(6) The authorisation is effective only if:
    (a) any requirement as to the quorum at the meeting at which the matter is considered is met without counting the director in question or any other interested director, and
    (b) the matter was agreed to without their voting or would have been agreed to if their votes had not been counted.
(7) Any reference in this section to a conflict of interest includes a conflict of interest and duty and a conflict of duties.

The related common law and equitable principles

A director must account to the company for any personal profit he may make in the course of his dealing with the company's property (which includes not only physical assets of the company but also commercial information and opportunities). This is now embodied in ss 175 and 177 of the Companies Act 2006. Thus, if a director buys shares in the company at par when the issue price is greater, he must account to the company for the difference; where he has sold at a profit, he must account for the profit. Again, if a director receives gifts of money or shares from the promoters of the company or from persons selling property to it, he must account for these sums to the company. The reason for this is that there has been a *conflict of interest*.

A company director is expected to undertake negotiations with a view to securing the greatest benefit for the company, and he can hardly have done so if he was taking gifts from the other party. He must also account for commissions received from persons who supply goods to the company. In addition, a director who in the course of his employment obtains a contract for himself is liable to account to the company for the profit he makes, even if it can be shown that the company would not necessarily have obtained the contract. The accountability arises from the mere fact that a profit is made by the director; it is not a question of loss to the company.

 Industrial Development Consultants v Cooley [1972] 2 All ER 162

The defendant was an architect of considerable distinction and attainment in his own sphere. He was employed as managing director by Industrial Development Consultants who provided construction consultancy services for gas boards. The Eastern Gas Board were offering a lucrative contract in regard to the building of four depots and IDC was very keen to obtain the business. The defendant was acting for IDC in the matter and the Eastern Gas Board made it clear to the defendant that IDC would not obtain the contract because the officers of the Eastern Gas Board would not engage a firm of consultants. The defendant realised that he had a good chance of obtaining the contract for himself. He therefore represented to IDC that he was ill and because IDC were of the opinion that the defendant was near to a nervous breakdown, he was allowed to terminate his employment with them on short notice. Shortly afterwards the defendant took steps which resulted in his obtaining the Eastern Gas Board contracts for the four depots for himself. In this case IDC sued the defendant for an account of the profits that he would make on the construction of the four depots.

Held – by Roskill J – that the defendant had acted in breach of duty and must account. The fact that IDC might not have obtained the contract itself was immaterial. *Per* Roskill J:

Therefore it cannot be said that it is anything like certain that the [claimants] would ever have got this contract [. . .] on the other hand, there was always the possibility of the [claimants] persuading the

Eastern Gas Board to change their minds; and ironically enough, it would have been the defendant's duty to try and persuade them to change their minds. It is a curious position under which he should now say that the [claimants] suffered no loss because he would never have succeeded in persuading them to change their minds.

Comment

The High Court ruled in *Gencor ACP Ltd* v *Dalby* [2000] 2 BCLC 734 that the fact that a fiduciary, such as a director, has made a profit makes him liable to account for it to the company. Whether the company would or would not have obtained the profit is irrelevant.

Regal (Hastings) Ltd v *Gulliver* [1942] 1 All ER 378

The Regal company owned one cinema and wished to buy two others with the object of selling all three together. The Regal company formed a subsidiary so that the subsidiary could buy the cinemas in question but the Regal company could not provide all the capital needed to purchase them and the directors bought some of the shares in the subsidiary themselves thus providing the necessary capital. The subsidiary company acquired the two cinemas and eventually the shares in the Regal company and in the subsidiary were sold at a profit. The new controllers of the Regal company then caused it to bring an action to recover the profit made.

Held – by the House of Lords – that the directors must account to the Regal company for the profit on the grounds that it was only through the knowledge and opportunity they gained as directors of that company that they were able to obtain the shares and consequently to make the profit. In particular, the House of Lords stated that directors were liable to account to the company once it was established:

(a) that what the directors did was so related to the affairs of the company that it could properly be said to have been done in the course of their management and in utilisation of their opportunities and special knowledge as directors; and
(b) that what they did resulted in a profit to themselves.

Comment

(i) This same question was considered by the House of Lords in *Boardman* v *Phipps* [1967] 2 AC 46 where the *Regal* case was followed. It is generally felt that the fiduciary duty to account which was placed on the directors in these two cases is rather high. In the *Regal* case the directors did not have a majority of shares in the company. It would have been possible for them to obtain ratification of their acts by the company in general meeting. Furthermore, it was always conceded that they had acted in good faith and in full belief in the legality of their action, so that it had not occurred to them to obtain the approval of a general meeting. It is also true to say that the directors had not deprived the company of any of its property. The shares in the subsidiary were bought with their own money and those shares had never been the company's property on the facts as the court found them. It would seem that the mere possession of information which results from the holding of office as a director is sufficient to raise the duty to account.

(ii) A further case in point is *Re Bhullar Bros Ltd* [2003] All ER (D) 445 (Mar). The company was a family company running a grocery business from several properties. It also owned investment properties. The two families involved fell out. They decided not to buy any more investment properties and to divide the assets of the company between them. Negotiations came to nothing and one of the families asked the court to order the sale of the shares held by one family to the other family or to the company under s 459 (unfair prejudice). The court refused a buy-out order. However, it was discovered that two of the company's directors had, while the company was still trading, bought at an advantageous price two investment properties next to the company's existing investment properties on their own behalf. The Court of Appeal ruled that the directors concerned held the newly acquired properties on a constructive trust for the company. The Court of Appeal affirmed the ruling of the High Court that the properties should be transferred to the company at the price that was paid for them. As the appeal judgment says, whether the company could or would have taken the opportunity to acquire the properties had it been aware of the facts was not to the point. The existence of the opportunity was information that it was relevant for the company to have and the directors concerned were under a fiduciary duty to communicate it to the company.

A director is not accountable for the profits of a competing business which he may be running (*Bell* v *Lever Bros Ltd* [1932] AC 161), unless the articles or his service contract expressly so provide, but he will be accountable if he uses the company's property in that business, or if he uses its trade secrets, or induces the company's customers to deal with him. Furthermore, a director of two or more companies takes the risk of an application under s 994, CA 2006 (unfair prejudice) if he subordinates the interests of one company to those of the other (*Scottish CWS* v *Meyer* [1958] 3 All ER 66). A director is not allowed, either during or after service with a company, to use for his own purposes confidential information entrusted to him by the company (*Baker* v *Gibbons* [1972] 2 All ER 759).

The High Court has ruled that a director who, on leaving his company, persuaded former clients to transfer their advertising business to a new company run by him had acted in breach of his fiduciary duty. The diversion of clients was a misappropriation of the original company's property and the director was liable for profits derived from that property (see *CMS Dolphin Ltd* v *Simonet Ltd* [2001] 2 BCLC 704). The High Court has also ruled that a director who registered the company's name as his own trademark was in breach of a fiduciary duty to the company because the registration was in his own personal interest and in conflict with the interests of the company (see *Ball* v *Eden Project Ltd*, *Eden Project* v *Ball* [2001] 1 BCLC 313).

It is, of course, possible for a director's service contract to be so drafted as to debar him from running a competing business, allowing the company to seek an injunction if such a business was carried on. It might also justify dismissal if the contract was breached. By contrast, a shareholders' agreement may provide individuals who are both members and directors of a company with control over the direction which the company is to take. As such, as in the case of *Wilkinson* v *West Coast Capital* [2005] EWHC 3009, those directors may be able to deny that a new venture could be classed as a 'corporate opportunity'.

A director may keep a personal profit if the company consents, but the consent must be given by the members in general meeting and not by the board, and a resolution in general meeting may be rendered invalid as prejudicial to the minority, if the director concerned controls the voting in general meetings (*Cook* v *Deeks*, 1916, see Chapter 17 ◐). Shareholder approval can be given by the unanimous written resolution procedure though in such a case there would be no question of the abuse of minority rights.

However, a director may take advantage of a corporate opportunity on his own account if his company has considered the same proposition and rejected it in good faith.

 Peso Silver Mines Ltd (NPL) v Cropper (1966) 58 DLR (2d) 1

The board of directors of Peso was approached by a person named Dikson who wanted to sell to Peso 126 prospecting claims near to the company's own property. The board of Peso rejected this proposal after bona fide consideration. However, a syndicate was then formed by Peso's geologist to purchase Dikson's claim. A company called Cross Bow Mines Ltd was incorporated by the syndicate for the purpose. Cropper was a director of Peso and had taken part in the earlier decision of the Peso board and also become a shareholder in Cross Bow Mines. This action was brought claiming that Cropper was accountable to Peso for the Cross Bow shares which he had obtained.

Held – by the Supreme Court of Canada – that he was not bound to account. On the facts, Cropper and his co-directors had acted in good faith solely in the interest of Peso and with sound business reasons for rejecting the offer. There was no evidence that Cropper had any confidential or other information which he concealed from the board. The court also found that when Cropper was approached to join the syndicate it was not in his capacity as a director of Peso but as an individual member of the public whom the syndicate was seeking to interest as a co-adventurer.

Finally, a director may choose to resign from a company so as to take up a corporate opportunity on his own, raising the question as to whether this would amount to a conflict of interest. The answer is that directors may pursue private opportunities while working for a company, though these would be subject to the duties outlined in ss 175 and 177 CA 2006; in particular the requirement to declare their activities to the company. (The key message should always be, '*if in doubt, disclose*'.) A more common situation with which the courts are faced is where a director chooses to resign around the time that such a private venture is commenced so that they are able to devote their attention to it.

There are a number of important cases in this area including ***Industrial Development Consultants Ltd v Cooley*** [1972] 1 WLR 443, which involved an architect who pursued an opportunity in his private capacity. A more recent Court of Appeal case, ***Foster Bryant Surveying Limited v Bryant, Savernake Property Consultants Limited*** [2007] BCC 804, deals with a situation whereby a director resigned his position and subsequently commenced new work without breaching the conflicts rule. The judgment of Rix LJ also provides a good summary of the case law in this area.

Foster Bryant Surveying Limited v Bryant, Savernake Property Consultants Limited [2007] BCC 804

The appellant company (S) appealed against the decision that the respondent director (B) had not been in breach of his fiduciary duties before his resignation had taken effect. S had been set up by a chartered surveyor (F) who was the majority shareholder. S had an agreement to carry out all the surveying and project management work for its largest client (C). F persuaded B, another chartered surveyor, to join him as a director and shareholder of S. B's wife also worked for S. Two years later F had lost confidence in B and made B's wife redundant. As a result B had resigned his directorship. Before B's resignation took effect C requested B to work for it under a retainer arrangement. C offered to share its work between B and S but F declined. S brought a claim against B. The judge found that B had been excluded from his role as director after his resignation, that there had been no breach of fiduciary duty by B and that even if B had been in breach of fiduciary duty the company had suffered no loss as a result. S submitted that the judge had been wrong to find that B had been excluded from discharging his role as a director of the company as from his resignation, that he had been wrong not to recognise that what B did during his notice period between resignation and departure was a breach of fiduciary duty, and that once that breach was established, then a duty to account was inevitable and did not depend on the need to establish any loss. *Per* Rix LJ:

At trial it was common ground between the parties that the synthesis of principles expounded by Mr Livesey QC, sitting as a deputy judge of the High Court, in *Hunter Kane Ltd v Watkins* [2003] EWHC 186 (Ch), which Mr Livesey had himself taken largely from the judgment of Lawrence Collins J in *CMS Dolphin Ltd v Simonet* [2002] BCC 600 and the authorities there cited and discussed, accurately stated the law. In this court in *In Plus Group Ltd v Pyke* [2002] EWCA Civ 370; [2003] BCC 332 Brooke LJ described the *Simonet* analysis as 'valuable'. Mr Livesey said:

1 A director, while acting as such, has a fiduciary relationship with his company. That is he has an obligation to deal towards it with loyalty, good faith and avoidance of the conflict of duty and self-interest.

2 A requirement to avoid a conflict of duty and self-interest means that a director is precluded from obtaining for himself, either secretly or without the informed approval of the company, any property or business advantage either belonging to the company or for which it has been negotiating, especially where the director or officer is a participant in the negotiations.

3 A director's power to resign from office is not a fiduciary power. He is entitled to resign even if his resignation might have a disastrous effect on the business or reputation of the company.

4 A fiduciary relationship does not continue after the determination of the relationship which gives rise to it. After the relationship is determined the director is in general not under the continuing obligations which are the feature of the fiduciary relationship.

5 Acts done by the directors while the contract of employment subsists but which are preparatory to competition after it terminates are *not necessarily* in themselves a breach of the implied term as to loyalty and fidelity.

6 Directors, no less than employees, acquire a general fund of skill, knowledge and expertise in the course of their work, which is plainly in the public interest that they should be free to exploit it in a new position. After ceasing the relationship by resignation or otherwise a director is in general (and subject of course to any terms of the contract of employment) not prohibited from using his general fund of skill and knowledge, the 'stock in trade' of the knowledge he has acquired while a director, even including such things as business contacts and personal connections made as a result of his directorship.

7 A director is however precluded from acting in breach of the requirement at 2 above, even after his resignation where the resignation may fairly be said to have been prompted or influenced by a wish to acquire for himself any maturing business opportunities sought by the company and where it was his position with the company rather than a fresh initiative that led him to the opportunity which he later acquired.

8 In considering whether an act of a director breaches the preceding principle the factors to take into account will include the factor of position or office held, the nature of the corporate opportunity, its ripeness, its specificness and the director's relation to it, the amount of knowledge possessed, the circumstances in which it was obtained and whether it was special or indeed even private, the factor of time in the continuation of the fiduciary duty where the alleged breach occurs after termination of the relationship with the company and the circumstances under which the breach was terminated, that is whether by retirement or resignation or discharge.

9 The underlying basis of the liability of a director who exploits after his resignation a maturing business opportunity 'of the company' is that the opportunity is to be treated as if it were the property of the company in relation to which the director had fiduciary duties. By seeking to exploit the opportunity after resignation he is appropriating to himself that property. He is just as accountable as a trustee who retires without properly accounting for trust property.

10 It follows that a director will not be in breach of the principle set out as point 7 above where either the company's hope of obtaining the contract was not a 'maturing business opportunity' and it was not pursuing further business orders nor where the director's resignation was not itself prompted or influenced by a wish to acquire the business for himself.

11 As regards breach of confidence, although while the contract of employment subsists a director or other employee may not use confidential information to the detriment of his employer, after it ceases the director/employee may compete and may use know-how acquired in the course of his employment (as distinct from trade secrets – although the distinction is sometimes difficult to apply in practice).

In the present proceedings the principles with which we are most concerned are 1, 2, 4, 5, 7, 8, 9 and 10 . . .

It may be observed that the factual situation presented by this case falls uneasily between the scenarios dealt with in that jurisprudence. This is not a case where a director has used corporate property. It is not a case where a director has resigned in order to make use of a corporate opportunity. It is not a case where a director has solicited corporate business in competition with his company. It is not a case where a director has acted in bad faith, deceitfully or clandestinely. It is, however, at any rate arguably, a case where, by agreeing, while still a director, to work for Alliance after he ceased to be a director, Mr Bryant was still obtaining for himself a business opportunity, possibly even existing business, of the company, or putting himself in a position of conflict with the company, before he was free to do so. Moreover, these events happened at a time of transition, after a forced resignation but before the resignation had taken contractual effect, in circumstances where both parties might be said to be in need of protection. It is possibly above all when a director is leaving that a company needs the protection which the law relating to directors' fiduciary duties provides. But it is also when a director is forced out of his own company that he needs the protection that the law allows to someone who has thereafter to earn his living. Many of these considerations are discussed in the jurisprudence, but not in our particular setting.

Regal (Hastings) Ltd v *Gulliver* [1967] 2 AC 134n; [1942] 1 All ER 378 is perhaps in many ways still the leading case. It was decided in the war and not reported otherwise than in the All England Reports until it was printed in the Law Reports as a note to *Boardman* v *Phipps* [1967] 2 AC 46. It is well described in *Gower and Davies' Principles of Modern Company Law* (7th edn, 2003, Sweet & Maxwell) at pp 417–418, where the observation is made that the decision illustrates the extreme severity of the law but also that it possibly carries equitable principles to an inequitable conclusion . . .

It would thus seem that even though the directors had in fact been proved to have been acting honestly, and even though it had been in fact proved that the company had suffered no loss, the position must in law be regarded, for the safety of mankind, as though they had been acting secretly and dishonestly, to the loss of their company, and no inquiry otherwise was to be permitted.

In other respects, however, that was a straightforward case where the directors had acquired their personal profits by reason of and in the course of acting as directors of their company. As Viscount Sankey said (at p 139E): 'At all material times they were directors and in a fiduciary position, and they used and acted upon their exclusive knowledge acquired as such directors.' Lord Russell pointed out that they acquired their shares 'by reason and in course of their office of directors' (at p 145F, see also at p 149F). Lord Macmillan said that the critical findings of fact which the claimant company had to establish were '(i) that what the directors did was so related to the affairs of the company that it can properly be said to have been done in the course of their management and in utilisation of their opportunities and special knowledge as directors; and (ii) that what they did resulted in a profit to themselves' (at p 153F). Lord Wright said that the stringent rule was that a director must account to his company 'for any benefit which he obtains in the course of and owing to his directorship' (at p 156C). Lord Porter said that the shares were obtained by the directors 'by reason of their position as directors' (at p 158C) and that the relevant rule was that 'one occupying a position of trust must not make a profit which he can acquire only by use of his fiduciary position' (at p 158F).

Twenty-five years later a majority of the House of Lords applied *Regal (Hastings) Ltd* v *Gulliver* to a somewhat similar situation in *Boardman* v *Phipps* [1967] 2 AC 46, save that the defendants there were a trustee and the solicitor of a trust rather than directors of a company, and the shares bought by the defendants were bought from third parties. The defendants obtained a profit for themselves as well as for their beneficiaries in buying shares where the trust would not have been able or willing to do so, and had acted openly and honourably albeit mistakenly. On this occasion, however, their Lordships, although agreed on the principle to be applied, were divided in its application. Lord Cohen said that information was not property in the strict sense and that it did not follow that because an agent acquired information and opportunity while acting in a fiduciary capacity he is accountable to his principals for any profit that comes his way as the result of the use he makes of that information and opportunity; that must depend on the facts of the case; but here in buying the shares the defendants were acting on behalf of the trust and its beneficiaries and they had put themselves in a position of conflict or possible conflict with the interests of those whom they were bound to protect (at pp 102–104). Lord Hodson thought that information could properly be described as property, albeit each case must be decided on its own facts (at p 107). Lord Guest thought the same (at p 115). However, Viscount Dilhorne and Lord Upjohn saw the matter differently, although they were agreed on the great principles at stake.

In both those cases, what happened was that the defendants obtained a profit for themselves out of property of their trust while acting as fiduciaries. However, the application of the underlying principles, that fiduciaries must not profit from their role nor put themselves in a position of conflict of interest, has raised problems in circumstances where a director resigns and reaps his profit after resignation. A number of cases, considered by the judge below, have illustrated the problems . . .

The defendants were castigated as 'faithless fiduciaries'. It was again irrelevant that the company might not have obtained the contract, for the defendants' liability was their gain rather than the company's loss. *Gower and Davies* comment (at p 420) that in that passage Laskin J seems to have favoured a flexibility greater than English case law allows. However, the decision on the facts appears best encapsulated in the following extract from his judgment (at p 382):

> An examination of the case law . . . shows the pervasiveness of a strict ethic in this area of the law. In my opinion, this ethic disqualifies a director or senior officer from usurping for himself or diverting to another person or company with whom or with which he is associated a maturing business opportunity which the company is actively pursuing; he is also precluded from so acting even after his resignation where the resignation may fairly be said to have been prompted or influenced by a wish to acquire for himself the opportunity sought by the company, *or* where it was his position with the company rather than a fresh initiative that led him to the opportunity which he later acquired . . .

In *CMS Dolphin Ltd* v *Simonet* [2002] BCC 600 the relevant jurisprudence was carefully considered by Lawrence Collins J, as he then was. The director there resigned (without any notice) in order to profit from the claimant company's business. Having made plans in advance of resignation, after his departure he immediately set up in competition, first in partnership and subsequently through a new company. He approached the claimant's staff and clients, to draw them both to him. Before long, the claimant had no staff and no clients. The director was found to be in breach of fiduciary duty and liable to account. By resigning, he had exploited the maturing business opportunities of the claimant, which were to be regarded as its property. The case made by the claimant and accepted by Lawrence Collins J was that the director had been prompted or influenced to resign by a wish to acquire for himself or his company the business opportunities which he had previously obtained or was actively pursuing with the claimant's clients and had now actually diverted to his own profit.

Lawrence Collins J considered the legal principles at [84]–[97]. Having referred to *Regal (Hastings)* v *Gulliver*, he said that the case before him concerned the question of how far the principle of that case, which concerned directors who were in office at the time of acquisition of the shares, extended to: 'a director who resigns his office to take advantage of a business opportunity of which he has knowledge as a result of his having been a director'.

He concluded:

> In English law a director's power to resign from office is not a fiduciary power. A director is entitled to resign even if his resignation might have a disastrous effect on the business or reputation of the company. So also in English law, at least in general, a fiduciary obligation does not continue after the determination of the relationship which gives rise to it (see *A-G* v *Blake* [1998]

Ch 439, at p 453, varied on other grounds [2001] 1 AC 268 (HL)). For the reasons given in *Island Export Finance Ltd* v *Umunna* a director may resign (subject, of course, to compliance with his contract of employment) and he is not thereafter precluded from using his general fund of skill and knowledge, or his personal connections, to compete . . . In my judgment the underlying basis of the liability of a director who exploits after his resignation a maturing business opportunity of the company is that the opportunity is to be treated as if it were property of the company in relation to which the director had fiduciary duties.

In my judgment, Lawrence Collins J was not saying that the fiduciary duty survived the end of the relationship as director, but that the lack of good faith with which the future exploitation was planned while still a director, and the resignation which was part of that dishonest plan, meant that there was already then a breach of fiduciary duty, which resulted in the liability to account for the profits which, albeit subsequently, but causally connected with that earlier fiduciary breach, were obtained from the diversion of the company's business property to the defendant's new enterprise.

In Plus Group Ltd v *Pyke* [2002] EWCA Civ 370; [2003] BCC 332, a rare case in this court, presents a somewhat novel position. There the claimant company sought over a period of many months, but without success, to force the defendant director to resign following a bout of severe illness. The relationship between him and his partner in the company completely broke down, and he was deprived of any remuneration or information; he was also refused the repayment of his loans to the company. But he steadfastly refused to resign. In this state, but while still a director, the defendant set up his own company and began competing with the claimant, even to the extent of working for its major client. Both trial court and this court held that there was no breach of fiduciary duty . . .

Finally, there have been two further cases in which the essence of the finding of a breach of fiduciary duty has consisted in what the directors had done while directors, rather than in post-resignation competition. Thus in *British Midland Tool Ltd* v *Midland International Tooling Ltd* [2003] EWHC 466 (Ch); [2003] 2 BCLC 523, the director who merely resigned in order to compete was not in breach, but his three former colleague directors who remained and thereafter conspired with him to poach the claimant's employees were in breach (Hart J, whose recent death is much mourned). And in *Shepherds Investments Ltd* v *Walters* [2006] EWHC 836 (Ch); [2007] 2 BCLC 202 the directors were found to have breached their fiduciary duties by reason of what they did while still directors in anticipation of the competition they planned after their resignations. In the latter case, Etherton J said:

> What the cases show, and the parties before me agree, is that the precise point at which the preparations for the establishment of the competing business by a director become unlawful will depend on the actual facts of any particular case. In each case, the touchstone for what, on the one hand, is permissible, and what, on the other hand, is impermissible unless consent is obtained from the company or employer after full disclosure, is what, in the case of a director, will be in breach of the fiduciary duties to which I have referred or, in the case of an employee, will be in breach of the obligation of fidelity. It is obvious, for example, that merely making a decision to set up a competing business at some point in the future and discussing such an idea with friends and family would not of themselves be in conflict with the best interests of the company and the employer. The consulting of lawyers and other professionals may, depending on the circumstances, equally be consistent with a director's fiduciary duties and the employee's obligation of loyalty. At the other end of the spectrum, it is plain that soliciting customers of the company and the employer or the actual carrying on of trade by a competing business would be in breach of the duties of the director and the obligations of the employee . . .

The jurisprudence which I have considered above demonstrates, I think, that the summary is perceptive and useful. For my part, however, I would find it difficult accurately to encapsulate the circumstances in which a retiring director may or may not be found to have breached his fiduciary duty. As has been frequently stated, the problem is highly fact sensitive. Perhaps for this reason, appeals have been rare in themselves, and, of all the cases put before us, only *Regal (Hastings)* v *Gulliver* (not a case about a retiring director) demonstrates success on appeal. There is no doubt that the twin principles, that a director must act towards his company with honesty, good faith, and loyalty and must avoid any conflict of interest, are firmly in place, and are exacting requirements, exactingly enforced. Whether, however, it remains true to say, as James LJ did in *Parker* v *McKenna* (cited in *Regal (Hastings)* v *Gulliver*) that the principles are (always) 'inflexible' and must be applied 'inexorably' may be in doubt, at any rate in this context. Such an inflexible rule, so inexorably applied might be thought to have to carry all before it, in every circumstance. Nevertheless, the jurisprudence has shown that, while the principles remain unamended, their application in different circumstances has required care and sensitivity both to the facts and to other principles, such as that of personal freedom to compete, where that does not intrude on the misuse of the company's property whether in the form of business opportunities or trade secrets. For reasons such as these, there has been some flexibility, both in the reach and extent of the duties imposed and in the findings of liability or non-liability. The jurisprudence also demonstrates, to my mind, that in the present context of retiring directors, where the critical line between a defendant being or not being a director becomes hard to police, the courts have adopted pragmatic solutions based on a common-sense and merits-based approach.

In my judgment, that is a sound approach, and one which reflects the equitable principles at the root of these issues. Where directors are firmly in place and dealing with their company's property, it is understandable that the courts are reluctant to enquire into questions such as whether a conflict of interest has in fact caused loss. Even so, considerations that equitable principles should not be permitted to become instruments of inequity have been voiced: see for instance *Murad* v *Al-Saraj* [2005] EWCA Civ 959; [2005] WTLR 1573 at [82]–[84], [121]–[123], [156]–[158]; and see the solutions discussed in *Gower and Davies* at pp 420–421. Where, however, directors retire, the circumstances in which they do so are so various, as the cases considered above illustrate, that the courts have developed merits-based solutions. At one extreme (*In Plus Group* v *Pyke*) the defendant is director in name only. At the other extreme, the director has planned his resignation having in mind the destruction of his company or at least the exploitation of its property in the form of business opportunities in which he is currently involved (*IDC, Canaero, Simonet, British Midland Tool*). In the middle are more nuanced cases which go both ways: in *Shepherds Investments* v *Walters* the combination of disloyalty, active promotion of the planned business, and exploitation of a business opportunity, all while the directors remained in office, brought liability; in *Umunna*, *Balston* and *Framlington*, however, where the resignations were unaccompanied by disloyalty, there was no liability.

On which side of the line does Mr Bryant fall?

Mr Bryant's resignation had no ulterior purpose. In human terms, and even though there was no repudiation of the shareholders' agreement, it was forced on him by Mr Foster's hostile and truculent manner and the sacking of Mrs Bryant. As soon as he was told that his wife was to be made redundant, Mr Bryant, not unreasonably, reacted by announcing his resignation. At that time his intention was to find employment with a firm of chartered surveyors, in other words to retrace his steps. In this important aspect, Mr Bryant's case has no connection or similarity with, for instance, *Canaero*'s 'faithless fiduciaries'.

All that Mr Bryant did was to agree to be retained by Alliance after his resignation became effective. He did nothing more. His resignation was not planned with an ulterior motive. He did not seek employment, or a retainer, or any business from Alliance. It was offered to him, it might be said pressed upon him . . .

Moreover, in considering the claim for loss and damage, the judge was unable to identify any existing projects which had actually been subsequently transferred to Mr Bryant or his new company . . .

As for the extent of his fiduciary duties, it seems to me that the judge's realistic findings as to the position within the company after Mr Bryant's resignation makes it very arguable that, so long as he remained honest and neither exploited nor took any property of the company, his duties extended no further than that. To demand more while he is excluded from his role as a director appears to me to be unrealistic and inequitable. As for the innocence of his resignation, although the matter may not be free of doubt, it again seems well arguable on the authorities that it is critically opposed to liability to account, where there is no active competition or exploitation of company property while a defendant remains a director. And as for a reassignment of projects, I have already pointed out that the judge was unable to find that any existing company projects had been reassigned.

Held – appeal dismissed.

Duty not to accept benefits from third parties

The statutory duty

Section 176 of the Companies Act 2006 provides that:

(1) A director of a company must not accept a benefit from a third party conferred by reason of:
   (a) his being a director, or
   (b) his doing (or not doing) anything as director.
(2) A 'third party' means a person other than the company, an associated body corporate or a person acting on behalf of the company or an associated body corporate.
(3) Benefits received by a director from a person by whom his services (as a director or otherwise) are provided to the company are not regarded as conferred by a third party.
(4) This duty is not infringed if the acceptance of the benefit cannot reasonably be regarded as likely to give rise to a conflict of interest.
(5) Any reference in this section to a conflict of interest includes a conflict of interest and duty and a conflict of duties.

Furthermore, according to s 170(2)(b), a person who ceases to be a director continues to be subject 'to the duty in section 176 (duty not to accept benefits from third parties) as regards things done or omitted by him before he ceased to be a director'.

Duty to declare interest in proposed transaction or arrangement

The statutory duty

Section 177, CA 2006 requires a director to declare any interest he or she may have in a proposed transaction or arrangement. The declaration goes to the nature and extent of the interest but is only required if the director is aware of the interest.

(1) If a director of a company is in any way, directly or indirectly, interested in a proposed transaction or arrangement with the company, he must declare the nature and extent of that interest to the other directors.
(2) The declaration may (but need not) be made:
   (a) at a meeting of the directors, or
   (b) by notice to the directors in accordance with:
       (i) section 184 (notice in writing), or
       (ii) section 185 (general notice).
(3) If a declaration of interest under this section proves to be, or becomes, inaccurate or incomplete, a further declaration must be made.
(4) Any declaration required by this section must be made before the company enters into the transaction or arrangement.

(5) This section does not require a declaration of an interest of which the director is not aware or where the director is not aware of the transaction or arrangement in question. For this purpose a director is treated as being aware of matters of which he ought reasonably to be aware.

(6) A director need not declare an interest:

(a) if it cannot reasonably be regarded as likely to give rise to a conflict of interest;

(b) if, or to the extent that, the other directors are already aware of it (and for this purpose the other directors are treated as aware of anything of which they ought reasonably to be aware); or

(c) if, or to the extent that, it concerns terms of his service contract that have been or are to be considered:

(i) by a meeting of the directors, or

(ii) by a committee of the directors appointed for the purpose under the company's constitution.

This is supported by s 182, which deals with existing contracts (as distinct from proposed transactions or agreements), and provides that:

(1) Where a director of a company is in any way, directly or indirectly, interested in a transaction or arrangement that has been entered into by the company; he must declare the nature and extent of the interest to the other directors in accordance with this section.

This section does not apply if or to the extent that the interest has been declared under s 177 (duty to declare interest in proposed transaction or arrangement).

(2) The declaration must be made:

(a) at a meeting of the directors, or

(b) by notice in writing (see s 184), or

(c) by general notice (see s 185).

(3) If a declaration of interest under this section proves to be, or becomes, inaccurate or incomplete, a further declaration must be made.

(4) Any declaration required by this section must be made as soon as is reasonably practicable. Failure to comply with this requirement does not affect the underlying duty to make the declaration.

(5) This section does not require a declaration of an interest of which the director is not aware or where the director is not aware of the transaction or arrangement in question.

For this purpose a director is treated as being aware of matters of which he ought reasonably to be aware.

(6) A director need not declare an interest under this section:

(a) if it cannot reasonably be regarded as likely to give rise to a conflict of interest;

(b) if, or to the extent that, the other directors are already aware of it (and for this purpose the other directors are treated as aware of anything of which they ought reasonably to be aware); or

(c) if, or to the extent that, it concerns terms of his service contract that have been or are to be considered:

(i) by a meeting of the directors, or

(ii) by a committee of the directors appointed for the purpose under the company's constitution.

As may be noted from the provisions outlined above, if an interest has already been declared under s 177, CA 2006, s 182 does not apply.

The related common law and equitable principles

In many respects, the case law which is applicable to the interpretation and application of CA 2006, s 177 overlaps to a considerable extent with that discussed in relation to s 175. As such, it is recommended that the analysis undertaken earlier in this chapter is read in conjunction with this section of the Companies Act 2006.

Effects of a breach of duty

1 The extent of liability

A director cannot be made liable for the acts of co-directors if he has not taken part in such acts and he had no knowledge of them and the circumstances were not such as ought to have aroused his suspicion. The fact that he does not attend all board meetings will not in itself impose liability but habitual absence may do so and the duty may be higher for the executive directors and qualified or experienced non-executive directors (see the *Dorchester Finance* case, above).

A director who is involved in a breach along with others is jointly and severally liable with them and can be required to make good the whole loss with a contribution from his co-directors. There would be no contribution, of course, where money was misappropriated for his sole benefit.

As we have seen, the company can make a director account for any secret profit and a breach will usually entitle the company to avoid any contract it may have made with him. Property taken from the company can be recovered from the director if he still has it or from third parties to whom he may have transferred it unless they have taken the property in good faith and for value.

The court may also grant an injunction where a director's breach of duty is continuing or merely threatened.

2 The company may ratify the breach

The company may by ordinary (or written) resolution waive a breach of duty by a director. Thus, in *Bamford* v *Bamford* [1969] 2 WLR 1107 the directors allotted shares to a company which distributed their products. The object was to fight off a takeover bid because the distributors had agreed not to accept the bid. This was an improper exercise of the directors' powers but the allotment was good because the members (excluding the distributors' shares) had passed an ordinary resolution ratifying what the directors had done.

3 Company indemnity

By reason of the provisions of the CA 2006 the ability of the company to indemnify directors and managers (s 232) in regard to claims made against them was limited, indemnity could be given in these cases where a criminal or civil claim was successfully defended so that the person concerned had to bear his or her costs until the conclusion of the proceedings. Section 233 provides for the provision of insurance by the company to protect directors against the liability that might arise from s 232 and s 234 indicates that s 232(2) does not apply to qualifying third party indemnity provisions.

4 Relief by the court

The court has power to grant relief to a director who has acted honestly and reasonably and who ought, in all the circumstances, to be excused.

In Re Duomatic Ltd [1969] 1 All ER 161

The share capital of the company was made up of 100 £1 ordinary shares and 50,000 £1 non-voting preference shares. At one time E, H and T held all the ordinary shares between them and in addition were directors of the company. E and T did not consider that H was a good director. Although they could have voted him off the board, they decided instead to pay him £4,000 to leave the company perhaps largely because he was threatening to sue the company and generally to cause trouble if he was removed against his will. On payment of the £4,000 H left, transferring his shares to E. No disclosure of the payment of the £4,000 was made in the company's accounts.

It was also the practice for each director to draw remuneration as required and for the members to approve these drawings at the end of the year when the accounts were drawn up. The amounts drawn were as follows:

In period A (E, T and H sole directors and ordinary shareholders)	£10,151 paid to E £5,510 paid to H.
In period B (E and T sole directors and ordinary shareholders)	£9,000 paid to E but no final accounts agreed.
In period C (when additional persons had become shareholders)	E informally agreed to limit his drawings to £60 per week but in fact drew approximately £100 per week.

The company then went into voluntary liquidation and the liquidator began proceedings against E, H and T for:

(a) repayment of the sums paid to E and H as salaries on the ground that these had never been approved in general meeting;

(b) repayment of the £4,000 paid to H for loss of office; and

(c) declarations that E and T had been guilty of misfeasance.

Held – by Buckley J – that:

(i) repayment of the sums of £10,151 and £5,510 could not be ordered since they had been made with the approval of all the shareholders;

(ii) although E had not obtained the approval of all the shareholders to the payment of the £9,000, final accounts not having been agreed, in the circumstances and in view of the general practice E ought to be excused repayment of the £9,000;

(iii) since there had been no disclosure to the preference shareholders of the payment of £4,000 compensation to H as required by company legislation, E and T had misapplied the company's funds and were jointly and severally liable to repay the sums. Furthermore, H held the money on trust for the company and if necessary could be required to repay it. E and T had not acted reasonably in this matter and could not be excused.

Ministerial 'eight-point guidance'

The DTI (now known as Department for Business, Innovation and Skills) issued Ministerial Statements on the 'Duties of Company Directors' in June 2007. Included in these statements is an 'eight-point guidance' for company directors, which will not have the force of law. The points are of useful guidance to company directors who might not be fully familiar with the legal obligations set forth in the CA 2006:

1 Act in the company's best interests, taking everything you think relevant into account.
2 Obey the company's constitution and decisions taken under it.
3 Be honest, and remember that the company's property belongs to it and not to you or to its shareholders.
4 Be diligent, careful and well-informed about the company's affairs. If you have any special skills or experience, use them.
5 Make sure the company keeps records of your decisions.
6 Remember that you remain responsible for the work you give to others.
7 Avoid situations where your interests conflict with those of the company. When in doubt disclose potential conflicts quickly.
8 Seek external advice where necessary, particularly if the company is in financial difficulty.

Essay questions

1 'The rule of equity which insists on those who by use of fiduciary position make a profit, being liable to account for that profit, in no way depends on fraud . . . The profiteer, however honest and well-intentioned, cannot escape the risk of being called upon to account.' *Per* Lord Russell of Killowen in *Regal (Hastings) Ltd* v *Gulliver*.
Comment. *(University of Plymouth)*

2 (a) Give an account of the extent to which the common law fiduciary duties of company directors have been added to by statutory provisions.

(b) Henry is a non-executive director of Dreghorn plc. He also runs his own management consultancy business, Manpower & Co. Dreghorn is undergoing a process of internal restructuring. Without knowing of Henry's involvement with Manpower, one of the other directors proposes to the board of directors that Manpower & Co be engaged by the company to advise on recruitment of key staff. Henry, who happens to sit on the Staff Affairs Committee of the Board of Directors along with two other directors, mentions his connection with Manpower & Co at a meeting of that committee, but it is not minuted and is never mentioned again. The Board resolves to contract with Manpower & Co. Some months later, Henry's connection with Manpower comes to light.
Advise Henry as to his legal position. *(Napier University)*

3 A managing director is usually appointed by the other directors and his powers and duties will depend on his contract of service with the company.

(a) Explain and illustrate whether a director who has not been appointed as a managing director can bind the company as if he were managing director.

AND

(b) Explain the degree of skill and care which the law requires of a company director.

(Glasgow Caledonian University)

4 A director is in a fiduciary relationship with his company. Explain the meaning and effect of this statement with reference to decided cases. *(The Institute of Company Accountants)*

5 (a) What controls are there on the provision by a public company of loans to its directors and on other financial dealings with them?

(b) Eric, Frank and George are the directors of Happy Ltd. At a recent board meeting, Eric proposed that £50,000 be paid to Frank in recognition of his services in opening new trading opportunities for the company. The money has been paid to Frank although no vote was ever taken on the motion. George was away on holiday at the time of the meeting. Happy Ltd now wish to recover the £50,000 but Frank is insolvent. Can they recover it from either Eric or George? *(The Institute of Chartered Secretaries and Administrators)*

6 You have recently been appointed as company secretary to a large public company with a Stock Exchange listing for its securities. The board of directors has asked you for advice on certain matters relating to their duties as directors.

You are required to advise the board of directors on the legal aspects of the following three matters.

(a) The restrictions which exist upon the freedom of directors to issue company shares.

(b) The problems directors might encounter when they deal in the company's securities for their own personal gain.

(c) The restrictions which control the lending of funds by the company to directors to meet their business expenses. *(The Chartered Institute of Management Accountants)*

7 Landrut plc is a property company. Its principal activity is buying land, building private houses and selling those houses directly to the public.

Six directors form the board. The three executive directors are Jack, a solicitor, in charge of the legal department; Jeremy, a quantity surveyor, responsible for land buying; Philip, the third executive director, is in charge of advertising, marketing and house sales. The three non-executive directors are Joe (who founded the company 30 years ago with his brother Jim), Helen (Jim's widow) and Sam (a retired accountant). Joe is chairman of the board.

The following situations have arisen:

(i) The company recently purchased a small rectangular piece of building land for £500,000. Although the land was surrounded on three sides by existing development, it appeared on visual inspection to have access to the highway on the fourth. Jack dealt with the legal work necessary to complete the purchase. It now appears that a routine inspection of the title deeds would have revealed that a two-metre strip of land runs the length of the fourth side preventing access to the highway and making development impossible. The owner of this strip of land is willing to sell at a price of £100,000. Consider the liability to the company of Jeremy and Jack.

(ii) The company developed and sold a small site of town houses. The houses were marketed and quickly sold at £40,000 each. It is now clear that the houses were under-valued and would have easily sold at £45,000. While the company did not make a loss on the development, its profit was only marginal rather than substantial. Consider the liability to the company of Philip and Sam.

(iii) Jeremy asks the board to consider purchasing two building sites: Toddmoor for £750,000 and Rawsum for £500,000. After full discussion, the board decides to proceed with the purchase of Toddmoor and reject Rawsum. Joe later decides to buy Rawsum personally. He does so and immediately resells the site for £600,000. Sam and Helen who remain silent throughout the discussion are also the only directors and shareholders of a small land company, Helsam Ltd, which is concurrently negotiating for the purchase of Toddmoor. Helsam Ltd subsequently acquires Toddmoor. Consider the liability to the company of Joe, Sam and Helen.

(The Association of Chartered Certified Accountants)

Test your knowledge

Four alternative answers are given. Select ONE only. Circle the answer which you consider to be correct. Check your answers by referring back to the information given in the chapter and against the answers at the end of the text.

1 Mike has a service contract with Trent plc for a fixed term of 10 years which cannot be terminated by notice. The contract has not been considered in general meeting. What is the legal position?

   A The contract is valid.
   B The contract is void and the company can terminate it at any time by giving such notice as the company in general meeting may decide.
   C The contract is void and the company can terminate it at any time by the giving of reasonable notice.
   D The contract is void and the company can terminate it by giving six months' notice.

2 Joe is a director of Slow Ltd and has just unsuccessfully defended an action brought against him by a third party in regard to the affairs of Slow Ltd. Can Joe be indemnified in respect of the legal and judgment costs he incurred from the assets of Slow Ltd?

   A The company cannot indemnify Joe without the approval of the members.
   B The company cannot indemnify Joe in any circumstances.
   C The company can indemnify Joe if the court approves.
   D The company can indemnify Joe and the approval of neither the members nor the court is required.

3 Morgan is in breach of his fiduciary duty to the company. How may he be exempted from liability given that the breach is not a fraud on the minority?

   A By a written or an ordinary resolution of the members.
   B By a provision in the company's articles.
   C By a provision in the company's memorandum.
   D By a resolution of the board of directors.

4 Mostyn, who is a director of Test Ltd, has caused the company loss by negligent mismanagement. The company wishes to sue Mostyn but the articles of Test exempt the directors from

liability for negligence in the course of their duties. What is the legal position given that Mostyn has left the board?

A The company cannot claim since Mostyn is no longer a director.
B The company can make a claim since the article is void and of no effect.
C The company cannot claim because the articles are binding.
D The company can claim if the court makes an order overriding the articles.

5 The register of directors and secretaries must, so far as directors are concerned, give particulars in regard to each director of other directorships currently held and those which have been held in the previous:

A Three years B Two years C Fifteen years D Five years

6 Dee Ltd has net assets of £650,000. It intends to enter into a transaction with one of its directors involving a non-cash asset. At which of the following figures of non-cash asset value will it be necessary to attain member approval?

A £100,000 B £2,000 C £65,000 D £6,500

Answers to test your knowledge questions appear on p. 645.

Suggested further reading

Alcock, 'The case against the concept of shareholders' (1996) *Company Lawyer* 17, 177.

Alcock, 'An accidental change to directors' duties' (2009) *Company Lawyer* 30, 362.

Edmunds and Lowry, 'The continuing value of relief for director's breach of duty' (2003) MLR 66, 195.

Fisher, 'The enlightened shareholder – leaving stakeholders in the dark: Will section 172(1) of the Companies Act 2006 make directors consider the impact of their decisions on third parties?' (2009) *International Company and Commercial Law Review* 28, 10.

Grantham, 'The judicial extension of directors' duties to creditors' [1991] JBL 1.

Grantham, 'Can directors compete with the company?' (2003) MLR 66, 109.

Ireland, 'Company Law and the myth of shareholder ownership' (2005) MLR 62, 32.

Keay, 'Section 172(1) of the Companies Act 2006: An interpretation and assessment' (2007) *Company Lawyer* 28, 106.

Keay, 'The duty of directors to exercise independent judgment' (2008) *Company Lawyer* 29, 290.

Kershaw, 'No end in sight for the history of corporate law: The case of employee participation in corporate governance' (2002) *Journal of Corporate Law Studies* 2, 34.

Kershaw, 'Does it matter how the law thinks about corporate opportunities?' (2005) *Legal Studies* 25, 533.

Linklater, 'Promoting success: The Companies Act 2006' (2007) *Company Lawyer* 28, 129.

Lowry and Sloszar, 'Judicial pragmatism: Directors' duties and post-resignation conflicts of duty' [2008] JBL 83.

Miles, 'A philosophical basis for the "enlightened shareholder value" approach' (2012) *Company Law Newsletter* 308, 1.

Prentice and Payne, 'The corporate opportunity doctrine' (2004) LQR 120, 198.

Riley, 'The company director's duty of care and skill: The case for an onerous but subjective duty of care' (1999) MLR 62, 697.

Sealy, 'The director as trustee' [1967] CLJ 83.

Singla, 'The fiduciary duties of resigning directors' [2007] LQR 123, 21.

Wedderburn, 'Employees, partnership and Company Law' (2002) ILJ 31, 99.

22 Vacation of office, disqualification and personal liability

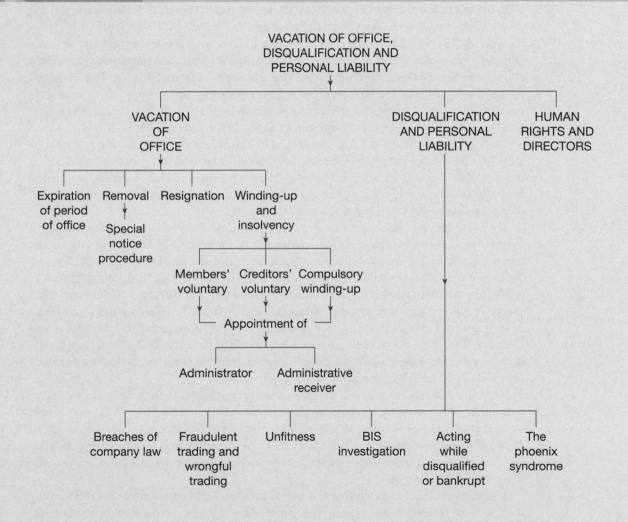

A director may vacate office for a variety of reasons.

Expiration of the period of office

The articles usually provide what the period of office shall be. *Table A* provides that at the first annual general meeting all the directors shall retire from office, and at the annual general meeting in every subsequent year one-third shall retire, or if their number is not three or a multiple of three, then the number nearest to one-third shall retire from office. If the company has only two directors one of them will retire every year if *Table A* applies because one is the nearest to two-thirds of the directors who are subject to the retirement by rotation rules. A sole director must retire every year (***Re David Moseley & Sons Ltd*** [1939] 2 All ER 791) (but see below). The directors retiring will be those longest in office since their last election. Difficulties may arise in the early years of the company's life if all the directors were appointed at the same time. If this is the case, those retiring must, by reason of *Table A*, be ascertained by agreement between the board and on agreement failing, by drawing lots. It should be noted that the model articles for private companies no longer demand retirement by rotation. Directors of public companies are still subject to this in the module articles.

Table A provides that a retiring director shall be eligible for re-election, and further provides that if the office vacated by a director *on retirement by rotation* is not filled, the retiring director shall, if he still offers himself for re-election, be deemed re-elected, unless the meeting expressly resolves not to fill the vacancy or unless the resolution for the re-election of such director has been put to the meeting and lost.

The board may fill casual vacancies and appoint additional directors up to the maximum in the articles. These persons must stand for re-election at the next AGM and do not count in the one-third retiring, but are additional to that number. If not re-elected, they vacate office under *Table A* at the end of the AGM. There is no deemed re-election as is the case with directors retiring by rotation. Furthermore, the managing director and directors holding any other executive office, e.g. finance director, do not retire by rotation. They are subject to the terms of their contracts but cannot be either managing director or executive director unless also directors. Therefore, they cannot continue in post if they are removed as directors by the members under s 168, CA 2006 or under a provision in the articles. They would normally have a claim for breach of contract.

Since the current *Table A* and previous ones make the AGM the lynchpin of director retirement and re-election, private companies now existing under *Table A* may no longer have retiring directors because CA 2006 no longer require a private company to hold an AGM. They will stay in post unless they voluntarily resign or a member calls for a meeting to be held, which is his right, at which to discuss the removal of a director, or a removal procedure in the articles is used (s 303(3)).

Alternatively, companies wishing to dispense with the AGM requirement but still wanting retirement by rotation would have to insert an article under which retirement by rotation was triggered in some other way, e.g. by a date, such as, say, one-third to retire on 31 March each year.

The Model Articles for Private Companies Limited by Shares did not make changes to the way in which private companies may appoint directors either by ordinary resolution of the shareholders or by decision of the directors. However, these Model Articles now cover the position where a sole director who is also the sole shareholder dies. Finally, there is no time limit for a director to retain office however they serve only until the next AGM on appointment by the board, as was the case under Article 79 of *Table A*.

In the Model Articles for Public Companies, public companies may appoint directors by ordinary resolution or by decision of the directors. In relation to the requirement for retirement of the directors by rotation, re-election takes place every three years to ensure consistency with the Combined Code.

In neither the draft Model Articles for Private Companies Limited by Shares nor the draft Model Articles for Public Companies is there a provision for the termination of a director's appointment for failure to attend meetings. Nor is there a more general provision under which the appointment will terminate when all the other directors decide that the particular director should be removed from office.

Removal – under statute

A company may by *ordinary resolution* in general meeting remove a director before the expiration of his period of office regardless of the way in which he was appointed and not-withstanding anything in its articles or in any agreement with him (CA 2006, ss 168 and 169), though weighted voting rights may render the section ineffective. The written resolution procedure is not available for this purpose because the director has a right to put his case against removal to the meeting (see below).

 Bushell v Faith [1969] 1 All ER 1002

Mrs Bushell, Mr Faith and their sister, Dr Bayne, each owned 100 shares in a family company which had an issued share capital of 300 fully paid shares of £1 each. The company had adopted *Table A* for its articles of association but a special Art 9 provided that, in the event of a resolution being proposed at a general meeting for the removal of a director, any shares held by that director should carry three votes per share.

Mr Faith's conduct as a director displeased his sisters and they requisitioned a general meeting at which an ordinary resolution was passed on a show of hands to remove him. Mr Faith demanded a poll, contending that, in accordance with Art 9, his 100 shares carried 300 votes and that therefore the resolution had been defeated by 300 votes to 200.

Mrs Bushell then claimed a declaration by the court that the resolution had been validly passed and an injunction restraining her brother from acting as a director. Ungoed-Thomas J, at first instance, granted the injunction *holding* that Art 9 was invalid because it infringed what is now CA 2006, s 168 and that therefore the resolution removing Mr Faith had been duly passed. The Court of Appeal did not agree with the decision at first instance and allowed Mr Faith's appeal. In particular, Russell LJ stated that a provision as to voting rights in the articles which has the effect of making a special resolution to alter the articles incapable of being passed if a particular shareholder or group of shareholders exercise his or their voting rights against it is not a provision depriving the company of the power to alter its articles or any of them by special resolution, and so does not contravene what is now s 9 and is valid. However, an article providing that no alteration shall be made in the articles without the consent of a particular person would be contrary to s 9 and so would be invalid.

Mrs Bushell's appeal to the House of Lords ([1970] 1 All ER 53) was also dismissed, their Lordships *holding* that the provisions of what is now CA 2006, s 168 did not prevent companies from attaching special voting rights to certain shares for certain occasions, e.g. to directors' shares on a resolution at a general meeting for the removal of a director.

Comment

In the House of Lords, Lord Reid pointed to what is now Reg 2 of *Table A* as justifying the weighted voting provisions. *Table A*, Reg 2 provides 'any share may be issued with such rights or restrictions as the company may by ordinary resolution determine'. This to Lord Reid indicated that there was no reason why shares should not have weighted voting rights if the company wished that to be the position.

Special notice of 28 days to the company is required of the intention to move the resolution. If the company calls a meeting for a date, say, 26 days after receipt of the special notice to foil the attempt to remove, the notice is nevertheless regarded as valid under CA 2006, s 312(4). Under s 312(4), the meeting at which the resolution to remove is to be considered must be called with at least 21 days' notice. It is not necessary that the person who served the special notice should propose the resolution. This could be done, for example, by another member.

Removal under the articles

This power is in addition to any other means of removal that may be provided in the articles, e.g. a power under which certain of the directors may remove others (*Bersel Manufacturing Co Ltd* v *Berry*, 1968, see below). Thus, shareholders who wish to remove a director have a choice: either they can proceed under CA 2006, s 168 or under a provision, if any, in the articles, and if the articles make removal more difficult, as where they require a special resolution, then s 168 will be used. On the other hand, where the articles allow the directors themselves to carry out the removal, as in *Bersel Manufacturing Co Ltd* v *Berry*, 1968 (see below), then, of course, it would be easier to do it through the power vested in the board, first because the articles do not require a members' resolution to effect the removal but perhaps just a letter signed by the company's chairman and secretary and, second, because the article is unlikely to give the director being removed rights of representation as s 168 does.

A quite common use of a clause in the articles setting out a means of removal of directors is to be found in the articles of subsidiary companies where a removal clause allows the holding company to remove the directors of the subsidiary, something which cannot be achieved under s 168 where removal must be by the members of the company of which the person removed is a director.

 ***Bersel Manufacturing Co Ltd* v *Berry* [1968] 2 All ER 552**

Berry and his wife were the first directors of a private company and were appointed permanent life directors by Art 11 of the company's articles of association. In addition, Art 16(H) provided that 'The permanent life directors shall have power to terminate forthwith the directorship of any of the ordinary directors by notice in writing.' Mr Berry's wife died in 1962. The question before the court in this case was whether or not the power given in Art 16(H) could only be exercised during the joint lives of Mr Berry and his wife and ceased to be exercisable when she died.

Held – by the House of Lords – that the power was not vested in the permanent life directors as recipients of a joint confidence but for the securing of their joint interests, and the principle that a bare power could not be exercised by the survivor of joint holders did not apply. Furthermore, the principle that a power annexed to an office passed to successive holders of the office was not conclusive since the office in question died with the death of the survivor of the two occupants of the power. Therefore, on a true construction of the articles the power conferred by Art 16(H) remained exercisable by Mr Berry after the death of his wife. In these circumstances it was possible for Mr Berry to terminate the directorship of any of the ordinary directors by a notice in writing.

Comment

The power to remove a director in the articles is effective even if the directors who exercise the power have acted with ulterior motives as in **Lee v Chou Wen Hsian** [1984] 1 WLR 1202 where a director who was asking for information about the company's dealings and not receiving all the information he wanted asked the secretary to convene a board meeting but was removed by the other directors two days before the meeting under a power in the articles. A removal under s 168 would seem to be effective in a similar situation.

Statutory removal – restrictions

If the s 168 procedure is followed the director concerned is allowed to put his case to the members by the circulation of his representations with the notice of the meeting, or if his representations are received too late for this, they are to be read out at the meeting. The company is required under s 169 to send a copy of the special notice to the director concerned forthwith.

The vacancy so created may be filled at the meeting, or if not so filled, may be filled as a casual vacancy and any person appointed in the place of a director removed under s 168 shall be deemed to hold office for as long as the director removed would have held it, and to retire when he would have retired.

Nothing in s 168 is to deprive a director so removed of any action he may have for dismissal, as where he has a contract outside the articles appointing him for a specified period which has not expired.

At first sight, s 168 appears to give any member of a company who is not satisfied with the way in which a director is carrying out his duties the right to ask the members as a whole to consider passing an ordinary resolution in general meeting to remove him.

Let us suppose, as would be usual, that X, a member of the company, chooses the annual general meeting for this purpose. Let us further suppose that he serves special notice on the company secretary in the proper manner of his intention to propose a resolution to remove the director or directors concerned. Are the directors obliged to place that resolution on the agenda and take it at the annual general meeting? According to the decision of Slade J in *Pedley* v *Inland Waterways Association Ltd* [1977] 1 All ER 209, the answer is no, unless, that is, X or persons joining with him satisfy the requirements of CA 2006, ss 314 *et al*.

This section provides that members representing not less than one-twentieth of the total voting rights of all members or 100 or more members holding shares in the company on which there has been paid up an average of not less than £100 per member can, by making a written requisition to the company, compel the company in effect to put a particular item of business up at the annual general meeting.

Therefore, if a particular member or members cannot satisfy, e.g. the one-twentieth voting rights provision, then the directors are not obliged to raise the question of the removal of one or more of their number at the annual general meeting. Thus, it would seem that the rights given by s 168, and indeed CA 2006, s 510 (power to remove auditors), are much more restricted than might hitherto have been thought. It is impossible to use these sections unless the member or members concerned can satisfy the requirements of CA 2006, s 338 (at least so far as the annual general meeting is concerned).

Although the *Pedley* case dealt only with matters regarding the removal of a director at the annual general meeting it would seem that an individual member is in a similar position if he wishes to remove a director between annual general meetings. Unless the board is willing to call an extraordinary general meeting, he or members joining with him will have to do so. This can be done under CA 2006, s 303, but only by members holding not less than one-tenth of such of the company's paid-up capital as carries voting rights at the general meetings of the company.

Resignation

A resignation need not be in writing; thus an oral resignation at a board meeting is effective. Once resignation has been made it cannot be withdrawn except with the consent of those persons who are entitled to appoint new directors.

Winding-up

The position is as follows:

(a) In a members' voluntary winding-up

Here the company is necessarily solvent and the directors' powers cease only on the appointment of a liquidator, not when the resolution to wind up is passed. However, the members or the liquidator may sanction the continuance of the directors' powers (Insolvency Act 1986, s 91). The directors may decide to resign, but if they do not their powers remain in suspense until they would have retired by rotation and obviously they cannot be re-elected (*Re Zinotty Properties Ltd* [1984] 3 All ER 754). Executive directors may claim redundancy or unfair dismissal as the case may be under the usual employment law rules. There could also be a claim for wrongful dismissal at common law.

(b) In a creditors' voluntary winding-up

Here the company is necessarily insolvent. The directors' powers cease on the appointment of a liquidator. They may resign but if not they vacate office as in (a) above. The position of executive directors is also as in (a) above.

If a resolution for a creditors' voluntary winding-up is passed without a liquidator being appointed, the directors' powers are limited under s 114 of the Insolvency Act 1986, e.g. to the disposal of perishable goods (see further Chapter 29 ◑).

Although the directors' powers cease on the appointment of a liquidator, the liquidation committee or, if none, the creditors can approve the continuance of the directors' powers in whole or in part (s 103 of the 1986 Act). To do so would be rare.

(c) In a compulsory winding-up

The directors' powers cease on the making of a winding-up order or on the earlier appointment of a provisional liquidator. There is no mechanism whereby the directors' powers can be continued. The position of executive directors is as in (a) above.

Appointment of an administrator/administrative receiver

A major change effected by the Enterprise Act 2002 is to restrict the right of a creditor with a full package of securities that includes a floating charge to appoint an administrative receiver. There are a number of exceptions to the prohibition under which the holder of a floating charge entered into after 15 September 2003 will retain the power to make such an appointment. (These will be dealt with in Chapter 27. ◑) However, it should be borne in mind that many lenders, particularly banks, hold floating charges entered into before the above date and may appoint administrative receivers as before. Thus for some time to come the law relating to administrative receivers will be relevant in business. For this reason the following materials have been retained at least for this edition.

On the appointment of an administrative receiver the powers of the directors effectively cease. They are not dismissed, however, though the administrative receiver is entitled to continue the company's business and realise its property without interference by the board (*Gomba Holdings UK Ltd* v *Homan* [1986] 3 All ER 94). There may be rather special situations in which the court will allow the directors to exercise their powers, as the following case shows.

Newhart Developments Ltd v *Co-operative Commercial Bank Ltd*
[1978] 2 All ER 896

A scheme for a housing development in North Wales was to be carried out by a company formed specially for the purpose and jointly owned by Newhart Developments Ltd (Newhart) and the Co-operative Commercial Bank Ltd (the bank), finance being provided by the bank. The scheme got into difficulties and the bank appointed a receiver of Newhart under the provisions of a debenture in common form. In particular, clause 2(c) provided that the company should not deal with its books or other debts or securities for money otherwise than by getting in and realising the same in the ordinary course of business. Clause 5 provided that the receiver should have power to take possession and collect and get in the property charged by the debenture and for that purpose to take any proceedings in the name of the company or otherwise. Newhart took the view that they might have a claim against the bank for breach of contract arising from the development scheme. They issued a writ (claim form) and the bank applied to the court to have it set aside because it had been issued by the directors of Newhart without the receiver's consent. The bank's application was successful in the High Court but Newhart appealed to the Court of Appeal which allowed the appeal thus enabling Newhart's claim to proceed to trial.

Shaw LJ said that the function of a receiver was to protect the interests of debenture holders; he was not like a liquidator whose function was to wind the company up. During a liquidation directors were divested of their powers but not so in a receivership. The fact that a receiver had been appointed did not prevent the directors of the company concerned from exercising their powers as the governing body of the company provided that their acts did not threaten the assets which were subject to the debenture holders' charge. In this case the receiver was put into a curious and unenviable position because the action by Newhart was against the bank which had appointed him. Nevertheless, where a receiver had in his discretion chosen to ignore an asset, such as a right of action, there was nothing in law to prevent the directors pursuing it in the company's name. A company might have creditors other than the debenture holders and those creditors were entitled to expect the directors to bring an action which, if successful, might provide a fund out of which to pay them. If the claim succeeded, the receiver would have an interest in the disposition of any money received, but if he decided not to pursue a claim of this kind, the directors could do so provided that nothing in the course of proceedings would influence the security of the debenture holders.

Under the Insolvency Act 1986 the directors have an obligation to co-operate with an administrative receiver, under the penalty of prosecution and a fine if they do not. Continued refusal can result in a fine on a daily basis.

Directors' powers are suspended during an administration. They must give way to the administrator and in addition the administrator may remove them from office and appoint new directors. However, they are not dismissed merely by the appointment of an administrator and retain some residual powers on the lines of the *Newhart* case. They retain their Companies Acts duties in regard to the keeping of records. An administrator has no statutory obligations in this regard.

Disqualification – generally

A director may become disqualified, and if so he automatically vacates office. The following are the reasons for disqualification:

(a) Under a provision in the articles

Table A provides that the office of director shall be vacated if the director:

(i)   ceases to be a director by virtue of any provision of the Act, e.g. removal under CA 2006, s 168; or becomes prohibited by law from being a director, e.g. is disqualified by the court; *or*

(ii) becomes bankrupt or makes any arrangement or compositions with his creditors generally; *or*

(iii) becomes of unsound mind; *or*

(iv) resigns his office by notice to the company; *or*

(v)   has for more than six months been absent without permission of the directors from meetings of the directors held during that period *and* the directors resolve that his office shall be vacated. Under *Table A* one counts from the last meeting he attended and not the first meeting that he missed. It should be noted also that this provision covers involuntary absence, as where the director is ill.

The articles may be altered to provide additional reasons for disqualification (*Shuttleworth* v *Cox Bros*, 1927, see Chapter 7 ➲), though an express contract is not affected by alterations in the articles and the director may bring an action for wrongful dismissal (*Southern Foundries* v *Shirlaw*, 1940, see Chapter 7 ➲).

A more current example would be where the company is involved in financial services and a director loses a licence or permission to act from a regulatory body such as the Financial Services Authority.

(b) Share qualifications

The office of director is vacated if the director does not within two months from the date of his appointment, or within such shorter time as may be fixed by the articles, obtain his qualification shares, or if after the expiration of that time he ceases at any time to hold his qualification where a qualification is required.

(c) Minimum age requirement

A director may become disqualified if his or her age is below the minimum age of 16 years. This matter has already been dealt with previously (CA 2006, s 159).

(d) Bankruptcy

Where a director is disqualified because of bankruptcy he does not automatically vacate office unless the articles provide as does *Table A.* Article 17 of the Model Articles for Private Companies Limited by Shares provides an undischarged bankrupt is disqualified (unless they have been given permission by the court to act for a particular company).

Disqualification by the court and personal liability

This section is based mainly on the provisions of the Company Directors Disqualification Act 1986 and section references are to that Act unless otherwise indicated.

Disqualification only

The following headings and their supporting paragraphs deal with areas where directors may be disqualified but personal liability for the company's debts is not involved.

Disqualification on conviction of an indictable offence (s 2)

The offence must be in connection with the promotion, formation, or management or liquidation of a company or with the receivership or management of a company's property. Disqualification is possible even though the indictable offence was tried summarily before magistrates rather than by a jury in the Crown Court.

The court which convicts the offender can make the disqualification order. There is no minimum period of disqualification. The maximum is five years in a magistrates' court and 15 years in a Crown or other court. There are no provisions relating to personal liability.

An example is *R v Corbin* [1984] Crim LR 302. C set up in business selling yachts through three companies. He obtained money and property by fraud, e.g. he obtained money from two finance companies to buy yachts by falsely representing that a deposit had been paid on them and took a part-payment for a yacht from a customer but the yacht never materialised. He was sentenced to two and a half years' imprisonment and disqualified from acting as a director for five years.

It should also be noted that there have been disqualifications in more recent times where a director has been tried and convicted of an indictable offence under the Health and Safety at Work Act 1974, for an infringement of health or safety requirements, which is a management offence within s 2.

Disqualification for persistent breach of company law (ss 3 and 5)

A person may be disqualified following persistent default under company legislation, e.g. in filing returns, accounts and other documents with the Registrar.

Persistent default is conclusively proved by three convictions (whether or not on the same occasion) within a period of five years.

There is no minimum period, but the maximum, whether in a magistrates' or other court, is five years. There are no provisions relating to personal liability.

Disqualification following the crime of fraudulent trading (s 4)

The court may make a disqualification order following an offence under CA 2006, s 993, (crime of fraudulent trading). There is no minimum period but the maximum is 15 years. There are no provisions for personal liability.

Disqualification for unfitness (ss 6, 7, 9 and Sch 1)

The court *must* disqualify a director (including a shadow director) on the application of the Department for Business, Innovation and Skills (BIS) through the medium of the Trade Secretary or the Official Receiver if the company concerned has become insolvent while the person concerned was a director (or subsequently) *and* his conduct makes him unfit to be concerned in the management of a company. Insolvency arises under the Act from insolvent liquidation or the making of an administration order or the appointment of an administrative receiver.

Liquidators, administrators and administrative receivers must report alleged unfitness to the BIS.

The minimum period of disqualification is two years and the maximum is 15 years. There is a time limit of two years from the date on which the company became insolvent, e.g. the date when the company went into insolvent liquidation, during which an application must be made, although the court can allow a later application.

The first check on the suitability of disqualification proceedings under these sections is the BIS. The BIS may, not must, apply for disqualification. The second check is with the court which must be satisfied as to unfitness. Schedule 1 sets out matters to be taken into account when determining unfitness.

The Schedule, which is long, reflects the experience of the government's insolvency service and the comments and experience of practitioners. It is concerned with the way in which the directors have managed the company. It includes matters usually found when a company has been badly managed by incompetent directors, e.g. failure to keep accounting records and failure to send the annual return and to keep necessary registers.

Schedule 1 is split into: Part I, matters applicable in all cases; and Part II, matters applicable where the company has become insolvent. This is to take care of disqualification after inspection (see below) where the company need not be insolvent.

There are no provisions relating to personal liability for the debts of the company.

The case law indicates that unfitness has become divided into three main areas, i.e. (1) commercial immorality; (2) recklessness in management; and (3) gross incompetence.

Disqualification following Secretary of State investigation (s 8)

If it appears to the Secretary of State: (a) from a report made by inspectors under s 437 of the Companies Act 1985 (provision for inspectors to make interim and final reports) or (b) from information or documents obtained under s 447 (power to require production of documents) or s 448 (regarding entry and search of premises) of the 1985 Act that (c) it is in the public interest that a disqualification order should be made against a person who is or has been a director or shadow director of any company, then (d) the Secretary of State may apply to the court for such an order. *The company need not be insolvent.* The court must be satisfied that the particular director's conduct makes him unfit to manage a company and Sch 1 applies.

There is no minimum period of disqualification. The maximum is 15 years. There are no provisions in s 8 relating to personal liability of directors.

Disqualification: some illustrative case law

The following cases in which the courts have interpreted the various sections of the Company Directors Disqualification Act 1986 are included in order to enable the student to give examples of the application of the Act in the business context.

Nationality, residence and domicile

The High Court decided in *Re Seagull Manufacturing Co (No 2)* [1994] 2 All ER 767 that a disqualification order may be made against a director regardless of his or her nationality and current residence and domicile. Furthermore, the conduct leading to the disqualification need not have occurred within the jurisdiction. In other words, you can run an English company badly from abroad. The director concerned was a British subject but at all material times he was resident and domiciled in the Channel Islands. Nevertheless, he could be disqualified under s 6 for unfitness. The relevant legislation contained no express jurisdiction requirement or territorial distinction.

Director/secretaries

The High Court also decided in *Re Pamstock Ltd* [1994] 1 BCLC 716 that a director who was also the secretary of the company could be disqualified as much for failure to perform his duties as secretary as those of a director. The company had two directors and one was also the company secretary. It traded beyond the point at which it should have ceased to do so and went into insolvent liquidation. The judge said that as the company secretary one of the directors had failed to ensure that accounts and returns were filed on time and that an adequate system of management was put in place. These were serious defaults which must be taken into account when dealing with the period of disqualification. This implies that it was the director's failure to carry out his duties as a secretary that was at the root of his disqualification for two years. There is, of course, no power to disqualify a company secretary from acting as such.

Inactive directors

It is also worth noting that it is not a defence to an application for a disqualification order that the director concerned was not an active participant in the business of the company. Thus, in *Re Park House Properties Ltd* [1997] 2 BCLC 530 the High Court disqualified three directors as unfit by reason of irresponsible trading leading to insolvency even though they were inactive in the running of the business. The company was run by a husband but his wife, son and daughter were also directors and shareholders but played no part in the running of the business and did not receive a salary or fees. Having disqualified the husband for four years, Neuberger J disqualified the other three directors for two years in each case, saying that a director has legal duties and could not escape liability by saying that he or she knew nothing about what was going on.

Conduct in collateral companies

The Court of Appeal has decided that in order to satisfy the requirements of s 6(1)(b) of the Company Directors Disqualification Act 1986 the director concerned must be a director of the lead company which must be insolvent. However, his conduct in relation to other companies of which he is or has been a director may be taken into account. This conduct does not have to be the same or similar to that in regard to the lead company, and the collateral companies do not have to be insolvent, although the lead company must be. See *Secretary of State for Trade and Industry* v *Ivens* [1997] BCLC 334.

Failure to keep proper accounting records and improper retention of monies due to HMRC, Customs and Excise and National Insurance contributions

The following case covers the above points and others and to that extent is probably one of the most seminal cases on disqualification for unfitness.

Re Firedart Ltd, Official Receiver v Fairall [1994] 2 BCLC 340

Mr Alan John Fairall was a director of Firedart which was an advertising agency. It began trading in 1984 and went into insolvent liquidation in 1988. The Official Receiver as liquidator applied to the court under s 6 of the Company Directors Disqualification Act 1986 (Unfit Directors) for Mr Fairall to be disqualified as a director. The main allegations against Mr Fairall were:

● failure to maintain accounting records as required by ss 386 and 387 of the Companies Act 2006 (formerly CA 1985, ss 221 *et seq.*);
● trading through the company while it was insolvent;
● the receipt of remuneration and benefits in kind which exceeded the level which the company could be expected to bear; and
● improper retention of monies due to the Inland Revenue, Customs and Excise and what is now the Contributions Agency (NI contributions).

In disqualifying Mr Fairall for six years, Mrs Justice Arden stated how essential it was for officers of a company to ensure that proper accounting records are maintained. She said:

> When directors do not maintain accounting records in accordance with the very specific requirements of s 221 of the Companies Act 1985 they cannot know their company's financial position with accuracy. There is, therefore, a risk that the situation is much worse than they know and that creditors will suffer in consequence. Directors who permit this situation to arise must expect the conclusion to be drawn in an appropriate case that they are in consequence not fit to be concerned in the management of a company.

Also raised was the responsibility for maintenance of accounting records. On this the judge said:

> Mr Fairall states that the company's accountants maintained its accounting records from 31 January 1987. The accountants however say that they were not responsible for writing up the books prior to August 1987. However that may be I accept the submission on behalf of the Official Receiver that it

was Mr Fairall who was responsible for providing information to the accountants to enable the accounting records to be maintained accurately and up to date. I further find that he did not provide all the necessary information and explanations, that there is no excuse for his failure to do so and that therefore he is responsible for the deficiencies in the accounting records even after the firm of accountants had been instructed to carry out the bookkeeping function for the company. According to Terence Anthony Price, a partner in or proprietor of Firedart's accountants, the flow of information from Mr Fairall was 'spasmodic' and Mr Fairall was always too busy to provide any necessary explanations. I accept this evidence.

Comment

(i) It is of interest that the court affirmed that it is the duty of the directors to keep and supply accounting information and that the duty cannot be avoided merely by employing accountants.

(ii) The necessity for directors to make use of and understand the company's accounts was also stressed in *Re Continental Assurance Co of London plc* [1996] 28 LS Gaz 29. The High Court disqualified a corporate financier from acting as a director for three years because in his role as a non-executive director he failed to read the company's accounts (which he would have understood) and so did not discover illegal loans made to acquire the company's own shares constituting illegal financial assistance contrary to s 151 of the Companies Act 1985 (now CA 2006, s 678).

(iii) The disqualification regime is important to lawyers and accountants engaged in insolvency practice. For those in business as directors the cases represent a 'warning order' as to what to avoid to prevent disqualification. For professionals in general and audit practice they are less important in that they will normally have resigned some time before insolvency proceedings take place. A wise professional will not stay long with a board that fails to keep accounting records and file accounts!

Pleas in mitigation

As regards pleas in mitigation by directors in connection with disqualification case law indicates that the following might be successful:

- reliance on professional directors; thus where a board contains say a qualified accountant the others being business amateurs, the court may excuse them while disqualifying the accountant though the court will not in any case excuse sheer incompetence;
- the effect on employees may be relevant in the sense that it will be difficult to run the company if the director is disqualified so that jobs may be lost.

Directors' undertakings not to act

It was held by the High Court in *Re Blackspur Group plc* [1997] 1 WLR 710 that an undertaking by a director not to act as such or in the management of a company was not acceptable to the court except possibly in exceptional circumstances. The court, therefore, would not prevent the Secretary of State from proceeding with an application for disqualification merely because the director concerned had given such an undertaking. A statutory amendment would be required to allow the court to accept such an undertaking on a general basis. However, the High Court did say that it would be desirable to amend the relevant legislation in order to give an undertaking the same status and effect as an order under the 1986 Act. In *Secretary of State for Trade and Industry* v *Cleland* [1997] 1 BCLC 437 the High Court did grant a stay of disqualification proceedings in return for an undertaking from a director that he would not work as a director in the future. There were special circumstances in that the director was 60 years of age and in poor health. Additionally, the Secretary of State's action was out of time and the BIS were asking for an extension of time. The action failed.

The Insolvency Act 2000

The relevant legislation was amended by s 6 of the Insolvency Act 2000. This allows the Secretary of State for Business, Innovation and Skills to accept from a director he considers unfit a consent to a period of disqualification without the need for court involvement. The director's undertaking suffices. The relevant periods of disqualification are as for those in court proceedings. The director concerned may subsequently apply to the court to vary the undertaking he has given. The Secretary of State is entitled to make acceptance of the undertaking conditional on there being a statement giving the basis on which the director admits he is unfit to be concerned in the management of a company (*In re Blackspur Group plc (No 3)* (2001) *The Times*, 5 July). The reasons for unsuitability will normally emanate from the insolvency practitioner concerned who has recommended the disqualification.

The decision in *Re Blackspur Group plc*, 1997 (above) is largely overtaken by the Act of 2000, as is *Cleland* since the normal procedure now would be to give an undertaking to the Secretary of State not the court. The material is retained as explanatory of the use of Insolvency Act 2000 procedure.

Disqualification and personal liability

Disqualification and personal liability for fraudulent and wrongful trading (s 10 CDDA 86)

The court may disqualify a director who has participated in fraudulent trading under s 213 of the Insolvency Act 1986 (IA 1986), or wrongful trading under s 214, IA 1986. There is no minimum period, the maximum being 15 years.

Fraudulent trading

The crime of fraudulent trading in s 993, CA 2006 is now separated from the personal liability section, which is in s 213, IA 1986. Criminal liability can arise whether the company is in liquidation or not. Civil liability arises only if the company is wound up.

In the case of fraudulent trading and wrongful trading (see below) only the liquidator may apply to the court for a declaration of civil liability, but all persons, knowingly parties (including the directors), may have civil liability under s 213, IA 1986: for example, a creditor or accountant or auditor of the company may be held liable if he has participated. Only directors and shadow directors are liable under s 214, IA 1986 for wrongful trading. There is thus no danger of auditors, bankers or other advisers who are merely mounting a rescue campaign for the company becoming involved under s 214, IA 1986 unless they participate in management more than is necessary to carry out their functions, when they might be regarded as shadow directors.

Since it is necessary to prove fraud under s 213, IA 1986, which is not an easy matter, whereas only proof of negligence is required under s 214, IA 1986, it would appear that s 214, which sets out the requirements for wrongful trading, will clearly become the main section for directors' personal liability.

There is no need for participation in the company's management or business. Liability for fraudulent trading and to contribute to the company's assets may be incurred by a creditor who accepts payment of his debt out of money that he knows has been obtained by the fraud of the directors (see *Morris* v *Banque Arabe et Internationale D'Investissement SA (No 2)* (2000) *The Times*, 26 October).

It is important to note that s 213, IA 1986 requires that the business has been carried on to defraud *creditors*. The fact that only one creditor has been defrauded does not satisfy the definition of fraudulent trading ruled the Court of Appeal in *Morphitis* v *Bernasconi* [2003] 2 BCLC 53. In that case it was only the company's landlord that was defrauded in regard to payment of rent.

Re Overnight Ltd (In Liquidation) [2010] BCC 796

The applicant liquidator applied under s 213 of the Insolvency Act 1986 for a declaration that the respondents were liable to make contributions to the insolvent company's assets. It was alleged that the company (X) was engaged in missing trader fraud in purchasing computer processing units for importation into the United Kingdom from Germany, so that no VAT was payable on the purchase, and then re-selling the goods within the UK at a price including VAT. X accrued a large VAT liability, but VAT was never paid to Revenue and Customs. The second respondent (C) was the director of X, and the first respondent (H) was the company secretary. H operated in his own name the bank account where all monies were received by X or paid out by X. X's activities ceased when Revenue and Customs obtained a freezing order against its assets. X was wound up and the only creditor was Revenue and Customs. H did not respond to the proceedings, but had submitted in an affidavit that he was never involved in X's affairs except for the operation of the bank account and that he had no awareness of what was really going on in the making of those payments. C gave evidence that he was an informant for Revenue and Customs via an intermediary and that he acted like a delivery boy for X, earning £500 per week. The third respondent (Z) had not been traced. Declaration granted.

(1) Since the only transactions in which X was engaged would have been carried out at a loss if VAT had been duly accounted for to Revenue and Customs, X's business must have been carried on with intent to defraud a creditor or with a fraudulent purpose within the terms of s 213(1), IA 1986. On that basis s 213(2), IA 1986 was engaged. On the basis of the undisputed facts regarding the movement of monies in and out of H's account, the court was satisfied that H either knew much more than he was prepared to admit or, at the least, deliberately chose not to make enquiries as to the basis on which those payments were being made and which he must have realised had the appearance of engagement in dishonest transactions. Accordingly, H's state of mind met the requirements of s 213(2). Based on all the evidence, C's story that he was an informant was incredible and untrue. C's account of his role within X was fundamentally inconsistent with the accounts given by other witnesses who said that C was heavily involved in setting up the transactions. C had also signed a questionnaire stating that he was involved in the day-to-day running of the business. The court concluded that C had the requisite knowledge that X's business was being carried out in a fraudulent manner. The case against Z was not established, as evidence against Z was lacking.

(2) On the question of what contributions H and C should be ordered to pay pursuant to s 213(2), the court had a wide jurisdiction under s 214, IA 1986 *Singer* v *Beckett* [2007] 2 BCLC 287 considered. It would be surprising if the 1986 Act sought to prescribe a different approach in a fraudulent trading case within s 213 from that in a wrongful trading case within s 214. The fact that immediately-adjacent provisions in the statute adopted almost identical wording was a strong indication that no such distinction was intended. It was clearly possible for the court to determine that several respondents should all be jointly and severally liable for the full loss caused to the

creditor. However, it was appropriate to make a separate assessment of the contribution of H and of C on the facts. C was paid only £500 a week but H drew large sums. It was appropriate for H to be liable to contribute to X's assets the full loss caused to Revenue and Customs as a creditor. The proper contribution from C was on a joint and several basis for 50 per cent of that loss.

Re D'Jan of London [1994] I BLCL 561

A director who failed to read an insurance proposal before signing it was liable to the company at common law in negligence. The director signed an insurance proposal filled in by another person without reading it. The proposal gave inaccurate information and enabled insurers to repudiate the policy. The liquidator brought an action against the director in negligence.

Hoffmann LJ held that a director's duty of care to the company at common law is the same as that set out in s 214 of the Insolvency Act 1986. By failing to read the proposal the director had been negligent and it could not be said that the shareholders had authorised the director's act since they did not give any thought to the manner in which the proposal was completed. The case was one where the court would exercise its discretion under s 727 of the Companies Act 1985 because the negligence was not gross and the only interests that were put at risk at the time of the proposal form were those of the director and his wife. The director would be ordered to compensate the company by an amount equal to any sum that he would receive by way of dividend in the liquidation of the company.

Wrongful trading generally

Section 214, IA 1986 sets out the requirements for wrongful trading. They are: (a) that the company has gone into insolvent liquidation; (b) that at some time before the commencement of the winding-up the person concerned knew or ought to have concluded that there was no reasonable prospect that the company would avoid going into insolvent liquidation; and (c) that the person concerned was a director or shadow director of the company at that time. The court cannot make a declaration of civil liability where the time mentioned in (b) above was before 28 April 1986.

If the requirements, (a) to (c) above, are satisfied the court may, on the application of the liquidator, declare the person concerned liable to make such contribution (if any) to the company's assets as the court thinks proper (see below).

The court will not make a declaration if satisfied that the person concerned took every step that he ought to have taken, with a view to minimising the potential loss to the creditors.

The section is concerned with liability for negligence and the court is required to take into account not only the director's own knowledge, skill and experience, but also the skill and experience that can be expected from a reasonably diligent director. The test is objective and not subjective. Thus, a director may be liable even if he does his best if he falls below the standard of the reasonably diligent director. The court will have to consider current practice.

In Re Produce Marketing Consortium Ltd [1989] 3 All ER I

The liquidator of Produce Marketing had asked the court for an order that Eric Peter David and Ronald William Murphy, who were directors of the company, should contribute to the company assets in his hands.

This followed a finding by the court that the two directors concerned were liable for wrongful trading on the basis that they had pressed on with their insolvent company's business in the unrealistic – but not fraudulent or dishonest – hope that it would eventually trade out of its difficulties.

Mr Justice Knox said the fact that wrongful trading was not based on fraud was not a reason for giving a nominal or low figure of contribution. Having taken into account all the surrounding circumstances – that the case was one of failure to appreciate what should have been clear rather than a dishonest course of wrongdoing, that there had been occasions when positive untruths were told, that a solemn warning from the company's auditors in February 1987 that it was insolvent was ignored – a contribution of £75,000 plus interest was an appropriate contribution for the directors to make. Mr David and Mr Murphy were jointly and severally liable for the payment of this sum and, in addition, they were liable for the costs of the case.

Comment

(i) This was the first case to deal with compensation to the company for wrongful trading. It was a significant breakthrough for creditors, since the assets available to them in the winding-up may be considerably increased by a personal contribution from directors if, of course, they can pay it. It does give a warning order to directors to take professional advice at the earliest possible date, since this could be much cheaper than having to face the possibility of making contributions of considerable amounts to the company's assets in the event of a winding-up.

(ii) In an earlier decision, **Halls v David and Another** (1989) *The Times*, 18 February, the court had decided that its power to forgive directors who had acted honestly and reasonably (see Chapter 19, p. 367) was not available in regard to wrongful trading.

Singla v Hedman [2010] BCC 684

A company director who had entered into an agreement with another company for production of a film, knowing that his company had insufficient funding to discharge its obligations under the agreement, had known or ought to have known that there was no reasonable prospect that his company could avoid going into insolvent liquidation and was guilty of wrongful trading under the Insolvency Act 1986 s 214.

The applicant liquidator (L) brought an action for wrongful trading against the first respondent company director (H). L also sought declarations against H and the second and third respondent companies (G and S) that certain alleged agreements were void and sought a declaration that the insolvent company (N) was entitled to an inquiry as to damages for copyright infringement. H was the director of N, which had been compulsorily wound up. Its sole creditor (O) had obtained judgment against it because N had failed to honour its obligations under an agreement which committed it to pay certain sums to O for the provision of production facilities for the making of a film. H had entered into the agreement whilst N had issued share capital of only £2 and no other assets. Production of the film had quickly terminated because N was unable to finance it and because the proposed main actor refused to agree to participate. H hoped to partly finance the production of the film with low-budget film tax relief but that had not been put in place. N acquired its rights to make the film from S under a licence which granted it exclusively and irrevocably, in perpetuity and throughout the universe, all rights it might have to the extent necessary to enable it to do so. Just after N had been wound up, H and S forged several documents, including a letter purporting to amend the terms of the licence to provide for certain termination events and a short-form assignment purporting to have N assign all its copyrights in the picture to S. When it became apparent that those documents were forgeries, H, G and S claimed that there had been an oral agreement to terminate N's rights under the licence. S subsequently granted a further licence for G to make the film, which it did. L argued that H ought not to have entered into the agreement knowing that

N had insufficient funding and had not agreed terms with the proposed lead actor. H, G and S accepted that the forged documents were void and of no effect but submitted that the licence was merely a licence for N to make one film and did not prohibit S from granting a parallel licence to a third party.

Application granted, declarations granted in favour of applicant.

(1) H had taken a casual approach to his duty as director to look to the best interests of N and, if N did not have assets to pay creditors, the duty that he owed to those creditors to minimise their losses. By committing N to its obligations under the agreement without being able to procure the necessary finance or the participation of the principal actor, he knew or ought to have known that there was no reasonable prospect that N could avoid going into insolvent liquidation, for the purposes of the Insolvency Act 1986 s 214(2)(b). He had no reasonable prospect of being satisfied that the lead actor would sign and no reasonable prospect of being satisfied that N would secure the necessary finance to honour its obligations under the agreement. He had been prepared to sign because he perceived that he was not at risk and had been prepared to transfer the risks onto creditors. The requirements of wrongful trading were satisfied and the claim under s 214 was made out, subject to being reduced by any recovery against G or S by N.

(2) It was quite clear that the forged documents had been produced because H and S wanted to have G produce the film. All the participants in the preparation of the false documents did so to create a false title trail which would be shown to backers of G to show that N had no rights because the licence had been terminated pursuant to contractual rights. It was therefore an attempt to defraud the backers of G and deprive the creditors of N of a valuable asset. H had told various lies and the responses of G and S to the claim had been evasive. The contention that there had been any variation of the licence could not be believed. The amendment letter and any alleged oral agreement to vary the licence were void and of no effect under s 238 and s 423 of the 1986 Act.

(3) It was difficult to accept that N would have committed itself to the expense of making a film when it only had a licence. The only possible indication that S had granted a licence rather than an assignment was the fact that it was labelled as a licence but labelling was not necessarily conclusive and was insufficient to displace the other factors. The wording of the licence was far more consistent with a partial assignment which had the effect that as long as the licence subsisted the only body which had the copyright to make the film was N. The copyright therefore remained vested in N. It followed that the subsequent film produced by G was an infringement of N's rights and relief could be sought against G and S.

 ### *Roberts v Frolich* [2011] 2 BCLC 625

The claimant liquidator (L) sought declarations that the defendant directors (D) of a company (O) were guilty of misfeasance and breach of fiduciary duty and of wrongful trading. D had created O as a special purpose vehicle to acquire land worth approximately £900,000 for development as industrial trading units. It acquired the land on June 24, 2004. O borrowed the money for the transaction, including £437,000 from a bank (B). The funding from B was obtained on the basis that the construction of the units was under a fixed-price contract and that a number of units had been pre-sold. That overstated the position. There was a dispute between D and the main contractors (F) for the development as to whether the contract was a fixed-price or a cost plus contract, which was not resolved. F suspended further work on November 27, 2004 having undertaken work and acquired materials. B was not informed that work had been suspended and honoured further payments made by D. Administrators were appointed. O went into liquidation and L was appointed. L contended that D had (1) caused, procured or permitted O to commence and continue the development when they had known or ought to have known that it was speculative, inadequately funded and bound to fail; (2) wrongfully traded as they had known or ought to have concluded on or around July 1, 2004 or, alternatively, by September 1, 2004 that there was no reasonable prospect that O would avoid going into liquidation.

Declaration granted.

(1) D had honestly believed when the acquisition of the site was completed that it was in O's interests to go through with the transaction, and it was beneficial for O as it secured itself a paper profit which, if realised, would have enabled it to pay off existing creditors and still make a profit, *Regentcrest Plc (In Liquidation) v Cohen* [2001] BCC 494 applied. Although D had misrepresented the true position to B regarding the fixed-price contract and pre-sales, the bank had not relied on those representations. D were not acting in breach of their fiduciary duty at the beginning of July 2004; they honestly believed that when the time came for payment there was a good chance that the money would be available. However, the position was different by early September 2004. F had already undertaken work to a value exceeding the sum available and the only proper inference to be drawn was that D could not honestly have believed that continuing with the work was in O's interests. It could only have been a deliberate decision not to enquire or consider the position lest an unpalatable truth be exposed. The only honest thing to do at that stage would have been to stop the development, at least temporarily, for a review of existing and intended commitments and for B to be fully appraised. From mid-September 2004, D were not acting bona fide in the best interests of O and its creditors, *Colin Gwyer & Associates Ltd v London Wharf (Limehouse) Ltd* [2003] BCC 885 applied. D had also breached their duty to O to exercise reasonable care and skill. If O's solvency was in doubt the functions of its directors fell to be performed in that context. The acts which a competent director might justifiably undertake in relation to a solvent company might be wholly inappropriate in relation to a company of doubtful solvency where a long-term view was unrealistic, and no reasonably competent director would have continued with the development after early to mid-September 2004. They would have appreciated that the time horizon for the company was extremely short, that significant further liabilities were about to be incurred and that O had no cash resources. They would have appreciated that to carry on and pretend that there was no problem rather than stopping and assessing the response to marketing was not proper or viable. The more difficult question was whether D were liable for such breach of duty at any earlier date and it was clear that D could not be held as negligent at the beginning of July 2004. L had not demonstrated that they were incompetent in permitting orders to be placed. Allowing the development to continue at that point required a judgement regarding what was likely to happen in the future and it had not been established that no reasonably competent director could have made the judgement made by D.

(2) D ought to have concluded by 1 September 2004 that there was no realistic prospect of avoiding an insolvent liquidation and that continuing with the development constituted wrongful trading, *Produce Marketing Consortium (In Liquidation) Ltd, Re (No 2)* (1989) 5 BCC 569 followed.

Re Idessa Ltd [2012] 1 BCLC 80

The first applicant liquidator (B) and second applicant company in liquidation (C) applied for relief against the respondents (M and P) in respect of alleged misfeasance and wrongful trading. M was alleged by B to have been a *de facto* director of C, and P was a statutory director for more than four years until just before C was compulsorily wound up on a creditor's petition in November 2007. C was engaged in the development and implementation of electronic tools used in electoral registration and election management. P held one-third of the issued share capital, as did two other directors. M did not hold shares. There were other companies closely associated with C, one in the United Kingdom, others in the US, of which M and/or P were directors. B alleged that M and P had made or authorised a number of payments in breach of fiduciary duty which he was entitled to recover on behalf of C and its creditors pursuant to the Insolvency Act 1986 s 212, and that they were liable for wrongful trading within the meaning of s 214 of the Act in that they knew or ought to have concluded by around June 2005 that there was no reasonable prospect that it would avoid insolvency. B submitted that a lucrative US contract was in fact a contract with C, even though payment for it was made to another company's US bank account, and that the money held in that account was held on trust for C and should not have been used as it was.

Application granted in part.

(1) M had acted as a *de facto* director of C from incorporation until its liquidation, *Revenue and Customs Commissioners v Holland* [2010] UKSC 51, [2010] 1 WLR 2793 followed. He had exercised real influence over its affairs and had acted on an equal footing with P such that he was fairly to be regarded as part of its corporate governance.

(2) Contrary to P's assertions, C was at all times balance sheet insolvent.

(3) There was clear evidence that the US bank account was used extensively to fund expenditure on behalf of C as well as for three other companies, and that M and particularly P did not draw any clear boundaries between the companies. That was in sharp contrast with P's evidence that there was no relationship between the companies. The lucrative US contract was undertaken by C; the company actually contracted to do the work was no more than a vehicle to facilitate perceived tax efficiencies. M and P had acted in breach of their fiduciary duties and for improper purposes in causing or procuring C to pay various sums of remuneration to themselves. They were paid from the US bank account to avoid accounting for PAYE and national insurance. Further payments from the US account to M and P were unexplained. They were unable to explain various payments made to them from C's bank account, so the inference was that they were not authorised by C and were not for proper purposes. Numerous company credit card payments were for the personal use of M and P and were not legitimate company expenses. Pursuant to s 212(3)(a) they were directed to repay all of those sums, and they were liable under s 212(3)(b) to repay sums to C in relation to unpaid or underpaid tax and national insurance. Various other payments using company funds were made or authorised by M and P for improper purposes and/or in breach of their fiduciary duties.

(4) By the end of June 2005 it was clear, and M and P should have concluded, that the combined loss of income from external investors and the lucrative US contract meant there was no reasonable prospect that C would avoid insolvent liquidation. There was no evidence that M and P thereafter took any steps to minimise the potential loss to creditors; in fact they continued to use, and often abuse, the company's money as before. They were liable for wrongful trading.

(5) The applicants could recover in respect of the wrongful trading to the extent of the difference between the net deficiency in June 2005, when M and P should have concluded that C was insolvent, and the net deficiency in November 2007, when it actually went into liquidation. They were liable in respect of the s 212 claims up to June 2005; recovery under that head after June 2005 would correspondingly reduce the quantum of the claims under s 214 to avoid duplication, *DKG Contractors Ltd, Re* [1990] BCC 903 applied. Recovery under the pre-June 2005 s 212 claims would be taken into account in calculating the overall net deficiency.

The amount payable

In cases of wrongful trading the court may declare that the director(s) concerned should make a personal contribution to the company's assets if the liquidator of the company makes an application. The amount of the contribution depends on the facts in each particular case and the court is given a wide discretion. However, the general approach is that the directors' personal contributions should be the amount by which the company's assets have been depleted by their conduct. As we have seen, the court can also make a disqualification order. *However, if the court does not make a declaration regarding personal liability, it cannot make a disqualification order.*

Time limits

Section 214 does not straightforwardly contain any time limit on the liquidator's ability to bring such proceedings. The Court of Appeal has decided that it is six years from the cause of action, i.e. the time at which the relevant ingredients of wrongful trading could have been established on the basis of the evidence.

Moore v *Gadd* [1997] 8 LSG 27

The liquidators of Farmizer (Products) Ltd brought proceedings under s 214 of the Insolvency Act 1986 against Mr Richard Gadd and Mrs Ada Gadd, the directors of the company, for a declaration that they knew or ought to have concluded that there was no reasonable prospect that the company would avoid going into insolvent liquidation and that they should make a contribution to the assets of the company. The proceedings were brought more than six years after the cause of action, i.e. the time when the relevant ingredients of wrongful trading could have been established on the basis of the evidence. Counsel for the liquidators contended that the section did carry a limitation period and, indeed, it does contain almost at the beginning, the phrase 'if in the course of winding-up'. Therefore, it was contended that so long as the company was in the course of winding-up, which it was, the liquidators could ask the court for the declaration. The Court of Appeal did not accept this contention on the basis that limitation periods are normally specific and the expression 'in the course of winding-up' was markedly dissimilar to any other prescribed period of limitation. The Court of Appeal went on to conclude that s 214 proceedings were proceedings for the recovery of a sum of money which the court declared the delinquent director(s) liable to contribute to the assets of the company. This fell within s 9(1) of the Limitation Act 1980 which applies to proceedings to 'recover any sum recoverable by virtue of any enactment' (in this case the Insolvency Act 1986). The six-year limitation provision of s 9(1) of the 1980 Act applied and therefore the liquidators' proceedings was struck out as time barred.

Comment

It should be noted that this case has no effect on the absence of time limits in cases of disqualification for unfitness already considered.

The 'every step' defence

Directors may have a defence against personal liability for wrongful trading if they can show that they took 'every step' that a reasonably diligent person would have taken to minimise the potential loss to creditors, once they knew (or ought to have known) that the company was unlikely to avoid going into insolvent liquidation. If the directors can establish such a defence, the court cannot make an order against them.

It may be difficult to satisfy the court that a particular director took 'every step' or even most of the steps and the court will have to take a view of conduct in all the circumstances of the case. Taking every step may well involve immediate cessation of trading or, if the business can be sold, it could mean the appointment of an administrator who will keep the company going until it is sold. Certainly directors of companies which are in danger of insolvent liquidation should take competent professional advice at the earliest possible opportunity.

Abilities of a director

As we have seen, wrongful trading is concerned with liability for negligent mismanagement, not dishonesty, though a dishonest person will, in most, if not every, case have been guilty also of negligent mismanagement. The court has to assess what steps a director took (or ought to have taken) when considering whether to apply the relief from liability. The court must take into account the director's conduct by the standard of a reasonably diligent person who has the following abilities.

(a) General ability, i.e. the general knowledge, skill and experience that can reasonably be expected of a person carrying out the same functions as the director. This is the lowest standard allowed. Nevertheless, general incompetence will not be sanctioned. Thus directors may be liable even if they have done their best if their best was not good enough for the office they held. Furthermore, it is no defence for directors to say that in fact they did not carry out any functions such as attending board meetings because they will be judged by the functions of the office with which they have been entrusted. The general knowledge, skill and experience to be expected for a director of a small company with limited operations will be less than for the directors of bigger and more sophisticated organisations, although the courts have already decided that there are basic minimum standards to be applied to everyone.

(b) Actual ability, i.e. the standard of a reasonably diligent person with the general knowledge, skill and experience that the director actually has. In this case the actual ability of the director will be assessed. This introduces a higher standard for talented and professionally qualified or experienced directors. However, the reverse will not apply and directors with less than average ability will be judged by the general standard even if they are personally below it.

In summary, talented directors are judged by their own standards while incompetent directors are judged by the standard of reasonably competent directors. The court will consider current standards of business practice.

Wrongful trading: profitable but undercapitalised companies

When discussing the matter of a director's knowledge at a particular time of the company's insolvency and yet continuing to trade it is important to note the decision of the Court of Appeal in *Secretary of State for Trade and Industry* v *Creegan* [2002] 1 BCLC 99. It deals essentially with what is meant by insolvency for this purpose. There are two forms of insolvency. One is balance sheet insolvency, i.e. the company's liabilities exceed its assets. The second is cash flow insolvency, i.e. where the company does not have sufficient funds coming in to pay its creditors as they fall due. The Court of Appeal made clear in the above case that both tests of insolvency must be satisfied and the director must know or ought to know that these tests are not satisfied and yet continue to trade. Therefore, a company that is undercapitalised but has at the particular time no cash flow problem can continue trading without the directors being under threat of wrongful trading proceedings even though the situation may not be desirable in general business terms.

Action by directors

There are several actions which directors can take to avoid disqualification and personal liability if an insolvency were to ensue:

(a) Make sure that the board has up-to-date and adequate financial information. A mitigating factor for the court in deciding whether to disqualify directors or find them personally liable is whether the board has considered regular budgets and whether forecasts were produced carefully, even if they turned out to be inaccurate.

(b) Seek professional accounting advice if there are any doubts about the financial position of the company. If things have gone too far, an insolvency practitioner should be asked to give advice on alternative insolvency procedures. If there is still hope for the company, an administration order might be the solution so that ultimately there may be no need for liquidation. The most common applicants for administration orders are directors who hope that the appointment of an administrator may save their companies.

(c) Early warnings from the company's auditors must be heeded. Directors have generally found greater difficulty when asking the court for relief if they have not acted upon warnings from the company's auditors about the financial state of the company.

(d) Any difficulties should be discussed fully at frequent board meetings and the board should try to act unanimously. If one or two directors wish to stop trading but are overruled by the majority who wish to carry on, then the majority may have difficulty later on in justifying their decision to continue trading.

(e) The proceedings of board meetings should be minuted properly. Although board minutes are not normally conclusive, they can be good evidence that a board exercised its functions properly.

(f) Resignation from the board is not usually an adequate response to a problem within the company because a director must take 'every step' to protect creditors. A director who feels, however, that the rest of the board is inadvisedly but implacably determined to continue trading in spite of insolvency or impending insolvency might usefully write to the board giving his view. If this produces no change and he resigns, the court might well accept that resignation was the only course open to him. However, the High Court has decided that a director of an insolvent company whose recommendations regarding necessary economies had been disregarded by the controlling directors was not necessarily to be treated as unfit to be concerned in the management of a company under s 6(1)(b) of the Company Directors Disqualification Act 1986 simply because he failed to resign from the board.

Re a Company (No 004803 of 1996) (1996) *The Times*, 2 December

Mr Taylor was employed as a bookkeeper of a company at an annual salary of £8,000 and was also a director and 10 per cent shareholder of the company. As a result of a letter from the company's bankers in October 1991, Mr Taylor had made recommendations to the company for specific economies which would have given it a reasonable chance of trading out of its difficulties. However, the other directors had refused to implement these recommendations. In September 1993 the company went into voluntary liquidation with a deficiency in excess of £100,000. The Secretary of State had argued that Mr Taylor ought to have resigned his directorship by the end of 1992 and, in failing to do so, he should be treated as unfit to be concerned in the management of a company under s 6(1)(b) of the Company Directors Disqualification Act 1986. The district judge did not agree, though he thought that perhaps Mr Taylor would have been wiser to resign since by continuing to act as a director of an insolvent company he had exposed himself to potential liability under s 214 of the Insolvency Act 1986 (wrongful trading). However, Mr Justice Chadwick said that the district judge, against whose decision the BIS appealed, had properly considered the question of Mr Taylor's personal responsibility. He had seen and heard both Mr Taylor and the company's auditor. A director who protested against further trading, because he thought that there was no reasonable prospect of avoiding insolvency, was entitled to remain on the board using his influence to try to bring trading to an end. It was necessary to consider the purpose of a director remaining in that capacity. If it could be shown that the only reason why he remained a director was to draw his fee or preserve his status, then a court might think he lacked an appreciation of a director's duties and was unfit to be concerned in a company's management. In this case the district judge in the lower court had not found Mr Taylor lacking in this way and therefore the original decision was upheld. Mr Taylor was not disqualified.

(g) The court is bound to look more favourably on directors who have acted honestly and have not tried to benefit themselves at the expense of creditors. The court is also likely to take into account the willingness of directors to make a financial commitment to the company. The court will also consider relevant personal circumstances, such as matrimonial difficulties or more general factors such as recession.

Creditors

If a company becomes insolvent these days, its creditors have a better chance than ever of gaining access to the private assets of the directors in order to increase the amount which they are likely to receive. At the various creditors' meetings, which must be held in insolvent liquidation, creditors can impress upon the liquidator their wish to pursue the recovery of money from the directors personally. Any cash received will be available for distribution to the creditors and improve their position in terms of the dividend which the liquidator can pay.

Disqualification in other capacities (s 1)

It is worth noting that the Company Directors Disqualification Act 1986 provides that when making a disqualification order the court can disqualify a person not only from acting as a director but also from acting as a liquidator or administrator of a company, or from acting as administrative receiver, or from being concerned in any way directly or indirectly in the promotion, formation or management of a company. The legislation could, therefore, bear very hard on accountant/directors who could be disqualified not only from membership of the board but also from certain of their professional activities.

In this connection the Insolvency Act 2000 amended s 1 of the CDDA 1986 by providing that an individual who is the subject of a disqualification order or undertaking cannot obtain leave of the court to act as an insolvency practitioner. He may ask the court for leave to act as a director.

Competition violation: disqualification of directors

The Enterprise Act 2002 applies and inserts new provisions into s 9 of the CDDA 1986. A competition violation involves engaging in conduct that infringes any of the following:

- Chapter I of the Competition Act 1998 (agreements preventing, restricting or distorting competition, e.g. restricting retail outlets for goods);
- Chapter II of the 1998 Act (abuse of a dominant position, e.g. monopoly trading); and
- Articles 81 and 82 of the EC Treaty that carry similar prohibitions.

The Office of Fair Trading makes application to the court for a disqualification order.

Register of disqualification orders

This register is kept by the Registrar of Companies. The public can inspect the register and see the names of those currently disqualified from acting as directors. Obviously, the name is removed at the end of the period of disqualification.

Personal liability only

Acting while disqualified or a bankrupt

By reason of s 15 a person who is disqualified and/or an undischarged bankrupt who becomes involved in the management of a company is jointly and severally liable with the company and any other person who is liable for the company's debts under s 15 or under some other section for such debts and other liabilities of the company as are incurred while the person concerned was involved in management.

In order to prevent disqualified persons and undischarged bankrupts from running a company through nominee managers, s 15 provides that anyone who acts or is willing to act (without leave from the court) on instructions given by a person whom he knows, at the time of acting or being willing to act, to be in either or both of the above categories, is also jointly and severally liable for debts and other liabilities incurred while he was acting or willing to act.

The phoenix syndrome (IA 1986, s 216)

The purpose of this section is to prevent a practice under which company directors may contrive to mislead the public by utilising a company name which is the same as or similar to one of a failed company of which they also were directors in order to conduct a virtually identical business.

The provisions used to prevent this forbid a director or shadow director of the failed company from being a director or shadow director of a company with the same or similar name and business to the failed company for five years. If they infringe the above rules, they commit a criminal offence and under s 217 of the IA 1986 are personally liable jointly and severally for the debts of the second company during the period for which they managed it. If they manage through nominees who are aware of the circumstances, the nominees are also jointly and severally liable with the directors and shadow directors.

The court can, as in *Penrose v Official Receiver* [1996] 2 All ER 96, give exemption from the above requirements and the business and its name can be sold by an insolvency practitioner and run by a new management. There is no objection to this.

Disqualification: can violation of s 216 be taken into account?

The High Court has ruled that when deciding whether to disqualify a director for unfitness under s 6 of the CDDA 1986 the court may take into account the unauthorised use of a liquidated company's name even though breach of s 216 does not appear in Sch 1 of the CDDA 1986. Schedule 1 was not exhaustive in terms of what the court could take into account (*In re Migration Services International Ltd* [2000] 1 BCLC 666).

Directors and National Insurance contributions

The Social Security Act 1998 contains two powers to deal with problems caused by unscrupulous directors who fail to pay employees' National Insurance contributions, as follows: those found guilty of the new criminal offence could be imprisoned for up to seven years, or the NIC debt can be transferred to the fraudulent or negligent directors as a personal debt. (See s 64 of the Social Security Act 1998, inserting ss 121C and 121D into the Social Security and Administration Act 1982.)

Liability as a signatory, CA 2006, ss 82–85

Although the sanction of personal liability has been removed for failure to state the company's name correctly on cheques, such a failure is not devoid of civil consequences, though they are now visited wholly on the company.

Leave to act while disqualified

Section 17 of the CDDA 1986 gives the court power to grant leave to directors to act while disqualified. In *Re Westmid Services Ltd, Secretary of State for Trade and Industry* v *Griffiths* [1998] 2 All ER 124 the Court of Appeal gave guidance as to the exercise of the court's discretion under s 17. This includes:

- the age and state of health of the director;
- the length of time he has been disqualified;
- whether the offence was admitted;
- the general conduct before and after the offence;
- the periods of disqualification of the co-directors;
- the responsibilities that the disqualified director wishes to take on.

It can also be helpful to a submission to the court for leave to act if a professional such as a qualified accountant has joined or will join the board. A helpful case in ascertaining the attitude of the court in the matter of granting or refusing leave appears below.

Re China Jazz Worldwide plc [2003] All ER (D) 66 (Jun)

The director concerned had been disqualified for five years for unfitness in regard to his directorship of China Jazz. He was a part-time director and had been for less than two years. There was no remuneration. He was also employed as a director of four companies in the FM Group but could not carry on in view of the disqualification. His duties in China Jazz had been undertaken in his spare time. It was accepted that he had acted throughout with honesty and not for personal gain. He asked the High Court to grant him leave to continue acting as a director of the FM Group companies and to have an involvement in the management of other companies. His application was granted. The judge referred to relevant circumstances as follows:

- He had not been disqualified for *more* than five years. If he had it would have been unlikely that leave would have been granted.
- He had acted honestly. Leave will not normally be granted otherwise.
- The FM Group had procedures in place to ensure proper accountability. Leave is unlikely to be granted otherwise.

- There was evidence that the companies needed the services of the director and that he needed to continue his career. Although there is case law suggesting that these matters are not a requirement of granting leave China Jazz affirms that they are important and should be included in an application for leave in appropriate circumstances.

Comment

Those who have given disqualification undertakings can also apply to the court to cancel or reduce the period of disqualification. Presumably the above principles will guide the court in these applications.

Human rights and directors

The Human Rights Act 1998 came into force on 2 October 2000. It incorporates the European Convention on Human Rights into UK law. The major impact is to allow human rights issues to be brought before UK courts as distinct from a former requirement to take them to the European Court of Human Rights (ECtHR) in Strasbourg. Importantly, UK courts are required to interpret legislation in a way that is compatible with Convention rights. The likely effect upon proceedings against directors is set out below.

Public authority

The 1998 Act makes it unlawful for a public authority to conduct its affairs in a way that is incompatible with a Convention right. The expression 'public authority' is defined widely and includes government departments and regulators such as the Financial Services Authority as well as courts and tribunals within the UK. The activities of these bodies insofar as they affect directors will provide the major impact in this area.

Right to a fair trial (Art 6)

Article 6 of the Convention gives a right to access to justice and a fair trial in civil and criminal matters by an independent and impartial tribunal within a reasonable time. Impact on directors here will certainly take the form of protection against self-incrimination. In *Saunders* v *UK* (1997) 23 EHRR 313 the European Court of Human Rights held that protection against self-incrimination was at the heart of fair procedure. Mr Saunders had been compelled to give BIS inspectors information regarding the takeover by Guinness, of which he was a director, of the Distillers Company. There were, among other things, allegations of market abuse in the form of loans to individuals to buy Guinness shares so as to increase the market price and make them more attractive to the shareholders of Distillers. When criminal proceedings were later brought against Mr Saunders, the prosecution sought to bring in the information as evidence but the ECHR decided that this would be contrary to Art 6.

It can be seen from the *Saunders* case that Art 6 extends to cover the use of statements made by the Financial Services Authority and the Serious Fraud Office acting under statutory powers, such as the Financial Services and Markets Act 2000. However, Art 6 does not apply where the BIS investigation is not 'adjudicative' in the sense that it reaches conclusions as to liability. Thus in *Fayed* v *UK* (1994) *The Times*, 11 October, a report by BIS inspectors into the takeover of the House of Fraser by the Fayed brothers stated that they lied about their origins, but the European Court of Human Rights held that the report was not unlawful under Art 6 because it was investigative rather than adjudicative, or administrative rather than judicial, and in any case the limits of acceptable criticism of business people involved in the affairs of large companies were wider than in cases involving private persons.

Article 6 also prohibits undue delay in investigating and determining proceedings. Thus, in *EDC* v *UK* [1998] BCC 370 the ECtHR ruled that disqualification proceedings that had taken five years to conclude infringed Art 6 on the ground of unacceptable delay. In this context it is worth noting that Art 6 may apply to BIS investigations which also take many years to conclude.

The employment dimension

Employment law is thought by many to be the area of law where the 1998 Act will have most impact. Directors should be aware of these ramifications as managers of staff. The most significant rights of the Convention that are likely to be involved are in the following areas:

Prohibition of discrimination (Art 14)

The Convention may have the effect of widening the scope of discrimination in relation to sexual orientation, religion, age and sexual identity.

Right to respect for private and family life (Art 8)

This area will, it seems, have the greatest impact on the employer/employee relationship, involving access to medical records and employee surveillance.

Right to freedom of thought, conscience and religion (Art 9)

This may mean that employers will have to allow employees to hold controversial religious or political beliefs and to have time off for religious purposes. Such rights, however, are subject to the employment contract which, if freely negotiated, may exclude time off, as in *Stedman* v *UK* (1997) 23 EHRR CD 168 where the ECtHR rejected a claim by a Christian required to work on Sunday on the grounds that she had signed a contract requiring her to work on that day.

Right to freedom of expression (Art 10)

Employers will be able to insist that confidential information about the business is not disclosed though 'whistleblowers' will be protected. It seems also that the employer will be allowed to place reasonable restrictions on the clothes worn by and hairstyles of employees as part of a dress code.

Essay questions

1   Melchester FC Ltd was incorporated by Albert Arkwright and Bertie Boozer in 1950. The company was set up to take over the running of Melchester FC, a Lancashire football club, who were founder members of the Football League. Arkwright, at the age of 70, is still a director and shareholder of the company. Bertie has since died with his shares passing on to his family who

have recently sold out to Loadsamoney and two associates, all three becoming directors of the company.

Arkwright is deeply passionate about football and in particular has a strong affection for Melchester FC, having spent a great deal of his childhood and adult life associated with the club. Loadsamoney has expansionist plans for the club and is considering ways of merging Melchester FC with Ambridge United, a rival team, and also to start up a professional basketball team, both of which will require a heavy investment.

Arkwright objects to Loadsamoney's plans but finds himself outvoted on the board. Loadsamoney considers that Arkwright can no longer serve a useful purpose. He decides to remove him as director by securing an ordinary resolution at the next general meeting. Despite his removal, Arkwright is still able to raise objections as a shareholder. His objections, however, go unheard and he receives minimal co-operation from the board in response to his requests for information on the company's plans. Loadsamoney, annoyed with Arkwright's interference, decides to make an offer to Arkwright to buy out his shareholding at a price fixed by the board. Arkwright declines Loadsamoney's offer, but finds himself faced with a proposal, at an extraordinary meeting of the company, that the company's articles be changed so that any member can be requested by the board to transfer their shares to a nominated person at a fair value.

Advise Arkwright. *(University of Greenwich)*

2 'The combined effect of the Insolvency Act 1986 and the Company Directors Disqualification Act 1986 is to give a clear signal to directors that to allow their companies to continue trading and to incur debts at a time when the position is hopeless is both a costly and foolhardy thing to do. In particular, the temptation to use money owed to the Crown to keep their companies afloat must be avoided at all costs.' Discuss.

(The Institute of Chartered Secretaries and Administrators)

3 D was appointed director and managing director of X Ltd. The terms of his service contract provided that he should hold office for eight years and this term was also stated in the articles of association of X Ltd. The other directors of the company decided that D should be removed from his directorship and managing directorship. They placed a resolution before the shareholders in general meeting that D be removed from office and it was duly passed. D was at that meeting and made a statement that he intended to take legal advice for he was certain that he could not be removed in breach of the articles of association and of his service contract. The directors of X Ltd have asked your advice.

You are required to draft a statement for the board of directors explaining whether the shareholders had the authority to pass the resolution and suggesting what legal redress D might have. *(The Chartered Institute of Management Accountants)*

4 Mini-mo Ltd is a registered company whose main activity is the production of animal feedstuffs. The company has a fully issued share capital of 10,000 £1 shares. The three directors, George, Sheila and Robert, each hold 1,000 shares and the remaining shareholders Emily and Maurice hold 5,200 and 1,800 shares respectively. The articles provide that in the event of a resolution being proposed at a general meeting for the removal of a director any shares held by that director should carry three votes per share. Maurice is a director of another company, Plucko Ltd, whose main activity is also the production of animal feedstuffs. The directors wish to alter the articles of the company to give them power to require any member who engages in any competing business to transfer his shares at a fair value to the directors' nominees. Emily agrees to support the proposed alteration.

(a) Advise the directors on the statutory procedures which must be observed to effect the change in the articles.

The articles are altered accordingly. Emily is then surprised to find that the three directors have appropriated and allocated Maurice's shares equally between themselves. She decides to take action to remove George, Sheila and Robert as directors.

(b) Advise Maurice as to whether he can successfully challenge the alteration to the articles.

(c) Advise Emily on (i) the procedures she must follow if she wishes to remove the directors from office, and (ii) her chances of success.

(The Association of Chartered Certified Accountants)

5 Harold was appointed managing director of Aire Ltd with a service contract for a term of four years. A group of shareholders is dissatisfied with Harold's conduct of the company's affairs and wishes to remove him from office.

Advise the shareholders.   *(The Institute of Chartered Accountants in England and Wales)*

6 The following situations have arisen in the affairs of Harbottle Ltd:

(a) The company's managing director and founder member wishes to retire and move permanently to the south of France. For this purpose he needs capital. He owns 900,000 shares in the company which he needs to dispose of. Other members of the company are willing and able to purchase between them 600,000 of his shares. There is no other way of purchasing his remaining 300,000 shares without resorting to the company's capital. The directors propose to use the company's capital to purchase the shares.

(b) The company has a class of preference shares entitled to 8 per cent cumulative dividend. Dividends have not been declared for the last four years as the company has not been making significant profits. This year the company has made substantial profits large enough to pay the arrears of dividend. The directors propose to transfer the profits to reserve.

(c) The company owns a luxury villa in the south of France. Because of the property boom the villa has trebled in price. The directors of the company, however, resolve to sell the villa to the managing director's wife at its original price.

Discuss the legal validity of the above transactions.   *(University of Plymouth)*

7 'A modern company secretary is not a mere clerk but an officer of the company with extensive duties and responsibilities and he has ostensible authority to sign contracts in connection with the administration side of a company's affairs.'

Discuss this statement.   *(The Institute of Company Accountants)*

Test your knowledge

Four alternative answers are given. Select ONE only. Circle the answer which you consider to be correct. Check your answers by referring back to the information given in the chapter and against the answers at the end of the text.

1 A director can be removed at a general meeting of his company. What kind of resolution is required?

A An ordinary resolution following special notice to the company.
B An ordinary resolution.
C A special resolution following special notice to the company.
D A special resolution.

2 The following directors of Julius Ltd have been disqualified for two years following their miscon- duct while directors of the company – Jane, Harry, Mary and James. Jane is now working as a secretary with Julius Ltd; Harry has taken a management consultancy appointment with Archer Ltd; Mary has formed a new company in a different kind of business; and James has returned to his accountancy practice and has recently accepted an appointment as an administrative receiver. Which one of them is complying with the disqualification order?

A James   B Mary   C Harry   D Jane

3 The court is about to disqualify the directors of Blue Ltd for unfitness. How long may the order last?

A A maximum of 15 years with no minimum.
B A minimum of two years with a maximum of 15 years.
C A minimum of two years with a maximum of five years.
D A minimum of five years with a maximum of 15 years.

4 Unless the articles of a company carry a contrary provision directors must retire from office:

A Every five years but may be re-elected any number of times.
B Every three years with re-election any number of times.
C Every three years with re-election only three more times.
D Every five years with re-election only three more times.

5 Harry has been found guilty of persistent default in sending various documents and returns to the Registrar. What is the maximum period for which he may be disqualified?

A Five years   B Ten years   C Three years   D Fifteen years

6 Joe has been found guilty of wrongful trading. What is the maximum period for which he can be disqualified?

A Fifteen years   B Five years   C Ten years   D Three years

Answers to test your knowledge questions appear on p. 645.

23

Meetings and resolutions

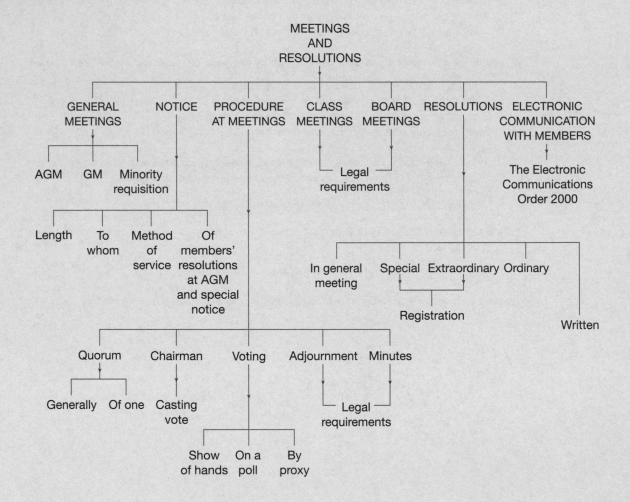

A company may be required to hold certain meetings of shareholders, i.e. annual general meetings and ordinary meetings. The articles of a company provide for the holding of general meetings, the relevant provisions of *Table A* being in Regs 36 and 37.

Once the principles of meetings and resolutions in terms of paper communication have been grasped, the reader will find it necessary to refer to the material relating to the introduction of new technology in terms of changes to the law to allow electronic communication with shareholders.

General meetings of the company

1 Annual general meeting

The requirement for private companies to hold an annual general meeting has been abolished. Rather than holding a general meeting, private companies can use the written resolution procedure set out in Chapter 2 of Part 13 of the CA 2006. In relation to private companies which are not traded companies, the CA 2006 does not require them to hold annual general meetings. As the CA 2006 does not prohibit such a meeting, a company will only need to hold annual general meetings where required to do so by its articles. This issue will exist for private companies formed prior to 1 October 2007 who may wish to amend their articles or adopt new ones to avoid the requirement to hold annual general meetings. A private company that is a traded company is now required to hold annual general meetings.

CA 2006 makes separate provision for annual general meetings for public companies. Section 336 has a requirement that the annual general meeting of a public company must be held within six months of the end of a public company's financial year (that is in each period of six months beginning with the day following its accounting reference date) in addition to any other meetings held during the period. This replaces the requirement that not more than 15 months must elapse between the date of one annual general meeting and the next, but so long as a company holds its first annual general meeting within 18 months of its incorporation it need not hold it in the year of its incorporation or in the following year.

CA 1985, s 367 provided that, on the application of any member of a company, the Secretary of State had the power to call, or direct the calling of, an annual general meeting where the company had failed to hold an annual general meeting in accordance with section 366 of CA 1985. This provision has not been included in CA 2006.

There is no statutory provision which deals with the business which may be conducted at the annual general meeting and *Table A* contains no such provision.

A matter that may be overlooked arises as a result of the provisions of Sch 13, Part IV para 29 which states that the register of directors' interests must be produced at the commencement of the meeting and remain open and accessible during the continuance of the annual general meeting to any person attending the meeting. This has now been repealed in 2007 and not replaced.

The meeting is a safeguard for the shareholders in that it provides them with an opportunity of questioning the directors on the accounts and reports, which are usually, but not necessarily, presented to the annual general meeting, and on general matters. Moreover, it is a meeting which must be held whether the directors wish it or not, unless in a private company an elective resolution has been passed to dispense with the need to hold it.

2 General meetings

The CA 2006 does not refer to 'extraordinary general meetings' as such a general meeting which is not an annual general meeting should simply be referred to as a general meeting. The court has power under CA 2006, s 306 (formerly CA 1985, s 371) to call a general meeting if it is impractical to call one in the usual way, and the court may direct that one member of the company present in person or by proxy shall be deemed to constitute a valid meeting.

An example of the use of CA 1985, s 371 is to be found in the following case.

Re British Union for the Abolition of Vivisection (1995) *The Times*, 3 March

It appeared that in 1994 an EGM had been so disrupted that a near riot had broken out as a result of animosity between opposing factions within the Union and no business had been done. The Union's articles stated that no votes by proxy were allowed at AGMs or EGMs, but the committee members of the Union wished to change that provision, allowing proxies so that it would be possible for members to vote without actually attending the meeting. The committee members asked the court to direct them to hold an EGM at which only the 13 committee members would be present, i.e. 13 out of 9,000 members. The change to proxy voting could then be resolved upon at the meeting. The court made the necessary direction under s 371. It was clearly not practical to hold a meeting in the normal way or, in fact, at all.

Comment

(i) It may seem that the case is likely to apply in rather special and isolated situations but it could be useful as a precedent where, in a private family company, opposing factions within the family were making it difficult to do business. However, it should be borne in mind that the courts are unlikely to use the section to suppress genuine and orderly debate.

(ii) Section 371 is not available to sort out disputes between shareholders simply because they have equal shareholdings. It is available for quorum disputes as where A and B are the only share-holders in Boxo Ltd and, say, A will not attend general meetings so that there is no quorum and business cannot proceed. In such a case the court can, under s 371, authorise a valid meeting with only B present. However, if the problem is deadlock as where A and B each own 50 per cent of the voting shares and business cannot proceed because A votes one way and B another, s 371 is not available to enable the court to make an order allowing B to outvote A or vice versa (see *Ross v Telford* [1998] 1 BCLC 82). Such a deadlock will, unless it can be resolved by agreement between the parties, generally result in the liquidation of the company.

(iii) The decision in *Ross* may be contrasted with *Re Whitchurch Insurance Consultants Ltd* [1993] BCLC 1359 where the shareholdings were unequal. The issued capital was 1,000 shares, of which the husband held 666 and the wife 334. Their personal and business relationship had broken down. The wife would not attend board and general meetings so that there was no quorum and the husband could not remove his wife from the board. The court ordered that a general meeting be held without the wife because otherwise a minority shareholder would prevent the majority share-holder from exercising majority power.

In addition, an auditor has the right to requisition a meeting on his resignation. Under CA 2006, s 518 where a resigning auditor has given a statement of the circumstances connected with his resignation (in accordance with s 519), that auditor is entitled to call on the directors of the company to convene a general meeting for the purposes of receiving and considering an explanation of those circumstances (see Chapter 25 ○), and a meeting must be called by a plc if there is a serious loss of capital pursuant CA 2006 s 656 (see Chapter 10 ○).

Convening of general meetings

General meetings are normally convened by the board of directors (CA 2006, s 302), though, as noted above, the court has power to do so in certain circumstances. CA 2006, s 306 gives the court power to order a meeting of the company and to direct the manner in which that meeting is called, held and conducted. The court can order a general meeting on its own motion or on the application of any director or any member who would be entitled to vote at the meeting: section 306(2). If the articles contain provisions relating to the directors' ability to call general meetings, these cannot supersede CA 2006 by preventing the board from calling general meetings.

The company secretary or other executive has no power to call general meetings unless the board ratifies his act of doing so (*Re State of Wyoming Syndicate* [1901] 2 Ch 431).

As regards the time and place at which the meeting is to be held, this is in general terms a matter for the directors. However, it must be reasonably convenient for the members to attend and this probably prevents general meetings being held overseas. In addition, the directors must act in good faith when they call a meeting. Thus, in *Cannon v Trask* (1875) LR 20 Eq 669 the directors called the annual general meeting at an earlier date than was usual for the company to hold it in order to ensure that transfers of shares to certain persons who opposed the board would not be registered in time so that they would be unable to vote. An action for an injunction to stop the meeting succeeded. It should also be noted that once the directors have called the meeting they cannot postpone it and the meeting may be held even though the directors try to postpone or cancel it (*Smith v Paringa Mines Ltd* [1906] 2 Ch 193). With the consent of the majority of those present and voting it could, however, once held, be adjourned.

Rights of minorities to requisition general meetings

The articles of a company usually provide that, apart from annual general meetings, meetings of the company can be convened by the directors whenever they think fit. The directors are, therefore, seldom under any obligation to call general meetings at which minority grievances can be put forward. However, under CA 2006, s 303 *et seq.* (formerly CA 1985, s 368) members holding not less than one-tenth of such of the company's paid-up capital as carries voting rights at the general meetings of the company can requisition a meeting. Thus, where a company has 200,000 £1 A ordinary shares, 50p paid, and (say) 50,000 B ordinary shares of £1 each, fully paid, and all the shares carry voting rights, the requisitionists must have paid up on their shares, whether A or B ordinary, one-tenth of £150,000, i.e. £15,000. Where the company does not have a share capital, members of the company representing not less than one-tenth of the total voting rights of all the members having a right to vote at general meetings of the company may make a requisition. The required percentage becomes 5 per cent in the case of a private company in which more than 12 months has elapsed since the end of the last general meeting (s 303(3)).

The requisitionists must deposit at the company's registered office a signed requisition stating the objects for which they wish a meeting of the company to be held. The directors must then convene a *general meeting*, and if they have not done so within 21 days after the deposit of the requisition, the requisitionists, or any of them representing more than one-half of their total voting rights, may themselves convene the meeting so long as they do so within three months of the requisition. The requisitionists can recover reasonable expenses so incurred from the company, and the company may in turn recover these from the fees of the defaulting directors (see CA 2006, ss 304 and 305).

To ensure that the directors do not call the meeting for a date so far in the future as to frustrate the minority's aims the Act provides that the directors are deemed not to have duly convened the meeting if they call it for a date more than 28 days after the notice convening it. If they infringe this rule, the requisitionists' power to call the meeting arises.

The company's articles cannot deprive the members of the right to requisition a meeting although they can provide that a *smaller number* of persons may requisition, e.g. one-twentieth. An article would not be effective if it required a larger number than one-tenth.

It should be noted that CA 2006, s 303 uses the plural expression 'members' throughout so that the section basically requires two or more members holding the one-tenth share or voting requirement. One member would not suffice even though he held the one-tenth requirement. This requirement is presumably to ensure that there will be a quorum at the requisitioned meeting.

CA 2006, s 306(2) allows one member to ask the court to call a meeting and says so but there is no quorum problem here because the court when calling a meeting can fix the quorum even at one if it wishes.

CA 2006, ss 303–305 provide the method by which members may demand a general meeting. Section 303 requires the directors to call a general meeting once the company has received requests for companies with a share capital, from members representing at least 5 per cent of such of the paid-up capital of the company as carries the right of voting at general meetings of the company (excluding any paid-up capital held as treasury shares) and for companies without a share capital, from members who represent at least 5 per cent of the total voting rights of all the members having a right to vote at general meetings.

A member may request a general meeting in hard copy or electronic form pursuant to CA 2006, s 303(6)(a). However, the request must be authenticated under CA 2006, s 303(6)(b). CA 2006, s 303(4)(a) necessitates that the request must state the general nature of the business to be dealt with at the meeting so, for example, the text of a resolution to be presented at the meeting might be included in the general nature statement. CA 2006, s 304 requires the directors to call a general meeting with 21 days of receiving a valid request under s 303 and that the general meeting to be held on a date not more than 28 days after the date of the notice of meeting. Under CA 2006, s 304(2), if the members' request for a general meeting identifies a resolution intended to be moved at the meeting, the notice of meeting must include notice of this resolution.

CA 2006, s 305 (Power of members to call meeting at company's expense) provides that the members who requisitioned the meeting or any of them representing more than half of the total voting rights of the requisitionists may themselves call the meeting where the directors are required to call a meeting under s 303 but fail to do so within the requisite time period set out in s 304. CA 2006, s 305(2) provides that where the members' meeting request identified a resolution intended to be moved at the meeting, the notice of meeting must include notice of this resolution. CA 2006, s 305(3) provides that the meeting must be called for a date not more than three months after the date on which the directors became subject to the requirement to call a meeting. CA 2006, s 305(6) states that members shall be reimbursed their reasonable expenses by the company with CA 2006, s 305(7) requiring that the directors who are in default in relation to calling the meeting having such expenses deducted by the company from their directors' fees or other remuneration due to them.

Notice of meetings

Regulations relating to notice of meetings are usually laid down in the company's articles and these must be referred to, although there are certain statutory provisions with regard to notice which must not be overlooked.

Length of notice

The company's articles must be followed, but CA 2006, s 307 (formerly CA 1985, s 369) provides that any provision in the company's articles is void if it provides for the calling of a meeting of the company (other than an adjourned meeting) by a shorter notice than:

(a) in the case of the annual general meeting not less than 21 days' notice in writing; and
(b) in the case of a meeting other than an annual general meeting, 14 days' notice in writing.

Where the company's articles do not make provision, the above periods apply. The Combined Code that applies to public limited companies but is an indicator of good practice in all companies generally recommends 20 working days for annual general meeting notice and papers.

Short notice

It should be noted that a meeting of a company, if called by a shorter period of notice than that prescribed in the CA 2006 or by the company's articles, shall be deemed *validly called* if:

(a) in the case of the annual general meeting, *all the members entitled to attend and vote* there at *agree* (CA 2006, s 337(2)); and
(b) in the case of any other meeting, *it is agreed by a majority in number* of the members having a right to attend and vote at the meeting, being a majority together *holding not less than 95 per cent in nominal value of the shares* giving a right to attend and vote at the meeting; *or* in the case of a company not having a share capital, a majority representing *95 per cent of the total voting rights* at the meeting (CA 2006, ss 307(5) and (6)).

Since in both (a) and (b) above *all* the members of the company with voting rights would have to be in attendance the concession is in practice confined to meetings of private companies. Furthermore, it was held in **Re Pearce Duff Co Ltd** [1960] 3 All ER 222 that the mere fact that all the members are present at the meeting and pass a particular resolution, either unanimously or by a majority holding 95 per cent of the voting rights, does not imply consent to short notice and anyone who voted for a resolution in these circumstances can later challenge it. In practice a document setting out the agreement of the members to short notice should be signed by members at the meeting if all are present or, if not, consent can be given by means of a number of documents sent out to members and returned by post. There would appear to be no reason why this should not be done after a meeting called by inadequate notice has taken place.

The days of notice must be 'clear days', i.e. exclusive of the day of service and the day of the meeting (CA 2006, s 360).

Persons to whom notice must be given

CA 2006, s 310 sets forth persons entitled to receive notice. Notice of a general meeting must be sent to every member of the company and every director. Section 310 has effect subject to any enactment or provisions of the company's articles. For instance, *Table A* provides that notice of general meetings shall be given to all the members, to all persons entitled to a share in consequence of the death or bankruptcy of a member, and to the directors and auditors. Notice of every general meeting must be given to the auditors, and if notice of a meeting is not given to every person entitled to notice, the proceedings and any resolution passed at the meeting will be invalid.

Young v *Ladies Imperial Club* [1920] 2 KB 523

Mrs Young, who was a member of the club, was expelled by a resolution passed by the appropriate committee. The Duchess of Abercorn, who was a member of the committee, was not sent a notice of the meeting, it being understood that she would not be able to attend. In fact, she had previously informed the chairman that she would not be able to attend. Nevertheless, in this action which was concerned with the validity of the expulsion, it was *held* – by the Court of Appeal – that the failure to send a notice to the Duchess invalidated the proceedings of the committee and rendered the expulsion void. *Per* Scrutton LJ:

> Every member of the committee ought, in my view, to be summoned to every meeting of the committee except in a case where summoning can have no possible result, as where the member is at such a distance that the summons cannot effectively reach the member in time to allow him or her to communicate with the committee. Extreme illness may be another ground, though I should myself require the illness to be extremely serious, because a member of the committee receiving a notice to attend may either write to ask for an adjournment of the meeting or express his views in writing to the committee, and I should require the illness to be such as to prevent that form of action being taken on receiving notice of such a meeting.

However, under CA 2006, s 313 the *accidental omission to give notice* of a meeting, or the non-receipt of notice of a meeting by any person entitled to receive notice, *does not invalidate the proceedings at that meeting* and any resolutions passed.

Re West Canadian Collieries Ltd [1962] Ch 370

The company failed to give notice of a meeting to certain of its members because their plates were inadvertently left out of an addressograph machine which was being used to prepare the envelopes in which the notices were sent. The proceedings of the meeting were not invalidated, it being *held* in the High Court to be an accidental omission within an article of the company similar to *Table A*.

Musselwhite v *C H Musselwhite & Sons Ltd* [1962] Ch 964

The company failed to give notice of a general meeting to certain persons who had sold their shares but had not been paid and remained on the register of members. The directors believed that the mere fact of entering into a contract of sale had made them cease to be members.

Held – in the High Court – the proceedings of the general meeting were invalidated since the error was one of law and not an accidental omission within an article of the company similar to *Table A*.

In the absence of a provision to the contrary in the articles, preference shareholders without the power to vote have no right to be summoned to general meetings (*Re Mackenzie & Co Ltd* [1916] 2 Ch 450). Where the company has share warrants, some arrangements will have to be made to advertise the meeting if the holders of the warrants have any right to attend under the articles.

CA 2006, s 307 sets out, as we have seen, certain minimum periods of notice for general meetings. This makes it impossible and therefore unnecessary to send notice to persons becoming members after the notice is sent out. Such persons, do, however, have the right to attend and vote at the meeting or appoint a proxy and if this causes difficulty legal advice should be sought on the drafting of an article which states expressly that notice need not be sent to such persons and also that they cannot attend and vote at the meeting.

Method of service

CA 2006, s 308 designates how notice of a general meeting of a company must be given. CA 2006, s 309 indicates when a website notice is appropriate. *Table A* provides for service of notice and this sort of procedure is generally followed. These provisions are as follows:

(i) A notice may be given by the company to any member or his representative either personally or by sending it by post to his registered address.

(ii) A notice may be given to *joint holders* by giving notice to the first joint holder named in the register of members.

The minimum number of days which must intervene between the day of posting the notice and the day of the meeting is not affected by the length of time which it takes for the Post Office to deliver the notice. The articles must, of course, be looked at but under Reg 115 of *Table A* service of a notice of meeting is deemed to have been effected 48 hours after posting. Thus under *Table A* an annual general meeting due to be held on 25 March would be validly convened by notices sent on 1 March whether by first or second class mail. It will be recalled that days of notice must be 'clear days'.

However, such a provision will not always be applied. In *Bradman* v *Trinity Estates plc* [1989] BCLC 757, the High Court refused to accept deemed delivery of notices posted to shareholders outside London during a postal dispute. Those who attended the meeting were members with London addresses who received their notices by courier. Mr Bradman, a shareholder, asked for and obtained an injunction to prevent the company from acting on a resolution passed at the meeting.

If the letter containing the notice has clearly not been delivered, as where it is returned to the company, notice would under *Table A*, Reg 115 still be regarded as having been given. Evidence of proper posting is, under that regulation, 'conclusive' evidence that notice was given and this cannot be rebutted as is the case with all evidence which is regarded as conclusive. Other articles may not carry a provision regarding the conclusive nature of receipt of notice and evidence of non-delivery would prevent the deeming provisions from applying. These points were decided in *Re Thundercrest* (1994) *The Times*, 2 August.

Contents of notice

CA 2006, s 311 sets forth the contents of notices of a general meeting. The notice of a general meeting must state the time and date of the meeting and the place of the meeting. Notice of a general meeting of a company must state the general nature of the business to be dealt with at the meeting. *The articles generally specify what the notice must contain*, but *Table A* provides that it must specify the time and place of the meeting, and the general nature of the business to be transacted.

If the meeting is the annual general meeting of a public company, the notice must under CA 2006, s 337 say so. If it is convened to pass a special resolution, it must say so and the resolution(s) must be set out verbatim (*McConnell v Prill* [1916] 2 Ch 57), as must ordinary resolutions of which special notice is required and resolutions put on the agenda of the annual general meeting by shareholders (see below) (see CA 2006, s 339). In addition, the notice must be adequate to enable members to judge whether they should attend the meeting to protect their interests. Thus in *McConnell v Prill* [1916] 2 Ch 57 a notice of a meeting called to increase the nominal capital of the company did not say by how much. It was held that the notice was invalid because the eventual issue of the new shares (and there were no pre-emption rights then) could affect the rights of existing shareholders and they were therefore entitled to know by how much the nominal capital was to be increased.

Under CA 2006, s 325 the notice must clearly state the right of a member to appoint a proxy.

Notice of members' resolutions at the Annual General Meeting

Members representing not less than one-twentieth of the total voting rights of all the members, or 100 or more members holding shares in the company on which there has been paid up an average sum of not less than £100 per member, can, under CA 2006, s 314, by making a written requisition to the company, *compel the company*:

(a) to give to members who are entitled to receive notice of the next annual general meeting, *notice of any resolution* which may be properly moved and which they intend to move at that meeting; and

(b) to circulate to members who are entitled to have notice of any general meeting sent to them, any *statement* of not more than 1,000 words with respect to the matter referred to in any proposed resolution or the business to be dealt with at the meeting.

The amount which has been paid up on the shares is not material so, assuming that a company has 300,000 £1 ordinary shares 50p paid and 100,000 £1 preference shares fully paid all with voting rights, then the requisition could be made by the holders of 80,000 shares. If made by 100 requisitionists, then the amount paid up on their shares if added together would have to come to at least £10,000.

The requisition must be made and deposited in accord with CA 2006, s 314(4) governing procedures for circulation of resolutions for annual general meetings.

Under s 316(1) of the CA 2006, the expenses of the company do not need to be paid by the members who requested the circulation of the statement if (a) the meeting to which the requests relate is an annual general meeting of a public company; and (b) requests are sufficient to require the company to circulate the statement received before the end of the financial year preceding the meeting. Section 316(2) goes on to state that otherwise the expenses of the company must be paid by the members who requested the circulation of the statement unless the company resolves otherwise, and unless the company has previously so resolved, it is not bound to comply with that section unless there is deposited with or tendered to it, not later than one week before the meeting, a sum reasonably sufficient to meet its expenses in doing so.

The company is not bound by the above provisions if, on application to the court by the company or any person affected, the court is satisfied that they are being abused in order to secure needless publicity for defamatory or abusive behaviour (CA 2006, s 317). The above procedures are confined to resolutions to be proposed at the annual general meetings.

Special notice

An ordinary resolution of which *special notice* has been given is required in the following cases:

(a) under CA 2006, s 168, to remove a director before the expiration of his period of office, regardless of any provision in the articles or in any agreement with him. If it is intended to *replace* the director if he is removed, special notice must be given of that also. The section does not prevent companies from attaching special voting rights to certain shares on this occasion (*Bushell v Faith*, 1969, see Chapters 7 and 22 ◯); *or*

(b) removing an auditor before the expiration of his term of office (CA 2006, s 511).

Under CA 2006, s 312, where special notice is required, the resolution is not effective unless notice of the intention to move it has been given to the company not less than 28 days before the meeting at which it is to be moved. The notice should be posted or delivered to the registered office of the company. The company must give its members notice of any such resolution at the same time and in the same manner as it gives notice of the meeting or, if this is not possible, must give them notice of it either by advertisement in a newspaper having an appropriate circulation or by any other method allowed by the articles, *not less than 14 days before the meeting*. If a meeting is called for a date 28 days or less after the notice has been given, the notice, though not given in time under the section, shall be deemed to have been properly given.

The above provision is designed to protect shareholders who give notice, e.g. to remove a director or auditor, in case the board calls the meeting of members deliberately at less than 28 days so as to frustrate the removal of the director or auditor.

Procedure at meetings – legal aspects

A consideration of the legal, as distinct from the company secretarial, aspects of procedure once the meeting has been convened involves a discussion of the matter of quorum, voting, proxies, the position of the chairman and the recording of minutes.

Quorum: generally

The concept of quorum relates to the minimum number of persons suitably qualified who must be present at a meeting in order that business may be validly transacted.

If the articles do not lay down the quorum required for general meetings, CA 2006, s 318 provides that in the case of both public and private companies two members *personally* present shall be a quorum.

Therefore, as a general rule and in the absence of a provision in the articles at least two members *present in person* are required to constitute a meeting. The position in regard to single-member companies has already been considered (see Chapter 1) but the quorum there is one member present in person or by proxy.

Sharp v *Dawes* (1876) 2 QBD 26

The Great Caradon Mine was run by a mining company in Cornwall and was carried on on the cost-book system, being controlled by the Stannaries Act 1869. The company had offices in London, and on 22 December 1874 notice of a general meeting was properly given. The meeting was held, but only the secretary, Sharp, and one shareholder, a Mr Silversides who held 25 shares, attended. Nevertheless, the business of the meeting was conducted with Silversides in the chair. Among other things, a call on shares was made and the defendant refused to pay it. He was sued by the secretary, Sharp, who brought the action on behalf of the company, and his defence was that calls had to be made at a meeting and there had been no meeting on this occasion.

Held – by the Court of Appeal – the call was invalid. According to the ordinary use of the English language, a meeting could not be constituted by one shareholder.

In Re London Flats Ltd [1969] 2 All ER 744

The company was in liquidation and a meeting was called under what is now the Insolvency Act 1986 to appoint a successor to the liquidator who had died. At the meeting X, one of the only two shareholders, proposed that he be appointed liquidator and put forward an amendment to the resolution before the meeting which substituted his own name in the resolution for the person named therein who was a chartered accountant. The other shareholder, Y, left the meeting saying, 'I withdraw from the meeting, you now have no quorum.' The meeting continued and the amended resolution was put to the vote. There being one vote in favour and none against, X as chairman declared the amendment carried, thus making himself liquidator. Y made application to the court for the removal of X and the appointment of a liquidator by the court on the ground that the appointment of X was invalid, the meeting having consisted of only one shareholder.

Held – by Plowman J – that the appointment of X was invalid. The matter was then referred to chambers for the appointment of an independent liquidator. An accountant unconnected with the parties was appointed.

CA 2006, s 318 calculates the quorum by reference to the numbers of 'qualifying persons' who are present at the meeting. This term includes an individual who is a member of the company; a person authorised under section 323 to act as the representative of a corporation; and a person appointed as proxy of a member. CA 2006 establishes that proxies and corporate representatives will usually count as part of a quorum. In the case of single-member companies, one qualifying person present at a meeting is a quorum. In any other case, subject to the provisions of the company's articles, two qualifying persons present at a meeting are a quorum, unless: they are both a qualifying person as the representative of a corporation, and they are representatives of the same corporation; or they are both a qualifying person as proxy of a member, and they are proxies of the same member.

CA 2006, s 334 provides that the necessary quorum for a variation of class rights meeting is, for a meeting (other than an adjourned meeting), two persons present holding at least one-third in nominal value of the issued shares of the class in question (excluding any shares of that class held as treasury shares) and, for an adjourned meeting, one person present, holding shares of the class in question. Where a person is present by proxy or proxies, she is treated as holding only the shares in respect of which those proxies are authorised to exercise voting rights. CA 2006, s 334 confirms the position regarding proxies in that they apply equally to class meetings as they would to general meetings.

Article 30 of the Model Articles of Association for Public Companies states, and Article 38 of the Model Articles of Association for Private Companies states, that no business other than the appointment of the chairman of the meeting is to be transacted at a general meeting if the persons attending it do not constitute a quorum (*Companies (Model Articles) Regulations 2008*). In *Table A*, Reg 40 sets the number of persons required to satisfy a quorum for *Table A* companies.

Quorum of one

Where an annual general meeting or other general meeting is called by the court, the court, as the case may be, may decide upon the quorum which may even be one member present in person or by proxy.

 Re El Sombrero Ltd [1958] 3 All ER 1

The applicant in this case held 90 per cent of the shares of the company which was a private company. The company's two directors held 5 per cent of the shares each. The company's articles provided that the quorum for general meetings was two persons present in person or by proxy, and if within half an hour from the time appointed for holding a meeting a quorum was not present, the meeting, if convened on the requisition of the members, was deemed dissolved. On 11 March 1958, the applicant requisitioned an extraordinary general meeting to pass a resolution removing the two directors and appointing others in their place. The directors did not comply with the requisition, so the applicant himself convened an extraordinary general meeting for 21 April 1958. The two directors deliberately failed to attend, and since no quorum was present, the meeting was dissolved. The applicant took out a summons asking for a meeting to be called by the court to pass a resolution removing the two directors, and for a direction that one member of the company should be deemed to constitute a quorum at such meeting. The application was opposed by the directors.

Held – by the High Court – since in practice a meeting of the company could not be convened under the articles, the court had a jurisdiction to order a meeting to be held, and for one member to constitute a quorum, and such an order was made. The applicant was entitled to enforce his statutory right to remove the directors by ordinary resolution, and the directors had refused to perform their statutory duty to call a meeting for the sole reason that, if a meeting was held, they would cease to be directors.

Comment

This case was followed in *Re HR Paul & Son Ltd* (1973) *The Times*, 17 November, where Brightman J ordered a general meeting to take place with a quorum of one where a 90 per cent shareholder could not get alterations in the articles because the minority had refused to attend general meetings. In cases such as this it is often impossible for the major shareholder to transfer a few shares to a nominee in order to make a quorum, either because there are pre-emption provisions in the articles or the remaining members are also directors who have a majority on the board and refuse to register the necessary transfers.

CA 2006, ss 334 and 335 are concerned with the matter of quorum at class meetings, fixing it at two persons holding or representing by proxy at least one-third in nominal value of the issued share capital of the class in question. At an adjourned class meeting the required quorum is one person holding shares of the class in question or his proxy. In addition, in *East v Bennet Bros Ltd* [1911] 1 Ch 163 it was held by Warrington J that *one* member who held *all* the shares of a class constituted a valid class meeting.

The position in single-member private companies has already been considered.

Quorum of one: committees of directors

Table A, Reg 72 authorises delegation by the board to one director acting as a committee of the board. The court accepted in *Re Taurine Co* (1883) 25 Ch D 118 that under a similar provision in articles a director meeting alone constituted a valid meeting of the committee.

Effect of no quorum

Unless there is a quorum present, the meeting is null and void, but the articles must be looked at in order to ascertain whether a quorum is required throughout the meeting or only at the beginning. For instance, *Table A* provides that a quorum is required throughout the meeting but if the articles are silent on this particular point the better view is that a quorum need only be present at the beginning and need not be present throughout, though no valid resolutions can be passed if the number of persons present falls to one (*In Re London Flats Ltd*, 1969, but see above).

Table A provides that if within half an hour from the time appointed for the meeting a quorum is not present, the meeting shall stand adjourned to the same day in the next week at the same time and place, or to such other day and at such time and place as the directors may determine. The same provision applies if there ceases to be a quorum during the course of the meeting. There must be a quorum of two at the adjourned meeting or it is similarly adjourned until there is. Ultimately, application to the court would be necessary.

The chairman

It is his duty to preserve order, to call on members to speak, to decide points of order, such as the acceptability of amendments, and to take the vote after a proper discussion in order to ascertain the sense of the meeting. However, he is not bound to hear everyone. He must be fair to the minority but as Lindley MR said in *Wall v London Northern & Assets Corporation* [1898] 2 Ch 469, the majority can say: 'We have heard enough. We are not bound to listen until everybody is tired of talking and has sat down.' Under CA 2006, s 319 the members present at the meeting may elect one of their number as chairman unless the articles otherwise provide.

Table A provides that the chairman (if any) of the board of directors shall preside as chairman at every general meeting of the company, or if there is no such chairman, or if he is not present within 15 minutes after the time appointed for the holding of the meeting, or if he will not act, the directors present shall elect one of their number to be chairman of the meeting, and if there is only one director present and willing to act he shall be chairman.

If no director is present, or no director present is willing to act within 15 minutes after the time appointed for holding the meeting, the members present must choose one of their number to be chairman of the meeting.

Voting

Unless the articles provide to the contrary, voting is by show of hands only. Articles usually allow an initial vote by show of hands, particularly for routine matters, and each member has only one vote, regardless of his shareholding. Under CA 2006, s 324 there cannot be any voting in respect of proxies held, unless the articles provide. On controversial issues it is usual to demand a poll on which members can vote according to the number of shares they hold and proxy votes can be used. *Table A* allows a poll to be demanded before a vote on a show of hands is taken. The provisions of *Table A* state that in the case of joint holders the person whose name appears first in the register of members shall be allowed to cast the vote in respect of the shares, and no member shall be entitled to vote at any general meeting unless all moneys presently payable by him in respect of the shares have been paid. *Table A* also provides that objections to the qualification of a voter can only be raised at the meeting at which the vote is tendered. Objections are to be referred to the chairman of the meeting whose decision is final and conclusive.

It should also be noted that a shareholder, even if he is a director, can vote on a matter in which he has a personal interest subject to the rules relating to prejudice of minorities (see Chapter 18 ◗). Furthermore, a bankrupt shareholder may vote and give proxies if his name is still on the register, though he must do so in accordance with the wishes of the trustee (***Morgan v Gray*** [1953] Ch 83).

If no poll is demanded, the vote on the show of hands as declared by the chairman and recorded in the minutes is the decision of the meeting and under *Table A* his declaration is *conclusive*, without proof of the number of votes cast for or against the resolution, unless there is an obvious error, as where the chairman states: 'There being a majority of 51 per cent on the show of hands, I hereby declare that the special resolution to alter the articles has been passed.' The chairman's declaration would not be conclusive either if he had improperly refused a poll.

The articles may set out the provisions governing the demand for a poll, but CA 2006, s 321 lays down that such provisions in the company's articles shall be *void* in certain circumstances:

(a) *They must not exclude* the right to demand a poll at a general meeting on any question other than the election of the chairman or the adjournment of the meeting.
(b) *They must not try* to stifle a demand for a poll if it is made by:
    (i) *not less than five members* having the right to vote at the meeting; *or*
    (ii) a member or members representing not less than one-tenth of the total voting rights of all the members having the right to vote at the meeting; *or*
    (iii) a member or members holding shares in the company which confer a right to vote at the meeting and on which an aggregate sum has been paid up equal to not less than one-tenth of the total sum paid up on all such shares. For example, if the share capital of the company was 10,000 shares of £1 each with 50p per share paid, the company would have received £5,000 from the shareholders and those wishing to demand a poll under this head would have had together to have paid up £500.

Thus, the articles cannot prevent a fairly sizeable group of members from demanding a poll, and under CA 2006, s 329 the holder of a proxy can join in demanding a poll. As such, a proxy for five members could in effect demand a poll on his own. The right of a proxy to demand a poll (CA 1985, s 373(2)) is restated at CA 2006, s 329. CA 2006, s 322 has now replaced CA

1985, s 374. A proxy will be entitled to vote on a show of hands as well as on a poll (CA 2006, s 324(1)). The current version of Reg 54 of *Table A* provides that every member present by proxy has a vote on a show of hands. Versions of *Table A* in force prior to 1 October 2007 only provided for a member present in person to be able to vote on a show of hands (and not a proxy).

Table A provides that the chairman can demand a poll, and indeed it would be his duty to do this if he felt it necessary to ascertain the sense of the meeting. It also ensures that the board can exercise its full voting rights. *Table A* also provides that two members present in person or by proxy can demand a poll, and no provision in the special articles can increase this number beyond five, as we have already seen.

Taking the poll

A poll, if demanded, is usually taken straight away, the result being announced at the end of the meeting, but the articles may allow the poll to be taken at a later date. *Table A* provides that on any issue, other than the election of a chairman or on the adjournment of the meeting, a poll may be taken at such time not being more than 30 days after the poll is demanded, as is directed by the chairman who then proceeds to the next business.

Persons not actually present at the first meeting may vote on the subsequent poll. Under *Table A* in the case of a poll taken more than 48 hours after it is demanded, the proxies must be deposited after the poll has been demanded and not less than 24 hours before the time appointed for the taking of the poll. Where the poll is not taken forthwith but is taken not more than 48 hours after it was demanded, proxies must be delivered at the meeting at which the poll was demanded to the chairman or to the secretary or to any director and an instrument of proxy which is not deposited or delivered in a manner so permitted is invalid.

Even where a poll is taken immediately, the result may not be declared until a future date, because of the problems involved in checking the votes and the right of the members to cast them. Postal votes are not acceptable. Under CA 2006, s 322, where a proxy holder is acting for several principals, he need not use all the votes in the same way on a poll. This enables him to vote in the way each principal directs. Section 322A provides that a company's articles can provide for votes to be cast in advance of a meeting.

Chapter 5 of Part 13 of CA 2006 sets out new requirements for quoted companies if a poll is taken (quoted company is defined in CA 2006, s 385 which applies to Part 13 as a result of CA 2006, s 361). CA 2006, s 341 mandated a quoted company to disclose on a website the result of any poll taken at a general meeting. A quoted company must, as a minimum, disclose the following: the date of the meeting; the text of the resolution or a description of the subject matter of the poll; the number of votes cast in favour; and the number of votes cast against. Non-compliance does not invalidate the poll but is an offence punishable by fine.

CA 2006, s 342 allows members of a quoted company to require the directors to obtain an independent report of any poll taken, or to be taken, at a general meeting of the company. The report may be demanded by members holding not less than 5 per cent of the voting rights or by not less than 100 members who hold shares in the company on which there has been paid-up an average sum per member of not less than £100. The request must be received by the company not less than one week after the poll was taken.

If an independent report is requested, the directors must appoint an independent assessor pursuant to CA 2006, s 343. Such appointment must be made within one week of the request for a report. The assessor must be independent in accordance with CA 2006, s 344. He must not be an officer or employee (or partner or employee of such person, or a partnership of which such person is a partner) of the company or any associated undertaking of the company and there must not be some other connection (of any description as may be specified by regulations made by the Secretary of State) between the person or his associate and the company or associated undertaking of the company. The company's auditor is considered to be independent. A person also cannot act if he has another role on any poll on which he is to report.

The independent assessor is entitled to attend the meeting at which the poll may be taken and any subsequent proceedings in connection with the poll pursuant to CA 2006, s 348. He may access the company's records relating to any poll on which he is to report or the meeting at which the poll or polls may be, or were, taken pursuant to CA 2006, s 349. CA 2006, s 351 provides that the independent assessor's identity, a description of the subject matter of the poll to which his appointment relates and a copy of his report must be made available on a website that is maintained by or on behalf of the company in question or which identifies the company in question. The minimum information the independent report must contain is set forth in CA 2006, s 347. The report must give the assessor's reasons for the opinions stated and, if he is unable to form an opinion on any of the matters, record that fact and state the reasons.

CA 2006, s 341 requires quoted companies to disclose poll results on their websites.

Chairman's casting vote

Chairmen of companies incorporated prior to 1 October 2007 (excluding traded companies) and if permitted by the articles, have a casting vote. For traded companies incorporated at any time and non-traded companies incorporated after 1 October 2007, the articles may no longer give the chairman a casting vote as CA 2006, s 282 requires an ordinary resolution to be passed by a simple majority. For non-traded companies incorporated prior to 1 October 2007, the CA 2006 provides that if the articles gave the chairman a casting vote such provision would continue to have effect notwithstanding CA 2006, ss 281(3) and 282.

The chairman is not bound to exercise his casting vote and may declare that the resolution has not been passed or exercise the casting vote for or against it. He ought normally to vote against it so that it is clearly lost because since those who want the resolution passed and those who want it to fail are equal in number it would not be fair to pass the resolution in the face of such opposition. The most common use of a casting vote is by a chairman on a show of hands, in favour of the resolution, where he knows that there are a lot of proxies in favour of the resolution.

Proxies

The right to appoint proxies is governed by CA 2006, ss 284, 285 and 324–331. It must be noted that the Government issued a Ministerial Statement on 6 November 2008 indicating that it will propose to repeal CA 2006, ss 327(2)(c) and 330(6)(c) of the CA 2006 which were not commenced with the rest of Part 13. CA 2006, s 324(1) gives members the right to appoint a proxy to attend, speak and vote at general meetings. This section, of course, countermands any provision to the contrary that may be contained in a company's articles. Under CA 2006, s 324 *et seq.* every member of a company having a share capital and entitled to vote at a meeting may appoint a proxy, and the person appointed need not be a member of the company. However, the proxy should have full legal capacity and the appointment of a minor is probably void; certainly the Insolvency Rules 1986 (SI 1986/1925) exclude minors as proxies in meetings concerned with winding-up (see Rule 8.1(3)). In addition, the notice of the meeting must make it clear that proxies can be appointed and failure to do will result in a fine on every officer of the company in default but even so the meeting is valid (CA 2006, s 325).

CA 2006, s 324(2) allows members to appoint multiple proxies provided that that a proxy must be appointed in relation to at least one share or different £10, or multiple of £10, of stock. This is a baseline standard, however, and articles are free to provide for additional rights. Accordingly if a member holds two ordinary shares, he will only be permitted by s 324(2) to appoint one or two proxies but the company's articles could permit the member to appoint more than two proxies. In public companies a member may appoint two or more proxies, but in a private company only one unless the articles provide to the contrary. *Table A* allows two or more in both public and private companies. Under CA 2006, s 327, companies may set a cut-off point by which time a member must have lodged his proxy appointment in order for it to be valid. It also provides that any provision of the company's articles which requires any appointment of a proxy to be received by the company more than 48 hours before the time of the meeting is void. In CA 2006, s 327(2) different cut-off periods for proxy appointments where a poll is taken are provided. Finally, CA 2006, s 327(3) provides that in calculating the periods pursuant to subsection (2) of CA 2006, s 327 'no account shall be taken of any part of a day that is not a working day'.

The expression 'proxy' also refers to the document by which the voting agent is appointed. The articles frequently set out the form of a proxy but a written appointment in reasonable form will suffice (*Isaacs v Chapman* (1916) 32 TLR 237). Furthermore, minor errors which do not seriously mislead will not make a proxy invalid. Thus in *Oliver v Dalgleish* [1963] 3 All ER 330 a proxy form gave the correct date of the meeting but said it was the annual general meeting and not an extraordinary general meeting as it in fact was. It was held by the High Court that the proxy was nevertheless valid.

Table A and the Model Articles (Art 45(3)) provides for two-way proxies, as distinct from appointing a person to exercise the vote, under which a member can indicate whether he wishes to vote for or against a particular resolution. The articles of association must not forbid two-way proxies if the Stock Exchange is to give a listing or the shares are to be dealt in on the AIM. It is uncertain whether the company is bound by a two-way proxy as regards the choice of vote but the better view is that it is bound so that if a proxy tried to cast his votes differently from the way in which the member had indicated the company ought not to accept the change (*Oliver v Dalgleish* [1963] 3 All ER 330).

Listed companies now use three-way which provides for an option to abstain from voting. Additionally, some listed companies provide for four-way voting which allow the proxy discretion to decide whether and how to vote (or withhold their vote). In the absence of such an option, the proxy retains such discretion if no specific voting instruction has been given by the member.

Following on from the discussion above on polling, CA 1985 provided that proxies had the right to vote on a poll but there was no automatic right to vote on a show of hands. Now CA 2006, s 285(1) provides that on a vote on a resolution on a show of hands at a meeting, every proxy present who has been duly appointed by one or more members entitled to vote on the resolution has one vote. However, subsection (2) provides an exception in that a proxy has one vote for and one vote against the resolution if he has been duly appointed by more than one member entitled to vote on the resolution; and instructed by one or more of those members to vote for the resolution and by one or more other of those members to vote against it. The fallback provision provided for in CA 2006, s 285(5) is that the articles can override the position set forth in subsections (1) and (2).

CA 2006, s 326 requires that where the company offers that a particular person (or persons), such as the chairman of the meeting, will act as a proxy (or proxies), that offer must be made to all members. CA 2006, s 328 allows that a proxy may be elected to be the chairman of a general meeting by resolution of the company passed at a meeting so long as this is not contrary to any existing provision in the company's articles.

CA 2006, s 331 authorises a company's articles to give more extensive rights regarding proxies than the minimum set out in the CA 2006, ss 324 to 330 (proxies).

The board may circulate proxy forms in favour of the board to members and meet the expense from the company's funds (*Peel* v *L & NW Railway* [1907] 1 Ch 5). However, these forms must be sent to all members entitled to attend and vote. This provision prevents the directors merely soliciting the votes of those who are likely to vote in favour of the board's proposals. In addition, the directors may also send circulars with the notice of the meeting putting forward their views on various resolutions and pay for the circularisation out of the company's funds (*Peel* v *L & NW Railway* [1907] 1 Ch 5). However, the circular must be issued in good faith to inform the members of the issues involved and must not be unduly biased in favour of the directors' views.

The right to appoint a proxy would be useless if it had to be made many weeks before the meeting. So, whatever the articles may provide, a proxy is valid if lodged not later than 48 hours before the meeting. If the articles do have an earlier requirement, it is void and it appears that the company cannot then require any period of lodgement at all so that if the proxy turns up at the meeting with his form and votes his vote must be accepted.

The law relating to faxed proxies is unclear. The court may not regard a fax as 'executed' (signed) by the member as *Table A*, Reg 60 requires, and perhaps also as not 'deposited with the company' as Reg 62 requires. Also the proxy remains with the member and the company does not get 'deposit' of it but only a 'copy' of it (but see *PNC Telecom plc* v *Thomas* [2003] BCC 202 that seems to support the view that a fax will be 'deposited' as the law requires). However, in the last analysis it is up to the chairman of the meeting to decide whether or not to accept a proxy, and he would be wise to accept a faxed proxy rather than risk a challenge in the courts as to the validity of the meeting brought by the shareholder whose faxed proxy was rejected.

It is worth noting that the acceptance of a faxed proxy is reinforced by the decision of the High Court in *Re a Debtor (No 2021 of 1995), ex parte IRC* v *Debtor* [1996] 2 All ER 345 where Laddie J held that a faxed proxy form was signed for the purposes of a creditors' meeting in a proposed voluntary arrangement and under Rule 8.2(3) of the Insolvency Rules of 1986 if it bore upon it some distinctive or personal marking which had been placed there by or with the authority of the creditor. When a creditor faxed a proxy form to the chairman of a creditors' meeting he transmitted the contents of the form and the signature applied to it. The receiving fax was instructed by the transmitting creditor to reproduce his signature on the proxy form which was itself being created at the receiving station. It followed that the received fax was a proxy form signed by the principal. The judge did, however, make clear that his decision was on the Insolvency Rules and that different considerations may apply to faxed documents in relation to other legislation. To avoid any doubt, special articles could be drafted so as to specifically allow faxed proxy forms to be accepted. Obviously, faxed proxies are acceptable where the company has set up electronic communication systems with the consent of the relevant member(s).

The Model Articles for both private companies limited by shares and public companies each contain just two articles relating to proxies (Articles 31 and 32 in the case of the Model Articles for private companies and Articles 45 and 46 in the case of the model articles for public companies). These articles cover the content of proxy notices as well the delivery of proxy notices. The Model Articles require certain information to be included in proxy forms and permit the company to require use of a particular form instead of indicating precise wording. However, it must be noted that many matters concerning proxies are to be found in the CA 2006 as opposed to the Model Articles.

Electronic communications

These are governed by CA 2006, ss 308, 309, 333 and 1143 to 1148 and Schedules 4 and 5 to the CA 2006. Moreover, CA 2006, ss 1144(2) and (3), requires that documents or information sent or supplied by a company (including notices) must be sent or supplied in accordance with Schedule 5. CA 2006, s 333(1) provides that where a company has given an electronic address in a notice of general meeting it is deemed to have agreed that any document or information relating to proceedings at the meeting (this appears to cover proxy forms) may be sent by electronic means to that address subject to any conditions or limitations specified in the notice. Additionally, CA 2006, s 333 also contains similar deemed acceptance provisions specifically relating to proxy forms.

CA 2006, s 309 provides for publication of notices of meeting on website. In these circumstances, where a member has agreed, or is deemed to have agreed, to website publication of documents, the notice of meeting does not have to be sent to that person in hard copy but the member must be notified of the presence of the notice on the company's website. Notification by hard-copy (always good) or by electronic communications (such as by email) when the member has specifically agreed to accept this type of communication will suffice.

CA 2006, s 333A requires an electronic address to be provided for receipt of 'any document or information relating to proxies for a general meeting'. CA 2006, s 333A(4) states that documents relating to proxies include a proxy appointment, any document necessary to show the validity of, or otherwise relating to, the appointment of a proxy including a copy of a power of attorney showing authority to appoint a proxy on behalf of the member and notice of the termination of the authority of a proxy. Under s 333A, 'electronic address' has the meaning given by s 333(4) of the CA 2006: any address or number used for the purposes of sending or receiving documents or information by electronic means.

Euroclear UK (formerly known as CRESTCo) provides a system enabling registered holders of securities in CREST to appoint and instruct a proxy by electronic means through the CREST system. CREST is the UK's real-time electronic settlement system for UK and international shares, and UK government bonds (Gilts). Allowing proxy appointments to be made through CREST constitutes an electronic appointment. Typically a service offering members the ability to appoint and terminate a proxy electronically will be provided by the company's registrars. Section 333A does not require electronic appointment to be available to all members.

CA 2006, s 324A mandates that a proxy must vote in accordance with any instructions given by the member by whom the proxy is appointed. As regards revocation of a proxy, since the proxy is merely an agent of the member this can be done expressly by telling the proxy not to vote or by the member exercising his right to vote in person, in which case his personal vote will override that of the proxy if the latter votes (*Cousins* v *International Brick Co Ltd* [1931] 2 Ch 90). No statutory provision to the contrary exists in CA 2006. There is also automatic revocation of a proxy if the member who made the appointment dies or becomes bankrupt or of unsound mind. It should be noted that revocation is impossible if the proxy has an interest. Thus where L lends money to B and takes B's share certificates in X Ltd as security but is not registered it may be part of the agreement that L should always be appointed B's proxy at meetings of X Ltd. If so, the appointment of L as proxy is irrevocable until the loan is repaid.

All that is said in the above paragraph is subject to the articles of the company concerned (*Spiller* v *Mayo (Rhodesia) Development Co (1908) Ltd* [1926] WN 78). *Table A* provides that a vote given or poll demanded by a proxy or by the duly authorised representative of a corporation shall be valid notwithstanding the previous determination of the authority of the person voting or demanding a poll unless notice of the determination was received by the company at the office or at such other place at which the instrument of proxy was duly deposited before the commencement of the meeting or adjourned meeting at which the vote is given or the poll demanded or (in the case of a poll taken otherwise than on the same day as the meeting or adjourned meeting) the time appointed for taking the poll. Thus, under *Table A* the acts and votes of a proxy are valid *unless the company knows* of any revocation.

Corporate representatives

Where a company is a member of another company, the member company is entitled under CA 2006, s 323 to appoint by resolution of its directors a representative to attend meetings. If the member company is in liquidation, the liquidator may also make the appointment (*Hillman* v *Crystal Bowl Amusements* [1973] 1 All ER 379). The representative is not a proxy and has the full rights of a member; thus he always counts towards the quorum, can move resolutions and amendments, can speak, even if the company is a public one, and can always vote on a show of hands. It is of some advantage to a company to appoint a representative, though if the meeting is not controversial a proxy will do just as well. CA 2006, s 323 provides that a corporate representative is entitled to exercise the same powers on behalf of the corporation as that corporation could exercise if it were an individual shareholder.

A corporate representative is entitled to exercise the same powers on behalf of the corporation as that corporation could exercise if it were an individual shareholder (CA 2006, s 323(2)). If the corporation authorises more than one person, this same section sets for the law to be followed with respect to such representative in the case of a show of hands or on a poll.

Adjournment of the meeting

A meeting may be adjourned for various reasons, e.g. where the business cannot be completed on that day, or where there is no quorum. The adjourned meeting is deemed to be a resumption of the original meeting and the articles may provide as to the amount of notice required for it, but no business may be transacted at an adjourned meeting except that which was left unfinished at the original meeting.

Where a resolution is passed at an adjourned meeting of the company, or at a class meeting or a meeting of the directors, the resolution shall be deemed for all purposes to have been passed on the date when it was in fact passed and not at the date of the earlier meeting. The section is thus important in deciding on what date to file a resolution which has to be filed within so many days of its being passed.

The articles usually determine who shall decide to adjourn, whether the members or the chairman. A chairman must not adjourn frivolously, and if he does so the members may elect a new chairman and proceed with the meeting. *Table A* provides that the chairman may (and *shall* if so directed by the meeting), with the consent of the meeting, adjourn the meeting from time to time and from place to place. Model Articles 41(5) (private companies) and 33(5) (public companies) also cover adjournment.

The chairman can, of course, adjourn under the common law without any resolution of the members where there is disorder at the meeting. However, he must exercise the power properly. Thus, if he adjourns the meeting immediately upon the outbreak of disorder without waiting to see whether it will subside, the adjournment will be invalid and the meeting may continue (*John v Rees* [1969] 2 All ER 274).

Another example of an invalid adjournment is to be found in *Byng v London Life Association Ltd* (1988) *The Times*, 22 December. A meeting of London Life was called to be held at the Barbican Centre in London. The main meeting place was not large enough to hold all those who wished to attend and the audio-visual linking system in the overflow rooms had broken down. The chairman adjourned the meeting without the consent of the meeting as London Life's articles required. His adjournment was challenged by Mr Byng, a shareholder, because the members had not consented. However, the Court of Appeal held that even so the chairman could use his common law right to adjourn in the difficult circumstances of the case. However, he had not exercised it reasonably. He had adjourned the meeting only until the afternoon of the same day at the Café Royal. He must have known that many people who had tried to attend the meeting at the Barbican would be unable to attend at the Café Royal in the afternoon at such short notice. Accordingly resolutions passed at the Café Royal by the much diminished number of people who did attend were invalid. Incidentally the court also held that a meeting may be validly held even though not everyone is in the same room, as where some are using audio-visual equipment in overflow rooms.

Minutes

Under CA 2006, s 248 every company must keep minutes of all proceedings of directors' meetings, whether they be meetings of the full board or a committee of the board, and enter these into a minute book. If a minute is signed by the chairman of the meeting or of the next succeeding meeting, the minutes are prima facie evidence of the proceedings. This means that although there is a presumption that all the proceedings were in order and that all appointments of directors, managers or liquidators are deemed to be valid, evidence can be brought to contradict the minutes. Thus, in *Re Fireproof Doors* [1916] 2 Ch 142 a contract to indemnify directors was held binding though not recorded in the minutes. On the other hand, if the articles provide that minutes duly signed by the chairman are *conclusive* evidence, they cannot be contradicted. Thus, in *Kerr v Mottram* [1940] Ch 657 the claimant said that a contract to sell him preference and ordinary shares had been agreed at a meeting. There was no record in the minutes and since the articles of the company said that the minutes were conclusive evidence the court would not admit evidence as to the existence of the contract.

Under CA 2006, s 358 the minute books are to be kept at the registered office of the company, and the minutes of general meetings are open to the inspection of members free of charge. Copies or extracts from the minutes must be supplied and a charge may be made. The copy must be given within seven days of the request. The auditor of the company has a right of inspection at all times. Minute books may be kept on a loose-leaf system so long as there are adequate precautions to prevent fraud. However, it seems that some sort of visual record is required and the Companies Acts would not appear to envisage tapes being used.

Many companies keep their statutory registers on computer using one of the software packages available and this is permitted by CA 2006, s 1135.

CA 2006, s 355 requires every company to keep records comprising copies of all resolutions of members passed otherwise than at general meetings, minutes of all proceedings of general meetings and details provided to the company in accordance with s 357 (decisions of sole members). These records must be kept for at least 10 years from the date of the resolution, meeting or decision (as appropriate). These records relating to the previous 10 years must be kept available for inspection at the company's registered office in the UK or at a place designated under regulations issued by the Secretary of State pursuant to CA 2006, s 1136.

We have already referred to the need in one-member companies for the member to supply the company with a written record of decisions made at general meetings unless they are by written resolution (see Chapter 1 ⊙).

Class meetings

The provisions of CA 2006, Chapter 3 of Part 13 (Resolutions at meetings) are applicable to meetings of the holders of a class of shares and, for companies without a share capital, for meetings of a class of members as they do to general meetings (ss 334(1) and 335(1)) subject to the following certain exceptions:

- Shareholders and members may require directors to call a general meeting of the company (CA 2006, ss 303–305) but these provisions do not apply to the calling of class meetings (CA 2006, s 334(2)(a)).
- The court has the power to call a meeting of the company (CA 2006, s 306) but this power does not apply to the calling of a class meeting (CA 2006, s 334(2)(b)).

In connection with a variation of class rights meeting, the following differences must be noted:

- A poll may be demanded by any holder of shares of the class or, for companies without a share capital, any member of the class present (CA 2006, ss 334(6) and 335(5)).
- The quorum (other than an adjourned meeting) is two persons present holding at least one-third in nominal value of the issued shares of the class (excluding any shares held as treasury shares) or, for companies without a share capital, two members of the class present (in person or by proxy) who together represent at least one-third of the voting rights of the class.
- The quorum for an adjourned meeting is one person present holding shares of the class or, for companies without a share capital, one member of the class present (in person or by proxy) (CA 2006, ss 334(4) and 335(4)).

Company meetings and the disabled

The Equality Act 2010 places a duty on those who provide goods, facilities and services not to discriminate against disabled people. The Act applies to any person, organisation or entity which is concerned with the provision in the UK of goods, facilities or services *to the public or a section of the public*. The Act will therefore apply, it would seem, if a company meeting can be described as a meeting involving the public. In the case of a plc which is also listed, the annual general meeting would seem to be a public meeting and consideration would have to be given, for example, to access for the disabled and the provision of reports and accounts in Braille, together with systems designed to enable the deaf to participate in the meeting. However, since in this connection private companies provide the overwhelming majority of corporate structures in the UK (many with five or fewer members), it is unlikely that the Act would apply in this context. Of course, it does a company no harm to give proper consideration to its disabled members, if any.

Board meetings

CA 2006, s 248 provides in relevant part that every company must cause minutes of all proceedings at meetings of its directors to be recorded and kept for at least 10 years from the date of the meeting. If a company fails to comply with these requirements an offence is committed by every officer of the company who is in default (a fine not exceeding level 3 on the standard scale and, for continued contravention, a daily default fine not exceeding one-tenth of level 3 on the standard scale). CA 2006, s 249 provides that minutes recorded in accordance with CA 2006, s 248, if purporting to be authenticated by the chairman of the meeting or by the chairman of the next directors' meeting, are evidence of the proceedings at the meeting. Where minutes have been made in accordance with the proceedings of a board of directors, CA 2006, s 249(2) provides that until the contrary is proved the meeting is deemed duly held and convened, all proceedings at the meeting are deemed to have duly taken place and all appointments at the meeting are deemed valid.

The provisions of the Model Articles for private companies limited by shares contain several articles of note with respect to Directors' Meetings. These articles of note are also found in the provision of the Model Articles for private companies limited by guarantee as well. **Article 7** requires that decision-making by directors must be either a majority decision at a meeting or by unanimous decision when taken in accordance with **Article 8**. If the company only has one director, and no provision of the articles requires it to have more than one director, the general rule does not apply, and the director may take decisions without regard to any of the provisions of the articles relating to directors' decision-making. **Article 8** requires that a decision of the directors is taken in accordance with this article when all eligible directors indicate to each other by any means that they share a common view on a matter. It also requires that a decision may not be taken in accordance with **Article 8** if the eligible directors would not have formed a quorum at such a meeting.

Article 9 provides for the specifics of calling a directors' meeting which is done by any director or directors giving notice of the meeting to the directors or by authorising the company secretary (if any) to give such notice. The notice of the meeting must indicate: (a) its proposed date and time; (b) where it is to take place; and (c) if it is anticipated that directors participating in the meeting will not be in the same place, how it is proposed that they should communicate with each other during the meeting. Notice of a directors' meeting must be given to each director, but need not be in writing. Notice of a directors' meeting need not be given to directors who waive their entitlement to notice of that meeting, by giving notice to that effect to the company not more than 7 days after the date on which the meeting is held. Where such notice is given after the meeting has been held, that does not affect the validity of the meeting, or of any business conducted at it.

Article 10 provides for participation in directors' meetings. Subject to the articles, directors participate in a directors' meeting, or part of a directors' meeting, when the meeting has been called and takes place in accordance with the articles, and they can each communicate to the others any information or opinions they have on any particular item of the business of the meeting. In determining whether directors are participating in a directors' meeting, it is irrelevant where any director is or how they communicate with each other. If all the directors participating in a meeting are not in the same place, they may decide that the meeting is to be treated as taking place wherever any of them is.

Article 11 provides that unless a quorum is participating, no proposal is to be voted on, except a proposal to call another meeting. The quorum for directors' meetings may be fixed from time to time by a decision of the directors, but it must never be less than two, and unless otherwise fixed, it is two. If the total number of directors for the time being is less than the quorum required, the directors must not take any decision other than a decision to appoint further directors, or to call a general meeting so as to enable the shareholders to appoint further directors.

Article 12 allows that directors may appoint a director to chair their meetings who for the time being is known as the chairman. The directors may terminate the chairman's appointment at any time. If the chairman is not participating in a directors' meeting within 10 minutes of the time at which it was to start, the participating directors must appoint one of themselves to chair it.

Article 13 allows for casting vote procedures, namely, that if the numbers of votes for and against a proposal are equal, the chairman or other director chairing the meeting has a casting vote. However, this does not apply if, in accordance with the articles, the chairman or other director is not to be counted as participating in the decision-making process for quorum or voting purposes.

Article 14 provides that if a proposed decision of the directors is concerned with an actual or proposed transaction or arrangement with the company in which a director is interested, that director is not to be counted as participating in the decision-making process for quorum or voting purposes. However, a director who is interested in an actual or proposed transaction or arrangement with the company is to be counted as participating in the decision-making process for quorum and voting purposes.

Finally, pursuant to **Article 15**, the directors must ensure that the company keeps a record, in writing, for at least 10 years from the date of the decision recorded, of every unanimous or majority decision taken by the directors. **Article 16** allows directors the discretion to make further rules: 'any rule which they think fit about how they take decisions, and about how such rules are to be recorded or communicated to directors.'

With respect to the Model Articles for Public Companies, there are many similarities to the Model Articles for Private Companies except that there are some additional provisions respecting the more formal decision-making processes of public companies.

Article 12 provides that (unlike in the private companies), the directors may appoint other directors as deputy or assistant chairmen to chair directors' meetings in the chairman's absence which are terminable at any time. If neither the chairman nor any director appointed generally to chair directors' meetings in the chairman's absence is participating in a meeting within 10 minutes of the time at which it was to start, the participating directors must appoint one of themselves to chair it.

Article 15 provides that a director who is also an alternate director has an additional vote on behalf of each appointor who is not participating in a directors' meeting and would have been entitled to vote if they were participating in it.

Article 16 provides that if a directors' meeting, or part of a directors' meeting, is concerned with an actual or proposed transaction or arrangement with the company in which a director is interested, that director is not to be counted as participating in that meeting, or part of a meeting, for quorum or voting purposes. A director who is interested in an actual or proposed transaction or arrangement with the company is to be counted as participating in a decision at a directors' meeting, or part of a directors' meeting, relating to it for quorum and voting purposes when the company by ordinary resolution disapplies the provision of the articles which would otherwise prevent a director from being counted as participating in, or voting at, a directors' meeting; the director's interest cannot reasonably be regarded as likely to give rise to a conflict of interest; or the director's conflict of interest arises from a permitted cause. A 'permitted cause' includes: (a) a guarantee given, or to be given, by or to a director in respect of an obligation incurred by or on behalf of the company or any of its subsidiaries; (b) subscription, or an agreement to subscribe, for shares or other securities of the company or any of its subsidiaries, or to underwrite, sub-underwrite, or guarantee subscription for any such shares or securities; and (c) arrangements pursuant to which benefits are made available to employees and directors or former employees and directors of the company or any of its subsidiaries which do not provide special benefits for directors or former directors.

Article 17 provides that any director may propose a directors' written resolution but the company secretary must propose a directors' written resolution if a director so requests. A directors' written resolution is proposed by giving notice of the proposed resolution to the directors indicating the proposed resolution, and the time by which it is proposed that the directors should adopt it. The notice must be given in writing to each director and any decision which a person giving notice of a proposed directors' written resolution takes regarding the process of adopting that resolution must be taken reasonably in good faith.

Article 18 provides that a proposed directors' written resolution is adopted when all the directors who would have been entitled to vote on the resolution at a directors' meeting have signed one or more copies of it, provided that those directors would have formed a quorum at such a meeting. It is immaterial whether any director signs the resolution before or after the time by which the notice proposed that it should be adopted. Once a directors' written resolution has been adopted, it must be treated as if it had been a decision taken at a directors' meeting in accordance with the articles. The company secretary must ensure that the company keeps a record, in writing, of all directors' written resolutions for at least 10 years from the date of their adoption.

The powers of the directors must be exercised collectively at a board meeting and not individually, though an informal agreement made by them all will bind the company. This is envisaged by *Table A* which provides that a resolution in writing signed by all the directors entitled to receive notice of a meeting of directors or of a committee of directors shall be as valid and effectual as if it had been passed at a meeting of directors or (as the case may be) a committee of directors duly convened and held and may consist of several documents in the like form each signed by one or more directors; but a resolution signed by an alternate director need not also be signed by his appointor and if it is signed by a director who has appointed an alternate director, it need not be signed by the alternate director in that capacity.

A meeting of the board can be called by any director unless the articles otherwise provide. *Table A* provides that a director may, and the secretary shall at the request of a director, summon a meeting of the board. *Regulations 88–98 Table A (Proceedings of Directors)* remains unchanged since the passage of the CA 2006 as there are no comparable provisions in the CA 2006.

Notice of board meetings

Notice of a board meeting should normally be given to all the directors and the time must be reasonable. This may be a matter of days, hours, or even minutes, depending on the circumstances. It has been held that three hours' notice to directors who had other business to attend to was insufficient, even though their places of business and the place where the board meeting was to be held were all in the City of London (*Re Homer District Consolidated Gold Mines Ltd, ex parte Smith* (1888) 39 Ch D 546). On the other hand, five minutes' notice to a director was held sufficient where neither distance nor other engagements prevented him from attending (*Browne v La Trinidad* (1887) 37 Ch D 1). Notice of a board meeting need not be given to a director whose whereabouts are unknown because, for example, he is travelling, and *Table A* provides that notice need not be sent to a director who is for the time being absent from the United Kingdom, e.g. where he is absent on business; but unless the articles are in the form of *Table A*, notice must be given to all directors if their whereabouts are known.

The effect of failure to give proper notice is uncertain, but it is the better view that it does not render resolutions passed at the meeting void. The law is not entirely clear, but in *Re Homer*, etc. (above) it was held that all resolutions passed at the meeting were void, whereas in *Browne v La Trinidad* (above) it was held that failure to give proper notice to a director merely entitles him to require that a second meeting be held if he does not attend the first. If he does not require a second meeting to be held within a reasonable time, then he waives his right to ask for it and the resolutions passed at the first meeting are then valid. The notice need only specify when and where the meeting is to be held. It is not necessary to set out the business to be transacted but in practice it is usual to do so.

Quorum

This is normally fixed by the articles, and *Table A* provides that the quorum shall be fixed by the directors and unless so fixed shall be two. A private company may have only one director, and if this is intended to be so in practice the articles should provide for a quorum of one. Alternatively, the sole director could presumably fix the quorum at one and minute the decision.

A person who holds office only as an alternate director shall, if his appointor is not present, be counted in the quorum. This does not, of course, apply to a private company with only one director. Certainly no business can be validly transacted without a quorum, and the quorum must if the articles so require (*Re Greymouth Point Elizabeth Rail & Coal Co Ltd* [1904] 1 Ch 32) consist of directors who are not personally interested in the business which is before the meeting, although in such a case interested directors are entitled to notice of the meeting and may attend and speak but not vote.

As regards personal interest, *Table A* provides as follows. A director shall not vote at a meeting of directors or of a committee of directors on any resolution concerning a matter in which he has, directly or indirectly, an interest or duty which is material and which conflicts, or may conflict, with the interest of the company unless his interest or duty arises only because the case falls within one or more of the following areas:

(a) the resolution relates to the giving to him of a guarantee, security or indemnity in respect of money lent to, or an obligation by him for the benefit of, the company or any of its subsidiaries;

(b) the resolution relates to the giving to a third party of a guarantee, security or indemnity in respect of an obligation of the company or any of its subsidiaries for which the director has assumed responsibility in whole or part and whether alone or jointly with others under a guarantee or indemnity or by the giving of security;

(c) his interest arises by reason of his subscribing or agreeing to subscribe for any shares, debentures, or other securities of the company or any of its subsidiaries, or by reason of his being, or intending to become, a participant in the underwriting or sub-underwriting of an offer of any such shares, debentures or other securities by the company or any of its subsidiaries for subscription, purchase or exchange;

(d) the resolution relates in any way to a retirement benefit scheme which has been approved, or is conditional upon approval, by HMRC for taxation purposes.

For the purposes of *Table A* an interest of a person who is, for any purpose of the Companies Act, connected with a director shall be treated as an interest of the director and in relation to an alternate director, an interest of his appointor shall be treated as an interest of the alternate director in addition to his own interests. A director shall not be counted in the quorum present at a meeting in relation to a resolution on which he is not entitled to vote. A director may vote on the appointment of a fellow director to an office of profit under the company, but not on his own appointment. The company may by ordinary resolution suspend or relax to any extent, either generally or in respect of any particular matter, any provision of the articles prohibiting a director from voting at a meeting of directors or of a committee of directors. If the company is to have a listing on the Stock Exchange, the rules of the Stock Exchange require that the company's articles follow the above provisions of *Table A* in terms of directors' interests, otherwise a listing will not be granted.

Voting at board meetings

The voting at board meetings is usually governed by the articles and is normally one vote per director, but *Table A* provides, as we have seen, that directors with a personal interest in the business before the meeting are not allowed to vote. A majority of one will carry a resolution, though an equality of votes means that the resolution is lost, unless the position is resolved by the use of the chairman's *casting vote* if he is given one under the articles. *Table A* gives the directors power to appoint a chairman to preside at board meetings and give him a casting vote.

Minutes

Every company must keep minutes of all proceedings at directors' meetings, and where there are managers all proceedings at meetings of managers must be entered in books kept for that purpose. When the minutes are signed by the chairman of the meeting, or by the chairman of the next succeeding meeting, they are prima facie evidence of the proceedings. The members have no general right to inspect the minutes of directors' meetings (*R* v *Merchant Tailors Co* (1831) 2 B & Ad 115), but the directors have.

Meetings by telephone

As we have seen, *Table A* allows written resolutions of directors to be as effective as resolutions passed in a board meeting. Therefore, *Table A* does not require a 'face to face' meeting either in the 1985 version or the 1948 version (see Part I, Art 106 – plcs; and Part II, Arts 1 and 5 – private companies).

Thus, if the relevant provisions were altered to allow valid decisions to be taken by telephone, either by the chairman obtaining the agreement of the majority of the board having contacted them all by telephone or by means of a 'conference' call, there would be no need for a meeting of the board. Impersonation of a director could arise but should not in general be a serious problem. A record equivalent to minutes would have to be kept. As regards general meetings of members, this does not have the same impact for change in the articles as in the case of board meetings. In view of the written resolution procedure and the infrequency of general meetings compared with board meetings, there is obviously less point in such a change. After all, a unanimous written resolution is effective as soon as the last member has signed his copy and a telephone call to each member to ascertain this means that the business which was the subject matter of the resolution can be proceeded with. There is no need to wait until the separate copies are returned (though they must be) and collated in one place.

Resolutions – generally

First, it must be noted that written resolutions under Chapter 2 of Part 13 of CA 2006 are exclusively for the use of private companies. CA 2006, s 281 limits the ways in which resolutions can be passed and has the effect that written resolutions can only be passed using the procedure set out in Chapter 2 of Part 13. While the common law principle of unanimous consent does continue to apply under CA 2006, s 1(4), CA 2006, s 300 provides that the articles of a private company cannot override the ability to pass written resolutions under Chapter 2 of Part 13 of CA 2006. As such, despite whatever a private company's articles might say, Chapter 2 of Part 13 of CA 2006 predominates. Again it is critical to note that the statutory written resolution procedure cannot be used by public companies at all pursuant to CA 2006, s 281(2). Moreover, the common law position on unanimous consent also known as the *Duomatic* principle (see below) remains in effect under CA 2006, s 281(4).

At the same time, there are limitations on the use of written resolutions for private companies (CA 2006, s 288 (2)). Such a mechanism, for instance, cannot be used to remove a director from office before the expiration of his term in office under s 168; or the auditors from office before the expiration of their term in office under s 510. Instead, both of these decisions require actual meetings of the company's members to be held and require the special notice provisions as set out in CA 2006, s 312.

1 Special resolutions

A special resolution is one passed by a majority of not less than three-quarters of such members as are entitled to and do vote in person, or, where proxies are allowed, by proxy, at a general meeting of which notice specifying the intention to propose the resolution as a special resolution has been duly given (CA 2006, s 283). CA 2006, s 307 removed one of the big differences between special and ordinary resolutions for non-traded companies that existed under CA 1985. CA 1985 required 21 clear days' notice for a meeting at which a special resolution was proposed to be passed and 14 clear days' notice was required for a meeting at which an ordinary resolution was to be passed.

CA 2006, s 307(1) now provides that any general meeting of a non-traded private company (other than an adjourned meeting) must be called by notice of at least 14 days (subject always to shorter notice being agreed by the members). The notice period no longer depends on the type of resolutions being proposed and is 14 days for all general meetings of non-traded private companies (and 14 days for all general meetings of non-traded public companies apart from annual general meetings of public companies, where the notice period remains 21 days under CA 2006, s 307(2)). CA 2006, ss 29 and 30 mandate the requirement for copies of all special resolutions that are passed to be filed with the Registrar of Companies within 15 days of the resolutions being passed. This requirement is carried over from CA 1985, s 380.

CA 2006, s 281 states that where any provision of CA 2006 requires a resolution of a company or its members and it does not specify what kind of resolution, an ordinary resolution will be required unless the company's articles require a higher majority or unanimity. When a provision specifies that an ordinary resolution is required, the articles will not be able to specify a higher majority.

CA 2006, s 283 defines a special resolution as a resolution passed by a majority of not less than 75 per cent. Section 283 distinguishes between a special resolution passed at a meeting on a show of hands and a special resolution passed on a poll taken at a meeting. CA 2006, s 283(4) provides that a resolution passed at a meeting on a show of hands is passed by a majority of at least 75 per cent if it is passed by not less than 75 per cent of the votes cast by those entitled to vote. CA 2006, s 283(5) provides a resolution passed on a poll taken at a meeting is passed by a majority of at least 75 per cent if it is passed by members representing 75 per cent (or more) of the total voting rights of members who, being entitled to vote, do so in person or by proxy.

CA 2006, s 283 deals with the situation of special resolutions passed by means of a written resolution. CA 2006, s 283(2) provides that a written resolution is passed by a majority of at least 75 per cent if it is passed by members representing at least 75 per cent of the total voting rights of eligible members. CA 2006, s 283(3) provides that where a resolution of a private company is passed as a written resolution, the resolution will not be a special resolution unless the written resolution states that the resolution was proposed as a special resolution. Accordingly, if the written resolution states that it was proposed as a special resolution, it may only be passed as such. Thus, it is now clear that a written resolution is specifically required to state on its face that it is intended as a special resolution for it to qualify as a special resolution. This brings written resolutions into alignment with special resolutions passed in general meetings which expressly require the statement in the notice of general meeting that the resolution is proposed as a special resolution.

CA 2006, s 283(6) indicates what is to be required to be included in a notice of general meeting at which a special resolution is proposed to be passed. Chiefly, the notice of general meeting must specify the intention to propose the resolution as a special resolution but also specifies that the text of the special resolution must be included in the notice.

2 Ordinary resolutions

CA 2006, s 281 provides that, where any provision of CA 2006 requires a resolution of a company or its members and it does not specify what kind of resolution, an ordinary resolution will be required unless the company's articles require a higher majority or unanimity. When a provision specifies that an ordinary resolution is required, the articles will not be able to specify a higher majority. Extraordinary resolutions – found in the CA 1985 – was not incorporated into the CA 2006.

Ordinary resolutions are defined in CA 2006, s 282 as a resolution that is passed by a simple majority. The same section also distinguishes between an ordinary resolution passed at a meeting on a show of hands and an ordinary resolution passed on a poll taken at a meeting. Additionally, CA 2006, s 282(2) covers a written resolution that is passed by a simple majority if it is passed by members representing more than 50 per cent of the total voting rights of eligible members.

For companies incorporated before 1 October 2007, the Fifth Commencement Order (paragraph 2(5), Schedule 5) provides that if, immediately before 1 October 2007, the articles of a company provided for the chairman to have a casting vote in the event of equality of votes (whether on a show of hands or on a poll) on an ordinary resolution proposed at a general meeting and that provision has not been removed from the articles, it continues to have effect notwithstanding ss 281(3) and 282. In addition, if there was such a provision in the articles immediately before 1 October 2007 and it was removed from the articles on or after 1 October 2007, the company may, at any time, restore that provision and it will be effective notwithstanding ss 281(3) and 282. For traded companies only, this saving provision for the casting vote was removed from 3 August 2009, by the Companies (Shareholders' Rights) Regulations 2009.

CA 2006, s 282(5) provides that anything that may be done by ordinary resolution may also be done by special resolution.

Sections 29 and 30 (which came into force on 1 October 2007) provide that a copy of every resolution affecting a company's constitution must be forwarded to the Registrar of Companies within 15 days after it is passed. This includes resolutions to which the requirement applies by virtue of 'any enactment' (which could include ordinary resolutions if they affect a company's constitution).

There was no change made by the CA 2006 to the requirement for special notice of at least 28 days in respect of an ordinary resolution to remove a director before the expiration of his period of office (CA 2006, s 168) or remove an auditor before the expiration of his term of office (CA 2006, s 511).

Seconding resolutions

The chairman can put any resolution to the meeting without its being seconded though not if the articles forbid it (*Re Horbury Bridge Coal, Iron & Wagon Co* (1879) 11 Ch D 109). Whether a resolution requires a seconder and whether that seconder must be a member depends upon the articles. *Table A* does not require a seconder at all so that the motion or resolution could be put to the meeting after proposal and no seconder is required at common law (see *Re Horbury Bridge Coal, Iron & Wagon Co*, 1879, above).

Registration of resolutions

Special resolutions must be registered with the Registrar of Companies. This is achieved under CA 2006, s 30 by sending a printed copy of the resolution to the Registrar within 15 days after its passing. It is not necessary to send a *printed* copy of the resolution to the Registrar if instead the company forwards a copy in some other form approved by him. A copy of each such resolution must also be embodied in or attached to every copy of the articles of association issued after the passing of the resolution.

It has already been noted (see Chapter 13 ◯) that if shares in a public company are forfeited or surrendered to the company, the company must see to it that the shares are disposed of and if this has not been done within three years it must cancel the shares. If the result of this is that the company's issued share capital is brought below the authorised minimum, the company will have to apply for re-registration as a private company, and a resolution of the directors is sufficient to change the company's memorandum of association to prepare it for re-registration. That resolution of the directors is registrable with the Registrar within 15 days of its being passed.

The Electronic Communications Order 2000 enables the Registrar to direct that any document required to be delivered to him under the Companies Act or the Insolvency Act 1986 may be delivered electronically in a manner decided by him.

Ordinary resolutions requiring special notice

An ordinary resolution of which *special notice* has been given is required in the following cases:

(a) to remove a director before the expiration of his period of office (CA 2006, s 168). The section does not prevent companies from attaching special voting rights to certain shares on this occasion (*Bushell* v *Faith*, 1969, see Chapter 22 ◯); or

(b) to remove an auditor before the expiration of his term of office (CA 2006, s 511).

It should be noted that the actual resolution need not be moved at the meeting by the same member who served the special notice.

Amendments

As regards amendments to resolutions, which must be set out verbatim, such as special and extraordinary resolutions, it is often suggested that no amendment is possible since the Companies Acts require *notice* of the resolution and some say, by implication, of any amendment, because if the resolution is changed by an amendment then proper notice has not been given of that part of it which was amended. It is generally believed that this view is too strict, and indeed in *Re Moorgate Mercantile Holdings* [1980] 1 All ER 40 Mr Justice Slade decided that such a resolution could depart in some respects from the text of the resolution set out in the notice, e.g. on account of correction of grammatical or clerical errors, or the use of more formal language. However, apart from alterations of form of this kind, there must be no alterations of substance; otherwise only where all the members (in the case of an annual general meeting) or a majority in number and 95 per cent in value of members (in the case of any other meeting) have waived their rights to notice, could a special resolution be validly passed. The judge also decided that in the case of notice of intention to propose a special resolution nothing is achieved by the addition of such words as 'with such amendments and alterations as shall be determined on at the general meeting'.

The facts of the case were that the company wished to reduce its share premium account on the grounds that it had been lost in the course of trade. The share premium account to be cancelled was stated in the notice to be £1,356,900 48p. That figure included the sum of £321 17p which had been credited to the share premium account under an issue of shares made on the acquisition of the outstanding minority interest in a subsidiary. This share premium could not be regarded as lost. At the meeting the chairman proposed to amend the special resolution and, although not all the members of the company were present, a special resolution was passed in the following form: 'That the share premium account of the company amounting to £1,356,900 48p be reduced to £321 17p.' The court was then asked to agree to the reduction and the judge refused to do so on the grounds that the special resolution had not been validly passed.

Subject to what has been said above, once a resolution has been moved and, if the articles require, seconded, any member may speak and move amendments. No notice of the amendments is required unless the amendment effects a substantial change in the original resolution, i.e. is the change such that a reasonable man who had decided to absent himself from the meeting would have decided to come if he had received notice of the amended resolution? This is a decision which the chairman must take and hope that if his decision is questioned in court the judge will agree with him. For example, in *Re Teede and Bishop Ltd* (1901) 70 LJ Ch 409 it was held that at a meeting to resolve that A Ltd should be sold to B Ltd and then that A Ltd should be wound up, it was not in order to accept an amendment that A Ltd be wound up without the sale to B Ltd unless notice had been given of it.

Amendments must be put to the vote before the resolution is voted upon. Improper refusal by the chairman to put an amendment renders the main resolution void (*Henderson* v *Bank of Australasia* (1890) 45 Ch D 330).

Resolutions and the '*Duomatic* principle' of unanimous consent

Where all the shareholders of a company assent to a matter that could be brought into effect by a resolution in general meeting the unanimous consent of the shareholders without a formal meeting is enough. This is called the '*Duomatic* principle' from the case in which it was most famously canvassed, i.e. *Re Duomatic Ltd* [1969] 1 All ER 161. Alterations in the articles can be achieved in this way and in this connection the *Duomatic* principle has been applied to changes in shareholders' agreements that are often used in private companies to supplement the articles in confidential areas of governance (see *Euro Brokers Holdings Ltd* v *Monecor (London) Ltd* [2003] 1 BCLC 506).

Written resolutions for private companies (s 288, CA 2006 *et seq.*)

Written resolutions no longer have to be agreed by all members, but merely a simple majority or a three-quarters majority as appropriate depending on whether a resolution is ordinary or special (CA 2006, ss 281(2) and 283(2)). Two types of resolution for which the written resolution is not permissible are the resolution to remove a director (CA 2006, s 168) and the resolution to remove an auditor (CA 2006, s 510). These two exceptions are in effect even for a private company and nothing in the articles of any company may preclude these provisions requiring a meeting (CA 2006, s 510). CA 2006, s 288(4) and (5) contain saving provisions for those written resolutions entered into before Chapter 2 comes into force. CA 2006, s 296 sets forth the procedure for a member to signify his agreement to a proposed written resolution. CA 2006, s 291 governs written resolutions proposed by directors while CA 2006, s 292 governs written resolutions proposed by members. CA 2006, s 298 governs situations involving electronic communications with respect to written resolutions.

There are some cases where the written resolution procedure cannot be used, e.g. the removal of a director or auditor by ordinary resolution after special notice to the company. The ordinary resolution must be passed at a meeting of the company because the director or auditor concerned is allowed to make representations as to why he should not be removed, either in writing with the notice of the meeting, or orally at the meeting.

The company is required to keep a record of written resolutions and the signatures of those members who signed them in a record book which is, in effect, a substitute for what would, in the case of a meeting, be the minutes.

Written resolutions: special adaptations

Schedule 15 of the CA 1985 formerly contained special adaptations to the written resolution procedure in certain circumstances, e.g. where documents have to be available at the meeting at which the resolution is passed, if that method were followed instead of a written procedure where there is no meeting, as in approval of a director's service contract exceeding five years, where the contract must be supplied to members before or at the time of signing the resolution instead of being available at the meeting where a non-written resolution is passed. These can now be found in the CA 2006: ss 571(7), 573(5), 695(2), 698(2), 696(2), 699(2), 717(2), 718(2) and 188(5).

Filing of written resolutions

There is no general need to file a written resolution with the Registrar unless it takes effect, e.g. as a special or elective resolution or an ordinary resolution increasing authorised share capital. Even where a written resolution does have to be filed, there is no requirement to file the original. A copy can be filed and the signed copy kept in the minute book. In connection with the filing of written resolutions, Companies House states that it has received copies of 'written special resolutions'. There is, of course, no such thing. There are written resolutions *which take effect as special resolutions*. It would be a better approach to indicate on the filed copy and minute copy of the resolution that it took effect as a special resolution.

Involvement of auditors

CA 2006, s 502, replacing CA 1985, s 390, requires an auditor to receive much of the information that members of the company are entitled to receive including information concerning written resolutions of a private company and notices of and communications relating to a general meeting of a company.

Meetings of single-member companies

The amendments of the law relating to meetings to accommodate the single-member company have already been considered (see Chapter 1 ➲).

Electronic communications – CA 2006

The electronic communications provisions of Companies Act 2006, namely, ss 1143–1148, Schedules 4 and 5 have now been implemented. It should be noted at first that these provisions apply to all types of companies. The earlier distinctions made between companies whose shares are traded on a stock exchange and those whose shares were not traded have been eliminated. CA 2006 allows any information or documents to be communicated in electronic form, provided that the requirements of the CA 2006 are met.

Definitions of electronic form and electronic means (CA 2006, s 1168)

A document sent in 'electronic form' means that the document or information is sent or supplied by electronic means (for example, by email or fax) or by any other means while in electronic form (for example, sending a disk by post). The same section also states that a document or information is sent by 'electronic means' if it is sent initially and received at its destination by means of electronic equipment for the processing or storage of data or entirely transmitted, conveyed and received by wire, radio, optical means or other electromagnetic means. A document or information sent by 'electronic means' must also be sent in such a form that the sender or supplier *reasonably considers* will enable the recipient to read it and retain a copy of it. In CA 2006, s 1169 'read' means that the document or information can be read with the naked eye, or, if it consists of images, pictures, maps, plans or drawings, etc., it can be seen with the naked eye.

CA 2006 – Schedules 4 and 5

CA 2006 makes a distinction between communications by a company (Schedule 4) and communications to a company (Schedule 5). Please note, however, that in the situation where there are two companies communicating, e.g. a proxy fight, it is only the rules relating to communications by a company that are applicable.

Schedule 4 – Communications to a company

If the company agrees, documents may be sent to or served on it by electronic means. The address is that specified by the company and so, for example, it could be an email address or fax number. In some situations, the company is deemed to have consented to receiving documents electronically. For example if it publishes an electronic address in a notice convening a general meeting, CA 2006 provides that the company is deemed to have consented to receiving documents relating to that meeting, such as proxies, at that electronic address. If a document is sent in electronic form by hand or by post (e.g. a CD-ROM or floppy disk) then it must be sent to the company's registered office or to the address provided by the company for receipt of hard copy correspondence. The company may also agree to receive documents in a form other than hard copy or electronic form.

Schedule 5 – Communications by a company

Schedule 5 provides a method for communications in both hard copy form and electronic form. With respect to communications in electronic form, if the recipient agrees, the company may supply information and documents in electronic form to the address provided for that purpose by the recipient. If the document or information is sent in electronic form by post or delivered by hand (for instance on a computer disk or CD-ROM), it must be handed to the intended recipient or sent or supplied to an address to which it could be validly sent if it were in hard copy form.

Communications by means of a website (Part 4 of Schedule 5 to CA 2006)

A company may communicate via its website with its members if its members have resolved that the company may communicate with members through a website or the company's articles must contain a provision to this effect. The resolution must be filed at Companies House. Each member must be individually asked by the company to consent to communication by means of a website (either generally or in relation to specific documents). The company's request must clearly state the effect of a failure to respond by the member (for instance, that he or she would be deemed to have consented if he or she does not reply within 28 days starting with the date on which the request is sent). The company's request must not be sent less than 12 months after a previous request made to that member in respect of a similar class of documents. If the company satisfies all of this, it can communicate via a website with any members who consent or who fail to respond within 28 days starting with the date on which the request is sent. If a member says he or she does not want to be communicated with via a website, the company must wait 12 months before it asks the member again for consent in relation to the specific documents for which consent was originally sought.

Procedures to be followed after consent is obtained (Schedule 5)

Once needed consents are obtained (from all or some of the members), the company must take the following steps:

- A document or information on a website must be made available in a form, and by a means, that the company reasonably considers will enable the recipient to read it and retain a copy of it.
- The company must notify the intended recipient of the presence of a document or information on a website, the address of the website, the place on the website where it may be accessed and how to access the document or information.
- Unless the member has also consented to being contacted by electronic means, this means that this information must be provided in hard copy form such as letter.
- The company must make the document or information available on the website throughout the period specified by any applicable provision of the Companies Acts or, if no such period is specified, the period of 28 days beginning with the date on which the notification that the document is available on the website is sent to the person in question.

Right to request hard copy form (CA 2006, s 1145)

If the member so requests, the company must provide a hard copy form of any document sent by electronic means or made available on a website, within 21 days of receipt of the request and for no charge. Failure of a company to comply with this requirement means that the company and every officer in default commits an offence and are liable to a fine and a daily fine while the contravention continues.

CA 2006, s 1146 – authentication of electronic communications

Section 1146 provides that an electronic communication is authenticated if the identity of the sender is confirmed in the manner specified by the company or, in the absence of such specification, the document contains statement of the identity of the sender and the company has no reason to doubt the truth of the statement.

Conclusions

We live in an age where we use the Internet and email to communicate with each other ever more often. The electronic communications reforms are designed to save companies significant postage and printing costs while contributing to increased sustainability of the planet by reducing the use of paper. However, a company's use of emails and websites for communications is entirely dependent on consent of the member which can be withdrawn at any time. In addition, if a website is to be used as a basis to communicate with members, special procedures such as agreement to a resolution authorising such communications must be obtained as well. In short, while it may be environmentally friendly, it may not be feasible to expect that a large company will be able to communicate with all its members electronically at all times. Some members will always feel more comfortable with receiving 'snail-mail' instead.

Essay questions

1 (a) Explain how and in what circumstances a general meeting of a company will be called.

AND

(b) Explain what minimum period of notice must be given to call an extraordinary general meeting and whether and how such period may be shortened/lengthened.

AND

(c) Explain how many members must be present for a quorum at a general meeting of a company and whether and how the quorum may fall below the required minimum.

(Glasgow Caledonian University)

2 (a) What members' meetings are held by registered companies?

(b) Name and define the different kinds of resolution which may be passed by such companies in general meeting. In the case of each kind of resolution give one example of business for which such a resolution is necessary. *(The Institute of Company Accountants)*

3 You are required to explain the following issues relating to company meetings.

   (a) What is an extraordinary resolution and when is such a resolution required under the Companies Act 2006?

   (b) What is proxy voting? State whether such voting is always possible at company meetings.

   (c) What is a poll vote and who may demand such a vote?

   (d) What is special business? Identify two matters which would be included under such business.

   (e) What is a requisitioned circular? Who may demand it and who bears the cost?

(The Chartered Institute of Management Accountants)

4 Maurice, a shareholder of Traders plc, has informed the company secretary that he intends to propose a resolution at the forthcoming annual general meeting that the company should discontinue its business activities in a particular overseas country.

   The directors have instructed the secretary not to include the proposed resolution on the agenda for the meeting.

   Advise Maurice.   *(The Institute of Chartered Accountants in England and Wales)*

5 Directors owe their company a duty to exercise their powers only for a 'proper purpose'. Explain what is meant by 'proper purpose' and discuss the nature and scope of this duty. Illustrate your answer with references to decided cases, particularly those dealing with the power to issue shares.   *(The Association of Chartered Certified Accountants)*

6 XY Bank plc is the subject of a takeover bid by Able Securities plc. In order to frustrate the takeover bid, the board of directors take the following action:

   (a) they allot one million unissued shares to Lionel who will vote against the takeover bid by Able Securities plc. Lionel does not have enough money to pay for the shares but secures a loan from XY Bank plc to cover the payment;

   (b) they make a payment of £1 million to Computer Security Services Ltd as an advance payment on a contract that has been negotiated between the two companies. Computer Security Services Ltd is informed by the directors that it should buy shares in XY Bank plc if it wants to make a quick profit and keep the contract. Computer Security Services Ltd buy £1 million of shares in XY Bank plc;

   (c) they decide that XY Bank plc should buy its own shares as a good investment and £10 million of shares are purchased.

The shares rise in value and all purchasing parties make a profit. The takeover bid is frustrated. Advise the directors as to the legality of their actions and of any proceedings that could be brought against them or the company.   *(University of Central Lancashire)*

Test your knowledge

Four alternative answers are given. Select ONE only. Circle the answer which you consider to be correct. Check your answers by referring back to the information given in the chapter and against the answers at the end of the text.

1 In what circumstance may the members of a company who have requisitioned an EGM call the meeting themselves?

   A If the directors do not call a meeting to be held within 21 days of the deposit of the requisition.

   B If the directors do not within 21 days from the date of the deposit of the requisition call a meeting for a date not more than 28 days after the notice calling the meeting.

C   If the directors take action to call a meeting within 21 days but the date of the meeting is set at a date more than three months from the date of the deposit of the requisition.

D   If the directors fail to call a meeting to take place within 28 days of the date of the deposit of the requisition.

2   Felicity is a member of Wash plc. She has appointed Thomas as her proxy for the next AGM. Thomas will be able:

A   To vote on a show of hands and speak at the meeting.

B   To vote on a show of hands but not speak at the meeting.

C   To vote but only on a poll and speak at the meeting.

D   To vote only on a poll but not speak at the meeting.

3   Cunnane Ltd was incorporated on 1 February 2004. What is the latest date on which it must hold its first AGM?

A   31 July 2005   B   31 December 2005   C   31 March 2006   D   31 December 2006

4   Thames Ltd wishes to pass a special resolution of the members to change the articles. What length of notice is required, and how many of the company's members present and voting in person or by proxy are needed to pass the resolution?

A   21 days' notice and over 50 per cent.

B   28 days' notice and over 50 per cent.

C   21 days' notice and 75 per cent.

D   28 days' notice and 75 per cent.

5   What is the minimum period of notice which must be given to the members of a limited company who are entitled to be present and vote in person or by proxy at an EGM to pass an ordinary resolution?

A   28 days   B   21 days   C   14 days   D   7 days

6   What quorum is required for a general meeting of a multi-member registered company?

A   Two persons who are either members or proxies for members.

B   Three persons who are members or proxies for members.

C   Two persons who are members.

D   Three persons who are members.

Answers to test your knowledge questions appear on p. 645.

24

Debentures and charges

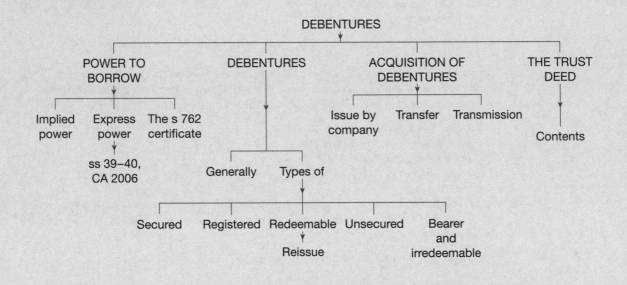

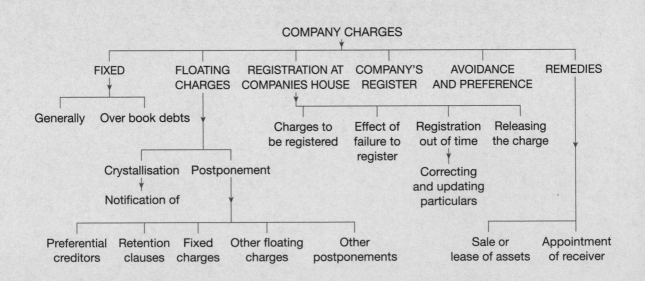

In this chapter we shall be concerned with a company's loan capital and the means of securing loans by charging the company's assets.

Power to borrow

A trading company has implied power to borrow (*General Auction Estate and Monetary Co v Smith* [1891] 3 Ch 432). Nevertheless, prior to the CA 2006, it was usual for an express power to be given in the memorandum, and such express powers may impose some limit on the company's borrowing by stating a fixed sum beyond which the company cannot borrow, or by limiting the borrowing, say, to one-half of the issued share capital. A non-trading company has no implied borrowing powers and must take express power to borrow in its constitution.

A power to borrow, whether express or implied, carries with it by a further implication of law a power to give a security for the loan and to pay interest upon it (*General Auction Estate & Monetary Co v Smith*, 1891, above). Once again, it is usual for the company's constitution to give an express power to do these things, though an express power cannot override the Companies Act. Thus, it would not be possible to charge the company's reserve capital since this is expressly forbidden by the provisions of the Act, which renders such capital incapable of being called up except on a winding-up (see Chapter 9 ◑).

As regards the directors, *Table A* gives the board all powers to manage and there is no need for a *specific* power to borrow. There is no limit on the amount the directors can borrow so long as they remain within the company's power. However, in view of the provisions of CA 2006, s 39 and s 40 (see Chapter 10 ◑), borrowing by the directors beyond the provisions of the company's constitution is much less likely to affect a contract of loan with an outsider such as a bank.

The directors must obtain member approval before allotting convertible debentures, i.e. debentures which carry rights of conversion into share capital. As we have seen, a public company should not borrow money until it has received a CA 2006, s 762 certificate allowing it to trade, though this does not affect the enforceability of the loan (see Chapter 4, p. 77 ◑).

Debentures – generally

The most usual form of borrowing by companies is by means of debentures. The debenture also gives a charge on the company's property. The word 'debenture' has its origin in a Latin word for 'owing'.

As regards a definition, a debenture is a document executed by a company as a deed in favour of a creditor, providing the creditor with security over the whole or substantially the whole of the company's assets and undertaking, normally creating a fixed charge over fixed assets such as land and buildings and a floating charge over the rest of the company's assets such as stock and giving the creditor power to appoint an administrative receiver with extensive authority to collect in the assets, run the company's business and dispose of the assets either one at a time or as part of a sale of the business as a going concern. Under the Companies Acts, debenture includes debenture stock, bonds and other securities of a company, whether or not constituting a charge on the assets of the company.

Debenture holders are creditors (but consider the position under a trust deed) and not members of the company, and are entitled to interest on their debentures whether the company earns profits or not. Holders are provided with a safe if limited income, and debentures appeal to a cautious investor.

Debentures may also be *convertible* which means that they are issued with an option, tenable for a certain period of time, to exchange them for shares in the company. Debentures can be issued at a discount without restriction, but the issue of convertible debentures must not be allowed to operate as a device to issue shares at a discount as would be the case if a debenture for £100, issued at £90, were later to be exchanged for 100 shares of nominal value of £1 each. This would in effect be an issue of shares at a discount which is forbidden by the Companies Acts.

Types of debentures

Debentures may be issued in a series, e.g. where there is a public offer, or alternatively they may be issued singly, e.g. to secure a bank loan or overdraft. They may also be issued in respect of either an existing debt or a fresh loan.

In the case of a public offer the admission of debentures to listing must comply with Part VI of the Financial Services and Markets Act 2000. The Public Offers of Securities Regulations 1995, which regulated a public offer of unlisted debentures, was repealed in 2005. (These matters are considered in Chapter 12. ◐)

Where debentures are issued in a series, it is usual to provide expressly that they are to rank *pari passu*, i.e. equally. This is essential because loans rank for priority according to the time they are made, and if such an express provision were not made, the debentures in the series would rank for priority of payment and security according to the date of issue, and if all were issued on the same day, they would rank in numerical order.

Gartside v Silkstone and Dodworth Coal and Iron Co Ltd (1882) 21 Ch D 762

The company issued 150 debentures of £100 each on the same day. They were issued in two lots, one lot being numbered 501–600 and the second lot 601–650. Each of the debentures contained a provision that it was to rank *pari passu* with the others, but the first group referred to the amount of £10,000 and the second to £5,000, this being the only difference in the respective provisions. Nevertheless, this suggested that they were independent issues. The company was in liquidation and the question of priority arose. When two deeds are executed on the same day, the court must inquire which of them was executed first, but if there is anything in the deeds to show such an intention, they may take effect *pari passu*.

Held – by the High Court – the company could, therefore, choose to give security in the form of a second floating charge of the kind outlined, and this was valid and did rank equally with the first charge because they were expressed to be *pari passu*.

Where debentures rank *pari passu*, there can be no action at law brought by an individual debenture holder merely in respect of his own rights, and any such action brought by him is deemed to be a representative action on behalf of all the debenture holders of the series.

Debenture stock may be issued so long as the stock is fully paid, and this affects transfer. A debenture must be transferred as a whole unit whereas debenture stock can be transferred in part, though the articles or the terms of issue usually fix a minimum amount which can be transferred, e.g. £1.

Debentures are usually *secured, registered* and *redeemable*, though they may be unsecured, unregistered (i.e. bearer debentures) and irredeemable.

Secured debentures

These are normally secured by a charge on the company's assets, either by a provision to that effect in the debenture itself, or by the terms of the trust deed drawn up in connection with the issue. Sometimes a provision appears in both documents.

Registered debentures

These are recorded in the register of debenture holders. Such debentures are transferable in accordance with the provisions of the terms of issue, but transfer is usually effected by an instrument in writing in a way similar to that of shares. The transferee of a debenture takes it subject to equities, and this includes claims which the company has against the transferor. However, the company's claims are normally excluded by the terms of issue of the debentures, these terms usually stating that the money secured by the debentures will be paid without regard to any equities between the company and previous holders.

Re Goy & Co Ltd, Farmer v Goy & Co Ltd [1900] 2 Ch 149

In a voluntary winding-up of the company WH Doggett had been appointed liquidator and also receiver. At this point, Chandler, a former director, transferred £600 of debentures to GD Robey by way of security for a loan. The conditions of the debentures provided that on complying with certain formalities, the principal and interest secured by the debentures would be paid without regard to any equities between the company and the original or intermediate holder. After Robey had taken the transfer, it was discovered that Chandler had been guilty of misfeasance and he was ordered by the court to pay £300 to the liquidator. Robey, who had no notice of this cross-claim, sent his transfer to the liquidator, for registration. The liquidator declined to register it, and claimed the right to deduct the £300 owed by Chandler.

Held – by the High Court – the right to transfer and have the transfer registered was not affected by the winding-up or by the court order against Chandler, and Robey was entitled to have the debentures registered without deduction.

It should also be noted that when a company sets up a register of debenture holders, the CA 2006, ss 743–748 provisions relating to no notice of trust do not apply to it, and the company would be bound by any notice of trust or other equity over the debentures. It is, therefore, usual to provide in the terms of issue that the company shall not be bound to recognise anyone other than the registered holder.

Redeemable debentures

Debentures are usually redeemable, and the company may provide a fund for their redemption. The annual amount so provided must be charged whether profits are made or not, though in some cases the terms of issue may stipulate that the fund shall be provided only out of profits, if made.

Debentures may be redeemed in the following ways:

(a) *By drawings by lot*, either at the company's option or at fixed intervals.

(b) *By the company buying them in the market*, and if the debentures are bought in the market at a discount, the consequent profit to the company is a realised profit available for dividend unless the articles otherwise provide.

(c) *By the company redeeming them either out of a fund or possibly by a fresh issue of debentures.* A fresh issue is useful to the company where rates of interest have fallen, because the old debentures can be redeemed and the money reborrowed by the fresh issue at lower rates of interest. Where redemption is by a fresh issue, it is usual to allow the existing debenture holders to exchange the old debentures for the new ones if they so wish.

The company will redeem at a fixed future date, but usually has an option to redeem on or after a given earlier date, and this allows the company to choose the most convenient time for redemption.

Redemption may be at the issue price or at a higher price, and debentures may be issued at (say) 80 and redeemed at 100, or issued at 100 and redeemed at 110, thus giving the debenture holders a capital gain in addition to the interest payments made.

Reissue

CA 2006, s 752 allows the company to reissue debentures which it has redeemed unless the company has resolved that the debentures shall not be reissued, or unless there are provisions in the articles or terms of issue of the original debentures that they shall not be reissued. A person to whom debentures are reissued has the same priorities as had the original debenture holder.

The articles and/or the trust deed under which the debentures are issued invariably forbid reissue, and if there was a reissue in that situation the purchasers of the reissued debentures would be deferred to other persons holding debentures at that time.

Where a company has issued debentures to secure advances made from time to time on a current account such as a bank overdraft, the debenture shall not be considered redeemed by reason only of the account ceasing to be at a certain point in debit so long as the debentures are still deposited with the person making the advances. They are a valid security for fresh advances.

Unsecured debentures

Such a debenture is no more than an unsecured promise by the company to repay the loan. The holder can, of course, sue the company on that promise, but is only an ordinary creditor in a winding-up, although, since he is a creditor, he can petition the court for a winding-up.

Bearer debentures

These are negotiable instruments and are transferable free from equities by mere delivery and it is not necessary to give the company notice of transfer.

Interest is paid by means of coupons attached to the debenture, these coupons being in effect an instruction to the company's banker to pay the bearer of the coupon a stated sum on presentment to the bank after a certain date. The company can communicate with the holders of bearer debentures only by advertisement, and it is often provided that the holders of such debentures may exchange them for registered debentures.

Irredeemable debentures

A debenture which is issued with no fixed date of redemption is an irredeemable debenture, though such debentures are redeemable on a winding-up, and the liquidator is empowered to discharge them. In addition, irredeemable debentures always empower the debenture holders to enforce their security should the company, for example, fail to pay interest on the loan and such enforcement will result in the payment of the debenture debt. CA 2006, s 735 provides that such debentures may be issued, and this provision is necessary because otherwise the general rule of equity, that redemption of a mortgage cannot be postponed for too long a time, would apply. The result is that a company can create long mortgages over its land and other property by means of debentures, whether irredeemable or for a long contractual period prior to redemption.

Knightsbridge Estates Trust Ltd v *Byrne* [1940] AC 613

The claimants owned a large freehold estate close to Knightsbridge. This estate was mortgaged to a Friendly Society for a sum of money which, together with interest, was to be repaid over a period of 40 years in 80 half-yearly instalments. The company wished to redeem the mortgage before the expiration of the term, because it was possible for it to borrow elsewhere at a lower rate of interest.

Held – by the House of Lords – the company was not entitled to redeem the mortgage before the end of the 40 years because the effect of what is now the Companies Act 2006 was to remove the application of the equitable doctrine of no postponement of the right of redemption from mortgages given by companies. Therefore, Knightsbridge was not entitled to redeem the mortgage except by the half-yearly instalments as agreed.

A debenture with no fixed date for redemption, but which gives the company the right to repay it at its option, is properly called a *perpetual* and not an irredeemable debenture (CA 2006, s 739).

Acquisition of debentures

Debentures may be acquired either from the company itself or by transfer or transmission.

Issue by the company

A company may issue debentures either individually or in a series. The provisions of the Companies Act 2006 forbidding the allotment of shares at a discount do not apply to debentures, and accordingly they may be allotted at par, at a discount, or at a premium, unless this is forbidden by the company's articles. However, if debentures are issued at a discount together with a right to exchange them for shares at par value, the debentures are good but the right to exchange is void (*Mosely* v *Koffyfontein Mines Ltd* [1904] 2 Ch 108). The share premium provisions do not apply to an issue of debentures and so if they are issued at a premium there is no need to open the equivalent of a share premium account.

If a person agrees to take a debenture from the company in return for a loan, the contract may be enforced by both the lender and the company by *specific performance*. CA 2006, s 740 gives this right because, in the absence of such statutory provision, equity would not specifically enforce a loan.

A private company cannot offer securities including debentures to the public.

The company must have certificates ready within two months after allotment or transfer, unless the terms of issue otherwise provide. (But note the position on transfer through the Stock Exchange system – see Chapter 14. ◗)

Transfer

Registered debentures are transferable in accordance with the method laid down in the terms of issue, usually a stock transfer form as for shares. The company cannot refuse to register a properly stamped transfer, provided the terms of issue allow transfers and contain no restrictions, but a proper instrument of transfer must be produced to the company except, for example, in cases of transmission. Where the company refuses to register a transfer, it must send a notice to this effect to the transferee within two months of the transfer being lodged.

Certification by the company of an instrument of transfer has the same effect in the case of debentures as it has in the case of shares, i.e. it is a representation that documents have been produced to the company which show a prima facie title in the transferors.

In the case of bearer debentures, transfer is by mere delivery and the company is not involved.

Transmission

As in the case of shares, debentures pass by operation of law (a) to the holder's personal representatives on *death*, and (b) to the holder's trustee on *bankruptcy*, and the rights of such persons are similar to their rights when shares pass by operation of law (see Chapter 14 ◗).

The trust deed

When debentures are offered for public subscription, the company enters into a trust deed with trustees, being a trust corporation such as an insurance company. The charge securing the debentures is made in favour of the trustees who hold it on trust for the debenture stock holders. The trustees are usually appointed and paid by the company to act on behalf of the debenture stock holders.

Debenture stock holders, unlike debenture holders, are not creditors of the company. Thus, in *Re Dunderland Iron Ore Co Ltd* [1909] 1 Ch 446 it was held that the holder of debenture stock secured by a trust deed could not present a petition to wind up the company since he was not a creditor. The trustees are the creditors for the whole debenture debt, and the stockholder is an equitable beneficiary of the trust on which they hold that debt. Consequently, his remedies are against the trustees, but by suing them, on behalf of himself and the other debenture holders, to compel them to exercise their remedies against the company, he can indirectly enforce the same remedies against the company as the holder of a single debenture can enforce directly.

The creation of a trust deed has the following advantages:

(a) *It enables a legal or equitable mortgage on specific assets of the company to be created.* The deeds of property can be held by the trustees, and where there is a legal mortgage the legal estate can be vested in them. It could not be vested in hundreds or possibly thousands of debenture holders because, since the property legislation of 1925, the legal estate in land cannot be vested in more than four persons.

(b) *There is also the matter of priorities.* A mortgage, in general terms, ranks in the order of its creation, so without a trust deed, in an issue to the public, the holder of the first certificate to be issued would rank in front of the second and so on. Holder number one would be entitled to payment from the company's assets *in full* before the second certificate holder got anything. Certificate holder, say, 1,000 might get nothing if the company's assets were insufficient. Under the trust deed the trustees have the charge and can, for example, sell the company's assets and distribute the proceeds equally so that all the stockholders get the same amount even if it is not a payment in full. Distribution is *pari passu*, which is a term commonly used of this procedure.

(c) *The interests of the debenture holders are better safeguarded* by the employment of a professional trust corporation, or by a small number of expert trustees, than they would be if left to the debenture holders themselves. The latter are often widely dispersed and often lack the knowledge required to safeguard their interests properly.

Trustees usually have the power to call meetings of the debenture holders to inform them of matters of particular concern to them.

(d) *The trust deed usually gives the trustees power to sell the property charged* without the aid of the court, and to appoint an administrative receiver should the company default, for example, in the payment of interest or repayment of the principal sums borrowed.

(e) The trust deed usually gives the trustees power to see that the security is properly maintained and repaired and insured.

Where debentures are issued under a trust deed, the debentures themselves refer to the deed and thereby incorporate its terms.

Contents of the trust deed

The main clauses of a trust deed are as follows:

(a) *The nature of the security.* Details of the assets charged are given, and it sets out the powers of the trustees to deal with them on default by the company and on a winding-up.

(b) *The nature of the charge.* The deed will state whether the charge is a fixed or a floating charge. Usually there is a combination of both, i.e. a fixed charge on certain of the company's assets and a floating charge on the rest. There will also be a provision relating to the company's power to create other charges ranking equally with, or in priority to, the present charge.

(c) *The kind of debentures to be issued.* This clause will state whether the debentures are to be registered or bearer, or whether debenture stock is to be issued; and if stock, the minimum amount which can be transferred.

(d) *The method of redemption*. The clause will state whether there is to be an ordinary redemption by the company, or whether redemption is to be made by drawings or in the market, and when the redemption is to take place. This clause will also give details of any fund which the company proposes to set up to provide for the redemption of the debentures.

A copy of any trust deed for securing any issue of debentures must be forwarded to every holder of any such debentures on payment of a fee.

The Act prevents a trust deed from exempting the trustees from liability for breach of trust on grounds of negligence. It can, however, permit subsequent release from such liability by a majority of not less than three-quarters in value of the debenture holders present and voting at a meeting summoned for the purpose.

Company charges

Part 25, CA 2006, ss 860–894 covers company charges.

Debentures may be secured by a fixed or by a floating charge, or by a combination of both types of charge. The expression 'mortgage debenture' normally denotes a debenture secured by a fixed charge.

Fixed (or specific) charge

Such a charge usually takes the form of a legal mortgage over specified assets of the company, e.g. its land and buildings and fixed plant. The mortgage is usually created by a charge by deed expressed to be by way of legal mortgage under s 85(1) of the Law of Property Act 1925. The major disadvantage from the company's point of view is that it cannot dispose of the asset or assets subject to the charge without the consent of the debenture holder. However, there is a major advantage for the directors in a fixed charge because they will almost always have personally guaranteed the company's overdraft, and in an insolvency it is important to them that the bank gets as much as possible from the debenture securing the overdraft so that their liability is extinguished or reduced. In this connection it is worth noting that a fixed charge is not postponed to preferential creditors and other creditors as is a floating charge, and the bank will get more from the security on realisation. This will not apply if the fixed charge is, by agreement between lenders, to rank behind a floating charge, in which case the second ranking fixed charge is subject to the floating charge and ranks after it *and the claims of the preferential debts, e.g. wages and salaries, upon it* (see *Re Portbase (Clothing) Ltd, Mond v Taylor* [1993] 3 All ER 829).

Where the company has no land, buildings or fixed plant, a bank can be asked to take a fixed charge over book debts.

The words used by the parties are not conclusive. If the court finds on the facts that the charge is a floating charge, it will not be persuaded that the charge is a fixed charge merely because the parties have said that it is (*Re ASRS Establishment Ltd* [1999] *The Times*, 17 November).

Floating charge

This is a charge which is not attached to any particular asset(s) identified when the charge is made. Instead it attaches to the company's assets as they then are, if and when the charge crystallises. The company is in the meantime free to dispose of its assets, and any new assets which the company may acquire are available to the debenture holder should the charge crystallise. Because such a charge does not fix at the time of its creation upon any particular asset it is equitable by nature, and this is relevant when considering the question of priority of charges when more than one has been created over the assets of the company.

Fixed charges over book debts

The advantage to the directors, and to the bank as debenture holder, of such a charge has already been considered. However, since a charge over book debts is over after-acquired property, the legal position was not absolutely settled, though it had been held in England that such a charge was valid (see *Siebe Gorman & Co Ltd* v *Barclays Bank Ltd* [1979] 2 Lloyd's Rep 142), and this decision was affirmed by the Irish Supreme Court in *Re Keenan Bros Ltd* [1985] 1 RLM 641, and again by the English Court of Appeal in *Re New Bullas Trading Ltd* [1994] 1 BCLC 485.

There are procedures to be set up by the bank in order to safeguard its position as a fixed charge holder but these are not considered here because they are a matter for the bank's legal advisers. Those advising the company can only suggest the fixed charge and point out to the directors its advantage to them in terms of their guarantees to the bank.

It is, however, of interest to note that the High Court has held that the terms of a debenture which contained provisions for a lending bank to have control of the borrowing company's book debts and other debts over which it had taken a specific charge, were essential to protect the validity of such a charge. Although the terms restricted the company's commercial use of its book and other debts, they were not anti-competitive, nor contrary to Arts 81 and 82 of the Treaty of Rome (*Oakdale (Richmond) Ltd* v *National Westminster Bank plc* [1997] 1 BCLC 63).

A major difficulty arose in connection with fixed charges over book debts following the ruling of the Privy Council in *Agnew* v *Inland Revenue* [2001] All ER (D) 21 (the *Brumark* case).

This ruling came out of an appeal from New Zealand and represented the usual sort of challenge to the fixed charge. If it is a fixed charge it will, as we have noted, rank before the preferential creditors. HMRC (formerly Inland Revenue) is now no longer a preferential creditor but ranks with the unsecured trade creditors but the Revenue often tried to attack the fixed charge over book debts hoping that it would be regarded as a floating charge which is postponed to preferential creditors.

The difficulty with *Brumark* was that the Privy Council ruled that the lender must have systems in place to exercise control over the book debts both collected and uncollected. In *Brumark* the charge left the company free to collect and use the book debts in the ordinary course of its business. This in the view of the Privy Council made the charge floating not fixed by reason of the lender's lack of sufficient control.

The *Brumark* decision was of course only persuasive as are decisions of the Privy Council but it added a new strand worrying to business because businessmen and women had always understood that if a debenture took a fixed charge over book debts under what was known as the *Siebe Gorman* formula the court would treat it as a fixed charge. The *Siebe Gorman* charge merely:

- prohibits the borrower from disposing (as by sale) of its book debts before collection; and
- requires the proceeds of the book debts to be paid into an account with the lending bank. *It does not prevent use of the proceeds by the company in its business.*

In the latest case in the saga, *In Re Spectrum Plus Ltd (in Liquidation)* [2004] NLJR 890, the Court of Appeal refused to follow *Brumark* and restored the *Siebe Gorman* formula to validity.

However, in June 2005, the House of Lords allowed the appeal, holding that it was possible to create a fixed charge over book debts. The essential characteristic of a floating charge is that the asset subject to the charge is not finally appropriated as a security for the payment of the debt until the occurrence of some future event. In the meantime, the chargor is left free to use the charged asset and to remove it from the security, *Brumark Investments Ltd, Re* applied. Where the chargor remains free to remove the charged assets from the security, the charge should, in principle, be categorised as a floating charge. It was not possible to create a charge on book debts which was fixed while they were uncollected but floating in respect of the proceeds when collected, *Re New Bullas Trading Ltd* overruled. The House of Lords went on to overrule the decision in *Siebe Gorman*.

Crystallisation of floating charges

A floating charge crystallises:

(a) In the circumstances specified in the debenture. This means that crystallisation can take place by agreement between the parties and the particular debenture must be looked at. However, most usually where the loan is repayable on demand, as in the case of an overdraft, the charge will crystallise automatically when the bank calls in the overdraft which the company cannot pay. The bank may then appoint an administrative receiver. However, the High Court has decided that where a bank has lent a company money that is repayable on demand with a security over the company's assets, the timing of the bank's appointment of an administrative receiver is governed, where the company has the means to repay by the time it needs to set the mechanics of repayment in motion. If the company has made it clear that it cannot pay, the bank may make the appointment straightaway as could any other secured creditor (see *Sheppard and Cooper Ltd* v *TSB Bank plc* [1996] 2 All ER 654). Other circumstances specified include failure of the company to pay interest or the principal sum when due as agreed. These may also result in automatic crystallisation. In some cases the charge may be stipulated to crystallise when the company exceeds a specified borrowing limit.

(b) Automatic crystallisation occurs on the appointment of a receiver under a fixed charge or an administrative receiver under a fixed/floating charge, or if the company commences to wind up and on cessation of its business (*Re Woodroffes (Musical Instruments)* [1985] 2 All ER 908).

Once a floating charge crystallises, the assets subject to the charge pass into the eventual control of the receiver and pass out of the control of the company immediately. Any disposition of those assets by the company after the charge crystallises means that the purchaser from the company takes the assets subject to the charge, i.e. the right of the debenture holder to proceed against them to satisfy the debt.

Note: The appointment of administrative receivers is now much restricted.

Postponement of floating charges

A person who lends money on the security of a fixed charge over the company's property is always entitled to repayment of his loan from the proceeds of sale of the mortgaged property before any other creditor, except a creditor with a prior fixed charge. A person who takes a floating charge is not so secure. There are cases in which his receiver will have to yield priority to other classes of creditors. The detailed law in this area is not considered because it is relevant only in an insolvency and is therefore more within the specialist province of the insolvency practitioner. It is not likely to be examined in detail in a general paper on company law. However, an outline of the position is given below.

Preferential creditors

Once a floating charge has crystallised the owner of the charge, e.g. the bank, is entitled to repayment of the loan out of the assets to which the charge has attached before the company's unsecured creditors. However, there is one statutory exception to this, which is that when a floating charge crystallises the claims which would be preferential in a winding-up rank in front of the debenture holder in respect of realisation of assets under the floating charge. The debenture debt is postponed only to preferential payments accrued at the date of the appointment of an administrator and not to those which accrue subsequently. Schedule 6 to the Insolvency Act 1986, as amended by the Enterprise Act 2002 applies, and there are no provisions for payment of interest on these debts until payment. Schedule 6 should be referred to if necessary for further detail, but the main preferential debts are as follows:

(a) Wages or salaries of employees due within four months before the relevant date, up to a maximum of £800 for each employee. The fees of non-executive directors are not preferential, though executive directors will normally be regarded as employees (see further Chapter 19 ⊃) to the extent of the remuneration paid to them in respect of their duties as executives, except where they are also controlling shareholders (see e.g. *Buchan* v *Secretary of State for Employment* (1997) 565 IRLB 2). A practice has developed of regarding the £800 as a gross sum, thus reducing the amount payable to the relevant preferential creditor. The legislation does not specify net or gross.
(b) All accrued holiday remuneration of employees.
(c) Unpaid pension contributions.

It should be noted that if a bank has provided funds to pay wages and salaries *before* the administration that debt becomes preferential under the rule of subrogation. The justification for the subrogation principle which is contained in Sch 6, para 11 to the 1986 Act is that the protection it offers to banks and other lenders may encourage them to advance further money for the payment of wages at a critical time in the debtor company's affairs so as to enable it to continue trading and possibly avoid insolvency leading to the appointment of an administrator or liquidator.

The main advantage of being a secured or preferential creditor in an administration (administrative receiverships being largely abolished under Enterprise Act 2002 amendments to the Insolvency Act 1986) is that the administrator's proposals for achieving the purposes of the administration must preserve the rights of the preferential creditors to prior payment of their debts. The priority of secured creditors such as floating chargeholders in terms of payment must also be preserved though in this case payment is subject to a ring-fenced fund for payment of unsecured creditors of a percentage that shall not be distributed to floating chargeholders. These matters are further considered in the chapters on corporate insolvency.

Protection of employees

Under ss 167–170 of the Employment Rights Act 1996 (as amended), an employee who loses his job when his employer becomes insolvent can claim through the National Insurance Fund certain payments which are owed to him rather than relying on the preferential payments procedure. The administrative receiver will normally calculate what is due and obtain authorisation through the Department for Business, Innovation and Skills. In so far as any part of this payment is preferential, the rights and remedies of the employee concerned are transferred to the Department for Business, Innovation and Skills, which becomes preferential in respect of them. Major debts covered are:

(a) arrears of pay for a period not exceeding eight weeks up to a maximum of £350 per week;
(b) pay in respect of holidays taken and accrued holiday pay up to £350 per week up to a limit of six weeks in the last 12 months of employment;
(c) payments in lieu of notice at a rate not exceeding £350 per week up to the statutory minimum entitlement of a particular employee under the Employment Rights Act 1996;
(d) any payment outstanding in regard to an award by an employment tribunal of compensation for unfair dismissal, limited to the amount of the basic award;
(e) reimbursement of the whole or part of any fee or premium paid by an apprentice or articled clerk;
(f) certain unpaid contributions to an occupational or a personal pension scheme. The amount of £350 refers throughout to the employee's gross wage.

There is a provision in s 167 of the Employment Rights Act 1996 for the Department for Business, Innovation and Skills to make payments relating to redundancy direct to the employee where the employer is insolvent. The Department will normally claim against the employer, but such a claim is unsecured and does not concern the receiver in terms of preferential payments. There is no qualifying period of employment for claimants on the National Insurance Fund, though, of course, certain periods of employment will have been necessary before an award for unfair dismissal and redundancy would be made.

The Employment Appeal Tribunal has decided that in the above situation the statutory insolvency provisions apply including the right to set-off. Thus if the employee owes money to the employer, this must be set off against the payment and only the balance paid to the employee (see *Secretary of State for Employment* v *Wilson* (1996) 550 IRLB 5 – decided when the Employment Secretary was responsible for these payments).

Employees working outside the UK: who pays?

Where within the EU an employee works in the UK for an Irish company which is wound up in Ireland, the BIS is responsible for the insolvency payments described above (see *Everson* v *Secretary of State for Trade and Industry* [2000] All ER (EC) 29). The case is to the effect that the country in which the claimant works is the payee. This may depend, however, on the number of employees employed in the country alleged to be liable to pay. Where there is only an insignificant number of employees, the country in which the employing company is being wound up may be liable instead (see the *Danmarks/Bosbaek Case* [1998] All ER (EC) 112 where only one employee was involved). In *Everson* the Irish company had a registered branch at Avonmouth employing over 200 people. The above rulings are from the European Court, UK law being silent on the matter.

Retention of title clauses

These clauses have as their purpose the retention of the seller's ownership in goods supplied until the buyer has paid for them, even though the buyer is given possession of the goods and may resell them or use them in the manufacture of other goods which will be resold. These clauses may also extend to the proceeds of sale.

If the clause is valid and if the purchasing company goes into an administrative receivership (where this is still possible) or liquidation, then the seller may try to recover the goods which the purchasing company still has in stock, and sometimes even the proceeds of resale by the purchasing company, on the basis that the purchaser is a mere *bailee* of the goods and not the owner, the seller being the owner and bailor.

In an administration, a valid retention clause is subject to a stay on creditors' remedies under Insolvency Act 1986, Sch B1 so the creditors' rights under the clause cannot generally be enforced and the administrator may dispose of the retained property free of the proprietory interest of creditors with the consent of the court.

The *Romalpa* case

The decision in *Aluminium Industrie Vaassen BV* v *Romalpa Aluminium* [1976] 2 All ER 552 was the first UK decision to alert the accountancy and legal professions to the problems which these clauses might cause in insolvency practice. The claimants in that case were successful in recovering aluminium foil supplied under a retention clause, together with the proceeds of resale of the foil which the clause also covered.

It should be noted, however, that any interest which the seller may claim in the proceeds of resale will, in view of more recent case law, be regarded by the courts as a charge on book debts which will be void under CA 2006, ss 860 *et seq.* if not registered at Companies House. The relevant authorities are *Modelboard Ltd* v *Outer Box Ltd (in Liquidation)* [1993] BCLC 623 and *Compaq Computers Ltd* v *Abercorn Group Ltd (t/a Osiris)* [1993] BCLC 603.

It does not matter what the seller's retention clause says, e.g. proceeds to be held 'on trust', the buyer acts as 'agent' of the seller, and so on. The courts have in recent times looked beyond the language to the reality and regarded the relationship as that of debtor (buyer) and creditor (seller), which is not an equitable fiduciary relationship, so that the equitable remedy of tracing is not available and recovery of the proceeds of sale is not possible without the creation and registration of a charge over what are, in effect, book debts. Those in equitable relationships, such as trustee and beneficiary, can trace trust property without the need for registration.

The recovery of the proceeds in *Romalpa* has been looked on in more recent times as not significant since the receiver in that case conceded the proceeds and did not contest their recovery, so the court did not have to rule on the matter.

Subsequent cases

Since the decision in the *Romalpa* case the courts have, broadly speaking, had to deal with two main types of actions, as follows:

(i)   Those cases where the supplier has been solely concerned to implement that part of his retention clause to retain title over goods supplied under a contract of sale where the goods have not been changed or added to in a process of manufacture, as was the situation in *Romalpa*. These actions will probably succeed and insolvency practitioners will normally release the stock to the supplier provided the goods can be identified with invoices unpaid. Otherwise, the insolvency practitioner faces an action in conversion by the supplier. However, should the insolvency practitioner believe that either the clause has not been properly communicated and is therefore not part of the contract of sale (see below), or that the goods have not been properly identified, he cannot be prevented from selling them as part of the realisation of assets. It is clear from the decision of the House of Lords in *American Cyanamid Co v Ethicon* [1975] AC 396 that an application for an injunction to prevent sale will fail because the supplier has an alternative claim for damages in conversion, if his contention that the retention clause is enforceable is correct.

(ii) Those cases in which the supplier is trying to use a retention clause to cover goods supplied to be used in manufacture, as in *Borden (UK) Ltd v Scottish Timber Products Ltd* [1979] 3 All ER 961 (seller's resin used in making chipboard and mixed with the company's material). In these cases the supplier may well have difficulty in recovering even those goods in stock and not yet used by the purchaser in the manufacturing process, because it is difficult to construe a bailment where the purchaser can use the goods in manufacture. This must give the company some sort of ownership of them. Without the relationship of bailment, there can be no recovery of the goods.

Where the goods have been mixed with the purchaser's goods, or where the purchaser's workforce has added value by skill and effort, the clause will not work unless the retention clause is registered at Companies House as a charge over the purchasing company's assets. Such a charge is in fact registrable under the Companies Acts. An example is provided by *Re Peachdart Ltd* [1983] 3 All ER 204, where the seller's leather was converted into handbags by the skill of the purchaser's workforce and the purchaser supplied handles and other decoration. The stock of leather was not recoverable, nor were the finished handbags or work in progress, even though the retention clause purported to extend to finished products and work in progress.

Other points to be borne in mind regarding retention clauses are:

(a) the need to ensure that the clause has become part of the contract of sale. It is not enough to include the clause on an invoice, because the contract has already been made by the time the invoice is issued and new terms cannot be introduced unless there have been previous dealings, including retention clauses, which can be incorporated;

(b) the need to identify the goods which it is sought to recover. Where goods have been supplied over a period of time it is essential to be able, for example, by serial numbers on the goods and unpaid invoices, to identify which goods have not been paid for.

Fixed charges

A fixed charge, whether legal or equitable and whenever created, takes priority over the equitable floating charge on the asset(s) concerned. The only exception is where the floating charge expressly prohibits the creation of charges in priority to the floating charge (called a negative pledge clause) and the person taking the fixed charge knew this to be so. At the present time this has to be actual knowledge, because registration of the charge at Companies House gives only constructive notice of the charge but not its particulars (see *Wilson v Kelland* [1910] 2 Ch 306). However, ss 860–877 of the CA 2006 provide that registration of the charge gives constructive notice also of its contents or particulars. The effect would be that the negative pledge clause would be constructively communicated and *Wilson* overruled.

There may be agreement between lenders that a particular floating charge shall rank in front of a particular fixed charge. Where this is so the first ranking floating charge remains subject to preferential debts and the second ranking fixed charge is subject to the prior ranking floating charge and the calls of the preferential debts on it (*Re Portbase (Clothing) Ltd, Mond* v *Taylor* [1993] 3 All ER 829).

Other floating charges

If a company is to have power to create a second floating charge over its undertaking ranking before the first, the debenture securing the first charge must so provide. Otherwise floating charges rank for priority in the order in which they were created.

In this connection, it is worth noting that in *H & K Medway Ltd, Mackay* v *IRC* [1997] 2 All ER 321 the High Court decided that if a company grants two floating charges over its assets in favour of two different debenture holders and the second ranking debenture holder appoints a receiver first, the preferential creditors of the first ranking debenture holder are entitled to be paid before the first ranking debenture holder even though that debenture holder is not the person appointing the receiver.

Garnishee orders (now called third-party debt claims for procedural purposes)

A garnishee order *nisi* may be issued on behalf of a judgment creditor as a method of enforcing judgment. It may attach to debts owed to the judgment debtor by others. Service of a garnishee order *nisi* operates as an equitable charge on the debt preventing the debt from being paid to anybody except the judgment creditor. However, the judgment debtor's funds in the hands of a third party, e.g. a bank, cannot in law be actually paid over to the judgment creditor until the garnishee order is made absolute. Between order *nisi* and absolute the judgment debtor may bring evidence to the court as to why the funds should not be paid over to the judgment creditor, which will normally be difficult since the creditor has gone to judgment. If the funds are paid over while the order has not been made absolute, the third party, e.g. a bank, must replace the funds of the judgment debtor even though a debt of the judgment debtor has, in effect, been paid because the bank has no authority to make the payment (see *Crantrave Ltd (in Liquidation)* v *Lloyds Bank plc* [2000] 3 WLR 877, CA where a liquidator recovered a sum of money paid by the company's bankers to the judgment creditor at a time when the relevant garnishee order was not absolute).

Other postponements

Judgment creditors may, in certain circumstances, be able to retain the proceeds of sale of the company's goods taken in execution by bailiffs. Finance companies may be able to recover goods which the company has taken on hire-purchase.

However, in the case of an administration which will be the normal insolvency procedure followed by holders of floating charges now that administrative receivership is restricted to special cases that will be considered in the chapters on corporate insolvency, a moratorium prevents execution by judgment creditors who have not actually taken property and sold it through the bailiff system. A finance company would be prevented by the moratorium from recovering goods on hire-purchase and the administrator can ask the court for an order to sell the goods provided the proceeds are applied to paying the sums payable under the hire-purchase agreement plus any additional sum to make the proceeds up to market value where the sale has been below market value. This is to assist the administrator to rescue the company by selling it as a going concern without having to ask permission of owners of goods such as finance companies to sell them.

As regards landlords who may seek to enforce non-monetary remedies to deal with any liabilities outstanding under the company's lease, para 43(4) of Sch B1 to the Insolvency Act 1986 prevents a landlord or other person to whom rent is payable from exercising any right of forfeiture except with the leave of the court or the consent of the administrator.

Validity of charges

Consideration will now be given to how a charge may be made invalid by failure to register particulars of it, or where it is a floating charge by avoidance under the Insolvency Act 1986 or because the charge is regarded under the same Act as a preference.

Registration of charges

The CA 2006 provides for the registration of certain charges created by companies over their assets. Accordingly, the secured debenture given typically to a bank to secure an overdraft must be registered at Companies House. CA 2006, ss 860 and 861 apply.

Charges to be registered

These are as follows:

1 A charge on land or any interest therein belonging to the company and wherever situate, other than a charge on rent payable by another in respect of the land.
2 A charge on the company's goods where the company is to retain possession of the goods. If the lender takes possession of the goods, as in a pawn or pledge, or takes a document of title to them so that the borrower cannot dispose of them effectively, the charge need not be registered.
3 Charges on the following intangible movable property of the company:
   (a) goodwill;
   (b) intellectual property – this covers any patent, trade mark, service mark, registered design, copyright or design right, or any licence under or in respect of any such right. In the case of a trade mark the charge is ineffective unless the charge is also registered at the Trade Mark Registry under s 25 of the Trade Marks Act 1994. This is just as important as registration at Companies House;
   (c) book debts, whether originally owing to the company or assigned to it;
   (d) uncalled share capital of a company or calls made but not paid;
   (e) charges for securing an issue of debentures;
   (f) floating charges on the whole or part of the company's property.

It should be noted that (e) and (f) above are 'sweep-up' provisions, and (e) above would cover an investment company whose only assets were shares and debentures of other companies.

Such a company would have to register a charge over those assets to secure a debenture even though the securities which are its assets are not included specifically under other headings.

So far as (f) above is concerned, this would cover a floating charge which was not part of the issue of a debenture, and so a charge over mixed goods by means of a retention clause would be registrable under this head.

Contractual liens

The High Court has decided that a contractual possessory lien, i.e. the right to retain another's property until he has met a debt due in respect of that property coupled with an eventual right of sale of the relevant property, does not amount to a charge that requires registration (*Re Hamlet International plc: Re Jeffrey Rogers (Imports) Ltd* [1998] 95 (16) LSG 24).

Thus, A sells goods to B and takes a contractual possessory lien over the goods until B pays for them. There is also a power for A to sell the goods if B fails to pay. B goes into administration as in the *Hamlet* case. The administrator of B claims the goods regarding the lien as a type of floating charge which is void against the administrator because it is unregistered. In this case the lien (which is not a charge) is valid since registration is not required of such an arrangement. A keeps the goods and does not have to deliver them into an insolvent company's assets and take the very great risk of receiving payment. If A has delivered the goods to B, then, of course, the lien being possessory is lost and the administrator may deal with the goods.

Charges by banks over customer deposits

It was held by the House of Lords in *Re Bank of Credit and Commerce International SA (No 8)* [1997] 4 All ER 568 that a bank could take a charge over its customers' deposits, thus doubting and refusing to follow the decision in *Re Charge Card Services Ltd* [1986] 3 All ER 289 which had regarded this as a 'conceptual impossibility'. The decision was because a deposit with a bank was a debt owed by the bank to the customer concerned, and as such was an asset in the customer's hands which could be charged by him to anyone. The case is of significance to banks since it extends their options in taking security over third-party deposits. Banks may be enabled in future to use deposits of subsidiary companies as assets to be set off against loans made to parent companies. Until this decision, banks have had to rely on special contractual arrangements which have not always survived the liquidation process. The decision in *BCCI (No 8)* raises the question of whether charge-backs should be registered. The House of Lords left this matter open but given that a charge is void unless registered the safest course would be to submit the charge for registration as an equitable floating charge.

Registration at Companies House

CA 2006, ss 866 and 870 state that it is the duty of the company to deliver particulars of a charge within 21 days of its creation. CA 2006, s 870 clarifies how the 21-day registration period is measured:

- If the charge is created in the UK, with the day after the day on which the charge is created.
- If the charge is created outside the UK, with the day after the day on which the instrument by which the charge was created or evidenced (or a copy of it) could, in due course of post (and if despatched with due diligence), have been received in the UK.

- If the charge is on property which is acquired by a company, with the day after the day on which the acquisition is completed.
- If the charge is on property outside the UK which is acquired by a company and the charge is created outside the UK, with the day after the day on which the instrument by which the charge was created or evidenced (or a copy of it) could, in due course of post (and if despatched with due diligence) have been received in the UK.

CA 2006, s 881 also applies, and in general the date of creation of the charge is when the instrument involved is signed on behalf of the company. The delivery of particulars can be made by 'any person interested in the charge' such as the lender, and the document creating the charge must also be filed. It is an offence for a company and every officer in default to fail to deliver particulars of a charge within the specified time.

Re Advantage Healthcare (T10) Ltd [1999] All ER (D) 1294

In this case the High Court held that although in the normal course the applicant for registration of a charge is required to include correctly the company's number, that number is not a particular of the charge to be registered. Thus failure to give the correct number does not constitute a breach of s 395 of the 1985 Act and the registration is valid.

Comment

The inclusion of the wrong company number, if not detected and changed, does, of course, affect those who search the register for the chargor. Presumably such cases are rare. The High Court was appraised of this problem but nevertheless found the charge valid.

The lender will usually take responsibility for the registration process because of the protection it obtains: first because the charge is registered and therefore not void, and secondly because registration establishes priority since charges registered earlier have priority over those registered later.

The Registrar will, under CA 2006, s 885, check the particulars and issue a certificate of registration which is currently conclusive evidence that the requirements of registration have been satisfied.

Effect of non-registration

If a charge is not registered as required by the CA 2006, it is void as against a liquidator or an administrator and any creditor of the company. Thus the holder of the charge becomes an unsecured creditor on a winding-up. However, the charge is not void against the company while it is a going concern and can be enforced, for example, by a sale of the assets charged. Such a sale cannot be set aside in the event that a liquidation takes place afterwards. In addition, when the charge becomes void, all sums including any interest payable become payable immediately on demand.

It will be noted that under the CA 2006 an unregistered charge is not void where exceptionally there is an administrative receivership.

However, the charge is void against a company when it is in administration or liquidation. Although CA 2006, ss 860 *et seq.* refers to an unregistered charge being void 'against the liquidator or administrator', this means only that the relevant insolvency practitioner can employ the assets in the process of liquidation or administration for insolvency purposes. Yet, if a person holding an unregistered charge removes the property charged then unless the provisions of ss 860 *et seq.* can be construed as making the charge void also against the company, a liquidator or administrator cannot sue for damages for conversion in a personal capacity because the asset is not his. Assets do not vest into the ownership of insolvency practitioners and ownership is essential in most cases for a successful action in conversion. If the charge is also void against the company then the insolvency practitioner can bring a claim in conversion on behalf of the company, as the administrator did successfully in *Smith (Administrator of Coslett (Contractors) Ltd)* v *Bridgend County Borough Council* [2001] UKHL 58, [2002] 1 All ER 292 where the House of Lords decided that CA 1985, s 395 must be regarded at least in an insolvency as making an unregistered charge void also against the company.

Registration out of time

It is necessary to ask the court to allow registration out of time. A usual condition imposed by the court is that late registration is to be allowed but 'without prejudice to the rights of any parties acquired prior to the time when the charge was registered'. In effect, then, the charge ranks for priority from the date of its late registration.

Registration out of time and insolvency

Except in very exceptional circumstances the court will not grant late registration where a liquidation has commenced. The court is also reluctant to give permission where liquidation is imminent (*Re Ashpurton Estates Ltd* [1982] 3 All ER 665). However, late registration was allowed in *Barclays Bank* v *Stuart London Ltd* [2001] 2 BCLC 316 where the order provided in effect that if winding-up commenced before the end of the extension time the liquidator could set it aside on application to the court thus reducing the holder of the charge to an unsecured creditor.

Releasing the charge: Companies House

Under CA 2006, s 887 and on application being made to him by the company that the charge has been released or redeemed the Registrar will enter a memorandum of satisfaction on the register.

Releasing the charge: act of parties

A security over property may be released by act of parties. An example is provided by *Western Intelligence Ltd* v *KDO Label Printing Machines Ltd* [1998] BCC 472 where the High Court held that when goods were transferred with the consent of the bank from a company in financial difficulties to a new company controlled by the same directors, the goods were released from a debenture granted by the original company to the bank.

Company's register

Sections 877 and 892 of the CA 2006 enable a company to keep its instruments creating charges and mortgages and its register of charges and mortgages in a place other than its registered office. Section 1136 of CA 2006 gives the Secretary of State power to make provisions by regulations specifying places other than a company's registered office at which a company's records, including its registers required to be kept available for inspection, may be kept. The company must enter in the register a short description of the property charged, the amount of the charge and the names of the persons entitled to the charge, except in the case of securities to bearer.

The Companies (Company Records) Regulations 2008 (SI 2008/3006) specify the inspection location which may be used as an alternative to the registered office, for those company records referred to in CA 2006, s 1136(2), which includes instruments creating charges and mortgages and the register of charges and mortgages. The alternative location is a single location that is situated in the same part of the UK (for example, England, Wales, Scotland or Northern Ireland) as the company's registered office. This is sufficiently flexible for a company to select an alternative location appropriate to its business.

The Companies (Trading Disclosures) Regulations 2008 provide that where a company has specified an alternative inspection location, it is required to disclose the address of that place and the type of records kept at that place to any person it deals with in the course of business who makes a written request for such information. The company is required to send a written response to that person within five working days of receiving the request.

As regards failure to register a charge in the company's register, there is a default fine on any officer of the company who is in default as well as upon the company itself, but the charge is still valid. In other words, it is only failure to register at Companies House which affects the validity of the charge.

The company must keep a register of debenture holders but only if the terms of issue of the debentures require it. The register, if it exists, must be kept at the registered office or the place where it is made up so long as it is within the country in which the company is registered. The register may be inspected free of charge by those who are registered holders of debentures and, in addition, shareholders in the company, and by other persons on payment of a fee. Members, registered holders of debentures and other persons may acquire a copy of the register on payment of a fee. The register of directors' interests must show their debenture holdings also. (This register is dealt with more fully in Chapter 16. ◑)

Because a power of inspection exists a company must maintain the register even though there are no entries in it if only to indicate that this is so.

Avoidance of floating charges

Under s 245 of the Insolvency Act 1986, a floating charge created by a company within one year before the commencement of its winding-up or the making of an administration order is void as a security for any debt other than cash paid or goods supplied to the company in consideration of the charge at the time the charge was created or subsequently, with interest, if any, thereon as agreed. The above provisions do not apply if the company was solvent immediately after the creation of the charge.

It was held in *Power* v *Sharp Investments Ltd* [1993] BCC 609 that no moneys paid to the company *before* the execution of the debenture would qualify for the invalidity exemption in s 245 unless the interval between the payment and execution of the debenture was minimal and could be regarded as contemporaneous.

If the person in whose favour the charge was created was connected with the company, e.g. a director or shadow director (see further Chapter 19 ◑), the period is two years, and the charge is void even though the connected person gave consideration at the time or subsequently, and even though the company was solvent immediately after the charge was given.

The purpose of the section is to prevent a company which is unable to pay its debts from, in effect, preferring one of its unsecured creditors to the others by giving him a floating charge on its assets. There is no objection to the creation of a floating charge where the company actually receives funds or goods at the time or afterwards because these may assist it to carry on business, and indeed avoid winding-up or administration. The charge only extends to the value of the funds or goods supplied after it was given and does not secure the existing debt to the unsecured creditor. As regards goods supplied, the charge extends only to the price which could reasonably have been obtained for them in the ordinary course of business at the time when they were supplied. The security would not extend to the whole of the value of goods supplied at an artificially high price.

Practical points arising

(i) Most importantly, a floating charge is valid as a security for loans made after the date it was created if the lender promised to make such loans (covenanted loans), and even if the lender did not (uncovenanted loans) (*Re Yeovil Glove Co Ltd* (1965), see below). Consequently, advances made to an insolvent company by its bank on an overdraft facility during the year before it is wound up are validly secured in the winding-up (or administration if relevant) by a floating charge given before the advances were made. The debenture creating the charge must expressly cover covenanted and uncovenanted loans, i.e. agreed loans and other loans not agreed at the time.

Re Yeovil Glove Co Ltd [1965] Ch 148

The company was in liquidation and had an overdraft of £67,000 with the National Provincial Bank Ltd. The overdraft was secured by a floating charge given less than 12 months prior to winding-up at a time when the company was insolvent. The charge was therefore void under what is now s 245 of the Insolvency Act 1986. However, the company had paid in some £111,000 and the bank had paid cheques out to the amount of some £110,000. The Court of Appeal held that under *Clayton's Case* (1816) 1 Mer 572, under which the earliest payments into an account are set off against the earliest payments out and vice versa, the overdraft, which was not validly secured, had been paid off and the floating charge attached to the money drawn out because the company had received consideration for this. It did not matter that the floating charge did not require the bank to make further advances. It did, however, expressly secure uncovenanted loans.

Comment

The Cork Committee said that this case defeated the object of what is now s 245. They thought it should be repealed by statute so that for the purposes of s 245 payments into the account should be treated as discharging debit items incurred after the creating of the floating charge before those incurred before it (see Cmnd 8558, para 1562).

(ii) The period of one (or two) year(s) from the creation of the floating charge is calculated from the date when the instrument imposing the charge is executed and not from the date of the issue of the debenture which may be later.

(iii) If an unsecured creditor takes a new loan to the company on the security of a floating charge on the understanding that the loan will be applied immediately in paying off his existing unsecured debt, the floating charge will normally be invalid unless the company is solvent immediately after the charge is given (*Re Destone Fabrics Ltd* [1941] 1 All ER 545).

(iv) Floating charges are invalidated only if the company is wound up or goes into administration, and so if before either of those events it redeems a floating charge which would have been invalid in those situations, the liquidator or administrator cannot require the owner of the charge to repay what he has received (*Re Parkes Garage (Swadlincote) Ltd* [1929] 1 Ch 139). However, if the redemption takes place within six months (two years if the debenture holder is a connected person) before the winding-up or administration it may be a preference of the debenture holder, in which case the relevant insolvency practitioner can recover the amount paid to the debenture holder under s 239 of the Insolvency Act 1986 (see below).

The s 245 avoidance provisions do not apply to fixed charges, but the preference provisions of s 239 do (see below).

Preference

A liquidator or an administrator may avoid a fixed or floating charge as a preference under s 239 of the Insolvency Act 1986 if:

(a) in giving the charge the company was influenced by a desire to better the position of a creditor or surety. Thus, to give a charge to a lender where the directors had personally guaranteed the loan would be a preference (see *Re Kushler* [1943] 2 All ER 22). However, the giving of a charge to an unsecured creditor about to levy execution on the company's goods may very well not be, because it would be given to preserve the company's assets at market value, bearing in mind that sheriff sales are often at throwaway prices;

(b) the company was insolvent when the charge was given; and

(c) the charge was given within the six months preceding the commencement of the winding-up or administration.

Where the creditor preferred is a connected person, e.g. a director or shadow director, the time period is two years and (a) above is presumed.

In this connection, the High Court decided in *Weisgard* v *Pilkington* [1996] CLY 3488 that a company's transfer by lease of certain of its assets (six flats) to two of its directors before it went into insolvent liquidation – ostensibly in discharge of a debt the company owed them – was a preference to connected persons so that the transfer must be reversed and the flats returned to the company. The directors had not displaced the presumption under s 239 that the transfers constituted a preference to connected persons. The transfers had put the directors in a better position than they would have been in given an insolvent liquidation. This was so even in regard to two of the flats which were charged to a bank to secure an overdraft since the charge operated to reduce the directors' liabilities as guarantors of that overdraft.

Most recently, in the case of *Re Harmony Care Homes Ltd* [2010] BCC 358, the joint administrative receivers of a company applied to the Chancery Division for a direction pursuant to s 35 of the Insolvency Act 1986 as to whether the book debt proceeds collected by them during the course of the administrative receivership should be subject to fixed charges to the holders of the debentures, or as subject to floating charges to the preferential creditors under s 40 of the 1986 Act. It was the judge's conclusion from the opening of a designated account the company could not make and did not make any use of the money paid into the account without the chargee's written instructions to the bank. It thus appeared that all book debts collected in by the company from the inception of the debenture were subject to the chargee's control and that from the outset, the status of the security over the book debts was specific and ascertained. Thus there was never a moment from when the company was entitled to remove the charged assets from the security. The effect of the debenture and the arrangements the parties put in place was to disentitle the company from using the proceeds of the book debts as a source of its cash flow or for any other purpose. The security granted in respect of the book debt realisations was a fixed charge.

Remedies of secured debenture holders

Where the debentures are secured on the assets of the company the following main remedies are available:

(a) the property charged may be sold or leased;
(b) a receiver may be appointed to take possession of the property.

Where the debenture is secured by a fixed charge, these remedies are available under s 101 of the Law of Property Act 1925. However, since a floating charge may not be covered by s 101 (see *Blaker* v *Herts & Essex Waterworks* (1889) 41 Ch D 399 under earlier similar legislation), the remedies are invariably given in the debenture.

After sale of the assets in a receivership any surplus, after paying off the debenture holders and the cost of realisation and receivers' costs and charges, belongs to the company.

BIS consultation

In March 2010, the Department for Business, Innovation and Skills (BIS) commenced a consultation exercise on the registration of company charges. The consultation document states that it makes proposals to revise the current scheme for the registration of company charges under the Companies Act 2006 based on the 2001 recommendations of the Company Law Review and the subsequent advice of the Law Commission. They involve possible changes to: which charges must be registered; how charges may be registered including the introduction of electronic registration at Companies House; and the consequences of registering and not registering a registrable charge.

Essay questions

1 Richard is the founder, managing director and controlling shareholder of RST Ltd. For some years Richard kept the company afloat by making a number of unsecured loans to it. At the last tally the company owed him £20,000, and yet needed a further loan of £5,000. Richard is willing to advance the money, but realising that the company is very likely to go into liquidation, and with a view to salvaging something for himself from the company's assets, causes the company to execute in his favour a deed of debenture secured by a floating charge over all the assets of the company. The floating charge is stated to secure not only the £5,000 paid to the company at the time the charge was executed but also the £20,000 outstanding debt owed him by the company.

 The company goes into insolvent winding-up three months after the floating charge is executed. Its assets are estimated at a little over £25,000, and its unsecured debts add up to £20,000.

 Discuss the competing claims of Richard, who is a secured creditor, and the company's unsecured creditors. *(University of Plymouth)*

2 In January 2003 Jones made an unsecured loan of £3,000 to a company of which he was a director. In January 2005 the directors resolved that in consideration of a further loan of £2,000 Jones should be issued with a debenture for £5,000, secured by a floating charge on the assets and undertaking of the company. Jones made this further loan and the debenture was issued. The company was wound up four months later.

 Advise the liquidator as to the points to bear in mind regarding this transaction. Would your answer be different if the debenture had been secured by a fixed charge on the company's factory? *(The Institute of Company Accountants)*

3 Compare and contrast equity shares and debentures as alternative forms of investment, explaining also the difference between fixed and floating charges. *(Kingston University)*

4 'A person who lends on the security of a specific mortgage of a company's property is always entitled to repayment on his loan out of the proceeds of sale of the mortgaged property before any other creditor. A person who takes a floating charge is not in as secure a position.' *Pennington*.

 Why is the holder of a floating charge in a less favourable position?
(The Institute of Chartered Accountants in England and Wales)

5 (a) What are the statutory requirements in respect of calling an annual general meeting? What is the usual business at an annual general meeting of a company?

 (b) What is an extraordinary general meeting? When must the directors call such a meeting? What consequences may follow the directors' failure to call such a meeting?

 (c) The directors of Fireworks Ltd, a company whose articles are regulated by *Table A*, wish to give effect to the following matters:

 (i) to change the company's name to Chatterbox Ltd;
 (ii) to increase the company's share capital to £30,000.

 Explain to the directors the requirements of the Companies Act 1985 in relation to both the calling of a meeting and the passing of resolutions to give effect to these proposals.
(The Association of Chartered Certified Accountants)

6 (a) Distinguish between (i) ordinary, (ii) special and (iii) extraordinary resolutions. Indicate, in particular, the length of notices and matters in respect of which each resolution is required.

AND

(b) Fred is a managing director of Pine Wood Ltd. He also owns 25 per cent of the company's ordinary shares which carry voting rights. It has just been discovered by the other directors that Fred is acting as a consultant to another company which is in direct competition with Pine Wood Ltd. The other directors wish to propose an alteration of articles to restrict Fred's powers.

Advise the directors on whether and how they may alter the articles.

(Glasgow Caledonian University)

Test your knowledge

Four alternative answers are given. Select ONE only. Circle the answer which you consider to be correct. Check your answers by referring back to the information given in the chapter and against the answers at the end of the text.

1 Ouse Ltd has borrowed £10,000 from the Barchester Bank which is secured by an equitable charge over the company's freehold land. The charge, which states that it will rank in front of subsequent charges including fixed charges, has been registered. Later on Ouse granted a fixed charge over the freehold land to Onslow who had made it a loan. Onslow has not examined the Register of Charges at Companies House and has no other knowledge of the bank's equitable charge. Which charge has priority?

A The equitable charge taken by the bank because the first in time prevails.
B The equitable charge taken by the bank since registration is equivalent to notice of the contents of the charge.
C Onslow's legal charge because legal charges take priority to equitable charges.
D Onslow's legal charge since he had no notice of the equitable charge.

2 Thames Ltd is insolvent and is being wound up. The bank has a floating charge over its assets in regard to an overdraft which has not been registered. What is the effect of this?

A The charge is void against the liquidator and the bank proves as an ordinary creditor.
B The debt is void as against the liquidator and the bank will get nothing.
C The charge is voidable by the liquidator if the company was insolvent when the charge was created.
D The charge is void against subsequent secured creditors and the bank loses its priority accordingly.

3 Tay Ltd has assets of £10,000. Its trade creditors are worth £20,000 and it has an unsecured overdraft with the Barchester Bank of £20,000. Tay wants to increase the overdraft facility to £30,000. The bank has agreed and has been given a floating charge over Tay's assets to secure the overdraft. Tay Ltd is now in liquidation. Given that the overdraft is repayable on demand, how much is the bank entitled to as a secured creditor?

A £30,000   B £20,000   C Nothing   D £10,000

4 Within how many days of its creation must a charge over the assets of a company be registered?

A Twelve days   B Twenty-one days   C Fifteen days   D Fourteen days

5 The Barchester Bank has just taken a floating charge over the assets of Derwent Ltd, a manufacturing company. Who can be appointed by the bank to safeguard its security should circumstances require this?

A The trustee for the debenture holder.
B The Official Receiver.
c An administrator.
D An administrative receiver.

The answers to test your knowledge questions appear on p. 645.

Suggested further reading

Atherton and Mokal, 'Charges over chattels: Issues in the fixed/floating jurisprudence' (2005) *Company Lawyer* 26, 163.

Pennington, 'Recent developments in the law and practice relating to the creation of security for companies' indebtedness' (2009) *Company Lawyer* 30, 163.

Worthington, 'An unsatisfactory area of the law: Fixed and floating charges yet again' (2004) *International Corporate Rescue* 175.

25 Accounts and audit

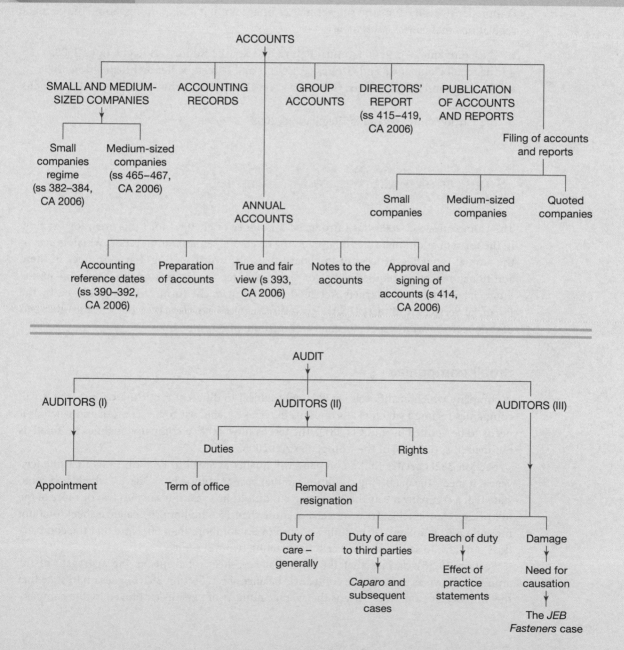

In this chapter we shall consider the main underlying principle of company law in regard to a company's accounts, which is to achieve disclosure of a company's financial affairs for the benefit of those who have invested in it and those who do business with it. The purpose of an audit by independent accountants is to add credibility to the financial statements forming part of the annual accounts and to ensure that they comply with regulations and give a true and fair view though small companies may take exemption from audit.

The keeping of accounts, the audit and filing with the Registrar are the price which the members and directors of a limited company must pay for limited liability. As we have seen, a freestanding unlimited company does not have to file accounts though its directors have a duty to see that annual accounts are prepared and audited (see further Chapter 1 ❍).

Only matters of company law have been included. No attempt has been made to give a comprehensive survey of the subject matter of accounting and auditing. Some of the main regulations that concern this area:

- The Companies Act 2006 (Annual Return and Service Addresses) Regulations 2008;
- The Small Companies and Groups (Accounts and Directors' Report) Regulations 2008;
- The Large and Medium-sized Companies and Groups (Accounts and Reports) Regulations 2008; and
- The Partnerships (Accounts) Regulations 2008.

Small and medium-sized companies

The Companies Act 2006 has introduced a number of changes into this area, for example in the form of additional rules relating to the directors' remuneration report which is part of the annual reporting process of the board. It is also worth noting that a number of these additional reporting requirements for public limited companies are to be found in the Financial Services and Markets Act 2000 (FSMA) or in the form of rules produced by the Financial Services Authority (FSA). However, changes have also taken place at the other end of the spectrum with respect to small and medium-sized companies.

Small companies

A company which qualifies as small is now subject to different reporting regime (the 'small companies regime') which is less onerous in terms of what has to be reported and whether it needs to be verified by audit (s 381). The test as to whether a company qualifies as 'small' is outlined in ss 382–384 of the Companies Act 2006.

Section 382(1) states that a company will qualify as small in relation to its first financial year if it meets the qualifying conditions in that year as outlined in s 382(3), which goes on to state that a company meets the qualifying conditions in a year if it satisfies two or more of the following requirements: (i) turnover not more than £5.6 million; (ii) balance sheet total not more than £2.8 million; (iii) number of employees not more than 50. Note that the company does not have to satisfy all three criteria, meeting two will suffice.

Section 382(5) clarifies that the term 'balance sheet total' means the aggregate of the amounts shown as assets in the company's balance sheet. Section 382(6) goes on to state that the 'number of employees' means the average number of persons employed by the company in the year, determined as follows: (a) find for each month in the financial year the number of persons employed under contracts of service by the company in that month (whether throughout the month or not); (b) add together the monthly totals; and (c) divide by the number of months in the financial year.

Section 382(2) sets down that a company will qualify as small in relation to a subsequent financial year if the qualifying conditions are met in that year and the preceding financial year; if the qualifying conditions are met in that year and the company qualified as small in relation to the preceding financial year; if the qualifying conditions were met in the preceding financial year and the company qualified as small in relation to that year. The purpose of these rather complex rules is to prevent a potentially small company from moving in and out of the 'small companies regime' if performance differs year-on-year, thus providing greater flexibility within the system to cater for such changes.

It is also worth noting that s 382(7) states that this test is subject to the requirements of s 383, which focuses on whether parent companies may qualify as small companies for the purpose of the CA 2006. Section 383(1) states that a parent company qualifies as a small company in relation to a financial year only if the group headed by it qualifies as a small group, the test for which is outlined in s 383(3) as follows:

> A group qualifies as small in relation to a subsequent financial year of the parent company: (a) if the qualifying conditions are met in that year and the preceding financial year; (b) if the qualifying conditions are met in that year and the group qualified as small in relation to the preceding financial year; (c) if the qualifying conditions were met in the preceding financial year and the group qualified as small in relation to that year.

Section 383(4) sets down the qualifying conditions for a group to qualify as small and states that a group must satisfy two or more of the following requirements in a year: (i) aggregate turnover not more than £5.6 million net (or £6.72 million gross); (ii) aggregate balance sheet total not more than £2.8 million net (or £3.36 million gross); (iii) aggregate number of employees not more than 50.

Importantly, s 383(6) goes on to clarify the term 'net' with respect to the aggregate figures for turnover and balance sheet total, stating that it means after any set-offs and other adjustments made to eliminate group transactions: (a) in the case of Companies Act accounts, in accordance with regulations under s 404; (b) in the case of IAS accounts, in accordance with international accounting standards. Section 383(6) also notes that 'gross' means without those set-offs and other adjustments. A company may satisfy any relevant requirement on the basis of either the net or the gross figure.

Finally, it is necessary to refer to s 384 which sets out those companies which are excluded from this regime. Section 384(1) states that the regime does not apply to a company that is, or was at any time within the financial year to which the accounts relate: (a) a public company; (b) a company that (i) is an authorised insurance company, a banking company, an e-money issuer, an ISD investment firm or a UCITS management company; or (ii) carries on insurance market activity; or (c) a member of an ineligible group (see s 384(2)).

Medium-sized companies

A company which qualifies as medium is also subject to different reporting regime and for some reason is outlined in ss 465–467 of the Companies Act 2006. The general test as to whether a company qualifies as 'medium' is outlined in s 465 which states that a company qualifies as medium-sized in relation to its first financial year if the qualifying conditions are met in that year (s 465(1)). These qualifying conditions are outlined in s 465(3) which states that a company meets them in a year in which it satisfies two or more of the following requirements: (i) turnover not more than £22.8 million; (ii) balance sheet total not more than £11.4 million; (iii) number of employees not more than 250.

Section 465(5) clarifies that the term 'balance sheet total' means the aggregate of the amounts shown as assets in the company's balance sheet. Section 465(6) goes on to state that the 'number of employees' means the average number of persons employed by the company in the year, determined as follows: (a) find for each month in the financial year the number of persons employed under contracts of service by the company in that month (whether throughout the month or not); (b) add together the monthly totals; and (c) divide by the number of months in the financial year.

Section 465(2) sets down that a company will qualify as medium-sized in relation to a subsequent financial year if the qualifying conditions are met in that year and the preceding financial year; if the qualifying conditions are met in that year and the company qualified as medium-sized in relation to the preceding financial year; if the qualifying conditions were met in the preceding financial year and the company qualified as medium-sized in relation to that year.

It is worth noting that s 465(7) once again states that this test is subject to the requirements of s 466, which focuses on whether parent companies may qualify as medium-sized companies for the purpose of the CA 2006.

Finally, it is necessary to refer to s 467 which sets out those companies which are excluded from the medium-sized company regime. Section 467(1) states that the regime does not apply to a company that is, or was at any time within the financial year to which the accounts relate: (a) a public company; (b) a company that: (i) has permission under Part 4 of the Financial Services and Markets Act 2000 (c. 8) to carry on a regulated activity; or (ii) carries on insurance market activity; or (c) a member of an ineligible group (s 467(2)).

Accounting records

Under s 386 of the Companies Act 2006, the directors of a company must keep adequate accounting records sufficient to show and explain the company's transactions (s 386(1)) and to disclose with reasonable accuracy, *at any time* throughout the financial year, the financial position of the company *at that time* (s 386(2)). They must also enable the directors to ensure that any accounts required to be prepared comply with the requirements of the Companies Act 2006 and the IAS Regulation (s 388(3)(b)).

In addition to this, s 386(3) goes on to state that the records must contain (a) entries from day to day of all sums of money received and expended with details of transactions; and (b) a record of assets and liabilities.

Equally, under s 386(4) a company dealing in goods must keep statements of stock held at the end of the financial year, and of stocktaking from which the year-end statement is made up and of all goods sold and purchased, other than retail trade transactions, showing goods, buyers and sellers, so as to allow identification.

Under s 388(1) accounting records must be kept at its registered office or such other place as the directors think fit, and must be open for inspection by the officers of the company at all times. Section 388(4) goes on to note that these records must be kept for six years (public company) and three years (private company) from the date on which they are made (s 388(4) (a) and (b)).

As regards statements of work in progress, the Act does not specifically require these to be kept, on the grounds that many small companies have little or no work in progress and those for whom it is significant will have to keep statements as part of the general requirement to keep records sufficient to disclose the financial position of the company and to enable accounts to be prepared.

Under s 387(1) failure to keep accounting records as required is an offence for which officers of the company in default are liable. The offence is punishable with a maximum of two years' imprisonment and/or a fine (s 387(3)). In addition, under s 388(1) if a company fails to comply with s 388(1) to (3) of the Act, an offence is committed by every officer of the company who is in default.

Annual accounts

The term 'annual accounts' is commonly used in business and is now in fact an expression used in company legislation. For legal purposes it can be taken to mean the year end balance sheet together with the related profit and loss account and directors' and auditors' reports. Section 475(1) of the Companies Act 2006 provides that a company's annual accounts for a financial year must be audited in accordance with this Part 16 of the Act unless the company is exempt from audit under s 477 (small companies), s 480 (dormant companies), or is exempt from the requirements of Part 16 of the Act under s 482 (non-profit-making companies subject to public sector audit). Section 475(2) goes on to state that a company is not entitled to any such exemption unless its balance sheet contains a statement by the directors to that effect. A company is not entitled to exemption under any of the provisions mentioned above unless its balance sheet contains a statement by the directors to the effect that (a) the members have not required the company to obtain an audit of its accounts for the year in question in accordance with s 476; and (b) the directors acknowledge their responsibilities for complying with the requirements of the Companies Act 2006 with respect to accounting records and the preparation of accounts (s 475(3)).

Accounting reference dates

Sections 390 to 392 outline the company's financial year which depends upon the company's 'accounting reference period' (ARP) and its 'accounting reference date' (ARD) which is the date on which the company's ARP ends in each calendar year.

Section 390(2) states that a company's first financial year begins with the first day of its first accounting reference period, and ends with the last day of that period or such other date, not more than seven days before or after the end of that period, as the directors may determine. Section 390(3) goes on to note that the company's subsequent financial years begin with the day immediately following the end of the company's previous financial year, and end with the last day of its next accounting reference period or such other date, not more than seven days before or after the end of that period, as the directors may determine.

Section 391 defines in greater detail the ARD of companies incorporated in Great Britain and divides them between those incorporated before 1 April 1990 and those incorporated on or after 1 April 1990. Section 391(2) states that the ARD of a company incorporated in Great Britain before 1 April 1996 is: (a) the date specified by notice to the Registrar in accordance with s 224(2) of the Companies Act 1985; or (b) failing such notice: (i) in the case of a company incorporated before 1 April 1990, 31 March; and (ii) in the case of a company incorporated on or after 1 April 1990, the last day of the month in which the anniversary of its incorporation falls. Section 391(4) goes on to note that the ARD a company incorporated in Great Britain on or after 1 April 1996 and before the commencement of the Companies Act 2006, or after the commencement of this Act, is the last day of the month in which the anniversary of its incorporation falls.

Section 391(5) goes on to outline that a company's first accounting reference period is the period of more than six months, but not more than 18 months, beginning with the date of its incorporation and ending with its accounting reference date. Its subsequent accounting reference periods are successive periods of 12 months beginning immediately after the end of the previous accounting reference period and ending with its accounting reference date (s 391(6)).

However, a company may choose a new ARD for its current, future and previous ARPs under s 392(1) of the Companies Act 2006 by giving notice to the Registrar specifying a new ARD. Section 392(2) states that the notice must state whether the current or previous accounting reference period (a) is to be shortened, so as to come to an end on the first occasion on which the new accounting reference date falls or fell after the beginning of the period; or (b) is to be extended, so as to come to an end on the second occasion on which that date falls or fell after the beginning of the period.

It should be noted that s 391(5) places a restriction on this process, stating that an accounting reference period may not be extended so as to exceed 18 months and a notice under this section is ineffective if the current or previous accounting reference period as extended in accordance with the notice would exceed that limit. Equally, s 391(4) provides that a notice under this section may not be given in respect of a previous accounting reference period if the period for filing accounts and reports for the financial year determined by reference to that accounting reference period has already expired.

Preparation of accounts: form and content

Directors must prepare accounts for each financial year under s 394 of the Companies Act 2006 and are referred to as the company's 'individual accounts'. Section 395(1) provides that a company's individual accounts may be prepared: (a) in accordance with s 396 ('Companies Act individual accounts'); or (b) in accordance with international accounting standards ('IAS individual accounts').

Section 395(3) goes on to state that after the first financial year in which the directors of a company prepare IAS individual accounts ('the first IAS year'), all subsequent individual accounts of the company must be prepared in accordance with international accounting standards unless there is a relevant change of circumstance. There is a relevant change of circumstance if, at any time during or after the first IAS year: (a) the company becomes a subsidiary undertaking of another undertaking that does not prepare IAS individual accounts; (b) the company ceases to be a company with securities admitted to trading on a regulated market in an EEA State; or (c) a parent undertaking of the company ceases to be an undertaking with securities admitted to trading on a regulated market in an EEA state (s 395(4)).

Section 396(1) goes on to provide that Companies Act individual accounts must comprise: (a) a balance sheet as at the last day of the financial year; and (b) a profit and loss account.

Section 396(2) goes on to state that the accounts must: (a) in the case of the balance sheet, give a true and fair view of the state of affairs of the company as at the end of the financial year; and (b) in the case of the profit and loss account, give a true and fair view of the profit or loss of the company for the financial year. Furthermore, the accounts must comply with provision made by the Secretary of State by regulations as to: (a) the form and content of the balance sheet and profit and loss account; and (b) additional information to be provided by way of notes to the accounts (s 396(3)).

Section 397 of the CA 2006 deals with the requirements for IAS individual accounts and provides that where the directors of a company prepare IAS individual accounts, they must state in the notes to the accounts that the accounts have been prepared in accordance with international accounting standards.

True and fair view

Section 393(1) of the Companies Act 2006 provides that the directors of a company must not approve accounts unless they are satisfied that they give a true and fair view of the assets, liabilities, financial position and profit or loss (a) in the case of the company's individual accounts, of the company; (b) in the case of the company's group accounts, of the undertakings included in the consolidation as a whole, so far as concerns members of the company.

This is an overriding principle and as such, s 396(4) provides that if compliance with the regulations, and any other provision made by or under the Companies Act as to the matters to be included in a company's individual accounts or in notes to those accounts, would not be sufficient to give a true and fair view, the necessary additional information must be given in the accounts or in a note to them. This is repeated under s 404(4) with respect to group accounts discussed below.

Equally, s 396(5) goes on to state that if, in special circumstances, compliance with any of those provisions is inconsistent with the requirement to give a true and fair view, the directors must depart from that provision to the extent necessary to give a true and fair view. Furthermore, particulars of any such departure, the reasons for it and its effect must be given in a note to the accounts. Once again, this is repeated in s 404(5) with respect to group accounts.

Notes to the accounts

Section 472(1) provides that information required by Part 15 of the Companies Act 2006 to be given in notes to a company's annual accounts may be contained in the accounts or in a separate document annexed to the accounts. Section 472(2) goes on to state that references in Part 15 of the Act to a company's annual accounts, or to a balance sheet or profit and loss account, include notes to the accounts giving information which is required by any provision of this Act or international accounting standards, and required or allowed by any such provision to be given in a note to company accounts.

Section 411 of the CA 2006 provides that in the case of a company not subject to the small companies regime, the following information with respect to the employees of the company must be given in notes to the company's annual accounts: (a) the average number of persons employed by the company in the financial year; and (b) the average number of persons so employed within each category of persons employed by the company.

In addition, s 413(1) states that in the case of a company that does not prepare group accounts, details of: (a) advances and credits granted by the company to its directors; and

(b) guarantees of any kind entered into by the company on behalf of its directors, must be shown in the notes to its individual accounts. Section 413(2) goes on to provide that in the case of a parent company that prepares group accounts, details of: (a) advances and credits granted to the directors of the parent company, by that company or by any of its subsidiary undertakings; and (b) guarantees of any kind entered into on behalf of the directors of the parent company, by that company or by any of its subsidiary undertakings, must be shown in the notes to the group accounts.

Approval and signing of accounts

Section 414(1) provides that a company's annual accounts must be approved by the board of directors and signed on behalf of the board by a director of the company. Under s 414(2), the signature must be on the company's balance sheet. Section 414(3) goes on to state that if the accounts are prepared in accordance with the provisions applicable to companies subject to the small companies regime, the balance sheet must contain a statement to that effect in a prominent position above the signature.

Section 414(4) goes on to provide that if annual accounts are approved that do not comply with the requirements of the Companies Act 2006 (and, where applicable, of Art 4 of the IAS Regulation), every director of the company who: (a) knew that they did not comply, or was reckless as to whether they complied; and (b) failed to take reasonable steps to secure compliance with those requirements or, as the case may be, to prevent the accounts from being approved, commits an offence.

Small company accounts

The statutory format for the Companies Act accounts of a small company is simpler than that outlined above and is set out in the Small Companies and Groups (Accounts and Directors' Report) Regulations 2008 (SI 2008/409).

Group accounts

If a company has subsidiaries, s 399(2) of the Companies Act 2006 provides that group accounts showing the state of affairs and profit or loss of the company and the subsidiaries must be prepared. Section 404 goes on to provide details of the requirements for Companies Act group accounts, while s 406 deals with IAS groups accounts.

Section 404(1) states that Companies Act group accounts must comprise: (a) a consolidated balance sheet dealing with the state of affairs of the parent company and its subsidiary undertakings; and (b) a consolidated profit and loss account dealing with the profit or loss of the parent company and its subsidiary undertakings. Section 404(2) goes on to provide that the accounts must give a true and fair view of the state of affairs as at the end of the financial year, and the profit or loss for the financial year, of the undertakings included in the consolidation as a whole, so far as concerns members of the company.

The accounts must comply with provision made by the Secretary of State by regulations as to: (a) the form and content of the consolidated balance sheet and consolidated profit and loss account; and (b) additional information to be provided by way of notes to the accounts (s 404(3)).

Section 405(1) provides that where a parent company prepares Companies Act group accounts, all the subsidiary undertakings of the company must be included in the consolidation, subject to the exceptions outlined in s 405(2) and (3). Section 405(2) notes that a subsidiary undertaking may be excluded from consolidation if its inclusion is not material for the purpose of giving a true and fair view. Additionally, under s 405(3) a subsidiary undertaking may be excluded from consolidation where: (a) severe long-term restrictions substantially hinder the exercise of the rights of the parent company over the assets or management of that undertaking; or (b) the information necessary for the preparation of group accounts cannot be obtained without disproportionate expense or undue delay; or (c) the interest of the parent company is held exclusively with a view to subsequent resale.

Section 407 deals with the consistency of financial reporting within a group, with s 407(1) providing that the directors of a parent company must secure that the individual accounts of: (a) the parent company; and (b) each of its subsidiary undertakings, are all prepared using the same financial reporting framework, except to the extent that in their opinion there are good reasons for not doing so.

Finally, ss 400–401 of the Companies Act 2006 set out exemptions for companies included in EEA and non-EEA group accounts of larger companies.

The directors' report

The directors are required under s 415(1) to prepare a directors' report for each financial year of the company. Failure to comply with this requirement is an offence committed by every person who was a director of the company immediately before the end of the period for filing accounts and reports for the financial year in question, and failed to take all reasonable steps for securing compliance with that requirement (s 415(4)).

Section 416 goes on to set down the general contents of directors' report, with s 416(1) providing that the directors' report for a financial year must state the names of the persons who, at any time during the financial year, were directors of the company, and the principal activities of the company in the course of the year. Section 416(3) states that except in the case of a company subject to the small companies regime, the report must state the amount (if any) that the directors recommend should be paid by way of dividend.

Furthermore, according to s 417 of the Companies Act 2006, unless the company is subject to the small companies' regime, the directors' report must contain a business review. The purpose of the business review, set down in s 417(2), is to inform members of the company and to help them assess how the directors have performed their duty under s 172 (duty to promote the success of the company). Section 417(3) provides that the business review must contain: (a) a fair review of the company's business; and (b) a description of the principal risks and uncertainties facing the company. In this regard, s 417(4) goes on to state that the review required is a balanced and comprehensive analysis of the development and performance of the company's business during the financial year, and the position of the company's business at the end of that year, consistent with the size and complexity of the business. This is extended under s 417(5) for quoted companies which must, to the extent necessary for an understanding of the development, performance or position of the company's business, include:

(a) the main trends and factors likely to affect the future development, performance and position of the company's business; and

(b) information about:
  (i) environmental matters (including the impact of the company's business on the environment),
  (ii) the company's employees, and
  (iii) social and community issues, including information about any policies of the company in relation to those matters and the effectiveness of those policies; and
(c) subject to subsection (11), information about persons with whom the company has contractual or other arrangements which are essential to the business of the company.

In addition, s 417(6) provides that the review must, to the extent necessary for an understanding of the development, performance or position of the company's business, include: (a) analysis using financial key performance indicators, i.e. factors by reference to which the development, performance or position of the company's business can be measured effectively; and (b) where appropriate, analysis using other key performance indicators, including information relating to environmental matters and employee matters. This provision is relaxed slightly for companies which qualify as medium-sized. Under s 417(7), the directors' report for the year need not comply with the requirements of s 417(6) so far as they relate to non-financial information.

The review must, where appropriate, include references to, and additional explanations of, amounts included in the company's annual accounts (s 417(8)). However, this section does not require the disclosure of information about impending developments or matters in the course of negotiation if the disclosure would, in the opinion of the directors, be seriously prejudicial to the interests of the company (s 417(10)).

Section 418 goes on to provide details of the statement as to disclosure to auditors and applies to a company unless under s 418(1) it is exempt for the financial year in question from the requirements of Part 16 as to audit of accounts, and the directors take advantage of that exemption. Otherwise, according to s 418(2), the directors' report must contain a statement to the effect that, in the case of each of the persons who are directors at the time the report is approved: (a) so far as the director is aware, there is no relevant audit information of which the company's auditor is unaware (i.e. information needed by the company's auditor in connection with preparing his report); and (b) he has taken all the steps that he ought to have taken as a director in order to make himself aware of any relevant audit information and to establish that the company's auditor is aware of that information. In order to discharge the obligations arising under this subsection, a director must show that he has taken all the steps that he ought to have taken as a director in order to do the things mentioned (i.e. made such enquiries of his fellow directors and of the company's auditors for that purpose, and taken such other steps (if any) for that purpose, as are required by his duty as a director of the company to exercise reasonable care, skill and diligence) (s 418(4)).

Section 418(5) goes on to provide that where a directors' report containing the statement required by this section is approved but the statement is false, every director of the company who (a) knew that the statement was false, or was reckless as to whether it was false; and (b) failed to take reasonable steps to prevent the report from being approved, commits an offence.

Finally, with respect to the approval and signing of the directors' report, s 419(1) states that it must be approved by the board of directors and signed on behalf of the board by a director or the secretary of the company. If the report is prepared in accordance with the small companies regime, it must contain a statement to that effect in a prominent position above the signature (s 419(2)).

Publication of accounts and reports

A company is under a duty to circulate copies of its annual accounts and reports for each financial year to every member of the company, every holder of the company's debentures, and every person who is entitled to receive notice of general meetings (s 423(1)). Section 426 of the Act though provides that a company may provide a summary financial statement instead of copies of the accounts and reports required to be sent out in accordance with s 423. Section 426(4) goes on to state that a summary financial statement must comply with the requirements of s 427 (form and contents of summary financial statement: unquoted companies), or s 428 (form and contents of summary financial statement: quoted companies). However, if default is made in complying with any provision of s 426, 427 or 428, or of regulations under any of those sections, an offence is committed by the company, and every officer of the company who is in default (s 429).

With respect to a company's annual accounts and reports, s 424(2) provides that a private company must comply with s 423 not later than the end of the period for filing accounts and reports, or if earlier, the date on which it actually delivers its accounts and reports to the Registrar. A public company must comply with s 423 at least 21 days before the date of the relevant accounts meeting (i.e. the accounts meeting of the company at which the accounts and reports in question are to be laid) (s 424(3)). Section 424(4) goes on to provide that if a public company sends out copies later than this they shall, despite that, be deemed to have been duly sent if it is so agreed by all the members entitled to attend and vote at the relevant accounts meeting.

If the company defaults in sending out copies of its accounts and reports, then under s 425 an offence is committed by the company, and every officer of the company who is in default.

Requirements in connection with publication of accounts and reports

Section 433 of the Companies Act 2006 provides that every copy of a document that is published by or on behalf of the company must state the name of the person who signed it on behalf of the board. In the case of an unquoted company, this applies to copies of the company's balance sheet, and the directors' report (s 433(2)). In the case of a quoted company, this section applies to copies of the company's balance sheet, the directors' remuneration report, and the directors' report (s 433(3)). If a copy is published without the required statement of the signatory's name, then an offence is committed under s 433(4) of the Act by the company, and every officer of the company who is in default.

Section 434 states that if a company publishes any of its statutory accounts, they must be accompanied by the auditor's report on those accounts (unless the company is exempt from audit and the directors have taken advantage of that exemption). The term 'statutory accounts' is defined by s 434(3) as a company's accounts for a financial year as required to be delivered to the Registrar under s 441 (see below).

Section 435 deals with the requirements in relation to non-statutory accounts, which must be published with a statement indicating: (a) that they are not the company's statutory accounts; (b) whether statutory accounts dealing with any financial year with which the non-statutory accounts purport to deal have been delivered to the Registrar; and (c) whether an auditor's report has been made on the company's statutory accounts for any such financial year, and if so whether the report: (i) was qualified or unqualified, or included a reference to any matters to which the auditor drew attention by way of emphasis without qualifying the report; or (ii) contained a statement under s 498(2) (accounting records or returns inadequate or accounts or directors' remuneration report not agreeing with records and returns); or s 498(3) (failure to obtain necessary information and explanations). Section 435(2) goes on to provide that the company must not publish with non-statutory accounts the auditor's report on the company's statutory accounts.

Finally, it is worth noting that under s 436(2) the term 'publication' is defined as the publishing, issuing or circulating of a document or otherwise making it available for public inspection in a manner calculated to invite members of the public generally, or any class of members of the public, to read it.

Filing of accounts and reports

Section 441 of the Companies Act 2006 states that the directors of a company are under a duty to deliver to the Registrar for each financial year the accounts and reports required by: (i) s 444 (filing obligations of companies subject to small companies regime); (ii) s 445 (filing obligations of medium-sized companies); (iii) s 446 (filing obligations of unquoted companies); or (iv) s 447 (filing obligations of quoted companies). The period allowed for the directors of a company to comply with their obligation to deliver accounts and reports for a financial year to the Registrar is referred to as the 'period for filing'. Section 442(2)(a) states that for a private company, the period for filing is nine months after the end of the relevant accounting reference period (i.e. the accounting reference period by reference to which the financial year for the accounts in question was determined), while according to s 442(2)(b) for a public company, it is six months after the end of that period. This is subject to s 442(3) (a company's first relevant accounting reference period) and s 442(4) (shortened relevant accounting period due to notice given under s 392: alteration of accounting reference date).

Filing obligations: small companies

Section 444 sets out the filing obligations of companies subject to small companies regime. Section 444(1) notes that the directors must deliver to the Registrar for each financial year a copy of a balance sheet drawn up as at the last day of that year, and may also deliver to the Registrar (i) a copy of the company's profit and loss account for that year; and (ii) a copy of the directors' report for that year. Under s 444(2) they must also deliver to the Registrar a copy of the auditor's report on those accounts and on the directors' report, though this does not apply if the company is exempt from audit and the directors have taken advantage of that exemption. Section 444(4) goes on to state that if abbreviated accounts are delivered to the Registrar the obligation to deliver a copy of the auditor's report on the accounts is to deliver a copy of the special auditor's report required by s 449.

According to s 444(5), where the directors of a company subject to the small companies regime deliver to the Registrar IAS accounts, or Companies Act accounts that are not abbreviated accounts, and in accordance with this section (a) do not deliver to the Registrar a copy of the company's profit and loss account; or (b) do not deliver to the Registrar a copy of the directors' report, the copy of the balance sheet delivered to the Registrar must contain in a prominent position a statement that the company's annual accounts and reports have been delivered in accordance with the provisions applicable to companies subject to the small companies regime.

Copies of the balance sheet and any directors' report delivered to the Registrar must, under s 444(6), state the name of the person who signed it on behalf of the board. Furthermore, s 444(7) provides that the copy of the auditor's report must state the name of the auditor and (where the auditor is a firm) the name of the person who signed it as senior statutory auditor, or if the conditions in s 506 (circumstances in which names may be omitted) are met, state that a resolution has been passed and notified to the Secretary of State in accordance with that section.

Filing obligations: medium-sized companies

With respect to medium-sized companies, s 445(1) states that the directors must deliver to the Registrar a copy of the company's annual accounts, and the directors' report. They must also deliver to the Registrar a copy of the auditor's report on those accounts (and on the directors' report), though this does not apply if the company is exempt from audit and the directors have taken advantage of that exemption (s 445(2)).

Where the company prepares Companies Act accounts, s 445(3) provides that the directors may deliver to the Registrar a copy of the company's annual accounts for the financial year that includes a profit and loss account in which items are combined in accordance with regulations made by the Secretary of State, and that does not contain items whose omission is authorised by the regulations.

Copies of the balance sheet and directors' report delivered to the Registrar must, under s 445(5), state the name of the person who signed it on behalf of the board. Section 445(6) goes on to provide that the copy of the auditor's report must state the name of the auditor and (where the auditor is a firm) the name of the person who signed it as senior statutory auditor, or if the conditions in s 506 are met, state that a resolution has been passed and notified to the Secretary of State in accordance with that section.

Filing obligations: quoted companies

Finally, the filing obligations of quoted companies are covered by s 447 of the Companies Act 2006. According to s 447(1) the directors must deliver to the Registrar for each financial year of the company a copy of the company's annual accounts, the directors' remuneration report, and the directors' report. They must also deliver a copy of the auditor's report on those accounts (and on the directors' remuneration report and the directors' report) under s 447(2). Section 447(3) goes on to provide that the copies of the balance sheet, the directors' remuneration report and the directors' report delivered to the Registrar under this section must state the name of the person who signed it on behalf of the board. Furthermore, under s 447(4) the copy of the auditor's report delivered to the Registrar under this section must state the name of the auditor and (where the auditor is a firm) the name of the person who signed it as senior statutory auditor, or if the conditions in s 506 are met, state that a resolution has been passed and notified to the Secretary of State in accordance with that section.

Failure to file accounts and reports

Under s 451(1) of the Companies Act 2006, if a company fails to file a copy of its annual accounts and reports with the Registrar before the end of the period for filing those accounts and reports, then every person who immediately before the end of that period was a director of the company commits an offence. It is a defence for a person to prove that he took all reasonable steps for securing that those requirements would be complied with before the end of that period (s 451(2)), though it is not a defence to prove that the documents in question were not in fact prepared as required by this Part of the Act (s 451(3)).

Section 452 goes on to provide that if a company fails to comply with the requirements of s 441 and the directors fail to make good the default within 14 days after the service of a notice on them requiring compliance, the court may, on the application of any member or creditor of the company or of the Registrar, make an order directing the directors to make good the default within such time as may be specified in the order.

Finally, where the requirements of s 441 are not complied with in relation to a company's accounts and reports for a financial year before the end of the period for filing those accounts and reports, the company is liable to a civil penalty under s 453. This is in addition to any liability of the directors under s 451. Furthermore, the penalty may be recovered by the Registrar and is to be paid into the Consolidated Fund (s 453(3)).

Auditors

An audit is a process which is concerned to establish and confirm confidence in the accounting information yielded by the company's records and systems so that an opinion may be given upon the accounts which have been prepared by the company from those records and systems. The audit is carried out primarily for the shareholders as a check upon the directors' stewardship, but it is obviously also of benefit to creditors and potential investors. The statute law relating to auditors in terms of their appointment, rights, remuneration, removal and resignation are to be found in ss 485 to 526 of the 2006 Companies Act.

Appointment of auditors: public companies

At each general meeting at which accounts in respect of an accounting reference period are laid, usually the annual general meeting, the members must appoint auditors who will hold office until the conclusion of the next general meeting at which accounts in respect of an accounting reference period are laid.

In this regard, s 437 of the 2006 Act provides that the directors of a public company must lay before the company in general meeting copies of its annual accounts and reports and this must be complied with not later than the end of the period for filing the accounts and reports in question. Section 438 goes on to provide that if these requirements are not complied with before the end of the period allowed, every person who immediately before the end of that period was a director of the company commits an offence.

Returning to the issue of appointment, s 489 states that an auditor or auditors of a public company must be appointed for each financial year of the company, unless the directors reasonably resolve otherwise on the ground that audited accounts are unlikely to be required. Under s 489(4) the members may appoint an auditor or auditors by ordinary resolution: (a) at an accounts meeting; (b) if the company should have appointed an auditor or auditors at an accounts meeting but failed to do so; (c) where the directors had power to appoint under s 489(3) but have failed to make an appointment. Section 489(2) goes on to provide that for each financial year for which an auditor or auditors is or are to be appointed (other than the company's first financial year), the appointment must be made before the end of the accounts meeting of the company at which the company's annual accounts and reports for the previous financial year are laid. Furthermore, the directors may appoint an auditor or auditors of the company (a) at any time before the company's first accounts meeting; (b) following a period during which the company (being exempt from audit) did not have any auditor, at any time before the company's next accounts meeting; (c) to fill a casual vacancy in the office of auditor (s 489(4)).

According to s 491, the auditor or auditors of a public company hold office in accordance with the terms of their appointment, subject to the requirements that they do not take office until the previous auditor or auditors have ceased to hold office, and they cease to hold office at the conclusion of the accounts meeting next following their appointment, unless reappointed.

If no appointment is made by a public company, then under s 490, the Secretary of State may appoint one or more persons to fill the vacancy.

Term of office of auditors of public company

According to s 491(1), the auditors of a public company hold office in accordance with the terms of their appointment, subject to the requirements that: (a) they do not take office until the previous auditor or auditors have ceased to hold office; and (b) they cease to hold office at the conclusion of the accounts meeting next following their appointment, unless reappointed. Section 491(2) goes on to provide that this is without prejudice to the provisions of this Part of the Act as to removal and resignation of auditors.

Removal and other special notice requirements

The members of a company may remove the auditors before the expiration of their office under s 510 of the Companies Act 2006. If this is done the Registrar must be informed within 14 days of removal in accordance with s 512 of the 2006 Act. As regards procedure, s 511 provides that special notice is required for an ordinary resolution at a general meeting.

Section 511(3) states that the auditor may make representations in writing to the company and request their notification to the members of the company. Section 511(4) goes on to provide that the company must: (a) in any notice of the resolution given to members of the company, state the fact of the representations having been made; and (b) send a copy of the representations to every member of the company to whom notice of the meeting is or has been sent. If a copy of any such representations is not sent out as required because it was received too late or because of the company's default, the auditor may require that the representations be read out at the meeting in accordance with s 511(5). However, s 511(6) states that copies of the representations need not be sent out and the representations need not be read at the meeting if, on the application either of the company or of any other person claiming to be aggrieved, the court is satisfied that the auditor is using the provisions of this section to secure needless publicity for defamatory matter.

Resignation

An auditor of a company may, under s 516 of the Companies Act 2006, resign his office at any time by depositing at the registered office of the company a notice in writing to that effect.

The notice is not effective unless it is accompanied by the statement required by s 519 of the Act. The date of his resignation is the date of the notice or such later date as may be specified in the notice (s 516(3)). According to s 519, the notice of resignation must contain a statement of the circumstances connected with his ceasing to hold office.

Section 520 goes on to state that where the statement deposited under s 519 states the circumstances connected with the auditor's ceasing to hold office, the company must within 14 days of the deposit of the statement either (a) send a copy of it to every person who under s 423 is entitled to be sent copies of the accounts; or (b) apply to the court. If the company applies to the court, then under s 520(3), it must notify the auditor of the application. Section 520(4) goes on to state that if the court is satisfied that the auditor is using the provisions of s 519 to secure needless publicity for defamatory matter: (a) it shall direct that copies of the statement need not be sent out; and (b) it may further order the company's costs on the application to be paid in whole or in part by the auditor, even if he is not a party to the application. However, if no such direction is made, then under s 520(5) the company must send copies of the statement to the persons mentioned in subsection (2)(a) within 14 days of the court's decision or, as the case may be, of the discontinuance of the proceedings.

On receiving the auditor's notice of resignation, s 517 of the 2006 Act provides that the company must send a copy of it to the Registrar within 14 days. In addition, if the notice contains a statement of circumstances connected with his resignation, s 521 states that a copy must also be sent to the Registrar within 21 days.

Finally, s 523 provides that where an auditor ceases to hold office before the end of his term of office, the company must notify the appropriate audit authority and the notice must inform the appropriate audit authority that the auditor has ceased to hold office, and be accompanied by: (i) a statement by the company of the reasons for his ceasing to hold office; or (ii) if the copy of the statement deposited by the auditor at the company's registered office in accordance with s 519 contains a statement of circumstances in connection with his ceasing to hold office that need to be brought to the attention of members or creditors of the company, a copy of that statement. Section 523(3) provides that this must be later than 14 days after the date on which the auditor's statement is deposited at the company's registered office in accordance with s 519. Similarly under s 522, a duty is placed on the auditor to notify the appropriate audit authority. The notice must inform the appropriate audit authority that he has ceased to hold office, and be accompanied by a copy of the statement deposited by him at the company's registered office in accordance with s 519. If the auditor fails to comply with this provision then he commits an offence under s 522(5) of the 2006 Act.

Duties of auditors

An auditor has *two main duties*: (1) *to audit* the accounts of the company; and (2) *to report* to the members of the company on the accounts, i.e. on every balance sheet and profit and loss account and all group accounts, if any, laid before the company in general meeting during his tenure of office. The auditor's report must be open to inspection by any member.

As regards the role of the auditor *in combating corporate fraud*, expectations which the public and some in business have of the auditor often go beyond their role as auditors. Although the term 'fraud' is often mentioned, there is in fact no crime of that name and if auditors are to be responsible for exposing it or reporting on it, then there must first be legislation to define what it is they are to report upon. There are some specific reporting duties in the field of money laundering in connection with drugs or terrorism set out in the Criminal Justice Act 1993. Reporting duties also exist in areas where organisations take deposits of the public's money, e.g. banking, insurance and investment funds, and, in particular, there is a duty on the auditors to a pension scheme to report to the Occupational Pensions Regulatory Authority if they have reasonable grounds to believe that any duty imposed upon the scheme trustees, the employer or any professional adviser is not being complied with and is of material significance. Sections 47 and 48 of the Pensions Act 1995 contain these 'whistleblowing' provisions.

In this connection, workers are protected in terms of whistleblowing on matters arising during their employment by the Public Interest Disclosure Act 1998. In relation to this and to the receipt of information in this way generally, the Institute of Chartered Accountants in England and Wales has issued a discussion paper, i.e. TECH 5/98, *Receipt of Information in Confidence by Auditors* (and see below).

Rights of auditors

The auditors are given wide statutory rights and powers to enable them to obtain whatever information they require for the purposes of their audit. In particular:

(a) they have a right of access at all times to the books, accounts and vouchers of the company and are entitled to require from the officers of the company such information and explanation as they think necessary for the performance of their duties as auditors;

(b) it is a criminal offence for any officer of a company knowingly or recklessly to make a statement which is misleading, false or deceptive in a material particular;

(c) they have a right to receive notices of and other communications relating to general meetings and to attend them. They also have a right to be heard at any general meeting which they attend on any part of the business which concerns them as auditors.

Information and the Companies (Audit, Investigations and Community Enterprise) Act 2004

This Act entitles an auditor to require information from employees and to that extent widens the auditor's sources of information. The right applies to subsidiary companies including those that are non-GB where the parent company carries the responsibility for obtaining the information.

In addition, it is a criminal offence to fail to provide information or explanations required by the auditor.

The 2004 Act also requires the directors' report to state that so far as *each* director is aware there is no relevant information of which the company's auditors are unaware and that each director has taken all the steps that he ought to have taken as a director in order to make himself aware of any relevant audit information and to ensure that the company's auditors were aware of it.

'Relevant audit information' is defined as information needed by the company's auditors in connection with the preparation of their report.

It is a criminal offence if a false statement is made applying to each director who knew or was reckless as to the existence of undisclosed information. It does not seem possible for the directors to make a qualified report.

Duty of care of the auditor

When carrying out their duties, auditors must exercise skill and care and the degree of skill and care to be shown in particular in relation to the depth of the investigation and the sorts of check to be made is to be found in judicial decisions. The relevant case law is summarised below.

(a) It is not their duty to see that the business is being run efficiently or profitably or to advise on the conduct of the business. The auditors' concern is to ascertain the true financial position of the company at the time of the audit. However, an auditor is not an insurer and does not guarantee that the accounting records show the true state of the company's affairs. Nevertheless, he must be honest and not certify what he does not believe to be true and must take reasonable care and skill before he believes that what he certifies is true.

Re London and General Bank [1895] 2 Ch 166

The greater part of the capital of the bank, which was being wound up, had for some years been advanced to four of the 'Balfour' companies and a few special customers on securities which were insufficient and difficult of realisation. The auditors drew attention to the situation in a confidential report to the directors, stressing its gravity, and ending by saying – 'We cannot conclude without expressing our opinion unhesitatingly that no dividend should be paid this year.' The chairman, Mr Balfour, persuaded the auditors to strike this sentence out before the report was officially laid before the board of directors. The certificate signed by the auditors and laid before the shareholders at the annual general meeting stated that 'the value of the assets as shown on the balance sheet is dependent on realisation'. As originally drawn, it also said – 'And on this point we have reported specifically to the board.' But again Mr Balfour persuaded them to withdraw this statement by promising to mention this in his speech to the shareholders which he did without drawing special attention to it. The directors declared a dividend of 7 per cent.

Held – by the Court of Appeal, affirming the decision of Vaughan Williams J – that the auditors had been guilty of misfeasance, and were liable to make good the amount of dividend paid. It is the duty of an auditor to consider and report to the shareholders, whether the balance sheet exhibits a correct view of the state of the company's affairs, and the true financial position at the time of the audit. He must take reasonable care to see that his certification is true, and must place the necessary information before the shareholders and not merely indicate the means of acquiring it. In the course of his judgment Lindley LJ said:

An auditor [. . .] is not an insurer; he does not guarantee that the books correctly show the true position of the company's affairs; he does not even guarantee that his balance sheet is accurate according to the books of the company [. . .] but, he must be honest, i.e. he must not certify what he does not believe to be true, and he must use reasonable care and skill before he believes that what he certifies is true. What is reasonable care in any particular case must depend upon the circumstances of the case.

Theobald, the auditor, stated the true position to the directors, and if he had done the same to the shareholders, his duty would have been discharged.

(b) As we have seen, there is no statutory duty upon an auditor to detect fraud but if suspicions are aroused the auditor has a duty to investigate matters. A standard issued by the Auditing Practices Board (SAS 110) states that an auditor's prime duty is to ensure that the company's accounts give a true and fair view of its position and not to detect fraud. Nevertheless, says the standard, material fraud can distort a company's accounts and auditors should be alert to the possibility of its existence. Other guidelines issued by the APB state that auditors may be barred from auditing financial services companies if they detect fraud and fail to report on it to the relevant regulator, e.g. the Financial Services Authority.

(c) An auditor may have to value shares and in this connection it should be noted that if on the facts of the case the court takes the view that the auditor was employed in the capacity of arbitrator rather than expert there is no liability in negligence. However, in most cases the auditor will be regarded as valuing as an expert because the parties are seldom in dispute with regard to the value of the shares and are simply seeking a professional valuation. Where the auditor values as an expert he will be liable in negligence under the rule in *Hedley Byrne & Co* v *Heller & Partners* [1963] 2 All ER 575 if he reaches a valuation without the exercise of proper skill and care. In addition, the auditors' valuation of shares is generally binding on the parties even if it is wrong. The courts are reluctant to set aside a professional valuation in the absence of fraud, or collusion (*Baber* v *Kenwood Manufacturing Co* [1978] 1 Lloyd's Rep 175), and this makes the remedy against the auditors more attractive provided, of course, negligence can be established.

(d) The auditor should be familiar with the company's constitution, i.e. its memorandum and articles (*Re Republic of Bolivia Exploration Syndicate Ltd* [1914] 1 Ch 139) and must, of course, check and verify the company's accounts (*Leeds Estate, Building and Investment Co* v *Shepherd* (1887) 36 Ch D 787).

(e) The auditor is not under a duty to take stock and can accept as honest any statements made by the company's officers and servants so long as he acts reasonably in so doing and the circumstances are not suspicious (*Re Kingston Cotton Mill Co* (1896), below). In other words, he must act as a reasonably careful and competent auditor would.

Re Kingston Cotton Mill Co [1896] 2 Ch 279

The directors of a company were enabled to pay dividends out of capital because the stock in trade of the company was overstated for several years. The auditors had not required the production of the stock records but had accepted the certificate of the company's manager regarding the value of the stock.

Held – by the Court of Appeal – the auditors were not liable. It was stated that an auditor is 'a watchdog not a bloodhound'. He can assume that the company's servants are honest and can rely upon statements they make unless there are suspicious circumstances which would give reason for distrust. *Per* Lopes LJ:

It is the duty of an auditor to bring to bear on the work he has to perform that skill, care and caution which a reasonably competent, careful and cautious auditor would use. What is reasonable skill, care and caution must depend on the particular circumstances of each case. An auditor is not bound to be a detective, or, as was said, to approach his work with suspicion, or with a foregone conclusion that there is something wrong. He is a watchdog, but not a bloodhound. He is justified in believing tried servants of the company in whom confidence is placed by the company. He is entitled to assume that they are honest and to rely upon their representations, provided he uses reasonable care. If there is anything calculated to excite suspicion, he should probe it to the bottom; but in the absence of anything of that kind he is only bound to be reasonably cautious and careful [. . .] It is not the duty of an auditor to take stock; he is not a stock expert; there are many matters on which he must rely on the honesty and accuracy of others.

Comment

The rule laid down in the above case has been modified by subsequent cases. In *Westminster Road Construction and Engineering Company Ltd* (1932) unreported, a company paid dividend out of profits which were overstated by reason of the overvaluation of work in progress. This figure was supplied by the manager and secretary and it was held that the auditor was liable to repay the money paid out as dividend because he had accepted the certificate given by them without making proper enquiries which would have revealed that the valuation was inflated.

See also *Re City Equitable Fire Insurance Co Ltd*, 1925 (Chapter 21, p. 409 ⬤).

It should be borne in mind, however, that the cases relating to the general duty of care of the auditor are rather old and that professional standards have risen since they were decided. Thus, it is now generally accepted that an auditor should not rely on the accuracy and honesty of other persons even in the matter of stocktaking, and that he should carry out a check on at least one or more sample items. The standard of care required of an auditor at the present time was probably more accurately expressed by Lord Denning in *Fomento (Sterling Area) Ltd* v *Selsdon Fountain Pen Co Ltd* [1958] 1 WLR 45 at p 61 where he said:

An auditor is not confined to the mechanics of checking vouchers and making arithmetical computations. He is not to be written off as a professional 'adder-upper and subtractor'. His vital task is to take care to see that errors are not made, be they errors of computation, or errors of omission or commission, or downright untruths. To perform this task properly he must come to it with an enquiring mind – not suspicious of dishonesty [. . .] – but suspecting that someone may have made a mistake somewhere and that a check must be made to ensure that there has been none.

This higher duty of care was to some extent applied in the following case.

Re Thomas Gerrard & Son Ltd [1968] Ch 455

The managing director of the company had falsified the accounts by three methods one of which involved including non-existent stock and altering invoices. The auditors who were put on inquiry by alterations of invoices negligently failed to investigate the matter and gave a falsely favourable picture of the profits of the company as a result of which it declared dividends it would not otherwise have declared which in turn resulted in extra tax being payable. The company was wound up and in misfeasance proceedings under what is now s 212 of the Insolvency Act 1986 against the auditors they claimed that they had not been given enough time to do their work.

Held – this was no defence and the auditors must repay the dividends, the cost of recovering the extra tax and any of the extra tax not recoverable. In the course of his judgment Pennycuick J made the following points:

(i) if directors do not allow the auditors adequate time to make proper investigations, they must either refuse to make a report at all or qualify it;

(ii) while leaving open the question whether the auditors would have been in breach of duty had the only fraud been falsification of stock, the judge held that once they were on notice of the altered invoices, they had a duty to make an exhaustive inquiry. Having failed to do so, they were liable to the company under what is now s 212 of the Insolvency Act 1986.

Auditors' liability

The liability of auditors can be brought under three headings as set out below.

By statute

As we have seen in *Re Thomas Gerrard* (above) an auditor may be liable in a winding-up for misfeasance or breach of any fiduciary or other duty in relation to the company. Under this provision an order may be made to repay money or to make compensation as the court thinks just.

In contract

An auditor has a contract with the company and if he is in breach of his duty in regard to the work he has agreed to do for the company, which is normally set out in a 'letter of engagement', he can be sued by the company for damages.

In tort

The claim here will normally be in negligence. It is unlikely that a professional person would make statements which he *knew* to be false in order dishonestly to deceive a party, but if he did the claim would be in the tort of deceit.

To succeed in a claim for negligence, the claimant must show that the defendant auditor owed him a duty of care, that the auditor was in breach of that duty, and finally that the breach caused the damage to the claimant.

Duty of care

The duty of care in regard to negligent misstatements by auditors has been considered in a number of cases since the early 1950s. However, the present position has been the subject of comprehensive analysis by the House of Lords in *Caparo Industries plc v Dickman* [1990] 1 All ER 568 and by the High Court in *Al Saudi Banque v Clarke Pixley* [1989] 3 All ER 361.

From these decisions and important later ones the position would appear to be as follows:

(a) Auditors do not owe a duty of care to potential investors in the company, e.g. those who rely on the audited accounts when contemplating a takeover bid. The fact that the accounts and auditors' report might foreseeably come into their hands and be relied on is not enough to create a duty of care. In addition, it was decided in *James McNaughton Paper Group v Hicks Anderson* [1991] 1 All ER 134 that even if an auditor knew that the audited accounts would be used by a bidder as the basis of a bid, he would not be liable if he reasonably believed and was entitled to assume that the bidder would also seek the advice of his own accountant.

(b) Auditors do not owe a duty of care to potential investors even if they already hold shares in the company since, although they are shareholders and auditors are under a statutory duty to report to shareholders, the duty of the auditors is to the shareholders as a whole and not to shareholders as individuals.

(c) Even where the auditors are aware of the person or persons who will rely upon the accounts, they are not liable unless they also know what the person or persons concerned will use them for, e.g. as the basis for a takeover.

(d) Where there is knowledge of user and use, then in that restricted situation the Court of Appeal held in *Morgan Crucible Co plc* v *Hill Samuel Bank Ltd* [1991] 1 All ER 148 that a duty of care would exist in regard to the user. However, even in such a situation the auditor will not be liable if, in the circumstances, he was entitled to assume that the user would also seek the advice of his own accountant and not rely solely on the audited accounts (see the *McNaughton* case, above).

(e) A case which appears to widen the liability of auditors beyond misstatements to mere omissions is *Coulthard* v *Neville Russell* [1998] 1 BCLC 143, where the Court of Appeal held that as a matter of principle auditors have a duty of care to advise that a transaction which the company and its directors intend to carry out might be a breach of the financial assistance provisions of the Companies Act (see also Chapter 10, p. 200 ⬤).

(f) In addition, the High Court ruled in *Abbott* v *Strong* (1998) *The Times*, 9 July, that a circular issued by a company to its shareholders in connection with a rights issue and allegedly containing misleading profit forecasts by the directors together with an allegedly negligent letter from the company's accountants and management consultants affirming that the forecast statement was properly compiled and in accordance with the company's accounting policies did not lead to the accountants having a duty of care in negligence to the shareholders who acquired shares in the rights issue so that their attempt to claim against the accountants failed. Mr Justice Ferris ruled that the accountants did not owe a duty of care to the shareholders individually for their alleged loss. The judge proceeded by analogy with the issue of shares under listing particulars or prospectus. In such cases, as we have seen, there is a requirement that any statement by accountants should make clear that it has been given with their consent and that the consent has not been withdrawn. This shows that the accountants *adhere to or are part of* the issue process and, of course, in that situation they can be liable for their misstatements. There was, said the judge, no such statement in this case. Once again, the court has decided that there is no duty of care in those advising companies to the individual shareholders, maintaining the *Caparo* line. There were in fact 200 claimants in this case, so the decision may be based on public policy, bearing in mind the problems of obtaining indemnity insurance.

(g) The High Court has ruled that two companies that invested venture capital in a shopfitting company that later went into receivership were entitled to damages from the company's auditors on the basis of negligent misstatements by the auditors in the company's accounts and in letters sent by the auditors to the investing companies. The auditors owed those companies a duty of care (see *Yorkshire Enterprises Ltd* v *Robson Rhodes New Law Online* (1998) 17 June, Transcript Case No 2980610103 approved judgment). A main problem had been that the provision for bad debts was inadequate. The court was saying in summary that if the auditors had carried out the audit work thoroughly, they would have found certain bookkeeping errors and would have made a greater and more appropriate provision for bad debt (or qualified the accounts). In consequence, the auditors were liable in damages. The facts of the case showed that the auditors were aware of the user of their statements and the use to which they would be put.

Breach of duty

An auditor will not be liable if, given a duty of care, he is not in breach of it. An auditor is not likely to be in breach of duty if he follows Auditing Standards and Guidelines, Statements of Standard Accounting Practice and Financial Reporting Standards devised and issued by the profession. If he does that, he will at least have the advantage of the judgment of McNair J in *Bolam* v *Friern Hospital Management Committee* [1957] 2 All ER 118. He said in connection with doctors: 'A doctor is not guilty of negligence if he has acted in accordance with a practice accepted as proper by a responsible body of medical men skilled in that particular art . . . merely because there is a body of opinion who would take a contrary view.' The statement is of course equally applicable to other professions including that of accountant and auditor.

In addition, the explanatory foreword to the profession's Auditing Standards and Guidelines states that 'a court of law may, when considering the adequacy of work of an auditor, take into account any pronouncements or publications which it thinks may be indicative of good practice. Auditing standards and guidelines are likely to be so regarded.'

The importance of professional pronouncements was also stressed in *Lloyd Cheyham* v *Littlejohn* [1987] BCLC 303 where Woolf J remarked that 'while SSAPs are not conclusive so that a departure from their terms necessarily involves a breach of duty of care and they are not rigid rules, they are very strong evidence as to what is the proper standard which should be adopted and unless there is some justification a departure will be regarded as constituting a breach of duty'.

This statement would, of course, apply with equal force to the more recent Financial Reporting Standards.

The effect of the decision in *Bolitho* v *City and Hackney Health Trust* [1997] 4 All ER 771 was considered earlier in the text (see Chapter 11 ⊙) in relation to company distributions and should be referred to again at this point by way of revision.

Damage

It must be shown that the breach caused the damage. Thus, in *JEB Fasteners Ltd* v *Marks Bloom & Co* [1983] 1 All ER 583, the accounts of BG Fasteners were prepared by the defendants who were the auditors of BG. Unknown to the auditors, they were handed to the directors of JEB by the directors of BG as part of a takeover discussion. JEB took over BG and then complained through its directors that it had paid too much for BG and that this was the result of relying on the defendants' accounts which, it was alleged, were negligently prepared and showed BG to be a better proposition than it actually was.

In the High Court it was decided that the auditors should have foreseen the use of the accounts by JEB in the takeover and that this was enough to establish the duty of care. This part of the decision cannot now be supported in view of the requirement of *knowledge of use and user* in *Caparo* and subsequent cases. However, the High Court went on to hold that the auditors were not liable because it appeared in evidence that a major motive in taking over BG was to obtain the technical services of its two directors. It was admitted that JEB would have taken over BG anyway, regardless of the accuracy or otherwise of BG's annual accounts. The auditors' alleged negligence did not cause the damage and they were not liable.

Developments in exclusion of liability

The case of *Royal Bank of Scotland plc* v *Bannerman Johnstone Maclay (a Firm)* (2003) SLT 181 raised issues in regard to auditors' liability and also their ability to exclude that liability.

The bank lent money to a company APC Ltd on the strength of accounts audited by the defendants. It was alleged by the claimant that the audited accounts were less than adequately informative in terms, for example, of the going concern factor. The bank had later to appoint a receiver to the company which was insolvent.

The auditors had notice that under overdraft facility letters the bank was entitled to see management accounts and annual audited accounts. However, they contended that the claimant had to prove that as auditors they *intended* the bank to rely on the accounts to make further loans or advances. The auditors said in effect 'when auditing the accounts our only intention was to carry out Companies Act duties to audit the accounts'. The Scottish Court of Session (Outer House) in this case, equally applicable in England and Wales, ruled that the case law did not support a requirement of intention. The compelling effect of the authorities was that knowledge of user and use formed the basis of a duty of care for those making information or advice available. The auditors had the requisite knowledge and therefore owed a duty of care.

On appeal to the Inner House of the Court of Session in May 2005, it was held that the element of positive intention was not a *sine qua non* of the existence of a duty of care and the pursuers were entitled to inquiry on the averments made. The absence of a disclaimer might be a relevant circumstance pointing to an assumption of responsibility in respect of the information or advice tendered. A major matter relating to this case was that *the auditors had not disclaimed liability to third parties such as the bank*. In this connection, the Institute of Chartered Accountants in England and Wales has stated that it is clear that auditors assume responsibility for the contents of the audit report to shareholders as a body under s 495 of the Companies Act 2006. It also states that the absence of a disclaimer may in some cases enable a court to draw an inference that the auditors have assumed responsibility for the audit report to a third party such as the bank in this case. *The ICAEW recommends* that auditors include the following wording in audit reports to clarify their duty of care to third parties by indicating that no such duty is owed.

> This report is made solely to the company's members as a body, in accordance with s 495 of the Companies Act 2006. Our audit work has been undertaken so that we might state to the company's members those matters we are required to state to them in an auditor's report and for no other purpose. To the fullest extent permitted by law, we do not accept or assume responsibility to anyone other than the company and the company's members as a body, for our audit work, for this report, or for the opinions we have formed.

Capping liability

For the larger firms of accountants providing audit services indemnity insurance adequate to cover potential liability is not available. The sums of damages potentially involved are of Armageddon proportions. In consequence the profession continues to lobby the government for a statutory cap on their liability. Failure by the government to respond may result in the larger groups of companies and public authorities being unable to obtain audit services.

Essay questions

1 Detail the provisions of the Companies Act 2006 relating to the qualifications, method of appointment and procedures for the removal of a company auditor.

(The Institute of Company Accountants)

2 (a) How may a company remove an auditor from the position he holds before the expiration of the term of his office? What can the auditor do if he is removed?

(b) What can a company do if it considers that the auditor has been negligent in his duties to the company?

(c) Can an individual shareholder sue an auditor if he carries out his duties negligently?

(The Chartered Institute of Management Accountants)

3 Lagjet Ltd has a fully issued authorised share capital of £40,000 divided into 40,000 ordinary £1 shares; 75p has been paid up on each share. The shares are allocated as follows:

the directors, Constance, Alan and Jack, each hold 6,500 shares;
James holds 9,500 shares; Alfred and Florence each hold 5,500 shares.

The board wishes to call an extraordinary general meeting to pass the following resolutions:

1 to reduce the company's share capital by extinguishing the liability of shareholders in respect of the unpaid capital on their shares;
2 to appoint a new auditor, Bill, to fill a casual vacancy caused by the sudden death of the auditor appointed at the last annual general meeting.

James, who is owed £5,000 by the company for goods supplied, is opposed to the proposal to reduce the share capital. Alfred and Florence are opposed to the choice of Bill as auditor.

(a) Advise the board on the following matters:

(i) the statutory provisions relating to length of notice before such resolutions can be validly presented to an extraordinary general meeting;
(ii) the number of votes which must be secured before the above resolutions can be passed;
(iii) any further action it can take to secure the appointment of Bill as auditor if it fails to obtain the necessary majority at an extraordinary general meeting.

(b) In the event of the resolution to reduce the company's share capital being passed, advise:

(i) the board as to any further action it must take to make the reduction effective;
(ii) James who is still determined to prevent the reduction becoming effective until he has obtained repayment of his debt.

(c) What possible difference (if any) would it have made if BOTH Florence had not received notice of the meeting due to an error on the part of the company secretary and in consequence had failed to attend the meeting AND Jack had been unable to attend the meeting and had failed to appoint a proxy? *(The Association of Chartered Certified Accountants)*

4 (a) Examine the nature of 'floating charges' as security for moneys lent or credit given to registered companies.

(b) Multifix plc borrowed £1,000,000 from Moneybags giving as security a floating charge over all its undertakings. A clause in the contract provided that the company was not to create any other charges over its assets ranking in priority to or *pari passu* with the floating charge created in favour of Moneybags. Multifix purchased land and several buildings for development and resold most of the properties for substantial profits. A fixed charge was created over the unsold properties valued at £1,500,000 in favour of Finance Limited to secure moneys borrowed from the latter. Multifix has now gone into insolvent liquidation.

Advise the liquidator as to the respective rights of Moneybags and Finance Limited if in the event the assets of the company are insufficient to pay both parties in full.

Would your answer be different if in the contract with Moneybags there was a term to the effect that any attempt by the company to create any other charge over the assets subject to the floating charge, without the consent of Moneybags, would result in the immediate crystallisation of the floating charge? *(University of Plymouth)*

Test your knowledge

Four alternative answers are given. Select ONE only. Circle the answer which you consider to be correct. Check your answers by referring back to the information given in the chapter and against the answers at the end of the text.

1 Morgan Ltd has just delivered its accounts to 31 December 2004 to the Registrar. The accounting records for that period must under the Companies Act 2006 be kept until:

A 31 December 2005.
B 31 December 2006.
C 31 December 2007.
D 31 December 2008.

2 Plush plc has prepared its accounts for the financial year ended 31 December 2004. What is the last date by which the accounts must be laid before a general meeting and filed with the Registrar?

A 31 July 2005.
B 31 October 2005.
C 31 December 2005.
D 31 March 2005.

3 The following resolutions may all be moved at a general meeting of a company:

(i) appointing a person as auditor other than a retiring auditor;
(ii) filling a casual vacancy in the office of auditor;
(iii) removing an auditor before the expiration of his term of office.

Which of these resolutions requires the special notice procedure?

A (i)   B (iii)   C (i) and (iii)   D (i), (ii) and (iii)

4 Which one of the following qualifications does a person require in order to seek the designation 'Registered Auditor'?

A A member of the Chartered Institute of Management Accountants.
B A member of the Chartered Institute of Public Finance and Accountancy.
C A member of the Association of Chartered Certified Accountants.
D A member of the Association of Accounting Technicians.

5 There are provisions in the Companies Act 2006 which relate to the appointment of auditors in the following situations:

(i)   where the first auditors are to be appointed before the first general meeting at which the company's accounts are laid;

(ii) where there is a casual vacancy in the office of auditor;

(iii) where a general meeting at which accounts were laid did not appoint an auditor.

In which of the above situations have the directors of a company power to appoint auditors?

A (i) only   B (i) and (ii)   C (i) and (iii)   D (ii) and (iii)

6 The directors of Tomos Ltd want to change their auditors and are putting the relevant resolution before a general meeting. What statutory rights have the auditors got to make representations to the shareholders of Tomos?

A They may speak at the meeting but cannot communicate with the shareholders in writing.

B They may communicate in writing with the shareholders before the meeting but cannot speak at it.

C The auditors may communicate in writing directly with shareholders and speak at the meeting.

D The auditors may communicate in writing through the company with the shareholders before the meeting and can speak at it.

Answers to test your knowledge questions appear on p. 645.

26

Amalgamations, reconstructions and takeovers

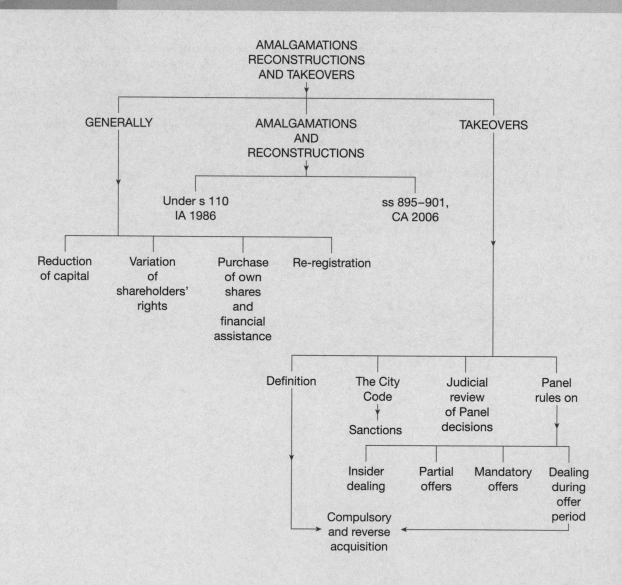

Generally

The ways in which companies can alter their structures are set out below.

Objects clause

This is less of a problem after CA 2006 s 31 which now provides that unless a company's articles specifically restrict the objects of a company, its objects are unrestricted.

Reduction of capital

If the company merely wishes to reduce its share capital it may do so under the procedures discussed earlier (see Chapter 10 ○). Sections 641–651 of the CA 2006 govern how a company may reduce its share capital.

Companies limited by shares – dual regime

There are two methods for companies limited by shares to reduce their share capital:

1 Court approved reduction of capital: available to both private and public companies limited by shares.
2 Reduction of capital supported by a solvency statement: only available to private companies limited by shares.

Unlimited companies

Unlimited companies are free to reduce their share capital by members' resolution without needing either court approval or a solvency statement (provided they have the power to do so in their articles of association).

The default position under the CA 2006 is that a company limited by shares is free to reduce capital by special resolution of its members (supported by either court approval or, for private companies only, a solvency statement) provided such a reduction is not prohibited by its articles (s 641(6)).

Section 641 of the CA 2006 does not apply to unlimited companies. Therefore, an unlimited company should not undertake a reduction of capital unless it has an article giving it express authority to do so.

Variation of shareholders' rights under the memorandum and articles or under the Companies Acts

If the company wishes to alter the rights of shareholders, this can be effected by the approval of the variation at class meetings followed by a special resolution of the company. There is, of course, always the possibility that dissentients within the class will apply to the court (see further Chapter 9 ○).

The relevant sections apply only to registered companies and in addition do not enable any variation to be made in the rights of creditors, including debenture holders. Often, however, the trust deed of an issue of debentures will contain a similar variation clause under which the rights of debenture holders can be varied. In such a case, however, the only remedy of dissenting debenture holders is to plead a general fraud on the minority.

Purchase of own shares and financial assistance

As we have seen, the Companies Acts allow the purchase by a company of its own shares (see further Chapter 10 ◕), and lays down procedures under which a company may give, in appropriate circumstances, financial assistance for the acquisition of its shares (see further Chapter 10 ◕).

Re-registration

It should also be borne in mind that a private limited company may now re-register as unlimited, but only with the consent of all the members, and that an unlimited company may re-register as a private limited company, though with the preservation of the liability of former members (Insolvency Act 1986, s 77).

Other methods of changing corporate structures

In addition to the areas of reconstruction described above, for most of the transactions which a company wishes to enter into, the powers of the board combined with the approval of 51 per cent of the members in general meeting will suffice. Why, then, is it necessary to include in the CA 2006, ss 895, 896 and 899 and in the Insolvency Act 1986, ss 110 *et seq.* provisions to deal with arrangements and reconstructions?

The reason is that the provisions referred to above do not permit a company to *compel* a shareholder to sell or otherwise dispose of his shares, except as part of a reduction when he is, for example, paid off, or under CA 2006, ss 979(1)–(4) in a takeover (see below). Nor do they allow the rights of creditors to be affected or enable the liability of members to be increased without their individual consent. Nor, again, do they provide a means of amalgamating two or more companies or the transfer of the undertaking of one company to another, or the demerger or partition of a company into separate management in another company or companies.

Sections 895, 896 and 899 of the CA 2006 and s 110 of the Insolvency Act 1986 provide procedures for these kinds of changes to be made in a corporate structure.

In addition, there are some companies which cannot remedy internal problems by the use of the specific procedures referred to above. For example, the provisions allowing variation of shareholders' rights do not apply to companies which do not have a share capital. Therefore, if the rights of members are to be varied, ss 895, 896 and 899 will be used.

The provisions on schemes of arrangements and reconstructions in ss 425–427 of CA 1985 are now contained in Part 26 of the CA 2006 and the provisions on mergers and divisions in s 427A of public companies are now contained in Part 27 of the 2006 Act. Parts 26 and 27 came into force on 6 April 2008 as a result of The Companies Act 2006 (Commencement No. 5, Transitional Provisions and Savings) Order 2007 (SI 2007/3495). The sections in Part 26 of CA 2006 restate the provisions of ss 425–427 of the CA 1985, with some drafting amendments and consequential changes as a result of changes to provisions in other Parts of the CA 2006.

Part 27 of the CA 2006 restates the provisions contained in s 427A and Sch 15B to the CA 1985. However, the provisions have been reorganised into a separate chapter for each of mergers and divisions, thereby making the provisions more accessible, depending on the structure chosen by a public company for the scheme of arrangement.

Sections 895 and 896 restate ss 425(1) and (6) of the CA 1985 and grant the power for a company; any of the company's creditors or members; or a liquidator or administrator (if the company is being wound up or an administration order is in force in relation to it), to apply to the court to sanction a compromise or arrangement, as well as providing for the convening of the relevant meetings by the court.

Section 897 restates s 426 of the CA 1985 and prescribes the details that must be contained in the statement that accompanies a notice convening a meeting of creditors or members. The duty of directors and trustees to provide information to the company for the purposes of the statement (section 426(7), CA 1985) has been restated in section 898 of CA 2006.

Section 899 restates s 425(2) of the CA 1985 and sets out the condition that must be satisfied before the court can sanction a compromise or agreement, namely if, at a meeting properly summoned, a majority in number, representing 75 per cent in value of the creditors or class of creditors or members or class of members (as the case may be), agree to the compromise or arrangement. Section 899(2) provides that the persons who may apply for a court order sanctioning a compromise or arrangement are the same as those who may apply to the court for an order for a meeting (under s 896(2)). Section 899 also restates the first part of s 425(3) of the CA 1985, which provides that the court's order has no effect until a copy of it has been delivered to the Registrar (s 899(4)).

Section 900 restates ss 427(1) to (6) of the CA 1985 and provides powers for the court to make provisions to facilitate a reconstruction or amalgamation and requires a copy of any court order made pursuant to the court's powers to make provisions to facilitate a reconstruction or amalgamation to be delivered to the Registrar within seven days of the making of such court order.

Section 901 restates part of ss 425(3) and 425(4) of the CA 1985, but with consequential amendments to reflect the new provisions under the CA 2006 relating to a company's memorandum and articles of association. The requirement in s 425(3) of the CA 1985 for a copy of the court's order to be annexed to every copy of the company's memorandum is replaced with a requirement to annexe a copy of any order under s 899 (order sanctioning a compromise or arrangement) and any order under s 900 (order facilitating reconstruction or amalgamation) that alters the company's constitution to every copy of the company's articles issued after the order has been made, unless the effect of the order has been incorporated into the articles by amendment (s 901(3)). A reference to the company's articles includes the memorandum, so the order must be attached to both.

In addition, if the order amends the company's articles or any resolution or agreement affecting the company's constitution, the copy of the order delivered to the Registrar must be accompanied by a copy of the company's articles or the relevant resolution or agreement, as amended. These changes have been included for consistency with other provisions in the CA 2006 concerning such orders.

Re NFU Development Trust Ltd [1973] 1 All ER 135

The company was limited by guarantee without a share capital and had 94,000 members. All members could vote at general meetings and in the event of a winding-up had a right to the surplus assets of the company in such proportions as the directors should determine. The company proposed a scheme of arrangement where in order to reduce the expense of administration in sending out notices and other communications to the 94,000 members, the number of members of the company would be reduced to seven, all the other members being deprived of their membership. At a meeting to consider the scheme 85 per cent of the votes were cast in favour of it. Application was then made to the court to sanction the scheme.

Held – by Brightman J – that the scheme would not be approved. It was not a compromise or arrangement within the terms of s 425. The rights of members were being expropriated without any compensating advantage and in this sense it could not be said that they were entering into a compromise or arrangement with the company.

Comment

The CA 1985, s 425 (ss 895 *et seq.* in the CA 2006) had to be used here, albeit unsuccessfully, because the company did not have a share capital, which meant that the usual variation of rights procedure was not available. Brightman J suggested that the solution was that members who were not interested in receiving, e.g. reports and accounts, should be asked to resign.

Amalgamations and reconstructions

The term 'reconstruction' is not defined by company legislation. However, it may be said that in a reconstruction the undertaking of the company concerned is preserved and is carried on *after* reconstruction by substantially the *same people* as it was before.

The contrast with an 'amalgamation' is that while a reconstruction consists of the reorganisation of one company or group, an amalgamation involves two or more companies (e.g. A and B) being brought together under one. That one may be either a new company, C, to absorb both A and B, or one of the companies, say B, may absorb the other, A.

Nevertheless, CA 2006, ss 900 *et seq.*, which is the major reconstruction section of the 2006 Act, can be used to effect an amalgamation by takeover by one company of another.

The takeover

Section 110 of the Insolvency Act 1986 is useful in obtaining mergers where the boards of the companies concerned are willing for the merger to take place. If they face opposition from members and/or creditors, then CA 2006, ss 895 *et seq.* would be the better approach.

In a takeover proper, the board of the company to be acquired, say B, is not willing to cooperate so that the company seeking to acquire is forced to address an offer direct to the shareholders of B.

In an amalgamation or takeover involving A and B where A and B are in a similar line of business or are complementary, as where A makes the goods and B markets them, there is potentially a monopoly. In such a case the Secretary of State for BIS may, on the recommendation of the Director of Fair Trading, refer the merger to the Competition Commission under the Competition Act 1998. The merger will not then proceed until the Commission agrees that it should.

When a merger has been referred to the Commission, the parties are prohibited, for the duration of the inquiry, from acquiring shares in any of the other parties without the consent of the Secretary of State.

The Secretary of State is permitted to accept legally binding undertakings for part of the merged business to be disposed of, as an alternative to reference to the Commission.

Formerly these undertakings had to involve agreements to dispose of parts of the business. The Competition Act 1998 now provides for the acceptance of a wider range of undertakings, such as agreements for the future conduct of the business.

The Coalition Government announced as of 15 October 2010 that it will merge the Competition Commission into the Office of Fair Trading.

Amalgamation (or reconstruction) under the Insolvency Act 1986, s 110

Section 110 gives a liquidator power to accept shares as consideration for the sale of the property of a company, so that if A is in voluntary liquidation it may empower its liquidator by special resolution to sell its business and assets to B in exchange for B's shares.

The section would be used where there was no real opposition to an *amalgamation* by the members of A and no compromise with creditors was necessary. There are no provisions for variation of creditors' rights. Creditors are still entitled to prove in the liquidation of A.

If, in order to effect a *reconstruction*, the transfer of the undertaking of one company, A, to another, B, is to be associated with the liquidation of A, the scheme may be carried out under s 110 provided no compromises are required. For example, the section may be used to *demerge*, as where the various business activities of one large company, A, are placed under separate management in a number of other companies, B, C and D, and A is wound up. It may also be used to *partition* companies, as where a family company, E, is carrying on various activities and certain members of the family wish to carry on the activities separately through independent companies, F, G and H, and E is to be wound up.

Procedure

This is as follows:

(a) The company proposing to be wound up voluntarily will pass a special resolution for winding-up and appoint a liquidator.

(b) It will authorise the liquidator by special resolution to transfer the company's assets to a new company in return for shares in the new company. The new company may be one formed for the purpose or it may be an existing company.

(c) Such shares will be distributed among the members of the old company.

(d) Any member who did not vote in favour of the resolution can express his dissent by serving a written notice on the liquidator within seven days requiring him either:

    (i) to abstain from carrying the scheme into effect; or

    (ii) to purchase his shares at a price to be fixed by agreement or by arbitration, and the company must not be wound up until any such dissentient has been paid off, so that opposition from too many members could be costly.

(e) In *Payne* v *The Cork Co Ltd* [1900] 1 Ch 308 it was held that any provision in the articles preventing a member from dissenting was void.

(f) If an order for the compulsory winding-up of the company is made within a year, the special resolution authorising the transfer is void unless the leave of the court is given.

(g) It should be noted that in the case of a creditor's voluntary winding-up, the consent of the liquidation committee (if any) or the court is necessary. Apart from this there is no provision for a compromise with creditors.

Amalgamation (or reconstruction) under the CA 2006, s 895

If on a company *reconstruction* any compromise or arrangement is proposed between the company and its members or creditors s 895 must be used. The use of s 900 (as well) is essential for *amalgamation* where rights of members, debenture holders and creditors are to be compromised.

Procedure

This is as follows:

(a) The court has to be consulted at the outset and must be asked to direct the holding of meetings of members, creditors and debenture holders to discuss the proposed scheme. At this first stage the court will not exercise its discretion to call the meetings if, having regard to the opposition to the scheme by the holders of the majority of the votes, the meetings will serve no useful purpose. In addition, the court is concerned to see that the meetings are properly constituted. For example, a class meeting of shareholders may not be enough if there are groups within each class with different interests (*Re Hellenic and General Trust Ltd*, 1975; see further Chapter 9 ◐). The same problems can exist with creditors who may have different interests, e.g. some may have securities and others not.

However, in *Anglo-American Insurance Ltd* [2001] 1 BCLC 755 the High Court ruled that separate meetings of creditors were not required even though some were short term and some long term or resident in the USA. It appeared that they all had the same substantial rights under the scheme. The problems presented by a challenge to the suitability of the meetings held should not occur unless the company's creditor and/or member *structure* is significantly diverse. This view is supported by the decision in *Re Hawk Insurance Co Ltd* [2001] All ER (D) 289 (Feb) which is to the effect that unless significant and substantial differences in rights exist all creditors/members are capable of consulting together. The decision prevents unreasonable and oppressive complaints by minority interests but it has also, some say, significantly reduced the consideration and protection of minority concerns.

If the court agrees, the meetings will be summoned and full details of the scheme presented. The scheme may involve a winding-up of the company and a transfer of assets under CA 2006, ss 895, 896 and 899 (see below) or it may be an internal reconstruction of the kind seen in *NFU Development Trust Ltd*, 1973. In particular, the scheme must disclose the effect of the amalgamation upon directors, especially where it involves the retirement of some of them and payment to them of compensation for loss of office. This must be disclosed in the notices and sanctioned by the members.

Where the rights of debenture holders are affected, a reference to the material interests, if any, of the trustees for the debenture holders must be disclosed as for directors.

(b) The scheme must be approved by a majority in number and three-quarters in value of the members, creditors and debenture holders. For example, if a company has 100 members and A has got 901 shares of £1 each, and the other 99 members have one share each, then the rest cannot force a scheme on A. Equally, A plus 49 of the rest cannot force a scheme on the remainder but A plus 50 of the rest can force the scheme on the others. The same rules apply to creditors and debenture holders. The court must then be asked to consent to the scheme as approved. The court will have to be satisfied in particular that creditors are not being prejudiced by the scheme of arrangement proposed by the company; and creditors have not only the right to hold their own meeting before the court hearing, as we have seen, but also to be represented in court on the issue of the court's approval. In practice, the company will make sure at a very early stage that creditors are fully satisfied with the proposed scheme and will not raise objections. Furthermore, the court must be satisfied that there is a genuine 'compromise or arrangement' within the meaning of CA 2006, s 895; this implies some element of accommodation on each side, so that a scheme involving the total surrender of the rights of one side will not be approved (see *NFU Development Trust Ltd*, 1973).

(c) If the court approves the scheme it will do so by order and a copy of the court order certified is delivered to the Registrar at which point the scheme becomes binding on all concerned (s 901, CA 2006).

Although any member or creditor can ask the court to convene meetings under CA 2006, s 895, provided some compromise or arrangement is proposed, it appears that the court cannot do this unless the company has generated, or at least approves of, the scheme. Thus in *Re Savoy Hotel Ltd* [1981] 3 All ER 646, Trusthouse Forte had made a bid for the shares of Savoy but could not get acceptance from the major class of voting shareholders. Trusthouse Forte asked the court to convene a meeting of those shareholders under former CA 1985, s 425 so that the bid might be discussed with them, and hopefully they might be convinced to accept it. The judge held that he had no power to convene the meeting because the Savoy Company had not generated the scheme, nor did the board or the voting members appear to approve of it.

However, where the board and the majority of the shareholders of the company to be acquired wish to accept the bid a scheme under CA 2006, s 899 is useful, because s 899 only requires a majority in number and 75 per cent in value of the shareholders attending a meeting and voting in favour of the acquisition of their company to bind any dissenting minority, whereas under a normal takeover offer 90 per cent of the shareholders of the victim company must accept the bid before the predator company can compulsorily acquire the rest.

The provisions of the CA 2006, s 900 (formerly CA 1985, s 427)

Where a scheme under CA 2006, s 900 involves a winding-up, either to an internally reconstructed new company having the same members, debenture holders and creditors, or to a new or existing company as part of a merger, the court may by order:

(a) transfer assets to the other company;
(b) allot shares or debentures to members and debenture holders of the old company;
(c) allow the old company's actions to be brought in the name of the other company;
(d) dissolve the old company without a winding-up;
(e) provide for dissentients otherwise than outlined in the scheme, e.g. by requiring them to be paid off.

Orders made under s 900 must be filed with the Registrar (CA 2006, s 901).

Examples of schemes of internal reconstruction approved by the court under the CA 2006, s 900

Where s 900 is used internally, it represents a means by which a company can enter into a compromise or arrangement with its creditors and/or members without going into liquidation. Schedule 4, Part I of the Insolvency Act 1986 allows a compromise with creditors in the context of a winding-up, though Part I of the 1986 Act also provides a procedure for compromise with creditors, even though the company concerned is not in the course of winding-up. These provisions are considered in more detail later.

The court has approved the following types of internal reconstructions under ss 427(1) to (6) of the CA 1985 (which has been restated in CA 2006, s 900):

(a) Debenture holders have given extension of time for the payment of their loan capital.
(b) Debenture holders have accepted a cash payment less than the par value of the debentures.
(c) Debenture holders have given up their security, thus releasing it to secure further loans.
(d) Debenture holders have exchanged their debentures for shares.
(e) Creditors have taken cash in part payment of their debt and the balance in shares.
(f) Preference shareholders have given up their right to arrears of dividend.
(g) To simplify the capital structure of companies within a group, as where H is the holding company of several partly owned subsidiaries, all of which have old-fashioned complex capital structures comprising many types of shares carrying widely varying rights. The capital structure of the group has been simplified by exchanging all the subsidiary companies' shares held by minority shareholders for ordinary shares or even loan stock in the holding company by means of a scheme of arrangement.

As (g) above shows, reconstruction does not necessarily involve compromising with creditors, nor is it always set in a context of financial difficulty. It is, for example, a technique used for demerging and incentives to dismantle a large group of companies are given, as we have seen, by the Companies Acts in terms of share premium (see Chapter 15 ⊙).

An example of a demerger attracting share premium relief appears in Figures 26.1 and 26.2. The activities of the companies are indicated, as is the holding of H in each.

(a) A allots 1,000 £1 ordinary shares (valued at £6.00 per share) to H.
(b) H transfers its 75 per cent holding in B to A.
(c) C allots 1,000 £1 ordinary shares (valued at £6.00 per share) to H.
(d) H transfers its 65 per cent holding in D to C.
(e) H is then wound up, its holdings in A and C being sold, e.g. by a public placing.

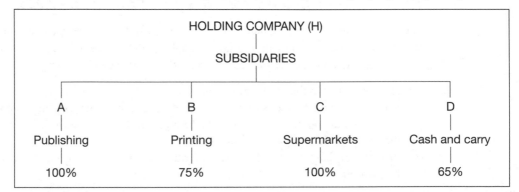

Figure 26.1 **Old ground structure**

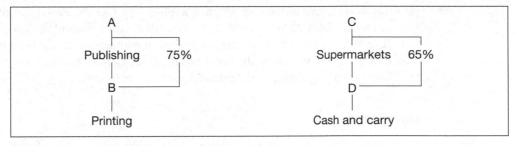

Figure 26.2 **New demerged structure**

Share premium relief: CA 2006, s 611 (formerly CA 1985, s 132)

A and C need only transfer to share premium the 'minimum premium value'. This is the amount, if any, by which the base values of the shares in B and D exceed the aggregate nominal value of the shares A and C allotted to H.

Base value is the lower of the cost to H of the shares in B and D and the amount at which the shares of B and D were stated immediately prior to the transfer in the accounting records of H.

Example

(i) Shares in B and C cost H £4,000 in each case but stood in the accounting records of H at £3,000: base value £3,000.

(ii) Nominal value of shares allotted by A and C was £1,000, so minimum premium value is £2,000. This goes to a share premium account in the books of A and C, but not the true value of the consideration received from B and D by allotting shares to H. The true value, of course, is the total value of the assets of B and D which could run into many thousands or millions of pounds.

It should be noted that share premium relief under s 611 is available where the consideration for the issue of the shares consists of any *non-cash assets* of the company providing the consideration and not merely of shares in another subsidiary of the holding company.

Takeovers

Section 942 of the Companies Act 2006 confers certain statutory powers upon the Takeover Panel but does not seek to regulate the constitution of the Panel itself. The composition of the Panel is to be found not in the legislation but in the Takeover Code.

This area of corporate activity is covered by the law of the Panel on Takeovers and Mergers. The Panel has been designated as the supervisory authority to carry out certain regulatory functions in relation to takeovers under the EC Directive on Takeover Bids (2004/25/EC). Its statutory functions are set out in and under Chapter 1 of Part 28 of the Companies Act 2006. Additionally, there are now criminal penalties for insider dealing generally and during a takeover, under the Criminal Justice Act 1993. If applicable, one must also consider the Unregistered Companies Regulations 2009.

The majority of the rules relating to takeovers are still contained in the Takeover Code, which was given a statutory basis by Part 28 of the CA 2006 in relation to all offers and other statutory merger transactions to which it applies. The General Principles and Code Rules were amended in CA 2006 to implement certain of the provisions of the Takeovers Directive as well as to bring into effect a number of other amendments that had been the subject of a public consultation process by the Panel and the Code Committee, including the abolition of the Rules Governing Substantial Acquisitions of Shares (SARs).

Definition

On the assumption that A plc is acquiring B plc, a takeover may be defined as an offer to all the shareholders of B or one or more classes of shareholders of B, to buy their shares for cash and/or securities in A, the purpose being that A will obtain control of B. A's offer is normally conditional upon sufficient acceptances to ensure control.

A takeover proper occurs when the directors of B do not support the bid. In such a situation A must deal direct with the shareholders of B. As we have seen, if the directors of B do support a merger with A, then they can call the necessary meetings and in general terms organise an amalgamation by methods set out in s 110 of the Insolvency Act 1986 or the CA 2006, s 895 which have already been dealt with.

Why the City Code?

The City Code on Takeovers and Mergers and the Takeover Panel which administer it provide legal control in regard to some of the following:

(a) The offer document

This is used to convey the offer to the shareholders of the company to be acquired, in this case B, is a prospectus and governed by the rules of the Financial Services and Markets Act 2000 and the Stock Exchange Listing requirements.

However, the documents issued by the offeror (or the offeree board, giving, for example, advice to its members whether or not to accept) are also governed by section J of the City Code, Rules 23–27. The full details are beyond the scope of a book of this nature. However, Rule 23 expresses the general standard of care in regard to documents from the offeror and offeree board as follows:

> Shareholders must be given sufficient information and advice to enable them to reach a properly informed decision as to the merits or demerits of an offer. Such information must be available to shareholders early enough to enable them to make a decision in good time. The obligation of the offeror in these respects towards the shareholders of the offeree company is no less than an offeror's obligation towards its own shareholders.

Of major importance is the requirement to give stated financial information about the offeror company (see Rule 24.2). This includes, for the last three financial years for which information has been published, turnover, net profit or loss before and after taxation, the charge for tax, extraordinary items, minority interests, the amount absorbed by dividends and earnings and dividends per share.

(b) Partial bids

In the absence of the City Code there would be nothing to prevent a company making a partial bid in order to achieve control of a company 'on the cheap' as it were. It is not in practice necessary to acquire 50 per cent or more of the voting power of a company in order to control it. The making of partial bids is controlled by the Code and there are provisions under which a mandatory bid must be made for the remainder of the shares of the company to be acquired once a certain number of shares in that company has been obtained. These matters will be considered in more detail later.

(c) Insider dealing

The Code deals with insider trading in quoted companies and the Takeover Panel can publish reprimands in respect of those who deal inside. These are extra-legal sanctions, the Criminal Justice Act 1993 providing for criminal sanctions. The contribution in this field made by the Financial Services and Markets Act 2000 on market abuse under the control of the Financial Services Authority has already been noted (see Chapter 15 ○).

(d) Misleading profit forecasts

Directors and other officers of companies do, from time to time, make public statements as to the future profits of companies which are misleading. The Panel has been active in this area in requiring the publication of corrections of misleading statements.

In addition, when a forecast of profit before taxation appears in a document addressed to shareholders, there must be included forecasts of taxation, extraordinary items and minority interests.

(e) Tactics of directors

The directors of the company to be acquired have in the past used tactics to frustrate the bid and retain control. The Panel takes action on the basis of the Code's general principle 7 which states:

> At no time after a bona fide offer has been communicated to the board of the offeree company or after the board of the offeree company has reason to believe that a bona fide offer might be imminent may any action be taken by the board of the offeree company in relation to the affairs of the company, without the approval of the shareholders in general meeting, which could effectively result in any bona fide offer being frustrated or in the shareholders being denied an opportunity to decide on its merits.

In the past, directors' tactics used to frustrate a bid have often consisted of the issue of additional shares to a company or person(s) who would not accept the bid, without consulting the shareholders of the victim company as to whether this tactic of the directors was acceptable. Obviously general principle 7 would apply to such a situation but now the 2006 Act provides, as we have seen, that the authority of the company is required before the allotment of certain securities by the directors (see Chapter 13). This is reinforced by Rule 21 which carries a similar provision regarding the issue of shares but extends to the making of other contracts otherwise than in the ordinary course of business.

However, there are some situations where general principle 7 and Rule 21 would be the only sanction, for example where the directors lease off the company's property to put it beyond the control of the bidder so that he does not continue with his bid. If we assume that company B, our victim company, owns the freehold of a large block of flats which a bidder for company B wishes to demolish in order to develop the site, then if the directors of B were to lease out the block of flats for, say, 99 years, thus preventing the bidder, even if he were successful, from demolishing the premises for that period so that he did not proceed with his bid, then such a tactic would, unless approved by ordinary resolution of the members, infringe general principle 7 and Rule 21 and the 'proper purpose' rule and could be the basis of a complaint to the Panel and action by it to prevent infringement of the Code.

Statutory Authority of the Panel and the City Code

The Panel is an independent body, established in 1968, whose main functions are to issue and administer the City Code (sometimes referred to as the Code or the Takeover Code) and to supervise and regulate takeovers and other matters to which the Code applies in accordance with the rules set out in the Code. It has been designated as the supervisory authority to carry out certain regulatory functions in relation to takeovers pursuant to the Directive on Takeover Bids (2004/25/EC) (the 'Directive'). Its statutory functions are set out in and under ss 942 to 963 of CA 2006. Rules are set out in the Code. Further information relating to the Panel and the Code can be found on the Panel's website at **www.thetakeoverpanel.org.uk**.

In addition, the membership of the Panel covers a wide range of services within the City and therefore a flagrant flouting of the Code could lead to problems in addition to the loss of the Stock Exchange market for purchase and sale of securities. The Code is issued on the authority of the Takeover Panel.

Membership of the Panel

The chairman, deputy chairmen and certain members of the Panel used to be appointed by the Governor of the Bank of England under earlier editions of the Code, reflecting the historical reality of how the self-regulatory process was initiated. However, the Governor no longer has a formal role in the Panel's composition, rather these individuals are appointed by the Panel itself. In addition, its membership comprises individuals nominated by the following bodies, all of which are committed to support its activities:

The Association of British Insurers;
The Association of Investment Trust Companies;
The Association of Private Client Investment Managers and Stockbrokers;
The British Bankers' Association;
The Confederation of British Industry;
The Institute of Chartered Accountants in England and Wales;
The London Investment Banking Association (with separate representation for its Corporate
     Finance Committee and Securities Trading Committee);
The National Association of Pension Funds;
The Investment Management Association;
London Investment Banking Association Securities Trading Committee.

Each of the bodies listed above may also nominate designated alternates.

In addition, the Panel publishes reprimands which may even appear in the professional press. The publication of this sort of information should have some effect upon practitioners for publication leads to knowledge by their colleagues that they have transgressed the ethics of the Code. Published public reprimands are rare because of the devastating effect such statements may have on companies operating within the financial sector.

It is the nature and purpose of the City Code to ensure that shareholders are treated fairly and are not denied an opportunity to decide on the merits of a takeover. In particular, shareholders of the same class must be afforded equivalent treatment by an offeror under the City Code. The City Code however is not concerned with the financial or commercial advantages or disadvantages of a takeover which are matters for the company and its shareholders. Additionally, competition policy is outside of its remit.

CA 2006, s 952 allows the Panel to impose sanctions on a person who breaches the rules. These sanctions can be enforced by the Panel seeking enforcement by the court pursuant to s 955, CA 2006. Hearings and appeals (including the establishment of an independent Takeover Appeal Board) are provided for in s 951, CA 2006.

Judicial review

In *R v Panel on Takeovers* [1987] 1 All ER 564 the Court of Appeal decided that, having regard to the public consequences of non-compliance with the Code, e.g. that a bid by one company for another could be declared invalid if the procedures of the Code were infringed, an application to the High Court to consider a Panel ruling by way of judicial review would be available in an appropriate case. The courts are not, however, anxious to intervene because judicial review of a Panel decision introduces an element of delay which is undesirable in the takeover situation.

All that now remains is to consider some of the major steps in a takeover bid and see how the various rules of the Code affect the position. In addition, we must give special consideration to the duties of directors in takeovers since this is not only the greatest area of practical problems but is also most likely to be required for examination purposes.

In all situations company A is attempting to acquire company B.

Secrecy during negotiations: insider dealing

The relevant provisions, which are set out in Rules 2 and 4, are designed to prevent insider dealing and they are *extra-legal* in their operation. The *legal* provisions, under which insider dealing may, in certain circumstances, be a criminal offence punishable by a fine and/or imprisonment, are set out in the Criminal Justice Act 1993 (see Chapter 15 ○).

There are, as we have seen, additional *civil* sanctions for market abuse in the Financial Services and Markets Act 2000 that are administered by the Financial Services Authority.

> *Rule 2*, which is concerned with keeping bids secret before public announcement, states: 'The vital importance of absolute secrecy before an announcement must be emphasised.'
>
> *Rule 4*, which is concerned with dealings before and during the offer, requires all persons who have confidential price-sensitive information concerning an offer or contemplated offer to treat it as secret and not pass it on to anyone else unless it is necessary to do so, as where it is part of a person's work to pass it on as, for example, by one member of an audit team to another as part of the audit function.

Additionally, there must not be dealings in securities of the offeree or the offeror company by persons (other than the offeror) who have price-sensitive information prior to the announcement of an approach by a bidder, or an actual bid, or of the termination of negotiations. Dealing is allowed in the shares of the offeror company where the bid will not significantly affect the value of the offeror's shares, which may often be the case. It is the shares of the offeree company which are most likely to be affected by a bid.

If those involved in the negotiations feel that secrecy cannot be maintained, they should ask the Stock Exchange for a temporary halt in dealings.

Failure to comply with Rules 2 and 4 may result in a reprimand from the Panel which may be published.

The rules of the Code are now preventive and information suggesting that insider dealing has taken place which might be revealed by dealings on the Stock Exchange would be passed by the Stock Exchange and by the Panel to the Financial Services Authority for investigation.

Offer document and response of offeree board

The rules derive from section J (consisting of Rules 23–27) of the City Code. It is worth referring again to the general object of the detailed contents of the offer document and any documents issued by the offeree board which is stated in Rule 23.

More important than the contents of the offer document is what an individual shareholder can do if he is misled by the contents of the offer document. While accepting that this branch of the law is not well developed, the judgment of Brightman J in *Gething* v *Kilner* [1972] 1 WLR 337 would seem to justify the following statement:

> If an offer document or a recommendation circulated by the directors of the offeree company contains a false or misleading statement made knowingly, or presumably, if such a document omits information known to the persons issuing it which the law or good practice requires it to contain, any shareholder of the class to whom the bid is addressed may apply to the court for an injunction to restrain the offeror from proceeding with the bid or declaring it unconditional.

Partial offers and mandatory offers

In this connection a knowledge of Rule 36 (partial offers) and Rule 9 (mandatory offers) is of importance. However, before considering the rules relating to partial offers which can result in a bidder obtaining control of a company 'on the cheap', as it were, the nature of a partial bid should be understood. If we take three shareholders of the target company and their holdings to be Mr A (100 shares), Mr B (50 shares), and Mr C (40 shares), then a 50 per cent partial bid will involve, for example, an offer to take 50 of A's shares, 25 of B's shares, and 20 of C's. When this sort of bid is being contemplated, Rule 36 must be followed. Under the rule the Panel's consent is required for any partial offer.

In addition, the following subrules of Rule 36 should be noted.

In the case of an offer which would result in the offeror holding shares carrying less than 30 per cent of the voting rights of a company, consent will normally be granted (Rule 36.1).

Any offer which would result in the offeror holding shares carrying 30 per cent or more of the voting rights of a company must normally be conditional, not only on the relevant number of acceptances being received, but also on approval of the offer, normally signified by means of a separate box on the Form of Acceptance and Transfer, being given by shareholders holding 50 per cent of the voting rights not held by the offeror and persons acting in concert with it. This requirement may on occasion be waived if over 50 per cent of all voting rights of the offeree company are held by the shareholder (Rule 36.5).

Where an offer is made for a company with more than one class of equity share capital which would result in the offeror holding shares carrying 30 per cent or more of the voting rights, a comparable offer must be made for each class (Rule 36.8).

In connection with mandatory offers, the following subrules of Rules 2 and 9 should be noted.

Mandatory offers

A mandatory bid must be made unless the Panel gives its consent:

- by a person who acquires whether by a series of transactions over a period of time or not shares which taken together with shares held or acquired by persons acting in concert with him carry 30 per cent or more of the voting rights of the company;
- by a person who together with people acting in concert with him holds not less than 30 per cent but not more than 50 per cent of the voting rights of a company if there is *any increase at all* in the percentage level of that holding.

Previously in such situations a person or a group acting in concert could acquire in any 12-month period additional shares carrying up to 1 per cent of the voting rights without making a general offer for the company. The change was made following criticism of the ability of a person or concert party to achieve control over a period of time without making a formal bid as where the holding was, say, 48 per cent and the 1 per cent acquisitions eventually brought over 50 per cent and thereby basic control.

The second rule is to deal with persons who have made a bid that has failed to achieve control but which has left the bidder with, say, a 35 per cent holding. Although the City Code consists of extra-legal rules, the High Court applied the 30 per cent mandatory bid rule in effect by the decision in *Philip Morris Products Inc* v *Rothmans International Enterprises Ltd (No 2)* (2000) *The Times*, 10 August.

Immediately upon an acquisition of shares which gives rise to an obligation to make an offer under this rule, the offeror shall make an announcement of its offer giving the information required by the Code. The announcement of an offer under this rule should include confirmation by a financial adviser or other appropriate independent party that resources are available to the offeror sufficient to satisfy full acceptance of the offer (Rule 2.5(c)).

An important exception to the requirement to make a mandatory bid occurs when there is a rescue operation. If company B is in financial difficulties but company A is willing to invest in the share capital of B in order to save it, then if A takes an issue of shares in B which gives A, say, 35 per cent of the share capital of B, the Panel will consider waiving the mandatory bid requirement for the rest of B's shares.

Except with the consent of the Panel, no nominee of the offeror or persons acting in concert with it shall be appointed to the board of the offeree company, nor shall the offeror and persons acting in concert with it transfer, or exercise the votes attaching to, any shares in the offeree company, until the offer document has been posted (Rule 9.7).

The Code defines 'acting in concert' as follows: 'Persons acting in concert comprise persons who, pursuant to an agreement or understanding (whether formal or informal), actively cooperate, through the acquisition by any of them of shares in a company, to obtain or consolidate control of that company.'

Then follows a list of persons who will be presumed to be persons acting in concert with others in the same category unless the contrary is established. These include a company, its parent, subsidiaries, and fellow-subsidiaries, and their associated companies.

For this purpose, ownership or control of 20 per cent or more of the equity share capital of the company will be regarded as a test of associated company status. Other persons presumed to be acting in concert are a company with any of its directors (together with their close relatives and related trusts); a company with any of its pension funds; a person with any investment company, unit trust or other funds whose investments such person manages on a discretionary basis; a financial adviser with his client where the financial adviser has shares in the client company; and finally, directors of a company which is subject to an offer or where the directors have reason to believe a bona fide offer for their company may be imminent.

It should be noted that although an interest of under 30 per cent does not constitute control in the Takeover Panel's eyes, the Office of Fair Trading may take the view that it could constitute a merger giving the Office of Fair Trading power to make a reference to the Competition Commission with a view to preventing the takeover going ahead if it is thought by the Competition Commission to be undesirable in the public interest. The relevant provisions are contained in the Competition Act 1998 and the Enterprise Act 2002.

Compulsory acquisition

CA 2006, s 979 (formerly CA 1985, s 429) is a section which can be used but only by a corporate bidder who has made a bid to acquire compulsorily the shares of a small minority who have not accepted the offer. The provisions of the section are as follows:

(a) Where A already has not more than 10 per cent of B or no holdings in B at all, then if 90 per cent of B's shareholders, or other shareholders, have accepted the offer within four months A may within two months after the reaching of the 90 per cent threshold serve a notice on dissentients that it intends to acquire their shares. The dissentients have six weeks from the date on which the notice was given to appeal to the court. If there is no appeal or the court does not order otherwise, A acquires the shares.

(b) Where A has more than 10 per cent of B, then under s 979 of the 2006 Act, three-quarters in number and 90 per cent in value of B's other shareholders must accept within four months of the offer.

The court will seldom interfere if the offer is fair but will not allow the section to be used for improper purposes such as the expulsion of a minority.

Re Bugle Press Ltd [1960] 3 All ER 791

Holders of 90 per cent of the shares in a company formed a new company which made an offer for the shares of the old company. As was to be expected, 90 per cent of the shareholders accepted the offer and the new company then served notice on the holder of the other 10 per cent of the shares stating that it wished to purchase his holding.

Held – by the Court of Appeal – that in substance the new company was the same as the majority shareholders, and the scheme was in effect an expropriation of the minority interest. 'What the section is directed to is a case where there is a scheme or contract for the acquisition of a company, its amalgamation, reorganisation or the like, and where the offeror is independent of the shareholders in the transferor company, or at least independent of that part or fraction of them from which the 90 per cent is to be derived.' *Per* Evershed MR.

The High Court (affirmed by the Court of Appeal) has ruled that CA 2006, s 979 allows a bidder who holds 90 per cent in value of the shares in the victim following a bid to compulsorily acquire the shares of the remaining members even though they did not receive the offer documents.

In Re Joseph Holt plc Winpar Holdings Ltd v Joseph Holt Group plc [2000] 97 (44) LSG 44. Appeal case available at **www.lawtel.com**, under Case Law-CO100109

In March 2000, Inhoco 1849 plc, now the Joseph Holt Group plc, announced that it was making an offer to acquire all the issued share capital of Joseph Holt plc. The offer document was sent to most of Joseph Holt plc's existing shareholders, and an advertisement was placed in the London edition of the *Financial Times*. The offer document was not sent to shareholders whose addresses were in Australia, Canada, Japan or the USA because complying with the securities laws of those countries was difficult and costly.

By April 2000, Joseph Holt Group plc had received acceptances which, together with the shares it already held, amounted to over 90 per cent in value of Joseph Holt plc.

Notices of compulsory acquisition under s 429(1) were sent to the remaining shareholders. Once notices are sent, the bidder is entitled to, and must, acquire the outstanding shareholdings under s 430(2).

A s 429(1) notice was sent to Winpar Holdings Ltd in Australia. The company objected on the ground that the notice was invalid since it had not received the offer documents.

The High Court ruled (later affirmed by the Court of Appeal) that the offer was to acquire all the shares as required by s 428. The fact that the offer was not communicated to a particular shareholder was not fatal to the offer and the subsequent proceedings under s 429(1). For the compulsory acquisition procedure to apply, it was necessary only that an offer for all the shares was made: it was not necessary that such an offer was received by or known to a particular shareholder. The offer made by Joseph Holt Group related to Winpar's shares, even though Winpar was not aware of it. The offer documentation was a general and not a limited process, and in addition the offer did not exclude the shares of those resident in Australia. The s 429(1) notice to Winpar was therefore valid and the compulsory purchase procedure applied to its shares.

Comment

Transfer of the acquired shares is effected by an instrument of transfer executed on behalf of the shareholder by a person appointed by the offeror (CA 2006, s 981).

Reverse acquisition

This is a takeover method used by a private company to go public without undertaking all the regulatory hurdles that going public usually requires. The private company acquires majority ownership in a publicly listed company that has no assets or liabilities (called a shell), changes the company's name, and installs its management and board of directors.

Directors' duties in a takeover by general offer

Suppose that in a bid situation the directors bargain for additional payments to themselves, what can the other shareholders do?

Apart from the provisions of the City Code, if the directors of B retire from office, 'golden handshakes' are covered by the Companies Acts and such sums are held in trust for those shareholders who sold their shares as a result of the offer, if the payments were not disclosed and approved by ordinary resolution of the members.

If they do not retire, the Companies Acts do not apply and additional payments made to directors are not recoverable. Thus if no change is made in the directorship but, for example, the board are paid £100,000 to persuade them to recommend the offer to the other shareholders, or are paid an increased price for their shares because they hold a large block, it seems there can be no recovery under the Acts.

It will be apparent, therefore, that there are situations in which the directors, in connection with a takeover bid, may receive additional payments without being liable to account for them under the statute.

The Code also applies and provides that unless the Panel consents the offeror, or persons acting in concert, may not make arrangements to deal or buy or sell shares of the offeree company during an offer or when one is in contemplation, if those arrangements have attached to them favourable conditions not being extended to all shareholders.

The City Code and the supervision of the Panel should in most cases prevent this occurring in the case of public companies but it could still occur in the case of private ones where in fact some of the worst abuses have occurred in the past. Where a private company is concerned or, in the case of a public company if the Panel is not effective, the most hopeful line, in terms of getting the money back from the directors, is to allege a breach of their fiduciary duties towards the company. The general equitable principle exemplified in *Regal (Hastings) Ltd* v *Gulliver*, 1942 (see Chapter 21 ○) could apply. However, the action is not straightforward because the wrong covered in that case is basically one to the company and payments made to directors to secure favourable recommendation to the shareholders in a bid situation seem merely to be a payment to them in their capacity as directors, no corporate action being involved, though the extra money received is, of course, an undisclosed benefit or profit from office and is recoverable by the company on the basis of a breach of fiduciary duty.

However, it is somewhat futile to allow the company to recover in cases where those who are really wronged are the other shareholders who have sold. The Companies Act provides that moneys paid as a result of retirement are held on trust for the shareholders but the judge-made equitable rules as seen in the *Regal* case do not necessarily extend to shareholders. Presumably, the s 175 CA 2006 which codifies the duties of a director to avoid conflicts of interest such as misuse of corporate opportunities for personal gain might now replace the general equitable principle stated in *Regal*.

Dealings in shares during offer period

Another problem which can arise if the directors have been offered incentives to recommend a bid is that the bid price for the shares may be lower than it should be. Where this is so, the offeror company (A) may, in order to enhance its chances of successful control, purchase shares in B on the market at a price higher than the bid price.

Since it is not desirable to fetter the market in shares, Rule 8.1 of the Code provides that dealings in relevant securities by the parties to a takeover and by any associates, for their own account, or the account of discretionary investment clients, must be disclosed daily to the Stock Exchange (Company Announcements Office), the Panel and the press (discretionary) not later than 12 noon on the business day following the date of the transaction. Such disclosures must state the total of all relevant securities of any offeror or the offeree company purchased or sold on any day during the offer period, in the market or otherwise, and the prices paid or received.

In this connection, Rule 6.2 provides that if the offeror or persons acting in concert purchase securities during the offer period at above the offer price, then it shall increase its offer to not less than the highest price paid for the securities so acquired. Rule 7.1 provides that an announcement of any such purchase and the consequent increased offer must be made immediately.

The Code provides that a person with a significant commercial interest in the outcome of an offer should not, without the consent of the Panel, deal in the shares of an offeror or an offeree company during an offer period.

Recent amendments and developments

The Code was amended on 14 January 2008 to cover transactions implemented by way of a scheme including the addition of a new Appendix 7 to the Code explaining how the provisions of the Code apply to schemes (and listing those which do not apply where a scheme is used). Rule 26 of the Code (documents on display) was amended on 25 January 2010 (among other things) to provide that all documents required by that Rule to be put on display should also be available for inspection on a website.

On 1 July 2009, legislation was put in place in Jersey, Guernsey and the Isle of Man, putting the Takeover Panel's regulation of takeovers and mergers of companies registered in those jurisdictions on a statutory footing. As a result, the Takeover Panel now has powers and duties in the Channel Islands and the Isle of Man equivalent to those imposed on and granted to it in the UK by the Companies Acts 2006.

Two important changes were made to the Code's disclosure rules which came into effect on 19 April 2010: (a) first, to require that a person subject to the Code's disclosure regime (including a person with a gross long interest of 1 per cent or more in any relevant securities of any party to an offer, other than a cash offeror) should disclose his long interests and short positions in relevant securities of an offeree company by no later than the tenth business day after the commencement of the offer period (and, in the case of a securities exchange offer, in relevant securities of the offeror by no later than the tenth business day after the announcement that first identifies it as an offeror), regardless of whether he has dealt in the relevant securities of the party concerned (the 'opening position disclosure' requirement); and (b) secondly, to require that a person who has a gross long interest of 1 per cent or more in any relevant securities of a party to an offer (other than a cash offeror) should disclose any dealing by him in any relevant securities of any party to the offer (other than a cash offeror) – i.e. not only dealings in relevant securities of the party to the offer in which he has a gross long interest of 1 per cent or more; and also that any person making a disclosure under the Code should disclose details of all his long interests and short positions in relevant securities of all parties to the offer (other than a cash offeror) – i.e. not only the party to the offer in whose relevant securities the dealing occurred (the 'extended composite disclosure' requirement).

Essay questions

1 In order to raise additional finance Devonia Trust plc, a holding company, intends to make a rights issue. Its subsidiaries have their own classes of share capital with different voting and dividend rights. With a view to simplifying the capital structure of the group it is proposed to exchange all the subsidiary companies' shares held by minority shareholders for ordinary shares in the holding company itself.

    Advise Devonia Trust plc as to how its objective could be achieved, the steps necessary to be taken and the implications of any such scheme.   *(University of Plymouth)*

2 Write notes on TWO of the following:

(a) promoters;

(b) redeemable shares;

(c) disqualification of directors;

(d) schemes of arrangement.   *(The Institute of Chartered Secretaries and Administrators)*

3 Zed Ltd wish to acquire the undertaking of a company which is in members' voluntary liquidation but still trading. Zed Ltd cannot afford cash for the purchase and suggest they should issue their own shares to the value required. How can this suggestion be implemented?
(The Institute of Chartered Accountants in England and Wales)

4 Beefy Farm Ltd was incorporated in 2005. Its articles of association appointed Peter and Richard as directors for life. The objects clause of the company's memorandum of association provided that the company should carry on the business of beef breeding with any other activities reasonably incidental thereto. The objects clause included a power to borrow money and a provision that no object or power should be deemed subsidiary to any other.

In November 2005 Beefy Farm Ltd unexpectedly received what appeared to be an attractive proposition from an Italian company to manufacture their ice cream under licence. The Italian company encouraged them to use the farm's milk in the manufacture. Beefy Farm Ltd borrowed £100,000 from National Bank plc to get started with the new business but subsequently refused to repay it on the ground that the loan was *ultra vires*.

(a) Advise National Bank plc on their legal position.

AND

(b) How far, if at all, would your answer to (a) differ if the bank had a copy of Beefy Farm Ltd's memorandum of association at the time of lending the money?

AND

(c) How far, if at all, would your answer to (a) differ if Richard alone negotiated the loan agreement and Peter knew nothing about it?   *(Glasgow Caledonian University)*

5 B Ltd held a general meeting including the following alterations to the articles which were duly passed:

(a) 'a member shall, upon the request of the board, transfer his shares to a person nominated by the board';

(b) 'a director shall vacate office upon the written request of all other directors';

(c) 'upon the death of a director his/her shares shall be forthwith registered in the name of his/her spouse or other next of kin notwithstanding any testamentary disposition to the contrary';

(d) 'a member wishing to sell his shares shall inform the directors who shall buy them at a fair valuation made by the auditors'.

Henry has been a director for five years and was appointed by the articles. He has no service contract, but the articles appointed him for life. He has been asked to resign under (b) above.

John, who holds 1,000 shares, and is also a shareholder in a rival company with which he now trades (having formerly traded with B Ltd), has been requested under (a) above to transfer his shares to Alice, the daughter of one of the directors.

Sally is executor of Jim, a deceased director who by his will bequeathed his shares to his daughter Lyn. The board has refused to transfer his shares to Lyn saying they have been registered under (c) above in the name of Rebecca, Jim's widow, from whom he had been separated but not divorced for 40 years.

Vera has informed the board that she wishes to sell her shares, but two months have elapsed and the board has taken no action at all.

Advise Henry, John, Sally and Vera of any legal remedies which may be open to them.

(Kingston University)

Test your knowledge

Four alternative answers are given. Select ONE only. Circle the answer which you consider to be correct. Check your answers by referring back to the information given in the chapter and against the answers at the end of the text.

1 Thames plc is in financial difficulties and wants its debenture holders to exchange their debentures for shares in order to get rid of the requirement to pay interest on the debentures. How should Thames proceed?

   A Under s 110 of the Insolvency Act 1986.
   B Under s 895 of the Companies Act 2006.
   C By a reduction of capital.
   D By unilaterally altering the terms of issue of the debentures.

2 Developer plc wishes to take over Hotels Ltd in order to develop the sites on which various hotels belonging to Hotels Ltd stand as supermarkets. Developer's bid is likely to be accepted by a majority of Hotels' shareholders. The directors of Hotels Ltd have sold the various hotels to a subsidiary of Hotels Ltd and taken a lease back off them. The lease restricts the use of the various premises to the hotel business. Developer has now withdrawn its bid. What is the position of the directors of Hotels Ltd?

   A They are only in breach of the 'proper purpose rule'.
   B They are not in breach of any fiduciary duty.
   C They are in breach of the 'proper purpose rule' and the City Code.
   D They are liable for breach of warranty of authority.

3 Tay plc is to make a bid for shares in Uncle plc. If the bid is successful it will result in Tay holding 20 per cent of the shares in Uncle. What is the position under the City Code?

   A The Panel must consent and will normally do so.
   B There is no need for the Panel to be involved.
   C The Panel must consent and is unlikely to do so.
   D The City Code does not allow this sort of bid.

4 Toys plc is in financial difficulties. Cycles plc is prepared to inject new capital into Toys, which when completed will leave Cycles with 35 per cent of the share capital of Toys. What is the position under the City Code?

   A Cycles is required to make a bid for the rest of Toys' shares.
   B The City Code provides for rescue bids to go through without recourse to the Panel.

c The City Code is not concerned with rescue bids.

D The Panel may in the case of a rescue bid waive the normal requirements for a mandatory bid.

5 Fred, a financier, has made a personal bid for the equity shares of Brick plc. He has acquired 92 per cent of the shares in Brick and intends to compulsorily acquire the rest. What is the legal position?

A Fred will be able compulsorily to acquire the shares under the Companies Act 2006.

B Fred cannot compulsorily acquire the shares under the Companies Act 2006 because he did not get 95 per cent.

c There are no legal provisions which allow compulsory acquisition.

D The compulsory acquisition provisions of the Companies Act 2006 do not apply in this situation.

6 Before incorporation of a company called Alfredo Ltd its promoter, Mostyn, made a contract on behalf of the company. Who will be liable if the contract is not performed by Alfredo Ltd?

A Alfredo Ltd.

B Mostyn.

c The directors of Alfredo Ltd.

D The shareholders of Alfredo Ltd.

Answers to test your knowledge questions appear on p. 645.

Suggested further reading

Boardman, 'What the takeover directive means for the UK' (2006) *International Financial Law Review* 25, 174.

Mejucq, 'The European regime on takeovers' (2006) *European Company & Financial Law Review* 3, 222.

Walters, 'Corporate restructuring under schedule B1 of the Insolvency Act 1986' (2005) *Company Lawyer* 26, 97.

27

Corporate insolvency – company rescue

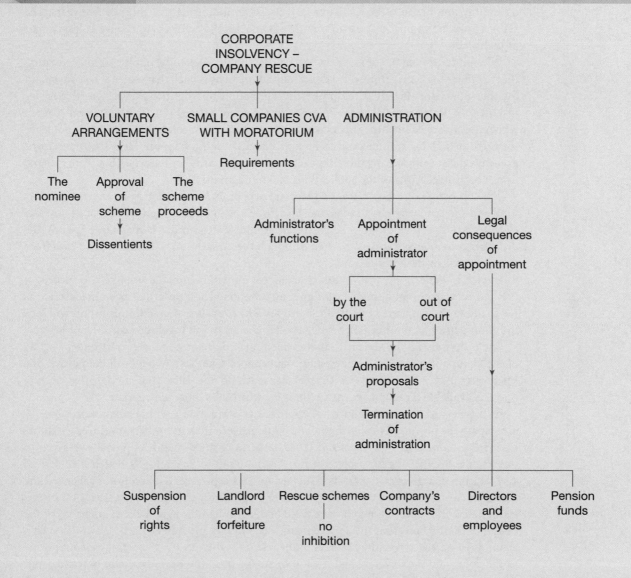

I n this chapter we shall consider those aspects of insolvency law which are designed to rescue the company and prevent winding-up.

Voluntary arrangements

Sections 1 to 7 of the Insolvency Act 1986 provide for a type of voluntary arrangement which is concerned to prevent a company from being wound up. In general terms, a company voluntary arrangement (CVA) is a contract made between the company and its creditors. The contract freezes the existing debts at an agreed date. The company carries on trading and pays a monthly amount into the CVA over an agreed period, usually of three to five years. The CVA allows the company to go on trading but enables the creditors to receive at least a part of their debt.

When interpreting the terms of a CVA contract, courts generally opt for an interpretation that supports the CVA. However, a court may adopt an approach that may not be convenient for the supervisors if that is the proper interpretation of what the parties agreed. See, for instance, *In Re Energy Holdings (No 3) Ltd (In Liquidation)* [2010] EWHC 788 (Ch) in which the court held that the supervisors must apply the terms of the CVA and thus not leave the creditor's claim in limbo and lacking an effective right of appeal. Here the supervisors' excessive delay from leaving these claims unadjudicated cost them dearly! They were ordered to pay both sides' costs of the applications on an indemnity basis.

The company's directors can initiate formal proposals for a voluntary arrangement at any time and the company need not actually be insolvent though it often will be, or at any rate close to it. Once a winding-up begins or an administration order is made (see below), the directors can no longer initiate a scheme, though the initiative may come in such a case from the liquidator or the administrator.

In fact, in general terms a voluntary arrangement will be much more likely to succeed if it is put forward by an administrator after an administration order has been made since as we shall see the suspension of creditors' rights which occurs in an administration will give the administrator/nominee (see below) a better chance to put together a considered scheme.

The proposals will be similar to those which must be referred to the court under Part 26 of the Companies Act 2006, e.g. creditors agreeing to take, say, 50 pence in the pound. The Insolvency Act 1986 provides a simpler approach to the 2006 Act, though that section remains available for major reconstructions for which it is more appropriate.

In this regard, the High Court has approved as a voluntary arrangement a proposal by a company to pay nil pence in the pound to its preferential and other unsecured creditors (see *IRC v Adams and Partners Ltd* [1999] 2 BCLC 730). Creditor approval was given to the scheme because it gave a better return to the Bank of Scotland plc which held a fixed and floating charge over the assets. The Revenue, as a preferential creditor, challenged the arrangement on the basis that it was not an arrangement permitted by the 1986 Act but its claim failed. The Revenue might have fared better if it had brought a claim under s 6 of the 1986 Act on the basis that the arrangement was 'unfairly prejudicial' to it. However, such a claim must be brought within 28 days of the results of the creditors' meeting being reported to the court and the Revenue had left it too late for this. The Revenue could only challenge it on the basis that it was an arrangement of a type not permitted by the Act, and on this contention the Revenue failed.

Re NT Gallagher Ltd [2002] EWCA Civ 404

S and H, the liquidators of N, appealed against the decision of the judge ([2002] 1 BCLC 224) giving directions in relation to a company voluntary arrangement, CVA. The issue for determination was whether trusts created by a CVA in relation to a company were brought to an end by the termination of the CVA through the company going into liquidation.

Held – allowing the appeal in part, that where a CVA or an individual voluntary arrangement provided for money or assets to be paid to, or held for the benefit of, the respective creditors, a trust was created for those creditors and the subsequent liquidation of a company or bankruptcy of an individual, although bringing the voluntary arrangement to an end, would not terminate the trust created under it unless there was specific provision in the voluntary arrangement for such termination. If the trust continued, the creditors of the voluntary arrangement would be entitled to prove in the liquidation or bankruptcy for so much of their debts as remained after payment of what had been or would be recovered under the trust.

The nominee

The directors must appoint a nominee, though in an administration or liquidation the administrator or liquidator will act as nominee. The nominee must be an authorised licensed insolvency practitioner.

Certain professional bodies recognised by the Secretary of State for Business, Innovation and Skills (Secretary of State) may authorise their members to act as insolvency practitioners. The bodies currently recognised for England and Wales are: The Chartered Association of Certified Accountants, The Insolvency Practitioners Association, The Institute of Chartered Accountants in England and Wales, and The Law Society. Persons not authorised by a professional body may apply to the Secretary of State for authorisation. The relevant professional association is the Insolvency Practitioners Association.

In this connection, s 4 of the Insolvency Act 2000 authorises persons other than licensed insolvency practitioners (IPs) to act as nominees or supervisors of company (or individual) voluntary arrangements, provided that such persons are members of bodies that are recognised by the Secretary of State. The change seems designed to let in members of bodies such as the R3, the Association of Business Recovery Professionals, and other turnaround specialists and maybe to provide more competition in the market where there are only some 1,200 IPs at present taking appointments.

The nominee will investigate the scheme and report to the court, within 28 days after he is given notice of the proposed scheme, as to whether the scheme is likely to be viable so that meetings of members and creditors should be called to approve it. If the nominee is already an administrator or liquidator, there is no need to report to the court. Unless the court orders otherwise, where a report is made to it, the nominee will order meetings of creditors and members to be called to consider the proposals for a voluntary arrangement and to approve it.

In order to assist him with his report, he is entitled to a statement of affairs from the directors. Where a nominee is required to report to the court, he must state in his report whether in his opinion the proposed company voluntary arrangement (CVA) has a reasonable prospect of being approved and implemented (Insolvency Act 2000, Sch 2). As we have seen, such a report is not necessary where the nominee is an administrator or liquidator.

Approval of scheme: by members and creditors

Approval requires a simple majority in value of the members voting in person or by proxy (or by written resolution) and a three-quarters majority in value of creditors voting in person or by proxy at a creditors' meeting. Every creditor of the company of whose claim and address the nominee is aware is entitled to attend.

A resolution will fail if at the creditors' meeting more than half in value of the creditors who are not connected with the company, i.e. who are not director creditors or directors' relatives who are creditors, vote against it.

If the meetings approve the arrangement, it becomes binding on all ordinary creditors, but not on preferred or secured creditors, unless they agree, who can pursue their claims against the company.

In *Re Cancol Ltd* [1996] 1 BCLC 100 the High Court decided that a person who was entitled to a future or contingently payable debt such as future payments of rent to fall due under an existing lease was a 'creditor' for the purposes of insolvency legislation and was bound by a company voluntary arrangement approved at a meeting of creditors of which he had notice and at which he was entitled to vote.

The approval of the scheme is reported to the court which may discharge an administration order or a winding-up order.

The decision in *Re Cancol* (1996) is now reinforced by the Insolvency Act 2000 which provides that a CVA will bind all of the company's creditors, including unknown creditors, who are then able to claim from the company only the dividends they would have received if they had come to light after the CVA had been completed. Such creditors may also make an application to the court on the ground that their interests are unfairly prejudiced by the voluntary arrangement that is approved (see Sch 2, paras 6 and 7). Preferential creditors retain their priority, of course, and secured creditors will rely on their security unless they have consented to surrender it to the company and become ordinary creditors when the above provisions of the IA 2000 will apply if, for example, they fail to attend a meeting and vote even where no notice was given.

The case of *Mourant & Co Trustees Ltd* v *Sixty (UK) Ltd* [2010] BCC 82 should also be noted. In this instance a landlord had leased two retail properties to a company, whose liabilities were guaranteed by its parent company. A subsequent company voluntary arrangement was set aside as it was unfairly prejudicial to the interests of the landlord as the effect of the CVA was to release the parent company from all liability under the guarantees.

Mourant & Co Trustees Ltd v *Sixty (UK) Ltd* [2010] BCC 82

The applicant landlords (M) applied for the revocation of a creditors' meeting to approve a company voluntary arrangement (CVA) proposed by the respondent tenants (S) and their administrators. S had leased two retail properties from M. S's liabilities were guaranteed by its Italian parent company (X). S went into administration and a CVA was prepared. The effect of the CVA was to release X from all liability under the guarantees upon payment of a sum of £300,000 to M. The sum was said to represent 100 per cent of S's estimated liability to M on a surrender of the leases. The effect was that M were ostensibly to receive full compensation on the basis of a notional surrender of the leases, but they were to be deprived of any recourse against X as guarantor during the remainder of the leases, which had approximately seven and a half years to run. Under the terms of the CVA all creditors, with the exception of M and landlords of two other closed stores, would be paid in full. M applied under the Insolvency Act 1986 s 6(1) for the revocation of the CVA. M submitted that the CVA was unfairly prejudicial to their interests as creditors of S. Application granted.

(1) On a vertical comparison, in liquidation M would still have had the benefit of the guarantees for the remainder of the term of the leases. The contractual rights were of obvious commercial value to M and formed an important part of the consideration for the package of incentives negotiated with S. Neither S nor X could unilaterally alter any of those contractual provisions and, but for the CVA, it would have been open to M to continue to enforce the guarantees against X. It was unreasonable and unfair in principle to require M to give up their guarantees, *Prudential Assurance Co Ltd* v *PRG Powerhouse Ltd* [2007] EWHC 1002 (Ch), [2007] Bus. LR 1771 applied.

(2) Even if that conclusion was wrong, the sum of £300,000 was inappropriate as, on the evidence, a sum in the region of £1 million was the least that could fairly be regarded as appropriate. The sum of £300,000 was not a genuine estimate but was dictated to the administrators by X, who stood to benefit from the release of the guarantees. The administrators appeared to have abdicated their responsibilities as office holders and put forward a proposal for the CVA, which they must have known could not be objectively justified, *Sisu Capital Fund Ltd* v *Tucker* [2005] EWHC 2170 (Ch), [2006] BCC 463 considered.

(3) On a horizontal comparison, there was no sufficient justification for the difference between the treatment of M and other creditors.

(4) The purpose of the CVA was to compel M to give up their rights for a fraction of their value and to improve the group's negotiating position by forcing M either to accept the CVA or to embark on lengthy and expensive proceedings to set it aside. It was the duty of administrators, or other office holders, in such circumstances to maintain an independent stance, to act in good faith, and only to propose a CVA if they were satisfied that it would not unfairly prejudice the interests of any creditor, member or contributory of the company. Accordingly, the CVA was fatally flawed and had to be set aside.

It is an offence under the IA 2000 for an officer of a company to try to obtain approval of the members or creditors to a proposed CVA by making a false representation or fraudulently doing or failing to do anything (Sch 2, paras 8 and 12). The nominee or supervisor is required under para 10 of Sch 2 to report suspected offences to the Secretary of State. The Secretary of State is granted powers to investigate such suspected offences (para 10).

Dissentients

Dissenting members and creditors may apply to the court to set aside the scheme on the grounds of unfair prejudice or material irregularity. This must be done within 28 days of the nominee reporting the approval of the scheme to the court. The time limit cannot be extended.

The High Court considered the phrase 'material irregularity' in *In re Trident Fashions plc* [2004] *The Times*, 23 April. The application was brought against the company's three joint administrators and the company which employed them. The material irregularity relied on was the failure by one of the administrators to disclose to the meeting the existence of certain offers to purchase the company. It appeared that at the meeting the administrator concerned mentioned only one formal offer without saying that there had been two other offers as well. The judge concluded from this that there had been a relevant irregularity. However, the decision of the Court of Appeal in *Cadbury Schweppes plc* v *Somji* [2001] 1 WLR 615 had to be looked at. It laid down a test in this sort of case which was that if the truth had been told at the meeting it would be likely to have made a material difference to the way in which the creditors would have assessed the terms of the proposed voluntary arrangement: was there a substantial chance that the creditors would not have approved the arrangement? The fact that the meeting might have been adjourned for a few days was not enough. The judge said that in the circumstances it was unlikely that the meeting would have been adjourned but even if it had been adjourned for a few days there was no real prospect that it would have affected the approval of the voluntary arrangement. On the matter of omission of material at the meeting the court could interfere with the arrangement only if the omission was one which no reasonable practitioner would have made. The creditors' application was dismissed.

Approval by creditors only

A decision by the creditors' meeting to approve a proposed CVA will prevail where this conflicts with the decision made by a meeting of the company, subject to the right of a member to challenge this on an application to the court (Insolvency Act 2000, Sch 2, para 5).

If the scheme proceeds

If the scheme proceeds beyond the above stages, the nominee becomes the supervisor and implements the scheme. At any stage in the implementation of the scheme, and as it proceeds, the creditors can challenge the supervisor's decisions in front of the court and, equally, the supervisor may ask the court for directions.

Subsequent liquidation

In *Re Arthur Rathbone Kitchens Ltd* [1997] 2 BCLC 280 the High Court ruled that s 84 of the Insolvency Act 1986 (circumstances in which a company may be wound up voluntarily) allowed members of the company to resolve that the company be wound up voluntarily even though the directors had proposed an approved voluntary arrangement that was still in progress or capable of fulfilment or not, even though this might mean that the members had broken the terms of the arrangement.

Here the decision of the High Court in *Re Brelec Installations Ltd* (2000) *The Times*, 18 April, is of interest. BI had entered into a 'trading out' voluntary arrangement whereby regular payments of a set amount were paid to the supervisors over a fixed period. Some six months later the company failed to pay its debts as they fell due and later went into liquidation. The issue between the supervisors and liquidator was the monies paid by the company to the supervisors prior to the liquidation. Was it available to the supervisors or the liquidator? The court ruled in favour of the supervisors. It was not appropriate to scrutinise the company's trading to determine when default first occurred so as to pinpoint the date from which payments to the supervisors were to be regarded as held for the benefit of the company rather than for the arrangement. The monies received by the supervisors prior to the liquidation remained subject to the trusts of the voluntary arrangement.

The High Court also ruled in *Re Kudos Glass Ltd (in liquidation)* [2001] 1 BCLC 390 that sums held by the supervisor of a creditors' voluntary arrangement are in the event of a compulsory winding-up order made in regard to a non-CVA debt held by the supervisor on trust solely for the CVA creditors. The court ruled that if the petitioner had been the supervisor or a CVA creditor, it would have found that the petitioner had elected to end the scheme and the funds would be transferred to the liquidator.

Small companies: a CVA with a moratorium option

The following provisions of the Insolvency Act 2000 are relevant. Section 1 introduces Sch 1 to the Act, which makes the option of applying for a short moratorium of 28 days available to a small company where its directors intend to put a proposal to the company's creditors for a company voluntary arrangement.

Small companies are not obliged to use this procedure but can proceed under the standard procedure if they wish.

Eligible companies

To be eligible a company must satisfy *two* or more of the conditions for being a small company within s 247(3) of the CA 1985 (repealed and replaced by Companies Act 2006, ss 382 and 465 consolidating). Certain other companies that are involved in financial markets where the modifications to former law are designed to ensure that financial markets continue to function in the event of the insolvency of one of the participants are also included. Those ineligible are companies that are subject to formal insolvency proceedings, as where a winding-up is in progress, or where in the previous 12 months a moratorium has failed.

Nominee's statement

Directors who want a moratorium must provide information to the nominee as follows:

- a document setting out the terms of the proposed CVA;
- a document giving details of the company's assets, debts and other liabilities, together with any other information that the nominee may request.

Given that the nominee considers that the proposal has a reasonable prospect of success in terms of being approved and implemented and that sufficient funding is available and that meetings of the company and creditors should be held, he must provide the directors with a statement to that effect. In reaching conclusions, the nominee may rely on the information provided by the directors unless he has reason to believe it may be inaccurate.

Documents to be submitted to the court

In order to obtain a moratorium, the directors must file certain documents with the court. These are set out in Sch 1, para 7 and include the terms of the proposed CVA and a statement of the company's affairs.

Duration of moratorium

Schedule 1, para 8 deals with this and provides that the moratorium will come into force when the documents referred to above are filed with the court. The maximum initial moratorium is 28 days. This period can be extended or reduced by order of the Secretary of State. A meeting of the company and creditors held within the initial period may decide to extend the moratorium by up to a further two months. The Secretary of State may by order increase or decrease that period of two months. The moratorium may be brought to an end by a decision of the meetings of creditors and company to approve a CVA. Alternatively, it may be brought to an end:

- by the court;
- by the nominee's withdrawal of his consent to act;
- by a decision of meetings of creditors and the company other than to approve a CVA;

- at the end of the 28-day minimum period if *both* of the first meetings of the company and creditors have not taken place;
- if there is no decision of the above meetings to extend it.

Notification of the beginning of the moratorium

The directors have a duty to inform the nominee that a moratorium has come into force. When a moratorium comes into force and when it ends, the nominee must advertise that fact and notify the Registrar of Companies and the company. When the moratorium comes into force, he must also notify any creditor who has petitioned for a winding-up and, when it ends, any creditor of whose claim he is aware.

Effect of moratorium on creditors

Except for an 'excepted petition', i.e. a petition by the Secretary of State that winding-up is in the public interest under s 124A of the IA 1986, no petition to wind up the company can be commenced nor can any other insolvency proceedings. No steps may be taken to enforce any security over the company's property or repossess any goods in the company's possession under any hire-purchase agreement, nor can any other proceedings, execution or other legal process be commenced or continued, or distraint, e.g. by a landlord, be levied. No meeting of the company may be held or requisitioned without the consent of the nominee or of the court.

Winding-up petitions presented prior to the moratorium are stayed during the period but not 'public policy' petitions which continue unaffected.

Section 127 of the IA 1986 rendering void dispositions of the company's property after presentation of a winding-up petition does not apply.

Securities given during the moratorium

These are unenforceable unless given with reasonable grounds that they would benefit the company.

Company invoices

All invoices and orders and letters where the name of the company appears must give the name of the nominee and state that a moratorium is in force. The officers of the company commit an offence if this provision is breached in the absence of reasonable excuse.

Obtaining credit

During the moratorium the company may not obtain credit to the value of £250 or more without first telling the person giving the credit that a moratorium is in force. This includes payments in advance for the supply of goods and services. There are criminal penalties on the company's officers for breach.

Disposals and payments

While the moratorium is in force the company may only dispose of any of its property or pay a debt that existed at the start of the moratorium if there are reasonable grounds for believing that it will benefit the company and the moratorium committee gives approval. If there is no committee, approval must be given by the nominee. There is nothing to prevent the sale of property in the ordinary course of business as where, for example, a farming supplies company sells a tractor as part of its retail trade. Again, officers of the company commit an offence on breach.

Disposal of charged property

The Schedule allows the disposal by the company during the moratorium of charged property and any goods in its possession under an HP agreement, provided the holder of the security or the owner agrees. The holder of a fixed charge and the owner of goods on HP are entitled to have the proceeds of sale applied to repayment of the loan or debt but the holder of a floating charge retains a charge of equal priority to his original charge over the proceeds of the sale or disposal of the charged property.

Monitoring of company's activities

The Schedule imposes a duty on the nominee to monitor the company's affairs during the moratorium in order to form a judgment as to the viability of a CVA and the company's ability to carry on during the moratorium. The directors have a duty to provide the nominee with information.

Withdrawal of consent to act by nominee

The Schedule provides that a nominee may withdraw his consent to act if:

- he considers that the CVA proposal (or modifications communicated to him) no longer has a reasonable prospect of being approved or implemented; or
- he considers that the company has insufficient funds now and during the moratorium to enable it to continue in business throughout the moratorium; or
- he becomes aware that on the date of filing the company was not eligible for a moratorium; or
- the directors are not providing him with relevant information on request.

On withdrawal of the nominee's consent, the moratorium ends. The above are the only grounds on which the nominee may withdraw his consent and he must give notice to various parties, i.e. the court, the Registrar of Companies, the company and creditors of whom he is aware. He commits an offence by not doing so.

Challenging the nominee's actions

Any creditor, director or member of the company or any other person affected by the moratorium who is not satisfied by any decision or act of the nominee may apply to the court for relief. The court may confirm, reverse or modify any such decision or act and give directions to the nominee or make any order it sees fit either during or after the moratorium.

Where the acts of the nominee have caused the company loss and the company appears not to be taking any action, creditors may apply to the court which, if it thinks that the acts of the nominee were unreasonable, may order the company to make a claim against the nominee or authorise a creditor to do so.

Replacement of the nominee by the court

Where it is, for example, impracticable or inappropriate for the nominee to continue, the court may direct that the nominee be replaced by a qualified person who consents.

Summoning of meetings and their conduct

Schedule 1, paras 27 and 28 deal with this and provide, among other things, that the nominee may call meetings of creditors and of the company whenever he sees fit.

These meetings decide whether or not to approve the proposed CVA with or without modification. These modifications may not affect the rights of secured creditors or preferential creditors unless they consent.

Moratorium committee

In a case where the moratorium is extended, there is provision for the setting up of a moratorium committee to exercise functions conferred on it by the meetings referred to above. The meetings must approve an estimate of the committee expenses.

Members and creditors: conflicting decisions

If the decisions of the members and creditors are conflicting, the decision of the creditors prevails but a member may apply to the court for an order that the members' decision should prevail.

Effect of the CVA

The CVA, when approved, binds all creditors of the company including unknown creditors. That includes those creditors who, having followed the insolvency rules, were not served with notice of the relevant meeting(s). Such persons can apply to the court on the grounds of unfair prejudice and the court may, for example, revoke or suspend the approval of the CVA. Otherwise, these creditors are entitled to the dividends payable under the arrangement only. On approval of the CVA, the nominee becomes the supervisor.

Challenge of directors' actions during the moratorium

Any member or creditor can apply to the court for relief on the grounds that the directors are acting in a way unfairly prejudicial to the interests of creditors or members. The court may make an order regulating matters or bring the moratorium to an end. This form of action applies in relation to the acts of directors during the moratorium. The application may be made during or after the moratorium. If made afterwards, the court's order will be to regulate matters and obviously not to bring the moratorium to an end.

Offences by officers of the company

The Schedule provides that if during the 12 months prior to the start of the moratorium an officer of the company has committed certain acts, e.g. fraudulently removed the company's property worth £500 or more or falsified the company's records in relation to its property, he commits an offence, as does an officer who so acts during the moratorium.

It is also an offence for an officer of the company to try to obtain a moratorium or an extension of it by making false statements or fraudulently doing or not doing anything.

Void provisions in floating charge documents

Schedule 1 provides that any provision in a floating charge is invalid if the charge is to crystallise (and therefore become a fixed charge) on the obtaining of, or any action to obtain, a moratorium.

The remainder of the Schedule makes consequential amendments to various parts of the IA 1986, e.g. so that suppliers of gas, water and electricity are not permitted to require a nominee to pay outstanding debts for supply as a condition for supply during the moratorium. There is also a provision that the relevant date for determining preferential claims is the date on which the moratorium comes into force.

Trading with companies that are in a CVA

It is not unusual for creditors to carry on trading with a CVA company. Any new debts will not be covered by the CVA and become, in effect, new liabilities of the CVA company. There are, of course, some concerns about a continuation of trade since, if the company cannot meet its CVA requirements, it will almost certainly be forced into liquidation and the new liabilities, if not paid, may not be met. Set out below are some precautions that a creditor can take in such circumstances:

- where goods are supplied a retention of title clause could be used in the contract of supply to ensure that the seller retains ownership of the goods until they are paid for and if they are still in stock;
- the contract of sale could require cash on delivery;
- an attempt should be made to obtain personal guarantees of the new liabilities from the directors;
- ascertain from the CVA supervisor whether or not the company is up to date with its payments under the CVA;
- it is obviously not wise to carry on trading on the old terms; the terms of trade should be renegotiated.

Following the implementation of the Insolvency (Amendment) Rules 2010, Companies House prescribes the use of the following Insolvency forms within Registrar's Rules for the first time. The forms listed below are to be filed with the Registrar, for all corporate voluntary arrangements:

1 Notice to Registrar of Companies of voluntary arrangement taking effect;
2 Notice to Registrar of Companies of order of revocation or suspension of voluntary arrangement;
3 Notice to Registrar of Companies of supervisor's progress report; and
4 Notice to Registrar of Companies of completion or termination of voluntary arrangement.

The initiation or termination of insolvency procedures involving a European company (SE), or any decision to continue operating the SE, must be notified to Companies House on Form SE WU01.

Administration

The current law concerning administration was introduced with effect from 15 September 2003. Under this regime, a company will usually be described as being 'in administration' – under the old regime a company would be described as subject to an 'administration order'.

Administrator's functions

The functions of an administrator are now contained in Insolvency Act 1986, Sch B1, para 3 (as inserted by Enterprise Act 2002 Part 10). The administrator now has the function of carrying out a single statutory purpose, that is:

- to rescue the company as a going concern;
- if this is not reasonably practicable, to achieve a better result for the company's creditors as a whole than would be likely if the company were wound up (without first being in administration) – an example would be to allow the company to trade on in administration for long enough to complete a large order; or

● if neither of the above is reasonably practicable and the administrator does not unnecessarily harm the interests of the creditors as a whole, realising the company's property to make a distribution to one or more secured or preferential creditors. Nevertheless, even if there are insufficient funds to pay unsecured creditors the administrator must not unnecessarily harm their interests.

Schedule 1 gives an administrator full management powers which are not available to a liquidator. The case of *Re Consumer and Industrial Press Ltd* [1988] BCLC 177, made under previous legislation, gives an example of the second aspect of the single statutory purpose. The company had since 1949 published a magazine. Net liabilities were judged by accountants to be too great to trade out of trouble. The Inland Revenue petitioned for a compulsory winding-up but the directors asked the court to make an administration order which the court did. Administrators were appointed to manage the company so that at least one more issue of the magazine could be published. The court thought that the company might be saved by a voluntary arrangement which an administrator may propose but even if not it would get a better price for the title if publication continued than if it were sold in a liquidation. This would obviously be to the benefit of creditors.

Comment The expression 'unnecessarily harming' the interests of the creditors as a whole is not defined and its practical effect is not clear. Presumably if the secured creditors wanted an immediate sale of the secured assets (bearing in mind that in the developed future they will not be able to appoint an administrative receiver) but the administrator takes the view that the market is rising giving a better future realisation for the creditors as a whole, would an immediate sale unnecessarily harm the interests of the creditors as a whole? If the administrator had insufficient funds to carry on the administration and so had to sell the assets presumably he would be in the clear. We may see more applications to the court by administrators seeking the court's assistance. The court will, however, be reluctant it seems to interfere with what is, in the end, a business decision (see *T & D Industries plc* [2000] 1 All ER 333: comments made in that case).

Appointment of an administrator by the court

The Enterprise Act 2002 retains with some minor modifications the court route into administration. The court route can be used by the company (by ordinary resolution of the members or a unanimous written resolution), by the directors (by a majority decision at a board meeting or by a unanimous written resolution) or by one or more creditors with no minimum value of debt. A holder of a floating charge must be able to satisfy the requirements of a 'qualifying floating charge'. The most usual applicants for an administration order are the company's directors.

The qualifying floating charge

The requirements are set out in Enterprise Act 2002, Sch 16 which inserts Sch B1 to the IA 1986. Under para 14 of Sch B1:

(i)   A qualifying floating charge (QFC) must be created by an instrument that:
   ● states that para 14 applies to the floating charge;
   ● purports to empower the holder to appoint an administrator; or
   ● purports to empower the holder to appoint an administrative receiver.

Note: even those pre-Enterprise Act 2002 floating charges that give power to appoint an administrative receiver will thus give power to apply for an administration order.

(ii) A person will be regarded as holding a qualifying floating charge if he holds one or more debentures of the company secured:

- by a qualifying floating charge that relates to the whole or substantially the whole of the company's property;
- by a number of QFCs that together relate to the whole or substantially the whole of the company's property; or
- by charges (including fixed charges) which together relate to the whole or substantially the whole of the company's property and at least one of which is a QFC.

What is required to satisfy the court in making the order?

The court must be satisfied that the company is, or is likely to become, unable to pay its debts and that the order is reasonably likely to achieve the purpose of administration. A qualifying floating charge holder (QFCH) need only show that the charge is enforceable.

The process is initiated by filing a prescribed form of application with the court. There is no requirement for what was known as a 'Rule 2.2 Report' in support of the application. This form of application replaces the former procedure by petition. The matter of the company's insolvency and whether the order, if made, reasonably achieves the purpose of the administration is expressed in a single-page statement from the proposed administrator. This replaces the old Rule 2.2 Report. The application must be served on the holder of any QFC.

If others apply to the court for an order can a QFCH intervene?

A QFCH can intervene and appoint an administrative receiver (if entitled to do so) or administrator or make a request that a person specified by the QFCH be appointed administrator in the application (see IA 1986, Sch B1, para 36). The court may accept or refuse the QFCH's nominee as administrator (see IA 1986, Sch B1, para 36(2)). In practice the court is unlikely to refuse, especially where the QFCH has chosen an insolvency practitioner from one of the large accountancy firms. However, in this connection the High Court ruling in *Re Colt Telecom Ltd* (20 December 2002, unreported), HC is of interest, though not based specifically on the Enterprise Act 2002 provisions. In the case, Jacob J refused to make an administration order because the company was not actually in default to the creditor who was applying to the court. Nevertheless, he went on to say that even if he had had jurisdiction to make the order he would not have done so because the accountant who had made the report to the court in connection with the order was not impartial – he would stand to gain significantly in fees if his report was accepted and he was appointed administrator.

Furthermore, there was a potential conflict of interest in that the firm involved had previously given the company tax advice. The judge also stated that the appointment of an administrator who lacked specialised knowledge of the telecoms industry which was possessed by the company's management would 'almost certainly stop the business in its tracks' and would increase its running costs.

Comment The judge's comments may become highly relevant in regard to challenges to the appointment of administrators under IA 1986, Sch B1, para 36.

Are there any special features in an application to the court by a QFCH?

A QFCH can make an application to the court for an administration order without having to show that the company is, or is likely to become, unable to pay its debts (IA 1986, Sch B1, para 35).

The court must, however, be satisfied that the floating charge is a QFC and has become enforceable. The court may also make an administration order on the application of a QFCH, even where the company is in compulsory liquidation so that the administration takes over.

It is also now open for *any* liquidator to make application to the court for the discharge of the liquidation and the appointment of an administrator.

The fact that creditors object to the making of an administration order is not necessarily a bar. In **Structures and Computers Ltd** v **Ansys Inc** (1997) *The Times*, 3 October the High Court held that where it is satisfied that there is a real prospect of an administration order achieving one or more of its purposes, the court has a jurisdiction to make the order under s 8 of the Insolvency Act 1986 despite the fact that it is opposed by more than half of the company's unsecured creditors.

Notice of application for order

Notice of the application must be given to any person entitled to appoint a QFCH who may intervene (see above).

Notification of appointment

An administrator must:

- advertise the court order of his appointment in the *London Gazette* and in a newspaper circulating in the area where the company has its principal place of business; and
- send a copy of the court order to the Registrar of Companies within seven days with the appropriate forms.

The *Gazette* is published by the Stationery Office, and these notices are included in the *Company Law Official Notifications Supplement* to the *Gazette* which is published on micro-fiche. Copies may be seen at Companies House search rooms and some of the larger public libraries have copies.

Statements in support of an administration order: restriction orders

Under the Insolvency Rules 1986 Rule 2.2, a petition for an administration order was supported by a report of an independent person to the effect that the appointment of an administrator for the company is expedient. This report could be inspected by creditors and members of the company concerned under Rule 7.31. The report might contain sensitive material and so the court could, under Rule 7.31(5), make an order restricting inspection of the whole or part of the report. The same problems may now apply to the shorter statement by the would-be administrator. Application may be made by the Official Receiver or an insolvency practitioner or any other person having an interest. Under a Practice Direction issued in April 2002 (see [2002] 3 All ER 95) the High Court stated that good reason must be shown for a restriction order otherwise it will not be made. The statement lists as appropriate grounds for a restriction order: information about the perceived market for any assets of the company which it is anticipated could be sold in the administration or the period for which it is anticipated that trading of the company would be continued by any administrator and the prospects for such trading.

The business application This occurs where, for example, the directors of a company are seeking an administration order and have a supporting statement. They may wish to ensure that their legal and other advisers address the matter of a restriction order on matters that the directors think are sensitive at what is after all *a very early stage* in the proceedings.

Appointment of an administrator out of court

Out of court appointments may be made by qualified floating charge holders and by the company or its directors. Ordinary creditors must seek an appointment through the court. The requirements are as follows:

(a) Appointment by a QFCH

A QFCH must give two business days' written notice to any prior QFCH. This notice is not required if the relevant QFCH has consented to the making of the appointment.

This notice of intention to appoint may be filed in court but this is optional.

What must be filed in court following appointment? The QFCH must file in court:

(i)   a notice of appointment;
(ii) a statutory declaration by the appointing QFCH that:
- he is a QFCH;
- the floating charge was enforceable when the appointment was made;
- the appointment accords with the requirements of Insolvency Act 1986, Sch B1.

There must also be filed:

(iii) a statement by the administrator that:
- he consents to the appointment;
- the purpose of the administration is reasonably likely to be achieved.

When is the appointment effective? The appointment takes effect once the above filing requirements have been satisfied. In the case of a QFCH, such as a bank, this filing requirement can be achieved out of court hours by fax.

Notification to the administrator The fact that the court filing requirements set out above have been complied with must be notified by the QFCH as soon as practicable after completion of filing.

Comment A lender commits a criminal offence if, in the statutory declaration referred to above, it makes a statement that it does not reasonably believe to be true (see IA 1986, Sch B1, para 18(6)).

(b) Appointment by the company or the directors

Where the appointment is to be by the company or by its directors five business days' notice in writing of intention to appoint must be given to:

- persons having the right to appoint an administrative receiver (where an exception applies);
- persons having a right to appoint an administrator under Sch B1, para 14, i.e. a QFCH (IA 1986, Sch B1, para 26).

The notice of intention to appoint must be filed in court along with a statutory declaration by the appointer that:

- the company is likely to become unable to pay its debts;
- the company is not in liquidation;
- the appointment is not prevented because the company has been in administration instigated by the company or its directors, or subject to a moratorium in regard to a failed company

voluntary arrangement in the previous 12 months and that there arc no outstanding winding-up petitions in respect of the company and that there is not an administrator or administrative receiver in office.

What else must be filed in court?

- A notice of the appointment; and
- a statutory declaration by the appointer that:
  - (a) the appointer is entitled to make the appointment;
  - (b) the appointment is in accordance with IA 1986, Sch B1;
  - (c) the statements in the statutory declaration filed with the notice of intention to appoint are still accurate.
- a statement by the administrator that:
  - (a) he consents to the appointment; and
  - (b) that the purpose of the administration is reasonably likely to be achieved. In this connection the administrator may rely on information supplied by the directors unless there is reason to doubt its accuracy.

When is the appointment effective? The appointment of the administrator becomes effective when the above-mentioned filing requirements are completed satisfactorily.

Minmar (929) Ltd v *Khalatschi* [2012] 1 BCLC 798

The applicant (C) applied for an order setting aside the appointment of the respondents (K) as administrators of the company (M) of which he was a director. A resolution appointing the interveners (X) as additional directors of M had been signed on behalf of M's sole shareholder. X purportedly appointed K as administrators under the Insolvency Act 1986 Sch B1 Pt 4 para 22, claiming to have constituted a majority of the board when doing so. Contrary to the terms of M's articles, no notice of the meeting at which the appointment was made had been given to the existing directors and only one person had been present at the meeting. The issues were (i) whether Schedule B1 para 105, which referred to a 'majority decision of directors', was intended to give effect to the views of the majority, however reached, or whether the majority were required to comply with the company's rules of internal management before making a valid decision; (ii) whether K's appointment was invalidated as a result of the failure to give M notice of the intention to appoint them as administrators.

Application granted.

(1) The terms of Sch B1 para 105 gave to an act of the majority the same validity as would be accorded to an act of the directors as a whole but if the act in question had still to be an act of the majority of such directors, there was no reason why the reduction in the requisite number of directors should also cause the usual rules of internal management to be dispensed with. That would give greater effect to a provision of general application than was to be derived from the words used, the context in Sch B1 in which they were used and the previous case law, *Re Emmadart Ltd* [1979] Ch 540, *Re Instrumentation Electrical Services Ltd* (1988) 4 BCC 301 *and Re Equiticorp International Plc* [1989] 1 WLR 1010 considered. Accordingly, Schedule B1 para 105 did not validate K's appointment. It was plain that the so-called meeting was not a valid meeting of the board. No notice had been given to the existing directors and there was only one person present, so there was no quorum or indeed any meeting. It followed that K's appointment was invalid and ought to be set aside.

(2) As to the obligation under Schedule B1 para 26 to give notice of an intention to appoint administrators, there was no reason why all those enumerated in the Insolvency Rules 1986 Part 2 (4)

r 2.20(2), including the company itself, should not receive such notice. It had not been suggested that any notice of X's intention to appoint K as administrators had been given to M. Their appointment was therefore invalid for that reason also.

Notification to the administrator The fact that the court filing requirements set out above have been satisfactorily completed must be notified to the administrator as soon as is practicable.

Comment

i   Where directors or the company use the out of court route there is a requirement, as we have seen, that notice of intention to appoint an administrator is given to a QFCH. Such a holder then has a period of five business days to appoint its own administrator if it does not consent to the company's or the directors' choice of administrator (IA 1986, Sch B1, paras 14, 26). If the QFCH does not make its own appointment of an administrator the company or the directors can carry on with making their own appointment of an administrator using the out of court route. Nevertheless, *an interim moratorium* on action by creditors including action to enforce a security will commence when notice is given by the company or the directors of their intention to appoint an administrator, i.e. earlier than the actual appointment of the administrator (IA 1986, Sch B1, para 44). However, the moratorium will not prevent the appointment of an administrative receiver where one of the exceptions to the general prohibition on these appointments applies.

ii   The company or the directors cannot make an out of court appointment if a winding-up petition has been filed. A QFCH is not affected and may proceed with an appointment with the petition being suspended (though not dismissed) if an administration is commenced out of court. By contrast, where the court makes an administration order, the court is required to dismiss an outstanding winding-up petition.

Statement of affairs Following appointment the administrator will request the company's officers and employees (where necessary) to supply a statement of affairs. This must be done within 11 days of the request. It will be appreciated that the statement of affairs is the starting point of the administration as indeed it is of any corporate insolvency procedure although much of the information may be known in outline at least before the appointment of an administrator. The statement gives particulars of the company's assets and liabilities and details of its creditors and although it is basically the responsibility of the company's directors it is often prepared by the company's accountants.

Administrator's proposals

The following paragraphs of IA 1986, Sch B1 (as inserted by Enterprise Act 2002, Sch 16) apply to the administrator, *however appointed*.

1   As soon as is reasonably practicable, and in any case within eight weeks of the company going into administration (not three months as previously), the administrator must make proposals as to how the purpose of the administration is to be achieved. The statement is sent to the Registrar of Companies, the members of the company and all known creditors (para 49).

2   The administrator must call an initial creditors' meeting as soon as is reasonably practicable, and in any case within ten weeks of the company going into administration, to consider

the proposals (para 51). The meeting need not be called if the administrator thinks that there is insufficient property to make a distribution to unsecured creditors over and above the ring-fenced asset distribution referred to below.

3 If there is a request by creditors whose debts amount to at least 10 per cent of the total debts of the company, the administrator must convene a meeting even if the administrator considers that there will be no distribution to unsecured creditors (para 52).

4 Where the meeting is held, the creditors will vote on whether to accept the proposals or whether to modify or reject them. A simple majority in value will decide.

5 The relevant times for sending proposals and convening the initial meeting of creditors may be extended by court order or by the consent of all the secured creditors and more than 50 per cent of the unsecured creditors (para 108(2)). It is an offence for an administrator to fail to comply with the above time periods.

6 Secured creditors vote in terms of the value of any shortfall between the debt and the value of the security but the administrator's proposals cannot include action affecting the right of the secured creditors to enforce the security, unless the secured creditor(s) consent (para 73).

Comment Since the fact of the administration prevents enforcement of the security without the consent of the administrator or the court, this provision will mean that the administrator will need the consent of the secured creditors before putting the proposals to the initial creditors' meeting.

There is no need for secured creditor consent in regard to those proposals (if any) that relate to a company voluntary arrangement under IA 1986 or a scheme of arrangement under the Companies Acts 2006 Part 26 (ss.895–901) and Part 27 (special rules for public companies).

As reference to these procedures will show, there is secured-creditor protection built into both of them.

Powers and duties of the administrator

The powers and duties contained in IA 1986, Sch 1 are retained, as is the power to act as the company's agent (para 69). In addition, an administrator is an officer of the court *whether appointed by the court or out of court* (para 5).

An administrator may make distributions to secured creditors and preferential creditors and, with the consent of the court, to unsecured creditors (paras 65, 66). This provides a contrast to previous legislation that did not give preference to Crown and employee claims in an administration as was, and is, the case in an administrative receivership and a liquidation. The Crown preference is abolished but employee claims and contributions to an occupational pension scheme will have priority over the claims of a QFCH (para 65(2)).

An administrator retains the right to dispose of property subject to a floating charge as if the charge did not exist. The expenses of the administration rank ahead of the claims of the floating charge holder as regards the proceeds of sale. Other secured assets and property on hire-purchase can be disposed of with the consent of the court (paras 70–72).

Administrator's expenses

These continue to rank in front of the claims of floating charge holders and also have priority over preferential claims. This will relate mainly to employee claims and contributions to an occupational pension fund.

Goldacre (Offices) Ltd v Nortel Networks UK Ltd [2010] Ch 455

The applicant landlord (G) applied for the rent of business premises to be paid as an expense of the administration of the respondent company (N). There were two long leases, both predating the date of the administration. The premises had, since the date of the administration, been used to an extent by the administrators for the more efficient conduct of the administration. The administrators were only using a relatively small part of the premises. There were sub-tenants in respect of other parts. Those rents were being received by or being passed to G. G submitted that once the administrators decided to continue to use any part of the properties for the beneficial outcome of the administration they were liable to pay the rent as it fell due in full as an administration expense. The administrators submitted that a disbursement could only be regarded as necessary if the administrators chose to make it or if the court, founding itself upon some proper jurisdictional basis, ordered it; there was also a distinction between the rules applying to liquidations and those applying to administrations; they should only pay a proportionate amount of the rent attributable to the floor space that they occupied, and G was free to have the rest.

Application granted.

(1) It had been decided as a matter of principle that liquidators were liable to pay rent as a liquidation expense where they made use of or retained, for the benefit of the liquidation, possession of leasehold premises, *Re Lundy Granite Co* (1870–71) LR 6 Ch App 462 considered. The Insolvency Rules applicable to liquidations had been construed to include debts which, under the *Lundy Granite* principle, were deemed to be expenses of the liquidation, *Re Toshoku Finance UK Plc (in Liquidation)* [2002] 1 WLR 671 considered. The wording of the Insolvency Rules 1986 r 2.67(1)(a) relating to administration was similar to that of r 4.218(1)(a) relating to liquidation considered in *Toshoku*. The expenses regime set out in the rules had been held to be mandatory in the case of administrations as well as liquidations, *Exeter City Council v Bairstow* [2007] EWHC 400 (Ch) considered. The matter was to be considered exclusively by reference to the relevant Insolvency Rules and if the rental liability fell within the rules, then it was payable as a matter of mandatory obligation, not as a matter of discretion, either on the part of the administrators or on the part of the court. There was no discretion to declare something to be or not to be a liquidation or administration expense.

(2) If the rent was not an expense within r 2.67(1)(a), it fell within r 2.67(1)(f) as a necessary disbursement. Whatever the precise extent of the meaning of the word 'necessary', it was plainly apt to extend to a case where the *Lundy Granite* principle applied, *Re Lehman Brothers International (Europe) (in Administration)* [2009] EWHC 2545 (Ch) considered. The reasons advanced by the administrators for not regarding rent as an administration expense were not accepted. The *Lundy Granite* principle applied, and the court's jurisdiction to order payment derived from the relevant rules which, properly construed in accordance with the *Lundy Granite* principle, compelled payment.

(3) As the rent falling due on the next quarter day was a payment in advance, it was not subject to the Apportionment Act 1870 from which it followed that the quarter's rent became payable in full from that date as one of the costs and expenses of the administration and would not fall to be apportioned should the administrators vacate the premises during that quarter, *Ellis v Rowbotham* [1900] 1 QB 740 followed and *Shackell & Co v Chorlton & Sons* [1895] 1 Ch 378 not followed. A liquidator electing to hold leasehold premises could do so only on the terms and conditions contained in the lease, and any liability incurred while the lease was being enjoyed or retained for the benefit of the liquidation was payable in full as a liquidation expense and the same principle applied in an administration, *Powdrill v Watson* [1995] 2 AC 394 applied. The court had no discretion to consider how much it would be fair for the administrators to pay in this case, *Sunberry Properties Ltd v Innovate Logistics Ltd (in Administration)* [2009] BCC 164 considered.

Bloom v Pensions Regulator [2011] EWCA Civ 1124

The appellant administrators of companies in two groups (L and N) appealed against a decision ([2010] EWHC 3010 (Ch)), made in the context of the financial support direction (FSD) regime created by the Pensions Act 2004, holding that when a relevant target company was in administration, the liability under a contribution notice was not a provable debt in the administration, but was payable as an expense of the administration. The FSD regime enabled the Pensions Regulator to impose, by the issue of an FSD to associated companies of a corporate employer, an obligation to provide reasonable financial support to the employer's underfunded occupational pension scheme. It further enabled the regulator to deal with non-compliance with that obligation by imposing by contribution notice a specific monetary liability, payable by the associated, or 'target', company to the trustees of the employer's pension scheme. Following their entry into administration, companies in L and N had been notified that the regulator had decided to issue them with FSDs. N's administrators argued that the liability under any contribution notices was not an expense, but created a provable debt. L's administrators argued that the liability was only payable after all other creditors had been paid in full.

Appeals dismissed.

(1) The critical question in determining whether the liability under a contribution notice was a provable debt was whether it was within the terms of the Insolvency Rules 1986 r 13.12(1)(a) or (b) at the date the company went into administration, if neither the notice nor a financial support direction had yet been issued. The question under r 13.12(1)(b) was whether the liability under a notice issued after the start of the insolvency process was one to which, as at that start date, the company could become subject by reason of an obligation incurred before that date. The judge had been right to find that, without a pre-existing legal obligation such as was referred to in r 13.12(1)(b) or the Insolvency Act 1986 s 382(1)(b), a liability could not qualify as a contingent liability so as to be provable under those provisions, *Glenister v Rowe (Costs)* [2000] Ch 76, *R (on the application of Steele) v Birmingham City Council* [2006] 1 WLR 2380 and *Day v Haine* [2008] EWCA Civ 626 followed. He had also been right to find that, even on the basis that the circumstances which might give rise to the use of the FSD regime would exist at a date before inception of any insolvency proceedings, nevertheless, there would at that stage be no more than the possibility that the regime would be invoked in relation to any particular company. The judge had been right to decide that he was bound by the Court of Appeal decisions to the effect that a prior legal obligation was essential to establish that a liability which had matured after the commencement of an insolvency process was, at the outset of that process, already a contingent liability, so that it was provable in the process. The existence of the FSD regime did not show that any company which might be made the subject of an FSD or contribution notice was then under a legal obligation for the purposes of r 13.12(1)(b).

(2) The judge had correctly rejected the submission that *Re Toshoku Finance UK Plc (in Liquidation)* [2002] UKHL 6, [2002] 1 WLR 671 only showed a liability to be an expense if it was not merely a liability of the company but also one as to which it could be seen that the intention of the legislation was that the relevant office-holder was bound to discharge it. He had correctly stated that Toshoku had established that where Parliament imposed a liability that was not a provable debt on a company in an insolvency process then, unless it constituted an expense under another provision of the expenses regimes for administration and liquidation, it would constitute a necessary disbursement; the rejected submission was not consistent with that, Toshoku followed. It was not necessary to find a positive indication of statutory intention that the liability was one with which the company was bound to perform. Such a statutory liability was at any rate likely to be found to be one which was binding on the company and one with which it was the obligation of the office-holder to comply. The 2004 Act accordingly had to be examined to see what obligation it imposed and in what circumstances. The FSD regime applied to target companies undergoing an insolvency process,

and if action was taken under that regime in relation to such a company, it would not be free to ignore the relevant obligation. That obligation, and, if it was not complied with, the liability created by a contribution notice, was created by statute and was not a provable debt, nor was it an expense under any other provision of the expenses regimes for liquidation and administration. Parliament had therefore imposed a financial liability on a company in an insolvency process which constituted a necessary disbursement of the administrator. The judge had been right to conclude that the liability was payable as an expense of the administration or liquidation, despite various anomalies that that gave rise to.

The accountability of an administrator

The accountability of an administrator is as follows:

Creditors and members of the company in administration These persons can make application to the court where the administrator acts or proposes to act in a way that could unfairly harm their respective interests or where the applicant believes that the administrator is not carrying out relevant functions as efficiently or as quickly as is reasonably practicable (para 74).

Any interested party These persons can make application to the court where it is alleged that the administrator has misapplied or retained the property of the company or is guilty of misfeasance or in breach of fiduciary duty. So far this aspect of accountability is similar to that under IA 1986, s 212 but now an application can be made while the company is still in an administration instead of waiting until the company has gone into liquidation.

Cessation of an administration

The exit from administration may be achieved in the following ways:

- *Automatic cessation.* The appointment of the administrator will come to an end automatically 12 months after the date on which the appointment took effect.
- *Extension of appointment.* The period of 12 months can be extended *once only* by a period of up to six months with the consent of the creditors or any number of times by the court on the application of the administrator for such period as the court may determine. Creditor consent means the consent of all the secured creditors and more than 50 per cent in value of the unsecured creditors. Consent may be written or expressed by resolution at a meeting. The above majorities disregard any creditor who does not respond to an invitation to give or withhold consent. The above materials are contained in IA 1986, Sch B1, paras 76–78.

Administration: a timetable of major events

- *Seven days after appointment*: notice of appointment filed at Companies House.
- *Eleven days after administrator's request*: company's officers and employees to provide administrator with statement of affairs.
- *Eight weeks after appointment*: administrator sends proposals to members, creditors and Companies House.
- *Ten weeks after appointment*: first creditors' meeting held unless not required.
- *One year after appointment*: automatic end of the appointment of administrator subject to extension.

Termination of administration through notice to Registrar of Companies

If the company is not rescued, the exit routes from administration are streamlined by provisions relating to voluntary liquidation and dissolution as follows:

(a) *Where funds are available after payment of secured and preferential creditors.* The company can go directly into a creditors' voluntary winding-up. The administrator gives notice to Companies House and the creditors, and files a copy with the court. There is no need to hold a meeting of creditors and the administrator becomes the liquidator unless the creditors put forward a different nomination. The intention is that these procedures will reduce the number of compulsory liquidations that have followed administration.

(b) *If no funds are available for distribution to creditors.* The administrator must, unless the court otherwise orders, give notice to that effect to Companies House. Copies must be sent to creditors and the court. The company will be deemed dissolved after three months from registration of the notice at Companies House, unless an interested person, e.g. a member who believes the company has a good claim for damages against a third party, makes application to the court.

The above provisions are to be found in IA 1986, Sch B1, paras 83–84.

Replacement of administrator

Where a QFCH has used the out of court route, and in the event that there was a prior ranking floating chargeholder entitled to make the appointment, then the prior charge holder can apply to the court for the replacement of the administrator by his own nominee for the office (IA 1986, Sch B1, para 96).

Abolition of Crown preference

Enterprise Act 2002, s 251 abolishes the preferential status of Crown debts. These are debts due to the Inland Revenue, Customs and Excise and social security contributions. Employee claims continue to be preferential, as do contributions to an occupational pension fund. IA 1986, Sch 6 is amended accordingly.

Ring-fencing mechanism for unsecured creditors

In order to ensure that the benefit of the abolition of Crown preference does not go solely to floating chargeholders the Enterprise Act 2002 sets up a mechanism for ring-fencing assets where there is a floating charge that was created after the 2002 Act provisions came into force. The abolition of Crown debts and the ring-fencing applies to all corporate insolvencies, not merely to administration, though it is convenient to deal with it here. The ring-fence arrangements do not apply where the fund is below a minimum to be prescribed and the insolvency practitioner considers that the costs in distributing it would be disproportionate to the benefits. The provision may also be disapplied by the terms of a company voluntary arrangement or by a scheme of arrangement under Part 26 of the CA 2006 (note the changes under ss 899(2) and 901). The court may also disapply it on the application of the insolvency practitioner if he wishes to take this route.

Ring-fencing: the prescribed percentage

Under the Insolvency Act 1986 (Prescribed Part) Order 2003 the following thresholds apply:

- minimum fund for distribution – £10,000;
- prescribed percentage to be calculated on the basis of a sliding scale as follows: 50 per cent of the first £10,000 of floating charge realisations; 20 per cent of floating charge realisations after that;
- up to a maximum ring-fenced fund of £600,000.

The ring-fencing provisions apply to relevant amounts of the company's 'net property'. Net property is defined in Insolvency Act 1986, s 176A(5) (as inserted by Enterprise Act 2002) as the amount of property which would, but for the ring-fencing provisions, be available for the floating chargeholder. Thus, it represents any floating charge realisations.

Important business application

Lenders should check all existing documents to ensure that they cover the new out of court route into administration rather than, for example, referring merely to administration orders and petitions.

Administrator: legal consequences of appointment

Consideration has been given to the appointment of an administrator both in court and out of court. The following materials deal with the main legal consequences of the appointment together with case law on earlier provisions that carries through to illustrate the law.

Suspension of rights

From the presentation of a petition for an administration order and during the period of the administration:

(i) no resolution to wind up the company may be passed nor may the court make a winding-up order (IA 1986, Sch B1, para 40);

(ii) there can be no enforcement of fixed charges or other security over the company's property except with the consent of the administrator or leave of the court (IA 1986, Sch B1, para 43);

(iii) there can be no recovery of property which the company has under a hire-purchase agreement or leasing arrangement and retention clauses are not enforceable except with the consent of the administrator or the court (IA 1986, Sch B1, para 43);

(iv) no other legal proceedings can be commenced against the company except with the consent of the administrator or leave of the court (IA 1986, Sch B1, para 43).

The Court of Appeal has ruled that the administrator's consent or leave of the court is necessary to commence or continue criminal as well as civil proceedings against a company in administration (see *Re Rhondda Waste Disposal Ltd (in Administration)* [2000] EGCS 25). In this case the Environmental Agency wished to prosecute for failure to comply with one of the conditions of a waste management licence. The court gave leave because the pollution was serious.

Consent or leave is also required even if a civil action is not being brought by a creditor but by a claimant suing for alleged breach of a patent (see *Biosource Technologies Inc v Axis Genetics plc (in Administration)* [2000] 1 BCLC 286).

In regard to (iii) above the High Court ruled in *Razzaq v Pala* [1997] 1 WLR 1336 and *Re Lomax Leisure Ltd* [1999] 1 All ER 22 that a landlord's right to forfeit a lease is not in the nature of a security over a company's property in a legal sense. Therefore the moratorium preventing anyone from taking steps to enforce a security over the property of a company while in administration does not bind a landlord. The cases had considerable significance for creditors who initiate an administration, particularly the larger scale administrations where there may be a number of leaseholds among the assets of the company. They have no way of knowing whether the objects of the administration will be achieved since the landlords will be able to frustrate the purpose of the administration by forfeiting leases or by requiring payment of rents for not doing so. Thus placing themselves in a superior position to other creditors since they can achieve payment of arrears of rent or forfeit the lease and market it elsewhere even during the course of the administration.

Landlord's right of forfeiture

IA 1986, Sch B1, para 43(4) prohibits a landlord's right to re-entry by forfeiture of the lease except by leave of the court. Once an administration order has been made or is in force, re-entry by forfeiture continues to be barred except by permission of the administrator or leave of the court.

No inhibition of rescue schemes

In order to prevent the administrator's schemes to save the company or to conduct the company as near as possible as a going concern until liquidation as in *Re Consumer and Industrial Press Ltd* (1988), it is sometimes necessary to deal with persons who have charges or other rights over the property of the company and whose consent is required before the property is sold. A rescue package may very well involve such sales.

In this connection IA 1986, Sch B1, paras 70 and 71 provide as follows:

(a) Assets subject to a floating charge can be sold by the administrator and the proceeds used in the business. The permission of the chargeholder is not required nor is it necessary for the administrator to obtain the permission of the court. However, the chargeholder has the same priority as he had before over the assets generally as they may be from time to time and this would include the proceeds of sale and other assets which might be purchased with the proceeds because these would be included in the general assets of the company (para 70).

(b) Assets held on hire-purchase or subject to a fixed charge can be sold but court approval must be obtained and the proceeds *must* be used to pay off the chargeholder or owner. In addition, and so as to ensure that the administrator gets the market price, IA 1986, Sch B1, para 71 provides that the administrator must make up any difference between the sale price and the market price.

The company's contracts

Following the refusal of administrators to complete a contract entered into by the company before their appointment, the High Court was asked to consider in that context its powers of intervention (see *C E King Ltd (in Administration)* [2000] 2 BCLC 297).

The judge decided that in general terms it would be inappropriate to make an order requiring the administrators to perform the relevant contract. Administrators were appointed (and expected) to make commercial decisions and where necessary take legal advice. In the end, however, the matter of performing (or not) the company's contracts remains a commercial decision to be taken by the administrators.

Directors and employees

The directors are not dismissed by the appointment of an administrator. However, their powers are suspended and the administrator may remove any director of the company and appoint any person to be a director of it whether to fill a vacancy or as an additional director.

The appointment of an administrator does not operate to dismiss the company's employees. The reason for this is that under IA 1986, Sch B1, para 69 he is said to act as an agent of the company and so there is no change in the personality of the employer. However, an administrator can terminate contracts of employment.

Employees' contracts and the provisions of the Enterprise Act 2002

The provisions of the Insolvency Act 1986 which were relevant stated, in s 19, that nothing done or omitted to be done within 14 days of appointment (of an administrator and by the administrator) shall be construed as 'adoption' (of employment contracts by the administrator). The position where contracts of employment are adopted by an administrator is that sums outstanding called 'qualifying liabilities', i.e. wages or salaries including sickness and holiday pay and contributions to occupational pension funds incurred after the adoption of an employment contract, are payable in priority to the claims of preferential creditors and holders of floating charges and if, at the end of the administration, there are qualifying liabilities unpaid and there are insufficient funds to pay them and the administrator's remuneration and expenses, the outstanding amount is payable in full before the administrator's remuneration and expenses (see below).

A problem for administrators has been whether failure to act during the first 14 days can be regarded as 'adoption' of employment contracts leading to the above mentioned loss of remuneration and expenses. The matter was raised in the High Court under the old law (see *Antal International Ltd* [2003] EWHC 1339 (Ch), [2003] 2 BCLC 406).

In this case the administrators asked the court for directions on the matter of the alleged adoption of the contracts of a group of French workers. The company, its auditors and the administrators had originally thought the 12 workers were employed by a subsidiary company but it emerged that they were in fact employees of Antal. This was discovered 16 days after the administrators' appointment. Had the contracts been adopted by inactivity in the last two days? The High Court ruled that they had not. Adoption would only occur when the administrators had done something that amounted to choosing to adopt. The mere keeping on of employees did not amount to adoption. Once the administrators became aware of the French employees they took immediate steps to terminate their contracts under French law.

Antal and Enterprise Act 2002 changes

The Enterprise Act 2002 inserts new provisions in the 1986 Act as Sch B1. Paragraph 99 of that Schedule applicable to administrations on or after 15 September 2003 states that '*action taken within the period of 14 days after an administrator's appointment shall not be taken to amount or contribute to the adoption of a [contract of employment]*'. This seems to cut out all failure to act and is in line with the decision of the House of Lords in *Powdrill* v *Watson* [1995] 2 AC 394 (see below).

The decision in *Powdrill* v *Watson*

In *Powdrill* v *Watson* [1995] 2 AC 394 the House of Lords ruled that inaction by the administrators after the 14-day period could not amount to 'adoption' of employment contracts.

However, their Lordships did also rule that administrators could not actively retain employees after the 14-day period and avoid liability by sending each employee a letter disclaiming adoption. Such a letter was of no effect. That this was the case was also held by the Court of Appeal and that merely allowing employment to continue after 14 days could amount to adoption. This latter ruling, however, was not acceptable to the House of Lords which ruled that some conduct amounting to an election to adopt an employment contract was required.

The position in case law and under insolvency legislation would appear now to be the same.

Pension funds

The High Court has decided that the duty of an administrator to manage the 'company's affairs' – as referred to in Insolvency Act 1986, Sch B1, paras 59 and 68 – includes the trustee-ship of any employees' pension funds where the company had previously been the trustee. Furthermore, the administrator could only be reimbursed those costs out of the pension fund to which the company would have been entitled but could make a claim for any costs or expenses incurred in actually running the scheme as costs of the administration generally and not as a specific charge against the trust fund (see *Polly Peck International plc (in Administration) v Henry* [1999] 1 BCLC 407). Mr Justice Buckley so ruled when dismissing an application by the administrators of Polly Peck International (PPI) for a new trustee, i.e. the Trustee Corporation Ltd to be appointed as trustee of the two pension funds set up by PPI.

IA 1986, Sch B1, para 68 provides that, where an appointment is made in court, the administration order is an order directing that during the period for which the order is in force, the affairs, business and property of the company shall be managed by a person (the administrator) appointed for the purpose by the court. IA 1986, Sch B1, para 59(c) provides that the administrator of the company may do all such things as may be necessary for the management of the affairs, business and property of the company.

Essay questions

1 The prime intention of the Insolvency Act 1986 with regard to companies is to provide various alternatives to the winding-up of an insolvent company.
   Discuss.   *(The Institute of Chartered Secretaries and Administrators)*

2 Corporate entity and limited liability do not always provide complete protection from personal liability for company directors and shareholders.
   You are required to discuss the situations where such persons may be personally liable.
                                               (The Chartered Institute of Management Accountants)

3 Plym plc is a holding company whose several subsidiaries are all exclusively private companies. The capital structure of the subsidiaries consists of ordinary shares, several classes of preference shares, and debentures. Because of the administrative difficulties caused by the diverse nature of the capital structure of the subsidiaries, the board of directors of Plym plc wish to introduce a simplified system whereby Plym would purchase the minority shares and debentures for cash or in the alternative issue fully paid equity shares in Plym in exchange for the said shares and debentures at an agreed ratio. Preliminary inquiries indicate that there is a substantial minority of members who would neither sell nor exchange their securities for shares in Plym plc.

Advise the directors of Plym plc as to how, if at all, they could achieve their objective in spite of the minority's anticipated refusal to cooperate.   *(University of Plymouth)*

4 Discredit Bank plc is a large merchant bank situated in the City of London. The Chairman and Managing Director of the company is Dan, a high-powered executive who is well-respected in the City. Seven other directors sit on the board, including Maggie, the Finance Director. Dan and Maggie, together with some of the other directors, have a shareholding but they do not represent the majority.

Last year, Dan purchased property on Discredit's behalf from Chivers-Benson plc of whom Dan is a director. The property, which was valued by Chivers-Benson, was bought by Discredit for £400,000. Within two weeks of Discredit buying the property, it was sold to Briac Ltd, a subsidiary company of Chivers-Benson, for £100,000.

Last month Dan was approached by Homestore plc for the financing of new shop development in London. Dan informed Homestore that Discredit was not in a position to provide Homestore with financial backing but that he, himself, could provide the finance through the setting-up of a separate company. He persuades Maggie to assist him in the incorporation of Quick Loan Ltd, which, owing to Dan's influence in the City enabling the finance to be provided to Homestore, makes a profit of £70,000 on the deal. Both Dan's and Maggie's shares in Quick Loan have increased in value.

These activities have come to the attention of TCR plc, a minority shareholder. Dan has become aware of TCR's interest and, in anticipation of TCR raising these activities at the next general meeting, he decides to publish a report, addressed to all shareholders, claiming that all the relevant transactions and decisions involving Discredit were carried out for strict commercial reasons and for the benefit of the company.

Advise TCR, which doubts the accuracy of Dan's statements and considers the report to be misleading, a factor which TCR is convinced is not known to other shareholders who are likely, as far as TCR is concerned, to accept the report's contents.   *(University of Greenwich)*

Test your knowledge

Four alternative answers are given. Select ONE only. Circle the answer which you consider to be correct. Check your answers by referring back to the information given in the chapter and against the answers at the end of the text.

1 Bloggs Ltd has recently been made the subject of an administration order. John had previously presented a winding-up petition in regard to Bloggs. What will the effect of the administration order be on John's winding-up petition?

A It will be heard by the court.
B It will be dismissed by the court if the administrator applies to it.
C It will be postponed for 12 months.
D It will be automatically dismissed.

2 Which of the following must be given notice of the intention to appoint an administrator out of court by the directors?

A Unsecured creditors and the company.
B Anyone entitled to appoint an administrative receiver.
C Unsecured creditors.
D Anyone entitled to appoint an administrative receiver or an administrator.

3 Who can fill the office of administrator if there is a vacancy?

   A The court.

   B The creditors.

   C Anyone entitled to appoint an administrative receiver.

   D Anyone entitled to appoint an administrative receiver provided the court approves of the appointee.

4 An administrator is taken to have adopted contracts of employment within a stated period after his employment. The period is:

   A 28 days   B 15 days   C 14 days   D 21 days

5 A qualifying floating chargeholder is seeking to petition the court for an administration order. Which of the following statements is correct?

   A A QFCH cannot petition the court for an order.

   B A QFCH can petition but must satisfy the court that the company is unable to pay its debts.

   C A QFCH can petition but must satisfy the court that the purposes of an administration can be achieved.

   D A QFCH can petition and need only show that the charge is enforceable.

6 Once the court has received a petition for an administration order, when can a liquidator be appointed? He may:

   A be appointed if the court consents.

   B be appointed if the creditors consent.

   C be appointed if the Official Receiver consents.

   D not be appointed.

The answers to test your knowledge questions appear on p. 645.

28

Corporate insolvency – procedures other than rescue

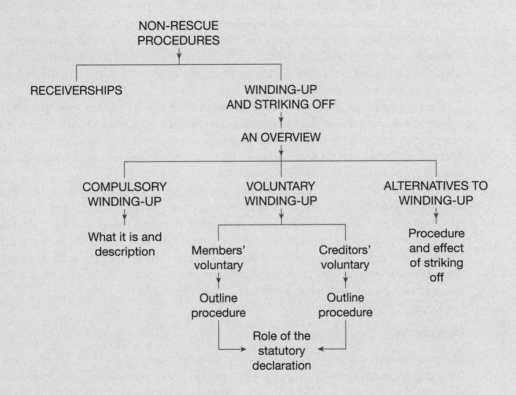

In this chapter we take an overview of corporate insolvency procedures that are not in their major aims concerned to rescue a company from an insolvency situation.

Receiverships

Administrative receivers: the demise of

An administrative receiver was the usual appointment of a bank when a company with an overdraft and/or a loan was in financial difficulties. The bank invariably held a floating charge on the company's undertaking and the function of this type of receiver was to undertake such procedures with the company as would pay off the bank. These receivers were not primarily concerned with company rescue as an administrator is. What is more the existence of the office of administrative receiver inhibited the rescue procedures of an administration because if the company or its creditors tried to make an appointment of an administrator the bank, which had to be notified, would often immediately appoint an administrative receiver and this would in law veto the administration.

The Enterprise Act 2002 inserted provisions into the Insolvency Act 1986 that prevent the holder of a floating charge such as a bank from appointing an administrative receiver except in a restricted number of organisations such as some companies involved in financial market operations. These are beyond the scope of this text and are unlikely to be raised in examinations in corporate law at a non-specialist level.

However, it should be recognised that the ban on the appointment of administrative receivers will not be complete for some time since the relevant provisions of the Enterprise Act 2002 did not come into force until September 2003 and banks that had taken floating charges over continuing overdrafts before that date are still able to appoint such practitioners. However, it is most unlikely that an examiner would see the need or the sense in asking questions on the detail of the law relating to administrative receivers. The office is from the student point of view redundant and no more will be said about it in this text.

Receivers

The practice of appointing receivers without management powers by those who have taken fixed charges over corporate property will continue. These practitioners are in no sense managers appointed to deal with the borrowing company's business and pay off the debt. They are appointed merely to sell the charged property to pay the debt or, for example, to collect income such as rent from the company's tenants (if any) until the debt is paid. They do not have to be authorised insolvency practitioners and the practice is to appoint chartered surveyors to do this work.

Winding-up or striking off

A company's life can be brought to an end by a process known as *winding-up*. This process is carried through by a *liquidator* whose functions are:

(a) to settle the list of contributories;

(b) to collect the company's assets;

(c) to discharge the company's liabilities to its creditors;

(d) to redistribute the surplus (if any) to the contributories according to the rights attaching to their shares of the company's capital.

There are two methods of winding-up:

(i) a compulsory winding-up by the court;

(ii) a voluntary winding-up, which may be either a members' winding-up or a creditors' winding-up.

We shall now proceed to examine the general characteristics of these various types.

Compulsory winding-up

A company may be wound up by the court when a number of situations occur – the most common being when the company is unable to pay its debts.

A petition for winding-up may be presented by the company or by the Department for Business, Innovation and Skills (BIS), but is normally presented by a creditor.

When there is a petition for winding-up, the court is not forced to make an order, but if it does, a liquidator is appointed who realises the assets and pays the creditors, handing over the surplus (if any) to the shareholders. When the company's affairs are fully wound up, the court will make an order dissolving the company. The order is registered with the Registrar of Companies by the liquidator, and the Registrar makes an entry on the Register dissolving the company from the date of the court order.

Voluntary winding-up

A company may apply to the Registrar of Companies to be struck off the Register and dissolved. The company can do this if it is no longer needed. For example, the directors may wish to retire and there is no one to take over from them; or it is a subsidiary whose name is no longer needed; or it was set up to exploit an idea that turned out not to be feasible. This may not happen however if the Registrar of Companies has already started dissolution action under s 1000 (power to strike off company not carrying on business or in operation). This procedure is not an alternative to formal insolvency proceedings where these are appropriate. Even if the company is struck off and dissolved, creditors and others could apply for the company to be restored to the Register.

Sections 1004 and 1005 of the Companies Act 2006 set out the circumstances in which the company may not apply to be struck off. For example, the company may not make an application for voluntary strike off if, at any time in the last three months, it has traded or otherwise carried on business, changed its name, made a disposal for value of property or rights that, immediately before ceasing to trade or otherwise carry on business, it held for the purpose of disposal for gain in the normal course of trading or otherwise carrying on business. A company cannot apply to be struck off if it is the subject, or proposed subject, of any insolvency proceedings (such as liquidation, including where a petition has been presented but has not yet been dealt with); or a s 895 scheme (that is a compromise or arrangement between a company and its creditors or members). However, a company can apply for strike off if it has settled trading or business debts in the previous three months.

A company may be wound up voluntarily:

(a) When the period, if any, fixed for the duration of the company by the articles expires, or the event, if any, occurs, on the occurrence of which the articles provide that the company is to be dissolved, and the company in general meeting has passed an *ordinary resolution* requiring the company to be wound up voluntarily. A limitation on a company's duration is in practice very rare.

(b) If the company resolves by *special resolution* that the company be wound up voluntarily for any cause whatever.

(c) If the company resolves by *extraordinary resolution* to the effect that it cannot by reason of its liabilities continue its business, and that it is advisable to wind up.

When a company has passed a resolution for voluntary winding-up, it must give notice of the resolution by an advertisement in the *London Gazette* within 14 days. The voluntary winding-up is deemed to commence at the time of the passing of the resolution.

Withdrawal of application

If the directors wish to withdraw an application, they must withdraw it by sending the 'Withdrawal of striking off application by a company', Form DS02 if they change their mind or the company ceases to be eligible for striking off. This may be because, after applying to be struck off, the company trades or otherwise carries on business, changes its name, for value, disposes of any property or rights except those it needed in order to make or proceed with the application:

● becomes subject to formal insolvency proceedings or makes a s 900 application (a compromise or arrangement between a company and its creditors);

● engages in any other activity, unless it was necessary to make or proceed with a striking off application, conclude those of its affairs that are outstanding because of the need to make or proceed with an application (such as paying the costs of running office premises while concluding its affairs and then finally disposing of the office);

● and comply with a statutory requirement.

Any director of the company may complete and sign the 'Withdrawal of striking off application by a company', Form DS02, and send it to the Registrar. Section 1009 of the 2006 Act contains the full circumstances that mean you must withdraw an application for strike off and question 12 contains information on the offences for failure to withdraw an application.

Objections

Objections or complaints to a voluntary winding-up application must be in writing and sent to the Registrar with any supporting evidence, such as copies of invoices that may prove the company is trading.

Some of the reasons could include:

- if the company has broken any of the conditions of its application for example, it has traded, changed its name or become subject to insolvency proceedings during the three-month period before the application, or afterwards;
- if the directors have not informed interested parties;
- if any of the declarations on the form are false;
- if some form of action is being taken, or is pending, to recover any money owed (such as a winding-up petition or action in a small claims court);
- if other legal action is being taken against the company;
- if the directors have wrongfully traded or committed a tax fraud or some other offence (see ss 1004 and 1005 of the 2006 Act).

Offences

It is an offence:

- to apply when the company is ineligible for striking off;
- to provide false or misleading information in, or in support of, an application;
- not to copy the application to all relevant parties within seven days;
- not to withdraw application if the company becomes ineligible.

The offences attract a fine of up to a maximum of £5,000 on summary conviction (before a magistrates' court or Sheriff Court) or an unlimited fine on indictment (before a jury). If the directors breach the requirements to give a copy of the application to relevant parties and do so with the intention of concealing the application, they are also potentially liable to not only a fine but also up to seven years' imprisonment. Anyone convicted of these offences may also be disqualified from being a director for up to 15 years.

Declaration of solvency

Where it is proposed to wind up a company voluntarily, the directors, or a majority of them if there are more than two, may at a meeting of the board make a statutory declaration that they have made a full enquiry into the affairs of the company and have formed the opinion that it will be able to pay its debts in full within a stated period of not more than 12 months from the beginning of the winding-up. To be effective, such declaration must be made within the five weeks before the passing of the winding-up resolution or on that date but before the resolution was passed, and must be delivered to the Registrar of Companies for registration, and must embody a statement of the company's assets and liabilities as at the latest practicable date before the making of the declaration, though errors and omissions will not necessarily render the statement invalid. Thus, in *De Courcy* v *Clements* [1971] 1 All ER 681, the statement of the company's assets and liabilities was held to be valid even though it omitted to state that a debt of £45,000 was owed by the company to a third party. Megarry J observed that what is now the Insolvency Act 1986 did not require absolute perfection since, among other things, a liquidator who forms the opinion that the company will not be able to pay its debts in full within the period specified in the declaration of solvency must forthwith summon a creditors' meeting and put the matter to them. The creditors can petition for a compulsory winding-up, notwithstanding the voluntary liquidation, and might therefore be regarded as adequately protected. Directors making such a declaration without reasonable grounds are liable to heavy penalties.

The advantage to the company of such a declaration is that the winding-up is then a 'members' voluntary winding-up'. In the absence of such a declaration, it must be a 'creditors' voluntary winding-up'.

Commonly HMRC (which is no longer a preferential creditor) has not completed its tax assessments on the company and has not therefore been paid. Nevertheless, if funds are available to pay HMRC when liability (which has been approximated) is ascertained, a members' voluntary winding-up may continue and there is no need to convert to a creditors' voluntary, nor are the directors liable for a false declaration that the company's debts will be paid during the stated period of not longer than 12 months.

Members' voluntary winding-up

The company in general meeting, and by ordinary resolution, must appoint one or more liquidators for the purpose of winding up the company and distributing its assets, and may fix the remuneration to be paid to him or them. The appointment may be made at the same meeting at which the resolution for winding-up was passed.

On the appointment of the liquidator all the powers of the directors cease, except in so far as their continuance is sanctioned either by the company in general meeting or by the liquidator. However, a resolution for voluntary winding-up does not automatically dismiss all employees but if the liquidator does not carry on the business, which he may do for beneficial winding-up, e.g. to complete work in progress so that the finished articles may be sold more profitably, then employees are dismissed (*Reigate* v *Union Manufacturing Co (Ramsbottom)* [1918] 1 KB 592).

If a liquidator dies, resigns, or otherwise vacates his office, the company may in general meeting and subject to any arrangement with its creditors, fill the vacancy. Such a meeting may be convened by any contributory or, if there were more liquidators than one, by those continuing. However, as a general rule a single shareholder cannot constitute a meeting for the purpose of making a valid appointment of a liquidator (*In Re London Flats Ltd*, 1969, see Chapter 22 ◑), except in the case of the single-member company.

Meetings

If the liquidator at any time forms the opinion that the company will be unable to pay its debts in full within the period stated in the statutory declaration, he must forthwith summon a meeting of creditors. When the liquidator calls the meeting of creditors the company is deemed to be in a creditors' voluntary scheme, and that meeting may exercise the same powers as a creditors' meeting at the beginning of a liquidation which is initiated as a creditors' winding-up, including appointing their nominee as liquidator and a liquidation committee.

In any event, if the winding-up continues for more than a year, the liquidator must summon a general meeting of the company at the end of the first year and of each succeeding year, or at the first convenient date within three months from the end of the year, or such longer period as the BIS may allow. He must lay before the meeting an account of his acts and dealings, and the conduct of the winding-up during the preceding year.

As soon as the affairs of the company are fully wound up, the liquidator must make up an account of the winding-up showing how it has been conducted, and how the property of the company has been disposed of, and then call a general meeting of the company in order to lay the account before it and explain it. The meeting is called by advertisement in the *London Gazette*, specifying the time, place and object of the meeting. The advertisement must be published at least one month before the meeting.

Within one week after the meeting the liquidator must send to the Registrar of Companies a copy of the account, and make a return to him of the holding of the meeting and its date. If no quorum was present at the meeting, the liquidator makes a return to the effect that the meeting was duly summoned and no quorum was present, and this is deemed to constitute compliance. The Registrar must publish in the *London Gazette* notice of the receipt by him of the return of the holding of the meeting.

The Registrar then registers the account and return as to the meeting and three months after such registration the company is deemed to be dissolved. The liquidator or any interested person may apply to the court for the deferment of dissolution and, if the grounds seem adequate, the court may defer the date as it thinks fit. The court may, after the dissolution, make an order declaring the dissolution void, again on the application of the liquidator or any interested person being someone who has a claim against its assets, e.g. a creditor.

In the case of creditors, and others generally, the court cannot order restoration to the Register after two years, but in the case of those wishing to make claims for personal injury against the company, the time can be extended for a longer period up to the maximum time allowed for bringing the claim under the Limitation Act 1980. For example, where the injury was not apparent at the time of an accident the time is three years after the injury did become apparent. Thus, if there is an injury to the head which later is seen to have caused blindness, the time would be three years after discovering the blindness; so a company responsible for the initial injury could be restored to the Register, so that a claim could be made against it some years after it had been dissolved. These restoration provisions apply regardless of the method of winding-up. This will enable a person to get a judgment and make a claim on the company, the claim then being, in effect, met by the company's insurers. It is, however, necessary to make the claim against the company before the insurance indemnity is triggered and the above provisions enable this to be done.

Where the liquidator has been obliged to call a meeting of creditors because of insolvency, these procedures are modified and those appropriate to a creditors' voluntary winding-up apply.

Creditors' voluntary winding-up

Where a company proposes to wind up voluntarily and the directors are not in a position to make the statutory declaration of solvency, the company must call a meeting of its creditors not later than the fourteenth day after the members' meeting at which the resolution for voluntary winding-up is to be proposed. Notices of this meeting are to be sent by post to creditors not less than seven days before the day of the creditors' meeting.

The company must advertise a notice of the creditors' meeting once in the *London Gazette* and once at least in two local newspapers circulating in the district where it has its registered office or principal place of business.

The directors must place before the creditors' meeting a full statement of the company's affairs, together with a list of creditors and the estimated amount of their claims, and appoint a director to preside at the meeting. The notice of the meeting must give the name and address of an insolvency practitioner who will give creditors information about the company or state a place where a list of creditors can be inspected.

Appointment of liquidator

The creditors and the company at their respective meetings may nominate a liquidator. If the creditors do not nominate one, the company's nominee becomes the liquidator. If the creditors and the company nominate different persons, the person nominated by the creditors has preference. However, where different persons are nominated, any director, member or creditor of the company may, within seven days after the date on which the nomination was made by the creditors, apply to the court for an order to appoint the company's nominee to act either instead of or in conjunction with the creditors' nominee, or alternatively to appoint some other person.

At the same meeting the creditors may, if they think fit, appoint a liquidation committee to act with the liquidator. On the appointment of a liquidator all the powers of the directors cease, except in so far as the liquidation committee, or, if there is no such committee, the creditors sanction their continuance. The position of employees is the same as in a members' voluntary winding-up.

If a vacancy occurs, by death, resignation or otherwise, in the office of liquidator, other than a liquidator appointed by or by the direction of the court, the creditors may fill the vacancy.

Where the winding-up continues for more than a year, the liquidator must summon a general meeting of the company and a meeting of the creditors at the end of the first and each succeeding year, or within three months of that time, and lay before the meetings an account of the conduct of the winding-up during the preceding year. The BIS may allow modifications to the time limit.

Centrebinding

In the past, when no particular qualifications were required to undertake insolvency work, it was possible for the members in a creditors' voluntary to appoint a liquidator from among a group of unscrupulous persons prepared to participate in fraud. The person appointed would then proceed to dispose of the company assets and dissipate the proceeds often into other enterprises of the directors or their associates. This was done without the holding of a creditors' meeting to affirm the appointment of the liquidator, and by the time the creditors became aware of the liquidation it was too late to do anything about it. The difficulty was that the disposal of the assets by the members' liquidator was quite legal. The court so decided in *Re Centrebind* [1966] 3 All ER 889 and the procedure became known as 'centrebinding'.

The practice has been brought to an end for two reasons as follows:

(a) the requirement of qualified insolvency practitioners; *and*
(b) because of s 166, which provides that until a meeting of creditors has been called to approve the company's liquidator, that liquidator has power only to take control of the company's property and to sell perishable goods. Any other dispositions of the company's property are invalid.

Final meetings and dissolution

As soon as the affairs of the company are fully wound up, the liquidator makes an account of the winding-up, and calls a general meeting of the company and a meeting of the creditors to lay before them the account and give an explanation of it. This meeting must be advertised in the *London Gazette*, specifying the time and place and object, the advertisement being published one month at least before the meeting.

Within one week after the date of the meeting or, if they are not held on the same date, after the date of the later meeting, the liquidator must send to the Registrar a copy of the account and a return of the holding of the meetings and their dates. If a quorum is not present at either meeting, the return should specify that the meeting was duly summoned and that no quorum was present and this will suffice. As with a members' voluntary liquidation, the Registrar registers the returns and the company is dissolved at the end of three months, subject to the rights of the liquidator or of interested persons to apply for the date to be deferred. The Registrar must cause to be published in the *London Gazette* notice of the receipt by him of the return of the holding of the meeting.

Applications to court

The liquidator or any contributory or creditor may apply to the court to determine any question arising in the winding-up of a company, or to exercise, as respects the enforcing of calls or any other matter, all or any of the powers which the court might exercise if the company were being wound up by the court, and the court may accede to these requests and make such orders as it thinks just. A copy of any such order must be sent forthwith by the company, or otherwise as may be prescribed, to the Registrar of Companies for minuting in his books relating to the company.

Rights of creditors and contributories

Notwithstanding the fact that the company is being wound up voluntarily, a creditor or contributory may still apply to have it wound up by the court, but the court must be satisfied that, in the case of a contributory, the rights of the contributories will be prejudiced by a voluntary winding-up.

Alternatives to winding-up

There are two ways in which a company can be dissolved without following winding-up procedures.

Striking off at the instigation of the Registrar: defunct companies

The dissolution here results where the Registrar has a reasonable cause to believe that a company is not carrying on business or is not in operation. This jurisdiction, which has been with us for many years, is currently to be found in s 1000 of the 2006 Act. The Registrar may act because, for example:

(a) he has not received documents from the company which should have been sent to him; or
(b) correspondence sent to the company's registered office by the Registrar has been returned undelivered.

The Registrar will enquire if the company is still in business or operation. If he is satisfied that it is not, he will publish a notice in the *London Gazette* of his intention to strike the company off the Register. The Company Law Official Notifications Supplement to the *London Gazette* publishes weekly notices in microfiche form. A copy notice is placed on the company's public record.

The Registrar will take into account representations from the company and other interested parties, such as members and creditors, but unless cause to the contrary is shown, the Registrar will strike the company off not less than three months after the date of the notice. The company is, in fact, dissolved on publication of a further notice to that effect in the *London Gazette*. It will be seen, therefore, that if the company is to remain in business, it is important for the company to reply promptly to any formal letter of inquiry from the Registrar and to deliver any outstanding documents. Failure to deliver the documents required may result in the directors being prosecuted.

Assets of dissolved company

From the date of dissolution any assets held by a dissolved company will be *bona vacantia* (property without an owner). This means that they belong to the Crown. The main source of enquiry in regard to *bona vacantia* property is the Treasury Solicitor (BV), One Kemble Street, London WC2B 4TS (see http://www.bonavacantia.gov.uk). If the company's registered office is in Lancashire, enquiries should be addressed to the Solicitor to the Duchy of Lancaster, 66 Lincoln's Inn Fields, London WC2A 3LH. Where the registered office is in Cornwall or the Isles of Scilly, enquiries should be made to the Solicitor to the Duchy of Cornwall, 10 Buckingham Gate, London SW1E 6LA.

Applications for striking off

A private company which is not trading but which is sending relevant documents and returns to the Registrar may apply to the Registrar to be struck off the Register. The procedure is useful, for example, for companies formed to pursue what was thought to be a good project but which has failed. Nevertheless, the directors may be in a position to deal with its assets and liabilities and ensure that the company's affairs are brought to a conclusion without the cost of employing an insolvency practitioner as liquidator. Until the company is struck off the Register, though, the directors are burdened with duties under the Companies Acts, such as filing accounts and annual returns. Accordingly, the Deregulation and Contracting Out Act 1994, s 13 and Sch 5 introduce new ss 652A–652F into the Companies Act 1985 to provide for the application procedure. These sections are now contained in ss 1000–1011 of the Companies Act 2006.

Application is made by the directors or a majority of them under s 1003 of the CA 2006. The application is returned to the Registrar and copies must be sent to notifiable parties (see below). In general terms, the company should have concluded its affairs, though even after making application it can conclude its outstanding affairs where necessary or expedient to make or proceed with an application, e.g. paying the costs of running office premises while concluding its affairs and disposing of the office.

It is important to note that in the previous *three months* the company must not have:

- changed its name;
- traded or carried on its business;
- made a disposal for value of property that it held immediately prior to ceasing to trade, for the purpose of disposal for gain in the normal course of business or otherwise carrying on business; or
- engaged in any other activity except for the purposes of making the application, concluding the affairs of the company complying with any statutory requirement or as specified by the Secretary of State by order for the purpose of s 1004(1); furthermore

- any property which has not been transferred out of the company will be regarded as *bona vacantia* (goods without an owner) and will become the property of the Crown. There should therefore be no assets or liabilities at the time of dissolution. The potential liability of the directors to members and creditors remains.

A company cannot apply to be struck off if it is the subject, or proposed subject of:

- any insolvency proceedings such as liquidation and including a situation where a petition has been presented but has not yet been dealt with; or
- a scheme under Part 26 of the 2006 Act (section 895), i.e. a compromise or arrangement between the company and its creditors or members.

However, a company can apply for strike off if it has settled trading or business debts in the previous three months. Further circumstances in which an application cannot be made can be found in ss 1004 and 1005 of the Companies Act 2006.

When the company meets all of the above criteria for striking off, an application (DS01) can be completed, signed by the majority of directors and submitted with a £10 fee to Companies House. The form must be signed and dated by:

- the sole director, if there is only one;
- by both, if there are two; or
- by all, or the majority of directors, if there are more than two.

Notifiable persons

A copy of the application must be sent within seven days of making the application to:

- members, usually the shareholders;
- creditors, including all contingent (existing) and prospective (likely) creditors such as banks, suppliers, former employees if the company owes them money, landlords, tenants (for example, where a bond is refundable), guarantors and personal injury claimants;.
- employees;
- managers or trustees of an employees' pension fund; and
- any directors who have not signed the form (see s 1006(1)).

These notifiable persons can object to the court against the striking off for up to 20 years after the publication by the Registrar of the striking off in the *London Gazette*. Such an objection might be raised because a notifiable person was owed money by the company and is taking action in court to recover it or because the conditions for application for striking off have been breached.

In addition to persons notifiable under s 1006, other interested parties should be informed such as the local authority where there have been planning disputes and health and safety issues. HMRC should be informed in advance of an application to strike off. HMRC is the main objector in the striking-off process and can hold up the procedure for some time. It is better therefore to clear matters with HMRC and other interested parties before making the application. Consideration must also be given to notifying the Department for Work and Pensions if there are outstanding, contingent or prospective liabilities that would be of concern to this agency.

Safeguards exist for those who are likely to be affected by a company's dissolution. Loose ends, such as closing the company's bank account, the transfer of any domain names should all be taken care of before applying for voluntary wind up. In addition to notifying HMRC, a company may want to notify local authorities, especially if the company is under any obligation involving planning permission or health and safety issues, training and enterprise councils and government agencies.

Finally it should be noted that from the date of dissolution, any assets of a dissolved company will belong to the Crown. The company's bank account will be frozen and any credit balance in the account will pass to the Crown.

The company's directors must also send a copy of the application to any person who, after the application has been made, becomes a director, member, creditor or employee of the company, or a manager or trustee of any employee pension fund of the company. This must be done within seven days of the person becoming one of these. They must also send a copy of the application to any person who becomes one of the above at any time after the day the company made the application for voluntary strike off. This obligation continues until the dissolution of the company or the withdrawal of the application.

A copy of the 'Striking off application by a company' Form DS01 can be left at the last known address (if an individual) or the principal/registered office (if a company or other body). It is also permissible to make a creditor of the company aware of the application by leaving a copy of it at, or posting a copy of it to, the place of business with which the company has had dealings in relation to the current debts, for example, the branch from where goods were ordered or invoiced. However, if there is more than one such place of business, Companies House advises that a copy of the application be delivered to each of those places. They also suggest that it is advisable to keep proof of delivery or posting.

Companies House will examine the form and if it is acceptable will register the information and put it on the company's public record. If the Registrar has already started dissolution action under s 1000 (power to strike off company not carrying on business or in operation), Companies House will not accept the application. However, if the application is acceptable Companies House will send an acknowledgement to the address shown on the form and will also notify the company at its registered office address to enable it to object if the application is bogus.

The Registrar will publish notice of the proposed striking off in the *London Gazette* to allow interested parties the opportunity to object. A copy of this notice will be placed on the company's public record. If there is no reason to delay the Registrar will strike the company off the Register not less than three months after the date of the notice. The company will be dissolved on publication of a further notice stating this in the relevant *London Gazette*.

Restoration to the Register by court order

Unless a company is administratively restored to the Register, the Registrar can only restore a company if he receives a court order. Any company which is restored to the Register is deemed to have continued in existence as if it had not been struck off and dissolved. Companies struck off under s 1000 and the new application arrangements can be restored to the Register for up to 20 years after dissolution (see above). A court order is necessary and application to the court can be made by interested parties such as creditors, particularly those who did not receive a copy of the company's application for striking off.

An interested party may also sometimes be a person who wishes to bring a personal injury claim against the company. The company will normally have been insured against such claims, but unless a judgment is obtained against the company, the liability of the insurer to meet the claim does not arise. The Secretary of State may also restore a company to the Register if he considers this to be in the public interest. An application for restoration may be made by any of the following:

- any former director, member, creditor or liquidator;
- any person who had a contractual relationship with the company or who had a potential legal claim against the company;
- any person who had an interest in land or property in which the company also had an interest, right or obligation;
- any manager or trustee of the company's former employees' pension fund; or
- any other person who appears to the court to have an interest in the matter.

Except in cases of personal injury, an application for restoration must be made within six years of the date of dissolution. In the case of bringing a claim for damages for personal injury, an application for restoration may be made at any time, but the court may not make an order for restoration where it appears that the claim would fail due to legal time limits placed on it.

It was thought that interested parties who may apply for restoration to the Register must 'feel aggrieved' at the strike off *at the time of strike off*. It followed, therefore, that a director who had agreed with the board's decision to apply for strike off and who had been instrumental in bringing about the company's dissolution could not successfully ask the court to restore the company to the Register (see *Conti* v *Ueberseebank AG* also cited *Conti, Petitioner* [1998] 11 CL 581).

This decision was reversed on appeal (see *Conti* v *Ueberseebank AG* [2000] 4 CL 698) where it was held that a member applying for restoration did not have to show that he had been aggrieved at the date of striking off so long as he could establish *a grievance at the time of his application* to restore the company, such as the possibility of a legal claim.

Outline procedure

Restoration to the Register is a matter for the Companies Court, local district registries and county courts that have jurisdiction to wind up companies. The Registrar of Companies must also consent and applications for restoration must be served on him at least 10 days before the court hearing. In this connection, it is important to note that it is the normal practice of the Registrar to require delivery of outstanding accounts, annual returns and any other documents in acceptable form before the hearing, before giving his consent to the application. These documents must be delivered to the Registrar at least five working days before the hearing. A member of the company must be joined in the application to give any undertakings required by the Registrar and to be responsible for his costs of the application. If the company to be restored was registered in England or Wales, one must apply by completing a Part 8 claim form (this is the standard form that starts proceedings). The Registrar of the Companies Court in London usually hears restoration cases in chambers once a week on Friday afternoons. Cases are also heard at the District Registries. Alternatively, you can make an application to a County Court that has the authority to wind up the company.

Delay in application to restore to Register

Where there is an application to restore a company to the Register so that a claim can be brought against it the claimant should bear in mind that delay in regard to the making of a petition to the court for restoration may mean that the Limitation Act 1980 has applied so that the claim is statute-barred and restoration will not be granted. The period from the company's dissolution until the bringing of the restoration proceedings is taken into account by the court in deciding this issue (see *Whitbread (Hotels) Ltd Petitioners* 2002 SLT 178).

Offences and penalties

The application provisions must not be used to defraud creditors or for any other wrongful purpose. Most offences under the new provisions attract a fine of up to £5,000 on conviction before magistrates and an unlimited fine in the Crown Court. If directors deliberately conceal the application from interested parties, they are liable not only to a fine but up to seven years' imprisonment. There may also be disqualification from being a director, the maximum period being 15 years.

Name of restored company

The Registrar will normally restore a company with the name it had before it was struck off and dissolved. However, if at the date of restoration the company's former name is the same as another name on the Registrar's index of company names, the Register cannot restore the company with its former name. If the name is no longer available, the court order may state another name by which the company is to be restored. As an alternative, the company may be restored to the Register as if its registered company number is also its name. The company then has 14 days from the date of restoration to pass a resolution to change the name of the company. It is an offence if the company does not change its name within 14 days of being restored with the number as its name.

When a company has been restored, the general effect is that a company is deemed to have continued in existence as if it had not been dissolved or struck off the Register. The court may give directions or make provision to put the company and all other persons in the same position as they were before the company was dissolved and struck off. A notice must also be placed in the *London Gazette*.

Administrative Restoration

This is when, under certain conditions, where a company was dissolved because it appeared to be no longer carrying on business or in operation, a former director or member may apply to the Registrar to have the company restored. If the Registrar restores the company it is deemed to have continued in existence as if it had not been dissolved and struck off the Register. Section 1025 of the 2006 Act gives details of the requirements relating to Administrative Restoration.

Administrative Restoration is available where the company was struck off under: s 652 of the 1985 Act; s 603 of the Companies Consolidation (Consequential Provisions) (Northern Ireland) Order 1986 (SI 1986/1035 (NI 9); or ss 1000 and 1001 of the 2006 Act. Only a former director or former member of the company, who was a director or member at the time the company was dissolved, can apply. To be eligible for Administrative Restoration, the company must have been struck off the Register under the above sections cited and dissolved for no more than six years as of the date the application for restoration has been received by the Registrar.

If a company meets the above criteria, an application for restoration may be made if it meets the following conditions:

- it must have been carrying on business or in operation at the time it was struck off; and
- if any property or rights belonging to the company became *bona vacantia*, the applicant must provide the Registrar with a statement in writing from the relevant Crown Representative giving consent to the company's restoration.

If the Registrar decides to restore the company, the restoration will take effect from the date the Registrar sends the notice. The notice will include the company's registered number and the name of the company. If the company is restored under a different name or with the company number as its name, both that name and the former name shall appear on the notice.

(Authors' note: Questions on winding-up can be found at the end of Chapter 29. ◐)

Suggested further reading

Ferran, 'The duties of an administrative receiver to unsecured creditors' (1998) *Company Lawyer* 9, 58.

Finch, 'Corporate rescue in a world of debt' [2008] JBL 8, 756.

Kastrinou, 'An analysis of the pre-pack technique and recent developments in the area' [2008] *Company Lawyer* 29, 259.

Keay, 'The duty of directors to take account of creditors' interests: Has it any role to play?' [2002] JBL 379.

29 Corporate insolvency – winding-up in context

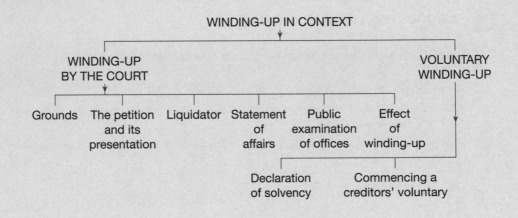

WINDING-UP IN CONTEXT

WINDING-UP BY THE COURT

- Grounds
- The petition and its presentation
- Liquidator
- Statement of affairs
- Public examination of offices
- Effect of winding-up

VOLUNTARY WINDING-UP

- Declaration of solvency
- Commencing a creditors' voluntary

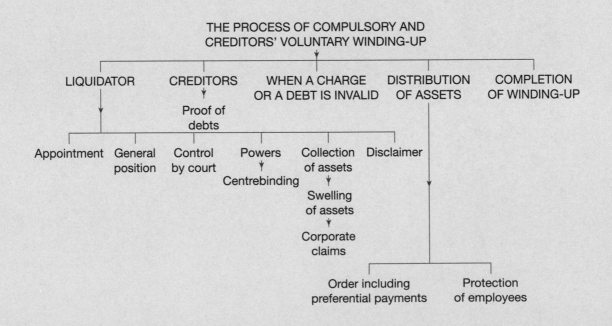

THE PROCESS OF COMPULSORY AND CREDITORS' VOLUNTARY WINDING-UP

- LIQUIDATOR
- CREDITORS
  - Proof of debts
- WHEN A CHARGE OR A DEBT IS INVALID
- DISTRIBUTION OF ASSETS
- COMPLETION OF WINDING-UP

- Appointment
- General position
- Control by court
- Powers
  - Centrebinding
- Collection of assets
  - Swelling of assets
  - Corporate claims
- Disclaimer

- Order including preferential payments
- Protection of employees

Having outlined the methods of winding-up in terms of a broad overview, we now consider in this chapter the likely course of a winding-up.

Let us assume that we are dealing with a small manufacturing company which has suffered from a recession in trade and is now in difficulties in terms that its creditors are pressing for payment which it cannot make. In addition, let us consider the problem from the point of view of the unsecured or trade creditors who do not wish to appoint an administrator.

Two courses are open to them as follows:

1 To initiate a winding-up by the court. This is slow and expensive.
2 To convince the directors that the company cannot continue in business and that it would be advantageous to initiate a creditors' voluntary winding-up.

Both procedures will be considered in turn. Section references are to the Insolvency Act 1986 unless otherwise stated.

Winding-up by the court

Grounds

The grounds for compulsory winding-up under s 122 are as follows:

(a) a special resolution by the members to wind up;
(b) failure to start business within one year of incorporation or suspension of business for a whole year;
(c) if the number of members falls below two, though not in the case of a single-member company;
(d) if the company is unable to pay its debts;
(e) if it is just and equitable that the company be wound up.

In addition, a newly incorporated public company may be wound up if it does not obtain a certificate under CA 2006, s 761 within one year of incorporation. The petition may be presented by the Secretary of State. We have already considered the more important cases under (e) above (see Chapter 18 ◖).

It is only the fourth ground (which is the commonest and most important) that will be dealt with in any detail here.

A company's inability to pay its debts is defined by s 123 as follows:

(a) If a creditor to whom the company is indebted in a sum *exceeding £750* has served a demand in writing for payment and within three weeks the company has failed to pay the sum due (or given a security or entered into a compromise acceptable to the creditor). A statutory demand cannot be based on a statute-barred debt, e.g. a contract debt that is more than six years old, so an action cannot be brought upon it (*Re a Debtor (No 50A SD/95)* [1997] 2 All ER 789). A statutory demand cannot be based upon a contingent debt as where a contract debt is unlikely to be paid but has not yet become due under the contractual provisions for payment (see *JSF Finance & Currency Exchange Co Ltd* v *Akma Solutions Inc* [2001] 2 BCLC 307).

Note that it is not merely the failure to pay the debt which gives the ground for winding-up. Thus, if a company can satisfy the court that it has a defence to the claim a winding-up order will not be made. In consequence it is advisable for a creditor to sue the company to judgment before serving a demand for payment of the judgment debt, though this is not a legal requirement.

(b) If a judgment creditor has tried to enforce his judgment by execution on the company's property and the execution has failed to satisfy the debt.

(c) If the court is satisfied that the company is unable to pay its debts. The following case provides an example.

Taylors Industrial Flooring Ltd v *M & H Plant Hire (Manchester) Ltd* [1990] BCLC 216

M & H supplied plant to Taylors, who were building contractors, in December 1988. M & H invoiced Taylors in mid-January 1989 but by 14 April 1989 the invoice had not been paid, nor had the second invoice which was issued in February 1989. M & H petitioned for the compulsory winding-up of Taylors on 14 April. The Court of Appeal *held* that the petition could proceed. Section 123 was satisfied. Taylors had no grounds to dispute the debt, and the fact that they might not wish to pay it was no defence.

Comment

This is a useful decision in modern times when companies have collapsed so quickly that the wait of three weeks for the statutory demand to trigger has seen the company's assets dissipated.

Petitioners

For our purposes, six classes of persons can present a petition as follows:

1 the company itself;
2 the Official Receiver who can present a petition even after the commencement of a voluntary winding-up;
3 the Department for Business, Innovation and Skill (BIS), following an investigation;
4 a contributory;
5 a creditor;
6 the Secretary of State for BIS (Secretary of State) where a public company does not obtain a s 762 (CA 2006) certificate in time.

Only a petition by a contributory or creditor will be considered in any detail here.

(a) Contributory

The following points should be noted:

(i) A contributory is defined as meaning everyone who is liable to contribute to the assets of the company should it be wound up.

(ii) Although at first sight the term would appear to cover only shareholders whose shares are partly paid, it applies also to holders of fully paid shares since all members are liable to contribute subject to any limits on their liability provided for by s 74 of the Insolvency Act 1986 (*Re Anglesey Colliery Co* (1886) 1 Ch App 555). The section provides that a person who has fully paid shares is not liable to contribute but nevertheless he is within the definition of a contributory. So 'contributory' is merely another name for 'member' under s 124.

(iii) Under s 124 a contributory cannot petition unless (a) the number of members is reduced below two, but not in the case of a single-member company; or (b) he took his shares as an original allottee; or (c) by transmission from a deceased shareholder; or (d) he had held the shares for six out of the last 18 months. This is presumably a precaution to prevent the purchase of shares with a view to an immediate wrecking operation on the company.

(iv) Finally, a contributory cannot petition unless he has an interest in the process, e.g. it must be likely that there will be surplus assets. Thus, if a company is insolvent, a contributory cannot petition, though he can and has an interest if, because of the potential liability for the company's debts in a multi-member company, the membership is below the statutory minimum of two.

(b) Creditors

The following points should be noted:

(i) The creditor is the most usual petitioner. A creditor is a person who is owed money by the company and who could enforce his claim by an action in debt.

An unliquidated (or unascertained) claim in contract or tort is not enough. Thus it is better for the creditor petitioner to have the debt made precise as to amount by suing the company to judgment before winding-up. Then on petition the company cannot, by reason of the judgment, deny that it owes the money, or that it is an unliquidated sum.

(ii) The debt owed to the creditor to be *at least* £750. If it is not, he will no doubt find other creditors to make a joint petition with him so that the total debt is at least £750.

The figure of £750 has been adopted by the judiciary from the amount specified in s 123 of the Insolvency Act 1986 though that section does say: 'exceeding £750'.

(iii) Even if the debt on which the petition is based is not disputed, but there are some creditors who think that their best chance of recovering their money lies in the company continuing business, then the court may, in its discretion, refuse a winding-up order. Section 195 gives the court power to have regard to the wishes of the creditors, which in practice usually means the wishes of the majority in value.

Thus, in *Re ABC Coupler & Engineering Ltd* [1961] 1 All ER 354 a judgment creditor for £17,540 petitioned as his debt was not paid. He was opposed by various creditors whose debts were slightly more, namely £18,328. The company had extensive goodwill, orders worth £110,000 and its assets were worth almost £700,000 more than its liabilities. The court found that the wishes of the majority for the company to continue were reasonable.

Presentation of the petition

As soon as a petition is presented, the court may under s 135 take charge of the company's affairs by appointing a provisional liquidator. This is usually the Official Receiver.

It is a somewhat drastic measure to appoint a liquidator before the court has made a winding-up order, but if the company's assets are at risk of being dissipated by the directors it may be done. The role of the Official Receiver as provisional liquidator is to take possession of the assets and accounting records until the hearing of the petition. Normally the directors will also be relieved of the company's cheque books.

Avoiding property dispositions in compulsory winding-up

If a winding-up order is made on a petition for compulsory winding-up the commencement of the winding-up is deemed to be the date of presentation of the petition under what is known as the principle of 'relation back'. If there have been dispositions of the company's property during that period the liquidator may ask the court for an order restoring the property to the company. The directors may have made such dispositions after the petition but before the making of the order. These dispositions are void under s 127, Insolvency Act 1986 whether the recipient of the property is aware of the presentation of the petition or not. Those who are aware of it and wish genuinely to deal with the company should ask the court for a validating order which if given will make the relevant transaction legally enforceable and the property irrecoverable. In *Oxford Pharmaceuticals Ltd, Re* [2009] EWHC 1753 (Ch); [2009] 2 BCLC 485, the court concluded that a breach of s 127 is likely to constitute misfeasance on the part of a company director. Nonetheless, this point must be explicitly alleged otherwise a failure to do that will preclude a remedy under s 127 against a director unless the director was the beneficiary of the disposition.

Liquidator

Under s 136 the Official Receiver becomes the liquidator of any company ordered to be wound up by the court. Section 136 prescribes the steps to be taken to secure the Official Receiver's replacement as liquidator by an insolvency practitioner. For this purpose he may summon meetings of the company's creditors and members to choose a person to replace him and, under s 141, to decide whether to establish a liquidation committee to supervise the performance by the liquidator of his functions in the winding-up. Alternatively, the Official Receiver may ask the Secretary of State to make an appointment of a liquidator. If one-quarter in value of the company's creditors request him at any time to call the meetings of creditors and members referred to above the Official Receiver must do so.

Under s 139, if the members and creditors nominate different persons to be liquidators, the creditors' nominee becomes liquidator. Where a winding-up order follows immediately upon the discharge of an administration order, the court may under s 140 appoint the former administrator to be liquidator.

Statement of affairs

Under s 131, where the court has made a winding-up order or appointed a provisional liquidator, the Official Receiver may require the submission of a statement of affairs of the company giving, e.g. particulars of its assets and liabilities and details of its creditors.

The persons who will most usually be called upon to make the statement are the directors or other officers of the company. However, the 1986 Act empowers the Official Receiver to require other persons connected with the company to produce or assist in the production of the statement, e.g. employees or those employed within the last 12 months.

Investigation by the Official Receiver

Section 132 places a duty on the Official Receiver to investigate the affairs of the company and the reasons for its failure and to make such report, if any, to the court as he thinks fit.

Public examination of officers

Under s 133 the court has power on the application of the Official Receiver to require the public examination of persons connected with the company, e.g. its officers or an administrator. Those who without reasonable excuse fail to attend the examination may be arrested and books or papers in their possession seized.

Effect of winding-up

This is as follows:

(a) Immediately an order is made all actions for debt against the company are stopped (s 130). Actions in tort, e.g. for personal injury from negligence, continue.
(b) The company ceases to carry on business except with a view to a beneficial winding-up. For example, it may be necessary to carry on the company's business for a while in order to realise its assets at a better price, as by completing work in progress, but realisation must not be long delayed.
(c) The powers of the directors cease (*Fowler* v *Broads Patent Night Light Co* [1893] 1 Ch 724).
(d) Employees are automatically dismissed (*Chapman's Case* (1866) LR 1 Eq 346), though the liquidator may have to re-employ some of them until the winding-up is completed.

The EC Regulation on Insolvency Proceedings

The EC Regulation on Insolvency Proceedings came into force on 31 May 2002. It is directly applicable in the UK but a number of amendments were required to UK law to accommodate it. These appear below.

Before the coming into force of the Regulation it was possible to wind up a foreign company with assets in the UK in a UK court. Now *the main proceedings* are to be conducted where the company has its centre of main interests. In most cases this will be where the registered office is. Courts of other member states can open proceedings called *territorial proceedings* where the company carries on a non-transitory economic activity with human means or goods. These proceedings are restricted to assets situated in that member state. The proceedings affected are winding-up by the court, voluntary winding-up (with confirmation of the court), administration and voluntary arrangements.

Comment

(i) When an insolvency relates only to a person or entity with all of his or its assets in the same jurisdiction, the Regulation will have no application. In other cases the Regulation effects a most significant change to insolvency practice and merits careful study.
(ii) Although, under the above rules, courts throughout the EU (except Denmark) will be forced to recognise and assist insolvency practitioners from other countries, there are some difficulties, as follows:
   - The rules do not apply to the insolvencies of a group of companies. Since this is the most common way in which international businesses are structured where there are operations in different countries, the regulations may not come into effect that often.
   - There will also be arguments over whether the company has its 'centre of main operations' in a particular country.

- The provisions do not apply to insolvency practitioners appointed out of court – such as administrative receivers – and although these appointments are to be phased out under the Enterprise Act 2002, that Act does carry provisions under which an administrator may be appointed out of court, e.g. by the directors, and these appointments may not be covered.

The regulations seem to require a court involvement before proceedings are covered.

UK regulations to ensure compatibility

The UK regulations made to ensure the compatibility of the EC Regulation with UK law are: the Insolvency Act 1986 (Amendment) (No 2) Regulations 2002 (SI 2002/1240) and the Insolvency (Amendment) Rules 2002 (SI 2002/1307).

The regulations: an illustration

If the debtor (corporate or individual) has all the business interests in, say, Chester, proceedings will be commenced in the Chester County Court, or the High Court in the case of a corporate debtor with a share capital in excess of £120,000. These will be *main proceedings*. If, however, the debtor has main interests in, say, Paris, with some assets in Chester, the proceedings will be commenced as above but they will be *territorial proceedings* and confined to Chester assets.

The regulations: case law

The High Court has ruled that it could make an administration order against a company incorporated outside the European Union under the above-mentioned regulations if the centre of the company's main interests was in England (see *In Re Brac Rent-A-Car International Inc* [2003] EWHC 128 (Ch), [2003] All ER (D) 98 (Feb)). Certain judgment creditors challenged the jurisdiction of the court on the grounds that the company (which was the petitioner for administration) was incorporated in Delaware and had its registered address in the USA. The court accepted that there was no specific reference to companies outside the EU but since the jurisdiction was defined only in terms of where the petitioner's main interest lay the court had jurisdiction. The company's operations were conducted almost entirely in England and its trading contracts were governed by English law. Its employees worked in England and their contracts were governed by English law.

Comment

(i) It would appear that a UK court will, conversely, be denied its traditional jurisdiction to proceed to total winding-up where the company's centre of interest is not in the UK and be restricted to territorial proceedings confined to local assets.

(ii) Case law is still somewhat confusing on the interpretation to be put on the expression 'centre of main interests'. In the *Brac Rent-a-Car* case the court seems to have laid stress on where the employees were based and where trading took place and operations were put into effect, i.e. England. More recently the High Court has reached a conclusion that would have given the English court jurisdiction because key personnel, e.g. chairman, CEO, chief financial officer and chief operating officer, were based in London. The headquarters function played less of a role in the *Brac Rent-A-Car* case. A future case will hopefully sort out whether high level decision making or lower administration or back office functions are most important (see *King* v *Crown Energy Trading* [2003] EWHC 163 (Comm), [2003] All ER (D) 133 (Feb) which favoured high level decision making).

Byers v *Yacht Bull Corp* [2010] EWHC 133 (Ch); [2010] BCC 368 held that a claim asserted by joint liquidators to the ownership of an asset did not fall within the insolvency exception in the Judgments Regulation (44/2001) (see Art 1(2)(b)) and as such, the French courts had jurisdiction over this claim. Nonetheless, a secondary transactional avoidance claim that relied entirely on provisions contained in the Insolvency Act 1986 did with the end result that the English courts enjoyed jurisdiction over this transactional avoidance claim by virtue of the EC Regulation on Insolvency Proceedings (1346/2000) even though this jurisdiction could not be exercised until the French courts had determined the primary ownership issue. This position is consistent with the European Court of Justice ruling in *Seagon* v *Deko Marty Belgium NV (C-339/07)* [2009] BCC 347; [2009] 1 WLR 2168.

Voluntary winding-up

This is a more common method of winding-up. If in our situation the directors can be persuaded to take the view that the company has no future and agree it would be best if its existence came to an end, then a voluntary winding-up would be a cheaper method of achieving this purpose.

What sort of voluntary winding-up is applicable?

If we want a members' voluntary winding-up the directors would, as we have seen, have to make a *statutory declaration of solvency*, as it is called, in the five weeks before the special resolution for winding-up was passed, or on that date but before the resolution was passed (s 89). In the declaration they would have to say that in their opinion the company will be able to pay its debts in full plus interest within a stated period of time which must not be longer than 12 months, and a statement of assets and liabilities must be attached. Since the directors and the members control the process in a members' voluntary winding-up, there is a strong temptation for the directors to make a declaration, even if it is not fully justified.

The rate of interest is the rate, if any, in the contract with a creditor, or the interest paid on unpaid judgments under the Judgments Act 1838, which is currently 8 per cent. This rate has been in force since 1 April 1993 (see SI 1993/564). The interest is payable from the commencement of the winding-up until payment and can only be paid if all creditors have been paid the principal sum of their debt in full – in other words, it is payable from surplus assets which would normally belong to shareholders. If the contract provides for interest, this, along with the principal sum, will be proved for in the liquidation in the ordinary way.

False declarations – what are the penalties?

Under s 89, if the declaration is made without reasonable grounds the directors are liable to imprisonment and/or an unlimited fine; *and* if the debts are not in fact paid within the stated period it is *presumed* that the directors did not have reasonable grounds so that they will have to prove that they did, which is not an easy matter.

However, this does not apply to debts which are not fully ascertained. Commonly HMRC has not completed its assessments and cannot be paid. Nevertheless, if funds are available to pay such debts when ascertained, the members' winding-up continues and there is no need to convert to a creditors', nor are the directors liable for a false declaration.

However, if during a members' voluntary winding-up the liquidator is of the opinion that the company will not be able to pay its ascertained debts although a declaration of solvency has been given, s 95 provides that he must summon a meeting of creditors within 28 days of that opinion and put before it a statement of assets and liabilities.

As from the date when the liquidator calls the meeting of creditors, the company is deemed to be in a creditors' voluntary, and that meeting may exercise the same powers as a creditors' meeting at the beginning of a liquidation which is initiated as a creditors' winding-up, including appointing their nominee as liquidator and a liquidation committee.

If he does not follow this procedure, the liquidator is liable to a fine; and if he does, then the directors are liable to penalties for making a declaration of solvency without reasonable grounds.

The liquidator who has been nominated by the company on the basis that there would be a members' voluntary winding-up can, between the date of summoning the meeting and the meeting taking place, act only with the sanction of the court, except for taking all property under his control to which the company appears entitled. He may also dispose of perishable goods and do all such other things as may be necessary for the protection of the company's assets but no more.

Filing the declaration of solvency

The declaration must be filed with the Registrar before the expiry of the period of 15 days immediately following the date on which the resolution for winding up the company is passed. The company must give the usual 21 days' notice to its members of the extraordinary general meeting to consider the special resolution to wind up voluntarily.

If the statutory declaration is not delivered within the 15-day period, the liquidation remains a members' voluntary liquidation but the company and its officers are liable to a default fine under s 89.

Can we use a members' voluntary winding-up?

Unfortunately, our directors are only too well aware that the company will not be able to pay its debts within 12 months, so we shall have to have a creditors' voluntary winding-up and proceed as follows under s 84:

(a) Summon an extraordinary general meeting.
(b) Pass an extraordinary resolution that the company cannot by reason of its liabilities continue in business.
(c) It is the resolution which marks the start of a voluntary winding-up.
(d) The liquidator is appointed by the company if it is a members' voluntary winding-up; in a creditors' voluntary winding-up, though the members may by ordinary resolution have nominated their choice, the creditors have powers to override and appoint their own nominee, subject to the right of any member or creditor to appeal to the court within seven days.

However, even though the members may appoint their choice of liquidator he has only very limited powers until such time as the creditors have met and confirmed him in office or not. He can take the company's property under his control and dispose of perishable goods and generally protect the company's assets but *no more*.

If the company nominates five persons for what is called the liquidation committee, both in a voluntary winding-up and also in a compulsory winding-up, the creditors can now nominate five more and veto the company's nominees, subject again to a right of appeal to the court.

Purpose of liquidation committee

The purpose of such a committee is to provide a small representative body to help the liquidator. Moreover, if there is a major creditor, who regards the assets of the company as virtually his own, the committee may provide him with a useful safety valve. The liquidator becomes involved in many kinds of businesses but a major creditor, with his knowledge of the trade, can control the committee, and supervise the winding-up, and see that the run-down of the company is carried out to the best advantage. Since a liquidation committee can exercise certain powers, such as, for example, approving payment to any class of creditors, it will save the liquidator the necessity of calling a full meeting of creditors, whose approval would otherwise be necessary.

From now on we will combine consideration of the compulsory and voluntary winding-up process.

The duties of a liquidator

Appointment

The following points should be noted:

(a) If it is a compulsory winding-up, the Official Receiver, who automatically became provisional liquidator on the winding-up order (if not earlier on the presentation of the petition), will commonly continue as the liquidator.

(b) In the case of a voluntary winding-up, a person, other than a corporate body or a bankrupt, can be appointed, provided he is a qualified insolvency practitioner (see further Chapter 28 ⊙). The liquidator is usually an experienced accountant.

(c) In a voluntary winding-up, the liquidator will have to notify his appointment to the Registrar of Companies and publish it in the *London Gazette*, both within 14 days.

General position of the liquidator

Section 143 states that the functions of the liquidator of a company *which is being wound up by the court* shall be to ensure that the assets of the company are got in, realised and distributed to the company's creditors, and, if there is a surplus, to the persons entitled to it.

Beyond this there is no clear definition of his role; it is a mixture of common law and statutory duties and obligations. He partakes partly of the nature of a trustee, partly of an agent of the company and partly of an officer of the company.

(a) As a trustee

A liquidator is clearly not a trustee in the sense of the Trustee Act 1925, because the property of the company does not automatically vest in him as does trust property in trustees, although the court can make an order so vesting it. However, he takes over the powers of directors who equally, without being trustees, owe fiduciary duties to the company. His duty, like that of the directors, is owed to the company as a whole and not to individual contributories. Also, like a trustee, he cannot, by reason of the Insolvency Rules 1986 (which have been in part amended by The Insolvency (Amendment) Rules 2010 (SI 2010 No 686)), buy the company's property without leave of the court, or make a profit out of sales to the company. Moreover, he is in a more vulnerable position than a lay trustee because he is always paid to assume his responsibility and in *Re Home & Colonial Insurance Co* [1929] All ER Rep 231 the court referred to the 'high standard of care and diligence' required from him. 'His only refuge was to apply to the court for guidance in every case of serious doubt or difficulty.'

Furthermore, although it has not been definitely decided, it does not appear that the liquidator can claim the protection of s 61 of the Trustee Act 1925 if he has acted honestly and reasonably and ought to be excused. In *Re Windsor Steam Coal Ltd* [1929] 1 Ch 151 the Court of Appeal held on the facts that the liquidator had not acted reasonably in paying a claim without the directions of the court, but left open the question of whether s 61 was available as a defence.

(b) As an agent

The liquidator can be described as an agent for the company in that he can make contracts on behalf of the company for winding-up purposes.

He has, of course, the paid agent's obligation to bring reasonable skill to his duties. However, he is not a true agent in that he controls the actions of his so-called principal, the company.

(c) As an officer

The liquidator is treated as an officer of the company in s 30(4), CA 2006. He or she is also named in s 212 of the Insolvency Act 1986 as a person against whom proceedings may be taken for misfeasance, which will be referred to again later. Neither is it certain that he or she is entitled to the protection of the Companies Acts whereby the court can relieve any officer who, though negligent or in breach of trust, has acted honestly and reasonably and ought to be relieved. We have already seen an example of this section in operation in *In Re Duomatic Ltd* (1969) (see Chapter 23, p. 493 ●).

Control by the court

Finally, the liquidator is subject to constant control by the court because any person aggrieved by an action or decision of a liquidator in a winding-up may apply to the court. However, it would seem that the court is not anxious to upset his acts. Thus, in *Leon v York-O-Matic* [1966] 3 All ER 277, where the liquidator was charged by a member of the company with selling assets at an undervalue, the judge said that in the absence of fraud there could not be interference in the day-to-day administration of the liquidator, nor a questioning of the exercise by the liquidator in good faith of his discretion, nor a holding him accountable for an error of judgement.

Powers of the liquidator

The following points should be noted:

(a) In a compulsory winding-up, s 167 provides that something like half of his powers can only be exercised with the approval of the court or of the liquidation committee, e.g. to bring or defend actions, to carry on the business of the company so far as may be necessary for its beneficial winding-up, and to pay any class of creditors in full. Otherwise he can do most acts on his own authority, e.g. sell the company's property or raise money on the security of the company's assets.

(b) In a creditors' voluntary winding-up, he can exercise all the powers on his own except three which need the sanction of the court, the liquidation committee or the creditors. These powers are: to pay creditors; to make a compromise with creditors; and to compromise calls and debts (s 165).

(c) While the liquidator in a voluntary winding-up has a freedom from supervision by the court which is not available in a compulsory winding-up, he can always get support and guidance by applying to the court on any matter arising out of the winding-up (s 112).

Centrebinding

In the past, when no particular qualifications were required to undertake insolvency work, it was possible for the members in a creditors' voluntary to appoint a liquidator from among a group of unscrupulous persons prepared to participate in fraud. The person appointed would then proceed to dispose of the company assets and dissipate the proceeds often into other enterprises of the directors or their associates. This was done without the holding of a creditors' meeting to affirm the appointment of the liquidator, and by the time the creditors became aware of the liquidation it was too late to do anything about it. The difficulty was that the disposal of the assets by the members' liquidator was quite legal. The court so decided in *Re Centrebind* [1966] 3 All ER 889 and the procedure became known as 'centrebinding'.

The practice had been brought to an end for two reasons as follows:

(a) the requirement of qualified insolvency practitioners; *and*

(b) because of s 166, which provides that until a meeting of creditors has been called to approve the company's liquidator, that liquidator has power only to take control of the company's property and to sell perishable goods. Any other dispositions of the company's property are invalid.

Collection of the assets

(a) The liquidator will take charge of all assets which can be physically brought under his control, including money in the bank.

(b) He will not be able to touch money subject to a trust. Thus, in *Re Kayford* [1975] 1 All ER 604 a mail order company in anticipation of liquidation had put customers' deposits for goods which the company might not be able to supply in a special 'Customer Trade Deposit Account' and it was held that these deposits were returnable to the customers and did not come under the control of the liquidator. However, if there are any other assets in the hands, for example, of a sheriff, who is intending to sell the goods as part of a judgment creditor's execution, the liquidator will be able to recover these assets if the process of sale has not been completed before the winding-up commenced.

(c) The liquidator will normally in a compulsory winding-up pay all money into the Insolvency Services Account at the Bank of England, but in a voluntary winding-up he need not do so unless he has in his hands assets unclaimed or undistributed for six months.

(d) He can bring actions to enforce debts due to the company.

(e) He will settle the list of contributories and he can ask the court to exercise its powers under s 237 to order an officer or any person who has previously held office as administrator or liquidator of the company or as an administrative receiver and any trustee for or any banker or agent or officer of the company to hand over any property or money or books, papers or records of the company under his control. Set-off is not allowed to a contributory until all the creditors have been paid in full. In the unlikely event of there being uncalled capital, he can call it up, and will settle the A list of present members and the B list of persons who have been members in the 12 months preceding winding-up. The B list members will only be liable for debts contracted while they were members to the extent that their successors failed to pay the balance due on their shares.

Officers: co-operation with liquidator

It was held by the Court of Appeal Criminal Division in *R* v *McCredie* [2000] BCLC 438 that the company's directors and other officers are required by s 208(1) of the Insolvency Act 1986 to co-operate with the liquidator in terms of the ascertainment and delivery up of the company's property, not merely in a reactive manner but proactively. The requirement to deliver up does not depend on a prior request from the liquidator. It is a continuing and not a once-for-all-time duty. Failure to act in a proactive way can, as this case decides, be a criminal offence under s 208 punishable with imprisonment or a fine.

Swelling the assets

It is the duty of the liquidator, subject to the problems outlined below, to swell the assets by recovering any sums due from the directors or officers of the company. His ability to recover may arise under a number of headings as follows:

(a) Secret profits

It may be that the directors have made an unauthorised profit out of their position. As we saw in *Regal (Hastings) Ltd* v *Gulliver*, 1942, the directors had helped the parent company out by putting up money for shares in a subsidiary company, but were made to repay to the parent company a profit on those shares when they were sold. Alternatively, the directors may have paid themselves unauthorised salaries which may be recovered. As we have seen, officers of the company can be summoned before the court for examination if they are suspected of having property of the company in their possession.

(b) Wrongful and fraudulent trading

The company's officers, and others, may be held personally liable for certain debts of the company under the rules relating to wrongful and fraudulent trading. If the liquidator recovers money under the above heads, it goes into a fund for all the creditors (*Re William C Leitch Ltd (No 2)* [1933] Ch 261). In the past if an individual creditor, such as the Revenue, was paid his debt by the directors as a result of his bringing an application for, say, fraudulent trading, then he could keep the money (*Re Cyona Distributors* [1967] 1 All ER 281). This will not arise now because only the liquidator may apply, under the relevant sections.

(c) Power to conduct examinations

Section 212 allows the court on the application of the Official Receiver, the liquidator, a creditor or a contributory to examine the conduct of any promoter, past or present director, manager, liquidator, administrator, administrative receiver or officer of the company. If it appears that such a person has misapplied or retained or become liable or accountable for any money or property of the company, or been guilty of any misfeasance or breach of trust in relation to the company, the court can order him to repay or restore or to contribute to the assets of the company by way of compensation such a sum as the court thinks just.

Corporate claims in liquidation

Although, in general terms, a liquidator will wish to swell the assets by recovering sums under the headings mentioned above, it should be noted that it is, generally speaking, unwise for a liquidator to enter into litigation for the company. First, because legal aid has been abolished in civil matters (except for family and clinical negligence cases). In addition, the Access to Justice Act 1999 specifically provides in s 6 and Sch 2, para 1(g) that the new Legal Services Commission shall not fund 'matters of company or partnership law', or under para 1(h) 'other matters arising from the carrying on of a business'. Second, because the Court of Appeal ruled in *Mond* v *Hammond Suddards* [2000] Ch 40 that the cost of an unsuccessful litigation will not be treated as an expense of the liquidation, even though the liquidator had not acted in any way improperly in defending a claim by the company's receiver in regard to title to certain of the company's property. As regards conditional fee arrangements (the no-win no-fee concept), these require security for costs by the litigant or the making of a single premium insurance arrangement which admittedly is recoverable from the defendant (if he has funds) where the action is successful but not otherwise. So costs remain a problem even where the lawyer receives no fee if the claim is lost. 'Lawyer' means the solicitor in the case. Separate arrangements are required with a barrister to take the case in court unless the solicitor is also an advocate. Thus cases that have a good chance of success will continue to be brought if funded by creditors but perhaps rarely otherwise. Litigation funding agreements are dealt with by s 28 of the Access to Justice Act 1999, which inserts a new s 58B into the Courts and Legal Services Act 1990.

The ruling in the *Mond* case was affirmed in *Lewis* v *Inland Revenue Commissioners* (2000) *The Times*, 15 November. The Court of Appeal ruled in that case that a liquidator had no automatic right to recoup litigation costs. A company's liquidator attempting to use the company's realised funds for the purpose of taking proceedings against directors for wrongful trading or the recovery of a preference could not automatically regard the cost as an expense of the liquidation and payable before all other claims under s 115, IA 1986. The liquidator's right to recoup was subject to making an application to the court, under s 112 (voluntary liquidation) or s 156 (compulsory liquidation), for the court to exercise its power under those sections as relevant to dictate a different order of priority of payment in terms of allowing recoupment of litigation costs at the court's discretion.

Comment

The law is obviously anxious to look at each case on its merits. Even where the case is good, litigation is, after all, unpredictable and can be a very quick way to lose the company's funds.

Creditors – proof of debts

The following points should be noted:

1 The liquidator will normally have written to every known creditor on first appointment, sending him a copy of the statement of affairs, and he will advertise in the *London Gazette* and a local newspaper (Insolvency Rules 1986) for details of debts to be submitted within a definite period, and he will normally require debts to be verified by affidavit. Then he will examine and decide on every debt, and a rejected creditor can appeal to the court.

2 The admission of debts will depend on whether the company is solvent or not. If the company is solvent, all debts can be proved which could have been enforced against the company if it had not gone into liquidation. However, statute-barred debts are only payable if all the members agree, and future debts are payable subject to a rebate of 5 per cent per annum because they are paid early.

3 If the company is insolvent, the following rules apply and certain debts are non-provable as follows:

   (a) Claims for unliquidated damages in tort. Damages for breach of contract or trust are provable on an estimate. Thus, if a claim can be framed in either contract or tort, as might be the case where injury was caused to a person by the negligence of a company driver, it may be possible to include the claim as one of contract rather than of tort. This is a useful rule for a liquidator because in a compulsory liquidation he does not have to await the outcome of tort proceedings before winding up the company, though, as we have seen, an order can be made by the court restoring it to the Register so that a formal claim may be made against it to trigger its insurance company's duty to indemnify the company against the claim. However, in *Re Islington Metal and Plating Works* [1983] 3 All ER 218, Harman J decided that if a company which started liquidation as insolvent later became solvent, where, as in this case, an action by the liquidator on behalf of the company against its directors for misfeasance might succeed, debts of all descriptions could be proved. In such a situation, once the claims of the undoubted creditors were satisfied and the costs provided for, the tort claimants would be entitled to make claims before distribution of any surplus. Members' and creditors' voluntaries must be kept open while tort claims are quantified.

   (b) Debts incurred after notice of a transaction at undervalue or preference (see below), or if the company could not pay its debts as they fell due and had suspended payment of debts.

   (c) Contingent debts when the value cannot be fairly estimated. In *Re Patent Floor Cloth Co* (1872) 26 LT 467, two persons Dean and Gilbert were employed by the company as travellers for a period of three years on commission. In the first year they made £400 each and then the company was wound up. The court held that an estimate could be made of their entitlement to commission for the purposes of the winding-up but this would have been impossible if there had not been a first year commission on which to base it.

   (d) Debts barred by the Limitation Act 1980 at the commencement of winding-up are not enforceable, though time stops running on the commencement of the liquidation and if the debt is not statute-barred then it will not become so because of delay in payment arising out of the liquidation.

   (e) Illegal debts and unenforceable debts are not provable. For example, a debt on a contract for the sale of land which is not in writing as is required by the Law of Property

(Miscellaneous Provisions) Act 1989 is not provable. Nor would an illegal debt be provable as where a builder has built premises for a company knowing that there was no planning permission.

If a debt cannot be proved, the creditor gets no dividend and has no rights as a creditor, e.g. to attend and vote at meetings.

There are also certain *deferred debts*. These are provable but no dividend is payable nor is there a right to vote until all provable debts have been paid with interest (see below). The deferred debts are as follows:

(a) loans under a written agreement that the lender is to receive a rate of interest varying with the profits of the company; and

(b) where the vendor of a business sold to the company is receiving a share of the profits as payment.

The Third Parties (Rights Against Insurers) Act 1930 as amended by The Third Parties (Rights Against Insurers) Act 2010

A method of circumventing a liquidation by a creditor is to be found in the above Act, which has been the subject of a Law Commission consultation paper. If a worker is injured by his employer's negligence and the employer is a company that goes into liquidation, the 1930 Act allows the injured worker to make a claim against the company's insurer, thus avoiding a proof in the company's liquidation which might only produce a small payment covering only part of the claim.

However, the claim against the insurer is by no means straightforward since the insurer is only liable to indemnify the company. Therefore, the worker must sue the company to establish its liability before the insurance company is obliged to pay. This may mean an action at law to restore the company to the register if it has been struck off on liquidation and another action against the company to establish its liability. It may then be necessary to bring a legal action against the insurance company if it disputes liability.

The Law Commission and the Scottish Law Commission published a joint report (Law Com No 272/Scot Law Com No 184) on 31 July 2001. The report recommended the repeal of the Third Parties (Rights Against Insurers) Act 1930 and its replacement with a new Act that would make it easier for a third party to obtain a remedy as well as provide that the third party should not have to take legal proceedings to restore a company to the Register.

The Law Commissions' recommendations were accepted by Government in 2002, and the Third Parties (Rights Against Insurers) Bill was introduced in Parliament in November 2009. The Bill proceeded through Parliament via a trial procedure for Law Commission bills, and received Royal Assent on 25 March 2010.

The key changes made by Third Parties (Rights Against Insurers) Act 2010 are:

● A new court procedure is available to third parties. The third party has a right to seek declarations as to the insured's liability to them and as to the insurer's potential liability under the insurance contract in one set of proceedings. If the court or tribunal makes such declarations, it will be able to make an appropriate judgment which is likely to be a money judgment. This mechanism is optional; the third party may alternatively bring proceedings against the insured before commencing proceedings against the insurer (as at present).

● The third party will no longer be obliged to join the insured in proceedings against the insurer; but if this is not done where a declaration is made regarding the insured's liability to the third party, it will not bind the insured.

Position of secured creditors

As regards secured creditors, a secured creditor must state in his proof that he is a secured creditor and either:

(i) surrender the security and prove for the whole debt as an unsecured creditor; *or*
(ii) value the security and prove for the balance which then remains as an unsecured creditor.

If the creditor values the security and proves for the balance, then the liquidator may (a) redeem the security by paying the creditor the amount of the valuation, or (b) require the security to be sold by auction to establish its value.

The creditor may at any time after lodging his proof by notice in writing require the liquidator to choose between (a) and (b) above. The liquidator then has six months from receipt of the notice to make a choice. If he does not make a choice, the creditor owns the security at his valuation and may prove for the balance as an unsecured creditor.

Under s 189 the surplus remaining in any winding-up after payment in full of proved debts is to be applied in the payment of interest to the extent specified on the amount of those debts before it is available for members. The rate of interest payable under the section in respect of any debt is whichever is the greater of:

(a) the rate specified in s 17 of the Judgments Act 1838 on the day on which the company went into liquidation (currently 8 per cent per annum (SI 1993/564)); and
(b) the rate applicable to that debt apart from the winding-up, e.g. the contract rate of interest, if any.

The court may on the application of the liquidator vary or set aside any extortionate credit transaction between the company and a creditor.

Provisions which may invalidate a charge or debt

There are various provisions, some of which have been considered briefly already, which may invalidate a charge granted by the company or any other disposition it has made or any debt which it has incurred. These are as follows:

(a) A charge will be invalid against the liquidator or creditors if it is not registered under the Companies Act 2006 within 21 days with the Registrar. If it is invalid the holder falls to the level of an unsecured creditor.
(b) Section 241 enables the court on the application of the liquidator to make orders for restoring the position of the company and its creditors to what it would have been if the company had not entered into a transaction at an undervalue or given a preference to a creditor before the commencement of the winding-up. Preferences within six months from the commencement of winding-up can be set aside. The period is two years if with a connected person, e.g. a director. Transactions at undervalue made up to two years before can be set aside whether the recipient was connected with the company or not.

The Act applies to the creation of a charge and to any delivery of goods or the payment of money. A simple example from previous legislation of a preference is *Re Kushler* [1943] 2 All ER 22, where ordinary creditors were ignored but the company paid some £700 into the bank merely to clear the overdraft guaranteed by the directors. Repayment was ordered.

(c) As we have seen, a floating charge created by a company within the year before the commencement of its winding-up or within two years if given to a connected person, e.g. a director, may be void.

The purpose of this section appears to be similar to a preference to prevent a company, while it is unable to pay its debts, from preferring an unsecured creditor by giving him a floating charge on its assets.

(d) Consider the impact that ss 39–40 of CA 2006 (a company's capacity and powers of directors to bind a company) will have to eliminate the availability of a liquidator claiming a debt is invalid because it is *ultra vires*. The problem of an *ultra vires* obligation will fall to the wayside in the future to the extent that post-2006 Act companies will not have memorandums with object clauses in them anyhow. An *ultra vires* debt is invalid and the liquidator need not pay it, though the creditor may follow and trace his property into the company's assets. See the recent case of ***Progress Property Co Ltd* v *Moore*** [2010] UKSC 55.

Progress Property Co Ltd v *Moore* [2010] UKSC 55

The appellant company (P) appealed against a decision ([2009] EWCA Civ 629) that there had not been an unlawful distribution of capital when the whole issued share capital of its subsidiary company (Y) was sold to the respondent company (M). All three companies were indirectly controlled by the same holding company. The sale price was calculated on the basis of Y's open market value, subtracting liabilities for creditors and a further sum in respect of an indemnity believed to have been given by P for a repairing liability. It transpired that P had no such indemnity liability to be released from and that there was no justification for the reduction in Y's value. P alleged that the transaction had been at a gross undervalue, relying on what the Court of Appeal referred to as 'the common law rule', devised for the protection of creditors, that a distribution of a company's assets other than in accordance with specific statutory procedures constituted a return of capital which was unlawful and *ultra vires*. The Court of Appeal upheld the High Court's decision that the transaction had been genuine and not *ultra vires* despite being at an undervalue. P contended that an objective approach was required and that any such transaction which resulted in a transfer of value not covered by distributable profits, regardless of its purpose, constituted an unlawful return of capital. Appeal dismissed. Whether a transaction infringed the common law rule against unlawful distributions was a matter of substance, not form. The label attached to the transaction by the parties was not decisive, ***Ridge Securities Ltd* v *Inland Revenue Commissioners*** [1964] 1 WLR 479, ***Aveling Barford Ltd* v *Perion Ltd*** (1989) 5 BCC 677 and ***Re Halt Garage (1964) Ltd*** [1982] 3 All ER 1016 applied. The essential issue therefore was how the sale of Y was to be characterised. A relentlessly objective rule would be oppressive and unworkable and would cast doubt on any transaction between a company and a shareholder, even if negotiated at arm's length and in good faith, where the company proved with hindsight to have got significantly the worst of the transaction (para 24). If it was a stark choice between a subjective and an objective approach, the least unsatisfactory option would be the latter but the court's real task was to inquire into the true purpose and substance of the impugned transaction. That approach called for an investigation of all the relevant facts, which could include the state of mind of the persons orchestrating the transaction. That state of mind could be totally irrelevant. A distribution described as a dividend but actually paid out of capital would be unlawful however technical the error and well-meaning the intention. However, the participants' subjective intentions would sometimes be relevant and a distribution disguised as an arm's length commercial transaction was the paradigm example. If a company sold to a shareholder, at a low value, assets which were difficult to value precisely but were potentially very valuable, the transaction might call for close scrutiny. The company's financial position and the motives and intentions of its directors would be highly relevant. If the conclusion was that it was a genuine arm's length transaction then it would stand even if it appeared with hindsight to have been a bad bargain. If it was an improper attempt to extract value by the pretence of an arm's length sale, it would be held unlawful. It would depend on a realistic assessment of all the relevant facts, not simply an isolated retrospective valuation exercise, *Clydebank Football Club Ltd* v *Steedman* 2002 SLT 109 applied. In the instant case, there had been concurrent findings that the sale of Y was a genuine commercial sale.

The Companies Act 2006 will now operate to render most transactions valid. The position under the 2006 Act was considered in Chapter 5 ⬤.

(e) If the liquidator can prove fraudulent trading or wrongful trading against, for example, a director or officer under the Insolvency Act 1986, which have already been considered, the court may order that person to become personally liable for the debt. (Note also management by disqualified persons; see Chapter 22 ⬤.)

(f) Finally, the liquidator has a very powerful weapon in the right to disclaim given to him by ss 178 and 179. The sections allow him to disclaim property, e.g. stock or shares, unprofitable contracts, property unsaleable or not readily saleable or land burdened with onerous covenants. As regards the latter, an illustration is provided by *Re Nottingham General Cemetery Co* [1955] 2 All ER 504 where contracts between the company and the owners of the grave plots prevented its use for a purpose other than a cemetery. The liquidator can, of course, disclaim such land, and if he does it vests in the Crown subject to the right of any interested party, e.g. a local authority, to ask that the land be vested in him.

The liquidator must disclaim in writing within 12 months (this does not apply if he is the Official Receiver) and if he hesitates, anyone concerned can ask him to decide within 28 days what he will do. If he fails to tell the court within 28 days that he intends to disclaim he will lose his right. The court can assist persons affected by the disclaimer because, although they can no longer prove as creditors in the liquidation, they are entitled to damages. These damages may or may not equal the full amount of the debt. An illustration taken from the law of bankruptcy, which is the same on this point, is set out below.

Re Hooley, ex parte United Ordnance and Engineering Co Ltd [1899] 2 QB 579

Hooley's trustee in bankruptcy disclaimed certain unpaid shares which Hooley held in the company, the shares being of low value. Hooley owed £25,000 under the contract to take the shares. The court assessed the damages payable to the company on the basis of the company's indebtedness. It appeared that the gross amount owed by the company was £16,169. The court deducted from this the cash in hand of £4,000 and directors' fees owing of £1,669, leaving a balance of £10,500.

Held – this was the measure of damages which the company could prove for in the bankruptcy.

Distribution of assets

The liquidator is now able to distribute the assets. The order laid down for a compulsory winding-up under the Insolvency Rules is usually followed. The order is as follows:

1 First come the costs of the winding-up. In broad terms these cover the costs of getting in the assets, of the petition, of making the statement of affairs, the liquidator's remuneration and the expenses of the committee of inspection.

2 Then come the preferential debts (see Insolvency Act 1986, Sch 6). These debts rank equally between themselves so that if the property of the company is not sufficient to pay them all in full they will have to abate proportionately. The preferential debts are as follows:

(a) wages or salaries of employees due within four months next before the relevant date up to a maximum of £800 for each employee;

(b) all accrued holiday remuneration of employees;

(c) it should be noted that assessed taxes are no longer preferential and also that if a bank has provided funds to pay wages and salaries that debt becomes preferential under the rule of subrogation;

(d) contributions to an occupational pension fund.

3 Next come charges, secured by a floating charge, which take second place to preferential creditors. Fixed chargeholders are not subject to the claims of preferential creditors.

4 These are followed by the unsecured ordinary creditors. It should be noted that secured creditors are paid before the unsecured creditors if the liquidator is allowed to sell the assets charged. This is, however, rare because secured creditors, e.g. fixed chargeholders, normally appoint a receiver to sell the assets charged, returning any surplus after sale to the liquidator. If there is a shortfall and the proceeds of sale do not cover the debt, the secured creditors prove for the balance as unsecured creditors, as they do if they surrender the security to the liquidator.

In order to ensure that the abolition of the preferential status of Crown debts does not go solely to floating chargeholders the Enterprise Act 2002 set up a mechanism for *ring-fencing a percentage of assets for unsecured creditors*. The reform made under the Enterprise Act 2002 substantially restricts the use of receivership and channels the enforcement of floating charges into the administrative procedure, a general procedure for handling insolvent companies that is not specific to enforcement of a floating charge. These provisions that apply in all corporate insolvencies have already been detailed in the materials on administration (see Chapter 27 ○).

5 Lastly come the deferred debts. These have already been referred to but one could add at this stage sums due to members in their capacity as members, such as dividends declared but not paid.

If there is money left at this stage, the company is solvent and debts such as unliquidated damages in tort will be admitted and paid when quantified by the court.

Finally, any surplus will be distributed among members according to their rights under the articles or the terms of issue of their shares.

Insolvency: protection of employees

Under ss 166–168 of the Employment Rights Act 1996 an employee who loses his job when his employer (in this case a company) becomes insolvent can claim through the National

Insurance Fund arrears of wages, holiday pay and certain other payments which are owed to him, rather than rely on the preferential payments procedure.

Any payments made must be authorised by the Secretary of State and the legal rights and remedies in respect of the debts covered are transferred to the Secretary of State, so that he can try to recover from the assets of the insolvent employer the costs of any payments made, up to the preferential rights the employees would have had. Major debts covered are as follows:

(a) Arrears of wages for a period not exceeding eight weeks up to a rate of £380 per week. The definition of wages includes the same items as are mentioned above.

(b) Pay in respect of holidays actually taken, and accrued holiday pay up to a rate of £380 per week, up to a limit of six weeks.

(c) Payments in lieu of notice at a rate not exceeding £380 a week, up to the statutory minimum entitlement of a particular employee under the Employment Rights Act 1996 (one week after one calendar month's service rising to one week per year of service up to a maximum of 12 weeks (new earnings will be taken into account)).

(d) Any payment outstanding in regard to an award by an employment tribunal of compensation for unfair dismissal.

(e) Reimbursement of any fee or premium paid by an apprentice or articled clerk.

There is no qualifying period before an employee becomes eligible and virtually all people in employment are entitled.

Completion of winding-up

The final stages of the winding-up are as follows:

(a) *Compulsory winding-up.* Once the liquidator has paid off the creditors and distributed the surplus (if any) and summoned a final meeting of the company's creditors, under s 146 he may vacate office and obtain his release. The company is dissolved at the end of three months from the receipt by the Registrar of the liquidator's notice that the final meeting of creditors has been held and that the liquidator has vacated office.

(b) *Voluntary winding-up.* In a voluntary winding-up the liquidator will call final meetings of the company and creditors for approval of his accounts. Within a week he will file with the Registrar his accounts and a return of the meetings, and under s 201, two months later the company is dissolved.

Whether it is a compulsory or voluntary liquidation, the court can restore the company to the Register. The law relating to this has already been considered (see Chapter 28 ◉).

We have now completed a consideration of the two main methods of winding-up. However, it is possible for a company which is in voluntary liquidation to be compulsorily wound up and this is referred to in the next section.

Compulsory winding-up by a company in voluntary liquidation

The following points should be noted:

(a) A voluntary winding-up does not by reason of s 116 bar the right of a creditor or con-tributory to have the company wound up by the court, though it is necessary to show one of the grounds for a compulsory winding-up. If a creditor applies to the court, the court will take into account the wishes of all the creditors and the majority view would almost certainly prevail. In the case of contributories, the Act provides that the court must be satisfied that the rights of contributories will be prejudiced by a voluntary winding-up and that a compulsory order would be justified if, for example, the voluntary winding-up was being conducted in a fraudulent manner or there were suspicious circumstances and a searching investigation was required.

(b) Under s 124 the Official Receiver may present a petition but the court will not order winding-up unless it is satisfied that the voluntary winding-up cannot be continued with due regard to the interests of the creditors and contributories. Thus, in **Re Ryder Installations** [1966] 1 All ER 453 the liquidator in a voluntary winding-up had not after eight years called a meeting of creditors and he had five convictions for failing to make the appropriate returns. Here the court ordered a compulsory winding-up by the court.

(c) The Secretary of State can also present a petition for a compulsory winding-up after a voluntary winding-up has been started. Thus, in **Lubin, Rosen & Associates** [1975] 1 All ER 577 the Secretary of State for Trade and Industry petitioned because an investigation suggested there had been fraud and the company, formed to build flats in Spain, never had sufficient share capital for its activities. In the event, 198 creditors with claims totalling £540,000 opposed compulsory winding-up. Megarry J held that while such opposition by creditors was a formidable obstacle, the petition of the Secretary of State carried great weight and that when there were circumstances of suspicion it was highly desirable that the winding-up should be by the court with all the safeguards that that provided. Consequently, he ordered a compulsory winding-up.

Essay questions

1 Insolvent Ltd is in compulsory liquidation and its assets are insufficient to meet its liabilities in full.

Advise the liquidator as to what action he should take in respect of the following matters:

(a) Three months before the commencement of the winding-up Insolvent Ltd created a floating charge over all its assets to its bank, to secure its overdraft, and this charge was duly reg-istered. Immediately after this the bank allowed the overdraft to be increased by £50,000, which was used in paying wages to company employees.

(b) A private individual has put in a claim for an allegedly slanderous statement made by the managing director in the course of his duties.

(c) 18 months prior to the winding-up and at a time when the company was solvent a floating charge was created in favour of Grab Ltd which is controlled by a director of Insolvent Ltd.

(d) The following debts, *inter alia*, are due from the company:
   (i) 12 months' VAT;
   (ii) 12 months' corporation tax;
   (iii) £20,000 arrears of salary due to 10 employees.

(e) A 20-year lease on a factory which had to be shut down as being unprofitable.

(University of Plymouth)

2 Deadloss plc has gone into insolvent winding-up. The petition was presented on 1 April 2005 and the winding-up order was made on 30 May 2005. The liquidator is uncertain as to the priorities and whether the following transactions are binding on him:

(a) Deadloss created a floating charge on its undertaking and assets on 1 January 2004 to secure a loan of £500,000 from Financings Ltd. The charge contained a clause restricting Deadloss from creating any further charges ranking in priority or *pari passu* with it. This charge was duly registered within the requisite period.

(b) On 1 June 2004 Deadloss created a fixed charge over its land and buildings in favour of Easymoney to secure a loan of £200,000. The charge was not dated and, owing to an over-sight, not registered either. The oversight was discovered on 10 July 2004. The secretary of Deadloss promptly filled in the date as 10 July 2004 and had the charge registered, obtaining a certificate of registration from the Registrar of Charges.

(c) Deadloss had accumulated a debt of £100,000 with Suppliers Ltd. In order to ensure un-interrupted supplies of raw materials and to prevent an anticipated petition for winding up the company, Deadloss created a floating charge over its assets on 10 January 2005, in favour of Suppliers Ltd. The charge was duly registered within 21 days of execution.

(d) The following debts are, among many others, owed by Deadloss:
   (i)   Twelve months' VAT amounting to £10,000.
   (ii) Eight months' PAYE amounting to £12,000.
   (iii) One hundred employees of the company are each owed £900 in wages for the three months prior to the winding-up order.
   (iv) Twelve months' corporation tax is due to Inland Revenue.

   Write a report advising the liquidator on each of the above transactions.

(University of Plymouth)

3 (a) What kinds of liquidation or windings-up are there and what distinguishes them from each other?

 (b) In what order must a liquidator distribute the assets?

 (c) Distinguish between fraudulent trading and wrongful trading and say what consequences may follow if a person is found guilty of either of them. *(Kingston University)*

4 On the liquidation of Technix plc the assets and liabilities of the company are stated as follows:

Assets	£	Liabilities	£
Factory	350,000	Alpha plc	300,000
Finished products	70,000	Beta plc	200,000
Computer components	20,000	Delta Bank plc	20,000
Vehicle fleet	30,000	In. Rev. & employees	30,000
Machinery	50,000	Trade creditors	25,000
		Managing Director	10,000
	520,000		585,000

The liquidator of Technix seeks your advice as to the priority of each of the company's creditors. You are given the following additional information:

(i) In 2003 a charge was created over all the company's assets and undertaking, both present and future, in favour of Alpha.

(ii) In 2004 finance was provided by Beta with the company's factory being used as security.

(iii) In 2005 a second charge was created over the company's entire undertaking in favour of Delta, in order to secure the company's overdraft facility of £20,000. The instrument creating the charge specified that Delta was to have priority over any earlier charge.

(iv) Six months prior to the winding-up, the Managing Director secured a specific charge over the company's vehicle fleet as security for loans made in the past which remain unpaid. Owing to an administrative error, his charge was not registered.

(v) Of the trade creditors, Psion Ltd claim that the contract, under which microchips were supplied to Technix at a cost of £10,000, for which Psion has not received payment, contained a reservation of title clause. *(University of Greenwich)*

5 You are required to discuss the following liquidation matters.

(a) An allegation by a creditor of a company during a winding-up that the directors of the company continued trading when business debts could not be met.

(b) A view reached by a company liquidator that certain directors of the company ought to be restricted in their intention to form a new company operating in the same business area as soon as liquidation is complete.

(c) The order of priority which a liquidator should afford to claims from company employees for backdated wages, unsecured trade creditors for unpaid goods supplied to the company, and debenture holders secured by way of floating charge for repayment of their loans. *(The Chartered Institute of Management Accountants)*

Test your knowledge

Four alternative answers are given. Select ONE only. Circle the answer which you consider to be correct. Check your answers by referring back to the information given in the chapter and against the answers at the end of the text.

1 A company may go into a members' voluntary winding-up if the directors or a majority of them make a declaration to the effect that the company will be able to pay its debts in full within a period not exceeding:

A One year B Six months C Two years D Three years

2 The members of a solvent company may resolve to wind it up following the passing of:

A An ordinary resolution after special notice.
B An ordinary resolution.
C An extraordinary resolution.
D A special resolution.

3 Thames Ltd is in a creditors' voluntary winding-up. The members and the creditors have nominated different persons as liquidators. What happens?

A An application must be made to the court to decide who shall act.
B The creditors' nominee becomes liquidator but any director, member or creditor may apply to the court to appoint the members' nominee.

C The creditors' nominee becomes liquidator in any event.

D The members' nominee will become liquidator but any creditor may apply to the court to appoint the creditors' nominee.

4 Tees Ltd is insolvent and its directors have made a payment to one of its creditors which is designed to improve the position of that creditor in the event of a liquidation. The creditor is not connected with the company. The company is now in liquidation. The liquidator can recover the payment if it was made within:

A Two years of the winding-up.

B Twelve months of the winding-up.

C Six months of the winding-up.

D Eighteen months of the winding-up.

5 What kind of resolution is required to commence a voluntary winding-up when no declaration of solvency can be given?

A Special B Extraordinary C Ordinary D Ordinary with special notice

6 When does a voluntary winding-up, whether members' or creditors', commence?

A When the relevant resolution is passed.

B When notice of the passing of the resolution is received by the Registrar.

C When the resolution is approved by the court.

D When notice of the resolution is published in the *London Gazette*.

Answers to test your knowledge questions on p. 645.

Suggested further reading

Mokal, 'What liquidation does for secured creditors and what it does for you' (2008) MLR 71, 699.

Schillig, '"Deepening insolvency" – liability for wrongful trading in the United States?' [2009] *Company Lawyer* 30, 298.

Answers to test your knowledge questions

Chapter 1
1 (D)
2 (B)
3 (C)
4 (D)

Chapter 4
1 (D)
2 (D)
3 (B)
4 (B)
5 (B)
6 (B)

Chapter 5
1 (A)
2 (C)
3 (C)
4 (B)

Chapter 6
1 (C)
2 (C)
3 (C)
4 (C)

Chapter 8
1 (C)
2 (A)
3 (A)
4 (B)

Chapter 9
1 (B)
2 (A)
3 (D)
4 (A)
5 (C)

Chapter 10
1 (C)
2 (A)
3 (B)

4 (D)
5 (C)

Chapter 11
The relevant questions and answers appear at pp. 219–221.

Chapter 12
1 (C)
2 (C)
3 (A)
4 (A)
5 (A)
6 (C)

Chapter 13
1 (D)
2 (B)
3 (C)
4 (B)
5 (C)
6 (B)

Chapter 14
1 (B)
2 (D)
3 (A)
4 (C)
5 (B)
6 (C)

Chapter 15
1 (C)
2 (C)
3 (A)
4 (B)
5 (D)
6 (A)

Chapter 16
1 (D)
2 (B)

3 (A)
4 (C)
5 (C)

Chapter 18
1 (D)
2 (A)
3 (C)
4 (D)
5 (A)

Chapter 19
1 (C)
2 (B)
3 (A)
4 (A)
5 (A)
6 (C)

Chapter 20
1 (B)
2 (D)
3 (C)
4 (C)
5 (A)

Chapter 21
1 (C)
2 (D)
3 (A)
4 (B)
5 (D)
6 (C)

Chapter 22
1 (A)
2 (D)
3 (B)
4 (B)
5 (A)
6 (A)

Chapter 23
1 (B)
2 (D)

3 (A)
4 (C)
5 (C)
6 (A)

Chapter 24
1 (D)
2 (A)
3 (D)
4 (B)
5 (C)

Chapter 25
1 (C)
2 (A)

3 (D)
4 (C)
5 (B)
6 (D)

Chapter 26
1 (B)
2 (C)
3 (A)
4 (D)
5 (D)
6 (B)

Chapter 27
1 (D)

2 (D)
3 (A)
4 (C)
5 (D)
6 (D)

Chapter 29
1 (A)
2 (D)
3 (B)
4 (C)
5 (B)
6 (A)

Companies (Model Articles) Regulations 2008, SI 2008/3229

SCHEDULE 1 Model Articles for Private Companies Limited by Shares

Part 1: Interpretation and limitation of liability

Defined terms

1. In the articles, unless the context requires otherwise –

'articles' means the company's articles of association;

'bankruptcy' includes individual insolvency proceedings in a jurisdiction other than England and Wales or Northern Ireland which have an effect similar to that of bankruptcy;

'chairman' has the meaning given in article 12;

'chairman of the meeting' has the meaning given in article 39;

'Companies Acts' means the Companies Acts (as defined in section 2 of the Companies Act 2006), in so far as they apply to the company;

'director' means a director of the company, and includes any person occupying the position of director, by whatever name called;

'distribution recipient' has the meaning given in article 31;

'document' includes, unless otherwise specified, any document sent or supplied in electronic form;

'electronic form' has the meaning given in section 1168 of the Companies Act 2006;

'fully paid' in relation to a share, means that the nominal value and any premium to be paid to the company in respect of that share have been paid to the company;

'hard copy form' has the meaning given in section 1168 of the Companies Act 2006;

'holder' in relation to shares means the person whose name is entered in the register of members as the holder of the shares;

'instrument' means a document in hard copy form;

'ordinary resolution' has the meaning given in section 282 of the Companies Act 2006;

'paid' means paid or credited as paid;

'participate', in relation to a directors' meeting, has the meaning given in article 10;

'proxy notice' has the meaning given in article 45;

'shareholder' means a person who is the holder of a share;

'shares' means shares in the company;

'special resolution' has the meaning given in section 283 of the Companies Act 2006;

'subsidiary' has the meaning given in section 1159 of the Companies Act 2006;

'transmittee' means a person entitled to a share by reason of the death or bankruptcy of a shareholder or otherwise by operation of law; and

'writing' means the representation or reproduction of words, symbols or other information in a visible form by any method or combination of methods, whether sent or supplied in electronic form or otherwise.

Unless the context otherwise requires, other words or expressions contained in these articles bear the same meaning as in the Companies Act 2006 as in force on the date when these articles become binding on the company.

Liability of members

2. The liability of the members is limited to the amount, if any, unpaid on the shares held by them.

Part 2: Directors

Directors' powers and responsibilities

Directors' general authority

3. Subject to the articles, the directors are responsible for the management of the company's business, for which purpose they may exercise all the powers of the company.

Shareholders' reserve power

4. – (1) The shareholders may, by special resolution, direct the directors to take, or refrain from taking, specified action.

(2) No such special resolution invalidates anything which the directors have done before the passing of the resolution.

Directors may delegate

5. – (1) Subject to the articles, the directors may delegate any of the powers which are conferred on them under the articles –

(a) to such person or committee;

(b) by such means (including by power of attorney);

(c) to such an extent;

(d) in relation to such matters or territories; and

(e) on such terms and conditions;

as they think fit.

(2) If the directors so specify, any such delegation may authorise further delegation of the directors' powers by any person to whom they are delegated.

(3) The directors may revoke any delegation in whole or part, or alter its terms and conditions.

Committees

6. – (1) Committees to which the directors delegate any of their powers must follow procedures which are based as far as they are applicable on those provisions of the articles which govern the taking of decisions by directors.

(2) The directors may make rules of procedure for all or any committees, which prevail over rules derived from the articles if they are not consistent with them.

Decision-making by directors

Directors to take decisions collectively

7. – (1) The general rule about decision-making by directors is that any decision of the directors must be either a majority decision at a meeting or a decision taken in accordance with article 8.

(2) If –

(a) the company only has one director, and

(b) no provision of the articles requires it to have more than one director,

the general rule does not apply, and the director may take decisions without regard to any of the provisions of the articles relating to directors' decision-making.

Unanimous decisions

8. – (1) A decision of the directors is taken in accordance with this article when all eligible directors indicate to each other by any means that they share a common view on a matter.

(2) Such a decision may take the form of a resolution in writing, copies of which have been signed by each eligible director or to which each eligible director has otherwise indicated agreement in writing.

(3) References in this article to eligible directors are to directors who would have been entitled to vote on the matter had it been proposed as a resolution at a directors' meeting.

(4) A decision may not be taken in accordance with this article if the eligible directors would not have formed a quorum at such a meeting.

Calling a directors' meeting

9. – (1) Any director may call a directors' meeting by giving notice of the meeting to the directors or by authorising the company secretary (if any) to give such notice.

(2) Notice of any directors' meeting must indicate –

(a) its proposed date and time;

(b) where it is to take place; and

(c) if it is anticipated that directors participating in the meeting will not be in the same place, how it is proposed that they should communicate with each other during the meeting.

(3) Notice of a directors' meeting must be given to each director, but need not be in writing.

(4) Notice of a directors' meeting need not be given to directors who waive their entitlement to notice of that meeting, by giving notice to that effect to the company not more than 7 days after the date on which the meeting is held. Where such notice is given after the meeting has been held, that does not affect the validity of the meeting, or of any business conducted at it.

Participation in directors' meetings

10. – (1) Subject to the articles, directors participate in a directors' meeting, or part of a directors' meeting, when –

(a) the meeting has been called and takes place in accordance with the articles, and

(b) they can each communicate to the others any information or opinions they have on any particular item of the business of the meeting.

(2) In determining whether directors are participating in a directors' meeting, it is irrelevant where any director is or how they communicate with each other.

(3) If all the directors participating in a meeting are not in the same place, they may decide that the meeting is to be treated as taking place wherever any of them is.

Quorum for directors' meetings

11. – (1) At a directors' meeting, unless a quorum is participating, no proposal is to be voted on, except a proposal to call another meeting.

(2) The quorum for directors' meetings may be fixed from time to time by a decision of the directors, but it must never be less than two, and unless otherwise fixed it is two.

(3) If the total number of directors for the time being is less than the quorum required, the directors must not take any decision other than a decision –

(a) to appoint further directors, or

(b) to call a general meeting so as to enable the shareholders to appoint further directors.

Chairing of directors' meetings

12. – (1) The directors may appoint a director to chair their meetings.

(2) The person so appointed for the time being is known as the chairman.

(3) The directors may terminate the chairman's appointment at any time.

(4) If the chairman is not participating in a directors' meeting within ten minutes of the time at which it was to start, the participating directors must appoint one of themselves to chair it.

Casting vote

13. – (1) If the numbers of votes for and against a proposal are equal, the chairman or other director chairing the meeting has a casting vote.

(2) But this does not apply if, in accordance with the articles, the chairman or other director is not to be counted as participating in the decision-making process for quorum or voting purposes.

Conflicts of interest

14. – (1) If a proposed decision of the directors is concerned with an actual or proposed transaction or arrangement with the company in which a director is interested, that director is not to be counted as participating in the decision-making process for quorum or voting purposes.

(2) But if paragraph (3) applies, a director who is interested in an actual or proposed transaction or arrangement with the company is to be counted as participating in the decision-making process for quorum and voting purposes.

(3) This paragraph applies when –

(a) the company by ordinary resolution disapplies the provision of the articles which would otherwise prevent a director from being counted as participating in the decision-making process;

(b) the director's interest cannot reasonably be regarded as likely to give rise to a conflict of interest; or

(c) the director's conflict of interest arises from a permitted cause.

(4) For the purposes of this article, the following are permitted causes –

(a) a guarantee given, or to be given, by or to a director in respect of an obligation incurred by or on behalf of the company or any of its subsidiaries;

(b) subscription, or an agreement to subscribe, for shares or other securities of the company or any of its subsidiaries, or to underwrite, sub-underwrite, or guarantee subscription for any such shares or securities; and

(c) arrangements pursuant to which benefits are made available to employees and directors or former employees and directors of the company or any of its subsidiaries which do not provide special benefits for directors or former directors.

(5) For the purposes of this article, references to proposed decisions and decision-making processes include any directors' meeting or part of a directors' meeting.

(6) Subject to paragraph (7), if a question arises at a meeting of directors or of a committee of directors as to the right of a director to participate in the meeting (or part of the meeting) for voting or quorum purposes, the question may, before the conclusion of the meeting, be referred to the chairman whose ruling in relation to any director other than the chairman is to be final and conclusive.

(7) If any question as to the right to participate in the meeting (or part of the meeting) should arise in respect of the chairman, the question is to be decided by a decision of the directors at that meeting, for which purpose the chairman is not to be counted as participating in the meeting (or that part of the meeting) for voting or quorum purposes.

Records of decisions to be kept

15. The directors must ensure that the company keeps a record, in writing, for at least 10 years from the date of the decision recorded, of every unanimous or majority decision taken by the directors.

Directors' discretion to make further rules

16. Subject to the articles, the directors may make any rule which they think fit about how they take decisions, and about how such rules are to be recorded or communicated to directors.

Appointment of directors

Methods of appointing directors

17. – (1) Any person who is willing to act as a director, and is permitted by law to do so, may be appointed to be a director –

(a) by ordinary resolution, or

(b) by a decision of the directors.

(2) In any case where, as a result of death, the company has no shareholders and no directors, the personal representatives of the last shareholder to have died have the right, by notice in writing, to appoint a person to be a director.

(3) For the purposes of paragraph (2), where 2 or more shareholders die in circumstances rendering it uncertain who was the last to die, a younger shareholder is deemed to have survived an older shareholder.

Termination of director's appointment

18. A person ceases to be a director as soon as –

(a) that person ceases to be a director by virtue of any provision of the Companies Act 2006 or is prohibited from being a director by law;

(b) a bankruptcy order is made against that person;

(c) a composition is made with that person's creditors generally in satisfaction of that person's debts;

(d) a registered medical practitioner who is treating that person gives a written opinion to the company stating that that person has become physically or mentally incapable of acting as a director and may remain so for more than three months;

(e) by reason of that person's mental health, a court makes an order which wholly or partly prevents that person from personally exercising any powers or rights which that person would otherwise have;

(f) notification is received by the company from the director that the director is resigning from office, and such resignation has taken effect in accordance with its terms.

Directors' remuneration

19. – (1) Directors may undertake any services for the company that the directors decide.

(2) Directors are entitled to such remuneration as the directors determine –

(a) for their services to the company as directors, and

(b) for any other service which they undertake for the company.

(3) Subject to the articles, a director's remuneration may –

(a) take any form, and

(b) include any arrangements in connection with the payment of a pension, allowance or gratuity, or any death, sickness or disability benefits, to or in respect of that director.

(4) Unless the directors decide otherwise, directors' remuneration accrues from day to day.

(5) Unless the directors decide otherwise, directors are not accountable to the company for any remuneration which they receive as directors or other officers or employees of the company's subsidiaries or of any other body corporate in which the company is interested.

Directors' expenses

20. The company may pay any reasonable expenses which the directors properly incur in connection with their attendance at –

(a) meetings of directors or committees of directors,

(b) general meetings, or

(c) separate meetings of the holders of any class of shares or of debentures of the company,

or otherwise in connection with the exercise of their powers and the discharge of their responsibilities in relation to the company.

Part 3: Shares and distributions

Shares

All shares to be fully paid up

21. – (1) No share is to be issued for less than the aggregate of its nominal value and any premium to be paid to the company in consideration for its issue.

(2) This does not apply to shares taken on the formation of the company by the subscribers to the company's memorandum.

Powers to issue different classes of share

22. – (1) Subject to the articles, but without prejudice to the rights attached to any existing share, the company may issue shares with such rights or restrictions as may be determined by ordinary resolution.

(2) The company may issue shares which are to be redeemed, or are liable to be redeemed at the option of the company or the holder, and the directors may determine the terms, conditions and manner of redemption of any such shares.

Company not bound by less than absolute interests

23. Except as required by law, no person is to be recognised by the company as holding any share upon any trust, and except as otherwise required by law or the articles, the company is not in any way to be bound by or recognise any interest in a share other than the holder's absolute ownership of it and all the rights attaching to it.

Share certificates

24. – (1) The company must issue each shareholder, free of charge, with one or more certificates in respect of the shares which that shareholder holds.

(2) Every certificate must specify –

(a) in respect of how many shares, of what class, it is issued;

(b) the nominal value of those shares;

(c) that the shares are fully paid; and

(d) any distinguishing numbers assigned to them.

(3) No certificate may be issued in respect of shares of more than one class.

(4) If more than one person holds a share, only one certificate may be issued in respect of it.

(5) Certificates must –

(a) have affixed to them the company's common seal, or

(b) be otherwise executed in accordance with the Companies Acts.

Replacement share certificates

25. – (1) If a certificate issued in respect of a shareholder's shares is –

(a) damaged or defaced, or

(b) said to be lost, stolen or destroyed,

that shareholder is entitled to be issued with a replacement certificate in respect of the same shares.

(2) A shareholder exercising the right to be issued with such a replacement certificate –

(a) may at the same time exercise the right to be issued with a single certificate or separate certificates;

(b) must return the certificate which is to be replaced to the company if it is damaged or defaced; and

(c) must comply with such conditions as to evidence, indemnity and the payment of a reasonable fee as the directors decide.

Share transfers

26. – (1) Shares may be transferred by means of an instrument of transfer in any usual form or any other form approved by the directors, which is executed by or on behalf of the transferor.

(2) No fee may be charged for registering any instrument of transfer or other document relating to or affecting the title to any share.

(3) The company may retain any instrument of transfer which is registered.

(4) The transferor remains the holder of a share until the transferee's name is entered in the register of members as holder of it.

(5) The directors may refuse to register the transfer of a share, and if they do so, the instrument of transfer must be returned to the transferee with the notice of refusal unless they suspect that the proposed transfer may be fraudulent.

Transmission of shares

27. – (1) If title to a share passes to a transmittee, the company may only recognise the transmittee as having any title to that share.

(2) A transmittee who produces such evidence of entitlement to shares as the directors may properly require –

(a) may, subject to the articles, choose either to become the holder of those shares or to have them transferred to another person, and

(b) subject to the articles, and pending any transfer of the shares to another person, has the same rights as the holder had.

(3) But transmittees do not have the right to attend or vote at a general meeting, or agree to a proposed written resolution, in respect of shares to which they are entitled, by reason of the holder's death or bankruptcy or otherwise, unless they become the holders of those shares.

Exercise of transmittees' rights

28. – (1) Transmittees who wish to become the holders of shares to which they have become entitled must notify the company in writing of that wish.

(2) If the transmittee wishes to have a share transferred to another person, the transmittee must execute an instrument of transfer in respect of it.

(3) Any transfer made or executed under this article is to be treated as if it were made or executed by the person from whom the transmittee has derived rights in respect of the share, and as if the event which gave rise to the transmission had not occurred.

Transmittees bound by prior notices

29. If a notice is given to a shareholder in respect of shares and a transmittee is entitled to those shares, the transmittee is bound by the notice if it was given to the shareholder before the transmittee's name has been entered in the register of members.

Dividends and other distributions

Procedure for declaring dividends

30. – (1) The company may by ordinary resolution declare dividends, and the directors may decide to pay interim dividends.

(2) A dividend must not be declared unless the directors have made a recommendation as to its amount. Such a dividend must not exceed the amount recommended by the directors.

(3) No dividend may be declared or paid unless it is in accordance with shareholders' respective rights.

(4) Unless the shareholders' resolution to declare or directors' decision to pay a dividend, or the terms on which shares are issued, specify otherwise, it must be paid by reference to each shareholder's holding of shares on the date of the resolution or decision to declare or pay it.

(5) If the company's share capital is divided into different classes, no interim dividend may be paid on shares carrying deferred or non-preferred rights if, at the time of payment, any preferential dividend is in arrear.

(6) The directors may pay at intervals any dividend payable at a fixed rate if it appears to them that the profits available for distribution justify the payment.

(7) If the directors act in good faith, they do not incur any liability to the holders of shares conferring preferred rights for any loss they may suffer by the lawful payment of an interim dividend on shares with deferred or non-preferred rights.

Payment of dividends and other distributions

31. – (1) Where a dividend or other sum which is a distribution is payable in respect of a share, it must be paid by one or more of the following means –

(a) transfer to a bank or building society account specified by the distribution recipient either in writing or as the directors may otherwise decide;

(b) sending a cheque made payable to the distribution recipient by post to the distribution recipient at the distribution recipient's registered address (if the distribution recipient is a holder of the share), or (in any other case) to an address specified by the distribution recipient either in writing or as the directors may otherwise decide;

(c) sending a cheque made payable to such person by post to such person at such address as the distribution recipient has specified either in writing or as the directors may otherwise decide; or

(d) any other means of payment as the directors agree with the distribution recipient either in writing or by such other means as the directors decide.

(2) In the articles, 'the distribution recipient' means, in respect of a share in respect of which a dividend or other sum is payable –

(a) the holder of the share; or

(b) if the share has two or more joint holders, whichever of them is named first in the register of members; or

(c) if the holder is no longer entitled to the share by reason of death or bankruptcy, or otherwise by operation of law, the transmittee.

No interest on distributions

32. The company may not pay interest on any dividend or other sum payable in respect of a share unless otherwise provided by –

(a) the terms on which the share was issued, or

(b) the provisions of another agreement between the holder of that share and the company.

Unclaimed distributions

33. – (1) All dividends or other sums which are –

(a) payable in respect of shares, and

(b) unclaimed after having been declared or become payable,

may be invested or otherwise made use of by the directors for the benefit of the company until claimed.

(2) The payment of any such dividend or other sum into a separate account does not make the company a trustee in respect of it.

(3) If –

(a) twelve years have passed from the date on which a dividend or other sum became due for payment, and

(b) the distribution recipient has not claimed it,

the distribution recipient is no longer entitled to that dividend or other sum and it ceases to remain owing by the company.

Non-cash distributions

34. – (1) Subject to the terms of issue of the share in question, the company may, by ordinary resolution on the recommendation of the directors, decide to pay all or part of a dividend or other distribution payable in respect of a share by transferring non-cash assets of equivalent value (including, without limitation, shares or other securities in any company).

(2) For the purposes of paying a non-cash distribution, the directors may make whatever arrangements they think fit, including, where any difficulty arises regarding the distribution –

(a) fixing the value of any assets;

(b) paying cash to any distribution recipient on the basis of that value in order to adjust the rights of recipients; and

(c) vesting any assets in trustees.

Waiver of distributions

35. Distribution recipients may waive their entitlement to a dividend or other distribution payable in respect of a share by giving the company notice in writing to that effect, but if –

(a) the share has more than one holder, or

(b) more than one person is entitled to the share, whether by reason of the death or bankruptcy of one or more joint holders, or otherwise,

the notice is not effective unless it is expressed to be given, and signed, by all the holders or persons otherwise entitled to the share.

Capitalisation of profits

Authority to capitalise and appropriation of capitalised sums

36. – (1) Subject to the articles, the directors may, if they are so authorised by an ordinary resolution –

(a) decide to capitalise any profits of the company (whether or not they are available for distribution) which are not required for paying a preferential dividend, or any sum standing to the credit of the company's share premium account or capital redemption reserve; and

(b) appropriate any sum which they so decide to capitalise (a 'capitalised sum') to the persons who would have been entitled to it if it were distributed by way of dividend (the 'persons entitled') and in the same proportions.

(2) Capitalised sums must be applied –

(a) on behalf of the persons entitled, and

(b) in the same proportions as a dividend would have been distributed to them.

(3) Any capitalised sum may be applied in paying up new shares of a nominal amount equal to the capitalised sum which are then allotted credited as fully paid to the persons entitled or as they may direct.

(4) A capitalised sum which was appropriated from profits available for distribution may be applied in paying up new debentures of the company which are then allotted credited as fully paid to the persons entitled or as they may direct.

(5) Subject to the articles the directors may –

(a) apply capitalised sums in accordance with paragraphs (3) and (4) partly in one way and partly in another;

(b) make such arrangements as they think fit to deal with shares or debentures becoming distributable in fractions under this article (including the issuing of fractional certificates or the making of cash payments); and

(c) authorise any person to enter into an agreement with the company on behalf of all the persons entitled which is binding on them in respect of the allotment of shares and debentures to them under this article.

Part 4: Decision-making by shareholders

Organisation of general meetings

Attendance and speaking at general meetings

37. – (1) A person is able to exercise the right to speak at a general meeting when that person is in a position to communicate to all those attending the meeting, during the meeting, any information or opinions which that person has on the business of the meeting.

(2) A person is able to exercise the right to vote at a general meeting when –

(a) that person is able to vote, during the meeting, on resolutions put to the vote at the meeting, and

(b) that person's vote can be taken into account in determining whether or not such resolutions are passed at the same time as the votes of all the other persons attending the meeting.

(3) The directors may make whatever arrangements they consider appropriate to enable those attending a general meeting to exercise their rights to speak or vote at it.

(4) In determining attendance at a general meeting, it is immaterial whether any two or more members attending it are in the same place as each other.

(5) Two or more persons who are not in the same place as each other attend a general meeting if their circumstances are such that if they have (or were to have) rights to speak and vote at that meeting, they are (or would be) able to exercise them.

Quorum for general meetings

38. No business other than the appointment of the chairman of the meeting is to be transacted at a general meeting if the persons attending it do not constitute a quorum.

Chairing general meetings

39. – (1) If the directors have appointed a chairman, the chairman shall chair general meetings if present and willing to do so.

(2) If the directors have not appointed a chairman, or if the chairman is unwilling to chair the meeting or is not present within ten minutes of the time at which a meeting was due to start –

(a) the directors present, or

(b) (if no directors are present), the meeting,

must appoint a director or shareholder to chair the meeting, and the appointment of the chairman of the meeting must be the first business of the meeting.

(3) The person chairing a meeting in accordance with this article is referred to as 'the chairman of the meeting'.

Attendance and speaking by directors and non-shareholders

40. – (1) Directors may attend and speak at general meetings, whether or not they are shareholders.

(2) The chairman of the meeting may permit other persons who are not –

(a) shareholders of the company, or

(b) otherwise entitled to exercise the rights of shareholders in relation to general meetings,

to attend and speak at a general meeting.

Adjournment

41. – (1) If the persons attending a general meeting within half an hour of the time at which the meeting was due to start do not constitute a quorum, or if during a meeting a quorum ceases to be present, the chairman of the meeting must adjourn it.

(2) The chairman of the meeting may adjourn a general meeting at which a quorum is present if –

(a) the meeting consents to an adjournment, or

(b) it appears to the chairman of the meeting that an adjournment is necessary to protect the safety of any person attending the meeting or ensure that the business of the meeting is conducted in an orderly manner.

(3) The chairman of the meeting must adjourn a general meeting if directed to do so by the meeting.

(4) When adjourning a general meeting, the chairman of the meeting must –

(a) either specify the time and place to which it is adjourned or state that it is to continue at a time and place to be fixed by the directors, and

(b) have regard to any directions as to the time and place of any adjournment which have been given by the meeting.

(5) If the continuation of an adjourned meeting is to take place more than 14 days after it was adjourned, the company must give at least 7 clear days' notice of it (that is, excluding the day of the adjourned meeting and the day on which the notice is given) –

(a) to the same persons to whom notice of the company's general meetings is required to be given, and

(b) containing the same information which such notice is required to contain.

(6) No business may be transacted at an adjourned general meeting which could not properly have been transacted at the meeting if the adjournment had not taken place.

Voting at general meetings

Voting: general

42. A resolution put to the vote of a general meeting must be decided on a show of hands unless a poll is duly demanded in accordance with the articles.

Errors and disputes

43. – (1) No objection may be raised to the qualification of any person voting at a general meeting except at the meeting or adjourned meeting at which the vote objected to is tendered, and every vote not disallowed at the meeting is valid.

(2) Any such objection must be referred to the chairman of the meeting, whose decision is final.

Poll votes

44. – (1) A poll on a resolution may be demanded –

(a) in advance of the general meeting where it is to be put to the vote, or

(b) at a general meeting, either before a show of hands on that resolution or immediately after the result of a show of hands on that resolution is declared.

(2) A poll may be demanded by –

(a) the chairman of the meeting;

(b) the directors;

(c) two or more persons having the right to vote on the resolution; or

(d) a person or persons representing not less than one tenth of the total voting rights of all the shareholders having the right to vote on the resolution.

(3) A demand for a poll may be withdrawn if –

(a) the poll has not yet been taken, and

(b) the chairman of the meeting consents to the withdrawal.

(4) Polls must be taken immediately and in such manner as the chairman of the meeting directs.

Content of proxy notices

45. – (1) Proxies may only validly be appointed by a notice in writing (a 'proxy notice') which –

(a) states the name and address of the shareholder appointing the proxy;

(b) identifies the person appointed to be that shareholder's proxy and the general meeting in relation to which that person is appointed;

(c) is signed by or on behalf of the shareholder appointing the proxy, or is authenticated in such manner as the directors may determine; and

(d) is delivered to the company in accordance with the articles and any instructions contained in the notice of the general meeting to which they relate.

(2) The company may require proxy notices to be delivered in a particular form, and may specify different forms for different purposes.

(3) Proxy notices may specify how the proxy appointed under them is to vote (or that the proxy is to abstain from voting) on one or more resolutions.

(4) Unless a proxy notice indicates otherwise, it must be treated as –

(a) allowing the person appointed under it as a proxy discretion as to how to vote on any ancillary or procedural resolutions put to the meeting, and

(b) appointing that person as a proxy in relation to any adjournment of the general meeting to which it relates as well as the meeting itself.

Delivery of proxy notices

46. – (1) A person who is entitled to attend, speak or vote (either on a show of hands or on a poll) at a general meeting remains so entitled in respect of that meeting or any adjournment of it, even though a valid proxy notice has been delivered to the company by or on behalf of that person.

(2) An appointment under a proxy notice may be revoked by delivering to the company a notice in writing given by or on behalf of the person by whom or on whose behalf the proxy notice was given.

(3) A notice revoking a proxy appointment only takes effect if it is delivered before the start of the meeting or adjourned meeting to which it relates.

(4) If a proxy notice is not executed by the person appointing the proxy, it must be accompanied by written evidence of the authority of the person who executed it to execute it on the appointor's behalf.

Amendments to resolutions

47. – (1) An ordinary resolution to be proposed at a general meeting may be amended by ordinary resolution if –

(a) notice of the proposed amendment is given to the company in writing by a person entitled to vote at the general meeting at which it is to be proposed not less than 48 hours before the meeting is to take place (or such later time as the chairman of the meeting may determine), and

(b) the proposed amendment does not, in the reasonable opinion of the chairman of the meeting, materially alter the scope of the resolution.

(2) A special resolution to be proposed at a general meeting may be amended by ordinary resolution, if –

(a) the chairman of the meeting proposes the amendment at the general meeting at which the resolution is to be proposed, and

(b) the amendment does not go beyond what is necessary to correct a grammatical or other non-substantive error in the resolution.

(3) If the chairman of the meeting, acting in good faith, wrongly decides that an amendment to a resolution is out of order, the chairman's error does not invalidate the vote on that resolution.

Part 5: Administrative arrangements

Means of communication to be used

48. – (1) Subject to the articles, anything sent or supplied by or to the company under the articles may be sent or supplied in any way in which the Companies Act 2006 provides for documents or information which are authorised or required by any provision of that Act to be sent or supplied by or to the company.

(2) Subject to the articles, any notice or document to be sent or supplied to a director in connection with the taking of decisions by directors may also be sent or supplied by the means by which that director has asked to be sent or supplied with such notices or documents for the time being.

(3) A director may agree with the company that notices or documents sent to that director in a particular way are to be deemed to have been received within a specified time of their being sent, and for the specified time to be less than 48 hours.

Company seals

49. – (1) Any common seal may only be used by the authority of the directors.

(2) The directors may decide by what means and in what form any common seal is to be used.

(3) Unless otherwise decided by the directors, if the company has a common seal and it is affixed to a document, the document must also be signed by at least one authorised person in the presence of a witness who attests the signature.

(4) For the purposes of this article, an authorised person is –

(a) any director of the company;

(b) the company secretary (if any); or

(c) any person authorised by the directors for the purpose of signing documents to which the common seal is applied.

No right to inspect accounts and other records

50. Except as provided by law or authorised by the directors or an ordinary resolution of the company, no person is entitled to inspect any of the company's accounting or other records or documents merely by virtue of being a shareholder.

Provision for employees on cessation of business

51. The directors may decide to make provision for the benefit of persons employed or formerly employed by the company or any of its subsidiaries (other than a director or former director or shadow director) in connection with the cessation or transfer to any person of the whole or part of the undertaking of the company or that subsidiary.

Directors' indemnity and insurance

Indemnity

52. – (1) Subject to paragraph (2), a relevant director of the company or an associated company may be indemnified out of the company's assets against –

(a) any liability incurred by that director in connection with any negligence, default, breach of duty or breach of trust in relation to the company or an associated company,

(b) any liability incurred by that director in connection with the activities of the company or an associated company in its capacity as a trustee of an occupational pension scheme (as defined in section 235(6) of the Companies Act 2006),

(c) any other liability incurred by that director as an officer of the company or an associated company.

(2) This article does not authorise any indemnity which would be prohibited or rendered void by any provision of the Companies Acts or by any other provision of law.

(3) In this article –

(a) companies are associated if one is a subsidiary of the other or both are subsidiaries of the same body corporate, and

(b) a 'relevant director' means any director or former director of the company or an associated company.

Insurance

53. – (1) The directors may decide to purchase and maintain insurance, at the expense of the company, for the benefit of any relevant director in respect of any relevant loss.

(2) In this article –

(a) a 'relevant director' means any director or former director of the company or an associated company,

(b) a 'relevant loss' means any loss or liability which has been or may be incurred by a relevant director in connection with that director's duties or powers in relation to the company, any associated company or any pension fund or employees' share scheme of the company or associated company, and

(c) companies are associated if one is a subsidiary of the other or both are subsidiaries of the same body corporate.

SCHEDULE 3
Model Articles for Public Companies

Part 1: Interpretation and limitation of liability

Defined terms

1. In the articles, unless the context requires otherwise –

'alternate' or 'alternate director' has the meaning given in article 25;

'appointor' has the meaning given in article 25;

'articles' means the company's articles of association;

'bankruptcy' includes individual insolvency proceedings in a jurisdiction other than England and Wales or Northern Ireland which have an effect similar to that of bankruptcy;

'call' has the meaning given in article 54;

'call notice' has the meaning given in article 54;

'certificate' means a paper certificate (other than a share warrant) evidencing a person's title to specified shares or other securities;

'certificated' in relation to a share, means that it is not an uncertificated share or a share in respect of which a share warrant has been issued and is current;

'chairman' has the meaning given in article 12;

'chairman of the meeting' has the meaning given in article 31;

'Companies Acts' means the Companies Acts (as defined in section 2 of the Companies Act 2006), in so far as they apply to the company;

'company's lien' has the meaning given in article 52;

'director' means a director of the company, and includes any person occupying the position of director, by whatever name called;

'distribution recipient' has the meaning given in article 72;

'document' includes, unless otherwise specified, any document sent or supplied in electronic form;

'electronic form' has the meaning given in section 1168 of the Companies Act 2006;

'fully paid' in relation to a share, means that the nominal value and any premium to be paid to the company in respect of that share have been paid to the company;

'hard copy form' has the meaning given in section 1168 of the Companies Act 2006;

'holder' in relation to shares means the person whose name is entered in the register of members as the holder of the shares, or, in the case of a share in respect of which a share warrant has been issued (and not cancelled), the person in possession of that warrant;

'instrument' means a document in hard copy form;

'lien enforcement notice' has the meaning given in article 53;

'member' has the meaning given in section 112 of the Companies Act 2006;

'ordinary resolution' has the meaning given in section 282 of the Companies Act 2006;

'paid' means paid or credited as paid;

'participate', in relation to a directors' meeting, has the meaning given in article 9;

'partly paid' in relation to a share means that part of that share's nominal value or any premium at which it was issued has not been paid to the company;

'proxy notice' has the meaning given in article 38;

'securities seal' has the meaning given in article 47;

'shares' means shares in the company;

'special resolution' has the meaning given in section 283 of the Companies Act 2006;

'subsidiary' has the meaning given in section 1159 of the Companies Act 2006;

'transmittee' means a person entitled to a share by reason of the death or bankruptcy of a shareholder or otherwise by operation of law;

'uncertificated' in relation to a share means that, by virtue of legislation (other than section 778 of the Companies Act 2006) permitting title to shares to be evidenced and transferred without a certificate, title to that share is evidenced and may be transferred without a certificate; and

'writing' means the representation or reproduction of words, symbols or other information in a visible form by any method or combination of methods, whether sent or supplied in electronic form or otherwise.

Unless the context otherwise requires, other words or expressions contained in these articles bear the same meaning as in the Companies Act 2006 as in force on the date when these articles become binding on the company.

Liability of members

2. The liability of the members is limited to the amount, if any, unpaid on the shares held by them.

Part 2: Directors

Directors' powers and responsibilities

Directors' general authority

3. Subject to the articles, the directors are responsible for the management of the company's business, for which purpose they may exercise all the powers of the company.

Members' reserve power

4. – (1) The members may, by special resolution, direct the directors to take, or refrain from taking, specified action.

(2) No such special resolution invalidates anything which the directors have done before the passing of the resolution.

Directors may delegate

5. – (1) Subject to the articles, the directors may delegate any of the powers which are conferred on them under the articles –

(a) to such person or committee;

(b) by such means (including by power of attorney);

(c) to such an extent;

(d) in relation to such matters or territories; and

(e) on such terms and conditions;

as they think fit.

(2) If the directors so specify, any such delegation may authorise further delegation of the directors' powers by any person to whom they are delegated.

(3) The directors may revoke any delegation in whole or part, or alter its terms and conditions.

Committees

6. – (1) Committees to which the directors delegate any of their powers must follow procedures which are based as far as they are applicable on those provisions of the articles which govern the taking of decisions by directors.

(2) The directors may make rules of procedure for all or any committees, which prevail over rules derived from the articles if they are not consistent with them.

Decision-making by directors

Directors to take decisions collectively

7. Decisions of the directors may be taken –

(a) at a directors' meeting, or

(b) in the form of a directors' written resolution.

Calling a directors' meeting

8. – (1) Any director may call a directors' meeting.

(2) The company secretary must call a directors' meeting if a director so requests.

(3) A directors' meeting is called by giving notice of the meeting to the directors.

(4) Notice of any directors' meeting must indicate –

(a) its proposed date and time;

(b) where it is to take place; and

(c) if it is anticipated that directors participating in the meeting will not be in the same place, how it is proposed that they should communicate with each other during the meeting.

(5) Notice of a directors' meeting must be given to each director, but need not be in writing.

(6) Notice of a directors' meeting need not be given to directors who waive their entitlement to notice of that meeting, by giving notice to that effect to the company not more than 7 days after the date on which the meeting is held. Where such notice is given after the meeting has been held, that does not affect the validity of the meeting, or of any business conducted at it.

Participation in directors' meetings

9. – (1) Subject to the articles, directors participate in a directors' meeting, or part of a directors' meeting, when –

(a) the meeting has been called and takes place in accordance with the articles, and

(b) they can each communicate to the others any information or opinions they have on any particular item of the business of the meeting.

(2) In determining whether directors are participating in a directors' meeting, it is irrelevant where any director is or how they communicate with each other.

(3) If all the directors participating in a meeting are not in the same place, they may decide that the meeting is to be treated as taking place wherever any of them is.

Quorum for directors' meetings

10. – (1) At a directors' meeting, unless a quorum is participating, no proposal is to be voted on, except a proposal to call another meeting.

(2) The quorum for directors' meetings may be fixed from time to time by a decision of the directors, but it must never be less than two, and unless otherwise fixed it is two.

Meetings where total number of directors less than quorum

11. – (1) This article applies where the total number of directors for the time being is less than the quorum for directors' meetings.

(2) If there is only one director, that director may appoint sufficient directors to make up a quorum or call a general meeting to do so.

(3) If there is more than one director –

(a) a directors' meeting may take place, if it is called in accordance with the articles and at least two directors participate in it, with a view to appointing sufficient directors to make up a quorum or calling a general meeting to do so, and

(b) if a directors' meeting is called but only one director attends at the appointed date and time to participate in it, that director may appoint sufficient directors to make up a quorum or call a general meeting to do so.

Chairing directors' meetings

12. – (1) The directors may appoint a director to chair their meetings.

(2) The person so appointed for the time being is known as the chairman.

(3) The directors may appoint other directors as deputy or assistant chairmen to chair directors' meetings in the chairman's absence.

(4) The directors may terminate the appointment of the chairman, deputy or assistant chairman at any time.

(5) If neither the chairman nor any director appointed generally to chair directors' meetings in the chairman's absence is participating in a meeting within ten minutes of the time at which it was to start, the participating directors must appoint one of themselves to chair it.

Voting at directors' meetings: general rules

13. – (1) Subject to the articles, a decision is taken at a directors' meeting by a majority of the votes of the participating directors.

(2) Subject to the articles, each director participating in a directors' meeting has one vote.

(3) Subject to the articles, if a director has an interest in an actual or proposed transaction or arrangement with the company –

(a) that director and that director's alternate may not vote on any proposal relating to it, but

(b) this does not preclude the alternate from voting in relation to that transaction or arrangement on behalf of another appointor who does not have such an interest.

Chairman's casting vote at directors' meetings

14. – (1) If the numbers of votes for and against a proposal are equal, the chairman or other director chairing the meeting has a casting vote.

(2) But this does not apply if, in accordance with the articles, the chairman or other director is not to be counted as participating in the decision-making process for quorum or voting purposes.

Alternates voting at directors' meetings

15. A director who is also an alternate director has an additional vote on behalf of each appointor who is –

(a) not participating in a directors' meeting, and

(b) would have been entitled to vote if they were participating in it.

Conflicts of interest

16. – (1) If a directors' meeting, or part of a directors' meeting, is concerned with an actual or proposed transaction or arrangement with the company in which a director is interested, that director is not to be counted as participating in that meeting, or part of a meeting, for quorum or voting purposes.

(2) But if paragraph (3) applies, a director who is interested in an actual or proposed transaction or arrangement with the company is to be counted as participating in a decision at a directors' meeting, or part of a directors' meeting, relating to it for quorum and voting purposes.

(3) This paragraph applies when –

(a) the company by ordinary resolution disapplies the provision of the articles which would otherwise prevent a director from being counted as participating in, or voting at, a directors' meeting;

(b) the director's interest cannot reasonably be regarded as likely to give rise to a conflict of interest; or

(c) the director's conflict of interest arises from a permitted cause.

(4) For the purposes of this article, the following are permitted causes –

(a) a guarantee given, or to be given, by or to a director in respect of an obligation incurred by or on behalf of the company or any of its subsidiaries;

(b) subscription, or an agreement to subscribe, for shares or other securities of the company or any of its subsidiaries, or to underwrite, sub-underwrite, or guarantee subscription for any such shares or securities; and

(c) arrangements pursuant to which benefits are made available to employees and directors or former employees and directors of the company or any of its subsidiaries which do not provide special benefits for directors or former directors.

(5) Subject to paragraph (6), if a question arises at a meeting of directors or of a committee of directors as to the right of a director to participate in the meeting (or part of the meeting) for voting or quorum purposes, the question may, before the conclusion of the meeting, be referred to the chairman whose ruling in relation to any director other than the chairman is to be final and conclusive.

(6) If any question as to the right to participate in the meeting (or part of the meeting) should arise in respect of the chairman, the question is to be decided by a decision of the directors at that meeting, for which purpose the chairman is not to be counted as participating in the meeting (or that part of the meeting) for voting or quorum purposes.

Proposing directors' written resolutions

17. – (1) Any director may propose a directors' written resolution.

(2) The company secretary must propose a directors' written resolution if a director so requests.

(3) A directors' written resolution is proposed by giving notice of the proposed resolution to the directors.

(4) Notice of a proposed directors' written resolution must indicate –

(a) the proposed resolution, and

(b) the time by which it is proposed that the directors should adopt it.

(5) Notice of a proposed directors' written resolution must be given in writing to each director.

(6) Any decision which a person giving notice of a proposed directors' written resolution takes regarding the process of adopting that resolution must be taken reasonably in good faith.

Adoption of directors' written resolutions

18. – (1) A proposed directors' written resolution is adopted when all the directors who would have been entitled to vote on the resolution at a directors' meeting have signed one or more copies of it, provided that those directors would have formed a quorum at such a meeting.

(2) It is immaterial whether any director signs the resolution before or after the time by which the notice proposed that it should be adopted.

(3) Once a directors' written resolution has been adopted, it must be treated as if it had been a decision taken at a directors' meeting in accordance with the articles.

(4) The company secretary must ensure that the company keeps a record, in writing, of all directors' written resolutions for at least ten years from the date of their adoption.

Directors' discretion to make further rules

19. Subject to the articles, the directors may make any rule which they think fit about how they take decisions, and about how such rules are to be recorded or communicated to directors.

Appointment of directors

Methods of appointing directors

20. Any person who is willing to act as a director, and is permitted by law to do so, may be appointed to be a director –

(a) by ordinary resolution, or

(b) by a decision of the directors.

Retirement of directors by rotation

21. – (1) At the first annual general meeting all the directors must retire from office.

(2) At every subsequent annual general meeting any directors –

(a) who have been appointed by the directors since the last annual general meeting, or

(b) who were not appointed or reappointed at one of the preceding two annual general meetings,

must retire from office and may offer themselves for reappointment by the members.

Termination of director's appointment

22. A person ceases to be a director as soon as –

(a) that person ceases to be a director by virtue of any provision of the Companies Act 2006 or is prohibited from being a director by law;

(b) a bankruptcy order is made against that person;

(c) a composition is made with that person's creditors generally in satisfaction of that person's debts;

(d) a registered medical practitioner who is treating that person gives a written opinion to the company stating that that person has become physically or mentally incapable of acting as a director and may remain so for more than three months;

(e) by reason of that person's mental health, a court makes an order which wholly or partly prevents that person from personally exercising any powers or rights which that person would otherwise have;

(f) notification is received by the company from the director that the director is resigning from office as director, and such resignation has taken effect in accordance with its terms.

Directors' remuneration

23. – (1) Directors may undertake any services for the company that the directors decide.

(2) Directors are entitled to such remuneration as the directors determine –

(a) for their services to the company as directors, and

(b) for any other service which they undertake for the company.

(3) Subject to the articles, a director's remuneration may –

(a) take any form, and

(b) include any arrangements in connection with the payment of a pension, allowance or gratuity, or any death, sickness or disability benefits, to or in respect of that director.

(4) Unless the directors decide otherwise, directors' remuneration accrues from day to day.

(5) Unless the directors decide otherwise, directors are not accountable to the company for any remuneration which they receive as directors or other officers or employees of the company's subsidiaries or of any other body corporate in which the company is interested.

Directors' expenses

24. The company may pay any reasonable expenses which the directors properly incur in connection with their attendance at –

(a) meetings of directors or committees of directors,

(b) general meetings, or

(c) separate meetings of the holders of any class of shares or of debentures of the company,

or otherwise in connection with the exercise of their powers and the discharge of their responsibilities in relation to the company.

Alternate directors

Appointment and removal of alternates

25. – (1) Any director (the 'appointor') may appoint as an alternate any other director, or any other person approved by resolution of the directors, to –

(a) exercise that director's powers, and

(b) carry out that director's responsibilities,

in relation to the taking of decisions by the directors in the absence of the alternate's appointor.

(2) Any appointment or removal of an alternate must be effected by notice in writing to the company signed by the appointor, or in any other manner approved by the directors.

(3) The notice must –

(a) identify the proposed alternate, and

(b) in the case of a notice of appointment, contain a statement signed by the proposed alternate that the proposed alternate is willing to act as the alternate of the director giving the notice.

Rights and responsibilities of alternate directors

26. – (1) An alternate director has the same rights, in relation to any directors' meeting or directors' written resolution, as the alternate's appointor.

(2) Except as the articles specify otherwise, alternate directors –

(a) are deemed for all purposes to be directors;

(b) are liable for their own acts and omissions;

(c) are subject to the same restrictions as their appointors; and

(d) are not deemed to be agents of or for their appointors.

(3) A person who is an alternate director but not a director –

(a) may be counted as participating for the purposes of determining whether a quorum is participating (but only if that person's appointor is not participating), and

(b) may sign a written resolution (but only if it is not signed or to be signed by that person's appointor).

No alternate may be counted as more than one director for such purposes.

(4) An alternate director is not entitled to receive any remuneration from the company for serving as an alternate director except such part of the alternate's appointor's remuneration as the appointor may direct by notice in writing made to the company.

Termination of alternate directorship

27. An alternate director's appointment as an alternate terminates –

(a) when the alternate's appointor revokes the appointment by notice to the company in writing specifying when it is to terminate;

(b) on the occurrence in relation to the alternate of any event which, if it occurred in relation to the alternate's appointor, would result in the termination of the appointor's appointment as a director;

(c) on the death of the alternate's appointor; or

(d) when the alternate's appointor's appointment as a director terminates, except that an alternate's appointment as an alternate does not terminate when the appointor retires by rotation at a general meeting and is then reappointed as a director at the same general meeting.

Part 3: Decision-making by members

Organisation of general meetings

Members can call general meeting if not enough directors

28. If –

(a) the company has fewer than two directors, and

(b) the director (if any) is unable or unwilling to appoint sufficient directors to make up a quorum or to call a general meeting to do so,

then two or more members may call a general meeting (or instruct the company secretary to do so) for the purpose of appointing one or more directors.

Attendance and speaking at general meetings

29. – (1) A person is able to exercise the right to speak at a general meeting when that person is in a position to communicate to all those attending the meeting, during the meeting, any information or opinions which that person has on the business of the meeting.

(2) A person is able to exercise the right to vote at a general meeting when –

(a) that person is able to vote, during the meeting, on resolutions put to the vote at the meeting, and

(b) that person's vote can be taken into account in determining whether or not such resolutions are passed at the same time as the votes of all the other persons attending the meeting.

(3) The directors may make whatever arrangements they consider appropriate to enable those attending a general meeting to exercise their rights to speak or vote at it.

(4) In determining attendance at a general meeting, it is immaterial whether any two or more members attending it are in the same place as each other.

(5) Two or more persons who are not in the same place as each other attend a general meeting if their circumstances are such that if they have (or were to have) rights to speak and vote at that meeting, they are (or would be) able to exercise them.

Quorum for general meetings

30. No business other than the appointment of the chairman of the meeting is to be transacted at a general meeting if the persons attending it do not constitute a quorum.

Chairing general meetings

31. – (1) If the directors have appointed a chairman, the chairman shall chair general meetings if present and willing to do so.

(2) If the directors have not appointed a chairman, or if the chairman is unwilling to chair the meeting or is not present within ten minutes of the time at which a meeting was due to start –

(a) the directors present, or

(b) (if no directors are present), the meeting,

must appoint a director or member to chair the meeting, and the appointment of the chairman of the meeting must be the first business of the meeting.

(3) The person chairing a meeting in accordance with this article is referred to as 'the chairman of the meeting'.

Attendance and speaking by directors and non-members

32. – (1) Directors may attend and speak at general meetings, whether or not they are members.

(2) The chairman of the meeting may permit other persons who are not –

(a) members of the company, or

(b) otherwise entitled to exercise the rights of members in relation to general meetings,

to attend and speak at a general meeting.

Adjournment

33. – (1) If the persons attending a general meeting within half an hour of the time at which the meeting was due to start do not constitute a quorum, or if during a meeting a quorum ceases to be present, the chairman of the meeting must adjourn it.

(2) The chairman of the meeting may adjourn a general meeting at which a quorum is present if –

(a) the meeting consents to an adjournment, or

(b) it appears to the chairman of the meeting that an adjournment is necessary to protect the safety of any person attending the meeting or ensure that the business of the meeting is conducted in an orderly manner.

(3) The chairman of the meeting must adjourn a general meeting if directed to do so by the meeting.

(4) When adjourning a general meeting, the chairman of the meeting must –

(a) either specify the time and place to which it is adjourned or state that it is to continue at a time and place to be fixed by the directors, and

(b) have regard to any directions as to the time and place of any adjournment which have been given by the meeting.

(5) If the continuation of an adjourned meeting is to take place more than 14 days after it was adjourned, the company must give at least 7 clear days' notice of it (that is, excluding the day of the adjourned meeting and the day on which the notice is given) –

(a) to the same persons to whom notice of the company's general meetings is required to be given, and

(b) containing the same information which such notice is required to contain.

(6) No business may be transacted at an adjourned general meeting which could not properly have been transacted at the meeting if the adjournment had not taken place.

Voting at general meetings

Voting: general

34. A resolution put to the vote of a general meeting must be decided on a show of hands unless a poll is duly demanded in accordance with the articles.

Errors and disputes

35. – (1) No objection may be raised to the qualification of any person voting at a general meeting except at the meeting or adjourned meeting at which the vote objected to is tendered, and every vote not disallowed at the meeting is valid.

(2) Any such objection must be referred to the chairman of the meeting whose decision is final.

Demanding a poll

36. – (1) A poll on a resolution may be demanded –

(a) in advance of the general meeting where it is to be put to the vote, or

(b) at a general meeting, either before a show of hands on that resolution or immediately after the result of a show of hands on that resolution is declared.

(2) A poll may be demanded by –

(a) the chairman of the meeting;

(b) the directors;

(c) two or more persons having the right to vote on the resolution; or

(d) a person or persons representing not less than one tenth of the total voting rights of all the members having the right to vote on the resolution.

(3) A demand for a poll may be withdrawn if –

(a) the poll has not yet been taken, and

(b) the chairman of the meeting consents to the withdrawal.

Procedure on a poll

37. – (1) Subject to the articles, polls at general meetings must be taken when, where and in such manner as the chairman of the meeting directs.

(2) The chairman of the meeting may appoint scrutineers (who need not be members) and decide how and when the result of the poll is to be declared.

(3) The result of a poll shall be the decision of the meeting in respect of the resolution on which the poll was demanded.

(4) A poll on –

(a) the election of the chairman of the meeting, or

(b) a question of adjournment,

must be taken immediately.

(5) Other polls must be taken within 30 days of their being demanded.

(6) A demand for a poll does not prevent a general meeting from continuing, except as regards the question on which the poll was demanded.

(7) No notice need be given of a poll not taken immediately if the time and place at which it is to be taken are announced at the meeting at which it is demanded.

(8) In any other case, at least 7 days' notice must be given specifying the time and place at which the poll is to be taken.

Content of proxy notices

38. – (1) Proxies may only validly be appointed by a notice in writing (a 'proxy notice') which –

(a) states the name and address of the member appointing the proxy;

(b) identifies the person appointed to be that member's proxy and the general meeting in relation to which that person is appointed;

(c) is signed by or on behalf of the member appointing the proxy, or is authenticated in such manner as the directors may determine; and

(d) is delivered to the company in accordance with the articles and any instructions contained in the notice of the general meeting to which they relate.

(2) The company may require proxy notices to be delivered in a particular form, and may specify different forms for different purposes.

(3) Proxy notices may specify how the proxy appointed under them is to vote (or that the proxy is to abstain from voting) on one or more resolutions.

(4) Unless a proxy notice indicates otherwise, it must be treated as –

(a) allowing the person appointed under it as a proxy discretion as to how to vote on any ancillary or procedural resolutions put to the meeting, and

(b) appointing that person as a proxy in relation to any adjournment of the general meeting to which it relates as well as the meeting itself.

Delivery of proxy notices

39. – (1) Any notice of a general meeting must specify the address or addresses ('proxy notification address') at which the company or its agents will receive proxy notices relating to that meeting, or any adjournment of it, delivered in hard copy or electronic form.

(2) A person who is entitled to attend, speak or vote (either on a show of hands or on a poll) at a general meeting remains so entitled in respect of that meeting or any adjournment of it, even though a valid proxy notice has been delivered to the company by or on behalf of that person.

(3) Subject to paragraphs (4) and (5), a proxy notice must be delivered to a proxy notification address not less than 48 hours before the general meeting or adjourned meeting to which it relates.

(4) In the case of a poll taken more than 48 hours after it is demanded, the notice must be delivered to a proxy notification address not less than 24 hours before the time appointed for the taking of the poll.

(5) In the case of a poll not taken during the meeting but taken not more than 48 hours after it was demanded, the proxy notice must be delivered –

(a) in accordance with paragraph (3), or

(b) at the meeting at which the poll was demanded to the chairman, secretary or any director.

(6) An appointment under a proxy notice may be revoked by delivering a notice in writing given by or on behalf of the person by whom or on whose behalf the proxy notice was given to a proxy notification address.

(7) A notice revoking a proxy appointment only takes effect if it is delivered before –

(a) the start of the meeting or adjourned meeting to which it relates, or

(b) (in the case of a poll not taken on the same day as the meeting or adjourned meeting) the time appointed for taking the poll to which it relates.

(8) If a proxy notice is not signed by the person appointing the proxy, it must be accompanied by written evidence of the authority of the person who executed it to execute it on the appointor's behalf.

Amendments to resolutions

40. – (1) An ordinary resolution to be proposed at a general meeting may be amended by ordinary resolution if –

(a) notice of the proposed amendment is given to the company secretary in writing by a person entitled to vote at the general meeting at which it is to be proposed not less than 48 hours before the meeting is to take place (or such later time as the chairman of the meeting may determine), and

(b) the proposed amendment does not, in the reasonable opinion of the chairman of the meeting, materially alter the scope of the resolution.

(2) A special resolution to be proposed at a general meeting may be amended by ordinary resolution, if –

(a) the chairman of the meeting proposes the amendment at the general meeting at which the resolution is to be proposed, and

(b) the amendment does not go beyond what is necessary to correct a grammatical or other non-substantive error in the resolution.

(3) If the chairman of the meeting, acting in good faith, wrongly decides that an amendment to a resolution is out of order, the chairman's error does not invalidate the vote on that resolution.

Restrictions on members' rights

No voting of shares on which money owed to company

41. No voting rights attached to a share may be exercised at any general meeting, at any adjournment of it, or on any poll called at or in relation to it, unless all amounts payable to the company in respect of that share have been paid.

Application of rules to class meetings

Class meetings

42. The provisions of the articles relating to general meetings apply, with any necessary modifications, to meetings of the holders of any class of shares.

Part 4: Shares and distributions

Issue of shares

Powers to issue different classes of share

43. – (1) Subject to the articles, but without prejudice to the rights attached to any existing share, the company may issue shares with such rights or restrictions as may be determined by ordinary resolution.

(2) The company may issue shares which are to be redeemed, or are liable to be redeemed at the option of the company or the holder, and the directors may determine the terms, conditions and manner of redemption of any such shares.

Payment of commissions on subscription for shares

44. – (1) The company may pay any person a commission in consideration for that person –

(a) subscribing, or agreeing to subscribe, for shares, or

(b) procuring, or agreeing to procure, subscriptions for shares.

(2) Any such commission may be paid –

(a) in cash, or in fully paid or partly paid shares or other securities, or partly in one way and partly in the other, and

(b) in respect of a conditional or an absolute subscription.

Interests in shares

Company not bound by less than absolute interests

45. Except as required by law, no person is to be recognised by the company as holding any share upon any trust, and except as otherwise required by law or the articles, the company is not in any way to be bound by or recognise any interest in a share other than the holder's absolute ownership of it and all the rights attaching to it.

Share certificates

Certificates to be issued except in certain cases

46. – (1) The company must issue each member with one or more certificates in respect of the shares which that member holds.

(2) This article does not apply to –

(a) uncertificated shares;

(b) shares in respect of which a share warrant has been issued; or

(c) shares in respect of which the Companies Acts permit the company not to issue a certificate.

(3) Except as otherwise specified in the articles, all certificates must be issued free of charge.

(4) No certificate may be issued in respect of shares of more than one class.

(5) If more than one person holds a share, only one certificate may be issued in respect of it.

Contents and execution of share certificates

47. – (1) Every certificate must specify –

(a) in respect of how many shares, of what class, it is issued;

(b) the nominal value of those shares;

(c) the amount paid up on them; and

(d) any distinguishing numbers assigned to them.

(2) Certificates must –

(a) have affixed to them the company's common seal or an official seal which is a facsimile of the company's common seal with the addition on its face of the word 'Securities' (a 'securities seal'), or

(b) be otherwise executed in accordance with the Companies Acts.

Consolidated share certificates

48. – (1) When a member's holding of shares of a particular class increases, the company may issue that member with –

(a) a single, consolidated certificate in respect of all the shares of a particular class which that member holds, or

(b) a separate certificate in respect of only those shares by which that member's holding has increased.

(2) When a member's holding of shares of a particular class is reduced, the company must ensure that the member is issued with one or more certificates in respect of the number of

shares held by the member after that reduction. But the company need not (in the absence of a request from the member) issue any new certificate if –

(a) all the shares which the member no longer holds as a result of the reduction, and

(b) none of the shares which the member retains following the reduction,

were, immediately before the reduction, represented by the same certificate.

(3) A member may request the company, in writing, to replace –

(a) the member's separate certificates with a consolidated certificate, or

(b) the member's consolidated certificate with two or more separate certificates representing such proportion of the shares as the member may specify.

(4) When the company complies with such a request it may charge such reasonable fee as the directors may decide for doing so.

(5) A consolidated certificate must not be issued unless any certificates which it is to replace have first been returned to the company for cancellation.

Replacement share certificates

49. – (1) If a certificate issued in respect of a member's shares is –

(a) damaged or defaced, or

(b) said to be lost, stolen or destroyed,

that member is entitled to be issued with a replacement certificate in respect of the same shares.

(2) A member exercising the right to be issued with such a replacement certificate –

(a) may at the same time exercise the right to be issued with a single certificate or separate certificates;

(b) must return the certificate which is to be replaced to the company if it is damaged or defaced; and

(c) must comply with such conditions as to evidence, indemnity and the payment of a reasonable fee as the directors decide.

Shares not held in certificated form

Uncertificated shares

50. – (1) In this article, 'the relevant rules' means –

(a) any applicable provision of the Companies Acts about the holding, evidencing of title to, or transfer of shares other than in certificated form, and

(b) any applicable legislation, rules or other arrangements made under or by virtue of such provision.

(2) The provisions of this article have effect subject to the relevant rules.

(3) Any provision of the articles which is inconsistent with the relevant rules must be disregarded, to the extent that it is inconsistent, whenever the relevant rules apply.

(4) Any share or class of shares of the company may be issued or held on such terms, or in such a way, that –

(a) title to it or them is not, or must not be, evidenced by a certificate, or

(b) it or they may or must be transferred wholly or partly without a certificate.

(5) The directors have power to take such steps as they think fit in relation to –

(a) the evidencing of and transfer of title to uncertificated shares (including in connection with the issue of such shares);

(b) any records relating to the holding of uncertificated shares;

(c) the conversion of certificated shares into uncertificated shares; or

(d) the conversion of uncertificated shares into certificated shares.

(6) The company may by notice to the holder of a share require that share –

(a) if it is uncertificated, to be converted into certificated form, and

(b) if it is certificated, to be converted into uncertificated form, to enable it to be dealt with in accordance with the articles.

(7) If –

(a) the articles give the directors power to take action, or require other persons to take action, in order to sell, transfer or otherwise dispose of shares, and

(b) uncertificated shares are subject to that power, but the power is expressed in terms which assume the use of a certificate or other written instrument,

the directors may take such action as is necessary or expedient to achieve the same results when exercising that power in relation to uncertificated shares.

(8) In particular, the directors may take such action as they consider appropriate to achieve the sale, transfer, disposal, forfeiture, re-allotment or surrender of an uncertificated share or otherwise to enforce a lien in respect of it.

(9) Unless the directors otherwise determine, shares which a member holds in uncertificated form must be treated as separate holdings from any shares which that member holds in certificated form.

(10) A class of shares must not be treated as two classes simply because some shares of that class are held in certificated form and others are held in uncertificated form.

Share warrants

51. – (1) The directors may issue a share warrant in respect of any fully paid share.

(2) Share warrants must be –

(a) issued in such form, and

(b) executed in such manner,

as the directors decide.

(3) A share represented by a share warrant may be transferred by delivery of the warrant representing it.

(4) The directors may make provision for the payment of dividends in respect of any share represented by a share warrant.

(5) Subject to the articles, the directors may decide the conditions on which any share warrant is issued. In particular, they may –

(a) decide the conditions on which new warrants are to be issued in place of warrants which are damaged or defaced, or said to have been lost, stolen or destroyed;

(b) decide the conditions on which bearers of warrants are entitled to attend and vote at general meetings;

(c) decide the conditions subject to which bearers of warrants may surrender their warrant so as to hold their shares in certificated or uncertificated form instead; and

(d) vary the conditions of issue of any warrant from time to time,

and the bearer of a warrant is subject to the conditions and procedures in force in relation to it, whether or not they were decided or specified before the warrant was issued.

(6) Subject to the conditions on which the warrants are issued from time to time, bearers of share warrants have the same rights and privileges as they would if their names had been included in the register as holders of the shares represented by their warrants.

(7) The company must not in any way be bound by or recognise any interest in a share represented by a share warrant other than the absolute right of the bearer of that warrant to that warrant.

Partly paid shares

Company's lien over partly paid shares

52. – (1) The company has a lien ('the company's lien') over every share which is partly paid for any part of –

(a) that share's nominal value, and

(b) any premium at which it was issued,

which has not been paid to the company, and which is payable immediately or at some time in the future, whether or not a call notice has been sent in respect of it.

(2) The company's lien over a share –

(a) takes priority over any third party's interest in that share, and

(b) extends to any dividend or other money payable by the company in respect of that share and (if the lien is enforced and the share is sold by the company) the proceeds of sale of that share.

(3) The directors may at any time decide that a share which is or would otherwise be subject to the company's lien shall not be subject to it, either wholly or in part.

Enforcement of the company's lien

53. – (1) Subject to the provisions of this article, if –

(a) a lien enforcement notice has been given in respect of a share, and

(b) the person to whom the notice was given has failed to comply with it,

the company may sell that share in such manner as the directors decide.

(2) A lien enforcement notice –

(a) may only be given in respect of a share which is subject to the company's lien, in respect of which a sum is payable and the due date for payment of that sum has passed;

(b) must specify the share concerned;

(c) must require payment of the sum payable within 14 days of the notice;

(d) must be addressed either to the holder of the share or to a person entitled to it by reason of the holder's death, bankruptcy or otherwise; and

(e) must state the company's intention to sell the share if the notice is not complied with.

(3) Where shares are sold under this article –

(a) the directors may authorise any person to execute an instrument of transfer of the shares to the purchaser or a person nominated by the purchaser, and

(b) the transferee is not bound to see to the application of the consideration, and the transferee's title is not affected by any irregularity in or invalidity of the process leading to the sale.

(4) The net proceeds of any such sale (after payment of the costs of sale and any other costs of enforcing the lien) must be applied –

(a) first, in payment of so much of the sum for which the lien exists as was payable at the date of the lien enforcement notice,

(b) second, to the person entitled to the shares at the date of the sale, but only after the certificate for the shares sold has been surrendered to the company for cancellation or a suitable indemnity has been given for any lost certificates, and subject to a lien equivalent to the company's lien over the shares before the sale for any money payable in respect of the shares after the date of the lien enforcement notice.

(5) A statutory declaration by a director or the company secretary that the declarant is a director or the company secretary and that a share has been sold to satisfy the company's lien on a specified date –

(a) is conclusive evidence of the facts stated in it as against all persons claiming to be entitled to the share, and

(b) subject to compliance with any other formalities of transfer required by the articles or by law, constitutes a good title to the share.

Call notices

54. – (1) Subject to the articles and the terms on which shares are allotted, the directors may send a notice (a 'call notice') to a member requiring the member to pay the company a specified sum of money (a 'call') which is payable in respect of shares which that member holds at the date when the directors decide to send the call notice.

(2) A call notice –

(a) may not require a member to pay a call which exceeds the total sum unpaid on that member's shares (whether as to the share's nominal value or any amount payable to the company by way of premium);

(b) must state when and how any call to which it relates it is to be paid; and

(c) may permit or require the call to be paid by instalments.

(3) A member must comply with the requirements of a call notice, but no member is obliged to pay any call before 14 days have passed since the notice was sent.

(4) Before the company has received any call due under a call notice the directors may –

(a) revoke it wholly or in part, or

(b) specify a later time for payment than is specified in the notice,

by a further notice in writing to the member in respect of whose shares the call is made.

Liability to pay calls

55. – (1) Liability to pay a call is not extinguished or transferred by transferring the shares in respect of which it is required to be paid.

(2) Joint holders of a share are jointly and severally liable to pay all calls in respect of that share.

(3) Subject to the terms on which shares are allotted, the directors may, when issuing shares, provide that call notices sent to the holders of those shares may require them –

(a) to pay calls which are not the same, or

(b) to pay calls at different times.

When call notice need not be issued

56. – (1) A call notice need not be issued in respect of sums which are specified, in the terms on which a share is issued, as being payable to the company in respect of that share (whether in respect of nominal value or premium) –

(a) on allotment;

(b) on the occurrence of a particular event; or

(c) on a date fixed by or in accordance with the terms of issue.

(2) But if the due date for payment of such a sum has passed and it has not been paid, the holder of the share concerned is treated in all respects as having failed to comply with a call notice in respect of that sum, and is liable to the same consequences as regards the payment of interest and forfeiture.

Failure to comply with call notice: automatic consequences

57. – (1) If a person is liable to pay a call and fails to do so by the call payment date –

(a) the directors may issue a notice of intended forfeiture to that person, and

(b) until the call is paid, that person must pay the company interest on the call from the call payment date at the relevant rate.

(2) For the purposes of this article –

(a) the 'call payment date' is the time when the call notice states that a call is payable, unless the directors give a notice specifying a later date, in which case the 'call payment date' is that later date;

(b) the 'relevant rate' is –

(i) the rate fixed by the terms on which the share in respect of which the call is due was allotted;

(ii) such other rate as was fixed in the call notice which required payment of the call, or has otherwise been determined by the directors; or

(iii) if no rate is fixed in either of these ways, 5 per cent per annum.

(3) The relevant rate must not exceed by more than 5 percentage points the base lending rate most recently set by the Monetary Policy Committee of the Bank of England in connection with its responsibilities under Part 2 of the Bank of England Act 1998(1).

(4) The directors may waive any obligation to pay interest on a call wholly or in part.

Notice of intended forfeiture

58. A notice of intended forfeiture –

(a) may be sent in respect of any share in respect of which a call has not been paid as required by a call notice;

(b) must be sent to the holder of that share or to a person entitled to it by reason of the holder's death, bankruptcy or otherwise;

(c) must require payment of the call and any accrued interest by a date which is not less than 14 days after the date of the notice;

(d) must state how the payment is to be made; and

(e) must state that if the notice is not complied with, the shares in respect of which the call is payable will be liable to be forfeited.

Directors' power to forfeit shares

59. If a notice of intended forfeiture is not complied with before the date by which payment of the call is required in the notice of intended forfeiture, the directors may decide that any share in respect of which it was given is forfeited, and the forfeiture is to include all dividends or other moneys payable in respect of the forfeited shares and not paid before the forfeiture.

Effect of forfeiture

60. – (1) Subject to the articles, the forfeiture of a share extinguishes –

(a) all interests in that share, and all claims and demands against the company in respect of it, and

(b) all other rights and liabilities incidental to the share as between the person whose share it was prior to the forfeiture and the company.

(2) Any share which is forfeited in accordance with the articles –

(a) is deemed to have been forfeited when the directors decide that it is forfeited;

(b) is deemed to be the property of the company; and

(c) may be sold, re-allotted or otherwise disposed of as the directors think fit.

(3) If a person's shares have been forfeited –

(a) the company must send that person notice that forfeiture has occurred and record it in the register of members;

(b) that person ceases to be a member in respect of those shares;

(c) that person must surrender the certificate for the shares forfeited to the company for cancellation;

(d) that person remains liable to the company for all sums payable by that person under the articles at the date of forfeiture in respect of those shares, including any interest (whether accrued before or after the date of forfeiture); and

(e) the directors may waive payment of such sums wholly or in part or enforce payment without any allowance for the value of the shares at the time of forfeiture or for any consideration received on their disposal.

(4) At any time before the company disposes of a forfeited share, the directors may decide to cancel the forfeiture on payment of all calls and interest due in respect of it and on such other terms as they think fit.

Procedure following forfeiture

61. – (1) If a forfeited share is to be disposed of by being transferred, the company may receive the consideration for the transfer and the directors may authorise any person to execute the instrument of transfer.

(2) A statutory declaration by a director or the company secretary that the declarant is a director or the company secretary and that a share has been forfeited on a specified date –

(a) is conclusive evidence of the facts stated in it as against all persons claiming to be entitled to the share, and

(b) subject to compliance with any other formalities of transfer required by the articles or by law, constitutes a good title to the share.

(3) A person to whom a forfeited share is transferred is not bound to see to the application of the consideration (if any) nor is that person's title to the share affected by any irregularity in or invalidity of the process leading to the forfeiture or transfer of the share.

(4) If the company sells a forfeited share, the person who held it prior to its forfeiture is entitled to receive from the company the proceeds of such sale, net of any commission, and excluding any amount which –

(a) was, or would have become, payable, and

(b) had not, when that share was forfeited, been paid by that person in respect of that share,

but no interest is payable to such a person in respect of such proceeds and the company is not required to account for any money earned on them.

Surrender of shares

62. – (1) A member may surrender any share –

(a) in respect of which the directors may issue a notice of intended forfeiture;

(b) which the directors may forfeit; or

(c) which has been forfeited.

(2) The directors may accept the surrender of any such share.

(3) The effect of surrender on a share is the same as the effect of forfeiture on that share.

(4) A share which has been surrendered may be dealt with in the same way as a share which has been forfeited.

Transfer and transmission of shares

Transfers of certificated shares

63. – (1) Certificated shares may be transferred by means of an instrument of transfer in any usual form or any other form approved by the directors, which is executed by or on behalf of –

(a) the transferor, and

(b) (if any of the shares is partly paid) the transferee.

(2) No fee may be charged for registering any instrument of transfer or other document relating to or affecting the title to any share.

(3) The company may retain any instrument of transfer which is registered.

(4) The transferor remains the holder of a certificated share until the transferee's name is entered in the register of members as holder of it.

(5) The directors may refuse to register the transfer of a certificated share if –

(a) the share is not fully paid;

(b) the transfer is not lodged at the company's registered office or such other place as the directors have appointed;

(c) the transfer is not accompanied by the certificate for the shares to which it relates, or such other evidence as the directors may reasonably require to show the transferor's right to make the transfer, or evidence of the right of someone other than the transferor to make the transfer on the transferor's behalf;

(d) the transfer is in respect of more than one class of share; or

(e) the transfer is in favour of more than four transferees.

(6) If the directors refuse to register the transfer of a share, the instrument of transfer must be returned to the transferee with the notice of refusal unless they suspect that the proposed transfer may be fraudulent.

Transfer of uncertificated shares

64. A transfer of an uncertificated share must not be registered if it is in favour of more than four transferees.

Transmission of shares

65. – (1) If title to a share passes to a transmittee, the company may only recognise the transmittee as having any title to that share.

(2) Nothing in these articles releases the estate of a deceased member from any liability in respect of a share solely or jointly held by that member.

Transmittees' rights

66. – (1) A transmittee who produces such evidence of entitlement to shares as the directors may properly require –

(a) may, subject to the articles, choose either to become the holder of those shares or to have them transferred to another person, and

(b) subject to the articles, and pending any transfer of the shares to another person, has the same rights as the holder had.

(2) But transmittees do not have the right to attend or vote at a general meeting in respect of shares to which they are entitled, by reason of the holder's death or bankruptcy or otherwise, unless they become the holders of those shares.

Exercise of transmittees' rights

67. – (1) Transmittees who wish to become the holders of shares to which they have become entitled must notify the company in writing of that wish.

(2) If the share is a certificated share and a transmittee wishes to have it transferred to another person, the transmittee must execute an instrument of transfer in respect of it.

(3) If the share is an uncertificated share and the transmittee wishes to have it transferred to another person, the transmittee must –

(a) procure that all appropriate instructions are given to effect the transfer, or

(b) procure that the uncertificated share is changed into certificated form and then execute an instrument of transfer in respect of it.

(4) Any transfer made or executed under this article is to be treated as if it were made or executed by the person from whom the transmittee has derived rights in respect of the share, and as if the event which gave rise to the transmission had not occurred.

Transmittees bound by prior notices

68. If a notice is given to a member in respect of shares and a transmittee is entitled to those shares, the transmittee is bound by the notice if it was given to the member before the transmittee's name has been entered in the register of members.

Consolidation of shares

Procedure for disposing of fractions of shares

69. – (1) This article applies where –

(a) there has been a consolidation or division of shares, and

(b) as a result, members are entitled to fractions of shares.

(2) The directors may –

(a) sell the shares representing the fractions to any person including the company for the best price reasonably obtainable;

(b) in the case of a certificated share, authorise any person to execute an instrument of transfer of the shares to the purchaser or a person nominated by the purchaser; and

(c) distribute the net proceeds of sale in due proportion among the holders of the shares.

(3) Where any holder's entitlement to a portion of the proceeds of sale amounts to less than a minimum figure determined by the directors, that member's portion may be distributed to an organisation which is a charity for the purposes of the law of England and Wales, Scotland or Northern Ireland.

(4) The person to whom the shares are transferred is not obliged to ensure that any purchase money is received by the person entitled to the relevant fractions.

(5) The transferee's title to the shares is not affected by any irregularity in or invalidity of the process leading to their sale.

Distributions

Procedure for declaring dividends

70. – (1) The company may by ordinary resolution declare dividends, and the directors may decide to pay interim dividends.

(2) A dividend must not be declared unless the directors have made a recommendation as to its amount. Such a dividend must not exceed the amount recommended by the directors.

(3) No dividend may be declared or paid unless it is in accordance with members' respective rights.

(4) Unless the members' resolution to declare or directors' decision to pay a dividend, or the terms on which shares are issued, specify otherwise, it must be paid by reference to each member's holding of shares on the date of the resolution or decision to declare or pay it.

(5) If the company's share capital is divided into different classes, no interim dividend may be paid on shares carrying deferred or non-preferred rights if, at the time of payment, any preferential dividend is in arrear.

(6) The directors may pay at intervals any dividend payable at a fixed rate if it appears to them that the profits available for distribution justify the payment.

(7) If the directors act in good faith, they do not incur any liability to the holders of shares conferring preferred rights for any loss they may suffer by the lawful payment of an interim dividend on shares with deferred or non-preferred rights.

Calculation of dividends

71. – (1) Except as otherwise provided by the articles or the rights attached to shares, all dividends must be –

(a) declared and paid according to the amounts paid up on the shares on which the dividend is paid, and

(b) apportioned and paid proportionately to the amounts paid up on the shares during any portion or portions of the period in respect of which the dividend is paid.

(2) If any share is issued on terms providing that it ranks for dividend as from a particular date, that share ranks for dividend accordingly.

(3) For the purposes of calculating dividends, no account is to be taken of any amount which has been paid up on a share in advance of the due date for payment of that amount.

Payment of dividends and other distributions

72. – (1) Where a dividend or other sum which is a distribution is payable in respect of a share, it must be paid by one or more of the following means –

(a) transfer to a bank or building society account specified by the distribution recipient either in writing or as the directors may otherwise decide;

(b) sending a cheque made payable to the distribution recipient by post to the distribution recipient at the distribution recipient's registered address (if the distribution recipient is a holder of the share), or (in any other case) to an address specified by the distribution recipient either in writing or as the directors may otherwise decide;

(c) sending a cheque made payable to such person by post to such person at such address as the distribution recipient has specified either in writing or as the directors may otherwise decide; or

(d) any other means of payment as the directors agree with the distribution recipient either in writing or by such other means as the directors decide.

(2) In the articles, 'the distribution recipient' means, in respect of a share in respect of which a dividend or other sum is payable –

(a) the holder of the share; or

(b) if the share has two or more joint holders, whichever of them is named first in the register of members; or

(c) if the holder is no longer entitled to the share by reason of death or bankruptcy, or otherwise by operation of law, the transmittee.

Deductions from distributions in respect of sums owed to the company

73. – (1) If –

(a) a share is subject to the company's lien, and

(b) the directors are entitled to issue a lien enforcement notice in respect of it,

they may, instead of issuing a lien enforcement notice, deduct from any dividend or other sum payable in respect of the share any sum of money which is payable to the company in respect of that share to the extent that they are entitled to require payment under a lien enforcement notice.

(2) Money so deducted must be used to pay any of the sums payable in respect of that share.

(3) The company must notify the distribution recipient in writing of –

(a) the fact and amount of any such deduction;

(b) any non-payment of a dividend or other sum payable in respect of a share resulting from any such deduction; and

(c) how the money deducted has been applied.

No interest on distributions

74. The company may not pay interest on any dividend or other sum payable in respect of a share unless otherwise provided by –

(a) the terms on which the share was issued, or

(b) the provisions of another agreement between the holder of that share and the company.

Unclaimed distributions

75. – (1) All dividends or other sums which are –

(a) payable in respect of shares, and

(b) unclaimed after having been declared or become payable,

may be invested or otherwise made use of by the directors for the benefit of the company until claimed.

(2) The payment of any such dividend or other sum into a separate account does not make the company a trustee in respect of it.

(3) If –

(a) twelve years have passed from the date on which a dividend or other sum became due for payment, and

(b) the distribution recipient has not claimed it,

the distribution recipient is no longer entitled to that dividend or other sum and it ceases to remain owing by the company.

Non-cash distributions

76. – (1) Subject to the terms of issue of the share in question, the company may, by ordinary resolution on the recommendation of the directors, decide to pay all or part of a dividend or

other distribution payable in respect of a share by transferring non-cash assets of equivalent value (including, without limitation, shares or other securities in any company).

(2) If the shares in respect of which such a non-cash distribution is paid are uncertificated, any shares in the company which are issued as a non-cash distribution in respect of them must be uncertificated.

(3) For the purposes of paying a non-cash distribution, the directors may make whatever arrangements they think fit, including, where any difficulty arises regarding the distribution –

(a) fixing the value of any assets;

(b) paying cash to any distribution recipient on the basis of that value in order to adjust the rights of recipients; and

(c) vesting any assets in trustees.

Waiver of distributions

77. Distribution recipients may waive their entitlement to a dividend or other distribution payable in respect of a share by giving the company notice in writing to that effect, but if –

(a) the share has more than one holder, or

(b) more than one person is entitled to the share, whether by reason of the death or bankruptcy of one or more joint holders, or otherwise,

the notice is not effective unless it is expressed to be given, and signed, by all the holders or persons otherwise entitled to the share.

Capitalisation of profits

Authority to capitalise and appropriation of capitalised sums

78. – (1) Subject to the articles, the directors may, if they are so authorised by an ordinary resolution –

(a) decide to capitalise any profits of the company (whether or not they are available for distribution) which are not required for paying a preferential dividend, or any sum standing to the credit of the company's share premium account or capital redemption reserve; and

(b) appropriate any sum which they so decide to capitalise (a 'capitalised sum') to the persons who would have been entitled to it if it were distributed by way of dividend (the 'persons entitled') and in the same proportions.

(2) Capitalised sums must be applied –

(a) on behalf of the persons entitled, and

(b) in the same proportions as a dividend would have been distributed to them.

(3) Any capitalised sum may be applied in paying up new shares of a nominal amount equal to the capitalised sum which are then allotted credited as fully paid to the persons entitled or as they may direct.

(4) A capitalised sum which was appropriated from profits available for distribution may be applied –

(a) in or towards paying up any amounts unpaid on existing shares held by the persons entitled, or

(b) in paying up new debentures of the company which are then allotted credited as fully paid to the persons entitled or as they may direct.

(5) Subject to the articles the directors may –

(a) apply capitalised sums in accordance with paragraphs (3) and (4) partly in one way and partly in another;

(b) make such arrangements as they think fit to deal with shares or debentures becoming distributable in fractions under this article (including the issuing of fractional certificates or the making of cash payments); and

(c) authorise any person to enter into an agreement with the company on behalf of all the persons entitled which is binding on them in respect of the allotment of shares and debentures to them under this article.

Part 5: Miscellaneous provisions

Communications

Means of communication to be used

79. – (1) Subject to the articles, anything sent or supplied by or to the company under the articles may be sent or supplied in any way in which the Companies Act 2006 provides for documents or information which are authorised or required by any provision of that Act to be sent or supplied by or to the company.

(2) Subject to the articles, any notice or document to be sent or supplied to a director in connection with the taking of decisions by directors may also be sent or supplied by the means by which that director has asked to be sent or supplied with such notices or documents for the time being.

(3) A director may agree with the company that notices or documents sent to that director in a particular way are to be deemed to have been received within a specified time of their being sent, and for the specified time to be less than 48 hours.

Failure to notify contact details

80. – (1) If –

(a) the company sends two consecutive documents to a member over a period of at least 12 months, and

(b) each of those documents is returned undelivered, or the company receives notification that it has not been delivered,

that member ceases to be entitled to receive notices from the company.

(2) A member who has ceased to be entitled to receive notices from the company becomes entitled to receive such notices again by sending the company –

(a) a new address to be recorded in the register of members, or

(b) if the member has agreed that the company should use a means of communication other than sending things to such an address, the information that the company needs to use that means of communication effectively.

Administrative arrangements

Company seals

81. – (1) Any common seal may only be used by the authority of the directors.

(2) The directors may decide by what means and in what form any common seal or securities seal is to be used.

(3) Unless otherwise decided by the directors, if the company has a common seal and it is affixed to a document, the document must also be signed by at least one authorised person in the presence of a witness who attests the signature.

(4) For the purposes of this article, an authorised person is –

(a) any director of the company;

(b) the company secretary; or

(c) any person authorised by the directors for the purpose of signing documents to which the common seal is applied.

(5) If the company has an official seal for use abroad, it may only be affixed to a document if its use on that document, or documents of a class to which it belongs, has been authorised by a decision of the directors.

(6) If the company has a securities seal, it may only be affixed to securities by the company secretary or a person authorised to apply it to securities by the company secretary.

(7) For the purposes of the articles, references to the securities seal being affixed to any document include the reproduction of the image of that seal on or in a document by any mechanical or electronic means which has been approved by the directors in relation to that document or documents of a class to which it belongs.

Destruction of documents

82. – (1) The company is entitled to destroy –

(a) all instruments of transfer of shares which have been registered, and all other documents on the basis of which any entries are made in the register of members, from six years after the date of registration;

(b) all dividend mandates, variations or cancellations of dividend mandates, and notifications of change of address, from two years after they have been recorded;

(c) all share certificates which have been cancelled from one year after the date of the cancellation;

(d) all paid dividend warrants and cheques from one year after the date of actual payment; and

(e) all proxy notices from one year after the end of the meeting to which the proxy notice relates.

(2) If the company destroys a document in good faith, in accordance with the articles, and without notice of any claim to which that document may be relevant, it is conclusively presumed in favour of the company that –

(a) entries in the register purporting to have been made on the basis of an instrument of transfer or other document so destroyed were duly and properly made;

(b) any instrument of transfer so destroyed was a valid and effective instrument duly and properly registered;

(c) any share certificate so destroyed was a valid and effective certificate duly and properly cancelled; and

(d) any other document so destroyed was a valid and effective document in accordance with its recorded particulars in the books or records of the company.

(3) This article does not impose on the company any liability which it would not otherwise have if it destroys any document before the time at which this article permits it to do so.

(4) In this article, references to the destruction of any document include a reference to its being disposed of in any manner.

No right to inspect accounts and other records

83. Except as provided by law or authorised by the directors or an ordinary resolution of the company, no person is entitled to inspect any of the company's accounting or other records or documents merely by virtue of being a member.

Provision for employees on cessation of business

84. The directors may decide to make provision for the benefit of persons employed or formerly employed by the company or any of its subsidiaries (other than a director or former director or shadow director) in connection with the cessation or transfer to any person of the whole or part of the undertaking of the company or that subsidiary.

Directors' indemnity and insurance

Indemnity

85. – (1) Subject to paragraph (2), a relevant director of the company or an associated company may be indemnified out of the company's assets against –

(a) any liability incurred by that director in connection with any negligence, default, breach of duty or breach of trust in relation to the company or an associated company,

(b) any liability incurred by that director in connection with the activities of the company or an associated company in its capacity as a trustee of an occupational pension scheme (as defined in section 235(6) of the Companies Act 2006),

(c) any other liability incurred by that director as an officer of the company or an associated company.

(2) This article does not authorise any indemnity which would be prohibited or rendered void by any provision of the Companies Acts or by any other provision of law.

(3) In this article –

(a) companies are associated if one is a subsidiary of the other or both are subsidiaries of the same body corporate, and

(b) a 'relevant director' means any director or former director of the company or an associated company.

Insurance

86. – (1) The directors may decide to purchase and maintain insurance, at the expense of the company, for the benefit of any relevant director in respect of any relevant loss.

(2) In this article –

(a) a 'relevant director' means any director or former director of the company or an associated company,

(b) a 'relevant loss' means any loss or liability which has been or may be incurred by a relevant director in connection with that director's duties or powers in relation to the company, any associated company or any pension fund or employees' share scheme of the company or associated company, and

(c) companies are associated if one is a subsidiary of the other or both are subsidiaries of the same body corporate.

Companies (Tables A to F) Regulations 1985 (SI 1985/805) as amended by SI 2007/2541 and SI 2007/2826

Table A

Regulations for management of a (public) company limited by shares

1. In these regulations –

'the Act' means the Companies Act 1985 including any statutory modification or re-enactment thereof for the time being in force and any provisions of the Companies Act 2006 for the time being in force;

'the articles' means the articles of the company;

'clear days' in relation to the period of a notice means that period excluding the day when the notice is given or deemed to be given and the day for which it is given or on which it is to take effect;

'communication' means the same as in the Electronic Communications Act 2000;

'electronic communication' means the same as in the Electronic Communications Act 2000;

'executed' includes any mode of execution;

'office' means the registered office of the company;

'the holder' in relation to shares means the member whose name is entered in the register of members as the holder of the shares;

'the seal' means the common seal of the company;

'secretary' means the secretary of the company or any other person appointed to perform the duties of the secretary of the company, including a joint, assistant or deputy secretary;

'the United Kingdom' means Great Britain and Northern Ireland.

Unless the context otherwise requires, words or expressions contained in these regulations bear the same meaning as in the Act but excluding any statutory modification thereof not in force when these regulations become binding on the company.

Share capital

2. Subject to the provisions of the Act and without prejudice to any rights attached to any existing shares, any share may be issued with such rights or restrictions as the company may by ordinary resolution determine.

3. Subject to the provisions of the Act, shares may be issued which are to be redeemed or are to be liable to be redeemed at the option of the company or the holder on such terms and in such manner as may be provided by the articles.

4. The company may exercise the powers of paying commissions conferred by the Act. Subject to the provisions of the Act, any such commission may be satisfied by the payment of cash or by the allotment of fully or partly paid shares or partly in one way and partly in the other.

5. Except as required by law, no person shall be recognised by the company as holding any share upon any trust and (except as otherwise provided by the articles or by law) the company shall not be bound by or recognise any interest in any share except an absolute right to the entirety thereof in the holder.

Share certificates

6. Every member, upon becoming the holder of any shares, shall be entitled without payment to one certificate for all the shares of each class held by him (and, upon transferring a part of his holding of shares of any class, to a certificate for the balance of such holding) or several certificates each for one or more of his shares of any class, to a certificate for the balance of such holding) or several certificates each for one or more of his shares upon payment for every certificate after the first of such reasonable sum as the directors may determine. Every certificate shall be sealed with the seal and shall specify the number, class and distinguishing numbers (if any) of the shares to which it relates and the amount or respective amounts paid up thereon. The company shall not be bound to issue more than one certificate for shares held jointly by several persons and delivery of a certificate to one joint holder shall be a sufficient delivery to all of them.

7. If a share certificate is defaced, worn-out, lost or destroyed, it may be renewed on such terms (if any) as to evidence and indemnity and payment of the expenses reasonably incurred by the company in investigating evidence as the directors may determine but otherwise free of charge, and (in the case of defacement or wearing-out) on delivery up of the old certificate.

Lien

8. The company shall have a first and paramount lien on every share (not being a fully paid share) for all moneys (whether presently payable or not) payable at a fixed time or called in respect of that share. The directors may at any time declare any share to be wholly or in part exempt from the provisions of this regulation. The company's lien on a share shall extend to any amount payable in respect of it.

9. The company may sell in such manner as the directors determine any shares on which the company has a lien if a sum in respect of which the lien exists is presently payable and is not paid within fourteen clear days after notice has been given to the holder of the share or to the person entitled to it in consequence of the death or bankruptcy of the holder, demanding payment and stating that if the notice is not complied with the shares may be sold.

10. To give effect to a sale the directors may authorise some person to execute an instrument of transfer of the shares sold to, or in accordance with the directions of, the purchaser. The title of the transferee to the shares shall not be affected by any irregularity in or invalidity of the proceedings in reference to the sale.

11. The net proceeds of the sale, after payment of the costs, shall be applied in payment of so much of the sum for which the lien exists as is presently payable, and any residue shall (upon surrender to the company for cancellation of the certificate for the shares sold and subject to a like lien for any moneys not presently payable as existed upon the shares before the sale) be paid to the person entitled to the shares at the date of the sale.

Calls on shares and forfeiture

12. Subject to the terms of allotment, the directors may make calls upon the members in respect of any moneys unpaid on their shares (whether in respect of nominal value or premium) and each member shall (subject to receiving at least fourteen clear days' notice specifying when and where payment is to be made) pay to the company as required by the notice the amount called on his shares. A call may be required to be paid by instalments. A call may, before receipt by the company of any sum due thereunder, be revoked in whole or part and payment of a call may be postponed in whole or part. A person upon whom a call is made shall remain liable for calls made upon him notwithstanding the subsequent transfer of the shares in respect whereof the call was made.

13. A call shall be deemed to have been made at the time when the resolution of the directors authorising the call was passed.

14. The joint holders of a share shall be jointly and severally liable to pay all calls in respect thereof.

15. If a call remains unpaid after it has become due and payable the person from whom it is due and payable shall pay interest on the amount unpaid from the day it became due and payable until it is paid at the rate fixed by the terms of allotment of the share or in the notice of the call or, if no rate is fixed, at the appropriate rate (as defined by the Act) but the directors may waive payment of the interest wholly or in part.

16. An amount payable in respect of a share on allotment or at any fixed date, whether in respect of nominal value or premium or as an instalment of a call, shall be deemed to be a call and if it is not paid the provisions of the articles shall apply as if that amount had become due and payable by virtue of a call.

17. Subject to the terms of allotment, the directors may make arrangements on the issue of shares for a difference between the holders in the amounts and times of payment of calls on their shares.

18. If a call remains unpaid after it has become due and payable the directors may give to the person from whom it is due not less than fourteen clear days' notice requiring payment of the amount unpaid together with any interest which may have accrued. The notice shall name the place where payment is to be made and shall state that if the notice is not complied with the shares in respect of which the call was made will be liable to be forfeited.

19. If the notice is not complied with any share in respect of which it was given may, before the payment required by the notice has been made, be forfeited by a resolution of the directors and the forfeiture shall include all dividends or other moneys payable in respect of the forfeited shares and not paid before the forfeiture.

20. Subject to the provisions of the Act, a forfeited share may be sold, re-alloted or otherwise disposed of on such terms and in such manner as the directors determine either to the person who was before the forfeiture the holder or to any other person and at any time before sale, re-allotment or other disposition, the forfeiture may be cancelled on such terms as the directors think fit. Where for the purposes of its disposal a forfeited share is to be transferred to any person the directors may authorise some person to execute an instrument of transfer of the share to that person.

21. A person any of whose shares have been forfeited shall cease to be a member in respect of them and shall surrender to the company for cancellation the certificate for the shares forfeited but shall remain liable to the company for all moneys which at the date of forfeiture were presently payable by him to the company in respect of those shares with interest at the rate at which interest was payable on those moneys before the forfeiture or, if no interest was so payable, at the appropriate rate (as defined in the Act) from the date of forfeiture until payment but the directors may waive payment wholly or in part or enforce payment without any allowance for the value of the shares at the time of forfeiture or for any consideration received on their disposal.

22. A statutory declaration by a director or the secretary that a share has been forfeited on a specified date shall be conclusive evidence of the facts stated in it as against all persons claiming to be entitled to the share and the declaration shall (subject to the execution of an instrument of transfer if necessary) constitute a good title to the share and the person to whom the share is disposed of shall not be bound to see to the application of the consideration, if any, nor shall his title to the share be affected by any irregularity in or invalidity of the proceedings in reference to the forfeiture or disposal of the share.

Transfer of shares

23. The instrument of transfer of a share may be in any usual form or in any other form which the directors may approve and shall be executed by or on behalf of the transferor and, unless the share is fully paid, by or on behalf of the transferee.

24. The directors may refuse to register the transfer of a share which is not fully paid to a person of whom they do not approve and they may refuse to register the transfer of a share on which the company has a lien. They may also refuse to register a transfer unless –

(a) it is lodged at the office or at such other place as the directors may appoint and is accompanied by the certificate for the shares to which it relates and such other evidence as the directors may reasonably require to show the right of the transferor to make the transfer;

(b) it is in respect of only one class of shares; and

(c) it is in favour of not more than four transferees.

25. If the directors refuse to register a transfer of a share, they shall within two months after the date on which the transfer was lodged with the company send to the transferee notice of the refusal.

26. The registration of transfers of shares or of transfers of any class of shares may be suspended at such times and for such periods (not exceeding thirty days in any year) as the directors may determine.

27. No fee shall be charged for the registration of any instrument of transfer or other document relating to or affecting the title to any share.

28. The company shall be entitled to retain any instrument of transfer which is registered, but any instrument of transfer which the directors refuse to register shall be returned to the person lodging it when notice of the refusal is given.

Transmission of shares

29. If a member dies the survivor or survivors where he was a joint holder, and his personal representatives where he was a sole holder or the only survivor of joint holders, shall be the only persons recognised by the company as having any title to his interest; but nothing herein contained shall release the estate of a deceased member from any liability in respect of any share which had been jointly held by him.

30. A person becoming entitled to a share in consequence of the death or bankruptcy of a member may, upon such evidence being produced as the directors may properly require, elect either to become the holder of the share or to have some person nominated by him registered as the transferee. If he elects to become the holder he shall give notice to the company to that effect. If he elects to have another person registered he shall execute an instrument of transfer of the share to that person. All the articles relating to the transfer of shares shall apply to the notice or instrument of transfer as if it were an instrument of transfer executed by the member and the death or bankruptcy of the member had not occurred.

31. A person becoming entitled to a share in consequence of the death or bankruptcy of a member shall have the rights to which he would be entitled if he were the holder of the share, except that he shall not, before being registered as the holder of the share, be entitled in respect of it to attend or vote at any meeting of the company or at any separate meeting of the holders of any class of shares in the company.

Alteration of share capital

32. The company may by ordinary resolution –

(a) increase its share capital by new shares of such amount as the resolution prescribes;

(b) consolidate and divide all or any of its share capital into shares of larger amount than its existing shares;

(c) subject to the provisions of the Act, sub-divide its shares, or any of them, into shares of smaller amount and the resolution may determine that, as between the shares resulting from the sub-division, any of them may have any preference or advantage as compared with the others; and

(d) cancel shares which, at the date of the passing of the resolution, have not been taken or agreed to be taken by any person and diminish the amount of its share capital by the amount of the shares so cancelled.

33. Whenever as a result of a consolidation of shares any members would become entitled to fractions of a share, the directors may, on behalf of those members, sell the shares representing the fractions for the best price reasonably obtainable to any person (including, subject to the provisions of the Act, the company) and distribute the net proceeds of sale in due proportion among those members, and the directors may authorise some person to execute an instrument of transfer of the shares to, or in accordance with the directions of, the purchaser. The transferee shall not be bound to see to the application of the purchase money nor shall his title to the shares be affected by any irregularity in or invalidity of the proceedings in reference to the sale.

34. Subject to the provisions of the Act, the company may by special resolution reduce its share capital, any capital redemption reserve and any share premium account in any way.

Purchase of own shares

35. Subject to the provisions of the Act, the company may purchase its own shares (including any redeemable shares) and, if it is a private company, make a payment in respect of the redemption or purchase of its own shares otherwise than out of distributable profits of the company or the proceeds of a fresh issue of shares.

General meetings

37. The directors may call general meetings and, on the requisition of members pursuant to the provisions of the Act, shall forthwith proceed to convene a general meeting in accordance with the provisions of the Act. If there are not within the United Kingdom sufficient directors to call a general meeting, any director or any member of the company may call a general meeting.

Notice of general meetings

38. An annual general meeting shall be called by at least twenty-one clear days' notice. All other general meetings shall be called by at least fourteen clear days' notice but a general meeting may be called by shorter notice if is so agreed –

(a) in the case of an annual general meeting, by all the members entitled to attend and vote thereat; and

(b) in the case of any other meeting by a majority in number of the members having a right to attend and vote being a majority together holding not less than ninety-five per cent in nominal value of the shares giving that right.

The notice shall specify the time and place of the meeting and the general nature of the business to be transacted and, in the case of an annual general meeting, shall specify the meeting as such. Subject to the provisions of the articles and to any restrictions imposed on any shares, the notice shall be given to all the members, to all persons entitled to a share in consequence of the death or bankruptcy of a member and to the directors and auditors.

39. The accidental omission to give notice of a meeting to, or the non-receipt of notice of a meeting by, any person entitled to receive notice shall not invalidate the proceedings at that meeting.

Proceedings at general meetings

40. No business shall be transacted at any meeting unless a quorum is present. Two persons entitled to vote upon the business to be transacted, each being a member or a proxy for a member or a duly authorised representative of a corporation, shall be a quorum.

41. If such a quorum is not present within half an hour from the time appointed for the meeting, or if during a meeting such a quorum ceases to be present, the meeting shall stand adjourned to the same day in the next week at the same time and place or to such time and place as the directors may determine.

42. The chairman, if any, of the board of directors or in his absence some other director nominated by the directors shall preside as chairman of the meeting, but if neither the chairman nor such other director (if any) be present within fifteen minutes after the time appointed for holding the meeting and willing to act, the directors present shall elect one of their number to be chairman and, if there is only one director present and willing to act, he shall be chairman.

43. If no director is willing to act as chairman, or if no director is present within fifteen minutes after the time appointed for holding the meeting, the members present and entitled to vote shall choose one of their number to be chairman.

44. A director shall, notwithstanding that he is not a member, be entitled to attend and speak at any general meeting and at any separate meeting of the holders of any class of shares in the company.

45. The chairman may, with the consent of a meeting at which a quorum is present (and shall if so directed by the meeting), adjourn the meeting from time to time and from place to place, but no business shall be transacted at an adjourned meeting other than business which might properly have been transacted at the meeting had the adjournment not taken place. When a meeting is adjourned for fourteen days or more, at least seven clear days' notice shall be given specifying the time and place of the adjourned meeting and the general nature of the business to be transacted. Otherwise it shall not be necessary to give any such notice.

46. A resolution put to the vote of a meeting shall be decided on a show of hands unless before, or on the declaration of the result of, the show of hands a poll is duly demanded. Subject to the provisions of the Act, a poll may be demanded –

(a) by the chairman; or

(b) by at least two members having the right to vote at the meeting; or

(c) by a member or members representing not less than one-tenth of the total voting rights of all the members having the right to vote at the meeting; or

(d) by a member or members holding shares conferring a right to vote at the meeting being shares on which an aggregate sum has been paid up equal to not less than one-tenth of the total sum paid up on all the shares conferring that right;

and a demand by a person as proxy for a member shall be the same as a demand by the member.

47. Unless a poll is duly demanded a declaration by the chairman that a resolution has been carried or carried unanimously, or by a particular majority, or lost, or not carried by a particular majority and an entry to that effect in the minutes of the meeting shall be conclusive evidence of the fact without proof of the number or proportion of the votes recorded in favour of or against the resolution.

48. The demand for a poll may, before the poll is taken, be withdrawn but only with the consent of the chairman and a demand so withdrawn shall not be taken to have invalidated the result of a show of hands declared before the demand was made.

49. A poll shall be taken as the chairman directs and he may appoint scrutineers (who need not be members) and fix a time and place for declaring the result of the poll. The result of the poll shall be deemed to be the resolution of the meeting at which the poll was demanded.

51. A poll demanded on the election of a chairman or on a question of adjournment shall be taken forthwith. A poll demanded on any other question shall be taken either forthwith or at such time and place as the chairman directs not being more than thirty days after the poll is demanded. The demand for a poll shall not prevent the continuance of a meeting for the transaction of any business other than the question on which the poll was demanded. If a poll is demanded before the declaration of the result of a show of hands and the demand is duly withdrawn, the meeting shall continue as if the demand had not been made.

52. No notice need be given of a poll not taken forthwith if the time and place at which it is to be taken are announced at the meeting at which it is demanded. In any other case at least seven clear days' notice shall be given specifying the time and place at which the poll is to be taken.

Votes of members

54. Subject to any rights or restrictions attached to any shares, on a show of hands every member who (being an individual) is present in person or by proxy or (being a corporation) is present by a duly authorised representative or by proxy, unless the proxy (in either case) or the representative is himself a member entitled to vote, shall have one vote and on a poll every member shall have one vote for every share of which he is the holder.

55. In the case of joint holders the vote of the senior who tenders a vote, whether in person or by proxy, shall be accepted to the exclusion of the votes of the other joint holders; and seniority shall be determined by the order in which the names of the holders stand in the register of members.

56. A member in respect of whom an order has been made by any court having jurisdiction (whether in the United Kingdom or elsewhere) in matters concerning mental disorder may vote, whether on a show of hands or on a poll, by his receiver, curator bonis or other person authorised in that behalf appointed by that court, and any such receiver, curator bonis or other person may, on a poll, vote by proxy. Evidence to the satisfaction of the directors of the authority of the person claiming to exercise the right to vote shall be deposited at the office, or at such other place as is specified in accordance with the articles for the deposit of instruments of proxy, not less than 48 hours before the time appointed for holding the meeting or adjourned meeting at which the right to vote is to be exercised and in default the right to vote shall not be exercisable.

57. No member shall vote at any general meeting or at any separate meeting of the holders of any class of shares in the company, either in person or by proxy, in respect of any share held by him unless all moneys presently payable by him in respect of that share have been paid.

58. No objection shall be raised to the qualification of any voter except at the meeting or adjourned meeting at which the vote objected to is tendered, and every vote not disallowed at the meeting shall be valid. Any objection made in due time shall be referred to the chairman whose decision shall be final and conclusive.

59. On a poll votes may be given either personally or by proxy. A member may appoint more than one proxy to attend on the same occasion.

60. The appointment of a proxy shall be executed by or on behalf of the appointor and shall be in the following form (or in a form as near thereto as circumstances allow or in any other form which is usual or which the directors may approve) –

'............ PLC/Limited .... I/We, ..., of ...., being a member/members of the above-named company, hereby appoint .... of ...., or failing him, ... of ...., as my/our proxy to vote in my/our name[s] and on my/our behalf at the annual/any other general meeting of the company to be held on .... 19............., and at any adjournment thereof.

Signed on .... 19.............:

61. Where it is desired to afford members an opportunity of instructing the proxy how he shall act the appointment of a proxy shall be in the following form (or in a form as near thereto as circumstances allow or in any other form which is usual or which the directors may approve) –

'............ PLC/Limited .... I/We, ..., of ...., being a member/members of the above-named company, hereby appoint .... of ...., or failing him .... of ...., as my/our proxy to vote in my/our name[s] and on my/our behalf at the annual/any other general meeting of the company, to be held on .... 19............., and at any adjournment thereof.

This form is to be used in respect of the resolutions mentioned below as follows:

Resolution No. 1 *for *against
Resolution No. 2 *for *against.

*Strike out whichever is not desired.

Unless otherwise instructed, the proxy may vote as he thinks fit or abstain from voting.

Signed this .... day of .... 19.............:

62. The appointment of a proxy and any authority under which it is executed or a copy of such authority certified notarially or in some other way approved by the directors may –

(a) in the case of an instrument in writing be deposited at the office or at such other place within the United Kingdom as is specified in the notice convening the meeting or in any instrument of proxy sent out by the company in relation to the meeting not less than 48 hours before the time for holding the meeting or adjourned meeting at which the person named in the instrument proposes to vote; or

(aa) in the case of an appointment contained in an electronic communication, where an address has been specified for the purpose of receiving electronic communications –

(i) in the notice convening the meeting, or

(ii) in any instrument of proxy sent out by the company in relation to the meeting, or

(iii) in any invitation contained in an electronic communication to appoint a proxy issued by the company in relation to the meeting,

be received at such address not less than 48 hours before the time for holding the meeting or adjourned meeting at which the person named in the appointment proposes to vote;

(b) in the case of a poll taken more than 48 hours after it is demanded, be deposited or received as aforesaid after the poll has been demanded and not less than 24 hours before the time appointed for the taking of the poll; or

(c) where the poll is not taken forthwith but is taken not more than 48 hours after it was demanded, be delivered at the meeting at which the poll was demanded to the chairman or to the secretary or to any director;

and an appointment of proxy which is not deposited, delivered or received in a manner so permitted shall be invalid.

In this regulation and the next, 'address', in relation to electronic communications, includes any number or address used for the purposes of such communications.

63. A vote given or poll demanded by proxy or by the duly authorised representative of a corporation shall be valid notwithstanding the previous determination of the authority of the person voting or demanding a poll unless notice of the determination was received by the company at the office or at such other place at which the instrument of proxy was duly deposited or, where the appointment of the proxy was contained in an electronic communication, at the address at which such appointment was duly received before the commencement of the meeting or adjourned meeting at which the vote is given or the poll demanded or (in the case of a poll taken otherwise than on the same day as the meeting or adjourned meeting) the time appointed for taking the poll.

Number of directors

64. Unless otherwise determined by ordinary resolution, the number of directors (other than alternate directors) shall not be subject to any maximum but shall be not less than two.

Alternate directors

65. Any director (other than an alternate director) may appoint any other director, or any other person approved by resolution of the directors and willing to act, to be an alternate director and may remove from office an alternate director so appointed by him.

66. An alternate director shall be entitled to receive notice of all meetings of directors and of all meetings of committees of directors of which his appointor is a member, to attend and vote at any such meeting at which the director appointing him is not personally present and generally to perform all the functions of his appointor as a director in his absence but shall not be entitled to receive any remuneration from the company for his services as an alternate director. But it shall not be necessary to give notice of such a meeting to an alternate director who is absent from the United Kingdom.

67. An alternate director shall cease to be an alternate director if his appointor ceases to be a director; but, if a director retires by rotation or otherwise but is reappointed or deemed to have been reappointed at the meeting at which he retires, any appointment of an alternate director made by him which was in force immediately prior to his retirement shall continue after his reappointment.

68. Any appointment or removal of an alternate director shall be by notice to the company signed by the director making or revoking the appointment or in any other manner approved by the directors.

69. Save as otherwise provided in the articles, an alternate director shall be deemed for all purposes to be a director and shall alone be responsible for his own acts and defaults and he shall not be deemed to be the agent of the director appointing him.

Powers of directors

70. Subject to the provisions of the Act, the memorandum and the articles and to any directions given by special resolution, the business of the company shall be managed by the directors who may exercise all the powers of the company. No alteration of the memorandum or articles and no such direction shall invalidate any prior act of the directors which would have been valid if that alteration had not been made or that direction had not been given. The powers given by this regulation shall not be limited by any special power given to the directors by the articles and a meeting of directors at which a quorum is present may exercise all powers exercisable by the directors.

71. The directors may, by power of attorney or otherwise, appoint any person to be the agent of the company for such purposes and on such conditions as they determine, including authority for the agent to delegate all or any of his powers.

Delegation of directors' powers

72. The directors may delegate any of their powers to any committee consisting of one or more directors. They may also delegate to any managing director or any director holding any other executive office such of their powers as they consider desirable to be exercised by him. Any such delegation may be made subject to any conditions the directors may impose, and either collaterally with or to the exclusion of their own powers and may be revoked or altered. Subject to any such conditions, the proceedings of a committee with two or more members shall be governed by the articles regulating the proceedings of directors so far as they are capable of applying.

Appointment and retirement of directors

73. At the first annual general meeting all the directors shall retire from office, and at every subsequent annual general meeting one-third of the directors who are subject to retirement by rotation or, if their number is not three or a multiple of three, the number nearest to one-third shall retire from office; but, if there is only one director who is subject to retirement by rotation, he shall retire.

74. Subject to the provisions of the Act, the directors to retire by rotation shall be those who have been longest in office since their last appointment or reappointment, but as between persons who became or were last reappointed directors on the same day those to retire shall (unless they otherwise agree among themselves) be determined by lot.

75. If the company, at the meeting at which a director retires by rotation, does not fill the vacancy the retiring director shall, if willing to act, be deemed to have been reappointed unless at the meeting it is resolved not to fill the vacancy or unless a resolution for the reappointment of the director is put to the meeting and lost.

76. No person other than a director retiring by rotation shall be appointed or reappointed a director at any general meeting unless –

(a) he is recommended by the directors; or

(b) not less than fourteen nor more than thirty-five clear days before the date appointed for the meeting, notice executed by a member qualified to vote at the meeting has been given to the company of the intention to propose that person for appointment or reappointment stating the particulars which would, if he were so appointed or reappointed, be required to be included in the company's register of directors together with notice executed by that person of his willingness to be appointed or reappointed.

77. Not less than seven nor more than twenty-eight clear days before the date appointed for holding a general meeting notice shall be given to all who are entitled to receive notice of the meeting of any person (other than a director retiring by rotation at the meeting) who is recommended by the director for appointment or reappointment as a director at the meeting or in respect of whom notice has been duly given to the company of the intention to propose him at the meeting for appointment or reappointment as a director. The notice shall give the particulars of that person which would, if he were so appointed or reappointed, be required to be included in the company's register of directors.

78. Subject as aforesaid, the company may by ordinary resolution appoint a person who is willing to act to be a director either to fill a vacancy or as an additional director and may also determine the rotation in which any additional directors are to retire.

79. The directors may appoint a person who is willing to act to be a director, either to fill a vacancy or as an additional director, provided that the appointment does not cause the number of directors to exceed any number fixed by or in accordance with the articles as the maximum number of directors. A director so appointed shall hold office only until the next following annual general meeting and shall not be taken into account in determining the directors who are to retire by rotation at the meeting. If not reappointed at such annual general meeting, he shall vacate office at the conclusion thereof.

80. Subject as aforesaid, a director who retires at an annual general meeting may, if willing to act, be reappointed. If he is not reappointed, he shall retain office until the meeting appoints someone in his place, or if it does not do so, until the end of the meeting.

Disqualification and removal of directors

81. The office of a director shall be vacated if –

(a) he ceases to be a director by virtue of any provision of the Act or he becomes prohibited by law from being a director; or

(b) he becomes bankrupt or makes any arrangement or composition with his creditors generally; or

(c) he is, or may be, suffering from mental disorder and either –

(i) he is admitted to hospital in pursuance of an application for admission for treatment under the Mental Health Act 1983 or, in Scotland, an application for admission under the Mental Health (Scotland) Act 1960, or

(ii) an order is made by a court having jurisdiction (whether in the United Kingdom or elsewhere) in matters concerning mental disorder for his detention or for the appointment of a receiver, curator bonis or other person to exercise powers with respect to his property or affairs; or

(d) he resigns his office by notice to the company; or

(e) he shall for more than six consecutive months have been absent without permission of the directors from meetings of directors held during that period and the directors resolve that his office be vacated.

Remuneration of directors

82. The directors shall be entitled to such remuneration as the company may by ordinary resolution determine and, unless the resolution provides otherwise, the remuneration shall be deemed to accrue from day to day.

Directors' expenses

83. The directors may be paid all travelling, hotel, and other expenses properly incurred by them in connection with their attendance at meetings of directors or committees of directors or general meetings or separate meetings of the holders of any class of shares or of debentures of the company or otherwise in connection with the discharge of their duties.

Directors' appointments and interests

84. Subject to the provisions of the Act, the directors may appoint one or more of their number to the office of managing director or to any other executive office under the company and may enter into an agreement or arrangement with any director for his employment by the company or for the provision by him of any services outside the scope of the ordinary duties of a director. Any such appointment, agreement or arrangement may be made upon such terms as the directors determine and they may remunerate any such director for his services as they think fit. Any appointment of a director to an executive office shall terminate if he ceases to be a director but without prejudice to any claim to damages for breach of the contract of service between the director and the company. A managing director and a director holding any other executive office shall not be subject to retirement by rotation.

85. Subject to the provisions of the Act, and provided that he has disclosed to the directors the nature and extent of any material interest of his, a director notwithstanding his office –

(a) may be a party to, or otherwise interested in, any transaction or arrangement with the company or in which the company or in which the company is otherwise interested;

(b) may be a director or other officer of, or employed by, or a party to any transaction or arrangement with, or otherwise interested in, any body corporate promoted by the company or in which the company is otherwise interested; and

(c) shall not, by reason of his office, be accountable to the company for any benefit which he derives from any such office or employment or from any such transaction or arrangement or from any interest in any such body corporate and no such transaction or arrangement shall be liable to be avoided on the ground of any such interest or benefit.

86. For the purposes of regulation 85 –

(a) a general notice given to the directors that a director is to be regarded as having an interest of the nature and extent specified in the notice in any transaction or arrangement in which a specified person or class of persons is interested shall be deemed to be a disclosure that the director has an interest in any such transaction of the nature and extent so specified; and

(b) an interest of which a director has no knowledge and of which it is unreasonable to expect him to have knowledge shall not be treated as an interest of his.

Directors' gratuities and pensions

87. The directors may provide benefits, whether by the payment of gratuities or pensions or by insurance or otherwise, for any director who has held but no longer holds any executive office or employment with the company or with any body corporate which is or has been a subsidiary of the company or a predecessor in business of the company or of any such subsidiary, and for any member of his family (including a spouse and a former spouse) or any person who is or was dependent on him, and may (as well before as after he ceases to hold such office or employment) contribute to any fund and pay premiums for the purchase or provision of any such benefit.

Proceedings of directors

88. Subject to the provisions of the articles, the directors may regulate their proceedings as they think fit. A director may, and the secretary at the request of a director shall, call a meeting of the directors. It shall not be necessary to give notice of a meeting to a director who is absent from the United Kingdom. Questions arising at a meeting shall be decided by a majority of votes. In the case of an equality of votes, the chairman shall have a second or casting vote. A director who is also an alternate director shall be entitled in the absence of his appointor to a separate vote on behalf of his appointor in addition to his own vote.

89. The quorum for the transaction of the business of the directors may be fixed by the directors and unless so fixed at any other number shall be two. A person who holds office only as an alternate director shall, if his appointor is not present, be counted in the quorum.

90. The continuing directors or a sole continuing director may act notwithstanding any vacancies in their number, but, if the number of directors is less than the number fixed as the quorum, the continuing directors or director may act only for the purpose of filling vacancies or of calling a general meeting.

91. The directors may appoint one of their number to be the chairman of the board of directors and may at any time remove him from that office. Unless he is unwilling to do so, the director so appointed shall preside at every meeting of directors at which he is present. But if there is no director holding that office, or if the director holding it is unwilling to preside or is not present within five minutes after the time appointed for the meeting, the directors present may appoint one of their number to be chairman of the meeting.

92. All acts done by a meeting of directors, or of a committee of directors, or by a person acting as a director shall, notwithstanding that it be afterwards discovered that there was a defect in the appointment of any director or that any of them were disqualified from holding office, or had vacated office, or were not entitled to vote, be as valid as if every such person had been duly appointed and was qualified and had continued to be a director and had been entitled to vote.

93. A resolution in writing signed by all the directors entitled to receive notice of a meeting of directors or of a committee of directors shall be as valid and effectual as it if had been passed at a meeting of directors or (as the case may be) a committee of directors duly convened and held and may consist of several documents in the like form each signed by one or more directors; but a resolution signed by an alternate director need not also be signed by his appointor and, if it is signed by a director who has appointed an alternate director, it need not be signed by the alternate director in that capacity.

94. Save as otherwise provided by the articles, a director shall not vote at a meeting of directors or of a committee of directors on any resolution concerning a matter in which he has, directly or indirectly, an interest or duty which is material and which conflicts or may conflict with the interests of the company unless his interest or duty arises only because the case falls within one or more of the following paragraphs –

(a) the resolution relates to the giving to him of a guarantee, security, or indemnity in respect of money lent to, or an obligation incurred by him for the benefit of, the company or any of its subsidiaries;

(b) the resolution relates to the giving to a third party of a guarantee, security, or indemnity in respect of an obligation of the company or any of its subsidiaries for which the director has assumed responsibility in whole or part and whether alone or jointly with others under a guarantee or indemnity or by the giving of security;

(c) his interest arises by virtue of his subscribing or agreeing to subscribe for any shares, debentures, or other securities of the company or any of its subsidiaries, or by virtue of his being, or intending to become, a participant in the underwriting or sub-underwriting of an offer of any such shares, debentures, or other securities by the company or any of its subsidiaries for subscription, purchase or exchange;

(d) the resolution relates in any way to a retirement benefits scheme which has been approved, or is conditional upon approval, by the Board of Inland Revenue for taxation purposes.

For the purposes of this regulation, an interest of a person who is, for any purpose of the Act (excluding any statutory modification thereof not in force when this regulation becomes binding on the company), connected with a director shall be treated as an interest of the director and, in relation to an alternate director, an interest of his appointor shall be treated as an interest of the alternate director without prejudice to any interest which the alternate director has otherwise.

95. A director shall not be counted in the quorum present at a meeting in relation to a resolution on which he is not entitled to vote.

96. The company may by ordinary resolution suspend or relax to any extent, either generally or in respect of any particular matter, any provision of the articles prohibiting a director from voting at a meeting of directors or of a committee of directors.

97. Where proposals are under consideration concerning the appointment of two or more directors to offices or employments with the company or any body corporate in which the company is interested the proposals may be divided and considered in relation to each director separately and (provided he is not for another reason precluded from voting) each of the directors concerned shall be entitled to vote and be counted in the quorum in respect of each resolution except that concerning his own appointment.

98. If a question arises at a meeting of directors or of a committee of directors as to the right of a director to vote, the question may, before the conclusion of the meeting, be referred to the chairman of the meeting and his ruling in relation to any director other than himself shall be final and conclusive.

Secretary

99. Subject to the provisions of the Act, the secretary shall be appointed by the directors for such term, at such remuneration and upon such conditions as they may think fit; and any secretary so appointed may be removed by them.

Minutes

100. The directors shall cause minutes to be made in books kept for the purpose –

(a) of all appointments of officers made by the directors; and

(b) of all proceedings at meetings of the company, of the holders of any class of shares in the company, and of the directors, and of committees of directors, including the names of the directors present at each such meeting.

The seal

101. The seal shall only be used by the authority of the directors or of a committee of directors authorised by the directors. The directors may determine who shall sign any instrument to which the seal is affixed and unless otherwise so determined it shall be signed by a director and by the secretary or by a second director.

Dividends

102. Subject to the provisions of the Act, the company may by ordinary resolution declare dividends in accordance with the respective rights of the members, but no dividend shall exceed the amount recommended by the directors.

103. Subject to the provisions of the Act, the directors may pay interim dividends if it appears to them that they are justified by the profits of the company available for distribution. If the share capital is divided into different classes, the directors may pay interim dividends on shares which confer deferred or non-preferred rights with regard to dividend as well as on shares which confer preferential rights with regard to dividend, but no interim dividend shall be paid on shares carrying deferred or non-preferred rights if, at the time of payment, any preferential dividend is in arrear. The directors may also pay at intervals settled by them any dividend payable at a fixed rate if it appears to them that the profits available for distribution justify the payment. Provided the directors act in good faith they shall not incur any liability to the holders of shares conferring preferred rights for any loss they may suffer by the lawful payment of an interim dividend on any shares having deferred or non-preferred rights.

104. Except as otherwise provided by the rights attached to shares, all dividends shall be declared and paid according to the amounts paid up on the shares on which the dividend is paid. All dividends shall be apportioned and paid proportionately to the amounts paid up on the shares during any portion or portions of the period in respect of which the dividend is paid; but, if any share is issued on terms providing that it shall rank for dividend as from a particular date, that share shall rank for dividend accordingly.

105. A general meeting declaring a dividend may, upon the recommendation of the directors, direct that it shall be satisfied wholly or partly by the distribution of assets and, where any difficulty arises in regard to the distribution, the directors may settle the same and in particular may issue fractional certificates and fix the value for distribution of any assets and may determine that cash shall be paid to any member upon the footing of the value so fixed in order to adjust the rights of members and may vest any assets in trustees.

106. Any dividend or other moneys payable in respect of a share may be paid by cheque sent by post to the registered address of the person entitled or, if two or more persons are the holders of the share or are jointly entitled to it by reason of the death or bankruptcy of the holder, to the registered address of that one of those persons who is first named in the register of members or to such person and to such address as the person or persons entitled may in writing direct. Every cheque shall be made payable to the order of the person or persons entitled or to such other person as the person or persons entitled may in writing direct and payment of the cheque shall be a good discharge to the company. Any joint holder or other person jointly entitled to a share as aforesaid may give receipts for any dividend or other moneys payable in respect of the share.

107. No dividend or other moneys payable in respect of a share shall bear interest against the company unless otherwise provided by the rights attached to the share.

108. Any dividend which has remained unclaimed for twelve years from the date when it became due for payment shall, if the directors so resolve, be forfeited and cease to remain owing by the company.

Accounts

109. No member shall (as such) have any right of inspecting any accounting records or other book or document of the company except as conferred by statute or authorised by the directors or by ordinary resolution of the company.

Capitalisation of profits

110. The directors may with the authority of an ordinary resolution of the company –

(a) subject as hereinafter provided, resolve to capitalise any undivided profits of the company not required for paying any preferential dividend (whether or not they are available for distribution) or any sum standing to the credit of the company's share premium account or capital redemption reserve;

(b) appropriate the sum resolved to be capitalised to the members who would have been entitled to it if it were distributed by way of dividend and in the same proportions and apply such sum on their behalf either in or towards paying up the amounts, if any, for the time being unpaid on any shares held by them respectively, or in paying up in full unissued shares or debentures of the company of a nominal amount equal to that sum, and allot the shares or debentures credited as fully paid to those members, or as they may direct, in those proportions, or partly in one way and partly in the other: but the share premium account, the capital redemption reserve, and any profits which are not available for distribution may, for the purposes of this regulation, only be applied in paying up unissued shares to be allotted to members credited as fully paid;

(c) make such provision by the issue of fractional certificates or by payment in cash or otherwise as they determine in the case of shares or debentures becoming distributable under this regulation in fractions; and

(d) authorise any person to enter on behalf of all the members concerned into an agreement with the company providing for the allotment to them respectively, credited as fully paid, of any shares or debentures to which they are entitled upon such capitalisation, any agreement made under such authority being binding on all such members.

Notices

111. Any notice to be given to or by any person pursuant to the articles (other than a notice calling a meeting of the directors) shall be in writing or shall be given using electronic communications to an address for the time being notified for that purpose to the person giving the notice.

In this regulation, 'address', in relation to electronic communications, includes any number or address used for the purposes of such communications.

112. The company may give any notice to a member either personally or by sending it by post in a prepaid envelope addressed to the member at his registered address or by leaving it at that address or by giving it using electronic communications to an address for the time being notified to the company by the member. In the case of joint holders of a share, all notices shall be given to the joint holder whose name stands first in the register of members in respect of the joint holding and notice so given shall be sufficient notice to all the joint holders. A member whose registered address is not within the United Kingdom and who gives to the company an address within the United Kingdom at which notices may be given to him, or an address to which notices may be sent using electronic communications, shall be entitled to have notices given to him at that address, but otherwise no such member shall be entitled to receive any notice from the company.

In this regulation and the next, 'address', in relation to electronic communications, includes any number or address used for the purposes of such communications.

113. A member present, either in person or by proxy, at any meeting of the company or of the holders of any class of shares in the company shall be deemed to have received notice of the meeting and, where requisite, of the purposes for which it was called.

114. Every person who becomes entitled to a share shall be bound by any notice in respect of that share which, before his name is entered in the register of members, has been duly given to a person from whom he derives his title.

115. Proof that an envelope containing a notice was properly addressed, prepaid and posted shall be conclusive evidence that the notice was given. Proof that a notice contained in an electronic communication was sent in accordance with guidance issued by the Institute of Chartered Secretaries and Administrators shall be conclusive evidence that the notice was given. A notice shall be deemed to be given at the expiration of 48 hours after the envelope containing it was posted or, in the case of a notice contained in an electronic communication, at the expiration of 48 hours after the time it was sent.

116. A notice may be given by the company to the persons entitled to a share in consequence of the death or bankruptcy of a member by sending or delivering it, in any manner authorised by the articles for the giving of notice to a member, addressed to them by name, or by the title of representatives of the deceased, or trustee of the bankrupt or by any like description at the address, if any, within the United Kingdom supplied for that purpose by the persons claiming to be so entitled. Until such an address has been supplied, a notice may be given in any manner in which it might have been given if the death or bankruptcy had not occurred.

Winding up

117. If the company is wound up, the liquidator may, with the sanction of a special resolution of the company and any other sanction required by the Act, divide among the members in specie the whole or any part of the assets of the company and may, for that purpose, value any assets and determine how the division shall be carried out as between the members or different classes of members. The liquidator may, with the like sanction, vest the whole or any part of the assets in trustees upon such trusts for the benefit of the members as he with the like sanction determines, but no member shall be compelled to accept any assets upon which there is a liability.

Indemnity

118. Subject to the provisions of the Act but without prejudice to any indemnity to which a director may otherwise be entitled, every director or other officer or auditor of the company shall be indemnified out of the assets of the company against any liability incurred by him in defending any proceedings, whether civil or criminal, in which judgment is given in his favour or in which he is acquitted or in connection with any application in which relief is granted to him by the court from liability for negligence, default, breach of duty or breach of trust in relation to the affairs of the company.

Index

abuse
  of the corporate form 38–40
  market abuse 281–3, 565, 567
accountants
  company 353, 375
  and director disqualification 453
  and shadow directors 354
accounting reference date (ARD) 531–2
accounting reference period (ARP) 531
accounting standards
  and realised profits 208–9
  and share premiums 278
Accounting Standards Board 209, 278
accounts 527–53
  accounting records 530–1
    and director disqualification 442–3
  annual 531–4
  and auditors 540–50
  directors' report on 535–6
  filing of 538–40
    failure to file 539–40
  group accounts 534–5
  and limited liability 528
  medium-sized companies 529–30, 539
  publication of 537–8
  small companies 528–9, 538–9
  see also IAS accounts
acquisitions 277
administration 587–602
  appointment of an administrator
    by the court 588–90
    out of court 591–7
  automatic cessation of 597
  ban on appointment of administrative
    receiverships 606
  changing corporate structures 556–7
  and company charges
    avoiding as a preference 522–3
    floating 510, 513–14, 515–16
  and director disqualification 437–8, 453
  extension of appointment 597
  functions of administrators 587–8
  legal consequences of appointment 599–601
    company contracts 600

directors 601
employees 601–2
landlord's right of forfeiture 600
no inhibition of rescue schemes 600
suspension of rights 599–600
  and pension funds 594, 602
  and receiverships 606
  termination of through notice to Registrar of
    Companies 598–9
  timetable of major events 597
Administrative Restoration 618–19
agency
  company contracts and rules of 144–7
    defective authority and insiders 149–50
  and the corporate veil 37, 42–3
alternate directors 357–8
Alternative Investment Market (AIM)
  and the EU Prospectus Directive 231, 232
  offers of unlisted securities 228
  and purchase of treasury shares 189
amalgamations and reconstructions 557,
    558–63
  and the Companies Act (2006) 558, 560–3
  defining 558
  schemes of internal reconstruction 562–3
  takeovers 558–9, 563–73
annual accounts 531–4
  approval and signing of 435
  filing of 538–40
  form and content 532–3
  notes to the accounts 533–4
  publication of 537–8
  as a true and fair view 533
Annual General Meetings (AGMs) 370, 463
  and director retirement and re-election
    432, 433
  notice of 467, 470
    members' resolutions 470–1
  quorum 473
annual returns 295–7
  information in 296
  LLPs 60
  sanctions if return not made 296–7
ARD (accounting reference date) 531–2

'Armageddon' legal claims 56
ARP (accounting reference period) 531
articles of association 62, 88, 103–22
    alteration of 124–37
        breaches of contract arising out of 133–5
        by the court 135–6
        and entrenched positions 126
        expulsion of members 128–31
        and majority rule 126, 128
        and the objective test 126–7, 127–8
    and capital reduction 173, 179
    and the Companies Act (2006) 104, 105,
        108–10
    and the Contracts (Rights of Third Parties) Act
        (1999) 117–18
    and directors 353, 355, 365
        disqualification of 359, 438
        duties of 406
        removal of 434–5
    dormant companies 24–5
    and General Meetings 104, 105, 106–7, 108
    and insider/outsider rights 105, 113–17
    legal effect of 108–12
    and the objects clause 94, 96
    and shareholders' agreements 118–21
    and shares 237
        allotment of 239
        calls on 245
        certificates 241
        forfeiture of 249
        transfer of 255, 265–6
    and the statutory contract 109–10
    traditional division of powers under 106–8
    and variation of shareholders' rights 555
    see also Model Articles
asset strippers
    and financial assistance for the purchase of
        shares 191
assets
    acquisition of non-cash 26
    and capital maintenance
        financial assistance for the purchase of
            shares 193–4, 195
        loss of and capital reduction 177–81
    compensation payments to directors 387
    and debentures 500
    distribution of 26, 206–7, 210
    and floating charges 508–9
    and shares 237
    winding-up
        collection of 631–2

    distribution of 639
    swelling of 632–3
assistant secretary 375
associated companies
    and fair dealing by directors 388
Auditing Practice Board 545
auditors 540–50
    and accounts
        directors' report on 536
        filing of auditor's report 539
    appointment of 365, 540–2
    and capital maintenance 200, 211–12, 216
    duties of 542–3
    duty of care 544–5, 547–8
    Information and the Companies (Audit,
        Investigations and Community
        Enterprise) Act (2004) 543–4
    liability of 547–50
        and breach of duty 549
        capping 550
        developments in exclusion of 550
    removal of and special notice requirements 541
    resignation of 541–2
    rights of 543
    term of office 541
    and written resolutions 494
auditor's report
    on payments out of capital 185
authorised capital 96, 97

bank charges
    over customer deposits 517
Bank of England 4
bankruptcy
    and director disqualification 348–9, 439, 455
    of a partner 53
    and share transfers 265, 288
    and share transmissions 266–7
    and termination of membership 293
    and transmission of debentures 506
bearer debentures 504–5, 506, 507
bearer shares 243–4
BIS (Department of Business, Innovation and Skills)
    amalgamations and reconstructions 558
    consultation on company charges 523
    and CVA contracts 579
    and director disqualification 440
    and redundancy payments to employees 512
    and winding-up 607, 612
blank transfers
    and equitable mortgages of shares 246–7

board of directors
  amalgamations and reconstructions 561
  appointment of directors 356, 359–60
  and articles of association 106–7
  board unable or unwilling to act 368–70
  chairman 370, 371, 474
  and company contracts 140–50
  and the company secretary 374
  disclosure of material transactions in board
    minutes 394–5
  dissension between members of the board
    369–70
  and general meetings 465
  and interim dividends 214
  meetings 484–9
    chairman 485, 486
    minutes 488–9
    notice of 484–5, 487
    participation in 485
    quorum 368, 370, 485, 487–8
    telephone meetings 489
    voting at 485, 488
  and members
    delegation of powers 368
    division of power 365–70
  private companies 353
  and the promoters 69
  public companies 353
  selection process 5
  and shares
    allotment of 240
    forfeiture of 248–9
  see also directors
bonus shares 195, 217–18
book debts
  fixed charges over 509–10
  registration of 516
brokerage 231
Bullock Report (1977) 5
Business Names Act (1985) 55

calls of shares 244–5
capacity to contract 52–3
capital 153–70
  authorised capital 96, 97
  consolidation of 165
  and forfeiture of shares 249
  repayment of, and preference shares 159–61
  statements of capital and initial shareholdings
    75–6, 86–7, 296
  see also share capital; shares

capital maintenance 171–221
  acquisition of own shares 181–2
  financial assistance for the purchase of shares
    191–201
  and promoters 69
  reduction of capital 172–81
    and minority shareholder protection 331
  rule 208, 211
  see also company distributions; purchase of
    own shares
capital redemption reserve 218
capitalising profits 217–18
cash
  issue of equity shares for 239
  payment of shares in 271
centrebinding 612, 631
chairman
  board of directors 370, 371, 474
  board meetings 485, 486
  general meetings 474, 477, 482
charges 507, 508–23
  avoiding as a preference 522–3
  provisions invalidating 636–8
  registration of 516–20
  and trust deeds 507
  validity of 516
  see also fixed (specific) charges; floating
    charges
charities
  and the objects clause 96
Chartered Directors 356
citation as partner 52
City Code on Takeovers and Mergers 564–70,
  572–3
Civil Procedure Rules
  and derivative actions 314
class meetings 483
Cohen Committee
  and minority shareholder protection 326
Companies (Acquisition of Own Shares)
    (Treasury Shares) Regulations 2003 (SI
    2003/1116) 189
Companies Act (1844) 109
Companies Act (1929) 191
Companies Act (1948) 5, 180
Companies Act (1985)
  articles of association 104, 105, 108, 109
  capital maintenance
    company distributions 212, 217
    reduction of capital 173, 174, 555
  constitution of a company 88

Companies Act (1985) (*continued*)
  directors
    disqualification of 441
    fair dealing by 390
    and substantial shareholdings 294
  and incorporation 65, 74
  and LLPs 58–9
  memorandum of association 88, 94
  and shares 237
    ordinary shareholders 161
    variation or abrogation of class rights 163
  winding-up, alternatives to 614
Companies Act (2006) 2, 4
  accounts
    accounting records 530–1
    annual 531–4
    directors' report on 535–6
    filing of 538–40
    group accounts 534–5
    publication of 537–8
    small and medium-sized companies 528–30
  administrative orders 594
  alteration of share capital 165
  amalgamations and reconstructions 558,
    560–3
  annual returns 295–7
  articles of association 104, 105, 108–10
    alteration of 125, 126, 127
    insider/outsider rights 115
    Model Articles 75
    shareholders' agreements 118, 119
  auditors, appointment of 540–2
  board meetings 484, 487, 488
  and brokerage 231
  capital maintenance
    acquisition of own shares 181–2
    company distributions 206, 207, 208, 210,
      211, 212, 214, 215, 216
    financial assistance for the purchase of
      shares 192–3, 196, 200
    purchase of own shares 183–7, 189, 190
    reduction of capital 172–5
  changing corporate structures 556–8
  class meetings 483
  company members
    acquiring membership 288
    register of 289–92
  company registration 65
  and the company secretary 373–5
  constitution of a company 88, 104, 109
  CVA contracts 578, 583

debentures 500
  acquisition of 505–6
  charges 508, 518–20
  convertible 502
  irredeemable 505
  and power to borrow 501
  registered 503
  reissued 503
directors
  appointment of 355–6, 359, 360
  and company contracts 140–1, 143, 144
  and company indemnity 424–5
  compensation for loss of office 386
  contracts of employment 361, 362
  defining 353
  disqualification of 438, 439, 440
  duties of 398–9, 402, 406, 407, 412–13, 415,
    416, 422–4, 426
  fair dealing by 387–90, 388–90, 391, 393,
    394–5
  and members 365, 366–7
  publicity in connection with 371–3
  removal of 433, 434, 436
  remuneration 381–2, 383–4
  shadow directors 354–5
  share qualification 365, 439
and the EC Transparency Directive 223
electronic communications 495–7
general meetings 464–6
  AGMs 463
  chairman 474
  and electronic communications 480–1
  minutes 482–3
  notice of 467–71
  proxies 477–9, 480–1
  quorum 472–3, 474
  voting 475–7
incorporation 74–6, 78
  electronic 78
  pre-incorporation contracts 73
and internal flexibility 62
investigation of interests 295
lifting the corporate veil 47–8
memorandum of association 88–9, 109
minority shareholders 301
  derivative actions 312, 313–16
  exceptions to the rule in *Foss* v *Harbottle*
    304–5
  petitions for winding-up 347
  protection against unfair prejudice 326,
    329–31, 335, 336

names of companies 92
and the objects clause 94–6, 555
partnerships
   LLPs 56, 57, 58–61
   ordinary 52
private companies 14, 17, 29
   small and medium-sized 18, 19, 20, 23
promotion and rules of capital maintenance 69
resolutions 489–92, 494
and the rule in *Foss* v *Harbottle* 301
and share premiums 276–9
and shares
   allotment of 238, 239, 240
   calls on 245
   certificates 241–2
   class rights 155, 156, 161–2
   defining 237
   forfeited and surrendered 250
   lien on 247
   payment for 271, 273–5, 275–6
   redeemable 166
   return of allotments 240–1
   share warrants or bearer shares 243
   transfer of 258, 258–9
and the statement of capital 96–7
and substantial share interests 294
takeovers 563–4, 570, 572
underwriting 230
and unlimited companies 29
and voluntary winding-up 607–8
winding-up
   alternatives to 614–15
   provisions invalidating a charge or debt 636–7, 638
Companies Bill (1973) 73
Companies (Company Records) Regulations (2008) 520
Companies (Cross-Border Mergers) Regulations (2007) 59
companies *de jure* 78
Companies House
   and administrative orders 590, 597, 598
   incorporation 74
   LLP registration 55–6
   re-registration process 80
   registration of charges 517–18, 519, 520
   and return of share allotments 241

Companies (Share Capital and Acquisition by Company of its Own Shares) Regulations (2009) 238–9
Companies (Shareholders' Rights) Regulations (2009) 491
Companies (Trading Disclosures) Regulations (2008) 520
company charges *see* charges
Company Directors Disqualification Act (1986) 5, 61, 358–9, 439–41, 442, 453, 454, 455, 456
company distributions 205–21
   audit considerations 211–12
   capitalising profits 217–18
   consequences of unlawful distribution 215–17
   defining 206
   and dividends 206
      declaration and payment of 212–15
      directors failing to declare 215
      interim dividends 213–14
   realised profits 208–9, 210, 211
   related statutory rules 209–11
   relevant accounts 211
   reserves 218
   restrictions on distribution by public companies 207–8
   special cases 211
company flotations 222–35
   brokerage 231
   offer of unlisted securities 228
   procedures for issuing shares 229–30
   reform
      the EU Prospectus Directive 231–2
      FSA Listing Rules review 231, 232–3
   remedy of rescission 229
   sub-underwriting contracts 231
   system for listing securities 223–8
   underwriting 230–1
Company Law Review
   and company charges 523
   and share certificates 241
   Steering Groups, and the objects clause 94
Competition Act (1998) 454, 558
Competition Commission 558–9
competition violation
   and director disqualification 454
compliance, statement of
   altering articles of association 126
   incorporation 76, 80, 81

compulsory winding-up 559, 607, 621–7
  avoiding property dispositions 624
  companies in voluntary liquidation 640–1
  completion of 640
  EC Regulation on Insolvency Proceedings
    625–6
    and UK law 626
  effect of 625
  grounds for 621–2
  investigation by the Official Receiver 624
  liquidators 624
    duties of 629, 631
  petitioners 622–3
  public examination of officers 625
  statement of affairs 624
computers and company records 289
concurrent powers
  of directors and members 366
connected persons
  and fair dealing by directors 388, 391
contracts (company) 138–52
  and administrative orders 600
  and capital maintenance, purchases of own
    shares 184–5
  and the company secretary 373
  directors and fair dealing 393–4
  directors and others as agents 140–50
    acts of individual directors and other
      officers 144–7
    defective authority and insiders 149–50
    and forged company documents 149
    indoor management rule 142–3
    non-executive directors and employees
      148
    proper purpose rule 143–4
  of minors 288–9
  public companies and the s 761 certificate 139
  s 33 statutory contract 301, 302
  and shares 237
  see also CVA contracts
contracts (employment)
  and administrative orders 601
  directors 360, 361–3, 372, 381–2, 384–5
Contracts (Rights of Third Parties) Act (1999)
  articles of association 117–18
  and pre-incorporation contracts 70, 72–3, 74
  and shares 237
contractual liens
  registration of 517
contributories
  and compulsory winding-up 622–3

corporate representatives at general meetings
  481
corporate structure
  methods of changing 555–8
corporate veil 35–49
  lifting 13
  and the judiciary 35–47, 48
  limits on 48
  statutory provisions for 47–8
corporation aggregate 6
corporation sole 5–6
corporations
  classification of 5–13
  distinguishing features of 2
County Court Rules
  and registered company offices 98
court orders
  disqualification of directors 359
  and minority shareholders, rule in Foss v
    Harbottle 303–4
  restoration of companies to the register
    616–18
courts
  appointment of an administrator 588–90
  and articles of association, alteration of 135–6
  compulsory winding-up 621–7
Courts and Legal Services Act (1990) 633
credit transactions
  fair dealing by directors 387, 388–90
creditors
  and administrative orders 588, 590, 597
    exit from 598–9
    meeting of 593–4
    unsecured creditors 594, 597, 598–9
  amalgamations and reconstructions 560–1,
    562
  and capital maintenance 172
    company distributions 206, 212
    creditor's buffer 167, 229
    purchase of own shares 186
    reduction of capital 173, 174–5
  and compulsory winding-up 607, 621–2, 623
  and CVA contracts 580, 585–6
    approval by creditors only 582
    dissenting 581–2
    trading with companies in a CVA 586–7
  and directors
    duties of 407–8
    fraudulent trading 444–5
    insolvency 454
    voluntary winding-up 436, 611

and floating charges
    preferential creditors 511
    unsecured creditors 522
  judgment 515–16
  and liquidators
    position of secured creditors 636
    proof of debts 634–5
  and the objects clause 94
  protection of, and unfair prejudice 343
  and voluntary winding-up 436, 610–11, 613
  see also debenture holders
CREST system
  and communication of general meetings
    480
  and the doctrine of estoppel 242–3
  transfer of listed shares 257–8
Criminal Justice Act (1993) 279–81, 282, 283,
    404, 543
  and insider dealing 565, 567
criminal penalties
  company restoration offences 618
  and financial assistance for the purchase of
    shares 191, 197
  right to a fair trial 457–8
  voluntary winding-up offences 609
CVA contracts 578–87
  approval by members and creditors 580–2
  dissentients 581–2
  nominees 579, 581, 582, 583, 585
  small companies and moratorium option
    583–6
  and subsequent liquidation 582

damages
  claims for unliquidated damages in tort 634
  and derivative claims 312
death
  deceased shareholders/members and unfair
    prejudice 327, 336
  of a liquidator 610, 612
  of a partner 53
  and termination of membership 293
  and transfers of shares 259, 265, 288
  and transmission of debentures 506
  and transmission of shares 266
debenture holders 502, 555
  amalgamations and reconstructions 560, 561,
    562
  and qualifying floating charges 589
debentures 500–26
  acquisition of 505–6

certificates 241
charges 507, 508–23
company charges 507, 508–23
  avoiding as a preference 522–3
  registration of 516–20
  and trust deeds 507
  validity of 516
  see also fixed (specific) charges; floating
    charges
convertible 500, 502
defining 500–1
discounted issues 275
letter of rights 237
and power to borrow 500
promoters of companies and holders of 68
ranked *pari passu* 502–3, 507
reissued 503
remedies of secured debenture holders 523
stock 503, 506, 507
transfers of 255, 258, 506
transmission of 506
and trust deeds 506–8
types of 502–5
underwriting 230
and unrealised profits 209
declaratory judgments 311
Deeds of Partnership 52
deferred debts 635
deputy secretary 375
Deregulation and Contracting Out Act (1994)
    614
derivative actions 301, 304, 305, 311, 312, 313–23
  defining 313–14
  and duties of directors 398–8
  permission to continue 314–23
development costs
  as a realised loss 211
directors 352–461
  abuse of power by 93
  and accounts
    annual 533–4
    report on 535–6
  and administrative orders 591–2, 601
  amalgamations and reconstructions 560
  and annual returns 296
  appointment of 355–64
    alternate directors 357–8
    contracts of employment 360, 361–3
    contractual rights to appoint 356–7
    controlling members as employed directors
      363–4

directors (*continued*)

    persons who cannot be appointed 358–9

    and qualifications 356

    statutory employment claims 364

    to executive posts 371

  and articles of association 105, 106–8

    subsidiary companies 104

  and capital maintenance

    company distributions 206, 213–14, 215–18

    financial assistance for the purchase of

      shares 197, 200

  and the company accountant 353

  and the company secretary 353, 373, 374

  compensation for loss of office 386–7

  and contracts 140–50

  and CVA contracts 578

  defining 353–5

  disqualification of 353, 354, 365, 438–57

    acting while disqualified or a bankrupt 455

    and competition violation 454

    on conviction of an indictable offence

      439–40

    following Secretary of State investigation

      441, 443

    and fraudulent trading 439, 440, 444–54

    leave to act while disqualified 456–7

    offences relating to restored companies 618

    for persistent breach of company law 440

    and personal liability 439, 444–55

    and the phoenix syndrome 455

    pleas in mitigation 443

    under a provision in the articles 438

    for unfitness 440

  division of power with members 365–70

  duties of 397–430

    avoiding conflicts of interest 378, 412–21

    effects of a breach of duty 424–5

    Ministerial Statement on 426

    not accepting benefits from third parties

      378, 422

    in a takeover by general offer 571–2

    to act within powers 399–402

    to declare interest in proposed transaction

      or arrangement 422–4

    to exercise independent judgement 408

    to exercise reasonable care, skill and

      diligence 408–12, 536

    to promote the success of the company

      402–8

  and employment law 359–61

  executive directors 310, 355, 362, 409

fair dealing by 387–95

  board minutes 394–5

  and connected persons 388, 391

  contracts with the company 393–4

  property transactions 394

  treatment of directors' loan accounts

    391–3

and human rights 457–8

inactive 441–2

incorporation 78

  ready-made companies 79

  statement of proposed directors 76

listed companies, Model Code for Securities

    Transactions by 283–4

loans to 26

managing directors 370–1

minimum age requirement 358, 439

and minority shareholders 301, 303

  derivative actions 214

  petition for winding-up 346

  protection against unfair prejudice 327–8,

    336, 340

Model Code of Directors' Dealings 190

and National Insurance contributions 456

non-executive directors 370

private companies 25, 26

public companies 25, 26

publicity in connection with 371–3

purchases of own shares

  civil liability 189

  statements on permissible capital payments

    185–6

  treasury shares 190

remuneration 379–84

service contracts 372–3, 385

  and appointment 360, 361–3

  duty to declare interest 423

  remuneration through 381–2

shadow directors 314, 354–5, 372, 373

  fair dealing by 391

share qualification 364–5, 439

and shares 237

  allotment of 238

  calls on 244, 245

  certificates 241

  companies whose articles restrict transfer

    260–1, 263

  forfeited or surrendered 250–1

  liens on 248

  rejection of 263–4

  rejection of transfer 264–5

surrender of 240
transfer of 255, 256
and substantial shareholdings 293–5
and takeovers 565–6, 571–2
termination of directorship 360
and *ultra vires* actions 93
vacation of office 423–8
appointment of administrator/
administrative receiver 437–8
dismissal 361
expiration of period of office 423–3
removal by members 366–7, 373, 436
removal under the articles 434–5
resignation 416–21, 436, 453
sole directors 423
statutory removal 433–4, 435–6
winding-up 436–7, 632
wrongful trading 410, 446–54
abilities of directors 452
action to avoid disqualification 452–3
profitable but undercapitalised companies 452
see also board of directors; executive directors
Disability Discrimination Act (1995) 484
disclosure of dealings
in treasury shares 190
Disclosure and Transparency Rules (DTR) 294
discounted shares
prohibition on issue of 275–6
discrimination legislation
directors 361, 458
meetings 484
dissentient shareholders/creditors
and purchase of own shares 186
dissolution
of a partnership 53
distributions *see* company distributions
dividend warrants 214, 244
dividends
declaration and payment of 212–15
directors failing to declare 215
and directors' loan accounts 391–2
and distributions 206
interim 213–14
liens on 248
and mortgages of shares 247
and preference shares 157–9
procedure for payment of 214–15
domicile
and director disqualification 441
dormant companies 22, 23–5
agency arrangements 25

articles of association 24–5
form of dormant accounts 24
and ineligible companies 23–4
loss of exemption 24
provisions of company law applicable to 25
DTI (Department of Trade and Industry)
and directors' contracts of service 362–3, 385
Ministerial Statements on the Duties of
Company Directors 426
due diligence
and market abuse 283
Duomatic principle 62, 120

East India Company 3, 4
electronic communications 495–7
authentication of 497
and general meetings 480–1
right to request hard copy form 497
Electronic Communications Order (2000) 492
electronic incorporation 78
employees
and administrative orders 601
and company contracts 148
unfair prejudice 340–1
director decision-making in the interests of
405–6
insider dealing 281
insolvency and the protection of 512, 639–40
management buy-outs 191–2
and the Model Code for Securities
Transactions 284
participation
and company directors 5
and SEs 29–30
share schemes 238, 239
and voluntary winding-up 612
working outside the UK 512
Employment Appeal Tribunal 512
employment law
and directors 359–61
and human rights 458
Employment Rights Act (1996) 361, 362, 512,
639–40
Employment Rights (Increase of Limits) Order
(2008) 364
Enterprise Act (2002) 2, 511, 588–9, 593
and administrative orders 588–9, 593,
598
employees' contracts 601–2
and floating charges 606
and winding-up 639

equal shareholdings
   and unfair prejudice provisions 331–2
equitable interest in shares
   effect of transfer of 262–3
equitable mortgages of shares 246–7, 248, 292
equity *see* shares
estoppels 244
European company law
   insolvency proceedings and registered
      company offices 99–100
   and private companies founded on personal
      relationships 46
   and share capital requirements 200–1
   the *Societas Europaea* (SE) 5, 29–30
European Convention on Human Rights 30–1,
   282–3
European Court of Human Rights 458
European Court of Justice
   insolvency proceedings and registered
      company offices 99–100
European Economic Area Stock Exchange
   and purchase of treasury shares 189
European Public Limited-Liability Company
   Regulations (2004) 29
European Union
   Directives 5
      EC Transparency Directive 223
      Prospectus Directive 231–3
      Transparency Directive (TD) 294–5
      EC Regulation on Insolvency Proceedings
      625–6
executive directors 355, 362
   and company contracts 148
   purchase of own shares 183
   standards of care 409–10
executive posts, appointment of directors to 371
experts
   Listing Rules and statements by 226
extraordinary resolutions
   and voluntary winding-up 608

face-to-face transactions 280
family companies
   and capital maintenance, purchase of own
      shares 183
   and management buyouts 191–2
Family Law Reform Act (1969) 289
faxed proxies 479–80
fees for directors 379–80
financial assistance
   for the purchase of shares 191–201

and the company 192–3
and European law 200–1
and management buy-outs 191–2, 195, 200
meaning of 193–4
previous position 191
problems created by previous legislation
   191–2
sanctions for breach of rules 196–7
when it is lawful 195–200
Financial Reporting Standard for Smaller Entities
   (FRSEE) 19
Financial Reporting Standards (FRSs) 209, 549
Financial Services Authority (FSA)
   and capital maintenance
      company distributions 215
      purchases of shares 183, 190
   Code of Market Conduct 282–3
   and director disqualification 438
   Disclosure and Transparency Rules (DTR)
      223, 233, 294
   and the Human Rights Act 457
   and market abuse 281–3
   Model Code for Securities Transactions 283–4
   Prospectus Rules 224, 225, 228, 233
   see also Listing Rules (LR)
Financial Services and Markets Act (2000) 20, 21
   accounting rules 528
   and debentures 502
   directors and substantial shareholdings 294
   and market abuse 281–2, 567
   and promoters 65
   (Regulated Activities) (Amendment) (No 3)
      Order 2003 190
   system for listing securities 223–7
   and takeovers 564, 565
Financial Services and Markets Tribunal 224
fixed (specific) charges 508
   avoiding as a preference 522–3
   and floating charges 514–15
   over book debts 509–10
   and trust deeds 507
Fixed-Term Employees (Prevention of Less
   Favourable Treatment) Regulations
   (2002) 360
floating charges 62, 508–9
   and administrative receivers 606
   avoidance of 520–2
      as a preference 522–3
   crystallisation of 509, 510
   and the distribution of assets 639
   postponement of 510–16

and fixed charges 514–15
    retention clauses 513–14
QFCH (qualifying floating charge holder)
        589–90, 591, 593, 594, 598
qualifying (QFC) 588–90
registration of 516, 517
second 515
and trust deeds 507
void 637
flotations *see* company flotations
foreign companies
    UK courts and insolvency proceedings 100
forfeited shares 248–9
    reissue of 249
    and termination of membership 293
    treatment of in public companies 250–1
forged company documents 149
forged transfers of shares 259–60
fraud
    and auditors' duties 542–3, 545
    and debenture holders 555
    and director disqualification 439, 440, 444–54
    fraudulent trading and LLPs 60
    and minority shareholders 305–11, 347–8
    and termination of membership 293
    winding-up and fraudulent trading 632–3
FSA *see* Financial Services Authority (FSA)

garnishee orders 515
general meetings 463–83
    adjournment of 481–2
    and articles of association 104, 105, 106–7, 108
        alteration of 125
    chairman 474, 477, 482
    convening of 465
    and directors
        appointment of 355–6
        pay 383–4
        power of 366
        removal of 433, 435–6
    and electronic communications 480–1
    and minority shareholders 303, 309
    minutes of 482–3
    notice of 467–71
        contents of notice 469–70
        length of notice 467
        method of service 469
        persons to whom notice must be given
            468–9
        short notice 467
    proxies 475–6, 477–81

right to demand a poll 475–6
    quorums 471–4
    and shares 237
        calls on 245
    voting 475–7
        chairman's casting vote 477
        independent assessors 476–7
    see also Annual General Meetings (AGMs);
        resolutions
gift, share transfers by way of 293
Gladstone, William 4
good faith
    and company contracts 141
Great Depression 5
group accounts 534–5
group reconstructions 278–9
groups of companies
    lifting the corporate veil 40–5
        and the concept of agency 42–3
        the human and commercial reality of the
            group 40–2
    naming 89
    small and medium-sized 20–2
    see also subsidiary companies
guarantee
    companies limited by 27–8
    statement of 76
Guernsey 573

Harassment Act (1997) 2
Health and Safety at Work Act (1974) 439–40
holding companies
    amalgamations and reconstructions 562
    capital maintenance
        acquisition of own shares 182
        company distributions 212
        financial assistance for the purchase of
            shares 195–6
        management buyouts 191
    directors
        contracts of employment 361–2
        fair dealing by 388
    and share premiums 279
holding out 144–7
human rights 30–1
    and directors 457–8
Human Rights Act (1998) 30–1, 457–8

IAS accounts 208, 529, 530
    filing of 538
    individual accounts 532–3

illegal and immoral businesses
    refusal to incorporate 77, 79–80
illegality
    and the corporate veil 43–5
inactive directors 441–2
incorporation 74–84
    and articles of association 75, 104
    and company names 89
    documents 74–5, 89
    effect of 78–9
    electronic 78
    fees for registration 75
    of LLPs 55–6, 62
    publicity in connection with 80
    re-registration procedures (post-
        incorporation) 80–4, 556
    ready-made companies 79
    registration procedure 74–5, 77–8
    statements
        of capital and initial shareholdings 75–6,
            96–7
        of compliance 76, 80, 81
        of guarantee 76
        of proposed officers 76
    see also promoters
indemnity rights
    and unlawful distribution 216
individual shareholders
    and fraud 307, 308–9
indoor management rule 142–3
Industrial Revolution 4
Information and the Companies (Audit,
        Investigations and Community
        Enterprise) Act (2004) 543–4
injunctions 311, 424
insider dealing 279–81, 565, 567–8
insolvency 2
    and company charges 510–16, 519
    and company distributions 206, 216
    company rescue 578–604
        administration 587–602
        voluntary arrangements 578–87
    and directors
        contracts of employment 363
        disqualification of 441–2, 452–3
        duties of 406–8
        irregular acts 367
        loan accounts 391–2
    EC Regulation on Insolvency Proceedings
        625–6
    and the objects clause 94

proceedings, and registered company offices
        98–100
    see also liquidation; winding-up
Insolvency Act 1986 (Amendment) (No 2)
        Regulations 100
Insolvency Act 1986 (Prescribed Part) Order
        (2003) 598–9
Insolvency Act (1986) 2, 5, 27
    and administrative orders 587–8, 590, 591,
        598–9
        employees' contracts 601
    amalgamations and reconstructions 558, 559
    capital maintenance 175, 189, 195
    changing corporate structures 556
    and companies incorporated for unlawful
        purposes 79
    company charges
        avoiding as a preference 522–3
        floating 511, 513, 516, 520–2
        validity of 516
    and the company secretary 374
    compulsory winding-up 621–5
    and CVA contracts 578, 582, 583–6
    directors
        disqualification of 444
        duties of 406–8, 410
        removal of 436, 438
    duties of a liquidator 632, 634
    and floating charges 606
    and general meetings, proxies at 478, 479
    and LLPs 58, 61
    minority shareholders 301
        petition for winding-up 345, 348
    promoters of companies 68
    re-registered companies 84
    redeemable shares 167
    and registration of resolutions 492
    termination of membership 293
    transfer of shares 256
    transmission of shares 267
Insolvency Act (2000) 444
    and CVA contracts 579
Insolvency Amendment Rules (2010) 630
insolvency practitioners
    and voluntary winding-up 611, 612
Institute of Chartered Accountants in England
        and Wales 543
Institute of Directors 356
insurance companies 211, 229, 257
intellectual property 516
interim dividends 213–14

International Accounting Standards Board 278
internet
  website communications 496
investment companies 211
irredeemable debentures 505

Jenkins Committee on Company Law Reform
    73
  and unfair prejudice 326, 335–6
Jersey 573
Joint Stock Companies Acts 3, 4
judgment creditors 515–16
  and mortgages of shares 247
Judgments Act (1838) 636
judicial review
  and takeover bids 567
the judiciary
  lifting the corporate veil 35–47
    abuse of the corporate form 38–40
    groups of companies 40–3
    illegality 43–5
    limits on 48
    and the personal relationship company 45–7

Large and Medium sized Limited Liability
    Partnerships (Accounts) Regulations
    (2008) 58
The Large and Medium-sized Companies and
    Groups (Accounts and Reports)
    Regulations (2008) 383
Law Commission
  and debentures 523
  Joint Consultation Paper on Partnership Law
    Reform 54–5
Law of Property (Miscellaneous Provisions) Act
    (1989) 634–5
legal mortgages of shares 246, 247
legal personality
  and partnerships 54
Legal Services Commission 633
liability
  of auditors 547–50
  for breaches of contract, arising out of
    alteration of articles of association 133–5
  capital maintenance
    company distributions 208, 209, 216, 218
    purchase of own shares 189
    reduction of capital 174, 175, 176–7
  and company distributions 206
  and CVA contracts 580
  and director disqualification 439, 444–57

director liability 141, 189, 358–9, 410–12, 439,
    442
  and forfeited shares 249
  and incorporation 75
    re-registered companies 73–4
  LLPs, personal liability of the partners 57
  ordinary partnerships 51, 52–3, 55
  promoters and pre-incorporation contracts
    73–4
  share transfers and certification 258–9
  underwriters 231
  unlimited 28–9
  see also limited liability; negligence liability
lien on shares 247–8
Limitation Act (1980) 611, 617–18, 634
limited companies
  capital maintenance
    acquisition of own shares 182
    purchase of own shares 183
    reduction of capital 172–5
  conversion of
    private limited company to private
      unlimited company 83
    private unlimited company to private
      limited company 83–4
  limited by guarantee 27–8
  limited by shares 26–7
  naming 88
  private single-member 14–17
  reduction of share capital 166, 555
  and share allotments 241
  see also plc (public limited companies)
limited liability 26–8, 61
  and account-keeping 528
  background to 3–5
  capital maintenance 172
  and company names 88
  and LLPs 62
  and the personal relationship company 46
  removing protection of (lifting the corporate
    veil) 13
  and the Salmon principle 6–9, 13
  see also LLPs (limited liability partnerships)
Limited Liability Act (1855) 4
limited liability partnerships see LLPs (limited
    liability partnerships)
Limited Liability Partnerships Act (2000) 2–3,
    51, 54, 55–8
Limited Liability Partnerships (Applications of
    Companies Act 2006) Regulations 2009
    58–61

Limited Liability Partnerships Regulations (2001)
3, 46
limited partnerships 51
Limited Partnerships Act (1907) 51, 53
liquidation
and company distributions 212
compulsory winding-up by a company in
voluntary liquidation 640–1
corporate claims in 633
CVA contracts and subsequent 582
and directors 365
disqualification 440, 450–1
duties of 410
loan accounts 391–2
duties of a liquidator 629–40
and promoters of companies 68
and purchase of own shares 186–7
financial assistance for 191
and redeemable shares 168
and the remedy of rescission 229
and voluntary winding-up 608, 610–11
see also winding-up
listed shares
Model Code for Securities Transactions
283–4
transfer of 255, 257–60
Listing Rules (LR) 223–8, 230
Model Code for Securities Transactions 283–4
review 231, 232–3
listing securities 223–8
applications for listing 223–4
common law claims on 227–8
compensation for false or misleading
statements 226
dealings in the after-market 227
default sanctions 225
discontinuance and suspension of listing 224
FSA Listing Rules (LR) 223–8, 230, 231, 232–3
listing particulars and other documents 224–6
general duty of disclosure in 224
negligence claims 228, 229
supplementary particulars 225
persons responsible for listing 227
prospectuses 224, 225
remedy of rescission 229
sponsors 225–6
statements by experts 226
statutory defences 226
litigation
and the company secretary 374
and minority shareholders 302, 311–12

and partnerships 55
and pre-incorporation contracts 70, 72
LLPs (limited liability partnerships) 2–3, 51, 53,
54, 55–62
accounts and audit exemptions 61
advantages and disadvantages of incorporation
62
agreements 62
annual returns 60
disadvantage of financial disclosure 61
formation 55–6
and fraudulent trading 60
incorporation document 55–6
and internal flexibility 62
membership agreements 57–8
names of 57
and ordinary partnerships 58
and private limited companies 61–2
protection of members from unfair prejudice
60–1
register of members 59–60
registered company offices 57
status at law 56
loans
fair dealing by directors 387–95
treatment of loan accounts 391–3
trading certificates and loan repayments 139
see also debentures
London Gazette
and administrative orders 590
certificates of incorporation 80
re-registration 83
notice of striking off companies 613–14,
615
publication of payments out of capital 186
restoration of companies 618
and winding-up
creditors and proof of debts 634
voluntary 608, 611, 612, 613
London Stock Exchange
capital maintenance
dividend payments 215
purchases of treasury shares 184, 189, 190
and the EU Prospectus Directive 231, 232–3
and the FSA Listing Rules review 232–4
and liens on shares 247–8
and market abuse 282
Model Code for Securities Transactions
405
and takeovers 564
transfer of listed shares 255, 257–60

majority rule
and the articles of association 126
Man, Isle of 573
management
and partnerships 52
management buy-outs 191–2, 195, 200
managing directors 370–1
market abuse 281–3, 565, 567
market purchase of shares 183–4
medium-sized companies *see* small and medium-sized companies
meetings 463–99
board meetings 484–9
class meetings 483
creditors
and administrative orders 593–4
and voluntary winding-up 610–11, 628–9
and the disabled 484
electronic communications 480–1, 495–7
resolutions 489–94
of single-member companies 16–17
voluntary winding-up, final meetings and dissolution 612–13
see also general meetings
members (company) 287–99
acquiring membership 288
and capacity 288–9
controlling members as employed directors 363–4
and CVA contracts 580, 586
dissenting 581–2
and derivative actions 313–14
and directors
appointment of 355–6
division of power 365–70
removal of 366–7, 373, 436
service contracts 372, 381–2
and substantial shareholdings 293–5
voluntary winding-up 436
and dividends
declaration of 212–13
interim 214
and general meetings 465–6
register of 289–93
rights of
and the articles of association 105, 110
directors acting beyond their powers 141
insider (membership) rights and non-membership rights 113–17
and the objects clause 95
and shares 237

certificates 243
purchases of own shares 183–4
waivers of pre-emption rights 263
termination of membership 293
and unfair prejudice 340–1
voluntary winding-up 610–11, 627, 628–9
see also shareholders
memorandum of association 74–5, 78, 87–102
and the articles of association 88
and the Companies Act (2006) 88–9, 109
company names 88–92
and directors 355, 365
duties of 406
and membership of a company 288
the registered office 97–100
and shares 237
allotment of 238, 239
calls on 245
statement of capital 75–6, 96–7
and variation of shareholders' rights 555
see also the objects clause
Mental Health Act patients
and transmission of shares 266
mergers 277–8
minimum wage (NMW)
and director's pay 384–6
minority shareholders 300–51
and articles of association 121
altering 127–8
capital maintenance
company distributions 215
reduction of capital 173
derivative actions 301, 304, 305, 313–23
protection of 325–51
against unfair prejudice 326–48
rule in *Foss* v *Harbottle* 301, 302–13
exceptions to the rule 301, 304–11
s 33 statutory contract 301, 302
shareholders' agreements 302
and voting at general meetings 475
minors, capacity of 288–9
minutes
board meetings 488–9
general meetings 482–3
Model Articles 75, 104, 105, 106, 118, 144
and board meetings 484–7
and the company chairman 370
and the company secretary 373
and directors 353, 365
appointment of 356, 358
disqualification of 439

Model Articles (*continued*)
    expiration of period of office 432–3
    managing directors 371
    and members 367, 368
    remuneration 379, 380, 381
   for Private Companies Limited by Shares 241
   and proxies at general meetings 478, 480
   for Public Companies 241, 243, 245, 248–9,
    249, 250
money laundering 543
mortgages
   of shares 246–7, 248, 292
   and trust deeds 507
mortgage debentures 508
multiple voting rights (shares) 154

names of companies 88–92
   changing 91–2
    by special resolution 82
    conversion of companies from private to
     public 80
   limited companies 88
   LLPs 57
   and passing off claims 89–90
   prohibited names 88–9
   public companies 25
   restored 618
   use of first names/nicknames 91
National Insurance contributions
   and directors 456
nationality
   and director disqualification 441
negligence liability
   of auditors 547–9
   and company distributions 209, 216
   directors 410–12
   listing securities 227, 228, 229
   LLPs 56
   minority shareholders and fraud 310–11
   ordinary partnerships 53
net assets
   and financial assistance for the purchase of
    shares 193–4
non-executive directors 370
   and company contracts 148
non-voting shares 154
Northern Ireland 75

the objects clause 92–6, 555
   and agent's lack of authority 92
   altering 96

   and charities 96
   and the company's capacity 95
   and the rights of members 95
   and the *ultra vires* rule 92–3, 94, 95
Occupational Pensions Regulatory Authority
   543
Ofex 228
off-market purchases of shares 183, 184–5
Office of Fair Trading 454
officers (company)
   and company contracts 144–7
   statement of proposed 76
Official Receiver
   and administrative orders 590
   and the company secretary 374
   and compulsory winding-up 623, 624–5
    of a company in voluntary liquidation 641
   and director disqualification 440
   and the duties of a liquidator 633
Official Solicitor 6
ordinary partnerships 51–4
   as business organisations 53
   capacity to contract 52–3
   citation as partner 52
   formation 52
   lack of continuity 53
   and LLPs 58
   not a persona at law 54
   number of partners 52
ordinary resolutions 491, 493–4
   requiring special notice 492
ordinary shares 154
   advantages and disadvantages of 157
   company distributions 218
   pre-emption rights 238–40
   and preference shares 158, 161

Partnership Act (1890) 51, 52, 54, 55, 58
Partnership Agreements 52, 53
partnerships 51–63
   compared with companies 2
   law reform proposals 54–5
   limited 51
   and minority petitions for winding-up 345
   ordinary 51–4, 58
   and the personal relationship company 45–7
   and shareholders' agreements 302
   see also LLPs (limited liability partnerships);
    quasi-partnerships
payments out of capital 185–6
PCPs (permissible capital payments) 185, 187–9

pension funds
  and administrative orders 594, 602
Pensions Act (1995) 543
permissible capital payments (PCPs) 185, 187–9
perpetual debentures 505
perpetual succession 2
persona at law 2
  and incorporation 78
  and minority shareholders 303
  and partnerships 54
phoenix syndrome 455
plc (public limited companies)
  accounts 528
  capital maintenance 175, 182
  corporate abuse 301
  directors
    appointment of 358
    power of members and 366, 367
  managing directors 371
  minority shareholders 304
    protection against unfair prejudice 334–5
  naming 88
  shares
    acquisition of own shares 182
    articles restricting transfer 261
    transfer of 255
postal services
  and registered company offices 98
pre-emption rights 238–40, 261, 262–3,
    265
  disapplication of 366
  and listed companies 229
  on purchase of treasury shares 190
  waiver of 239–40, 263
pre-incorporation contracts 70–4
preference shareholders
  and general meetings 469
preference shares 154, 157–61
  allotment of 239
  capital maintenance 172
    company distributions 218
    purchases of own shares 187
    reduction of capital 173, 174
  redeemable 166, 168
  and winding-up
    arrears of preference dividend 158–9
    repayment of capital 159–61
preferential creditors
  and crystallised floating charges 511
  and CVA contracts 580
private companies 14–26

annual returns 296
articles of association 104
  new Model Articles 105, 106
board meetings 484–5
capital maintenance
  company distributions 207, 213, 214, 215
  purchases of own shares 183, 185–6
  reduction of capital 173, 175–6
and company distributions 211
company secretary 373
conversion of
  private limited company to private
    unlimited company 83
  private unlimited company to private
    limited company 83–4
  to public companies 69, 80–1
directors 353, 379
  expiration of period of office 423–3
dormant 22, 23–5
and financial assistance for the purchase of
  shares 196
founded on personal relationships 45–7
minority shareholder protection 302, 303
  and unfair prejudice 327–8, 331–2
power of directors and members 366
and public companies 25–6
public companies converting to 82
reduction of share capital 166
resolutions 489–94
  written 493–4
secretary 355
shares
  allotment of 238, 239
  articles restricting transfer 261
  payment of 271–3
  transfer of 255–7, 262
single-member 14–17
small and medium-sized 18–25
  groups of 20–2
unfair prejudice in 327
private limited companies
  and LLPs 61–2
  managing directors 371
  power of members and directors 367
  share capital requirements and European law
    200–1
profits
  capitalising 217–18
  directors 380, 413–15
  distribution of 205–21
    public and private companies 26

profits (*continued*)

  and promoters of companies 66–8

  sharing in ordinary partnerships 51

prohibited company names 88–9

promoters 65–74

  dealings with the prospective company and rules of capital maintenance 69

  defining 65

  duties of 66–9

  payments to 69–70

  pre-incorporation contracts 70–4

  see also incorporation

PROOF Scheme (protected on-line filing) 56

proper purpose rule 143–4, 368–9

property transactions

  and fair dealing by directors 394

Prospectus Rules/Regulations 224, 225, 228, 233

  the EU Prospectus Directive 231–3

proxies

  general meetings 475–6, 477–81

    corporate representatives 481

    faxed 479–80

public companies

  annual returns 296

  appointment of auditors 540–2

  board meetings 485–6

  capital maintenance 69

    company distributions 207–8, 213, 214, 215

    financial assistance for the purchase of shares 192–3, 196

    purchases of own shares 183–5

  company secretary 373, 374

  defining 14

  directors 353, 379, 423

    expiration of period of office 432, 433

    power of 366

  Model Articles for 241, 243, 245, 248–9

  names of 25

  and private companies 25–6

  promotion and incorporation 66

  proxies at general meetings 478

  re-registration

    as an unlimited company 83

    from private to public 69, 80–1

    as a private company 82

  restrictions on distribution 207–8

  and the s 761 certificate 139

  secretaries 25

  shares

    allotment of 239, 240

    payment of 273–5

    treatment of forfeited and surrendered 250–1

  see also plc (public limited companies)

Public Interest Disclosure Act (1998) 543

Public Offers of Securities Regulations (1995) 502

Public Trustee Office 5–6

purchase of own shares 183–91, 556

  civil liability of past shareholders and directors 189

  dissentient shareholders/creditors 186

  failure by company to purchase shares 186–7

  financial assistance for 191–201

  market purchase 183–4

  off-market purchases 183, 184–5

  permissible capital payments (PCPs) 185, 187–9

  and private companies 185–6

  provisions to ensure preservation of capital 187

  publicity for 186

  reasons for purchase 183

  treasury shares 189–91

QFC (qualifying floating charge) 588–90

QFCH (qualifying floating charge holder) 589–90, 591, 593, 594, 598

quantum meruit 380

quasi-loans

  fair dealing by directors 387–8

quasi-partnerships 5, 52

  and articles of association 113, 116, 119

  and unfair prejudice 340

  winding-up 348

quorum

  board meetings 485, 487–8

  class meetings 483

  general meetings 471–4

    effect of no quorum 474

    of one 473–4

re-registration (post-incorporation) 80–4, 556

ready-made companies

  incorporation of 79

realised profits and losses

  provisions for depreciation 208–11

receiverships 606

  see also administration

Recognized Investment Exchanges 295

reconstructions *see* amalgamations and reconstructions

redeemable debentures 503–4
redeemable shares 166–8
    failure to redeem shares 167–8
    financing the redemption 166–7
    issue of 166
    redemption of 166
    and reduction of capital 173
    time of redemption 167
reduction of capital 166, 172–81, 555
    general procedure for 173–5
    payment of shareholders on reduction 177–81
    and private companies 175–6
    types of reduction 176–7
redundancy payments to employees 512
register of directors 372
register of members 289–93
    and annual returns 296
    inspection of 290
    notice of trusts 291–3
    obsolete entries 290
    rectification of 290–1
registered companies
    classification of 14–30
    nature of 6–13
registered company offices 97–100
    and insolvency proceedings 98–100
    LLPs 57
    location and address 75, 97, 98
    purpose of 98
registered debentures 503, 506, 507
Registrar of Companies
    and accounts 532, 537
        filing of 539–40
    and administrative orders 593
    and alternate directors 358
    amalgamations and reconstructions 561
    applications for registration 74–5
    and articles of association 125
    capital maintenance
        purchases of own shares 184
        reduction of capital 175, 176
    changing company names 91
    and company charges 518
    and compulsory winding-up 607
    and CVA contracts 587
    and directors
        disqualification 359, 440, 455
        service contracts 372
    effect of registration 78
    and forfeited or surrendered shares 250–1
    and the Listing Rules 224, 225

LLPs 55–6
    and payment for shares 274, 275
    post-incorporation re-registration procedures
        80–1, 83
    public companies and the s 761 certificate 139
    and redemption of shares 168
    refusal to register 77
    and registered company offices 97, 98
    registration process 77
    and resolutions 491, 492, 494
    restoration to the register 616–19
    and share allocations 240
    and special resolutions 490
    statement of capital 96
    striking off defunct companies 613–16
    and termination of administrative orders
        598–9
    and voluntary winding-up 607, 608, 609, 611,
        613
    see also Companies House
registration (company)
    legal personality of partnerships dependent on
        54
    LLPs 55–6
    re-registration (post-incorporation) 80–4, 556
    restoration to the register 616–19
registration of company charges
    bank charges over customer deposits 517
    contractual liens 517
    effect of non-registration 518–19
    and insolvency 519
    out of time 519
    releasing the charge 519
Regulatory Reform (Removal of 20 Member
        Limit in Partnerships) Order (2002) 52
remuneration of directors 379–86
    contract of service 381–2
    fees 379–80
    listed companies and reporting on directors'
        pay 382–4
    and loan accounts 392
    power to pay 384–6
    report on 537, 538, 539
    waiver of 382
reports
    filing of 538–40
    publication of 537–8
reserves
    company distributions 218
residence
    and director disqualification 441

resolutions 489–94
  amendments to 492–3
  extraordinary 608
  notice of
    members' resolutions at the Annual General
     Meeting 470–1
    special notice 471, 489
  ordinary 491, 493–4
    requiring special notice 492
  registration of 491, 492, 494
  seconding 491
  special 490–1, 492, 494, 608
  and voluntary winding-up 608
  see also written resolutions
restoration to the register 616–19
restriction orders 590

s 761 trading certificates 139
Salmon principle
  articles of association and insider/outsider
    rights 113
  and the corporate veil 35
  and limited liability 6–9, 13
SARs (Rules Governing Substantial Acquisitions
  of Shares) 564
Scottish Law Commission 54
Scottish Registrar of Companies 75, 97
scrip issue 217
SE (*Societas Europaea*) 5, 29–30
secretaries (company) 353, 373–5
  and annual returns 296
  appointment 373
  assistant and deputy secretary 375
  authority 374
  and board meetings 486
  and director disqualification 441
  incorporation
    re-registration procedure 81
    ready-made companies 79
  private companies 355
  public companies 25
  qualifications 374
  removal 375
  and share certificates 241
  statement of proposed 76
Secretary of State
  and accounting rules 533, 534–5
  and AGMs 463
  and annual returns 297
  appointment of auditors 541
  and company names 88–9
  and compulsory winding-up 641
  and director disqualification 441, 443, 444
  and insolvency, payments to employees
    640
  and registration of charges 519–20
  reporting on directors' pay 382
  restoration of companies to the register
    616–17
  and share certificates 242
  and trading certificates 139
secured creditors 594
secured debentures 503
securities
  purchase and sale of by directors 294
  see also listing securities; unlisted securities
shadow directors 314, 354–5, 372, 373
  fair dealing by 391
share capital 237
  alteration of 165–6
  companies limited by guarantee 27–8
  and company distributions 206, 208,
    213
  and debentures 500
  and directors 365
  and general meetings 465
  as a liability 237
  and non-distributable reserves 167
  public and private companies 25–6
  and re-registration procedures 80, 81–2
  reduction of 166, 172–81, 555
  and registration of members 289
  and s 761 trading certificates 139
  unlimited companies 28–9
  see also capital maintenance
share certificates 241–3
  and the doctrine of estoppel 242–3
  and equitable mortgages 246–7
  forfeiture of 249
  transfer of shares 257–8
    liability arising out of certification
     258–9
share premium accounts 230, 249
  and resolutions 493
share premium relief 563
share premiums 249, 276–9
  acquisitions 277
  and debentures 506
  group reconstructions 278–9
  mergers 277–8
share warrants 214, 243–4, 365
  and general meetings 469

shareholders 237
 and AGMs 463
 and articles of association 104, 106–8
  alteration of 126–7
 and calls on shares 245
 capital maintenance 172
  dividend payments 213, 214, 216–17
  purchases of own shares 189
  reduction of capital 173, 177–81
 and the City Code on Takeovers and Mergers
  566–7
 and company contracts 141
 and credit transactions by directors 389–90
 and liens on shares 247–8
 and misstatements in listing particulars,
  remedy of rescission 229
 and the objects clause 94
 pre-emption rights of 229
 purchase of own shares 186, 189
 rights issues to existing 229–30
 shareholder democracy 5
 shareholders' agreements 118–21
 statement of capital and initial shareholdings
  75–6, 96–7
 transfer of shares 257–60
  death of a holder in a joint account 260
 transmission of shares 266–7
 in two-member companies 15
 variation of rights 555
 see also minority shareholders
shares 236–86
 acquiring company membership 288
 allotment of 238–40
  authority to issue 238
  pre-emption rights 238–40
  public companies and the 25 per cent rule
   240
  return of an allotment 240–1
 calls 244–5
 capital maintenance
  acquisition of own shares 181–2
  purchase of own shares 183–201
 class rights 154–6
  capital maintenance 172, 173
  variation and abrogation of 161–5, 173
 common or securities seal 241, 242, 243
 defining the term 237
 directors' share qualification 364–5
 directors and substantial shareholdings
  293–5
 forfeiture of 248–9, 293

and incorporation, statement of capital and
 initial shareholdings 75–6
insider dealing 279–81
joint holders of 245
lien 247–8
limitation of liability by 27
and LLPs 3
market abuse 281–2
mortgages of 246–7, 248
non-voting 154
ordinary 154, 157, 158, 161
payment for 27–9
 prohibition on allotment of shares at a
  discount 275–6
 public and private companies 26
and perpetual succession 2
redeemable 166–8
reissue of forfeited shares 249
share warrants (or bearer shares) 243–4
and stock 237
subdivision of 165–6
subscribers' contract 237
surrender of 250–1, 293
and takeovers, dealings during offer period
 572–3
transfer of 255–66, 288
 and articles of association 105
 companies whose articles restrict transfer
  260–6
 forged transfers 259–60
 legal transactions 256
 listed shares 257–60
 rejection of transfers 263–6
 and termination of membership 293
 unlisted shares 255–7
transmission of 266–7
trustees of 293
voting rights 154
see also company flotations; debentures;
 pre-emption rights; preference shares;
 share capital
shelf companies
 capital and initial shareholdings 96
 route to incorporation 79
single-member companies 14–18
 accounts and audit 16
 contracts with sole member/director 17
 conversion to single-member status 16
 death of sole member/director 17
 meetings of 16–17
 private limited 14–16

single-member companies (*continued*)
quorum 472
registration of 16
Small Companies and Groups (Accounts and
Directors' Report) Regulations (2008)
528, 534
Small Limited Liability Partnerships (Accounts)
Regulations (2008) 58
small and medium-sized companies 18–20
accounting exemptions 18–19
disclosure in annual report and accounts
22–3
inapplicable 20
ineligible companies 23–4
LLPs 61
loss of exemption 24
accounts 528–30, 534
filing obligations 538–9
CVA contracts and small companies
583–6
definitions of 19
dormant 22, 23–5
financial reporting standard for 19
small and medium-sized groups of companies
20–2
audit exemption and small groups 22
criteria for exemption 21–2
exemptions inapplicable 21
Social Security Act (1998) 456
Societas Europaea (SE) 5, 29–30
solvency statements 166
South Sea Company 3–4
special resolutions 490–1, 492, 493–4
and voluntary winding-up 608
specialty debts 245
sponsors
and Listing Rules 225–6
SSAPs (Statements of Standard Accounting
Practice) 209
statutory derivative actions *see* derivative
actions
Stock Exchange *see* London Stock Exchange
Stock Transfer Act (1963) 256–7
stock transfer forms 256–7, 267
stop notices
and mortgages of shares 247
sub-underwriting contracts 231
subsidiary companies
accounting rules 535
amalgamations and reconstructions
562

and articles of association 104
capital maintenance, acquisition of own shares
182
and the corporate veil 37, 42–3
directors
contracts of employment 361–2
duties of 406
and financial assistance for the purchase of
shares 192–3
and management buyouts 191
share premiums 278
small and medium-sized 20
Supply of Goods and Services Act (1982)
411
Supreme Court Rules
and mortgages on shares 247
and persona at law 54

Takeover Panel 282, 563, 564, 570, 573
membership 566–7
and purchase of treasury shares 190–1
takeovers 563–73
amalgamation by takeover 558–9
City Code on Takeovers and Mergers 564–70,
572
compulsory acquisition 570–1
dealings in shares during offer period 572–3
defining 465
directors' duties in takeovers by general offer
571–2
and insider dealing 565, 567–8
and judicial review 567
mandatory offers 568–70
misleading profit forecasts 565
offer document 564
and response of offeree board 568–70
partial offers 564–5, 568
recent amendments and developments
573
reverse acquisition 571
tactics of directors 565–6
takeover bids and unfair prejudice 340
telephone meetings 489
Third Parties (Rights Against Insurers) Act
(2010) 635–6
third-party debt claims 515
Trade and Companies Board 201
trade creditors
and promoters of companies 68
Trade Union and Labour Relations
(Consolidation) Act (1992) 22

trading certificates 139
treasury shares, purchase of 189–91
  and the City Takeover Panel 190–1
  companies dealing in 190
  disclosure of dealings in 190
  pre-emption rights 190
trust deeds 506–8
trust of land 54
Trustee Act (1925) 267, 630
trustees
  and transmission of shares 267
trusts
  and the register of members 291–3
two-member companies 15

UK Listing Authority (UKLA) 223, 231
ultra vires transactions 56, 88, 92–3, 94, 95
  and company contracts 143
  and company distributions 212
  and directors 367
  and minority shareholders 304
  and winding-up, provisions invalidating 637
underwriting shares/debentures 230–1
unfair dismissal of directors 361, 364
unfair prejudice, protection against 218
  limited liability partnerships 60–1
  minority shareholders 326–48
    abuse of procedure 332–3
    equal shareholdings 331–2
    illustrative case law 336–45
    public limited companies 334–5
    winding-up petitions 345–8
  and promoters of companies 68
unlimited companies
  conversion and re-registration of 83–4
  reduction of share capital 555
  special features of 28–9
unlisted securities
  and insider dealing 280
  offer of 228
unsecured creditors
  and administrative orders 594, 597, 598–9
  and floating charges 522
  and winding-up 621
unsecured debentures 504

veil of incorporation *see* corporate veil
voluntary winding-up 559, 607–13, 627–9
  applications to be struck off 607–8
  applications to court 613
  centrebinding 612, 631

completion of 640
declaration of solvency 609–10, 627
  penalties for false declarations
    627–8
liquidation committee 629
liquidators 610–11, 612
  duties of 629, 631
members 610–11, 627, 628–9
objections to 608–9
offences 609
resolutions for 608
rights of creditors and contributories 613
withdrawal of application 608
voting
  board meetings 485, 488
  general meetings 465, 475–7
    chairman's casting vote 477
    independent assessors 476–7
voting rights (shares) 154
  and disclosure requirements 295
  forfeited or surrendered shares 250
  and holders of share warrants 244
  members and the removal of directors
    366–7
  and minority shareholders 304
    wrongdoer control 308–9
  multiple 154
  and transmission of shares 266

winding-up 606–44
  and administrative orders 593, 599
  alternatives to 613–19
    restoration to the register 616–19
    striking off defunct companies 613–16
  capital maintenance
    company distributions 215
    payment of shareholders on reduction of
      capital 177, 180
    purchase of own shares 186–7, 189
  distribution of assets 206
  duties of directors 406–8
  duties of a liquidator 629–40
    co-operation of officers 632
    collection of the assets 631–2
    completion of winding-up 640
    control by the court 630
    and corporate claims 633
    creditors and proof of debts 634–5
    distribution of assets 639
    position of secured creditors 636
    powers 631

winding-up (*continued*)
    provisions invalidating a charge or debt
      636–8
    as a trustee, agent or officer 630
  functions of a liquidator 606–7
  methods of 607
  minority petition for a just and equitable
    345–8
  and preference shares
    arrears of preference dividend 158–9
    repayment of capital 159–61
  and redeemable shares 167–8
  and the register of members 290
  removal of directors 436–7

and shares 237
  transfer of 256, 265
see also compulsory winding-up; voluntary
  winding-up
written resolutions 366, 367, 493–4
  board meetings 486, 489
  filing of 494
  general meetings 483
  involvement of auditors in 494
  special adaptations 494
  use of 489
wrongful trading
  and directors 410, 446–54
  duties of a liquidator 632–3